HANDBOOK OF DEFENSE ECONOMICS
VOLUME 2
DEFENSE IN A GLOBALIZED WORLD

HANDBOOKS
IN
ECONOMICS

12

Series Editors

KENNETH J. ARROW
MICHAEL D. INTRILIGATOR

AMSTERDAM · BOSTON · HEIDELBERG · LONDON
NEW YORK · OXFORD · PARIS · SAN DIEGO
SAN FRANCISCO · SINGAPORE · SYDNEY · TOKYO
North-Holland is an imprint of Elsevier

ELSEVIER

HANDBOOK OF DEFENSE ECONOMICS

DEFENSE IN A GLOBALIZED WORLD

VOLUME 2

Edited by

TODD SANDLER

Vibhooti Shukla Professor of Economics and Political Economy,
University of Texas at Dallas, USA

and

KEITH HARTLEY

Director, Centre for Defence Economics, University of York, UK

ELSEVIER

AMSTERDAM · BOSTON · HEIDELBERG · LONDON
NEW YORK · OXFORD · PARIS · SAN DIEGO
SAN FRANCISCO · SINGAPORE · SYDNEY · TOKYO
North-Holland is an imprint of Elsevier

North-Holland is an imprint of Elsevier
Radarweg 29, PO Box 211, 1000 AE Amsterdam, The Netherlands
The Boulevard, Langford Lane, Kidlington, Oxford OX5 1GB, UK

First edition 2007

Notice
No responsibility is assumed by the publisher for any injury and/or damage to persons or property as a matter of products liability, negligence or otherwise, or from any use or operation of any methods, products, instructions or ideas contained in the material herein. Because of rapid advances in the medical sciences, in particular, independent verification of diagnoses and drug dosages should be made

Library of Congress Cataloging-in-Publication Data
A catalog record for this book is available from the Library of Congress

British Library Cataloguing in Publication Data
A catalogue record for this book is available from the British Library

ISBN-13: 978-0-444-51910-8

ISSN: 0169-7218 (Handbooks in Economics series)
ISSN: 1574-0013 (Handbook of Defense Economics series)

For information on all North-Holland publications
visit our website at books.elsevier.com

Printed and bound in Great Britain

07 08 09 10 11   10 9 8 7 6 5 4 3 2 1

INTRODUCTION TO THE SERIES

The aim of the *Handbooks in Economics* series is to produce Handbooks for various branches of economics, each of which is a definitive source, reference, and teaching supplement for use by professional researchers and advanced graduate students. Each Handbook provides self-contained surveys of the current state of a branch of economics in the form of chapters prepared by leading specialists on various aspects of this branch of economics. These surveys summarize not only received results but also newer developments, from recent journal articles and discussion papers. Some original material is also included, but the main goal is to provide comprehensive and accessible surveys. The Handbooks are intended to provide not only useful reference volumes for professional collections but also possible supplementary readings for advanced courses for graduate students in economics.

KENNETH J. ARROW and MICHAEL D. INTRILIGATOR

*To the memory of Jack Hirshleifer and Herschel I. Grossman,
two innovators and guiding lights in the study of conflict and defense*

CONTENTS OF THE HANDBOOK

VOLUME 1

Chapter 1
Introduction
KEITH HARTLEY and TODD SANDLER

Chapter 2
Defense Economics and International Security
MARTIN C. MCGUIRE

Chapter 3
World Military Expenditures
MICHAEL BRZOSKA

Chapter 4
The Demand for Military Expenditure
RON SMITH

Chapter 5
Military Alliances: Theory and Empirics
JAMES C. MURDOCH

Chapter 6
Arms Races and Proliferation
DAGOBERT L. BRITO and MICHAEL D. INTRILIGATOR

Chapter 7
Theorizing About Conflict
JACK HIRSHLEIFER

Chapter 8
Insurrections
HERSCHEL I. GROSSMAN

Chapter 9
Terrorism: Theory and Applications
WALTER ENDERS and TODD SANDLER

viii

Chapter 10
Defense Expenditure and Economic Growth
RATI RAM

Chapter 11
Military Expenditure and Developing Countries
SAADET DEGER and SOMNATH SEN

Chapter 12
Incentive Models of the Defense Procurement Process
WILLIAM P. ROGERSON

Chapter 13
The Economics of Military Manpower
JOHN T. WARNER and BETH J. ASCH

Chapter 14
The Defense Industrial Base
J. PAUL DUNNE

Chapter 15
Economics of Defense R&D
FRANK R. LICHTENBERG

Chapter 16
Industrial Policies in the Defense Sector
KEITH HARTLEY

Chapter 17
Regional Impact of Defense Expenditure
DEREK BRADDON

Chapter 18
Economics of Arms Trade
CHARLES H. ANDERTON

Chapter 19
The Economics of Disarmament
JACQUES FONTANEL

VOLUME 2

Chapter 20
Defense in a Globalized World: An Introduction
TODD SANDLER and KEITH HARTLEY

Chapter 21
Economics of Defense in a Globalized World
MARTIN C. MCGUIRE

Chapter 22
Economics of Conflict: An Overview
MICHELLE R. GARFINKEL and STERGIOS SKAPERDAS

Chapter 23
Civil War
PAUL COLLIER and ANKE HOEFFLER

Chapter 24
Political Economy of Peacekeeping
BINYAM SOLOMON

Chapter 25
Terrorism: A Game-Theoretic Approach
TODD SANDLER and DANIEL G. ARCE

Chapter 26
Terrorism: An Empirical Analysis
WALTER ENDERS

Chapter 27
The Political Economy of Economic Sanctions
WILLIAM H. KAEMPFER and ANTON D. LOWENBERG

Chapter 28
The Econometrics of Military Arms Races
J. PAUL DUNNE and RON P. SMITH

Chapter 29
Arms Trade and Arms Races: A Strategic Analysis
MARÍA D.C. GARCÍA-ALONSO and PAUL LEVINE

Chapter 30
Arms Industries, Arms Trade, and Developing Countries
JURGEN BRAUER

Chapter 31
Trade, Peace and Democracy: An Analysis of Dyadic Dispute
SOLOMON W. POLACHEK and CARLOS SEIGLIE

Chapter 32
New Economics of Manpower in the Post-Cold War Era
BETH J. ASCH, JAMES R. HOSEK and JOHN T. WARNER

Chapter 33
The Arms Industry, Procurement and Industrial Policies
KEITH HARTLEY

Chapter 34
Success and Failure in Defense Conversion in the 'Long Decade of Disarmament'
MICHAEL BRZOSKA

Chapter 35
A Survey of Peace Economics
CHARLES H. ANDERTON and JOHN R. CARTER

CONTENTS OF VOLUME 2

Introduction to the Series	v
Dedication	vi
Contents of the Handbook	vii

Chapter 20
Defense in a Globalized World: An Introduction
TODD SANDLER and KEITH HARTLEY

TODD SANDLER and KEITH HARTLEY	607
Abstract	608
Keywords	608
1. Introduction	609
2. Defense economics: Then and now	611
3. Our decision on what to include in Volume 2	615
4. Organization of the book	615
5. Concluding remarks	620
References	620

Chapter 21
Economics of Defense in a Globalized World
MARTIN C. MCGUIRE

MARTIN C. MCGUIRE	623
Abstract	624
Keywords	624
1. Overview	625
1.1. Defense economics: The agenda – Update on a field in transition	625
1.2. Economics as the source of conflict	626
1.3. Political economy – international public choice: Fight and grab or work and trade	626
1.4. Governance and economic calculus of war	627
1.5. Core economics of resource allocation remains central	630
2. World trends and big picture security themes	630
2.1. Technology driven globalization: A source of new threats, risks, opprortunities, and resources	631
2.2. Great world prosperity: Greater costs and benefits of conflict	631
2.3. Governments paradoxically overshadowed	633
2.4. US hegemony: A fading monopoly	634
2.5. A new frequency distribution of violence/conflict	635
2.6. Whither defense? Warring alliance blocks? Criminal disorder? Partitioned global security?	637

3. Defense: A normative problem in economics   638
4. New century salients in defense economics   639
    4.1. Carry-over or legacy issues from Cold War   639
    4.2. Security issues of traditional geopolitical origin: China   639
    4.3. Culture driven conflicts   640
    4.4. Defense and the media   640
    4.5. Moral-political limits on the military instrument   641
5. Tasks for defense economics: Two special and timely topics   641
    5.1. Rogue states, WMD, and failed states: Economic analyses of predation and tyranny   641
    5.2. New dimensions of alliance cooperation   642
6. Some examples of economic method applied to defense   643
7. Conclusions: Future direction of defense economics   645
References   646

Chapter 22
Economics of Conflict: An Overview
MICHELLE R. GARFINKEL and STERGIOS SKAPERDAS   649
Abstract   650
Keywords   651
1. Introduction   652
2. Technologies of conflict   654
3. Representative models of conflict and the determinants of power   658
    3.1. Competing for a resource   659
    3.2. Guns versus butter   662
4. Settlement in the shadow of conflict   667
    4.1. Sources of the preference for settlement   668
    4.2. How much arming? Settlement under different rules of division   671
5. Why fight?   677
    5.1. Traditional explanations: Asymmetric information, misperceptions, irrationality   677
    5.2. Incomplete contracting in the shadow of the future   677
6. Trade, insecurity, and conflict   682
    6.1. Secure autarky versus insecure exchange   683
    6.2. Insecure resources, trade restrictions and other market interventions 685
7. Coalitions and group formation   690
    7.1. Stage 1: Inter-group conflict   692
    7.2. Stage 2: Intra-group conflict   693
    7.3. Equilibrium allocations   694
    7.4. The level of conflict under different symmetric group structures   696
    7.5. Requirements of stability and equilibrium group structures   698
8. Dynamics and growth   699
9. Conflict management and the state   701
    9.1. Hierarchical governance   702
    9.2. Modern governance   703

10. Concluding remarks   704
References   705

Chapter 23
Civil War
PAUL COLLIER and ANKE HOEFFLER   711
Abstract   712
Keywords   712
1. Introduction   713
2. Concepts and data   713
   2.1. Definition of civil war   713
   2.2. Quantitative measures of the severity of civil wars 714
3. Causes of civil war   718
   3.1. Motivation and feasibility   718
   3.2. Theories of rebellion   719
   3.3. Evidence on the causes   721
4. Duration   723
   4.1. Theories   723
   4.2. Evidence   724
5. Consequences of civil war   725
   5.1. Economic consequences   725
   5.2. Social consequences   727
   5.3. Psychological damage of civil war   728
   5.4. Political consequences   730
6. Post-conflict   731
   6.1. Theories of post-conflict recovery and relapse   731
   6.2. Evidence   732
7. Policy interventions   733
   7.1. Policies for prevention   733
   7.2. Policies for ending conflict   734
   7.3. Policies for maintaining post-conflict peace   735
8. Conclusions and research agendas   736
References   737

Chapter 24
Political Economy of Peacekeeping
BINYAM SOLOMON   741
Abstract   742
Keywords   742
1. Introduction   743
2. Background   744
   2.1. Peacekeeping assessment scales   747
   2.2. Peacekeeping trends and stylized facts   748

3. Financial arrangements and burden sharing   752
    3.1. Financial reforms and revenue sources   752
    3.2. Peacekeeping alliances and burden sharing   755
4. Economic assessment of peacekeeping, intervention and policy implications   762
    4.1. Theoretical models   762
    4.2. Empirical results   764
5. Peacekeeping in theatre and policy implications   766
    5.1. Economic impacts   767
    5.2. Policy implications   769
6. Summary and future directions   769
    6.1. Future directions   771
References   772

Chapter 25
Terrorism: A Game-Theoretic Approach
TODD SANDLER and DANIEL G. ARCE   775
Abstract   776
Keywords   777
1. Introduction   778
2. A brief look at the early literature   780
3. Counterterrorism: Normal-form representations   782
    3.1. Proactive versus defensive measures: 2×2 canonical representations   782
    3.2. A 3×3 deterrence–preemption game   784
    3.3. Asymmetric targets and preempting   785
    3.4. Other cases   787
4. Counterterrorism: Extensive-form games   789
    4.1. Preemption versus deterrence in a continuous choice scenario   793
5. Alternative externalities   795
6. Pitfalls of international cooperation   799
    6.1. Specific examples: Freezing terrorist financial assets   800
    6.2. Specific example 2: Safe havens   802
7. Game theory and never conceding to terrorist demands   803
    7.1. Conventional wisdom evaluated   805
    7.2. Reputation   806
8. Asymmetric information   806
    8.1. Signaling extensions: Alternative forms of regret   810
9. Concluding remarks   811
References   812

Chapter 26
Terrorism: An Empirical Analysis
WALTER ENDERS   815
Abstract   816
Keywords   816

1. Introduction 817
2. Statistical properties of the terrorist incident types 818
   2.1. Comparison of data sets 824
3. Counterterrorism policy: The substitution effect 832
   3.1. Testing the HPF model 834
4. Terrorism since 9/11 840
   4.1. Effects on the attack modes 841
   4.2. Effects on the location of incidents 845
5. Measuring the economic costs of terrorism 849
   5.1. Case studies 853
   5.2. Microeconomic consequences of terrorism 855
6. Measuring the economic determinants of terrorism 859
7. Conclusions and assessment 862
References 864

Chapter 27
The Political Economy of Economic Sanctions
WILLIAM H. KAEMPFER and ANTON D. LOWENBERG 867
Abstract 868
Keywords 868
1. Introduction 869
2. Economic effects of sanctions 872
3. The political determinants of sanctions policies in sender states 879
4. The political effects of sanctions on the target country 884
5. Single-rational actor and game theory approaches to sanctions 889
6. Empirical sanctions studies 892
7. Political institutions and sanctions 898
8. Conclusions and avenues for further research 903
References 905

Chapter 28
The Econometrics of Military Arms Races
J. PAUL DUNNE and RON P. SMITH 913
Abstract 914
Keywords 914
1. Introduction 915
2. Data 916
3. Theoretical issues in specification 920
4. Action–reaction models 924
5. A game theory model 929
6. Panel and cross-section models 932
7. Conclusions 937
References 939

Chapter 29
Arms Trade and Arms Races: A Strategic Analysis
MARÍA D.C. GARCÍA-ALONSO and PAUL LEVINE   941
Abstract   942
Keywords   942
1. Introduction   943
2. Products and data: The facts   944
3. Demand for arms imports   947
4. Supply: The arms industry   948
5. Regulation   949
6. An non-technical review of the arms trade models   952
    6.1. Supplier objectives and the benefits of coordination   952
    6.2. Demand for imports and responses to regulation   954
    6.3. The arms industry   955
7. A formal model of the arms trade   957
    7.1. The basic model   958
    7.2. Collective action problems   961
    7.3. Domestic production   963
    7.4. Industry and market structure   963
8. Concluding remarks   967
References   969

Chapter 30
Arms Industries, Arms Trade, and Developing Countries
JURGEN BRAUER   973
Abstract   974
Keywords   974
1. Introduction   975
2. Major conventional weapons   977
    2.1. Arms transfers   977
    2.2. Arms production   982
    2.3. Transnationalization of arms production and trade   987
    2.4. A theory of arms production   989
3. Small arms and light weapons   993
    3.1. Definition, data, and market characteristics   994
    3.2. Trade values, production volumes, stockpiles, and prices 995
    3.3. Supply, technology, diffusion   998
    3.4. The demand for small arms and light weapons   1000
4. Non-conventional weapons   1002
    4.1. Atomic weapons   1002
    4.2. Biological weapons   1004
    4.3. Chemical weapons   1005
    4.4. Missile technology and space-based activities   1007

   4.5. ABC-weapons production and entry/exit theory   1008
5. Conclusion   1010
References   1011

Chapter 31
Trade, Peace and Democracy: An Analysis of Dyadic Dispute
SOLOMON W. POLACHEK and CARLOS SEIGLIE   1017
Abstract   1018
Keywords   1019
1. Introduction   1020
   1.1. The setting: Monadic versus dyadic analysis   1020
   1.2. Defining peace: A trade theory perspective   1021
   1.3. Requirement for peace: A lasting peace – Notions of a stable equilibrium   1021
2. Modeling how trade affects conflict and cooperation   1023
   2.1. An economics model of the "peace-through-trade" liberal hypothesis   1023
   2.2. Alternative conflict–trade theories   1028
3. Testing the theory   1031
   3.1. Data   1031
   3.2. Statistical analysis: Testing the trade–conflict theory   1041
4. An application – The democratic peace: Why democracies do not fight each
   other   1051
   4.1. The issue   1051
   4.2. The evidence   1053
   4.3. Conclusions from the trade–conflict model regarding the democratic peace 1054
5. Extensions of the conflict–trade model   1057
   5.1. Commodity-specific trade   1058
   5.2. Foreign direct investment   1058
   5.3. Country size   1059
   5.4. Multilateral interactions   1061
6. Conclusion   1065
References   1066

Chapter 32
New Economics of Manpower in the Post-Cold War Era
BETH J. ASCH, JAMES R. HOSEK and JOHN T. WARNER   1075
Abstract   1076
Keywords   1076
1. Introduction   1077
2. Supply of defense manpower in the post-Cold War era   1078
   2.1. Enlistment supply   1080
   2.2. Retention: Models and recent evidence   1091
   2.3. Deployment: Theory and evidence   1097
   2.4. Spouses and families: Effect of military on the earnings of spouses   1103

3. Demand for manpower and force management in post-Cold War era   1105
   3.1. Personnel productivity and efficient force mixes   1105
   3.2. Personnel management in the post-Cold War era   1109
4. Issues in compensation   1112
   4.1. Pay adequacy to attract a quality force   1112
   4.2. Gaining added pay flexibility   1115
   4.3. Civilian earnings of military retirees   1117
   4.4. Rising cost of entitlements   1118
   4.5. Addressing obstacles to compensation reform   1120
5. New contributions to the economics of the draft   1120
   5.1. Recent contributions   1121
   5.2. Ending conscription in Europe   1127
6. Summary   1131
References   1133

Chapter 33
The Arms Industry, Procurement and Industrial Policies
KEITH HARTLEY   1139
Abstract   1140
Keywords   1140
1. Introduction   1141
2. Arms industries   1141
   2.1. Definitions   1141
   2.2. Facts on the world's arms industries   1144
   2.3. The economics of arms industries   1148
   2.4. Market conduct: Competition and the military–industrial complex   1151
   2.5. Market performance   1156
3. Procurement: Theory and policy issues   1161
   3.1. Assessing arms industries: Benefit–cost analysis   1166
   3.2. Some policy issues and challenges   1168
4. Industrial policies   1171
5. Conclusion   1173
References   1174

Chapter 34
Success and Failure in Defense Conversion in the 'Long Decade of Disarmament'
MICHAEL BRZOSKA   1177
Abstract   1178
Keywords   1178
1. Introduction   1179
2. Elements for the analysis of defense conversion   1180
   2.1. Definitions of defense conversion   1180
   2.2. Post-Cold War resource release   1181

    2.3. Conversion as a class of transformations 1184
    2.4. Measures of conversion 1186
    2.5. Conversion and grand theories of economics 1188
3. Economic benefits and costs of conversion after the Cold War 1190
    3.1. Reorientation of government budgets 1190
    3.2. Reuse of military know-how as well as research and development facilities 1192
    3.3. Industrial conversion on the level of the firm 1194
    3.4. Re-employment of former soldiers and military personnel 1199
    3.5. Base conversion 1200
    3.6. Regional conversion effects 1201
    3.7. Net costs of weapons destruction 1202
4. Government policies for conversion 1203
5. Conclusions 1205
References 1206

Chapter 35
A Survey of Peace Economics
CHARLES H. ANDERTON and JOHN R. CARTER 1211
Abstract 1212
Keywords 1212
1. Introduction 1213
2. Nature and scope of peace economics 1213
    2.1. Definition of peace economics 1213
    2.2. Patterns of conflict in the international system 1216
3. Determinants of interstate armed conflict 1221
    3.1. Conflict cycle 1221
    3.2. Wittman's expected utility model of war 1223
    3.3. Assessing the risk of interstate armed conflict 1224
    3.4. Assessing war duration 1227
4. Arms rivalry, proliferation, and arms control 1229
    4.1. Definitions 1229
    4.2. Models of arms rivalry 1229
    4.3. Selected empirical studies of arms rivalry and proliferation 1234
5. Technological and geographic dimensions of conflict 1236
    5.1. The inherent propensity toward peace or war 1236
    5.2. Lanchester theory and the inherent propensity toward peace or war 1236
    5.3. Offense/defense theory and evidence 1240
6. Appropriation and exchange theory 1242
    6.1. Edgeworth box model of vulnerable trade 1242
    6.2. General equilibrium model of production, appropriation, and exchange 1245
7. Experiments in peace economics 1247
    7.1. Experimental methods 1247
    7.2. Early experiments 1248

7.3. Recent experiments   1250
8. Concluding remarks   1251
References   1254

Author Index of Volume 2   I-1

Subject Index of Volume 2   I-17

Chapter 20

DEFENSE IN A GLOBALIZED WORLD: AN INTRODUCTION

TODD SANDLER[1]

School of Economic, Political and Policy Sciences, University of Texas at Dallas, Green Building, Richardson, TX 75083-0688, USA
e-mail: tsandler@utdallas.edu

KEITH HARTLEY[2]

Centre for Defence Economics, University of York, Heslington, York YO10 5DD, England, UK
e-mail: kh2@york.ac.uk

Contents

Abstract	608
Keywords	608
1. Introduction	609
2. Defense economics: Then and now	611
3. Our decision on what to include in Volume 2	615
4. Organization of the book	615
5. Concluding remarks	620
References	620

[1] Todd Sandler is the Vibhooti Shukla Professor of Economics and Political Economy.
[2] Keith Hartley is the Director of the Centre of Defence Economics.

Handbook of Defense Economics, Volume 2
Edited by Todd Sandler and Keith Hartley
DOI: 10.1016/S1574-0013(06)02020-5

Abstract

Since the end of the Cold War, the world remains a dangerous place with new threats: regional conflicts, transnational terrorist networks, rogue states, and weapons of mass destruction (i.e., chemical, biological, radiological, and nuclear). The second volume of the *Handbook of Defense Economics* addresses defense needs, practices, threats, agents, and policies in the modern era of globalization. This new era involves novel technologies, new business practices, and enhanced cross-border flows. Such ever-growing flows mean that military armaments and armies are less equipped to keep out unwanted intruders.

This introductory chapter sets the stage for this volume in three ways. First, the chapter identifies how threats have changed since the Cold War. For example, the end of the superpower arms race has brought forth new issues, such as the quelling of local conflicts, the role of economic sanctions, and the challenge of asymmetric warfare. There are also new concerns about military manpower and the role of reservists and civilian contractors during a time when most countries have downsized their forces. Second, the chapter indicates the choice of topics and how these topics differ from those in Volume 1. In particular, we selected chapters on topics not covered in Volume 1 (e.g., civil wars, peacekeeping, trade and peace, and economic sanctions); chapters on past topics where there has been significant advances in knowledge (e.g., conflict, terrorism, arms races, and military manpower); and chapters on topics that reflects the influence of globalization and new threats (e.g., terrorism, trade and peace, and arms industries). Third, the chapter provides a brief overview of each chapter in the volume.

Keywords

Armed Forces, arms trade, arms races, collective action, conflict, defense industries, globalization, new technology, peacekeeping, procurement, terrorism

JEL classification: D74, C72

1. Introduction

In the early 1990s, many people wondered why we decided to edit the first volume of the *Handbook of Defense Economics* in light of the end of the Cold War, significant progress in reducing nuclear arsenals, the fall in arms sales, and the promise of a more peaceful world. Back then, interest focused on the so-called peace dividend as money from the defense sector was being redirected to the civilian sector, including social programs. In the 1980s, defense spending as a percent of gross domestic product (GDP) was 4.5%; by 2000, it had fallen to 2.5% [NATO (2000)]. The nature of the security threat has indeed changed since the Cold War, but the world remains a dangerous place with myriad security concerns. During the decade since the publication of the first volume, the terrorist attacks on 11 September 2001 (henceforth, 9/11), the rise of rogue states, and the prevalence of intra-state wars have underscored security issues despite the end of the nuclear confrontation between the superpowers and the demise of the former Soviet Union and the Warsaw Pact.

The second volume of the *Handbook of Defense Economics* addresses defense needs, practices, threats, and policies in the modern era of globalization. New technology in the form of the information revolution has contributed to creating a global economy and a revolution in military affairs (e.g., electronic warfare and unmanned air vehicles). Defense contractors have become international companies and are increasingly using global supply chains. Globalization emphasizes the enhanced cross-border flows of all kinds (e.g., capital and labor flows, ideas, and goods) including the spillovers of benefits and costs associated with public goods and transnational externalities (i.e., uncompensated interdependencies affecting two or more nations). Such ever-growing flows mean that military armaments and armies are less able to keep out unwanted intruders. Borders are porous to sleeper cells, pollutants, diseases, political upheavals, conflicts, computer viruses, and insidious pests. These enhanced cross-border transmissions bring with them new defense and security needs and implications. Even increased trade and financial flows imply novel security challenges and defenses. Globalization also underscores the importance of a new set of institutions (e.g., the European Union, other regional pacts, global governance networks, transnational defense contractors, and multilateral agencies) and agents (e.g., nongovernmental organizations and terrorist networks) that influence ever-increasing transfrontier flows. Globalization blurs the distinction between domestic and transnational security concerns. Thus, a civil war in a remote African country may cut off the supply of strategic resources (e.g., titanium), foster the start of a pandemic, or impact neighboring countries' economies [Murdoch and Sandler (2002, 2004)].

Globalization not only spreads security concerns but also provides nations with a greater rationale to act collectively. The difficulty arises because nations are not inclined to sacrifice their autonomy over security matters for the collective good. Thus, globalization presents a host of collective security challenges – e.g., preempting a common terrorist threat, curbing nuclear proliferation and the spread of chemical and biological weapons among rogue nations, forgoing profitable arms trade, upholding an arms boycott, contributing to peacekeeping operations, and reducing civil wars in developing countries – that are extremely difficult to address. Although today's security exigencies may not threaten apocalyptic consequences, as did the superpower confrontation during the Cold War, these challenges are nevertheless a security concern that can be as costly as nuclear confrontation to eliminate. Since the end of the Cold War, the world clearly remains a dangerous place. World order needs guarding and in the absence of a guardian, disorder is likely. There is a view that currently and for the foreseeable future, the United States is the only possible guardian and the guardian will look to its national interest while possibly seeking to serve the "general good" [Gray (2004)]. The longer-term challenge is whether the United Nations can develop into an effective organization for maintaining and enforcing world peace [McNamara (1992)]. Given its past record, it is doubtful that the United Nations will fulfill this role.

The events of 9/11 demonstrate that today's threats can assume novel and ghastly forms. If weapons of mass destruction (WMDs) were to get into terrorists' hands, then 9/11 may seem tame compared with the carnage and economic consequences of a WMD terrorist attack. In the United States, the Department of Homeland Security's (DHS) budget is now over $40 billion, which does not include about the same amount spent on terrorist-related intelligence [Enders and Sandler (2006)]. Proactive measures taken by the US military and its allies in Afghanistan and Iraq account for many billions more (conflict and peacekeeping operations are costly) [Sandler and Hartley (2003)]. Security measures by US states, cities, and local jurisdictions and similar measures in other countries cost still more billions of dollars. Billions are also spent in lost time waiting at airports to clear security and there are further costs through losses of liberty and freedom. Terrorism leads to spending that can continue to escalate without ever guaranteeing that a terrorist attack will not occur. Terrorists can attack anywhere in the target-rich environment of liberal democracies; yet, a country cannot afford to equally secure every potential target. As a consequence, softer targets must exist that will draw the attack, with terrorists always seeking new and novel methods of attacks (terrorist policy resembles the squeezing of a balloon). Addressing nuclear proliferation also poses costly collective action problems, where even a single nonparticipant can spoil the cumulative efforts of the cooperating nations. Each of today's security challenges confronts governments with costly and difficult-to-achieve countermeasures and even more challenges in developing effective collective action responses.

The purpose of this volume is to analyze the security challenges in this new age of globalization, where conflicts involve novel tactics, new technologies, asymmetric warfare (among mismatched adversaries), new agents, different venues, and frightening weapons. Some of these threats are less discriminate than traditional warfare and put civilians in harm's way. In addition, this volume addresses changes in the defense sector that involves arms trade, arms races, arms industries, and military manpower concerns. With today's leaner military, procurement practices are changing as reflected by the increased concentration in some defense industries. The Iraq War and its aftermath illustrates some essential lessons in today's strategic environment. First, modern-day, high-technology weapons can only substitute to a limited extent for military manpower.

Second, casualties may be far greater after "victory" owing to an insurgency requiring substantial peacekeeping operations. By accepting defeat quickly, a losing side can maintain more of its military assets to carry on the insurgency. Third, the most expensive military assets can still be defeated by inexpensive improvised munitions or countermeasure (e.g., a Stinger missile shot at an Apache helicopter), thus underscoring Hirshleifer's (1991) paradox of power. The latter refers to a strategic advantage that the weak has over the strong. Fourth, the United States needs to reassess the adequacy of its military manpower if it intends to confront "rogue nations" and proliferation threats (e.g., with the need to develop expeditionary forces capable of worldwide operations). Fifth, private contractors have an increasing role to play in future conflicts and in the peace-time military (i.e., military outsourcing).

2. Defense economics: Then and now

Defense economics applies the tools of economics to the study of defense and defense-related issues including defense policies and industries, conflict, arms races, disarmament, conversion, peacekeeping, insurgencies, civil wars, and terrorism. When applying these tools, defense economists must tailor economic methods, both theoretical and empirical, to defense issues and policies, while taking account of institutional aspects that characterize the defense section. In, say, the defense industries, the development and manufacture of new weapons possess factors, not characteristic of many other industries. For example, a government may be a monopsony that may be unsure about a weapon's intended combat role with a contractor required to commit costly and defense-specific resources to the program; and where both parties will have to agree on a suitable contract providing efficiency incentives, an acceptable profit, and guarantees about paying a contractor's costs. A study of the procurement practices in the United States must include the relevant participants – the Congress, the defense contractors, the military, and the constituency of weapon-building districts – and how they vie for strategic advantage. As such, game theory has an increasing role in the study of defense economics. Game theory also plays a role in the study of conflict, insurgencies, peacekeeping, economic sanctions, arms races, and arms trade.

In addition to institutional details, defense economics must account for the nature of the agents. If, for example, terrorists or insurgents are weak compared with their government adversaries, then the implications of this relative weakness must be addressed. This can show up with the high soldier to rebel ratios (sometimes higher than 100 to 1) that characterize insurgencies, where the government is still unable to put down the rebellion (e.g., Columbia and Peru). Key agents include networked terrorist groups, third-party interveners into civil wars, private contractors, insurgents, reservists, arms runners, and Diaspora supporters. Agents may display novel tastes and possess information unknown to their counterparts. Nevertheless, they are modeled as maximizing an objective subject to one or more constraint that may be influenced by the choices of others. That is, government efforts to harden potential terrorist targets change the price of various terrorist modes of attacks – i.e., the relative price of skyjackings and kidnappings leading terrorists to substitute cheaper for costlier methods of attacks (e.g., kidnapping, assassinations, or bombings replacing skyjackings).

During the decade or so between the publication of Volumes 1 and 2 of the *Handbook*, the definition of defense economics has not altered. Rather, there has been a changing mix of agents that now include failed states, rogue nations, transnational terrorist networks, rapid deployment forces, and alliance-backed peacekeepers. Technological change has presented new threats (e.g., the ability of terrorists to coordinate operation by the Internet) and challenges (e.g., the need for governments to monitor Internet traffic). On the military side, precision-guided munitions have changed war fighting and pilotless drones harbor the increasing substitution of capital for manpower. With these new agents, there is a change in the nature of threats. The fear of a nuclear holocaust fought between the superpowers of the Cold War has given way to threat of a rogue nation resorting to nuclear blackmail. Other worries involve WMDs (i.e., chemical, biological, radiological, or nuclear weapons) falling into the hands of terrorists or insurgents, who may plant them in a major city. A common scenario is a radiological device or dirty bomb that consists of radiological material dispersed by a conventional bomb. Such a device could cause billions of dollars of losses if exploded at a major harbor, such as Los Angeles. The rise of intra-state wars from the late 1980s on has increased the risk to neighboring countries from either an expanding conflict or negative economic consequences. In most cases, an inflow of refugees from the conflict-torn country creates hardships to recipient countries. Cost may also stem from the spillover of border skirmishes that can destroy infrastructure and create the need for border patrols and fortification [Collier et al. (2003)].

During the last decade, the nature of conflict has also changed drastically. Contrary to the democratic peace doctrine, the United States invaded two sovereign states: Afghanistan in October 2001 and Iraq in March 2003. In the former case, the invasion was to punish and dismantle al-Qaida for its role in 9/11 and global terrorism; in the latter case, the invasion was to disarm Saddam Hussein and his alleged WMDs. Both interventions were costly for the United States, its allies, Afghanistan, and Iraq. Moreover, costs were incurred not only during the conflict, but also during the subsequent peace-keeping missions. Estimates suggest that the US military expense for these conflicts exceeded $400 billion to 2006 (i.e., not including costs to the US civilian economy). Since the mid 1990s, there is a heightened prevalence of asymmetric warfare between adversaries of vastly different abilities. Asymmetric warfare makes obsolete some of the weapons of the Cold War, including the B-2 bomber and M-1 tanks. There is also a growing concern over civil wars, insurrections, transnational terrorism, and rogue nations. Nations must reconfigure their defenses to counter these new contingencies. This reconfiguration involves not only weapons, but also manpower and its necessary training.

Another change concerns new institutional relationships that include a much expanded NATO with Russia as a partner and some Eastern Europe and former Warsaw Pact nations as allies (e.g., East Germany, Hungary, and Poland). Given NATO's unanimity voting rule, military response to crises is anticipated to be slower in the future as deals must be struck to get holdout allies to agree to an action. This raises questions about the "optimal" size of NATO, which requires an assessment of the benefits and costs of expanded memberships for both existing and new members. The future of NATO has also to be assessed against the development of the European Union's Security and Defense Policy, including its efforts to create a Single European Market for defense equipment. Further changes have affected the defense industry, which has experienced a growing importance of the electronics industry and increased concentration among large defense contractors [Hartley and Sandler (2003)]. The emergence of national monopolies means the loss of domestic competition in procurement and the possible need to treat defense contractors as regulated firms. Some contractors are transnational with plants on both sides of the Atlantic; such development makes government control more difficult as the contractor maintains autonomy over some component plants. Fewer contractors make competition over competing new designs for innovative weapon systems and platforms more difficult, thereby giving governments less leverage and this loss of leverage is reinforced through the increasing trend to global chains. Yet another change involves the emergence of loosely linked terrorist networks, which makes it more problematic for government efforts to infiltrate a terrorist group. More important, hierarchically organized governments may be ill-suited to battle nonhierarchically organized terrorist organizations. For military manpower, the reliance on reservists for combat roles has not only hurt recruitment but also raised issues of the heavy use of reservists in extended duty in combat zones. Similar problems arise with military outsourcing and the increasing substitution of civilian contractors for military personnel to undertake activities traditionally provided by "in-house" units (e.g., catering, training, and transport). Changed threats and new technology create the need for new weapons, altered force structures, and novel procurement practices, which presents a challenge to the Armed Forces, often reluctant to change owing to vested interests (i.e., each service seeks to maintain its monopoly property rights over land, sea, and air domains).

The post-Cold War era has brought forth new issues [Chapters 21 (M.C. McGuire) and 22 (M. Garfinkel and S. Skaperdas)]. The end of the superpower confrontation and their use of surrogates for localized conflict have implications for the conversion of both the Armed Forces and defense industries [see Chapters 33 (K. Hartley) and 34 (M. Brzoska)]. With fewer surrogate-directed conflicts, the arms trade assumed a smaller importance. In the post-Cold War era, the spread of democracy has its implications not only for trade but also for world peace [Chapters 31 (S.W. Polachek and C. Seiglie) and 35 (C.H. Anderton and J.R. Carter)]. Enhanced trade flows foster links among countries that limit the gains from conflict. The increase in intra-state conflict, which really began in the latter 1980s, and the need for peacekeeping have put stress on UN peacekeeping capacity [Chapter 24 (B. Solomon)]. This has resulted in a greater role for regional alliances, especially NATO and the developing peacekeeping roles of the EU. Peacekeeping raises issues of burden sharing and allocative efficiency since such efforts have strong public good components. Similar burden-sharing issues arise with economic sanctions, which are a means by which the international community can change a nation's behavior [e.g., Iraq or Iran; see Chapter 27 (W.H. Kaempfer and A.D. Lowenberg)].

There are also new concerns about military manpower and the role of reservists and civilian contractors [Chapter 32 (B.J. Asch, J.R. Hosek, and J.T. Warner)]. The latter constitutes the growing interest in military outsourcing. Given the prolonged Iraq War and its bloody aftermath, there is a possible return to the draft in the United States. Following the Cold War, arms races have assumed a more localized form between re-gional adversaries – e.g., India and Pakistan nuclear arms race [Chapters 28 (J.P. Dunne and R.P. Smith) and 29 (M.C. Garcia-Alonso and P. Levine)], which is particularly worrying given their longstanding hatred. With the rise of intra-state conflicts, small arms and light weapons assume an enhanced importance [Chapter 30 (J. Brauer)]. Such weapons often dominate local conflicts and are difficult to police internationally [also see Chapter 23 (P. Collier and A. Hoeffler)]. Another concern is over the proliferation of WMDs to nonstate actors, particularly terrorists. Terrorists pose a few concerns: (1) the escalating cost of homeland security; (2) the failing efforts to coordinate governments' counterterrorism; (3) growing carnage in terrorist attacks [Chapters 25 (T. Sandler and D.G. Arce) and 26 (W. Enders)]; and (4) the effectiveness of traditional military forces against terrorism (i.e., asymmetric warfare).

The post-Cold War period has made nations acutely aware of the guns-versus-butter tradeoff. Enhanced military budgets must come at the expense of social welfare spend-ing as many governments are trying to downsize in terms of the share of GDP devoted to government. With limited budgets and rising military input costs (e.g., the unit costs of new fighter jets), difficult choices must be made by defense policymakers. Examples of such choices include a re-assessment of a nation's military commitments (e.g., the costs of a world role); a search for "efficiency improvements" (e.g., competitive procure-ment policy and contractorization); role specialization and substitutions between forces (e.g., air power replacing some land forces; cruise missiles replacing bomber aircraft); reservists and civilians replacing regular personnel; and imported equipment replac-ing arms bought from a national defense industrial base. The move to all-volunteer armies has also increased the cost of defense. New security challenges have required new weapon systems that are expensive to develop, especially in light of smaller pro-duction runs [see Chapter 33 (K. Hartley)]. Today's threats require the Armed Forces to assume new roles, which in turn give rise to transformation costs: it requires both time and costs to change the traditional roles of the Armed Forces, especially in peacetime. Typically, the drivers for change for the Armed Forces are wars and new threats (in-cluding defeat in battle), new technology, budget cuts, and (occasionally) an innovative Secretary of Defense (e.g., McNamara). But the Armed Forces lack the incentive and market structures that are the feature of private industry, where consumers are continu-ally demanding new products and lower-cost suppliers emerge to satisfy such demands. However, the Armed Forces differ from private markets in their lack of competition, the absence of a profit motive, and the absence of a capital market. For industries, capital markets act as a policing mechanism through takeovers and the threat of bankruptcy.

3. Our decision on what to include in Volume 2

Three considerations drove our decisions on Volume 2's coverage. First, we wanted to include topics that were not covered in Volume 1. Thus, this volume contains chapters on civil wars, peacekeeping, economic sanctions, and the econometrics of arms races. New topics also involve trade, peace, and democracy, the study of conversion, and a survey of peace economics. Second, we allowed for chapters on past topics where there had been a significant advancement of knowledge since Volume 1. There are, thus, chapters on conflict, terrorism, arms races, arms trade, military manpower, and arms industries. Each of these areas witnessed an explosion of literature over the last decade. Third, we commissioned chapters that reflect the influence of globalization and the changing threats (e.g., terrorism, civil wars, and weapon proliferation). In some cases, a topic is included because it fulfilled two or more of these criteria (e.g., terrorism).

In terms of the first two criteria, the increased incidence of civil wars and other forms of conflict have resulted in myriad contributions in economics and political science [see, e.g., Chapter 23 (P. Collier and A. Hoeffler)]. The World Bank and other institutions funded some of this research. Not surprising, 9/11 greatly expanded both theoretical and empirical analyses of terrorism; hence, we included chapters that review and evaluate recent theoretical [Chapter 25 (T. Sandler and D.G. Arce)] and empirical analyses [Chapter 26 (W. Enders)]. Advances in the study of arms races have also been empirical and theoretical in nature; thus, Chapters 28 (J.P. Dunne and R.P. Smith) and 29 (M.C. Garcia-Alonso and P. Levine) present these two aspects in separate studies. Recent breakthroughs in econometric methods allow for more accurate study of the dynamics of arms races. Important environmental and/or institutional changes are associated with the role of manpower in the Armed Forces and the arms industry. For the former, there is a substitution of capital for manpower [Chapter 32 (B.J. Asch, J.R. Hosek, and J.T. Warner)], while for the latter, there is an unprecedented consolidation of producers [Chapter 33 (K. Hartley)]. In terms of the third criterion, we are not only interested in the changing nature of threats [Chapter 21 (M.C. McGuire)] but also the impact of these threats on military spending.

4. Organization of the book

The remainder of the book consists of fifteen chapters. The next chapter sets the stage for this volume. Chapter 21 (M.C. McGuire) argues that the nature of defense changed drastically since the end of the Cold War. Security challenges are now more diverse and involve terrorism, rogue states, WMDs, localized conflicts, and invisible invaders (e.g., bacteria and viruses). Although McGuire sees the unitary role of the United States in confronting these challenges in the near-term, he envisions a new "multi-polar power configuration" for the future. McGuire lays out the meaning and role of defense economics in understanding the new security exigencies. McGuire also shows the influence of globalization in this transformation of defense economics.

The following three chapters address various aspects of conflict. In Chapter 22, Garfinkel and Skaperdas provide an up-to-date review and overview of the economics of conflict, which is a fast growing field of inquiry. These authors indicate how conflict is modeled as a contest between self-interested adversaries who expend resources to augment their likelihood of winning the confrontation. The root of conflict theory is rent-seeking behavior. This conflict research agenda was spearheaded by Jack Hirshleifer and Herschel Grossman. Garfinkel and Skaperdas explore the essential ingredients of the conflict paradigm, which includes the "contest success function" and the "technologies of conflict". Myriad aspects of conflict – endogenous production, war damage, risk aversion, and discount rates – are investigated. Chapter 23 (P. Collier and A. Hoeffler) analyzes conflict in the form of civil wars that may be motivated by greed, grievance, or both. In the post-Cold War era, inter-state wars gave way to intra-state wars, which are primarily based in developing countries. As such, development efforts are severely hampered in conflict-torn countries and their neighbors owing to collateral damage. Collier and Hoeffler review both econometric and theoretical studies. At the outset, the authors offer a clear definition of civil wars and then turn to available datasets on intra-state conflicts. Severity measures may hinge on either deaths or duration. The authors investigate the causes, consequences, and duration of civil wars. With the increased incidence of civil wars has come the need for greater peacekeeping efforts by the United Nations, NATO, other regional alliances, and the United States. Chapter 24 (B. Solomon) investigates the economics of peacekeeping. In particular, he reviews not only alternative financial arrangements for peacekeeping, but also past burden-sharing behavior. The post-Cold War expansion in peacekeeping meant a greater role for NATO in complex missions in Bosnia and Kosovo where NATO's vital interests are at stake. Moreover, NATO altered its force structure to respond to peacekeeping demands.

Chapters 25 (T. Sandler and D.G. Arce) and 26 (W. Enders) address the economics of terrorism. Sandler and Arce apply game-theoretic methods to the study of terrorism. At the outset, they explain a government's choice between defensive and proactive policies against a terrorist threat. For transnational terrorism where two or more countries face a common threat, there is a proclivity to spend too much on defensive measures and too little on proactive measures. Defensive action represents a "commons" problem with public costs and private benefits, while a proactive response action represents a public good provision problem with public benefits and private costs. For asymmetric targets where one country attracts the most attacks, the prime-target country will take offensive action that affords a free ride on other target countries. A more optimal mix of defensive and proactive measures characterizes domestic terrorism, insofar as externalities from action are internalized in the host country. This chapter displays the study of counter-terrorism in terms of normal-form (matrix) and extensive-form games. For the latter, Sandler and Arce show the importance of leadership for defensive and proactive scenarios. The extensive-form game is applied to investigate the effectiveness of a pledge never to concede to hostage-taking terrorists. In Chapter 26, Enders provides a fresh review of the application of econometrics to the study of terrorism. Much has been written since 9/11 using a host of different techniques – e.g., time series, panel estimation, and spectral analysis. Enders begins by introducing the reader to various event-based terrorism data sets, which he uses to display the changing nature of terrorism since the 1990s. In particular, terrorism has become more deadly following the dominance of fundamentalist terrorism. He also displays some differences between the data sets. Next, Enders examines the effectiveness of select past counterterrorism measures – e.g., metal detectors in airports, heightened embassy security, and the Libyan retaliatory raid. In the case of barriers such as metal detectors, he emphasizes the substitution phenomenon, where terrorists respond to policy-engineered changes in the relative prices of modes of attacks by substituting into relatively cheaper attack modes. The last third of the chapter evaluates recent studies on the economic impact of terrorism on the general economy and on specific sectors (e.g., tourism and foreign direct investment).

Chapter 27 (W.H. Kaempfer and A.D. Lowenberg) surveys the literature on the use of economic sanctions, which poses an interesting collective action problem because even a single noncompliant nation can greatly compromise the accomplishment of sanction-imposing nations. Following the Gulf War of 1991, economic sanctions was imposed against Saddam Hussein's regime with mixed results. Iran's recent defiance in pursuing nuclear weapons may bring new economic sanctions against it. As indicated by Kaempfer and Lowenberg, economic sanction represents a means, short of war, by which the international community can coerce an action by some recalcitrant nation. The authors examine not only the redistributive influence of sanctions but also their efficacy. In so doing, they stress game-theoretic strategic aspects and the importance of political institutions. Kaempfer and Lowenberg point to the consensus that smart sanctions – designed to impose selective costs on a specific group – have better success than more broad-based sanctions. Chapter 27 also reviews the empirical literature on the use of sanctions. In so doing, they highlight a number of issues of estimation associated with gauging the effectiveness of sanctions.

The next two chapters concern arms races. Chapter 28 (J.P. Dunne and R.P. Smith) investigates econometric issues surrounding military arms races among adversaries. To provide a balanced econometric approach, these authors consider the underlying theory, data, and statistical specifications. As enduring rivalries between pairs of hostile countries or alliances, arms races represent a dynamic interaction that is particularly difficult to investigate from a statistical standpoint. A primary issue concerns the arms race variable: is it military spending, military assets, manpower, or some combination? Another issue involves how much the arms variable must increase each year to constitute a "race". The authors present four alternative econometric paradigms for arms races: time-series estimation of a Richardson action–reaction model; Markov switching estimation of a discrete game-theory model; cross-section estimation model; and panel (time-series, cross-section) estimation model. The time-series Richardson model is tested for India and Pakistan, while the Markov switching estimation is tested for Greece and Turkey. Both of these dyads represent localized arms races that characterize the post-Cold War era of globalization. This chapter adds greatly to the Brito and Intriligator (1995) chapter in Volume 1, which did not investigate econometric issues. The empirical concerns raised by Smith and Dunne also apply to other econometric exercises – e.g., the impact of defense spending on economic growth. In Chapter 29, Garcia-Alonso and Levine present a game-theoretic-based study of arms trade and arms races. The authors note that arms trade has positive and negative consequences. On the positive side, arms exports may add to GDP while bolstering the security of allies; on the negative side, arms exports may decrease security while fueling conflict in unstable regions. Moreover, arms can fall into the hands of enemies. In short, arms exports have positive and negative externalities. The authors display some intertemporal models with a demand and supply side for the arms trade and account for strategic interactions among the agents. According to the authors, the resulting Nash equilibrium will be inefficient owing to coordination failures that neglect externalities. The more likely scenario is too much arms trade that can fuel local arms races, with negative consequences for the world community. Possible regulatory regimes are also discussed to ameliorate a host of collective action problems.

In Chapter 30, J. Brauer focuses on arms industries and the arms trade in developing countries. An important insight of this chapter is its recognition of the transnationalization of arms industries and its implications for developing countries. Namely, developing countries contribute components to a wide range of arms even though some other country may, at times be credited with the production of the weapon platform. Brauer notes that some developing countries – e.g., Brazil, China, India, Russia, and South Africa – produce arms on a par with some developed countries – e.g., Australia, Sweden, and Canada. Brauer also points to the failure of nonproliferation as ideas, know-how, and technologies transcend borders in an age of globalization. In the latter portion of the chapter, the market for small arms and light weapons is analyzed. These weapons cause many deaths in civil-war-torn developing countries. Additionally, proliferation issues are addressed in terms of how they pertain to developing countries.

Chapter 31 (S. Polachek and C. Seiglie) represents a new topic for the *Handbook of Defense Economics* that weds ideas from economics and political science. In essence, Polachek and Seiglie investigate whether trade linkages make for less conflict by forging profitable interactions (i.e., gains from trade) that could be destroyed by conflict and disagreements. This chapter builds a theoretical underpinning as to how trade between countries affects conflict and cooperation. Conflict or "trade gone awry" can result from the failure to profit from trading opportunities, nontrading countries competing over a trade opportunity, or the perception of inequitable terms of trade. These authors also review past empirical tests of trade as an impediment to conflict by displaying many issues of estimation, including data availability. A host of empirical models – time-series, cross-section, and panel estimates – are reviewed. In addition, Polachek and Seiglie consider the "democratic peace" literature that views democracies as seldom fighting with other democracies or initiating wars. If this viewpoint is correct, then efforts to promote democracy may result in a more peaceful world.

Much has changed regarding military manpower since J.T. Warner and B.J. Asch contributed to Volume 1 of the *Handbook of Defense Economics*. First, there has been a significant reduction in personnel in the NATO allies – e.g., US military manpower fell from 2.2 million in 1985 to 1.4 million in 2004; Germany's military manpower fell from 495,000 to 252,000 over the same period; and France's military manpower fell from 560,000 to 357,000 over the same period [NATO (2005)]. Second, there have been significant deployments of US troops to combat zones in Afghanistan and Iraq. Third, NATO supported complex and lengthy peacekeeping missions in Bosnia and Kosovo. Fourth, more European countries shifted to volunteer forces. Fifth reservists have played an integral role in Iraq. In Chapter 32, B.J. Asch, J.R. Hosek, and J.T. Warner present the new economics of manpower in the light of these and other changes in the post-Cold War era. Among the topics addressed, the authors investigate the ability of the United States to recruit high-quality personnel in the light of longer tours of duty and mounting casualties in Iraq. Manpower enlistment supply is related to advertising, bonuses, educational benefits, and other considerations. Chapter 32 provides a balanced presentation of the supply and demand for manpower in the post-Cold War era. Issues of compensation – i.e., pay, retirement benefits, and entitlement – are discussed. In addition, the authors consider the possible return of the draft.

In Chapter 33, K. Hartley examines the defense industrial base, procurement practices, and industrial policies in light of developments since the end of the Cold War. Mergers have significantly reduced competition and have left just one or two domestic producers for some large defense systems. To take advantage of economies of scale during an era of smaller production runs, some governments (e.g., the United States) encouraged these mergers. There are challenges and costs in maintaining a defense industrial base during peaks and troughs in orders, as well as issues in maintaining competition for domestic procurement. Topics addressed include military outsourcing, the performance of joint ventures, the internal efficiency in the Armed Forces, and the profitability of defense industries. A globalized world with increased international competition has profound implications for procurement practices and the future of defense firms. Hartley indicates how defense industries are adjusting to globalization, new technologies, and new threats.

Chapter 34 (M. Brzoska) analyzes conversion (i.e., the switch of inputs from defense to civilian production) during the post-Cold War era, as the share of GDP devoted to defense plunged in most countries. Brzoska begins with a careful analysis of the meaning of conversion and the many different ways that conversion and its "success" can be measured. Although the author's prime focus is on the general concept of conversion and its measurement during the last decade, he refers to numerous case studies to support his arguments. In places, he presents enlightening comparisons and contrasts in conversion experience between countries in the West and the East. Government policies for fostering conversion are also highlighted and evaluated. Conversion involves reallocation of lands, labor, research capacity, and capital – each of which has its unique issues. The chapter also assesses the impact and implications of conversion for both the Armed Forces and defense industries.

In Chapter 35, C.H. Anderton and J.R. Carter provide a survey of peace economics that identify seminal and current contributions. The authors begin by distinguishing between defense economics and peace economics in terms of topics and orientation. Next, they examine data sources on conflict that have greatly fostered econometric studies of civil wars, inter-state wars, and nonconventional conflict (e.g., terrorism). These data are used by the authors to show recent trends in conflict. A sizable portion of the chapter is devoted to an analysis of the seminal work of arms rivalry by Richardson (1960), Lanchester (1916), and Intriligator (1975). Many fascinating extensions of these models are displayed. In the latter portion of the chapter, the authors consider models that account for appropriation and exchange – standard economic models focus on exchange and production, and ignore appropriation. Finally, the authors review experiments in peace economics dating back to the 1950s.

5. Concluding remarks

As with Volume 1, it is our intention that Volume 2 of this *Handbook* will serve as a reference source, a teaching tool, and a stimulant for future research. The intended audience includes academics, researchers, and graduate students in economics, political science, and military sciences. The book should also interest defense policymakers in the Armed Forces, national defense ministries, Department of Homeland Security, NATO, the EU, and the United Nations; staff and decision makers in defense industries; and personnel in peace organizations.

The military downsizing set in motion at the end of the Cold War is still playing itself out. Hence, further research is needed on changing manpower needs and the restructuring of the defense industry. Weapon proliferation continues to present a difficult collective action problem that must be addressed. Globalization will further change business practices which will affect defense industries. Although many national defense markets are highly protected, there will continue to be barriers to the creation of an open and global defense market (e.g., EU nations protect their national defense industries through the application of Article 296). In defense procurement, preferential purchasing and tariff protection represent government-created market failures. Finally, asymmetric warfare and the rising threat of terrorism present countries with force restructuring issues that have not been adequately handled. Today's threats require radical change and departures from traditional methods of warfare. Such transformations will be difficult and costly.

References

Brito, D.L., Intriligator, M.D. (1995). "Arms races and proliferation". In: Hartley, K., Sandler, T. (Eds.), Handbook of Defense Economics, vol. 1. North-Holland, Amsterdam, pp. 109–164.

Collier, P., Elliott, V.L., Hegre, H., Hoeffler, A., Reynal-Querol, M., Sambanis, N. (2003). Breaking the Conflict Trap: Civil War and Development Policy. World Bank and Oxford University Press, Washington, DC.

Enders, W., Sandler, T. (2006). The Political Economy of Terrorism. Cambridge University Press, Cambridge.

Gray, C.S. (2004). The Sheriff: America's Defense of the New World Order. University Press of Kentucky, Lexington, KY.

Hartley, K., Sandler, T. (2003). "The future of defense firm". Kyklos 56, 361–380.

Hirshleifer, J. (1991). "The paradox of power". Economics and Politics 3, 177–200.

Intriligator, M.D. (1975). "Strategic considerations in the Richardson model of arms races". Journal of Political Economy 83, 339–353.

Lanchester, F. (1916). Aircraft in Warfare, the Dawn of the Fourth Arm. Constable, London.

McNamara, R.S. (1992). "The post-Cold War world: Implication for military expenditure". In: World Bank (Ed.), Proceedings of the World Bank Annual Conference on Development Economics 1991. World Bank, Washington, DC, pp. 95–125.

Murdoch, J.C., Sandler, T. (2002). "Economic growth, civil wars and spatial spillovers". Journal of Conflict Resolution 46, 91–110.

Murdoch, J.C., Sandler, T. (2004). "Civil wars and economic growth: Spatial dispersion". American Journal of Political Science 48, 137–150.

NATO (2000). Financial and economic data relating to NATO defence. NATO Press Release M- DPC-2 (2000) 107. NATO headquarters, Brussels, Belgium.

NATO (2005). NATO–Russia compendium of financial and economic data relating to defence. NATO Press Release (2005) 161. NATO headquarters, Brussels, Belgium.

Richardson, L.F. (1960). Arms and Insecurity: A Mathematical Study of the Causes and Origins of War. Homewood, Pittsburgh.

Sandler, T., Hartley, K. (Eds.) (2003). The Economics of Conflict, vols. I–III. Elgar, Cheltenham, UK.

Chapter 21

ECONOMICS OF DEFENSE IN A GLOBALIZED WORLD

MARTIN C. MCGUIRE[*,1]

Department of Economics, University of California-Irvine, Irvine, CA 92697, USA
e-mail: mcmcguir@uci.edu

Contents

Abstract	624
Keywords	624
1. Overview	625
1.1. Defense economics: The agenda – Update on a field in transition	625
1.2. Economics as the source of conflict	626
1.3. Political economy – international public choice: Fight and grab or work and trade	626
1.4. Governance and economic calculus of war	627
1.5. Core economics of resource allocation remains central	630
2. World trends and big picture security themes	630
2.1. Technology driven globalization: A source of new threats, risks, opportunities, and resources	631
2.2. Great world prosperity: Greater costs and benefits of conflict	631
2.3. Governments paradoxically overshadowed	633
2.4. US hegemony: A fading monopoly	634
2.4.1. US privileged economic and security stature dissolving	634
2.4.2. Debt and world influence	634
2.5. A new frequency distribution of violence/conflict	635
2.6. Whither defense? Warring alliance blocks? Criminal disorder? Partitioned global security?	637
3. Defense: A normative problem in economics	638
4. New century salients in defense economics	639
4.1. Carry-over or legacy issues from Cold War	639
4.2. Security issues of traditional geopolitical origin: China	639
4.3. Culture driven conflicts	640
4.4. Defense and the media	640
4.5. Moral-political limits on the military instrument	641
5. Tasks for defense economics: Two special and timely topics	641
5.1. Rogue states, WMD, and failed states: Economic analyses of predation and tyranny	641

[*] I thank Keith Hartley and Todd Sandler for insightful criticisms and suggestions.
[1] Heinz Professor for Economics of Global Peace and Security.

Handbook of Defense Economics, Volume 2
Edited by Todd Sandler and Keith Hartley
© 2007 Elsevier B.V. *All rights reserved*
DOI: 10.1016/S1574-0013(06)02021-7

    5.2. New dimensions of alliance cooperation   642
6. Some examples of economic method applied to defense   643
7. Conclusions: Future direction of defense economics   645
References   646

Abstract

In a world continuously beset by conflict and violence, the positive study of international security and defense has developed rapidly over the past decade as a cohesive discipline within economics. Part of the cause for this trend is the revolutionary effects of globalization and its new challenges to world security and stability. The challenges to security now come from new sources; they threaten new dangers, and require new instruments and concepts from us. The field of play for defense economics has thus greatly increased, but the opportunity to exploit new insights from throughout economics grown accordingly.

This essay aspires to show how the recent developments in models of international political economy relate to study of this phenomenal evolution of the world's strategic situation and challenges to its safety. Here I give one perspective on the contributions expected of defense economics in a globalized world where old patterns of thinking risk obsolescence. Emphasis is focused on (a) how the field is changing, and the relation between new security challenges and required new analytic approaches, (b) how developing ideas about conflict, predation and governance have entered into and greatly influenced defense economics, and (c) how this raises questions over what should be retained from study of earlier eras and what discarded.

Keywords

alliances, conflict, debt, deterrence, globalization, governance, risk, threat

JEL classification: D72, D74, H56, H87

1. Overview

1.1. Defense economics: The agenda – Update on a field in transition

As most agree, getting the question right is more important than providing precise answers. A-propos of this aphorism defense economics has departed an era when the questions seemed clear, to a new phase where defining the issue itself is central. Whereas in Cold War days defense economics involved the study of how to achieve pretty clearly pre-defined given objectives, it now is much more engaged in helping to define the new objective itself. At the publication of Volume 1 of this *Handbook* ten years ago, soon after the collapse of the USSR, the degree of change required in policies, forces, and other instruments of defense was yet to be recognized. We now see that changes in the sources, structure and diversity of the world's security problem are great indeed, challenging our ability to refocus and to identify the instruments required to combat the new challenges and to re-shape our way of thinking about them. Thus economics, as the study of how agents do and should react to incentives, to resource scarcities, to information and to each other has become of relevance not only in the management of world security but also in its definition. A perusal of the foci of the chapters to follow attests to the diversity of problems that the scholarly and analytic community must address to shape a new definition of security and conflict management.

Defense economics can no longer represent merely effective self-serving defense resource allocations by Western countries. This is partly as a consequence of the terror attacks of September 11, 2001. Deeper than this though we can now see that the end of the Cold War marks a tectonic change: after centuries, the territorial security-status of European countries seems basically settled. But this is not the case for the other parts of the globe, from Taiwan south and west to the steppes of Asia and so on. This tells me that we should regard the present period of solitary US power and minimal overt great power conflict as one of transition, to some new phase where new powers will struggle over resources and spheres of influence and territory. A major task, therefore, for a volume such as this is to identify the economic and strategic incentives by which rational calculation may lead to new fault lines in security of countries and their defense.

The problem overlaps two rather distinct though interconnected time frames: for the medium term while the US continues to have unquestionably unique power, issues such as: containment of terrorism, dealing with rogue states, controlling weapons of mass destruction, and reform of failed states predominate. But for the longer term, transition to a new multi-polar power configuration and shared or partitioned spheres of influence is probable, and how to manage the transition across time frames without major war is preeminent. For the long run, neither the US alone nor the West in aggregate will retain a monopoly of force as today; relative economic dynamics will not permit this. But for the interim, before zones of supremacy or spheres of influence are re-established, US security, by default, has become inherently global. And precisely because this global monopoly permits US interventionism in all manner of internal conflicts and civil strife it becomes incumbent on defense economics to help identify when intervention is wise –

to develop criteria for when positive involvement is good. This is not made easier at all by the fact that Cold War arsenals, logistics and thought processes are uniquely unqualified to address the new exigencies, including especially to know when to refrain from intervention.

For the moment in this transitional world the front rank security issues are neither primarily presented nor resolved by large scale force-on-force military component of defense. But those days may well return. Thus the requirements for defense paradoxically have expanded compared to Cold War requirements. In this epoch where the US security commitment and responsibility is worldwide, it is even more necessary to understand the motives and incentives of threatening adversaries, troublemakers, wobbly allies, and false friends. Defense economics with its emphasis on incentives is thus more central than ever. A security challenge notably amenable to economic analysis, concerns how to evolve relationships of trust with others and how to merit trust from others.

1.2. Economics as the source of conflict

For recognizing/understanding the sources of conflict both on the immediate horizon and over the longer sweep of the future, economics is utterly crucial. Territorial issues have receded, at least temporarily, and economic issues have replaced them. Examples of these economic sources include:
- binding resources scarcities brought on by surges in global demand;
- incidence, restriction, and repair of environmental degradation and health;
- import/export monopoly and monopsony injustices;
- migrations of persons and capital with ensuing redistribution of rents;
- International monetary system, capital markets, and transfers of risks.

Here the role of defense economics is to understand how these trends and structures lead to international conflict and military insecurity. Consider the health example. The role of defense in this case is not to cure or treat disease, but it can be to control national borders when international population movements, ignited by health hazards require more control by force than police can provide. Or as a second example take the case of monetary instability and wealth transfer as causes of power redistribution and security conflict.

1.3. Political economy – international public choice: Fight and grab or work and trade

The new challenges to world security, thus, have their roots in political economy of our 21st century world. These roots include the deepening inequality and elevated volatility/turbulence of the world economy, the evolving vagaries for creation of surplus rents within societies and their capture by privileged elites vs. more equitable distribution among the citizenry. Consequently, to become more deeply involved in the definition of international security, economics of defense must be related much more intimately with political economy and international public choice. Ignorance of the structure and dynamics of autocratic societies for instance may lead to ineffective policy and self-defeating decisions, e.g., the invasion of Iraq, 2003 and its aftermath. Contemporary challenges to peace and those just over the horizon – more convoluted than for the old NATO–Warsaw Pact paradigm – are tightly bound up with globalization and the inter-penetrations of commerce-culture-security. Examples abound, including the inter-dependence of finance, trade, political development and strategic salience that is the Taiwan–China tangle.

Serendipitously, building on the work of pioneers [Boulding (1962), Grossman (2002), Grossman and Kim (1996), Grossman and Mendoza (2004), Hirshleifer (1988, 1989, 1994, 2001), Olson and Zeckhauser (1966), Polachek (1980), Sandler (2000), Schelling (1960, 1966, 1967), and Tullock (1974)] the economics of conflictual systems has advanced substantially in the past decade. The challenge now to defense economics is to exploit these conceptual advances – how to make them practical in a policy context. For example consider the voluntary public good model. How practically can we help induce the diverse bureaucracies of the world to overcome tendencies to free ride, not merely in established groups but with respect to incentives to form security promoting clubs in the first place? Could this be achieved by crafting Stackelberg-strategies, or by bundling? Practical analysis is needed for how to achieve this in many realms: finance, environment, population migrations, disease control, terror, etc.

Or as another example: economists agree that property right protection is essential to growth and success of a society while corruption undermines necessary legitimacy and trust [Tullock (1974), Konrad and Skaperdas (2005), Olson (1981), McGuire and Olson (1996), Tanzi (1998)]. So how can defense allocations and policies of emerging countries cultivate governance of the *right quality*, supporting property protection with required/sufficient force without spilling over into corruption and confiscation? Performance on this dimension influences our defense directly (as, say, in Central America) and indirectly via its impact on international stability generally.

1.4. Governance and economic calculus of war

But possibly the foremost example of how the economic study of defense should include political economy concerns the impact of the system of governance itself upon so many defense issues. One entry point for the political economy of war and defense should be Immanuel Kant (1795) for his introduction of the notion of a positive connection between the institutions of governance – specifically democratic representative institutions – and incentives for peace. Although many following Kant have endorsed this idea, it has been the role of economists to derive the connection between quantitative differences in the incidence of costs and benefits of war and the governance systems of adversarial parties. The recognition of this as an economic phenomenon may first be due to Angell (1910) for the idea that in a perfect consensual and representative democracy all the citizens share in the country's costs of war and all of them share in its benefits. Pursuing this logic, unanimous consensual democracies should avoid those wars where the country loses on balance, since if the country loses every citizen loses, and war-decisions are made by the citizens [Anderton (1999), Thompson (1974), Thompson and Hickson (2001)]. This assumedly would include (a) avoiding wars that would be lost, *and* (b) those that it is not worth winning even though winnable [McGuire (2002)]. On the other hand, for the polar opposite unrepresentative society an autocrat pays nothing (or only a small fraction) of the costs of a war if he wins it and reaps all the benefits, so an autocrat is more likely to enter wars that it will win even those that are "unprofitable" for "his" society as a whole. And what of wars he could lose? Although the autocrat may lose everything, his country's loss is much greater. This idea is summarized in Table 1 where costs and benefits are assigned.

Table 1

System of governance: Determines definition of costs and benefits	War outcome	
	Win	Lose
Monolithic autocracy		
Autocrat's costs	0	0
Autocrat's gain	R_F	$-R_H$
Unanimous consensual democracy		
Society's costs	C	C
Society's benefit	0^*	$-R_H$

C = home country's social costs of war. R_F = surplus rent autocrat acquires from defeated foreigners. R_H = surplus rent that autocrat collects from his domestic subjects. He foregoes this amount in the event of a loss. I assume this to be the same as the amount a winner would extract from the home democratic society after conquest.

*How much a consensual democracy benefits from winning a war could be some positive amount, other than the prevention of the loss from losing should some synergism exist between winning a war and internal productivity following merger or trade.

The entries of Table 1 represent only one side in a quarrel, and the table assumes without evidence that a democracy would not exercise its claim to booty if it wins. But even though other tableaux may reflect other assumptions and even though this table may be incomplete it raises a rich menu of research issues germane to defense economics. For example:

- Is a potential war situation in the aggregate (among all affected parties and interests) zero sum or positive sum? The answer to this will depend on which parties and interests are recognized when counting values – entire societies, two autocrats, elites and proletariat?
- For comparing the incentives for cooperative, Pareto optimal seeking, and war averting resolutions with those for non-cooperative more violent behaviors, what is the role of alliances, information, and commitment in conditioning incentives on opposing sides to fight or negotiate?
- Can outside intervention (e.g., side payments) influence/reverse incentives for fighting, and if so does autocratic or democratic organization favor resolution in this manner?

- Do geographical and/or inter-temporal patterns of benefits/cost make committed agreement to work-invest-produce-and-trade hard to sustain, and do such incentives vary systematically with the style of governance?

This is only a short list, but the point is that the defense economics research agenda should extend to the effects of *institutions* and their organization on peace and war fighting. Fortunately many of these questions are the focus of our thriving literature on the new institutional economics [e.g., Thompson and Hickson (2001)] and economic logic of political predation [Anderton (2000), Grossman and Kim (1996), Skaperdas (1992), Skaperdas and Syropoulos (2002)]. But Kant's idea that rent redistribution underlies all rational calculation of war is not always affirmed by modern analysis. His principles relate closely to similar concepts in modern public economics, and those suggest that an economic approach to war should distinguish wars as instruments of redistribution among states and as instruments of redistribution within states. Those schooled in the mentality of WWII and the Cold War have often tended to think of wars as patriotic, or public good wars supported voluntarily by an entire nation, and representing the will or welfare of its entire people. For this category everyone benefits or possibly everyone avoids a loss (of being conquered), and costs are broadly shared in some reasonable and justifiable fashion. Such opinion of war obviously no longer dominates the consensus within Western societies but it could return and impact war calculus in the future.

A second category of war is founded on redistribution within adversaries – a war for the private benefit of some privileged subgroup in the country, to its rulers (and their support) or opposing insurgents as foreshadowed by Eisenhower's "military industrial complex". A conviction that US defense initiatives of the past fifty years has these as sources represents a good fraction of current opinion. Or in the inverse of this Orwellian case, suppressed factions may foment wars hoping that their rulers will be defeated and overturned, such being the assumption behind the idea that modern terrorism is really a type of civil war that partisans can only pursue outside of their country's borders. While it risks politicizing defense economics – undesirable to be sure – a careful identification of the costs and benefits of war within countries and its incidence should help to identify motives and thus clarify the true nature of terrorism and insurrection especially in African and Muslim worlds.

This way of looking at international conflict has proven of increasingly insightful over the past couple of decades, as it relates to when wars may be rational for both parties, and not the result of some sort of mistake. It also can show how alternatives of acquiring the capability short of actual resort to arms may produce outcomes that are Pareto superior. In fact such results show that bilateral, "public good", democratic wars are quite possible as an expression of non-cooperative equilibrium pursued to resolve information deficits, or because binding future bargains cannot be struck due to transaction costs or various commitment problems [Garfinkel and Skaperdas (2000), Garfinkel (2004)]. Such studies show for example, that trade concessions, economic assistance, offer of asylum or other instruments will have different impacts depending on the economic structure of the conflict. They show and the consensus opinion among economists trained in Public Choice reflects that conflict, war, and governance contain an intertwined economic structure. These are in the vanguard of defense economics as it will develop to incorporate and exploit the insights of political economy and public choice.

1.5. Core economics of resource allocation remains central

While augmenting the field of defense economics in this fashion and incorporating new insights from political economy of institutions it is well to remind ourselves again of what the ECONOMIC approach uniquely brings to the problem. One wants to take care not to neglect the core of the subject – not to abandon the established framework of defense economics. Without the anchor of resource scarcity, "utility" or net benefit maximization, individual interactions (whether competitive or strategic), information and rational incentives, the jumble of problems would cast us intellectually adrift. Our task – advanced by the essays in this book – is to adapt the tools and ideas created in an earlier and simpler environment to the more complex world of contemporary insecurity not to throw them out. Any contributions we can make to understanding defense and security whether national or global will involve application of these principles:

- First and above all, even defense is ruled by the iron law of scarcity of resources, and even for the "richest" group of countries. "Pay any price, bear any burden" will not suffice to judge how much defense really is too much [Enthoven and Smith (1971)].
- Second, defense or security economics as a normative project will always include a concern for *efficiency* and the many attendant conceptual, measurement, and implementation questions surrounding it.
- Third, economics of defense must be always alert to the role of incentives, our own, an ally's, an adversary's – and to the possibilities of influencing those incentives for our long run benefit. A special instance of incentives especially relevant to security and defense is the interdependence among own and others actions in small interacting groups as distinct from the conventional large competitive markets.

2. World trends and big picture security themes

The end of the Cold War marks more than the terminus of an historic confrontation. As the downfall of the Iron Curtain dissolved our adversarial presuppositions, the parameters that define where national security terminates have dissolved and muddied. And on the heels of the Cold War comes the phenomenon of globalization. The new environment thus consists of a mix of these two factors. A result has been painful and groping efforts at reorganization by the national defense establishments worldwide, the temporary resignation by most countries to a world of a solitary superpower, and jarring adjustments demanded of armed forces and defense industries alike. In particular, the need for at the ready *standby* Warriors has evolved to a need for *on-the-job* Peacekeepers. The adjustments of defense industries have also been dramatic with the relentless pressures are to down-size, discard, and replace formerly critical weapons systems, as well as the pressures to exploit new technologies created by the modern digital revolution. Associated with the shift to peacekeepers has been a shift in the distribution of the security threat. Rather than one quite improbable but overwhelming threat of unspeakable catastrophe, we face much higher chances of unwelcome but still qualitatively lesser, repetitive, or continuing violence. The US has become increasingly involved in undertaking actual operations on an ongoing basis rather than holding back all out retaliatory forces on the stand-by and hoping never to use their capabilities. The proliferation of regional and sub-regional conflicts that can require peacekeeping action seems a new, if regrettable, fixture of defense most unlikely to subside or even attenuate in the foreseeable future or until once again the world is partitioned into antagonistic blocks. Here I merely sketch out selected parameters that I think will characterize this evolving conflict-security environment and condition any economic analysis of it.

2.1. Technology driven globalization: A source of new threats, risks, opportunities, and resources

Swift changes in technology, culture, and the devolution of power, have fed new needs for security while simultaneously provided new resources for defense. But significantly these new factors can restrict the tools we have to employ against new threats and/or the uses to which old tools can be put. An example is the inability to construct a policy of "retaliation". I am struck by the difference in defense response from the 1960s where the US announced it would blatantly slaughter about 200 million innocent civilians if it were attacked by Cuba, while official announcements of punitive retaliation after September 11, 2001 were low keyed at most. Although military action was taken against the Taliban after September 11, its purpose seems to have been preventive rather than a promise of future punitive retribution for any future attacks. At the time, absence of a pre-announced policy of retaliation is not surprising – a policy that would harm terrorists in terms they understand. It is noteworthy though that even today since it seems so very difficult to know in advance who would be responsible for future attack or to hold a governmental or quasi-government entity responsible in advance, we continue to have no policy of retribution and no public debate on its merits. That such a policy by Israel against terror bombers seems to have been ineffective may explain why the US has none.

2.2. Great world prosperity: Greater costs and benefits of conflict

Within this new threat environment, it is useful to remind ourselves that the lives of a good majority of humanity have become more secure and richer over the past few decades where the green revolution and wide spread conquest of primary disease have benefited billions. How this affects the incentive to fight/thieve vs. produce/trade is at once highly relevant and hard to judge.

Globalization has made us all richer but more vulnerable to interruption by attack. By expanding the scale of production and exchange and communications the need for greater insurance, mutual protection, and defense has increased. Thus, a requirement has arisen for conflict management institutions on a grander scale. In the same vein, communication and targeting advances have made precise wars more possible, but under the watchful and distorting eye of the media. Other vulnerabilities point especially to Internet dependence or international indebtedness as a reflection of peacetime prosperity but an albatross for nations who might require outside financial support in emergencies. Or consider the obvious benefits of migration as a source of labor and manning for armed forces but co-mingled with the concomitant costs of security vulnerability. The upshot of these effects, I believe, is that net opportunity costs of conflict across countries are greater now, even as within some countries these net costs have diminished for many groups. I say this because on average productivity has increased so much relative to the payoff from war-theft, that returns to work under peaceful circumstances seems to have far outpaced returns from fighting, conquest, and oppression. The high productivity and growth of modern tech driven society is simply unobtainable from suppressed or enslaved populations.

These trends and processes – with sources in both technological change and globalization – have several implications for defense and the design of forces. (1) They have invoked changes in the relative costs to an enemy of imposing damages vs. the damage imposed or of our costs of deterring, of defending, and of defeating, or recovering from destruction. Therefore, these trends induce changes in cost effective methods available to us for combating them. For example, at the scale of terrorism we have hitherto experienced, a dollar's worth of damage can be imposed by the enemy at a cost to him of very much less than one dollar (though this may well change at greater scales). And to defeat or defend against one dollar's worth of damage may require more than one dollar of our expenditures, making such defense pointless, and stimulating needs for other methods of dissuasion such as deterrence, retribution and punishment. (2) Analysis and clarification of these impacts of globalization should surely be a major program for defense economics. It would seem for instance that the cost to terrorists is vastly less even relative to their limited resource levels, than our costs of defense. (3) How has globalization influenced the relative cost effectiveness of protection, retribution, insurance, etc.? That is, how do our diverse options to combat terror compare on a cost effectiveness basis? (4) The same question arises for evaluating protection against conventional threats from conventional states such as how to share costs and missions between Japan and the US for combined security of Japan–China–US – it being understood that the *defensive* security of China is in the interest of all three.

The above trends also have caused lightening dispersal of information, rumor, hope, fear, with ensuing challenges to government's media management (e.g., China and SARS), to such a degree that the role of the media in national and international security deserves to be a new study area, included under intelligence. Thus might one hope to avoid domino effects, such as preceded WWI. Co-mingled with revolutions in cultural attitudes, the modern avalanche of information has fed a vast media machine that limits governmental action, provokes fear, and may inflame hatreds – all told, troubling issues of instability. A clear implication for defense studies in this environment is that the government function of understanding and then leading public opinion has grown immensely. So again, analysis of the intelligence and public opinion leading agencies of governments has become much more important and a proper focus for defense economics. And when success requires steady enduring commitment from elites and the public at large, a decline in the power of governments if it extends to incompetence in leadership and persuasion has a special even ominous impact.

2.3. Governments paradoxically overshadowed

All of these developments imply significant new responsibilities for individual governments and for multi government organizations, and therefore needs for new effective power at diverse strata of enforcement and coordination. But ironically, the powers of governments have been subject to challenge and dilution by the very same forces. Combined with gigantic changes in technology and culture, globalization has modified the roles of borders among countries, and other groups. Borders have become porous to people, commercial goods and services, information, money, weapons, laws and to ideas. This aspect of globalization has put great pressure on governments, raising demands for performance by way of relief from economic and security impacts, but undermining the powers of government at the same time. Border and institutional porosity, for example, undermines government power to control terrorist finance. Government at all levels must have resources and power to tax. But the multi-national corporation and ease of population movement and communication reduce governments' powers to capture the resources, by taxes or conscription necessary to fight. Such shifting foundations of security have yielded a dilution of government ability to manage global dangers. Because of the emergence of so many alternative foci of organized power (such as the modern multinational corporation, Internet finance, the modern subversive interest group) it has become inherently more difficult to control and direct resources, and to control information, opinion, movements of people, and how groups are organized. Paradoxically then, governments enjoy unprecedented technological tools and may have more raw power in some sense but less control over events. Globalization, it seems, has induced new limits on power to control from the center, even though governance is central to conflict management.

But this genre of problem is not new to economists. The economic theory of clubs – and of nation-states as a particular form of club – has always seen a need to balance scale economies in private sector (and therefore the required reach of private regulation by collective authority) with diseconomies of scale in the governance mechanism itself Olson (1969). Thus, one way to conceive the multi-national governance problem is that of a mismatch between optimal scales of public and private organization between regulator and regulated [Alesina and Spolaore (1997, 2003)].

2.4. US hegemony: A fading monopoly

2.4.1. US privileged economic and security stature dissolving

The present mode of unbounded hegemony is surely transitional. The future, I believe, will record that the past ten years and the coming 20 as transitional, toward a new era where centers of rival Asian populations, economic strengths, and strategic power set the parameters of global war and peace. The world seems happy to sit back, to free ride and to enjoy the benefits of American hegemony, while the US pays. But once unable to foot the bill, America will no longer call the shots. Basic cultural features also will strongly influence the situation for the next generation such as trends in military conscription vis-à-vis mercenary armed forces. Such factors as these make new strategic configurations especially hard to anticipate yet essential for deriving our near future strategic force requirements.

Some influences on the other hand seem quite predictable over the medium term, such as population trends and national/international debt. Similarly a highly fixed factor is geography and in particular the influence of the Pacific Ocean, on natural spheres of influence. Consequently, the heightened strategic significance of South America seems quite predictable and conflict over a Monroe Doctrine of the Pacific not implausible. Why South America? To capture the idea of a strategic shrinkage of the Pacific Ocean due to technologic change imagine that the longitudinal displacement from Shanghai to San Francisco were 30° rather than 120°. The strategic importance of South America then as a potential forward base against North America becomes rather clear.

2.4.2. Debt and world influence

Is it coincidental that for the past several years the entire US military budget has, in effect, been financed by borrowings from abroad? History shows unmistakably that borrowing capacity is necessary to conduct war [Neal (1994), Grossman and Han (1993)]. Contrasting this historical fact with Table 2 gives one good cause for discomfort. The table shows net US private and public holdings abroad minus foreign private and public

Table 2
International investment position of the United States (billions of USD) [US Department of Commerce (2005)]

	1976	1985	1995	2004
1. Net balance*	+165	+54	−458	−2,484
2. US-owned assets abroad	457	1,287	3,486	9,053
3. Foreign-owned assets in the US	292	1,233	3,945	11,537

*Row 1 = Row 2 minus Row 3 except for rounding error.

holdings of US assets real and financial. For some scenarios gross figures may be more representative of vulnerability or more telling as estimates of assets at risk.

However the current and astonishing debt position of the US plays out (it is projected to grow exponentially), its existence will greatly constrain US capabilities to confront new emerging great powers in the future. Although the international debt position may not much influence abilities vis-à-vis Iraq, once inflated by a magnitude of 2 or 3, it will most certainly influence capabilities vis-à-vis China sometime down the road. "It may be our debt but their problem," will not wash if in the future the US should require trillions to outgun a new adversary in an arms race. Whether or not the US can reverse its gigantic foreign indebtedness without destroying itself and others, the monstrous size of that debt suggests that the creation of financial alliances will assume far greater importance than ever. They will be at the heart of long run western strategy and thus of the future of defense economics – alliances first because management of such debt is indeed a collective international security problem, but also because more equal collaborative partnerships will surely replace US hegemony as it is weakened by its indebtedness. Without debt forgiveness foreigners will have to dramatically increase their imports from the US whereas they have spent a generation building capacity for sending exports to the US.

2.5. A new frequency distribution of violence/conflict

Compared to the Cold War another dramatic change that we face concerns the threat profile. I refer to the shift from rare catastrophic perils (i.e., super power nuclear war), to more probable, frequent, ongoing and less ultimate threats (e.g., suicide bombers, air hijackings, Internet "strikes"), most prominently terrorism from sub-state groups, and lesser threats. The military and readiness consequences of protracted violent *actualization* of conflict needs more serious exploration from the defense economics community. For example, the effect of this change on the comparative roles of regular forces, reserve and home guard forces, and police needs examination and the susceptibility it poses to manipulation from the media.

Rather than being ever-ready for a 500 division war in Europe we are going to have to actually conduct continuous ongoing peacekeeping. Rather than a 1/100% risk of 100 million casualties, we face actual losses ranging say from 1000 to 200,000 annually (depending on who is counted as a casualty of conflict, whether only soldiers or also bystanders and/or refugees also). Even as the source of disease or pandemic, these threats if realized are incomparably less grave than thermonuclear annihilation. That is, an important feature/principle of our new security environment is that our primary concern is no longer the prevention of one unspeakable cataclysm. This concern may resurface but for these transition years, world conflict (like in Iraq), will basically disrupt commerce and population movements, and may be characterized by engagements of a few hundred thousands of soldiers, guerillas, peacekeepers, partisans and criminals more or less continuously. Without wishing to minimize the tragedy, misery and unacceptability of such an equilibrium as a steady state, its difference from the threat of thermonuclear war deserves emphasis. Even recurring low yield nuclear events cannot be omitted from our menu of today's world threats. These would indeed set a new milestone in human catastrophe, and thus they demand determined opposition to nuclear proliferation. Nevertheless such threats are altogether different from the world of Herman Kahn (1959).

With a broader spectrum of threat we should reasonably expect a greater and more diverse need for defense resources. Because the American defense establishment is driven by estimates of threats, this may explain American "extravagance" in military spending. Yet, critics may come to conclude that the reason others can afford to spend so little, is precisely because the US spends so much. Irrespective of polemics, it is not extravagant to assume that the broader spectrum of defense need will create increasing resource pressures in future years, more than off-setting savings from Cold War programs.

Just to visualize this point suppose one could measure worldwide violent damages in dollars, and the likelihood of violence occurring. Then Figure 1 illustrates my meaning about a change in the distribution of threatened damage as between the Cold War compared to the present. Using number strictly to illustrate, the figure depicts the idea that during the Cold War we confronted a small chance of nuclear disaster (2%) and a strong chance (98%) of non-violent "peaceful" standoff. Contrasted with this in today's world the risks of protracted low intensity fighting are quite great (50% for illustration) and of minor nuclear event not at all negligible (10%) so that genuine non-violence is not very likely (40%). Our plans, readiness, and above all psychology are governed by this: whereas the confrontation with the Soviet Union threatened horrific damage with a very small likelihood, our present situation threatens much lesser damage with much much

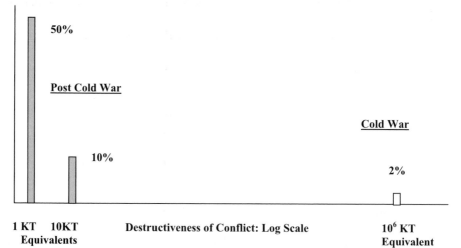

Figure 1.

greater probability. The diagram pictures low yield nuclear events or equivalent conventional shocks, disasters that in no way equate with the cataclysm of thermonuclear exchange that informed all defense policy for 40 years. Such a revision in the threat probability profile summarizes the transformation of our defense/security challenge from that focused over 1950–1990 on a pin-point catastrophe to its present multi-layered fuzzy unfocused fog.

But this raises a crucial issue for defense economics: does deterrence have a role in this new environment and if so what is it? Deterrence, dissuades enemy actions in a specific fashion: it works on an adversary's incentives and motives, *in advance* as it credibly promises punishment for transgression. But deterrence assumes that a responsible entity can be identified, and that it is some sort of government. Now for the distribution given by the diagram the challenge seems more and more to be to *defeat* attack, or limit its damage and disruption to our population and assets, knowing pretty well that some continuing and repeated losses are highly likely.

The option to punish the attacker (if we know who he is and he has not achieved sanctuary) may prove elusive. Of course it is axiomatic that we want to dissuade attack. If we face a rational and calculating enemy we may achieve dissuasion by preventing attack, defeating it, deflecting it. But should we try to deter attacks by promise of punishment?

Should deterrence in the future focus on a specific restricted range of contingencies or on the greater part of the spectrum of violent threat? This raises the interesting question whether strategic arms inventories should be multi-purpose. Or should future deterrence be designed for a more specific narrow range of contingencies – merely to combat the residual threat of nuclear attack from nuclear weapon armed states? (The Cold War nuclear arsenal was the ultimate single-purpose weapon, and deterred only a very narrow range of threats.) If the future of nuclear forces is for highly specific/single defense only then downsizing of Western nuclear forces will continue with capability diminishing possibly to levels only needed to dissuade other's attempts to leapfrog [Nalebuff (1988), O'Neill (2001)].

But then can an effective *non-nuclear* deterrent be created? It could easily turn out that the broader more diverse spectrum of threats as suggested by Figure 1 will require more diverse and specialized defense resources in response, and in the aggregate higher resource demands compared to Cold War. The only conclusion now sustainable seems to be that future deterrence will differ greatly from the Cold War variety.

2.6. Whither defense? Warring alliance blocks? Criminal disorder? Partitioned global security?

Aside from knowing that "splendid isolation" is no longer possible just how population, resources, technology, wealth and governance patterns will evolve to configure the international system over the next generation it is not for an economist to guess. Speculation that terrorism, or more generally finely disaggregated and uncoordinated population-to-population violence will displace nation-state confrontations seems to me to be a bad bet. What will endure though is the economic insight that this system is driven by incentives, incentives to collaborate or compete, build or destroy, produce or prey upon others. For the American, European, and Eastern friends the creation of new alliances to counterbalance the strength of emerging Asiatic powers will become crucial, with the purpose to make the preferred option for all sides to continue with investment, production, and trade rather than violent quarrel. Most intriguing is to speculate how the world's great powers in 50 years will manage the competition, and whether the vast space of the Pacific Ocean will serve as a barrier to Sino-American conflict, or instead be bridged by ever advancing technology.

3. Defense: A normative problem in economics

This lengthy and disperse list of changes to security makes it harder to think through and organize the normative defense problem in the aftermath of the Cold War, where all objectives are no longer merged into the goal of containment. But the goal still remains achievement of a good overall Pareto resolution of risk and conflict.

Even though the underlying environment has changed a lot, in a way the same normative imperatives endure. Assuming armed force can advance these objectives, the old imperatives include:

- Avoid/minimize global or great power war but prevail if it occurs.
- Avert/minimize nuclear war but suffer least and prevail in the event.
- Prevent/minimize nuclear, chemical, biologic terror, or other large ongoing criminal events.
- Facilitate peaceful political and economic development favorable to democratic ideals, and the interest of democratic countries.
- Manage/minimize "free lance" inter-state violence in its many forms.
- Suppress or diminish intra-state violence where desirable to do so.

The objective of "prevail" remains essential even if it places defense economics on one side of a quarrel. The normative problem of defense economics then involves (a) how to specify these (and others since the list is incomplete) goals, (b) how to measure and weight them, (c) recommend the extent to achieve them and (d) do this at least cost (comprehensively defined). At this level of national and international policy the academic community of defense experts remains on the fringes. Moreover, economics has competition: the entire discipline of international relations is devoted to understanding the deeper roots of conflict. Yet economics retains an important role even at this level of grand strategy – the role of identifying relationships among policies and objectives, and searching for efficient resolutions. A good example for economists here would be the work of Rosendorff and Sandler (2004) warning of unintended implications for terrorist recruitment of excessive counterterror pressure from the biggest most prominent target in the international system.

4. New century salients in defense economics

Hoping to proceed beyond generalities, I now attempt to itemize a list of concerns, more structured and based on the history of international conflict and violence, although the categories are by no means exhaustive.

4.1. Carry-over or legacy issues from Cold War

Certain aspects of the Cold War conflict continue as questions for analysis, and as threats that require vigilance and absorb resources. And some problems originate in the termination of the Cold War rather than as an extension or residual of it. An example of this would be non-proliferation security which has become more difficult to control than when the globe was divided into two rival camps. This is closely related to retirement and destruction of excess and dangerous warhead stockpiles of both the USSR and the US and thus prevention of unwanted ownership of them. A useful economic analysis in this area should calculate the benefits and costs of various components such Nunn-Lugar activities so as to prioritize among different programs. Such would include, for example, purchase then destruction of redundant Soviet nuclear weapons and delivery systems, subsidy of Russian nuclear weapons dismantlement projects, safeguarding of weapons useable atomic energy facilities and stockpiles, and collaborative programs for monitoring criminal activity connected to nuclear safety.

Another example concerns the status of inherited institutions, including notably the composition and function of NATO. The military function of NATO grows increasingly uncertain. Though the political, economic, and financial function remains of high consequence its role in international defense, including how to re-employ NATO for global security seems open. How can economic concepts of comparative advantage be useful to NATO/US coordination and collaboration in a new strategic era where their policies interests overlap less and less?

Still another example of legacy issues would be grand cost effectiveness analyses of US forward basing (itself essentially an artifact of the Cold War). This more generally would be an instance of the need for ongoing skeptical economic critique of capabilities requirements for conventional wars. Such continuing issues would center on the needs for continental ground war capabilities in Asian and Mid-East contexts, and the implied changes in force structures, especially programs for combined force integration.

4.2. Security issues of traditional geopolitical origin: China

As the large populous states of Asia develop, issues will arise as to whether international conflict over territory and spheres of influence will re-emerge as a norm – resource driven competitions created by changes in scarcities and other economic factors. These fault lines could soon displace terrorism as the issue of ongoing priority.

Here the major foreseeable security challenge that the world faces concerns coexistence between China and the US – so tightly bound to the western political net, to the US–Japan alliance, and to international trade and finance. Who can project whether paths of economic growth and technical progress will make Taiwan more or less critically important to China's vital strategic interests? China is a nuclear power, with growing strategic power and reach. In this realm, the old tension between deterrence and defense will reassert itself, and debates regarding nuclear war come up again. For Western interests a continued ability to deter and defeat nuclear attack will re-emerge. But this need and the implied requirement – to keep abreast along so many independent dimensions at once – may well increase the gigantic resource cost of maintaining a dominant defense capability. This burden on the US will eventually be unsustainable. Can it be shared among friendly powers? The answer boils down to an unaccustomed degree of power sharing by the US.

4.3. Culture driven conflicts

Worldwide Islamicist and psycho-terrorist threats come first to mind under this category [Huntington (1993)]. Can economics enhance our understanding of how to manage these conflicts, and especially of how to decide when entanglement is justified? The presumption should be for non-involvement by regular forces – a lesson to be learned from Iraq 2003. These conflicts place special demands on an extended role for unconventional forces, covert action, and intelligence – missions that segue into police and border security functions, enhancing the need for police, anti-narcotic, anti-terror skills/capabilities. Again such threats may burden free societies with new and onerous costs – costs measured in loss of privacy and free movement, empowerment of continuous surveillance mechanisms and a prolonged struggle in the shadows where economic analysis is needed for uncovering the full costs of protection and defense. Although economists have occasionally entered this milieu, [Nordhaus (2002)] more is needed.

4.4. Defense and the media

Ruled by the iron law of scarcity, governments require resources to provide defense. In a democratic decentralized economy this depends on government's abilities to tax and when necessary and possible to conscript. Complementary to this requirement in a modern society is government's need to influence or to mould public opinion to unify, rally support, and otherwise employ its favored advantage in scale of communications. This means that for Western style democracies the world media is both a resource for and a constraint on security. As an area for study, the field of "media and defense" deserves closer analysis: for media is often the source of demands for governments to take action, yet a restriction on its behavior. This interplay of constraint and instrument, I believe, will assume ever greater relevance. For example, the strength as well as the weakness of the North Korean dictatorship lies in the isolation of its supporting population. Break that communication monopoly and one will have gone a long way to break the grip of the tyrant.

4.5. Moral-political limits on the military instrument

A novel factor in such an inventory of emerging salients in defense economics concerns new limits on the use of the military. These have been created by education and globalization of culture. Events which generations ago would have provoked swift military response – including reprisal – do so no longer. Military responses have evolved to become more and more police-like, requiring specialized management. Consequently, the need for closer scrutiny of such questions as when does advance preparation for war provoke hostility, and when is payback counterproductive? [Rosendorff and Sandler (2004)]. A far more self-critical comparison of the carrot vs. the stick in applications of military force would seem to be needed.

5. Tasks for defense economics: Two special and timely topics

5.1. Rogue states, WMD, and failed states: Economic analyses of predation and tyranny

Where news reports often focus on gee-whiz technologies of WMD or disaster spectacles, economics focuses on the incentive driven behavior of those who threaten their use. Developing conflict theory puts at our disposal some clue as to how such behavior could vary as between alternative forms of governance (e.g., autocrats, oligarchies, representative governments, and non-governmental groups). Recent work on Hirshleifer's (1991) "paradox of power" should, for instance, shed light on how the structure *over time* of gains/losses from "fight", versus "produce" identifies levers for dealing with pariah states. With a better understanding of the incentives that operate we may be able to fashion better instruments to counter these threats.

An important application of conflict and property-right models should be to discern how much and what type of force must a well run government posses [e.g., Hegre and Sandler (2002)]. So-called failed states even with elements of tyranny may lack power to police their own populations which may diminish any ability to control extragovernmental violence originating within their boundaries. Some of these states have emerged in the fall-out from other battles: Cold War, WWI and II. What can our economic models of dictatorship, kleptocracy, and predation and of the incentive structures they embody yield in the way of useful policies for dealing with dictators and with failed states?

Economics has special contribution to make to analyses of rogue states which act outside the bounds of acceptable norms, trafficking in drugs, counterfeit currency, kidnapping foreigners or exploiting its own populations. Typically these will be states that can be influenced by economic incentives – economic carrots or sticks. Rewarding atrocious action with carrots runs the risk of stimulating more, or other copycats. Punishing the perpetrators can be agonizing because of the shield they create with their own people. How can we leapfrog and enlist support of dis-enfranchised oppressed within rogue states? All is not lost though; some rogue states have been restored (Cambodia, Libya, Viet Nam possibly). One hopes that governments can learn for the future from these lessons.

5.2. New dimensions of alliance cooperation

The rogue states example is also a development with particular relevance to new issues for alliance formation and governance because of the strong multifaceted temptation it offers for an alliance member to free ride. Covert cooperation with the pariah may be highly lucrative for private interests in an "ally", more than merely saving the costs of cooperative action which will often only accrue to a government from free riding. Building on seminal contributions [Sandler (1977)] and more recent ones [Sandler (1999), Sandler and Hartley (2001)] how can we economists help in the design of future alliance arrangements? Can our model for incentive mechanism design help? Bailey (2001) would say most definitely yes. Will the US lose the role of the unchallenged leader, or can we help in devising systems of shared governance? Creativity in building incentive structures to hold groups together should have an especially high payoff. New, single function alliance-like agreements may evolve among countries with rather little in common along the axis of defense. These include agreements concerning intelligence acquisition and sharing, financial security, corporate crime, narcotics control and human rights abuses, prisoner management, and world health, or space exploration to take a few examples. Consider the role of the International Energy Authority in oil stockpile releases following hurricane Katrina in 2005. Where economic alliances are successful, strategic conflicts may be more trustingly resolved. Alternatively, in the approaching era of return to multiple centers of power, benefits of economic cooperation could be a necessary cement to sustain military collaboration. Thus, from the viewpoint of defense economics, economic collaborations between countries and groups may generate crucial external economies along diverse dimensions; success along one dimension may presage a more formal alliance. The idea that alliance-generated common goods should be funded by contributions according to comparative advantage is heard often [McGuire (1990)]. If we write the standard pure public good model with i denoting countries, Y_i the endowed numeraire income, and C_i each country's contribution to the pure collective good, denoted by X then the alliance members' welfares U^i can be written:

$$U^i\left[(Y_i - C_i), X\left(\sum C_i\right)\right]. \tag{1}$$

And allowing for comparative advantage in different contributions changes this to:

$$U^i\left[(Y_i - C_i), X(C_1, C_2, C_i, \ldots, C_N)\right]. \tag{2}$$

Equation (2) simply represents the case of "non-summation" consumption–aggregation technology inaugurated by Hirshleifer's (1983) "weakest link", and "best shot", innovations and developed extensively in such textbooks as Cornes and Sandler (1996) or

Mueller (2003). Less standard but no less worth as a representative is the mirror image of comparative advantage in contribution, where common contributions governed by non summation aggregation generate different goods $X_i = f^i(C_1, C_2, C_i, \ldots, C_N)$ for different countries as in

$$U^i\big[(Y_i - C_i), f^i(C_1, C_2, C_i, \ldots, C_N)\big], \quad i = 1, \ldots, n. \tag{3}$$

As in the IEA case another good example of economic collaboration with strong externalities for security can be international risk management. This includes crafting insurance against supply disruptions – an especially good example which asks economics to incorporate its large corpus of knowledge about risk reduction, insurance, and risk sharing, into models of collective action. And here the dynamics and limits of groups that insure each other may be quite different than groups that improve their *common risk profile* [Ihori and McGuire (2006)]. More generally, the challenge for defense economics is to include the insights from public finance [Ihori (1996)], public choice and international relations to evolve a better understanding of the new century's groupings of states, including criteria for when to limit membership, or when to exclude some agents altogether. Examples include applying the theory of clubs, principal agent theory, theories of rent seeking behavior, as well as recent developments in risk analysis and insurance theory to interactions among states. Applications of Ehrlich and Becker's (1972) analysis of self-protection, self-insurance, and market insurance to alliance formation, allocative behavior, and stability would be especially timely [Ihori and McGuire (2006)].

6. Some examples of economic method applied to defense

Just as a decade (1955–1965) was required to work out our governing Cold War deterrent-defense strategy (in the final analysis successful), similarly, we have yet to form a comprehensive new strategy that incorporates (1) new constraints, resources, instruments, (2) new objectives attainable, and (3) new hazards and losses that we are willing to risk. Here, the relative isolation of academe from defense analysts is particularly unfortunate. The academic specialist's focus should be on how to bring the recent insights of research to bear on policy problems. There have indeed been significant advances in our understanding in may areas of economics of particular relevance to security studies. Many of these concern discovery of new structures of incentives, such as in the analysis of asymmetric information and its impact on markets. Other areas include developments in management of financial risk, and the entire new field of financial engineering, or advances in understanding the structure of incentives when agents are only partially, boundedly, rational. Yet another example is our improved grasp on the mixed structure of incentives as between productive trading activities and expropriating predating ones, together with deeper understandings of the interactions among wealth, security, and forms of governance. These should all serve better to illuminate such weighty questions as how to defang terrorists, how to induce local security collaboration from developing countries, how better to organize and interpret intelligence, or when to punish defection and when to bribe cooperation.

To be specific, consider the carrot vs. stick problem. We hear the terms often. Can economics help identify when a carrot or a stick is more effective? We should try to shed some light. Charles Wolfe Jr. has suggested to me that there is a *prima facie* assumption against carrots and in favor of sticks! If an agent's utility $U(X)$ improves with his wealth X at a diminishing rate, then increasing his wealth by $\$\Delta$ as a promise or a reward should have less effect than decreasing his wealth by the same amount $-\$\Delta$ as a threat or punishment. With $U'' < 0$ if the costs *to "us"* of $+\Delta$ and $-\Delta$ are equal, we achieve less influence with the carrot than with the stick. This of course is just the beginning because the cost to us may not be the same and the simple $U(X)$ formulation may need to further distinguish gainers-from-the-carrot from losers-from-the-stick. Rewards vs. punishments may impact different agents in that country whose behavior we desire to influence, and different agents will have different responsiveness to incentives. So one should not favor punishment over bribery too swiftly. Nevertheless this suggests comparisons of carrot and stick instruments as a useful project for defense economics. Moreover, in principal agent analysis we have a ready made structure for thinking of this problem.

As another example consider this defense economic approach to homeland security, structurally having some similarity to defense against nuclear attack. One often hears as a counsel of pessimism that for protection against terror attacks we cannot protect everything, or that terrorists will simply strike targets that we have not protected. Historically, once standard analytic techniques of defense economics [e.g., McGuire (2004)] actually have a lot to contribute to dealing with such problems. To illustrate how to mine solutions to earlier problems for insight into current issues, let us focus for concreteness on protection of a country's transportation net. Any dispersed infrastructure system will serve just as well for illustration.

A defender's, π's, problem of protecting (i.e., defeating, not deterring, or punishing) his rail and air infrastructure against terrorist or other enemy, γ's, attack. Table 3 shows damages depending on what is attacked and what is defended. Only "pure" concentrated allocations are shown to simplify the illustration.

Table 3

$L_{JK}^{\pi} = \pi$'s loss when π defends target J and γ attacks target K		Attacker(s) $= \gamma$	
		Attackers budget $= M^{\gamma}$	
Defender $= \pi$		$K = 100\%$ Air	$K = 100\%$ Rail
Defender's budget $= M^{\pi}$	$J = 100\%$ Airport/plane protection	L_{AA}^{π}	L_{AR}^{π}
	$J = 100\%$ Railway protection	L_{RA}^{π}	L_{RR}^{π}

The entries L^{π}_{JK}, J, K = Air or Rail, depend not only on the technical factors and relative costs mentioned but also on resource availabilities or budgets. An important economic issue, therefore, concerns how the defenders should allocate a budget of M^{π} dollars. (If γ were an organized society with its own infrastructure so that in-kind retaliation was a possibility then similar matrix could be obtained for γ as defender and π as attacker, but that is unlikely in the context of terror threats.)

The analytics of this problem as a game are available in an extensive literature originating in the early days of the Cold War MAD [Everett (1963), Pugh (1964)], with solutions depending on information distribution and timing, move sequence, etc. In addition to providing solutions to the allocation problem, the set-up raises important questions about how to defend, answers to which are highly context dependent. For example: are the defender's losses just the negative of the attacker's gains (consider the London bombings of 2005)? The answer is "probably not" in the current context. Would attacker and defender agree on the symbolic value (lost or protected) of some special targets (World Trade Center)? Could it be wiser for the defender to create costs for the attacker by making certain of the special targets more expensive to attack by imposing costs along another dimension such as promised retaliation against "his" village [Schelling (1967)]? Must an attacker have the last move, and if so how can a defender utilize this fact? How should the defender weigh losses L against budget costs (to defeat a 5% risk of loss of $200 Bil, how much is it rational for a society to spend?)? How does the problem change if the attacker is irrational/random? While answers to such questions may vary dramatically the issues they raise recur in any application of game theory to conflict.

This is just one instance of the fact that there is a large knowledge base available to proceed with a reasonable analysis of homeland security and defense against terror – technical, economic, demographic, and strategic information [e.g., Enders and Sandler (1999, 2004)]. As this information is assembled it will become clearer how and what it is efficient to protect. Defense economics has much to contribute to such analysis, including the insight that simply because protection cannot be perfect is no reason to neglect it.

7. Conclusions: Future direction of defense economics

As I hope this essay makes clear, "defense economics" is vital and evolving. But it differs markedly from those other fields in economics that one might denominate as "pure" – like micro theory, or public finance, or international trade – in two important respects.

First, its object of study is strongly conditioned by events outside the discipline itself. Major developments in the economics of international trade, for example have originated from economic ideas about oligopoly inherent to economics itself. But challenges to defense economics have originated significantly from external events, such as the loss in Viet Nam, the End of the Cold War, or the attacks of September 11, 2001.

Second, economics makes a vital contribution to defense, but is not the decisive intellectual player. Defense, security, war, and peace are not the domain of economics in the manner that monetary or trade policy is. To the contrary, international relations and political science form the core of defense study. In the same way, economics is not the core of a nation's health systems delivery; medicine is.

So in a sense, the issues and problems for defense economics are not of its own internal evolving choice, but are given to it; the object of study shifts around. Nevertheless, in pursuit of a moving target, defense economics has many vital contributions to offer. The economic model of rational behavior with its focus on measurement, on calculated benefits and costs, on incentives and calculated goal maximization together with competition among participant-actors continues to provide essential insight into how we can deal with the dilemmas of war and peace.

References

Alesina, A., Spolaore, E. (1997). "On the number and size of nations". Quarterly Journal of Economics 112, 1027–1056.

Alesina, A., Spolaore, E. (2003). The Size of Nations. MIT Press, Cambridge, MA.

Anderton, C.H. (1999). "Appropriation possibilities in a simple exchange economy". Economic Letters 63, 77–83.

Anderton, C.H. (2000). "Exchange of goods or exchange of blows? New directions in conflict and exchange". Defense Economics 11, 55–71.

Angell, N. (1910). The Great Illusion: A Study of the Relation of Military Power in Nations to Their Economic and Social Advantage. Heinemann, London.

Bailey, M.J. (2001). Constitution for a Future Country. Palgrave Press, London.

Boulding, K. (1962). Conflict and Defense. Harper Torchbooks, New York.

Cornes, R., Sandler, T. (1996). The Theory Externalities, Public Goods, and Club Goods, second ed. Cambridge University Press, New York.

Ehrlich, I., Becker, G. (1972). "Market insurance, self-insurance, and self-protection". Journal of Political Economy 80, 623–648.

Enders, W., Sandler, T. (1999). "Transnational terrorism in the post-Cold War era". International Studies Quarterly 43, 145–167.

Enders, W., Sandler, T. (2004). "An economic perspective on transnational terrorism". European Journal of Political Economy 20, 301–316.

Enthoven, A., Smith, W.Y. (1971). How Much Is Enough, Shaping the Defense Program, 1961–1969. Harper & Row Publishers, New York.

Everett, H.M. (1963). "Generalized Lagrange multiplier method for solving problems of optimum allocation of resources". Operations Research 11, 399–417.

Garfinkel, M.R. (2004). "Stable alliance formation in distributional conflict". European Journal of Political Economy 20, 829–852.

Garfinkel, M.R., Skaperdas, S. (2000). "Conflict without misperceptions or incomplete information: How the future matters". Journal of Conflict Resolution 44, 793–807.

Grossman, H. (2002). "Make us a king': Anarchy, predation, and the state". European Journal of Political Economy 18, 31–46.

Grossman, H., Han, T. (1993). "A theory of war finance". Defence Economics 4, 33–44.

Grossman, H.I., Kim, M. (1996). "Predation and accumulation". Journal of Economic Growth 1 (3), 333–351.

Grossman, H.I., Mendoza, J. (2004). "Annexation or conquest? The building of the Roman empire". Mimeo. Brown University.

Hegre, H., Sandler, T. (2002). "Economic analysis of civil wars". Defence and Peace Economics 13, 429–433.

Hirshleifer, J. (1983). "From weakest-link to best-shot: The voluntary provision of public goods". Public Choice 41, 371–386.

Hirshleifer, J. (1988). "The analytics of continuing conflict". Synthese 76, 201–233.

Hirshleifer, J. (1989). "Conflict and rent-seeking success functions". Public Choice 63, 101–112.

Hirshleifer, J. (1991). "The paradox of power". Economics and Politics 3, 177–200.

Hirshleifer, J. (1994). "The dark side of the force". Economic Inquiry 32, 1–10.

Hirshleifer, J. (2001). The Dark Side of the Force, 2001. Cambridge University Press, New York.

Huntington, S.P. (1993). The Clash of Civilizations and the Remaking of World Order. Simon and Schuster, New York.

Ihori, T. (1996). "International public goods and contributions of productivity differentials". Journal of Public Economics 61, 139–154.

Ihori, T., McGuire, M.C. (2006). "Collective risk control and group security: The unexpected consequences of differential risk aversion". Meetings of the American Economic Association, Boston, MA, January 5–8.

Kahn, H. (1959). On Thermonuclear War. Princeton University Press, Princeton.

Kant, I. (1795). "Perpetual peace: A philosophical sketch". In: Reiss, H. (Ed.), Kant's Political Writings. Cambridge University Press, Cambridge, pp. 93–130 (1970).

Konrad, K.A., Skaperdas, S. (2005). "The market for protection and the origin of the state". Mimeo. University of California-Irvine.

McGuire, M.C. (1990). "Economic models of nation specific vs. alliance wide benefits of defense contributions to NATO". Defence Economics 1, 17–35.

McGuire, M.C. (2002). "Property distribution and configurations of sovereign states: A rational economic model". Defence and Peace Economics 13, 251–270.

McGuire, M.C. (2004). "Economics of strategic defense and the global public good". Defence and Peace Economics 15, 1–24.

McGuire, M.C., Olson, M. (1996). "The economics of autocracy and majority rule: The invisible hand and the use of force". Journal of Economic Literature 34, 72–96.

Mueller, D. (2003). Public Choice III. Cambridge University Press, New York.

Nalebuff, B. (1988). "Minimal nuclear deterrence". Journal of Conflict Resolution 32, 411–425.

Neal, L. (1994). War Finance. Edward Elgar Publishing, Brookfield, VT.

Nordhaus, W. (2002). "The Economic consequences of a war with Iraq". Mimeo. Yale University.

O'Neill, B. (2001). "Risk aversion in international relations theory". International Studies Quarterly 45, 617–640.

Olson, M. (1969). "The principle of fiscal equivalence". American Economic Review: Papers and Proceedings 59, 479–487.

Olson, M. (1981). The Rise and Decline of Nations. Yale University Press, New Haven.

Olson, M., Zeckhauser, R. (1966). "An economic theory of alliances". Review of Economics and Statistics 48, 266–279.

Polachek, S.W. (1980). "Conflict and trade". Journal of Conflict Resolution 24, 55–78.

Pugh, G.E. (1964). "Lagrange multipliers and the optimal allocation of defense resources". Operations Research 12, 543–567.

Rosendorff, B.P., Sandler, T. (2004). "Too much of a good thing?: The proactive response dilemma". Journal of Conflict Resolution 49, 171–182.

Sandler, T. (1977). "Impurity of defense: An application to the economics of alliances". Kyklos 30, 443–460.

Sandler, T. (1999). "Intergenerational public goods: Strategies, efficiency and institutions". In: Kaul, I., Grunberg, I., Stern, M.A. (Eds.), Global Public Goods: International Cooperation in the Twenty-First Century. Oxford University Press, New York, pp. 20–50.

Sandler, T. (2000). "Economic analysis of conflict". In: Sandler, T. (Ed.), Journal of Conflict Resolution 44, 723–729.

Sandler, T., Hartley, K. (2001). "Economics of alliances: The lessons for collective action". Journal of Economic Literature 39, 869–896.

Skaperdas, S. (1992). "Cooperation, conflict, and power in the absence of property rights". American Economic Review 82, 720–739.

Skaperdas, S., Syropoulos, C. (2002). "Insecure property and the efficiency of exchange". Economic Journal 112, 133–146.

Schelling, T.C. (1960). The Strategy of Conflict. Harvard University Press, Cambridge, MA.

Schelling, T.C. (1966). Arms and Influence. Yale University Press, New Haven.

Schelling, T.C. (1967). "The strategy of inflicting costs". In: McKean, R.N. (Ed.), Issues in Defense Economics. Columbia University Press, New York, pp. 105–127.

Tanzi, V. (1998). "Corruption around the world: Causes, consequences, scope, and cures". IMF Staff Papers 45(4).

Thompson, E.A. (1974). "Taxation and national defense". Journal of Political Economy 82, 755–782.

Thompson, E.A., Hickson, C. (2001). Ideology and the Evolution of Vital Institutions: Guilds, The Gold Standard, and Modern International Cooperation. Kluwer, Amsterdam.

Tullock, G. (1974). The Social Dilemma, Economics of War and Revolution. Center for Study of Public Choice, University of Virginia, Charlottesville.

US Department of Commerce (2005). "Net investment position of the United States". Bureau of Economic Analysis. News release, June 30.

Chapter 22

ECONOMICS OF CONFLICT: AN OVERVIEW[*]

MICHELLE R. GARFINKEL and STERGIOS SKAPERDAS

Department of Economics, University of California, Irvine, Irvine, CA 92697-5100, USA
e-mails: mrgarfin@uci.edu; sskaperd@uci.edu

Contents

Abstract	650
Keywords	651
1. Introduction	652
2. Technologies of conflict	654
3. Representative models of conflict and the determinants of power	658
3.1. Competing for a resource	659
3.2. Guns versus butter	662
3.2.1. Symmetric outcomes	664
3.2.2. Asymmetric outcomes	665
4. Settlement in the shadow of conflict	667
4.1. Sources of the preference for settlement	668
4.1.1. Destruction and additional costs of open conflict	668
4.1.2. Risk aversion and the uncertainty of conflict	669
4.1.3. Complementarities in production and consumption	670
4.2. How much arming? Settlement under different rules of division	671
4.2.1. Equilibrium under open conflict	672
4.2.2. Equilibrium under settlement: Division by winning probabilities	673
4.2.3. Equilibrium under settlement: Split-the-surplus rule of division	674
4.2.4. Discussion: Rules of division and norms of conduct	676
5. Why fight?	677
5.1. Traditional explanations: Asymmetric information, misperceptions, irrationality	677
5.2. Incomplete contracting in the shadow of the future	677
5.2.1. Preliminaries: The second-period outcome	679
5.2.2. Settlement or war? First-period choices	680

[*] The authors are grateful to Francisco Gonzalez, Ragnar Torvik and Karl Wärneryd, as well as to the editors of this volume, for their valuable comments on previous drafts of this chapter. Skaperdas thanks the Center for Global Peace and Conflict Studies and the Center for the Study of Democracy, both at UC Irvine, for financial support.

Handbook of Defense Economics, Volume 2
Edited by Todd Sandler and Keith Hartley
© 2007 Elsevier B.V.   All rights reserved
DOI: 10.1016/S1574-0013(06)02022-9

6. Trade, insecurity, and conflict   682
   6.1. Secure autarky versus insecure exchange   683
   6.2. Insecure resources, trade restrictions and other market interventions   685
        6.2.1. Outcomes under autarky   686
        6.2.2. Outcomes under trade   687
        6.2.3. The relative appeal of free trade   688
        6.2.4. Other implications   690
7. Coalitions and group formation   690
   7.1. Stage 1: Inter-group conflict   692
   7.2. Stage 2: Intra-group conflict   693
   7.3. Equilibrium allocations   694
   7.4. The level of conflict under different symmetric group structures   696
   7.5. Requirements of stability and equilibrium group structures   698
8. Dynamics and growth   699
9. Conflict management and the state   701
   9.1. Hierarchical governance   702
   9.2. Modern governance   703
10. Concluding remarks   704
References   705

Abstract

In this chapter, we review the recent literature on conflict and appropriation. Allowing for the possibility of conflict, which amounts to recognizing the possibility that property rights are not perfectly and costlessly enforced, represents a significant departure from the traditional paradigm of economics. The research we emphasize, however, takes an economic perspective. Specifically, it applies conventional optimization techniques and game-theoretic tools to study the allocation of resources among competing activities – productive and otherwise appropriative, such as grabbing the product and wealth of others as well as defending one's own product and wealth. In contrast to other economic activities in which inputs are combined cooperatively through production functions, the inputs to appropriation are combined adversarially through technologies of conflict.

A central objective of this research is to identify the effects of conflict on economic outcomes: the determinants of the distribution of output (or power) and how an individual party's share can be inversely related to its marginal productivity; when settlement in the shadow of conflict and when open conflict can be expected to occur, with longer time horizons capable of inducing conflict instead of settlement; how conflict and appropriation can reduce the appeal of trade; the determinants of alliance formation and the importance of intra-alliance commitments; how dynamic incentives for capital accumulation and innovation are distorted in the presence of conflict; and the role of governance in conflict management.

Keywords

anarchy, bargaining, conflict technology, economic growth, exchange, governance, group formation, open conflict, power, shadow of the future

JEL classification: D30, D70, D72, D74, H56, O17

1. Introduction

Conflict is difficult to comprehend from a traditional economic perspective. The difficulty arises from the emphasis that the discipline places on the win–win aspects of exchange and the gains from trade, at the expense of neglecting environments with imperfectly specified and imperfectly enforced property rights. These latter environments are precisely the ones in which conflict typically arises. In this chapter we will review and synthesize recent research that takes an economic perspective to study conflict. This research shares with traditional economics the assumption of self-interested behavior on the part of economic agents. However, contrary to traditional economics, there is no presumption that agents can only produce and trade to make a living. They can also engage in appropriation, grabbing the production of others or defending what they themselves have produced.

Central to the economic analysis of conflict and its consequences, which we emphasize in this chapter, is the tradeoff between production and appropriation. To the best of our knowledge, Haavelmo (1954) was the first economist to model the basic choice between production and appropriation, and did so in a general equilibrium setting. Haavelmo was interested in incorporating appropriation into economic modelling because he thought it was important for understanding economic development. It seems, however, that other scholars in economics did not share his vision. For his work in this area, in sharp contrast to his research in econometrics, has had no discernible impact. Yet, over the past fifteen years or so, we have witnessed a growing research effort, spearheaded largely by Jack Hirshleifer and Herschel Grossman, to try to put "conflict and appropriation" squarely within the scope of discourse and inquiry of the economics discipline, and what we cover in this chapter owes as much to their direct contributions as to their inspiration.

Another important feature of the economic analysis of conflict, which we also emphasize in this chapter, lies in the modelling of conflict as a contest – that is, a game in which participants expend resources on arming so as to increase their probability of winning if conflict were to actually take place. Actual, overt conflict does not necessarily have to occur but arming can be used, as is often in reality, as a bargaining tool and as a deterrent within a larger economic context.

We explore the key ingredient of contests, "contest success functions" or "technologies of conflict" in Section 2. These technologies show how probabilities of winning vary with the different levels of arming of those potentially engaged in conflict. For the theory of conflict and appropriation they are the analog of production functions in production theory and utility functions in consumption theory. We discuss the different classes of functional forms that have been used and review their axiomatic foundations or stochastic derivations.

In Section 3 we examine two basic models of conflict, one that involves fighting for an exogenous prize and another in which all production is endogenous and contested by the contending parties. Here we derive some comparative static results of the models in the equilibrium determination of power, to show how allowing for conflict and appropriation can change many of the standard findings from traditional economic theory.

In the subsequent sections, we review a number of advances that have been made recently in this area of research, based largely on variations of one of the two basic models. Section 4 reviews the various factors, such as the destructive effects of war, risk aversion and complementarities in production as well as consumption, that could give adversaries a short-run preference for bargaining and settling instead of fighting. Because commitments are not possible, open conflict can not be ruled out. Hence, settlement takes place in the *shadow of conflict*. But arming also provides one with a better bargaining position. We show that the bargaining rules in place and the norms shared by the parties to potential conflict are crucial for the level of arming that emerges under settlement.

Although there are many reasons to expect adversaries to settle in the short-run, we often observe open conflict and fighting. Typically, conflict is considered the outcome of incomplete and asymmetric information or, even, a result of misperceptions and irrationality. In Section 5, we bring attention to another potentially important hypothesis for the emergence of open conflict. In particular, it seems reasonable to suppose that fighting changes the strategic positions of the adversaries well into the future and in ways that sequential short-run settlements do not. In this case, a party who views the future as being important might choose to fight, despite the short-run benefits of settling. Such a choice would be consistent with rational, forward-looking behavior, based on complete information. If one or more of the parties views the future as being sufficiently important, we would expect the outbreak of war.

Section 6 examines how exchange and trade affect and are affected by insecurity and conflict. When trade across national borders is insecure, but trade within the nation (or autarky) is not, parties may very well choose autarky, even if doing so limits their productive opportunities, because the costs of enforcement under trade are too high. But, in this section we explore, in more detail, the implications of another form of insecurity – that is, where a contested resource can be traded. Trade and autarky in the presence of contested resources generally induce different levels of arming; and, comparing welfare under trade and under autarky is far from being straightforward, for the gains from trade can be outweighed by the additional costs of arming that trade might induce. Thus, the presence of insecurity and conflict can help to explain some types of restrictions on exchange and market interventions that cannot be explained when property rights are perfectly and costlessly enforced.

In Section 7, we turn to explore some issues that arise when appropriative activities are carried out not by unitary actors, but by individuals organized into groups. We find that, relative to the case where individuals compete on their own for the contested resource, group formation tends to reduce the overall severity of conflict, though that severity varies with different group structures. If we were to assume that groups could somehow commit in advance to a rule to share the prize in case they won, then the severity of conflict would be decreasing in the size of groups, and the grand coalition (a single group consisting of all individuals) would be the efficient structure. But, here we suppose instead that conflicts over the distribution of the prize within groups cannot be resolved so easily. Even factoring in this additional source of conflict, stable group formation reduces the severity of conflict. Nevertheless, as long as there is some cost involved in managing within-group conflict, the grand coalition will generally not emerge as the efficient structure. Whether a structure with larger or smaller groups can be sustained in equilibrium depends crucially on whether groups possess any advantage in managing conflict relative to individuals, and if so to what degree.

Sections 8 and 9 review some dynamic effects of conflict and appropriation, and the role of the state in conflict management. Many of the static inefficiencies we examine in the earlier sections become magnified in dynamic settings, with incentives distorted toward appropriative investment and against innovation. The reduction and management of conflict is briefly reviewed in view of recent research on state organization and institutions. Traditional hierarchical governance tends to reduce internal conflict but displace conflict at a higher, more organized level between autocratic rulers. Modern governance may provide more durable solutions to conflict, yet research about how it functions and interacts with economic growth has essentially only just begun. We conclude our overview in Section 10.

2. Technologies of conflict

A key ingredient of conflict has been, and still is, the use of weapons: swords, pikes, cannons, bombs, guns, and so on. From an economic perspective, weapons can be thought of as inputs into conflict. However, unlike the case of ordinary economic production, in which inputs are combined cooperatively in order to produce useful output, the inputs of conflict are contributed by each party in an *adversarial* fashion against other parties. Instead of useful production, the output of conflict can reasonably be thought to be wins and losses. How inputs in conflict – weapons – translate into wins and losses for the different parties involved in conflict is thus the first topic that we examine.

Hirshleifer (1989) was first to call such functions "technologies of conflict", a term which we will be using ourselves throughout this chapter. Consider two contending parties, labelled $i = 1$ and $i = 2$, and denote their choice of weapons as G_1 and G_2 (for "guns"). For any given combination of guns, we can expect each party to have a probability of winning and a probability of losing. (The probability of an impasse or "draw" is considered to be zero, but we briefly mention the case when this assumption does not hold below.) Denote the probability of party $i = 1$ winning as $p_1(G_1, G_2)$ and the probability of party $i = 2$ winning as $p_2(G_1, G_2)$.

For $p_i(G_1, G_2)$, $i = 1, 2$, to be probabilities, they need to take on values between 0 and 1 and add up to 1, or equivalently they must satisfy the following: $0 \leqslant p_2(G_1, G_2) = 1 - p_1(G_1, G_2) \leqslant 1$. Moreover, we can expect an increase in one party's guns to increase her own winning probability and reduce the winning probability of her opponent; that is, $p_1(G_1, G_2)$ should be increasing in G_1 and decreasing in G_2.

A wide class of technologies that has been examined takes the following additive form:

$$p_1(G_1, G_2) = \begin{cases} \frac{f(G_1)}{f(G_1)+f(G_2)} & \text{if } \sum_{i=1}^2 f(G_i) > 0; \\ \frac{1}{2} & \text{otherwise,} \end{cases} \tag{1}$$

where $f(\cdot)$ is a non-negative, increasing function. This class has been employed in a number of fields, including in the economics of advertising [Schmalensee (1972)], sports economics [Szymanski (2003)], rent-seeking [Tullock (1980), Nitzan (1994)], and contests in general [see Konrad (2005) for a recent survey]. Luce (1959) axiomatizes such probabilistic choice functions in relation to utility theory, while Skaperdas (1996) provides an axiomatization in relation to contests. Key to both axiomatizations is an *Independence of Irrelevant Alternatives* property. In the context of conflict, this property requires that the outcome of conflict between any two parties depend only on the amount of guns held by these two parties and not on the amount of guns held by third parties to the conflict.

One unique and appealing feature of the class of conflict technologies in (1) is that it naturally extends to the case of conflict between more than two parties. Thus, if there were n parties to the conflict, denoting the gun choice of party i by G_i and the vector of gun choices of all other agents $j \neq i$ by G_{-i}, the winning probability of i would be as follows:

$$p_i(G_i, G_{-i}) = \begin{cases} \frac{f(G_i)}{\sum_{j=1}^n f(G_j)} & \text{if } \sum_{j=1}^n f(G_j) > 0; \\ \frac{1}{n} & \text{otherwise.} \end{cases} \tag{2}$$

Although we will touch upon the case of more than two parties in Section 7, everywhere else, including in the rest of this section, we will focus on the simple case with $n = 2$.

The most commonly used functional form is the one in which $f(G_i) = G_i^m$, where $m > 0$ (and often, for technical reasons, $m \leq 1$), so that

$$p_1(G_1, G_2) = \frac{G_1^m}{G_1^m + G_2^m}. \tag{3}$$

Sometimes referred to as the "power form" or as the "ratio form", this functional form is that which was employed by Tullock (1980) and the ensuing voluminous literature on rent-seeking. It is also the workhorse functional form used in the economics of conflict. As Hirshleifer (1989) has noted, the probability of winning in this case depends on the *ratio* of guns of the two parties, $\frac{G_1}{G_2}$. To put it differently, this technology of conflict is *homogeneous of degree zero* in guns. For the general case with an arbitrary number of parties (n), $p_i(tG_i, tG_{-i}) = p_i(G_i, G_{-i})$ for all $t > 0$. This property of (3) is rather convenient analytically, and could account for much of its popularity in applications, like the Cobb–Douglas form in the case of production functions.

Another well-known functional form is the following "logistic" specification, in which $f(G_i) = e^{kG_i}$, where $k > 0$, so that

$$p_1(G_1, G_2) = \frac{e^{kG_1}}{e^{kG_1} + e^{kG_2}} = \frac{1}{1 + e^{k(G_2 - G_1)}}. \tag{4}$$

Again as Hirshleifer (1989) has noted and as is evident from the expression above, this specification implies the probability of winning depends on the *difference* in guns between the two parties. Thus, in general, the probabilities are invariant to the addition of a constant C to the guns of each party – i.e., $p_i(G_i + C, G_{-i} + C) = p_i(G_i, G_{-i})$ for all C such that $G_j + C > 0$ for all j.[1] Though the logistic or difference form also has analytical advantages, it has not been used as much as the power form shown in (3). The reason is that, for a number of well-specified models (including the one we examine in Section 3.1 below, which is analogous to the basic rent-seeking model), no pure-strategy, Nash equilibrium exists.

But, an appealing feature of (4), one that accounts for its popularity in econometric studies of discrete choice, is that it can be derived stochastically.[2] In particular, suppose each party's "guns" allocation is a noisy predictor of "performance" in battle so that the performance of party i equals $G_i + \varepsilon_i$, where ε_i is a stochastic error term. If the error term is distributed according to a specific distribution (namely, the extreme value distribution) and the outcome of the battle depends on which party performs best (or, more precisely, $p_1(G_1, G_2) = \text{Prob}\{G_1 + \varepsilon_1 > G_2 + \varepsilon_2\}$), then (4) is the resultant functional form.

No similar stochastic derivation of the power form in (3) existed, to our knowledge, until Hirshleifer and Riley (1992). On pp. 380–381 of their book, Hirshleifer and Riley include an exercise that asks the reader to prove that the power form in the case of $n = 2$ players, as shown in (3) but with $m = 1$, can be derived when the performance of party i is now $\theta_i G_i$, where θ_i is a multiplicative error term with an exponential distribution: $\text{Prob}\{\theta_1 G_1 > \theta_2 G_2\} = \frac{G_1}{G_1 + G_2}$. Only recently has this result been extended beyond the case where $m = 1$ and $n = 2$. In particular, Jia (2005) derives (3) more generally for $m > 0$ and $n \geq 2$, assuming that the probability density function for the error, θ is given by $g(\theta) = am\theta^{-(m+1)} \exp(-a\theta^{-m})$, where $a > 0$ and $\theta > 0$. Jia shows how m can be interpreted as a "noise" parameter, with a greater value of m inducing less noise in the determination of the winner of a contest. That is, higher values for m, and given a certain level of guns for the parties, make for a closer contest. Therefore, from the viewpoint of an adversary, it is cheaper in terms of the cost of guns to increase her probability of winning when m is higher rather than lower. The level of m has been variously identified with "decisiveness" or "effectiveness" of conflict. In the remainder of this chapter, we will be using the latter term.

---

[1] Hirshleifer (1989) as well as Section 4 of Hirshleifer (1995b) and Hirshleifer (2000) provide many insightful discussions of the technologies of conflict and comparisons of the functional forms in (3) and (4).

[2] See McFadden (1984) and many econometrics textbooks.

Thus, both the "power" functional form in (3) and the "logistic" form in (4) can be derived axiomatically as well as stochastically. We should mention that the *probit* function – derived under the assumption $p_1(G_1, G_2) = \text{Prob}\{G_1 + \varepsilon_1 > G_2 + \varepsilon_2\}$ with ε_i, $i = 1, 2$, normally distributed – has not been used in the literature that we review, most likely because there is no analytical functional form to express it.

The class in (1) and the specific forms in (3) and (4) have the property of symmetry or anonymity, in the sense that only the amount of guns possessed by a party and her adversaries matters for the outcome. Consequently, when two parties hold the same amount of guns, they have equal probabilities of winning and losing. The cost of producing guns might differ across parties, thereby inducing strategic asymmetries between them and resulting in an asymmetric solution for guns (i.e., $G_1 \neq G_2$); nevertheless, for each gun held by the parties, the technology of conflict does not favor one party over the other.

There are circumstances, however, in which one party might be favored over another though they hold the same amount of guns. An obvious setting conducive to such an asymmetry is where one party is in a defensive position vis a vis her opponent. The defender typically, but not always, has the advantage. A simple way to extend (1) to admit the possibility of such asymmetries is shown in the following form:

$$p_1(G_1, G_2) = \frac{\varphi f(G_1)}{\varphi f(G_1) + (1 - \varphi) f(G_2)}, \tag{5}$$

where $\varphi \in (0, 1)$.[3] Note that when the parties hold equal amounts of guns, $G_1 = G_2 > 0$, party $i = 1$'s probability of winning equals φ and party $i = 2$'s probability of winning is $1 - \varphi$. Thus, when $\varphi > \frac{1}{2}$, party $i = 1$ has an advantage, whereas when $\varphi < \frac{1}{2}$ party $i = 2$ has the advantage, and the closer φ is either to 0 or 1, the greater is the advantage that one party has over another. Clark and Riis (1998) have axiomatized this asymmetric form for the case of the power function (i.e., where $f(G) = G^m$), and Grossman and Kim (1995) have employed that form in order to distinguish between offense and defense.

For the technologies of conflict we have reviewed to this point, the sum of the winning probabilities of all parties involved equals 1. But there are circumstances under which a draw or an impasse might be a reasonable outcome. That is, a battle could very well leave the adversaries in the same relative bargaining position as they were before the battle. Blavatsky (2004) axiomatizes the following reasonable extension of (1) as well as (5), which captures such a possibility:

$$p_1(G_1, G_2) = \frac{f_1(G_1)}{1 + f_1(G_1) + f_2(G_2)}, \tag{6}$$

---

[3] It would seem arbitrary to assume, along the lines of the specification in (1) that, in this asymmetric case, $p_i(G_1, G_2) = \frac{1}{2}$ for $i = 1, 2$, whenever $\sum_{i=1}^{2} f(G_i) = 0$. An alternative and more palatable specification would be $p_1(G_1, G_2) = \varphi$ which would then imply $p_2(G_1, G_2) = 1 - p_1(G_1, G_2) = 1 - \varphi$.

where $f_1(\cdot)$ and $f_2(\cdot)$ are non-negative increasing functions. According to this general formulation, the probability of a draw, given by

$$1 - p_1(G_1, G_2) - p_2(G_1, G_2) = \frac{1}{1 + f_1(G_1) + f_2(G_2)},$$

is always positive. Also note that having $f_1(\cdot) = \varphi f(\cdot)$ and $f_2(\cdot) = (1 - \varphi) f(\cdot)$ yields a straightforward generalization of the asymmetric form in (5). The "1" that appears in the denominator of (6) does not have any special significance, because if we were to multiply the numerator and denominator of (6) by any positive number we would get an equivalent functional form. One way of thinking about (6) is to consider a third party, say "Nature", that has a constant endowment of "guns", G', which is defined by $f(G') = 1$ (where $f(\cdot)$ is non-negative and increasing). When Nature "wins", there is a draw. Blavatsky (2004) has extended (6) to more than 2 parties but not in the straightforward way that (2) extends (1).

The technologies of conflict we have reviewed in this section have been derived either axiomatically or stochastically and, thus, are comparable in terms of the foundations to production functions and utility functions. Yet, unlike the case of production functions, to our knowledge there have not been empirical estimates of the technologies of conflict. This is a topic, then, that could be taken up in future research.

3. Representative models of conflict and the determinants of power

In this section, we present two basic models of conflict, both of which embed the conflict technology presented above into an economic framework of optimizing behavior. This approach to modelling conflict effectively envisions the relations between individual parties as anarchic in the sense that, like sovereign states, there is no higher authority to which they must answer.[4] Without a higher authority, contracts between parties can be meaningful only if those parties can enforce the contracts themselves. But, since the power of enforcement ultimately derives from the credible threat of using force, under anarchy individual parties cannot write enforceable contracts that would eliminate arming and preclude the use of violence. As these implications indicate, the approach of this research departs sharply from a long tradition in neoclassical economics that largely ignores any imperfections in contracts and views property rights as perfectly and costlessly enforced. However, the approach is much in line with the fundamental assumption of self-interest, for a genuine *Homo economicus* would not refrain from using force, if by doing so, he could enhance her material well-being.

Laws, institutions and norms would be expected to emerge to limit and shape the use of force by economic agents, as they pursue their self interests.[5] Nevertheless, under anarchy, an individual's holding of guns would seem paramount in determining her

---

[4] While this research has important implications for the interactions between nations, such interactions are not our primary focus or concern.

[5] See Section 4.2.4.

position relative to others and thus in influencing the terms of transactions. Of course, this influence comes at a cost, for the production of guns necessarily diverts valuable resources from other uses and the use of guns can have other more direct negative consequences on welfare.

The model we present in the first subsection abstracts from individual parties' production decisions, and hence might be considered a partial equilibrium framework. Nevertheless, it is closely related to the basic rent-seeking model – see, e.g., Nitzan (1994) – and its simplicity allows us to highlight the logic of the interactions between individuals as they contest a given resource. In the subsequent subsection, we present an extended model where the contested pie is endogenous to the decisions that the adversaries make between production and appropriation. This extension shifts the focus of the analysis more squarely on the trade-off between guns and butter, allowing us to make the opportunity cost of guns explicit. Overall, our central objective here is to highlight the implications of abandoning the assumption of neoclassical economic theory that property is secure for (i) the equilibrium determination of income and (ii) the distribution of that income or equivalently, in this model, the determination of power.

3.1. Competing for a resource

Consider an environment populated by two identical, risk-neutral agents. These agents can be thought of as either individuals or collections thereof – for example, tribes or nations. However, we abstract from all problems of collective action and put aside, for now, any issues that may arise with group formation.[6] Here, we treat each agent as a unitary actor, and suppose that they contest $\bar{R} \equiv 2R$ units of a resource, which can be consumed directly. Each agent might claim the rights to half or even more of the resource. However, due to imperfect institutions of governance and enforcement, any such claim can be settled only by overt conflict or, equivalently, in this setting under the threat of conflict, through the production of "guns" or "arms" (G_i). In particular, following the approach outlined in Section 2, we model the conflict over $\bar{R}$ as a *winner-take-all contest*: $p_i(G_1, G_2)$ denotes the probability that agent i emerges as the winner and thus is able to claim the entire resource $(\bar{R})$ as her prize, leaving nothing for her opponent $j \neq i$ for $i = 1, 2$. To fix ideas, assume that $p_i(G_1, G_2)$ is symmetric, taking the functional form shown in (3).

Consistent with the general class of conflict technologies discussed in Section 2, this specification implies that agent i's likelihood of winning the resource $\bar{R}$, $p_i(G_1, G_2)$, is increasing in her choice of guns, G_i, and decreasing in that of her opponent $j \neq i$, G_j, for $i = 1, 2$. Thus, each agent's expected gross winnings, $p_i(G_1, G_2)\bar{R}$, is similarly increasing in her own production of guns, G_i and decreasing in that of her opponent, G_j, $j \neq i$ for $i = 1, 2$. However, the production of guns is not costless. In particular, as noted above, producing guns diverts the flow of valuable resources from useful, welfare

---

[6] We take up these issues in Section 7, where we consider the possibility of coalition formation explicitly.

enhancing activities.[7] This cost of producing guns is borne by the agent whether or not she wins the contest. Thus, agent i's expected payoff, $V_i(G_1, G_2)$, can be written as follows:

$$V_i(G_1, G_2) = p_i(G_1, G_2)\overline{R} - G_i, \quad i = 1, 2,$$ (7)

where $p_i(G_1, G_2)$ is given by (3). Note that under the alternative, non-probabilistic interpretation of (3), where agents are envisioned as dividing the contested resource according to their respective winning probabilities $p_i(G_1, G_2)$ given their choices of guns, the expected payoff shown above would be equivalent to the agent's ex post pay-off. Note further that this interpretation is equivalent to our probabilistic interpretation of (3) as a winner-take-all contest. This equivalence, which arises under various sets of assumptions (including the assumption of risk neutrality specified here), implies, in turn, that the agents are indifferent, in an ex ante sense, between the two contests as a way of distributing the resource, $\overline{R}$. However, the actual outcomes and the corresponding payoffs obtained under each could be very different.[8]

Subject to the conflict technology (3) and treating her opponent's choice of guns as given, each agent i chooses G_i to maximize her expected payoff (7). The conflict technology implies generally that, if agent i's opponent were to make no appropriative effort ($G_j = 0$, $j \neq i$), agent i could seize all of $\overline{R}$ with near certainty by producing an infinitesimally small quantity of guns. But, neither agent would leave such an opportunity unexploited. As such, the "peaceful" outcome where $G_i = 0$ for $i = 1, 2$ cannot be an equilibrium outcome, and agent i's optimizing guns choice satisfies the following first-order condition:

$$\frac{\partial V_i(G_1, G_2)}{\partial G_i} = \frac{\partial p_i(G_1, G_2)}{\partial G_i} \overline{R} - 1 = 0, \quad i = 1, 2.$$ (8)

The first term on the left-hand side (RHS) of the condition represents the marginal benefit of guns. By producing an additional gun, holding everything else constant, agent i enhances her chances of winning the prize ($\overline{R}$) or equivalently her *power*. From (3), it is straightforward to verify that this marginal effect, given $G_j > 0$, equals

$$\frac{\partial p_i(G_1, G_2)}{\partial G_i} = \frac{mG_i^{m-1}G_j^m}{(G_1^m + G_2^m)^2}, \quad j \neq i, \ i = 1, 2.$$ (9)

The second term on the RHS of (8) represents the marginal cost of guns, a constant and equal to 1 for both players.[9]

---

[7] In a more fully articulated setting such as in the model presented in the following section, this opportunity cost could be modelled more explicitly as a reduction in the production of goods available for current consumption and/or for future consumption.

[8] Moreover, as discussed in some detail below, the ex ante equivalence breaks down under reasonable conditions, implying a preference for negotiated settlement under the shadow of conflict [see Section 4].

[9] It might be more reasonable to suppose that the marginal cost is increasing due to diminishing returns. Although assuming a constant marginal cost of appropriative activity is not critical here, it could matter where, as discussed below, we admit the possibility of group formation. Also see Esteban and Ray (2001).

Under our specifications for the players' expected payoffs (7) and the conflict technology (3), the first-order conditions shown in (8) combined with (9) for $i = 1, 2$ define a unique, symmetric pure-strategy (Nash) equilibrium:

$$G_i^* = G^* = \frac{m}{2} R, \quad i = 1, 2, \tag{10}$$

implying that each party i has an equal chance of winning $\bar{R}$: $p_i^* = p^* = \frac{1}{2}$ for $i = 1, 2.$[10] Thus each player's expected winnings equals $p^* \bar{R} = R$, where $R = \frac{1}{2}\bar{R}$ measures the contested resource in per capita terms, as previously defined. But, the players' expected payoffs are also negatively affected by the guns they produce. To be more precise, by substituting the solution G^* into (7) with $\bar{R}$ replaced by $2R$, one can verify that the payoff expected by agent i, $V_i(G^*)$, in this symmetric equilibrium is given by

$$V_i(G^*) = V^* = \left[1 - \frac{m}{2} \right] R, \quad i = 1, 2. \tag{11}$$

Since, by assumption, $m \in (0, 1]$, this expression shows that each player has an incentive to participate in the contest, even factoring in the cost of producing guns.

One result that follows immediately from these solutions is that a larger "prize", R in per capita terms, induces greater allocations to guns and hence induces more conflict. But, the increased cost of conflict is swamped by an accompanying increase in each side's gross expected winnings. That is, the net effect of an increase in R on each agent's expected payoff is positive, $\frac{dV^*}{dR} = 1 - \frac{m}{2} > 0$. The solutions show further that the conflict effectiveness parameter, m, has a positive influence on the players' optimizing guns choice, G^*, and thus a negative influence on the payoff each agent expects to obtain in the symmetric equilibrium, $V(G^*)$. The spillover effects of the contenders' choices give rise to the possibility that some coordination of choices could make them both better off. In particular, if the two players could enter into a credible agreement to share $\bar{R}$ equally with no the threat of conflict (i.e., without guns, $G^* = 0$), then the payoff to each would be, $V(0) = \frac{1}{2}\bar{R} = R$, implying a gain of $V(0) - V(G^*) = \frac{m}{2} R$, which is precisely the cost of conflict borne by each agent. However, the potential here for mutually beneficial gains is not itself sufficient to induce a better outcome. The critical departure of this research from the long-standing neoclassical approach that rules out the possibility of contracting by agents to eliminate conflict and arming, at the same time, raises important questions about the feasibility of realizing such gains. Below we return to this issue, exploring alternative ways in which agents could possibly limit arming under anarchy.

---

[10] See Skaperdas and Syropoulos (1997) for conditions and proofs under more general specifications for production.

3.2. Guns versus butter

A fundamental premise of the economics literature on conflict is that economic agents often face a tradeoff between producing goods and grabbing what others have produced. Indeed, the tradeoff between production and appropriation is central to the study of interaction between individual parties under anarchy. In this section we extend the model developed above, incorporating production as well as appropriation to study this tradeoff more formally.[11] This extension enables us to make explicit the opportunity cost of guns and to highlight its role in the determination of the distribution of power between the two agents.

In this model of conflict, each agent i, $i = 1, 2$, possesses R_i units of a secure primary resource. This resource, which can be thought of as a composite of labor and land, cannot be consumed directly. Instead, it is allocated among two sorts of activities: (i) usefully productive activities that eventually yield goods for consumption (i.e., butter) and (ii) appropriative activities that ultimately determine the distribution of those consumption goods among them. To be more precise, each agent i transforms her initial resource (R_i) into guns (G_i) on a one-to-one basis and into an intermediate input (X_i) at a rate of β_i-to-one, as follows:

$$R_i = G_i + X_i/\beta_i, \quad i = 1, 2. \tag{12}$$

As will become obvious below, β_i measures agent i's marginal product in the production of butter. Rearranging (12) shows that her production of X_i depends positively on her initial resource, R_i, net of what she allocates to appropriation, G_i, as well as positively on the productivity parameter, β_i:

$$X_i = \beta_i[R_i - G_i], \quad i = 1, 2. \tag{13}$$

To fix ideas, we suppose henceforth that $\beta_1 \geqslant \beta_2$. Thus, agent $i = 1$ ($i = 2$) is the more (less) productive contender.

Given these allocations, the two sides, $i = 1$ and 2, combine their intermediate inputs, X_i, in a joint production process that delivers $\overline{B}$ units of butter for consumption, according to the following specification:

$$\overline{B} \equiv F(X_1, X_2) = \sum_{i=1}^{2} \beta_i[R_i - G_i]. \tag{14}$$

---

[11] An early form of this model was first presented in Hirshleifer (1988) and can be found in his subsequent publications, including Hirshleifer (1989, 1991, 1995a). However, the very first general equilibrium model of this sort appeared in the often neglected work of Haavelmo (1954, pp. 91–98). Other contributors to the more recent literature include Garfinkel (1990), Grossman (1991), Skaperdas (1992), Grossman and Kim (1996), Esteban and Ray (1999), Wittman (2000), and Mehlum, Moene and Torvik (2003). Also see Skaperdas (2003) for a detailed review of the literature.

As we have specified the units and the technology of transformation of the initial resource in (12), the quantity of the intermediate good, X_i, that agent i contributes to
the joint production of butter, $i = 1, 2$, coincides with the compensation that the agent
would receive in a competitive world if property rights were well defined and perfectly
enforced. This hypothetical compensation is increasing in the agent's own marginal
product, β_i, as well as that part of her initial resource she chooses to devote to usefully productive activities, $X_i = R_i - G_i$.[12] [In what follows where there is no risk
of confusion, we will write $F(X_1, X_2)$ as $F(G)$ to emphasize the dependence of this
function on the agents' gun choices as represented by the vector, G, while economizing
on notation.]

However, in the anarchic environment we are studying here, the output from the two
agents' joint production, $\overline{B} \equiv F(G)$, is subject to dispute, which we suppose is resolved
in a winner-take-all contest, with each agent's probability of winning depending on her
relative holdings of guns. This method of distributing the yield from their joint efforts
in production motivates the agents to devote some of their initial resource to guns production, thereby making the tradeoff between appropriation (G) and useful production
(X) embedded in (12) relevant. Specifically, subject to the conflict technology (3) and
her production technology (13), each agent i chooses G_i, taking the other agent's guns
choice (G_j) as given, to maximize her expected payoff, which equals the prize that
goes to the sole winner – i.e., the aggregate quantity of butter they produce jointly –
weighted by the probability that she wins the conflict. Using the specification for total
output shown in (14), this expected payoff can be written as

$$V_i(G_1, G_2) = p_i(G_1, G_2) \sum_{j=1}^{2} \beta_j [R_j - G_j], \quad i = 1, 2, \tag{15}$$

where $p_i(G_1, G_2)$ is given by (3).[13]

---

[12] One could assume a more general specification for the joint production technology, $F(X_1, X_2)$, which is
similarly linearly homogeneous and increasing, but is also strictly concave in each input and, exhibits some
degree of complementarity between them: $F_i > 0$, $F_{ii} < 0$, and $F_{ij} > 0$ for $j \neq i, i = 1, 2$, where subscripts
represent partial derivatives. Skaperdas (1992), Neary (1997), and Skaperdas and Syropoulos (1997) provide
such more general treatments of the model presented in this subsection. Here, since the specification for total
output shown in (14) assumes that production is separable in the two inputs, X_1 and X_2, that representation
could be viewed simply as total production which depends on two separate and independent technologies,
one for each agent.

[13] Given our assumptions that (i) the players are risk neutral and (ii) the total quantity of production is linearly homogeneous and separable in the two factors, X_i, our interpretation of conflict as a winner-take-all
contest is again equivalent to the non-probabilistic interpretation, which views the winning probabilities as
consumption shares. Under the non-probabilistic interpretation, given our separable specification for aggregate production (14), one can think of agent i's consumption share, $p_i(G_1, G_2)$, as representing the fraction
of her own product, X_i, that she successfully defends and the fraction of the other agent's product, X_j, that
she confiscates with her choice of G_i, given G_j, $j \neq i$ [see footnote 12]. For an analysis that distinguishes
between defense and offense in appropriation, see Grossman and Kim (1995).

Although the conflict technology (3) implies, as before, that peace (i.e., $G_1 + G_2 = 0$) cannot be a Nash equilibrium outcome, variation in β_i and R_i across agents $i = 1$ and 2 means generally that we cannot rule out the possibility that one of the two agents will exhaust all of her initial resource in the production of guns, $G_i = R_i$, implying that $X_i = 0$, for $i = 1$ or 2.[14] However, to remain focussed on the central issues of concern, we will assume that the following first-order condition is satisfied at an interior optimum:

$$\frac{\partial V_i(G_1, G_2)}{\partial G_i} = \frac{\partial p_i(G_1, G_2)}{\partial G_i} \sum_{j=1}^{2} \beta_j [R_j - G_j] - \beta_i \, p_i(G_1, G_2) = 0, \quad i = 1, 2.$$
(16)

The first term on the LHS of the condition represents the marginal benefit of guns production, reflecting an increase in the likelihood of winning the contest when agent i produces an additional gun, which is shown in (9). As in the previous model, for both agents, the marginal effect of an increase in their production of guns is multiplied by the contested good to give an expression for the marginal benefit of guns to agent i as a function of the gun choices by both agents. However, in this model, what the agents are contesting – i.e., $\bar{B} = F(G)$ – is itself endogenous. The second term on the LHS of the condition represents the marginal cost to the agent of producing that additional gun – that is, the resulting reduction in butter output – weighted by the probability she will win the contest, as only in that case will she realize that (smaller) prize. The marginal cost to each agent i depends positively on her marginal product in the production of X_i, β_i. At an interior optimum, each agent i balances her marginal cost against her marginal benefit, such that the conditions in (16) implicitly define the equilibrium solutions for guns production, $G_i^* \in (0, R_i)$, for $i = 1, 2$.

3.2.1. Symmetric outcomes

In the special case where the agents are identical – i.e., $\beta_i = \beta = 1$ and $R_i = R$ for $i = 1, 2$, – these conditions imply a unique, pure-strategy symmetric Nash equilibrium in which $G_i = G^* < R$, and consequently each agent has an equal chance of winning the conflict: $p^* = \frac{1}{2}$ for $i = 1, 2$. To be more precise, using (3) with (16), it is straightforward to verify that

$$G_i^* = G^* = \frac{m}{m+1} R, \quad i = 1, 2,$$
(17)

which is increasing in the conflict effectiveness parameter (m) as well as in the initial resource (R). In turn, from Equation (14), we can find that the agents jointly produce

---

[14] To be sure, given our specifications for the payoff functions (15) and production (14), that a unique, pure-strategy equilibrium exists follows from our specification for the conflict technology (3). In particular, existence requires $p_i [\partial^2 p_i / \partial G_i^2] < (\partial p_i / \partial G_i)^2$, and uniqueness of that equilibrium follows from the general characteristics of (1) satisfied by our specification in (3). See Skaperdas and Syropoulos (1997).

$\overline{B} = F(G^*) = \frac{1}{m+1} 2R$ units of butter. Then, Equation (15) implies that, in this symmetric equilibrium, each agent i obtains an expected payoff, $V_i(G^*)$, equal to

$$V_i(G^*) = V^* = \frac{1}{m+1} R, \quad i = 1, 2, \tag{18}$$

which is decreasing in the conflict effectiveness parameter, m, but increasing in the initial resource each agent receives, R. These are precisely the implications of the simpler model of Section 3.1.

Even when we relax the symmetry assumption, and suppose instead that $R_1 \neq R_2$, but maintain the assumption that the two agents are equally productive, $\beta_1 = \beta_2 = 1$, a symmetric equilibrium obtains. That is, letting $\widetilde{R} \equiv \frac{1}{2}[R_1 + R_2]$ denote the mean value of the two players' initial resource and assuming an interior optimum,[15] the conditions in (16) imply the following solutions for guns:

$$G_i^* = G^* = \frac{m}{m+1} \widetilde{R}, \quad i = 1, 2. \tag{19}$$

In this case, since the parties make identical guns allocations ($G_1^* = G_2^*$) despite the difference in their initial endowments, the agents' expected payoffs, given by

$$V_i(G^*) = V^* = \frac{1}{m+1} \widetilde{R}, \quad i = 1, 2, \tag{20}$$

are identical, implying that insecurity neutralizes the effects of cross-sectional variation in the resource endowment on individual payoffs. Jack Hirshleifer (1991) attributes this tendency, which he coins the *paradox of power*, to the relatively poorer side viewing the marginal return from appropriation to be relatively higher than the marginal product from useful production.[16] Hence, the poorer side tends to devote a relatively greater share of her initial resource to appropriation. This result, however, does not necessarily extend to the more general specification for production, $F(X_1, X_2)$, which is similarly linearly homogeneous and increasing, but is also strictly concave in each input [see Skaperdas and Syropoulos (1997)].

3.2.2. Asymmetric outcomes

Now suppose that the agents differ with respect to both their initial resources, R_i, and their marginal products β_i. Suppose, in particular, to fix ideas that $\beta_1 > \beta_2$ such that agent 1 has a comparative advantage in useful production. Assume further that a fully

[15] The necessary and sufficient condition for an interior optimum, where neither player exhausts her entire resource on guns production, is the following: if $R_i > R_j$, then $R_j > \frac{m}{2+m} R_i$. This condition requires that the difference between the players' initial resource not be too large.
[16] Hirshleifer refers to the case where power (or consumption shares) is equalized across the players having different initial resources as the *strong form* of the paradox. He also takes note of a *weak form* in which the disparity in consumption shares is narrower than that in the initial endowments.

interior optimum exists.[17] Then taking the ratio of agent $i = 1$'s first-order condition to agent $i = 2$'s first-order condition, using (16) with (9), after some rearranging, shows

$$G_2^*/G_1^* = [\beta_1/\beta_2]^{\frac{1}{m+1}}, \tag{21}$$

or that $G_2^* > G_1^*$ if and only if $\beta_1 > \beta_2$. That is to say, the agent who is less effective in useful production will be the more powerful agent, in the sense that she has the greater chance of emerging as the winner of the conflict to take sole possession of total output, $\overline{B}$: $p_1(G_1^*, G_2^*) < p_2(G_1^*, G_2^*)$ or, equivalently, using (21) with (3),

$$p_1^* = \frac{1}{1 + (\beta_1/\beta_2)^{\frac{m}{m+1}}} < \frac{1}{2} < 1 - p_1^* = p_2^* = \frac{1}{1 + (\beta_2/\beta_1)^{\frac{m}{m+1}}}. \tag{22}$$

Further manipulation of the first-order conditions, (16) for $i = 1, 2$, gives us the following equilibrium solutions for guns:

$$G_1^* = \frac{\frac{m}{m+1}[\beta_1 R_1 + \beta_2 R_2]}{\beta_1[1 + (\beta_2/\beta_1)^{\frac{m}{m+1}}]} < G_2^* = \frac{\frac{m}{m+1}[\beta_1 R_1 + \beta_2 R_2]}{\beta_2[1 + (\beta_1/\beta_2)^{\frac{m}{m+1}}]}. \tag{23}$$

These solutions with the production specification in (14) imply further that the agents' joint production of butter equals $F(G^*) = \frac{1}{m+1}[\beta_1 R_1 + \beta_2 R_2]$. Then, one can easily verify that the payoff expected by agent i in equilibrium, which can be written as $V_i(G^*) = p_i^* F(G^*)$, $i = 1, 2$, with p_i^* equal to the appropriate solution shown in (22), is higher for the less productive player, $i = 2$, simply because $p_2^* > p_1^*$. It is important to note here that, with more general specifications for the production of butter than that assumed in (14), the inequality $\beta_1 > \beta_2$ need not indicate that agent $i = 1$ is relatively more productive. Nonetheless, where property is insecure, whoever is relatively more productive will have a smaller chance of enjoying the output she produced with her opponent.[18]

This result might seem surprising at first. After all, it stands in sharp contrast to the prediction of neoclassical economic theory, based on the assumption of well-defined and perfectly and costlessly enforced property rights, that agents are compensated according to their relative marginal productivities. However, the result here is entirely consistent with economic theory. Specifically, it is based on self-interest, as each agent exploits her own comparative advantage. Moreover, although the result has been shown within the context of a simple model, it is quite robust. In particular, it holds for a general class

---

[17] As illustrated in the previous example, an interior optimum where $X_i > 0$ holds for $i = 1, 2$ requires that any asymmetries present across agents i are relatively mild. In particular, assuming that $R_i > R_j$, a necessary and sufficient condition for the solutions shown in (23) to hold is that $[1 + (m + 1)(\beta_i/\beta_j)^{\frac{m}{m+1}}]\beta_j R_j > m\beta_i R_i$.

[18] For a detailed discussion and analysis which is related to the elasticity of substitution/complementarity between the agents' inputs, see Skaperdas and Syropoulos (1997).

of symmetric conflict technologies, with a more general specification for the production technology than that assumed here.[19]

Equation (21) reveals another striking result of this model, similar to the *paradox of power* mentioned above. That is, provided the resource constraint in guns production, $R_i - G_i \geqslant 0$ or $X_i \geqslant 0$, is not binding,[20] the equilibrium distribution of power depends only on the relative value of the players' marginal products β_i and the conflict effectiveness parameter m. The distribution of the initial resource R_i across the agents $i = 1, 2$ plays no role. This finding can be attributed to the combination of two assumptions: (i) the risk neutrality of economic agents; and (ii) the absence of complementarity in production (between input factors) or consumption (between different types of consumption goods). If either of these two assumptions were relaxed, asymmetries in the resource endowment would drive a wedge between the adversaries' guns choices and thus matter for the determination of power. An agent's probability of winning, in this case, would be positively related to the size of her endowment relative to that of her opponent.[21]

The inverse relationship between productivity and power helps us understand an empirical regularity for much of human history: those who enjoyed the highest material rewards also were, or had power over, specialists in violence. Kings, lords, knights, and warriors owed their material standard of living to the coercive power rather than their economic productivity. As Milgrom (1988) and Rajan and Zingales (2000) argue, a similar tendency may well exist within modern organizations in the absence of sufficient restraints on influence activities in such organizations.

Finally, the conflict effectiveness parameter, m, has the same qualitative influence in this setting as in the simpler model of the previous section. Specifically, a larger m implies a greater incentive to arm by all agents, and consequently less production of butter and material welfare.

4. Settlement in the shadow of conflict

In our presentation to this point, we have not distinguished between conflicts with probabilistic outcomes, in which each contending party has a probability of winning, and conflicts with deterministic outcomes, in which each party receives a share of what is under dispute. The equivalence of the probabilistic and deterministic interpretations of the representative models can be derived under the assumption of risk neutrality. However, risk neutrality is neither sufficient nor necessary. In practice, interactions under

---

[19] See Skaperdas and Syropoulos (1997). The implications of this result in a dynamic context for incentives to innovate are discussed below in Section 8.

[20] See footnote 17.

[21] Differences in resource endowments would matter in this case, regardless of whether the players are equally productive ($\beta_1 = \beta_2 = 1$) or not. See Skaperdas and Syropoulos (1997), who provide results in this spirit.

anarchy typically involve a great degree of accommodation by the interacting parties with open conflict (or warfare) being only a last resort, and the outcomes under conflict and under settlement are rather different.

To illustrate what sorts of conditions might be more conducive to settlement, where negotiations by the individual parties would be more likely to result in a division of the contested good (a "cold" war) instead of open conflict (a "hot" war), we envision the interactions between the players as a two-stage game with the following protocol of moves:

Stage 1. Parties independently and simultaneously make their guns choices.

Stage 2. Given those choices, they enter into negotiations about how to divide the contested good.

    2.1. If they agree on a division, they share the good accordingly.

    2.2. If they reach an impasse, their negotiations end in conflict, with the winner taking the entire prize, leaving nothing for the other party.

The decision of whether to fight is made in Stage 2. Obviously, both parties would have to agree on a particular division for settlement to emerge as the equilibrium outcome, but only one party has to decide to fight for open conflict to emerge as the outcome. There are a number of compelling reasons for both parties to prefer a settlement in Stage 2, and we discuss briefly some major ones below first. Then we characterize outcomes under settlement under various rules of division.

4.1. Sources of the preference for settlement

4.1.1. Destruction and additional costs of open conflict

Contrary to our implicit assumption in the models of the previous section, open conflict typically destroys output and resources, and requires the use of arms beyond those that would be necessary for the parties to negotiate a settlement. Under the reasonable assumption that fighting yields no other benefits, a negotiated settlement should be feasible – that is, provided, the parties have open channels of communication.

To illustrate, we return to the benchmark model of Section 3.2, where any particular choice of guns that might have been made in Stage 1, say G'_i, $i = 1, 2$, would, by the technology constraint in (14), result in the following production of butter: $F(G) = \sum_{i=1}^{2} \beta_i [R_i - G'_i]$. We suppose that, in this setting, if fighting were to occur, only a fraction, $\phi < 1$, of total butter output, $F(G)$, would be left for the winner with the remaining fraction, $1 - \phi$, destroyed in combat. Under settlement, by contrast, this output is divided in accordance with the winning probabilities. Then, given the technology of conflict (1), the expected payoff in the event of open conflict would be $p_i(G'_1, G'_2)\phi F(G)$, for $i = 1, 2$. Under settlement where the losses from fighting are avoided, the agents' payoffs are $p_i(G'_1, G'_2)F(G)$ for $i = 1, 2$. Provided that $\phi < 1$, both sides would have an incentive to agree on the division of the total pie in accordance with the winning probabilities. Note that this incentive emerges despite the assumption that the two players are risk neutral, suggesting that knowing their attitudes towards risk alone is not sufficient to determine their preference(s) for settlement relative to open conflict.

There would be, of course, many other ways to divide the pie, but the possibilities are limited by each player's option to shut down negotiations and fight instead. That is to say, each agent's expected payoff under open conflict, which depends on their holdings of guns chosen in advance, defines the minimum payoff the agent would be willing to accept under any division rule. At the same time, the agents' holdings of guns serve to enforce any settlement they reach. Hence, the feasibility of these agreements is not predicated on third-party enforcement, and thus could be supported under anarchy. As discussed below in the context of our model with both appropriation and production where the agents are identical, at least one rule of division among the set of rules that could be supported under anarchy (i.e., those rules that both agents find acceptable) strictly dominates the rule of division we have considered which is based on winning probabilities alone. Thus, here we have shown the possibility of a preference for settlement under conditions that are not most favorable to such a preference.

4.1.2. Risk aversion and the uncertainty of conflict

The outcome of open conflict is typically subject to much uncertainty. While we have captured this uncertainty in our models, we have, at the same time, maintained that the contending parties are risk-neutral – that they do not care about the risk entailed in the outcome of open conflict. But, the fact of the matter is that most people are risk averse, particularly when it comes to large uncertain events – such as wars – having much potential to affect their jobs, career paths, health, and more generally their lives. If possible, they would avoid risks, but if it is not possible to avoid these risks, individuals would try to insure against them. We would expect such attitudes toward risk to transfer to political and military leaders and to the risk preferences expressed at the country level. Because war is uncertain but a particular settlement is not, a range of negotiated settlements can be expected to be preferable by both parties.

This logic can be shown within our benchmark model of Section 3.2. Again consider any particular choice of guns that might have been made in Stage 1, say G'_i, $i = 1, 2$. Then the production specification in (14) implies the following total output of butter: $F(G) = \sum_{i=1}^{2} \beta_i [R_i - G'_i]$. To isolate the importance of risk aversion alone, we assume no destruction from fighting: $\phi = 1$. Strictly concave von-Neumann–Morgenstern utility functions – i.e., $U(\cdot)$ with $U_B > 0$ and $U_{BB} < 0$, where subscripts denote partial derivatives – reflect the agents' aversion to risk. Then, in the event of conflict, agent i's expected payoff would be $p_i(G'_1, G'_2)U[F(G)] + [1 - p_i(G'_1, G'_2)]U[0]$. By contrast, under settlement, where each party receives a share of butter that equals her winning probability or $p_i(G'_1, G'_2)F(G) + [1 - p_i(G'_1, G'_2)]0 = p_i(G'_1, G'_2)F(G)$, her payoff would be $U[p_i(G'_1, G'_2)F(G)]$. By the strict concavity of $U(\cdot)$, the payoff under settlement is strictly greater than the expected payoff under war for any given set of choices for guns, G'_1 and G'_2. Thus, risk aversion could motivate both sides to agree to a division of the pie according to their winning probabilities whereby they could avoid fighting.[22]

It would be quite reasonable to argue that, in practice, there are multiple sources of uncertainty, whereas we assume only one – who will win and who will lose – with the probabilities $p_i(G'_1, G'_2)$, $i = 1, 2$, known by both sides. Do our results, then, understate the agents' preference for settlement? It is true that assuming only one source of uncertainty imparts quite a bit of knowledge on both parties. It is not immediately obvious, however, that admitting additional sources of uncertainty (e.g., different expectations, unforeseen contingencies, and so on), would make risk averse players even more conservative and more willing to negotiate. To the best of our knowledge, no one has formally examined the effects of risk aversion in such complicated environments. And, there is a well-known finding related to the issue in hand that, in the presence of incomplete information, where each side has a different set of beliefs about the nature of their interaction, the contending sides are more likely to choose open conflict in equilibrium [see, e.g., Brito and Intriligator (1985) and Bester and Wärneryd (2006)].[23]

4.1.3. Complementarities in production and consumption

Another consequence of open conflict having winners and losers is that the distribution of what is being contested among the parties could easily be far from what would be optimal for production or consumption. Consider, for example, the situation where two agents contest some territory. In the case of war, the winner could get all the contested land minus its people who might become refugees on the loser's remaining territory. In this case, the winner would likely have too much land relative to its available labor force, whereas the losing country would have insufficient land relative to its available labor force. In a negotiated settlement, the two countries could avoid this imbalance, thereby making both sides better off than they would be in expected terms under war. Likewise, there are complementarities between final consumption goods and a similar line of reasoning that shows a preference for negotiated settlements applies.

To make this reasoning more explicit, we must consider a slightly different model of conflict. One possibility, which follows our discussion above, involves several modifications to the benchmark model presented in Section 3.2. In the modified model, the two agents, $i = 1, 2$, do not contest their output. Instead, as in the model presented in Section 3.1, they contest a productive resource, which we denote here by T for territory or land. Let T_i denote country i's holding of land, which would be realized with the outcome of Stage 2 of the negotiation process, whether it be under

---

[22] Again, for reasons made explicit below, dividing the pie according to the agents' winning probabilities need not be the best rule, such that the preference for settlement could be stronger than what these calculations would indicate.

[23] Risk aversion can also have distributional effects similar to those examined in the previous section. See Skaperdas (1991) and Konrad and Schlesinger (1997).

open conflict in a winner-take-all contest or under settlement by a division in accordance with the winning probabilities. At the same time, like the model of Section 3.2, this modified model supposes that each agent is endowed with a secure resource, $\widehat{R}_i$ units of human capital, which she allocates to appropriative activities (G_i) and productive activities (L_i), subject to the constraint, $\widehat{R}_i = G_i + L_i/\beta_i$.[24] Each agent i produces butter, B_i, with her inputs T_i and L_i, according to the following technology: $B_i = F(T_i, L_i)$, $i = 1, 2$, which is increasing and strictly concave in T_i and L_i (given G_i) and exhibits some degree of complementarity between its input factors, $F_{T_i L_i} > 0$, where subscripts denote partial derivatives. Now suppose again that in Stage 1, each agent chooses a certain quantity of guns, G_i', leaving $L_i' = \beta_i[\widehat{R}_i - G_i']$ units of labor for the production of butter. Then, under open conflict, agent i's expected payoff would be $p_i(G_1', G_2')F[T, L_i'] + [1 - p_i(G_1', G_2')]F[0, L_i']$. Under a negotiated settlement with each party receiving a share of the contested resource equal to her winning probability $T_i = p_i(G_1', G_2')T$, the payoff obtained by each agent i would be $B_i = F[p_i(G_1', G_2')T, L_i']$. While each agent is assumed to be risk neutral, the strict concavity of $F(\cdot, L_i)$ in land makes the players' payoffs under settlement strictly greater than their respective expected payoffs under war for any given choice of guns, G_i', $i = 1, 2$.

4.2. How much arming? Settlement under different rules of division

Based on a number of alternative two-stage models of conflict – largely, variations of the benchmark model presented in Section 3.2 – with the protocol of moves specified above, we have shown there exists a range of different scenarios that render settlement preferable to open conflict. Settlement would then be a part of any perfect equilibrium of games with the protocol of moves that we specified above. However, we have not even touched upon the implications of settlement for arming. Recall that, in this anarchic setting, the individual parties can make no firm commitments regarding their guns choices. Does the expectation of reaching a negotiated settlement in the future reduce the parties' choices relative to the case where they anticipate war? Furthermore, among the many possible negotiated settlements and rules of division that would be acceptable to both sides, which ones would the two sides be expected to use? Are there any rules of division that are "better" than others and, if so, in what sense? While we cannot answer all of these questions, in this subsection we illustrate how different rules of division affect arming and material welfare. In particular, we demonstrate the sensitivity of arming and welfare to the rule of division.

---

[24] It is important to distinguish not only between secure and insecure resource endowments, but given our interest here in complements in production, also between different types of factor inputs. Hence, whereas we view the secure resource, R, in the model of Section 3.2 as a composite of labor, land, capital and other inputs, we must view the secure resource $\widehat{R}$ of this modified framework more narrowly to exclude land, the insecure resource. That all land is insecure in this modified framework is not important for our purposes. But, if we were to relax this assumption, the quantity of agent i's secure land would be included in the measure T_i.

To proceed, we return to the benchmark model of Section 3.2, with one modification only, that open conflict is destructive.[25] Specifically, suppose that a fraction $1 - \phi$ of butter would be lost if fighting broke out. Assume further, for convenience, that both agents are identical with respect to their productivities: $\beta_1 = \beta_2 = 1$. We continue, however, to allow for differences in their initial resource: R_1 and R_2, with $\widetilde{R} \equiv \frac{1}{2}[R_1 + R_2]$ indicating the mean value. If open conflict were to break out in the second stage, the two parties' guns choices, indicated by the vector G, and the resulting production of butter, $\overline{B} = F(G)$, as dictated by (12) and (14) when $\beta_i = 1$ imply that the expected payoff for agent $i = 1, 2$ would be given by the total quantity of butter not destroyed in combat weighted by the probability of winning, $p_i(G_1, G_2)$, as specified in (3):

$$V_i^w = p_i(G_1, G_2)\phi[2\widetilde{R} - G_1 - G_2], \tag{24}$$

for $i = 1, 2$.

Under settlement, the two sides agree to divide their joint product, $\overline{B} = F(G)$, according to some rule, which will depend at least in part on their guns choices. For now, suppose that, by this rule, the share of total butter agent i receives is $\delta_i(G_1, G_2)$, implying the following payoff under settlement:

$$V_i^s = \delta_i(G_1, G_2)[2\widetilde{R} - G_1 - G_2], \tag{25}$$

for $i = 1, 2$.

4.2.1. Equilibrium under open conflict

For future comparisons, consider the outcome if both agents expect their negotiations to breakdown, resulting in open conflict in Stage 2. With this expectation, each agent i would choose G_i in Stage 1 to maximize her expected payoff, V_i^w, subject to the conflict technology (3), taking the other side's choice as given. The first-order conditions from the agents' optimization problems, assuming an interior optimum, are given by

$$\frac{\partial V_i^w}{\partial G_i} = \frac{\partial p_i(G_1, G_2)}{\partial G_i}\phi[2\widetilde{R} - G_1 - G_2] - \phi p_i(G_1, G_2) = 0, \quad i = 1, 2.$$

Observe that $\phi > 0$ can be factored out from both the first term – the marginal benefit of guns – and the second term – the marginal cost of guns – on the LHS of each agent's condition. Thus, the conditions above for $i = 1, 2$ simplify to those from the model of Section 3.2 (16), with $\beta_1 = \beta_2 = 1$. As can be easily confirmed using the conditions above with (3) and (9), the optimizing solutions, G_i^w, are given by

$$G_i^w = G^w = \frac{m}{m+1}\widetilde{R}, \quad i = 1, 2, \tag{26}$$

---

[25] As suggested by our discussion above, either risk aversion or complementarity in production or consumption would similarly create a short-term incentive for the parties to settle. Assuming that open conflict has a destructive element, however, makes the calculus much easier. For a comparison of alternative rules of division in the case of complementarities, see Anbarci, Skaperdas and Syropoulos (2002).

and are identical to those where war was assumed *not* to be destructive (19).[26] These solutions, in turn, imply an equal distribution of power: $p^{\mathrm{w}} = \frac{1}{2}$ for $i = 1, 2$. Then combining equations (26) and (14) shows that the quantity of butter available for consumption, after factoring in the destruction of warfare, would be $\phi F(G^{\mathrm{w}}) = \frac{2\phi}{m+1} \widetilde{R}$. Thus, the payoff that each party i could expect under war, V_i^{w}, is

$$V_i^{\mathrm{w}} = V^{\mathrm{w}} = \frac{\phi}{m+1} \widetilde{R}, \quad i = 1, 2, \tag{27}$$

which is decreasing in war's destruction $(1 - \phi > 0)$ and the effectiveness of conflict (m), but increasing in the mean value of the initial resource $(\widetilde{R} \equiv \frac{1}{2}[R_1 + R_2])$.

4.2.2. Equilibrium under settlement: Division by winning probabilities

Now we suppose that both sides expect that they will be able to agree in Stage 2 on a division of total output according to their winning probabilities: $\delta_i(G_1, G_2) = p_i(G_1, G_2)$, as specified in (3). Given that expectation, each party i in Stage 1 chooses G_i to maximize V_i^{s} subject to (3) taking the other agent's choice as given. The associated first-order conditions, in this case given by

$$\frac{\partial V_i^{\mathrm{ps}}}{\partial G_i} = \frac{\partial p_i(G_1, G_2)}{\partial G_i} [2\widetilde{R} - G_1 - G_2] - p_i(G_1, G_2) = 0, \quad i = 1, 2,$$

are identical to those in the case where war is anticipated, since ϕ drops out of the latter expressions, implying that the optimizing guns choices, denoted by G_i^{ps}, $i = 1, 2$, in this case, are identical to the optimizing choices when open conflict is anticipated in Stage 2: $G^{\mathrm{ps}} = G^{\mathrm{w}}$ as shown in (26).

This result should not be surprising. Given risk neutrality and the separability of production in its inputs, X_i, $i = 1, 2$, the marginal benefit of guns relative to their marginal cost under settlement with this rule of division, $\delta_i(G_1, G_2) = p_i(G_1, G_2)$, is identical to that under open conflict. With the incentive structure unchanged at the margin, both sides naturally allocate the same amount of resources to guns as they would under conflict, whereby each can ensure that her opponent gains no advantage in her bargaining position for their negotiations relative to their respective positions of power if they were to wage war. As a consequence, the quantity of intermediate goods each brings to the joint production process under settlement is identical to that under war, and the total amount of butter produced is also unchanged.

However, the equivalence of the players' allocation to guns when war is anticipated to that when settlement is anticipated should not be interpreted as an indication of the irrelevance of the damaging effects of warfare. Those effects do matter, as reflected in the difference between the size of total pie to be divided under settlement, $F(G^{\mathrm{ps}})$, and the size the pie contested under open conflict, $\phi F(G^{\mathrm{w}})$, given

---

[26] Thus, the condition for an interior optimum when war is destructive is identical to the condition which abstracts from war's destructive effects [see footnote 15].

by $F(G^{\mathrm{ps}}) - \phi F(G^{\mathrm{w}}) = \frac{2(1-\phi)}{m+1} \widetilde{R}$, which is positive by our assumption that war is destructive, $1 - \phi > 0$. Although the way in which the agents divide the pie under settlement coincides with that under open conflict ($p^{\mathrm{ps}} = p^{\mathrm{w}} = \frac{1}{2}$ for $i = 1, 2$), by allowing the agents to avoid the destructive effects of open conflict, settlement with $\delta_i(G_1, G_2) = p_i(G_1, G_2)$ brings both sides a higher payoff, V_i^{ps}, given by

$$V_i^{\mathrm{ps}} = V^{\mathrm{ps}} = \frac{1}{m+1} \widetilde{R}, \quad i = 1, 2, \tag{28}$$

which exceeds that which they could expect under war, V^{w}, as shown in (27). The difference, given by $\frac{1}{2}[F(G^{\mathrm{ps}}) - \phi F(G^{\mathrm{w}})]$ is positive, as argued above, and increasing in the mean value of the initial resource, $\widetilde{R}$ as well as war's destructive effects on output, $1 - \phi$, but decreasing in the effectiveness of conflict, m. The negative effect of m can be attributed to its equally negative influence on butter production under settlement and under war which is only in the latter case subject to destruction.

4.2.3. Equilibrium under settlement: Split-the-surplus rule of division

Still, one has to wonder if it would be possible for the agents to settle on a division of their joint product without diverting as many resources to the production of guns. One alternative division splits the surplus realized relative to the threat point of war equally; hence, it should not be surprising that this rule is referred to as *split-the-surplus*. Under risk neutrality, this rule coincides with the prescription of any symmetric bargaining solution, including the Nash bargaining solution, and is implementable non-cooperatively by a number of alternating-offers games [see Muthoo (1999) or Osborne and Rubinstein (1990)]. This rule can be found by simply setting $V_1^{\mathrm{s}} - V_1^{\mathrm{w}} = V_2^{\mathrm{s}} - V_2^{\mathrm{w}}$ for any given G_1, G_2, where $p_1(G_1, G_2) = p(G_1, G_2)$, $p_2(G_1, G_2) = 1 - p(G_1, G_2)$, $\delta_1(G_1, G_2) = \delta(G_1, G_2)$ and $\delta_2(G_1, G_2) = 1 - \delta(G_1, G_2)$:

$$\delta(G_1, G_2) = \phi p(G_1, G_2) + \frac{1}{2}(1 - \phi). \tag{29}$$

We continue to use the power functional form shown in (3). Each party's share of total output under settlement, δ for agent $i = 1$ and $1 - \delta$ for agent $i = 2$, is a weighted combination of two possible rules:
  (i) the probabilistic contest success function, $p(G_1, G_2)$; and,
  (ii) a 50–50 split of the output outright.
The relative weights are determined by the destruction parameter $1 - \phi$. When ϕ is smaller implying that more output is destroyed in warfare, the conflict technology plays a smaller role in the determination of the distribution of final output, and each side's choice of guns has a smaller impact on the settlement outcome.

The agents' optimizing choices for guns made in Stage 1, when they anticipate that they will agree in the second stage to divide their joint product based on (29), will again be symmetric, but not identical to their choices when they anticipate open conflict (or equivalently to their choices when they anticipate settlement where their joint product is divided according to their respective winning probabilities). In particular, from the first-order conditions to the optimization problems for agents $i = 1, 2$, given respectively in this case by

$$\frac{\partial V_1^{ss}}{\partial G_1} = \frac{\partial p(G_1, G_2)}{\partial G_1} \phi[2\tilde{R} - G_1 - G_2] - \delta(G_1, G_2) = 0,$$

$$\frac{\partial V_2^{ss}}{\partial G_2} = -\frac{\partial p(G_1, G_2)}{\partial G_2} \phi[2\tilde{R} - G_1 - G_2] - \left[1 - \delta(G_1, G_2)\right] = 0,$$

with $\delta(G_1, G_2)$ specified in (29), using (3) and (9), one can find the agents' allocations to guns in the symmetric equilibrium, denoted by G_i^{ss}:

$$G_i^{ss} = G^{ss} = \frac{\phi m}{\phi m + 1} \tilde{R}, \quad i = 1, 2. \tag{30}$$

Since $\phi < 1$, the allocation to guns under settlement with this rule is less than that under war: $G^{ss} < G^{ps} = G^w$. The smaller role played by the agents' guns choices in the split-the-surplus rule of division induces less equilibrium arming than that which would emerge either under open conflict or under settlement where $\delta_i = p_i$. Furthermore, as war becomes more destructive (i.e., as ϕ decreases), the importance of guns in $\delta(G_1, G_2)$ falls further, and, as a consequence, so does the equilibrium allocation to guns. Since the two agents produce the same quantity of guns, $p^{ss} = 1 - p^{ss} = \frac{1}{2}$, implying each is positioned to secure one-half of total output in their negotiations: $\delta = 1 - \delta = \frac{1}{2}$. With the production specification shown in (14), the agents' guns choices give us total output, $F(G^{ss}) = \frac{2}{\phi m + 1} \tilde{R}$, which exceeds that under war, $F(G^w)$, again provided that conflict is destructive $(1 - \phi > 0)$. This solution for output and its division according to $\delta = \frac{1}{2}$ implies that, under settlement with the split-the-surplus rule of division, party i can obtain a payoff, V_i^{ss}, equal to

$$V_i^{ss} = V^{ss} = \frac{1}{\phi m + 1} \tilde{R}, \quad i = 1, 2, \tag{31}$$

which is strictly greater than V^{ps} as well as V^w. The potential short-term gain from settlement in this case, given by $V^{ss} - V^w = \frac{m(1-\phi)}{(m+1)(\phi m+1)} \tilde{R}$, is increasing in the mean value of the initial resource $(\tilde{R})$ and in war's destructive element, $1 - \phi$, as before, but also increasing in the effectiveness of conflict (m). The positive influence of m can be attributed to the reduction in the players' incentive to arm under this particular rule of division given any m relative to the case of open conflict. That is, butter production is less sensitive to an increase in m under settlement than it is under open conflict. Although production under conflict and settlement both fall with m increases, any given increase in m causes $F(G^{ss})$ to fall by less than $F(G^w)$, thereby augmenting the possible gains under settlement.

4.2.4. Discussion: Rules of division and norms of conduct

There are a variety of other rules which differ with respect to their sensitivity to the agents' guns choices. In another, more complex environment, similar to that sketched above in Section 4.1.3, Anbarci, Skaperdas and Syropoulos (2002) examine the sensitivity of the parties' arming choices to rules of division under settlement generated by three alternative bargaining solution concepts. In their analysis, they find that the extent to which a rule depends on the players' threat points (i.e., their expected payoffs under conflict) has a positive influence on the extent to which the rule induces guns production under settlement, while leaving their relative bargaining positions unaffected, and thus has a negative effect on the players' payoffs.[27] Their findings suggest a positive role for *norms against threats* in anarchic settings. In particular, such norms can influence the conduct of the players in such a way so as to lower their incentive to arm, without substantively changing the terms of the settlement, thereby enhancing material welfare, even in the absence of a higher authority. Other norms and institutions similarly limit arming under anarchy, though we would not expect that they could substitute fully for guns. Guns will always be around, for they provide the "last-resort" means of conveying a credible threat to use force when all else fails. But arming could be supplanted, to a large extent, by diplomacy and politics, provided that the norms, institutions, and organizations are widely recognized as relevant to settling disputes.

In a related strand of the literature that can be traced back to Axelrod (1984), social scientists have modelled the evolution of norms, institutions and organizations as cooperative equilibria of indefinitely repeated supergames. In such games, the more individual parties value the future, the larger is the set of feasible outcomes (i.e., those which can be supported under anarchy), as alternatives preferred by all interested parties over open conflict. This approach, which exploits the repeated game setting with a dynamic strategy, could provide the rationale for the adoption of rules or *norms* that call for lower spending on guns, thereby leaving more resources for the production of butter.[28] However, Powell (1993) and Skaperdas and Syropoulos (1996a) have found, in different settings, that a longer shadow of the future could add to the players' incentive to arm under conflict. Moreover, as we shall see in the next section, a longer shadow of the future could reverse their preference ordering of settlement and war, to favor war.

---

[27] The rules analyzed include: (i) the split-the-surplus rule when there are cardinal preferences; (ii) the equal-sacrifice rule which splits the difference between the players' maximum, feasible payoffs and their respective payoffs under conflict; and, (iii) the Kalai–Smorodinsky rule which is effectively a weighted average of the first two rules. Among those rules, the equal-sacrifice rule induces the smallest amount of guns production, while the split-the-surplus rule falls at the other end of the spectrum, and the Kalai–Smorodinsky rule lies in between the two extremes. Anbarci, Skaperdas and Syropoulos (2002) suggest that these tendencies remain intact as we move away from the symmetric case, as long as the differences do not grow too large. In our simple setting, where the Pareto frontier is linear, all division rules yield the same solution.

[28] Garfinkel (1990) shows how, for a given rule of division, the set can be restricted by exogenous factors – namely, the mean and variance of the distribution from which the players' initial resource endowments are (identically) drawn. A larger mean increases whereas a mean-preserving spread reduces that set.

5. Why fight?

Given our discussion identifying a wide variety of factors that tend to create a short-term preference for settlement over open conflict, the emergence of inter-state and civil wars throughout history might seem puzzling. In what follows, we outline some of the longstanding and the more recent explanations for why we observe open conflict.

5.1. Traditional explanations: Asymmetric information, misperceptions, irrationality

War is often attributed to misperceptions, misunderstandings, or simply to irrationality and base instincts. But, those seeking an explanation consistent with *rational* behavior often appeal instead to the sorts of problems that can arise under asymmetric information, where the parties involved are assumed to know more about themselves in terms of their own valuation over what is being disputed and their willingness to bear the risks of war to fight for it as well as the strength of their own military forces than do their opponents. If the parties could communicate their privately held and otherwise unverifiable information to the opponent credibly during the bargaining process, they could facilitate a peaceful settlement. As discussed above, such an outcome would be preferable to open conflict. However, there are incentives to misrepresent that information. Specifically, each party would like to appear "tougher" than they truly are – not only in terms of their resolve to fight, but in terms of the strength of their military forces as well – to obtain a more advantageous position in the negotiations. Thus, any attempt to reveal this private information say through verbal communication is not likely to be very successful. But, Brito and Intriligator (1985) show in their seminal work that war can emerge in a separating equilibrium as a costly means of communication. Fearon (1995) suggests along similar lines that, in settings of asymmetric information, war could be chosen by a country, in a preemptive move, as a costly signal of its strength to others it may encounter in future negotiations. Sánchez-Pagés (2004) extends this line of reasoning to suppose that information about the adversaries' strength can be transmitted on the battlefield in limited conflict before and during negotiations until a final settlement is reached or negotiations breakdown, resulting in a full scale war. Azam and Mesnard (2003) and Bester and Wärneryd (2006) identify conditions under which, given asymmetric information, a peaceful agreement is not possible.[29]

5.2. Incomplete contracting in the shadow of the future

War can be rationalized, however, without appealing to problems of information at all. This alternative explanation, which has been proposed and examined recently by Fearon

---

[29] To be sure, there are circumstances where asymmetric information could alleviate conflict. In particular, Wärneryd (2003) shows that, if both parties are equally informed about the value of the prize they are contesting, the conflict between them can be more intense, thereby inducing more arming in equilibrium, than one would observe if only one of the two parties were fully informed about the value of the prize.

(1995), Powell (2006), and ourselves in Garfinkel and Skaperdas (2000), has two key components:

  (i) Although short-term contracts, conditional on arming and under the threat of conflict, can be written, adversaries are unable to enforce long-term contracts on arming.
 (ii) Open conflict changes the future strategic positions of the adversaries in different ways than a peaceful contract under the threat of conflict does.

To illustrate, we extend the one-period model of Section 3.1 to two periods, with period $t = 1$ representing today and period $t = 2$ representing the future, and assume that war is destructive, $\phi < 1$.[30] At the beginning of each of the two periods $t = 1, 2$, there are $\overline{R} = 2R$ units of a resource which can be consumed directly. The sequence of actions within each period is as specified in the previous section: In the first stage of period t, each side makes its guns choice; and, in the second stage of period t, given their choices of guns G_{it} for $i = 1, 2$, they decide whether to settle on a division of the resource, $\overline{R}$, or to go to war. We assume that, under settlement, the resource is divided in accordance with (29), which splits the surplus equally.[31] In the event of a war in $t = 1$, the winning party alone takes possession of the contested resource net of the war's destructive effects, $\phi \overline{R}$, for consumption, leaving nothing for the losing party. We assume further to emphasize war's longer term effects in the most convenient way, that the losing party is eliminated all together in the future.[32] In this case, the winning party is able to enjoy, on top of today's resource endowment, the future endowment, without any sort of conflict and, thus, without any need to arm.[33] However, both the current and future resource endowments are subject to the destructive forces of a war in the current period.

In this dynamic setting, actions taken in both stages of period $t = 1$ influence the amount of resources available to them in period $t = 2$. Rational, forward-looking parties

---

[30] In Garfinkel and Skaperdas (2000), we develop this argument within the context of the model of appropriation and production presented above in Section 3.2. In other related research, McBride and Skaperdas (2005) examine an infinite-horizon version of the model presented here, modified to allow for the possibility that the final winner of the conflict will have to win multiple battles. Based on related finite and infinite horizon models, Bester and Konrad (2004, 2005) extend the scope of the analysis to examine the effect of asymmetries between the rivals who contemplate whether or not to attack specific territories.

[31] In cases where the players are risk neutral and the opportunity cost of guns is constant such that the Pareto frontier is linear, all symmetric axiomatic bargaining solutions prescribe the same outcome, which is precisely that which is given by this rule.

[32] In a more general setting such as that of Skaperdas and Syropoulos (1997) where there is production and the production technology exhibits diminishing returns and complementarity in the two parties' inputs, the qualitative results of this logic would follow through with a less extreme assumption. All that would be required is that the defeated side's second-period initial resource is sufficiently small relative to that of the victor in the case of open conflict.

[33] Strictly speaking, the contest success function specified in (3) requires that the remaining party devote some resources to arming. However, it need only devote an infinitesimal amount to guns to gain full possession of $\phi \overline{R}$. But, to keep matters simple, we suppose that a party who receives nothing in the first period simply cannot participate in the second period of the game.

will take this influence into account when making their period $t = 1$ choices. But, to do so, they need to know what would occur in period $t = 2$ for each possible outcome (war and settlement) in period $t = 1$. This perspective accords with the notion of *sub-game perfection*, an appropriate equilibrium concept for such dynamic games. We therefore solve the model backwards, starting from the second and final period.

5.2.1. Preliminaries: The second-period outcome

In the second and final period of the game, neither side has to consider the effects of their choices for the future; there is no future beyond that period. Hence, the conditions and constraints effective in the second period are identical to those in the single-period model.

When there is settlement in the first period. When neither side has been eliminated by a war in period $t = 1$, the choices they face in period $t = 2$ will be identical to those within the context of a one-period model. That is, as confirmed below, the destruction caused by war creates a short-term preference for settlement. Accordingly, party i's choice of guns maximizes $V_{i2}(G_1, G_2) = \delta_i(G_1, G_2)\overline{R} - G_i$, $i = 1, 2$, where $\delta_1(G_1, G_2)$ is given by (29) and $\delta_2(G_1, G_2) = 1 - \delta_1(G_1, G_2)$. As can be easily verified, the solutions for guns are

$$G_{12}^s = G_{22}^s = \frac{\phi m}{2} R, \tag{32}$$

where as previously defined R measures the contested resource in per capita terms. This expression reveals that the optimizing choice for guns is increasing in the conflict effectiveness parameter, m, and the contested resource $R = \frac{1}{2}\overline{R}$. In addition, since the relevance of each player's guns choices for determining its respective share of the contested resource, by the specification of the division rule (29), is negatively related to the destructiveness of war, $-\phi$, guns production under settlement too is negatively related to $-\phi$. In fact, given the destructive effects of war ($\phi < 1$), the solution for guns under settlement with the split-of-surplus division rule (29) in this model, as in the model of Section 3.2 with production and appropriation, is less than that under war [see Equation (10)].

Since $G_{12}^s = G_{22}^s$, each party gets an equal share of the contested resource, $\delta = 1 - \delta = \frac{1}{2}$, which implies the following period $t = 2$ payoffs:

$$V_{12} = V_{22} = \left[1 - \frac{\phi m}{2}\right] R, \tag{33}$$

which for $\phi < 1$ is greater than the payoff each side expects under conflict (11). Thus, as claimed above, the short-term preference for settlement is present in this model too when war is destructive.

When there is war in the first period. Now when there is war in period $t = 1$, the winning party need not allocate any valuable resources to arming in period $t = 2$ to ensure a share of the resource, since by assumption the loser is eliminated, with a zero payoff. In eliminating the opponent, the winning party can avoid the period $t = 2$ cost of conflict. Still, the destructive effect of combat in period $t = 1$ carries over into period $t = 2$, such that there are only $\phi\overline{R} = \phi 2R$ units of the endowment (where $\phi < 1$) left for the winner to enjoy. These assumptions are summarized as follows: given that war breaks out in period $t = 1$, no choices are made in period $t = 2$ and the payoffs are given by:

$$V_{i2} = \begin{cases} \phi 2R & \text{if } i \text{ wins the war;} \\ 0 & \text{otherwise,} \end{cases} \tag{34}$$

for $i = 1, 2$. In this case, either $V_{12} > 0$ and $V_{22} = 0$ or $V_{12} = 0$ and $V_{22} > 0$.

5.2.2. Settlement or war? First-period choices

In the first period, each party cares about the sum of the payoffs it will receive over the two periods. That is, party i's two-period objective function is described by

$$W_i = V_{i1} + \lambda V_{i2}, \tag{35}$$

for $i = 1, 2$ where $\lambda \in (0, 1]$ represents the players' identical time preference. As revealed by Equations (33) and (34), the second-period payoffs depend on first-period choices in a discrete way. In effect, then, the two-period payoffs, W_i, depend on what occurs in the first period only – that is, on the party's first-period arming and war-or-settlement decisions.

When there is war.   Using (34) and (35) and letting $p(G_{11}, G_{21})$ denote side 1's probability of winning in period $t = 1$ and $1 - p(G_{11}, G_{21})$ denote side 2's probability of winning in period $t = 1$, the war payoffs, given $G_{i1}, i = 1, 2$, are:

$$\begin{aligned} W_1^w &= p(G_{11}, G_{21})\phi 2R - G_{11} + \lambda p(G_{11}, G_{21})\phi 2R \\ &= p(G_{11}, G_{21})\phi(1 + \lambda)\overline{R} - G_{11}, \end{aligned} \tag{36a}$$

$$\begin{aligned} W_2^w &= \left(1 - p(G_{11}, G_{21})\right)\phi 2R - G_{21} + \left(1 - p(G_{11}, G_{21})\right)\lambda\phi 2R \\ &= \left(1 - p(G_{11}, G_{21})\right)\phi(1 + \lambda)\overline{R} - G_{21}. \end{aligned} \tag{36b}$$

Keep in mind that these are expected payoffs: the winnings realized by party i in the event of a victory in the period $t = 1$ war, compounded over the two periods and weighted by the party's probability of winning.

When there is settlement.   As before, let $\delta(G_{11}, G_{21}) \in (0, 1)$ denote the share received by side 1 and thus $1 - \delta(G_{11}, G_{21})$ denote the share received by side 2 in Stage 2 of the first period, given G_{i1} for $i = 1, 2$ and the sharing rule negotiated in the second period under settlement.[34] Then, the two-period payoffs under settlement, using (33) and (35), can be written as

$$W_1^s = \delta(G_{11}, G_{21})2R - G_{11} + \lambda\left[1 - \frac{\phi m}{2}\right]R$$

$$= \left[\delta(G_{11}, G_{21}) + \frac{\lambda}{2}\left(1 - \frac{\phi m}{2}\right)\right]\bar{R} - G_{11}, \tag{37a}$$

$$W_2^s = \left(1 - \delta(G_{11}, G_{21})\right)2R - G_{21} + \lambda\left[1 - \frac{\phi m}{2}\right]R$$

$$= \left[1 - \delta(G_{11}, G_{21}) + \frac{\lambda}{2}\left(1 - \frac{\phi m}{2}\right)\right]\bar{R} - G_{21}. \tag{37b}$$

In contrast to the two-period payoffs under war (36a) and (36b), these payoffs are certain.

For any given combination of guns (G_{i1}, $i = 1, 2$), both sides would be willing to settle only if there exists at least one λ such that $W_i^s \geq W_i^w$ for both $i = 1, 2$. No such λ exists if $p = \frac{1}{2}$[35] and

$$\phi > \frac{1 + \lambda}{1 + \lambda + \lambda m/2}. \tag{38}$$

Now, in the limiting case when war is not destructive ($\phi = 1$), regardless of the values taken on by the other parameters ($m \in (0, 1]$ and $\lambda \in (0, 1] > 0$), this condition is always satisfied, implying an unequivocal long-term preference for war. The reasoning here is as follows: When $\phi = 1$, the war and settlement payoffs in the first period are identical. Going to war in period $t = 1$, however, effectively eliminates one of the opponents in the next period and, with it, the need to arm. In other words, waging war in period $t = 1$, when it has no destructive effects, yields both a net total and individual benefit.

More generally, the condition (38) shows that the long-term preference for war is limited by war's destructive effects. In addition, the condition reveals that the players' preference to wage war depends positively on the shadow of the future, λ. The idea here is as follows: In this dynamic model, war brings benefits to the winner over settlement not only in the current period but in the future. To the extent that the players tend to prefer current consumption relative to future consumption, they would discount those future benefits. But, a higher discount factor, which indicates that the players value the

---

[34] The determination of $\delta(G_{11}, G_{21})$ takes as given the share received by side 1 in period $t = 2$, $\delta^e = \delta(G_{12}, G_{22}) = \phi p(G_{12}, G_{22}) + \frac{1}{2}(1 - \phi)$, which we already found when we solved for the solutions of the period $t = 2$ sub-game, under the assumption that the parties settle in period $t = 1$: $\delta(G_{12}^*, G_{22}^*) = \frac{1}{2}$.

[35] As shown below and as was the case in the one-period model, $p = \frac{1}{2}$ always holds in equilibrium. When $p \neq \frac{1}{2}$ the conditions for finding such an λ are even more stringent.

future by more (i.e., discount the future by less) amplifies further the rewards of waging a war today relative to settlement.[36] The condition (38) shows, in addition, that the players' preference for war depends positively on the effectiveness of the conflict technology, m. The intuition here is that a more effective conflict technology induces more guns production under settlement as can be seen in (32), and magnifies the potential gains from eliminating one's opponent and not having to arm at all in the second period. Thus, both a longer shadow of the future (λ) and a more effective conflict technology (m) make each party more tolerant of war's destructive effects.

Although the destructive effects of war give the players a short-term incentive to settle, in an anarchic setting where writing long-term contracts on arms is not possible, the importance of the future and the compounding rewards of war enjoyed by the winner can induce the players to choose war over settlement. That is, waging war brings with it not simply the chance of taking all of the contested resource that remains after combat, but also the potentially even more appealing prospect of not having an opponent at all in the next period. The decision to fight does not ignore its downside risk – namely, the possibility of defeat and being eliminated in the future or more generally being weakened by the opponent and forced to take a much smaller piece of the pie in the future. Despite this downside risk, when initially the two parties are roughly equal, each side could expect a positive net benefit to fighting, due to the asymmetry fighting implies for their future relative positions and the consequent reduction in arming it brings. Hence, the choice to wage a war instead of settling can be rationalized without having to appeal to misperceptions, or incomplete information about the other side's preferences or capabilities.

6. Trade, insecurity, and conflict

Thus far, in each party's choice we have emphasized the trade-off between production and appropriation. Another way of making a living according to traditional economic analysis, however, is trade. That analysis is based on the assumption of perfectly secure endowments and perfect enforcement of these secure endowments. A key, then, to bringing in conflict into the study of trade is to relax that assumption and allow for imperfect or costly enforcement of property rights. Can trade be impeded by insecurity and the potential for conflict? Can restrictions on exchange, subsidies, taxes, and land reforms that re-allocate initial endowments ever be (constrained-)efficient in the presence of appropriation and conflict costs? Can autarky ever be superior to free trade under similar conditions? And getting closer to today's world, is globalization always beneficial in the presence of insecurity?

---

[36] We would obtain a similar effect if we were to extend the time horizon of the model, to make the shadow of the future even more important.

We will explore such questions in this section. The topic, once one confronts it with the right framework (which we believe we do here), easily reveals itself to be of immense empirical and historical significance, which unfortunately and curiously has been largely neglected by economists. In the short overview here, we will examine two settings and themes. First, we consider the case in which all tradeable goods are insecure, and each party has the choice between secure but less productive autarky versus insecure but more remunerative production for trade. Second, in the case of a model with an insecure resource, we explore the possibility that various restrictions on exchange and other measures viewed as inefficient in a first-best world can be efficient responses when the costs of conflict are taken into account. In that subsection we will touch upon substantive issues as varied as wage subsidies, land reform, and the effects of globalization in the presence of conflict.

6.1. Secure autarky versus insecure exchange

If parties expect to trade, but do not have completely secure possession of the goods they expect to trade, then they must take measures to guard against the theft of those goods by others. We suppose that they do so by arming. If, however, the cost of arming or more generally defense is sufficiently high, they might choose not to participate in the market, and refrain from trade.

To fix ideas we examine a modest extension of the model in Section 3.2. Suppose that, on top of the opportunities shown in (12) to produce guns (G_i) and butter (X_i), each player can produce Y_i, an inferior substitute for butter (say, margarine or just "leisure"). While inferior to butter, this consumption good is assumed to be immune to capture by the opponent. The resource constraint with identical parties ($R_i = R$ and $\beta_i = 1$ for both i's) can be expressed as follows:

$$R = G_i + X_i + Y_i/\gamma, \quad i = 1, 2, \tag{39}$$

where, to express the inferiority of Y to X, we have $\gamma < 1$. We can think of the total quantity of butter ($\bar{B} \equiv F(X_1, X_2) = 2R - G_1 - G_2$) as requiring the collaboration of, or an "exchange" between, the two parties so that *both* parties need to produce a positive quantity of butter for either party to be able to consume any quantity of it.[37] In a standard neoclassical world with perfect enforcement of property rights, where each party could reap the fruits of its own contribution to butter, there would be neither a need for guns nor an incentive to produce the inferior good, margarine. In this ideal case, each party would produce, and keep for its own consumption, R units of butter. We will refer to such outcomes as "Nirvana" or "no-conflict" outcomes.

With guns determining the distribution of butter and with margarine production being secure, party i can expect the following payoff:

$$V_i(G_1, G_2, Y_1, Y_2) = p_i(G_1, G_2)(2R - G_1 - G_2) + \gamma Y_i, \quad i = 1, 2. \tag{40}$$

---

[37] Of course, the main point of our example here would be reinforced, and be more convincing, with a more general function, $F(X_1, X_2)$, that allows for complementarity, but at considerably higher analytical cost.

In this setting, one of two qualitatively different outcomes can emerge in equilibrium:

(i) *Autarky.* Both parties produce only margarine: $Y^* = R$, thus implying $G^* = 0$ and $X^* = 0$. The payoffs in this symmetric equilibrium are $V_i^* = V^* = \gamma R$, $i = 1, 2$. Note that this is always a possible outcome, since both parties need to produce butter in order for either to consume any butter.[38] That is, given one party produces only margarine, the other party's best response it to produce only margarine as well. But, when $\gamma > \frac{1}{m+1}$, this outcome is the unique equilibrium.

(ii) *Exchange.* Both parties produce positive quantities of guns and butter as in the equilibrium of Section 3.2.1, $G_i^* = G^* = \frac{m}{m+1} R$ and $X_i^* = X^* = \frac{1}{m+1} R$, $i = 1, 2$, but no margarine, $Y_i^* = 0$, $i = 1, 2$. In this equilibrium, which emerges only when $\gamma \leqslant \frac{1}{m+1}$, the payoffs are $V_i^* = V^* = \frac{1}{m+1} R$, $i = 1, 2$.

The second type of equilibrium is the one in which there is exchange but it requires each side to have guns as back-up. To have such an equilibrium, though, requires that (i) autarky is sufficiently unproductive (γ is low enough) and (ii) conflict is not too effective (m is low enough). Otherwise, the only equilibrium is when each side engages in autarkic production and no exchange takes place. However, even when the conditions exist for an exchange equilibrium, it is not necessary for it to be implemented in practice, for autarky is always an equilibrium and, depending on the values of the various parameters, it could be the risk-dominant equilibrium.

Both types of equilibria of course yield payoffs lower than those of the Nirvana outcome with perfectly secure property rights. They are also consistent with much of history and this simple model helps us understand how traders were often indistinguishable from warriors, or at least that traders had to buy the protection of warriors. The European explorers of the fifteenth and sixteenth centuries who stumbled into the Americas or opened the way to the East around the Cape of Good Hope were hoping to discover riches that could come from plunder, from trade or both. To do so, they did have to have an ample supply of guns. The tendency for long-distance traders to be heavily armed, or for plunderers to engage in commerce on the side, has been hardly unique to the European explorers, however. The Classical Athenians, the Vikings, the Russians, the Genovese and the Venetians, the English and the Dutch East India companies all engaged in both trade and war. In other areas, Bedouins from the desert had plundered and engaged in long-distance trade before the advent of Islam, whereas afterwards Islam itself spread through the proselytizing zeal of merchant-warriors. And, the Chinese empire engaged in massive naval expeditions to East Africa and perhaps beyond, decades earlier than the much less impressive expeditions of the European explorers.

To be sure, the rationale for the possible absence of exchange is not simply, as has been emphasized, for example, in Dixit's (2004) recent influential synthesis, that the other party will cheat, either by not paying or by not delivering the promised goods.

---

[38] As suggested above, the same sort of result would obtain if we were to replace this assumption and the simple, linear specification for the total quantity of butter, with a more general functional form, $F(X_1, X_2)$, that allows for complementarity between X_1 and X_2.

The rationale here is based instead on the costly measures that the parties are induced to take to avoid being the victims of such cheating. That is to say, the costs of enforcing trade (with guns) could be quite high. This analytically and conceptually distinct reason for the difficulties with exchange has been explored by Rider (1993), Anderton, Anderton and Carter (1999), Hausken (2004), and Anderson and Marcouiller (2005). These papers present analyses, typically based on models that are more sophisticated than the one presented above, of a variety of factors that affect the emergence of exchange or its absence.

6.2. Insecure resources, trade restrictions and other market interventions

Instead of trade itself being insecure, insecurity and contestation of particular resources that are inputs in production is another form of insecurity. Such insecurity has been historically common, and continues to be prevalent today, both across and within countries. Oil, diamonds, and fresh water are examples of contested resources that have received attention lately [see Klare (2001)]. The oil of the Caspian Sea is not simply contested by the governments of the countries that surround it, but by the governments of countries and by private interests well beyond its shores as well as by various private interests within each of the surrounding countries. Here, we are interested in exploring the effects of the tradeability of such resources. Though tradeability confers the classical gains from trade, it can be expected to induce different – possibly higher – levels of arming. That is, to assess the effects of trade, we need to compare the gains from trade against the (possibly) excess levels of arming that trade may induce.

We illustrate the main ideas using a simplified version of the framework of Skaperdas and Syropoulos (2001) for the case of international conflicts and a simplified version of the framework in Garfinkel, Skaperdas and Syropoulos (2006) for the case of domestic conflicts. Consider as before two parties that can be, depending on the context, countries, groups or individuals. Suppose there are two factors of production, land and labor. The parties hold no secure claims to land. That is to say, all available land, denoted by T_o, is contested. Each party i, however, has a secure endowment of R units of labor, which can be transformed, on a one-to-one basis, into guns or used in conjunction with land to produce the final good valued for consumption. In keeping with the example we have used throughout this chapter, we suppose that this good is "butter", B. The following Cobb–Douglas function describes the production of output, B, given any input quantities of land T and labor L:

$$B = T^\alpha L^{1-\alpha} \quad \text{where } \alpha \in (0, 1). \tag{41}$$

The timing of actions is as follows:

Stage 1 Each party i chooses its allocation of labor to the production of guns, G_i, $i = 1, 2$, leaving $R - G_i$ for the production of butter or trade. The two parties make their choices simultaneously.

Stage 2 Given the choices of guns and the technology of conflict as described in (3) with $m = 1$, the contested land is divided according to the winning probabilities. At this point, party i's (new) endowment consists of $p_i(G_1, G_2)T_o$ units of secure land and $R - G_i$ remaining units of labor.

Stage 3 These new endowments can be traded domestically or, depending on the trade regime, internationally. Then, given the new quantities of inputs held, each party i produces butter according to (41). Each party aims to maximize its own production of butter.

Assume, for convenience, that the two parties treat the prices of land, labor, and guns as fixed. Taking labor – and guns too, since they are produced on a one-to-one basis from labor – as the numeraire, let π_{iT} denote the relative price of land measured in units of labor, butter, or guns relevant for party i. Under free trade, this price is given by world markets. Under autarky, it is determined endogenously by the appropriate domestic market-clearing condition. Given π_{iT} as determined in either trade regime, the value of each party's i's endowment at the beginning of Stage 3, following the division of T_o under the threat of conflict in Stage 2, can be written as

$$\pi_{iT} T_i + L_i = \pi_{iT} p_i(G_1, G_2)T_o + R - G_i. \tag{42}$$

Note how this value depends on the amount of guns chosen by *both* parties.

As can be verified, the solution to each party i's third-stage optimization problem of choosing T_i and L_i to maximize (41) subject to (42) given the gun choices made in Stage 1, yields the following value functions:

$$V_i(G_1, G_2; \pi_{iT}) = \eta(\pi_{iT})\big[\pi_{iT} p_i(G_1, G_2)T_o + R - G_i\big], \quad i = 1, 2, \tag{43}$$

where $\eta(\pi_{iT}) \equiv (1-\alpha)^{1-\alpha}[\alpha/\pi_{iT}]^\alpha$ denotes the marginal utility of income. With these value functions, which reflect the parties' optimizing third-stage choices, given their first-stage guns choices, we now turn to study those first-stage choices under autarky and free trade, whereby we can explore the implications of the two trading regimes for arming and welfare.

6.2.1. Outcomes under autarky

When barriers prevent trade across national borders, each party i in stage 1 chooses G_i to maximize its respective payoff, $V_i^T(G_1, G_2; \pi_{iT})$, shown in (43) with $\pi_{iT} = \pi_{iT}^A$ which is taken as given, subject to the conflict technology shown in (3) with $m = 1$ and the labor resource constraint $G_i \leqslant R$.

The specific market-clearing conditions that determine π_{iT}^A depend on whether the parties are countries (engaged in interstate conflict) or adversaries within a single country (engaged in domestic conflict). In the former case, the autarkic price for each party (or country) i would be determined endogenously as a function of the party's respective labor and land endowments: $\pi_{iT}^A = \frac{\alpha}{1-\alpha}[R - G_i]/T_i$, which would be identical for $i = 1, 2$ given our symmetry assumptions. When the parties are adversaries within a single country, the possibility of trade between them implies the autarkic price is determined endogenously by an aggregate domestic, market-clearing condition that is common to them: $\pi_T^A = \frac{\alpha}{1-\alpha}[2R - G_1 - G_2]/T_o$. Note, however, under our deterministic interpretation of the conflict technology – i.e., where T_o is divided according to the parties' winning probabilities – ex ante symmetry translates into ex post symmetry, such that no trade between domestic groups actually takes place under autarky. Accordingly, the two market-clearing solutions shown above yield the same equilibrium value for the autarkic price, as shown below.

The first-order condition to each party i's optimization problem in the absence of international trade is given by

$$\frac{\partial V_i^A}{\partial G_i} = \eta(\pi_{iT}^A)\left[\pi_{iT}^A T_o \frac{\partial p_i}{\partial G_i} - 1\right] = 0, \quad i = 1, 2, \tag{44}$$

where the marginal effect of party i's guns choice on its share of land is shown in (9) with $m = 1$. These conditions and either solution for π_{iT}^A – either that which applies to interstate conflict or that which applies to intrastate conflict – imply a unique interior symmetric solution for guns under autarky, G_i^A:

$$G_i^{A*} = G^{A*} = \frac{\alpha}{2 - \alpha} R, \quad i = 1, 2, \tag{45a}$$

$$\text{with } \pi_T^{A*} = \frac{4\alpha}{2 - \alpha} \frac{R}{T_o}. \tag{45b}$$

The optimizing guns choice for each party is proportional to its labor endowment, R, and also positively related to α, which measures the importance of land in the production of butter.

6.2.2. Outcomes under trade

When the barriers to trade are removed, each party i in Stage 1 chooses G_i, subject to the resource constraint $G_i \leqslant R$, to maximize its respective payoff as shown in (43), where $\pi_{iT} = \pi_T$, which is given in world markets. The first-order conditions to this problem for $i = 1, 2$, given by

$$\frac{\partial V_i^T}{\partial G_i} = \eta(\pi_T)\left[\pi_T \frac{\partial p_i}{\partial G_i} T_o - 1\right] = 0, \quad i = 1, 2, \tag{46}$$

with (9), are essentially the same as the first-order conditions ($i = 1, 2$) to the analogous problem under autarky (44). But, these conditions, in which π_T is exogenously given, imply the following equilibrium choices for guns:

$$G_i^{T*} = G^{T*} = \frac{1}{4}\pi_T T_o, \quad i = 1, 2. \tag{47}$$

Note how the optimizing choice of guns under trade is increasing in the value of the contested resource, $\pi_T T_o$, whereas the equilibrium choice of guns under autarky G^{A*} (45a) is not related at all to the contested resource but instead to the secure resource, R, and the parameter that indicates its relative importance in the production of butter. Thus, the incentives to arm in the two regimes are quite different. These qualitative differences, in turn, imply that the incentives to arm under trade tend to be greater than those under autarky when (i) the endowment of land is larger relative to that of labor (T_o/R), (ii) when the price of land is larger relative to labor (π_T), and (iii) when land is less important in production (α).

6.2.3. The relative appeal of free trade

When does trade induce a greater production of guns, and are the added costs of conflict in this case sufficiently large to swamp the gains from trade relative to autarky? To answer these questions, we now compare equilibrium welfare under the two regimes.

Combining the solution for guns (45a) and the market-clearing price (45b) with the payoff function (43), we can find the equilibrium payoff obtained by each party i under autarky, V_i^{A*}:

$$V_i^{A*} = V^{A*} = \left[\frac{1}{2}\right]^\alpha \left[\frac{2(1-\alpha)}{2-\alpha}\right]^{1-\alpha} T_o^\alpha R^{1-\alpha}, \quad i = 1, 2. \tag{48}$$

Similarly, combining (47) with (43) gives us the parties' equilibrium payoffs under trade, $V_i^{T*}(\pi_T)$:

$$V_i^{T*}(\pi_T) = V^{T*}(\pi_T) = \eta(\pi_T)\left[\frac{1}{4}\pi_T T_o + R\right], \quad i = 1, 2. \tag{49}$$

These equilibrium payoffs, like those obtained under the conventional assumption that all resources are secure, can be shown to be strictly quasi-convex in the price of land, π_T, reaching a minimum at a certain price, $\pi_T^{\min}$. As is well known, in the case that all resources are secure so that there is neither interstate nor intrastate conflict, this minimum price equals the autarkic price. However, where resources are insecure, this critical price is strictly greater than the autarkic price, π_T^{A*}.[39] Furthermore, given the strict quasi-convexity of $V^{T*}(\pi_T)$, there exists another price, $\pi_T' > \pi_T^{\min}$ defined uniquely by the condition, $V^{T*}(\pi_T^{A*}) = V^{A*} = V^{T*}(\pi_T')$.

With these critical values of π_T, the central results of the model are illustrated in Figure 1. Specifically, this figure depicts the parties' payoffs under free trade $(V^{T*}(\pi_T))$ relative to their payoffs under autarky (V^{A*}) as a function of the relative price of land (π_T).

   (i) For $\pi_T < \pi_T^A$ and $\pi_T > \pi_T'$, welfare under autarky is higher than welfare under trade $(V^{A*} > V^{T*}(\pi_T))$.
   (ii) For $\pi_T^A < \pi_T < \pi_T'$, welfare under trade is higher than welfare under autarky: $(V^{T*}(\pi_T) > V^{A*})$.

---

[39] Using (49), one can easily confirm that $\pi_T^{\min} = \frac{4\alpha}{1-\alpha}R/T_o > \pi_T^{A*} = \frac{4\alpha}{2-\alpha}R/T_o$.

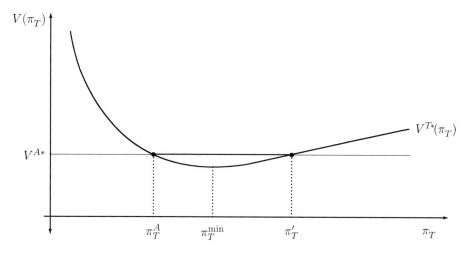

Figure 1. Free trade versus autarky in the presence of conflict.

The underlying logic here is straightforward: When the international price of land is sufficiently low (i.e., $\pi_T < \pi_T^A$), the two parties devote fewer labor resources into guns relative to what they would choose under autarky, since they know that they can use their labor in global markets to buy land cheaply in the third stage. As such, a shift away from the autarkic regime to free trade brings with it not only the familiar gains from trade, but also a reduction in the cost of conflict. When the price equals the autarkic price, $\pi_T = \pi_T^A$, the gains from trade are zero and the costs of conflict under autarky are identical to those under trade. But, when the international price of the contested resource is higher than its autarkic price, $\pi_T > \pi_T^A$, the stakes of the conflict are higher, thereby inducing the parties to allocate more labor resources to guns under the trade regime relative to the autarkic regime, and the additional cost of conflict more than offsets the gains from trade. In this case, a shift from autarky to trade induces a welfare loss. Only when the price of land is sufficiently high (i.e., $\pi_T > \pi_T'$) will the gains from trade again be greater than the additional costs of guns under trade.

Thus, trade can be welfare-reducing in the presence of conflict over valuable resources. The particular assumption of price-taking behavior is made for convenience only and can easily be relaxed without changing the main findings. Skaperdas and Syropoulos (2002), for example, allow for bargaining over the price of land, whereas Skaperdas and Syropoulos (1996b) allow for influence on the terms of trade. By the same token, the findings do not hinge on the particular way in which conflict has been modelled here. Findlay and Amin (2000), for instance, consider a trade model in which security is modelled as a public good and is increasing in one country's defense expenditures and decreasing in the defense expenditures of the other country. They similarly find that the gains from trade can be outweighed by the higher defense costs brought about by trade.

6.2.4. Other implications

As should be clear by now, the model we have just analyzed can apply to interstate as well as intrastate conflicts with minimal modifications. Interstate conflicts had been frequent and very costly up to World War II. World War I, in particular, took place just after the first big era of globalization, which was also an era of intense competition for colonies and resources between the Great powers. Since World War II, however, while the frequency of interstate wars has fallen, civil wars have increased in frequency. Indeed, most of the carnage and, arguably, much economic stagnation and even retrogression since World War II can be attributed to civil wars [see Collier et al. (2003)].

The approach we have taken here also provides an explanation for the "natural resource curse", the tendency of many resource-rich countries to have low or negative rates of growth despite the high prices of their exports. Trade not only makes exporters of contested resources worse off relative to the autarkic regime; it also leaves them vulnerable to declining welfare as increases in the prices for their exports would tend to increase the cost of domestic conflict. As Mehlum, Moene and Torvik (2006) argue, the key appears to be the security and governance of potentially contestable resources. Countries that have solved the problem of conflict over resources do well, whereas those that have not solved the problem can face declining welfare in the face of the seeming (and fleeting) prosperity that can come from higher oil or other export prices.

The comparison between autarky and complete trade openness is too stark for many contexts. In practice, there are a number of other instruments that countries, groups, or even individual actors could employ to minimize the potentially harmful conflict costs of greater openness to trade and exchange. Authors have argued in different but similar contexts that wage subsidies [Zak (1995) and Grossman (1995)], land reform [Horowitz (1993) and Grossman (1994)], and market interventions in general [Dal Bo and Dal Bo (2004)] can be optimal in the face of various types of conflict, from common crime, to low-level political conflict, to insurrections, civil wars, and interstate wars.

Another way to think of the conflict costs that we have explored in this section in relation to trade and exchange is as a large component of the often-discussed, yet rarely modelled or operationalized, concept of "transaction costs". Taking these costs into account indicates that exchange is neither likely to emerge nor necessarily optimal in a second-best world, and can explain many practices and institutions that would be difficult to comprehend in a world with zero enforcement and conflict costs.

7. Coalitions and group formation

The line of research we have reviewed in this chapter has made much progress in advancing our understanding of how conflict manifests itself in many different aspects of our economic lives. This research, however, leaves unanswered many questions about possible "solutions." For example, how can we explain the shift in the nature of conflict that occurred before and after the two world wars? Is this shift one that we can expect to persist or will it eventually reverse itself? Furthermore, why have only some countries been able to solve the problems of security and governance? While it might be overly optimistic or pretentious to believe that the approach adopted here could offer any useful insights into such important questions, it seems reasonable to suppose that a good starting point would be to develop a working theory of group formation in the presence of distributional conflict.

In models of conflict, the main parties are typically taken to be unitary actors. While this assumption simplifies matters tremendously, it prevents us from considering other issues that are directly related to the tradeoff between guns and butter. In thinking about why individuals would want to become allies, one might naturally suppose that there are cost-saving advantages that they can realize when they join forces in defending their property against a common enemy [Noh (2002)].[40] Or, along similar lines, one could suppose that the impact of pooled efforts is greater than the sum of the effects of individual efforts [Skaperdas (1998)]. In this case, individuals form groups to exploit increasing returns (or super-additivity) in the conflict technology. Of course, the benefits afforded by specialization and increasing returns in production would also provide some basis for group formation.

One could also argue, though, that individual incentives to free-ride would tend to undermine the effectiveness of collective action [Olson (1965)]. For example, where individuals come together in a group to contest some resource, each individual's willingness to contribute to the collective effort would be decreasing in the group's size, since whatever is contested, if won, would have to be shared with the other members, whereas the cost of the contribution is borne privately by the individual. To be sure, this reasoning suggests, at the same time, that the severity of conflict between groups would be diminished by group formation. Nevertheless, one has to acknowledge that, with group formation, there could be an additional source of conflict – namely, over how to allocate whatever the group produces and/or appropriates among the group's members. How does group formation and the ability of groups to manage conflict among their members influence the equilibrium severity of conflict? What sorts of group structures are more conducive to less severe conflict at both the aggregate and the group levels? Are such structures more or less likely to be stable in equilibrium – i.e., not subject to deviations?

Surprisingly, while there is a relatively large literature on military alliances[41] and more recently on endogenous group formation, very little has been written on group formation in the context of models of distributional conflict. In this section, we review the relevant literature, highlighting what advances have been made thus far in addressing these and related issues.

---

[40] Also see Sandler (1999). In a related though distinct line of research, Alesina and Spolaore (2006) consider the importance of international conflict in the equilibrium determination of the size and number of the nation-states.

[41] This literature dates back to Olson and Zeckhauser's (1966) seminal paper. See Sandler and Hartley (2001) for an update on the literature.

7.1. *Stage 1: Inter-group conflict*

We organize our discussion around a simplified model of sequential conflict, which builds on the framework presented in Section 3.1, along the lines of Wärneryd (1998) and Esteban and Sákovics (2003).[42] There are N identical, risk-neutral individuals, $\mathcal{I} = \{1, 2, \ldots, N\}$, who participate in a two-stage game. In the first stage, all individuals participate in a winner-take-all contest over a resource $\bar{R}$, which can be consumed directly. They participate either collectively with others or alone, as dictated by the structure of groups, which we take here as given. A group is defined as any subset of the population, $\mathcal{A}_k \subseteq \mathcal{I}$, with membership $n_k \geqslant 1$, where $k = 1, 2, \ldots, A$ and A denotes the total number of groups. For future reference, let the structure of groups be indicated by $S = \{n_1, n_2, \ldots, n_A\}$, with the groups ordered such that $n_1 \geqslant n_2 \geqslant n_3 \geqslant \cdots \geqslant n_A$. By definition, all individuals belong to a group. However, a group need not include more than one member. Moreover, this framework admits the possibility that everyone comes together to form a single group – the *grand coalition*: $\mathcal{A}_1 = \{1, 2, \ldots, n\}$.

For any given configuration of groups, each individual i, a member of some group k, chooses g_i, her contribution to her group's appropriative effort, $G_k \equiv \sum_{i \in \mathcal{A}_k} g_i$. Then, the probability that group k wins and successfully secures the entire resource, $\bar{R}$, depends on that group's allocation, G_k, relative to the allocation of all other groups, G_{-k}:

$$p_k(G_k, G_{-k}) = \begin{cases} \dfrac{G_k^m}{\sum_{j=1}^{A} G_j^m} & \text{if } \sum_{j=1}^{A} G_j^m > 0; \\[2ex] \dfrac{1}{A} & \text{otherwise,} \end{cases} \qquad (50)$$

for all k. This specification is based on the symmetric class of conflict technologies for the n-party case, shown in (2), taking the functional form $f(\cdot) = G^m$. To capture the special advantages that groups enjoy over individuals in appropriative activities, one could assume, following Skaperdas (1998), super-additivity in g so that $f(\sum_{i \in \mathcal{A}_k} g_i) > \sum_{i \in \mathcal{A}_k} f(g_i)$, or given $f(\cdot) = G^m$ that $m > 1$.[43] However, we abstract from any such advantages here, supposing instead that $m = 1$. This assumption simplifies the analytics considerably, allowing us to show more clearly how the presence of groups influences the structure of incentives and thus the aggregate intensity of conflict. One important influence relates to the public-good nature of arming in the contest for $\bar{R}$. In particular, appropriative efforts by different members of a given group are perfect substitutes for one another. Regardless of who provides additional effort, all members enjoy the increased probability of securing the resource it brings to the group.

---

[42] For an extended analysis based on a model that includes production, see Garfinkel (2004a, 2004b).

[43] Skaperdas (1998) shows, in the case where $n = 3$, that super-additivity is necessary to make individuals of the group strictly better off than they would be under individual conflict. Noh (2002) obtains a similar result with a slightly different (asymmetric) specification to admit the possibility that groups have some cost advantage in defense.

7.2. Stage 2: Intra-group conflict

To fix ideas, suppose that group k, with $n_k > 1$ emerges as the winner of the first-stage contest. Individuals not belonging to that group, $i \in A_{k'}$ where $k' \neq k$, receive nothing, implying that their first-stage efforts result only in a loss over the two stages.[44] However, each member of the winning group, $i \in A_k$, goes on to participate in a second-stage contest that determines the distribution of $\bar{R}$ among the group's members. In particular, assume that the *share* of that resource enjoyed by individual $i \in A_k$, σ_{ik}, depends on her effort s_i, distinct from g_i, and on the effort by everyone else in her group, s_j for $j \neq i \in A_k$ or s_{-i}. But her share need not depend entirely on those efforts. More formally, for $n_k > 1$, individual i's share is given by

$$
\sigma_{ik}(s_i, s_{-i}) = \begin{cases} \frac{1-\mu}{n_k} + \frac{\mu s_i}{\sum_{j \in A_k} s_j} & \text{if } \sum_{j \in A_k} s_j > 0; \\ \frac{1}{n_k} & \text{otherwise,} \end{cases} \tag{51}
$$

where $\mu \in (0, 1]$ for all $i \in A_k$. For groups having only one member ($n_k = 1$), there is no internal competition, implying that $s = 0$.

The assumption embedded in (51), that members of the group, with $n_k > 1$, must compete for a share of the prize ($\mu > 0$), departs from the assumption made by others – e.g., Baik and Lee (2001), Noh (2002) and Bloch, Sánchez-Pagés and Soubeyran (2006), that binding commitments to sharing rules between group members are possible.[45] However, this general formulation also admits the possibility that social institutions can mediate conflict within the group, and in doing so have implications for intergroup conflict.[46] In the context of this model, the fraction $1 - \mu \geqslant 0$ measures the effectiveness of existing mechanisms of conflict management to determine the distribution of the group's product without having to rely on the members' current appropriative activities. Put differently, smaller values of μ would reflect stronger social institutions to effect a less costly resolution of group conflict. In what follows, however, we abstract from such influences, and assume that $\mu = 1$, not only to keep matters simple but to emphasize the importance of continuing conflict among the members within the winning group.[47]

[44] As specified below, the individual's payoff would be $V_{ik'} = -g_i$. In other words, the first-stage conflict weakens individuals $i \in A_{k'}$ sufficiently such that it is not possible for them to try to steal the product from the winning group in the second-stage conflict.

[45] In those models, there is essentially no conflict after the first stage.

[46] Of course, this analysis can say nothing about the emergence of such institutions. Genicot and Skaperdas (2002) look specifically at individual investment in conflict management within groups. Related analyses which have considered more specifically the interrelations between democratic political institutions and international conflict, include Garfinkel (1994) and Hess and Orphanides (1995, 2001).

[47] For a more general analysis based on (51), see Garfinkel (2004b). Also see Niou and Tan (2005) who consider variations on (51) in the case of two alliances.

7.3. Equilibrium allocations

Each individual aims to maximize her expected payoff over both stages, given by

$$V_{ik}^e = p_k(G_k, G_{-k})\left[\sigma_{ik}(s_i, s_{-i})\overline{R} - s_i\right] - g_i, \tag{52}$$

subject to (50) with $m = 1$ and (51) with $\mu = 1$, where $G_k = \sum_{i \in A_k} g_i$, as previously defined. The terms inside the square brackets together represent the payoff to the individual, contingent on her group winning the first-stage contest. Accordingly weighted by the probability that her group wins that contest, this contingent payoff equals her share of the contested resource net of her efforts expended in securing that share. The second term is the utility cost of her contribution made in the first stage to the group's effort in that contest. In choosing her contribution to the group's effort, she will consider not only that cost – a cost she bears alone regardless of whether the group wins or loses the first-stage contest – but also the influence of that contribution on her second-stage choices through the conflict success function. Thus, we follow the strategy adopted earlier in this chapter in accordance with the equilibrium notion of sub-game perfection. That is, we solve the model backwards, starting with the second and final stage.

Second-stage outcome. Each individual i belonging to the winning group, k, chooses s_i to maximize $V_{ik} = \sigma_{ik}(s_i, s_{-i})\overline{R} - s_i - g_i$ subject to (51) with $\mu = 1$, taking the other group members' choices, s_{-i}, as given. The conflict technology (51) with $\mu > 0$ generally implies that $s_i = 0$ for all $i \in A_k$ cannot be an equilibrium outcome. As such, the following condition must be satisfied at an interior optimum:

$$\frac{\partial V_{ik}^e}{\partial s_i} = \frac{\sum_{j \neq i \in A_k} s_j}{[\sum_{j \in A_k} s_j]^2}\overline{R} = 1, \tag{53}$$

for $i \in A_k$. Symmetry of the group's membership, in turn, implies $s_i = s > 0$. With this result, (51) can be combined with (53), to verify the following Nash equilibrium of the second stage:

$$s(n_k) = \frac{n_k - 1}{n_k^2}\overline{R}, \tag{54a}$$

$$V_i(n_k) = \frac{1}{n_k^2}\overline{R} - g_i, \tag{54b}$$

for $i \in A_k$. In this equilibrium, each member of the winning group enjoys an equal share of the contest prize, $\sigma(n_k) = \frac{1}{n_k}$, which is decreasing in the size of the group, n_k. At the same time, a larger n_k implies a greater diversion of effort away from other (presumably valuable) activities towards security. As such, the payoff to the individual is decreasing in the square of the size of the group.

First-stage outcome. Now consider the first-stage conflict between groups, again with the structure of groups fixed. Each individual i belonging to group k chooses g_i to maximize the *expected* value of (54b), given by

$$V_i^e(n_k) = p_k(G_k, G_{-k}) \frac{1}{n_k^2} \overline{R} - g_i, \tag{55}$$

where $G_k = \sum_{i \in A_k} g_i$ subject to (50) with $m = 1$. Individuals in all A groups make their decisions simultaneously. The presence of the weight $\frac{1}{n_k^2}$ on the first term in (55) reflects the negative effects of group size mentioned above – the greater dilution of the prize, $\overline{R}$, and the greater diversion of valuable effort that is positively related to the prize as well. These effects detract from the benefits an individual expects to realize as a result of her contributions to the group's collective effort in the first-stage conflict. The cost to the individual of making such contributions, by contrast, is independent of her group's size. Accordingly, one would expect her choice of g_i to be negatively related to the size of her group.

Although the conflict technology (50) implies that $\sum_{j=1}^{A} \sum_{i \in A_j} g_i > 0$, a fully interior solution is not guaranteed for all configurations of groups when $A > 2$. That is to say, the members of one or more groups might choose $g_i = 0$. But, the stability of a given configuration requires that all groups actively participate in the second-stage conflict.[48] The analysis to follow, then, considers only such solutions. Accordingly, the individual's choice in the second-stage satisfies the following equality:

$$\frac{\partial V_i^e(n_k)}{\partial g_i} = \frac{\sum_{i' \notin A_k} g_{i'}}{[\sum_{j=1}^{A} \sum_{i' \in A_j} g_{i'}]^2} \frac{\overline{R}}{n_k^2} = 1. \tag{56}$$

Maintaining focus on the case of within-group symmetry,[49] one can find, based on (56), the equilibrium effort put forth by each individual belonging to group k of size n_k, given the structure of groups, $S = \{n_1, n_2, \dots, n_A\}$:

$$g(n_k, S) = \frac{A-1}{n_k H^2} [H - (A-1)n_k^2] \overline{R} \tag{57}$$

for all k, where $H \equiv \sum_{j=1}^{A} n_j^2$.[50]

---

[48] The basic idea is that, by participating in the intergroup conflict as a stand-alone group any individual can ensure herself a strictly positive expected payoff, which exceeds the zero payoff obtained by individuals belonging to those groups who do not participate at all. See Garfinkel (2004a).

[49] Since the probability of winning $\overline{R}$ depends on the group's effort G_k, not just the individual member's effort g_i for $i \in A_k$, only total effort by the group is uniquely determined; individual effort, g_i, is not. Our focus on within-group symmetry seems most natural given the assumption that individual members of the group are identical.

[50] Specifically, rewrite (56) as $\overline{R}(\overline{G} - n_k g_k) = \overline{G}^2 n_k^2$, where $\overline{G} \equiv \sum_{j=1}^{A} G_j$ denotes the aggregate effort to the first-stage contest, and sum over all groups, $k = 1, 2, \dots, A$ to obtain $A\overline{R}\overline{G} - \overline{R}\overline{G} = \overline{G}^2 \sum_{j=1}^{A} n_j^2$. Simplifying and rearranging shows that, in equilibrium, $\overline{G} = \overline{R}(A-1)/H$, which with the first expression above in g_k and $\overline{G}$, yields (57). Note our requirement that $g_k > 0$ for all k is satisfied provided that $H > (A-1)n_k^2$ holds for $n_k = n_1$, the number of members in the largest group.

For any given group structure with $g_k > 0$ for all k, the solution for $g(n_k, S)$ reveals that the equilibrium effort by the individual members of group k in the intergroup conflict is decreasing in the size of the group, n_k, as is the total effort by the group, $G_k = n_k g(n_k, S)$. Hence, the probability of winning the conflict in Stage 2, given by $p(n_k, S) = \frac{1}{H}[H - (A - 1)n_k^2]$ for $A > 1$, is also decreasing in the group size, n_k. Using this expression for $p(n_k, S)$, (55) and (57), the payoff expected by each individual member of group k at the beginning of stage one, $V^e(n_k, S)$, can be written as

$$V^e(n_k, S) = \frac{1}{n_k^2 H^2}[H - (A - 1)n_k^2][H - (A - 1)n_k]\bar{R} \tag{58}$$

for $k = 1, 2, \ldots, A$. Not surprisingly then, given any structure of groups, S, where $g_k > 0$ for $k = 1, 2, \ldots, A$, individuals belonging to larger groups expect a smaller payoff than the payoff expected by those belonging to smaller groups:

$$V^e(n_1, S) \leqslant V^e(n_2, S) \leqslant \cdots \leqslant V^e(n_A, S) \tag{59}$$

where by assumption $n_1 \geqslant n_2 \geqslant \cdots \geqslant n_A$.[51] Of course, this ranking says nothing about an individual's incentive to move from one group to another, as it does not account for the effect of the hypothetical move on the efforts levels g by anyone in the stage-two conflict or others' incentive to move in response. However, it should be clear that group formation in this setting generates positive spillover effects.

7.4. The level of conflict under different symmetric group structures

To give just a flavor for how the structure of groups can influence the intensity of conflict, we focus our attention on symmetric structures. In the case where all groups are of equal size $n \geqslant 1$, $S \equiv \hat{S} = \{n, \ldots, n\}$,[52] the solution shown in (57) simplifies to $g(n, \hat{S}) = \frac{N-n}{N^2 n^2}\bar{R}$. The two extreme symmetric cases of interest are (i) individual conflict where $n = 1$ and $A = N$, and (ii) the grand coalition where $n = N$ and $A = 1$. In the case of individual conflict, the solution simplifies even further to $g(1, \hat{S}) = \frac{N-1}{N^2}\bar{R}$. By contrast, when the grand coalition forms the solution is $g(n, \hat{S}) = 0$. As can easily be confirmed, under alternative, less extreme symmetric structures given $N(= An)$, $1 \leqslant n \leqslant N$, $g(n, \hat{S})$ is decreasing in n or equivalently increasing in A. However, to account for the effect of group structure on the level of conflict, we wish to factor in the conflict that takes place at both stages. In particular, we calculate the *expected* allocation to the intergroup and intragroup conflict for the representative group and then sum

---

[51] One might conjecture that this ranking depends on the assumption, commonly made in the literature as well as in this paper, of linear costs of effort in the intergroup conflict. Analyzing a model of collective action (with effectively just one layer of conflict), Esteban and Ray (2001) show that, if instead these costs are increasing sufficiently quickly in effort (or money as the case may be), then the group's probability of winning the conflict would be increasing in its size. Nevertheless, they also find that, if the prize is purely private as in the present analysis, the expected payoff to each member would be decreasing in group size.

[52] Ignoring integer problems in the symmetric case, $A = N/n$ and $H = Nn$.

across all A groups. Noting that, for symmetric group structures where $n_k = n$ for all k, we have that $p(n, N) = \frac{1}{A} = \frac{n}{N}$; and, from (54a), we have $s(n) = \frac{n-1}{n^2}\overline{R}$. Bringing these elements together after simplifying yields

$$A\left[ng(n, \widehat{S}) + np(n, N)s(n)\right] = \frac{1}{Nn^2}\left[N - n + Nn(n - 1)\right]\overline{R}. \tag{60}$$

As can be shown using this expression, given the total number of individuals N, the intensity of conflict is *increasing* monotonically in the size of groups, n, for $n > 1$. Hence, as we move from a structure with a small number of large groups towards individual conflict, the intensity of conflict decreases.

To be sure, using (58), one can verify that the payoff an individual could expect under a symmetric group structure with $n > 1$ is strictly greater than what she can expect under individual conflict (i.e., where $n = 1$). Nevertheless, this difference is decreasing in the size of each group ($n > 1$) and equals 0 when $n = N$ or $A = 1$. That is to say, the potential gains under the symmetric group structure are decreasing once individuals pair up, and continue to diminish as the groups grow, eventually disappearing – that is, once the group becomes as large as the population, or the grand coalition.

In the context of this simple model, the expected gains from (symmetric) group formation come in the form of a reduction in the severity of conflict over the contestable resource $\overline{R}$ for $1 < n < N$. No member of a group with $n > 1$ fully internalizes the benefits of her efforts in that conflict and so naturally devotes less effort to it. In the symmetric outcome, everyone else is doing just the same, so that, when compared to the case of individual conflict ($n = 1$), no one has gained an advantage in the conflict over $\overline{R}$ relative to anyone else, yet everyone has a greater chance of winning, $\frac{1}{A} > \frac{1}{N}$. However, as $n > 1$ increases and the first-stage conflict between groups weakens, the second-stage conflict over the distribution of $\overline{R}$ within the group intensifies; from an ex ante perspective, the increased costs associated with the intensifying intragroup conflict exceed the decreased costs associated with the weakening intergroup conflict. As n approaches N, the expected gains from group formation go to zero. Of course, the actual outcome under group formation with $n = N$ will differ from that under individual conflict by virtue of the difference in the nature of the conflict in the two outcomes. But, by our assumption that $\mu = 1$, the group is no more efficient in resolving conflict than individuals are on their own; therefore, assuming risk neutrality, shifting the entire conflict from one between $A = N$ groups of size $n = 1$ to a conflict within $A = 1$ group among $n = N$ members has no consequences in terms of expected payoffs.[53] Still, for $n < N$, the formation of symmetric groups on net enhances expected welfare.

---

[53] If the members of a group could credibly agree to share the product equally without arming ($s = 0$), the expected payoff under symmetric group formation, given in this case by $V^e(n, \widehat{S}) = \frac{1}{N^2 n}[N(n - 1) + n]X$, would be increasing in n, so that the expected gains under group formation relative to individual conflict, given by $\frac{n-1}{Nn}\overline{R}$, would also be increasing in n and be strictly positive when evaluated at $n = N$.

7.5. Requirements of stability and equilibrium group structures

Would that expected benefit be sufficient to render a symmetric group structure, $\hat{S}$, a stable equilibrium? In the absence of any specific benefits from belonging to a group (i.e., in terms of the conflict or production technologies), it should be fairly obvious that, for any given group structure S, each individual would have a large incentive to break away from her own group to form a stand-alone group. The logic here is quite simple. As discussed earlier, each member's incentive to contribute to her own group's collective effort in the first-stage contest over $\bar{R}$ is decreasing in the size of her group. Hence, once having broken away from her group to stand by herself, given the membership of all other groups and that of her former group, any individual would have an increased incentive to put forth some effort in the conflict over $\bar{R}$. At the same time, this deviation would likely decrease the effort made by members of groups not directly affected by the deviation. By forming a stand-alone group, the individual could, then, put herself in a very advantageous position to win the first-stage contest over $\bar{R}$ and she could keep it all for herself.

While this line of reasoning questions the stability of the original structure, one can go a step further to question the stability of the deviation itself, for other individuals too will have an incentive to break away from their respective groups. This is precisely the approach of the non-cooperative theory of endogenous coalition structures – see, e.g., Bloch (1996), Chwe (1994), Ray and Vohra (1999), and Yi (1997) – which has recently been applied to group formation in distributional conflict. This approach defines a stable equilibrium by imposing certain internal consistency requirements on possible deviations. One extreme possibility, based on Chwe's (1994) notion of *farsighted stability*, envisions individuals as looking at the ultimate outcome of a deviation. That is, in their evaluation of the potential gains from a given deviation, they factor in the possibility of all subsequent deviations by others and the resulting impact on expected payoffs. In the context of this model, although any individual would benefit, for example, by leaving her group to form a stand-alone group given the membership of the other groups and her former group, such deviations could ultimately trigger a reversion to individual conflict, leaving everyone, including the original deviator, worse off. Accordingly, such deviations themselves would be deemed unprofitable and, thus, would not pose a threat to the stability of the group structure under consideration. In effect, invoking the notion of farsighted stability expands the opportunities for "cooperation" among individuals who would behave otherwise in a non-cooperative way.

A common requirement of stability of the structure of groups in such settings with positive spillover effects is that the groups be of roughly the same size [Yi (1997)]. Asymmetric structures create larger incentives for deviations particularly for members of the larger groups, and more so when N is small. When there are only 3 individuals, a stable group structure is impossible [Esteban and Sákovics (2003)], unless the alliance enjoys some advantage in the conflict technology [Skaperdas (1998) and Noh (2002)]. More generally, in such settings for any N, the failure of the grand coalition to emerge as a stable group structure is common. However, this failure cannot be attributed to the positive spillover effects of group formation alone. For example, Bloch, Sánchez-Pagés and Soubeyran (2006) predict the emergence of the grand coalition despite the presence of such spillover effects. In fact, in that model, the grand coalition is the efficient outcome. The reason is because the solution concept, based on Bloch (1996), assumes that the members of a group can commit to an equal sharing rule of whatever they win, thereby abstracting from the intragroup conflict all together. By contrast, when resolving the conflict between members within a group is just as costly as resolving conflict between any other two individuals, smaller groups are more efficient [Garfinkel (2004a)]. Even when one supposes that groups have an advantage in conflict management ($\mu < 1$), there remains a tendency for structures with smaller groups to yield greater expected payoffs for all [Garfinkel (2004b)]. Though the grand alliance could be stable when groups are better able to manage conflict ($\mu < 1$), there are other structures that strictly dominate it from everyone's perspective.

Because scholars have only begun to study group formation and its effects on conflict and peace, there are many avenues for future research. Of special importance would be the study of conflict management within groups. One might adopt a dynamic approach, supposing that the survival of groups over time requires the creation and maintenance of "norms" and institutions that would allow the alliance members to effect a more "peaceful" distribution of output at a lower cost.[54] In addition, the literature has paid scant attention to asymmetries. Yet, the heterogeneity of individuals raises some important and interesting issues about the composition of alliances and about resolving conflicts therein, provided that a stable structure exists at all.

8. Dynamics and growth

Up to this point, Section 5.2 is the only place in which we have explicitly examined dynamic issues. Page constraints preclude us from developing a model in which we could examine most of the issues that have been analyzed in the literature. Instead, the following paragraphs summarize some of the central themes.[55]

The costs of conflict over time reduce welfare compared to the case without conflict. This finding, which is obvious, is present in all of the papers in this area, but is virtually absent from other models of growth that have dominated thinking in this area. Similarly, research on economic development has largely overlooked the costs of conflict and more generally the costs of unproductive activities [on which Sturzenegger and Tommasi (1994) and Barelli and Pessoa (2004) have focused]. This omission is rather

---

[54] See Genicot and Skaperdas (2002) who model conflict management as an investment decision in a dynamic setting.

[55] The interested reader should consult the relevant references, including Sturzenegger and Tommasi (1994), Hirshleifer (1995a), Zak (1995), Grossman and Kim (1996), Lee and Skaperdas (1998), Barelli and Pessoa (2004), and Gonzalez (2005, in press).

astounding given the obvious empirical importance of these costs, which has been recently corroborated by a World Bank study [Collier et al. (2003)] and the empirical analysis of Hess (2003).[56]

The incentives for productive innovation are severely reduced in the presence of conflict. Baumol (1990) has provided an intuitive discussion of the importance of secure property rights for productive innovation to flourish. But one can go beyond the basic intuition with the use of appropriate modelling to develop sharp insights. In particular, building on the result based on the benchmark model of Section 3.2, Gonzalez (2005) demonstrates that, where property is insufficiently insecure, an economic agent might choose not to adopt superior technologies (i.e., those with higher β_i's). The reason is not simply because the returns from innovation are expected to be partially expropriated. There is, in addition, a strategic element at play here. That is, the adoption of new technologies by one agent would be expected to induce greater relative guns production by the other agents, thereby placing the innovating agent in a disadvantaged position. Thus, even when superior technologies are available at zero cost, the effect of such innovations to make one more vulnerable to appropriation can lead to their rejection in favor of inferior technologies, an outcome that Gonzalez reasonably argues was relevant to many periods in history.

Productive versus appropriative capital accumulation. The tradeoff between production and appropriation exists not only for outputs with short-term durability. After all, guns typically last a number of years, as so do barracks, fortifications, or siege machines. Such objects can be considered an alternative form of capital, one that is non-productive and which we can call "appropriative" or "enforcive." It could even be argued that for much of history since the agricultural revolution, this type of capital has been quantitatively more important and technologically more sophisticated than ordinary productive capital. Certainly the technology of many castles and siege machines was far more advanced than anything that was available for civilian, material use. The same can be said for the organizational efficiency of standing armies, as no equivalent organizations existed in civilian affairs. Lee and Skaperdas (1998) explore this theme, in a setting where investments in appropriative capital compete with those in productive capital, finding that long-run economic performance can be hindered; and, as with technological choice, this effect can be expected to be dramatic. Thus, differences in governance can be expected to induce differences in capital accumulation. Such differences could, then, also account for the phenomenon of (financial, mobile) capital moving from poor

---

[56] Hess (2003), for example, estimates the welfare costs of conflict coming from its effects on consumption alone for 147 countries spanning the period 1960–1992 to be on average 8 percent of steady-state consumption. For some countries, the effect is lower (e.g., 3.2 percent for the United States), but the effect for others, especially the lower income countries, the estimated effect is considerably higher (e.g., 65 percent in Iraq and 40.5 percent in Angola).

countries to rich countries, the opposite movement one would expect under traditional modelling in which property rights are perfectly and costlessly enforced.

Among other themes that have been explored in dynamic models of conflict and appropriation are the effects of initial asymmetries in resource endowments [Sturzenegger and Tommasi (1994)] and of the degree of property rights enforcement [Gonzalez (in press)]. Consistent with the results in the static version of asymmetric contest models, Sturzenegger and Tommasi (1994) find that asymmetries in initial endowments tend to reduce the total resources devoted to appropriation and thus result in enhanced welfare relative to the case of symmetry. Since Sturzenegger and Tommasi's analysis is based on a deterministic model (which is common where structural dynamics are involved), it would be of interest to examine the case in which the technology of conflict has a probabilistic interpretation (i.e., a "winner-take-all-contest") and to suppose that the winner of the contest gains and maintains an advantage in future encounters.[57] Using a version of the asymmetric conflict technology in (5) to parameterize the security of property rights, Gonzalez (in press) shows how, at intermediate levels of security, welfare can be lower than when security is high or low. That is, welfare is non-monotonic in the degree of property right security. Thus, one should exercise caution in recommending improved property-rights enforcement, particularly when such improvements are to be made incrementally in middle income countries. At the same time, it would be worthwhile to examine alternative ways of measuring the security of property rights – for example, by identifying the degree of security by the fraction of one's output that is immune to capture by others.

Only the surface of the dynamic effects of conflict has been scratched. If politics and institutions are important for economic growth, as much recent research suggests, such effects through our dynamic models could further our understanding of what occurs when institutions are imperfect. However, ultimately the bigger question is how institutions and governance themselves evolve to reduce conflict and appropriation. Hirshleifer (1995a) suggests one factor that leads to the "breakdown" of anarchy: a conflict technology that is highly effective so that only one side emerges victorious. What would happen after one side is in charge, though, and presumably creates a monopolistic "state" is another important topic.

9. Conflict management and the state

How can conflict be reduced? That is an immensely important question, of course. The recent literature – which also reflects long-standing intellectual traditions in philosophy

---

[57] Another area of interest is the simultaneous examination of appropriative conflict and open-access resources. Reuveny and Maxwell (2001) have developed such a promising dynamic model. However, distinguishing between deterministic and probabilistic versions of the model necessitates numerical simulations, which do not appear to yield results that are independent of the parameters used in the particular simulations.

and the social sciences – describes two ways to reduce conflict. In Hirshleifer's terminology, conflict can be reduced or eliminated through (i) *vertical, Hobbesian contracts* or through (ii) *horizontal, Lockean contracts*. The former can be thought of as proprietary, for-profit, hierarchical governance and the latter as contractual mechanisms that are mostly associated with institutions of modern governance. Ultimately both types of governance rely on the strength of the state to impose a monopoly or near-monopoly in the means of violence, but they also reflect two different types of state.

9.1. Hierarchical governance

If one party were to defeat all of its adversaries decisively, so that it effectively gains the monopoly of force, then a long-term hierarchical contract could emerge between the winner and the losers. The winner would maintain a force that could put down or deter significant uprisings by the losers, the losers would not expend any resources on arming but would have to accept whatever material compensation their position allows while the winner would enjoy the greater material rewards the dominant coercive position confers. The overwhelming part of recorded history has been characterized by such hierarchical governance, with lords, kings, and emperors on top and masses of peasants at the bottom of the hierarchy. In polities where the monopoly of force has been stronger (or the state was stronger), the degree of conflict has appeared to be less severe. However, the historical record does not reveal an overall reduction in conflict associated with hierarchical governance. Rather, there seems to have been a migration to a different level: conflict with other states and internal succession struggles.

Findlay (1990) was, to our knowledge, the first author to model the state explicitly as a "proprietor", to use Grossman and Noh's (1994) characterization, with the motivation of modelling governance in many LDCs. Grossman and Noh (1994) provided a dynamic version of a similar model to examine the effect of the endogeneity of the ruler's survival and therefore the influence of the effective discount factor on economic policies. McGuire and Olson (1996) went further and argued for the possible effectiveness of autocracy in stimulating investment and economic growth, by likening a ruler to a "stationary bandit" who has an "encompassing interest" so as to limit extortionary taxation and, at the same time, provide high levels of public goods.

However, the incentives of a strong ruler with high extractive powers are not as clear cut as that. First, a long time horizon, necessary for the ruler to have an "encompassing interest", is far from being sufficient for the promotion of growth. As Robinson (1997) has argued, many such policies are often at the expense of their rule: promoting trade implies that merchants become richer and perhaps ask for more rights and a share of power; expanding education can make more of the population become increasingly conscious of its subservient status and therefore demand reforms and a change from the status quo; even building roads can make it easier for rebels to reach the capital and drive out the ruler. Stashing a few billions in Switzerland would be better for the ruler. Second, the extractive power of the ruler can be so high that commitment to a non-extortionary tax rate would be very difficult [Moselle and Polak (2001), Konrad and

Skaperdas (2005)]. Moreover, the time horizon of rule is shortened, and its uncertainty widened, by challenges to the ruler from within and without.

Overall, though traditional hierarchical rule could reduce conflict and provide other public goods, it often recreates the problems of conflict at a higher and more organized level. Indeed, tempted by the possible rents that can be extracted from their subjects, rulers have fought incessantly with neighboring rulers throughout history. Moreover, the problem of severely asymmetric coercive power between rulers and the ruled did not essentially solve many of the inefficiencies associated with conflict. In many ways it displaced the inefficiencies of high arming and destruction due to conflict with those of lower dynamic incentives for innovation and investment that absolutist rule tends to create. There was nobody to guard the guardians against arbitrary exactions. The type of governance that has intermittently appeared throughout history but has gained more ground over the past two centuries provides another model for reducing and managing conflict.

9.2. Modern governance

The alternative mechanism to hierarchical domination for the management of conflict is a contractual arrangement among equals. Note that such a contract is not like the settlement agreements that we examined in Sections 4 and 5, for those agreements are backed up by the bargaining power conferred by arming. The contracts that we are concerned with here entail partial or complete disarmament.[58] Since, ultimately, arming is the primary means of enforcement in settings with insecurity, such contracts pose a serious conundrum: How can the contract be enforced when the contract itself is about the means of its enforcement (i.e., arms)?

There is no complete or timeless solution to this conundrum, for someone somewhere is bound to be tempted to break and will eventually break such a contract at some point in time. Modern governance has partially solved the problem through an elaborate system of enforcement that changes the threat points from those that involve actual fighting to others that involve going to judicial courts, to the legislatures, to bureaucratic rulings, to the voters and so on. Separation of powers, checks and balances, the extension of the democratic franchise, the removal of discretion in ruled-based bureaucracies, and other mechanisms of modern states tend to create a wide dispersion of power and the multilateral sanctions that await anybody who attempts the illegitimate use of force.

Once a modern state has consolidated its main institutions, as in the rich countries of the West, it would be extremely difficult to have, say, a military coup. Protests, strikes, riots, other symptoms of social conflict still occur, of course, but organized warfare has virtually disappeared from within the modern state. How this has come about is still largely a mystery – or, a conundrum – but, a number of scholars have begun the immense task of unravelling the mystery.

---

[58] See Esteban and Sákovics (2006) for the derivation of a bargaining solution based on the threat of conflict but with no arming.

This research effort is beyond the scope of our review, but we should mention that conflict figures prominently in all examinations of the emergence of modern governance. Long periods of conflict and the threat of continued conflict have underpinned transitions to power-sharing arrangements in as varied places and conditions as Medieval Genoa [Greif (1998)], seventeenth-century England [North and Weingast (1989)], the extension of the democratic franchise in the West [Acemoglu and Robinson (2000)], and the transition from apartheid rule in South Africa [Rosendorff (2001)]. The role of conflict in the building of the institutions that facilitated modern economic growth also figures prominently in the survey of recent research in the area by Acemoglu, Johnson and Robinson (2004). We agree. The mystery of modern governance as well as the mystery of modern economic growth are siblings of the conundrum of the emergence of cooperation out of conflict.

10. Concluding remarks

We have provided an overview of the recent literature on appropriation and conflict that takes an economic perspective. Conflict is a natural consequence of the basic economic assumption of self-interest, yet it had been hardly examined from an economic perspective up until relatively recently. By accounting for conflict and appropriation in ordinary economic settings, we not only help explain issues that are related to conflict per se. We can also develop a better understanding of the sources of economic growth that concerned Haavelmo (1954) more than half a century ago as well as scholars currently working in the area of institutions and development. In closing, we would like to emphasize some of the more surprising and yet important implications of the research that we have reviewed:

- Conflict involves costs that are economically very important, ranging from the valuable resources diverted away from investment and consumption and instead allocated directly to arming and the resources destroyed in conflict to the reduction in trade and in the accumulation of productive capital. Estimates of the various costs by the World Bank [Collier et al. (2003)] and Hess (2003) are economically significant, especially for low-income countries; the costs of ordinary economic "distortions" pale in comparison. It is thus surprising, if not shocking, that economists have not paid any attention to these costs until very recently.
- The allocation of resources in the presence of conflict has also been shown to be, generally, very different than when conflict is not present or has no costs. Compensation can easily be inversely related to productivity; superior innovations available at zero cost might be rejected; incentives are often skewed in favor of non-productive investment. Thus, assuming compensation to be positively related to marginal productivity or that all investment is productive in settings that involve conflict in empirical research would be inadvisable.
- Trade in the presence of insecurity can be absent or suboptimal. Parties that face insecurity in trade may very well choose less productive but more secure alterna-

tives and thus forego trade. Those that do choose to trade would have to invest in defending their possessions, thereby leading to the common phenomenon in history of many merchants doubling as warriors. The costs of fighting over insecure resources can also preclude trade all together.

- A long shadow of the future need not facilitate peace. To the contrary, when fighting changes the long-term strategic positions of adversaries, a long-term horizon could very well induce conflict, despite conflict's short-term costs. This is a source of conflict that has been underemphasized compared with other sources like irrationality or asymmetric information.
- Very little is known about how to reduce, let alone eliminate, conflict. However, based on recent research on institutions and economic growth as well as group formation, we suspect that governance plays an important role. Moreover, conflict itself appears to play an important role in the emergence and evolution of governance. Conflict, governance, and economic growth are tied up in ways that economists and other social scientists have only began to tentatively unravel.

References

Acemoglu, D., Robinson, J.A. (2000). "Why did the West extend the franchise? Democracy, inequality and growth in historical perspective". Quarterly Journal of Economics 115, 1167–1199.

Acemoglu, D., Johnson, S., Robinson, J.A. (2004). "Institutions as the fundamental cause of long-run growth". Unpublished manuscript. Department of Economics, Massachusetts Institute of Technology, Cambridge, MA.

Alesina, A., Spolaore, E. (2006). "Conflict, defense spending, and the number of nations". European Economic Review 50, 91–120.

Anbarci, N., Skaperdas, S., Syropoulos, C. (2002). "Comparing bargaining solutions in the shadow of conflict: How norms against threats can have real effects". Journal of Economic Theory 106, 1–16.

Anderson, J., Marcouiller, D. (2005). "Anarchy and autarky: Endogenous predation as a barrier to trade". International Economic Review 46, 189–213.

Anderton, C.H., Anderton, R.A., Carter, J.R. (1999). "Economic activity in the shadow of conflict". Economic Inquiry 37, 166–179.

Azam, J.-P., Mesnard, A. (2003). "Civil war and the social contract". Public Choice 115, 455–475.

Axelrod, R. (1984). The Evolution of Cooperation. Basic Books, New York.

Baik, K.H., Lee, S. (2001). "Strategic groups and rent dissipation". Economic Inquiry 39, 672–684.

Barelli, P., Pessoa, S.D. (2004). "Rent-seeking and capital accumulation". Unpublished manuscript. Department of Economics, University of Rochester, Rochester, NY.

Baumol, W.J. (1990). "Entrepreneurship: Productive, unproductive, and destructive". Journal of Political Economy 98, 893–921.

Bester, H., Konrad, K. (2004). "Delay in contests". European Economic Review 48, 1169–1178.

Bester, H., Konrad, K. (2005). "Easy targets and the timing of conflict". Journal of Theoretical Politics 17 (2), 199–215.

Bester, H., Wärneryd, K. (2006). "Conflict and the social contract". Scandinavian Journal of Economics 108, 231–249.

Blavatsky, P. (2004). "Contest success function with the possibility of a draw: Axiomatization". Unpublished manuscript. University of Zurich, Switzerland.

Bloch, F. (1996). "Sequential formation of coalitions with fixed payoff division". Games and Economic Behavior 14, 90–123.

Bloch, F., Sánchez-Pagés, S., Soubeyran, R. (2006). "When does universal peace prevail? Secession and group formation in conflict". Economics of Governance 7, 3–29.

Brito, D., Intriligator, M. (1985). "Conflict, war and redistribution". American Political Science Review 79, 943–957.

Chwe, M.S.Y. (1994). "Farsighted coalition stability". Journal of Economic Theory 63, 299–325.

Clark, D.J., Riis, C. (1998). "Contest success functions: An extension". Economic Theory 11, 201–204.

Collier, P., Elliott, V.L., Hegre, H., Hoeffler, A., Reynal-Querol, M., Sambanis, N. (2003). "Breaking the conflict trap; Civil War and development policy". World Bank Policy Report. World Bank and Oxford University Press, Washington, DC.

Dal Bo, E., Dal Bo, P. (2004). "Workers, warriors and criminals: Social conflict in general equilibrium". Unpublished manuscript. Haas School of Business, University of California, Berkeley, CA.

Dixit, A. (2004). Lawlessness and Economics: Alternative Models of Governance. Princeton University Press, Princeton.

Esteban, J.M., Ray, D. (1999). "Conflict and distribution". Journal of Economic Theory 87, 379–415.

Esteban, J.M., Ray, D. (2001). "Collective action and group size paradox". American Political Science Review 95, 663–672.

Esteban, J.M., Sákovics, J. (2003). "Olson vs. Coase: Coalition worth in conflict". Theory and Decision 55, 339–357.

Esteban, J.M., Sákovics, J. (2006). "A theory of agreements in the shadow of conflict". Unpublished manuscript. University of Edinburgh, Edinburgh, UK.

Fearon, J.D. (1995). "Rationalist explanations for war". International Organization 49, 379–414.

Findlay, R. (1990). "The new political economy: Its explanatory power for the LDCs". Economics and Politics 2, 193–221.

Findlay, R., Amin, M. (2000). "National security and international trade: A simple general equilibrium model". Unpublished manuscript. Department of Economics, Columbia University, New York, NY.

Garfinkel, M.R. (1990). "Arming as a strategic investment in a cooperative equilibrium". American Economic Review 80, 50–68.

Garfinkel, M.R. (1994). "Domestic politics and international conflict". American Economic Review 84, 1292–1309.

Garfinkel, M.R. (2004a). "Stable alliance formation in distributional conflict". European Journal of Political Economy 20, 829–852.

Garfinkel, M.R. (2004b). "On the stable formation of groups: Managing the conflict within". Conflict Management and Peace Science 21, 43–68.

Garfinkel, M.R., Skaperdas, S. (2000). "Conflict without misperceptions or incomplete information: How the future matters". Journal of Conflict Resolution 44, 793–807.

Garfinkel, M.R., Skaperdas, S., Syropoulos, C. (2006). "Globalization and domestic conflict". Unpublished manuscript. Department of Economics, University of California, Irvine, CA.

Genicot, G., Skaperdas, S. (2002). "Investing in conflict management". Journal of Conflict Resolution 46, 154–170.

Gonzalez, F.M. (2005). "Insecure property and technological backwardness". Economic Journal 115, 703–721.

Gonzalez, F.M. (2006). "Effective property rights, conflict and growth". Journal of Economic Theory. In press.

Greif, A. (1998). "Self-enforcing political systems and economic growth: Late Medieval Genoa". In: Bates, R., Greif, A., Levi, M., Rosenthal, J.-L. (Eds.), Analytic Narratives. Princeton University Press, Princeton.

Grossman, H.I. (1991). "A general equilibrium model of insurrections". American Economic Review 81, 912–921.

Grossman, H.I. (1994). "Production, appropriation, and land reform". American Economic Review 84, 705–712.

Grossman, H.I. (1995). "Robin Hood and the redistribution of property income". European Journal of Political Economy 11, 399–410.

Grossman, H.I., Kim, M. (1995). "Swords or plowshares? A theory of the security of claims to property". Journal of Political Economy 103, 1275–1288.

Grossman, H.I., Kim, M. (1996). "Predation and accumulation". Journal of Economic Growth 1, 333–351.

Grossman, H.I., Noh, S.J. (1994). "Proprietary public finance and economic welfare". Journal of Public Economics 53, 187–204.

Haavelmo, T. (1954). A Study in the Theory of Economic Evolution. North-Holland, Amsterdam.

Hausken, K. (2004). "Mutual raiding and the emergence of exchange". Economic Inquiry 42, 572–586.

Hess, G.D. (2003). "The economic welfare cost of conflict: An empirical assessment". CESifo Working paper no. 852. Munich, Germany.

Hess, G.D., Orphanides, A. (1995). "War politics: An economic, rational-voter framework". American Economic Review 85, 828–846.

Hess, G.D., Orphanides, A. (2001). "War and democracy". Journal of Political Economy 109, 776–810.

Hirshleifer, J. (1988). "The analytics of continuing conflict". Synthese 76, 201–233.

Hirshleifer, J. (1989). "Conflict and rent-seeking success functions: Ratio vs. difference models of relative success". Public Choice 63, 101–112.

Hirshleifer, J. (1991). "The paradox of power". Economics and Politics 3, 177–200.

Hirshleifer, J. (1995a). "Anarchy and its breakdown". Journal of Political Economy 103, 26–52.

Hirshleifer, J. (1995b). "Theorizing about conflict". In: Hartley, K., Sandler, T. (Eds.), Handbook of Defense Economics, vol. 1. North-Holland, Amsterdam, pp. 165–189.

Hirshleifer, J. (2000). "The macrotechnology of conflict". Journal of Conflict Resolution 44, 773–792. December.

Hirshleifer, J., Riley, J. (1992). The Analytics of Uncertainty and Information. Cambridge University Press, New York, NY.

Horowitz, A.W. (1993). "Time paths of land reform: A theoretical model of reform dynamics". American Economic Review 83, 1003–1010.

Jia, H. (2005). "A stochastic derivation of contest success functions". Unpublished manuscript. Department of Economics, University of California, Irvine, CA.

Klare, M.T. (2001). Resource Wars: The New Landscape of Global Conflict. Henry Holt and Company, New York, NY.

Konrad, K.A. (2005). Strategy in Contests. WZB-Berlin, Germany (book manuscript in preparation).

Konrad, K.A., Schlesinger, H. (1997). "Risk aversion in rent-seeking and rent-augmenting games". Economic Journal 107, 1671–1683.

Konrad, K.A., Skaperdas, S. (2005). "The market for protection and the origin of the state". Unpublished manuscript. Department of Economics, University of California, Irvine, CA.

Lee, J., Skaperdas, S. (1998). "Workshops or barracks? Productive versus enforcive investment and economic performance". In: Baye, M.R. (Ed.), Advances in Applied Microeconomics, vol. 7. JAI Press, Greenwich, CT.

Luce, R.D. (1959). Individual Choice Behavior. Wiley, New York, NY.

McBride, M., Skaperdas, S. (2005). "Explaining conflict in low-income countries: Incomplete contracting in the shadow of the future". Unpublished manuscript. Department of Economics, University of California, Irvine, CA.

McFadden, D.L. (1984). "Econometric analysis of quantitative response models". In: Griliches, Z., Intriligator, M. (Eds.), Handbook of Econometrics, vol. 2. North-Holland, Amsterdam, pp. 1396–1456.

McGuire, M., Olson, M. (1996). "The economics of autocracy and majority rule: The invisible hand and the use of force". Journal of Economic Literature 34, 72–96.

Mehlum, H., Moene, K., Torvik, R. (2003). "Predator or prey? Parasitic enterprizes in economic development". European Economic Review 47, 275–294.

Mehlum, H., Moene, K., Torvik, R. (2006). "Institutions and the resource curse". Economic Journal 116, 1–20.

Milgrom, P. (1988). "Employment contracts, influence activities, and efficient organization design". Journal of Political Economy 96, 42–60.

Moselle, B., Polak, B. (2001). "A model of a predatory state". Journal of Law, Economics, and Organization 17, 1–33.

Muthoo, A. (1999). Bargaining Theory with Applications. Cambridge University Press, New York, NY.

Neary, H.M. (1997). "Equilibrium structure in an economic model of conflict". Economic Inquiry 35, 480–494.

Niou, E.M.S., Tan, G. (2005). "External threat and collective action". Economic Inquiry 43, 519–530.

Nitzan, S. (1994). "Modelling rent seeking contests". European Journal of Political Economy 10, 41–60.

Noh, S.J. (2002). "Resource distribution and stable alliance with endogenous sharing rule". European Journal of Political Economy 18, 129–151.

North, D.C., Weingast, B. (1989). "Constitutions and commitment: The evolution of institutions governing public choice in seventeenth-century England". Journal of Economic History 49, 803–832.

Olson, M. (1965). The Logic of Collective Action. Harvard University Press, Cambridge, MA.

Olson, M., Zeckhauser, R. (1966). "A theory of alliance formation". Review of Economics and Statistics 47, 266–279.

Osborne, M.J., Rubinstein, A. (1990). Bargaining and Markets. Academic Press, San Diego, CA.

Powell, R. (1993). "Guns, butter, and anarchy". American Political Science Review 87, 115–132.

Powell, R. (2006). "War as a commitment problem". International Organization 60, 169–203.

Rajan, R.G., Zingales, L. (2000). "The tyranny of inequality". Journal of Public Economics 76, 521–558.

Ray, D., Vohra, R. (1999). "A theory of endogenous coalition structures". Games and Economic Behavior 26, 286–336.

Reuveny, R., Maxwell, J.W. (2001). "Conflict and renewable resources". Journal of Conflict Resolution 45, 719–742.

Rider, R. (1993). "War, pillage, and markets". Public Choice 75, 149–156.

Robinson, J.A. (1997). "When is a state predatory?". Unpublished manuscript. Department of Economics, University of Southern California, CA.

Rosendorff, B.P. (2001). "Choosing democracy: The transition in South Africa". Economics and Politics 13, 1–29.

Sánchez-Pagés, S. (2004). "The use of conflict as a bargaining tool against unsophisticated opponents". Unpublished manuscript. University of Edinburgh, Edinburgh, UK.

Sandler, T. (1999). "Alliance formation, alliance expansion, and the core". Journal of Conflict Resolution 43, 727–747.

Sandler, T., Hartley, K. (2001). "Economics of alliances: The lessons for collective action". Journal of Economics Literature 39, 869–896.

Schmalensee, R. (1972). The Economics of Advertising. North-Holland, Amsterdam.

Skaperdas, S. (1991). "Conflict and attitudes toward risk". American Economic Review 81, 160–164.

Skaperdas, S. (1992). "Cooperation, conflict, and power in the absence of property rights". American Economic Review 82, 720–739.

Skaperdas, S. (1996). "Contest success functions". Economic Theory 7, 283–290.

Skaperdas, S. (1998). "On the formation of alliances in conflict and contests". Public Choice 96, 25–42.

Skaperdas, S. (2003). "Restraining the genuine homo economicus: Why the economy cannot be divorced from its governance". Economics and Politics 15, 135–162.

Skaperdas, S., Syropoulos, C. (1996a). "Can the shadow of the future harm cooperation?". Journal of Economic Behavior and Organization 29, 355–372.

Skaperdas, S., Syropoulos, C. (1996b). "Competitive trade with conflict". In: Garfinkel, M.R., Skaperdas, S. (Eds.), The Political Economy of Conflict and Appropriation. Cambridge University Press, New York, NY, pp. 73–95.

Skaperdas, S., Syropoulos, C. (1997). "The distribution of income in the presence of appropriative activities". Economica 64, 101–117.

Skaperdas, S., Syropoulos, C. (2001). "Guns, butter, and openness: On the relationship between security and trade". American Economic Review, Papers and Proceedings 91, 353–357.

Skaperdas, S., Syropoulos, C. (2002). "Insecure property and the efficiency of exchange". Economic Journal 112, 133–146.

Sturzenegger, F., Tommasi, M. (1994). "The distribution of political power, the costs of rent-seeking, and economic growth". Economic Inquiry 32, 236–248.

Szymanski, S. (2003). "The economic design of sporting contests". Journal of Economic Literature 41, 1137–1187.

Tullock, G. (1980). "Efficient rent seeking". In: Buchanan, J.M., Tollison, R.D., Tullock, G. (Eds.), Toward a Theory of the Rent Seeking Society. Texas A&M University Press, College Station, TX, pp. 3–15.

Wärneryd, K. (1998). "Distributional conflict and jurisdictional organization". Journal of Public Economics 69, 435–450.

Wärneryd, K. (2003). "Information in conflicts". Journal of Economic Theory 110, 121–136.

Wittman, D. (2000). "The wealth and size of nations". Journal of Conflict Resolution 44, 868–884.

Yi, S.-S. (1997). "Stable coalition structures with externalities". Games and Economic Behavior 20, 201–237.

Zak, P.J. (1995). "Institutions, property rights and growth". Unpublished manuscript. Department of Economics, Claremont Graduate School, Claremont, CA.

Chapter 23

CIVIL WAR

PAUL COLLIER and ANKE HOEFFLER

Department of Economics, University of Oxford, UK

Contents

Abstract   712
Keywords   712
1. Introduction   713
2. Concepts and data   713
   2.1. Definition of civil war   713
   2.2. Quantitative measures of the severity of civil wars 714
      2.2.1. Duration   716
      2.2.2. Human cost   716
      2.2.3. Geographic spread   717
3. Causes of civil war   718
   3.1. Motivation and feasibility   718
   3.2. Theories of rebellion   719
      3.2.1. Game-theoretic analyses   719
      3.2.2. The organization of rebellion   720
   3.3. Evidence on the causes   721
4. Duration   723
   4.1. Theories   723
   4.2. Evidence   724
5. Consequences of civil war   725
   5.1. Economic consequences   725
   5.2. Social consequences   727
   5.3. Psychological damage of civil war   728
   5.4. Political consequences   730
6. Post-conflict   731
   6.1. Theories of post-conflict recovery and relapse   731
   6.2. Evidence   732
7. Policy interventions   733
   7.1. Policies for prevention   733
   7.2. Policies for ending conflict   734

Handbook of Defense Economics, Volume 2
Edited by Todd Sandler and Keith Hartley
© *2007 Elsevier B.V. All rights reserved*
DOI: 10.1016/S1574-0013(06)02023-0

7.3. Policies for maintaining post-conflict peace   735
8. Conclusions and research agendas   736
References   737

Abstract

Civil wars are intricate social, political and psychological phenomena. However, economics can offer analytical insights which are useful alongside the more conventional approach of case-studies. Indeed, the policy conclusions drawn from economic analysis sometimes cast doubt on conventional advice. The use of economic theory and statistical evidence help to guard against excessive generalization from individual civil wars that inevitably suffer from both a surfeit of possible explanations and advocacy. Rigorous empirical study of civil war requires a precise definition of an imprecise and poorly observed phenomenon, a process that provides considerable room for legitimate disagreement. Hence, we begin by discussing the choices made in constructing the major data sets that describe the duration and severity of civil wars.

Ideological, religious or ethnic differences are conventionally regarded as the causes of civil war. Economic theory explains civil war in the framework of incentives and constraints rather than ideologies or identities. This framework enables economists to analyze the distinctive feature of civil war: the emergence and persistence of a rebel army: some conditions make rebellion both more attractive and more feasible than others. Consistent with this emphasis on incentives and constraints, statistical studies suggest that economic characteristics, notably the level, growth and structure of income, are important influences on the risk of war. In addition to the explanation of the initiation and duration of civil wars, economic methods can also generate estimates of their costs and consequences. This is an essential step towards the cost-benefit analysis of policy interventions.

Keywords

civil war, post-conflict, development, aid, natural resources, game theory, prevention, intervention, cost, data collection, panel data, health, refugee

JEL classification: C82, D74, J15, H56, O10, O13

1. Introduction

This chapter aims to cover the economic analysis of civil war. It focuses on the application of economic theory and econometrics to its causes, duration, consequences and costs. Much of the literature of civil war lies outside economics. While we have drawn on this literature, we do not aim to provide a comprehensive treatment of it. All civil wars are intricate social, political and psychological phenomena and each requires its own analysis. For example, conflicts invariably involve personalities: leadership matters. Nevertheless, modern economics can offer insights and explanations which are useful alongside such case-specific study. It helps to guard against excessive generalization from individual situations that inevitably suffer from both a surfeit of possible explanations and highly polarized advocacy.

Rigorous empirical study of civil war requires a precise definition of an imprecise and poorly observed phenomenon, a process that provides considerable room for legitimate disagreement. In Section 1 we discuss the choices made in constructing the major data sets that describe the dates and scale of civil wars. In Section 2 we turn to explanations of civil war, both theoretical and empirical. In Section 3 we consider the scale of conflict. Potentially, scale can be described in various dimensions, such as duration, mortality, and geographic spread, but as yet only the duration of conflict has been investigated sufficiently to warrant discussion. In the following two sections we consider the costs and consequences of civil war, and the processes of recovery or relapse that occur during the post-conflict decade. Section 6 discusses policy implications and their efficacy. In the final section we consider promising avenues for future research.

2. Concepts and data

'What is a civil war?' – this question is difficult to answer in a decisive way and we start with a presentation of the most commonly used definitions and data sets. We then discuss three measures of the severity of civil war: fatalities, duration and geographic spread.

2.1. Definition of civil war

The two most commonly used data sets are the Correlates of War (COW) project as described in Singer and Small (1982, 1994) and the more recently collected 'Armed Conflict Dataset' (ACD) by Gleditsch et al. (2002). Both data sources provide data on inter as well as intra state wars. Further significant data collection efforts are the State Failure Project,[1] as well as data sets collected by individual researchers such as for example Fearon and Laitin (2003). Typically the definition of civil war used in these

---

[1] Available at http://www.cidcm.umd.edu/inscr/stfail/sfdata.htm.

data sets is based on the use of violence and not on the aims of the protagonists or on the outcome of the conflict.

Both COW and ACD are huge data collection efforts and their distribution in electronic format has enabled many researchers to work with the data. The COW definition of civil wars is based on four main characteristics. It requires that there is organized military action and that at least 1000 battle deaths resulted. In order to distinguish wars from genocides, massacres and pogroms there has to be effective resistance, at least five percent of the deaths have been inflicted by the weaker party. A further requirement is that the national government at the time was actively involved. This excludes of a number of internal wars from the civil war definition, most notably wars of liberation from colonialism. Thus, Angola (1961–1975), Mozambique (1964–1975) and Western Sahara (1975–1983) are not defined as civil wars but are instead listed as 'extra-systemic wars'.

The definition of war as used by Gleditsch et al. (2002) has two main dimensions. First, they distinguish four types of violent conflicts according to the participants and location: (1) extra-systemic conflicts (essentially colonial or imperialist wars), (2) interstate wars, (3) intrastate wars and (4) internationalized intrastate wars. The second dimension defines the level of violence. *Minor* conflicts produce more than 25 battle related deaths per year, *intermediate* conflicts produce more than 25 battle related deaths per year and a total conflict history of more than 1000 battle related deaths and lastly *wars* are conflicts which result in more than 1000 battle related deaths per year.

Figure 1 uses these definitions and shows the global incidence of civil war. There is a marked upward trend in the incidence of violent internal conflict during the cold war, with a peak of 37 violent conflicts globally in 1992. Since then the number of violent conflicts has decreased to 21 in 2004.

The absolute number of deaths as a threshold criterion is commonly used to define conflicts. Relative thresholds, such as categorizing wars according to the proportion of a country's population killed in the conflict, are rarely used. A relative threshold would lead to categorizing conflicts of widely varying intensities as wars. In small countries only a few deaths would be interpreted as a civil war while a very large number of deaths would have to occur in larger countries.

These definitions leave one phenomenon as ambiguous, namely popular uprisings. Such uprisings can easily lead to mass fatalities but they differ from rebellions in lacking an organized rebel army and are unlikely to be prolonged. Examples include the Iranian revolution 1978–1979, and the revolutions in Romania and other East European countries in 1989. The theory of such uprisings has been analyzed by Kuran (1989, 1991), and Epstein (2002) presents an interesting simulation model. However, we do not consider the phenomenon further in this chapter.

2.2. Quantitative measures of the severity of civil wars

Closely related to the definition of civil war is the issue of measuring the severity of the civil war. As discussed above, most definitions of civil wars are based on the absolute

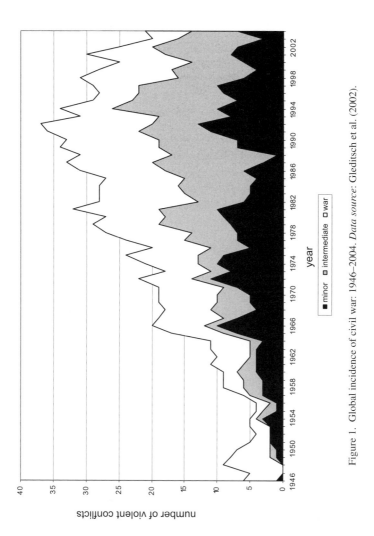

Figure 1. Global incidence of civil war: 1946–2004. *Data source:* Gleditsch et al. (2002).

number of battle related deaths. Fatalities are one measure of the severity of the civil war, however there are many other dimensions researchers may want to analyze. Here we concentrate on the duration, the human costs of conflict and the geographic spread.

2.2.1. Duration

Recent work [Fearon (2004), Collier, Hoeffler and Söderbom (2004)] analyzes the duration of civil war. Issues in the analysis of the duration of civil war are why some wars last much longer than others and whether the duration of conflict can be explained by the same determinants as the causes of conflict. Duration analysis of conflict requires that the start and the end of the conflict can be dated. Often trigger events can be dated and thus the beginning of the violence dated, e.g. the assassination of Rwanda's president on 6 March 1994 marks the start of the civil war in a number of data sets. However, often the violence escalates over some period of time before it reaches the relevant threshold and can thus be defined as a civil war. Wars end either with a military victory, settlement or truce. About half of all civil wars end in military defeat [Sambanis (2000)] which makes dating somewhat easier than using dates of peace agreements which may not have resulted in an end to all military action.

The duration of the war does not only depend on being able to date a start and end but also on the definition of violence thresholds. Data sets which define a civil war by 1000 battle related deaths per annum have on average shorter wars than data sets with lower thresholds. Take for example a war with more than 1000 battle related deaths during the first year, if the number of battle related deaths falls beneath the threshold in the second year but reaches it again during the third year a rigid application of the absolute threshold criterion leads to the classification of two conflicts for a high threshold definition and to the classification of one conflict for a low threshold definition. Thus, the problems with respect to dating the start and end of the conflict are not only of importance for the analysis of the duration of conflicts and peace but also for the analysis of the recurrence of civil wars. Walter (2004) defines recurrent civil wars as those fought by the same combatants for the same goals as the original war.

2.2.2. Human cost

As discussed in Section 2.1 the number of battle related deaths is one of the main defining characteristics of civil war. Exact numbers are difficult to obtain because both parties in the conflict tend to understate their fatalities and overstate the opponent's fatalities. Lacina and Gleditsch (2005) provide the best estimates for the human cost on an annual basis for all wars since 1946. They classify the human costs into three categories: 'combatant deaths', 'battle deaths' and 'war deaths'. Most other data sets only offer mortality statistics for the entirety of the conflict and do not clearly distinguish between battle and war deaths. Typically 'combatant deaths' can be used to assess strategic choices in warfare and are often quoted in order to evaluate normative questions such as the proportionality of the use of force. 'Battle deaths' include all people, military and civilian,

Table 1
Deaths in selected conflicts in Africa

Country	Years	Total war deaths	Battle deaths	Percentage battle deaths
Sudan (Anya Nya rebellion)	1963–1973	250,000–750,000	20,000	3–8%
Nigeria (Biafra rebellion)	1967–1970	500,000 to 2 million	75,000	4–15%
Angola	1975–2002	1.5 million	160,475	11%
Ethiopia (excluding Eritrean insurgency)	1976–1991	1–2 million	16,000	<2%
Mozambique	1967–1992	500,000 to 1 million	145,400	15–29%
Somalia	1981–1996	250,000 to 350,000 (to mid 1990s)	66,750	19–27%
Sudan	1983–2002	2 million	55,000	3%
Liberia	1989–1996	150,000–200,000	23,500	12–16%
Dem. Republic of the Congo	1998–2001	2.5 million	145,000	6%

Source: Lacina and Gleditsch (2005).

killed in combat. This measure is regarded as the most suitable to assess the scale, scope and nature of the military engagement. A more accurate account of the human cost of war also accounts for deaths due to increased violence as well as due to starvation and increased disease. Lacina and Gleditsch term this category 'war deaths'. A number of stylized facts can be drawn from their research. Since the end of the cold war most battle deaths were caused by civil wars of which a large number occur in Africa. As Table 1 illustrates the proportion of battle deaths in total war deaths is small, for example surveys in the Democratic Republic of Congo suggest that only about six percent of the war deaths were a result of direct military action.

There are a variety of reasons for the low proportion of battle deaths in total war deaths. Poorly equipped and organized armies may often not engage in direct battles with the opposing forces but government as well as rebel armies injure and kill civilians [see, for example, Herbst (2000), Cairns (1997)]. Most wars are fought in low income countries where a poor infrastructure and limited medical services increase the war related mortality rates. This is particularly tragic in countries where the war caused famines, such as in Ethiopia and the Sudan.

2.2.3. Geographic spread

A further measure of the severity of civil war is the geographic spread of the war. As a first step this requires to determine the country in which the conflict was fought. Data sets such as COW and Gleditsch et al. (2002) provide information on the primary participants and interventions as well as where the war was fought. Thus, making it possible to treat intervening countries differently from the countries in which the war was fought. However, there is very little information on the nature of the interventions, i.e. whether countries only supported the military intervention logistically or whether troops were sent.[2] For cases in which the rebellion spans several countries (e.g. the Kurdish rebellion) researchers assume two different war locations (in this example Turkey and Iraq).

Only very few data sets give some estimate of the geographic spread within the civil war country. The State Failure Project provides an ordinal indicator for the proportion of the country affected by fighting. However, the data set does not provide information on which part of the country was affected. Buhaug and Gates (2002) provide much more detailed geographic measures of the geography of war. Based on information on where military action took place they define the conflict center and area. The absolute scope of the conflict is measured by the circular area around the conflict center and the authors also provide the geographic distance between the conflict center and the capital city.

3. Causes of civil war

3.1. Motivation and feasibility

The distinctive feature of civil war is the emergence and persistence of a rebel army: this is the phenomenon that must be explained. A satisfactory explanation should include both motivation and feasibility, and in principle either could provide the bulk of explanatory power. Thus, civil wars may be rare because the circumstances which motivate the formation of private armies are rare, or because the circumstances in which such armies are feasible are rare.

In practice, there has been a greater focus on motivation than on feasibility. Within motivation, a recent and somewhat contentious distinction has been 'greed or grievance'. The rebel discourse invariably provides an account of motivation in terms of the need to redress objective grievances and this is often taken at face value. However, potentially, rebels may also be motivated by the opportunities that organized violence generates for private gain. A large number of studies provide a categorization of conflicts based on the different grievances. The 'issues of the conflict' are commonly seen as: territory, land and sea-borders, national independence or decolonization, ethnic, religious or regional autonomy, ideology and system conflicts, national power conflicts, international and geo-strategic power conflicts and conflicts over the access to and the distribution of resources. This type of classification into different types of conflict makes explicit but often uncontested assumptions about their causes. The motivation for violent conflict can sometimes be inferred as a revealed preference, providing at least some independent check on the rebel account of motivation. Further, alleged grievances can sometimes be measured: for example, it is to an extent possible to test whether societies that are more unequal are more prone to rebellion.

---

[2] Regan (2002) provides data on interventions and divides them into three categories: diplomatic, economic and military.

3.2. Theories of rebellion

There are a number of theoretical studies on the causes of violent conflict and a growing body of empirical literature. Economic theories of the causes of civil war follow two distinct approaches. The first approach focuses on motivation and applies game theory, usually with the rebels aggregated into one player and the government into the other. The second approach is to focus on feasibility and views the rebel group as an unusual type of business which can only prosper in special conditions. We consider them in turn.

3.2.1. Game-theoretic analyses

The standard game-theoretic model of civil war has its foundations in the work of Hirshleifer (1991, 1994, 2001). It postulates economic differences between agents that can generate predatory behavior. Typically, agents can be productive or unproductive in an output-generating activity, and strong or weak. Unproductive but strong agents then have an incentive to engage in predation against productive but weak agents. Such predation can be glossed as justice, equity, or extortion depending on the political perspective of the analyst, but the underlying structure is the same. Even within its own terms, this sort of model runs into several difficulties.

Since predatory behavior is costly, both agents can improve on redistribution-through-violence if the productive-but-weak agent engages in pre-emptive redistribution. In effect, the endowment differences should produce redistribution rather than rebellion, a line of analysis most closely associated with Azam (1995) and Roemer (1985). Within this framework the explanation of rebellion remains a challenge. There are three broad possibilities. One is to postulate asymmetric information: neither agent knows the military capabilities of the other. If both agents are over-optimistic, there may be no peaceful outcome that both recognize as mutually beneficial. Somewhat analogous to the 'winner's curse', once at war players discover that they have over-played their hand. A second possibility is to invoke hatred, and possibly reciprocal hatred, so that players get utility from inflicting harm on the other party. A third possibility is to introduce constraints upon the ability to make preemptive redistributions. The explanation for civil war then becomes not the differences in endowments but these additions.

A second area of difficulty is that each party to a civil war is comprised of a large group of actors. If rebellion generates costs that are borne by the rebel group and confers benefits that accrue to a much wider community, that is if the rebellion is aiming to generate a public good (a claim of many rebel groups), it will face a standard free-rider problem. In the absence of a government, public goods are radically undersupplied, and since government is not going to supply rebellion, those rebellions that are seeking to provide a public good will also be radically undersupplied: civil wars will be rare but bountiful. A way out of this difficulty is to think of rebellion as supplying a joint product, partly a public good and partly a private good which accrues only to participants.

3.2.2. The organization of rebellion

An alternative to the game-theoretic approach is to see civil war as the result of unusual conditions that enable a business organization – the rebel group – to be viable during what is typically a very long period of violent conflict. This need not imply that the organization is motivated by the profits to be made during the conflict. Indeed, the approach can be entirely agnostic as to motivation. In the limit it can hypothesize that where a rebel organization is viable it will develop, with the motive being whatever happens to be the agenda of the first group to occupy the available niche. Potentially, the conditions for viability might collapse the analysis back into a study of motivation: for example, rebellion might only be viable where a particular group had a sufficiently strong grievance to tolerate danger and hardship. However, the approach emphasizes rather different requirements for viability: the ability to equip and finance an army [Collier (2001)], and the ability to survive against a government army, an issue which has been extensively explored through the concept of contest success functions (see Chapter 22 of this *Handbook*).

Although the approach is agnostic about motivation, given that conflicts typically last many years it is natural to look to benefits that accrue during conflict. The most cynical interpretation of rebellion is to regard it as motivated by the opportunities for profit that accrue during violence. In a brilliant paper, Weinstein (2005) develops a theory of rebel recruitment. He shows that where there are opportunities for large profits, the composition of the rebel group will gradually shift towards those with an intrinsic motivation for private gain: the rebellion experiences adverse selection in intrinsic motivation. An alternative way of invoking intrinsic motivation is to recognize that rebellion is fundamentally about power through violence. Hence, it is likely to attract those who place an atypically high value on these features. Many rebellions depend upon child soldiers and drug addicts, features which are insufficiently recognized in economic models. Rebel leaders generally do well out of war, but cannot be bought off *ex ante* by government because they cannot be identified. Rebellion may therefore simply require the combination of child poverty, an initial supply of arms, and opportunities for continuing finance whether through predation or donations.

Gates (2002) and Grossman (1991, 1999) provide somewhat complementary microeconomic models of the rebel organization in which private gain motivates decisions. Gates takes the perspective of the rebel leader, emphasizing the agency problems that must be overcome. Grossman takes the perspective of the potential peasant recruit with households deciding how to allocate their labor time to production, soldiering, or participation in an insurrection. The interaction between the ruler and the peasants generates an equilibrium allocation of labor time and a probabilistic distribution of income from the various activities. One possible equilibrium outcome is a higher expected income if time is allocated to insurrections despite its opportunity cost.

Kuran (1989) investigates the likelihood of joining a rebel movement. Individuals with a strong preference for revolution are most likely to join first. Individuals with a less strong preference are more likely to join if the probability of success is higher. They are more likely to join if others have already joined. This 'bandwagon' effect is most likely to result in strong rebel support if preferences are uniformly distributed. Societies with clustered preferences are less likely to experience rebellion.

The issue of motivation and mobilization of national militaries has not received much attention. Herbst (2004) provides an analytical narrative for Africa. African armies are, by comparative standards, small but weak or failing states often have great difficulties to respond to the threat of civil war. Poor institutional environments and a lack of public finances contribute to the lack of intelligence and early warning systems. Once a civil war has started mobilization to mount a successful counter-insurgency is difficult and in a number of cases mobilization failed when faced with a credible internal threat. Herbst argues that additional sources of finance such as aid and income from natural resources (most notably from oil) can help to overcome mobilization problems.

3.3. Evidence on the causes

The most commonly cited causes of large scale violent conflict are probably differences due to religion, ethnicity and class/economic inequality. Examples include the 'Clash of Civilization' hypothesis [Huntington (2002)] and the assertion that 'the relation between inequality and rebellion is indeed a close one' [Sen (1973, Chapter 1)]. It is probably true that certain conflicts are due to some or a number of these causes but they may not be universal drivers of violence. Until recently none of these commonly held beliefs were subjected to empirical testing. A number of papers have tackled these issues [Fearon and Laitin (2003), Miguel, Satyanath and Sergenti (2004), Collier and Hoeffler (2004a)]. Due to the electronic availability of conflict data various researchers have coded civil wars as a dichotomous variable and analyzed the initiation of war using panel data analysis. While the debate on the determinants of civil war is ongoing there is a consensus regarding some of the factors which make countries more prone to civil war.

Collier and Hoeffler (2004a) find that a higher degree of ethnic and religious diversity makes a country *less* conflict prone. However, this is not the case if there is one dominant ethnic group, when there is a higher risk of civil war. Thus, the relationship between ethnic diversity and war is nonlinear. History is also important, countries with a past history of conflict are more likely to experience renewed conflict. This risk is about 44% during the immediate five post-conflict peace years. However, this conflict risk fades as the peace period continues, the risk of conflict is reduced by about one percent per year. Their most important finding is that economic factors such as the level, growth and structure of income to be significant in the analysis of war initiation. Poorer countries, countries with low growth rates and a high proportion of primary commodity exports in their GDP were more likely to experience war during 1960–1999.

The econometric analysis has moved from correlations to statements that can reasonably be seen as causal. For example, despite the evident reverse causality from conflict onto both growth rates and income, it has been possible to separate out that part of the correlation that is due to causal relationships from low growth and low income onto the risk of conflict. However, several interpretations of these causal relationships remain possible. One is that low incomes and growth rates indicate a lack of opportunities, thus making recruitment to rebel forces much easier. This is at least consistent with the evidence from the World Values Survey on reported preferences. Faster economic growth reduces the taste for revolution [Pezzini and MacCulloch (2004)].

The evidence that countries with a high proportion of primary commodity exports in their GDP are more prone to conflict is sometimes interpreted as evidence that rebels use these natural resources to fund their warfare. Financing a private army can be done in a number ways and looting natural resources is one of them. This result and its interpretation initiated a wide debate. Apart from the financing argument natural resource rich economies have specific policy characteristics and the reason for increased risk could be found in their political economy [see Humphreys (2005) and other articles in the same issue of Journal of Conflict Resolution (2005)]. Countries rich in natural resources suffer from a resource curse, they do not only have lower growth rates on average but also weaker institutions. At the core of the institutions' argument is the idea that leaders in resource rich economies do not have to tax the population and thus are less subject to electoral scrutiny [Bates (1981), Robinson, Torvik and Verdier (2002), Collier and Hoeffler (2005)]. Support is typically bought through patronage in the public sector. Both the financing as well as the political economy reasoning seem plausible. The work by Lujala, Gleditsch and Gilmore (2005) suggests that conflicts last longer if the rebels control naturally resource rich regions, i.e. presenting evidence for the rebel finance rather than for the weak state argument. In addition rebel recruitment may be affected by natural resources. Weinstein (2005) suggests that where resources permit, opportunistic rebel leaders crowd out ideological leaders. As a result these opportunistic rebellions are even less likely to produce economic and social development than ideologically motivated rebellions.

One of the most contested issues is the apparent lack of significance of some variables, particularly those that can most naturally be interpreted as proxying objective grievances. The degree of political rights is variously found to be either insignificant [Collier and Hoeffler (2004a)], or to have ambiguous effects. Some researchers suggest that the effect of political rights is non-monotonic, with 'anocracy' more dangerous than either autocracy or full democracy [Hegre et al. (2001), Gurr and Marshall (2005)]. However, these results have been questioned. Hegre (2003) finds that the effect of democracy is contingent upon the level of income, increasing the risk of conflict in low-income societies but reducing it in middle-income societies. Reynal-Querol (2005) suggests that representation is more important than level of democracy per se. Her results suggest that the design of political systems is important, violence is less likely in proportional representation systems. There is also some evidence that abuses of civil rights as monitored by Amnesty International are a leading indicator of violent conflict [Fearon (2004)], and political rights and civil liberties reduce the taste for revolution [Pezzini and MacCulloch (2004)].

Similarly, overall household inequality generally appears to have little effect on the risk of conflict despite the massive attention that it attracts. Stewart (2001) suggests that inequality between culturally defined groups, termed 'horizontal inequality', as opposed

Turning to the three explanations, there is considerable evidence for the difficulties of locking in to internal settlements. At the econometric level the strongest evidence is perhaps the high risk that conflicts restart: a risk that is much higher if conflicts are ended by settlements than if they are ended by outright military victory. However, the strongest evidence is probably from the interpretation of case studies [Walter (2001)]. She examines how the hazard of peace evolves over time. Since information should improve, the hazard of peace should gradually rise. In fact there is little sign that the hazard of peace follows such a pattern: typically it seems to be rather flat. While this is not decisive, it cautions against emphasis upon this explanation. The effect of the profitability of violence on the duration of conflict has received little empirical investigation. One study finds that in countries with substantial natural resource exports when the world price of these exports are high the chances of peace diminish, which is consistent with the explanation [Collier, Hoeffler and Söderbom (2004)].

5. Consequences of civil war

When translated into economic terms, the glorifying language of 'armed struggle' implies that rebellion is usually a socially productive investment. Whether this is a reasonable characterization depends upon the costs incurred during the conflict and the post-conflict consequences. The attempt to put civil war into a cost-benefit framework is still in its infancy, but there is sufficient evidence to challenge the presumption of 'armed struggle' as being fundamentally misleading. The legacy effects of civil war are usually adverse: rather than being viewed as an unavoidably costly but valuable investment, it is an avoidable calamity with highly persistent adverse effects. For example, the country tends to get locked into persistently high levels of military expenditure, capital continues to flow out of the country at an unusually high rate, and the incidence of infectious disease remains much higher. Even economic policies, political institutions and political freedom appear to deteriorate. Of course, it is always possible to find some modern civil wars that can reasonably be seen as ushering in social progress, but these are exceptional. On average, modern civil war has been development in reverse.

5.1. Economic consequences

Unsurprisingly, civil war reduces growth during the period of conflict. The most obvious economic costs arise from the direct destruction of infrastructure and other capital. Collier (1999) distinguishes four further effects. Public resources are diverted from productive activities to violence; there is an increase in opportunism as time horizons shorten; capital, both financial and human leaves the country; and there is a shift away from vulnerable economic activities towards those that are less vulnerable such as arable subsistence agriculture.

An estimate of the economic cost of the average civil war is presented in Collier and Hoeffler (2004c). They focus on the local and regional costs and their estimate should be interpreted as conservative since most of the global cost cannot be quantified. These global costs are massive in scale but difficult to assign a cost to. Three world scourges over the last 30 years have had civil conflicts as contributory factors: hard drug production, AIDS and international terrorism.

One year of conflict reduces a country's growth rate by around 2.2%. Since, on average, civil conflict lasts for seven years, by the end of the conflict the economy will be 15% smaller than if the war had not taken place. Post-conflict the economy recovers, at about one percent above its normal growth rate, although this effect probably peters out. Overall, it takes around 21 years to get back to the level of GDP that would have prevailed without the conflict, so that many of the costs accrue after the war has ended. The loss of GDP during these 21 years cumulates to a present value at the start of the conflict of 105% of initial GDP. The welfare of a country's population is further reduced because of increased military spending during and after the war. The present value of this additional cost is estimated at 18% of GDP.

At the regional level, the research indicates that the growth rate and military expenditures of neighboring countries are affected during and after the war.[4] On average, each country has 2.7 neighbors and applying the same concepts as detailed above the loss of income is 115% of the initial GDP of one country: greater than the direct effect in the conflict country itself. Due to neighborhood arms races the regions military expenditure will also rise, causing a cost of about 12% of one country's GDP.

Other costs which are too difficult to quantify are incurred both in the country at war and in the region as a whole, including forced migration and increased disease. With the proviso that the figures so far are therefore underestimated to some degree, the total cost of the "typical" civil war sums to around 250% of initial GDP. The average GDP of conflict-affected low-income countries just prior to war is around $20 billion, so that the cost of a single war is around $50 billion.

In addition to these direct economic costs, conflict has a severe effect on human health. One way of costing this effect is to express it in terms of Disability Affected Life Years (DALYs): An average war causes an estimated 0.5 million DALYs each year. Assuming a recovery period of 21 years gives a figure of 5 million DALYs as the net present value of health costs when hostilities start. If each DALY is valued at $1000 (roughly the per capita income in many at-risk countries), the economic cost of harm to human health in a typical war is around $5 billion.

A further layer of costs arise because of the "conflict trap": countries that have just experienced a civil war are more likely to have further conflict.[5] Among the 21 countries in which wars started and ended in the period 1965–1999, the risk of conflict over the five years before the war averaged 22.3%, but rose to 38.6% post-war. Over the 15 year

---

[4] For a detailed analysis of the spatial effects of civil wars see Murdoch and Sandler (2002, 2004). For estimates of regional arms race effects see Collier and Hoeffler (in press).

[5] The dynamics of conflict traps are also analyzed in Bloomberg and Hess (2002). An important addition to the conflict trap analysis is presented in Murdoch and Sandler (2004). They do not only investigate conflict risk for one country over time but extend the analysis of temporal aspects to neighboring countries.

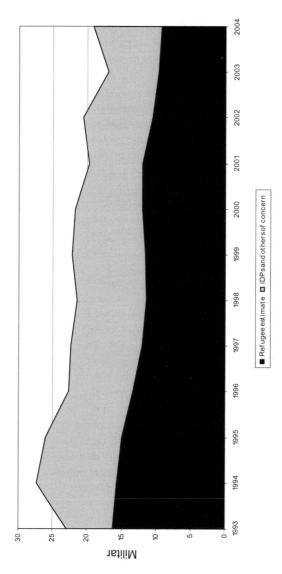

Figure 2. Refugees, IDPs and others of concern. *Data source:* UNHCR Statistical Yearbook (various issues).

not end when shooting or bombing stops, but continues after wars. Moreover, living in a refugee camp or transitory settlement can constitute a "secondary wound". The majority of individuals will experience low-grade but long lasting mental health problems [McDonald (2002)]. Russett, Ghobarah and Huth (2003) find an indirect effect of civil wars on suicides of woman of childbearing age. This probably reflects the trauma of rape.

5.4. Political consequences

Another persistent adverse legacy is the loss of social capital: civil war can have the effect of switching behavior from an equilibrium in which there is an expectation of honesty, to one in which there is an expectation of corruption. Once a reputation for honesty has been lost, the incentive for honest behavior in the future is much weakened. Clearly, civil war is not the only way in which a society can become corrupted; the point is simply that the costs inflicted by the loss of honesty and trust are likely to persist long after the conflict is over.

For civil war to have some redeeming features the most hopeful areas would be policies, political institutions, and human rights. The impact of civil war on each of these

Table 2
Is civil war a catalyst for change?

	Peaceful countries	Five years prior to the war	Five years post war
Per capita GDP growth (%)[a]	1.73	0.82	3.64
Life expectancy (in years)[a]	62.85	57.79	54.97
Democracy (0–10)[b]	2.99	2.66	2.38
Political rights (1–7)[c]	4.03	4.67	5.12
Civil liberties (1–7)[c]	4.01	4.81	5
% of seats held by minority parties[d]	21.1	19.84	19.86
Human rights violations (1–5)[e]	2.50	3.15	3.58
Assassinations (total deaths)[f]	0.09	0.35	0.30
Proportion of countries with religious freedom[g]	0.66	0.63	0.60

Note: Authors' calculations. *Data sources*:
[a]World Development Indicators 2005.

[b]Polity IV, http://www.cidcm.umd.edu/inscr/polity/.
[c]Freedom House, http://www.freedomhouse.org/ratings.

[d]Prio and Vanhanen, http://www.prio.no/page/Project_detail//9244/42504.html.
[e]Corbett and Gibney (2004).

[f]Banks (2002).
[g]Cingranelli and Richards (2004).

can, to an extent, be measured. In Table 2 we present some political and economic indicators. As a benchmark we report the values for countries that remained peaceful throughout the period 1960–2004. On average peaceful countries experienced an annual increase in their per capita GDP of 1.7 percent. For countries in which a war broke out we measure average growth rates in the five years prior to the start of the war and in the last column we present the values for the five post war years. Prior to a war growth rates are less than half of the peaceful countries, growth averages only about 0.8 percent. During the five post war years the average growth rate is substantially higher, at about 3.6 percent. This demonstrates that post-conflict economies have the potential to reap a substantial peace dividend. Life expectancy indicates that health problems continue to cut people's lives short even after the war has ended. The average life expectancy is about three years shorter after the war. This exemplifies the need for economic and political change in post-conflict societies. In Table 2 we also present the values for political systems and institutions. Our measure for the extent to which political institutions are democratic is the standard political science index – 'Polity IV'. The typical peaceful aid recipient country has a score of 2.99 and war countries average 2.66 prior to their civil war. Countries in the first five years of post-war peace average a score of only 2.38. Hence, on average civil war leads to a deterioration rather than an improvement in political institutions. A related measure is an index of political rights compiled by Freedom House. This is a seven point scale in which, unlike the other indices, a low score is better than a high score. The comparable numbers are 4.67 before war and 5.12 after war. Hence, again civil war leaves a legacy of reduced rather than increased rights. Likewise, civil war does not increase representation of minorities, the proportion of parliamentary seats held by minority parties is the same before and after the war. Human rights violations have been measured on a scale of 1 to 5. Again, civil wars make things worse, there are more human rights violations after the war than before the war. Post-conflict societies tend to be also much more violent, the average number of assassinations is considerably higher than in countries that never experienced civil war. The last row of Table 2 shows that civil war does not increase the proportion of societies that grant their citizens religious freedom. To summarize, although peace after a civil war can potentially generate considerable economic benefits it does not seem to be the case that civil war can be interpreted as a catalyst for policy improvement but rather for policy deterioration.

6. Post-conflict

6.1. Theories of post-conflict recovery and relapse

Post-conflict situations are distinctive both in their risk of conflict and in their economic growth. Their risk of conflict is far above average. Their rate of growth is typically high but subject to wide variations. Hence, post-conflict situations warrant theories both of the risk of repeat conflict and of the process of economic recovery.

Theories of why the risk of repeat conflict is so high include fixed effects and legacy effects: risks might be high because the country has underlying and unchanging characteristics that make it prone to conflict, or because the conflict increases the risks. Clearly, only the latter explanation warrants distinct theorizing. One such explanation is that preferences are endogenous: violence leaves a legacy of hatred. However, we have noted that hatred does not seem in general to be a very powerful explanation of large-scale organized violent conflict. Another explanation is that prolonged conflict reconfigures interests: organizations develop that have capital and skills that are useful only in the context of continuing violence. It is difficult to maintain transfers to all these groups so that they have a continuing interest in peace. For example, the new peace in Southern Sudan must contend against the problem that there are thirty separate armed groups. A third explanation has already been set out in our discussion of duration: peace settlements are fragile because the relative power of rebel groups erodes and so the government has an incentive to renege. In effect, settlements are liable to be time-inconsistent. Potentially, this gives the government the scope to signal its intentions through locking in to choices which diminish the risk of further conflict such as sharp reductions in military spending [Collier and Hoeffler (2006)].

Theories of economic recovery focus on reversing the specific effects of conflict on the economy discussed in Section 5: for example, there is a gradual reintegration of the rural economy into the market. However, these effects are inevitably related to the high risk of repeat conflict. For example, given such a risk, investment will be strongly influenced by the perceived risk of conflict. If the risk is seen to be high, the capital flight that is typically substantial during conflict is likely to continue unabated [Collier et al. (2003)], whereas if it is seen to be low the very fact of substantial past capital flight provides a major opportunity for rapid recovery.

6.2. Evidence

The evidence on the risk of repeat conflict suggests that the high risk is typically approximately equally divided between that due to long term proneness and that due to the legacy of the previous conflict. The latter appears to decay over time, but its rate of decay has not yet been adequately measured. There is evidence that in response to the high risk of further conflict post-conflict governments adopt high levels of military spending. Typically, spending during the post-conflict decade is much closer to a war situation than to peace. Consistent with the signaling theory noted above, controlling for endogeneity, such high military spending appears to cause an increase in the risk of repeat conflict [Collier and Hoeffler (2006)]. There is also some evidence that, controlling for endogeneity, the existence of a large diaspora in developed countries increases post-conflict risks. This is consistent with evidence that diasporas tend to be more extreme than the home population, in part perhaps because they do not bear the cost of a reversion to conflict. However, considering that half of all civil wars are post-conflict collapses, the evolution of post-conflict risk warrants much more quantitative empirical work than the subject has yet received.

The evidence on economic recovery is also rudimentary. Analysis of how the structure of the economy evolves, for example, investment and the return to the market, have only been investigated at the level of case studies. The relationship between overall growth, policy choices and aid has been the focus of only one quantitative study [Collier and Hoeffler (2004b)]. Using time dummies in a panel data analysis they find that while growth rates tend to be higher during the post-conflict decade, the main surge is in the middle of the decade rather than right after the end of conflict.

7. Policy interventions

Much of the previous analysis has implications for policy, both for governments in conflict-prone countries and for external actors. In some ways the key implication is that the costs of civil war are typically very high, and that many of these costs are external to the active participants, borne either by neighbors or the next generation. The high costs and dismal consequences of most civil wars suggest that those who launch them are usually fooling either themselves or others in claiming that they are means of social progress. Civil wars are best avoided. Because of the large externalities, external actors have a legitimate interest in promoting peace. Evidently, prevention is better than cure. However, whether the opportunities for prevention offer more scope for conflict reduction than the opportunities for ending current conflicts and reducing the risk of their rapid recurrence is less clear. Because many societies face some risk that conflict can occur, prevention policies are highly diffuse. In contrast, interventions to end conflicts and to reduce the risks in post-conflict situations, can be highly focused on a few countries. Around half of all civil wars have been due to post-conflict relapses.

7.1.   Policies for prevention

Policies for conflict prevention, outside the context of post-conflict, can be grouped into three categories: those which target the grievances of likely rebel groups; those that target the material feasibility of successful rebellion; and more general policies of economic and political development.

Governments at risk sometimes address grievances, but perhaps a more commonly suggested strategy is to buy off the leaders of potential rebel groups as they emerge. This strategy is for example presented in a formal way by Azam (2000). However, there is likely to be a trade off between buying off a rebel group and economy wide growth. Buying off now may secure current peace but compromises longer term growth. Not buying off threatens current peace but may enable the economy to grow and thus achieve peace in the longer run. A further problem with the buying off strategy is that it is not always obvious who should be bought off. *Ex post* it is obvious which rebel organization became a serious threat to the state, but *ex ante* it is often not clear which groups to buy off if there are several rebel organizations.

One illustrative example is the case of Chad, the country's small army has sixty generals, a structure better understood by this strategy than by operational military needs. Redistributions to entire groups are more common where there is a credible threat of secession, as in oil-rich regions. Evidently, the core reason for redressing the legitimate grievances of particular groups is built into the definition of the concept. It is more controversial whether such redressal also significantly reduces the risk of civil war. Groups with legitimate grievances may be too weak to rebel: powerful groups with manufactured grievances may be the most likely rebels. Our own view is that the apparent link between legitimate grievance and rebellion has been exaggerated.

The other extreme to appeasement is repression. There is some weak evidence that this is effective: autocratic societies are sometimes found to have lower risks of rebellion than partial democracies. However, correcting for the endogeneity implied by the dependence of military spending upon the risk of rebellion, there appears to be no significant deterrence effect of military spending [Collier and Hoeffler (2006)]. While the governments of countries at risk may thus have relatively little scope for effective deterrence, international actors may have considerable scope to reduce the feasibility of rebellion, through curtailing finance and armaments. These opportunities are just beginning to filter into international policy.

The surest prevention strategy is economic development. Recall that the level, growth and structure of income are all significant risk factors. Rapid economic development reduces the risk of rebellion directly through the growth rate, cumulatively through the level of income, and indirectly, through diversification of the economy. Bad governance may matter for conflict more because it closes off opportunities for economic development than because of the grievances that it generates. Aid to low-income countries has some pay-off in terms of conflict prevention in addition to its more conventional benefits of poverty reduction. Aid appears to have no systematic direct effect on the risk of conflict, but through its effect on growth it is beneficial [Collier and Hoeffler (2002)]. However, an attempt to quantify the payoff suggests that it is fairly modest relative to the cost of the aid, and so is unlikely to be the core rationale for aid to low-income countries [Collier and Hoeffler (2004c)].

7.2. Policies for ending conflict

Governments in conflict end them either through victory or compromise. The evidence suggests that military victory, where feasible, leads to a more secure peace. However, the investment in victory may involve temporary very large increases in military spending. For example, the government of Angola reached peace by raising its military spending to around 20% of GDP, at which point the massive rebel group UNITA collapsed. By contrast, the government of Colombia, has set its military spending at around 2% of GDP and is still fighting the much smaller FARC despite four years of negotiations and concessions which included ceding part of the country to the rebel group.

International interventions to end civil war are evaluated in Collier, Hoeffler and Söderbom (2004). They find that neither military nor economic interventions have had any significant systematic effects, although they have presumably been effective in individual instances. The time-consistency problem, discussed above, suggests that international interventions to guarantee the terms of a settlement could potentially make an important contribution as long as they are credible and long term, a combination that is difficult.

7.3. Policies for maintaining post-conflict peace

Given the importance of economic growth in building peace, and the highly variable post-conflict economic outcomes, it seems likely that the policy choices of post-conflict governments are particularly important. This is consistent with the results of Collier and Hoeffler (2004b) that growth is particularly sensitive to policy during the post-conflict decade. They also find some evidence that policy priorities should be distinctive, with greater attention to social inclusion relative to macroeconomic stability than in other situations.

Aid has long been seen as being important for post-conflict recovery. Indeed, the initial rationale for the World Bank was as an agency for postwar reconstruction. The same study finds that aid is atypically effective in the growth process during post-conflict, although the peak period for absorption may be around the middle of the decade rather than right at the beginning, which is when donors currently provide the bulk of their aid.

Given that the risk of reversion to conflict is so high, it is unsurprising that the typical post-conflict government reacts by maintaining high levels of military spending. Post-conflict spending looks much closer to wartime than to peacetime. One study investigates whether such spending is effective, controlling for the evident endogeneity of spending to war risk. It finds that far from being effective, high military spending in post-conflict situations significantly and substantially increases the risk of further conflict [Collier and Hoeffler (2006)].

Since economic recovery even if well-managed typically takes around a decade to deliver substantial reductions in risk, some temporary remedy is needed to maintain the peace. If domestic military spending is counterproductive, the only remaining option is external military stabilization. The record here is mixed. An attempt to provide a cost-benefit analysis of the external military intervention in post-conflict Sierra Leone, based upon the estimated risk of reversion to conflict that it has suppressed, concluded that it was highly cost-effective [Collier and Hoeffler (2004c)]. However, external interventions are only likely to be successful in particular conditions.

The paths to post-conflict recovery are currently under-researched. Thus, donors tend to apply their general programs designed for poor countries irrespective of whether the country has a recent experience of war or not. The relative importance of various macroeconomic reforms and their sequencing is not well understood. Although there is a growing awareness of the relationship between security, conflict and development, there seems to be a lack of attention to security issues when designing policy instruments to promote economic growth and development in post-conflict societies. Chalmers (2005) is one of the few to advise treating security as an important service provision to poor people in fragile states alongside other essential services such as the provision of health, infrastructure and education.

Given the extraordinary weakness of most post-conflict governments, there is usually an important role for international intervention across the spectrum of economic, political and military assistance. To date, international actors have met these needs without an adequate framework for coordination [Sandler (2004, Chapter 9)]. This problem was recognized in the decision of the UN in 2005 to establish a Peacebuilding Commission. The precise role of the Commission, and its effectiveness, will become important research issues.

8. Conclusions and research agendas

The economic analysis of civil war has undoubtedly challenged some anthropological pieties. At the theoretical level it has placed decisions into the framework of incentives rather than ideologies or identities. At the empirical level it has questioned whether the factors most emphasized in past literature can be correct depictions of the events they purport to analyze. Economic analysis can never be the whole story, yet there remains scope for far more economic work, both theoretical and empirical.

There is also scope for more work with other disciplines. To date, the study of civil war has been dominated by political scientists. Yet this prejudges the phenomenon as being essentially political. Many rebel movements are not, however, much like political parties or protest movements. One non-political analogy, between rebel groups and organized crime, has already been explored. Others may also be fruitful. For example, rebel groups may resemble the fringe religious communities in which gullible recruits are trapped to the point of their own death by charismatic autocrats, as in Jonestown and Waco. Economists may need to link with psychologists to study the process of selection according to intrinsic motivation. There may also be scope to link with historians. Civil wars are often explained in terms of long histories of violence and animosity. We suspect that since most societies have some history of violent conflict there is no significant causal relationship from distant history. Rather, where current conditions favor rebellion, leaders will trawl through the past to endow their cause with the trappings of historical legitimacy. This could be formally tested once global historical data are suitably codified.

At the theoretical level, the most productive area may be more game-theoretic analysis that disaggregates each side. Indeed, *ex ante*, in civil war there is no rebel side: potentially anyone can recruit a small private army. To give two examples, Weinstein's work, discussed above is pioneering the rebel recruitment process. At the other end of the time spectrum of rebellion, there is new research on why in post-conflict political contexts voters tend to favor extremists.

At the empirical level progress is also likely to come through disaggregation. One obvious dimension is spatial: there is as yet little work analyzing the location of rebellions within countries. Another dimension is temporal: there is little work analyzing the evolution of risk in post-conflict situations. There would be a high pay-off to quantitative on-the-ground observation, something which is understandably rare. Weinstein's insightful analysis of the rebel recruitment process depended upon such direct observation of rebel organizations. Analogous to the celebrated analysis of a Chicago drug gang [Levitt and Venkatesh (2000)], this probably implies collaboration with anthropologists.

In the end, the correct analysis of civil war matters. We estimate the social costs to be of the order of $100 bn per year. Policies, both by governments in risk-prone countries, and by international actors, have been informed by little more than popular prejudices. Yet this is surely a phenomenon akin to smallpox that with research-informed efforts will be eradicated during this century.

References

Addison, T., Murshed, S.M. (2002). "Credibility and reputation in peacemaking". Journal of Peace Research 39, 487–501.

Azam, J.-P. (1995). "How to pay for the peace? A theoretical framework with references to African countries". Public Choice 83, 173–184.

Azam, J.-P. (2000). "Looting and conflict between ethnoregional groups: Lessons for state formation in Africa". Journal of Conflict Resolution 46, 131–153.

Banks, A. (2002). "Cross national time-series data archive". Retrieved 12 September 2005, from http://www.databanks.sitehosting.net.

Bates, R. (1981). States and Markets in Tropical Africa: The Political Basis of Agricultural Policy. Series on Social Choice and Political Economy. University of California Press, Berkeley.

Bloomberg, S.B., Hess, G.D. (2002). "The temporal links between conflict and economic activity". Journal of Conflict Resolution 46, 74–90.

Buhaug, H., Gates, S. (2002). "The geography of civil war". Journal of Peace Research 39, 417–433.

Cairns, E. (1997). A Safer Future: Reducing the Human Cost of War. Oxfam Publications, Oxford.

Carballo, M., Solby, S. (March 2001). "HIV/Aids, conflict and reconstruction in Sub Saharan Africa". Paper presented at the conference: Preventing and Coping with HIV/Aids in Post-Conflict Societies: Gender Based Lessons from Sub-Saharan Africa, Durban, South Africa.

Chalmers, M. (2005). "Supporting security in fragile states". Mimeo. Department of Peace Studies, University of Bradford. http://www.brad.ac.uk/acad/peace/tmp/staff/chalmers_m/.

Cingranelli, D., Richards, D. (2004). "The Cingranelli–Richards human rights coder manual". Retrieved 4 October 2005, from http://ciri.binghamton.edu/web_version_7_31_04_ciri_coding_guide.pdf.

Collier, P. (1999). "On the economic consequences of civil war". Oxford Economic Papers 51, 168–183.

Collier, P. (2001). "Rebellion as a quasi-criminal activity". Journal of Conflict Resolution 44, 839–853.

Collier, P., Hoeffler, A. (2002). "Aid, policy and peace". Defence and Peace Economics 13, 435–450.

Collier, P., Hoeffler, A. (2004a). "Greed and grievance in civil wars". Oxford Economic Papers 56, 663–695.

Collier, P., Hoeffler, A. (2004b). "Aid, policy and growth in post-conflict countries". The European Economic Review 48, 1125–1145.

Collier, P., Hoeffler, A. (2004c). "Conflicts". In: Lomborg, B. (Ed.), Global Crises, Global Solutions. Cambridge University Press, Cambridge, UK.

Collier, P., Hoeffler, A. (2005). "Democracy and natural resource rents". Mimeo.

Collier, P., Hoeffler, A. (2006). "Military expenditure in post-conflict societies". Economics of Governance 7, 89–107.

Collier, P., Hoeffler, A. (in press). "Unintended consequences: Does aid promote arms races?". Oxford Bulletin of Economics and Statistics.

Collier, P., Elliot, L., Hegre, H., Hoeffler, A., Reynal-Querol, M., Sambanis, N. (2003). "Breaking the conflict trap: Civil war and development policy". World Bank Policy Research Report. Oxford University Press, Oxford, UK.

Collier, P., Hoeffler, A., Söderbom, M. (2004). "On the duration of civil war". Journal of Peace Research 41, 253–273.

Corbett, L., Gibney, M. (2004). "Political repression and human rights abuse". Mimeo. University of North Carolina at Asheville.

Elbadawi, I., Sambanis, N. (2002). "How much civil war will we see? Explaining the prevalence of civil war". Journal of Conflict Resolution 46, 307–334.

Epstein, J.M. (2002). "Modeling civil violence: An agent-based computational approach". Proceedings of the National Academy of Science 99. 14 May 2002 Supplement: 7243–7250.

Fearon, J. (2004). "Why do some wars last so much longer than others?". Journal of Peace Research 41, 275–301.

Fearon, J., Laitin, D. (2003). "Ethnicity, insurgency, and civil war". American Political Science Review 97, 75–90.

Gates, S. (2002). "Recruitment and allegiance: The microfoundations of rebellion". Journal of Conflict Resolution 46, 111–130.

Gleditsch, N.P., Wallensteen, P., Eriksson, M., Sollenberg, M., Strand, H. (2002). "Armed conflict 1946–2001: A new dataset". Journal of Peace Research 39, 615–637.

Grossman, H.I. (1991). "A general equilibrium model of insurrections". American Economic Review 81, 912–921.

Grossman, H.I. (1999). "Kleptocracy and revolutions". Oxford Economic Papers 51, 267–283.

Guha-Sapir, D., van Panhuis, W.G. (2002). Mortality Risks in Recent Civil Conflicts: A Comparative Analysis. CRED.

Gurr, T.R., Marshall, M. (2005). "Peace and Conflict: A Global Survey of Armed Conflicts, Self-determination Movements, and Democracy". Center for International Development and Conflict Management, University of Maryland.

Hegre, H. (2003). "Disentangling democracy and development as determinants of armed conflict". Paper presented at the Annual Meeting of the International Studies Association, 27 February 2003, Portland, Oreg.

Hegre, H., Sambanis, N. (2004). "Sensitivity analysis of the empirical literature on civil war onset". Mimeo.

Hegre, H., Ellingsen, T., Gates, S., Gleditsch, N.P. (2001). "Towards a democratic civil peace?". American Political Science Review 95, 33–48.

Herbst, J.I. (2000). States and Power in Africa: Comparative Lessons in Authority and Control. Princeton University Press, Princeton, NJ.

Herbst, J.I. (2004). "African militaries and rebellion: The political economy of threat and combat effectiveness". Journal of Peace Research 41, 357–369.

Hirshleifer, J. (1991). "The technology of conflict as an economic activity". American Economic Review, Papers and Proceedings 81, 130–134.

Hirshleifer, J. (1994). "The darker side of force". Economic Inquiry 32, 1–10.

Hirshleifer, J. (2001). The Dark Side of the Force: Economic Foundations of Conflict Theory. Cambridge University Press, Cambridge, UK.

Humphreys, M. (2005). "Natural resources, conflict and conflict resolution: Uncovering the mechanisms". Journal of Conflict Resolution 49, 508–537.

Huntington, S.P. (2002). The Clash pf Civilizations: And the Remaking of World Order. Free Press, London.

Keely, C.B., Reed, H.E., Waldman, R.J. (2000). "Understanding mortality patterns in complex humanitarian emergencies". In: Keely, C.B., Reed, H.E. (Eds.), Forced Migration and Mortality: Roundtable on the Demography of Forced Migration. National Academy Press, Washington, DC.

Kuran, T. (1989). "Sparks and prairie fires: A theory of unanticipated political revolution". Public Choice 61, 41–74.

Kuran, T. (1991). "The East European revolution of 1989: Is it surprising that we were surprised?". American Economic Review, Papers and Proceedings 81, 121–125.

Lacina, B., Gleditsch, N.P. (2005). "Monitoring trends in global combat: A new dataset of battle deaths". European Journal of Population 21, 145–166.

Levitt, S.D., Venkatesh, S.A. (2000). "An economic analysis of a drug selling gang's finances". Quarterly Journal of Economics 115, 755–789.

Lujala, P., Gleditsch, N.P., Gilmore, E. (2005). "A diamond curse? Civil war and a lootable resource". Journal of Conflict Resolution 49, 538–562.

McDonald, L. (2002). "The international operational response to the psychological wounds of war: Understanding and improving psychosocial interventions". Working Paper no. 7. Feinstein International Famine center, Tufts University.

Miguel, E., Satyanath, S., Sergenti, E. (2004). "Economic shocks and civil conflict: An instrumental variables approach". Journal of Political Economy 112, 725–753.

Murdoch, J.C., Sandler, T. (2002). "Economic growth, civil wars, and spatial spillovers". Journal of Conflict Resolution 46, 91–110.

Murdoch, J.C., Sandler, T. (2004). "Civil wars and economic growth: Spatial dispersion". American Journal of Political Science 48, 138–151.

Pezzini, S., MacCulloch, R., (2004). "The role of freedom, growth and religion in the taste for revolution". Tanaka Business School Discussion Paper TBS/DP04/26, London.

Regan, P.M. (2002). "Third-party interventions and the duration of intrastate conflicts". Journal of Conflict Resolution 46, 55–73.

Reynal-Querol, M. (2002). "Ethnicity, political systems and civil war". Journal of Peace Research 4, 29–54.

Reynal-Querol, M. (2005). "Does democracy preempt civil wars?". European Journal of Political Economy 21, 445–465.

Robinson, J.A., Torvik, R., Verdier, T. (2002). "Political foundations of the resource curse". CEPR Discussion Paper no. 3422.

Roemer, J.E. (1985). "Rationalizing revolutionary ideology". Econometrica 53, 85–108.

Ross, M. (2005). "Booty futures". Mimeo. UCLA.

Russett, B., Ghobarah, H., Huth, P. (2003). "Civil wars kill and maim people – long after the shooting stops". American Political Science Review 97, 189–202.

Sala-i-Martin, X. (1997). "I just ran two million regressions". American Economic Review 87, 178–183.

Sambanis, N. (2000). "Partition as a solution to ethnic war: An empirical critique of the theoretical literature". World Politics 52, 437–483.

Sambanis, N. (2004). "What is a civil war? Conceptual and empirical complexities". Journal of Conflict Resolution 48, 814–858.

Sandler, T. (2004). Global Collective Action. Cambridge University Press, Cambridge, MA.

Sen, A.K. (1973). On Economic Inequality. Clarendon Press, Oxford.

Singer, D.J., Small, M. (1994). Correlates of War Project: International and Civil War Data, 1816–1992. Inter-University Consortium for Political and Social Research, Ann Arbor, Michigan.

Small, M., Singer, J.D. (1982). Resort to Arms: International and Civil War, 1816–1980. Sage, Beverly Hills.

Stewart, F. (2001). "Horizontal inequality: A neglected dimension of development". 2001 Wider Annual Lecture. UN WIDER, Helsinki.

UNHCR Statistical Yearbook (various issues). Geneva.

Walter, B.F. (2001). Committing to Peace: The Successful Settlement of Civil Wars. Princeton University Press, Princeton, NJ.

Walter, B.F. (2004). "Does conflict beget conflict? Explaining recurring civil war". Journal of Peace Research 41, 371–388.

Weinstein, J.M. (2005). "Resources and the information problem in rebel recruitment". Journal of Conflict Resolution 49, 598–624.

WHO (World Health Organization) (2001). World Health Statistics Annual. Geneva.

Chapter 24

POLITICAL ECONOMY OF PEACEKEEPING

BINYAM SOLOMON*

Defence Research and Development Canada-Centre for Operational Research and Analysis, National Defence Headquarters 6ST, 101 Colonel By Drive, Ottawa, ON K1A 0K2, Canada
e-mail: Solomon.b@forces.gc.ca

Contents

Abstract	742
Keywords	742
1. Introduction	743
2. Background	744
2.1. Peacekeeping assessment scales	747
2.2. Peacekeeping trends and stylized facts	748
3. Financial arrangements and burden sharing	752
3.1. Financial reforms and revenue sources	752
3.2. Peacekeeping alliances and burden sharing	755
3.2.1. Burden sharing-other contributions	759
4. Economic assessment of peacekeeping, intervention and policy implications	762
4.1. Theoretical models	762
4.2. Empirical results	764
5. Peacekeeping in theatre and policy implications	766
5.1. Economic impacts	767
5.2. Policy implications	769
6. Summary and future directions	769
6.1. Future directions	771
References	772

* Helpful comments received from Keith Hartley and Todd Sandler are gratefully acknowledged. The opinions and assertions contained herein are those of the author and do not necessarily reflect the views or position of the Canadian Department of National Defence.

Handbook of Defense Economics, Volume 2
Edited by Todd Sandler and Keith Hartley
© 2007 Elsevier B.V. *All rights reserved*
DOI: 10.1016/S1574-0013(06)02024-2

Abstract

The study of peacekeeping from an economics perspective is a fairly recent phenomenon. This chapter surveys three research areas pursued by economists in analyzing
peacekeeping. The first research strand examines the theory and empirics of peacekeeping financing and burden sharing, while the second strand focuses on the efficacy of
third-party intervention in reducing conflict. The last strand utilizes case studies to generalize on the economic consequences of peacekeeping on host nations.

   In general, the research shows that peacekeeping has a relatively large share of purely
public benefits, which leads to a more sub-optimal allocation of resources to peacekeeping from a global perspective. The studies on third party intervention fail to provide
definitive answers to the research question. Specifically, theoretical models on interventions showed that intervention may or may not result in the reduction of conflict since
the strategic interactions among the warring parties and the intervener bring indirect
impacts that are not always clear.

   The empirical studies were equally ambiguous. On the one hand, multi-dimensional
peacekeeping/peace building missions tended to significantly improve the chances for
peace, while traditional peacekeeping (such as observer mission) did not. More recent
studies showed that intervention by international organizations was not a significant
factor in reducing the duration of conflict, while others found early intervention by the
UN to significantly reduce conflict.

   The final research question on the costs and benefits of peacekeeping was addressed
through a case study on Haiti, a peacekeeping host nation. The analysis can be generalized to other peacekeeping host nations. For example, host nations may perceive the
UN mission much as a military base is perceived in a small economically weak community, as a source of income and employment. This may lead to perverse incentive and
increase instability if such an economic source is reduced or removed.

Keywords

peacekeeping, United Nations, burden sharing, joint product model, perverse
incentives, sub-optimality

JEL classification: D74, H56

1. Introduction

Although it was never explicitly stated nor envisioned in the United Nations (UN) Charter, peacekeeping has become an integral and highly visible component of UN operations. Some of these operations have been successful such as the UN mission in Bosnia and Herzegovina (1995–2002) and the United Nations Transitional Administration in East Timor (1999–2002). Both missions provided the structures for sustainable governance and the rule of law. However, missions such as the United Nations Protection Force in the former Yugoslavia (1992–1995) and United Nations Operation in Somalia (1992–1993) were notable failures due to, among other factors, the lack of manpower, political will, and unclear or inadequate mandates [UN (2005b)].

United Nations (UN) sponsored peacekeeping operations have been taking place for over four decades, but it is more recently in the post-Cold War period that these operations have become more numerous, complex and costly. In financial terms, for example, the annual UN peacekeeping cost before the end of the Cold War was typically around $200 million per year (in constant 2000 dollars). But since then it has averaged about $2 billion. In 1994, peacekeeping costs peaked at $3.7 billion (all in constant 2000 dollars: see Figure 1).[1] While the increase is phenomenal, in relative terms the expenditures are still modest. In the context of other operations, peacekeeping expenditures are roughly equal to police or fire department budgets of most large developed metropolitan cities.

While the economic research agenda is motivated mostly because of the multifold increase in the peacekeeping budget, the interpretation of the problem and the subsequent methodology employed varies considerably in the literature. One strand, motivated by the end of the Cold War, looked at bolstering the UN through new financing schemes, a standing army or other mechanisms. Most of these studies are normative in nature

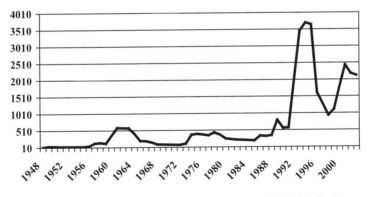

Figure 1. Trend in peacekeeping expenditures (constant 2000 US dollars).

---

[1] All figures are in US dollars unless otherwise indicated.

and search for solutions of self-sufficiency for the international body. Other researchers employ traditional economic tools and conclude that the financial problem or "crisis" is a combination of the increase in activity and the inability or unwillingness of member states to pay their financial obligations on time. In essence, the UN system is structured in such a way that any benefits achieved by the efforts of one (or a few) of its members to unilaterally bring about peace and stability is shared equally by all member nations (i.e., pure public good). However, the cost of this unilateral action is borne entirely by the initiating country(ies).

A second strand in the literature looked at the efficacy of the UN intervention. The assessment of efficacy of course is dependent on the definition of what constitutes success. Notwithstanding the definitional constraints, researchers in this strand attempt to generalize, theoretically, the implications of third-party intervention on the reduction of conflict by examining various facets of the problem. For example, does the third-party need to be impartial or biased? Is early intervention optimal?

The last strand is based on case studies and narrowly focused issues. These studies provide a necessary link between general theoretical studies and case studies in a way that reveals some qualitative aspects that may be missing from a general theoretical framework. For instance, why do nations participate in peacekeeping operations (PKOs)? What are the costs and benefits of PKOs to providers and host nations? In addition, the case studies can reveal why certain interventions did not work or what factors facilitated quick resolution of conflict.

All three strands or research questions are critically examined in subsequent sections of the chapter. In particular, Section 3 critically examines the theory and empirics of peacekeeping financing and burden sharing while Section 4 assesses issues related to the efficacy of third-party intervention in reducing conflict. Section 5 presents case studies to quantify the benefits and costs of peace missions to host countries and providers. Section 6 summarizes the chapter and suggests future directions for the unanswered and emerging research questions. Before the formal examination of the literature, however, the next section briefly presents definitions, stylized facts and institutional aspects of peacekeeping.

2. Background

In a report to the Security Council, Boutros-Ghali (1992) provided the following definition of peacekeeping and the related components:
  - *Peace making* is action to bring hostile parties to agreement, essentially through such peaceful means as those foreseen in Chapter VI of the Charter of the United Nations [Boutros-Ghali (1992)].
  - *Peacekeeping* is the deployment of a United Nations presence in the field, hitherto with the consent of all the parties concerned, normally involving United Nations military and/or police personnel and frequently civilians as well. Peacekeeping is a

technique that expands the possibilities for both the prevention of conflict and the making of peace [Boutros-Ghali (1992)].

– *Peace building* involves post-conflict action to identify and support structures, which will tend to strengthen and solidify peace in order to avoid relapse into conflict.

It is also important to identify the two chapters in the UN charter that deal with international conflict in order to provide context [UN (1945)]. Chapter VI of the charter states that:

VI. Article 33

1. *The parties to any dispute, the continuance of which is likely to endanger the maintenance of international peace and security, shall, first of all, seek a solution by negotiation, enquiry, mediation, conciliation, arbitration, judicial settlement, resort to regional agencies or arrangements, or other peaceful means of their own choice.*

2. *The Security Council shall, when it deems necessary, call upon the parties to settle their dispute by such means.*

If the parties fail to reach settlement as indicated above they can refer to the Security Council. The Security Council in turn can recommend the terms of settlement, as it may consider appropriate. Chapter VI can be considered as preventative diplomacy and a form of peace making. Chapter VII on the other hand, is geared towards a situation much like the Gulf War. In particular, Chapter VII articles include:

VII. Article 39

The Security Council shall determine the existence of any threat to the peace, breach of the peace, or act of aggression and shall make recommendations, or decide what measures shall be taken in accordance with Articles 41 and 42, to maintain or restore international peace and security.

The above is then followed by sanction and severance of diplomatic ties (Article 41) and if this is considered inadequate:

VII. Article 42

Should the Security Council consider that measures provided for in Article 41 would be inadequate or have proved to be inadequate, it may take such action by air, sea, or land forces as may be necessary to maintain or restore international peace and security. Such action may include demonstrations, blockade, and other operations by air, sea, or land forces of Members of the United Nations.

The graduated response to threat from Article 39 to 42 while logical is open to interpretation and the will of the Security Council to act. Furthermore, peacekeeping as we know it today and in the definition set out in the Agenda for Peace does not appear in the Charter. Chapter VII is more of *peace enforcement* and does not necessarily require the consent of the belligerents while Chapter VI is the classic definition of peace making. Multidimensional missions tend to have a large civilian component to monitor elections, train or monitor police, monitor human rights, and sometimes temporarily to administer the country. Because the civilian component includes Non-Governmental Organizations (NGO), international and regional organizations, it is on occasion referred to as a multidisciplinary mission. Because they represented a development not envisioned in the Charter, peacekeeping missions are sometimes referred to as Chapter VI and half.

The first peacekeeping mission originated in the 1956 Suez crisis when the Egyptian President Nasser decided to nationalize the Suez Canal much to the dismay of France and the United Kingdom (UK). The move by France and UK to seize the Canal (to "prevent it from suffering damage during the Israeli invasion") was opposed by nations including the United States and Canada. In order to avoid escalation of hostilities, the Canadian foreign Minister of the time (L.B. Pearson) suggested implementing an immediate cease-fire and providing "substantial police forces stationed on the Israel-Arab borders to keep peace" [United Nations Security Council (1956)]. The Security Council adopted the suggestion and the United Nations Emergency Force (UNEF) was established.

Multidimensional missions can also be considered peace-building activities [Doyle and Sambanis (2000)]. Peace-building brings special challenges to the military called "mission creep". There are two types of mission creep,[2] namely, horizontal and vertical. Horizontal mission creep occurs when the military contingent is asked to engage in activities outside their mandate of maintaining security (requiring additional equipment and mix of military personnel other than infantry). These activities include building schools, transporting food and providing medical help. For example, the UN mission in Haiti's original mandate was to assist the government in maintaining order and stability but soon included escorting food convoys, undertaking important improvements of the main supply routes and undertaking and completing some 330 small-scale community projects [Solomon (1998)].

Vertical mission creep is the extension of the mandate while the troop number remains the same (size of troops may not be adequate and rules of engagements become vague). For example, the forces may now be authorized to guard convoys, protect elected officials or add additional zones of responsibility. The UN Protection Force in the former Yugoslavia was faced with the protection of citizens in larger zones of responsibility without a proportionate increase in manpower and equipment, which led to the 1995 massacre in Srebrenica. These challenges have economic dimensions in terms of resource allocation, competition among various peace players, and perverse economic incentives to the host country production process (for example, food aid will disrupt production in the short term).

---

[2] This definition is attributed to Alex Morrison and his staff at the Pearson Peacekeeping Centre.

2.1. Peacekeeping assessment scales

Studies on the financing aspects, burden sharing and resource allocations of peace-keeping begin with some discussion on the efficacy of the UN peacekeeping assessment system. Almost all UN peacekeeping missions established after 1974 (except UNGOMAP–UN mission in Afghanistan and Pakistan in 1988) are financed through an assessment account based on the UN scale of assessments for the regular budget. Attempts to finance missions through voluntary contribution proved unworkable [Durch (1993)]. Each peacekeeping operation is assessed separately and is based on the UN scale of assessments for the regular budget.

The assessment account is based on an apportionment of the expenses on an ability to pay criterion. Payments to these accounts are in addition to the annual membership costs. The financing of peacekeeping operations is based on the scale of assessments for the regular budget of the UN but includes a complicated, albeit, transparent adjustment to account for the member states ability to pay. As shown in Table 1, member states are placed in one of ten groups, arranged alphabetically from A to J. Group A is reserved for the permanent members of the Security Council and these members are assessed at a higher rate than for the regular budget of the UN. On average, group A member states pay about 22% higher than their regular budget rates [UN (2001, 2003)].

Most of the industrialized nations are grouped in B and their assessment scale for peacekeeping is the same as their regular budget rates. In effect these nations get zero discount. Group C countries are assessed roughly 7.5% below their regular budget rates. The least developed countries (group J) pay only 10% of their regular budget rates.

Table 1
Peacekeeping assessment scales for selected member states

Member state	Average assessment (%) 2004–2006	Regular budget (%)	Per capita income US$ (2004–2006)	Group
United States	26.832	22.00	N/A	A
Japan	19.629	19.629	N/A	B
Kuwait	0.1508	0.163	N/A	C
Republic of Korea	1.4464	1.808	<10 188	D
Barbados	0.006	0.01	<9169	E
Saudi Arabia	0.2876	0.719	<8150	F
Argentina	0.2892	0.964	<7131	G
Poland	0.1392	0.464	<6112	H
Pakistan	0.0112	0.056	<5094*	I
Ethiopia	0.0004	0.004	N/A	J
G7	77.9	70.4		–
NATO	67.6	59.9		–

Source: UN (2001, 2003).
*$5094 is the average per capita Gross National Income of all member states for the period 1996–2001.

Those countries in groups D to I pay between 80% to 20% of their regular budget rates, respectively. All "discounts" resulting from adjustments to the regular budget assessment rates of member states in levels C through J are borne on a pro rata basis by the permanent members of the Security Council.

The classification of member states into the ten groups is based on the annual average per capita gross national product of all members for the period 1996–2001. This average is $5094. Member states, with per capita income less than 2 times the average or $10188, are placed in group D while member states with per capita income less than the average are placed in group I. The thresholds in US dollars for groups E to H are based on a range 1.8 to 1.2 times the member states' average per capita income [UN (2001)]. The seven largest industrialized nations contribute approximately 80% of the peacekeeping budgets while NATO member states are apportioned about 70% of the budget.

The cost of UN peacekeeping missions includes not only the reimbursement of troop contribution (at a rate of $ 1000 per month per troop), but also reimbursing member states for use of own equipment, letter of assistance and death and disability costs. The "Letter of Assistance (LOA)" is often used if the resources the UN provide are not adequate or if the member states convince the UN that its own resources are better suited for the particular mission at hand. The LOA will be later used to bill the UN. There is considerable time lag between the incurring of costs and reimbursement mostly as a result of non-payment of regular dues and peacekeeping assessments. Note that the UN has no authority to charge interest on late payment, and the only sanction for non-payment is the loss of a vote in the General Assembly (Article 19 of the UN Charter is discussed briefly in Section 3.2).

2.2. Peacekeeping trends and stylized facts

During the Cold War, the frequency and size of the peacekeeping missions were modest. The increase in activity was partially motivated by the optimism of a stronger international body as a result of a less divisive Security Council after the end of the Cold War and the increased enthusiasm for peacekeeping and the broadening of international intervention to include aspects of human rights protection, humanitarian and economic development initiatives [Boutros-Ghali (1992)]. In addition to the increasing financial strain caused by the complexity of recent peacekeeping missions, there has been a similar rise in peacekeepers fatalities. Figure 2 illustrates the trend in fatalities from 1948 to 2005. The 2005 data are to August only. About 60% of the fatalities occurred during the post-Cold War period. There is a spike in 1961 coinciding with the operation in Congo, which most observers consider a peace enforcement mission. Although there have been over 50 missions with fatalities during the period 1948–2005, half of the fatalities occurred in only five missions, almost all in the post-Cold War era. These were, in addition to the operation in Congo, missions to (UNPROFOR), Lebanon, Sierra Leone and Somalia. The causes of these fatalities include accidents (42%), hostile acts (30%) and illness and other incidents (28%).

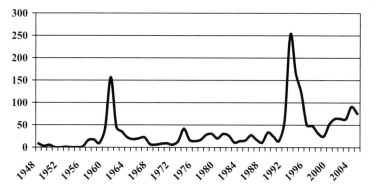

Figure 2.   UN peacekeeping fatalities 1948–2004.

In addition to the increase and complexity of peacekeeping missions, there are other developments that require some discussion. First, there is growing concern that the disproportionate representation of developing nations' troops in UN peace missions is an indication that industrialized nations are abdicating the role of peacekeeping primarily to developing nations [Seiglie (2005)]. There are a number of reasons why the developing nations are contributing more troops to UN missions than wealthier nations. As will be discussed in subsequent sections, wealthier nations, particularly NATO member nations are increasingly involved in peace missions in non-UN financed roles such as in Bosnia, Kosovo and Afghanistan. Also, Seiglie (2005) points out that valuation of life in wealthier nations predicates lesser troop contribution and more technological emphasis in peace missions. Bobrow and Boyer (1997), and Durch (1993) indicate that the $1000 per troop per month payment is attractive to a number of developing nations and, as such, the UN is subsidizing developing country troops during peacekeeping operations.

This latter assertion has yet to be analyzed in detail. Indeed as Sandler and Shimizu (2002, 2003) point out, the data on developing nations' troop costs and other defense expenditures are not readily available. Table 2 uses the Sandler and Shimizu (2002, 2003) ratio defense expenditures to total troop strength to proxy troop cost and to assess the benefit, if any, of troop contribution to UN missions by developing nations.[3] Obviously, the use of the entire defense budget overestimates the personnel budget.

The five nations shown in Table 2 have been frequent top 10 contributors for the period 1996–2005. For example, Bangladesh has been in the top 10 for the entire 10-year period examined while Ghana and India have been in the top ten list 9 times. Even with a favourable troop cost proxy, the UN reimbursement more than compensates their paid assessment and annual troop costs. In contrast, the costs of peace missions for developed nations are considerably higher. For example, Canada, a frequent peacekeeping mission

---

[3] Shimizu and Sandler (2003) have used this type of proxy to estimate the cost of non-UN financed missions the study and its implications to burden sharing are discussed later in the chapter.

Table 2
Top troop contributors for UN missions 1996–2005

Member state	Frequency in top-10	Estimated troop costs in 2003 US$M	Paid PK assessment 2003 US$M	Estimated reimbursement by UN 2003 US$M	Surplus US$M
Bangladesh	10	23.5	0.029	54.8	31.3
Ghana	9	2.1	0.074	12.7	10.5
India	9	7.1	3.5	26.1	15.5
Jordan	6	29.6	0.77	30.4	0.03
Pakistan	8	10.6	0.46	14.5	3.4

Source: UN (2003, 2005a) and author's calculation (surplus is calculated by subtracting paid assessment and estimated troop cost from UN reimbursement).

participant, is assessed at approximately 3% of the UN peacekeeping budget. In 2003 this amounted to $78 million while Canada's troop contribution to UN missions in 2003 was roughly 200 personnel. The estimated reimbursement received from the UN was about $2.4M. Canadian paid assessment in 2003 was more than the combined estimated troop costs of the five nations presented in Table 2.

As mentioned earlier, not all UN costs borne by the contributing nations are personnel compensation. In the Canadian case, the annual incremental costs associated with peace missions including non-UN financed missions were $600 million. Note that *incremental* personnel costs, for example, include rations, accommodations, communication support, transportation (deployment, redeployment, rotation, in theatre), etc.

While Table 2 provides a first approximation of the financial advantage of troop contribution for developing nations, there are other, albeit, non-quantitative aspects of benefits that accrue to troop contributors. For example, India may be motivated by the need to enhance its international identity and political image. The fact that the Cold War years saw little activity in peacekeeping, perhaps as a result of the Security Council indecisiveness due to the superpowers' veto, may have forced middle power countries such as Canada and Norway to assume a disproportionate share of the relative NATO peacekeeping burden. An alternative explanation for Canadian, Scandinavian and other Western nations' peacekeeping participation is that UN peace mission participation may be considered a prerequisite for "middle power" status in the UN. In essence, peacekeeping, especially during the Cold War displayed most of the characteristics of a "club good". The qualitative nature of some of the perceived country-specific benefits of peacekeeping has so far prevented an empirical validation. In Section 5, the survey of selected missions presents counter factual evidence to impute likely benefits of peacekeeping.

The complexities and frequency of the missions in the post-Cold War period has strained the UN and has exposed its inability to adjust to the ever-changing geo-strategic environment. Consequently, there has been an increase in peace missions led by regional organizations such as the European Union (EU) and the North Atlantic Treaty Organi-

Table 3
Non-united nations financed peace support operations

Mission*	Duration	Location
Multinational force and observers:	1982–	Egypt/Sina
• ISAF (International Security Assistance Force):	2001–	Afghanistan
KFOR (NATO-led Kosovo Force	1999–	Kosovo
• SFOR (NATO-led Stabilization Force):	1996–	Bosnia
NATO Albania Force	1999	Albania
Multinational Protection Force	1997	Albania
International Force in East Timor	1999	East Timor
• Russian/CIS Peacekeeping Force:	1992–	Georgia/Abkhazia
United task force in Somalia	1992–1993	Somalia
European Union: Operation Concordia	2003	Macedonia
EU (European Union) Military Operation in DRC	2003	Democratic Republic of Congo
EU military operation in Macedonia	2003	Macedonia
EU mission in Ituri	2003	Democratic Republic of Congo
African mission in Burundi	2003–	Burundi
Mission Interafricaine de Surveillance des Accords de Bangui	1997	Central African Republic
ECOMICI (Economic Community of West African States Mission in Cote d'Ivoire)	1990–1998; 2003	Cote d'Ivoire
Economic Community of West African States (ECOWAS) Military Observer Group	1998–2000	Sierra Leone
Economic Community of West African States (ECOWAS)	2003	Liberia
SANDF Operation Boleas	1998–2000	Lesotho
• Operation Northern/Southern Watch ("No-fly zone"):	1992–2003	Iraq

*Missions with military personnel strength in excess of 1000.

zation (NATO). In addition to paying a large portion of the UN peacekeeping costs, developed nations are also financing and contributing troops to these non-UN led missions. As shown in Table 3, the majority of these missions started in the 1990s and span the globe. If recent trends in NATO members' procurement towards force projection capabilities (such as air and sealift) is any indication, the organization, and particularly the larger members, can be expected to support more non-UN financed operations and consequently assume ever-increasing peacekeeping burdens [Shimizu and Sandler (2002, 2003)]. Note that Table 3 does not include all non-UN-financed missions. See Shimizu and Sandler (2002) for a detailed list.

In addition to the regional organizations discussed above, there are some discussions on whether the private sector or individual nations can effectively undertake peacekeeping missions. Some aspects of privatizations and possible research areas are discussed in Section 6 of this chapter. Having established some of the background information and stylized facts about peacekeeping, the next section addresses the first research question of peacekeeping financing and burden sharing in particular.

3. Financial arrangements and burden sharing

The surge in peacekeeping activity and the reasons are articulated by Boutros-Ghali (1992) when he observed that since the creation of the United Nations in 1945, over 100 major conflicts around the world have left some 20 million dead. The United Nations was rendered powerless to deal with many of these crises because of the vetoes – 279 of them – cast in the Security Council. He then points out that with the end of the Cold War there have been no such vetoes since 31 May 1990 [Boutros-Ghali (1992)]. Most papers published in the early 1990s tended to look at the UN peacekeeping budget and financing largely from a normative perspective with little or no discussion on the mechanics of the implementation. These papers are discussed briefly below.

3.1. Financial reforms and revenue sources

McNamara (1992) echoes Boutros-Ghali's guarded optimism of a stronger international body as a result of a less divisive Security Council after the end of the Cold War. Mc-Namara's (1992) vision of a new world order saw great opportunity for world peace and a stronger international body at the end of the Cold War that may facilitate the reduction of defense expenditures in developing countries. In addition, McNamara suggests the UN providing security globally and developed nations using aid as a means of reducing arms or defense spending (tied-aid). The view is somewhat idealistic, however, as shown from an economics perspective. Hartley (1992) comments on the challenges and myth surrounding "the new world order" and the "peace dividend". In particular Hartley (1992) points out that international organizations face the challenges of dealing with flexibility, as the UN body needs to develop a rapid-reaction capability while at the same time addressing inherent problems of collective action such as free riding and the possible changes to voting structure in the UN Security Council (moving from unanimity to majority voting or veto).

   McNamara's (1992) also suggests controlling exports of arms to and from developing nations but failed to examine the potential consequence of the development of domestic defense industries. In addition, monitoring arms sales is difficult as the police replaces the military and dual products such as chemicals, nuclear power and vehicles can easily be integrated within the civilian industrial structures [Hartley (1992)].

   Morrison (1993) warns about the problem of implementing large-scale structural change to an international body. For example, Morrison (1993) points out several potential difficulties in setting up a UN army including: unwillingness of participating nations to allow their military to fall under a UN commander, finding the "right" racial and geographical balance of the army, and, establishing an effective military headquarters, employment equity guidelines and pay scales [Morrison (1993)].

Funding the increasing cost of peacekeeping operations through potential sources of revenue attracted the attention of the UN and many researchers. Henderson and Kay (1995) suggest the formation of a UN Security Insurance Agency (a country will decide to buy insurance from the UN if the cost of insurance is less than the cost of maintaining its own force), while Felix (1995) and Mendez (1995) propose a Tobin Tax (a small uniform tax to be levied on foreign exchange transactions in at least all the major currencies). None of the studies, however, provide rigorous analysis on how to achieve consensus and implement these international taxes.[4]

Klein and Marwah (1996) look at the economic impact of establishing a UN standing force of approximately 1 million military personnel with an annual operating budget of $50 billion. The financing of this military force will be such that, according to the authors, no country will pay more than 0.5 percent of its Gross Domestic Product (GDP). The authors also provide an econometric analysis of the effects of the force on world macroeconomic indicators (i.e., inflation, growth, trade, etc.). For example, the authors claim that early deployment of a portion of the standing army in the former Yugoslavia would have stopped the internal fighting and by 1997 world exports would have increased by $16 billion. Apart from Morrison's (1993) valid criticisms of the administrative and logistical difficulties of establishing a UN standing army, the empirical examples also present problems. First, the Gross World Product is not equally distributed in the world. A quarter of the world GDP is accounted for by a single country, namely the US. While an annual expenditure of $50 billion may be incremental for the larger economies, there are countries that are unable to finance even the smallest fraction of the current $2–3B price tag of a peace mission. A progressive taxation scheme could be suggested and this is discussed below.

Second, Klein and Marwah (1996) do not provide sufficient evidence that a UN standing army is a superior solution than other arrangements such as the existing stand-by arrangements with selected member nations. Parai (1998) looks at the Danish proposed Stand-by Forces High Readiness Brigade (SHIRBRIG), and concludes that a stand-by arrangement with member countries is economically more efficient than a standing force. The argument is based on the fact that military resources of Member States contributing to UN peacekeeping would be utilized more efficiently since the military forces of contributing Member States are doing double duty of serving a country and peacekeeping missions.

In trying to address the immediate problem for the UN, countries' unwillingness to pay their allotted dues on time, and most importantly, the lack of guidelines on the principle of apportionment dues, Klein and Marwah (1997) examine some objective criteria for apportionment of financial burden among the members. The authors look at various taxation schemes that will bring a measure of progressivity and equity recognizing that the ability to pay (proxied by GNP) of the 180 nations varies considerably.[5] The

---

[4] Other similar papers on revenue sources include Isard and Fischer (1997) and Fischer and Hattori (1999).

[5] The existing system charges the five permanent members of the Security Council 56% of the total allotment while 78 developing countries are expected to pay 0.001%. Canada, a member of the seven large economies, is charged about 3.1%.

authors first examine a tax scheme where minimum and maximum bands are set based on a country's share of the World Gross Product (WGP). The maximum, set at 25% of allotment, was slightly higher than US share of WGP at over 20% and the minimum was set at 0.001%, the share of the world's poorest nations. The rest of the countries pay a flat or lump sum tax between the bands.

The authors bring progressivity into the taxation system using a quadratic function mainly to maintain ease and transparency in the calculation of allotments and six payment scenarios ranging from a flat tax system to more complicated non-linear functions to account for progressivity [Klein and Marwah (1997)]. The authors do achieve apportionment criteria that are objective, easy to use and transparent. However, one can argue that another alternative is the recalculation of the existing group assignments. Reducing the moving average calculation of economic growth from the current 7–10 years to three years will accurately capture the countries that are growing faster and consequently capable of paying a larger share. This is not a new idea, and the UN has now implemented this in the peacekeeping assessment scales.

The key here is not that we can improve on the payment schemes but that there are other underlying factors such as free-riding [Khanna and Sandler (1997)] and the impure public good characteristics of peacekeeping [Khanna et al. (1998), Bobrow and Boyer (1997)] that need to be acknowledged to tackle the problems of financing the UN's peacekeeping missions. In addition, as pointed out by Hartley and Sandler (1999) the peacekeeping burden may have shifted to NATO's larger allies as the organization continues to engage in peacekeeping activities and the UN may have to increasingly rely on the force projection capabilities of the NATO members.

Solomon (1998, 1999a) looked at the possibility of contracting-out a UN mission to a single country to avoid the cost of set-up and operational compatibility issues associated with a multi-force mission. The author argues that if the Security Council gives the consent, the authority of the nation should be enhanced. These nations may be willing to undertake peace missions if their middle power status is enhanced by the activity. However, there are some limiting factors that need to be recognized. First, the sub-contracted country has to have considerable experience and reputation before hand however, as the recent case in Sierra Leone has shown. The Indian led mission in Sierra Leone, while not a case of a sub-contracted country, fell victim to terrorist attacks due to insufficient training and the credibility problem of the force commander and troops. Second, it can also lead the "sub-contracted" nations into a position where they are able to dictate the post-conflict environment in the region (such as Australia in East Timor or NATO in Bosnia and Kosovo). Related to this issue, there is concern about the ethnic mix of some regional groups. Given the multi-ethnic nature of most unstable regions in Africa, an African Union led mission may not be perceived impartial if the force includes members from the ethnic group in conflict.

The loss of business with countries in conflict, or the high insurance premiums imposed on shipments traveling through dangerous air, water and ground routes may induce corporations to finance some portion of a UN peace mission. However, conflicts do not necessarily impede international trade since countries can continue to do business through third countries or dummy corporations.

3.2. Peacekeeping alliances and burden sharing

Peacekeeping activities can be characterized as purely public, especially when considering operations that contain a conflict or allow an unfettered access to humanitarian aid for those in need. As such, the provision of peace by an international community or some nation will suffer from the problems associated with these "goods", namely, free riding by member states of the international system. The benefits of global peace achieved by the efforts of a nation or the international body is shared equally by all member states but the cost of the action is borne entirely by the peacekeeping nation or international body. The framing of the peacekeeping expenditures and member states' unwillingness to pay as a burden sharing issue has led to a number of theoretical and empirical research and policy implications.

For ease of exposition, the subsection begins with the work of Khanna and Sandler (1997) and the follow up research of Khanna, Sandler and Shimizu (1998) and the demand for peacekeeping model [Khanna, Sandler and Shimizu (1999)]. Khanna and Sandler (1997) is one of the earliest researches to empirically test the burden sharing implications of peacekeeping to NATO. The research covers the time period starting from mid-1970s to 1994 and uses additional burden sharing measures such as foreign aid, peacekeeping contribution and conscription-adjusted data. The latter is to test whether allies that supplement their forces in whole or in part on conscripted forces usually assume a larger defense burden than their defense spending indicates, because military personnel are paid below their true opportunity cost.

Khanna and Sandler (1997) show that there is no evidence of free riding in NATO during the era of flexible response even after adjusting the data for conscription. In regards to peacekeeping, however, the paper finds some evidence of free riding.[6] Given that the size of the expenditures devoted to foreign aid and peacekeeping is substantially smaller than a typical ally's defense burden, the authors conclude that over-contribution to peacekeeping and foreign aid did not offset under-contribution in defense [Khanna and Sandler (1997)].

Khanna, Sandler and Shimizu (1998) extend the joint-product model, which was articulated within the context of an international organization such as NATO by Sandler and Forbes (1980) among others. Khanna et al. (1998) hypothesize that there are multiple outputs of peacekeeping (support for joint product model) such as gains in status as promoter of peace[7], or that contributors near the region of instability will derive country – specific benefit. The authors also point out that "over contribution" in peacekeeping

---

[6] Hartley and Sandler (1999) and Sandler and Murdoch (2000) note that from a peacekeeping perspective, the current crisis-response stance of NATO may imply the UN is free riding on NATO.

[7] Kammler (1997) and Hartley (1997) discuss the need to consider positional goods (power status) as a distinct incentive for states.

might be politically and financially expedient to the government if the electorate did not examine the magnitudes involved. The empirical portion of their study is designed along the same line as previous burden sharing studies, that is, by looking at a non-parametric rank correlation between burdens (in this study peacekeeping contribution as a proportion of GDP:PK/GDP) and GDP. However, Khanna et al. (1998) did not include troop contribution to overall peacekeeping burden. Ideally, the total cost of peacekeeping should have included payments as well as troop contributions. Unfortunately, the lack of detailed data on for the sample period precluded the inclusion of the burden measure [Khanna et al. (1998)]. The authors contend that the inclusion of troop contribution will only magnify the fact that larger countries shoulder even larger burdens.

Alternate burden sharing proxies were considered including PK contributions and per capita contributions. Khanna et al. (1998) assert that since GDP and contributions are institutionally based, the high correlation results were not informative. The authors test the hypothesis of pure public good (association between a country's GDP and burden PK/GDP) and found no rank correlation for the period 1976–1990 and a significant relationship for selected years in the 1990s. The authors conclude that in the 1990s there is evidence of disproportionate burden sharing in UN peacekeeping payments. The authors also consider non-UN financed operations such as Ops Deny Flight, IFOR, SFOR and the Gulf War with necessary adjustments to the heavy contributors such as the US, UK, France, etc. The inclusion of NATO-led and financed peacekeeping shows a more pronounced relationship between GDP and peacekeeping. The authors stress that transporting troops and equipment anywhere and time in the future will stretch the limits of the UN and may have to rely on NATO thus exacerbating the disproportionate burden sharing for NATO allies.

The Khanna et al. (1998) paper provides a basis for informed policy-making on the burden-sharing question among the UN members as well as the associated implications for NATO. If peacekeeping benefits can be quantified, relative burden-benefit analysis may be very informative especially given the fact that qualitative benefits such as status tend to be the overriding motivation for the so-called "middle power" nations.

Khanna, Sandler and Shimizu (1999) extend the joint product model to empirically test a reduced form demand equation for UN peacekeeping from 1975–1996. Peacekeeping activity is assumed to produce two joint products a nation-specific output or characteristic (x), and a global purely public characteristic (z). These are produced under a fixed-proportion technology so that:

$$x^i = \alpha q^i, \tag{1}$$
$$z^i = \beta q^i, \tag{2}$$

where $i = 1, \ldots, n$ in both Equations (1) and (2) and α, β are positive parameters. Note also that the public characteristic Z can be due to the nation's own peacekeeping contributions and those of the other $n - 1$ nations [Khanna et al. (1999)]. Thus:

$$Z = z^i + \widetilde{Z}^i, \tag{3}$$

where $\widetilde{Z}^i = \sum_{i \neq j}^n z^j$ denotes the spill-ins of global stability from peacekeeping activity. If other private and nation specific activity is denoted as y^i and the ith nation's utility function is

$$U^i = U^i(y^i, x^i, Z, E), \tag{4}$$

E represents a taste-shifting parameter. In Khanna et al. (1999) total trade is used as a taste parameter to assess whether trade-dependent nations are more willing to support peacekeeping. By substituting (2) into (3), the public good characteristic of Z can be expressed as

$$Z = \beta(q^i + \widetilde{Q}^i), \tag{5}$$

again where $\widetilde{Q}^i = \sum_{i \neq j}^n q^j$ and denotes the sum of peacekeeping activities of nations other than i. Each nation faces a budget constraint when choosing among peacekeeping and other activities:

$$I^i = y^i + p^i q^i. \tag{6}$$

Note that p^i is the ith nations relative price of peacekeeping and I^i is the ith country's income (GDP).

Substituting Equations (1) and (5) into (4) and using (6), the non-cooperative or Nash maximization problem for each nation can be represented as

$$\max_{y^i, q^i} = \{U^i[y^i, \alpha q^i, \beta(q^i + \widetilde{Q}^i), E] \mid I^i = y^i + pq^i\}. \tag{7}$$

Each nation's utility function is assumed increasing and strictly concave. Nash equilibrium is achieved when each nation satisfies its first order conditions:

$$\alpha MRS^i_{xy} + \beta MRS^i_{zy} = p, \tag{8}$$

where the first *MRS* is the marginal willingness to pay for the private, nation-specific peacekeeping activity and the second is the marginal willingness to pay for purely public benefits of peacekeeping. The sum of these weighted marginal valuations is equated to the relative price of peacekeeping activity. Depending on the values of α and β it can be shown that peacekeeping can range from purely private ($\alpha = 1$ and $\beta = 0$) to purely public ($\alpha = 0$ and $\beta = 1$). Thus, the joint product model provides a plausible and comprehensive assessment of both the nation-specific and global benefits of peacekeeping provision [Khanna et al. (1999)].

The econometric specification corresponding to the demand equation Q is

$$Q_{it} = f(GDP, Spill, Q_r, Tr, e). \tag{9}$$

Q_r is the residual peacekeeping spending by other non-sample countries, Tr is total trade and e is the residual. Note that a taste shifting parameter (total trade for this particular exercise) is also added to the utility function to account for any factor that can influence the demand for peacekeeping [Khanna et al. (1999)]. The rationale for the trade variable is that countries that are trade-reliant tend to support peace missions mainly to protect trade routes and to some extent to gain from "trade following the flag".

Non-discretionary and discretionary peacekeeping spill-ins are exogenous with the former held constant (best response level for other nations) and the latter treated as constant by the authors. Security Council members may be willing to under-contribute their peacekeeping dues since their group assessment for the regular budget is more favourable and consequently shirking their peacekeeping responsibilities.

Based on the underlying theory, the authors hypothesize the sign of the estimated variables:

- Jointly produced public and nation specific outputs of peacekeeping may be complementary and as such the coefficient of the *Spill* term may be positive.
- The coefficient of Q_r (residual contribution by non-sample countries) may be positive if it is complementary with other goods. Negative implies free riding.
- A positive sign with GDP implies peacekeeping is a normal good. However, given the size of peacekeeping contribution, as a proportion of GDP is relatively small, it may be impossible to find any statistical association.
- Trade (sum of exports and imports) is used as a taste parameter to capture other influences that will trigger nation-specific response to global stability and the sign is expected to be positive given nations with a large stake in world trade are more concerned about global stability [Khanna et al. (1999)].

The estimation procedure is augmented to account for the fact that the *Spill* variable is not independent of the demand equation (all countries essentially demand the same total discretionary contribution). An instrumental variable estimation procedure is utilized to get rid of the bias and is estimated as a function of all exogenous variables [Khanna et al. (1999)]. In order to have parsimonious representation the authors also test for substitutability of variables, especially between *Spill* and Q_r (GDP and trade which are expected to differ across the sample countries due to varied economic and political development). The relationship between *Spill* and Q_r may be related across countries, especially if tested within groupings based on UN assessment scales. Countries in the same scale may exhibit the same incentive to free ride or face comparable peacekeeping responsibilities. Khanna et al. (1999) divide the sample into three groups: the Security Council members; those countries whose peacekeeping assessment is the same as the regular budget; and the last group whose peacekeeping assessment is below the regular budget.

The 25 sample countries include the 16 member countries of NATO plus Austria, Australia, China, Finland, Ireland, Japan, an augmented USSR, Sweden and New Zealand (these nations account for 95% of the assessed peacekeeping dues). The peacekeeping contributions used are the sum of actual and voluntary contributions. All the variables have been converted into real dollars using the 1987 US price deflator.

The findings indicate that GDP is not a significant determinant of peacekeeping contribution. Khanna et al. (1999) argue that as peacekeeping contributions become larger the income effect will be reversed (become positive). *Spill-in* is found to be the most important variable explaining peacekeeping contribution as 19 out of the 25 countries in the sample show significant positive relationships (0.05 significance level and one additional country at 0.10 significance). This result is an indication of the complementarity between jointly produced private and public benefits. Trade is significant and positive for six of the 25-country sample, while two countries showed negative and significant coefficients. The hypothesis test that the parameter estimates for Q_r (residual contributions) and *Spill* are the same was rejected for the full sample although it was not rejected for the groupings (i.e., Security Council, group B, etc.). This led the authors to restrict the Spill variable within the groupings to increase the efficiency of the estimates. The re-estimated model shows that trade again is significant and positive for six of the 25 countries and significant and negative for three countries. In addition, relative assessment shares also play a role and thus all peacekeeping financing should be done through assessment accounts. Source of funding makes a difference (assessment accounts seen as overcoming free-riding incentives even though many nations did not annually meet their obligations) given the weaker response to residual contribution but a relatively stronger response to assessment spill-ins.

There are a number of issues not addressed in this important paper by Khanna et al. (1999). First, the lack of significant association between GDP and peacekeeping should be explored more. It is conceivable that for nations, peacekeeping may not be a normal good. Contributions become necessary only if additional benefits such as status or pressures from within and outside the country force commitment. Second, the results for the trade (imports and exports) variable were not as strong as the authors expected. If countries with open and trade-intensive economies are motivated to contribute to peacekeeping then the appropriate variable should be trade outside its region (for example 80% of Canada's total trade is with the US and should be excluded). Third, there is an obvious structural break in the series as pointed out by the authors: peacekeeping costs really became an issue after the 1990s when the size and complexities of the mission increased considerably partly as a result of the end of the Cold War.

As such, a more detailed time-series analysis is required once sufficient data are available. For example peacekeeping contributions may be affected by inertia (commitments are never short term and that once a record of commitment is established it is more or less expected in the future) a test for causality may be informative.

3.2.1. Burden sharing-other contributions

In addition to the contribution by Khanna et al. (1998, 1999) discussed above, others such as Bobrow and Boyer (1997) (B&B) conduct the burden sharing analysis by examining the contributors and their motivation as well as by inferring from general UN statistics on contribution trends. The authors suggest that PKOs are a public good but there may be private, country specific benefits. The authors articulate the fact that PKOs may not be purely public good by identifying for example: thinning of benefits in the sense that the benefit occurs in a region with immediate beneficiaries (e.g., adjoining states) while the contributors tend to benefit (through global stability or promotion of values) marginally and indirectly with a time lag. In addition, they point out that combatants who benefit from the peace maintained obtain in a sense a private good as well as those small states that make "profit" (as shown in Table 2 earlier) from the PKO participation.

Until recently, some nations particularly Japan and Germany had long standing policies against sending troops outside their borders. Similarly, Australia and New Zealand may wish to refrain from troop contribution to areas that are a considerable distance from their base for obvious logistical and hence cost reasons. B&B mentioned the UN financial assessment, particularly the fact that the Security Council members pay a large proportion of the allotment as one of the reasons for the unwillingness to pay.

Of particular interest is the observation by B&B on the persistent presence of selected countries in the over-contributor side of PKO. The authors suggest that the activity is habit forming (it may also override domestic and international circumstances). If previous commitments lead to future engagements then a model of peacekeeping demand should incorporate and at least test the significance of a lagged endogenous variable. In addition, why does it become a habit? Are there elements within the country that benefit from PKO participation? Are PKOs not only private to a country but also private to a group within a country?

PKO may be habit forming because commitments are never short term, and once a record of commitment is established, it is more or less expected in the future. Some elements of the defense establishment may find peacekeeping enhancing their visibility and thus may lobby for more missions, and hence higher budgets, suggesting a public choice explanation. Alternatively, a nation may acquire expertise that may lead to a comparative advantage in peace missions. An ethnic group within a nation may benefit from a peace mission if they successfully lobby for a peace mission in their former country.

Other more recent burden sharing papers have focused on non-UN financed missions and the associated implications for peacekeeping burdens. Shimizu and Sandler (2002, 2003) indirectly estimate the cost of non-UN financed missions by converting available troop contribution numbers into expenditures. Specifically, the authors use a number of proxies ranging from member country's share of its active personnel budget to a country's share of its entire military budget. Obviously the use of personnel budget under-estimates a member country's support of non-UN missions as it apportions peacekeeping troops expenses only, ignoring associated costs such as equipment and operations and maintenance. Using the entire defense expenditure, on the other hand, overestimates the costs. As an additional proxy, Shimizu and Sandler (2003) use the average of the two extremes in the assessment of burden sharing. Given the lack of information on developing nations' military costs and resource allocation strategy, the proxies are the best available.

The finding of these recent studies point to the fact that peacekeeping is assuming a larger share of purely public benefits. Consequently, the larger NATO allies carry a greater burden and given the complexity of the missions over time, this may lead to more sub-optimal allocation of peacekeeping resources. In an interesting analysis of the UN peacekeeping assessment system, Shimizu (2005) indicated that the existence of assessment in itself increases a country's contributions by increasing its contributor-specific benefits. For example, according to Article 19 of the UN Charter, a member state may lose its vote in the General Assembly if the amount of its arrears equals or exceeds the amount it owes the UN for the preceding two full years. Given the fact that unpaid UN peacekeeping assessments have been growing along with peacekeeping expenditures, the assessment system and Article 19 do not provide the member states with enough incentives to make timely payments. However, Shimizu (2005) points out that the assessment system is not necessarily ineffective especially when considering the seven largest economies which together account for 75–80% of the total assessed amount and between them held a small amount of accumulated debt. In addition, Shimizu (2005) compared the assessment to a voluntary system and concluded that the assessment system is effective in revealing the contributor-specific benefits or under contributor-specific damage. Khanna et al. (1999) also found some empirical evidence supporting the fact that the assessment account overcomes free-riding incentives.

The under-contributor damage, which may take the form of strained relation with allies or trade partners, is difficult to avoid since the assessment system effectively turns the 191-country organization into the seven wealthiest countries plus all the rest [Shimizu (2005)]. This under-contribution impact is incorporated into a standard utility maximization model to show a theoretical possibility of increasing a country's contribution through assessment redistribution [Shimizu (2005)]. While the Shimizu (2005) study does not provide a workable proxy to reveal a country's true valuation of benefits, it does illustrate the impure public good aspects of peacekeeping and the role of benefits in the re-formulation of the UN financial arrangements.

While Shimizu (2005) suggests ways to improve the financial system to reveal the preferences of member states, Seiglie (2005) proposes a system of marketable or tradable obligations to increase peacekeeping troop contributions. Seiglie's proposal while couched in public economics arguments, also focuses on developed nations' aversion to casualties as causing the under-provision of optimal peacekeeping troops. Assuming the military seeks to minimize costs associated with the production of a given level of national defense, the optimization problem is one of the marginal assessments of the costs associated with labour (soldier) and capital (weapons and stock of weapons employed). Seiglie (2005) makes the argument that as the relative value of labour (soldier) compensation rises, the optimal strategy for a given level of defense is to become more capital or weapon-intensive. Thus, developed nations have fewer incentives to send troops, or when necessary to engage in conflicts, they tend to use technology-intensive resources.

Seiglie (2005) also suggests a taxation policy that consists of elements from the ability-to-pay and the benefit principle. Such a policy will avoid the free-rider problem by allocating the cost of providing the service according to the ability of the user to pay and the distribution of the benefits according to individual preferences. For example, a nation that may benefit from a peace mission and if it is relatively well-off will be targeted for peace duties or financing while nations that benefit from a mission but cannot afford it will be required to provide assistance in kind (offer bases, air fields, troops, etc.). This is an interesting expansion of the burden sharing debate and the solution, at least theoretically is workable. In addition, the market for obligations can provide an explicit monetary value to risks inherent in different operations or the benefit to countries for establishing peace in their region. However, the assumption that the troop contributions mismatch between developed and developing nations is based on the risk aversion to casualties may not be accurate. As pointed out in Section 2 of the chapter, developed nations are increasingly involved in non-UN missions, using more troops and technology and deployed in missions that are complex and dangerous.

4. Economic assessment of peacekeeping, intervention and policy implications

The assessment of third-party intervention and peacekeeping intervention is the second research question addressed in this chapter namely, the efficacy of the UN or third-party intervention in reducing conflict. Third party intervention is a newer strand of research that relies on conflict models of Hirshleifer (1988), which proposes a general equilibrium framework to incorporate the full variety of conflicts with normal or peaceful economic interactions. Appropriation and the associated expenditures such as military forces, weaponry accumulation and conflict leading to violence, are just designed to secure resources of others or to defend against loss of resources to others. Hirshleifer sets up a model involving a resource partition function, a contestable-income production function, a combat power function and an income distribution function. Some of the papers reviewed below adapt the methodology to assess the utility of peacekeeping and the added dimension it brings to the conflict it is intended to suppress.

4.1. Theoretical models

Carment and Rowlands (1998, 2004), Seiglie (1999) and Siqueira (2003) best summarize the theoretical literature on third-party intervention. All these papers use a game with complete information and an objective function with the minimization of the aggregate cost of conflict. Seiglie (1999) does not directly assess peacekeeping intervention but the reasons and process by which a nation decides to intervene in a conflict either through aid or militarily. The amount of aid given is determined, according to the author, "by the preferences of the median voter" (in the donor nation).

Using this theoretical analysis, the author claims that foreign aid is positively correlated to the degree of altruism and the level of income of the median voter. It is also positively related to the number of civilian casualties resulting from the unrest. Foreign aid is inversely related to the size of the recipient country (holding the level of aid per household constant) and the rate that households in the recipient nation fail to receive the full amount of the aid provided [Seiglie (1999)].

The incentive to use own military forces in civil conflicts is also dependent on the median voter's welfare state. Thus, military intervention to establish order in the relief effort or a stable government is chosen if the welfare of the median voter is greater under such conditions or if the intervention's success rate is expected to be great. Furthermore, if the cost of the intervention is small or if the size and extent of the victimized group is greater, the greater the size of the transfer (aid) being provided by the donor nation [Seiglie (1999)].

Seiglie (1999), by explicitly modeling the behaviour of the median voter in the intervening nation, uncovers why the warring factions may correctly or incorrectly underestimate the resolve of the third party or why intervention may not occur immediately. The role of the median voter in the donor nation also provides possible rationale to some interesting empirical results discussed below (Section 4.2).

Siqueira (2003) utilizes a rent-seeking conflict model to investigate peacekeeping (third-party) intervention and adversaries in conflict. He makes the assumption that third party's commitment to actions and forces is credible according to the warring factions. Given a cost function for each faction (actor) that is convex and increasing in terms of effort and positive and exogenous shift perimeters that are determined by the third party, the objective function can be represented as

$$U_i = \frac{e_i}{\phi + e_i + e_j} R - C_i(e_i \alpha_i \beta_i), \tag{10}$$

where i and j represent factions that exert effort e to gain control of resource or rent R (there are two objective functions). The cost function for each is determined by positive shift parameters of the intervening party. Neutral policy by the third party is indicated by β and biased intervention by α. An economic sanction that increases the cost function of both factions is considered a neutral intervention while withdrawing aid to or attacking one of the factions is a type of biased intervention.

Siqueira (2003) adds an additional factor (ϕ) in the probability of winning of a fixed amount of rent or resource R to show that rebel factions need to exert some positive effort even if the government effort is zero. This accounts for the fact that the government is in essence "entrenched". Each faction's best response function for given levels of the other's effort is given by the first order conditions of maximizing (10). The Siqueira (2003) contribution is revealing when one considers the strategic reaction of one faction to the action of the other or, in terms of optimization parlance, the assessment of the "cross partials". In particular:

1. Whenever a particular faction has a higher probability of success the third party should "tailor" its policy to attack the weaker faction.
2. Targeting the weaker faction is superior than aiding the stronger faction if the intervener's intention is to lower overall fighting effort.
3. Neutral intervention or targeting both factions gives at best ambiguous results.

While the intriguing results are based on an approach where "just about anything can happen" the implications for the UN are sobering. Specifically, the Siqueira (2003) model is based on simple and restrictive assumptions of stable and balanced forces and a third-party that has the resolve and commitment. These are conditions that are very favourable for the UN and yet the results indicate that even in such scenarios, the reduction of conflict cannot be guaranteed [Siqueira (2003)].

A more sophisticated model by Amegashie and Kutsoati (2005) extends the Siqueira (2003) model by considering a game with both complete and incomplete information, an objective function that includes the minimization of the aggregate cost of conflict as a special case and differences in the abilities (technology, initial endowments, etc.) of the contestants. Their results generally point to the tailored response uncovered by Siqueira (2003), but the results are very sensitive to the intervener's intentions. For example, if the third-party cares equally about the warring factions and the rest of the population, then it will *not intervene*. If the third-party cares more about the warring factions, then it might intervene and will help the stronger faction unless it places a sufficiently higher weight on the welfare of the weaker faction. In addition, as pointed out by Seiglie (1999) the third party is likely to intervene if success in the conflict is extremely sensitive to effort. In the case of military intervention, we find that the third-party will intervene if it cares sufficiently about the rest of the population or cares about the net economic resources that will be left after the war [Amegashie and Kutsoati (2005)]. Thus, the more realistic the assumptions of the intervention model, the less clear the outcome or the reasons for intervention.

4.2. Empirical results

While the theoretical models of intervention proved both promising and frustrating, the empirical results are equally nebulous. For example, Doyle and Sambanis (2000) find that multi-dimensional peacekeeping/peace building missions significantly improve the chances for peace (success proxied as two years after conflict) while traditional peace-keeping, such as observer mission, has no effect on the chances for success. Regan (2002) finds that third-party interventions tend to *extend* the expected durations of conflict and intervention by international organizations is not a significant factor in reducing the duration of conflict. DeRouen (2003) on the other hand, finds that early intervention by the UN significantly reduces conflict.

Regan (2002) explicitly tests a number of hypotheses on the impact of third-party intervention on the duration of conflict. The hypotheses are derived from the existing literature on civil conflicts and factors that influence their duration (see Chapter 23, for examples). For the sake of simplicity and framing the role of intervention, Regan, like Siqueira (2003) makes the assumption that intervention is a form of conflict management. Specifically, that intervention attempts to maximize the expected utility of each actor for settling now versus continued fighting. Regan (2002) presents six propositions or hypotheses on factors that influence the duration of conflict:

1. Unilateral intervention that supports the government early in the conflict will shorten the expected duration of a conflict.
2. Early support to the rebel groups lengthens the duration.
3. Force by the intervener will shorten the expected duration of a conflict.
4. Early forceful intervention shortens conflict compared with late intervention by force.

5. Interventions that attract counter-interventions will increase the expected duration of a conflict, and

6. Neutral or multilateral interventions will lead to shorter expected duration of conflict [Regan (2002)].

For the first two propositions, Regan (2002) finds that regardless of the type and target, intervention tends to *increase* the duration of conflict. For Propositions 3 through 5, the empirical evidence is that the timing of an intervention has little impact on duration and opposing interventions tend to exacerbate conflict. And finally, the notion of impartiality and neutrality articulated in most UN mandates and hypothesized in 6 is associated with longer conflicts [Regan (2002)]. Clearly, this promising avenue of research is in its early stages and requires a well-integrated approach that combines testable theoretical specification, well-defined datasets and sophisticated statistical techniques to better understand and assess the impact of intervention.

The first factor that has not been adequately addressed in both the theoretical and empirical models is a thorough understanding of the UN as an institution and the reasons and decision processes for intervention. In some cases, UN intervention is broader than intervention in civil wars and includes intra-state, inter-state, etc. (civil wars exclude inter-state such as the Gulf War I and Korea). In addition, as DeRouen (2003) points out, factors that get the UN involved actually make it harder to achieve success. For example, the UN may purposefully select conflicts that are likely to have long durations because it expects settlements to be unlikely. Similarly, demand for intervention by the belligerents may increase due to conflict weariness. DeRouen (2003) employs a two-step process to correct for such selection and explain the counter-intuitive findings of Regan (2002) and others.

Second, studies on third-party intervention assume that conflict management is the primary goal of intervention. However, this is not the case for UN-led missions particularly those under the auspices of Chapter 7 of the Charter. Similarly, we can rule out conflict management for those non-UN financed or sanctioned missions, such as Afghanistan and the Gulf War II.

Third, the dataset used for the assessment of third-party interventions may not hold adequate number of observations for UN peace missions. Regan's (2002) assessment of third party intervention in civil wars may also suffer from limited observations, as UN and other international interventions in civil conflicts were quite rare during the Cold War. The following are examples of UN interventions in civil war during the Cold War: Congo (1960–1964), Lebanon (1958), Cyprus (1964) the Dominican Republic (1965–1966), and Zimbabwe (1966). In addition, how one defines duration and severity of conflict may also impact the empirical results. Recalling Seiglie (1999), if the median voter's behaviour is explicitly incorporated in intervention models then there is an inverse relationship between casualties and duration of missions. In essence, shorter mission duration is a sign of a failed intervention.

The methodological issues associated with conflict datasets and the definition and coding of civil wars is discussed in some detail in Chapter 23 and apply here as they relate to third-party intervention in civil conflicts. Like the joint product model discussed in the previous section, there is a need to have both the theory and the empirics harmonized. For example, if theoretical models feature motives and decisions to intervene then the empirical models should be based on datasets that measure severity and escalation of violence. In particular developments in operations research such as integer programming to cluster or group conflict types by severity may improve some of the data problems.

5. Peacekeeping in theatre and policy implications

This section looks at the economic aspects of PKO once in theatre. The section attempts to answer the third research question on the costs and benefits of PKOs to providers and host nations and derives policy implications to specific targeted groups such as the host country of a peace mission, a troop contributing country or a specific peace mission. These types of studies are common in defense economics literature, particularly, the early tradition of operation research based assessment of specific segments of the defense production process.

Case studies, despite their narrow focus on selected missions or countries, provide the basis for the design of performance measures on the efficacy of peacekeeping missions. For example, from a mission commander's perspective, success can be measured as progress towards "normalcy" (i.e., cession of hostilities and development of basic requirements for survival among the civilian population). Assuming there is a well-defined mandate from the Security Council or if it is a non-UN mission, an accord or framework, fulfillment of a majority of the mandate or framework can also be considered a measure of success.

During a typical peacekeeping operation the various peace partners such as the military and NGOs inject substantial funds into the local economy. Inevitably, this has a substantial impact on the local economy. In addition, the NGOs and UN agencies often duplicate their humanitarian and development projects. Dodd (1994) illustrates the problem of turf wars between aid agencies in Rwanda. For example, the NGOs and the UN refused to cooperate with the government and with each other causing duplication of efforts. According to the World Bank officials, the NGOs have flooded Rwanda with foreign exchange, inflating rents and wages [Dodd (1994)]. Typical spin-off effects from the NGO presence may not occur in the host country either. First, the NGOs do not pay taxes, denying the government financial resources to build much-needed infrastructure. Second, the staffs of these organizations prefer to exchange their salaries in the unofficial market causing further leakages from the economic system [Dodd (1994)].

Solomon (1998) examines the economic consequences of a PKO on the host country using the UN Mission in Haiti (UNMIH) as a case study and by employing a modified Input–Output (I–O) model. He acknowledges the need to modify an I–O methodology since the accuracy and vintage of I–O tables even in developed countries limits the usefulness of such models [Solomon (1998)]. This mode of inquiry is discussed in Section 5.1.

Sobel (1998) attempts to answer the question of how to measure the effectiveness of a peacekeeping mission through the examination of exchange rate movements caused by actual UN policies. Specifically, the magnitude of the exchange rate movement is used as a quantifiable measure of the effectiveness of UN policy. Since this exchange rate test requires that the host country have an independently floating exchange rate it unfortunately limited the sample size to two nations, namely, Lebanon and South Africa. Limit of sample size aside, the use of exchange rate markets is important as these markets are efficient and respond instantaneously to new information [Sobel (1998)]. The author uses a simple random walk specification to model the exchange rate, since many studies have shown that such models perform as well or even better than complicated models that account for prices, money supplies and interest rates [Sobel (1998)]. From a modeling perspective, the aim is to show significant correlation between the residual of the model and the UN intervention. The results show that in the case of Lebanon, the UN PKO caused a substantial long-term appreciation of the Lebanese currency. Since the Arab League (a regional organization) has also intervened during the crisis and caused a long-term appreciation of the currency during its mandate, it signals the fact that the UN has no comparative advantage in providing credible peacekeeping [Sobel (1998)]. The sanctions imposed on South Africa did not have any long-term impact. Public choice theories on sanctions have shown that nation-specific influences (sanctions that impose high costs on the sanctioning country are avoided) have interfered with the process and as such the results are not surprising [Sobel (1998)].[8]

Given that interventions are increasingly occurring in failed states and destabilized regions, the choice of a floating exchange rate for a variable is limiting. Sobel (1998) suggests the use of black market exchange rates. This variable is subject to multiple responses as is the exchange rate. For example, Sobel (1998) does not account for the possibility of the intervention force by their mere presence and other demand for goods and services might have caused the currency appreciation. Specifically, it is not clear whether the intervention, as a signal of future stability or peacekeepers and the UN demand for currency that affected the movement in exchange rates.

5.1. Economic impacts

To date the economic analysis of peace missions in theatre has been relatively neglected. Usually, the lack of detailed data on the host country is the contributing factor for the absence of empirical literature on the subject. Indeed, the political and economic upheavals, which precede peace missions, tend to distort the macroeconomic variables of interest such as GDP growth, inflation, balance of trade and fiscal balance. Given these limitations and general lack of quality data, two research questions are posed. First, what are the economic consequences of peace missions on the host country? Second, what are the policy implications to the UN, the host country and contributors?

---

[8] See Chapter 27 for a detailed discussions on economic sanctions.

Solomon (1998) utilizes the UN financial statistics as the starting point to estimate the direct flow of expenditures to Haiti. This methodology can be extended to any mission by incorporating UN and, when available, interview data. For example, the consumption pattern of the mission personnel from interview data [Solomon (1998)] indicated large savings (i.e., savings up to 66% of daily allowance); this level of saving is consistent with military personnel stationed for temporary duty in remote locations in Canada [Parai et al. (1996)]. Typically if the stay is temporary, purchases are limited to incidentals and basics.

Likewise, the lack of a developed industrial infrastructure in Haiti for the provision of resources for most of the Operations and Maintenance (O&M) requirements of the peace mission leads one to conclude that the indirect and induced economic impacts may be limited. Induced impacts are the increased in employment and incomes that occur as the consequences of direct and indirect impacts [Solomon (1998)].

Based on the general observations discussed above, Solomon (1998) estimated the likely economic impacts of the UNMIH shown in Table 4. The total UN expenses for the period amount to $134.6 million (all in current dollars). The largest expenses for the UN are the military and civilian personnel costs, which include the international police forces, UN volunteers, local staff and other civilian employees. This amount totalled approximately $95 million. According to the UN documents and interview data, about 80% of this amount goes back to the troop-contributing countries as standard troop cost reimbursement. Similarly high amounts of transportation and equipment expenditures are also leaked out or do not remain in the Haitian economy [Solomon (1998)]. After accounting for these additional leakages, an estimated $28.8 million dollars remain in the

Table 4
UNMIH economic impact summary (1 August 1995–29 February 1996)

Major cost item current dollars	Amount initially spent	Amount remaining in Haiti	As % of initial expenditures
Military and civilian pay	$95,445	$18,550	19%
Accommodation and infrastructure repairs	$3,227	$2,985	92%
Transportation	$13,357	$2,818	21%
Communications	$668	$75	11%
Equipment, supply and services	$17,932	$3,583	20%
Public information	$159	$159	100%
Air and surface freight	$937	$38	4%
Other UN administrative costs	$2,896	$579	20%
Total	$134,621	$28,785	21%
Percentage remaining in Haiti	21%		
Spin-off (multiplier 1.2)		$34,254	
Impact as % of GDP	2%		

Source: Solomon (1998), UN (1995, 1996).

Haitian economy for circulation. This is about 21 percent of the initial UN expenditures for the UNMIH (Table 4).

Considering the large leakage, Solomon (1998) compares Haiti's situation to a small isolated community in Canada with a military base and used a similar multiplier to estimate the spin-off effect of the peace mission. Thus, the direct, indirect and induced impact on the Haitian economy is estimated to amount to $34.5 million in 1995–1996 [Solomon (1998)].

In general the Solomon (1998) findings can be extended to other missions by utilizing UN financial data and by drawing some generalities about peace missions in developing nations and military installations in isolated communities of industrialized nations.

5.2. Policy implications

Regardless of the intentions of the UN or the mission mandate, the operation has an economic impact on the host country. The estimated $34.5 million that remained in Haiti is about 2 percent of its national GDP (Table 4).

If a country like Haiti without the necessary infrastructure managed to secure 2 percent of its annual GDP from a peace mission, other relatively developed nations like Croatia (UN expenditures have been in excess of current $5B and growing) can generate significant spin-offs from peace missions. This may lead to perverse incentives to keep the mission going. Thus, the host country develops economic activities that are at best temporary and external to its immediate economic needs. When peace missions successively reduce in scope and size, the host nation faces an economic crisis, which may lead to instability, conflict and another round of peace missions [Solomon (1998)].

Sobel (1998) used exchange rate history to assess the efficacy of peacekeeping missions in Lebanon. While Lebanon was ideal for the analysis, Haiti and most peacekeeping host nations are not. Alternatively, one can model selected macro variables within a random walk framework and, specifying a multi-period intervention model, one can assess the UN policy or action as either temporary or permanent. Temporary is defined by a significant but offsetting change in the variable under consideration (such as exchange rate, inflation, growth).

An empirical analysis using transfer function modeling can show whether the demand for scarce accommodation and skilled labour during the early stages of the peace mission tend to increase general price levels temporarily or permanently. In addition, a transfer function model can be used to assess the efficacy of economic and arms sanctions imposed on countries.

6. Summary and future directions

The study of peacekeeping from an economics perspective is a fairly recent phenomenon. The preceding three sections answered a number of economic issues related to the economics of peacekeeping. The main research questions addressed in the chapter were:

- Is peacekeeping a pure public good and what are the implications to burden sharing?
- Is peacekeeping or third party intervention efficient? Does intervention need to be impartial?
- Why do nations participate in peacekeeping operations (PKOs)? What are the costs and benefits of PKOs to providers and host nations?

The key finding of the financing and burden sharing research is that peacekeeping has a relatively large share of purely public benefits, which leads to a more sub-optimal allocation of resources to peacekeeping from a global perspective. The burden sharing implication is that the large nations will continue to shoulder a disproportionate share of the costs of peacekeeping. The burden sharing research also suggests that there are some country-specific benefits of peacekeeping (reduction of conflict in one's region, etc.) and thus it is theoretically possible to increase contribution by assessment redistribution or by designing marketable or tradable obligations to increase peacekeeping troop contributions

The studies on third party intervention attempted to answer the second research question on the efficacy of peacekeeping and the reasons why interventions succeed or fail. These studies, whether theoretical or empirical, failed to provide an adequate answer to the research question. Specifically, theoretical models on interventions showed that intervention may or may not result in the reduction of conflict since the strategic interactions among the warring parties and the intervener bring indirect impacts that are not always clear. The question of whether a third-party (a UN peacekeeping force) should be impartial or biased seemed to be resolved in favor of a biased intervention; however, such strategy requires complete information on the warring factions capabilities and the ability to "tailor" an intervention policy to attack the weaker faction.

The empirical studies were equally ambiguous. On the one hand, multi-dimensional peacekeeping/peace building missions tended to significantly improve the chances for peace, while traditional peacekeeping (such as observer mission) did not. More recent studies showed that intervention by international organizations was not a significant factor in reducing the duration of conflict, while others found early intervention by the UN to significantly reduce conflict.

The final research question on the costs and benefits of peacekeeping was addressed through a case study on Haiti, a peacekeeping host nation. The analysis can be generalized to other peacekeeping host nations. For example, host nations may perceive the UN mission much as a military base is perceived in a small economically weak community, as a source of income and employment. This may lead to perverse incentive and increase instability if such an economic source is reduced or removed. From a public choice perspective, citizens of peacekeeping host nations may demand more peacekeeping resources than would be efficient since the country did not pay the full cost of the international peacekeeping.

6.1. Future directions

Peacekeeping is an area that is rich in its potential for further research. The peacekeeping burden sharing research has benefited from the rich literature on alliances developed in defense economics. The application of the methods to peacekeeping was fruitful. However, the research also uncovered areas that demand more analysis. For example, peacekeeping may be habit-forming either because missions take more than a year to complete or bureaucratic self-interest sustains continued involvement. What is needed to effectively address the habit-forming aspect of peacekeeping is more time-series data to conduct a thorough econometric and Granger causality analysis.

The existence of a number of conflict datasets have helped foster the study of third-party interventions, in particular aspects such as the impact of intervention on duration. However, there is considerable variation on the interpretation of the data and the selection of performance measurement criteria for the efficacy and success of interventions. For example, a peacekeeping mission commander's criteria for success are considerably different than those of the UN, the host country or other international organizations such as the World Bank. As such, clearly specifying the research problem (does intervention reduce duration or intensity of conflict?), and identifying the appropriate metrics and research methodology (correcting for selection bias) may improve the ambiguous results uncovered in third-party intervention research.

While the case study on Haiti provides some important insights on the consequences of peacekeeping missions on the host country, the implications to contributors are yet to be directly tested. One simple framework for formally examining the contributors' benefits is through imputed costs and benefits, as well as counter-factual evidence. For example, Canada's involvement in Haiti may include a number of country-specific benefits such as the containment of instability in its region, assisting or contributing to its bi-lateral security arrangement with the US and status. Assuming the benefits at least equal the costs, the benefits to Canada can be estimated through its deployment and sustainment costs, its paid assessments to the specific mission(s) and economic or other type of grants. Similarly, the US may perceive or impute the benefit of Canada's participation through counter-factual evidence: for example, the cost to the US to deploy unilaterally, the cost of border patrols and other administrative costs from increased refugee traffic, etc.

There have been studies examining issues on the challenges and opportunities of cooperation between the various peace players such as NGOs and the military, but none from an economic perspective. Woodcock and Davis (1999) provide an operations research perspective while Solomon (1999b) employs decision support models to uncover some characteristics of collusion among NGOs when prioritizing missions. The increasing competition for funding among NGOs and the introduction of new players (competitors) to support humanitarian missions (which up to now was an exclusive domain of NGOs) have forced NGOs to re-organize and assume business processes and structures. This is well suited for economics based assessment. For instance, do NGOs collude in order to maximize available aid money? What are the impacts of NGOs on the host country and in fostering peace building?

Another peculiarity of most recent peacekeeping missions is the conspicuous presence of for-profit firms providing logistics and other support to the military and Non-Governmental Organizations (NGO) contingents in theatre. There is scope for further research on the costs and benefits of private provision of peacekeeping whether in the role of logistics support or security provision. For example, it is not clear whether private military companies are large enough to be involved in peacekeeping operations in a significant way. Another question for further research is the feasibility and cost effectiveness of private security provision. Of course, some of the political and administrative constraints, such as the International Convention against the "Recruitment, Use, Financing and Training of Mercenaries", need to be addressed as well. Recent studies such as Fredland (2004) use a transactions cost approach to suggest that the combat support role of firms is limited due to the inevitable contractual hazards.

References

Amegashie, J.A., Kutsoati, E. (2005). "(Non) Intervention in intra-state conflicts". University of Guelph economics discussion papers 2005-04.

Bobrow, D.B., Boyer, M.A. (1997). "Maintaining system stability: Contributions to PKO". Journal of Conflict Resolutions 41, 723–748.

Boutros-Ghali, B. (1992). An Agenda for Peace: Preventive Diplomacy, Peace-Making and Peacekeeping. United Nations, New York.

Carment, D., Rowlands, D. (1998). "Three's company: Evaluating third party intervention in intrastate conflict". Journal of Conflict Resolution 42, 572–599.

Carment, D., Rowlands, D. (2004). "Force and bias: Towards a predictive model of effective third party intervention". Mimeo. Earlier version available as BCSIA Working Paper 2001-08, JFK School of Government, Harvard University.

DeRouen Jr., K. (2003). "The role of the UN in international crisis termination, 1945–1994". Defence and Peace Economics 14, 251–260.

Dodd, R. (1994). "Do goodism is ruining this country". Gemini News Service, December 9.

Doyle, M.W., Sambanis, N. (2000). "International peace building: A theoretical and quantitative analysis". American Political Science Review 94, 779–801.

Durch, W.J. (1993). "Paying the tab: Financial crisis". In: Durch, W.J. (Ed.), The Evolution of UN Peacekeeping: Case Studies and Comparative Analysis. Macmillan Press, Pennsylvania, pp. 39–59.

Felix, D. (1995). "The Tobin tax proposal". Futures 27, 195–200.

Fischer, D., Hattori, A. (1999). "Economics of war and peace: Overview". In: Kurtz, L. (Ed.), Encyclopaedia of Violence. Peace and Conflict. Academic Press, San Diego.

Fredland, E. (2004). "Outsourcing military force: A transactions cost perspective on the role of military companies". Defence and Peace Economics 15, 205–219.

Henderson, H., Kay, A.F. (1995). "The flexibility of a United Nations security insurance agency: Update and summary". Report to the Global Commission to Fund the United Nations. United Nations, New York.

Hartley, K. (1992). "Comment on R.S. McNamara 'The Post Cold War World: Implications for Military Expenditures in the Developing Countries'". In: Proceedings of the World Bank annual conference in development economics. International Bank for Reconstruction and Development. The World Bank, Washington.

Hartley, K. (1997). "The Cold War, great-power traditions and military posture: Determinants of British defence expenditure after 1945". Defence and Peace Economics 8, 17–36.

Hartley, K., Sandler, T. (1999). "NATO burden sharing: Past and future". Journal of Peace Research 36, 665–680.

Hirshleifer, J. (1988). "The analytics of continuing conflict". Synthese 76, 201–233.

Isard, W., Fischer, D. (1997). "On financing and reorienting the United Nations". Peace Economics, Peace Science and Public Policy 4, 1–10.

Kammler, H. (1997). "Not for security only: The demand for international status and defence expenditure, An introduction". Defence and Peace Economics 8, 1–16.

Khanna, J., Sandler, T. (1997). "Conscription, peace-keeping, and foreign assistance: NATO burden sharing in the post-Cold War era". Defence and Peace Economics 8, 101–121.

Khanna, J., Sandler, T., Shimizu, H. (1998). "Sharing the financial burden for UN and NATO peacekeeping: 1976–1996". Journal of Conflict Resolution 42, 176–195.

Khanna, J., Sandler, T., Shimizu, H. (1999). "The demand for UN peacekeeping, 1975–1996". Kyklos 52, 345–368.

Klein, L., Marwah, K. (1996). "Economic aspects of peacekeeping operations". In: Gleditch, N.P., Bjerkholt, O., Chapplen, A., Smith, R.P., Dunne, J.P. (Eds.), The Peace Dividend. Elsevier Science, Amsterdam, pp. 533–553.

Klein, L., Marwah, K. (1997). Burden Sharing in Support of United Nations. United Nations Studies, Yale University.

McNamara, R.S. (1992). "The post Cold War World: Implications for military expenditures in the developing countries". In: Proceedings of the World Bank annual conference in development economics. International Bank for Reconstruction and Development. The World Bank, Washington, DC.

Mendez, R.P. (1995). "Harnessing the global foreign currency market: Proposal for a Foreign Currency Exchange (FXE)". In: Commission on Global Governance, Issues in Global Governance. Kluwer Law International, Amsterdam.

Morrison, A. (1993). "The fiction of a UN standing army". Unpublished paper. Pearson Peacekeeping Centre, Cornwallis Park.

Parai, L. (1998). The Benefits and Costs of Alternate Peacekeeping Arrangements. CSDRM Solicited Research, RMC, Kingston.

Parai, L., Solomon, B., Wait, T. (1996). "Assessing the socio-economic impacts of military installations on their host communities". Defence and Peace Economics 7, 7–19.

Regan, P. (2002). "Third-party intervention and the duration of intrastate conflicts". Journal of Conflict Resolutions 46, 55–73.

Sandler, T., Forbes, J.F. (1980). "Burden sharing, strategy, and the design of NATO". Economic Inquiry 18, 425–444.

Sandler, T., Murdoch, J.C. (2000). "On sharing NATO defence burdens in the 1990s and beyond". Fiscal Studies 21, 297–327.

Seiglie, C. (1999). "Altruism, foreign aid and humanitarian military intervention". Conflict Management and Peace Science 17, 207–223.

Seiglie, C. (2005). "Efficient peacekeeping for a New World Order". Peace Economics, Peace Science and Public Policy 11 (2). Article 2.

Siqueira, K. (2003). "Conflict and third-party intervention". Defence and Peace Economics 14, 389–400.

Shimizu, H. (2005). "An economic analysis of the UN peacekeeping assessment system". Defence and Peace Economics 16, 1–18.

Shimizu, H., Sandler, T. (2002). "Peacekeeping and burden sharing: 1994–2000". Journal of Peace Research 39, 651–668.

Shimizu, H., Sandler, T. (2003). "NATO peacekeeping and burden sharing: 1994–2000". Public Finance Review 31, 123–143.

Sobel, R.S. (1998). "Exchange rate evidence of the effectiveness of United Nations". Public Choice 95, 1–25.

Solomon, B. (1998). "The economic consequences of a peacekeeping mission on the host country: Haiti". In: Woodcock, A., Davis, D. (Eds.), Cornwallis III: Analysis for Peace Operations. Canadian Peacekeeping Press, Cornwallis, pp. 166–182.

Solomon, B. (1999a). "Economic analysis for a peacekeeping mission". Peace Economics Peace Science and Public Policy 5. Article 2.

Solomon, B. (1999b). "Prioritizing tasks in peace mission". In: Woodcock, A. Davis (Ed.), Cornwallis IV: Analysis of Civil–Military Interactions. Canadian Peacekeeping Press, Cornwallis, pp. 252–261.

United Nations (1945). The Charter of the United Nations. The United Nations, New York.

United Nations (1995). Report of the Secretary-General on the United Nations Mission in Haiti, S/1995/305. United Nations, New York.

United Nations (2001). Scale of assessments for the apportionment of the expenses of United Nations peace-keeping operations (A/55/712). United Nations, New York.

United Nations (2003). Implementation of general assembly resolutions 55/235 and 55/236 (A/58/157). United Nations, New York.

United Nations (2005a). Monthly summary of contributions (as of 31 August 2005). United Nations, New York.

United Nations (2005b). The official United Nations web site: http://www.un.org/Depts/dpko/glossary/p.htm, accessed February 21, 2005.

United Nations General Assembly (1996). Agenda Item 133: Financing of the United Nations Mission in Haiti A/50/363/Add.3. The United Nations, New York.

United Nations Security Council (1956). Resolution 118 (1956) [adopted by the Security Council at its 743rd meeting]. The United Nations, New York.

Woodcock, T., Davis, D. (Eds.) (1999). Cornwallis IV: Analysis of Civil–Military Interactions. Canadian Peacekeeping Press, Cornwallis.

Chapter 25

TERRORISM: A GAME-THEORETIC APPROACH[*]

TODD SANDLER[1]

School of Economic, Political and Policy Sciences, University of Texas at Dallas, Green Building, Richardson, TX 75083, USA
e-mail: tsandler@utdallas.edu

DANIEL G. ARCE[2]

Rhodes College, 2000 North Parkway, Memphis, TN 38112-1690, USA
e-mail: arce@rhodes.edu

Contents

Abstract	776
Keywords	777
1. Introduction	778
2. A brief look at the early literature	780
3. Counterterrorism: Normal-form representations	782
3.1. Proactive versus defensive measures: 2 × 2 canonical representations	782
3.2. A 3 × 3 deterrence–preemption game	784
3.3. Asymmetric targets and preempting	785
3.4. Other cases	787
4. Counterterrorism: Extensive-form games	789
4.1. Preemption versus deterrence in a continuous choice scenario	793
5. Alternative externalities	795
6. Pitfalls of international cooperation	799
6.1. Specific examples: Freezing terrorist financial assets	800
6.2. Specific example 2: Safe havens	802
7. Game theory and never conceding to terrorist demands	803
7.1. Conventional wisdom evaluated	805
7.2. Reputation	806
8. Asymmetric information	806
8.1. Signaling extensions: Alternative forms of regret	810

[*] The authors have profited from comments provided by Keith Hartley, Peter Matthews, and Kevin Siqueira on an earlier draft. Any shortcomings are the sole responsibility of the authors.
[1] Todd Sandler is the Vibhooti Shukla Professor of Economics and Political Economy.
[2] Daniel Arce is the Robert D. McCallum Distinguished Professor of Economics and Business.

Handbook of Defense Economics, Volume 2
Edited by Todd Sandler and Keith Hartley
© *2007 Elsevier B.V. All rights reserved*
DOI: 10.1016/S1574-0013(06)02025-4

9. Concluding remarks   811
References   812

Abstract

This chapter surveys the past applications of game theory to the study of terrorism. By capturing the strategic interplay between terrorists and targeted governments, game theory is an appropriate methodology for investigating terrorism and counterterrorism. Game theory has been used to examine the interaction among targeted governments, the interface between factions within a terrorist organization, and the interplay between diverse agents (e.g., rival terrorist groups). This chapter identifies a host of externalities and their strategic implications for counterterrorism policies. In addition, the chapter indicates novel directions for applying game theory to terrorism-related issues (e.g., cooperative collectives to strengthen borders).

For counterterrorism, we use normal-form games to distinguish proactive from defensive policies. Although both policy types can be represented with similar games, we identify essential strategic differences between these policy classes. When targeted governments must allocate resources among antiterrorism measures, there is generally a dominance of defensive over proactive countermeasures against transnational terrorism. The resulting outcome gives a suboptimal equilibrium. The policy prognosis is much better for domestic terrorism as a central government can internalize externalities among alternative targets.

For transnational terrorism, dilemmas also arise when counterterrorism is investigated for continuous choice variables. Too much action is associated with defensive measures, while too little action is associated with proactive measures. This follows because defensive responses are strategic complements, while proactive responses are strategic substitutes for targeted governments. These same strategic concepts are crucial for understanding the interaction among political and military wings of a terrorist group. Game-theoretic notions also inform about interdependent security choices where the safety achieved by one at-risk agent is dependent not only on its precautions but also on those of other agents. Coordination games are particularly appropriate for analyzing the pitfalls of numerous aspects of international cooperation – for example, freezing terrorist assets and denying safe havens. We identify many roadblocks to effective international cooperation.

For hostage negotiations, we show that the never-concede policy of governments hinges on at least five unstated assumptions that seldom hold in practice. Thus, even the staunchest proponents of the no-concession policy have reneged under the right circumstances. Ways to bolster adherence are indicated.

The chapter also investigates the influence of asymmetric information when terrorists are better informed about the strength of the governments than the other way around. A model is put forward that unifies two alternative approaches based on the terrorists' preferences for revenge or resolution. Recent contributions involving asymmetric information and terrorism are discussed.

Keywords

terrorism, Prisoners' Dilemma, counterterrorism, assurance game, externalities, hostage negotiations, asymmetric information, proactive measures, international cooperation, defensive measures, deterrence, interdependent risk

JEL classification: D74, C72, H56

1. Introduction

Terrorism is the premeditated use or threat of use of violence or force by individuals or subnational groups against noncombatants to obtain a political or social objective through the intimidation of a large audience beyond that of the immediate victim. Although definitions can vary in terms of the victim, perpetrator, and audience, all definitions agree on terrorists applying violence to achieve political or social goals [Enders and Sandler (2006a), Hoffman (1998), White (2003)]. Terrorists broaden their audience beyond the targeted victims by making their actions appear to be random so everybody feels anxiety. A series of street or public transport bombings makes everyone in a city feel at risk wherever they go even though the likelihood of becoming a victim is miniscule.

Terrorism comes in two basic varieties. *Domestic terrorism* is home grown with consequences for just the host country, its institutions, citizens, property, and policies. Moreover, domestic terrorism involves perpetrators, victims, and targets from the host country. Any demands associated with a domestic terrorist incident are issued to the people or institutions within the venue country. Through its victims, targets, supporters, terrorists, *or* implications, *transnational terrorism* concerns more than one country. The toppling of the World Trade Center (WTC) towers on 11 September 2001 (henceforth, 9/11) was a transnational terrorist event, because victims hailed from many countries, the mission had been planned abroad, the terrorists were foreigners, and implications (e.g., financial repercussions and subsequent security measures) of 9/11 were global. Transnational terrorist attacks represent a transnational externality where actions of the authorities (e.g., their policies) or terrorists of one country impose uncompensated costs or benefits on people or property of another country [see, e.g., Arce and Sandler (2005a), Enders and Sandler (2005a, 2006b), Heal and Kunreuther (2005), Kunreuther and Heal (2003), Sandler et al. (1983)]. Thus, a proactive response by one country that destroys training camps of a terrorist group that poses a threat to a number of countries provides positive externalities for all at-risk countries. Because positive and negative externalities are ubiquitous with terrorism, strategic considerations are essential in addressing the threat that it presents.

There are many reasons why game theory is an appropriate methodology for the study of terrorism. First, game theory captures the strategic interplay between terrorists and targeted governments, where actions are interdependent as each side responds to its adversary's action. Second, a game-theoretic framework captures the notion that terrorist scenarios concern interactions among rational agents that are trying to act according to how they think their counterparts will act and react. Interplay can be between factions within a terrorist organization, among terrorist groups, among targeted governments, or between terrorists and governments. Players may also be voters, the media, or an international organization. These players are rational in the sense that they optimize an objective subject to constraints. Third, game theory allows adversaries to issue threats and promises for strategic advantage – e.g., a no-negotiation pledge to limit hostage taking or a retaliation threat against state-sponsors to curb their support. Fourth, game-theoretic notions of bargaining are applicable to hostage negotiations and terrorist-campaign-induced negotiations over demands, such as autonomy for a province. The determinants of bargaining advantage and the length of negotiations inform policymakers of the likely consequences of alternative bargaining strategies. Fifth, game theory incorporates the uncertainty and learning in a strategic environment that characterizes all aspects of terrorism [see, e.g., Bueno de Mesquita (2005a)]. In a terrorism scenario, many agents interact with asymmetric information: e.g., the terrorists may know the government's capabilities, while the government may not know the terrorists' capabilities and must update beliefs based on past attack patterns [see Arce and Sandler (in press), Lapan and Sandler (1993), Overgaard (1994)].

As a weak adversary, terrorists must act in a strategic manner to be a formidable threat against a much stronger opponent. Terrorists have been adept at exploiting a host of asymmetries to gain advantage [see, e.g., Sandler (2005), Sandler and Enders (2004)]. Terrorists gain a second-mover advantage by identifying soft targets *after* the government has allocated defensive expenditures. Nations are target-rich; terrorists are target-poor. Terrorists overcome collective action barriers and form networks with other terrorist groups. In contrast, national governments are less inclined to cooperate with other national governments, even when confronted by the same terrorist threat. This collective action failure ensures plenty of soft targets, overspending on defensive measures, and underspending on proactive policies. Terrorists are less restrained than the liberal democracies that they attack [see, e.g., Hoffman (1998), Li (2005), Wilkinson (1986, 2001)]. Additionally, terrorists strategically choose their organizational structure of a loosely tied network to best confront the rigid hierarchical structure of targeted governments [Arquilla and Ronfeldt (2001)]. Terrorists also exploit their informational asymmetries, thereby leaving an opponent government uncertain about the requisite level of defense or whether resistance is the most appropriate response. This lack of information can result in government regret where it concedes to terrorists whose resources are modest (see Section 8).

This chapter has a number of purposes. The primary purpose is to review the relevant literature by presenting a number of game-theoretic applications to demonstrate through example how game theory has fostered our understanding of terrorism and antiterrorism policies. As such, the chapter investigates counterterrorism from alternative game-theoretic perspectives (see Sections 2–4, 6). This investigation indicates numerous pitfalls of international cooperation to curb terrorism. A secondary purpose is to identify alternative externalities and their implications for policy (see, e.g., Section 5). A tertiary purpose is to examine aspects of hostage taking using game theory (see Section 7). A fourth purpose is to investigate the role of information when terrorists confront a government (see Section 8). A final purpose is to highlight directions for future research (see Section 9).

2. A brief look at the early literature

Sandler et al. (1983) were the first to investigate terrorism with the use of game theory in which the terrorists' choice are constrained by governmental policies and government's choices are similarly constrained by the terrorists' actions. Terrorists divide their efforts between terrorist activities and legal protests, where the former involves making demands of a targeted government that is more apt to concede to low than to high demands. The terrorists confront a "chance constraint" that ensures that the probability of receiving a government concession of a given amount is greater than or equal to some probability. In contrast, the government chooses its concessions to terrorists in order to maximize its utility, subject to a budget constraint and an acceptable probability of being reelected. Granting concessions may lose or gain the government electoral support, depending on how voters evaluate the terrorism threat.

The authors describe the negotiation process in terms of Nash reaction paths where terrorists' demands are dependent on anticipated government concessions, which themselves are dependent on terrorists' demands. Changes in the underlying parameters of the model – e.g., the level of terrorist resources or the marginal costs of terrorist acts – are influenced by governmental policy choices that can shift the reaction paths and change a stalemate to a negotiated solution favoring one of the adversaries. Although the model is somewhat primitive, it clearly displays that neither opponent's decision could be examined in isolation, as had been the practice. Moreover, the authors highlighted the rationality on the part of the terrorists and how they respond in a predictable fashion to governmental policy decisions. Some of these responses are advantageous to the government, while others are not; thus, well-intended policies may have unintended consequences.

Next, Atkinson et al. (1987) employed a bargaining model to show that the duration of a hostage incident is dependent on bargaining actions such as bluffing (i.e., threatening an action that is not executed) or the difference between initial demands and concessions (i.e., the disagreement spread). These authors hypothesized that heightened bargaining costs cause the terrorists to reduce their demands and the government to raise its concessions. Moreover, an increase in bargaining costs to either side reduces the length of the incident. Atkinson et al. (1987) tested bargaining hypotheses based on real terrorist incidents.

Two subsequent papers also used game theory to investigate hostage-taking events. Selten (1988) presented an extensive form version of the hostage-taking game where terrorists first try to abduct hostages and, if successful, seek to extort ransom for the hostages' release. Once the hostages are secured, the incident can end with ransoms being paid and the hostages being released, or no ransom being paid and the hostages being killed. In Selten's model, the payoffs at the game's endpoints are known with certainty, so that the expected value of alternative pathways or decisions can be calculated. In a complete-information, deterministic setting, the solution of the game is known at the outset, since in the absence of ties, a finite game of perfect information has a unique subgame perfect equilibrium. Thus, the Selten representation does not offer a variety of outcomes.

In contrast, the Lapan and Sandler (1988) extensive-form representation of hostage taking left at least one endpoint payoff uncertain – i.e., the loss to the government from not capitulating to the terrorists' demands. This innovation means that the true equilibrium pathway cannot be known until this uncertainty is resolved (see Section 7). Such uncertainty can result in the government making a pledge – e.g., never to concede to terrorist demands – that they fail to honor for some realizations of the loss from not capitulating. As a consequence, the government may act in a *time inconsistent* fashion by pledging one course of action that they later abandon, once a decision node is reached and information is revealed.

In another contribution, Sandler and Lapan (1988) investigated terrorists' choice of targets for a three-player game involving two target venues and a common terrorist threat. The terrorists favor the target with the greater expected payoff. Defensive measures, taken by either venue, reduce the terrorists' logistical success probability and limit the terrorists' expected payoffs. Other things constant, increased defensive measures by one venue make the other venue appear to be "softer" and, hence, a relatively more attractive target. Their analysis is noteworthy because it was the first to identify a host of externalities associated with counterterrorist policies. A greater defensive response provides positive externalities by protecting visitors from the other venue and making any attack less likely. This defensive action also creates a negative externality by displacing the attack to another venue. The presence of positive and negative externalities means that more structure must be placed on the problem to gain unequivocal results. If, for example, an attack results in no collateral damage on visitors from the other venue, there is a tendency to overdefend [also see Sandler and Siqueira (2006)]. Other scenarios can result in other outcomes including too little defensive measures.

In an early game-theoretic paper on terrorism, Lee (1988) represented retaliation against a terrorist group as having pure public good properties that may lead to free riding. Lee (1988) relied on a 2×2 game matrix to depict his two-country case. If retaliation is purely public and no country is the target of the bulk of attacks, then Lee (1988) characterized the outcome as a Prisoners' Dilemma with neither country retaliating. If, however, one country receives most of the attacks and derives some country-specific benefits (e.g., from displacing the attack abroad), then Lee showed that the game is no longer a Prisoners' Dilemma. In particular, the targeted country has a dominant strategy to retaliate and the other country may then be best off following this response. Things become more complicated and interesting when Lee (1988) allowed for "paid riding" or the ability to "sell" the public good of retaliation by offering an accommodation to the terrorists, as Greece allegedly did for 17 November Organization and the French once did for the Basque terrorists. The paid-rider option dominates free riding and retaliating; hence, the final outcome is the least desirable with one country accommodating the terrorists and the other country failing to retaliate against the terrorists [also see Lee and Sandler (1989)]. Lee's (1988) analysis clearly recognized how targeted countries can work at cross-purposes by creating negative externalities when responding independently to the threat of terrorism. This study also demonstrated how actions by the terrorists may maximize this externality.

The first paper to allow for asymmetric information in a game-theoretic framework was Lapan and Sandler (1993). In their framework, the terrorists know the ability of the government, but the government does not know the strength of the terrorists and must update its priors based on the level of the first-period attacks. In the resulting perfect Bayesian equilibrium, a government may have regret by conceding to a weak terrorist group, whose first-period attacks mislead the government into inferring that the group is sufficiently strong to cause costly future attacks. Overgaard (1994) altered the Lapan–Sandler model to allow for less-vengeful terrorists who do not expend their remaining resources in endgame attacks when no concessions are granted. In Overgaard (1994), the terrorists are more political and less militant. We provide a unifying model for these two analyses in Section 8. In recent years, incomplete information has characterized a number of game-theoretic analyses of terrorism [e.g., Bueno de Mesquita (2005a, 2005b), Sandler and Arce (2003)]. Studies have relaxed standard notions of rationality to address the evolutionary dynamics of fundamentalist behavior and the role of liberal democracy for reducing violence [see, e.g., Arce and Sandler (2003)].

3. Counterterrorism: Normal-form representations

Two main classes of counterterrorism policies include proactive and defensive measures. Proactive or offensive policies take direct actions against the terrorists or their sponsors and include retaliating against a state-sponsor, destroying terrorist training camps, infiltrating a terrorist group, gathering intelligence, freezing terrorist assets, or preempting a planned attack. For transnational terrorism, a proactive response often gives rise to private (provider) costs and purely public benefits that favor all at-risk nations. If, however, the proactive measure is grievance generating, then it may also create purely public costs [Rosendorff and Sandler (2004)] that we address at a later point. In contrast, defensive or passive actions yield public costs as attacks get deflected to less-fortified venues [see, e.g., Enders and Sandler (1993, 2004, 2005a, 2006b)] and private (provider) benefits. These measures include erecting technological barriers (e.g., bomb-sniffing equipment and metal detectors), securing borders, stiffening penalties, improving surveillance, and fortifying targets. Defensive actions are intended to deter an attack by either making success more difficult or increasing the likely negative consequences to the perpetrator.

3.1. Proactive versus defensive measures: 2 × 2 canonical representations

In Figure 1a, we display a preemption game, representative of other proactive situations. Each of two targeted nations, denoted by 1 (row player) and 2 (column player), possesses two strategies: preempt or maintain the status quo. If, say, nation 1 preempts

nation 2

		Preempt	Status quo
nation 1	Preempt	$2B - c, 2B - c$	$B - c, B$
	Status quo	$B, B - c$	**0, 0**

$$(2B > c > B)$$

(a) 2×2 preemption game

nation 2

		Status quo	Deter
nation 1	Status quo	$0, 0$	$-C_1, b - C$
	Deter	$b - C, -C_2$	$b - C - C_1, b - C - C_2$

$$(C + C_i > b > C), i = 1, 2$$

(b) 2×2 deterrence game

Figure 1. Preemption and deterrence games in normal form.

while nation 2 does not, then nation 1 gains a net benefit of $B - c$ as it deducts its costs of c from the public benefit of B that it receives *along with* nation 2. Thus, nation 2 obtains a free-rider benefit of B. When the roles are reversed, so too are the payoffs. If both countries expend preemption effort, then each gains $2B$ from the cumulative action at an individual cost of c, so that net gains are $2B - c$ for both nations. No one preempting gives net gains of 0 to the nations. If we assume that $2B > c > B$, then a Prisoners' Dilemma applies with each country having a dominant strategy to do nothing. The Nash equilibrium, from which neither nation will unilaterally depart, is for nothing to be done at the mutual status quo outcome. Nash equilibrium payoffs are in boldface. Obviously, other game scenarios can apply to preemption depending on the relative ordering of $2B$, c, and B. For the present, we maintain the Prisoners' Dilemma.

In Figure 1b, we depict a 2×2 deterrence game, representative of other defensive cases, where deterrence by just nation i gives it a benefit of b at a cost of C in which $b > C$ by assumption. Moreover, passive country j endures a cost of $-C_j$ as it draws more attacks, since it becomes relatively softer in light of i's defensive measures. No action by either country gives no net gains, while mutual action gives each country a payoff of $b - (C + C_i)$, which is assumed to be negative [see, e.g., Arce and Sandler (2005a)]. This canonical deterrence game is also a Prisoners' Dilemma with a dominant strategy to deter and a Nash equilibrium of mutual deterrence with boldfaced payoffs.

		nation 2		
		Preempt	Status quo	Deter
nation 1	Preempt	$2B - c, 2B - c$	$B - c, B$	$B - c - C_1, B + b - C$
	Status quo	$B, B - c$	$0, 0$	$-C_1, b - C$
	Deter	$B + b - C, B - c - C_2$	$b - C, -C_2$	$b - C - C_1, b - C - C_2$

$(2B > c > B)$ and $(C + C_i > b > C)$, $i = 1, 2$

Figure 2. 3×3 Preemption–deterrence game.

Consider an alternative deterrence game where the payoffs are the same as those in Figure 1b, except that mutual deterrence gives a benefit of $\bar{b}$ (net of transference considerations) at a provision cost of C for each agent. This scenario has mutual deterrence as decreasing benefits so that $b > \bar{b}$, but $\bar{b}$ does not necessarily equal $b - C_i$ for $i = 1, 2$ as in Figure 1b. There *may* even be a net gain from mutual deterrence so that $\bar{b} - C > 0$. Most of the results displayed for Figures 2 and 3 will hold in this alternative case provided that $\bar{b} - C > -C_i$; i.e., mutual deterrence is better than becoming the softer target that draws the attack. With this assumption, the modified deterrence game is still a Prisoners' Dilemma with mutual deterrence as the Nash equilibrium. All of the results for Figures 2 and 3 hold if, in addition, $\bar{b} - C < 0$. Henceforth, we use the case depicted in Figure 1b unless indicated otherwise.

Even though the preemption and deterrence games may both be Prisoners' Dilemmas, differences arise. As depicted, the preemption game is analogous to the public good contribution game where action is desired but inaction is dominant; whereas, the deterrence game is analogous to the open-access commons game where inaction is desired but action is dominant [Arce and Sandler (2005b)]. The social optimum and Nash equilibrium are in opposite positions – i.e., mutual status quo is the social optimum for deterrence, while mutual action is the social optimum for preemption. Extending both games to n nations merely exacerbates the extent of suboptimality associated with the Nash equilibrium. For preemption, incentive-compatible bribes can be applied to motivate agents to view honest preference revelation as a dominant strategy. An analogous mechanism to induce inaction for the deterrence game is more problematic because penalties must be large to reflect the associated public costs [Sandler and Arce (2003)]. Moreover, agents tend to have an aversion to inhibiting their right to deterrence, even if such restrictions increase efficiencies.

3.2. A 3 × 3 deterrence–preemption game

We now allow each nation to have three strategies: preempt, status quo, and deter. In the 3×3 game matrix of Figure 2, the northwest 2×2 bold-bordered matrix depicts the previous 2×2 preemption game, while the southeast 2×2 bold-bordered matrix represents the earlier 2×2 deterrence game. If one nation preempts and the other deters, then the former receives $b - c - C_i$ and the latter receives $B + b - C$ as displayed in the two cells at the opposite ends of the off-diagonal of the 3×3 matrix. Based on the assumptions thus far, this matrix allows us to determine which counterterrorism policy choice dominates if each target can choose either policy or the status quo. For both nations, the dominant strategy is to deter since the payoffs are higher than the corresponding payoffs associated with the other two strategies owing to $b - C > 0 > B - c$. When both targeted nations adopt their dominant strategy, the Nash equilibrium of mutual deterrence with the boldfaced payoffs results. This outcome is like a "Prisoners' Dilemma squared" in which the *smallest summed payoff* of the nine cells *follows* – every other strategic combinations is preferred from an aggregate payoff standpoint. Of the two Nash equilibriums of the embedded overlapping 2×2 Prisoners' Dilemma games, the Pareto-inferior equilibrium reigns.[1]

When first confronted with this rather disturbing and fascinating result, one's intuition is to view it as merely following from the assumptions made thus far, but, in fact, it has resilience as assumptions are altered [Arce and Sandler (2005a)]. If, for example, we allow mutual inaction to cause negative payoffs so that the embedded preemption game is a *chicken* game, the dominant strategy is still to deter. The same mutual deterrence Nash equilibrium also follows when the preemption benefits are only achieved if both countries preempt so that the embedded preemption game is an assurance game. If we permit a fourth strategic option of *doing both* preemption and deterrence, then a 4×4 matrix (not shown for the extension of Figure 2) would apply. The northwest 3×3 embedded matrix would be Figure 2 [see Arce and Sandler (2005a)]. The four payoff pairs in the bottom row as well as the four payoff pairs in the right-most column can be easily computed. Given the assumptions of Figure 2, one can show that the deter strategy still dominates. In fact, any combination of deter and preempt is dominated by deter.

3.3. Asymmetric targets and preempting

We next turn to the northwest bold-bordered 3×3 matrix embedded in a 4×4 matrix game in Figure 3, where we initially ignore the doing both strategy. The payoffs in the 3×3 matrix are the same as Figure 2 except for those of nation 1 in the preempt row. The new storyline is that nation 1 is a prime target for the terrorists and attracts the lion's share of the attacks. This is true of the United States, whose people and property suffer 40% of transnational terrorist attacks, even though few occur on US soil. Suppose that nation 1 receives greater gains from its own preemption than it confers on nation 2. In particular, suppose that nation 1's preemption gives a benefit of $2B$ to itself and a

---

[1] When, however, we allow $\bar{b} - C > 0$ to be the mutual deterrence payoffs described earlier, the better of the two Nash equilibriums of the embedded overlapping 2×2 Prisoners' Dilemma games results. This case requires that benefits from defensive actions can exceed costs even when every target fortifies itself, thereby gaining no relative defensive advantage over other targets.

	nation 2			
nation 1	Preempt	Status quo	Deter	Both
Preempt	$3B - c, 2B - c$	$2B - c, B$	$2B - c - C_1, B + b - C$	$3B - c - C_1, 2B - c + b - C$
Status quo	$B, B - c$	$0, 0$	$-C_1, b - C$	$B - C_1, B - c + b - C$
Deter	$B + b - C, B - c - C_2$	$b - C, -C_2$	$b - C - C_1, b - C - C_2$	$B + b - C - C_1, B - c + b - C - C_2$
Both	$3B - c + b - C, 2B - c - C_2$	$2B - c + b - C, B - C_2$	$\mathbf{2B - c + b - C - C_1, B + b - C - C_2}$	$3B - c + b - C - C_1, 2B - c + b - C - C_2$

$(2B > c > B)$ and $(C + C_i > b > C)$, $i = 1, 2$

Figure 3.   Asymmetric dominance with three and four options.

spillover gain of B to nation 2. Everything else remains unchanged from the assumptions behind Figure 2 – i.e., preemption still costs c and nation 1 derives a preemption benefit of just B from nation 2's action. Moreover, the deterrence storyline and payoffs remain as before. Nation 1's payoffs in the top row of the 3×3 matrix follow from our new assumption and exceed the corresponding payoffs in Figure 2 by B. For this embedded game, nation 2's dominant strategy remains deter; hence, the only possible Nash equilibriums in this 3×3 game is (Preempt, Deter) or (Deter, Deter). The former holds provided that nation 1 gains more from preempting alone than from deterring alone – i.e., $2B - c > b - C$. In this scenario, the prime-target country is motivated to preempt because the terrorists direct more attacks against its interests. This pattern is in keeping with what we observe in the real world: prime-target countries, such as the United States and Israel, engage in proactive responses against transnational terrorists. Hence, asymmetric targeting by terrorists can induce a nation to resist the strong tendency to rely on defensive measures alone when confronting transnational terrorism.

This reliance on defensive measures is less characteristic of domestic terrorism. For domestic attacks, proactive measures do not confer spillover benefits on other countries because by their nature no other countries are being targeted. Additionally, a country will never get a free ride from the proactive measures of another country. Thus, countries engage in both defensive and proactive policies for domestic terrorism as all benefits are internalized.

Next, we consider the 4×4 game matrix in Figure 3, where a fourth option of doing both – deterrence and preemption – is allowed for each of the two countries. The seven new payoff pairs are computed as before. For example, suppose that nation 1 does both while nation 2 just preempts. Nation 1 then receives $3B - c$ from the two preempt responses and $b - C$ from its deterrence, while nation 2 receives $2B - c$ from the two preempt responses and $-C_2$ from nation 1's deterrence. The other six payoff pairs are calculated in a similar fashion. Although the matrix in Figure 3 appears complex, the unique Nash equilibrium is easy to locate. Nation 1 has a dominant strategy to do both since $2B - c > 0$, while nation 2 has a dominant strategy to deter since $B - c < 0$. As each nation plays its dominant strategy, the Nash equilibrium (Both, Deter) with the boldfaced payoffs results. We observe prime-target countries engaging in both defensive and proactive measures – e.g., the United States spends a lot on defensive homeland security while leading actions to destroy al-Qaida and its assets.

3.4. Other cases

Up until now, preemption is characterized as giving purely public benefits. A heavy-handed preemption may create grievances that give rise to public costs, C, as well as public benefits. The heavy-handed crackdown by the French in Algeria in the 1960s helped the terrorists to attract more recruits and shifted Algerian public opinion against the French forces as shown in the movie, *The Battle of Algiers*. We investigate this grievance scenario in Figure 4 for an asymmetric two-nation example, in which nation 1 is the prime target and gains $2B$ from its own preemption and B from nation 2's

		nation 2	
		Preempt	Status quo
nation 1	Preempt	$3B - c - 2C, 2B - c - 2C$	$2B - c - C, B - C$
	Status quo	$B - C, B - c - C$	$0, 0$

$$(2B > c + C > B)$$

Figure 4. Asymmetric dominance and preemption recruitment costs.

preemption. The preemptor must cover its provision costs of c. Each unit of preemption now generates public benefits, B, *and* public grievance costs, C. If nation 1 preempts alone, then it receives $2B - c - C$ as it accounts for its derived benefits $(2B)$ and the associated provision and grievance costs $(-c - C)$, while free-riding nation 2 obtains $B - C$ in terms of spillover benefits and costs. If nation 2 preempts alone, then it realizes $B - c - C$, while free-riding nation 1 receives $B - C$. Finally, mutual preemption gives nation 1 a payoff of $3B - c - 2C$, while it provides nation 2 with a smaller payoff of $2B - c - 2C$ since nation 2 derives only B from its own action.

We assume that $2B > c + C > B$ so that individual action yields a net gain to prime-target nation 1 but not to nonprime-target nation 2. Given these assumptions, nation 1's dominant strategy is to preempt, while nation 2's dominant strategy is to do nothing. The Nash equilibrium is for nation 1 to preempt alone. This is the outcome regardless of whether $B - C > 0$ or $B - C < 0$ provided that $2B > c + C$, as assumed. The dilemma posed by this case is that the proactive response by the prime-target country can result in a "forced ride" for nation 2 as its net welfare deteriorates because of nation 1's action if $B - C < 0$. This may have been the case for Spain following the backlash to the Abu Ghraib prison abuse scandal and the subsequent commuter train bombings on 11 March 2004 in reaction to Spain's participation as part of the "coalition of the willing" in Iraq.

Rosendorff and Sandler (2004) also allowed for proactive recruitment effects in a game-theoretic representation that involves a government and a terrorist group as the players. If the government responds too harshly, then its actions can trigger recruitment and result in a large-scale terrorist incident where many people perish. If, however, the government responds too mildly, the terrorists may also mount a large-scale event. To avoid these massive attacks, the government must choose a proactive response that is neither too small nor too large. These authors' analysis can be extended to allow for three players – two targeted governments and the terrorist group – and the presence of public benefits and costs arising from offensive choices. This extension highlights that some governments may be placed in jeopardy by overly zealous reactions of other governments.

A host of alternative game forms, including assurance and coordination can apply to proactive and defensive responses depending on the pattern of payoffs [Arce and Sandler (2005a), Sandler and Arce (2003)]. When, for example, two targeted governments are trying to infiltrate a terrorist group, infiltration by a single government is desirable to minimize risk and limit errors. As such, a coordination game applies where one nation needs to act and the other do nothing. Other examples are studied in greater detail in Section 6.

The varied game forms for counterterrorism are particularly apparent in Heal and Kunreuther's (2005) interesting study of interdependent risk and airline security. In their analysis, the risk that confronts each agent is determined by its own efforts and those of other agents to limit a catastrophic event that may be brought about by any agent who takes insufficient precautions. The authors gave the example of luggage in a plane's cargo hold, where bags are only screened on their flights of origin. Bags are not re-screened when transferred to other flights. Pan Am flight 103 exploded over Lockerbie, Scotland, on 21 December 1988 because of a bomb in a bag that was poorly screened in Malta and then transferred at Frankfurt to a London-bounded flight before being placed aboard Pan Am flight 103 in London's Heathrow Airport. In the 2×2 representation of interdependent risk, Heal and Kunreuther (2005) showed that many different game forms (e.g., assurance, coordination, and asymmetric dominance) may apply, depending upon security costs per trip, the associated probabilities of disaster, and the loss in the case of catastrophe. Their model shows that each airline does not fully internalize the associated negative externality that shoddy screening on their part imposes on other airlines. As airlines realize that their screening efforts may not be enough to divert disaster, their own incentives to exercise care may be reduced, particularly when their efforts have less of a safety impact. This problem is exacerbated as the number of airlines with shoddy procedures increases. A number of policy recommendations were offered, including identifying and changing the behavior of one or more airlines that can "tip" the system to a equilibrium with enhanced security precautions. Airlines with the most feeder flights fall into this category. Other public policy fixes were also discussed, such as the use of taxes, subsidies, and regulations. Their analysis highlight how externalities abound in the presence of terrorism. Moreover, the mix of public benefits and costs and private benefits and costs drives their result.

4. Counterterrorism: Extensive-form games

Dating back to Sandler and Lapan (1988) and Selten (1988), extensive-form games have also been associated with the practice of counterterrorism [see also Rosendorff and Sandler (2004), Sandler and Siqueira (2006)]. In Figure 5, we examine deterrence decisions by two domestic targets – a business target (B) and a tourist (T) target. The terrorists are assumed to stage their attack at a single venue in each period. Additionally, the terrorist group is assumed to be fanatical in the sense that it derives a positive gain even if the mission fails, so that the group will attack one of two venues. The model can be easily extended to allow for no attack – a fifth endpoint to the game – in some circumstances [Sandler and Lapan (1988)].

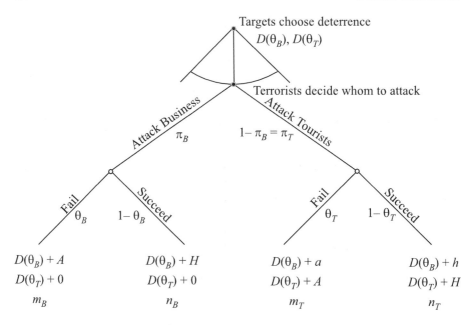

Figure 5. Deterrence game tree for domestic targets.

Figure 5 depicts the associated deterrence game tree where the alternative targets go first and choose their continuous levels of deterrence, D, or deterrence costs that, in turn, determines the terrorists' perceived likelihood of failure, θ_B, at the business venue and their perceived likelihood of failure, θ_T, at the tourist venue. Obviously, $1 - \theta_B$ and $1 - \theta_T$ are the probabilities of logistical success for attacks at these respective venues. Deterrence costs increase at an increasing rate with respect to the associated failure probability; thus, these costs are assumed to be convex. Deterrence represents an insurance policy that is paid regardless of the outcome.

The terrorists move second and decide which of the two targets to attack, in which the attack probability π_i against i (= B, T) depends on their perceived failure probabilities; i.e., $\pi_i(\theta_i, \theta_j)$ for $i, j =$ B, T and $i \neq j$. This probability function is assumed continuous with $\partial \pi_i / \partial \theta_i < 0$ and $\partial \pi_i / \partial \theta_j > 0$, so that information is incomplete with respect to terrorists' beliefs and value. We could allow nature to determine the terrorist type, where the endogeneity of the π_i functions is part of the model and the terrorists' pay-offs at the four endpoints have a random element [see Sandler and Siqueira (2006)]. The assumed partial derivatives for the π functions are consistent with target transference: i.e., efforts by target i to limit terrorist success merely displace the attack to target j, and vice versa. Target transference represents a negative externality where the terrorists attack the target with higher expected payoff. If both targets are equally attractive, then each target perceives a 50–50 chance of attack. The terrorists sit back and wait for the targets to deploy defensive measures so that they can take advantage of a second-mover advantage to attack the softer target.

The game ends in four outcomes: terrorist failure or success at the business target, or terrorist failure or success at the tourist target. In Figure 5, the payoffs to business, tourists, and the terrorists are displayed in descending order. Both targets experience costs that they desire to minimize, while the terrorists gain benefits that they want to maximize. Terrorists' payoffs m_i and n_i ($i = $ B, T) for failure and success are not necessarily known with certainty, so that terrorists must anticipate their values. Obviously, $n_i > m_i$ for either target as success rewards terrorists more than failure.

We focus on the actions of the target, leaving the terrorist choice to the interested reader [see Sandler and Siqueira (2006)]. In Figure 5, the targets must cover their deterrence costs in any realization. The displayed scenario assumes that there is no collateral damage on tourists at a business venue because tourists typically do not visit businesses. There is, however, collateral damage of a or h on business interests when a tourist venue is attacked. Thus, a terrorist attack on an airport is likely to affect both tourists and business personnel. Some symmetry of costs is assumed in which a direct attack on a business or tourist site causes damages of A for a failure and H for a success, where $H > A$. For collateral damage to business interests, terrorist success is more costly than failure so that $h > a$.

To compare the Nash equilibrium to the social optimum, we must first display the expected costs to business and tourist interests from attacks at the two venues while accounting for deterrence-determined failures and success probabilities. The expected costs to business concerns from a business attack is

$$l(\theta_B) = \theta_B A + (1 - \theta_B)H, \tag{1}$$

whereas the analogous costs to tourists from a tourist attack is

$$l(\theta_T) = \theta_T A + (1 - \theta_T)H. \tag{2}$$

The collateral damage from a tourist attack on business concerns is

$$v(\theta_T) = \theta_T a + (1 - \theta_T)h, \tag{3}$$

where as the collateral damage from a business attack on tourist concerns is

$$v(\theta_B) = 0. \tag{4}$$

Given our assumptions on the components of these cost expressions, $l(\theta_i)$ decreases as θ_i increases for $i = $ B, T while $v(\theta_T)$ decreases as θ_T increases since expected damages decline as terrorists are more apt to fail. When acting independently, business anticipates an expected cost, C_B, that satisfies:

$$C_B = D(\theta_B) + \pi_B l(\theta_B) + \pi_T v(\theta_T). \tag{5}$$

Because of the absence of collateral damage to tourist interests at business venues, the expected cost, C_T, to tourists satisfies:

$$C_T = D(\theta_T) + \pi_T l(\theta_T). \tag{6}$$

A Nash equilibrium corresponds to each target group minimizing its expected costs with respect to its deterrence variable while taking the other target's deterrence choice variable as given.

The social ideal is found by treating the decision maker for deterrence at the two locations as the same agent. Thus, θ_i, $i = $ B, T, is chosen to minimize the aggregate cost C:

$$C = D(\theta_B) + D(\theta_T) + \pi_B(\theta_B, \theta_T)[l(\theta_B)] + \pi_T(\theta_B, \theta_T)[l(\theta_T) + v(\theta_T)]. \qquad (7)$$

To ascertain the relative inefficiency of the Nash deterrence choice of business, we first find the first-order condition of minimizing C_B with respect to θ_B. The resulting expression includes marginal deterrence costs, the potential harm to business interests from an attack deflected to the tourist venue, and the marginal benefits of diverting an attack and limiting damage to its interests at home. Next, we minimize the social cost C in (7) with respect to θ_B. Last, we evaluate the social-cost first-order conditions at the θ_B that satisfies the Nash equilibrium where $\partial C_B / \partial \theta_B = 0$, denoted by θ_B^N. This evaluation results in:

$$l(\theta_T^N)\frac{\partial \pi_T}{\partial \theta_B} > 0, \qquad (8)$$

because there is no collateral damage on tourists at business venues. This term represents the external transference costs that enhanced business-site deterrence inflicts on a tourist venue. Given the convexity of the cost function, Equation (8) indicates that businesses are inclined to *overdeter*.

The case is less clear-cut for tourist deterrence decisions owing to opposing externalities stemming from collateral damage to business interests at a tourist venue. As defenses are increased at a tourist site, external costs are imposed on business interests through transference, while external benefits arise from protecting businessmen at tourist venues. The latter arises by making attacks less likely there and by limiting the damage from attacks. If we evaluate the cooperative first-order conditions at θ_B^N, we find:

$$\pi_T v'(\theta_T^N) + v(\theta_T^N)\frac{\partial \pi_T}{\partial \theta_T} + l(\theta_B^N)\frac{\partial \pi_B}{\partial \theta_T} \gtrless 0, \qquad (9)$$

whose sign is indeterminant without further assumptions. The external benefit is represented by the first two left-hand expressions in (9), while the external transference costs are captured by the third left-hand expression in (9). If, say, the transference externality is small compared with the absolute value of the first two terms, then the tourist venue will underdeter by not taking sufficient account of the protection that its efforts afford to businessmen.

For domestic terrorism, these externalities are likely to be internalized by the central government overseeing defensive measures, as the Transportation Security Administration (TSA) has done at US airports since its creation after 9/11. The externality is much more worrisome for transnational terrorism where the targets are venues in different countries and targeted countries engage in a deterrence race to shift an attack abroad or else underdeter by failing to protect foreign visitors, as first recognized by Lee (1988) and Lee and Sandler (1989). The game setup presented here can be applied to a wide variety of scenarios depending on the mix of external costs and benefits. Moreover, additional agents – e.g., more targeted countries – can be introduced.

For example, Bier et al. (in press) examined a model where the government has incomplete information about terrorists' preferences over multiple targets of opportunity. This analysis generalizes the "tragedy of the commons" analysis of defensive policies [Arce and Sandler (2005a) and Section 3] to the case where terrorists' reactions are no longer passive and confirms earlier findings that decentralized deterrence leads to overspending [Sandler and Lapan (1988)]. In Bier et al. (in press), the government moves first and allocates its defensive measures among various targets (subject to a budget constraint), thereby determining the associated success probabilities. Unlike Sandler and Siqueira (2006), there is no possibility of collateral damage. Given the success likelihoods, the terrorists (whose preferences over the targets are unknown) attack the target(s) with the greatest expected payoff(s). A couple of important findings follow. First, first-mover advantages are so great that the government prefers the case where its policies are public, compared to a simultaneous-move approach where they are secret. Second, even when the allocation of resources among targets is centralized, this does not mean that the government will (costlessly) reduce the vulnerability of a target to zero. The crucial consideration is the *relative* vulnerability of targets, so that the government may allow for some positive probability of success where terrorists attack less-damaging targets. This follows from the recognition of terrorists' best replies when the government acts as a Stackelberg leader. This insight is absent in studies that passively model terrorists' actions under deterrence.

4.1. Preemption versus deterrence in a continuous choice scenario

In a recent contribution, Sandler and Siqueira (2006) used an extensive-form game to contrast preemption and deterrence for transnational terrorism where a single terrorist network targets two countries. These authors associated only public benefits with preemption. In their scenario, each country's preemption against a common terrorist threat represents strategic substitutes. Let q^i, $i = 1, 2$, denote country i's preemption efforts. Because each country's preemption represents substitutes that contribute toward the pure public good of eliminating a common terrorist threat, each country's Nash reaction path in Figure 6a are downward sloping as displayed. N_1 denotes country 1's Nash reaction path, while N_2 indicates country 2's Nash reaction path. If preemption is a normal good, then N_1 must be steeper than a line with a slope of -1, while N_2 must be flatter than a line with a slope of -1 [Cornes and Sandler (1996)]. This outcome ensures that the Nash equilibrium at N is unique and stable, where country 1 contributes q^{1N} and country 2 contributes q^{2N} to preemption. The social optimum at, say, P must involve greater preemption than the Nash equilibrium by both countries, because neither includes the marginal benefits that its efforts confer on the other tar-

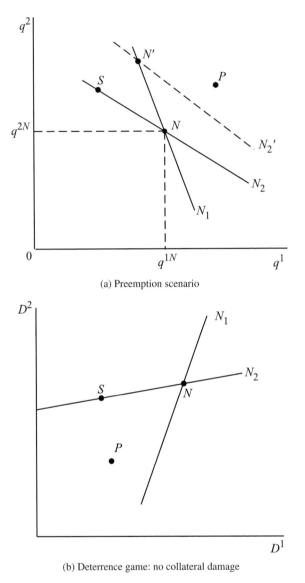

(a) Preemption scenario

(b) Deterrence game: no collateral damage

Figure 6. Counterterrorism continuous scenarios.

get when deciding its preemption level. If the terrorist threat were heightened to *just* country 2, then its Nash reaction path would shift out the dashed path N_2', where country 2 preempts to a greater amount for every preemption level of country 1. The new Nash equilibrium at N' has country 2 increasing its preemption by more than country 1 contracts its preemption; thus, the overall amount of preemption increases. The Pareto optimum (not shown) associated with Nash reaction path N_1 and N_2' involves more q^2 than the pre-threat optimum at P.

Next, we return to the original Nash reaction paths and inquire about the influence of leadership. Suppose that nation 1 assumes a leadership role because it attracts more terrorist attacks. Leadership implies that the leader takes the Nash reaction path of nation 2 as its constraint and finds a tangency between its U-shaped, income-constrained isoutility curves (not displayed) and nation 2's reaction path [see Sandler and Siqueira (2006) for details]. This tangency at S will be northwest of N on N_2. As a consequence, the leader nation is able to put more of the preemption burden on the follower as shown in panel (a) of Figure 6. Because the leader decreases its preemption by more than the follower increases its preemption, the aggregate level of preemption at the leader-follower equilibrium S falls. Thus, leadership is not a good thing for preemption when it yields purely public security gains. This conclusion may not apply if public grievance costs dominate.

If deterrence occurs in a situation when there is little or no collateral damage to foreign visitors, then deterrence is a strategic complement. An increase in one target's deterrence will then motivate the other target(s) to increase its (their) own deterrence so as not to attract the attack. Each target nation seeks to protect its own soil and to deflect the attack, thereby engaging in a deterrence race with too much deterrence. In panel (b) of Figure 6, this is reflected in two ways: by the positive slope of the Nash reaction paths and the relative position of the Nash equilibrium N, and the Pareto optimum, P. The Nash equilibrium indicates that both countries' deterrence, D^i ($i = 1, 2$), exceeds the level at the Pareto optimum at P.

For strategic complements, leadership has a completely different outcome than it had for strategic substitutes. Once again, suppose that nation 1 is the leader and nation 2 is the follower. The leader seeks a tangency between its hill-shaped, income-constrained isoutility curves (not displayed) and the follower's Nash reaction path. This leader-follower equilibrium, S, is displayed in panel (b) of Figure 6. Leader-follower behavior reduces the amount of the overdeterrence since S is nearer than N to P. This follows because the leader internalizes (recognizes) that its deterrence efforts will result in more effort by others and, thus, no necessary gain in security. At S, the overall level of deterrence falls relative to N. The welfare of both nations increases at S relative to N [Sandler and Siqueira (2006)]. After any major attack (e.g., 7 July 2005 London underground bombings), the host country assumes a leadership position and the above scenario applies.

5. Alternative externalities

For counterterrorism, government policy choices are shown in Section 4 to imply a host of externalities. Deterrence gives rise to transference externalities as attacks are deflected to softer targets, whereas preemption often yields positive externalities in the form of purely public benefits. Externalities, and the strategic behavior that they imply, arise from many other aspects of terrorism. Siqueira (2005) investigated the externalities between political and military wings of the same terrorist organization in which the actions of each faction generate faction-specific benefits along with organization-wide benefits (e.g., financing, advertising the cause) and costs (e.g., reduced constituency support). Four interactive scenarios for political and military wings are investigated that include mutually reinforcing actions and strategic complements, mutually reinforcing actions and strategic substitutes, reinforcing action by the political wing and detracting action by the militants, and reinforcing action by the militants and detracting action by the political wings. These scenarios lead to a variety of outcomes and policy recommendations. For strategic complements, Siqueira established that competition between two factions does not necessarily result in increased dissident activity, because independently acting factions tend to engage in less activity than groups whose factions coordinate efforts. Siqueira demonstrated that a faction may work at cross-purposes with the organization's goal when faction-specific gains are sufficiently strong. In such a scenario, an astute government can exploit this dissent.

His interesting analysis could be extended to a common agency problem [see, e.g., Bernheim and Whinston (1986)] where the terrorist group's leadership is the single agent and the two wings (i.e., political and military) are the two principals, who may have conflicting goals so that their ability to motivate the agent to act in their interests may result in inferior outcomes when the principal punishes the agent for pursuing the goals of the other principal. When this punishment and associated inefficiency surpass a threshold, the group fractures [e.g., Abu Nidal from the Palestine Liberation Organization (PLO) or Popular Front for the Liberation of Palestine (PFLP) from PLO]. Thus, Siqueira's analysis could be extended to explain how new groups split from old groups.

Siqueira's (2005) investigation brings a whole new dimension to the practice of counterterrorism. For reinforcing actions among factions in the presence of strategic complements, Siqueira demonstrated that piecemeal counterterrorism policy may be particularly effective. If, for example, the government's countermeasures effectively target just a single faction's activities, the other faction will also reduce its activities even when these activities are not limited per se by the government's action. Piecemeal counterterrorism policy, in which a single faction's efforts are targeted, may have undesirable consequences for the alternative of strategic substitutes. Siqueira (2005) succeeded in showing that counterterrorism prescriptions may have to account for strategic interactions among factions within terrorist organizations. The requisite information about such interactions requires an understanding of the terrorist group and its constituent parts. His investigation provides a novel insight to the practice of counterterrorism when a terrorist organization has factions whose actions may reinforce or oppose one another's goals – a situation that is not uncommon. Siqueira's results were illustrated with the help of diagrams, such as Figure 6, owing to the presence of strategic complements and substitutes.

Sandler and Arce (2003) also recognized that competing factions within a terrorist group can pose problems for conflict resolution. They analyzed a bargaining model where the government has incomplete information about the distribution of moderates and hard-liners within a terrorist organization's power structure. The government faces a tradeoff between the high benefits associated with appeasing violent hard-liners and the political costs of doing so. Furthermore, the government knows that both hard-liners and moderates will accept an offer that pacifies hard-liners, whereas only moderates will accept something less. If the costs of an acceptable offer to hard-liners are prohibitive, a smaller offer that only placates moderates results in an *adverse selection* as only hard-liner terrorists remain in the organization. Paradoxically, successful negotiations result in increased violence. In this model, hard-liner's own cost of violent action is the defining factor. When violent activities are subsidized (e.g., via a Diaspora or state sponsorship) the potential for an otherwise agreeable resolution of hostilities between hard-liners and the government may go unfulfilled.

In a different context, Bueno de Mesquita (2005b) also studied factions within a terrorist group and some associated externalities that are partly internalized through rewards. Rather than the direct interaction among rival factions, Bueno de Mesquita focused on the strategic interactions between a terrorist faction and the government. In his framework, the positive externality stems from the collaboration between these two agents in a game of moral hazard (i.e., hidden action) and learning. The government relies on the terrorist faction to help curb terrorism but does not know how hard it is working toward this goal. The skill of these collaborators in their counterterrorism role is unknown to the government, which uses observations on outcomes to update its priors about the terrorists' effectiveness. Through the threat of replacement and the promise of political concessions, the government motivates its terrorist confidant. In deciding concessions, the government trades off the marginal gain from motivating its collaborators with the associated marginal costs. The article neither investigated the strategic interaction between the collaborating terrorist factions and its public constituency, nor the interplay between the terrorist factions. The latter is particularly crucial because one faction's replacement value to the government imposes a negative externality on the cooperating faction. This is a rather essential externality that cries for analysis.

Two recent game-theoretic papers have investigated terrorist support and associated externalities. Bueno de Mesquita (2005c) put forward a three-player game with a targeted government, a terrorist group, and a population of potential terrorist sympathizers. Governmental counterterrorism measures can generate opposing externalities: i.e., reduced terrorist capabilities (a positive externality for society) and foment terrorist support (a negative externality for society). The latter arises from lost economic opportunities and enhanced anger among potential supporters of the terrorists. His analysis provide a theoretical framework for the observation that terrorist organizations tend "to screen volunteers for quality" (p. 515). Reduced economic opportunities stemming from recessions can also increase the pool of terrorist recruits, from which the highest quality individuals are then dispatched for missions. Siqueira and Sandler (2005) began with these same three agents, where a terrorist group and a besieged government vie for grass-roots support. Alternative scenarios were displayed where counterterrorism measures can have different net influences on the potential support for the terrorists. Leadership by either terrorists or government can reduce terrorism, compared with the simultaneous-move equilibrium, as terrorists curb attacks to keep from being overwhelmed by the government. In both scenarios, the weak player assumes the leadership. Siqueira and Sandler (2005) then showed that a fourth agent – an outside sponsor (e.g., a state sponsor or franchiser) can augment violence as both adversaries expend more effort. Sponsors can offset some natural limits to violence that competition for supporters offers.

In a recent paper, Siqueira and Sandler (2006) present a three-stage proaction game involving terrorists, elected policymakers, and voters. By so doing, these authors introduce domestic politics to the study of countermeasures by two countries, confronted by the same transnational terrorist threat. The median voter in each targeted country elects a policymaker in stage 1. This policy maker then decides a proactive response to the general terrorist threat in stage 2. In stage 3, the terrorists and any sympathizers fix their terrorist campaign against the two governments. Two considerations drive the voters' choice: free riding on the other country's countermeasures and limiting a reprisal terrorist attack to its country's proactive response. The game results in a smaller proactive level than usually presupposed. This outcome stems from a delegation problem where leadership by voters has a detrimental consequence on the well-being of targeted countries as they respond to augmented free-riding incentives. Domestic politics add a whole new inefficiency to addressing a common terrorist threat.

Myriad externalities are associated with *any* subset of agents tied to terrorism. Earlier, we highlighted the negative externalities that arise between airlines from interdependent risks when taking precautions about bombs on planes. In this situation, the externality is among the various targets. Another externality stems from the media and the terrorists, where the former can bolster the anxiety that the latter seeks through their reporting. Moreover, the media can unintentionally assist the terrorists spread their innovations while limiting the usefulness of governments' counterterrorism innovations through its reporting. For example, detailed accounts of how D.B. Cooper parachuted from a hijacked plane in 1971 with ransom money resulted in so many copycats that the rear door of DC-8s, DC-9s, and Boeing 727s had to be reengineered not to open in flight [Landes (1978)]. Reports on how commando raids gained entry to hijacked planes on a tarmac meant that terrorists guarded against those actions in all subsequent hijackings.

Externalities also abound among terrorists. For instance, terrorists can learn "best practice" or effective logistical innovations from one another. Begin's *The Revolt* contained practices applied by many future terrorist groups including Palestinian terrorists who attack Israel today; the Tupamaros in Uruguay (1968–1972) refined practices of urban warfare that other groups adopted [Enders and Sandler (2006a)]. Fortunately, this externality leads to the undersupply of terrorist innovations! Terrorists also try to free ride on one another's successful bombings so that multiple groups often claim credit for the same incident. This practice leads terrorists to develop distinguishing features to their attacks or calling cards to limit free riding. On the positive side, some terrorist groups have internalized training externalities by making their camps available to other terrorist groups – usually for fees – that share similar enemies.

Thus far, we considered contemporaneous externalities where actions today cause uncompensated interdependencies in the current period. Terrorism is also associated with intertemporal externalities where actions today can create uncompensated interdependencies that arise today and into the future. Any government (country) making concessions to terrorists' demands may induce terrorists to anticipate a greater probability of concessions by others. In response, terrorists associate a higher expected net gain from hostage taking and take more hostages. During 2004 in Iraq, concessions by the Philippine government to obtain the release of a Filipino truck driver (Angelo de la Cruz), threatened with beheading, caused the terrorists to raise their anticipated likelihood of concessions and abduct more hostages. Concessions were also made by the Spanish, Italian, and French governments. Intertemporal externalities also arise from logistical and technological innovations by either side. The development of effective bomb-sniffing equipment protects airline passengers for many years until a clever circumvention is devised. Clearly, plastic guns limited the effectiveness of metal detectors that could then be bypassed. Both terrorists and governments are keen to internalize innovations that help their respective sides.

Heavy-handed proactive measures by governments can sow grievances that may surface decades later when some relative of a slain terrorist takes up the cause. For example, the US bombardment of the hills of Lebanon on 8 February 1984 by *Battleship New Jersey* in retaliation for the bombing of the US Marine barracks resulted in an aggrieved relative conducting a US-directed incident years later [Mickolus et al. (1989)]. Thus, today's countermeasures can cause tomorrow's terrorist incidents. If the grievance is sufficiently held, the precipitating action can result in a large-scale or "spectacular" terrorist attack in the future. Moreover, a failed terrorist mission can be revisited: the 1993 bombing of the WTC failed to bring down the north tower; 9/11 completed the mission some eight years later. A spectacular event also creates an intertemporal externality because it stays in people's minds and gives rise to a long-term anxiety that is especially acute on anniversaries.

6. Pitfalls of international cooperation

Game theory is particularly useful in pointing to strategic dilemmas and cooperative failures faced by governments, targeted by the same terrorist groups. We have already explored the gaming aspects of defensive and proactive counterterrorism measures and focus here on other concerns. An ironic asymmetry arises as terrorists often address their collective difficulties in taking a united stance against targeted government, while governments typically fail to take united actions against the terrorists [Sandler and Enders (2004), Sandler (2005)]. Terrorist groups succeed to cooperate with their counterparts because terrorist leaders are tenured for life so that they view their interactions as continual with an uncertain endpoint. This means that their effective discount rate from losses sustained from not cooperating is low; thus, they are prone to cooperate. Moreover, the terrorists are weak relative to their adversaries and have little choice but to cooperate. Terrorists frequently concur on who is the enemy. In contrast, government's discount rates are high because office terms are so short and endpoints are frequently certain. Governmental officials do not put a lot of weight on future payoffs from cooperating unlike the citizens whom they represent. Moreover, governments see less need for cooperating with other governments because they view themselves are strong compared with the terrorists. Governments often disagree on what groups are terrorists – e.g., many governments do not consider Hamas or Hezbollah as terrorist groups.

This asymmetric cooperative response results in a *maximal externality*. Through their cooperation, terrorists can seek out the weakest link – i.e., the country with the least security – for their next attack and will dispatch their most capable team. Their cooperation allows them to mount the most formidable attack. By failing to cooperate, targeted nations will always present their common terrorist adversaries with attractive soft targets. Thus, terrorists can and do exploit governments' collective action failures to great advantage. This is particularly true today with some terrorist groups linked together in a global network with operative and sleeper cells dispersed worldwide.

6.1. Specific examples: Freezing terrorist financial assets

We present two cases of cooperative failures where targeted countries do not act in concert to counter a terrorist threat. The first example concerns freezing terrorist financial assets. If countries can reduce these assets, then this action shifts in the budget constraint of the terrorists and limits all types of terrorist attacks. Following 9/11, countries and world bodies (e.g., the United Nations and the International Monetary Fund) called for a freeze of terrorist assets. At first, many nations complied with the request and eventually $200 million of assets were frozen [White House (2003)]. Nevertheless, terrorists managed to find countries that did not go along with the freeze as well as ways of transferring money in small amounts to escape detection [Levitt (2003)].

To display the dilemma associated with freezing assets, we use a "Stag-Hunt" assurance game and begin with a two-country scenario where terrorists can sequester their assets in just two countries. Both nations are best off with payoffs of F when they institute identical measures to freeze assets. When one nation takes the action alone, this nation receives the smallest payoff, B, and the other nation, which does nothing, earns the second-largest payoff, E. Finally, no action all around gives the second-smallest payoff, A, where $F > E > A > B$. This game is displayed in Figure 7, with nation 1 as the row player and nation 2 as the column player. The relative ordering of payoffs where $E > A$ implies that the nation that does not go along with the freeze can make a profit from the terrorists and does not fear attacks on its interests at home or abroad. If, however, the noncooperating nation has its interests attacked, then $F > A > E > B$ may apply and the solution is different, as indicated later. For now, we stay with $E > A$.

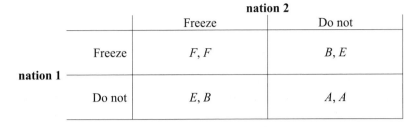

Figure 7. Freezing assets: symmetric game.

Given that $F > E$ and $A > B$, there is no dominant strategy for this assurance game. There are, however, two pure-strategy Nash equilibriums: both countries freeze assets or neither freezes assets. A third Nash equilibrium involves mixed strategies in which each pure strategy is played in a probabilistic fashion. To identify this mixed-strategy equilibrium, we calculate the probability q of nation 2 freezing terrorist assets *that makes nation 1 indifferent between freezing and doing nothing*. Similarly, we derive the Nash equilibrium probability p of action on the part of nation 1 that makes nation 2 indifferent between the two strategies. Once p and q are identified, equilibrium probabilities for maintaining the status quo by doing nothing equal $1 - q$ and $1 - p$ for nations 2 and 1, respectively. The calculation for q (or p not shown) goes as follows:

$$qF + (1 - q)B = qE + (1 - q)A \tag{10}$$

from which we get

$$q = (A - B)/[F - B + (A - E)]. \tag{11}$$

An identical expression holds for p owing to symmetry. When both p and q exceed this value, cooperation in the form of both countries freezing terrorist assets is the best strategic choice. If, for example, q exceeds the right-hand side of (11), then nation 1's best strategic choice is to freeze terrorist assets. The ratio in (11) represents the adherence probability that each nation requires of the other nation to want to institute its own freeze policy. A smaller equilibrium adherence probability favors successful coordination, because a nation then requires less certainty of its counterpart's intention to freeze assets in order to engage in its own freeze.

We can perform comparative static changes on q (or p) in (11) to ascertain whether a higher payoff for a particular strategic combination promotes or hinders cooperation. For example, a larger gain in F from a mutual freeze or a smaller status quo payoff of A promotes the freeze response by reducing the required adherence probability. A spectacular attack like 9/11 or the Madrid train bombings not only raises F but also lowers A as nations recognize the gains from limiting terrorist financial assets and the dire consequences from inaction. An increase in E raises the adherence requirements and makes a mutual freeze less likely. Finally, an increase in the payoff of B associated with acting alone increases the likelihood of cooperation by lowering p and q.

The real hurdle for an agreement to freeze assets is apparent when the game is generalized to n homogenous nations, where all n nations must freeze assets if each participant is to receive F. For less than n participants to the freeze, each adherent receives only B and nonadherents garner E. Because nations are uncertain about the intentions of other nations to abide by the freeze, freezing assets is a desirable policy whenever a nation believes that $n - 1$ required additional participants will follow through with a *collective probability* greater than q. Thus, each nation in this collective must be anticipated to freeze assets by at least the $(n - 1)$st root of q. Even for a modest sized group of, say, 10 nations *and* a q of 0.5, each nation must be perceived as being an adherent with near certainty [Sandler and Sargent (1995)]. This does not bode well for an effective freeze, especially when even one or two states can undo the efforts of the group. Moreover, these stringent adherence probabilities mean that many nations will not be attracted to a freeze unless persuaded by prime-target nations. Punishments doled out by such nations to induce compliance to the freeze increases $(A - E)$ so that p and q fall in value, thereby bolstering cooperation. There are at least two practical problems in punishing noncompliance: (i) identifying nations that accept terrorists' funds, and (ii) convincing freeze adherents to punish nonadherents. Nations hide their interactions with terrorists for fear of reprisals and lost reputation. Imposing punishment presents a Prisoners' Dilemma game with its own collective action issues. If a noncooperating nation has its interests attacked abroad by terrorists, then this reduces E and may result in $A > E$. As a consequence, the adherence probability falls [see the denominator in (11)]. Thus, terrorists must be careful not to cause collateral damage on nations that hide terrorists' assets.

The ability of even one nonparticipant to the freeze to undo the efforts of the cooperators is underscored when one realizes that terrorist events such as the 1993 bombing of the WTC costs very little. Nonetheless, freezes, no matter how universal, limit somewhat terrorists' ability to wage their campaigns and this has some positive payoff when enough nations prescribe. If this payoff is positive for at least k participants, where $k < n$, then a participating nation requires the adherence probability of other nations to be the $(k - 1)$st root of q. The smaller the value of k, the more hopeful is the prognosis that the freeze will have sufficient adherents to be worthwhile.

6.2. Specific example 2: Safe havens

The second example involves safe havens from which terrorists can stage their acts or take refuge to plan and train for future attacks. Afghanistan provided a safe haven for al-Qaida, while Syria afforded a safe haven for the Popular Front for the Liberation of Palestine-General Command (PFLP-GC). The game-theoretic analysis of safe havens is analogous to freezing assets. Each nation gains the most, denoted by N, when both deny a safe haven to the terrorists. The second greatest gain of S_i $(i = 1, 2)$ often derives from providing a safe haven alone if the terrorists agree not to attack its protector. The smallest payoff of E_i $(i = 1, 2)$ comes from denying the safe haven when the other nation accommodates the terrorists with a base of operations. Finally,

nation 2

		Deny haven	Safe haven
nation 1	Deny haven	*N, N*	E_1, S_2
	Safe haven	S_1, E_2	*S, S*

$$(N > S_i > S > E_i, i = 1, 2; S_2 > S_1; E_1 > E_2)$$

Figure 8. Safe havens: asymmetric game.

the next smallest payoff of S is associated with both nations offering safe havens to terrorists.

In Figure 8, we display the 2×2 asymmetric game matrix, where nation 2 gains more than nation 1 from acting alone to provide the safe haven (i.e., $S_2 > S_1$). Moreover, nation 2 gains less than nation 1 when it denies the safe haven alone (i.e., $E_1 > E_2$). As displayed, the game is an assurance game with no dominant strategy and two pure-strategy Nash equilibriums: to both deny safe havens or to both supply safe havens. Mutual denial Pareto dominates mutual supply. Let q represent nation 2's probability of denying a safe haven, and let p denote nation 1's probability of denying a safe haven. For the mixed-strategy equilibrium, the adherence probabilities are:

$$p = \frac{S - E_2}{N - S_2 + (S - E_2)} > \frac{S - E_1}{N - S_1 + (S - E_1)} = q. \tag{12}$$

This inequality follows because a larger S_i raises the adherence probability of denying a safe haven. Similarly, a smaller E_i raises the adherence probability of denying a safe haven. Since nation 2 gains relative to nation 1 from accommodating the terrorists, nation 2 is more inclined to do so as shown in (12). We could go so far as to allow nation 2 to earn the most from giving a safe haven to the terrorists. In this scenario, nation 2 then has a dominant strategy to offer a safe haven.

The analysis can allow for more nations with the result that more nations make the absence of a safe haven a near impossibility. This is especially true when some nations have sympathy with the terrorists or animosity with some prime-target countries. The certainty of safe havens is not a hopeful finding but concurs with what we observe since the late 1960s and the modern era of transnational terrorism. Even when antiterrorist treaties are consummated, their effectiveness has been very disappointing; e.g., treaties forbidding hostage taking or other terrorist tactics have had no significant effect [Enders et al. (1990a, 1990b)].

7. Game theory and never conceding to terrorist demands

In this section, we focus on the Lapan and Sandler (1988) study of hostage-taking events, since it still represents the most complete game-theoretic analysis to date. Their investigation is interesting because it highlights the implicit assumptions that must hold for a government to abide by a pledge never to concede to the demands of hostage takers. The desirability of the never-concede policy hinges on the conventional wisdom that if terrorists knew ahead of time that they have nothing to gain from concessions, then they will never abduct hostages. In essence, the conventional wisdom implies a subgame perfect equilibrium whereby the values at all endpoints are known beforehand and the payoffs are such that terrorists only gain from concessions.

The extensive-form game tree for a hostage event is depicted in Figure 9 where the government moves first and chooses a level of deterrence, D, that then determines the likelihood of a logistical failure by the terrorists – i.e., the probability, θ, that the terrorists will fail to secure their intended hostage(s). If hostages are successfully secured, the government must then decide whether or not to capitulate to the demands of the terrorists. The game can end in four ways: (i) no attack, (ii) an unsuccessful attack, (iii) a successful attack but failed negotiations, and (iv) successful attack and successful negotiations. At each endpoint, the top payoff is the costs to the government and the bottom payoff is the costs or benefits to the terrorists, who perceives the government's capitulation probability to be p.

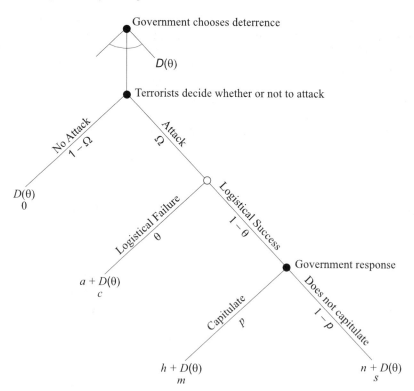

Figure 9. Game theory for hostage event.

In every contingency, the government must cover deterrence costs, which is like an insurance premium that must be paid regardless of the outcome. If the terrorists attempt an incident but fail, then the costs to the government is $D(\theta)$ plus a. The latter represents any expenditure incurred from putting down the incident – e.g., resources spent to stop the incident in the planning stage. When an incident succeeds, the government incurs an expense of h if they capitulate and an expense of n if they do not capitulate in addition to deterrence costs. The relative values of h and n depend, in part, on the value of the hostage(s) secured. The government is motivated to choose D to minimize its costs. From the terrorists' viewpoint, they receive nothing if they do not attack. A failed attack gives them c. If they capture hostages, then they get m for a negotiation success and s for a negotiation failure, where the payoffs are ordered as follows: $m > s > c$. Moreover, c is usually negative, while s may be positive or negative depending on how the terrorists value publicity for their cause. Media attention could conceivably result in a net positive benefit for the cause even when negotiations fail.

Based on the game tree, the terrorists will take hostages provided that they perceive there to be an expected positive benefit. That is, when the following inequality holds:

$$(1 - \theta) \times \left[pm + (1 - p)s \right] + c\theta > 0. \tag{13}$$

In (13), the expected gain from a logistical success exceeds the expected costs from a logistical failure. The former consists of the expected payoffs from either a negotiated success or failure. From (13), the likelihood of a terrorist attack increases as either the probability of logistical success, $(1 - \theta)$, or the perceived likelihood of a government capitulation, p, rises since $m > s$. Thus, the likelihood of an attack depends on θ and p, so that $\Omega = \Omega(\theta, p)$. Increases in concessions granted, m, or decreases in the consequences of a logistical failure, c, augment the chances of a terrorist mission by raising the left-hand side of the inequality, thereby increasing the chances that it will be positive.

7.1. Conventional wisdom evaluated

Suppose that terrorists believe the government's pledge never-to-concede to terrorist demands so that $p = 0$. The terrorists will only take hostages when

$$(1 - \theta)s + c\theta > 0, \tag{14}$$

based on (13). If the terrorists gain from a negotiation failure, then $s > 0$ and (14) may be satisfied so that the government's pledge may not deter hostage taking. Further suppose that $\theta = 1$ so that logistical failure is a certainty. Hostage attacks will still occur provided that even failure holds a benefit for the terrorists when $c > 0$. Unlike the conventional wisdom, hostage attacks cannot necessarily be eliminated even when the never-to-concede pledge is fully credible. A fanatical terrorist group considers self-sacrifice – martyrdom or imprisonment – as a positive payoff giving $c > 0$.

Obviously, hostage taking is even more attractive when the government's pledge is not fully believed by the terrorists. In this scenario, $p > 0$ and the relevant inequality is

(13) which exceeds the left-hand side of (14) by $(1-\theta) \times (pm - ps)$. When the expected payoff from a successful negotiation, $(1 - \theta)m$, is large, the government's pledge is not a sufficient deterrent. Thus, there are many instances where hostages are taken despite the government's pledge never to concede.

Because this is an interactive framework, we must next examine what the government will do when the terrorists are not deterred from capturing hostages. First suppose that the costs of capitulation, h, or not capitulating, n, are known with certainty and that $h > n$. In this case, the government maintains its pledge. When n or h is not known beforehand because the identity of the hostage(s) is not known, then the outcome may be different. If the revealed value of n exceeds h, the government will renege on its pledge. Thus the right hostage(s) – e.g., a CIA agent, schoolchildren, soldiers, or a member of parliament – may induce the government to give into the terrorists. Thus, the never-to-concede policy hinges on at least five implicit assumptions: (i) the government's deterrence is sufficient to stop all attacks; (ii) the government's pledge is fully credible to all potential hostage takers; (iii) the terrorists' gain from hostage taking only derives from fulfillment of their demands; (iv) there is no uncertainty concerning the costs to the government from having hostages abducted; and (v) the government's costs from making concessions always exceed holding firm.

7.2. Reputation

Lapan and Sandler (1988) also allowed for multiple periods where reputation conse-quences for capitulating is included. Reputation costs, R, augment the losses of the government from capitulation to $D(\theta) + h + R$, because concessions in one period increase the terrorists' perceived gains from hostage taking and encourage more ab-ductions. If hostages are secured, then the government will *not* capitulate when $h + R$ exceeds n. Anything that raises reputation costs – e.g., a negative reaction among voters in a liberal democracy – makes government concessions less likely than in the absence of these costs. The institution of rules that prohibit making concessions effectively in-creases R in the hopes of making $h + R$ greater than n for all its realizations, so that the government never gives in. Such rules make $p = 0$, thus limiting hostage taking to those groups that view logistical or negotiation failures as providing a positive payoff to the terrorists.

8. Asymmetric information

Lapan and Sandler (1993) and Overgaard (1994) investigated signaling models where governments update their beliefs about the type of terrorists that they face based upon the intensity of past attacks. Asymmetric information arises because terrorists can ob-serve government counterterrorism measures, but governments do not know the level of resources available to terrorists, which is the source of the incomplete information.

What differentiates the two models is the form of terrorists' preferences posited. In Lapan and Sandler (1993), terrorists are militant or vengeful because they will attack a government a second time if their initial attack does not result in concessions. Militant terrorists see a positive value in continuing to attack an obstinate government. This is also consistent with the current brand of fundamentalist terrorists who have intangible political goals and are unconstrained in their use of violence [Hoffman (1998)]. Alternatively, Overgaard (1994) examined the actions of politically motivated terrorists who receive a benefit for the political use of resources, not expended in an attack. If, moreover, an attack does not result in concessions, these terrorists revert to a purely political use of their resources. Each study focuses on the occurrence of *ex post* regret, in which the government concedes to a low-resource type that it would not concede to under complete information.

Figure 10 corresponds to a scenario where terrorists may employ an initially high level of attack to induce the government to make concessions. This approach unifies the Lapan and Sandler (1993) and Overgaard (1994) models, because it allows for both militant and politically motivated terrorists. The transformation from incomplete information about terrorists' resources to incomplete information about terrorists' preferences is possible because, in the Lapan–Sandler treatment, low-resource terrorists possess an initial level of resources to induce the government to concede if they attack with sufficient force (R^*). In Overgaard, politically motivated terrorists similarly have the requisite level of resources. As stated by Hoffman (1998), the most immediate challenge in countering or deterring (terrorists) is the problem of identifying them.

Incomplete information is modeled in Figure 10 by nature (N) moving first and selecting terrorists' type as either politically motivated (P) or militant (M). Terrorists have access to per-period resource levels R, where their type is defined by their preferences over the actions in this two-period model. In the first period, terrorists can attack at level A or a, in which $A > a$, $A \geqslant R^*$, and $R \geqslant R^*$. Attacks are zero-sum: the benefit to the terrorists is associated with an equivalent cost to the government (G).

The government does not know the terrorists' type and only observes the level of attack. The G_A or G_a nodes, connected by a dotted line, represent the government's information sets after an A- or a-level attack, respectively. At each information set, the government either concedes (C) or does not (D). Concession involves an additional cost of $S > 0$ to the government. If the government holds firm after the first-period attack, it is attacked in the second period by M-types and absorbs the discounted value βR of the attack, where β is the discount factor. This payoff structure is consistent with that in Lapan and Sandler (1993). In Overgaard (1994), G's payoffs are not specified; rather, a critical level of attack is given such that G concedes (R^* here).

Terrorists' activities in the second period differentiate their types. If G does not concede, P-types employ all second-period resources for political means, and the discounted second-period component of their payoff is βR. P-types' payoffs are therefore either $R - A + \beta R$ or $R - a + \beta R$, depending on the level of first-period attack. By contrast, M-types attack with all remaining resources. If, for example, G does not concede after an A-attack in the first period, M-types receive a total payoff of $A + \beta(R - A) + \beta R = (1 - \beta)A + 2\beta R$. Again, the consequences of an attack are zero-sum for G's payoffs. Finally, if the government concedes, terrorists receive νR, where

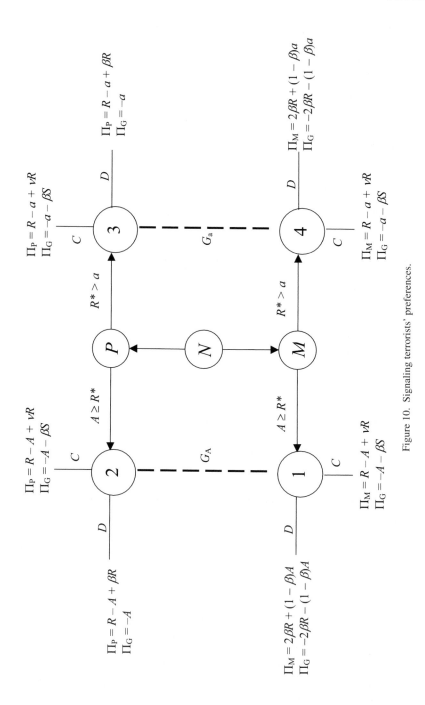

Figure 10. Signaling terrorists' preferences.

$v > \beta$ is a "victory" parameter for second-period resources. In the case of concessions, an attack is a cost to the terrorists in that it reduces the amount of resources that can be used for political purposes. This is true for either terrorist type. Concessions result in terrorist payoffs equal to $R - A + vR$ or $R - a + vR$.

Given the actions by M- and P-types, G has a set of beliefs, $\{\mu_i\}_{i=1,2,3,4}$ such that $\mu_1 + \mu_2 = 1$ at G_A and $\mu_3 + \mu_4 = 1$ at G_a. Along the equilibrium path, these beliefs are consistent with Bayes' rule. The government concedes at G_A if $E_G[C|G_A] = -(A + \beta S) \geqslant -[2\beta R + (1 - \beta)A]\mu_1 - A\mu_2 = E_G[D|G_A]$. Using the add-up condition on beliefs at G_A, we derive

$$\mu_1 \geqslant S/(2R - A). \tag{15}$$

The government concedes at G_A when its belief that it is facing an M-type meets or exceeds the lower bound on the right-hand side of (15). The properties of this lower bound are intuitive. First, as terrorists' overall resources $(2R)$ increase, the lower bound decreases, thereby increasing the likelihood of a concession. Second, if a government takes a hard-line stance against concessions, then S is increased, thereby decreasing the likelihood of acquiescence. Third, either terrorist type will set $A = R^*$ because A is a costly signal. By substitution, the lower bound is an increasing function of R^*, implying that hard-line governments will set a greater threshold for concessions. Note that G does not concede if (15) *is reversed*, a condition that we write as (~15).

The government concedes at G_a if $E_G[C|G_a] = -(a + \beta S) \geqslant -[2\beta R + (1 - \beta)a]\mu_4 - a\mu_3 = E_G[D|G_a]$. That is:

$$\mu_4 \geqslant S/(2R - a). \tag{16}$$

The lower bound for a concession at G_a, given by (16), is less that than for a concession at G_A, given by (15). This is due to the concern over an escalated attack by M-types that amass resources in the first period.

The focus of Lapan–Sandler and Overgaard is *ex post* regret subsequent to concessions, and the value of intelligence in order to avoid regret. We, therefore, examine equilibria possessing these features. For example, an A-pooling equilibrium occurs if (15) and (~16) hold, implying that G's (local) strategy at G_A is C and at G_a it is D, which is written as CD. For P-types, $\Pi_P(A, CD) = R - A + vR \geqslant R - a + \beta R = \Pi_P(a, CD)$, and for M-types $\Pi_M(A, CD) = R - A + vR \geqslant 2\beta R + (1 - \beta)a = \Pi_M(a, CD)$. These reduce to:

$$R \geqslant (A - a)/(v - \beta) \quad \text{and} \quad R \geqslant [A - (1 - \beta)a]/[(1 - \beta) + (v - \beta)], \tag{17}$$

respectively. By forward induction, P-types are more likely to send the out-of-equilibrium a-attack; hence, we set $a = 0$ because a is a pure cost for P-types. Substituting $a = 0$ into the inequalities in (17) and comparing the two, we have $R \geqslant A/(v - \beta)$ as the binding resource constraint. In this equilibrium, the potential for *ex post* regret exists because G could be conceding to P-types that it would not concede to under complete information.

An a-pooling equilibrium occurs if (15) and (16) hold, implying that G's strategy is CC. Clearly, $\Pi_P(a, CC) \geqslant \Pi_P(A, CC)$ and $\Pi_M(a, CC) \geqslant \Pi_M(A, CC)$ because $A > a$. The argument here is that the government concedes in order to avoid a larger second-period attack. Consequently, the potential for *ex post* regret also exists. The difference between *ex post* regret in Lapan–Sandler versus Overgaard is whether regret is associated with an A- or a-attack, respectively. As neither type of pooling equilibrium occurs in the other study, the model here is novel because it recognizes the potential for either form of *ex post* regret as a function of uncertainty over terrorists' types.

Lapan and Sandler (1993) argued that *ex post* regret identifies a standard for measuring the value of intelligence. This is also consistent with the statement from Hoffman (1998) above regarding the need to identify a terrorist group's type. The value of intelligence is the difference between the government's payoff for not conceding to P-types and its equilibrium payoff when it concedes. In either pooling equilibrium, this value equals βS. Only the government's hard-line stance towards concessions, S, matters. Terrorists' resources do not figure into this measure. This implies that a government that takes a firm stance against concessions must make a commensurate investment in intelligence in order to avoid *ex post* regret.

8.1. Signaling extensions: Alternative forms of regret

Arce and Sandler (in press) extended this model to allow for a government's response to an A-level attack by increasing its defensive posture, thereby decreasing the logistical likelihood of success of a subsequent attack. This approach generates an intertemporal substitution of terrorists' resources, and is indicative of the high- and low-terrorism periods empirically documented by Enders and Sandler (2002, 2005b). As escalated attacks can occur in equilibrium, a new form of *ex post* regret occurs in which nonconceding governments are subsequently attacked by M-types that they would have conceded to under complete information. For this form of regret, the value of intelligence is now influenced by the ability of the government to freeze assets (reduce R) and is *negatively* related to the governments' hard-line stance (S). This is because the hard-line stance is akin to a commitment to weather second-period attacks.

The possibility of *ex post* regret also arose in Basuchoudhary and Razzolini (2006), who investigated a model of terrorist deterrence (e.g., airline security) by using personal attributes such as clenched fists, attire (e.g., trench coats in the summer), race, name, country of origin, and so on to determine whether to subject individuals to a security check. They showed that racial profiling (or profiling based on any public signal) cannot survive as an equilibrium under forward induction; instead, security forces must randomize their searches and terrorists must mimic the general population. Terrorists' ability to "pass" scrutiny is limited by the costs of recruiting individuals who can exhibit the general populations' characteristics. For example, in the film, *The Battle of Algiers*, women with the ability to pass as westernized Arabs (or as European women) were used to smuggle armaments past checkpoints. These recruiting costs decrease the likelihood of *ex post* regret, now defined in terms of not searching an individual who later turns out to be a terrorist.

9. Concluding remarks

Given the strategic nature of the interaction between any agent associated with terrorism, game theory is an essential tool for investigating all aspects of terrorism. We illustrated this insight by investigating counterterrorism, alternative externalities, international cooperation, never-concede precommitments, and information asymmetries. Game theory often leads to surprising results: e.g., sharing information can exacerbate inefficiencies when governments do not jointly decide counterterrorism decisions [Enders and Sandler (1995), Sandler and Lapan (1988)]. Another unexpected outcome is that the mix of proactive and defensive responses can result in a more inefficient outcome than choosing just proactive measures. In general, game theory demonstrates that governments often work at cross-purposes when making counterterrorism decisions owing to a lack of coordination and a desire to maximize their own payoffs. Game-theoretic analyses teach that governments' independent actions result in too much defensive measures and too little offensive actions. To rectify such outcomes, governments must cooperate with respect to all counterterrorism policies. This cooperation may eventually take place once nations better appreciate the consequences of not cooperating as they afford terrorists the strategic advantage. Unfortunately, this realization may come only after a terrorist event more horrific than 9/11 occurs.

There are many additional issues that can be analyzed with game-theoretic tools. For example, there is currently no multiperiod analysis of terrorist campaigns where terrorists must choose the patterns of attacks for three or more periods; the signaling game analyses to date allow for just two periods. Additional unexplored environments for examining terror cycles and campaigns include repeated games with imperfect monitoring and the possibility of Stackelberg leadership for long-run terrorists who overlap with elected officials with shorter time horizons. Cooperative game theory has not been applied to investigate counterterrorism where targeted nations form collectively enforced perimeters to save on costs. The behavior of terrorist networks can also be examined with cooperative game theory.

Another area for future study involves the use of differential game theory to investigate how terrorist organizations – their personnel and resources – are influenced by successful and failed missions. By applying a differential game framework, the analyst can display the dynamics of the strategic choices of the terrorists and the government in which the underlying constraints capture the rate of change over time of resource supplies based on the terrorists' operations and the government's policy choices. The genesis and demise of terrorist groups can then be analyzed based on strategic considerations. If, for example, this demise is understood, then governments may better plan their antiterrorist policies.

Yet another direction for future research involves asymmetric information. Two-sided asymmetric information can be introduced so that adversaries are both ill-informed about their counterpart's resources and must use current period revealed actions to update their priors.

References

Arce, D.G., Sandler, T. (2003). "An evolutionary game approach to fundamentalism and conflict". Journal of Institutional and Theoretical Economics 159, 132–154.

Arce, D.G., Sandler, T. (2005a). "Counterterrorism: A game-theoretic analysis". Journal of Conflict Resolution 49, 183–200.

Arce, D.G., Sandler, T. (2005b). "The dilemma of the Prisoners' Dilemmas". Kyklos 58, 3–24.

Arce, D.G., Sandler, T. (2007). "Signaling and the value of intelligence", British Journal of Political Science 37. In press.

Arquilla, J., Ronfeldt, D. (Eds.) (2001). Networks and Netwars. RAND, Santa Monica.

Atkinson, S.E., Sandler, T., Tschirhart, J. (1987). "Terrorism in a bargaining framework". Journal of Law and Economics 30, 1–21.

Basuchoudhary, A., Razzolini, L. (2006). "Hiding in plain sight – Using signals to detect terrorists". Public Choice 128, 245–255.

Bernheim, B.D., Whinston, M. (1986). "Common agency". Econometrica 54, 923–942.

Bier, V., Oliveros, S., Samuelson, L. (2007). "Choosing what to protect: Strategic defensive allocation against an unknown attacker". Journal of Public Economic Theory. In press.

Bueno de Mesquita, E. (2005a). "Conciliation, commitment and counterterrorism: A formal model". International Organization 59, 145–176.

Bueno de Mesquita, E. (2005b). "The terrorist endgame: A model with moral hazard and learning". Journal of Conflict Resolution 49, 237–258.

Bueno de Mesquita, E. (2005c). "The quality of terror". American Journal of Political Science 49, 515–530.

Cornes, R., Sandler, T. (1996). The Theory of Externalities, Public Goods, and Club Goods, second ed. Cambridge University Press, Cambridge.

Enders, W., Sandler, T. (1993). "The effectiveness of anti-terrorism policies: A vector–autoregression–intervention analysis". American Political Science Review 87, 829–844.

Enders, W., Sandler, T. (1995). "Terrorism: Theory and applications". In: Hartley, K., Sandler, T. (Eds.), Handbook of Defense Economics, vol. 1. North-Holland, Amsterdam, pp. 213–249.

Enders, W., Sandler, T. (2002). "Patterns of transnational terrorism, 1970–1999: Alternative time-series estimates". International Studies Quarterly 46, 145–165.

Enders, W., Sandler, T. (2004). "What do we know about the substitution effect in transnational terrorism?". In: Silke, A. (Ed.), Research on Terrorism: Trends, Achievements and Failures. Frank Cass, London, pp. 119–137.

Enders, W., Sandler, T. (2005a). "After 9/11: Is it all different now?". Journal of Conflict Resolution 49, 259–277.

Enders, W., Sandler, T. (2005b). "Transnational terrorism 1968–2000: Thresholds, persistence, and forecasts". Southern Economic Journal 71, 467–482.

Enders, W., Sandler, T. (2006a). The Political Economy of Terrorism. Cambridge University Press, Cambridge.

Enders, W., Sandler, T. (2006b). "Distribution of transnational terrorism among countries by income classes and geography after 9/11". International Studies Quarterly 50, 367–393.

Enders, W., Sandler, T., Cauley, J. (1990a). "UN conventions, technology, and retaliation in the fight against terrorism: An econometric evaluation". Terrorism and Political Violence 2, 83–105.

Enders, W., Sandler, T., Cauley, J. (1990b). "Assessing the impact of terrorist-thwarting policies: An intervention time series approach". Defence Economics 2, 1–18.

Heal, G., Kunreuther, H. (2005). "IDS models of airline security". Journal of Conflict Resolution 49, 201–217.

Hoffman, B. (1998). Inside Terrorism. Columbia University Press, New York.

Kunreuther, H., Heal, G. (2003). "Interdependent security". Journal of Risk and Uncertainty 26, 231–249.

Landes, W.M. (1978). "An economic study of US aircraft hijackings, 1961–1976". Journal of Law and Economics 21, 1–31.

Lapan, H.E., Sandler, T. (1988). "To bargain or not to bargain: That is the question". American Economic Review Papers and Proceedings 78, 16–20.

Lapan, H.E., Sandler, T. (1993). "Terrorism and signalling". European Journal of Political Economy 9, 383–397.

Lee, D.R. (1988). "Free riding and paid riding in the fight against terrorism". American Economic Review Papers and Proceedings 78, 22–26.

Lee, D.R., Sandler, T. (1989). "On the optimal retaliation against terrorists: The paid-rider option". Public Choice 62, 141–152.

Levitt, M. (2003). "Stemming the flow of terrorist financing: Practical and conceptual challenges". Fletcher Forum of World Affairs 27, 59–70.

Li, Q. (2005). "Does democracy promote or reduce transnational terrorist incidents?". Journal of Conflict Resolution 49, 278–297.

Mickolus, E.F., Sandler, T., Murdock, J.M. (1989). International Terrorism in the 1980s: A Chronology of Events, 2 vols. Iowa State University Press, Ames.

Overgaard, P.B. (1994). "The scale of terrorist attacks as a signal of resources". Journal of Conflict Resolution 38, 452–478.

Rosendorff, B.P., Sandler, T. (2004). "Too much of a good thing? The proactive response dilemma". Journal of Conflict Resolution 48, 657–671.

Sandler, T. (2005). "Collective versus unilateral responses to terrorism". Public Choice 124, 75–93.

Sandler, T., Arce, D.G. (2003). "Terrorism & game theory". Simulation & Gaming 34, 319–337.

Sandler, T., Enders, W. (2004). "An economic perspective on transnational terrorism". European Journal of Political Economy 20, 301–316.

Sandler, T., Lapan, H.E. (1988). "The calculus of dissent: An analysis of terrorists' choice of targets". Synthèsis 76, 245–261.

Sandler, T., Sargent, K. (1995). "Management of transnational commons: Coordination, publicness, and treaty formation". Land Economics 71, 145–162.

Sandler, T., Siqueira, K. (2006). "Global terrorism: Deterrence versus preemption". Canadian Journal of Economics 39, 1370–1387.

Sandler, T., Tschirhart, J., Cauley, J. (1983). "A theoretical analysis of transnational terrorism". American Political Science Review 77, 36–54.

Selten, R. (1988). "A simple game model of kidnappings". In: Selten, R. (Ed.), Models of Strategic Rationality. Kluwer Academic, Boston, pp. 77–93.

Siqueira, K. (2005). "Political and militant wings within dissident movements and organizations". Journal of Conflict Resolution 49, 218–236.

Siqueira, K., Sandler, T. (2005), "Terrorists versus the government: Strategic interaction, support, and sponsorship". Unpublished manuscript. University of Southern California, Los Angeles, CA.

Siqueira, K., Sandler, T. (2006). "Terrorist Backlash, terrorism prevention, and policy delegation". Unpublished manuscript. University of Texas at Dallas, Richardson, TX.

White, J.R. (2003). Terrorism: 2002 update, fourth ed. Wadsworth/Thomson Learning, Belmont.

White House (2003). "Progress report on the global war on terrorism". At http://www.state.gov/s/ct/rls/rpt/24087.htm. Accessed 5 February 2004.

Wilkinson, P. (1986). Terrorism and Liberal State, revised ed. Macmillan, London.

Wilkinson, P. (2001). Terrorism Versus Democracy: The Liberal State Response. Frank Cass, London.

Chapter 26

TERRORISM: AN EMPIRICAL ANALYSIS

WALTER ENDERS

Department of Economics, Finance, and Legal Studies, Culverhouse College of Commerce & Business Administration, University of Alabama, Tuscaloosa, AL 35487-0024, USA
e-mail: wenders@cba.ua.edu

Contents

Abstract	816
Keywords	816
1. Introduction	817
2. Statistical properties of the terrorist incident types	818
2.1. Comparison of data sets	824
3. Counterterrorism policy: The substitution effect	832
3.1. Testing the HPF model	834
4. Terrorism since 9/11	840
4.1. Effects on the attack modes	841
4.2. Effects on the location of incidents	845
5. Measuring the economic costs of terrorism	849
5.1. Case studies	853
5.2. Microeconomic consequences of terrorism	855
5.2.1. Tourism	855
5.2.2. Net foreign direct investment (NFDI)	857
5.2.3. Trade influence	857
5.2.4. Financial markets	858
6. Measuring the economic determinants of terrorism	859
7. Conclusions and assessment	862
References	864

Handbook of Defense Economics, Volume 2
Edited by Todd Sandler and Keith Hartley
© 2007 Elsevier B.V.   All rights reserved
DOI: 10.1016/S1574-0013(06)02026-6

Abstract

The chapter surveys the empirical literature concerning the measurement of terrorism, effectiveness of counterterrorism policies, the economic consequences of terrorism, and the economic causes of terrorism. In Section 2, terrorist incidents are grouped according to incident type, victim, and location. It is shown that terrorism began a steady decline in all regions (except for Eurasia) during the early to mid-1990s. However, the severity of the typical incident has been increasing over time. Also, several different data sets are compared in order to judge the reliability of alternative methods of obtaining and coding the data. Section 3 discusses a number of empirical studies that measure the effects of counterterrorism policies on the overall level of terrorism and on the various sub-components of the overall series. In accord with the rational-actor model, an increase in the "relative price" of one type of terrorist activity induces a substitution out of that activity and into the now relatively less-expensive activity. Logistically similar activities display the greatest substitution possibilities. Moreover, periods of high-terrorism seem to be less persistent than periods with less terrorism. This is consistent with the notion that terrorists face a resource constraint. Section 4 pays special attention to the changes in terrorism due to the events of September 11, 2001 (9/11) and the resulting changes in counterterrorism policy. It is shown that the post-9/11 counterterrorism policies hampered al-Qaida's ability to direct logistically complex operations such as assassinations and hostage takings. The main influence of 9/11 has been on the composition, and not the overall level of terrorism. There has been a ratcheting-up of serious terrorist attacks against the US targets so that Americans are safer at home, but not abroad, following 9/11 and the enhanced homeland security. Section 5 surveys a number of empirical papers that attempt to estimate the macroeconomic and microeconomic costs of terrorism. Papers surveyed in the first part of the section indicate that the overall macroeconomic costs of terrorism are low. However, it is argued that the methodological complexities of estimating the macroeconomic costs of terrorism on a cross-section of widely disparate nations are nearly insurmountable. The macroeconomic costs of terrorism are best measured on a country-by-country basis. The second part of the section summarizes empirical studies of the microeconomic costs of terrorism on tourism, net foreign direct investment, international trade flows, and financial markets in selected countries. Section 6 considers the economic determinants of terrorism. Particular attention is paid to the common presumption that terrorism is caused by a lack of economic opportunities. Conclusions and directions for future research are contained in Section 7.

Keywords

counterterrorism, data set, rational-actor model, substitution effect, 9/11, al-Qaida, economic consequences, macroeconomic costs, tourism, domestic terrorism, and foreign direct investment

JEL classification: C51, C81, D74

1. Introduction

The purpose of this chapter is to survey the empirical literature concerning the effectiveness of counterterrorism policies, the economic consequences of terrorism, and the economic causes of terrorism. A precondition for any successful empirical study is to have a clear and consistent definition of the variables used in the analysis. Toward this end, it is useful to consider what is generally meant by the term "terrorism".

Terrorism is the premeditated use or threat of use of violence by individuals or subnational groups to obtain a political or social objective through the intimidation of a large audience beyond that of the immediate victims. For our purposes, there are two key ingredients in the definition. The first is that there needs to be a political or social motive for a crime to be defined as terrorism. Eric Harris and Dylan Klebold, the shooters in the Columbine HS rampage, were not terrorists because they had no political motive for their actions. The second is that the intent of the act must be to cause the intimidation of an audience beyond the immediate victims. Since terrorists undertake violent actions so as to pressure governments to grant political concessions, the motives of the individuals conducting the act are essential to the definition. John Wilkes Booth, the assassin of President Lincoln, was not a terrorist because he did not intend to intimidate a wide audience while Khalid Islambouli, the assassin of Anwar Sadat, was a terrorist because his actions were clearly geared to influence a worldwide audience. Terrorism is transnational when an incident in one country involves perpetrators, victims, institutions, governments, or citizens of another country.

Civil wars, insurgencies, and other forms of political violence may include terrorism as a tactic although this need not be the case. The usual distinction between warfare and terrorism is that attacks against armed forces and occupying armies are considered warfare while attacks against civilians are terrorism. There is a degree of ambiguity when peacekeepers and passive military targets are the intended victims of an attack. As such, there is not universal agreement about this important aspect of the definition. As discussed in Enders and Sandler (2006a), the US Department of Defense would include an attack against a roadside convoy in Iraq as a terrorist action. For our purposes, it is not especially important to focus on the most appropriate definition of terrorism. Instead, these ambiguities serve as a warning for empirical researchers using terrorism data. Regardless of the precise form of the definition actually used in a study, it is important to use a consistent definition across the entire span of the data. Pooling data from a source that uses a broad definition of terrorism with data from a source that uses a narrow definition is likely to result in biased results. Similarly, if a consistent definition is not used in a time-series study, the cyclical and trend components of the data are likely to be misidentified. For example, broadening the definition near the end of the sample period is likely to manifest itself in an apparent upward trend in terrorism.

Although the need for a consistent definition may seem obvious, coders of a particular data set may introduce a change in the definition in a number of subtle ways. For example, until 2003, the US Department of State (various issues) published a chronology of *significant* terrorist incidents in *Patterns of Global Terrorism* (PGT). However, the selection criteria were never clearly specified. What may be newsworthy or significant in one year may seem commonplace in another. For example, PGT reported no injuries on February 4, 1993 when a Molotov cocktail was thrown at a tour bus located outside of a hotel near Cairo, Egypt. It is not clear whether such an attack would appear in the chronology of a more recent issue. To be fair, any chronology of terrorism is necessarily faced with a host of coding problems. Such data sets rely on second-hand sources (i.e., newspaper and media accounts) so that incidents not deemed newsworthy are excluded from the counts. It is also the case that a number of terrorist actions, such as nonspecific threats, are unknown to the media so that these actions are excluded from the data set as well. Moreover, coders must use their judgment since it is not always clear whether a crime is actually terrorism. For example, it may not be clear that a crime has a political motive because the perpetrator's identity is unknown.

   The remainder of this chapter is organized as follows. Section 2 considers the statistical properties of a number of different measures of terrorism. When all terrorist incidents are grouped according to the incident type, victim, and location, it is possible to measure the changing nature of terrorism over time. Also, several different data sets are compared in order to judge the reliability of alternative methods of obtaining and coding the data. Section 3 discusses a number of empirical studies that measure the effects of counterterrorism policies on the overall level of terrorism and on the various subcomponents of the overall series. Section 4 pays special attention to the changes in terrorism due to the events of September 11, 2001 (9/11) and the resulting changes in counterterrorism policy. Section 5 discusses a number of empirical papers that attempt to estimate the macroeconomic and microeconomic costs of terrorism. The first part of the section shows that the methodological complexities of estimating the macroeconomic costs of terrorism on a cross-section of widely disparate nations are nearly insurmountable. The macroeconomic costs of terrorism are best measured on a country-by-country basis. The second part of the section summarizes empirical studies of the microeconomic costs of terrorism on tourism, net foreign direct investment, international trade flows, and financial markets in selected countries. Section 6 considers the economic determinants of terrorism. Particular attention is paid to the common presumption that terrorism is caused by a lack of economic opportunities. Conclusions and directions for future research are contained in Section 7.

2. Statistical properties of the terrorist incident types

Unless otherwise stated, the data used in this article draws on *International Terrorism: Attributes of Terrorist Events* (ITERATE) developed by Mickolus et al. (2004). Note that domestic terrorist incidents are explicitly excluded from the data set. Also excluded are actions involving insurgencies, attacks on occupying armies, guerrilla attacks on military targets, and declared wars. However, ITERATE does classify attacks against civilians, military contractors, or the dependents of military personnel as terrorist acts

Table 1
Number of incidents by type (1968–2004): ITERATE data

Incident type code	Incident type	Number of incidents
1	Kidnapping	1267
2	Barricade and hostage seizure	181
3	Occupation of facilities without hostage seizure	76
4	Letter or parcel bombing	452
5	Incendiary bombing, arson, Molotov cocktail	1018
6	Explosive bombing	4032
7	Armed attack involving missiles	48
8	Armed attack – other, including mortars and bazookas	1363
9	Aerial hijacking	363
10	Takeover of a nonaerial means of transportation	59
11	Assassination, murder	1101
12	Sabotage, not involving explosives or arson	32
13	Pollution, including chemical and biological agents	25
14	Nuclear-related weapons attack	1
15	Threat with no subsequent terrorist action	1127
16	Theft, break-in of facilities	111
17	Conspiracy to commit terrorist action	281
18	Hoax (for example, claiming a nonexistent bomb)	322
19	Other actions	402
20	Sniping at buildings, other facilities	130
21	Shoot-out with police	46
22	Arms smuggling	92
23	Car bombing	193
24	Suicide car bombing	40
25	Suicide bombing	30
	Unclassified	11
Cumulative total:		12 803

when such attacks are intended to create an atmosphere of fear to foster political objectives. The ITERATE coders rely on newspapers and electronic media to record critical aspects of each incident's date such as the incident date, starting location, ending location, type of attack, the number of wounded, the number of deaths, the nationality of the terrorists (if known), and the number and nationalities of the victims. At the time of this writing, the data set contains 12 803 incidents running from January 1, 1968 through December 31, 2004.

The classification of the incidents into twenty-five different types is reported in Table 1. Notice that there were 7176 total bombings (*Bombings*) (i.e., incident types 4–8 plus types 23–25), accounting for 56% of all recorded incidents. Kidnappings and hostage takings (incident types 1, 2, 9, and 10) account for almost 15% of the total.

Figure 1 shows the time series plots of the annual totals of selected incident series over the 1968 through 2004 period. Panel a shows the annual totals of all incident types (*All*) as well as the number of bombings. Since bombings are the largest component of

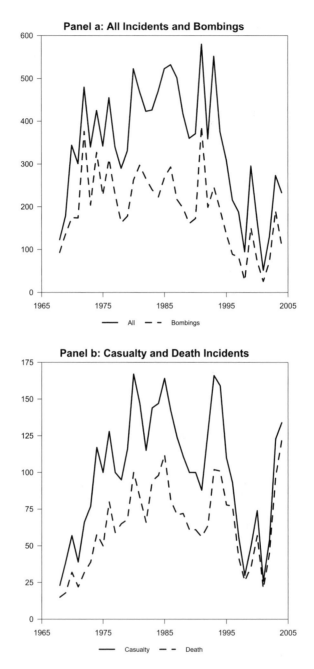

Figure 1. Terrorist incidents by type.

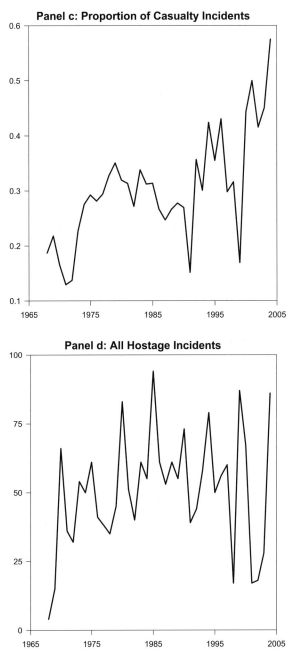

Figure 1. (*continued*)

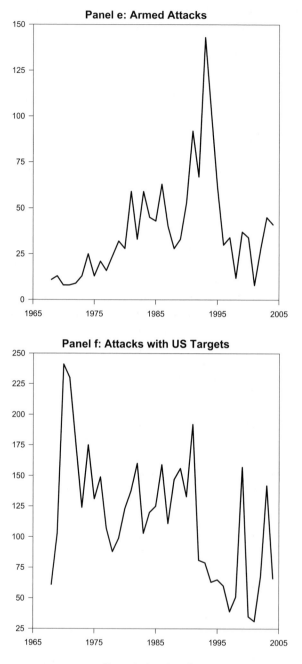

Figure 1. (*continued*)

the *All* series, it is not surprising that the two series track each other reasonably well. Although the incident totals have fallen since the 1980s, there is no clearly discernable downward trend in either series. Instead, it seems as if both series jumped in the early 1970s and fell sharply in the early 1990s. It is the case, however, that the proportion of bombings generally fell in the early 1970s through the late 1980s and then began to increase in 2001. For example, the proportion of bombings to all incidents was 67.8% from 1967–1977, 50.0% of all incidents from 1978–2000, and 55.6% of all incidents from 2001 to 2004.

Panel b of Figure 1 shows the number of incidents with at least one casualty (*Cas*) and the number of incidents with at least one death (*Death*). It is clear from examining Panel b that both series grew steadily throughout the 1970s, plunged in the early 1990s and jumped in 2003 and 2004. It is important to note that the typical incident has become more injurious over time. Beginning around 1995, the *Cas* and *Death* series virtually overlap suggesting that few incidents contain only wounded individuals. Moreover, the proportion of *Cas* incidents to *All* incidents, shown in Panel c, is far higher since the early 1990s than in previous periods. Panel d shows the time series of the number of incidents with a kidnapping or hostage taking; the series, labeled *Hostage*, is comprised by combining incident types $1+2+9+10$. Although the series behaves quite erratically, there are no discernable changes in the overall level of the series. In contrast, *Armed Attacks* (types $7 + 8$) does exhibit a number of structural breaks. After a gradual, but steady increase in the 1970s, the series reached a plateau lasting until the late 1980s. At that point, *Armed Attacks* increased sharply and, in the early 1990s, fell back to its earlier levels. In spite of the attention paid to attacks against the United States and it citizens, the number of attacks with a US target (*UStgts*) fell in the early 1990s. However, in 1999, *UStgts* jumped from 51 to 157 and in 2003, the number jumped from 68 to 142.

Table 2 shows the means and their standard errors for selected incident types, including suicide incidents, for several sample periods. As suggested by the discussion above, the subsample means of *All* for the 1980s and for the 2000–2004 period are significantly different from the overall sample mean of 345.73 incidents per year. It is interesting that the 2000–2004 subsample mean of the *Death* series is not significantly different from that of the overall period. However, the standard error of the mean for 2000–2004 ($\text{SE}(\bar{x}) = 18.19$) is far in excess of that for the overall period. This is due to the huge jump in *Death* incidents 2003 and 2004. Similar remarks can be made for the *Hostage, Bombings* and *UStgts* series in that the standard error of the mean is decidedly different from that of the overall period. Transnational suicide attacks (types 24 and 25) jumped to unprecedented levels, averaging 11 incidents per year, over the 2000–2004 period.

Figure 2 shows the regional breakdown of the *All* series using the identical regional breakdowns as in PGT. The regions are the Western Hemisphere, Africa (excluding North Africa), Asia (South and East Asia, Australia, and New Zealand), Eurasia (Central Asia, Russia, and the Ukraine), Europe (West and East Europe), and the Middle East (including North Africa). As such, most of the Islamic population falls into the

Table 2
Sample means of selected incident types (incidents per year)

		1968–2004	1968–1979	1980–1989	1990–1999	2000–2004
All	Mean ($\bar{x}$)	345.73	364.80	464.60	334.10	171.00
	SE($\bar{x}$)	22.59	20.55	18.03	47.86	38.80
Death	Mean ($\bar{x}$)	63.81	50.50	83.80	64.30	68.40
	SE($\bar{x}$)	4.63	5.91	5.28	8.14	18.19
Bombings	Mean ($\bar{x}$)	193.95	236.60	242.40	168.60	94.20
	SE($\bar{x}$)	14.63	23.82	13.68	31.71	27.62
Hostage	Mean ($\bar{x}$)	50.54	45.80	61.40	56.30	43.20
	SE($\bar{x}$)	3.53	3.67	5.00	6.49	14.05
Armed attacks	Mean ($\bar{x}$)	38.14	16.90	43.10	63.10	31.20
	SE($\bar{x}$)	4.72	2.61	4.18	12.51	6.49
Suicide attacks	Mean ($\bar{x}$)	1.89	0.00	1.10	0.40	11.00
	SE($\bar{x}$)	0.86	0.00	0.31	0.31	4.89
Proportion	Mean ($\bar{x}$)	0.305	0.248	0.293	0.307	0.477
	SE($\bar{x}$)	0.016	0.013	0.005	0.015	0.010
UStgts	Mean ($\bar{x}$)	115.89	152.00	134.20	92.00	68.40
	SE($\bar{x}$)	8.53	16.76	6.55	16.08	19.92

Notes: Mean ($\bar{x}$) denotes the sample (or subsample) mean of the series in question and SE($\bar{x}$) denotes the standard error of the mean.

Middle East, Eurasia, and Asia regions. The interesting feature to note about the figure is that terrorism began a fairly steady decline in all regions (except for Eurasia) during the early to mid-1990s. However, the number of African incidents spiked in the years 1999 and 2000. Terrorism in Asia and the Middle East jumped markedly in 2002 and has remained high.

2.1. Comparison of data sets

In addition to ITERATE, there are a number of other publicly available data sets record-ing terrorist incidents. The National Memorial Institute for the Prevention of Terrorism [MIPT (2005)] maintains an online data set that can be accessed without a fee. The data set begins in 1968 and is updated regularly. Like ITERATE, it is possible to ob-tain information about terrorist incidents by date, tactic, target, or the starting region. Beginning in 1998, the MIPT data set includes both domestic and transnational terror-ist incidents. One drawback of the data set is that it is possible to obtain information about the individual incident types on a regional basis, but not on a country-by-country basis.

Another online data set is maintained by The International Policy Institute for Coun-terterrorism [IPIC (2005)]. IPIC (2005) describes its 1427 terrorist incidents for 1986–

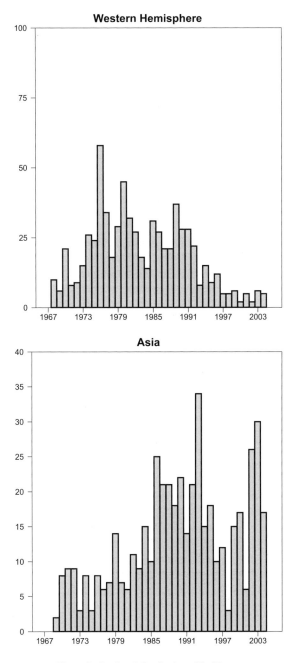

Figure 2. Regional distribution of incidents.

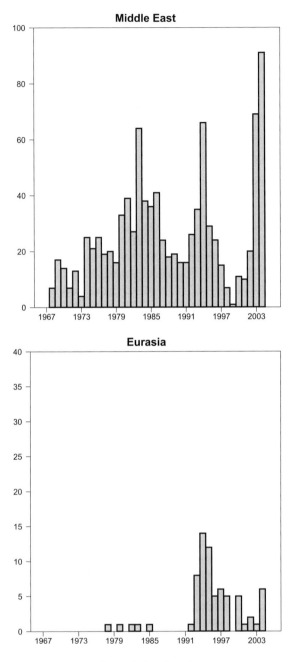

Figure 2. (*continued*)

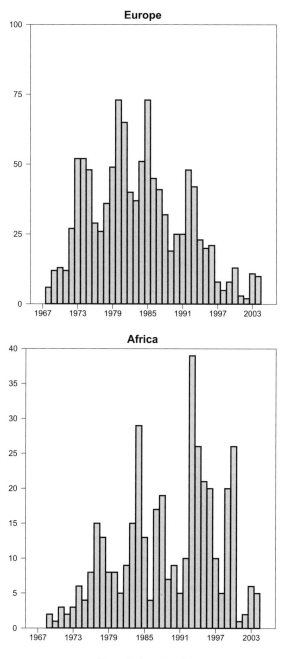

Figure 2. (*continued*)

2002 as "selected" transnational terrorist incidents. The IPIC website does not list its criteria for selecting which incidents to include and which to exclude. This is important because ITERATE and PGT record many times the number of incidents during the same period. For example, as compared to some of the ITERATE series shown in Figure 1, the IPIC (2005) data set lists only 22 incidents for 1988, 89 for 1989, and 26 for 1990, and 37 for 1991. Even though it excludes many incidents, the IPIC data set also has an over-reporting problem. Moreover, there seem to be a large number of incidents that might be crimes, rather than terrorism. Some Palestinian attacks in Israel are considered transnational even though the acts seem to be purely domestic. Consider an incident occurring on July 23, 1994. The description is "Two unknown Palestinians stabbed and seriously injured an American woman in the Arab quarter of the Old City of Jerusalem. The assailants escaped unharmed." Moreover, no one ever took responsibility for the act, and the group conducting the act is "Unknown". It is possible that this attack was a simple crime. In fact, IPIC data include a disproportionate number of incidents from the Middle East. This should not be too surprising since the data set is maintained by the Interdisciplinary Center Herziliya in Israel (http://www.ict.org.il).

As mentioned above, the US Department of State's (various years) *Chronology of Significant Terrorist Incidents* appeared as an appendix in each issue of *Patterns of Global Terrorism*. The State Department discontinued publication of GPT after a controversy surrounding the possible omission of some incidents in order to make it appear that the so-called 'War on Terror' is being won. Some of the disagreement concerned the issue of whether attacks on US troops in Iraq should be included in the 2004 totals. This was on the heels of a political embarrassment in June 2003 when the number of incidents and fatalities had to be revised substantially upward in the face of acknowledged omissions from the original report. The incident count for 2004 is unavailable and it is unclear how subsequent reporting of terrorism will be conducted. Title 22 of the United States Code, Section 2656f, requires the Department of State to provide Congress with a complete annual report on terrorism.

Figure 3 shows a comparison of the yearly ITERATE, MIPT and PGT incident totals. For comparability, the ITERATE totals shown in the figure have been purged of threats and hoaxes. The reason is that beginning in 1996 ITERATE no longer used the Foreign Broadcast Information Service *Daily Reports*. Thus, the totals following this date may not be directly comparable with those of earlier dates. Since most of the omitted incidents are likely to be threats and hoaxes, all threats and hoaxes are excluded from the ITERATE series shown in Figure 3.

The overall shapes of the three time series plots are somewhat similar. All rose from slightly over 100 annual incidents in 1968 and 1969 and reached their highest sustained levels in the 1980s. Beginning in 1991, all three series began to decline. Nevertheless there are enough differences among the series that the results of an empirical study might hinge on which of the three data sets is used. Notice that the values of PGT series generally exceed those of the other two series. This is especially true in the mid-1970s and in the 1980s. The gap remains quite sizable even if threats and hoaxes are added back to the ITERATE data. Also notice that the PGT data shows an increase

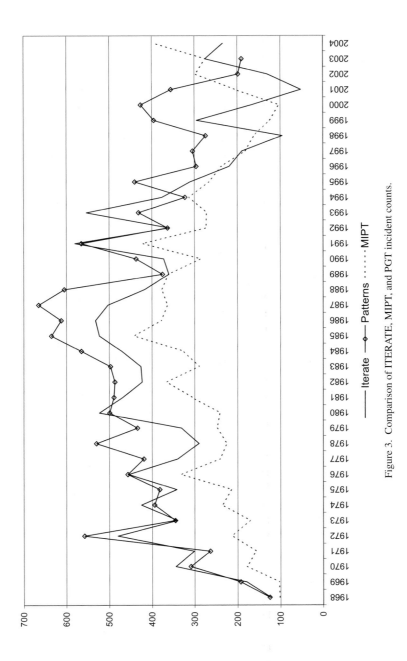

Figure 3. Comparison of ITERATE, MIPT, and PGT incident counts.

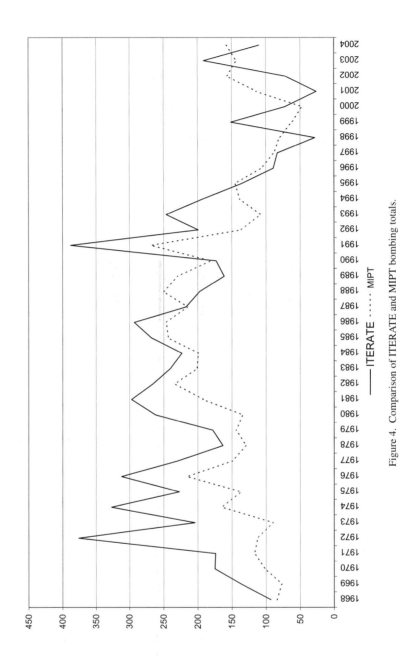

Figure 4. Comparison of ITERATE and MIPT bombing totals.

Panel a: MIPT Data Set

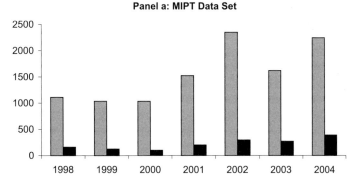

Panel b: Patterns of Global Terrorism

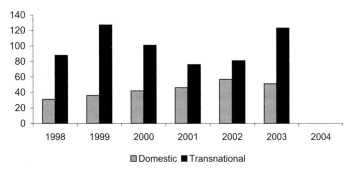

☐ Domestic ■ Transnational

Figure 5. Domestic and transnational incidents.

in terrorism in the late 1970s while the MIPT data and ITERATE show declines. The PGT data indicates a sharp decline in terrorism following 9/11 while the ITERATE data shows a sizable jump. The simple correlation coefficient between ITERATE and MIPT series is 0.66, and between ITERATE and PGT is 0.65. The simple correlation coefficient between MIPT and PGT is 0.78.

Comparison by type: It seems likely that major incidents get reported in any reasonable chronology. The main differences are likely to concern incident types such as bombings. Bombings usually account for approximately half of all incidents. However, it is unclear whether to record a letter-bombing campaign as a single incident or as the number of letter bombs actually received. Figure 4 records the annual incident totals of all bombings for ITERATE and for the MIPT data set through 1997. ITERATE reports far more incidents than the MIPT data set throughout the 1970s. The simple correlation coefficient between the two incident series is only 0.52.

Domestic versus transnational incidents. Although transnational terrorist attacks usually receive more media attention than domestic incidents, there are far more domestic incidents than transnational incidents. Panel a of Figure 5 shows the annual total of domestic and transnational incidents in the MIPT data set. The proportion of transnational to all incidents (both domestic and transnational) was 12.7% in 1998, fell to 9.1% in 2000, and rose to 14.9% in 2004. It should be clear that the relationship between domestic and transnational terrorism is not 1:1. Studies that use transnational terrorism as a 'proxy' for all terrorism may be seriously flawed. The problem is exacerbated using subcomponents of the series. For example, most incidents within continental Europe have been transnational while Israel has many domestic incidents relative to transnational incidents.

It is interesting to compare the 'selected' incident totals from the 1998–2003 *Patterns of Global Terrorism*. I coded the type of each PGT-listed incident using the same classification system as ITERATE.[1] The time paths of the numbers of domestic and transnational incidents are shown in Panel b Figure 5. Notice that there was a strong bias toward transnational incidents although the totals for domestic terrorism grew relative to those of transnational terrorism. In part, this growth reflected changes in the US State Department's preferences over the types of the various incidents. This shows the danger of using a data set containing "selected" incidents.

3. Counterterrorism policy: The substitution effect

Any counterterrorism policy that underestimates the wherewithal and resourcefulness of terrorists is doomed to fail. In order to predict new types of terrorist attack modes, the likelihood of an attack on a particular target or location, or the likely behavior of terrorists in response to a counterterrorism initiative, it is necessary to posit a theory of terrorist behavior. The rational-actor model leads to a number of straightforward predictions concerning the behavior of a terrorist network or cell. The hallmark of the rational-actor model is that terrorists use their scarce resources so as to maximize the expected value of their utility. This is not to say that the preferences of terrorists are, in any sense, laudable. Instead, the model posits that, for a given set of preferences, terrorists will make choices that are most likely to bring out their most preferred outcomes. In contrast, if terrorists are assumed to be completely irrational, there is no way of knowing how they will respond to future events. Moreover, the rational-actor model has a number of straightforward predictions that have proven to be consistent with the data.

Gary Becker (1971) developed the household production function (HPF) model to analyze decision making for a family group. Enders and Sandler (1993) formally extended the HPF model to study the behavior of rational terrorists. The basic premise of their model is that a terrorist group derives utility from a shared political goal. The shared goal could be the establishment of a religious state or the elimination of an unspecified grievance stemming from income inequality, racial or religious discrimination, ideological differences, or a lack of political or economic freedom. This shared goal can be obtained from the consumption of various basic commodities such as media attention, political turmoil, popular support for their cause, and the creation of an atmosphere of

---

[1] Ting Qin and Ashley Allen were especially helpful in preparing the data.

fear and intimidation. Each basic commodity can be produced using a number of alternative political and economic strategies. At one extreme, the group might simply choose legal activities such as advertising its cause, marching on the capitol, or running its own candidates for office. Alternatively, acts of civil disobedience might be undertaken by blocking entry to university or government buildings or by sit-ins at racially segregated lunch counters. At the other extreme, the group might resort to direct armed conflict or guerilla attacks. The point is that the group must select among the various ways that can be used to produce the basic commodities. If the group chooses to use terrorist tactics, it can choose among attack modes such as skyjackings, kidnappings, or suicide bombings.

The terrorist group has access to a finite set of resources including financial assets, weapons and buildings, personnel, and entrepreneurial abilities. Given its resources a rational terrorist group selects the set of activities that maximizes the expectation of its attaining the shared goal. Since terrorists can "save" their resources for future attacks, rational terrorists will time their attacks to enhance their overall effectiveness. Of course, groups such as the PLO and the IRA have used combinations of various legal and illegal means in an attempt to bring about their shared political goal.

The choices made by the group will be influenced by the prices of the various terrorist and nonterrorist activities. The full price of any particular attack mode includes the value of the resources used to plan and execute the attack, and the cost of casualties to group members. Certain attack modes are more likely to expose the group's membership to capture than others. The price of a suicide bombing includes the direct costs of the bomb, the costs of grooming the perpetrator to ensure that the attack takes place, and the cost to protect the group's security for failed attacks. At the other end of the spectrum, threats and hoaxes typically require few inputs.

The key feature of any antiterrorism policy is that it can influence the prices, resource supplies and the payoffs faced by terrorists. Enhanced airport security increases the logistical complexity of a skyjacking and raises its price. If, at the same time, governments do not increase security at ports-of-entry, attacks relying on contraband become relatively cheaper. Similarly, if immigration officials make it more difficult for terrorists to enter the United States, a terrorist group might attack US interests located abroad (for example, tourists and firms). Hence, a government policy that increases the price of one type of attack mode will induce a substitution away from that mode into other logistically similar incident types.

Enders and Sandler (1993, 2004) summarize the four key propositions of the model as:

PROPOSITION 1. *An increase in the relative price of one type of terrorist activity will cause the terrorist group to substitute out of the relatively expensive activity and into terrorist and nonterrorist activities that are now relatively less expensive.*

PROPOSITION 2. *Terrorist attack modes that are logistically similar and yield similar basic commodities will display the greatest substitution possibilities. Since the effects of complementary events are mutually reinforcing, an increase (decrease) in the price of one activity will cause that activity and all complements to fall (rise) in number.*

PROPOSITION 3. *An increase in the price of all terrorist activities or a decrease in the price of nonterrorist activities will decrease the overall level of terrorism.*

PROPOSITION 4. *For normal goods, an increase (decrease) in the resource base will cause a terrorist group to increase (decrease) the level of nonterrorist activities.*

3.1. Testing the HPF model

Enders and Sandler (1993) test Propositions 1 and 2 by examining how a number of counterterror measures induced substitutions across the various terrorism attack modes. Although they consider a number of substitution possibilities, it seems most useful to examine their five-variable 'Model 2' that uses skyjackings (*Sky*), incidents involving a hostage (*Hostage*), assassinations (*Assns*), threats and hoaxes (*Th*) and all other incident types (*OT*).[2] Since the data begins in the first quarter of 1968 (1968:1) and runs through 1988:4, it does not contain the period during which ITERATE stopped using information from *Daily Reports*. The policy interventions are dummy variables representing the installation of metal detectors in airports (*Metal*), two embassy fortifications (*Emb76* and *Emb85*) and the retaliatory raid on Libya (*Libya*). Specifically, in January 1973, metal detectors began to be installed in US airports and, shortly thereafter, in major international airports worldwide. *Emb76* refers to a more than doubling of US embassy security expenditures in 1976 and *Emb85* refers to another enhancement of embassy security in October 1985 resulting from Public Law 98-533. In April 1986, the US launched a retaliatory raid on Libya for its role in the terrorist bombing of the LaBelle Discotheque. Since the effects on the raid were temporary, *Libya* is a temporary dummy variable equal to one in 1986:2. Mathematical characterizations of the intervention variables are provided in Table 3.

Consider the standard vector autoregression (VAR) model augmented with dummy variables to capture the effects of the four interventions:

$$
\begin{bmatrix} Sky_t \\ Hostage_t \\ Assns_t \\ Th_t \\ Ot_t \end{bmatrix} = \begin{bmatrix} A_{11}(L) & \cdots & A_{15}(L) \\ A_{21}(L) & \cdots & A_{25}(L) \\ & \vdots & \ddots & \vdots \\ A_{51}(L) & \cdots & A_{55}(L) \end{bmatrix} \begin{bmatrix} Sky_{t-1} \\ Hostage_{t-1} \\ Assns_{t-1} \\ Th_{t-1} \\ Ot_{t-1} \end{bmatrix}
$$

$$
+ \begin{bmatrix} c_{11} & \cdots & c_{14} \\ c_{21} & \cdots & c_{24} \\ \vdots & \ddots & \vdots \\ c_{51} & \cdots & c_{54} \end{bmatrix} \begin{bmatrix} Metal \\ Emb76 \\ Emb85 \\ Libya \end{bmatrix} + \begin{bmatrix} \varepsilon_{1t} \\ \varepsilon_{2t} \\ \varepsilon_{3t} \\ \varepsilon_{4t} \\ \varepsilon_{5t} \end{bmatrix} \tag{1}
$$

[2] To avoid overlap in the series, all hostage events not involving a skyjacking were added together to form *Hostage*. The *OT* consists primarily of bombings.

Table 3
Interactions among the five incident series and the interventions

	Correlation matrix of the SUR residuals					Variance decompositions: 8-quarter horizon				
	Sky	Hostage	Assns	Th	OT	Sky	Hostage	Assns	Th	OT
Sky	1.000	0.103	−0.159	0.364	−0.129	85.2	4.90	5.38	2.54	2.00
Hostage		1.000	0.098	0.093	0.040	13.9	68.7	0.62	1.20	15.8
Assns			1.000	0.311	0.196	13.1	6.85	61.0	0.564	18.5
Th				1.000	0.211	34.4	7.97	11.4	35.7	10.5
OT					1.000	4.97	3.34	10.5	9.33	71.9
	Short-run effects of the interventions					*Long-run effects of the interventions*				
Metal	−14.1***	11.6***	6.58**	1.75	11.3	−13.0^a	5.3^a	4.1^a	−9.5^a	17.8^a
Emb76	2.51*	−1.41	3.56*	8.67***	−18.6*	0.98^a	−0.20^a	8.2^a	11.8^a	−21.1^a
Emb85	0.100	3.54**	−0.967	−5.31**	−2.81	0.52^a	5.4^a	−1.7	4.1^a	−5.4
Libya	−4.83	−1.62	1.57	50.5***	58.4**	NA	NA	NA	NA	NA

Description of the interventions:

  Metal: The United States began to install metal detectors in airports on 5 January, 1973. *Metal* = 0 for $t < 1973{:}1$ and = 1 otherwise.

  Emb76: A doubling of spending to fortify and secure US embassies beginning in October 1976. *Emb76* = 0 for $t < 1976{:}4$ and = 1 otherwise.

  Emb85: A significant increase in spending to secure US embassies was authorized in 1985:4. *Emb85* = 0 for $t < 1985{:}4$ and = 1 otherwise.

  Libya: In April, 1986, the US undertook a retaliatory raid against Libya for its involvement in the LaBelle Discothequet bombing. *Libya* = 1 in 1986:2 and = 0 otherwise.

[a] An intervention variable can significantly impact a series directly or have a significant indirect effect though the interaction of the variables in the VAR. At the 10% significance level, all of the long-run effects (except for *EMB85* on *Assns* and *OT*) are significant. By construction, *Libya* has only temporary effects.

  *Significance at the 10% level.

  **Idem, 5%.

  ***Idem, 1%.

where the expressions $A_{ij}(L)$ are polynomials in the lag operator L such that $A_{ij}(L)Sky_{t-1} = a_{ij}(1)Sky_{t-1} + a_{ij}(2)Sky_{t-2} + a_{ij}(3)Sky_{t-3} + \cdots$, the c_{ij} measure the influence of the contemporaneous effect of intervention j on incident type i; and the ε_i are the errors from the regression for incident type i.

The details of the estimation technique are described in Enders and Sandler (1993) and background on the VAR methodology is detailed in Enders (2004). For our purposes, it is sufficient to point out that ordinary least squares (OLS) provides efficient estimates of the coefficients $a_{ij}(k)$ and c_{ij} since all of the equations have the same set of regressors. It is important to note that a statistically significant value of c_{ij} means that intervention type j has a contemporaneous effect on incident type i. Also note that the presence of the various $A_{ij}(L)$ allow for a rich variety of interactions among the variables in that incident type j can have a lagged effect in incident type i. If, for example, any of the coefficients of $A_{12}(L)$ are statistically different from zero, then *Hostage* affects *Sky* with a lag. Finally, the contemporaneous interaction among incident types i and j are captured by the correlation coefficients between ε_i and ε_j.

The actual quarterly totals of *Sky*, *Hostage*, *Assns* and *OT* are shown as the dashed lines in Figure 6. The solid lines are the estimated time paths of the one-step-ahead forecasts of the series using the various interventions. As a visual aid, the vertical lines represent the starting dates of the four interventions.

From Figure 6, you can see the abrupt changes in *Sky*, *Hostage*, and *OT* beginning in 1973:1. As recorded in Table 3, on impact, metal detectors decreased skyjackings by 14.1 incidents per quarter. However, as predicted by the HPF approach, an increase in the price of a skyjacking induces substitutions into similar incident types. We found that the impact effect of *Metal* was to significantly increase *Hostage* incidents by 11.6 incidents per quarter and assassinations by 6.58 incidents per quarter. The impact effects of *Metal* on *Th* and *OT* were not statistically significant. Hence, there is strong evidence that terrorists substituted from skyjackings into logistically complex *Hostage* and *Assns* incidents.

The first embassy fortification (*Emb76*) shows few important effects. Threats and hoaxes showed a significant jump but none of the other series showed any significant changes at the 5% level. Of course, it is possible for *Th* to increase without changes in the levels of the other series since threats and hoaxes require few resources. Another interesting substitution was that the second embassy fortification (*Emb85*) acted to decrease threats by about by -5.51 incidents per quarter but to increase *Hostage* by about 3.54 incidents per quarter.

There seems to be a slight increase in *OT* following the installation of metal detectors, but this increase is not statistically significant. The embassy fortifications seemed to have no significant effects on any of the series. Other then the installation of metal detectors, the only significant intervention was the Libyan bombing, which caused the number of other incidents (*OT*) to jump sharply and then fall back to its pre-intervention mean. Since bombings, threats, and hoaxes are usually logistically simple and utilize few resources relative to the other types of incidents it is fairly easy to ratchet-up the number of such incidents.

The interactions among the various incident types can be obtained from the impulse response functions. The upper right-hand portion of Table 3 shows the impulse responses using an eight quarter forecasting horizon. Notice that *Sky* explains 85.2% of its own forecast error variance; no other incident type explains more than 5.38% of the movements in *Sky*. This is consistent with the presumption that skyjackings are logistically complex incidents that are not easily substituted for by the other types of incidents. Nevertheless, *Sky* explains 13.9, 13.1 and 34.4% of *Hostage*, *Assns*, and *Th*, respectively. Also note that *Hostage*, *Assns*, and *OT* explain 68.7, 61.0 and 71.9% of their own forecast error variance, respectively. In contrast, the low resource-intensive incident type, *Th*, is the only one that explains a small proportion (35.5%) of its own forecast error variance. The notion is that *Th* strongly responds to changes in the other incident types.

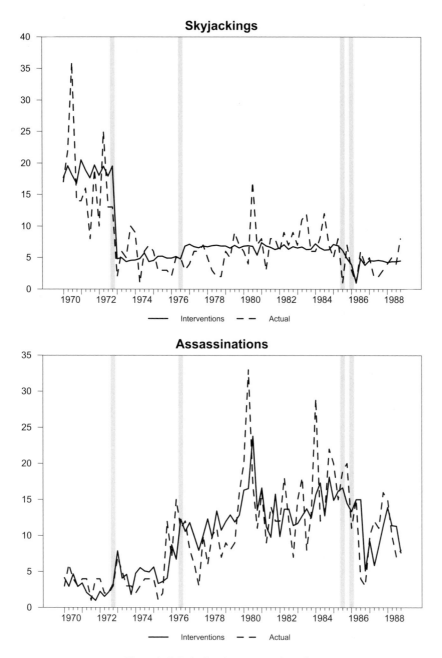

Figure 6. Substitutions between attack modes.

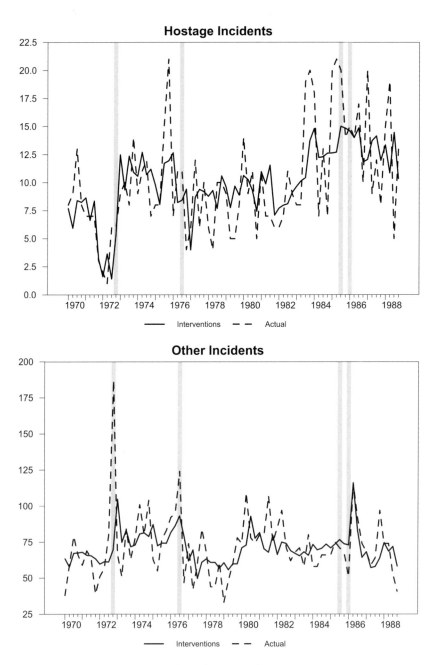

Figure 6. (*continued*)

Enders and Sandler (1993) did not report the cross-equation correlations of the residuals from their seemingly unrelated regressions (SUR) estimation. Nevertheless, as reported in Table 3, it is interesting to note the correlations of the residuals from the *Th* equation with those of the *Sky* and *Assns* equations are 0.364 and 0.311, respectively. Since there are 80 residuals from each equation, the *prob*-values are both less than 0.01. Hence, it appears that *Th* is complementary with *Sky* and *Assns* in that the innovations in each are positively correlated. The cross-correlation coefficient between *Th* and *OT* is marginally significant at the 5% level. None of the others are statistically different from zero at the 5% level.

In a separate study, Enders and Sandler (2005b) indirectly tested Proposition 4 by comparing the durations of high versus low periods of terrorist activity. The basic notion is that in relatively tranquil times, terrorists can replenish and stockpile resources, recruit new members, raise funds and plan for future attacks. Terrorism can remain low until an event occurs that switches the system into the high-terrorism regime. Because each terrorist attack utilizes scarce resources, high-terrorism states are not likely to exhibit a high degree of persistence. On the other hand, periods with little terrorism can be highly persistent to shocks since few resources are expended when terrorism is low.

For the 1968:1–2000:4 period, the *Cas* series seems to be well-estimated by the linear process (with t-statistics in parentheses):

$$Cas_t = \underset{(2.83)}{5.91} + \underset{(2.98)}{0.261\,Cas_{t-1}} + \underset{(3.59)}{0.310\,Cas_{t-2}} + \underset{(2.40)}{0.209\,Cas_{t-3}} + \varepsilon_t. \qquad (2)$$

Enders and Sandler (2005b) report that this linear specification seems adequate in that it satisfies the standard diagnostic tests, the coefficients are significant at conventional levels, pretests for a unit-root indicate that the *Cas* series is stationary, and the Ljung-Box Q-statistics indicate that the residuals are serially uncorrelated. As an alternative, they estimated the *Cas* series as a 2-regime threshold autoregressive (TAR) process. Consider:

$$Cas_t = [\underset{(3.19)}{17.87} + \underset{(1.83)}{0.189\,Cas_{t-1}} + \underset{(1.83)}{0.237\,Cas_{t-2}}]I_t$$
$$ + \left[\underset{(1.48)}{3.92} + \underset{(2.97)}{0.423\,Cas_{t-1}} + \underset{(3.12)}{0.398\,Cas_{t-3}}\right](1 - I_t) + \varepsilon_t; \qquad (3)$$

where $I_t = 0$ when $Cas_{t-2} < 25$ and $I_t = 1$ otherwise.

The TAR model allows for a low-terrorism regime and a high-terrorism regime. When terrorism is low (such that $Cas_{t-2} < 25$ incidents per quarter), $I_t = 0$ so that it is possible to write the equation for casualties as $Cas_t = 3.92 + 0.423Cas_{t-1} + 0.398Cas_{t-3}$. Instead, when terrorism is high (such that $Cas_{t-2} \geqslant 25$ incidents per quarter), $I_t = 1$ so that it is possible to write the equation for casualties as $Cas_t = 17.87 + 0.189Cas_{t-1} + 0.237Cas_{t-2}$.

The threshold model yields very different implications about the behavior of the Cas_t series than the linear model. Since the linear specification makes no distinction between high- and low-terrorism states, the degree of autoregressive decay is constant. Specifically, the degree of persistence is quite large as the largest characteristic root of the linear specification is 0.88. For the TAR specification, there is a different speed-of-adjustment in each of the two regimes. In the high-terrorism regime, the number of incidents gravitates toward the attractor 31.1 [= $17.87 \div (1 - 0.189 - 0.237)$]. As measured by the largest characteristic root, the speed of adjustment is 0.59: when terrorism is high, approximately 60% of each incident is expected to persist into the next period. In contrast, in the low-terrorism regime, the number of incidents gravitates toward 21.9 [= $3.92 \div (1 - 0.423 - 0.398)$]. The largest characteristic root is 0.88, indicating very persistent behavior following a shock. Thus, when the number of incidents is below the threshold value of 25, there is little tendency to return to a long-run mean value. As such, low-terrorism regimes are far more persistent than high-terrorism regimes. The explanation provided by Enders and Sandler (2005b) is that terrorists necessarily expend large quantities of their resources in the high-terrorism regime. As such, resources become scarce and terrorists need to wind-down their campaigns. In contrast, regimes in which the number of incidents is small can persist for long periods of time. They found similar patterns regarding the different rates of persistence in the *All*, *Death*, *Bomb*, *Assns*, and *Hostage* series. The only exception was for the *Th* series; for this series there is more persistence in the high-terrorism state than in the low terrorism state. Of course, this should not be too surprising since threats and hoaxes use relatively small quantities of resources. As such, the value of *Th* can remain high for long periods of time.

4. Terrorism since 9/11

The unprecedented attacks of 9/11 led to unprecedented counterterrorism measures. The US-led invasion of Afghanistan, the passage of the USA Patriot Act, and the formation of the Department of Homeland Security all affected the ability of terrorist groups to organize and function. For example, the USA Patriot Act created a counterterrorism fund, a Federal Bureau of Investigation (FBI) technical support center, a National Electronic Crime Task Force Initiative, and allowed the government greater latitude in intercepting and seizing communications including voice-mail messages. The act also encouraged collaboration among foreign and domestic law enforcement agencies and made money-laundering more difficult by mandating greater regulations of international money transfers. The creation of the Department of Homeland Security (DHS) merged the activities of 22 different agencies by bringing them together in a single cabinet-level department. As a result of this "war on terrorism", about two-thirds of al-Qaida leaders have either been killed or captured. Gerges and Isham (2003) report that more than 3400 al-Qaida suspects have been arrested since 9/11 and the White House (2003) reports that more than $200 million of the network's assets have been frozen since 9/11. At the same time, the War in Iraq has seemingly energized those with grievances against the United States and its Australian and UK allies. After successful al Qaida acts caused the Philippines and Spain to pull their troops from Iraq, it is expected that terrorist groups will be more vigorous in recruiting those willing to engage in terrorist acts.

4.1. Effects on the attack modes

Enders and Sandler (2005a) used several alternative methods to determine how the overall level of terrorism and the various attacks modes utilized changed since 9/11. For each attack mode considered, they estimated an intervention model in the form:

$$y_t = a_0 + A(L)y_{t-1} + \alpha_1 D_p + \alpha_2 D_L + \varepsilon_t, \tag{4}$$

where y_t is the series of interest, D_P and D_L are dummy variables representing September 11, 2001. In Equation (4), D_P is a dummy variable such that $D_P = 1$ if $t = 2001{:}3$ and $D_P = 0$ otherwise. This type of *pulse* variable is appropriate if the 9/11 attacks induced a temporary change in the $\{y_t\}$ series. The magnitude of α_1 indicates the initial effect of 9/11 on y_t and the rate of decay is determined by the largest characteristic root of $A(L)$. To allow for the possibility that 9/11 had a permanent effect on the level of $\{y_t\}$, the second dummy variable in Equation (4) is such that $D_L = 0$ for $t < 2001{:}3$ and $D_L = 1$ for $t \geqslant 2001{:}3$. The impact effect of the *level* dummy variable on $\{y_t\}$ is given by α_2 and the long-run effect of D_L on $\{y_t\}$ is given by $\alpha_2/(1 - \sum a_i)$. Without going into great detail concerning the estimation methodology, the key features of the estimated equation were such that the *pulse* dummies were not statistically significant for any of the attack modes considered. Hence, there were no statistically significant short-run effects in the behavior of any of the incident series that resulted from 9/11. Moreover, the level shift dummy was significant only for the *Hostage* series. The short-run effect is such that *Hostage* incidents fall by 6.05 incidents in 2001:3 and the long-run effect is a decline of approximately 9 incidents per quarter. However, even this finding is problematic because a careful inspection of the *Hostage* series (see Figure 1) shows that the sharp drop in hostage incidents actually occurred in 1999.

Although there is little evidence of shifts in the levels of the various attack modes, Enders and Sandler (2005a) used statistical methods to examine how the composition of the *All* series changed over time. Specifically, they estimated an intervention model in the form of Equation (4) for the ratio of each incident type to *All*. The pulse dummy variable was statistically significant for the proportion of *Death* to *All* (*P_Death*) and for the proportion of *Cas* to *All* (*P_Cas*). On impact, the proportion of incidents with deaths rose by 54 percentage points and the proportion of incidents with casualties rose by 48 percentage points. The level dummy variables, however, were not significant at conventional levels. Hence, the jumps in the *P_Death* and *P_Cas* were not permanent.

The *level* dummy variable was highly significant for the proportion of hostage incidents (*P_Hostage)* and the proportion of deadly incidents due to bombings (*P_Death_B*). The short-run effect reduced *P_Hostage* from approximately 13% to 4% of all incidents. After 9/11, the proportion of hostage incidents was estimated to be near zero. They also found evidence of a significant 16 percentage point decline in the proportion of assassinations to *All* (*P_Assns*) In contrast, the *P_Death_B* series was estimated to rise by 20 percentage points.

The conclusion was that the post-9/11 counterterrorism policies hampered al-Qaida's ability to direct logistically complex operations such as assassinations and hostage takings. However, the main influence of 9/11 has been on the composition, and not the level, of the *All* series. In particular, *P_Hostage* and *P_Assns* fell after 9/11 as terrorists substituted into deadly bombings. As a consequence, the proportion of deadly incidents due to bombings has increased as the proportion of hostage-taking and assassination attacks have decreased. The net result is that al-Qaida has substituted away from logistically complex attacks (e.g., hostage taking and assassinations) to logistically simpler bombings.

One possible weakness of these results is that there might be multiple structural breaks. Enders and Sandler (2000) reported significant changes in terrorism associated with the increase in religious fundamentalism and with the demise of the Soviet Union. The omission of any structural breaks from the estimating equation will result in a misspecified regression equation that might cloud the effects of 9/11. One research strategy is to reestimate Equation (4) by including dummy variables for all such breaks. However, Enders and Sandler (2005a) warn that this strategy can be problematic because there is a danger of *ex post* fitting if break points are selected as a result of an observed change in the variable of interest. In addition, the efficacy of the estimates cannot rely on the usual asymptotic properties of an autoregression because an increase in sample size does nothing to increase the number of points lying between two break points. As such, Enders and Sandler (2005a) go on to use a purely data-driven procedure to select the break dates. Bai and Perron (1998, 2003) developed a procedure that can estimate a model with an unknown number of structural breaks that occur at unspecified dates. The key feature of the Bai–Perron procedure is that the number of breaks and their timing are estimated along with the autoregressive coefficients. Bai and Perron (1998, 2003) also showed how to form confidence intervals for the break dates. This is important because there is visual evidence (see Figure 1) that key changes in some of the incident series actually began prior to 9/11. As such, it is desirable to ascertain whether the changes are due to 9/11 or to forces already in progress. The form of the Bai–Perron specification that was considered is the so-called partial change model:

$$y_t = \alpha_j + \sum_{i=1}^{p} a_i y_{t-i} + \varepsilon_t, \tag{5}$$

where $j = 1, \ldots, m + 1$, and m is the number of breaks. Equation (5) allows for m breaks that manifest themselves by shifts in the intercept of the autoregressive process. The notation is such that there are $m + 1$ intercept terms denoted by α_j. The first break occurs at t_1 so that the duration of the first regime is from $t = 1$ until $t = t_1$, and the duration of the second regime is from $t_1 + 1$ to t_2. Because the mth break occurs at $t = t_m$, the last regime begins at $t_m + 1$ and lasts until the end of the data set. In applied work, it is necessary to specify the maximum number of breaks; our estimation allowed for a maximum of five breaks. The procedure also requires that the minimum regime size (i.e., the minimum number of observations between breaks) be specified. Because

Table 4
Estimates of multiple structural breaks

Series	Break date	Lower	Upper	Initial mean	SR effect	LR effect
All	1994:3	1993:4	1996:4	106.62	−46.46	−62.63
Hostage	2000:3	2000:1	2002:3	13.79	−6.69	−9.94
Bombings	1994:1	1993:3	1996:1	61.50	−33.92	−40.43
Bomb_Cas[a]	1992:3	1989:4	1993:3	15.79	11.20	17.17
	1994:3	1994:1	1996:1		15.64	23.97
Deaths	1975:3	1973:2	1976:2	8.89	7.17	11.01
	1996:2	1994:2	1998:4		−5.81	−8.91

[a]*Bomb_Cas* denotes bombings with at least one casualty.

the data ran through the second quarter of 2003, a minimum break size of six was used in order to permit a break occurring as late as the first quarter of 2002. In principal, it would be possible to allow all coefficients (including the autoregressive coefficients) to change, but this would necessitate estimating a separate $AR(p)$ model for each regime. Since the data include only a small number of post-9/11 observations, this procedure was not possible. Instead, what Bai and Perron (1998, 2003) call the "partial change" model was adopted so that only one new coefficient (i.e., the intercept) was estimated for each regime.

For five selected series, Table 4 reports the point estimate of each break date, the lower and upper bounds of a 95 percent confidence interval around the break dates (lower and upper, respectively), the sample mean in the first regime (initial mean), and the short-run (SR) and long-run (LR) changes due to the break(s). The short-run effect of break j is measured by $\alpha_{j+1} - \alpha_j$ whereas the long-run effect is measured by $(\alpha_{j+1} - \alpha_j)/(1 - \sum a_i)$.

The results using the Bai–Perron procedure reinforce those found for the intervention model. For example, a single structural break, not at 9/11, was found for the *All* series. The most likely estimate of this break is 1994:3; a 95 percent confidence interval for the break date spans the period 1993:4 through 1996:4. The crucial point is that a 95 percent confidence interval for the break date does not include 9/11. Given that bombings constitute half of the *All* series, a similar structural break characterizes *Bombings* at 1994:1.

The *Hostage* series was found to have a single break after 2000:3 (i.e., the new regime begins in 2000:4). The short-run and long-run effects were estimated to be −6.69 and −9.94 incidents per quarter, respectively. Since the 95 percent confidence interval includes 2001:3, it can be claimed that the long-run decline in the mean number of *Hostage* incidents from 13.79 to about 3.85 (13.79 − 9.94 = 3.85) may be attributable to 9/11. There is no evidence of a break in the *Assns* series. Notice that none of the other series contained a break associated with 9/11. However, a careful examination of the table indicates the breaks seem to be associated with the rise of Islamic fundamentalism and the decline of the Cold War. The results for the various proportion series seemed to reinforce this pattern.

It is possible to update the study since the ITERATE data set is currently available through 2004:4. In the following analysis, the first two years of the data were eliminated in that there seemed to be relatively few incidents recorded in these early years (see Figure 1). When the Bai–Perron procedure is applied to the updated data, little of substance changed in the analysis. Instead of using the Bai–Perron procedure, it is possible to cautiously ignore the cautions of Enders and Sandler (2005a) and estimate the multiple intervention model:

$$y_t = a_0 + \sum_{i=1}^{p} a_i y_{t-i} + \alpha_1 FUND + \alpha_2 POST + \alpha_3 D_P + \alpha_4 D_L + \varepsilon_t, \tag{6}$$

where p is the number of lags, y_t is the number of incidents of a particular type in period t, c is a constant, the a_i's and α_i's are undetermined coefficients, and ε_t is an error term. Equation (6) is a standard autoregressive model augmented by four dummy variables. Again, D_P and D_L are dummy (intervention) variables representing potential impacts of 9/11. Equation (6) also includes dummy intervention variables to control for the rise of religious fundamentalism (*FUND*) and the post-Cold War era (*POST*). As identified by Enders and Sandler (2000), *FUND* is a dummy variable taking a value of 1 beginning in 1979:4, and *POST* is a dummy variable taking a value of 1 beginning in 1992:1. For each series, the lag length is determined by estimating the model using $p = 8$. If the pth lag was not significant at the 5% level, the value of p was reduced by one and the model was reestimated. The tests are performed without including time as a regressor, because there is no evidence of a deterministic trend in any of the incident series.

As shown in Table 5, the *pulse* dummy, but not the *level* dummy, is associated with a statistically significant reduction in the *All* series. The *Bombing, UStgts* and the *All* series purged of threats and hoaxes (All_{nt}) behave similarly. Notice that the *level* dummy variable is not statistically significant for any of the incident series. An examination of Panel *d* in Figure 1 reveals the reason why the *Hostage* series is no longer associated with a significant decline resulting from 9/11. It is clear that *Hostage* jumps to near-record levels in last quarter of the data set.

The proportion series, except for *P_Bombing*, also show no permanent effects resulting from 9/11 in that all of the coefficients for D_L are within 1.96 standard deviations from zero. In the *P_Bombing* equation, the coefficient for D_L is 0.12; since the sum of the autoregressive coefficients is about 0.26, the long-run increase is estimated to be 16.2 percentage points $[0.12/(1-0.26) \cong 0.162]$. The point is that controlling for other structural breaks in the data, there seems be few statistically significant changes in the terrorism attack modes that can be attributed to the time period beginning with 9/11.

Table 5
Updating Enders and Sandler (2005a) using an intervention model[a]

Series	Lags	DW	Intercept	FUND	POST	Pulse	Level
All	5	2.00	49.92	16.08	−31.12	−34.04	−2.98
			(3.76)	(1.80)	(−2.67)	(−4.28)	(−0.33)
All$_{nt}$	5	2.00	42.74	9.67	−23.45	−29.34	−0.49
			(3.53)	(1.30)	(−2.40)	(−3.84)	(−0.06)
Deaths	2	2.05	4.80	1.89	−1.56	−2.75	3.98
			(3.72)	(1.42)	(−1.12)	(−1.16)	(1.67)
Cas	2	2.13	8.09	2.14	−3.07	−4.34	3.19
			(3.58)	(0.95)	(−1.28)	(−1.57)	(1.09)
Bombing	5	2.00	35.43	2.03	−20.93	−18.67	2.55
			(4.04)	(0.32)	(−3.12)	(−3.50)	(0.46)
UStgts	1	2.04	33.45	0.04	−17.26	−16.51	4.82
			(7.51)	(0.01)	(−4.38)	(−4.22)	(1.12)
Arm	7	1.99	1.67	2.38	0.20	−1.34	−0.83
			(2.34)	(1.62)	(0.11)	(−0.66)	(−0.43)
Hostage	7	2.06	11.99	4.25	−0.98	−4.71	−4.87
			(5.38)	(2.98)	(−0.71)	(−1.25)	(−1.50)
			Proportion Series				
P_Deaths	8	2.15	0.07	0.00	0.04	0.52	0.08
			(2.85)	(−0.27)	(2.27)	(10.96)	(1.87)
P_Cas	4	1.88	0.13	0.00	0.05	0.44	0.06
			(3.51)	(−0.25)	(2.00)	(12.00)	(1.40)
P_Bombing	1	2.03	0.50	−0.09	−0.07	−0.05	0.12
			(8.55)	(−4.11)	(−2.69)	(−1.30)	(2.75)
P_UStgts	2	2.04	0.13	−0.03	0.02	−0.04	0.02
			(2.77)	(−0.93)	(0.51)	(−1.20)	(0.39)
P_Arm	1	2.07	0.04	0.04	0.07	−0.08	0.00
			(5.46)	(3.85)	(3.45)	(−4.15)	(0.19)
P_Hostage	4	1.97	0.07	0.00	0.07	0.13	−0.05
			(2.97)	(0.34)	(3.20)	(2.78)	(−1.24)

[a]*t*-statistics are in parentheses.

4.2. Effects on the location of incidents

Enders and Sandler (2006b) used a similar methodology to test for changes in the location of terrorist incidents within the six regional classifications shown in Figure 2. The specific types of incidents considered were the quarterly values of *All*, *Cas*, *UStgts* and casualty incidents with a US target (*CasUS*). In order to estimate the effects of 9/11 on the four types of incidents, they estimated each of these series using the intervention specification given by Equation (6). Since the series are counts and some of the series are thin, they also obtain the maximum likelihood estimates for thin series using a Poisson distribution. A normally distributed variable can be positive or negative and the likelihood function is symmetric about the mean. A benefit of using the Poisson distribution to model count data is that it rules out the possibility of negative realizations of y_t and always predicts a positive value for the conditional mean. Moreover, the Poisson distribution is better able to capture a series containing many zero or near-zero, realizations. Panel a of Figure 7 shows a Normal and a Poisson distribution having the same mean value of 3 and the same variance of 3. Although both seem somewhat similar, approximately 16% of area under the Normal distribution is in the region below zero. This illustrates the main problem with using a normal approximation for a variable that actually has a Poisson distribution since inference (such as t-tests and F-tests) concerning the estimated coefficients will be imprecise. However, this problem disappears as the mean of the variable in question increases since the distributions become increasingly similar. For example, in Panel b of Figure 7, the mean of each distribution is 7. The variance of the Normal distribution function has been kept constant at 3. Notice that there is very little difference between the Poisson and the Normal distributions in the right-hand portion of the figure. However, in applied work, one advantage of the Normal distribution is that it is possible to separately estimate the mean and the variance. In the Poisson, the mean and the variance are necessarily equal.[3]

Let x_t be the set of regressors $FUND$, $POST$, D_P, and D_L. Conditional on the set of regressors x_t, the Poisson model assumes that y_t is distributed with a probability density function:

$$f(y_t|x_t) = e^{-\mu_t}\mu_t/(y_t!),\tag{7}$$

where the conditional mean, μ_t, is modeled as

$$\mu_t = \exp\left[c + \sum_{i=1}^{p} a_i \ln(y_{t-i} + bI_{t-i})\right.$$
$$\left. + \alpha_1 FUND + \alpha_2 POST + \alpha_3 D_P + \alpha_4 D_L\right],\tag{8}$$

and I_{t-i} is an indicator function that equals 0 if $y_{t-i} > 0$ and 1 if $y_{t-i} = 0$.

The presence of lagged values in the equation for the conditional mean captures any persistence in the series. Since the natural logarithm function is undefined at nonpositive values of y_{t-i}, a small increment, b, is added to any values of y_{t-i} that are equal to zero. The standard practice to select the most appropriate value of b is to perform a grid search over the interval $0.1 \leqslant b \leqslant 0.9$. Select the value of b that provides the best fit.

Notice that Equations (6) and (8) are similar in that $FUND$, $POST$, D_P, and D_L can all affect the mean of y_t. Unlike Equation (6), we permit the mean to be influenced by $\ln(y_{t-i})$ instead of the level of y_{t-i}. The rationale for this specification is to prevent the $\{y_t\}$ sequence from becoming explosive.

---

[3] The negative binomial distribution has some of the advantages of the Poisson distribution. However, there are also estimations problems using the negative binomial.

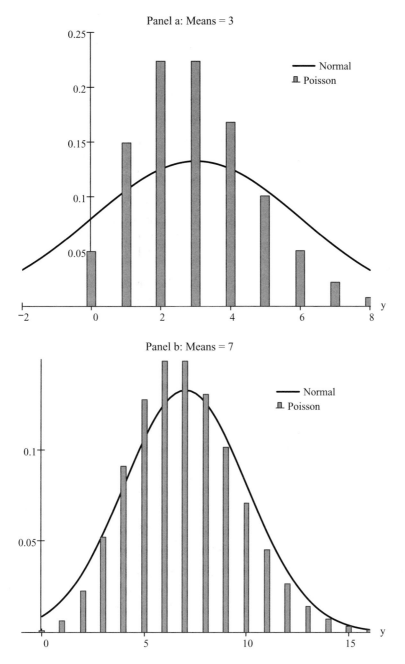

Figure 7. Comparison of the normal Poisson distributions.

Table 6
Analysis of selected incident types by location and income group[a]

Region	Model	Lags	c	FUND	POST	Pulse	Level	LR	F	Q(4)
				Cas incidents: Analysis by location						
West. Hem.	OLS	2	2.50	0.63	−2.25	3.64	−0.52	−1.14	0.00	0.85
			(4.55)	(0.75)	(−2.74)	(8.77)	(−1.06)			
Europe	OLS	3	2.70	0.26	−1.66	0.22	−0.53	−1.80	0.78	0.98
			(3.53)	(0.25)	(−1.39)	(0.42)	(−0.70)			
	Poisson	1	1.32	0.17	−0.42	1.18	−0.64		0.06	
			(13.62)	(2.32)	(−4.65)	(1.55)	(−2.20)			
Eurasia	Poisson	1	−3.35	1.29	2.50	−33.03	−0.91		0.23	
			(−3.28)	(1.15)	(4.54)	(0.00)	(−1.71)			
Africa	OLS	2	0.92	0.99	1.10	−1.13	−1.97	−3.08	0.00	0.58
			(3.18)	(2.17)	(1.29)	(−1.59)	(−1.83)			
Mid. East	OLS	1	2.07	1.88	−1.03	−6.64	3.75	7.28	0.00	0.21
			(3.66)	(2.38)	(−1.02)	(−3.17)	(1.69)			
Asia	OLS	1	1.16	1.53	0.12	−3.37	2.01	2.77	0.00	0.31
			(3.71)	(2.73)	(0.19)	(−3.03)	(1.57)			
				All incidents: Analysis by income group						
LICs	OLS	1	34.54	24.38	−16.90	−27.79	−11.92	−13.89	0.00	0.59
			(6.24)	(3.84)	(−2.77)	(−3.89)	(−1.41)			
HICs	OLS	2	22.13	2.87	−16.99	−1.99	−1.16	−2.27	0.54	0.97
			(4.91)	(0.77)	(−2.71)	(−0.76)	(−0.26)			
				Casualty incidents with a US target: Analysis by income group						
LICs	OLS	2	2.75	0.96	−1.31	−6.62	3.56	5.11	0.00	0.82
			(4.79)	(1.60)	(−1.90)	(−4.03)	(2.09)			
LICs	Poisson	1	1.24	0.28	−0.35	−33.52	0.75		0.00	
			(14.60)	(2.85)	(−3.22)	(0.00)	(4.99)			
HICs	Poisson	1	0.75	−0.10	−1.20	1.23	1.09		0.00	
			(7.26)	(−0.67)	(−4.58)	(2.29)	(3.11)			

[a] t-statistics are in parentheses.

Table 6 reproduces some of the findings for several selected series. The increase in fundamentalism was associated with a significant increase in casualty incidents in Africa, the Middle East, and Asia. Although there are sections in Africa with large Muslim populations, it is expected that the largest effects were in the Middle East and Asia. The post-Cold War ushered in a significant decline in casualty incidents in the Western Hemisphere and a significant rise in Eurasia. There is evidence that *POST* caused a decline in European casualty incidents; although the OLS estimate is insignificant at conventional levels, the Poisson estimate is negative and highly significant. For the Western Hemisphere, D_P is positive and highly significant so that it is possible to conclude that the Western Hemisphere experienced a temporary increase in casualty incidents during the post-9/11 period. The Middle East and Asia experienced a temporary drop in these events after 9/11. The OLS estimates show that no region displayed a permanent and significant change (at the 5% level) in casualty incidents following 9/11. The decline for Europe is only significant for the Poisson estimation. Enders and Sandler (2006b) also found that there is less evidence of a permanent 9/11-induced fall in casualty events compared with ALL events.

Enders and Sandler (2006b) also classified incidents according to the income level of the nation in which the attack occurred. Specifically, they grouped the 31 countries with the highest levels of per capita GNI according to the World Bank (2000) to the high income group (HIC) and all others to the low income group (LIC). These 31 HICs include most member states of the Organization of Economic Cooperation and Development (OECD) plus some other countries. As shown in the middle portion of Table 6, when countries were grouped in this way, FUND was associated with a large and statistically significant increase in transnational terrorism attacks in LICs of 24.38 incidents per quarter. Since the POST coefficient for the HICs was not significant, this grouping showed that the impact of fundamentalism was entirely based in the LICs. POST was associated with declines in terrorism in both income classes; the D_P dummy was negative and significant only for the LICs; and the D_L dummy was not significant for either group. The lower portion of Table 6 contains the empirical results for *Cas* incidents with a US target. The important feature to note is that the D_L dummy is positive and statistically significant for both income groups. As such 9/11 is associated with a ratcheting-up of serious terrorist attacks against the US. Americans are safer at home but not abroad following 9/11 and the enhanced homeland security.

5. Measuring the economic costs of terrorism

The direct costs of terrorism are probably the easiest to measure. According to the Bureau of Economic Analysis (2001), the direct costs of the 9/11 attacks on buildings and equipment were $16.2 billion. In conjunction with the clean-up costs of $10 billion and a $2.5 billion loss in wages in salaries due to the two-day work stoppage, the sub-total for total direct costs stands at $28.7 billion. Navarro and Spencer (2001) estimate the value of a human life to be $6.67 million. Given that almost 3000 died in the 9/11 attack, the total direct economic cost of 9/11 rises by another $20 billion. Yet, the US economy experienced a number of additional economic costs that are indirectly attributable to 9/11. The cost of pain and suffering and the value of lost output as a result of injuries are very difficult to value. Much of the federal government's current budget deficit is due to additional military and security expenditures necessary to fight the "War on Terror". Likewise, business firms had added new security measures and incurred additional insurance costs to protect themselves from another catastrophic terrorist attack. In a sense, the fear of terrorism acts like a tax on the entire economy. Given the impossibility of calculating and summing the various direct and indirect costs of terrorism, researchers have used other means. An alternative way to measure the full cost of terrorism is to compare the overall economic performance of countries or regions with high levels of terrorism to countries with low levels of terrorism. Of course, the comparison can also be done in a regression framework where terrorism is one of the variables affecting growth. To the extent that it is possible to control for all factors contributing to economic growth, the difference in growth rates between the high- and the low-terrorism nations is the estimated cost of terrorism.

Blomberg, Hess and Orphanides (henceforth BHO) (2004) used a cross section of 177 countries from 1968 to 2000 to measure the influence of various terrorist variables on real per capita GDP growth. In order to isolate the effects of terrorism on growth, they used dummy variables to control for the fact that African nations and non-oil commodity exporters tend to have low growth rates. The other control variables included each nation's initial level of income, the ratio of investment to real GDP, and dummy variables indicating whether the nation experienced internal and/or external conflicts. BHO found that if a country experienced transnational terrorist incidents on its soil in *each* year of the sample period, its per capita income growth fell by 1.587 percentage points over the *entire* sample period. As, each year of terrorism led on average to a fall in growth of only 0.048% ($= 1.587/33$) so that the overall impact of terrorism in any particular year is small.

BHO's initial terrorism measure (T_{it}) was such that $T_{it} = 1$ if country i experienced one or more transnational terrorist incidents in period t and $T_{it} = 0$ otherwise. Notice that this measure treats a country such as Israel (with many incidents in a year) in precisely the same way as a nation with only one isolated threat or hoax incident in a year. The point is that their specification does not allow the level or intensity of terrorism to affect growth. Moreover, the paper uses only *transnational* terrorism incidents even though some sample countries experienced a substantial amount of domestic terrorism. As shown in Figure 5, the number of domestic terrorism incidents greatly exceeds transnational incidents. As such, it is likely that the "internal conflict" dummy would capture some of the influence of domestic terrorism on growth. The overall effect is that the cost of terrorism is likely to be biased downward.

As a check for robustness, BHO grouped countries into panels and estimated models for nondemocratic countries, OECD countries, African countries, the Middle Eastern countries, and Asian countries. The findings were surprising in that the terrorism variable was not significant for any grouping except Africa. However, for the years covered in the sample, Africa had the lowest number of terrorist events per year (see Figure 2). Moreover, many African nations have experienced negative growth for reasons that have less to do with the presence of terrorism than with the presence of AIDS, open warfare, and economic mismanagement. It is also surprising that the full panel estimates (as compared to the cross-sectional estimates discussed above) indicated that terrorism in a single year reduced per capita GDP growth by *over a half a percent*. No reason was offered to explain why terrorism's average influence on growth for the entire sample is not reflected in *any* of the individual regions such as the Middle Eastern and Asian nations.

In another set of panel estimates, BHO (2004) used the per capita number of incidents within a country, rather than the dummy variable T_{it}, to measure the level of terrorism. The per capita measure means that a single incident in a country with a small population is somehow worse than the same incident in a more populous country. The results using this alternative measure are such that terrorism significantly affects per capita GDP growth for the full sample, the nondemocratic panel, the OECD panel, and the African panel. The impact of terrorism *varies widely* between the full sample and the subgroups so that there is no consistently measured cost of terrorism. Nevertheless, the authors provide an interesting explanation of the mechanism by which terrorism affects growth. In a second set of panel estimates, BHO found that terrorism increased government spending and decreased private investment. As such, they argue that increased security expenditures undertaken by the government to fight terrorism act to 'crowd out' private investment. The reduced level of investment limits growth in that the nation's capital stock is reduced.

Tavares (2004) also argues that the overall macroeconomic costs of terrorism are low. His estimating equation for a large, but unspecified, sample of countries over the 1987–2001 period is:

$$\Delta y_{it} = \beta_1 \Delta y_{it-1} + \beta_2 Y_{it} + \beta_3 \text{Terrorism}_{it} + \text{Control Variables} + \varepsilon_{it}, \tag{9}$$

where Δy_{it} is real per capita GDP growth of country i in period t, Y_{it} is i's level of real per capita GDP in t, and Terrorism$_{it}$ is either the total number of attacks per capita or the total number of casualties per capita. The Control Variables included a natural disaster index and a currency crisis index.

Given that Tavares (2004) obtained his terrorism measure from the IPIC, the results of his study are somewhat problematic because this data set is highly selective. Moreover, unlike BHO, Tavares (2004) does not control for internal conflicts. Nevertheless, using instrumental variables to correct for any simultaneity between terrorism and real per capita GDP growth, Tavares found that the terrorism variable had a negative impact on annual GDP growth of 0.038%. Note that the magnitude of this estimate is similar to that of BHO. Moreover, once additional determinants of growth (e.g., an education variable, trade openness, primary goods exports, and the inflation rate) were introduced into the estimating equation, the terrorism variable was not statistically significant and/or negative. It seems reasonable to believe that the first set of results is inappropriate since the additional variables are included in standard growth analyses. The finding that growth cost of terrorism is essentially zero is hard to believe. Of course, one explanation is that panel data estimates 'average out' the costs of terrorism for widely diverse nations. Another possible explanation is that terrorism is correlated with the education variable, trade openness, primary goods exports, and/or inflation so that coefficient magnitudes and the usual t-tests are misleading.

Tavares (2004) also compared the costs of terrorism in democratic versus nondemocratic countries. The key portion of his regression equation dealing with political rights is

$$\Delta y_{it} = 0.261 \Delta y_{it-1} - 0.029 T_{it} + 0.121 (T_{it} \times R_{it})$$
$$+ \text{ other explanatory variables}, \tag{10}$$

where R_{it} is a measure of political rights in country i in year t. R_{it} ranges from 0 to 1 with a sample mean of 0.53.

In contrast to Tavares' original specification given by (9), all of the coefficients in the equation with R_{it} are statistically significant. The positive coefficient on the interaction term $T_{it} \times R_{it}$, means that the effect of a typical terrorist attack decreases as the level of political freedom increases. The argument is that democracies are better able to withstand terrorist attacks than other types of governments with less flexible institutions. This is consistent with the view discussed in Enders and Sandler (2006a) that the cost of an attack in a democracy is lower than in other governmental forms because they rely on markets to allocate resources. The point estimates indicate that the growth effect of a single terrorist incident in country i in year t is $(-0.029 + 0.121R_{it})$ percentage points. Thus, for a nation with few political rights (so that R_{it} is near zero), terrorism reduces annual growth by -0.029 percentage points. Since the model is dynamic, this growth effect has some persistence. Nevertheless, the results are a bit problematic because the point estimates of the coefficients imply that terrorism can enhance growth. For a country with the average level of political rights (i.e., $R_{it} = 0.53$), the influence of a terrorist attack on growth is $+0.03513$ percentage points. It would have been interesting if results using T_{it}, R_{it} and $T_{it} \times R_{it}$ as explanatory variables were reported. In this way, the independent influence of R_{it} on growth could have been ascertained. Also, since the independent influence of R_{it} is excluded from the regression, the coefficient of $T_{it} \times R_{it}$ is probably biased upward.

Gupta et al. (2004) specifically analyzes the channel between economic growth, conflict, and government deficits using a simultaneous equation approach. If we modify their notation slightly, the growth equation can be written as

$$\Delta y_{it} = \beta_0 + \beta_1 Y_{it} + \beta_2 Edu_{it} + \beta_3 Def_{it} + \beta_4 Age_{it}$$
$$+ \beta_5 Conf_{it} + \beta_6 Inv_{it} + \varepsilon_{it}, \tag{11}$$

where y_{it} is real per capita GDP growth of country i in period t, Y_{it} is i's level of real per capita GDP in the initial year of the sample period, Edu_{it} is secondary school enrollment in the initial year of the sample period, Def_{it} is the share of defense spending in total government spending, Age_{it} is a measure of the age profile of the population, $Conf_{it} =$ a measure of internal conflict and terrorism, and Inv_{it} is total investment relative to GDP. Note that the time index references the four time periods 1980–1984, 1985–1989, 1990–1994, and 1995–1999 so that the estimates actually use 5-year averages of the variables.

The other two equations of the model specify the formulas for defense expenditures (Def_{it}) and tax revenues (Tax_{it}). Since they allow Def_{it} and tax revenues Tax_{it} to be functions of the conflict variable, there are actually two channels by which conflict can effect growth; conflict affects Δy_{it} directly and conflict affects Def_{it} which affects growth directly.

The equations are estimated using the generalized method of moments (GMM) in order to control for the possibility that $Conf_{it}$ is endogenous. In the base version of their model, Def_{it} has a negative and statistically negative effect on growth ($\beta_3 = -0.37$) and conflict significantly increases Def_{it}. However, their conflict measure is an aggregate that does not separate out the individual effects of terrorism on growth. As such, they simply report that terrorism significantly inhibits growth, but do not provide the actual cost estimates for any of the countries used in the study. Moreover, most macroeconomists would argue government deficits raise interest rates, reduce real investment and, thereby, reduce growth. Hence, it is not clear why Gupta et al. (2004) treat Inv_{it} as an independent variable.

In summary, there are few clear conclusions to be drawn from these studies. All of the papers use different control variables and measure terrorism differently from each other. In the world of econometric textbooks, omitted variables are not a problem if they are uncorrelated with the variable of interest. However, if the omitted variables are correlated with terrorism, the key results of the study will be biased. For example, if terrorism is more prevalent in liberal democracies (and democracy promotes growth), all cross-section and panel studies need to control for changing levels of democracy within countries. The same problem arises because the age profile and the level of education within a country can affect the growth rate and the terrorism. There seems to be little consensus on whether terrorism is measured as a (0, 1) dummy variable, by the number of incidents, the number of incidents on a per capita basis, or as part of an overall conflict variable. It does seem to be that case that more severe incident types (e.g., incidents with deaths or casualties) have larger effects than other types of incidents.

5.1. Case studies

Eckstein and Tsiddon (2004) used a four-equation VAR model to investigate the effects of terrorism (T) on real per capita GDP (GDP), investment (I), exports (EXP), and nondurable consumption (NDC) in Israel. The authors used quarterly data over the 1980–2003 period. Consider the following VAR:

$$
\begin{bmatrix} GDP_t \\ I_t \\ EXP_t \\ NDC_t \end{bmatrix} = \begin{bmatrix} A_{11}(L) & \cdots & A_{14}(L) \\ \vdots & \ddots & \vdots \\ A_{41}(L) & \cdots & A_{44}(L) \end{bmatrix} \begin{bmatrix} GDP_{t-1} \\ I_{t-1} \\ EXP_{t-1} \\ NDC_{t-1} \end{bmatrix}
$$
$$
+ \begin{bmatrix} c_1 T_{t-1} \\ c_2 T_{t-1} \\ c_3 T_{t-1} \\ c_4 T_{t-1} \end{bmatrix} + \cdots + \begin{bmatrix} \varepsilon_{1t} \\ \varepsilon_{2t} \\ \varepsilon_{3t} \\ \varepsilon_{4t} \end{bmatrix}, \tag{12}
$$

where the expressions $A_{ij}(L)$ are polynomials in the lag operator L, the c_i measure the influence of lagged terrorism on variable i, and the ε_i are the regression errors. Other right-hand side variables included the real interest rate and seasonal dummies.

The measure of terrorism is a weighted average of the number of Israeli fatalities, injuries, and noncasualty incidents due to both domestic and transnational attacks occurring in Israel. Experimentation with alternative lag lengths indicated that the initial impact of terrorism on economic activity was one quarter. Notice that the specification in (12) treats terrorism as a pre-determined variable that can affect the four endogenous macroeconomic variables simultaneously.

The largest influence of terrorism was found to be on exports and investment. Specifically, the impact of T_{t-1} on investment was three times larger than on nondurable consumption and two times larger than on GDP. This is consistent with the notion that in the face of a wave of terrorism, investors can readily transfer their funds to relatively safe localities. Given the point estimates of the various c_i, it is possible to estimate the costs of terrorism to the Israeli economy. Forecasts were conducted assuming either no subsequent terrorism or terrorism at the levels prevailing over 2000:4–2003:4. Eckstein and Tsiddon's (2004) first counterfactual exercise assumed that all terrorism actually ended in 2003:4 (so that all values of $T_j = 0$ for $j > 2003 : 4$). In this scenario, the annual growth rate of *GDP* was estimated to be 2.5% through 2005:3. Instead, if terrorism held steady at the 2000:4–2003:4 period average, the growth rate of *GDP* would have been zero. Thus, a steady level of terrorism would have cost the Israeli economy all of its real output gains.

Abadie and Gardeazabal (2003) estimated the per capita GDP losses from terrorism in the Basque region of Spain. The Euskadi Ta Askatasuna (ETA) and other smaller separatist groups, had waged a 25-year campaign against the Spanish government in order to achieve regional autonomy. Abadie and Gardeazabal (2003) argued that terrorism increases uncertainty and the expected return to investment. As such, open economies that are dependent on international capital flows should experience large losses from terrorism. In order to demonstrate their point, the authors construct a simulated economy that acts like the Basque region in all respects except that it experiences no terrorism. Specifically, this counterfactual Basque region is formed as a weighted average of other regions in Spain. The weights are chosen to yield values of real per capita GDP, the investment share of GDP, population density, and human capital measures that are nearly identical to those of the Basque region *prior* to the onset of terrorism. As such, the simulated region acts as a 'control' that allows the authors to compare actual Basque growth to what would have been attained in the absence of terrorism. It is important to note that the Basque region and the counterfactual region displayed similar per capita GDP values prior to the start of the terrorism campaign. Nevertheless, the counterfactual region had an average level of real per capita GDP exceeding that of the Basque region by about 10% over the 1976–1996 period. The gap widened to 12% during some high-terrorism periods and fell to about 8% during periods when terrorism was low. Abadie and Gardeazabal (2003) were also able to construct a portfolio of common stock consisting of companies with sizable business dealings in the Basque region. The value of this portfolio increased by 10.14% after a cease-fire was announced by ETA in late 1998. The same portfolio fell by 11.21% when the cease-fire collapsed 14 months later. A control portfolio, consisting of non-Basque stocks, experienced no noticeable movements corresponding to the cease-fire announcements.

5.2. Microeconomic consequences of terrorism

Regardless of the magnitude of the overall macroeconomic costs of terrorism, certain sectors of the economy feel the brunt of terrorism more than others. Since it can be problematic to combine data from very different industries, most of the studies measuring the economic costs of terrorism use time-series methods (as opposed to panel data) to analyze the microeconomic costs of terrorism.

5.2.1. Tourism

One reason terrorists attack popular tourist areas is to gather media attention and cause revenue losses as tourists redirect their vacation plans to relative safe areas. Enders and Sandler (1991) applied a VAR methodology to Spain for the 1970–1991 period, during which Euskadi Ta Askatasuna (ETA) and other groups had terrorist campaigns. During 1985–1987, ETA *directed* its bombs and threats against the Spanish tourist trade and even sent letters of warning to travel agents in Europe. Using monthly data, it was shown that the causation was unidirectional: terrorism affected tourism but not the reverse. Each transnational terrorist incident was estimated to dissuade over 140,000 tourists after all monthly impacts were included. This can translate into a sizable amount of lost revenue when multiplied by the average spending per tourist. Transnational terrorist attacks denote the appropriate terrorism measure, because much of the ETA terrorist campaign was transnational in order to chase away foreign tourists and FDI. Although Spain also experienced some domestic terrorism, data for ITERATE was used since the domestic attacks were performed away from tourist areas.

Enders et al. (1992) used a transfer function to investigate the impact of transnational terrorism on tourism in Austria, Spain, and Italy for 1974–1988 – three countries with highly visible transnational terrorist attacks against foreign tourists during this period. *Transfer function* analysis is particularly suited to estimate the short- and long-run effects of a terrorist attack on a country's tourist industry. Consider the following transfer function model of the effect of terrorism on Italian tourism:

$$y_t = A(L)y_{t-1} + B(L)x_t + C(L)\varepsilon_t, \tag{13}$$

where y_t is the logarithmic share of the Italy's tourism revenues in period t, x_t is the number of terrorist incidents in Italy in period t, L is the lag operator, and ε_t is the error term. This equation states that Italy's share of tourism revenues in any period is affected by its own past, $A(L)y_{t-1} + C(L)\varepsilon_t$, as well as the number of current and past values of terrorist events in Italy $B(L)x_t$. At first, the transfer function might look like the equation for y_t in a two-equation VAR. The essential difference is that the current value of x_t can appear in the transfer function because it is assumed to be independent of the current level of tourism. The coefficients of $A(L)$ and $C(L)$ capture any persistence in the level of tourism and the coefficients of $B(L)$ capture current and lagged effects of terrorism on tourism. All coefficients of $B(L)$ should be equal to zero if terrorism has no effect on tourism; certainly, the sum of the coefficients should be negative if terrorism reduces tourism.

Details concerning the estimation of a transfer function are contained in Enders (2004). The important point is that transfer function analysis can be used to estimate the indirect effects of terrorism of the tourism series. Once $A(L)$, $B(L)$ and $C(L)$ have been estimated, it is possible to perform a counterfactual analysis of what each value of y_t would have been in the absence of terrorism (i.e., all values of $x_{t-i} = 0$). Consider the final estimated equation for Italy[4]:

$$y_t = \frac{-0.0022x_{t-1}}{1 - 0.876L + 0.749L^2} + \frac{(1 + 0.293L^4)\varepsilon_t}{1 - 0.504 - 0.245L^2}. \tag{14}$$

It is possible to use Equation (14) to construct a counterfactual series for y_t by allowing the coefficient on x_{t-1} to be zero instead of the estimated value -0.0022. The difference between this counterfactual value and the actual value of y_t is then due to the effect of terrorism. It was found that terrorism had a significant negative lagged influence on these tourism shares that varied by country: one quarter for Italy, three quarters for Greece, and seven quarters for Austria. Since it takes time for tourists to revise plans, the lags are understandable. Losses varied by country: Austria lost 3.37 billion special drawing rights (SDRs); Italy lost 861 billion SDRs; and Greece lost 472 million SDRs. The authors also showed that some of the lost revenues left a sample of European countries for safer venues in North America.

Drakos and Kutan (2003) applied the Enders–Sandler–Parise methodology to Greece, Israel, and Turkey for 1991–2000. These authors used monthly transnational terrorism data, drawn from ITERATE. In addition to the home-country impacts, Drakos and Kutan were interested in cross-country or "spillover" effects – both positive and negative – that may arise if, say, a transnational attack in Israel shifts would-be Israeli tourists to safer venues in Italy, Greece, or elsewhere. They estimated a transfer function for each country's tourist shares, where, say, the share of tourism in Greece depends on: past tourist shares in Greece; current and past terrorist attacks in Greece; current and past terrorist attacks in Israel; and current and past terrorist attacks in Turkey. There was also an equation for tourist shares of Italy, which was a relatively safe haven. Based on transnational terrorist attacks, these authors calculated that Greece lost 9% of its tourism market share; Turkey lost over 5% of its tourism market share; and Israel lost less than 1% of its tourism market. Close to 89% of lost tourism due to terrorism in Europe flowed to safer tourist venues in other countries. Drakos and Kutan also uncovered significant spillover effects – low-intensity terrorist attacks in Israel reduced Greek tourism revenues.

---

[4] The estimated equation reported here is slightly different from the one actually reported in Enders et al. (1992). Enders (2004) reports the details of the estimation process.

5.2.2. Net foreign direct investment (NFDI)

Just as tourists avoid areas likely to suffer from a terrorist attack, international investors are likely to avoid high-terrorism areas. Obviously, a terrorist attack can destroy infrastructure and cause business disruptions. Firms also seek to avoid the increased costs necessary to protect a facility from potential attacks. Such costs include those of directly securing facilities, maintaining security clearances for employees, and additional insurance charges. Recruiting costs may rise since personnel from the home office may not wish to work in a terrorist-prone region. Moreover, terrorism augments the general level of uncertainty, which redirects NFDI to safer environs. The point is that terrorism raises the costs of doing business in a country; as such foreign firms will seek safer locations for their facilities and domestic firms will seek to locate abroad.

Enders and Sandler (1996) provided estimates of the effects of terrorism on NFDI in two relatively small European countries – Greece and Spain. Large countries – e.g., France, Germany, and the United Kingdom – draw their foreign capital inflows from many sources and appeared to endure attacks without a measurable aggregate diversion of inflows. Large countries are also better equipped to take defensive measures after an attack to restore confidence. Greece and Spain were selected as case studies insofar as both experienced numerous transnational terrorist attacks aimed at foreign commercial interests during the 1968–1991 sample period.

It turned out that a transfer function specification was appropriate for Spain because terrorism did not respond NFDI. However, a VAR model was used for Greece because of a potential endogeneity problem. For Spain, there was a long delay of 11 quarters between the advent of a terrorist incident and the response in NFDI. The counterfactual analysis indicated that a typical transnational terrorist incident in Spain was estimated to reduce NFDI by $23.8 million. On average, transnational terrorism reduced *annual* NFDI in Spain by 13.5%. For Greece, the story was similar, transnational terrorism curbed annual NFDI by 11.9%. These are sizable losses for two small economies that were heavily dependent on NFDI as a source of savings during the sample period.

5.2.3. Trade influence

In a recent contribution, Nitsch and Schumacher (2004) estimated the effects of transnational terrorism on bilateral trade flows using a standard trade-gravity model. In their model, trade flows between trading partners depended on terrorist attacks, the distance between the two countries, an income variable, an income per capita variable, and a host of dummy variables. They formally estimated the effects of terrorism within each country on all of the nation's trading partners. The data set consists of 217 countries and territories over the 1968–1979 period. Their terrorism data were drawn from IT-ERATE and only included transnational attacks, even though domestic terrorism would have also affected trade flows. The authors found that the first transnational terrorist attack reduced bilateral trade by almost 10%, which is a very sizable influence that may be picking up the effect of domestic terrorism. Nitsch and Schumacher also found that a doubling of the number of terrorist incidents reduced bilateral trade by 4%; hence, high-terrorism nations had a substantially reduced trade volume.

5.2.4. Financial markets

Chen and Siems (2004) applied an event-study methodology to investigate changes in average returns of stock exchange indices to 14 terrorist and military attacks that dated back to 1915. Their event study computed daily excess – negative or positive – following 14 occurrences, such as the Japanese attack of Pearl Harbor, the downing of Pan Am flight 107 and 9/11. Specifically, daily excess returns (AR_{jt}) for stock j on day t are computed as the difference between the stock's observed return on day t (R_{jt}) minus the average return that prevailed in the recent past $(\bar{R}_j)$:

$$AR_{jt} = R_{jt} - \bar{R}_j, \tag{15}$$

where the average return is calculated as

$$\bar{R}_j = 0.05 \sum_{t=-30}^{-11} R_{jt}. \tag{16}$$

The date on which the event occurs is normalized to be day 0 so that the average return is a 20-day mean of recent returns. Of course, if the event had no effect on stock prices, the return on day 0 should just equal the average return so that AR_{jt} should not be statistically different from zero. These authors showed that the influence of terrorist events on major stock exchanges, if any, is very transitory, lasting just one to three days for most major incidents. The sole exception is 9/11 where DOW values took 40 days to return to normal. These authors also showed that this return period varied according to the stock exchange – exchanges in Norway, Jakarta, Kuala Lampur, and Johannesburg took longer to rebound, while those in London, Helsinki, Tokyo, and elsewhere took less time to rebound. Most terrorist events had little or no impact on major stock exchanges. The paper goes on to claim that US capital markets are more resilient than in the past and recover sooner from terrorist attacks than other global capital markets. Although their argument that a more stable US financial sector has promoted stability is plausible, there is another explanation for the reason why recent market recoveries occur more quickly than in the past. The early events include the torpedoing of the Lusitania, the German invasion of France, the Pearl Harbor attacks, and the North Korean attacks on South Korea. Unlike the downing of an Air India flight (June 1985), a Korean Air flight (November 1987), and a Pan AM flight (December 1988), the earlier incidents signaled major long-term conflicts.

Eldor and Melnick (2004) applied time-series methods to ascertain the influence of the Israeli terror campaign following September 27, 2000 on the Tel Aviv 100 Stock Index (TA 100) and on the exchange rate. Given the continual nature of these terrorist attacks, the time-series method is clearly appropriate. As a preliminary check for the presence of a unit-root, Eldor and Melnick (2004) conducted augmented Dickey–Fuller tests on the data and found that stock prices and the exchange rate are both nonsta-tionary. As such, they estimated their equations using first-differences. Consider the specification:

$$\Delta x_t = \alpha + \beta f_t + \gamma_0 T_t + \gamma_1 T_{t-1} + \gamma_2 T_{t-2} + \varepsilon_t, \tag{17}$$

where x_t is either the log of the TA 100 or the exchange rate, f_t is a measure of the market fundamentals, and T_t is a measure of the level of terrorism in Israel in period t.

If any of the coefficients for the terrorism variable are statistically significant, it can be concluded that terrorism has important informational content for x_t. If the sum of the coefficients $\gamma_0 + \gamma_1 + \gamma_2$ is not statistically different from zero, terrorism has only a tran-sitory effect on x_t. Otherwise, the effect on terrorism on x_t is permanent. When x_t was the log of the TA 100, suicide attacks, attacks with deaths, and attacks with injuries all had permanent effects on the level of stock prices. However, when T_t measured attacks on transport or the overall level of attacks, the effects were only transitory. Analogous to the other time-series studies, they performed a counterfactual exercise to determine losses to the value of the TA 100 index by using the *estimated* time-series equation for returns but substituting a zero value in for terrorist attacks. Their analysis estimated that the TA 100 was 30% lower on June 30, 2003, owing to the terrorist campaign. However, they found little influence of any form of terrorism on the exchange rate.

Instead of looking at the effects of terrorism on a broad index of stocks, Drakos (2004) examined the effects of the 9/11 attacks on airline stocks. Let R_{it}, R_{ft} and R_{mt} denote the period t rate of return on airline stock i, on a risk-free asset, and on the market portfolio, respectively. His estimating equation is

$$(R_{it} - R_{ft}) = \beta_i (R_{mt} - R_{ft}) + \varepsilon_t. \tag{18}$$

The value of β_i shows how the excess return of stock i is correlated with the overall market rate of return over the risk free rate. If 9/11 had no effect on the systematic risk of the airline's stock, the pre-9/11 value of β_i should be equal to the post-9/11 value. Instead, if the average market participant perceived an increased risk of holding an airline's stock, β_i should rise to compensate asset holders for the increased risk. Similarly, if 9/11 had no effect on the stock's volatility, the pre-9/11 value of $Var(\varepsilon)$ should be equal to the post-9/11 value. Drakos (2004) found that eleven out of the thirteen stocks studies showed increased systematic risk in the post-9/11 period. Only KLM and Qantas (two non-US carriers) showed no increased systematic risk. Moreover, in nine of the cases the variance rose implying that risk of airline stocks increased.

6. Measuring the economic determinants of terrorism

In many instances, it is straightforward to point to the grievances of a particular group and designate those grievances as a cause of terrorism. The IRA was formed to achieve Irish independence, the Irgun was formed to achieve a homeland for the Jews, and the PLO was formed to fight against Israel and to achieve an independent Palestinian state.

Yet, social scientists want to know why some groups choose to fight using terrorist tactics while others do not. After all, some terrorist groups (such as the Red Brigades and Aum Shinrikyo) failed to achieve their ultimate ends while other groups using legal tactics have been successful. The real issue is to find out the underlying reasons why one group will seek to alleviate a grievance using terrorism instead of a host of other tactics.

Hoffman (1998) argues that liberal democracies are more prone to terrorism than other forms of government. In liberal democracies terrorists have the same freedoms as nonterrorists in that they can freely associate with each other, are free to communicate with each other and spread dissent, and have the same ability to obtain funding and weapons as any other member of society. Moreover, political pressures arising from terrorist attacks may induce the government to concede to some of the terrorists' demands. As such, there is more incentive for a group to resort to terrorism in a liberal democracy. Even though a number of studies, including those by Li (2005) and Weinberg and Eubank (1998), seem to verify this result, the issue seems to be straightforward and the policy implications are few. A more interesting issue is whether poverty and poor economic conditions breed terrorism.

If the motives for terrorism, rather than some political tactic, are purely economic, one might be tempted to conclude that the alleviation of poverty might reduce terrorism. However, there is little statistical evidence that poverty 'causes' terrorism. In an informal study, Sageman (2004) assembled biographical information on approximately 400 Salafi Mujahedin terrorists using publicly available information. The approximately seventy-five percent of the terrorists came from upper-class or middle class backgrounds and sixty-three percent attended college. Moreover, many had professional backgrounds and sixty-three percent were married. Since Sageman's (2004) sample of terrorists was not drawn scientifically, it is possible to argue that it is not representative of the large number of terrorists that were excluded from his data set. However, in a more formal study, Krueger and Maleckova (2003) find little relationship between the lack of market opportunities and terrorism. They begin be analyzing a public opinion poll conducted by the Palestinian Center for Policy Survey Research (PCPSR). From 19 December 2001 through 24 December 2001, the PCPSR surveyed 1357 Palestinians aged 18 or older living in the West Bank and Gaza Strip. The results of the survey are quite striking in that at least 72% of every educational and occupational group supported (or strongly supported) armed attacks against Israeli targets. It is particular interesting that the percentage supporting such attacks did not decrease with income or educational levels. In fact, support was especially strong among students and lowest among the unemployed. Corroborating evidence was provided by comparing the economic characteristics of 129 killed Hezbollah fighters with those from a similar population demographic in Lebanon. They found a 28% poverty rate for the militants compared with a 33% percent for the more general population. Moreover, the Hezbollah fighters were more likely to have attended secondary school.

Krueger and Maleckova (2003) used US State Department data to formally test for a relationship between terrorism and income. Let n_i denote the number of terrorist events perpetrated by individuals from each country i over the entire 1977–2002 period. In a very simple regression controlling only for population, they found a negative relationship between n_i and per capita GDP. Hence, in accord with the conventional wisdom, there tends to be a negative correlation between income and terrorism. However, the poorest countries tend to be those with low levels of civil liberties. When they included a measure of civil liberties in the regression equation, the GDP variable becomes statistically insignificant. Moreover, regardless of the form of the regression equation, the civil-liberties variable was always significant at better than the 0.02 level. The point they make is that it is the lack of political freedom, and not poverty, that spawns terrorism.

In a more recent paper, Blomberg, Hess, and Weerapana (BHW) (2004) estimate the relationship between economic conditions and the level of terrorism within a panel of 127 countries from 1968 to 1991. The intent is to measure the extent to which the business cycle helps to explain the level of terrorism within a country. Towards this end, BHW define a contraction as a period of negative per capita GDP growth and an expansion as a period of positive growth.[5] The terrorism variable, drawn from ITERATE, is a $(0, 1)$ measure of whether a nation was a target of a terrorist attack in year t. They show that there are some links between economic contractions and increased levels of terrorism in high-income and democratic countries. To explain, in any year t, there are four regimes depending on whether the economy was in a state of contraction or expansion and depending on whether the country experienced a terrorist attack. Let $P_{t-1} = 0$ if the country in question was in a state of peace in period $t - 1$, otherwise $P_{t-1} = 1$ (i.e., $P_{t-1} = 1$ if the country experienced at least one terrorists attack in $t - 1$). Also let $C_{t-1} = 1$ if the country in question was in a contraction in period $t - 1$, otherwise $C_{t-1} = 0$. As an example of the notations, for a country experiencing an expansion and no terrorism in year $t - 1$, $C_{t-1} = 0$ and $P_{t-1} = 0$. Thus, the four distinct regimes can be described by $(C_{t-1} = 0, P_{t-1} = 0)$, $(C_{t-1} = 0, P_{t-1} = 1)$, $(C_{t-1} = 1, P_{t-1} = 0)$ and $(C_{t-1} = 1, P_{t-1} = 1)$.

The issue is how readily countries switch between the four regimes. In other words, does a country in a high-terrorism, low-growth state tend to remain in that state while a country in a high-terrorism, high-growth state tends to switch into a low-terrorism, high-growth state? Let $PR(P_t | P_{t-1} = C_{t-1} = 1)$ denote the probability that the country experiences no terrorism in t given that P_{t-1} and C_{t-1} both equal 1. Analogously, $PR(C_t | P_{t-1} = C_{t-1} = 1)$ probability that the country has a contraction in t given that P_{t-1} and C_{t-1} both equal 1. If you follow the notation, it should be clear that $PR(T_t | P_{t-1} = C_{t-1} = 1) = 1 - PR(P_t | P_{t-1} \text{ and } C_{t-1})$ is the probability that the country is in the high-terrorism state given P_{t-1} and C_{t-1} both equal 1.

---

[5] Note that this is not the conventional way to define business cycle expansions and contractions. The typical definitions of recessions and expansions are measured relative to a long-term trend. Nations with sustained negative growth rates, such as many of the African nations, are generally not said to be experiencing a recession.

Table 7
The transition probabilities into the high-terrorism state

	All	Low income	High income
$\text{PR}(T_t \mid P_{t-1} = C_{t-1} = 1)$	0.197	0.171	0.252
$\text{PR}(T_t \mid P_{t-1} = 1, C_{t-1} = 0)$	0.196	0.177	0.211
$\text{PR}(T_t \mid P_{t-1} = 0, C_{t-1} = 1)$	0.694	0.577	0.782
$\text{PR}(T_t \mid P_{t-1} = C_{t-1} = 0)$	0.654	0.515	0.718

The various transition probabilities can be estimated by maximum likelihood methods. Some of the key BHW findings are summarized in Table 7. The first two rows of the table show that for all countries, transitions into the high-terrorism state from a state of peace are almost 0.20 regardless of whether or not the economy experiences a contraction. As such, there is an 80% chance that a country experiencing no terrorism in the current year experiences no terrorism in the subsequent year. The probability of switching into the high-terrorism state is slightly higher for the high-income countries than for the low-income countries. Moreover, since for the high-income nations $\text{PR}(T_t \mid P_{t-1} = C_{t-1} = 1) > \text{PR}(T_t \mid P_{t-1} = 1, C_{t-1} = 0)$, contractions are associated with terrorism for nations with already high income levels. The next two rows of the table show that the probability of remaining in a high-terrorism state is quite high regardless of whether or not the economy experiences a contraction. If the economy does not have a contraction, the probability is 65.4% and is 69.4% if there is a current contraction. Thus, both the terrorism state and the no-terrorism state are quite persistent. Also note that the probability of being in a high-terrorism state is always greater for the high-income nations. As such, there tends to be more terrorism in high-income nations than low-income nations. Finally, for the high-income nations $\text{PR}(T_t \mid P_{t-1} = 1, C_{t-1} = 0) > \text{PR}(T_t \mid P_{t-1} = 0, C_{t-1} = 1)$ so that it again follows that contractions are associated with terrorism for nations with already high income levels.

7. Conclusions and assessment

Assessing the state of the empirical literature on terrorism, it is clear that there is much to learn. In fact, the game-theoretic models of terrorism seem far more sophisticated than many of the empirical papers surveyed here. Part of the reason for the disparity is the nature of the available data measuring terrorism. Even though most definitions of terrorism involve the notion of a political crime committed against noncombatants, important differences in coverage, coding, and consistency appear in the available data sets. The ITERATE, PGT and MIPT data sets do seem to have similar long-run patterns. Chronologies of "selected" incidents, such as the IPIC data set, seem inappropriate for research purposes. Unfortunately, beginning with 2004, updates to the PGT data were suspended for political reasons. From an economic perspective, this makes little sense since the collection and widespread dissemination of information has public good aspects that typically involve some form of government subsidization. Although the MIPT data set is publicly available, it is difficult to use and does not contain country-specific breakdowns of terrorist incidents. The complete ITERATE data set is available for a fee large enough to dissuade some potential researchers from acquiring it. Although the number of domestic terrorist incidents far exceeds that of transnational incidents, there is not a long time series of domestic terrorism data.

In spite of the data problems, the implications of the rational-actor model of terrorism have been the subject of a number of empirical tests. Specifically, an increase in the relative price of one type of terrorist activity does induce a substitution out of that activity and into the now relatively less-expensive activity. Logistically similar activities do seem to display the greatest substitution possibilities. Moreover, periods of high-terrorism seem to be less persistent than periods with less terrorism. This is consistent with the notion that terrorists face a resource constraint. Terrorism can remain in an elevated state only as long as they have sufficient resources to sustain the struggle. Once resources have been sufficiently depleted, the intensity of terrorism will fall as the group replenishes its resources, funds and personnel.

Since 9/11, the nature of terrorism has changed in ways that are quite different from those typically reported in the media. There has not been a dramatic increase in the number of transnational terrorist incidents since 9/11. Instead, the post-9/11 counterterrorism policies have hampered al-Qaida's abilities to conduct resource-intensive and logistically sophisticated attacks. The proportion of bombings has increased at the expense of assassinations and hostage takings. Another change in the composition of the incident series is that there have also been increased efforts to attack US interests. However, Americans are safer at home, but not abroad, as a result of these terrorists' efforts and improved homeland security.

Far less is known about the macroeconomic costs of terrorism than the costs to specific countries and specific industries. The panel data estimates suggest that the costs of terrorism to overall economic growth are virtually zero. However, this is in direct contrast to the case studies of terrorism and the intuitive notion that the current macroeconomic climates in some countries (such as the US, Iraq, Philippines, Afghanistan, Pakistan, Spain, and the UK) would be very different had 9/11 never occurred. The appeal of cross-sectional and panel data studies of the macroeconomic costs of terrorism is obvious. Such studies can pool the experiences of a large number of countries at once to gain enhanced degrees of freedom. The fact that many countries experience widely different levels of terrorism can help in the statistical identification of the consequences of terrorism. However, these gains seem to be offset by a number of difficult problems. It is likely that some countries are too diverse to pool into a single regression equation. It is difficult to obtain adequate controls for the vast differences in institutions and governments that exist across the array of nations. As discussed in Enders and Sandler (2006a), countries with market economies and democratic governments will respond to terrorism very differently than countries with nonmarket economies and/or nondemocratic governments. The price system and economic freedoms allow a country to reallocate resources in such a way as to absorb the shocks of terrorist attacks. Similarly, large and diverse economies are better able to absorb shocks than small economies with only a small number of viable sectors. As such, it is not surprising the panel data studies of the macroeconomic costs of terrorism are sensitive to the particular groupings used in the panel. Moreover, the microeconomic studies of terrorism indicate that it may take several periods for the effects of terrorism to manifest themselves. Such delay factors are difficult to analyze in a cross-sectional framework.

A problem endemic in all studies trying to measure the costs of terrorism is that it is not clear how to measure the level and intensity of terrorism. Some studies, such as Enders and Sandler (1996) and Nitsch and Schumacher (2004), use the number of incidents occurring in a region to measure the level of terrorism. Eckstein and Tsiddon (2004) use a weighted average of the number of fatalities, injuries, and noncasualty incidents occurring in Israel. BHO (2004) alternatively used a (0, 1) dummy variable to indicate whether a country experienced an act of terrorism within a year and the per capita number of incidents within a country while Tavares (2004) alternatively used the number of attacks per capita and the total number of casualties per capita.

Measuring the economic determinants of terrorism seems to be the most problematic endeavor surveyed in this paper. It is certainly true that many of the individuals engaging in terrorism are not among the most impoverished people, high-income countries experience more terrorism than low-income countries, and noneconomic factors (such as the US presence in Saudi Arabia) sometimes motivate terrorists. Yet, it is instructive to consider the large existing literature on the relationship between poverty and (nonpolitical) crime. The consensus opinion among social scientists is that poverty alone does not cause crime. However, there are subtle linkages between the two (such as glaring income disparities between two otherwise similar groups). The riots in France during the fall of 2005 provide strong evidence that terrorist acts can result from the lack of economic opportunities for some members of society.

References

Abadie, A., Gardeazabal, J. (2003). "The economic cost of conflict: A case study of the Basque country". American Economic Review 93, 113–132.

Bai, J., Perron, P. (1998). "Estimating and testing linear models with multiple structural changes". Econometrica 66, 47–78.

Bai, J., Perron, P. (2003). "Computation and analysis of multiple structural change models". Journal of Applied Econometrics 18, 1–22.

Becker, G. (1971). Economic Theory. Alfred Knoff, New York.

Blomberg, S.B., Hess, G., Orphanides, A. (2004). "The macroeconomic consequences of terrorism". Journal of Monetary Economics 51, 1007–1032.

Blomberg, S.B., Hess, G., Weerapana, A. (2004). "Economic conditions and terrorism". European Journal of Political Economy 20, 463–478.

Bureau of Economic Analysis (2001). "Business situation". Survey of Current Business 81, 1–7.

Chen, A.H., Siems, T.F. (2004). "The effects of terrorism on global capital markets". European Journal of Political Economy 20, 249–266.

Drakos, K. (2004). "Terrorism-induced structural shifts in financial risk: Airline stocks in the aftermath of the September 11th terror attacks". European Journal of Political Economy 20, 436–446.

Drakos, K., Kutan, A.M. (2003). "Regional effects of terrorism on tourism in three Mediterranean countries". Journal of Conflict Resolution 47, 621–641.

Eckstein, Z., Tsiddon, D. (2004). "Macroeconomic consequences of terror: Theory and the case of Israel". Journal of Monetary Economics 51, 971–1002.

Eldor, R., Melnick, R. (2004). "Financial markets and terrorism". European Journal of Political Economy 20, 367–386.

Enders, W. (2004). Applied Econometric Time Series, second ed. John Wiley & Sons, Hoboken, NJ.

Enders, W., Sandler, T. (1991). "Causality between transnational terrorism and tourism: The case of Spain". Terrorism 14, 49–58.

Enders, W., Sandler, T. (1993). "The effectiveness of antiterrorism policies: A vector-autoregression-intervention analysis". American Political Science Review 7, 829–844.

Enders, W., Sandler, T. (1996). "Terrorism and foreign direct investment in Spain and Greece". Kyklos 49, 331–352.

Enders, W., Sandler, T. (2000). "Is transnational terrorism becoming more threatening? A time-series investigation". Journal of Conflict Resolution 44, 307–332.

Enders, W., Sandler, T. (2004). "What do we know about the substitution effect in transnational terrorism?". In: Silke, A. (Ed.), Research on Terrorism: Trends, Achievements and Failures. Frank Cass, London, pp. 119–137.

Enders, W., Sandler, T. (2005a). "After 9/11: Is it all different now?". Journal of Conflict Resolution 49, 259–277.

Enders, W., Sandler, T. (2005b). "Transnational terrorism 1968–2000: Thresholds, persistence, and forecasts". Southern Economic Journal 71, 467–482.

Enders, W., Sandler, T. (2006a). The Political Economy of Terrorism. Cambridge University Press, Cambridge.

Enders, W., Sandler, T. (2006b). "Distribution of transnational terrorism among countries by income classes and geography after 9/11". International Studies Quarterly 50, 367–393.

Enders, W., Sandler, T., Parise, G.F. (1992). "An econometric analysis of the impact of terrorism on tourism". Kyklos 45, 531–554.

Gerges, F.A., Isham, C. (2003). Sign of weakness? Do overseas terror strikes suggest al Qaeda inability to hit US? ABC News, November 22.

Gupta, S., Clements, B., Bhattacharya, R., Chakravarti, S. (2004). "Fiscal consequences of armed conflict in low- and middle-income countries". European Journal of Political Economy 20, 403–421.

Hoffman, B. (1998). Inside Terrorism. Columbia University Press, New York.

International Policy Institute for Counterterrorism (2005). Terrorism Database [http://ict.org.il], accessed December 15, 2005.

Krueger, A.B., Maleckova, J. (2003). "Education, poverty, and terrorism: Is there a causal connection?" Journal of Economic Perspective 17, 119–144.

Li, Q. (2005). "Does democracy promote transnational terrorist incidents?". Journal of Conflict Resolution 49, 278–297.

Mickolus, E.F., Sandler, T., Murdock, J.M., Flemming, P. (2004). International Terrorism: Attributes of Terrorist Events, 1968–2003 (ITERATE). Vinyard Software, Dunn Loring, VA.

National Memorial Institute for the Prevention of Terrorism (2005). MIPT Terrorism Database [http://www.mipt.org], accessed December 15, 2005.

Navarro, P., Spencer, A. (2001). "September 11, 2001: Assessing the costs of terrorism". Milken Institute Review 4, 16–31.

Nitsch, V., Schumacher, D. (2004). "Terrorism and international trade: An empirical investigation". European Journal of Political Economy 20, 423–433.

Sageman, M. (2004). Understanding Terror Networks. University of Pennsylvania Press, Philadelphia.

Tavares, J. (2004). "The open society assesses its enemies: Shocks, disasters and terrorist attacks". Journal of Monetary Economics 51, 1039–1070.

United States Department of State (various years). Patterns of Global Terrorism. US Department of State, Washington, DC.

The White House (2003). "Progress Report on the Global War on Terrorism" [http://www.state.gov/s/ct/rls/rpt/24087.htm], accessed 5 February 2004.

Weinberg, L.B., Eubank, W.L. (1998). "Terrorism and democracy: what recent events disclose". Terrorism and Political Violence 10, 108–118.

World Bank (2000). World Development Report. Oxford University Press, New York.

Chapter 27

THE POLITICAL ECONOMY OF ECONOMIC SANCTIONS[*]

WILLIAM H. KAEMPFER

Academic Affairs, Campus Box 40, University of Colorado, Boulder, Boulder, CO 80309-0040, USA
e-mail: william.kaempfer@colorado.edu

ANTON D. LOWENBERG

Department of Economics, California State University, Northridge, 18111 Nordhoff Street, Northridge,
CA 91330-8374, USA
e-mail: anton.lowenberg@csun.edu

Contents

Abstract	868
Keywords	868
1. Introduction	869
2. Economic effects of sanctions	872
3. The political determinants of sanctions policies in sender states	879
4. The political effects of sanctions on the target country	884
5. Single-rational actor and game theory approaches to sanctions	889
6. Empirical sanctions studies	892
7. Political institutions and sanctions	898
8. Conclusions and avenues for further research	903
References	905

[*] The authors thank Keith Hartley, Irfan Nooruddin and Todd Sandler for valuable comments. Derek Lowenberg provided technical assistance in preparation of the final manuscript. All errors remain the responsibility of the authors alone.

Handbook of Defense Economics, Volume 2
Edited by Todd Sandler and Keith Hartley
© 2007 Elsevier B.V. All rights reserved
DOI: 10.1016/S1574-0013(06)02027-8

Abstract

International economic sanctions have become increasingly important as alternatives to military conflict since the end of the Cold War. This chapter surveys various approaches to the study of economic sanctions in both the economics and international relations literatures.

Sanctions may be imposed not to bring about maximum economic damage to the target, but for expressive or demonstrative purposes. Moreover, the political effects of sanctions on the target nation are sometimes perverse, generating increased levels of political resistance to the sanctioners' demands.

The economic impacts of trade sanctions on the target country are reflected in their terms-of-trade effects, which are larger in the case of multilateral sanctions than unilateral. Investment sanctions initially raise the rate of return to capital in the target country, but eventually the decrease in the inflow of new capital from abroad constrains the target's growth.

Using an interest group model of endogenous policy, the level of sanctions imposed is shown to depend on the relative influences of competing interest groups within the sanctioning country. In the target country, normally only those sanctions that have differential effects on supporters and opponents of the ruling regime will induce the regime to alter its objectionable policy.

Game-theoretic models suggest that the success of sanctions depends on conflict expectations and levels of commitment. Many sanctions strategies end at the threat stage, without sanctions being implemented. Consequently, empirical studies using data on actually applied sanctions may exhibit selection bias. In general, the processes generating sanctions and the processes determining their outcome are intrinsically linked. Empirical work on sanctions has attempted to address this problem through the use of simultaneous equations methods. The empirical literature has also investigated the role of political regime type, specifically, democracy or the absence thereof, in determining nations' proclivities to impose sanctions and the success of the sanctions.

Keywords

economic sanctions, trade policy, trade sanctions, financial sanctions, interest groups, endogenous policy, game theory

JEL classification: F13, D72, D74

1. Introduction

International economic sanctions are often favored by nation states or by international organizations as a means of projecting power or influencing another government's behavior without resorting to military conflict. The utility of sanctions as an instrument of foreign policy is attested to both by their longevity as a staple of international diplomacy and by their growing popularity since the end of the Cold War. Historically, economic sanctions, which date back at least to the Megarian decree of Athens in 435 B.C., were used by Napoleon in the Continental System commencing in 1806, by Thomas Jefferson in the Embargo Act of 1807, and by the League of Nations against Italy in 1935. In recent times, the most encyclopedic taxonomy of sanctions episodes is that of Hufbauer et al. (1990), hereafter HSE, which records 116 cases since 1914. Following the collapse of the Soviet empire in 1990, there has been an acceleration of sanctioning activity that reflects their growing use by international organizations as well as by the one remaining world hegemon, the United States.[1]

The study of sanctions is, in essence, a part of the broader study of the mechanisms by which policy preferences in one nation or group of nations are transmitted to another, target, nation. How does a sender state, short of military intervention, bring about policy change in a target state? Clearly, economic pressure is one channel through which influence might be brought to bear on the international stage, others being diplomatic suasion and non-economic or cultural embargoes. Economic sanctions include trade sanctions, i.e., restrictions on imports from or exports to the target country; investment sanctions, which include restrictions on capital flows to the target or, in some cases, mandatory disinvestment; and more narrowly-targeted, so-called "smart", sanctions, such as freezing the offshore assets of individual members of the target nation's ruling elite, or travel bans on government officials and party cadres. In all cases, economic sanctions are supposed to work by imposing some kind of pain on the target country, and particularly on its ruling regime, which then alters its policies in order to comply with the sender's demands and thereby avoid further sanctions damage.[2]

---

[1] From 1945 to 1990, the UN Security Council imposed mandatory multilateral sanctions only against Rhodesia, and a much less-inclusive arms embargo against South Africa. During the 1990s, however, the Security Council implemented sanctions on no fewer than 13 occasions. The United States alone applied sanctions against 35 countries from 1993 to 1996 [Kaempfer and Lowenberg (1999), United Kingdom Parliament (1999)].

[2] As Kirshner (1997, p. 42) observes, the conventional view of how sanctions work is that, by inflicting damage on the target country, its ruling elite and core support groups, the sanctions will prompt the leadership to choose to change its objectionable policy in response to a straightforward cost-benefit calculus. It is assumed, in effect, that there is a rough proportionality between economic deprivation and political change in the target country – "the more value-deprivation, the more political disintegration" [Galtung (1967, p. 388)]. In the words of Mack and Khan (2000, p. 281), "[o]ne of the core assumptions of traditional sanctions theory is that the pain inflicted by sanctions on citizens of target states will cause them to pressure their government into making the changes demanded by the sanctioning body."

Although welfare-reducing in aggregate, sanctions, like any other restriction on the flow of goods or factors between countries, have redistributional effects in both sanctioning and target countries. These redistributional effects are important in determining both the nature of the sanctions imposed by the senders and the impact of the sanctions on the target. In regard to the latter, an important distinction needs to be made between the economic impact and the political impact. While there is no doubt that embargoes or restrictions on flows of goods and capital impose welfare costs on the target economy, or specifically on identifiable groups within the economy, there is considerable uncertainty as to how such costs are supposed to translate into policy change in the target, especially policy change in the direction desired by the sanctioner. Galtung (1967) was one of the earliest sanctions scholars to note that sanctions are often followed by increased levels of political integration in the target country, the so-called rally-around-the-flag effect that has captured the attention of many contributors to the sanctions literature. Thus Mayall (1984, p. 631) writes that sanctions "frequently have perverse effects, creating out of the siege mentality a sense of national cohesion and determination to triumph in adversity that was previously lacking. . . ." In such situations it is not uncommon for sanctions to increase popular support for the ruling regime in the target country [Mack and Khan (2000, p. 282)]. Moreover, as Galtung (1967) observes, sanctions can be counterproductive by giving rise to a new elite in the target nation that benefits from international isolation. For example, Selden (1999) notes that, in the long run, sanctions often foster the development of domestic industries in the target country, thus reducing the target's dependence on the outside world and the ability of sanctioners to influence the target's behavior through economic coercion.[3]

As far as the nature of the sanctions themselves are concerned, Galtung (1967) as well as several other theorists [Renwick (1981), Leyton-Brown (1987), Lundborg (1987), Tsebelis (1990)] have pointed out that sanctions are often imposed not for instrumental purposes, i.e., not to create the maximum pain for the target or to induce the target to comply with the sanctioner's demands, but for expressive or demonstrative purposes. For example, governments may impose sanctions in order to satisfy domestic groups within the sanctioning nations desirous of being seen to be "doing something" about the target's behavior without necessarily incurring a significant cost in the process. Alternatively, sanctions might be implemented as a signal of resolve or to establish a reputation in the eyes of foreign allies and enemies alike.[4]

---

[3] On the unintended long run consequences of sanctions, see also Doxey (1980, 1996).

[4] Renwick (1981, p. 85) argues that, in many cases in which sanctions have been applied, "demonstration of disapproval appears to have been the main purpose." A government may consider sanctions useful if they serve to "declare its position to internal and external publics or help win support at home or abroad" [Renwick (1981, p. 85)]. Similarly, Leyton-Brown (1987, p. 305) maintains that sanctions typically are not designed primarily to achieve compliance, but to "send a message both to the target nation and to one's own domestic population," where that message may be outrage, firmness, or solidarity. Tsebelis (1990) concurs that sanctions are often imposed to send a signal, especially to smaller nations, that a certain behavior will not be tolerated, rather than to accomplish a particular policy goal.

The importance of expressive sanctions raises a prickly conundrum for the sanctions literature, namely, how to judge whether a particular sanctions episode was successful in attaining its goals and, more importantly, whether sanctions in general actually work. The answer, of course, depends on what is meant by "work". Of the 116 episodes documented by HSE, 34 percent are rated by the authors as successful in achieving their political objectives. For some scholars, with an eye to the expressive motives for sanctions, such judgment is too harsh. Thus Baldwin (1985) offers a broad conceptualization of sanctions success, arguing that even if sanctions do not coerce the target into changing its objectionable policy they nevertheless can be an effective projection of influence by attaching costs to the target's behavior or by enhancing the sanctioner's international reputation.[5] Pape (1997, p. 97), by contrast, applies a much stricter definition of success, arguing that sanctions can only be deemed successful if the target country concedes to a significant part of the sanctioner's demands in the absence of any other internal or external pressures for change, i.e., there must be no other more-credible explanation for the target's change in behavior. Pape disputes HSE's finding, pointing out that, in almost all of the supposedly successful cases, there were other factors, such as military intervention, that contributed to the favorable outcome. According to Pape's definition of success, sanctions *by themselves* brought about political compliance in less than five percent of the episodes in the HSE database [Pape (1997, p. 93)].[6]

The literature on economic sanctions, a province of both economists and political scientists, has tackled all of the issues discussed above and many others. Not surprisingly, given the nature of the topic, the approach normally used in the literature is that

---

[5] Along similar lines, Rogers (1996) points out that simply because sanctions are usually unsuccessful in ending wars in progress does not mean that they are necessarily ineffective in attaining more modest goals. Verdier (2005) shows that sanctions can serve a useful informational function by helping to reveal an adversary's level of resolve. Nossal (1989, p. 315) maintains that sanctions can be considered a failure only if we expect them to achieve changes in policies or conduct of target nations, whereas "[r]etributive punishment, by its very nature always 'works.' " A sanction, after all, is intended to be a punishment inflicted on a deserving recipient, regardless of its subsequent effects [Hoffman (1967, p. 144)].

[6] Askari et al. (2003) concur that sanctions are rarely effective in achieving their political goals. A close examination of many sanctions episodes that are widely considered to have been successful often reveals that the sanctions were not in fact the main cause of policy change in the target country. Thus, for example, in a recent case study, Dadak (2003) demonstrates that the sanctions against Yugoslavia in the 1990s, which many credited with bringing an end to Serbian aggression in the Balkans, were ineffective due to widespread smuggling of goods into Yugoslavia through Bulgaria. According to Dadak, it was the NATO bombing campaign of 1995 and consequent setbacks on the battlefield, not sanctions, that induced the Serbs to accede to the Dayton agreement that ended the fighting. On the other hand, some authors [e.g., Cortright and Lopez (2000), O'Sullivan (2003)] view the UN sanctions against Libya as a case of a successful policy outcome. Cortright and Lopez (2000, p. 204) conclude that, although sanctions alone normally do not dramatically alter the behavior of a target nation, sanctions nevertheless should be considered a success "if they had a positive, enduring impact on bargaining dynamics or if they helped isolate or weaken the power of an abusive regime." Lopez and Cortright (2004) likewise point out that even if sanctions do not force a target government to change its objectionable policy, the sanctions may be effective tools of containment if they reduce the amount of resources available to the government. For example, in their opinion, the sanctions against Iraq, although ineffectual in getting Saddam Hussein to comply with UN resolutions, did play an important role in containing his ability to pursue aggressive policies toward his neighbors.

of political economy, and the present chapter follows in this tradition. The remainder of the chapter will be organized as follows. In Section 2 we briefly address the economic impacts of sanctions on the target country, focusing primarily on trade sanctions and disinvestment. In Section 3 we deal with the political origins of sanctions policies in sender states, characterizing sanctions as endogenous policy outcomes in the context of an interest group model of politics. Section 4 uses a similar interest group model to describe the political effects of sanctions within the target country, emphasizing the role of narrowly-targeted or selective sanctions. Section 5 considers single-rational actor and game-theoretic approaches to sanctions. Section 6 surveys the findings of empirical studies of sanctions, while Section 7 examines the impacts of political institutions, particularly regime type, on sanctions implementation and outcomes. Section 8 concludes with avenues for further research.

2. Economic effects of sanctions

We begin by considering the effects of trade sanctions. The extent of pre-sanctions trade between sanctioner and target is an important factor in determining the ease with which the target can find alternative sources of supply and alternative markets for its goods, and therefore in determining the terms-of-trade effects of the sanctions. A modeling device that is especially helpful in studying the effects of trade sanctions on relative prices of imports and exports is that of offer curves, used by Kaempfer and Lowenberg (1992b, 1999). Offer curves, or reciprocal demand curves, show the level of trade of imports for exports that some country would desire at various prices. By using offer curves to examine the consequences of trade sanctions, we can show not only the impact on the terms of trade for the relevant countries but we can also make inferences about the welfare effects of sanctions.

Figure 1 shows an initial offer curve equilibrium between a nation that is the potential target of multilateral economic sanctions, offer curve T, and its current trade partners comprising all other nations in the world, offer curve W. The horizontal axis measures quantities of the export good of country T, X_T, and the vertical axis shows quantities of country T's import good, M_T. Any point along T's offer curve shows some specific international trade equilibrium for country T, which is a welfare maximizing quantity of imports that would be acquired at the cost of a certain quantity of exports at some specific price ratio. That price ratio, or the terms of trade, is merely the ratio of exports to imports as represented by the slope of a ray from the origin to a point on the offer curve. Since, in general, as country T moves out from the origin along its offer curve it is able to buy more imports for a lower cost in terms of exports per import, i.e., its terms of trade improve, movement from the origin along a country's offer curve is welfare enhancing for that country.

Figure 1 also shows the composite offer curve for all other countries, W. This offer curve is essentially a composite of all world trade, net of the trade of the target country. As such, the world exports the good which the target country imports – the good on

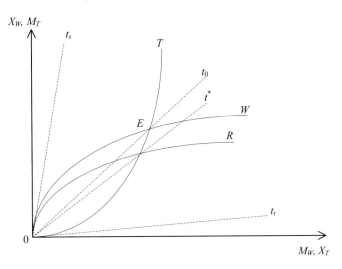

Figure 1. International trade equilibria with sanctions.

the vertical axis ($X_W = M_T$) – and it imports the export good of the target country on the horizontal axis ($M_W = X_T$). We make the simplifying assumption that the target country has a worldwide comparative advantage in the good on the horizontal axis, X_T. In other words, the target country, at least initially, is the only supplier of X_T on the world market, and all other countries are potential importers of this good and exporters of the second good, M_T. The intersection, E, between the two offer curves, W and T, is the international trade equilibrium in the two-good offer curve model. This intersection shows an equilibrium at which the given terms of trade, t_0, simultaneously equate supply and demand, i.e., exports and imports, in the markets for both goods.

Consider now the implications of multilateral sanctions imposed by W on country T. The easiest exercise for analysis in this case is to hypothesize a total embargo on trade between W and country T. Such an embargo, by eliminating the opportunity for trade between W and T, forces T from its trade equilibrium at E to a position of autarky at the origin, 0, and worsens the terms of trade in T from t_0 to t_t. However, Figure 1 also clearly shows the costs of the embargo to the sanctioning countries as well as to the target country. By imposing the sanction on its trading partner T, the world is also imposing autarky conditions on itself, vis-à-vis T, and forcing a deterioration of its terms of trade to t_s. This move from trade equilibrium is welfare worsening for the sanctioning countries as well as for the target in so far as the movement of the sanctioners' terms of trade, from t_0 to t_s, represents an increase in the price of their net importable good.[7]

---

[7] Within the trading coalition of countries belonging to W there might be considerable differences in the extent to which they individually suffer as a result of this terms-of-trade deterioration. Inside the group, some

But what factors determine the extent of this terms-of-trade swing? Essentially, how far the terms of trade move in a given situation depends on the amount of curvature in the offer curves, which is in turn a function of the price-elasticity of the offer to trade and the size of the trading countries. When a very large country enters trade, its economic size relative to the amount of trade that it undertakes ensures that the equilibrium terms of trade cannot be very different from the autarky terms of trade. Very large countries are self-sufficient enough to not reap very substantial gains from trade, but conversely they do not suffer extensively from abstaining from trade, following sanctions. Thus large-country offer curves have very little curvature, almost resembling linear rays from the origin. Small countries, however, tend to be much more dependent on trade. Their demands for and supplies of tradeable goods are price-inelastic and these countries can suffer greatly from the imposition of sanctions. Thus, small countries tend to have much more curvature in their offer curves than do large countries.

Let us now consider the economic effects of unilateral sanctions on the target country and on the rest of the world. With the imposition of sanctions by one sanctioning country, S, the rest of the world's offer to trade with the target is reduced to the new offer curve, R, in Figure 1, since the sanctioning country's offer is removed from W at each terms of trade. The elasticity of this residual offer curve is also reduced by the sanctioning country's withdrawal, meaning that the new offer curve, R, must have a greater degree of curvature than the original offer curve, W.[8] The opportunity to continue trading with those nations that are not participating in the sanctions, however, means that the target country is not reduced to autarky as it was in the first example. Rather, trade continues for the target at somewhat worsened terms of trade, t^*, where the degree of deterioration in the target's terms of trade depends on the magnitude of the shift from W to R, and on the trade elasticities involved. The greater the share of the target's pre-sanctions trade accounted for by the sanctioning country(ies), or the larger the number of sanctioning countries relative to non-sanctioners, the greater is the magnitude of the shift from W to R. As the number of sanctioning countries increases, we approach the multilateral case, with the target's terms of trade, t^*, approaching the autarky terms of trade, t_t. The less elastic is the rest-of-the-world offer curve, R, the greater the extent of the deterioration of the target's terms of trade.[9] Although not shown explicitly in Fig-

---

countries might actually become net exporters of the good formerly imported from the target, so that the sanctions actually benefit those nations. As a whole, however, the sanctions cannot cause a net improvement in W's terms of trade.

[8] The rest-of-the-world offer curve is constructed by summing up the import and export totals for all countries, except the target country, along each ray. This is the general equilibrium equivalent of adding up individual quantities supplied or demanded at each price in a supply-and-demand diagram in order to derive a market supply or demand curve. When the sanctioning country's offer curve is removed from the rest-of-the-world offer curve, the resulting residual offer to trade lies closer to the origin at each terms of trade and is less price-elastic.

[9] As more countries join in the sanctions, the elasticity of R is further reduced until we end up with the multilateral case.

ure 1, the deterioration of the target's terms of trade is also larger the more inelastic the target's offer curve.[10]

In the case of unilateral sanctions, the impact on the sanctioning country is similar to the impact on the sanctioning countries in the multilateral case. The imposition of sanctions eliminates, for S, an inexpensive source of imports and an attractive market for its exports. In the extreme case, if we assume that there are no alternative markets for S among the other members of R, the decision to apply sanctions against the target moves the sanctioning country to autarky: unable to obtain its desired import, the sanctioning country finds itself far worse off following sanctions than does the target, which retains a market among other countries albeit at worsened terms of trade.[11]

The trade model presented in Figure 1 indicates that both the sanctioning nation(s) and the target nation are, in general, made worse off by trade embargoes.[12] The degree to which the sanctions impose costs on these nations depends on the number and size of other countries willing to continue trading and on the elasticities of the trade offers of those countries. Unilateral sanctions create a smaller deterioration in the target's terms of trade than do sanctions involving a larger number of participant countries. Moreover, any distortion of prices of traded goods caused by sanctions inevitably creates opportunities for non-sanctioning third parties, transshippers and smugglers to capture rents by continuing to trade with the target (purchasing the target's exports below the world price and selling the target's imports above the world price). The magnitude of these rents, and therefore the incentive to engage in sanctions-busting activities, rises with the severity of the sanctions as reflected in their terms-of-trade-effects, and is consequently greater in the case of multilateral sanctions than unilateral sanctions [Kaempfer and Lowenberg (1999)]. While most of the sanctions rents under unilateral sanctions accrue to traders in non-sanctioning countries, under multilateral sanctions much of the

---

[10] On the effects of the target's domestic elasticities of demand and supply on the impact of sanctions, see Black and Cooper (1987), Dollery and Leibbrandt (1987), Kaempfer and Lowenberg (1988b) and van Bergeijk (1994).

[11] This result, of course, assumes no transshipment of the target's exports or imports through non-participating nations. If the goods traded among these countries were all perfectly fungible, then an embargo would leave all nations – target, sanctioner and others – exactly as they were before the embargo, less only the extra transaction costs involved in transshipping goods. Moreover, if both the sanctioning country and the target were members of larger groups of countries which participate on either side of the market, then the sanctions would not interfere with either country's ability to participate in some trade. Rather, both the sanctioner and the target would find their terms of trade worsened to some degree following sanctions, with the exact amount of damage depending on the trade elasticities of all parties involved. Harkness (1990) examines the case of sanctions that affect some, but not all, trade flows between sanctioner and target. He shows that the effects of such sanctions on the sanctioning country's terms of trade and trade balance depend on the elasticities of demand for its imports and exports.

[12] That trade sanctions impose costs on both the target and the sanctioner is one reason why sanctions are often viewed as less effective than other forms of diplomacy. For example, in a spatial bargaining model, Morgan and Schwebach (1997) show that sanctions are unlikely to alter significantly the outcome that has the highest joint probability of being accepted by both parties, essentially because the more costly the sanctions are to the target, the more costly they are to the sanctioner as well.

sanctions-busting activity is likely to involve traders in the target nation itself, thereby channeling a considerable portion of the rents into the very country that is supposed to be punished by the sanctions [Kaempfer and Lowenberg (1999)]. Sanctions rents might even, perversely, enrich the target country's own rulers if they are able to participate in the sanctions-busting trade.[13]

Turning now to the effects of investment sanctions, consider the balance of payments equation for a single-commodity economy that is a target of disinvestment,

$$P_X NX = F\{q, P_X MP_K(L, K)\}, \quad F_1 > 0, \ F_2 < 0, \tag{1}$$

where P_X is the price of the product X, NX is net exports of X, F is net capital outflows, q is the degree of disinvestment (discussed further below), L and K are the amounts of labor and capital employed in the target economy, which for present purposes are treated as exogenous, and MP_K is the marginal product of capital. The left-hand side of Equation (1) is net exports, the nominal value of exports net of the nominal value of imports. The right-hand side is an expression for net capital outflows, which is the outflow of investment funds net of foreign investment inflows. The left-hand side and the right-hand side must be equal to each other because of the way in which a country's balance of payments is defined: the foreign currency obtained as a result of selling more goods and services to foreigners than buying from them is used to finance the purchase of foreign financial and physical assets. In effect, the trade surplus provides the foreign currency to pay for the flow of investment abroad. If net exports were negative, i.e., if domestic residents were buying more goods and services from foreigners than selling to them, then the resulting trade deficit would need to be financed by a net capital inflow. In this case, investment funds from abroad would be providing the foreign currency required to finance the country's excess of imports over exports.

Net capital outflows, on the right-hand side of Equation (1), are a positive function of the degree of disinvestment, q, and a negative function of the value marginal product of the capital stock within the target economy, $P_X MP_K(L, K)$. Disinvestment means that foreigners are selling off assets that they own in the target country and repatriating the proceeds, which gives rise to a capital outflow from the target country. Or, if mandatory disinvestment prevents foreigners from investing in the target country in the first place, there will be a decrease in capital inflows. Either way, an increase in the degree of disinvestment causes an increase in net capital outflows from the target. The value marginal product of capital is simply the dollar value of output contributed by the last unit of capital employed. The greater the productivity of target-country capital assets, the greater the incentive to hold those assets on the part of both foreigners and domestic

---

[13] Thus, for example, Rowe (2001) documents the Rhodesian government's ability to exercise control over the marketing of the domestic tobacco crop. Saddam Hussein captured substantial revenues by adding illegal surcharges to the price of oil sold to intermediaries under the UN's oil-for-food program [Wall Street Journal (May 2, 2002, p. A1)] and the Milosevic regime was able to appropriate a large share of sanctions rents by creating state-run monopolies and centralizing the distribution of goods [Kaempfer and Lowenberg (1999)].

residents: more foreign capital will therefore flow into the country, while domestic residents will be more likely to employ their funds at home rather than send them abroad. Therefore an increase in the value marginal product of capital causes a decrease in net capital outflows.

The rate of return, r, on the target country's domestic assets is defined as follows:

$$r = \{P_X MP_K(L, K)\}/\{P_K(q, K)\}, \quad P_{K1} < 0, \ P_{K2} < 0, \tag{2}$$

i.e., the rate of return to capital is the ratio of the value marginal product of capital to the price of capital. The partial derivative, P_{K1}, measures the extent to which target-country assets are substitutable for foreign assets. Universal disinvestment by all countries would imply the sale of all foreign-owned assets in the target country. Because no foreign wealthholder would be allowed to own these assets, residents of the target country would acquire them at depressed prices. Thus, as indicated in Equation (2), $\partial r/\partial q = (\partial r/\partial P_K)P_{K1} > 0$. A rise in q causes a fall in P_K and a rise in r. This is a formalization of the "fire-sale" phenomenon, whereby disinvestment of foreign-owned assets raises the rate of return earned by domestic capital owners in the target country.[14]

If disinvestment occurred only on the part of a single country or a few countries, and if sufficient foreign wealthholders were indifferent between target-country and foreign assets, there would be no change in the price of target-country assets and no change in the rate of return. Intermediate cases are, of course, the most likely. In general, as the extent of disinvestment grows – from a few firms to many firms and from a mandated, fully binding policy in a few nations to most or even all nations – so the impact grows, because the degree to which target-country assets are only imperfectly substitutable for other assets rises.[15] This process has the effect of decreasing the price of target-country assets, which encourages their acquisition by domestic wealthholders. Such acquisition can be financed in two ways: by the sale of foreign assets owned by residents of the target country or by an increase in the target's net exports.[16]

Hence, the direct effect of disinvestment is that net capital outflows rise. But the rate of return in the target country increases due to the fall in the price of productive assets. This decrease in domestic asset prices slows the net capital outflow by making domestic assets more attractive. In other words, the increase in capital outflows caused by disinvestment can be offset either by an increase in the target country's net exports or by a decrease in the price of domestic capital assets, i.e., an increase in their rate

---

[14] For discussions of the fire-sale effect, see Kaempfer and Lowenberg (1986, 1992b, chapter 7) and Lowenberg and Kaempfer (1998, chapter 8).

[15] The degree of substitutability between assets of different national origin depends on several considerations, particularly differences in country risk. A schedule of substitutability might exist for every country such that, to some extent, the degree of capital mobility or asset substitutability might be almost perfect at the margin, but as asset markets are asked to handle large capital flows, this substitutability begins to break down.

[16] The terms-of-trade and exchange rate effects of sanctions are examined in more detail by Kaempfer and Moffett (1988).

of return, that is sufficient to induce target-country wealthholders to sell off their foreign assets in order to buy the cheaper domestic assets. To the extent that the target country's net exports cannot increase, perhaps due to a trade boycott that is imposed alongside the capital sanctions, the full burden of adjustment falls on domestic asset prices.

As pointed out by Kaempfer and Lowenberg (1986, 1992b) and Lowenberg and Kaempfer (1998), an implication that follows from the foregoing analysis is that disinvestment sanctions can have the perverse effect of enhancing the target country's ability to pursue its objectionable behavior. The existing foreign capital stock – the physical plant and capacity previously owned by foreigners – is purchased by domestic capital owners at reduced prices, causing yields to rise and prompting target-country residents to sell foreign assets and substitute into domestic assets with higher rates of return. The increase in the rate of return due to the acquisition of productive assets at fire-sale prices translates into a windfall gain to domestic capital owners, which increases the tax base available to the government to finance its policies, including those that attracted the sanctions in the first place.

In the longer run, if disinvestment were continued, the inflow of new capital goods from abroad would diminish as licensed techniques and patented processes of foreign firms were no longer available. In this case, the exogenous capital stock, K, will decrease. From Equation (2),

$$\partial r/\partial K = \left\{ P_X(\partial MP_K/\partial K)P_K(q, K) - P_X MP_K(L, K)P_{K2} \right\}/P_K(q, K)^2 > 0$$

$$\text{if } \left| (\partial MP_K/\partial K)P_K(q, K) \right| < \left| MP_K(L, K)P_{K2} \right|,$$

i.e., a decrease in K would both raise the marginal product of capital, MP_K, and raise the price of capital goods, P_K. These two effects work in opposite directions on the rate of return, r. A rising marginal product of capital raises r, but a rising price of capital depresses r. The above condition states that a fall in K will cause a fall in the rate of return if the impact on the marginal product of capital is less than the impact on the price of capital goods. As long as this condition holds, a decrease in K will cause a decrease in the rate of return, r, via an increase in the price of capital goods, P_K. In effect, firms in the target country will confront higher production costs and lower profits as a result of the increased scarcity of capital, thereby reducing the government's ability to extract tax revenue to finance its objectionable policy. However, as Porter (1979, pp. 590–591) points out, the long run impact of the withdrawal of international capital is essentially a growth-related phenomenon, which is difficult to capture in a static model. Although any decrease in the amount of new and depreciation investment can be expected to lower the growth rate of the target's per capita GDP, and therefore possibly hamper the target government's capacity to carry out its objectionable policy, the amount of damage depends ultimately on the difficulty experienced by the target country in replacing, or doing without, foreign sources of capital.

3. The political determinants of sanctions policies in sender states[17]

In this section we use an interest group model of endogenous policy to characterize the decision on sanctions implementation within a sender country.[18] According to this approach, the nature and extent of sanctions applied by the sanctioning state are determined by pressures brought to bear in the domestic political system by interest groups of differing motives. These pressures are the outcomes of private utility maximization on the part of individual members of the interest groups concerned. Although the groups are defined by commonality of interests, the political participation of any group member is tempered by a desire to free ride on the collective lobbying efforts of the group.

Consider some individual i, a member of the total population I of some country. This individual maximizes utility according to:

$$\text{Max} \quad U^i = U^i(Y^i), \quad U^i_1 > 0, \ U^i_{11} < 0$$
$$\text{subject to} \quad Y^i = Y^i(S), \quad Y^i(0) = Z^i, \quad Y^i_1 \gtrless 0, \ Y^i_{11} = 0, \tag{3}$$

where Y is income, Z is an initial endowment, and S is a non-negative, continuous variable measuring the level of sanctions applied. The sanctions are assumed to increase or decrease individual income at a fixed rate. Moreover, the sanctions, like any other trade restriction, generate distortions, i.e., $\sum_i Y^i_1 < 0$, although they increase the incomes of members of particular interest groups at the expense of others.

The change in utility produced by a change in the level of sanctions is:

$$\partial U^i / \partial S = U^i_1 Y^i_1 \gtrless 0. \tag{4}$$

Let $I = \{J, K\}$ such that for all $j, k \in J, K$ respectively, $Y^j_1 > 0, Y^k_1 < 0$, which allows separate demand functions for sanctions to be specified for those who benefit from them and for those who are hurt by them. For group J, all members' willingness to pay for an additional unit of sanctions can be summed to yield:

$$P_S = D^J(S) = \sum_j \partial U^j / \partial S = \sum_j U^j_1 Y^j_1, \quad D^J_1 < 0, \tag{5}$$

where P_S is the unit price of sanctions. This price is the dollar amount that individuals in group J would be willing to spend at the margin to achieve a certain level of utility enhancing sanctions through the political market.

Members of group K are willing to pay to avoid sanctions because $Y^k_1 < 0$. This implies a demand for reduced sanctions that, when expressed as a function of an increasing

---

[17] The material in this section and in the next section is adapted from Kaempfer and Lowenberg (1988a). See also Kaempfer and Lowenberg (1992b, chapters 4 and 8) and Lowenberg and Kaempfer (1998, chapter 5).
[18] The interest group model is based on the economic theory of regulation deriving from Stigler (1971), Peltzman (1976) and Becker (1983, 1985).

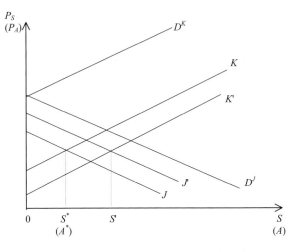

Figure 2. Endogenous policy equilibria.

level of sanctions, becomes:

$$P_S = D^K(S) = -\sum_k \partial U^k/\partial S = -\sum_k U_1^k Y_1^k, \quad D_1^K > 0. \tag{6}$$

This expression is defined as the negative of the sum of the marginal utilities of the change in Y from a change in S. In this case we interpret P_S as the amount that group K members would pay at the margin to keep sanctions from increasing.

Intuitively, the demand curve labeled D^J in Figure 2 shows the marginal utility to those interest groups that benefit from S associated with increased levels of S.[19] The curve labeled D^K is the marginal utility to opponents of S from reduced levels of S. (Ignore for now the variable A, which is also plotted on the horizontal axis in Figure 2; this variable is discussed in Section 4.) The height of the D^J curve reflects the amount of resources that the proponents of policy S are willing to spend to generate political influence in order to secure one more unit of S. Similarly, the height of the D^K curve is the willingness to pay on the part of opponents of S in order to prevent one more unit from being supplied.

Demanders of S are willing to pay for increments of the policy because the distributional effects of S raise the real incomes of the beneficiaries of the sanctions policy.[20] This willingness to pay is represented in a political market where the demanders "pay"

---

[19] By abstracting from income effects, we can interpret the marginal utility schedule as equivalent to a demand schedule.

[20] Individuals within the sanctioning country whose incomes are increased as a consequence of sanctions include producers of substitutes for proscribed imports as well as domestic consumers of exportables that previously went to the target country.

for S in a variety of ways, including political contributions or volunteer work for candidates who support policy S, a willingness to pay higher prices for goods made necessary
as a consequence of S, or to make side payments to groups not otherwise involved in
the issue. The demand curve has the traditional negative slope because, as the level of S
rises, additional benefits to the demanders decrease at the margin.

The D^K curve in Figure 2 is, in essence, a supply curve of S, showing the ability
of the government to implement policy S. Members of group K are made worse off
by higher levels of S.[21] This creates an incentive for them to engage in political activity which imposes costs on the government. These costs can come in the form of
increased support for opposition candidates or various forms of protest ranging from
non-violent dissent to civil disobedience. Group K's demand price for reduced levels
of S is therefore also the government's supply price for increases in S. The justification
for the upward sloping supply curve is that increases in S will cause increasing utility
losses at the margin for those made worse off.

The demand for sanctions must take into account the public good nature of this type
of policy. The demand functions (5) and (6) are derived by summing the maximum
willingness to pay for more sanctions or fewer sanctions over the members of groups
J and K. In an attempt to free ride on other group members, however, each member
has an incentive to reveal a lower willingness to pay. The extent to which this ability to
free ride diminishes the demand of a group determines the political effectiveness of that
group. The presence of free riding within groups requires a respecification of demand,

$$P_S = J(S, E^J), \quad J_1 < 0, \ J_2 < 0, \tag{5'}$$

$$P_S = K(S, E^K), \quad K_1 > 0, \ K_2 < 0, \tag{6'}$$

where E^J and E^K are shift parameters that reflect the degrees of free riding in groups J
and K and in turn determine the abilities of the two groups to produce political influence
[Becker (1983, 1985)]. Free riding is a function of the size of the group and other factors
that influence organization and enforcement costs [Olson (1965)]. The more severe the
free riding problem, the greater the magnitude of E^J and E^K. J_2 and K_2 are both
negative because free riding reduces willingness to pay in both groups and therefore
reduces their demand prices.

Equating the demand for more sanctions, (5) or (5'), with the demand for fewer sanctions, (6) or (6'), will clear the political market. Support-maximizing politicians clear
the market by raising the level of sanctions above its zero minimum until pressure for
higher sanctions at the margin is offset by pressure against higher sanctions. That is,
sanctions, like any other government regulation, are supplied up to the point where the
marginal utility to the beneficiaries, weighted by their political influence or effectiveness, is equal to the influence-weighted marginal disutility to the losers [Stigler (1971),

---

[21] Individuals within the sanctioning country whose incomes are reduced as a consequence of sanctions
include consumers of importables previously obtained from the target country as well as domestic producers
of proscribed exports.

Peltzman (1976), Becker (1983)]. A necessary condition for the existence of this equilibrium is that both interest groups display diminishing returns to political influence,
i.e., that the political pressure applied by each group increase at a decreasing rate as
the size of the wealth transfer to the group increases.[22] Figure 2 depicts such a political
market for sanctions, given the following additional assumptions. First, assume initially
that there are no output deadweight losses from sanctions. Thus the sanctions are merely
lump-sum redistributional transfers within the sanctioning polity, i.e., $\sum_i Y_1^i = 0$. Second, assume that marginal utilities of all individuals in the neighborhood of $S = 0$ are
identical. Third, assume that both groups of individuals are equally effective in controlling free riding and exerting political influence. Thus, for an infinitesimally small level
of sanctions, because the income gain of group J is assumed exactly equal to the loss
of group K, it follows that group J's willingness to pay for more sanctions is equal to
group K's willingness to pay for less sanctions. The political market therefore clears at
$D^K = D^J \Rightarrow S = 0$.

An increase in sanctions will be positively valued by group J along D^J, but at a
decreasing rate because the marginal utility of Y is assumed to be decreasing. Similarly,
group K is willing to pay increasing amounts to prevent sanctions from rising, again
due to the rising marginal disutility of falling Y. Because in this case sanctions are a
pure redistribution with no allocational effects, the political equilibrium is where the
marginal utilities of money income of J and K are equal, which occurs at a zero level
of sanctions.

Now assume that sanctions are market distorting interventions. Much like tariffs, quotas and other instruments of protection, they impose deadweight costs, i.e., $\sum_i Y_1^i < 0$.
Deadweight costs associated with redistributional policies generally have the effect of
increasing the amount of wealth that must be extracted from the losers while reducing
the amount transferred to the recipients. Thus for each increment in sanctions, members of group K must now forgo more wealth and members of group J now receive
less. Consequently, group K's willingness to pay to prevent each increment in sanctions
from being implemented is increased, while group J's willingness to pay to obtain each
increment is reduced. The D^K curve shifts up and the D^J curve shifts down, even
though we are continuing to assume that the two groups are equally effective in exerting political influence. The vertical distance between the D^K and D^J curves measures
the waste of resources generated as a result of the sanctioning policy, which arises because sanctions are a particularly inefficient way to redistribute income from group K
to group J, especially when compared to a simple cash subsidy.[23]

By causing an upward shift of the D^K curve and a downward shift of the D^J curve,
deadweight costs produce an equilibrium at a negative level of sanctions – precluded
by the assumption of non-negativity of S. The political market clearing level of sanctions is therefore zero. In effect, the pressure for sanctions by those individuals whose

---

[22] Diminishing returns to political influence might arise either from diminishing marginal utility of money
income, as in the present model, or from diminishing marginal product in the exertion of political pressure.

[23] On the inefficiency of regulatory transfers, see Tullock (1989, pp. 11–27).

incomes are increased by sanctions not only has to counter the pressure against sanctions by those individuals whose incomes are reduced but must also compensate for the allocational distortions and inefficiencies created by the sanctions. Moreover, if the government incurs an administrative cost of applying sanctions, this would further add to the output deadweight costs of the sanctioning policy and further increase the spread between the D^K and D^J curves.

Thus, without differences in the political effectivenesses of various interest groups, sanctions are unlikely to be applied by a government responding only to income maximizing political pressure. As Becker (1985, p. 344) points out, "...no policy that lowered social output would survive if all groups were equally large and skillful at producing political influence, for the opposition would always exert more influence than proponents." However, the political ineffectiveness of groups J and K will cause their respective demand curves, $J(S, E^J)$ and $K(S, E^K)$, to shift below D^J and D^K. If J is a small group, each member of which gains a significant share of the increase in income obtained from an increase in sanctions, e.g., manufacturers of substitutes for the exports of the target country, then J may be more politically effective than group K, comprising the consumers who lose from import restrictions.[24] Consequently, if E^J is smaller than E^K, the downward shift of $J(.)$ below D^J might be small enough relative to the downward shift of $K(.)$ below D^K to produce a political market clearing level of sanctions indicated in Figure 2 by S^*.

In general, however, political pressure for economic sanctions will arise not only because of the income effects of sanctions in terms of increased consumption opportunities for members of certain interest groups, but also because of utility enhancing attributes of the sanctions themselves.[25] That is, sanctions may be considered a public good (or bad) that directly contributes to individual utility (or disutility) by allowing individuals the satisfaction (or dissatisfaction) of experiencing their nation engaged in a foreign policy toward a certain goal. Some individuals might perceive their contributions to the sanctions policy as private goods, so that, in effect, sanctions jointly provide both public and private good attributes [Cornes and Sandler (1984)].[26] The possibility of direct

---

[24] This would be a classic case of concentrated benefits and dispersed costs which, in a majoritarian political system, so often leads to socially inefficient redistributional policies [see Kaempfer and Lowenberg (1992b, p. 28)].

[25] As already pointed out, in addition to the instrumental motive of imposing economic damage on the target country, embargoes can have an expressive value to sanctioners who feel obliged to act for moral or political reasons. Furthermore, sanctions that are perceived to be producing desirable results in the target country are likely to elicit growing support within the sanctioning country, while sanctions that appear not to be working, or hurting innocent groups, might be expected to attract less support.

[26] Cornes and Sandler (1984) demonstrate that certain standard propositions about public goods no longer hold in the presence of such jointly produced public and private outputs. For example, when the joint goods are Hicksian complements, free riding may actually diminish as the size of the group increases, i.e., agents' public expenditures may increase in response to increased public expenditures of others. Philanthropic activities, for instance, can generate private as well as public benefits to contributors.

effects of sanctions on individual utility suggests a respecified utility function:

$$U^i = U^i(Y^i, S). \tag{3'}$$

Differentiating this expression with respect to S implies a direct and an indirect effect on utility from imposing sanctions:

$$\partial U^i / \partial S = \partial U^i / \partial S| + U_1^i Y_1^i.$$
$$|Y_1^i = 0 \tag{7}$$

Assume initially that the direct effect, the first right-hand side term in Equation (7), is positive, which implies that pressure brought to bear by the pro-sanctions group J will increase, thereby shifting the demand for sanctions from J to J' in Figure 2. At the same time, although group K loses income from sanctions, its members obtain direct positive utility from the imposition of sanctions. Some individuals, for example, might be willing to forgo pecuniary income in order to desist from trading with an odious foreign regime. Under these circumstances, members of group K would be less willing to exert pressure against sanctions, which implies a downward shift of the demand curve for reduced sanctions from K to K' in Figure 2. Thus when all members of I derive utility directly from sanctions, the equilibrium level of sanctions will rise from S^* to S'.

The analysis in this section shows that the actual level of sanctions imposed by the sanctioning country is a function of the relative political influences of the pro-sanctions groups and the anti-sanctions groups within that country. The sanctions take the form of trade restrictions that are wealth reducing in aggregate but redistributional in nature. It follows that there is no reason why the sanctions should necessarily coincide with those required to induce maximum economic harm in the target country. It is to the target country that we now turn our attention.

4. The political effects of sanctions on the target country

We begin by assuming that the polity of the target country, like that of the sanctioning country, consists of two main interest groups. One of these, group J, exerts pressure through the political market in favor of a redistributional policy, which we will designate as A, and which is supplied by political support-maximizing politicians in the target country and is deemed objectionable by pro-sanctions interest groups in the sanctioning country. The other interest group, K, lobbies against A.[27] The interest group model used in this section is identical to that developed in the previous section, except that the endogenous policy outcome that emerges from the political market clearing process is the level of A instead of the level of sanctions.

---

[27] Examples of such interest groups might include pro- and anti-apartheid groups in South Africa, or supporters and opponents of the Milosevic regime in Serbia.

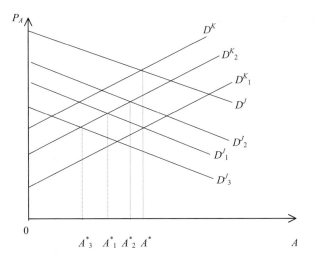

Figure 3. Effects of sanctions on equilibrium levels of policy A in the target country.

The political market clearing mechanism in the target country is described by Equations (3)–(6) and Figures 2 and 3, with the objectionable policy A replacing S. (S, the level of sanctions, was determined in Section 3. A, the level of the target country's objectionable policy, is the endogenous variable of interest in the present section. S and A are both plotted on the horizontal axis in Figure 2 only to economize on the number of figures.) Again, the curves J and K in Figure 2 are drawn to reflect the assumption that group J, the beneficiary of A, is more effective at producing political influence than group K. This assumption will result in a positive level of the equilibrium policy outcome, A^*. The relative political ineffectiveness of group K might be due to that group being politically repressed or excluded from the policy making process. The only options open to members of such a group are costly ones like insurrection or civil disobedience, which reduces their revealed willingness to pay for lower levels of A.

Figure 3 shows the possible effects of sanctions on the political market clearing level of A. We start out with the initial demand functions, D^J and D^K, and a political equilibrium at A^*. Both interest groups are now assumed to experience a decrease in income due to sanctions,[28] which lowers the demand price revealed by each, either for the policy A, in the case of J, or for reductions in A, in the case of K. With a fall in income, demanders of A will be less willing to pay for this policy, and the demand curve for A will shift down to D^J_1. However, the political costs to the government of supplying

---

[28] In general this need not be true. For instance, see Porter (1979) for a more detailed examination of the differential effects of sanctions on income groups within the target country. Sanctions restricting imports of the target country might increase the market power of producers of import substitutes [Selden (1999)]. As pointed out in Section 2, disinvestment sanctions can bring about a fire-sale selloff of foreign owned domestic assets, leading to a wealth transfer to those target country residents who acquire them at reduced prices.

A will also fall because of the negative income effect suffered by opponents of A. The decrease in incomes of individual members of the anti-A interest group reduces their ability to allocate resources to resistance activities. This fall in the government's supply price of providing A lowers the government's supply curve of A, which is group K's demand curve for reduced levels of A, to D_1^K. Both marginal utility curves have therefore shifted down from their original positions to D_1^J and D_1^K respectively and the effect on A^* is indeterminate because it depends on the relative magnitudes of the shifts. In Figure 3, A^* is unchanged. Clearly, however, it is conceivable that the income effect of sanctions might well entail an increase in A^* if group K experienced a greater reduction in income than group J. It follows that, in order to produce a diminution of the objectionable policy of the target country, sanctions should be designed to hurt the primary beneficiaries of that policy to a greater extent than those groups opposing it.[29]

However, in addition to their income effects, sanctions affect the political effectiveness parameters of the two groups, E^J and E^K. Members of the anti-A group, K, for example, might regard the imposition of sanctions as a signal of foreign support for their struggle against the A-producing government,[30] or as an indication of weakness on the part of the government.[31] In either case, free riding will diminish and group K will become more effective in exerting political influence. The resulting decrease in E^K will cause the demand schedule of group K in Figure 3 to shift up from D_1^K to D_2^K, leading to a fall in the equilibrium level of A from A^* to A_1^*. As Tullock (1971) has pointed out, anything that increases the probability of successful political resistance or lowers the expected costs to individuals of political participation will lead to an increase in resistance activities. Kaempfer and Lowenberg (1992a) use a threshold model of collective action to demonstrate how external pressure, such as sanctions, can generate widespread propagation of support for a group's cause among the domestic population.[32]

---

[29] However, if A is an inferior good for group J, then the negative income effect will induce an *upward* shift of D^J, leading to an increase in A^*. For example, sanctions that reduced the incomes of white workers in South Africa might have led to an increase in demand for regulations protecting them from black labor market competition, i.e., an increased demand for apartheid [Kaempfer et al. (1987)].

[30] Of course, this effect would depend on the identity of the sanctioner. If the sanctioning nation is not held in high regard by the populace in the target country, the sanctions could actually hinder the work of the domestic opposition.

[31] Such weakness, possibly in terms of financial resources or in terms of mass legitimacy, could be interpreted as a political opportunity by the anti-A group, mobilizing its members irrespective of whether or not they derive solace from the actions of foreign sanctioners.

[32] Kaempfer and Lowenberg's (1992a) analysis identifies several mechanisms linking sanctions with changes in political effectiveness of interest groups within a target nation. First, individuals might revise their private beliefs and preferences when they discover that foreigners publicly profess belief in some policy objective. The greater the number of people who appear to hold an opinion, the greater the extent to which private beliefs and preferences will be altered to accord more closely with that opinion. Second, foreign pressures could produce an increase in reputational benefits awarded to individuals who support certain domestic interest groups, by increasing the effectiveness of those groups in rewarding their supporters with selective incentives.

The impact of sanctions on the political effectiveness of the pro-A group, J, is ambiguous. One possibility is that members of group J might view sanctions as an unwelcome foreign encroachment on national sovereignty, in which case they will rally around the flag and the group as a whole will expend more resources on the production of political influence in favor of policy A. This rally effect makes it easier for the rulers to mobilize support for their policies. In effect, the incentive to free ride within group J will diminish, leading to a decrease in the group's political ineffectiveness parameter, E^J. The result is a shift to the right of the demand curve for A in Figure 3 from D_1^J to D_2^J and a rise in the resulting equilibrium level of A from A_1^* to A_2^*.

Alternatively, however, if individual members of group J are discouraged in their support for A by the income reducing impact of sanctions, their incentive to free ride in the production of pro-A pressure will increase. For example, individuals who normally support the ruling group might be deterred from doing so if foreign economic pressure is perceived to increase the probability of the ruling regime losing power, or if the sanctioners threaten even larger reductions in income in the future, or promise to remove the sanctions if the target regime rescinds its objectionable policy. Such discouragement of the regime's supporters causes E^J to increase and group J's demand curve in Figure 3 shifts down from D_1^J to D_3^J, leading to a reduction in the equilibrium level of A from A_1^* to A_3^*.[33]

The preceding analysis suggests that signal or threat effects of sanctions operate to bring about changes in A^* that are quite independent of the sanctions' impact on the income of the target country. In fact, sanctions that generate the greatest economic damage[34] need not necessarily produce a decrease in A^*, and might even precipitate an increase. A large negative income effect will cause a large downward shift of curves D^J and D^K in Figure 3, but unless group J is hurt proportionally more than group K so that D^J shifts down by more than D^K, there will be no reduction in A^*. If K's income falls by more that J's, then D^K will shift down by more than D^J, and A^* will actually increase. These economic impacts of sanctions thus have indeterminate and potentially perverse effects on the equilibrium level of A.

It follows from the interest group analysis of sanctions in this section that only those sanctions that have *selective* impacts on the supporters and opponents of A will lead to

Third, sanctions or foreign interest group lobbying might cause an increase in "collective sentiment" for the policies advocated by a domestic interest group, where collective sentiment, following Kuran (1989, p. 46), is defined as a representative individual's expectation about the share of the population adopting a given policy position. The perception that a threshold percentage of the population has already adopted such a position can create a bandwagon effect.

[33] An example is provided by Findlay and Lundahl (1987) who argue that white South African workers might have responded to disinvestment pressure from shareholder groups abroad by conceding to a diminution of apartheid in order to prevent erosion of their standard of living.

[34] As indicated in the previous section, the choice criteria for selecting sanctions need not necessarily include damage to the target country; rather, sanctions design reflects interest group preferences in the sanctioning countries. Sanctions that inflict the greatest economic damage would likely be broad-based multilateral trade embargoes, mandatory disinvestment or withdrawal of international credit.

policy changes in the target country. One way to bring about such selective impacts is to design the sanctions strategy with a view to its signal and threat effects rather than its income effects. A signal of support for the goals of the political opposition, and/or threats of further pain to supporters of the regime, will alter the political inefficiency parameters attaching to these two interest groups and thereby produce endogenous policy change in the desired direction. The interest group analysis therefore supports the smart sanctions strategy of aiming sanctions narrowly to impact specific groups within the target country. There is, in fact, considerable agreement in the sanctions literature on the value of pinpointing those groups most responsible for the objectionable policy. Morgan and Schwebach (1996), for example, argue that the impact of sanctions on the target country is best conceptualized in terms of their effect, direct or indirect, on the political elite.[35]

Kaempfer and Lowenberg (1999) maintain that non-economic or cultural sanctions are often more likely to have selective effects on narrowly-defined groups than are trade or investment sanctions whose income effects are typically quite indiscriminate. Moreover, symbolic sanctions, because they presuppose close cultural affinity between sanctioner and target, are necessarily unilateral rather than multilateral, or at least involve only a small group of sanctioners.[36]

---

[35] A similar view is taken by Alerassool (1993), Smith (1996), Dashti-Gibson et al. (1997) and Selden (1999). In the words of Cortright and Lopez (2000, p. 245), "[s]anctions are most likely to be effective when they target the decision-makers responsible for any wrong doing and deny the assets and resources that are most valuable to these decisionmaking elites." It is argued that smart sanctions are not only more effective than simply GNP reducing sanctions in achieving their objectives but are also less likely to impose "collateral damage" on innocent groups within the target country, such damage having the undesired effect of potentially strengthening the regime and retarding the emergence of a middle class and civil society [Haass (1998, p. 202)]. See also Weiss (1999), Cortright and Lopez (2000), Lopez (2001), Cortright, Lopez and Rogers (2002), Cortright, Millar and Lopez (2002) and Cortright and Lopez (2002a, 2002b). In a case study of US trade and financial sanctions against Iran, Torbat (2005) notes that these sanctions, while delivering a powerful economic blow, have had little political success. As an alternative, Torbat advocates the use of smart sanctions designed to exert pressure directly on the ruling clerics while avoiding negative impacts on the Iranian population as a whole. Kirshner (1997, pp. 56–63) offers a compelling example of how US sanctions against the Trujillo regime in the Dominican Republic in 1960–1962 provided vital support and encouragement to the domestic opposition. While the traditional view is that sanctions should be tailored to hurt the ruling elite and core support groups within the target country [Kirshner (1997, p. 42)] and to benefit, or at least avoid harming, the opposition, Major and McGann (2005) argue that, in some cases, relatively disinterested bystander groups ideally should feel the brunt of sanctions. These groups, because they attach little salience to the objectionable policy of the regime, will normally spend a very small proportion of their resources on lobbying either for or against this policy. Therefore sanctions that impose costs on such groups will produce a greater increase in lobbying expenditures against the objectionable policy than sanctions that target higher-salience groups such as either the elites or the counter-elites. A potential obstacle to evaluating the effectiveness of smart sanctions, however, lies in the difficulty of obtaining data to measure the impacts of these sanctions on targeted groups.

[36] Kaempfer and Lowenberg (1999) offer the example of the sports embargo on apartheid South Africa, imposed by a handful of rugby- and cricket-playing nations, which arguably had a greater impact on whites in that country, without hurting blacks much, than did many of the severest economic sanctions that were applied. On sanctions that entail proscriptions on cultural activities and sporting events, see Hanlon and Omond (1987, p. 225).

Smart sanctions are especially desirable in the case of an autocratic target regime, where the sanctions ideally should undermine the power of the autocrat, as well as diminish the resources available to the autocrat's key supporters, without imposing severe collateral damage on the repressed citizenry [Kaempfer et al. (2004)]. According to Wintrobe's (1990, 1998) model of dictatorship, an autocrat uses two inputs in the production of power, namely, repression and loyalty. Applying Wintrobe's model to sanctions, Kaempfer et al. (2004) show that sanctions can increase the budget of the dictator and thus strengthen his position if he is able to gain some of the rents accruing from changes in the terms of trade. If the sanctions harm the target country's economy to such an extent as to impoverish the public, the domestic opposition's ability to exert influence might be weakened. Furthermore, the capacity of the regime to repress dissent might be increased if a poor populace is more readily policed. In this case, the price of repression is lowered and the regime substitutes more repression for loyalty in the production of power. On the other hand, if the sanctions restrict the regime's access to instruments of repression, such as police and military equipment, or if the sanctions provide encouragement to opposition forces in organizing collective action, then the price of repression might rise. The effect of sanctions on the price of loyalty depends on the disposition of domestic interest groups at the time the sanctions are imposed. Groups that are close to the regime might be induced by the sanctions to increase their support in order to capture more of the sanctions rents for themselves. The price to the regime of obtaining loyalty from these groups is therefore reduced. However, the regime's opponents might allocate more effort toward resistance, or at least become less supportive of the regime, in which case the price to the regime of extracting loyalty from opposition groups is increased. A change in the quantity of repression also has an income effect on the quantity of loyalty supplied to the regime because repression is wealth-reducing in aggregate. Sanctions-induced changes in the price of power have both income and substitution effects on the dictator's budget constraint. The relative magnitude of these effects determines the impact of sanctions on the quantities of power and consumption chosen by the dictator to maximize his utility.

5. Single-rational actor and game theory approaches to sanctions

The previous two sections examined sanctioning behavior and the political effects of sanctions from the standpoint of an interest group theory of the political process. According to this theory, observed policies in international relations and their consequences are viewed as outcomes of the configurations of domestic interest group politics within sender and target nations. National governments are treated as more or less impartial arbiters of competing domestic interest group pressures; governments themselves have no independent policy preferences or agendas. This approach is consistent with the methodological individualism of neoclassical economics, in the sense that the behavior of interest groups is premised on utility maximization on the part of individual group members.[37]

However, many international relations scholars and economists have studied sanctions using a single-rational actor methodology, in which the relevant unit of analysis is no longer individual interest group members, voters or politicians, but entire nation-states. According to this approach, states are the main players on the international stage and decisions about whether and how to apply sanctions and whether to comply with or resist sanctions are made by states. Insights generated by single-rational actor theories are not necessarily inconsistent with those of interest group theories; rather, the two methodologies focus on different questions. The main concern of interest group models is to show how national policy choices reflect the interests of constituency groups within the polity. In single-rational actor models, however, the main purpose is to show how one country's international policy decisions both affect and are affected by other national governments' decisions. These decisions are usually strategic and game theory is often brought to bear in analyzing the behavior of states.

Thus, for example, Drezner (1998, 1999) explicitly rejects the domestic-politics approach in favor of a game-theoretic model of economic coercion in which both senders and targets of sanctions, viewed as nation-states, incorporate expectations of future conflict as well as the short-run opportunity costs of coercion into their decisions. Drezner identifies a "sanctions paradox" which is directly attributable to conflict expectations. The paradox is that sender states that anticipate frequent conflicts with the target state are more likely to initiate sanctions than states that anticipate few future conflicts, while target states that expect to be in conflict with the sender in the future are less likely to comply with the sender's demands for fear that concessions made in the present will be utilized in the future to threaten their security [Drezner (1998, p. 711)]. It follows that senders will be more likely to impose sanctions against adversaries than against allies but will get more significant concessions from allies because the latter are less concerned about the relative gains of holding out for a better bargaining position in the future, due to a low expected likelihood of future conflict. Drezner (1998, 2001) finds empirical evidence supporting the conflict expectations model. Moreover, Drezner (1999) dismisses domestic politics as a cause of the initiation of sanctions, finding evidence for his position in the fact that sanctions events are strongly correlated with crises in which states' interests are directly threatened; sanctions events tend not to be randomly distributed across *all* international crises as a domestic-politics hypothesis would predict.

Of game-theoretic treatments of sanctions, the most well-known in the literature are those of Eaton and Engers (1992, 1999). Using a theory of bargaining under incomplete information, Eaton and Engers (1999) demonstrate that success is more likely when the cost of a threatened sanction to the sender country is low relative to the gain to the sender

---

[37] On methodological individualism in international political economy, see Kaempfer and Lowenberg (1992b, chapter 3).

from changing the target's behavior, while the cost of the sanction to the target is high relative to the cost to the target of complying with the sanctioner's demands. Although this result is quite intuitive, the model does produce some interesting implications. In a world of perfect information, sanctions would never be implemented: if a threatened sanction were sufficiently effective, the target would comply immediately, obviating the need to impose the sanction, while if the sanction were ineffective, the sender would not threaten it in the first place. The fact that sanctions are observed means either that the sanctioner underestimated the target's cost of compliance, in which case the sanction fails, or that the target underestimated the sanctioner's resolve, in which case the sanction succeeds.

Although in many cases the mere threat of sanctions will be sufficient to induce compliance by the target, there could be instances of incomplete information in which the sender imposes sanctions and the target holds firm. For example, a sender might impose sanctions against a target for whom the cost of complying is greater than the cost of the sanction, either because the sender wishes to reinforce its reputation for toughness or because the sender cannot discriminate between a complaisant and a stubborn target [Eaton and Engers (1999)]. Lacy and Niou (2004) use a multistage game model to demonstrate that sanctions are most likely to be imposed precisely when they are not likely to succeed, while the sanctions that *are* likely to succeed will do so as threats, without having to be imposed at all. In the words of Eaton and Engers (1992, p. 902), "sanctions can be effective even if, in equilibrium, they are not actually used." An observer of actually applied sanctions would likely conclude that sanctions do not work, even though most sanctions are successful at the threat stage. Empirical studies based only on observed sanctions would then be biased against sanctions success. However, Eaton and Engers (1999) also point out that a resolute sanctioner might impose sanctions repeatedly, merely to demonstrate its resolve, thereby initiating a pattern of compliance on the part of targets over time which would lead an observer to conclude that sanctions are extremely effective. In this case, empirical analyses based on observations of actually implemented sanctions would be biased in favor of sanctions success. In general, sanctions that are actually imposed "constitute a very unrepresentative tip of an iceberg" [Eaton and Engers (1999, p. 410)]. We will return to the problem of selection bias in empirical sanctions studies in the next section.

In ongoing interactions characterized by a repeated game between sanctioner and target, Eaton and Engers (1999) show that the commitment of the sanctioner to actually impose sanctions if the target balks is an important determinant of the success of sanctions. By committing to always use sanctions rather than deciding on a case-by-case basis, the sender removes a target's incentive to balk in the hope of raising the probability that sanctions will be lifted in a future period [Eaton and Engers (1999, p. 413)].[38] The degree of compliance that a sanction is able to extract from a target

---

[38] Dorussen and Mo (2001), however, demonstrate that commitment strategies, by helping states improve their bargaining positions, make conflict resolution more difficult and therefore increase the duration of sanctions episodes.

depends not only on the cost of the sanction to each party but also on each party's patience. Eaton and Engers (1992) develop a measure of "toughness" based on a party's willingness to incur the cost of sanctions. The greater the target's impatience and the lower the cost to the sender, the more likely the sanction is to be successful. However, a patient sender and a high cost to the target could actually hinder compliance. Since the anticipation of such a high-cost sanction is enough to exact compliance, the threat to implement such a sanction every period is not credible. Because a patient sender will not apply sanctions with great frequency, the target can take advantage of the sender's patience by delaying compliance [Eaton and Engers (1992, p. 902)]. In this situation, a sanction that imposes less harm on the target (such as a symbolic sanction or a trade sanction affecting only a small share of the target's total trade), and is therefore more credible in repeated implementation, can sometimes be more effective.[39]

6. Empirical sanctions studies

There is a large literature that attempts to deal with the question of what factors determine whether or not sanctions are effective in bringing about their stated objectives. The starting point for this literature is the pioneering work of HSE, who assign to each sanctions episode in their database a success score ranging from 1 to 16.[40] HSE consider a sanction to be successful if its success score is greater than eight,[41] and then proceed to identify 18 potential correlates of sanctions success. Using a multiple regression model they test the impact of these correlates on the sanctions success score. However, the explanatory power and predictive success of the HSE model is weak, accounting for only 21 percent of the variation in success scores [Bonetti (1997), Leitzel (1987)]. One of the main reasons for these weak results is that HSE employ an ordinary least squares estimation technique that is not appropriate to the case of a limited dependent variable such as the sanctions success score [Bonetti (1997), van Bergeijk (1994)].[42] This

---

[39] However, Morgan and Schwebach (1996, 1997) argue that sanctions will have the greatest effect on the distribution of expected outcomes if the cost of the sanctions is sufficiently high relative to the values at stake. Specifically, Morgan and Schwebach's spatial bargaining model reveals that sanctions will be successful in attaining their political objectives in a target country only if they impose significant costs on politically powerful segments of the target society relative to the salience these segments attach to the issue in dispute.

[40] The outcome of each episode is ranked from one (failure) to four (success); the contribution of sanctions to this result is likewise ranked from one (none) to four (significant). The overall success score of the sanctions episode is then the product of the policy result score and the contribution score.

[41] However, as Bonetti (1997, pp. 334–335) points out, since the expected value of both the "result" score and the "contribution" score is 2.5, the expected success score for a random event where all results and contributions are equally probable is 6.25, which might be a more appropriate benchmark for sanctions success.

[42] The HSE regression analysis has also been criticized by van Bergeijk (1994, p. 73) and by Lam (1990, p. 241) for using as a dependent variable a measure of sanctions success that includes the importance of the sanction to the attainment of the goal. This measure requires prejudging the extent to which a given sanctions episode *caused* a change in the target's policy, which is precisely what is supposed to be estimated on the right-hand side of the regression equation.

problem has been addressed by various authors using discrete dependent variables estimators.[43]

The conclusions of this literature are quite mixed, the results being heavily dependent on model specification,[44] but a few regularities emerge, namely that the success of sanctions is positively correlated with political instability and economic weakness in the target country [HSE, Lam (1990), van Bergeijk (1989, 1994)] and with close, cordial ties between sanctioner and target prior to the sanctions being imposed [HSE, Lam (1990), Bonetti (1998)] – hence HSE's well-known dictum that it is better to sanction a friend than an enemy. Many, although not all,[45] empirical studies find a significant positive relationship between the cost of the sanctions to the target, measured as a percentage of the target's GNP, and the success of the sanctions [HSE, Lam (1990), Dehejia and Wood (1992), Dashti-Gibson et al. (1997), Drury (1998), Hart (2000)], while Lam (1990) also finds that the cost of sanctions to the sanctioner is negatively related to sanctions success. Several scholars have argued that a sanctioner's bargaining leverage, or its ability to impose costs on the target, depends on the extent of pre-sanctions trade linkages between the two countries [Miyagawa (1992), Dashti-Gibson et al. (1997), Bonetti (1998), Drury (1998), Hart (2000)]. Thus, for example, van Bergeijk (1994, pp. 77–87) finds that the potential welfare loss to the target, particularly as measured by proportional trade linkage – the sanctioner's trade flow to the target as a percentage of the target's GNP – is an important determinant of the success of sanctions. In Drury's (1998, p. 502) words, "closer ties with the target increase the sender's ability to visit damage on the target, and, according to the conventional wisdom, the greater the damage, the more effective the sanctions will be." However, Drury finds no significant effect of pre-sanctions trade flow on the sanctions outcome, leading him to conclude that while "pre-sanction trade was important in that it allows the sender to visit damage on the target . . . [i]t is this damage, measured by GNP cost, that increases sanction effectiveness" (1998, p. 507).

Although most studies find that multilateral cooperation among sanctioners has a negative impact on sanctions success,[46] Drury (1998) shows that this result holds only

---

[43] For example, van Bergeijk (1989, 1994), Drury (1998) and Dehejia and Wood (1992) use logit models, Lam (1990) and Hart (2000) use probit, and Bonetti (1998) uses logistic regressions to identify the circumstances in which high levels of success or failure are probable.

[44] For a recent survey of results, as well as a contribution of some new ones, see Jing et al. (2003).

[45] For a contrary finding, see Jing et al. (2003).

[46] See, for example, HSE and Bonetti (1996). This finding might seem counterintuitive because, as pointed out in Section 2, multilateral sanctions will generally have greater terms-of-trade effects on the target than unilateral sanctions. However, Kaempfer and Lowenberg (1999) argue that multilateral sanctions are actually less effective than unilateral sanctions precisely because the larger terms-of-trade effects generate sanctions rents that are often captured by the target regime. Also, the same large terms-of-trade effects create strong incentives for members of multilateral coalitions to cheat, trading with the target in contravention of the sanctioning agreement, thereby sending a counterproductive signal of support to the target government. Miers and Morgan (2002) implement a multidimensional spatial modeling approach to account for the higher failure rate of multilateral sanctions than unilateral.

if international organizations are not involved in the sanctions. Moreover, while assistance to the target from third countries is normally expected to reduce the probability of sanctions success [HSE, Bonetti (1998)], Drury (1998) finds that this is true only when the target was originally dependent on the sanctioner for its imports. Another correlate of sanctions success examined in the literature is the nature of the goal of the sanctions, with more ambitious goals generally shown to be negatively associated with success [Dashti-Gibson et al. (1997)], presumably because such goals are more difficult to achieve.[47] However, Drury (1998) finds no significant effect of the ambitiousness of the goal on the sanctions outcome. While countries that resort frequently to sanctions are found to be less successful on average than infrequent sanctioners [Paarlberg (1983), Dashti-Gibson et al. (1997)], the effect of duration of a given sanctions episode is controversial: Daoudi and Dajani (1983) and Brady (1987) argue that the welfare costs of sanctions increase with time, so that prolonged sanctions are more effective than short-lived sanctions,[48] whereas several other scholars find that sanctions duration is negatively correlated with success [Nincic and Wallensteen (1983), Leyton-Brown (1987), HSE, van Bergeijk (1989, 1994), Martin (1992), Miyagawa (1992), Bolks and Al-Sowayel (2000)].[49]

The empirical sanctions literature has been criticized for selection bias because the HSE data include only those episodes in which sanctions were actually applied. There are many other instances in which sanctions were considered or threatened but ultimately not used (since, as indicated in the previous section, a credible threat to sanction is, by itself, often enough to elicit compliance). In general, Fearon (1994) points out that samples of conflicts that are actually observed are drawn from an entirely different population than those of conflicts that are merely threatened. In the context of sanctions, Morgan and Miers (1999), Hart (2000) and Nooruddin (2002) argue that economic coercion is typically applied only in the most intractable of situations, in which irreconcilable differences between sanctioner and target make it unlikely that the sanctions will succeed in changing the target's behavior. It follows that the results of studies focusing on only those sanctions that are implemented will necessarily be biased against sanctions success. In order to address this problem, Drezner (2001, 2003) surveys cases in which sanctions were imposed in pursuit of economic or regulatory goals. In these categories of sanctions, threats are often made publicly before sanctions are implemented, providing an ideal test for selection bias. Consistent with Eaton and Engers'

---

[47] For example, a goal of overthrowing a ruling regime in some target country would be much more difficult to attain than simply bringing about a marginal change in the target government's policy.

[48] Galtung (1967) suggests that, as the costs of sanctions mount over time, threatening severe economic damage and political disintegration, the target is likely to eventually comply with the sanctioner's demands despite the prevalence of rally effects at lower levels of cost.

[49] This result might be due to the fact that the passage of time cracks the solidarity of international sanctioning coalitions [Martin (1992)] and hardens the resolve of the target [Miyagawa (1992), Bolks and Al-Sowayel (2000)] while enabling the target to find alternative markets and substitute imports [Renwick (1981, p. 81)], or because failed sanctioners are often reluctant to abandon their sanctions after recognizing a fiasco [Leyton-Brown (1987)].

(1992, 1999) and Lacy and Niou's (2004) theoretical analysis discussed in the previous section, Drezner's results show that the sanctions that generated significant concessions were most likely to end at the threat stage. Drezner interprets his findings to suggest that the significance of economic coercion might have been greatly undervalued, contradicting as they do much of the consensus in the recent literature that sanctions generally fail to achieve their political goals and that their continued use can be explained only by non-instrumental motives, such as domestic politics within the sanctioning countries. However, the view that empirical sanctions studies are biased *against* sanctions success is by no means universal. As noted in the previous section, a committed sanctioner might repeatedly apply sanctions, creating an incentive for targets to comply [Eaton and Engers (1999)]. Empirical studies based on observations of actually implemented sanctions would then be biased *in favor* of sanctions success. The same would be true if sender countries behaved strategically by imposing sanctions only when they believed them to have a good chance of working.

The problem of selection bias is part of a broader issue, namely that the factors determining whether sanctions are used are inherently connected to the factors determining their success [Smith (1996), Morgan and Miers (1999), Hart (2000), Bolks and Al-Sowayel (2000), Nooruddin (2002), Jing et al. (2003)]. This point is made clear by Eaton and Engers (1999, p. 413): "Any analysis of situations in which senders actually resort to taking measures can paint a misleading picture of the role of sanctions in the international order: a measure may be taken only in rare instances when a sender thinks that it can accomplish something, or in rare instances when a target fails to submit to the sender's will.... [A]ny attempt to quantify [sanctions'] effectiveness must consider the circumstances that lead to their use in the first place. Doing so requires an econometric approach more firmly embedded in theory."

From an empirical standpoint, the problem is that the choice of policy instrument, e.g., trade sanctions, financial sanctions, or military intervention, is endogenous to the political process and, in particular, to the policy outcome sought by the sanctioner.[50] But the choice of instrument also affects the outcome of the sanctions. Therefore some of the variables that explain the effectiveness of sanctions, e.g., the types of sanctions that are chosen or the design of the sanctions strategy, are themselves explained by other right-hand-side variables. Jing et al. (2003) address this endogeneity issue by estimating a simultaneous equations model in which the sanctions policy outcome and the probabilities of the sanctioner's adoption of different sanctions instruments are jointly determined.[51] Their results confirm some findings of the earlier literature but also reveal some key differences. Consistent with previous studies, sanctions are found to be

---

[50] Military intervention, for example, would normally be more costly to the sanctioner than either trade or financial sanctions, and would therefore most likely be implemented in pursuit of only the most ambitious, or highest-priority, policy outcome.

[51] Another two-stage estimation approach that has been used to deal with the problem of simultaneity of instrument choice and effectiveness is the censored probit model, exemplified by Nooruddin (2002), whose contribution is discussed further in the next section.

Table 1
Determinants of sanctions effectiveness: Dependent variable = sanctions success score

Independent variables	Hufbauer et al. (1990)	Lam (1990)	Dehejia and Wood (1992)	van Bergeijk (1994)	Dashti-Gibson et al. (1997)	Bonetti (1998)	Drury (1998)	Hart (2000)	Bolks and Al-Sowayel (2000)	Nooruddin (2002)	Jing et al. (2003)
Political instability of target	+	+		+							+
Economic weakness of target	+·	+		+							+
Cordial pre-sanctions ties	+	+				+					+
Cost of sanctions to target	+	+	+		+		+	+			
Cost of sanctions to sender		−									
Trade linkages between sender and target				+							
Multilateral cooperation among senders	−						−†				
Third-party assistance to target	−					−	−††				
Ambitiousness of sanctions goal					−						
Sender is frequent sanctioner					−						

(continued on next page)

Table 1
(continued)

Independent variables	Hufbauer et al. (1990)	Lam (1990)	Dehejia and Wood (1992)	van Bergeijk (1994)	Dashti-Gibson et al. (1997)	Bonetti (1998)	Drury (1998)	Hart (2000)	Bolks and Al-Sowayel (2000)	Nooruddin (2002)	Jing et al. (2003)
Size of sender relative to target											−
Trade versus financial sanctions*	−				−		−				
Duration of sanctions	−			−					−		
Democratic versus autocratic target**									+	+	

Note: + indicates a statistically significant positive effect of the independent variable on sanctions success; − indicates a statistically significant negative effect of the independent variable on sanctions success.

* + means trade sanctions are more effective than financial sanctions; − means financial sanctions are more effective than trade sanctions.

** + means sanctions are more effective against democratic targets than against autocratic targets.

[†] Only if international organizations are not involved in the sanctions.

[††] Only if the target is dependent on the sender for imports.

more effective the warmer the prior relationship between sanctioner and target and less effective the healthier the target, both economically and politically. However, contrary to some earlier studies, Jing et al. (2003) find that the larger the size of the sanctioner relative to the target the lower the likelihood of sanctions success and that the effectiveness of sanctions is not influenced significantly by third-country assistance to the target or by the costs of sanctions, to either sanctioner or target. Moreover, Jing et al.'s results reveal no unambiguous conclusions regarding the relative effectiveness of trade versus financial sanctions, contrary to HSE, Alerassool (1993), Dashti-Gibson et al. (1997), Drury (1998) and Selden (1999), all of whom maintain that financial sanctions are more effective than trade sanctions.[52]

The main empirical findings on the causes of sanctions success discussed in this section and the next section are summarized in Table 1.

7. Political institutions and sanctions

Another focus of inquiry in the sanctions literature, most prevalent among political scientists, is the role of domestic institutions and politics in determining both the likelihood that sanctions will be used and the political outcome of sanctions.[53] One of the most important aspects of domestic institutions is the nature of the political regime in both target and sanctioner, characterized as either democratic or non-democratic. The interest of sanctions scholars in regime type stems from the international relations literature on the so-called democratic peace, which is the theory that democratic dyads are less likely to enter into military conflict than non-democratic or mixed dyads.[54] One argument that is

---

[52] The expectation of greater effectiveness of financial sanctions may be attributable to the fact that financial sanctions often have more selective effects on particular groups within the target polity, notably the wealthy elite, than do trade sanctions.

[53] Thus, for example, Allen (2005) finds that domestic political structures in target states strongly influence their response to sanctions, while Bolks and Al-Sowayel (2000) show that a target country's institutions and the political vulnerability of its regime significantly affect the duration of sanctions episodes.

[54] For clear statements of the democratic peace hypothesis and empirical tests which confirm the pacific benefits of democracy, see Russett (1993), Dixon (1994), Oneal and Russett (1997), Mousseau (1998), Russett and Oneal (2001) and Dixon and Senese (2002). For reviews of the literature, see Russett and Starr (2000) and Weede (2004). For an analytical treatment of both the democratic peace argument and its various detractors, see Zinnes (2004). Mousseau (2003) demonstrates that the peace among democracies is limited to market-oriented states, which he ascribes to common interests derived from common economic structure. Indeed there is evidence that the conflict-reducing effect of democracy is conditional upon income levels. Mousseau (2000), for example, finds that this effect is about twice as strong among developed countries compared with other dyads and is not statistically significant among the poorest decile of jointly democratic conflict-prone contiguous dyads. A variant of the democratic peace theory is the liberal peace, which postulates a pacifying effect of trade [see Oneal and Russett (1997, 1999a, 1999b, 2001, 2003), Russett and Oneal (2001), Oneal (2003), Oneal et al. (2003)]. Trade exerts not only a direct influence on peace but also an indirect one, to the extent that it contributes to prosperity and democracy [Weede (2004, p. 170)]. For a critique of the view that trade causes peace, see Barbieri (1996, 2002), who notes that economic interdependence can potentially

typically made in support of this theory is that democratic political competition reveals information about a country's level of resolve, thereby avoiding escalation of disputes into violent conflict [Lektzian and Souva (2003, p. 647)].[55] A further argument is that accountability of democratic politicians to large constituencies gives them a greater incentive to conduct successful foreign policies and protect their citizens from the costs of war [Bueno de Mesquita et al. (1999, 2003)].[56] Autocrats, by contrast, are less concerned with overall public welfare and are therefore more likely to lead their nations into military conflict.

Bueno de Mesquita and Siverson (1995) find empirical evidence that engaging in war is hazardous to the survival in office of all types of leaders, but especially democrats. Along similar lines, McGillivray and Smith (2000) argue that domestically accountable politicians incur costs in the form of reduced levels of public support if they fail to cooperate with foreign nations. Leaders who can be easily replaced by their electorates if they cheat on international cooperative arrangements can credibly commit to cooperate [McGillivray and Smith (2005)]. Therefore the prospect of losing their jobs makes accountable leaders more trustworthy in the eyes of foreigners and fosters greater international cooperation. On the other hand, when replacing leaders is difficult, cooperation is less robust, which often leads to inter-state hostilities [McGillivray and Smith (2000)]. Moreover, as Bueno de Mesquita et al. (2003) point out, leaders of authoritarian states obtain support from narrow constituencies, with successive dictators normally relying on mutually exclusive groups of supporters. Consequently, leadership change results in different interests being represented, and policies are revised accordingly. Democratic leaders, however, must appeal to broader constituencies, the make-up of which does not change significantly with leadership turnover. As a result, it is unlikely that policies, including foreign economic policies, will change much with change in democratic

---

bring about *increased* frictions among trading partners. However, Barbieri's analysis has been challenged on the grounds that she fails to control for the relative capabilities of nations to wage war over considerable distances, while it has also been pointed out that her method of measuring trade shares biases her results in favor of a conflict-enhancing effect [Weede (2004, pp. 169–170)].

[55] It has also been hypothesized that the absence of liberal-democratic norms among leaders of non-democratic states creates an expectation of aggressive intentions and a presumption of enmity on the part of democratic leaders [see Farnham (2003)]. Gartzke (2000) attributes much of the lack of militarized disputes between democracies to preference similarity across democratic states, while Siverson and Emmons (1991) document a high rate of alliance formation among democracies.

[56] It is of course conceivable that the direction of causality might be quite the reverse, i.e., that the observed rarity of wars between democracies could be explained by a negative effect of war on democracy rather than vice versa. For example, it is plausible to suppose that nations become more autocratic as they prepare for impending wars. Mousseau and Shi (1999) test this hypothesis but find that disputant countries are in fact equally likely to become more democratic as they are to become more autocratic in the periods leading up to the outbreak of wars. James et al. (1999, 2000) reject single equation estimates of the relationship between democracy and war as merely ad hoc reduced forms, lacking in causal inference. In their view, a more appropriate methodology would be to identify a structural equation as part of a simultaneous system in which both democracy and conflict are treated as endogenous. Using a simultaneous equations model, Reuveny and Li (2003) find that dyadic militarized disputes reduce joint democracy while at the same time joint democracy reduces the probability of militarized disputes.

leadership [Major and McGann (2005, pp. 346–347)]. In an empirical study of trading relations, McGillivray and Smith (2004) confirm that the impact of leadership turnover on trade between democracies is much less pronounced than in the case of autocracies.[57]

The democratic peace theory is by no means uncontroversial, however, with some scholars disputing both the logical basis and the empirical evidence for it.[58] Nevertheless, it has clearly been influential in the sanctions literature. Thus Lektzian and Souva (2003) and Cox and Drury (2006) investigate whether there is an analogous "economic peace" between democracies, i.e., whether democracies are relatively unlikely to use economic sanctions against other democracies. The same factors that encourage peace among democracies – a greater ability to send clear signals of resolve and a greater dependence of democratic politicians on successful policies – are expected to operate in the realm of sanctions [Lektzian and Souva (2003, p. 647)]. Both Lektzian and Souva's (2003) and Cox and Drury's (2006) results show that democracies impose sanctions more often than other regime types. Lektzian and Souva hypothesize that this propensity to sanction is due to the fact that the ruling coalitions in democracies encompass a greater variety of interest groups that need to be satisfied (2003, pp. 644–645). Trade sanctions are useful particularly to democratic governments as a device to justify protection for domestic industries while still professing commitment to a liberal trading regime [Cox and Drury (2006)].[59] Cox and Drury add that democracies might choose sanctions over military action because non-violent measures generally attract less public attention and opposition.

At the same time, however, both Lektzian and Souva (2003) and Cox and Drury (2006) also find that democracies are more likely to sanction non-democracies than other democracies. Cox and Drury suggest that this result occurs because two of the

---

[57] These findings extend also to economic sanctions. Thus McGillivray and Stam (2004) show that leadership change in non-democratic sanctioning and target states is strongly related to the ending of sanctions, whereas leadership change in democratic states is unrelated to the duration of sanctions. Once sanctions are lifted, Lektzian and Souva (2001) find that jointly democratic dyads return to pre-sanctions levels of trade faster than non-democratic or mixed dyads, a result which they ascribe to the transaction cost-reducing and trust-promoting characteristics of democratic institutions.

[58] Hess and Orphanides (2001) for example argue that, because incumbent democratic leaders often have a need to hold on to power in the face of poor economic performance, they will sometimes have an incentive to initiate international conflict in order to salvage their domestic positions. Rosato (2003), after a critical examination of the causal logic underpinning the democratic peace theory, concludes that, while there is certainly peace among democracies, this peace may not be primarily due to the democratic nature of those states. Henderson (1999, 2002) attributes the post-World War II stability among democratic dyads not to joint democracy, but to the presence of an international security regime characterized by bipolarity, nuclear deterrence, alliance membership and trade links. Senese (1999) finds that regime maturity is just as important as regime type in determining dyadic conflict intensities.

[59] As Kaempfer and Lowenberg (1988a) point out, majoritarian democracies are especially vulnerable to pressure from interest groups to impose sanctions, sometimes motivated by moral outrage against the objectionable behavior of a foreign regime, but often driven by little more than thinly disguised protectionist interests in trade restrictions.

most common reasons that democracies impose sanctions – to promote democracy and to punish human rights violations – apply largely to autocratic targets; democratic states, by definition, are usually not the ones guilty of abusing their citizens' political or human rights. Moreover, according to Lektzian and Souva (2003, p. 648), given the strong imperative for democratic leaders to pursue successful foreign policies, they will typically prefer to pick on non-democratic targets on the grounds that a democratic target "will take all necessary means to offset or counter the sanctions in an effort to continue providing a stream of public goods to members of its broad winning coalition."[60]

The belief that democracies are more motivated than non-democracies both to use sanctions and to resist the demands of external sanctioners derives in part from Fearon's (1994) notion of audience costs. These are the costs in terms of forgone political support that are incurred by a nation's leaders when the public becomes disillusioned with their leaders' abilities. According to Fearon, a democracy, which faces high domestic audience costs, is always less likely to back down in a public confrontation during international crises than a non-democracy, whose audience costs are considerably lower and which consequently has greater flexibility to alter its policies in the face of foreign pressure.[61] It follows that a signal of resolve sent by a democratic target of sanctions will be more credible than one sent by an autocratic target, so that a potential democratic sanctioner, itself constrained by its own domestic political institutions to avoid foreign policy failures,[62] is less likely to initiate sanctions against a democratic target [Lektzian and Souva (2003, p. 648)]. Galtung (1967) lends further credence to the relative resilience of democratic targets by pointing out that democracies have greater legitimacy and are therefore more likely than autocracies to rally their citizens around the flag of resistance to sanctions.

However, like its political counterpart in the democratic peace literature, the economic peace hypothesis is contentious. In particular, the claim that a democratic target is less likely to concede to sanctions than a non-democracy is rejected by many scholars. For example, Nooruddin (2002, pp. 69–70) argues that, precisely because democratic political leaders are compelled to take into account their public's preferences, it is probable that a democratic target government would agree to the sanctioners' demands in order to get the sanctions lifted and relieve the suffering of its constituents. Similarly, Bolks and Al-Sowayel (2000) show that democratic governments typically do not resist sanctions for long because of the resulting domestic political costs that their

---

[60] Lektzian and Souva (2003) also find that, owing to incentives to achieve successful foreign policies and minimize harm to their publics, democratic regimes are more likely than non-democracies to use financial sanctions instead of trade sanctions. For the same reason, democracies are more likely to pursue minor foreign policy goals rather than attempt to bring about ambitious policy changes in target countries.

[61] In an empirical test of Fearon's theory, Partell and Palmer (1999) find that domestic political audiences do indeed exert a strong influence over which countries in a crisis are likely to achieve successful outcomes, although relative national capabilities are also found to be important.

[62] Hart (2000) suggests that democracies are generally more successful sanctioners than non-democracies because the audience costs confronted by democratic governments insure that they will initiate sanctions only if they are committed to holding out for success.

electorates would impose upon them. Much the same argument is proposed by Nossal (1999, p. 130), who notes that political leaders in target nations who fail to alter their behavior in order to put a stop to the economic pain caused by sanctions risk being ejected from office.[63] By contrast, in non-democracies, Pape (1997, p. 93) points out that unpopular ruling elites can often protect themselves and their supporters by shifting the economic burden of sanctions on to disenfranchised groups.[64] According to Bolks and Al-Sowayel (2000), when the leadership of a state is concentrated in the hands of a few, the leadership is better able to implement countermeasures that insulate the government from the economic hardships caused by sanctions. Non-democratic and illiberal regimes find it especially easy to hold out in the face of damaging sanctions because they can "simply pass on the costs of the sanctions to the governed and rely on armed forces to deter political opponents who are dissatisfied with policies" [Nossal (1999, p. 134)].[65] Moreover, pervasive nationalism often makes citizens of non-democratic states willing to endure considerable punishment rather than abandon policies that are seen to be in the national interest [Pape (1997, p. 93)]. Cortright and Lopez (2000, p. 214) argue that "sanctions provide authoritarian governments with leverage to create a 'rally-around-the-flag' effect as a means of suppressing domestic opposition."[66] Damrosch (1993, p. 299) contends that sanctions will almost inevitably benefit an autocratic regime because the regime will always be in a better position than the civilian population to control external transactions and the internal economy. In Damrosch's view, the creation and enrichment of a criminal class that profiteers from trading bootleg or scarce goods means that even the most skillfully targeted sanctions will serve only to entrench the power of the ruling elite.

Bolks and Al-Sowayel (2000) and Nooruddin (2002, p. 73) present empirical evidence that sanctions imposed against autocratic targets are less successful than those imposed against democracies. Nooruddin (2002, pp. 69–70) draws the logical conclusion that sanctioners are therefore more likely to sanction democracies than non-democracies precisely because democracies are more likely to concede.[67] A further argument supporting the claim that democracies, in particular, are inclined to use sanctions against

---

[63] Drawing on a large panel of cross-country and time-series data, Marinov (2005) finds empirical evidence for the destabilizing effect of economic pressure on the leadership of target countries.

[64] Pape (1997) cites the case of Iraq, which, despite facing the most damaging economic sanctions in history, with 48 percent of its GNP destroyed, did not acquiesce.

[65] Thus, in the literature on civil war, autocratic societies have been found to have somewhat lower risks of rebellion than partial democracies due to the ability of autocrats to successfully repress potential dissident groups. See Collier and Hoeffler (2007) (Chapter 23 in this *Handbook*).

[66] On the tendency of sanctions to strengthen the "hawks" and weaken the "doves", see Willett and Jalalighajar (1983/84).

[67] This finding does not necessarily refute the notion of an economic peace among democracies, however. The economic peace is a dyadic phenomenon [Lektzian and Souva (2003, p. 647)]; it requires that pairs of democratic countries be less likely to be involved in sanctions than pairs of non-democratic countries or mixed pairs. Although Nooruddin finds that democracies are more likely to be *targets* of sanctions, he does not test whether democracies are also more likely than non-democracies to *impose* sanctions. In fact, Nooruddin's data include only US-imposed sanctions (2002, pp. 63, 70).

Table 2
Summary of literature on regime type and sanctions

Autocracies more likely than democracies to concede to sanctions	Democracies more likely than autocracies to concede to sanctions	Democracies more likely than autocracies to impose sanctions	Sanctions imposed by democracies more successful than sanctions imposed by autocracies	Democracies more likely than autocracies to be targets of sanctions	Autocracies more likely than democracies to be targets of sanctions
Lektzian and Souva (2003)	Damrosch (1993)	Lektzian and Souva (2003)	Hart (2000)	Nooruddin (2002)	Lektzian and Souva (2003)*
	Pape (1997)	Cox and Drury (2006)			Cox and Drury (2006)*
	Nossal (1999)				
	Bolks and Al-Sowayel (2000)				
	Cortright and Lopez (2000)				
	Nooruddin (2002)				

*If the sender is democratic.

democratic adversaries is the observation that democracies prefer to substitute non-military coercion, including sanctions, for militarized tools of foreign policy when confronting other democracies in inter-state disputes [Palmer et al. (2002), Morgan and Palmer (2003)].[68]

Table 2 provides a summary of the contributions to the literature on sanctions and political regimes surveyed in this section.

8. Conclusions and avenues for further research

A number of areas of consensus have emerged in the sanctions literature. There is, for example, wide agreement on the utility of smart sanctions – those designed to have

---

[68] There is some evidence, however, that democracies favor the use of positive economic incentives rather than sanctions, especially in dealing with other democracies [Davidson and Shambaugh (2000), Drezner (2000)].

selective effects on specific groups within the target country. In addition, economists and political scientists alike have come to recognize that consideration of the political processes by which sanctioning policies emerge in the sender nations, as well as the political processes through which sanctions generate policy outcomes in a target country, is key to addressing the two main questions in the political economy of sanctions. These questions are (i) what factors determine when sanctions will be used as a preferred instrument of influence exertion in international relations and (ii) what factors determine the likelihood of success or failure of sanctions in achieving their policy objectives? Game-theoretic treatments of sanctions have contributed a clear understanding that these two questions are intrinsically linked: observed instances of sanctions represent only a small sub-sample of sanctions strategies, most of which end without sanctions actually being imposed. This understanding has carried over into the empirical literature, in which most practitioners now acknowledge the presence of potential selection bias in the data on observed sanctions episodes. Simultaneous equations approaches, geared to dealing with the problem of joint determination of instrument choice and success, have therefore become the norm. Moreover, scholars have increasingly recognized the importance of political institutions, within both sanctioning countries and target countries, in influencing the decision to implement sanctions and the effectiveness of the sanctions in attaining their goals.

Despite the fact that the body of knowledge about the processes generating sanctions and determining their success has undoubtedly expanded, and analyses of sanctions, both theoretical and empirical, have become considerably more sophisticated over the years, there are puzzles that still need to be resolved. Why, for example, has the use of sanctions accelerated so dramatically in the post-Cold War era, and why are some countries more frequent users of sanctions than others? The latter question applies with particular force to the United States, which is by far the premier sanctioner in the world.[69] Without further research on these questions, we can only speculate as to their answers. Perhaps the collapse of the Soviet Union initiated a spurt of sanctioning activity because sanctioners need no longer be concerned that their actions will exacerbate Cold War tensions between superpower blocs.[70] Perhaps the nations that are most likely to rely on sanctions are those without access to alternative avenues of pressure that could be brought to bear in a dispute, such as historical, colonial or cultural ties with potential targets.

In resolving these issues, consideration must necessarily be given to more than the standard economic and political factors that, thus far, have dominated the sanctions literature. We believe that cultural and historical characteristics of nations, which have been neglected in the literature, will need to be taken into account in future research on sanctioning behavior and effectiveness. Scholars of economic growth and development

[69] On the proclivity of the United States to resort to sanctions, see Hufbauer (1998).
[70] Verdier (2005) argues that, now that countries' allegiances are less transparent than they were during the Cold War, sanctions are useful in screening adversaries into "deterrable" and "undeterrable" types.

have increasingly applied political economy models to explain how cultural or normative attributes of states play an important role in determining institutions, policy choices
and economic performance.[71] Moreover, the democratic peace literature suggests that
countries that share participatory political institutions may be in a better position to
signal levels of resolve or commitment in international disputes than countries lacking
such institutions. In general, states with similar political and economic institutions can
be expected to have similar foreign policy preferences and therefore to be less likely
to enter into conflict with one another [Souva (2004)].[72] The same might conceivably
be said for other dimensions of national similarity, including culture and historical experience. Nations that share a range of cultural attributes may be supposed to be more
effective in communicating their collective preferences and intentions than culturally
dissimilar countries, thus mitigating conflict and increasing the likelihood of successful
resolution of inter-state disputes. A high priority for future extensions of the economic
sanctions research agenda will be to follow the broader emerging trend in economics,
specifically, to take into account a wider array of behavioral determinants than have
traditionally been applied in the study of sanctions.

References

Acemoglu, D., Johnson, S.H., Robinson, J.A. (2001). "The colonial origins of comparative development: An
empirical investigation". American Economic Review 91, 1369–1401.
Acemoglu, D., Johnson, S.H., Robinson, J.A. (2004). "Institutions as the fundamental cause of long-run
growth". NBER Working Paper No. 10481. National Bureau of Economic Research, Cambridge, MA.
Alerassool, M. (1993). Freezing Assets: The USA and the Most Effective Economic Sanction. St. Martin's
Press, New York.
Allen, S.H. (2005). "The determinants of economic sanctions success and failure". International Interac-
tions 31, 117–138.
Askari, H.G., Forrer, J., Teegen, H., Yang, J. (2003). Economic Sanctions: Examining Their Philosophy and
Efficacy. Praeger, Westport, CT.
Baldwin, D.A. (1985). Economic Statecraft. Princeton University Press, Princeton.
Barbieri, K. (1996). "Economic interdependence: A path to peace or a source of interstate conflict?". Journal
of Peace Research 33, 29–49.
Barbieri, K. (2002). The Liberal Illusion: Does Trade Promote Peace? University of Michigan Press, Ann
Arbor.
Becker, G.S. (1983). "A theory of competition among pressure groups for political influence". Quarterly
Journal of Economics 98, 371–400.
Becker, G.S. (1985). "Public policies, pressure groups and dead weight costs". Journal of Public Eco-
nomics 28, 329–347.
van Bergeijk, P.A.G. (1989). "Success and failure of economic sanctions". Kyklos 42, 385–404.
van Bergeijk, P.A.G. (1994). Economic Diplomacy, Trade and Commercial Policy: Positive and Negative
Sanctions in a New World Order. Edward Elgar, Aldershot.

---

[71] Examples include La Porta et al. (1999), Acemoglu et al. (2001, 2004), Rodrik and Subramanian (2003)
and Tabellini (2005).
[72] Souva's (2004) empirical results confirm that dyadic institutional similarity, especially similarity of economic institutions, reduces the probability of militarized conflict.

Black, P.A., Cooper, H. (1987). "On the welfare and employment effects of economic sanctions". South African Journal of Economics 55, 1–15.

Bolks, S.M., Al-Sowayel, D. (2000). "How long do economic sanctions last? Examining the sanctioning process through duration". Political Research Quarterly 53, 241–265.

Bonetti, S. (1996). "Predicting the outcome of economic sanctions". Working Paper. Department of Economics, University of St. Andrews, Scotland.

Bonetti, S. (1997). "The analysis and interpretation of economic sanctions". Journal of Economic Studies 24, 324–348.

Bonetti, S. (1998). "Distinguishing characteristics of degrees of success and failure in economic sanctions episodes". Applied Economics 30, 805–813.

Brady, L.J. (1987). "The utility of economic sanctions as a policy instrument". In: Leyton-Brown, D. (Ed.), The Utility of International Economic Sanctions. St. Martin's Press, New York, pp. 297–302.

Bueno de Mesquita, B., Siverson, R.M. (1995). "War and the survival of political leaders: A comparative study of regime types and political accountability". American Political Science Review 89, 841–855.

Bueno de Mesquita, B., Morrow, J.D., Siverson, R.M., Smith, A. (1999). "An institutional explanation for the democratic peace". American Political Science Review 93, 791–808.

Bueno de Mesquita, B., Smith, A., Siverson, R.M., Morrow, J.D. (2003). The Logic of Political Survival. MIT Press, Cambridge, MA.

Collier, P., Hoeffler, A. (2007). "Civil war". In: Sandler, T., Hartley, K. (Eds.), Handbook of Defense Economics. Defense in a Globalized World, vol. 2. Elsevier, Amsterdam. This volume.

Cornes, R., Sandler, T. (1984). "Easy riders, joint production, and public goods". Economic Journal 94, 580–598.

Cortright, D., Lopez, G.A. (2000). The Sanctions Decade: Assessing UN Strategies in the 1990s. Lynne Rienner Publishers, Boulder, CO.

Cortright, D., Lopez, G.A. (2002a). "Introduction: Assessing smart sanctions: Lessons from the 1990s". In: Cortright, D., Lopez, G.A. (Eds.), Smart Sanctions: Targeting Economic Statecraft. Rowman and Littlefield, Lanham, MD, pp. 1–22.

Cortright, D., Lopez, G.A. (2002b). Sanctions and the Search for Security: Challenges to UN Action. Lynne Rienner Publishers, Boulder, CO.

Cortright, D., Lopez, G.A., Rogers, E.S. (2002). "Targeted financial sanctions: Smart sanctions that do work". In: Cortright, D., Lopez, G.A. (Eds.), Smart Sanctions: Targeting Economic Statecraft. Rowman and Littlefield, Lanham, MD, pp. 23–40.

Cortright, D., Millar, A., Lopez, G.A. (2002). "Smart sanctions in Iraq: Policy options". In: Cortright, D., Lopez, G.A. (Eds.), Smart Sanctions: Targeting Economic Statecraft. Rowman and Littlefield, Lanham, MD, pp. 201–224.

Cox, D.G., Drury, A.C. (2006). "Democratic sanctions: Connecting the democratic peace and economic sanctions". Journal of Peace Research 43, 709–722.

Dadak, C. (2003). "The 1992–1996 Bulgarian trade data puzzle: A case of sanctions breaking?". Cato Journal 22, 511–532.

Damrosch, L.F. (1993). "The civilian impact of economic sanctions". In: Damrosch, L.F. (Ed.), Enforcing Restraint: Collective Intervention in Internal Conflicts. Council on Foreign Relations Press, New York, pp. 274–315.

Daoudi, M.S., Dajani, M.S. (1983). Economic Sanctions: Ideals and Experience. Routledge and Kegan Paul, London.

Dashti-Gibson, J., Davis, P., Radcliff, B. (1997). "On the determinants of the success of economic sanctions: An empirical analysis". American Journal of Political Science 41, 608–618.

Davidson, J., Shambaugh, G. (2000). "Who's afraid of economic incentives? The efficacy–externality trade-off". In: Chan, S., Drury, A.C. (Eds.), Sanctions as Economic Statecraft: Theory and Practice. Macmillan, London, pp. 37–64.

Dehejia, R.H., Wood, B. (1992). "Economic sanctions and econometric policy evaluation: A cautionary note". Journal of World Trade 26, 73–84.

Dixon, W.J. (1994). "Democracy and the peaceful settlement of international conflict". American Political Science Review 88, 14–32.

Dixon, W.J., Senese, P.D. (2002). "Democracy, disputes, and negotiated settlements". Journal of Conflict Resolution 46, 547–571.

Dollery, B.E., Leibbrandt, M.V. (1987). "On the welfare and employment effects of economic sanctions: Comment". South African Journal of Economics 55, 292–296.

Dorussen, H., Mo, J. (2001). "Ending economic sanctions: Audience costs and rent-seeking as commitment strategies". Journal of Conflict Resolution 45, 395–426.

Doxey, M.P. (1980). Economic Sanctions and International Enforcement, second ed. Oxford University Press, New York.

Doxey, M.P. (1996). International Sanctions in Contemporary Perspective, second ed. Macmillan, London.

Drezner, D.W. (1998). "Conflict expectations and the paradox of economic coercion". International Studies Quarterly 42, 709–731.

Drezner, D.W. (1999). The Sanctions Paradox: Economic Statecraft and International Relations. Cambridge University Press, Cambridge.

Drezner, D.W. (2000). "The trouble with carrots: Transaction costs, conflict expectations, and economic inducements". Security Studies 9, 188–218.

Drezner, D.W. (2001). "Outside the box: Explaining sanctions in pursuit of foreign economic goals". International Interactions 26, 379–410.

Drezner, D.W. (2003). "The hidden hand of economic coercion". International Organization 57, 643–659.

Drury, A.C. (1998). "Revisiting 'Economic Sanctions Reconsidered'". Journal of Peace Research 35, 497–509.

Eaton, J., Engers, M. (1992). "Sanctions". Journal of Political Economy 100, 899–928.

Eaton, J., Engers, M. (1999). "Sanctions: Some simple analytics". American Economic Review Papers and Proceedings 89, 409–414.

Farnham, B. (2003). "The theory of democratic peace and threat perception". International Studies Quarterly 47, 395–415.

Fearon, J.D. (1994). "Domestic political audiences and the escalation of international disputes". American Political Science Review 88, 577–592.

Findlay, R., Lundahl, M. (1987). "Racial discrimination, dualistic labor markets and foreign investment". Journal of Development Economics 27, 139–148.

Galtung, J. (1967). "On the effects of international economic sanctions, with examples from the case of Rhodesia". World Politics 19, 378–416.

Gartzke, E. (2000). "Preferences and the democratic peace". International Studies Quarterly 44, 191–212.

Haass, R.N. (Ed.) (1998). Economic Sanctions and American Diplomacy. Brookings Institution Press, Washington, DC.

Hanlon, J., Omond, R. (1987). The Sanctions Handbook. Penguin Books, Harmondsworth.

Harkness, J. (1990). "Marshall, Lerner & Botha: Canada's economic sanctions on South Africa". Canadian Public Policy 16, 155–160.

Hart, R.A. (2000). "Democracy and the successful use of economic sanctions". Political Research Quarterly 53, 267–284.

Henderson, E.A. (1999). "Neoidealism and the democratic peace". Journal of Peace Research 36, 203–231.

Henderson, E.A. (2002). Democracy and War: The End of an Illusion? Lynne Rienner Publishers, Boulder, CO.

Hess, G.D., Orphanides, A. (2001). "War and democracy". Journal of Political Economy 109, 776–810.

Hoffman, F. (1967). "The functions of economic sanctions: A comparative analysis". Journal of Peace Research 2, 140–160.

Hufbauer, G.C. (1998). "Sanctions-happy USA". Institute for International Economics, International Economics Policy Brief No. 98-4, Washington, DC.

Hufbauer, G.C., Schott, J.J., Elliott, K.A. (1990). Economic Sanctions Reconsidered: History and Current Policy, second ed. Institute for International Economics, Washington, DC.

James, P., Solberg, E., Wolfson, M. (1999). "An identified systemic model of the democracy–peace nexus". Defence and Peace Economics 10, 1–37.

James, P., Solberg, E., Wolfson, M. (2000). "Democracy and peace: Reply to Oneal and Russett". Defence and Peace Economics 11, 215–229.

Jing, C., Kaempfer, W.H., Lowenberg, A.D. (2003). "Instrument choice and the effectiveness of international sanctions: A simultaneous equations approach". Journal of Peace Research 40, 519–535.

Kaempfer, W.H., Lowenberg, A.D. (1986). "A model of the political economy of international investment sanctions: The case of South Africa". Kyklos 39, 377–396.

Kaempfer, W.H., Lowenberg, A.D. (1988a). "The theory of international economic sanctions: A public choice approach". American Economic Review 78, 786–793.

Kaempfer, W.H., Lowenberg, A.D. (1988b). "Determinants of the economic and political effects of trade sanctions". South African Journal of Economics 56, 270–277.

Kaempfer, W.H., Lowenberg, A.D. (1992a). "Using threshold models to explain international relations". Public Choice 73, 419–443.

Kaempfer, W.H., Lowenberg, A.D. (1992b). International Economic Sanctions: A Public Choice Perspective. Westview Press, Boulder, CO.

Kaempfer, W.H., Lowenberg, A.D. (1999). "Unilateral versus multilateral international sanctions: A public choice perspective". International Studies Quarterly 43, 37–58.

Kaempfer, W.H., Moffett, M.H. (1988). "Impact of trade sanctions on South Africa: Some trade and financial evidence". Contemporary Policy Issues 6, 118–129.

Kaempfer, W.H., Lehman, J.A., Lowenberg, A.D. (1987). "Divestment, investment sanctions, and disinvestment: An evaluation of anti-apartheid policy instruments". International Organization 41, 457–473.

Kaempfer, W.H., Lowenberg, A.D., Mertens, W. (2004). "International economic sanctions against a dictator". Economics and Politics 16, 29–51.

Kirshner, J. (1997). "The microfoundations of economic sanctions". Security Studies 6, 32–64.

Kuran, T. (1989). "Sparks and prairie fires: A theory of unanticipated political revolution". Public Choice 61, 41–74.

Lacy, D., Niou, E.M.S. (2004). "A theory of economic sanctions and issue linkage: The roles of preferences, information, and threats". Journal of Politics 66, 25–42.

Lam, S.L. (1990). "Economic sanctions and the success of foreign policy goals: A critical evaluation". Japan and the World Economy 2, 239–248.

La Porta, R., Lopez-de-Silanes, F., Shleifer, A., Vishny, R. (1999). "The quality of government". Journal of Law, Economics, and Organization 15, 222–279.

Leitzel, J. (1987). "Review of Hufbauer et al. (1985)". Kyklos 40, 286–288.

Lektzian, D., Souva, M. (2001). "Institutions and international cooperation: An event history analysis of the effects of economic sanctions". Journal of Conflict Resolution 45, 61–79.

Lektzian, D., Souva, M. (2003). "The economic peace between democracies: Economic sanctions and domestic institutions". Journal of Peace Research 40, 641–660.

Leyton-Brown, D. (1987). "Lessons and policy considerations about economic sanctions". In: Leyton-Brown, D. (Ed.), The Utility of International Economic Sanctions. St. Martin's Press, New York, pp. 303–310.

Lopez, G.A. (2001). "Toward smart sanctions on Iraq". Policy Brief No. 5. Joan B. Kroc Institute for International Peace Studies, University of Notre Dame, Notre Dame, IN.

Lopez, G.A., Cortright, D. (2004). "Containing Iraq: Sanctions worked". Foreign Affairs 83, 90–103.

Lowenberg, A.D., Kaempfer, W.H. (1998). The Origins and Demise of South African Apartheid: A Public Choice Analysis. University of Michigan Press, Ann Arbor.

Lundborg, P. (1987). The Economics of Export Embargoes: The Case of the US–Soviet Grain Suspension. Croom Helm, London.

Mack, A., Khan, A. (2000). "The efficacy of UN sanctions". Security Dialogue 31, 279–292.

Major, S., McGann, A.J. (2005). "Caught in the crossfire: 'Innocent bystanders' as optimal targets of economic sanctions". Journal of Conflict Resolution 49, 337–359.

Marinov, N. (2005). "Do economic sanctions destabilize country leaders?". American Journal of Political Science 49, 564–576.

Martin, L.L. (1992). Coercive Cooperation: Explaining Multilateral Economic Sanctions. Princeton University Press, Princeton.

Mayall, J. (1984). "The sanctions problem in international economic relations: Reflections in the light of recent experience". International Affairs 60, 631–642.

McGillivray, F., Smith, A. (2000). "Trust and cooperation through agent-specific punishments". International Organization 54, 809–824.

McGillivray, F., Smith, A. (2004). "The impact of leadership turnover on trading relations between states". International Organization 58, 567–600.

McGillivray, F., Smith, A. (2005). "The impact of leadership turnover and domestic institutions on international cooperation". Journal of Conflict Resolution 49, 639–660.

McGillivray, F., Stam, A.C. (2004). "Political institutions, coercive diplomacy, and the duration of economic sanctions". Journal of Conflict Resolution 48, 154–172.

Miers, A.C., Morgan, T.C. (2002). "Multilateral sanctions and foreign policy success: Can too many cooks spoil the broth?". International Interactions 28, 117–136.

Miyagawa, M. (1992). Do Economic Sanctions Work? McMillan Press, New York.

Morgan, T.C., Miers, A.C. (1999). "When threats succeed: A formal model of the threat and use of economic sanctions". Paper presented at the Annual Meeting of the American Political Science Association, Atlanta, GA.

Morgan, T.C., Palmer, G. (2003). "To protect and to serve: Alliances and foreign policy portfolios". Journal of Conflict Resolution 47, 180–203.

Morgan, T.C., Schwebach, V.L. (1996). "Economic sanctions as an instrument of foreign policy: The role of domestic politics". International Interactions 21, 247–263.

Morgan, T.C., Schwebach, V.L. (1997). "Fools suffer gladly: The use of economic sanctions in international crises". International Studies Quarterly 41, 27–50.

Mousseau, M. (1998). "Democracy and compromise in militarized interstate conflicts, 1816–1992". Journal of Conflict Resolution 42, 210–230.

Mousseau, M. (2000). "Market prosperity, democratic consolidation, and democratic peace". Journal of Conflict Resolution 44, 472–507.

Mousseau, M. (2003). "The nexus of market society, liberal preferences, and democratic peace: Interdisciplinary theory and evidence". International Studies Quarterly 47, 483–510.

Mousseau, M., Shi, Y. (1999). "A test for reverse causality in the democratic peace relationship". Journal of Peace Research 36, 639–663.

Nincic, M., Wallensteen, P. (Eds.) (1983). Dilemmas of Economic Coercion: Sanctions in World Politics. Praeger, New York.

Nooruddin, I. (2002). "Modeling selection bias in studies of sanctions efficacy". International Interactions 28, 59–75.

Nossal, K.R. (1989). "International sanctions as international punishment". International Organization 43, 301–322.

Nossal, K.R. (1999). "Liberal democratic regimes, international sanctions, and global governance". In: Väyrynen, R. (Ed.), Globalization and Global Governance. Rowman and Littlefield, Lanham, MD, pp. 127–150.

Olson, M., Jr. (1965). The Logic of Collective Action: Public Goods and the Theory of Groups. Harvard University Press, Cambridge, MA.

Oneal, J.R. (2003). "Empirical support for the liberal peace". In: Mansfield, E.D., Pollins, B.M. (Eds.), Economic Interdependence and International Conflict. University of Michigan Press, Ann Arbor, pp. 189–206.

Oneal, J.R., Russett, B.M. (1997). "The classical liberals were right: Democracy, interdependence, and conflict, 1950–1985". International Studies Quarterly 41, 267–294.

Oneal, J.R., Russett, B.M. (1999a). "The Kantian peace: The pacific benefits of democracy, interdependence, and international organizations, 1885–1992". World Politics 52, 1–37.

Oneal, J.R., Russett, B.M. (1999b). "Assessing the liberal peace with alternative specifications: Trade still reduces conflict". Journal of Peace Research 36, 423–442.

Oneal, J.R., Russett, B.M. (2001). "Clear and clean: The fixed effects of the liberal peace". International Organization 55, 469–485.

Oneal, J.R., Russett, B.M. (2003). "Modeling conflict while studying dynamics". In: Schneider, G., Barbieri, K., Gleditsch, N.P. (Eds.), Globalization and Armed Conflict. Rowman and Littlefield, Lanham, MD, pp. 179–188.

Oneal, J.R., Russett, B.M., Berbaum, M.L. (2003). "Causes of peace: Democracy, interdependence, and international organizations, 1885–1992". International Studies Quarterly 47, 371–393.

O'Sullivan, M.L. (2003). Shrewd Sanctions: Statecraft and State Sponsors of Terrorism. Brookings Institution Press, Washington, DC.

Paarlberg, R. (1983). "Using food power: Opportunities, appearances, and damage control". In: Nincic, M., Wallensteen, P. (Eds.), Dilemmas of Economic Coercion: Sanctions in World Politics. Praeger, New York, pp. 131–153.

Palmer, G., Wohlander, S.B., Morgan, T.C. (2002). "Give or take: Foreign aid and foreign policy substitutability". Journal of Peace Research 39, 5–26.

Pape, R.A. (1997). "Why economic sanctions do not work". International Security 22, 90–136.

Partell, P.J., Palmer, G. (1999). "Audience costs and interstate crises: An empirical assessment of Fearon's model of dispute outcomes". International Studies Quarterly 43, 389–405.

Peltzman, S. (1976). "Toward a more general theory of regulation". Journal of Law and Economics 19, 211–240.

Porter, R.C. (1979). "International trade and investment sanctions: Potential impact on the South African economy". Journal of Conflict Resolution 23, 579–612.

Renwick, R. (1981). Economic Sanctions. Center for International Affairs, Harvard University, Cambridge, MA.

Reuveny, R., Li, Q. (2003). "The joint democracy-dyadic conflict nexus: A simultaneous equations model". International Studies Quarterly 47, 325–346.

Rodrik, D., Subramanian, A. (2003). "The primacy of institutions (and what this does and does not mean)". Finance and Development 40, 31–34.

Rogers, E.S. (1996). "Using economic sanctions to control regional conflicts". Security Studies 5, 43–72.

Rosato, S. (2003). "The flawed logic of democratic peace theory". American Political Science Review 97, 585–602.

Rowe, D.M. (2001). Manipulating the Market: Understanding Economic Sanctions, Institutional Change, and the Political Unity of White Rhodesia. University of Michigan Press, Ann Arbor.

Russett, B.M. (1993). Grasping the Democratic Peace. Princeton University Press, Princeton.

Russett, B.M., Oneal, J.R. (2001). Triangulating Peace: Democracy, Interdependence, and International Organizations. W.W. Norton, New York.

Russett, B.M., Starr, H. (2000). "From democratic peace to Kantian peace: Democracy and conflict in the international system". In: Midlarsky, M. (Ed.), Handbook of War Studies, second ed. University of Michigan Press, Ann Arbor, pp. 93–128.

Selden, Z. (1999). Economic Sanctions as Instruments of American Foreign Policy. Praeger, Westport, CT.

Senese, P.D. (1999). "Democracy and maturity: Deciphering conditional effects on levels of dispute intensity". International Studies Quarterly 43, 483–502.

Siverson, R.M., Emmons, J. (1991). "Birds of a feather: Democratic political systems and alliance choices in the twentieth century". Journal of Conflict Resolution 35, 285–306.

Smith, A. (1996). "The success and use of economic sanctions". International Interactions 21, 229–245.

Souva, M. (2004). "Institutional similarity and interstate conflict". International Interactions 30, 263–280.

Stigler, G.J. (1971). "The theory of economic regulation". Bell Journal of Economics and Management Science 2, 3–21.

Tabellini, G. (2005). "Culture and institutions: Economic development in the regions of Europe". Working Paper. Innocenzo Gasparini Institute for Economic Research, Bocconi University, Milan, Italy.

Torbat, A.E. (2005). "Impacts of the US trade and financial sanctions on Iran". World Economy 28, 407–434.

Tsebelis, G. (1990). "Are sanctions effective? A game-theoretic analysis". Journal of Conflict Resolution 34, 3–28.

Tullock, G. (1971). "The paradox of revolution". Public Choice 11, 89–99.

Tullock, G. (1989). The Economics of Special Privilege and Rent Seeking. Kluwer, Boston.

United Kingdom Parliament (1999). http://www.publications.parliament.uk/pa/cm199900/cmselect/cmintdev/67/6707.htm#n12, London.

Verdier, D. (2005). "Sanctions as revelation mechanisms". Working Paper. Department of Political Science, Ohio State University, Columbus, OH.

Wall Street Journal (2002). May 2, p. A1.

Weede, E. (2004). "The diffusion of prosperity and peace by globalization". The Independent Review 9, 165–186.

Weiss, T.G. (1999). "Sanctions as a foreign policy tool: Weighing humanitarian impulses". Journal of Peace Research 36, 499–509.

Willett, T.D., Jalalighajar, M. (1983/84). "US trade policy and national security". Cato Journal 3, 717–727.

Wintrobe, R. (1990). "The tinpot and the totalitarian: An economic theory of dictatorship". American Political Science Review 84, 849–872.

Wintrobe, R. (1998). The Political Economy of Dictatorship. Cambridge University Press, Cambridge.

Zinnes, D.A. (2004). "Constructing political logic: The democratic peace puzzle". Journal of Conflict Resolution 48, 430–454.

Chapter 28

THE ECONOMETRICS OF MILITARY ARMS RACES[*]

J. PAUL DUNNE[1]

Bristol Business School, University of the West of England, Bristol, BS16 1QY, UK
e-mail: John2.Dunne@uwe.ac.uk

RON P. SMITH[2]

Department of Economics, Birkbeck College, University of London, Malet Street, London WC1E 7HX, UK
e-mail: R.Smith@bbk.ac.uk

Contents

Abstract	914
Keywords	914
1. Introduction	915
2. Data	916
3. Theoretical issues in specification	920
4. Action–reaction models	924
5. A game theory model	929
6. Panel and cross-section models	932
7. Conclusions	937
References	939

[*] We are grateful for comments on earlier versions from the editors Keith Hartley and Todd Sandler; our co-authors Maria Garcia-Alonso and Paul Levine; Jurgen Brauer, Walter Beckert and participants at the 9th Annual Conference on Economics and Security, Bristol, June 2005.

[1] Professor of Economics.

[2] Professor of Applied Economics.

Handbook of Defense Economics, Volume 2
Edited by Todd Sandler and Keith Hartley
© 2007 Elsevier B.V. *All rights reserved*
DOI: 10.1016/S1574-0013(06)02028-X

Abstract

Arms races – enduring rivalries between pairs of hostile powers, which prompt competitive acquisition of military capability – appear to be a pervasive phenomenon. From the past Cold War competition, between the US and the USSR, to present regional antagonisms, such as India and Pakistan, arms races remain a matter of continuing concern.

This chapter reviews the econometric issues involved in estimating models of military arms races, of the competitive acquisition of military capability by hostile powers. As econometrics involves the synthesis of theory, data and statistical methods, in reviewing the econometrics of arms races, as much attention is paid to theory and data as to statistical methods. After discussing the choice of data and the theoretical issues in specification, we then examine four types of model: time-series estimation of classical Richardson type action-reaction models, using India and Pakistan as an example; Markov switching estimation of game-theory type models, using Greece and Turkey as an example; cross-section models and panel models.

Our first general conclusion is that the theory suggests that the parameters of arms race interactions are unlikely to be constant over time and the empirical literature largely confirms this. Nonetheless, cross-section and panel estimates may be useful in that they allow estimation of average interaction effects, which may allow one to calculate the costs of the spill over effects of increases in military expenditure in one country.

Our second general conclusion is that globalization means that one cannot confine attention to a bivariate interaction between two countries without taking account of the wider strategic context. The emphasis in this literature is on quantitative-symmetric arms races, because those are easier to estimate, but this emphasis may be misleading, qualitative-asymmetric arms races, particularly between governments and their non-governmental opponents, may be much more important.

Keywords

arms race, econometric methods, game theory, measures of military capability

JEL classification: H56, C5, C7

1. Introduction

Arms races – enduring rivalries between pairs of hostile powers, which prompt competitive acquisition of military capability – appear to be a pervasive phenomenon. From the Cold War competition, between the US and the USSR, to regional antagonisms, such as those between Greece and Turkey, India and Pakistan, China and Taiwan or North and South Korea, arms races remain a matter of continuing concern. The concern arises because arms races consume scarce resources; because in a globalized world they can have repercussions for the whole international community, particularly when the arms are nuclear; and because of the danger that they may increase the probability of war. Gibler et al. (2005) provide a recent contribution to the empirical literature on whether arms races lead to war.

The question we address in this paper is how does one use data on military capabilities to estimate and test arms-race models. The focus of our review is on empirical papers that explain the mutual determination of military capabilities by two or more powers. There are different questions, such as about the effects of arms races, that take arms races for granted and provide criteria to define them. For example, Gibler et al. (2005) define an arms race as a case where both countries have increased their military spending or personnel by 8% or more in every year of a three year period and there was qualitative historical evidence that this build-up involved a competitive dynamic between the rivals. This is sensible given their purpose, but other definitions are possible.

Econometrics involves the synthesis of theory, data and statistical methods[1]: thus in reviewing the econometrics of arms races we will pay as much attention to theory and data as we do to statistical methods. Before we can consider estimation or testing, we need theory to provide the formal framework that defines what constitutes a model of an arms race. The theory of arms races comes in two main forms, a two-agent two-choice game, where each country has a discrete choice to arm or not to arm; and a Richardson type of dynamic action reaction process determining continuous measures of military capability. The theory of arms races is well surveyed by Gleditsch and Njolstad (1990), Brito and Intriligator (1995) and Intriligator and Brito (2000). Smith (1995) discusses estimation of demand functions for military expenditure, but largely treats foreign military expenditures as exogenous, whereas the central feature of arms race models is the mutual determination of military capabilities. Murdoch (1995) deals with alliance issues which overlap with arms races. In this volume, Garcia-Alonso and Levine, Chapter 29, and Brauer, Chapter 30, examine how arms races drive the arms trade and arms production. Smith et al. (2000a, 2000b) provide more detail on some of the technical time-series issues raised below. The literature is vast and our survey is far from comprehensive. There are also a number of statistical techniques that we do

---

[1] 'Econometrics may be defined as the quantitative analysis of actual economic phenomena based on the concurrent development of theory and observation, related by the appropriate methods of inference' [Samuelson et al. (1954)].

not discuss (e.g., Andreou et al. (2003) use genetically evolved fuzzy cognitive maps to study the Greek–Turkish arms race).

In evolutionary biology the idea of intra-species or inter-species arms races driving co-evolution has been empirically very fruitful. If you put 'arms race' into Google–Scholar, most of the hits are in biology. Robson (2005) provides a survey for economists. In contrast, the econometric evidence for military arms races has been less compelling. Sandler and Hartley (1995, chapter 4) in their review of the empirical analysis of arms races comment: 'To date, the empirical results can be best described as disappointing.' Brauer (2002) in a review of the literature on Greece and Turkey comments: 'The literature, as presently constituted, has reached the point of rapidly declining returns. Running more single or simultaneous regression equations, even when incorporating all the latest quirks of mathematical statistics, is unlikely to much advance our substantive knowledge.' Subsequent literature has not taken his advice. As teachers of 'the latest quirks in mathematical statistics', we would make a distinction between those who use arms race data to illustrate that they can implement the latest statistical model and those who ask which available statistical model best describes the data. The fact that we will be sceptical about the ability of the models to describe the data, should not be taken as scepticism about the need for statistical analysis of the data.

In evaluating such statistical analysis we need to consider three criteria by which econometric models may be judged [Pesaran and Smith (1985)]. The first is a relevance for a particular purpose. Different models are appropriate for different purposes – e.g., forecasting, policy analysis, or evaluating theories. The second is whether the model provides an adequate description of the data. This is not merely a matter of fit, but involves diagnostic testing to ensure that the assumptions required for the particular estimator to be appropriate are satisfied and comparison with alternative models. The third is the consistency of the model with theory, which allows us to interpret the results in a wider historical and analytic framework. Such theoretical interpretation often requires just-identifying assumptions, which by their nature cannot be tested. In practice, there are trade-offs between these criteria and alternative arms race models may have very similar fits but quite different theoretical interpretations or may explain different dependent variables for different purposes. This inevitably complicates evaluation.

Section 2 discusses the data and Section 3 the theoretical issues in specification. Section 4 examines time-series estimation of action–reaction models, using India and Pakistan as an example. Section 5 examines Markov switching estimation of game-theory type models, using Greece and Turkey as an example. Section 6 examines models for panel and cross-section data and Section 7 concludes.

2. Data

Probably the most important, though often least discussed, modelling issue is the choice of the measure of arms. Brauer (2002) discusses the issues in the case of Greece and

Turkey and reviews the various choices in that literature. In some cases the obvious measure is the number of a certain sort of weapon. Intriligator and Brito (2000, p. 46) note that until the East–West arms race of the Cold War, most arms races were naval: while armies were labor intensive, navies were capital intensive. Before World War I, Britain had a policy of matching competitors in numbers of major warships, giving rise to a typical Richardson type reaction function. This is a quantitative (numbers of battleships) symmetric (both acquired the same weapons) arms race. Craft (2000) examines the effect of the Washington Naval Agreement of 1922 on naval expenditure, suggesting that it caused diversion of resources to more advanced and expensive systems. McGuire (1977) analyzes another quantitative symmetric arms race, between the US and Soviet Union, using various measures of nuclear arsenals. Desai and Blake (1981) criticise his model and McGuire (1981) responds. This debate anticipates many of the time-series issues that are central to the subsequent literature: measurement of military capability, dynamic adjustment, specification sensitivity, existence and nature of long-run relationships and symmetric versus asymmetric models.

A qualitative and asymmetric arms race was that between fortifications and siege trains in the late medieval period, where there were evolutionary improvements in the technology of both, until the advent of gunpowder gave the besiegers an advantage the fortifiers could not counter. Markose (2005) discusses the way evolutionary arms races are characterized by this sort of feature: strategic innovations that change the structure of the dynamics. The current increasing returns to scale in military technology, emphasized by Intriligator and Brito (2000), leads to a virtual monopoly of military force by the US which gives its opponents incentives to choose asymmetric warfare and an asymmetric arms race.

Estimating qualitative asymmetric arms-races is inevitably difficult and we will largely confine out attention to quantitative symmetric arms races. This is a significant restriction, because what may be currently the most important arms race, between governments and terrorist opponents, is inherently qualitative and asymmetric. Data on preparations by terrorist groups, as distinct from actual attacks, are hard to come by. The 9/11 Commission[2] estimated that the cost of preparing the attack by the four planes was between $400,000 and $500,000; tiny compared to typical military expenditure numbers. In this volume, Sandler and Arce, Chapter 25, and Enders, Chapter 26, discuss models of the process by which terrorists substitute between different types of target in response to investments in defense. One reason the side with less resources may win is that they are rationally motivated to fight harder and invest more in conflict. Hirshleifer

---

[2] The National Commission on Terrorist Attacks Upon the United States (also known as the 9-11 Commission), was an independent, bipartisan commission created by congressional legislation and the signature of President George W. Bush in late 2002. It was chartered to prepare a full and complete account of the circumstances surrounding the September 11, 2001 terrorist attacks, including preparedness for and the immediate response to the attacks and to provide recommendations. On July 22, 2004 the Commission released its public report, which is available for download, http://www.9-11commission.gov/.

(2001, chapter 3) calls this the paradox of power. They may also have a second mover advantage, attacking where the richer side is vulnerable [Dunne et al. (2006)].

For a country involved in an enduring hostility the focus must be on military capability: the probability of prevailing in a conflict. This will be a function of its levels of forces, measured by military capital (troops, stocks of weapons, etc.), relative to those of its opponent. However, capability will also depend on how well those forces are used: a matter of strategy, tactics, training and leadership. Using a large sample of battles, Rotte and Schmidt (2003) show that relative force size is a poor predictor of victory. Instead, much quantitative analysis suggests that the strategy adopted by each side is the most important determinant of victory in war [Reiter (1999)].

Measuring military capability ex ante, before an actual conflict, is inherently problematic. Measuring forces is easier, but the long list of elements which go to make up a force structure cannot be well summarized by a single number. In particular, adding up spending on the different categories (personnel, research and development, R&D, procurement, etc.) may not be the appropriate form of aggregation. Dunne et al. (2004) suggest an aggregate of the form

$$ K_i = N^\nu \left[\sum_{j=1}^{N} (u_{ij} m_{ij})^\alpha \right]^{1/\alpha}, \tag{1} $$

where m_{ij} is the quantity of weapons system of type $j = 1, 2, \ldots, N$ that country i fields, u_{ij} the quality of the system and N is the total number of systems. The parameter α measures the elasticity of substitution between different types of system and the parameter ν measures the benefit of having a larger variety of systems. Thus, there are trade-offs between the number of systems in the inventory and the quality and quantity of each system. While useful theoretically, empirical implementation is difficult, though much military operational research does construct such force aggregates in the context of particular scenarios.

The level of forces reflects depreciated past stocks plus investment paid for by military expenditure. Payment for troops represents investment in human military capital. Again the conversion of military expenditure into effective forces is not a straightforward process, reflecting the efficiency of the arms production industries and personnel policies (e.g., the use of volunteers or conscripts). There are many cases where high military expenditures have not produced capable forces. Despite this, rather than using stocks of particular types of weapons, most empirical studies use measures based on military expenditures, either as levels: M_t; or shares of Gross Domestic Product, GDP: M_t/Y_t; or growth rates $(M_t - M_{t-1})/M_{t-1}$; or stocks calculated as $K_t = M_t + (1 - \delta)K_{t-1}$ where the rate of depreciation, δ, and initial stock, K_0, are either estimated or assumed. In principle, one can test between the alternative measures, but this is not often done.

Since the military expenditures of the two countries have to be in common units, there are issues about the choice of appropriate exchange rates and price indices. Measures of the levels of military expenditure can be very sensitive to these choices. For instance, the Stockholm International Peace Research Institute, SIPRI (2005), estimate that Chinese military expenditure was $35 billion at market exchange rates and $161 billion at purchasing power parity exchange rates. This is not an issue for shares, since they are pure ratios, but shares may be sensitive to the measurement of GDP. Most researchers use data from either SIPRI or the US government publication, World Military Expenditures and Arms Transfers, WMEAT, and there are often substantial differences between them [Lebovic (1999)]. In addition, the figures are often revised. Brauer (2002, p. 90) notes the big differences between the military expenditure series used in two studies of the Greek–Turkish arms race although both were based on the same SIPRI data source.

In principle, a government determines the level of military expenditure by first making a strategic assessment of the threat and of the effectiveness of military spending in countering the threat. It then balances the strategic assessment against the opportunity costs of the military spending, given available national output. The outcome of that political-economy calculation is the choice of a share of output to devote to military spending. The military may get a smaller share because the threat is thought to be less; or because military expenditure appears less effective at meeting the threat than alternative measures such as confidence building initiatives; or because the opportunity costs appear greater. While the share of military expenditures in output is clearly a measure of priorities not capabilities, arms races should be reflected in priorities, thus shares may be an interesting measure in certain contexts.

The issues are illustrated by the 1975 revision of estimated Soviet military spending by the US Central Intelligence Agency, CIA. The CIA calculated Soviet military spending by first estimating the number of goods and services purchased – number of troops, tanks, ships, soldiers, etc. – from intelligence sources. It then estimated what these would have cost the USA to get a dollar figure. This was then multiplied by an estimated rouble/dollar exchange rate, to get a rouble figure, which could then be expressed as a share of CIA estimates of Soviet GNP. In 1975, the CIA decided that the Soviet military industry was much less efficient than previously thought and altered the exchange rate to reflect this, raising the estimated share of military expenditure from 6–8% to 11–13%. Although this did not change their estimate of Soviet forces or the dollar figure for Soviet military expenditure, the revision to the estimated Soviet share of military expenditure was widely interpreted in the US as indicating an increased Soviet threat. With hindsight, we know the Soviet economy was even less efficient than the CIA thought, and the actual share was probably well over 20% of GNP.

Choice of a measure of military capability and the reliability of the data are both problematic and get less attention than they deserve. The data are undoubtedly poor and as Smith (1995) notes within the empirical literature there seem to be two responses to this. Some argue that given the known limitations of the data only the simplest models should be used. Others argue that only the most sophisticated techniques will be able to separate the signal from the background noise that dominates the data.

3. Theoretical issues in specification

The natural theoretical starting point for analysis of arms races is the Prisoner's dilemma or similar two-agent two-choice games and this is where Sandler and Hartley (1995, Section 4.1) start. A large variety of different types of games have been used in the theoretical arms-race literature, though fewer in the empirical literature. In the context of the Greek–Turkish arms race, Brauer (2002, p. 102) comments that 'the extant economics literature never addresses the disagreements and conflict from a game theoretic point of view.' Within the theoretical literature the arms-race game tends to be treated either as one stage of a more complex game – e.g., followed by decisions about war or preceded by negotiation [as in Baliga and Sjostrom (2004) who provide a review of this literature] or as a repeated game. Intriligator and Brito (2000) note that the existence of stocks means that arms races are not Markov processes, depending just on the state in the previous period. They suggest that the sufficient assumptions needed to transform this dynamic economic model into a repeated game are that the choice set is discrete, there are no income effects, and investment in weapons is reversible. We return to game theory models in Section 5.

Most empirical work has started from the model of Richardson (1960). This suggested that for some continuous measure of military preparedness of country $i = 1, 2$ at time t, $m_i(t)$, the arms race dynamics could be described by a pair of differential equations in continuous time:

$$\frac{dm_1(t)}{dt} = a_1 + b_1 m_2(t) - c_1 m_1(t),$$
$$\frac{dm_2(t)}{dt} = a_2 + b_2 m_1(t) - c_2 m_2(t). \tag{2}$$

Richardson interpreted the a_i as exogenous 'grievance' terms, b_i as 'reaction' or defense terms and c_i as 'fatigue' terms. The system can be written in discrete time as:

$$\Delta m_{1t} = a_1 + b_1 m_{2t} + c_1 m_{1,t-1},$$
$$\Delta m_{2t} = a_2 + b_2 m_{1t} + c_2 m_{2,t-1}, \tag{3}$$

where $b_i \geqslant 0$, $c_i \leqslant 0$. We return to the econometrics of this in the next section. The Richardson system is descriptive, in that it does not have behavioral foundations based on optimization or other explicit forms of decision-making and it does not include a budget constraint. There are many ways of providing those foundations, with Intriligator (1975) an early example. We will examine a model based on Levine and Smith (1995).

Consider two countries, $i, j = 1, 2$, each has a budget constraint in terms of national income, Y_{it}, consumption, C_{it}, investment in quantity of military goods and services, M_{it}, at relative price, P_{it}:

$$Y_{it} = C_{it} + P_{it} M_{it}. \tag{4}$$

The stock of arms accumulate according to:

$$K_{it+1} = (1 - \delta_i)K_{it} + M_{it}, \tag{5}$$

where δ_i is the rate of depreciation. Welfare in any period, W_{it} is a CES function of security S_{it} and consumption:

$$W_{it} = \left[(1 - a_i)C_{it}^{-\rho_i} + a_i S_{it}^{-\rho_i}\right]^{-1/\rho_i}, \tag{6}$$

where $\sigma_i = 1/(1+\rho_i)$ is the elasticity of substitution between security and consumption. Security is given by the difference between the forces that country j would need to make a successful attack on country i, a function of country i's forces: $\beta_i K_{it} + \alpha_i$, and the actual level of country j's forces:

$$S_{it} = \beta_i K_{it} + \alpha_i - K_{jt}. \tag{7}$$

Since welfare in each period is a function of stocks, we have a dynamic game, which requires an inter-temporal utility function:

$$U_i = \sum_{t=0}^{\infty} \mu_i^t W_{it}, \tag{8}$$

with discount rate μ.

The solution is a complete information open-loop Nash equilibrium as functions of the known path for the exogenous variables, incomes and prices. To evaluate the equilibrium, define a Lagrangian for country 1:

$$L_1 = \sum_{t=0}^{\infty} \lambda_1^t \left\{W_{1t} + \mu_{1t+1}\left[(1 - \delta)K_{1t} + M_{1t} - K_{1t+1}\right]\right\}, \tag{9}$$

which is maximized with respect to M_{1t}, K_{1t} and the costate variable μ_{1t} having eliminated C_{1t} using the budget constraint. This gives a set of first order conditions. From these one can solve for a non-linear difference equation determining S_{1t}. The set of equations determine the sequences K_{1t}, M_{1t} and C_{1t}, given Y_{1t}, P_{1t}, K_{2t} and the initial stock K_{10}. A similar set of equations holds for country 2. Solving the combined set of equations yields the open-loop Nash equilibrium as functions of the known paths for the exogenous variables P_{it}, Y_{it}.

To see the properties of the solution, abstract from the dynamics and consider a zero growth steady state, in which $S_{it} = S_i$, $C_{it} = C_i$, etc. In steady state the security consumption ratio is given by:

$$\frac{S_i}{C_i} = \left\{\frac{\beta_i a_i \mu_i}{(1 - a_i)[1 - \mu_i(1 - \delta)]P_i}\right\}^{\sigma_i} = \phi_i, \tag{10}$$

and the steady state equilibrium reaction functions by:

$$K_i = (\beta_i + \phi_i P_i \delta_i)^{-1}(-\alpha_i + K_j + \phi_i Y_i). \tag{11}$$

These correspond to the long-run relations derived from Richardson type equations, when adjustment through fatigue terms has been completed. They make the stock held by one country a function of the stock held by the other; with the difference that price and income appear explicitly, and the long-run coefficients to be estimated are complicated functions of the underlying parameters and price. Levine and Smith (1995) discuss the conditions for the existence of an internal solution.

This is a full information model, but in practice we have to allow for expectations. To introduce the issues, consider the case where only one of the countries is responding, say country one, while country two sets their military expenditure autonomously. Suppose the loss function for country one is forward looking with discount factor μ and penalises (a) the difference between the two countries military expenditure (this can be easily generalized as above) and (b) changes in its own military expenditure, because of adjustment costs. Assuming quadratic costs, this gives the function to be minimized as:

$$L_t = \sum_{i=0}^{\infty} \mu^i \left[\frac{1}{2}(m_{1t+i} - m_{2t+i})^2 + \frac{\theta}{2}\Delta m_{1t+i}^2 \right]. \tag{12}$$

The Euler equation takes the form:

$$\mu m_{1t+1} - \left(1 + \mu + \theta^{-1}\right)m_{1t} + m_{1t-1} = -m_{2t}\theta^{-1}. \tag{13}$$

Solving the Euler equation requires finding the two roots, $v_1 < 1 < v_2$ which are the solution to the characteristic equation:

$$\delta v^2 - \left(1 + \delta + \theta^{-1}\right)v + 1 = 0. \tag{14}$$

Calling the stable root (i.e., the one that is less than unity) v, the optimal policy is then given by the partial adjustment equation, of the same form as the Richardson equation above:

$$\Delta m_{1t} = (1 - v)(\hat{m}_{2t} - m_{1t-1}), \tag{15}$$

but with a forward looking target:

$$\hat{m}_{2t} = (1 - \mu v)E_t \left[\sum_{i=0}^{\infty}(\mu v)^i m_{2t+i} \right]. \tag{16}$$

If a time-series process is specified for m_{2t} an estimate of the expected value can be obtained in terms of observed values of m_{2t} and the parameters of the time-series process determining it. For instance, suppose:

$$\Delta m_{2t} = g(1 - \rho) + \rho\Delta m_{2t-1} + \varepsilon_t, \tag{17}$$

where g is the long run growth rate, then:

$$\Delta m_{1t} = \frac{\mu v(1 - v)(1 - \rho)g}{(1 - \mu v)(1 - \rho\mu v)} + \frac{1 - v}{1 - \rho\mu v}\Delta m_{2t} + (1 - v)(m_{2t-1} - m_{1t-1}). \tag{18}$$

This is an Error Correction Model, ECM, of the form commonly estimated. Notice that it differs from the Richardson equation in including m_{2t-1} in addition to m_{1t-1}. The estimated coefficients are functions not merely of the preference and adjustment parameters μ and ν, but of the parameters of the expectations process g and ρ. There is then the familiar Lucas Critique problem, if the expected behaviour of country two changes, (i.e., g or ρ change) then the parameters of country one's reaction function will change.

Given that strategic circumstances do show quite marked changes, this might make us sceptical of the likely structural stability of arms race models. Murdoch and Sandler (1984) discuss how the move from the doctrine of massive retaliation to flexible response affected the parameters of NATO alliance models, while Smith (1989) estimated structurally stable models of the UK and French shares of military expenditure as functions of US and Soviet shares, 1951–1987; but the equations, like the Soviet Union, collapsed a year after publication. Another form of structural instability could result from substitution between the arms being raced. For instance, if a country is losing the conventional forces race, it may switch to building nuclear weapons or supporting terrorism. Such substitutions may not show up particularly well in aggregate military expenditure data.

The leader–follower model above is particularly simple. If both countries react and have rational expectations the problem becomes more complex, because there may not be a unique solution. There may be an infinite number of rational expectations equilibria, in each of which both countries expectations prove self-fulfilling, all associated with different growth rates of military expenditure. Furthermore there may be transient 'bubbles', like those in markets for financial assets: periods when countries compete explosively, driven by the expectation that the others are arming; expectations which are confirmed by events. The form of the dynamics will reflect both expectations and adjustment lags and the theory gives little guidance on this, leaving it to be largely an empirical choice.

The models above are linear, primarily for mathematical convenience and because theory gives relatively little guidance about the appropriate functional forms. Non-linear reaction functions may intersect more than once, giving multiple equilibria with low and high levels of arms and zones of stability and instability [Brito and Intriligator (1995)]. One may then observe jumps from one equilibrium to another, which Richardson type models do not catch, and provide a role for arms control in stabilizing the system at a low expenditure equilibrium.

One conclusion from this very brief theoretical review is that one might question the likely structural stability of the underlying parameters. Some may be very stable (e.g., the elasticity of substitution between security and consumption or the discount rate), but many others may not be stable. Changes in military technology and tactical improvements will change the rate of depreciation, δ_i, and the parameters determining the forces country j needs to successfully attack country i: $\alpha_i + \beta_i K_i$. Changes in the strategic environment will change the country seen as a threat. Similar concerns arise with the parameters of the adjustment and expectations processes. In addition, as noted above, the evolutionary literature indicates that such hostile interactions are likely to generate strategic innovations that change the structure of the dynamics. As we shall see, structural instability is a pervasive feature of the econometric estimates of arms race models.

A second conclusion is that one may question the relevance of a purely bivariate framework, focussing on two countries in isolation. In an interdependent, globalized world, such rivalries take place in a wider strategic context, which needs to be addressed both in theoretical and empirical models.

4. Action–reaction models

The 'structural form' of the Richardson system introduced in the last section written in discrete time with the addition of a stochastic error term is:

$$\Delta m_{1t} = a_1 + b_1 m_{2t} + c_1 m_{1,t-1} + \varepsilon_{1t},$$
$$\Delta m_{2t} = a_2 + b_2 m_{1t} + c_2 m_{2,t-1} + \varepsilon_{2t}, \tag{19}$$

where it is usually assumed that:

$$E(\varepsilon_{it}) = 0; \quad E(\varepsilon_{it}^2) = \sigma_{ii}; \quad E(\varepsilon_{it}\varepsilon_{jt}) = \sigma_{ij};$$
$$E(\varepsilon_{it}\varepsilon_{j,t-s}) = 0, \quad s \neq 0; \; i, j = 1, 2.$$

As noted at the end of the last section, the rivalry takes place in a wider strategic context. Thus, these structural shocks, ε_{it}, will be driven partly by idiosyncratic factors (e.g., events in the Balkans for Greece and the conflict with the Kurds for Turkey) and partly by common factors (events in Cyprus or NATO for both). So, we would not expect the structural shocks to be independent of each other. They may also not be independent of the regressors and it is possible that systems like this may indicate an arms race between the two countries, when in fact the military expenditures of both are responding to common unobserved shocks.

The right-hand side military expenditures are endogenous, simultaneously determined and thus correlated with the error term. However, the system is just-identified and can be estimated by, for instance, two stage least squares. Of course, the plausibility of the just identifying restrictions ($m_{1,t-1}$ does not appear in the equation for Δm_{2t} and vice versa) may be questioned. For instance, the restriction does not hold in the ECM model derived above, Equation (18), which allowed for expectations. The interpretation of the coefficients is not straightforward. For instance, Richardson (1960) interpreted the c_i as fatigue terms, economists tend to interpret them as adjustment coefficients, political scientists as measures of bureaucratic inertia. We will follow the economic convention and write the model as:

$$\Delta m_{1t} = \lambda_1(\alpha_1 + \beta_1 m_{2t} - m_{1t-1}) + \varepsilon_{1t},$$
$$\Delta m_{2t} = \lambda_2(\alpha_2 + \beta_2 m_{2t} - m_{2t-1}) + \varepsilon_{2t}. \tag{20}$$

The model is stable as long as the adjustment parameters satisfy $-1 < \lambda_i < 1$, in which case there are two long-run reaction functions similar to (11), $m_i = \alpha_i + \beta_i m_j$, with static long run equilibria $m_i = (1 - \beta_i \beta_j)^{-1}(\alpha_i + \beta_i \alpha_j)$, which will exist as long as $\beta_i \beta_j \neq 1$. The reaction functions define two lines in the m_1, m_2 space, which will intersect once as long as they are not parallel. Non-linear reaction functions may intersect more than once.

This form is structural in that current values of the endogenous variables appear on the right hand side of the equation. Sets of equations with this general form can be derived from a variety of different theories. The structural coefficients will be functions of the underlying parameters of the system. For instance, in the theoretical model of the previous section, they are functions of prices (for which there are rarely data) and income, the depreciation rates for weapons, strategic parameters which describe the nature of conflict, discount rates, and the elasticity of substitution between security and consumption. Even if one can estimate the structural coefficients consistently, it may not be possible to recover the underlying parameters implied by the theory.

The reduced form of the system, in terms of predetermined, lagged, variables can be written in the VECM (Vector Error Correction Model) form of a first order VAR (Vector Autoregression) as:

$$\Delta m_{1t} = \frac{a_1 + b_1 a_2}{1 - b_1 b_2} + \frac{c_1 + b_1 b_2}{1 - b_1 b_2} m_{1t-1} + \frac{b_1(1 + c_2)}{1 - b_1 b_2} m_{2t-1} + \frac{\varepsilon_{1t} + b_1 \varepsilon_{2t}}{1 - b_1 b_2},$$

$$\Delta m_{2t} = \frac{a_2 + b_2 a_1}{1 - b_1 b_2} + \frac{c_2 + b_1 b_2}{1 - b_1 b_2} m_{1t-1} + \frac{b_2(1 + c_1)}{1 - b_1 b_2} m_{2t-1} + \frac{b_2 \varepsilon_{1t} + \varepsilon_{2t}}{1 - b_1 b_2}; \quad (21)$$

or

$$\Delta m_{1t} = \pi_{10} + \pi_{11} m_{1t-1} + \pi_{12} m_{2t-1} + u_{1t},$$

$$\Delta m_{2t} = \pi_{20} + \pi_{21} m_{1t-1} + \pi_{22} m_{2t-1} + u_{2t}; \quad (22)$$

with $E(u_{it}) = 0$, $E(u_{it}^2) = \omega_{ii}$, $E(u_{it} u_{jt}) = \omega_{ij}$, $E(u_{it} u_{j,t-s}) = 0$, $s \neq 0$, $i, j = 1, 2$. Each equation of the reduced form can be estimated consistently by least squares. There is Granger causality from m_1 to m_2 if $\pi_{21} \neq 0$ and from m_2 to m_1 if $\pi_{12} \neq 0$. Seiglie and Liu (2002) examine Granger causality in a number of arms races in the developing world. However, Granger causality may not correspond to economic causality. For instance, suppose $b_1 = 0$, country one is not arms-racing; m_1 will still Granger cause (help predict) m_2, as long as $c_2 \neq 0$. In addition, expectations mean that in economics effects can precede causes: weather forecasts Granger cause the weather. Unless one can identify the model, the reduced form is uninformative about contemporaneous interactions or expectations.

If the variables are I(1),[3] or equivalently contain a stochastic trend, then there is a danger of spurious regression. In a regression of one I(1) variable on another, the R^2

---

[3] A variable is said to be I(d), integrated of order d, if it must be differenced d times to become covariance stationary. A variable is said to be covariance stationary if its expected value, variances and auto-covariances are all constant, perhaps after the removal of a deterministic trend. An I(0) variable is thus stationary. If there is a linear combination of two I(1) variables which is I(0), the two variables are said to cointegrate.

tends to unity with the sample size and the t ratio to a non-zero value, even if the two series are unrelated. The requirement for the regression not to be spurious is that the two variables cointegrate. If this is the case then the process can be represented as a restricted form of the VECM above. If a long run relationship of the form $m_{1t} = \beta m_{2t}$ exists, then the disequilibrium or error correction term is measured by $z_t = m_{1t} - \beta m_{2t}$, which will be I(0). The VECM then takes the form:

$$\Delta m_{1t} = \pi_{10} + \alpha_1 z_{t-1} + u_{1t},$$
$$\Delta m_{2t} = \pi_{20} + \alpha_2 z_{t-1} + u_{2t}; \tag{23}$$

where the feedbacks are stabilizing if $\alpha_1 \leqslant 0$, $\alpha_2 \geqslant 0$, and at least one is non-zero. In the I(0) case, discussed above, there were two long-run reaction functions and both military expenditures tended to constants. In the I(1) cointegrating case, both military expenditures are driven by a single stochastic trend, so they can behave like random walks and go anywhere. But, because there is a single long-run relationship between them, the cointegrating vector, the series move together. Estimation and testing of the cointegrating vectors can be done in a number of ways, including within the maximum likelihood framework suggested by Johansen (1988).

Unit root tests, VARs and cointegration have been widely adopted in the defense economics literature and in the study of arms races. However, there are a number of problems with the techniques. Both the tests for unit roots (used to determine the order of integration) and the tests for cointegration tend to have low power, so determining the order of integration and cointegration is not straightforward. The tests are also sensitive to the choice of lag order, the treatment of the deterministic elements, the presence of structural breaks or non-linearities and various other factors. There are also questions of interpretation, since the order of integration is not a structural property of the series but a description of the time-series properties of a sample. Series which appear I(1) on short spans of data often appear I(0) on long spans, where span refers to the length in time of the series not the number of observations. Over centuries of data, the UK share of military expenditure is clearly I(0), over shorter spans it appears to be I(1). While cointegration allows us to estimate the long-run equilibrium, it does not help in identifying the short-run structural interaction.

As noted above, the Richardson model lacks a budget constraint, but this can be dealt with, as in the model of Section 3, by including GDP. Care needs to be taken in including extra variables within a VAR. The number of parameters grows very rapidly with the number of variables and large VARs can have very bad small sample properties. If there are m variables in the system and r cointegrating vectors, there are $m - r$ stochastic trends. When there are r cointegrating vectors r just-identifying restrictions are required on each cointegrating vector to interpret them. When $r = 1$, the restriction is just a normalization, choosing the dependent variable; when $r > 1$, it may be difficult to find just-identifying restrictions that allow the results to be interpreted.

Many papers have estimated VARs and VECMs for the Greek–Turkish arms race. Brauer (2002) provides a detailed review and concludes that the evidence for an action-reaction type arms race is, at best, mixed. Dunne et al. (2003a) describe an unsuccessful specification search. However, there is more evidence for an arms race between India and Pakistan. Deger and Sen (1990) obtained well-defined results and Ocal (2003) using data for the period 1949–1999 finds well-defined feedback. Ocal uses smooth transition regressions, which allow for non-linearities in the responses of the growth rates in military expenditure and may pick up structural changes.

Dunne et al. (2003a, 2003b) found that for SIPRI data, 1960–1996, various tests suggested a second order VAR in Indian and Pakistan real military expenditures (rather than logarithms or shares) and that GDP was Granger non-causal for military expenditures. Working with a VECM in the two military expenditure series, they found one cointegrating vector by both trace and eigenvalue tests, irrespective of the treatment of the deterministic elements. This was: $Z_t = MI_t - 2.0MP_t$. Indian military expenditure, MI_t, tends to a long-run relationship where it is twice Pakistan military expenditure, MP_t (plus a constant). The VECM showed significant feedbacks in both directions and interesting dynamics. The equations passed a variety of specification tests and in particular Cusum and Cusum-squared tests indicated that the equations were structurally stable.

When the data were updated to 1960–2003, using revised SIPRI data, re-estimation for 1962–1996, again gave one cointegrating vector, though it was slightly different: $Z_t = I_t - 2.51P_t$, perhaps as a consequence of rebasing and revision. The estimated VECM coefficients and the fit were very similar. When the data were extended to 1962–2003, there was much less evidence for cointegration. The extra seven years did not make a large difference to the estimated cointegration coefficient, but increased its standard error. The coefficients (standard errors) were -2.51 (0.09) for 1962–1996 and -3.04 (0.30) for 1962–2002. However, the dynamics changed substantially. The feedback coefficient on the error correction term in the Indian equation went from being large and significant, 1962–1996, to being small and insignificant, 1962–2003. None of the variables in the Indian equation are significant and it looks like a random walk. The feedback coefficient in the Pakistan equation went from 0.11 (0.04) to 0.05 (0.02) remaining significant. For the Indian equation, the Chow forecast accuracy test ($p = 0.02$) and the parameter equality test ($p = 0.009$) rejected structural stability after 1996. The equation estimated using data up to 1996 substantially underpredicted subsequent Indian military expenditure. The Pakistan equation also underpredicted subsequent expenditure, but not by as much, and the forecast accuracy test did not reject structural stability ($p = 0.08$), though the parameter equality test did ($p = 0.03$).

To investigate the nature of the change we allowed for a break in the intercept and a trend in 1996, when the break seemed to occur. This was done by including as exogenous variables in the cointegrating vector D_t, a dummy that was unity after 1996, and DT_t, a trend that started in 1996. This restored cointegration on both the trace and maximal eigenvalue tests. The cointegrating vector (standard errors) is

$$MI_t = 2.51MP_t + 921D + 272DT + Z_t. \tag{24}$$
$$\underset{(0.85)}{} \quad \underset{(437)}{} \quad \underset{(88)}{}$$

This is the long-run equilibrium relationship, and Z_t is the deviation from equilibrium. The coefficient on Pakistan military expenditure is very similar to the estimates for the earlier period and significant. Both the dummy and the broken trend are significant. The equation indicates that after 1996, Indian military expenditure was steadily increasing relative to the earlier equilibrium. Of course, including deterministic structural breaks is ad hoc, unless there is a theoretical explanation. One possible explanation is that the break was associated with the two countries preparations to test nuclear weapons.

The error correction equations are:

$$\Delta MI_t = 566 + 0.37\Delta MI_{t-1} + 0.14\Delta MP_{t-1} + 0.43 Z_{t-1},$$
$$\quad\;\;(132) \qquad (0.17) \qquad\quad (0.55) \qquad\qquad (0.13)$$

$$R^2 = 0.23, \qquad SER = 373, \tag{25}$$

$$\Delta MP_t = -57 - 0.07\Delta MI_{t-1} + 0.37\Delta MP_{t-1} - 0.12 Z_{t-1},$$
$$\quad\;\;(30) \qquad (0.04) \qquad\quad (0.12) \qquad\quad (0.03)$$

$$R^2 = 0.41, \qquad SER = 83. \tag{26}$$

Both error correction terms, Z_{t-1}, and the lagged changes in own military expenditure are significant, whilst lagged changes in the other countries military expenditure are not significant. The pattern of coefficients and fit are very similar to that for 1960–1996. The error correction equations show no sign of misspecification with respect to heteroskedasticity, normality or functional form, though the Pakistan equation just fails on a first order serial correlation test. Both equations pass Cusum and Cusum squared tests for structural stability, after allowing for the breaks.

The VECM approach described above is standard (though not unquestioned) in time-series methodology and flows naturally from the Richardson model. However, our conclusion from the review in this section is that it may not work well on arms race data for a variety of reasons. The first reason seems likely to be that structural stability may not be an appropriate assumption. The India-Pakistan example may be unusual in that their strategic relationship may have been bureaucratized, perhaps because of shared decision rules acquired from their common colonial heritage. But, even here the evidence for a structurally stable arms race is mixed and their acquisition of nuclear weapons may have changed their relationship. The second reason is that it ignores the wider strategic context. There is the danger that India may be responding to China and the apparent arms race is produced by common shocks as noted above. The quality of Chinese military expenditure data is such that it would be difficult to test this. Both countries operate in a wider strategic context: India has ambitions to be a wider regional naval power and Pakistan has been influenced by events in Afghanistan and neglecting this will produce misspecification. Thus, the time-series estimates support the two concerns that we expressed on the basis of the theoretical analysis.

5. A game theory model

As noted above, the natural theoretical starting point for analysis of arms races is the Prisoner's dilemma, and similar two-agent two-choice games and more complicated games have had a substantial influence on the theory. An empirical illustration of the estimation of a simple two-by-two game is Smith et al. (2000b) which analyzes the Greek–Turkish arms race. The paper models each country choosing either high or low military spending, with payoffs which depend on the choice of the other. This gives four possible states, with associated payoffs. Given the payoffs, the countries choose a strategy. This is a repeated or iterated game, played every year. One can imagine that during the annual budgetary cycle each country chooses its strategy, high or low military spending for the next year, knowing what its opponent chose for this year, but not what the opponent will do next year. The strategy they choose for the next year will be conditional on the state this year. A familiar example of a conditional strategy is tit for tat: begin by cooperating, and then do in the next period what your opponent did in this period. This can give good payoffs in a Prisoner's Dilemma game: it is nice, providing incentives for further cooperation; but not too nice, instantly retaliating to a defection.

Tit for Tat is a pure strategy, specifying either high or low for the next period conditional on the state in this period. But in repeated games, pure strategies are predictable and can be exploited. As an alternative, to reduce predictability, countries could follow mixed strategies, choosing high with some probability p and low with some probability $(1 - p)$. Mixed strategies are optimal for quite a wide range of games. The paper assumes countries play conditional mixed strategies, choosing a probability of being high or low next year depending on the current state, and tries to estimate these strategies to see what light they shed on the interaction between Greek and Turkish military expenditures. This is the reverse of the usual approach in game theory, which specifies the payoffs and then determines the optimal strategy. Here, the payoffs are not observed; but the strategies the players adopt are observed: whether they choose high or low. This allows inference about the nature of the game.

This game theory approach differs from the Richardson approach in a number of ways. Firstly, it naturally handles non-linearities and structural change – jumps from high to low – which the Richardson approach does not. Secondly, all the other factors, which are treated as deterministic influences in the regression approach, are treated stochastically: reflected in the conditional probabilities of choosing high or low. Thirdly, military expenditures are now discrete, taking two values high and low, rather than continuous as in the Richardson models. Obviously, this approach can only be applied where it is sensible to treat the outcomes as dichotomous. Therefore, it could not be applied to military expenditures which are trended upwards and there is no natural classification into high and low. However, it can be applied to shares of military expenditure or growth rates. It is clear that there have been marked changes both in the level of the Greek and Turkish shares and the relationship between them. To a first approximation, the series appear to be well described by variations around distinct high and low levels, so modelling them in terms of a simple high–low choice plus some random errors may not be too unrealistic.

Estimation of the strategies in a simple two-by-two game in which each side choses high or low can be done using the bivariate Hamilton (1989) discrete state switching model. There are four states or regimes: (1) both high, (2) Greece high, Turkey low, (3) Greece low, Turkey high and (4) both low. The parameters to be estimated are those for the two states, high and low, and the transition matrix. The state parameters are the high and low mean for each country, the variance for each country and the covariance between the shocks for each country, 7 in total. The evolution of the series is described by a four by four transition matrix, Π, the elements of which, π_{ij} give the probability of moving from state i in period t to state j in period $t + 1$, $i, j = 1, 2, 3, 4$. So π_{11} gives the probability of staying in state 1, both countries having high shares of military expenditure in the next period, given they both have high shares this period. Because the system must move to one of the four states in the next period, each of the four columns of the transition matrix sums to unity. Thus, the unrestricted transition matrix has 12 free probabilities, which together with the 7 state parameters gives 19 free parameters in total. The parameter estimates are obtained by maximizing the likelihood function. On the basis of the estimates, one can calculate the state probabilities for each year. This gives the probability of being in each of the four states, given the history of the process: for instance $P(s_t = 1)$ gives the probability of both countries being high in a particular year. If the four state model is a good description of the process, these probabilities should be close to one or zero, indicating a clear separation between the four regimes.

The unrestricted case allows unlimited dependence in the decisions of the two countries. The paper also considers three restricted transition matrices. The first assumes that each country determines its share of military expenditure independently. If two events A and B are independent, the probability of both happening is the product of the probabilities of each of them happening: $P(A \cap B) = P(A)P(B)$. Similarly, the probability of staying in state 1, both high, is just the product of the probability of Greece staying in the high state and the probability of Turkey staying in the high state: $\pi_{11} = \pi_{GH}\pi_{TH}$. With independence, there are only four free probabilities: that of Greece staying in a high state, π_{GH}; Turkey staying in the high state, π_{TH}; Greece staying in a low state, π_{GL} and Turkey staying in the low state, π_{TL}.

The second and third restricted versions assume that one country leads and the other plays tit-for-tat following the leader with a lag. The follower is always in the state that the leader was one period ago. In this case there are only two free probabilities, that of the leader staying in the high state or of the leader staying in the low state. Suppose Greece leads and Turkey plays tit for tat, then Turkey will always be in the state Greece was one period ago. There are then only two free probabilities, that represent Greek strategy, π_{GH} and π_{GL}. If Greece is high this period, Turkey will be high next period, so any state with Turkey low has zero probability. What drives the system is the probabilities of Greece staying in the high or low states. The analysis is similar if Turkey leads Greece.

This technique was applied to SIPRI annual data on Greek and Turkish shares of military expenditure 1958–1997. First, the unrestricted Markov structure is estimated, which allows for twelve free probabilities in the transition matrix. The Greece Low state has a mean military expenditure of 4.37% of GDP, the Greece High state has a mean 2.16 percentage points of GDP higher, and this shift is very significant, with a t ratio over 15. The Turkey Low state has a mean share of military expenditure of 3.86% with the Turkey High state 1.44 percentage points higher, again the difference between the high and low means is very significant. Turkey shows a higher variance around its means than does Greece: the standard deviations of the shocks are 0.43 for Greece and 0.55 for Turkey. Thus, the variations in the share of military expenditure around the means are about a half a percent of GDP. There is a positive covariance between the shocks, which is on the margin of significance at the 5% level.

The probabilities of being in each of the four regimes from the unrestricted, general, model show a very clear separation into regimes: the probabilities are close to zero or one, and match the impression of the time series. The series starts with both being low (state 4); switches in 1961 (about the time of a Turkish military coup) to Greece low, Turkey high (state 3); stays in that state till 1967 (the year of the Greek military coup), when it switches back to both low (state 4) until 1973. With 1974 (the invasion of Cyprus) it switches to both high (state 1) until 1983 (the end of a period of military rule in Turkey). From 1984–1988 Greece is High, Turkey Low (state 2). From 1989 (the end of the Cold War) to 1997 shares of military expenditure are in state 4 (both low). Although there is some correspondence, the division into states does not match up neatly with military rule: 1967 to 1974 for Greece and 1960–1961, 1971–1973 and 1980–1983 for Turkey.

The first restriction tested is that the probability of switching between states in each country is independent (i.e., each country has its own probabilities of switching, which does not depend on the state the other country is in). This reduces the number of free parameters in the transition matrix from 12 to 4, two for each country. This would be the case if each country was responding to its own domestic political economy or strategic concerns, which determined the probability of staying in the high state or the low state, without regard for whether the other was in a high or low state. Imposing independence reduces the maximized log-likelihood from 15.2 to 10.6, which is not a significant reduction at any conventional level. The likelihood ratio test would give LR $=$ 9.2 whereas the 5% critical value for $\chi^2(8)$ is 15.51. The estimates of the coefficients and the assignment of the sample into the four states are hardly changed by the restriction of independence. Furthermore, the estimates of the transition probabilities appear to be persistent and highly significant with values respectively given by $\pi_{GH} = 0.96$, $\pi_{GL} = 0.95$, $\pi_{TH} = 0.86$, $\pi_{TL} = 0.93$. If the two countries get into state 4 (low–low), there is a high probability of them staying there: $\pi_{44} = \pi_{TL}\pi_{GL} = 0.95 \times 0.93 = 0.88$. Independence of the two countries transition probabilities does not imply that the two series are independent or that they cannot change regime simultaneously. Because of the positive covariance through the error terms, shocks (e.g., Cyprus) hit them both in the same way.

The second and third restrictions tested were that one country determined its state independently and the other played tit for tat, playing what the leader had played in the previous period. The Greece leads Turkey or Turkey leads Greece restrictions lead to a large reduction in the maximized log likelihood. Using likelihood ratio tests both restrictions are rejected at the 1% level.

One could of course consider much more complicated games, but the simplicity of this two-by-two game allows us to test sharp hypotheses suggested by theory, which is difficult to do in a regression framework. The independence restriction can be interpreted either as the switches are determined by other factors than the Greece–Turkey antagonism, or that each country plays a mixed strategy that does not condition on the other side's behaviour. Neither interpretation provides much support for a traditional action-reaction type arms-race in which military expenditure is a response to an external threat represented by the other countries military spending. Instead, the estimates of the transition probabilities are more consistent with an internal explanation in which political or bureaucratic inertia mean that once either country gets into a particular state, high or low, there is a high probability that it will stay there.

It is also interesting that a very simple theoretical model translates into quite a complicated empirical model. To apply the simple unrestricted two by two game to data on observed choices requires 19 free parameters. However, these parameters can be related to game theory strategies in a straightforward way, which is not the case with regression-based arms race models. Theories about the possible strategies followed by the players, such as independence or tit for tat, can reduce the parameter space substantially. Such models, while useful in some cases, will only work where the observations can be divided into high and low, as in this case, and tend not to predict very well. Although it was not an issue in this case, the likelihood function in these models can be badly behaved, giving numerical problems in estimation, difficulty in obtaining convergence and sensitivity to choice of initial conditions. There are a variety of other regime-switching models, where transition depends on observed variables rather than latent states as in this case, which are likely to be a subject of further research.

6. Panel and cross-section models

There is a long tradition of estimating cross-section models which explain the military expenditures of one country by the military expenditure of their neighbours or antagonists as well as other economic and political variables. Rosh (1988) introduced the concept of a "Security Web", defined by neighbours and other countries (such as regional powers) that can affect a nation's security. Rosh calculates the degree of militarization of a nation's Security Web by averaging the shares of military expenditure in GDP of those countries in the web, finding it to have a significant positive effect on a country's military burden. Rather than average military shares, Collier and Hoeffler (2004) use the ratio of the sum of neighbouring nation's military expenditure to the sum of their GDPs. They give the example of India, which has borders with China and

Nepal, but the level of threat it faces is dominated by the military spending of China. More generally, spillover effects have been attracting increasing attention [e.g., Murdoch and Sandler (2002, 2004)]. Panel studies are fewer and more recent.

A natural objection is that a cross-section regression cannot be a model of an arms race, since it contains no dynamics. To analyse this issue, it is useful to start with a panel model. Suppose that we have data, $t = 1, 2, \ldots, T$, on a number of arms races between pairs of countries, $j = 1, 2, \ldots, J$ and they take the familiar Richardson form, augmented by exogenous variables:

$$\Delta m_{j1t} = \lambda_{j1}(\alpha_{j1} + \beta_{j1}m_{j2t} + \gamma_{j1}x_{j1t} - m_{j1t-1}) + \varepsilon_{j1t},$$
$$\Delta m_{j2t} = \lambda_{j2}(\alpha_{j2} + \beta_{j2}m_{j2t} + \gamma_{j2}x_{j2t} - m_{j2t-1}) + \varepsilon_{j2t}. \tag{27}$$

This gives us a panel of $N = 2J$ countries. Collier and Hoeffler (2004) include in the x_j measures of internal and external threats, log GDP per capita, log population (which may pick up scale or public good effects) and a measure of democracy. Whether there is any advantage in treating the J separate arms-races as a panel, depends whether there are any links between them. Those links may allow more efficient estimation using parameter equality restrictions, if the responses are similar between countries, or information in the covariances between the errors if common shocks hit all the countries.

Suppose the two countries had the same parameters, dropping the j and t subscripts, the equilibrium levels of military expenditure would be:

$$m_1 = \frac{\alpha}{1 - \beta^2} + \frac{\gamma}{1 - \beta^2}x_1 + \frac{\beta\gamma}{1 - \beta^2}x_2,$$
$$m_2 = \frac{\alpha}{1 - \beta^2} + \frac{\beta\gamma}{1 - \beta^2}x_1 + \frac{\gamma}{1 - \beta^2}x_2. \tag{28}$$

Thus, allowing for dynamics and interaction a unit increase in x_1 causes a long run increase in country one's military expenditure of $\gamma/(1 - \beta^2)$ and of $\beta\gamma/(1 - \beta^2)$ in that of country 2. We return to this issue below.

To examine what the cross-section measures, write the model for country one as:

$$m_{it} = a_i + b_i m_{kt} + c_i x_{it} + d_i m_{i,t-1} + \varepsilon_{it}, \tag{29}$$

where $i = j_1, k = j_2, a_i = \lambda_{j1}\alpha_{j1}, d_i = (1 - \lambda_{j1})$, etc. Then average the data over time for each country to give:

$$\bar{m}_i = a_i + b_i \bar{m}_k + c_i \bar{x}_i + d_i \bar{m}_{i-1} + \bar{\varepsilon}_i, \tag{30}$$

where $\bar{m}_i = \sum_{t=1}^{T} m_{it}/T, \bar{m}_{i-1} = \sum_{t=0}^{T-1} m_{it}/T$, etc. If we define $\Delta_T m_i = m_{iT} - m_{i0}$ and note that $\bar{m}_{i-1} = \bar{m}_i - \Delta_T m_i$ we can write this as:

$$\bar{m}_i = a_i + b_i \bar{m}_k + c_i \bar{x}_i + d_i (\bar{m}_i - \Delta_T m_i) + \bar{\varepsilon}_i. \tag{31}$$

Solving for $\bar{m}_i$, gives the long-run parameters as the coefficients:

$$\bar{m}_i = \frac{a_i}{1 - d_i} + \frac{b_i}{1 - d_i}\bar{m}_k + \frac{c_i}{1 - d_i}\bar{x}_i - \frac{d_i}{1 - d_i}\Delta_T m_i + \frac{\bar{\varepsilon}_i}{1 - d_i}, \tag{32}$$

$$\bar{m}_i = \alpha_i + \beta_i \bar{m}_k + \gamma_i \bar{x}_i - \psi_i \Delta_T m_i + \frac{\bar{\varepsilon}_i}{1 - d_i}, \tag{33}$$

where ψ_i is the mean lag. If we assume that the long run parameters are random, independent of the average levels of the regressors, with for instance, $\alpha_i = \alpha + \eta_{\alpha i}$ we obtain the standard cross-section regression on averaged data:

$$\bar{m}_i = \alpha + \beta \bar{m}_k + \gamma \bar{x}_i + u_i. \tag{34}$$

The error term is:

$$u_i = \eta_{\alpha i} + \eta_{\beta i} \bar{m}_k + \eta_{\gamma i} \bar{x}_i - \psi_i \Delta_T m_i + \frac{\bar{\varepsilon}_i}{1 - d_i}. \tag{35}$$

For large T, the growth terms $\Delta_T m_i$ are uncorrelated with the levels terms and if the parameters are random, the $\eta_{\cdot j}$ terms are independent of the regressors. If the x_{it} are strictly exogenous, $\bar{x}_i$ will be uncorrelated with $\bar{\varepsilon}_i$. Pesaran and Smith (1995) derive the small sample bias and consider various generalizations. Thus the only issue of concern is the covariance between $\bar{m}_k$ and $\bar{\varepsilon}_i$, which is certainly non-zero, as discussed in the time-series case. In the time-series case, lagged values of the variables provide possible instruments, but this is not the case here. However, the natural instruments for $\bar{m}_k$ would be $\bar{x}_k$. Thus, the average slope of the long-run reaction function in the arms race could be retrieved from the cross-section regression. Using these estimates one can calculate the average long-run effects of a change in an exogenous variable by one country on its own military spending, $\gamma/(1 - \beta^2)$ and on its rivals $\beta\gamma/(1 - \beta^2)$. Collier and Hoeffler (2004) use a similar approach to measure the effect of exogenous shocks on own military spending and other countries military spending.

There are obvious practical problems in running cross-section regressions: How to determine the pattern of threats and alliances? What time period to average over? Which measure of military capability to use? How to aggregate expenditures by groups of allies and groups of opponents? Dunne and Perlo-Freeman (2003a) estimate cross-section demand functions for developing countries using average data for Cold War (1981–1988) and post-Cold War (1990–1997) periods. The dependent variable was the log of the share of military expenditure. Significant explanatory variables were log of population (perhaps a proxy for public good effects); log of the sum of its potential enemies military expenditure; log of the sum of the military expenditures of countries in its security web (including potential enemies); a democracy measure; civil war; external war and region dummies. There was little evidence of a change in the underlying cross-section relationship with the end of the Cold War, though as we shall see this is not a robust conclusion.

Using cross-section data, rather than time-series for individual countries increases the sample size considerably and allows one to measure the effect of variables which tend not to vary very much within countries. The cost of this benefit is the assumption that the arms race and alliance parameters are the same across all countries or that the differences are random, independent of the right hand side variables. These assumptions are quite strong. If panel data are available, a separate model for each country can be estimated and the homogeneity or independence assumptions tested.

With panel data, one can employ a larger sample and allow for heterogeneity in the responses of different countries. The treatment and interpretation of heterogeneity in panels is a central issue and to focus on this, we will ignore the feedback issues discussed in Section 4, to concentrate on a single equation. When one allows for panel VARS and VECMs, the situation becomes more complicated, and is discussed in Fuertes and Smith (2005). Smith and Tasiran (2005) compare alternative panel estimators in an application to the demand for arms imports. Given the number of different ways to treat heterogeneity and between group dependence, there are a large number of different panel estimators.

A central issue in the choice of estimator is the relative size of N and T. The traditional panel literature deals with cases where N is large and T small, maybe only two or three time periods. Asymptotic analysis is done letting $N \to \infty$. The time-series literature deals with the case where T is large and N small and asymptotic analysis is done letting $T \to \infty$. Recently, there has been interest in panel time-series where N and T are of the same orders of magnitude and the asymptotic analysis is done letting both $N \to \infty$ and $T \to \infty$ in some way. What estimators are appropriate in the three cases differs.

Define the country and overall means as:

$$\bar{m}_i = T^{-1} \sum_{t=1}^{T} m_{it}; \qquad \bar{m} = (NT)^{-1} \sum_{i=1}^{N} \sum_{t=1}^{T} m_{it}. \tag{36}$$

The total variation in the dependent variable is the sum of the within country variation and the between country variation:

$$\sum_i \sum_t (m_{it} - \bar{m})^2 = \sum_i \sum_t (m_{it} - \bar{m}_i)^2 + T \sum_i (\bar{m}_i - \bar{m})^2, \tag{37}$$

similarly for the regressors. The main panel estimators differ in how they treat the within and between variation.

If the parameters are random, the within and between regressions will measure the same thing. However, if they are not random the cross-section (between country) estimates can be very different from the average time-series (within country) estimates. Country i may not respond to transitory variations in the military capability of country j, making the time-series estimate quite small. If the cross-section, using time-averages, picks up permanent components, the coefficient may be larger. The between estimate β_B and the within estimate β_W will differ if the α_i are correlated with the $\bar{x}_i$ and the two estimates may even be of opposite sign if countries that had traditionally been allies become antagonists.

Further issue arises with dynamic models. Consider the within (fixed effect, least squares dummy variable) estimator of:

$$m_{it} = a_i + b' x_{it} + c m_{it-1} + u_{it}, \tag{38}$$

where, the $(k \times 1)$ vector x_{it} contains other countries military expenditures and other variables. This assumes that the intercepts differ but the slopes are the same. The estimates are consistent for large T, but are not consistent for fixed T, large N. In this case the estimated coefficient of the lagged dependent variable, $\hat{c}$, is biased downwards. This is the standard small T bias of the OLS estimator in models with lagged dependent variables. There are a variety of instrumental variable estimators for this case. However, if the true model is heterogeneous:

$$m_{it} = a_i + b_i' x_{it} + c_i m_{it-1} + u_{it}, \tag{39}$$

and homogeneity of the slopes is incorrectly imposed, estimating

$$m_{it} = a_i + b' x_{it} + c m_{it-1} + v_{it}, \tag{40}$$

the within estimator is not consistent even for large T [Pesaran and Smith (1995)]. This is because the error term will be:

$$v_{it} = (b_i - b)' x_{it} + (c_i - c) m_{it-1} + u_{it}. \tag{41}$$

This will be serially correlated, even if the parameters are random. The estimated coefficient of the lagged dependent variable, $\hat{c}$, is biased upwards towards unity (assuming the regressors are positively serially correlated, as is usually the case). Comparison of the various estimators, which are subject to different biases, can allow us to infer which biases are most important.

Panel data allow for between group dependence arising from unobserved strategic factors that may influence all countries, which we have argued are important. Pesaran (2004) suggests that a simple and effective way to allow for such factors is to include the means for each year in a heterogeneous equation. Define $\bar{m}_t = \sum_{i=1}^{N} m_{it}/N$ and estimate the model including the cross-section means of the variables:

$$m_{it} = a_i + b_i' x_{it} + c_i m_{it-1} + d_{0i} \bar{m}_t + d_{1i}' \bar{x}_t + u_{it}. \tag{42}$$

The world average military expenditure captures global strategic effects. This estimator is consistent for large N and large T.

Gadea et al. (2004) estimate a heterogeneous panel model for the military expenditures of NATO countries (a) allowing for endogenously determined structural breaks and (b) using the Pesaran (2004) approach of including average shares of military expenditure which controls for between group residual dependence and acts as a proxy for the threat. They find a lot of structural breaks and the results for the individual countries are difficult to interpret. This is a common finding in other areas. In panel studies, where the number of time-periods is large enough to estimate a separate time-series model for each country, the pattern tends to be that while average effects are sensible there is a very large amount of heterogeneity in the country specific estimates, which may not appear sensible.

Dunne and Perlo-Freeman (2003b) estimate a very similar model to Dunne and Perlo-Freeman (2003a) explaining the log of the share of military expenditure with the same explanatory variables. The difference is that rather than averaging the data they use it as an unbalanced panel of annual data for 98 developing countries 1981–1997. The static fixed effects estimates are quite similar to those found in cross-section. However, when dynamics are allowed for, through a lagged dependent variable the results are very different. The estimates are obtained by first differencing the data to remove the fixed effect, then instrumenting the lagged change in the dependent variable, which becomes correlated with the error term from the differencing. In contrast to the cross-section results there is evidence of structural change, between Cold War and post-Cold War periods in the dynamic panel model.

Collier and Hoeffler (2004) use a pooled static panel of five-year averages explaining the share of military expenditure by measures of international war, civil war, external threat, democratic government, military expenditure by neighbours, a post-Cold War shift after 1995, log population, log GDP per capita, aid to GDP and a dummy for Israel. These are chosen after a specification search for significant variables. They find the effect of the military expenditure by neighbours to be quite large, which means that increases in military expenditure are escalated among neighbours, making them a regional public bad. They also investigate the endogeneity of a number of variables and find that once instrumented, military expenditure does not deter rebellions.

Having concluded in our review of time series models that we are unlikely to find structurally stable dynamic action-reaction systems, then for determining mutual military capabilities, persisting over long periods of time, cross-section and panel estimates may prove useful. In addition to providing larger samples and allowing for heterogeneity in the responses of different countries, they allow estimation of average interaction effects. This may allow the costs of the spill-over effects of increases in military expenditure in one country to be calculated, from which a variety of policy conclusions can be surmised. The approach is certainly worthy of further research.

7. Conclusions

Arms races are like bubbles in financial markets: most people agree they exist but it is remarkably difficult to define them unambiguously, estimate them or test for their existence. We have suggested two explanations for the difficulty: structural instability and globalization.

The theory does not suggest structural stability because the equations are interpreted as the optimal reaction functions for military capability by one government given the military capability of the other. The optimal response will depend on the perceived threat from the other government, the types of military capability available, their costs and relative effectiveness and the relevant budget constraints. It seems unlikely that all these factors, which determine the underlying parameters of an arms race models, would be constant over time. Hence, we would expect structural instability and the econometrics seems to confirm it. The one example of what looked like a stable action-reaction pattern, between India and Pakistan, has broken down since we last estimated it; though it could be rescued, to some extent, by a mechanical allowance for structural change. Of course, the apparent structural instability may be the product of misspecification and we would expect further research in that direction: experimenting with different specifications, functional forms, estimation methods, etc. In addition, there are a variety of models that allow for endogenous structural instability through regime switching with either smooth or abrupt transitions and with the transitions a function of observed variables or latent states. To be plausible, estimates from such models would need to have a clear theoretical basis and an historical interpretation rather than be a mechanical application of statistical techniques. There is also the danger that the literature is influenced by publication bias: only arms race models that 'work' get published.

A secondary explanation is globalization. As emphasized in the discussion, Greece and Turkey or India and Pakistan do not exist in bivariate isolation: they are influenced by a variety of other strategic factors. These act as omitted variables causing biased coefficients, with biases that change over time as strategic interactions change.

We are not claiming that there are no examples of equations where the military expenditure of antagonists, and allies, are significant in equations explaining the demand for military expenditure for particular countries over a particular sample. There are a lot of examples where this is certainly the case. What we are claiming is that one would not expect to see structurally stable dynamic action-reaction systems, determining mutual military capabilities, persist over long periods of time. Nonetheless, cross-section and panel estimates may be useful in that they allow estimation of average interaction effects, which may allow one to calculate the costs of the spill-over effects of increases in military expenditure in one country. Collier and Hoeffler (2004) draw a variety of policy conclusions from their estimates of such spill-over effects. Arms races have obvious implications for arms control, particularly where there are multiple equilibria, but the linear models common in the econometric literature do not allow for multiple equilibria.

The emphasis in this literature is on quantitative-symmetric arms races, because those are easier to estimate, but this emphasis may be misleading: qualitative-asymmetric arms races, particularly between governments and their non-governmental opponents, may be much more important. This is a lesson of the evolutionary literature that emphasises strategic innovation which changes the structural dynamics of the arms race [e.g., Markose (2005)]. This also seems historically important. Arreguin-Toft (2001) comments "material power is useful for theory building because it is quantifiable and measurable in a way that courage, leadership and dumb luck are not. ... The strategic interaction thesis makes clear, however, the limitations of relative material power by highlighting the conditions under which it matters more or less." The argument of Arreguin-Toft, like that of Reiter (1999) is that strategy matters and when combatants fight in the same way, the stronger wins, but when they fight in different ways, the weak has an advantage. We may be missing important arms races, where the opponents are preparing to fight in different ways.

References

Andreou, A.S., Mateou, N.H., Zombanakis, G.A. (2003). "The Cyprus puzzle and the Greek–Turkish arms race: Forecasting developments using genetically evolved fuzzy cognitive maps". Defence and Peace Economics 14, 293–310.

Arreguin-Toft, I. (2001). "How the weak win wars: A theory of asymmetric conflict". International Security 26, 93–128.

Baliga, S., Sjostrom, T. (2004). "Arms races and negotiations". Review of Economic Studies 71, 1–19.

Brauer, J. (2002). "Survey and review of the defense economics literature on Greece and Turkey: What have we learned?". Defence and Peace Economics 13, 85–108.

Brito, D.L., Intriligator, M.D. (1995). "Arms races and proliferation". In: Hartley, K., Sandler, T. (Eds.), Handbook of Defense Economics, vol. 1. North-Holland, Amsterdam, pp. 109–164.

Collier, P., Hoeffler, A. (2004). "Military expenditure: Threats aid and arms races". Unpublished manuscript. Department of Economics, University of Oxford.

Craft, C.B. (2000). "An analysis of the Washington Naval Agreement and the economic provisions of arms control theory". Defence and Peace Economics 11, 127–148.

Deger, S., Sen, S. (1990). "Military security and the economy: Defence expenditure in India and Pakistan". In: Hartley, K., Sandler, T. (Eds.), The Economics of Defence Spending. Routledge, London, pp. 189–227.

Desai, M., Blake, D. (1981). "Modelling the ultimate absurdity: A comment on 'A quantitative study of the strategic arms race in the missile age' ". Review of Economics and Statistics 63, 629–632.

Dunne, J.P., Perlo-Freeman, S. (2003a). "The demand for military spending in developing countries". International Review of Applied Economics 17, 23–48.

Dunne, J.P., Perlo-Freeman, S. (2003b). "The demand for military spending in developing countries: A dynamic panel analysis". Defence and Peace Economics 14, 461–474.

Dunne, J.P., Nikolaidou, E., Smith, R. (2003a). "Is there an Arms Race between Greece and Turkey?". Peace Economics, Peace Science and Public Policy 11 (2). Article 1. http://www.bepress.com/peps/vol11/iss2/1.

Dunne, J.P., Nikolaidou, E., Smith, R. (2003b). "Arms race models and econometric applications". In: Levine, P., Smith, R. (Eds.), Arms Trade, Security and Conflict. Routledge, London, pp. 178–187.

Dunne, J.P., Garcia-Alonso, M.D.C., Levine, P., Smith, R. (2004). "Military procurement, industry structure and regional conflict". University of Kent Working Paper 05/02.

Dunne, J.P., Garcia-Alonso, M.D.C., Levine, P., Smith, R. (2006). "Managing asymmetric conflict". Oxford Economic Papers 58, 183–208.

Fuertes, A.-M., Smith, R.P. (2005). "Panel time series, Cemmap course notes". http://www.econ.bbk.ac.uk/faculty/smith/.

Gadea, M.D., Pardos, E., Perez-Forniez, C. (2004). "A long run analysis of defence spending in the NATO countries (1960–1999)". Defence and Peace Economics 15, 231–250.

Gibler, D.M., Rider, T.J., Hutchison, M. (2005). "Taking arms against a sea of troubles: Conventional arms races during periods of rivalry". Journal of Peace Research 42, 131–148.

Gleditsch, N.P., Njolstad, O. (Eds.) (1990). Arms Races, Technology and Political Dynamics. Sage Publications, London.

Hamilton, J.D. (1989). "A new approach to the economic analysis of nonstationary time series and the business cycle". Econometrica 57, 357–384.

Hirshleifer, J. (2001). The Dark Side of the Force: Economic Foundations of Conflict Theory. Cambridge University Press, Cambridge.

Intriligator, M.D. (1975). "Strategic considerations in the Richardson model of arms races". Journal of Political Economy 83, 339–353.

Intriligator, M.D., Brito, D.L. (2000). "Arms races". Defence and Peace Economics 11, 45–54.

Johansen, S. (1988). "Statistical analysis of cointegrating vectors". Journal of Economic Dynamics and Control 12, 231–254.

Lebovic, J.H. (1999). "Using military expenditure data: the complexity of simple inference". Journal of Peace Research 36, 681–697.

Levine, P., Smith, R.P. (1995). "The arms trade and arms control". Economic Journal 105, 471–484.

Markose, S.M. (2005). "Computability and evolutionary complexity: Markets and complex adaptive systems". Economic Journal 115, F159–F192.

McGuire, M. (1977). "A quantitative study of the strategic arms race in the missile age". Review of Economics and Statistics 59, 328–339.

McGuire, M. (1981). "A quantitative study of the strategic arms race in the missile age: A reply". Review of Economics and Statistics 63, 632–633.

Murdoch, J.C. (1995). "Military alliances: Theory and empirics". In: Hartley, K., Sandler, T. (Eds.), Handbook of Defense Economics, vol. 1. North-Holland, Amsterdam, pp. 89–108.

Murdoch, J.C., Sandler, T. (1984). "Complementarity, free riding and the military expenditures of NATO allies". Journal of Public Economics 25, 83–101.

Murdoch, J.C., Sandler, T. (2002). "Economic growth, civil wars, and spatial spillovers". Journal of Conflict Resolution 46, 91–110.

Murdoch, J.C., Sandler, T. (2004). "Civil wars and economic growth: Spatial dispersion". American Journal of Political Science 48, 138–151.

Ocal, N. (2003). "Are the military expenditures of India and Pakistan external determinants for each other: An empirical investigation". Defence and Peace Economics 14, 141–149.

Pesaran, M.H. (2004). "Estimation and inference in large heterogeneous panels with a multifactor error structure". Unpublished manuscript. Faculty of Economics, University of Cambridge. Available on: http://www.econ.cam.ac.uk/faculty/pesaran.

Pesaran, M.H., Smith, R.P. (1985). "Evaluation of macroeconometric models". Economic Modelling 2, 125–134.

Pesaran, M.H., Smith, R.P. (1995). "Estimation of long-run relationships from dynamic heterogeneous panels". Journal of Econometrics 68, 79–114.

Reiter, D. (1999). "Military Strategy and the outbreak of international conflict: Quantitative empirical tests, 1903–1992". Journal of Conflict Resolution 43, 366–387.

Richardson, L.F. (1960). Arms and Insecurity: A Mathematical Study of Causes and Origins of War. Boxwood Press, Pittsburgh.

Robson, A.J. (2005). "Complex evolutionary systems and the Red Queen". Economic Journal 115, 211–224.

Rosh, R.M. (1988). "Third World militarisation: Security webs and the states they ensnare'". Journal of Conflict Resolution 32, 671–698.

Rotte, R., Schmidt, C.M. (2003). "On the production of victory: Empirical determinants of battlefield success in modern war". Defence and Peace Economics 14, 175–193.

Samuelson, P.A., Koopmans, T.C., Stone, J.R.N. (1954). "Report of an evaluative committee on Econometrica". Econometrica 22, 141–146.

Sandler, T., Hartley, K. (1995). The Economics of Defense. Cambridge University Press, Cambridge.

Seiglie, C., Liu, P. (2002). "Arms races in the developing world: Some policy implications". Journal of Policy Modeling 24, 693–705.

SIPRI (2005). Armaments, Disarmament and International Security, Stockholm International Peace Research Institute. Oxford University Press, Oxford.

Smith, R.P. (1989). "Models of military expenditure". Journal of Applied Econometrics 4, 345–359.

Smith, R.P. (1995). "The demand for military expenditure". In: Hartley, K., Sandler, T. (Eds.), Handbook of Defense Economics, vol. 1. North-Holland, Amsterdam, pp. 69–87.

Smith, R.P., Tasiran, A. (2005). "The demand for arms imports". Journal of Peace Research 42, 167–182.

Smith, R.P., Dunne, J.P., Nikolaidou, E. (2000a). "The econometrics of arms races'". Defence and Peace Economics 11, 31–44.

Smith, R.P., Sola, M., Spagnolo, F. (2000b). "The Prisoner's Dilemma and regime-switching in the Greek–Turkish arms race". Journal of Peace Research 37, 737–750.

Chapter 29

ARMS TRADE AND ARMS RACES: A STRATEGIC ANALYSIS[*]

MARÍA D.C. GARCÍA-ALONSO[1]

Department of Economics, The University of Kent, Canterbury, Kent CT2 7NP, UK
e-mail: m.c.garcia-alonso@kent.ac.uk

PAUL LEVINE[2]

Department of Economics, The University of Surrey, Guildford, Surrey GU2 7XH, UK
e-mail: p.levine@surrey.ac.uk

Contents

Abstract	942
Keywords	942
1. Introduction	943
2. Products and data: The facts	944
3. Demand for arms imports	947
4. Supply: The arms industry	948
5. Regulation	949
6. An non-technical review of the arms trade models	952
6.1. Supplier objectives and the benefits of coordination	952
6.2. Demand for imports and responses to regulation	954
6.3. The arms industry	955
7. A formal model of the arms trade	957
7.1. The basic model	958
7.1.1. Demand side	958
7.1.2. Supply side	960
7.2. Collective action problems	961
7.3. Domestic production	963
7.4. Industry and market structure	963
8. Concluding remarks	967
References	969

[*] The authors have profited from comments provided by Keith Hartley, Todd Sandler, Ron Smith and Asher Tishler on an earlier draft. The usual disclaimer applies.
[1] Lecturer in Economics.
[2] Professor of Economics.

Handbook of Defense Economics, Volume 2
Edited by Todd Sandler and Keith Hartley
© 2007 Elsevier B.V. All rights reserved
DOI: 10.1016/S1574-0013(06)02029-1

Abstract

In this chapter we present the main characteristics and problems involved in the study of the arms trade: product definition and data, strategic aspects of the arms trade and regulation. We illustrate these aspects using the latest theoretical and empirical literature on arms trade. The papers reviewed illustrate the complexity involved in studying the arms trade. The nature of the exporters interaction in setting export controls and export policies raises the benefits of coordination in both export control and industrial policies. A failure to coordinate in one of these two policies tends to increase the incentives to deviate from an agreement to coordinate in the other policy, therefore, highlighting the importance of a unified approach to arms trade regulation. Issues such as differences in the security perceptions of exporters, the home bias and the characteristics of the competition between exporter firms may all make the implementation of export controls ever more challenging. Interestingly, although uncertainty will generally make matters worse, it may not if it decreases the effort that exporter firms put into producing higher quality weapons. We argue that supply side regulation will not be enough to prevent arms proliferation among initially non-producer countries, even if supply side controls may have a positive impact on the importers' welfare.

In addition, we present a model of the arms trade which encompasses many of the strategic aspects of the problem. The model is mainly based on works by [Levine, P., Smith, R.P. (1995). "The arms trade and arms control". The Economic Journal 105, 471–484; Levine, P., Smith, R.P. (1997a). "The arms trade". Economic Policy, 337–370. October] and [Dunne, P., García-Alonso, M.D.C., Levine, P., Smith, R.P. (2005). "Military procurement, industry structure and regional conflict". Discussion Paper 0502, University of Kent]. It describes the process by which optimization by buyers and sellers within a particular supply regime will result in the determination of prices and quantities. Then the collective action problems suppliers face in establishing an arms export control regime are discussed. Finally, we generalize the model to allow for an endogenous number of firms producing distinct military technologies. We use this model to examine the determinants of market structure in the military sector and how this is affected by globalization in the form of an increasing willingness of governments in arms producing countries to import arms.

Keywords

defense industrial base, military procurement, market structure, arms trade, arms races

JEL classification: F12, H56, L10

1. Introduction

Within the Western Alliance during the Cold War military preparations had elements of a public good: the forces of one country had spillover benefits for other countries, thus arms transfers to allies could increase alliance capability and enhance inter-operability. In addition, having a domestic defense sector was seen as strategically important for home security. After the Cold War, security perceptions changed, with no clear adversaries and an increasingly costly domestic defense sector, there has been a tendency towards more concentration, rationalization and globalization of the defense industry. National champions now compete for a increasingly common exports market.[3] However, this process has not been identical in all countries. In some cases, such as in the former USSR, changing security needs have coincided with the difficulties in adapting to a whole new economic system.[4] Despite these changes, the defense industry is still unique in that arms exporters acknowledge that arms exports have a possibly negative impact on their national security. On the other hand, there is still a preference to maintain a domestic defense sector. Accordingly, the arms trade is heavily regulated with export controls and export subsidies often chasing contradictory objectives such as the promotion of a domestic defense industry and the limitation of arms exports and/or their quality so as to ensure national security. It is important to note that many weapon importers are involved in situations of conflict and arms races, another distinctive characteristic of the arms trade markets.

It is in this context that the arms trade literature has been developed. The economic analysis of the arms trade described in this chapter has focused mainly on major weapon systems. The international markets in these are mainly considered to be imperfectly competitive. Accordingly, this literature has used elements of new trade theory, industrial organization and regulation theory with the added elements of security perceptions and (home biased) procurement to analyze how export control policies and industrial policies impact on national security, the structure of the defense industry and the welfare of importer countries [Anderton (1995, 1996)]. The empirical literature has contributed to provide a picture of the post Cold War evolution of the arms trade markets and the security consequences of their existence.

The main research objectives within this literature have been (i) to provide a general framework for the analysis of arms trade markets that captures their main characteristics, such as, the strategic interaction between firms, governments of producer countries and decision-makers in importing countries, (ii) to assess the impact of changes in security perceptions on variables such as the volume of arms exports, domestic procurement and the concentration in the international defense industry, (iii) to analyze the impact of the changing relationship between governments and their national champions on the ability to implement arms export controls, (iv) to examine the benefits of

---

[3] Kinsella (2003) uses social network analysis to demonstrate that increasingly weapon exporters share and compete in a common market, also see Brzoska (2004a) and Markusen (2004).

[4] See Davis (2002) for an analysis of the Russian defense sector.

international coordination in security and industrial policies, and finally, (v) to analyze the impact of export controls on the welfare and proliferation incentives of importer countries.

This chapter is organized as follows. Sections 2 to 4 present the main stylized facts of the international defense industry through the main data sources and available empirical studies. Section 5 provides a general discussion of arms trade controls. Section 6 develops these regulation issues in the context of a non-technical overview of the recent arms trade models organized around research topics. Section 7 provides a technical presentation of a general model of the arms trade based on some of the reviewed papers. Finally, Section 8 presents some concluding remarks and possible future lines for research.

2. Products and data: The facts

The arms trade literature is generally concerned with trade in security sensitive products. These are all those goods, services and technologies, which have potential military applications currently or in the future. They can be roughly divided into Weapons of Mass Destruction (WMD), typically nuclear; biological and chemical (NBC); major weapons systems; small arms and light weapons; dual purpose goods, which have both military and commercial applications (NBC and others); and services including intangible technology transfer, such as training of military and industrial personnel. Major weapons systems are relatively easy to monitor and measure. For instance, the Congressional Research Service (CRS) (2005) reports that over the period 2001–2004 weapon deliveries by Major Weapon suppliers[5] to Near East Nations[6] included 1677 armoured vehicles, 156 warships, 101 supersonic combat aircraft and 1887 surface-to-air missiles. All the other categories are very difficult to monitor and measure. The difficulties arise partly from problems of defining a product or service as military (e.g., how to classify a high powered rifle as military or sporting); and partly because much of the trade is covert. Obtaining information on quantities of arms transferred is difficult enough; obtaining information on their prices is even worse. Arms may be transferred free to allies,[7] most contracts are very complicated including not only weapons, but also munitions, training, spares, etc., and involve countertrade (barter) arrangements, financing by suppliers, and various types of offsets.[8] Therefore, actual prices paid for weapons only partially reflect the real price of weapons. Arms transfers also tend to be 'lumpy', exports or imports may be large in a particular year just because of a particularly large delivery, so figures can fluctuate from year to year.

---

[5] These include US, Russia, China, European and all others, the disaggregated data can be found in CRS (2005).

[6] These are Algeria, Bahrain, Egypt, Iran, Iraq, Israel, Jordan, Kuwait, Lebanon, Libya, Morocco, Oman, Qatar, Saudi Arabia, Syria, Tunisia, United Arab Emirates and Yemen.

[7] Although this is now increasingly less frequent: see Brzoska (2004a).

[8] For a review and examples of the defense literature on offsets see Brauer and Dunne (2002, 2004).

Table 1

CRS (in value, millions constant 2004 US$) and SIPRI (in volume, millions constant 1990 US$) arms transfer deliveries 1997–2004

Year	CRS	SIPRI	Ratio
1997	51,581	24,832	2.08
1998	46,007	23,325	1.97
1999	45,964	21,257	2.16
2000	37,776	15,840	2.38
2001	30,567	16,618	1.84
2002	30,266	15,692	1.93
2003	35,629	17,178	2.07
2004	34,755	19,162	1.81

Two main sources have traditionally been used in the analysis of the arms trade markets, namely, the Stockholm International Peace Research Institute (SIPRI) and World Military Expenditure and the Arms Trade (WMEAT), previously provided by the US Arms Control and Disarmament Agency (ACDA), more recently by the Bureau of Verification and Compliance of the State Department. Both sources have advantages and disadvantages as discussed in Smith and Tasiran (2005). SIPRI provides yearly data on the volume of transfers of major weapons systems, not including transfers of small arms [SIPRI yearbook (2005)]. It is a volume measure because quantities are multiplied by trend indicator values not the prices actually paid. WMEAT provides value of transfers, therefore, taking account of prices actually paid, and includes small arms. Although WMEAT's data reports were discontinued in 2003, the reports from the US Congressional Research Service can be used as a substitute [CRS (2005)]. These reports offer up-to-date data on arms transfers to developing nations in value. The CRS report gives separate data on arms transfer agreements (i.e., arms orders) and arms transfer deliveries, whereas SIPRI focuses on arms transfer deliveries.

Table 1 compares value, from CRS, and volume, from SIPRI, of arms transfers in the period 1997–2004.[9] The third column gives a ratio between the two. Changes in this ratio could be seen as an indicator of changes in the price of transfers but could be treated as indicating measurement errors [Smith and Tasiran (2005)]. The ratio does not have any trend in it, ranging from 2.4 in 2000 to 1.8 in 2001. Both series tell a broadly similar story, with transfers tending to fall between 1997 and 2002, and increasing thereafter. Figures for exports or imports for individual countries tend to show larger differences.

Tables 2 and 3 give top world wide suppliers' arms transfer agreements and deliveries and the percentage of those transfers going to developing countries. It can be seen that the majority of arms transfers go to developing nations (58.90% of total agreements and

[9] Jurgen Brauer in Chapter 30 of this *Handbook* presents data on long-run trends in the arms trade over 1950–2004.

Table 2
2004 top world wide suppliers' arms transfer agreements (millions of constant 2004 US$)

Supplier	World wide agreements (value 2004)	Developing world (% of total)
United States	12,391	55.5
Russia	6,100	96.7
United Kingdom	5,500	58.2
France	4,800	20.8
China	600	100
Italy	600	100
Germany	200	0
All other European	4, 300	30.2
All others	2,500	92
TOTAL	36,991	58.9

Table 3
2004 top world wide suppliers' arms deliveries (millions of constant 2004 US$)

Supplier	World wide deliveries (value 2004)	Developing world (% of total)
United States	18,555	51.5
Russia	4,600	97.8
France	4,400	95.5
United Kingdom	1,900	68.4
Germany	900	55.6
China	700	85.7
Italy	100	100
All other European	1,200	41.7
All others	2,400	50
TOTAL	34,755	64.6

64.60% of total deliveries). Indeed, the relative importance of the developing countries as an importer market has been increasing in the past few years.[10] Both agreements and deliveries to developing countries in 2004 have been the highest total since 2000 [CRS (2005)]. In 2004, the United States ranked first in both arms transfer deliveries and agreements to the developing world, a market which has been jointly dominated by Russia and the US since 2001. Tables 4 provides data on the leading recipients of arms transfer deliveries in the developing world. Most of those countries are either involved

[10] This could be a sign of a lesser preference for domestic production together with the increasing costs of developing new generations of weapons. It could also be the result of an increase in conflict in developing countries relative to developed countries. As will be seen later, the arms trade literature tends to represent non-arms producer countries as being involved in an arms race with similar countries.

Table 4

Arms deliveries of developing nations in 2004 by leading recipients (in millions of current US$)

Rank	Recipient	Agreements value (2004)
1	U.A.E.	3,600
2	Saudi Arabia	3,200
3	China	2,700
4	India	1,700
5	Egypt	1,700
6	Israel*	1,500
7	Taiwan	1,100
8	Pakistan	900
9	South Korea	800
10	South Africa	500

*The CRS classification of Israel as a developing nation could be argued, at least in terms of its defense industry. Israel is a major weapons exporter and produces high tech weapon systems comparable to those of European countries and US [Shefi and Tishler (2005)].

in conflict or an arms race with a neighboring country.[11] To conclude, even though the available data are neither comprehensive nor perfect, it is clear that the international structure of the defense industry is such that a few developed countries are the main weapon exporters and producers and their production is at least in recent times increasingly dependent on imports from developing countries, many of which are involved in regional or internal conflicts.

3. Demand for arms imports

The demand for arms of various types is influenced by security perceptions of internal or external threats and by price and income, which determine what a state can afford. States then choose whether it is more cost effective to develop and produce the weapons domestically; develop and produce them in collaboration with other countries; to produce under license systems developed elsewhere; or to import the desired arms. The decision to import is not a one off: it generally implies agreement from the seller to provide technical assistance and therefore, it involves a certain dependence between importer and supplier. If they decide to import, they have to choose between competing systems available on the world market. Bribery and corruption are endemic in the arms market and a policy issue for supplier countries is to what extent they take anti-corruption measures [Gupta, De Mello and Sharan (2001), Berryman (2000)]. However, prices matter and the main factor constraining the proliferation of major weapons systems is that few

---

[11] The data on arms agreements provides a similar set of countries.

countries can afford them. Smith and Tasiran (2005) provide econometric estimates of the demand for arms imports as a function of domestic military expenditure (a proxy for the threat[12]), a measure of price[13] and the income of a country. On these estimates, demand is sensitive to price. For a constant threat, a one percent increase in price causes a roughly one percent fall in the quantity of arms imports demanded [also see Levine, Mouzakis and Smith (1998)].

Changes in demand side factors may affect the demand for weapons. The most common economic model used to model non-producer country demand for weapons is an arms race between two antagonists. A peace agreement or a decrease in perceived threats will reduce the demand for weapons.

4. Supply: The arms industry

Defense industries have the characteristics of both a military and economically strategic industry. They are economically strategic in terms of R&D intensity, spin-offs and decreasing unit costs reflecting both economies of scale and learning [Sandler and Hartley (1999) and Hartley and Sandler (2003)]. With high fixed R&D costs and decreasing unit production costs, output is a major determinant of unit total costs. Disarmament following the end of the Cold War resulted in fewer new projects and smaller national orders led to pressures for defense companies to seek export markets and reduce costs.[14]

Changes in the demand for domestic procurement happened at a time when technology and government attitudes towards domestic production and ownership were already leading to changes on the supply side. There was an increase in R&D as a proportion of total production costs within the companies, as companies responded to technological imperatives (i.e., the need to maintain a technological edge with respect to competitors and potential adversaries) and contracted-out component production to reduce costs. Changes in security perceptions led to the questioning of the strategic need for a domestic defense industrial base, making producer nations more willing to import, this forced defense firms to compete in an increasingly globalized arms trade market. Also, in response to cost pressures, arms producers have increasingly been using components that are commercial 'off-the-shelf' (COTS) products, produced by manufacturers that would not see themselves as part of the arms industry [Klein (2001) and Kulve and Smit (2003)].

As a consequence of the above changes, the structure of the defense industry also changed. Analyzing the data on the major arms producers, Dunne et al. (2003) show

---

[12] Domestic military expenditure will in general depend on the allies and adversaries' military expenditure, the perceived threat and the weight given to security in the welfare function, among other variables. The theoretical models of arms trade analyze some of these issues in detail.

[13] They use as a proxy for prices the ratio of value of exports (using data from WMEAT) to quantity of exports (using data from SIPRI).

[14] Kirkpatrick (1995, 2004) analyzes other factors behind the cost pressures in the defense industry.

that although at the end of the Cold War the international arms industry was relatively unconcentrated, concentration increased markedly in the 1990–1998 period, although this is proven not to be associated with increases in the average size of firms. Still, as argued in Dunne et al. (2003), the defense industry remains relatively unconcentrated if we compare it with other similar civilian industries.

At the same time, there have also been changes to the nature of the relationship between governments and the defense firms. In the past, it was common for national arms firms to be almost an extension of the state, and they were often publicly-owned. There has been a trend for increasing independence between governments and national arms firms, a move that was initially taken to improve the efficiency of weapons production. Such a situation has increased the importance of the strategic interaction between firm and government and the relevance of asymmetric information issues.

Strategic interaction between parties happens when the decisions of any one party affect the payoffs of the other party. In arms trade markets, strategic interaction happens not only between domestic firms and government but also between foreign firms and governments (foreign sales may affect both domestic firm profits and domestic security) and also between the different governments (other governments' regulations will affect domestic welfare).

Game theory models illustrate how information differences between the different parties to a transaction (asymmetric information) can lead to a range of market failures, cases where markets cannot be relied upon to allocate resources efficiently. As governments use domestic defense procurement contracts to interact with their increasingly independent domestic defense suppliers, uncertainty over the firm's costs and the quality of their production becomes an obstacle in the achievement of efficiency. Of course, even when the firm is owned by the state, the firm may capture the part of government nominally controlling it and producer interests come to determine policy. Also, there is still an asymmetric information problem between the public firm manager and the government. But, uncertainty becomes more of an issue as competition in the international arms market grows, defense firms become more internationalized, and collaborative projects between countries become more common. The relevance of uncertainty is then extended to the costs and quality (both produced and exported) of foreign firms and the weighting that other governments might give to security or firm profits when choosing their regulation tools.

It is these different interactions and the trade-offs with governments having to choose between support for their domestic defense industries and their concern with the possible impacts of arms exports on national security that makes the arms industry unique. The following section discusses such trade-offs.

5. Regulation

The arms trade is subject to more extensive controls than trade in most other goods. Producer countries use a number of instruments to regulate the arms trade: these are basically either arms export controls and industrial policies such as production, R&D and export subsidies.

Unilateral national export control systems are the foundation for multilateral controls, which vary from relatively informal clubs of suppliers, to very formal systems embodied in treaties and involving extensive monitoring systems like that associated with the nuclear Non-Proliferation Treaty (NPT).[15]

We can divide export controls into quantitative and qualitative controls.[16] Quantitative export controls include total or partial restriction of weapons exported to a single country or a group of countries. Qualitative export controls include controls on the transfer of state-of-the-art technologies that allow exporter countries to maintain a technological edge over potential adversaries, and controls on the transfer of very sensitive technologies.[17]

When regulating the arms industry, weapon producers have a variety of security and economic objectives, which are often in contradiction. Producer countries may see the exports market as a means of achieving profits that may help cover part of the increasingly high development costs of new weapons and retain a domestic defense sector. As security sensitive goods are exempted from WTO rules, countries are free to set whichever trade policies maximize their own objectives [Markusen (2004)]. The imperfectly competitive nature of the market in major weapon systems provides unilateral incentives to set strategic trade policies that often involve export subsidies. In addition, domestic procurement can also act as an indirect export subsidy by itself in the presence of increasing returns to scale. In other words, domestic production and exports would be complements rather than substitutes [García-Alonso (1999)]. However, the very existence of the arms exports market generates a potential negative impact on the national security of the exporter countries. For instance, an importing nation might be a future threat to the exporting nations either directly or through regional conflicts which involve the exporting nation (Iraq is just a recent example). In addition, arms transfers may create internal conflict and poverty that requires international help involving exporting nations [Blanton (1999), Craft and Smaldone (2003), Sanjian (2003), and Wang (1998)].[18]

---

[15] The SIPRI yearbooks provide updates on existing export control agreements. García-Alonso and Smith (in press) provide a non-technical review of the subject.

[16] See Panofsky (1990) for a similar classification.

[17] An example of this is that, when exporting advanced systems, the US often 'black-boxes' the software, not providing the source code, so the buyer cannot find out how the system works or change it. The UK Ministry of Defense could not use the Chinook HC3 helicopters because it was unable to verify the software [NAO (2004)].

[18] Kinsella (1998) argues that the dependency generated between client and supplier of weapons may counteract the negative effect of arms exports on regional conflict. However, as Kinsella himself acknowledges the post-Cold War common exports market predict a decrease in the importance of dependency as a conflict deterrent factor. Also see García-Alonso and Hartley (2000) for a discussion of captive markets on the ability to implement export controls.

The quality of the exported weapons, not just the quantity, may become a security issue for exporter countries. Already during the Cold War adversary powers extended their technological rivalries to the importers they chose to support, even though state of the art weapons were not transferred. The situation in the post-Cold War era has changed in many respects: arm suppliers face an economic profit incentive to compete for the now more globalized exports market. The 'unintended' security consequence of this situation is that competition in quality for export markets generates a further incentive to improve military technology so as to preserve the gap between domestic state of the art technology and exported technology. Buzan and Herring (1998) refer to the forces behind this process collectively as the 'technological imperative' [see also Kinsella (2001)]. In this sense, the restriction of exported quality is often chasing a moving target: the state-of-the-art technology. This makes the regulation of the arms trade ever more complex. In addition, the increasing use of dual-use technologies and military–civilian partnerships so as to rationalize arms production is making military goods more difficult to define and therefore, export controls more difficult to design and implement. A significant example is that of digital information technology. Most of the recent military developments in this field actually derive from initial civilian innovation, dissemination of this dual use technology is fast and difficult to control [Smith and Udis (2001) and Stowsky (2004)].

There has been a substantial debate about the extent to which arms export sales have been subsidized by supplier governments or in other words, how much the profit objective of producer countries has been given more weight than their security objectives. Ingram and Isbister (2004) argue that arms exports are bad for Britain, both because of the subsidies and the distortion of procurement choices. Chalmers et al. (2002) provide a detailed estimate of the benefits and costs of maintaining UK defense exports and suggest that even the economic effect of a reduction in arms exports are rather small and mainly a one-off [also see Martin (1999)]. However, Chalmers et al. (2002) argue that the impact of the arms exports industry on national welfare should include not only economic factors but also the impact of exports on security, and this empirical analysis is a much harder task to perform.

As already mentioned, industrial policies that aim to increase domestic firm export profits and export control policies that aim to increase domestic security are often in contradiction: whilst export controls tend to increase the cost of imports to the potential acquiring country, export and production subsidies do the opposite, therefore, encouraging arms exports. Also, R&D subsidies may exacerbate the technological imperative problem. However, there may be circumstances in which policies that aim to limit arms exports also enhance firm profits. Supplier cartels may have a positive impact on both export profits and the exporter security (via a reduction in exports). These issues will be further explored in Sections 6 and 7.

6. An non-technical review of the arms trade models

As discussed in Section 5, the arms trade problem involves a number of agents interacting in pursuit of different, sometimes contradicting, objectives. Whereas governments care for their domestic firms, they also have security objectives. The existence of intra-country and intra-firm strategic interaction usually leads to the global first best not being achieved, therefore, resulting in a need for the international coordination of national policies. Such coordination is difficult to achieve since enforcement of agreements is required but punishments are not always credible.

The New Trade literature illustrates the problems involved in countries independently aiming to support their own domestic imperfectly competitive industries. Multiple stage games portray governments that commit to a policy tool (e.g., an export subsidy or a production subsidy) prior to firms competing in the international market. The arms trade literature has tended to take this as a suitable framework for the analysis of markets for major weapon systems and possibly some dual use goods. There is the added difficulty involved in having a more complex imports demand side, often characterized by regional arms races, and also, by there being an added layer of strategic interaction between exporter governments who also want to optimize their security objectives.

The majority of arms trade models are characterized by multiple stage games in which first governments commit to arms control and industrial policies, second, firms aim to maximize profits by choosing either, prices, quantities or R&D investments and finally importer countries choose their imports, the market clears and world prices would be determined. Different models tend to focus on different aspects of the arms trade: the benefits of coordination, the impact of changes in the country's security perception on the arms trade and security itself, R&D policies, the impact of the exporter policies on importer governments welfare and decisions on home production or the determinants of the structure of the industry itself.

To summarize, global arms trade models covering industry exports and arms races must address and specify a large variety of model characteristics. Among them are: (i) the definition of security, (ii) the definition and scope of adversaries in the model, (iii) the relations between the governments and the defense firms in the arms-producing countries, (iv) the scope of the arms races among countries other than the arms-producing countries, (v) the procurement rules (methods of pricing of the defense goods) in arms-producing countries, (vi) the nature of the international market interaction between exporter firms, (vii) the variety of defense goods, and (viii) the decision rule that governments follow in determining their security level. In what follows, we provide a non-technical review of recent arms trade models organized around their research topics.

6.1. Supplier objectives and the benefits of coordination

Recent papers that study the arms trade tend to represent the welfare of supplier governments as a function of security, itself a negative function of arms exports and/or their quality. Arms exports are presented as generating a negative security externality on the exporter country and also a negative externality on other countries, although exports to allies may have positive externalities. Depending on the type of product to be studied, the arms trade models use different functions of international weapon exports and their quality to give a representation of security for the exporter country; also, security concerns may vary among exporters.

When producer countries decide on the amount or quality of weapons exported in a non-cooperative way, even if they share the same antagonists, they each export more than they would jointly have decided to export if they could have implemented cooperation. The reason is that countries only care about the negative impact that the exports have on their own security: in other words, they maximize their individual welfare functions. This is a typical characteristic of negative externalities which also arises in other contexts such as CO_2 emissions.[19] The added difficulty in the arms exports market is that these strategic interactions between exporters happen not only at the security level but also at the purely market competition level.

Countries competing in the exports market have unilateral incentives to give export or R&D subsidies so as to increase their market share. This may result in both less security and less welfare for both exporter countries and recipients. Dunne et al. (2005), García-Alonso (1999, 2000), García-Alonso and Levine (2005), and Levine and Smith (1995, 1997a, 2000b) provide examples of models that capture these interactions. An exporter may even create a technological arms race with itself, having to develop new generations of weapons that are superior to the ones that it previously exported. The inability of producer countries to coordinate in setting of export controls can sometimes lead to almost counter-intuitive situations. For example, a security concerned country might want to subsidize the development of sensitive technologies and then prohibit their exports. This would give their domestic firms a quality edge over firms in less security concerned countries. This quality edge would decrease the competitors' incentive to invest in new technologies since they would be likely to be "beaten" in the exports market should they decide to develop them anyway [García-Alonso (2000)].

Although the non-cooperative equilibrium among exporter countries is inefficient, cooperative agreements are often difficult to enforce. There are a number of specific factors affecting the incentives of individual countries to defect from multilateral export control agreements such as information asymmetries (within and between countries), the structure of the arms exports market (profits to be made out of weapons exports), asymmetry of security concerns among exporters, different discount rates of long-term security consequences, the number of countries having access to the restricted military product, the type of weapon to be controlled, the monitoring capability of the control system or the credibility of punishment strategies on defecting firms/countries [García-Alonso and Hartley (2000), Smith and Udis (2001), and Sandler (2000, 2004)].

---

[19] The externality discussed is also analogous to those associated with counterterrorism as shown in the Sandler and Arce Chapter 25 of this *Handbook*.

As mentioned in Section 5, agreements that decrease the quantity of weapons exported are not always export control agreements as such. Cooperative agreements among exporters such as cartels and international mergers would tend to increase export prices and therefore decrease exports in the same way as export taxes or direct export controls. Levine and Smith (1995, 1997a) provide an analysis of cartel agreements (see Section 7 for a technical presentation of these models). Mergers and cartelisation also reduce the number of potential deviators and decrease asymmetric information issues, therefore reinforcing export control agreements. However, it is important to note that these and other collaborative agreements among weapon producers, such as research joint ventures, might result in higher R&D investments. We then have higher levels of potential quality that could be exported. Therefore, cooperation between firms alone could result in more quality being exported unless combined with direct qualitative export controls [Dunne et al. (2005)].

Another example of an agreement that could in principle help export controls is for arms trade to be included within WTO rules prohibiting export subsidies. The fact that the arms industry has been exempted from WTO rules would tend to produce more arms exports than otherwise, as individual producer countries have incentives to give export subsidies. In addition, these subsidies may increase the incentives that individual producer countries would have to defect from standard export control agreements as a given deviation may then result in higher increases in profits [García-Alonso and Levine (2005)]. Finally, Brzoska (2004b) discusses the use of international taxation of arms exports as a means of reducing the arms trade. A multilateral exports tax will have similar effects to that of a cartel or a prohibition of export subsidies: higher export prices and therefore, less exports. The elimination of exports subsidies may be the easiest to rationalize from the suppliers' perspective, since it would also increase export profits, if done multilaterally, and would be consistent with already well-established trade rules. The arms export's tax suggested by Brzoska (2004b) would go a step further as revenues from taxation would go to an international fund. Such fund would be used to palliate some of the negative effects of conflict. This arrangement would be more difficult to implement as it would require a credible commitment to both taxation and revenue transfer to the fund. However, it exemplifies the idea that, like pollution, arms trade generates a negative externality on all countries, which the exporter countries must acknowledge.

Still, as we will see in the following section, supply side agreements will often not be enough to control arms proliferation.

6.2. Demand for imports and responses to regulation

The overall effect of export controls on the welfare of an importing country is complicated. Although qualitative or quantitative export controls may reduce conflict,[20] if

---

[20] Levine and Smith (1997b) show that the price of arms exports has an important influence on the stability of regional arms races among importers.

applied to all parties involved, the increase in the cost of acquiring these military products (sometimes prohibitory) will reduce consumption not just of weapons but also of other goods, especially if the price elasticity for weapon imports is low. However, the positive impact on security can offset the negative impact on consumption, so resulting in a positive welfare effect even though in some cases it must be combined with income transfers to importer countries [Levine and Smith (1995, 1997a, 2000b) and Dunne et al. (2005)].

Even if the welfare of importer countries was increased via export controls or exporter cartels, importer countries may still have an incentive to unilaterally search for alternative ways to build military capability that would give them an edge with respect to their adversaries. The problem, of course, being that their adversaries would do exactly the same resulting once again in conflict escalation. It is this situation that explains why export controls can sometimes have unintended consequences. States subject to embargo or control, or who fear that they may be subject to embargo in the future, may develop their own arms industry to produce the weapons that they cannot import. In addition, other potential exporters with less security concerns might have incentives to develop their own exports industry in face of other countries' export controls. For instance, the US embargoes on Latin American countries during the Carter Presidency proved a major incentive for countries like Brazil to set up their own industries, partly financed by exports. To try and avoid this, export control regimes are usually associated with measures to prevent the diffusion of the relevant technology to other states (e.g., the Missile Technology Control Regime). This raises the cost of acquiring domestic production, but rarely makes it completely impossible. Levine and Smith (2000a), Levine, Mouzakis and Smith (2000) and Mouzakis (2002) discuss the interaction between export controls and proliferation (see Section 7 for more details). Also, Golde and Tishler (2004) and Mantin and Tishler (2004) argue that an increase in world prices could crowd-out countries in the developing world from the market for modern weapon systems and may force them to develop and use 'cheap and dirty' weapon systems. The concern over the limited ability of export controls alone to deter proliferation is also voiced by Brauer (2000) who suggests that supply side controls alone are not enough to avoid proliferation[21]: they must be combined with measures to reduce the demand for weapons.

6.3. The arms industry

The arms trade literature has analyzed the changing security needs of exporter countries which have affected the characteristics of the international arms market and the ability of producer countries to implement export controls. Governments in exporter countries are increasingly treating defense providers as any other procurement provider. Arms trade models have reflected this by treating governments and defense firms as independent

---

[21] As an example of this, we have the French embargo on Israel, announced in 1967, as one important catalyst to the development of the Israeli defense industry [Shefi and Tishler (2005)].

decision makers who interact strategically with both competing firms and governments. Also, as previously said, governments now often face an information asymmetry, not only with respect to its own firms but also with respect to the firms and governments of other exporter countries. This issue has also been studied in the literature. The lack of transparency between governments and national champions over the quality exported generates incentives on the side of profit maximizing firms to export forbidden technologies or export to forbidden countries. This would force governments to introduce a penalty system strong enough to discourage firms from infringing export controls. However, the existence of limited liability on the side of possible infringers of export control regulations imposes constraints on the implementation of such punishments.[22] Governments may be unwilling to drive firms into bankruptcy[23]: therefore the expected value of cheating to the firm is increased, because the penalty if they are caught is smaller. Asymmetric information may not always have negative effects on the implementation of export controls. If the source of asymmetric information is the procurer government being unsure about the cost-effectiveness of the domestic firm, the quantity of exports may decrease. The reason for this is that it will be more difficult for the government to give incentives for firms to behave efficiently. This will result in costs being higher and therefore, optimal prices going up and equilibrium exports going down [Dunne et al. (2005)]. Another example of a positive effect of asymmetric information on export controls (broadly defined) would be the case when the importer government is unsure about the quality of the imported military product or whether future replacement needs will be covered [García-Alonso, Levine and Morga (2004)]. In principle, this will reduce imports demand; however, it may also increase the incentive to develop a domestic defense industry.

The changes in the concentration in the defense industry have also been studied in the arms trade literature. Dunne et al. (2005) construct a model of the global arms industry linking concentration, military procurement, international trade and regional conflict with endogenous market structure and quality. Concentration is proven to depend on the willingness of producers to import for their military needs and on the relative size of the external market of non-producers. Increases in concentration can be explained by either increases in openness or increases in the importance of the external market. In the data section, we observed an increase in the proportion of arms imports by developing countries, mainly non-producers, this could be identified with an increase in the importance of the external (non-producer) market relative to the developed producer countries, the decline in the demand for weapons could be one of the reasons behind this trend. The paper also analyzes other factors that influence the number of firms such as cooperation among producer countries and changes in R&D costs.[24]

---

[22] See Laffont (1995) for an analysis of this issue in the environmental literature context.

[23] This is an important issue for the defense sector where maintaining a domestic defense base is still seen as a matter of strategic importance, although increasingly less so.

[24] A version of this model is presented in Section 7.4 of this chapter.

Other papers analyze the structure of the global arms industry. Golde and Tishler (2004) analyze the international military markets with exogenous market structure. They conclude, using a two producer bloc multiple stage game model that net defense costs are lower when the number of defense firms is lower. Blume and Tishler (2000) provide a simple model of endogenous market structure for the military sector where firms produce homogeneous goods and the government exogenously decides to procure identical quantities from all domestic firms. They analyze the impact of different procurement pricing rules on world arms trade, net defense costs and government defense expenditure. They also conclude that a lower target security level results in a smaller number of defense firms. Mantin and Tishler (2004) model the interactions between the defense needs of the USA and Western Europe, which produce several heterogeneous defense goods and the defense industry market structure. They show that net defense costs of the USA and Europe are lower when the number of defense firms is small and when the world prices of the defense goods are high.

The papers reviewed in this section have illustrated the complexity involved in studying the arms trade. We have seen that the nature of the exporters interaction in setting export controls and export policies raises the benefits of coordination in both export control and industrial policies. We have also seen that a failure to coordinate in one of these two policies tends to increase the incentives to deviate from an agreement to coordinate in the other policy, therefore, highlighting the importance of a unified approach to arms trade regulation. Issues such as, differences in the security perceptions of exporters, the home bias and the characteristics of the competition between exporter firms may all make the implementation of export controls ever more challenging. Interestingly, although uncertainty will generally make matters worse, it may not if it decreases the effort that exporter firms put into producing higher quality weapons.

We have also argued that supply side regulation will not be enough to prevent arms proliferation among initially non-producer countries, even if, supply side controls may have a positive impact on the importers' welfare.

Finally, we have seen how some of the reviewed models provide a rationale for the evolution of the arms trade markets in the last few decades. A formal analysis is provided in the following section.

7. A formal model of the arms trade

Drawing upon the non-technical overview of the literature in the previous sections, we now present a formal model mainly based on work by Levine and Smith (1995, 1997a) and Dunne et al. (2005). We describe the process by which optimization by buyers and sellers within a particular supply regime will result in the determination of prices and quantities. Then the collective action problems suppliers face in establishing an arms export control regime are discussed. Finally, we generalize the model to allow for an endogenous number of firms producing distinct military technologies and we use this to examine the determinants of market structure in the military sector.

7.1. The basic model

Suppose the world can be divided into two groups of countries. There are a large number of buyers, each of whom are involved in a local arms race with a neighbor (e.g., India and Pakistan; Greece and Turkey). Buyers involved in arms races are indexed by $b = 1, 2, \ldots, r$. There are a small number of suppliers, indexed $s = 1, 2, \ldots, \ell$ who have the capability to build major weapons systems. The suppliers also have global security interests (e.g., through their foreign direct investment).

7.1.1. Demand side

On the demand side buyers maximize a multi-period discounted welfare U_{bt} from time t into the future[25]:

$$U_{bt} = \sum_{i=0}^{\infty} (1 + r_b)^{-i} W(C_{b,t+i}, S_{b,t+i}), \tag{1}$$

where $W(\cdot)$ is a single-period utility function of security, S, and consumption, C, and r_b is their discount rate. Their antagonist in the bth arms race, denoted by a star, has a similar welfare function determining U_{bt}^*. Security depends on the buyer's military capability and that of its antagonist. In general, military capability is a function of military personnel and the accumulated stock of arms. If there is little substitution between labor and arms then military capability is simply a function of the stock of arms and we can write the security function as:

$$S_{bt} = S(K_{bt}, K_{bt}^*), \tag{2}$$

with $\partial S / \partial K_b > 0$, $\partial S / \partial K_b^* < 0$. The stock of arms depends on investment in imported, M_b, and domestic weapons, D_b, and depreciated previous stock:

$$K_{bt} = f(D_{bt}, M_{bt}) + (1 - \delta) K_{b,t-1}. \tag{3}$$

$f(D_{bt}, M_{bt})$ measures the contribution to the military stock from imported and domestic arms, respectively.

A convenient general form of the military stock function is a *CES* form:

$$f(D_{bt}, M_{bt}) = \left[w_b D_{bt}^{\frac{\sigma-1}{\sigma}} + (1 - w_b) M_{bt}^{\frac{\sigma-1}{\sigma}} \right]^{\frac{\sigma}{\sigma-1}}, \tag{4}$$

where $\sigma \in (0, \infty)$ is the elasticity of substitution between domestically produced and imported arms. As σ approaches zero we tend to a Cobb–Douglas function $f(D_{bt}, M_{bt}) = D_{bt}^{w_b} M_{bt}^{1-w_b}$, indicating that they are imperfect substitutes, while as σ approaches unity they become perfect substitutes with $f(D_{bt}, M_{bt}) = w_b D_{bt} +$

---

[25] A similar model is used in Chapter 28 in this *Handbook*.

$(1 - w_b)M_{bt}$. The budget constraint is:

$$Y_{bt} = C_{bt} + p_{bt}D_{bt} + P_tM_{bt}, \tag{5}$$

where Y_{bt} is total output, p_{bt} and P_t are the per-unit cost of domestic and imported arms, respectively. The binding participation constraint for the domestic firm is:

$$p_{bt}D_{bt} - C(D_{bt}) = 0, \tag{6}$$

where $C(\cdot)$ is the cost function.[26]

The optimizing choices of the buyer and its antagonist, described in a similar way, then jointly determine a Nash equilibrium in arms subject to their available output and the price of imported and domestic weapons. This is discussed in Levine and Smith (1995) where following Anderton (1995), it is assumed that (2) is linear, and there is no domestic production by buyers engaged in local arms races. The steady state of the Nash equilibrium in this dynamic game is illustrated in Figure 1 for the case where there are positive fixed benefits from defense (i.e., the defender has an inherent advantage). BN and AN are the linear reaction functions[27] for countries 1 and 2, respectively, and N is the unique Nash equilibrium. The indifference curves of country 1 corresponding to the highest utility given K_b^2 are shown which map out BN. Similarly the indifference curves of country 2 corresponding to the highest utility given K_b^1 map out AN. The shaded area under the indifference curves of the two countries passing through N are points that raise welfare for both countries (i.e., are Pareto-improving) and the welfare-maximizing levels of military stock is zero at 0 in Figure 1, or total disarmament.[28]

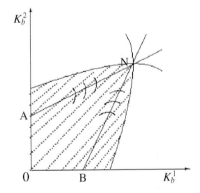

Figure 1. Nash equilibrium for importing countries.

---

[26] This specification of the cost function assumes the same good is produced for domestic use and exports, and that factor prices are given to suppliers when making decisions affecting arms production and trade (i.e., the model is of a partial equilibrium variety).

[27] If the reaction functions are non-linear there may be multiple equilibria.

[28] Complete disarmament is only the efficient outcome if there are fixed benefits from defense. If there are fixed benefits from attack so that the attacker has an inherent advantage, then although the Nash equilibrium

Thus, the Nash equilibrium will in general be inefficient because of coordination failure. Countries can increase their security by increasing military capability; but one country's security is its rival's insecurity. Security is a negative externality which both countries appreciate. The countries can do nothing to avoid this externality in the absence of a credible coordination mechanism. An arms control regime between regional rivals that jointly agreed on levels of military capability would internalize this externality and result in lower military expenditure and imports of arms, but given their antagonism they cannot agree to such a regime. With multiple equilibria there may be possibilities of moving from the highly armed to a lower armed Nash equilibrium.

This game generates a demand function by the buyers for imported arms as a function of price, the threat from the antagonist, and available output. Econometric estimates of such demand functions in Levine, Mouzakis and Smith (1998) using cross-section data estimate a significant negative price elasticity of demand. Price is also important for the dynamics of the arms race. If increasing demand increases price, the usual case, the feedbacks would tend to stabilize the arms race. If there were significant increasing returns to scale in weapons production, increased demand could reduce price causing destabilizing feedbacks or the multiple equilibria discussed by Brito and Intriligator (1999).

7.1.2. Supply side

On the supply side, seller governments maximize a similar welfare function:

$$U_{st} = \sum_{i=0}^{\infty} (1 + r_s)^{-i} W(C_{s,t+i}, S_{s,t+i}). \tag{7}$$

However, because of their global rather than regional concerns, their security depends on stocks of arms throughout the world (i.e., the stocks of each pair of buyers, $b = 1, 2, \ldots, r$ and each of the suppliers, $s = 1, 2, \ldots, \ell$) including itself:

$$S_{st} = S(\ldots, K_{bt}, K_{bt}^*, \ldots; \ldots K_{st}, \ldots). \tag{8}$$

In many post-Cold War situations (e.g., the Gulf War and former Yugoslavia) increased regional stocks of arms have a negative effect on supplier security, $\partial S_s / \partial K_b < 0$, and other suppliers are allies whose arms stocks have a positive effect, $\partial S_s / \partial K_s > 0$. In this case, from the suppliers point of view both arms exports and military expenditure, by itself and by the other suppliers, have security externalities. The decisions of producers involving domestic military capability and the exports of arms results is a public good in the form of their common regional security. It is non-excludable (no country can be

---

still sees the country spending too much on arms, total disarmament is no longer the efficient outcome [see Levine and Smith (1995)].

excluded from 'consuming' high regional security) and it is non-rival (its 'consumption' does not reduce the amount available for others).

Suppliers can also import arms so, as for buyers, stock is given by

$$K_{st} = f(D_{st}, M_{st}) + (1 - \delta)K_{s,t-1}.$$ (9)

The budget constraint is

$$Y_{st} = C_{st} + p_{st} D_{st} + P_t M_{st}.$$ (10)

Notice that the budget constraints (5) and (10) are balanced trade conditions.

Unlike buyers, suppliers export arms choosing a level of exports, X_{st}, and set the domestic price of arms, p_{st}, to maintain domestic production capability given their demand, export demands and costs. The participation constraint of the domestic firm is then:

$$p_{st} D_{st} + P_t X_{st} - C(D_{st} + X_{st}) = 0,$$ (11)

where $C(\cdot)$ is the cost function. For buyers, exports of the consumption good finance arms imports; for sellers arms exports finance imported consumption. Suppliers then jointly determine X_{st} and D_{st}, $s = 1, 2, \ldots, m$, subject to their outputs, demand and market structure. The world price of arms, P_t, then adjusts to clear the market so that:

$$\sum_{b=1}^{\ell+r}(M_{bt} + M_{bt}^*) = \sum_{s=1}^{\ell} X_{st}.$$ (12)

This framework is too general to get explicit analytical solutions, but a number of special cases have been considered in the literature. These use specific forms for the various functions and can be solved numerically for particular values for the parameters of those functions.

7.2. Collective action problems

Within the framework set out in the previous section a central issue is the form of market structure or international regime, which influences the determination of X_{st} and D_{st}. The form of regime is determined by the suppliers choice to cooperate or not to cooperate along three dimensions. Firstly, suppliers may or may not jointly regulate arms exports, operating as a suppliers cartel. Secondly, suppliers may or may not operate as allies, jointly determining their military expenditures. Thirdly, suppliers may or may not collaborate in production reducing $c(D_{st} + X_{st})$ by benefiting from learning curves, increasing returns to scale, and sharing fixed costs.

Under the assumptions above, $\partial S_s / \partial K_b < 0$, arms exports are a 'bad' within this framework, therefore monopoly (arms export control) is good, since it restricts supply and raises prices. This has two effects on the buyers. The first is a terms of trade effect which clearly reduces the buyers welfare: they pay more for their arms and have less for other uses. The second effect is for the higher price of arms to cause a switch from military expenditure into civil consumption. The reduction in arms stocks in response to the price rise shifts the reaction functions in the arms race. This moves the Nash equilibrium closer to the efficient consumption-military expenditure mix that pairs of buyers would choose if they could cooperate through some process of arms control. Such effect could outweigh the terms of trade loss, making the buyers better off as a result of the formation of the cartel and the higher prices. Suppliers also benefit from internalizing the regional stability externality if $\partial S_s / \partial K_b < 0$. These results suggest that the optimal market structure for the arms industry could be a cartel of cooperating producer countries. Under these assumptions, arms suppliers clearly have a common interest in forming a cartel. The results in Levine and Smith (1995) indicate that this could also be beneficial for recipients, particularly if combined with a tax on arms exports redistributed to recipients. Of course, the proposal for a supplier cartel plus transfers to recipients is both dependent on the specification of the model, particularly the form of the supplier security functions, and subject to obvious practical difficulties. Besides, any proposal for cooperation must inevitably address the collective action cartel stability problem of sustaining such a regime given the short-run incentives of any particular supplier to defect. Sandler (2000) discusses the collective action problem involved in verifying compliance and enforcing the rules of any cooperative regime. He discusses that while verification of compliance may improve over time, enforcing compliance will always remain as an issue to be addressed.

Suppose suppliers do solve the collective action problem and do cooperate in controlling the export of arms, acting as a joint monopolist. Then they face the credibility issues analyzed in Levine, Sen and Smith (1994). If buyers are forward looking as implied by Equation (1), and if some commitment mechanism[29] is in place so that the suppliers can credibly precommit to the quantities that they will export in the future, they can use these announcements to change the recipients behavior. However, if they cannot precommit, they are forced to adopt the less efficient time-consistent strategy: doing what is optimal in each period. In the arms trade the credibility of commitment to future supply or embargo is particularly important for the case of resupply of spares and munitions in a future conflict.

Finally, even if suppliers solve both the collective action and credibility problems, they face the problem that to the extent export controls are effective, driving up price or reducing quantity, they provide incentives for the buyers to create their own defense industrial base.

---

[29] These commitment mechanisms need careful consideration. One possibility is the desire to maintain a *reputation* for commitment in a world where there exists two types of policymaker: those (the vast majority) who behave opportunistically and seize the chance to improve their situation by reneging on any commitment promise and those who like to commit as a matter of principle. Reputational equilibria are then those where the first type of policymaker mimics the second.

7.3. Domestic production

Using a static version of the framework from Section 2, Levine, Mouzakis and Smith (2000) show that there is a threshold at which countries switch from depending completely on imports to establishing a domestic capability. A sufficiently high price can induce a pair of identical antagonistic buyers to switch from importing arms to domestic production. This switch causes higher levels of military expenditure, military capability, and inefficiency than had the antagonists relied on importing arms. Higher fixed costs of establishing domestic production increase the threshold level of military capability at which it is efficient to set up military production. The model assumes that domestic and imported arms are imperfect substitutes. The incentives for establishing a domestic industry also depend on the substitution between security and consumption. Levine and Smith (2000a) extend this analysis by introducing uncertainty and irreversible investment. Using real option theory[30] they find that greater uncertainty about future military demand and costs actually reduces the likelihood of a country investing in domestic production capability.

7.4. Industry and market structure

Up to now we have assumed that each supplier country produces a single homogeneous military good and different market structures only arise insofar as supplier countries collude in the production and exports of these goods. Following Dunne et al. (2005), we now extend the analysis by introducing differentiated goods and to allow for the free entry and exit of firms. Market structure now becomes endogenous. In this section we assume 100% depreciation per period ($\delta = 1$) so the model becomes static. For this reason the time subscript is superfluous. We also assume that the r buyer countries have no domestic military sector and are non-producers.

Consider the supplier country $s = 1$ which procures D_{1j}, $j = 1, 2, \ldots, n_1$, domestically produced military goods with quality q_{1j} and M_{1j}, $j = n_1 + 1, n_1 + 2, \ldots, N$, imported goods with quality u_{1j}. The latter can be less than the quality of the variety produced by the exporting country for internal use and this is one form that arms export controls can take. Military strength takes the form of a generalized Dixit–Stiglitz *CES* utility function of the form:

$$\left[w_1 n_1 + (1 - w_1)(N - n_1) \right]^{\nu}$$

$$\times \left[w_1 \sum_{j=1}^{n_1} (q_{1j} D_{1j})^{\frac{\sigma-1}{\sigma}} + (1 - w_1) \sum_{j=n_1+1}^{N} (u_{1j} M_{1j})^{\frac{\sigma-1}{\sigma}} \right]^{\frac{\sigma}{\sigma-1}}, \tag{13}$$

where $\sigma > 1$ is the elasticity of substitution and $\nu > 0$. In (13), which generalizes $f(D_{st}, M_{st})$ above, if we put $\nu = 0$ and $w = \frac{1}{2}$, (13) reduces to the familiar Dixit–Stiglitz utility function used in the new trade and endogenous growth literatures. But

---

[30] See Dixit and Pindyck (1994).

as Benassy (1996) points out, this form of utility is restricted in that it implies a one-to-one correspondence between the taste for variety and the elasticity of substitution. Introducing the extra parameter breaks this link. In addition, the parameter ν represents in a simple way the concept of integrative technology which refers to the ease with which different weapon systems work together to provide military capability [Setter and Tishler (2004)].[31]

The budget constraint for government in producer country 1 now becomes:

$$Y_1 = C_1 + \sum_{j=1}^{n_1} p_{1j} D_{1j} + \sum_{j=n_1+1}^{N} P_j M_{1j} \qquad (14)$$

and the binding participation constraint for each firm producing a single variety j of quality q_{1j}, of which D_{1j} is domestically procured and X_{1j} is exported is:

$$p_{1j} D_{1j} + P_{1j} X_{1j} - c(D_{1j} + X_{1j}) - F - f q_{1j}^{\beta} = 0. \qquad (15)$$

As before with (6), the first two terms in (15) consist of revenue from domestic procurement at price p_{1j} and from exports at price P_{1j}, respectively for producer $s = 1$. The third term and fourth terms are variable and fixed costs respectively. The final term is new and represents the costs of providing quality q_{1j}. We assume the R&D cost parameter $\beta > 1$ so these latter costs are convex. The model is then completed with a world market clearing condition for the exports and imports of each variety:

$$\sum_{b=1}^{\ell+r} (M_{bj} + M_{bj}^*) = \sum_{s=1}^{\ell} X_{sj}. \qquad (16)$$

To solve for the equilibrium of this model we need to specify the sequence of events:

1. Domestic procurement by producers. Given military expenditure, the government in producer country 1 sets and procures domestic goods of quantity D_{1j} and quality q_{1j} at price p_{1j}, for $j = 1, 2, \ldots, n_1$. It also formulates a plan to import goods M_{1j} of quality u_{1j}, for $j = n_1 + 1, n_1 + 2, \ldots, N$ at the world market equilibrium price P_{1j}. All decisions are subject to a budget constraint and a non-negative profit participation constraint for domestic firms. The procurement price may be greater or less than the international market price. Firms already participating in the international market will always accept domestic procurement as long as the procurement price exceeds the marginal cost. Given the procurement price, the participation constraint for each domestic firm then determines the number of such firms. Thus, in setting the procurement price the government in effect are choosing the number of domestic firms which is *endogenously determined* at this first stage of the game.

---

[31] Setter and Tishler (2004) define integrative technology as 'information and communication technologies that enable separate individual systems to work in a joint, coordinated, and synergistic fashion as a single holistic system.' In their paper, they endogenize the choice of integrative technology, they also use a different functional form. For simplicity, we keep it exogenous.

2. Monopolistic competition between firms. With a commitment to producing D_{1j}, in a price-setting equilibrium of this stage of the game, firms in producer country 1 set world prices P_{1j} and export quantity X_{1j} of quality u_{ij} to countries $i = 2, \ldots, \ell + r$. In general, the world market price can depend on procurement decisions at stage 1, but for large N (assumed in the analysis) we have monopolistic competition with the price given by $P_{1j} = P = \frac{\sigma c}{\sigma - 1}$ which depends only on the marginal cost c and the elasticity σ. Note that decisions on quality have been decided at stage 1 by the procuring governments.

3. Military spending by non-producers and demand for imports by all countries. Given the world market price P_j and quality u_{ij}, and military expenditure, governments in both producer and non-producer countries $i = 1, 2, \ldots, \ell + r$ procure imports of good, M_{ij}, $j = 1, 2, \ldots, N$, of quality u_{ij}, where $i \neq j$ for producer countries $i = 1, 2, \ldots, \ell$. Non-producers anticipating these decisions allocate resources between consumption and military expenditure.

This framework can be used to examine how the size of the defense industrial base is influenced by the degree of home bias for domestic production (the parameter w_s),

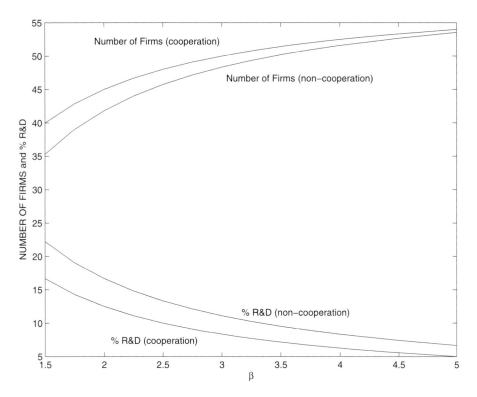

Figure 2. Number of firms per country as R&D cost parameter β increases: non-cooperation compared with cooperation.

R&D costs which determine the quality q_{sj} of system j, export controls captured by u_{sj} and the nature of regional arms races. Collective action problems relating to possible cooperation between suppliers in procurement, R&D and export control decisions can also be addressed with this framework. Figures 2 and 3 taken from Dunne et al. (2005) illustrate some insights provided by this model. We examine in these results a symmetric equilibrium in which all producer countries are identical in every respect and similarly for non-producers. The utility function across producers and cost conditions for firms are identical. The consequence of this is that procurement prices and firm numbers in each country are all equal.

In Figure 2 the endogenously determined number of firms in this symmetrical equilibrium is shown as a function of the R&D cost parameter β. This figure shows how there exists a *trade-off between quality and variety*: an increase in a cost parameter β increases barriers to entry and inhibits the emergence of new firms and varieties (since each firm produces a single variety in our set-up). Quality and R&D costs as a percentage of total costs falls with firms switching from quality to quantity. Figure 2 also demonstrates two effects of cooperation: the reduction of duplication in R&D invest-

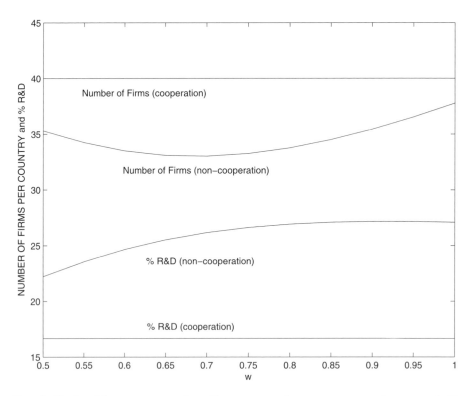

Figure 3. Number of firms per country as home bias parameter w increases: non-cooperation compared with cooperation.

ment and the increase in varieties. The latter occurs under cooperation because variety produced in each supplier country enters the utility of other producers as a positive externality.

In Figure 3 the endogenous number of firms in a symmetric equilibrium is plotted against the home bias parameter $w \in [0.5, 1]$. The fall in w from its value under autarky, $w = 1$, to the no home bias case, $w = 0.5$, can be seen as one aspect of the globalization of the international defense industry as countries are more willing to look to imports to provide for their military needs. Again, procurement cooperation increases variety and reduces R&D investment compared with non-cooperation. Furthermore, under cooperation, changes in home bias has no effect as it is internalized in the cooperative decision. With non-cooperation, as home bias increases the willingness to invest in both quality and variety rises (since there is less scope for importing these features). However in the vicinity of the no bias value $w = 0.5$, the R&D-variety trade-off sees more R&D investment at the expense of variety so firm numbers initially fall. As w increases further, the convex nature of R&D costs means that at some value (around $w = 0.7$) in Figure 3 the increase in R&D drops off and variety starts to increase. The prediction of the model then is for values of home bias w near the autarky value, globalization (a reduction in w) causes firm numbers to fall and thus international market concentration to increase.

The model can also predict that if quality and R&D expenditure are held fixed or indeed rise, then globalization in another sense of an increased relative size of the external market and greater willingness to export higher quality weapons will reduce the number of firms. Taken together our results then provide an explanation for the driving forces behind the recent increases in concentration in the defense industry [see Dunne et al. (2003)].

8. Concluding remarks

Recent developments in the arms trade literature have attempted to provide a suitable framework to analyze the strategic interactions of the arms trade. Elements of strategic trade theory and procurement theory have been brought together to capture a market structure which is complex for a number of reasons such as the insistence of producer governments in retaining a home defense industry, the web of subsidies and controls characteristic of this industry, the sometimes diverse security concerns of exporter countries and the arms race aspect of the demand for weapons in many importing countries.

Different models of the arms trade have focused on different aspects of the problem such as the impact of arms exports and arms export controls on arms races and arms proliferation, the importance of security perceptions for the structure of the defense industry and the benefits of coordination. The forces behind recent changes in the defense industry such as changes in concentration and asymmetries of information have also been analyzed.

We have also given a presentation of some of the formal models to provide an illustrative framework, integrating economic and security objectives, that allow the analysis of the institutions of the arms trade, particularly its national and international regulatory regimes and market structures. Of course, in any rational actor model such as those set out above, specifying the preferences or objectives of the actors is crucial. In this respect the specification of security is central. For buyers, the specification in terms of an arms race seems to capture very many important cases; though it does not cover actual war or internal threats. Supplier security is more problematical, but a specification which recognizes that they may come into conflict with buyers, perhaps in alliance with other suppliers, captures many important reasons for arms export controls.

The models include factors which are important but are often ignored. Budget constraints are clearly important as the fall in demand for arms after the 1985 oil price collapse and the 1997 East Asian crises indicates. Prices are important, as indicated both by econometric work and by the drop in prices for major weapon systems when demand fell in the 1990s for strategic reasons while supply did not. The formal models highlight a number of ways in which the military sector is fundamentally different from other industries. First, for buyers of arms involved in regional arms races price increases can actually be welfare enhancing by dampening arms races. From the viewpoint of these consumers, price competition between arms producers can therefore be detrimental and monopolistic market structures can be optimal. Second, home bias has been very high in this industry. A recent trend towards globalization (a reduction in home bias) can help to explain the observed drop in firm numbers in the military sector and the increase in concentration. Third, R&D plays an increasingly crucial role in the capability of major weapons systems. The trade-off between R&D and varieties then points to another factor that can explain the fall in firm numbers in this sector. Finally, the sector and the arms trade in particular, is subject to far more controls than other industries. However, regulatory regimes can generate perverse incentives. Controls can promote proliferation: by raising the price they increase the incentive for domestic production. By contrast uncertainty about the future supply of imported weapons, prices or quantities available, can reduce the probability of proliferation. This is a feature that does not seem widely recognized in the literature which has been more concerned with the need for sending clear signals.

Regarding future lines of research, it is apparent from our review that there is plenty of scope for empirical research that tests many of the hypotheses suggested in the theoretical literature. As seen in the product and data section, the lack of good and reliable data for arms trade could explain the relative lack of empirical studies in the area (with exceptions already quoted). A second reason though might be the difficult in measuring concepts such as the security of exporter countries or the degree of home bias or even the definition of arms product itself. This conceptual challenge has been enhanced by the emergence of terror and the decline in the prospect of inter-state wars. Related to this is the rise in importance of the so called dual use goods [Klein (2001), García-Alonso (2003), Kulve and Smit (2003), and Stowsky (2004)]. It is both in the understanding of the implications of these new trends and their implications for the defense industry, security and international cooperation that there lie a number of pressing issues for future research.

References

Anderton, C.H. (1995). "Economics of the arms trade". In: Hartley, K., Sandler, T. (Eds.), Handbook of Defense Economics, vol. 1. North-Holland, Amsterdam, pp. 523–590.

Anderton, C.H. (1996). "What can international trade theory say about the arms trade?". Peace Economics, Peace Science, and Public Policy 4, 7–30.

Benassy, J.P. (1996). "Taste for variety and optimum production patterns in monopolistic competition". Economic Letters 52, 41–47.

Berryman, J. (2000). "Russia and the illicit arms trade". Crime, Law and Social Change 33, 85–104.

Blanton, S.L. (1999). "Instruments of security or tools of repression? Arms imports and human rights conditions in developing countries". Journal of Peace Research 36, 233–244.

Blume, A., Tishler, A. (2000). "Security needs and the performance of the defense industry". CIC Working paper No. FS IV 00-04.

Brauer, J. (2000). "Potential and actual arms production: implications for the arms trade debate". Defence and Peace Economics 11, 461–480;
Reprinted in: Levine, P., Smith, R.P., Arms Trade Security and Conflict. Routledge, 2003, pp. 21–36.

Brauer, J., Dunne, J.P. (2002). Arming the South. Palgrave, Basingstoke.

Brauer, J., Dunne, J.P. (2004). Arms Trade and Economic Development: Theory, Policy, and Cases Studies in Arms Trade Offsets. Routledge, London.

Brito, D.L., Intriligator, M.D. (1999). "Increasing returns to scale and the arms race: The end of the Richardson paradigm". Defence and Peace Economics 10, 39–54.

Brzoska, M. (2004a). "The economics of arms imports after the end of the Cold War". Defence and Peace Economics 15, 111–123.

Brzoska, M. (2004b). "Taxation of the Global Arms Trade? An overview of the issues". Kyklos 57, 149–172.

Buzan, B., Herring, E. (1998). The Arms Dynamic in World Politics. Lynne Rienner, Boulder.

Chalmers, M., Davies, N., Hartley, K., Wilkinson, C. (2002). "The economic costs and benefits of UK defense exports". Fiscal Studies 23, 343–367.

Congressional Research Service (2005). Conventional Arms Transfers to Developing Nations, 1997–2004. CRS Report for Congress (downloadable from CRS Web).

Craft, C., Smaldone, J.P. (2003). "Arms imports in Sub-Saharan Africa: Predicting conflict involvement". Defence and Peace Economics 14, 37–49.

Davis, C. (2002). "Country survey XVI: The defense sector in the economy of a declining superpower: Soviet Union and Russia, 1965–2001". Defence and Peace Economics 13, 145–177.

Dixit, A.K., Pindyck, R.S. (1994). Investment Under Uncertainty. Princeton University Press, Princeton.

Dunne, J.P., García-Alonso, M.D.C., Levine, P., Smith, R.P. (2003). "Concentration in the international arms industry". University of the West of England Discussion Paper No. 03/01.

Dunne, P., García-Alonso, M.D.C., Levine, P., Smith, R.P. (2005). "Military procurement, industry structure and regional conflict". Discussion Paper 0502, University of Kent.

García-Alonso, M.D.C. (1999). "Price competition in a model of the arms trade". Defence and Peace Economics 10, 273–303.

García-Alonso, M.D.C. (2000). "The role of technology security in a model of trade with horizontal differentiation". International Journal of Industrial Organisation 18, 747–772.

García-Alonso, M.D.C. (2003). "National-security export quality restrictions in segmented and non-segmented markets". European Journal of Political Economy 19, 377–390.

García-Alonso, M.D.C., Hartley, K. (2000). "Export controls, market structure and international coordination". Defence and Peace Economics 11, 481–504.

García-Alonso, M.D.C., Levine, P. (2005). "Arms export control regimes, export subsidies and the WTO exemption". Scottish Journal of Political Economy 52, 305–322.

García-Alonso, M.D.C., Smith, R.P. (2006). "The economics of arms export controls". In: Joyner, D.H. (Ed.), The Future of Multilateral Non-proliferation Export Controls. Ashgate, Aldershot. In press.

García-Alonso, M.D.C., Levine, P., Morga, A. (2004). "Export credit guarantees, moral hazard and export quality". Bulletin of Economic Research 56, 311–328.

Golde, S., Tishler, A. (2004). "Security needs, arms exports, and the structure of the defense industry determining the security level of countries". Journal of Conflict Resolution 48, 672–698.

Gupta, S., De Mello, L., Sharan, R. (2001). "Corruption and military spending". European Journal of Political Economy 17, 749–777.

Hartley, K., Sandler, T. (2003). "The future of the defense firm". Kyklos 56, 361–380.

Ingram, P., Isbister, R. (2004). Escaping the Subsidy Trap, Why Arms Exports are Bad for Britain. Published jointly by BASIC, Saferworld and Oxford Research Group.

Kinsella, D. (1998). "Arms transfer dependence and foreign policy conflict". Journal of Peace Research 35, 7–23.

Kinsella, D. (2001). "Global arms transfers and regional security complexes: Some time-series evidence". Mimeo. School of International Service. American University.

Kinsella, D. (2003). "Changing structure of the arms trade: A social network analysis". Mimeo. Hartfiel School of Government, Portland State University.

Kirkpatrick, D. (1995). "The rising unit costs of defense equipment: the reason and the results". Defence and Peace Economics 6, 263–288.

Kirkpatrick, D. (2004). "Trends in the costs of weapon systems and the consequences". Defence and Peace Economics 15, 259–273.

Klein, H. (2001). "Technology push-over: defense downturns and civilian technology policy". Research Policy 30, 937–951.

Kulve, H., Smit, W.A. (2003). "Civilian-military co-operation strategies in developing new technologies". Research Policy 32, 955–970.

Laffont, J.J. (1995). "Regulation, Moral Hazard and Insurance of Environmental risks". Journal of Public Economics 58, 319–336.

Levine, P., Smith, R.P. (1995). "The arms trade and arms control". The Economic Journal 105, 471–484.

Levine, P., Smith, R.P. (1997a). "The arms trade". Economic Policy, 337–370. October.

Levine, P., Smith, R.P. (1997b). "The arms trade and the stability of regional arms races". Journal of Economic Dynamics and Control 21, 631–654.

Levine, P., Smith, R.P. (2000a). "Arms export controls and proliferation". Journal of Conflict Resolution 44, 885–895.

Levine, P., Smith, R.P. (2000b). "The arms trade game: from laissez faire to a common defense policy". Oxford Economic Papers 52, 357–380.

Levine, P., Smith, R.P. (2003). Arms Trade Security and Conflict. Routledge, London and New York.

Levine, P., Sen, S., Smith, R.P. (1994). "A model of the international arms market". Defence and Peace Economics 5, 1–18.

Levine, P., Mouzakis, F., Smith, R.P. (1998). "Prices and quantities in the arms trade". Defence and Peace Economics 9, 223–236.

Levine, P., Mouzakis, F., Smith, R.P. (2000). "Arms export controls and emerging domestic producers". Defence and Peace Economics 11, 505–530;
Reprinted in: Levine and Smith (2003).

Mantin, B., Tishler, A. (2004). "The structure of the defense industry and the security needs of the country: A differentiated products approach". Defence and Peace Economics 15, 397–419.

Markusen, A. (2004). "The arms trade as illiberal trade". In: Brauer, J., Dune, J.P. (Eds.), Arms Trade Offsets: Theory, Policy and Case Studies. Routledge, London (Chapter 5).

Martin, S. (1999). "The subsidy savings from reducing UK arms exports". Journal of Economic Studies 26, 15–37.

Mouzakis, F. (2002). "Domestic Procurement as an alternative to importing arms". In: Brauer, J., Dunne, J.P. (Eds.), Arming the South. Palgrave, Basingstoke, pp. 129–160.

NAO (2004). Battlefield Helicopters, HC486 National Audit Office.

Panofsky, W. (1990). "Barriers to negotiated arms control". In: Arrow, K., et al. (Eds.), Barriers to Conflict Resolution. Norton, London.

Sandler, T. (2000). "Arms trade, arms control and security: Collective action issues". Defence and Peace Economics 11, 533–548;
Reprinted in: Levine, P., Smith, R.P., Arms Trade Security and Conflict. Routledge, 2003, pp. 209–220.

Sandler, T. (2004). Global Collective Action. Cambridge University Press, Cambridge.

Sandler, T., Hartley, K. (1999). The Political Economy of NATO. Cambridge University Press, Cambridge.

Sanjian, G.S. (2003). "Arms transfers, military balances, and interstate relations. Modeling power balance versus power transition linkages". Journal of Conflict Resolution 47, 711–727.

Setter, O., Tishler, A. (2004). "The role of integrative technologies as a "force exponent" on military capability". Mimeo. University of Tel Aviv.

Shefi, Y., Tishler, A. (2005). "The effects of the world defense industry and US military aid to Israel on the Israeli defense industry: A differentiated products model". Defence and Peace Economics 16, 427–448.

SIPRI (2005). Armaments, Disarmament and International Security, Stockholm International Peace Research Institute Yearbook. Oxford University Press.

Smith, R.P., Tasiran, A. (2005). "The demand for arms imports". Journal of Peace Research 42, 167–182.

Smith, R.P., Udis, B. (2001). "New challenges to arms export control: whither Wassenaar?". The Nonproliferation Review 8, 81–92;
Reprinted in: Levine, P., Smith, R.P., Arms Trade Security and Conflict. Routledge, 2003, pp. 94–100.

Stowsky, J. (2004). "Secrets to shield or share? New dilemmas for military R&D policy in the digital age". Research Policy 33, 257–269.

Wang, T.Y. (1998). "Arms transfers and coups d'etat: A study on Sub-Saharan Africa". Journal of Peace Research 35, 659–676.

Chapter 30

ARMS INDUSTRIES, ARMS TRADE, AND DEVELOPING COUNTRIES*

JURGEN BRAUER

James M. Hull College of Business, Augusta State University, 2500 Walton Way, Augusta, GA 30904, USA
e-mail: jbrauer@aug.edu

Contents

Abstract   974
Keywords   974
1. Introduction   975
2. Major conventional weapons   977
   2.1. Arms transfers   977
   2.2. Arms production   982
   2.3. Transnationalization of arms production and trade   987
   2.4. A theory of arms production   989
3. Small arms and light weapons   993
   3.1. Definition, data, and market characteristics   994
   3.2. Trade values, production volumes, stockpiles, and prices   995
   3.3. Supply, technology, diffusion   998
   3.4. The demand for small arms and light weapons   1000
4. Non-conventional weapons   1002
   4.1. Atomic weapons   1002
   4.2. Biological weapons   1004
   4.3. Chemical weapons   1005
   4.4. Missile technology and space-based activities   1007
   4.5. ABC-weapons production and entry/exit theory   1008
5. Conclusion   1010
References   1011

* Part of this chapter was researched and written while the author was Visiting Professor at the University of New South Wales, Australian Defence Force Academy, Canberra, Australia. Assistance by the University, its School of Business, and its library is gratefully acknowledged. Björn Hagelin and Mark Bromley of the Stockholm International Peace Research Institute, Sweden, provided trend-indicator values for major conventional arms transfers, 1950–2004, and Phillip Killicoat of Oxford University, United Kingdom, provided data on AK47 black market prices, 1990–2005. Helpful comments received from Professors Charles Anderton, Keith Hartley, and Todd Sandler, and research assistance provided by Milos Nikolic, are gratefully acknowledged as well. All shortcomings are the sole responsibility of the author.

Handbook of Defense Economics, Volume 2
Edited by Todd Sandler and Keith Hartley
© 2007 Elsevier B.V. All rights reserved
DOI: 10.1016/S1574-0013(06)02030-8

Abstract

This chapter discusses developing (non-high income) states' participation in the production and trade of parts or whole units of major conventional weapons, their integration into a transnationalized global arms industry, and the underlying industrial prerequisites that make that participation and integration possible. Drawing on the vertical boundaries of the firm literature, the chapter provides a theory that explains some aspects of post-Cold War shifts in the composition and location of arms production. The chapter further discusses characteristics of the small arms and light weapons industry. A highly lethal industry with far-ranging adverse effects on public health, education, and institutions of law and order and therefore on work incentives and investment climate, it is suggested that the horizontal boundaries of the firm literature, especially the product-cycle hypothesis, may explain certain features of the spacial and temporal diffusion of small arms production, technology, and supply. Newly emerging literature on small-arms demand is also discussed. Furthermore, the chapter examines the widening presence of non-high income states in the production of weapons of mass destruction. Vertical contracting and R&D/patent-race literatures are applied to the case of nuclear weapons.

Major conclusions of the chapter include that data sources are poor, that arms production and trade theory is underdeveloped, and that although non-proliferation regimes may have slowed weapons proliferation, they have failed to stop it. We observe industry entry in all weapons categories and in future may expect to see further increases in industry participation by non-high income states, should they choose to do so. This is the natural consequence of the gradual development of non-high incomes states' production capacities. We also observe, however, that states sometimes exit the arms industry or choose not to participate in it, despite their capacity to do so.

Keywords

ammunition, arms industry, arms production, arms trade, arms transfers, developing states, major conventional weapons, small arms and light weapons, non-conventional weapons, offsets, weapons of mass destruction

JEL classification: D20, F14, H56, L64, O33

1. Introduction

The prospect of violent conflict induces people, as individuals and in groups such as states, to acquire arms. Arms acquisition takes place along a spectrum from self-production to trade, but acquisition by theft, especially of small arms, or by illegal transfer, including the clandestine transfer of critical production technology, is not uncommon. Although agricultural implements and hunting gear can and have been used as weapons, the bulk of the production of arms today is a specialized industrial activity carried out for a political purpose, namely the defense or conquest of a physical space or sphere of interest by threat of violence against enemy populations.

States are not self-sufficient in weapons production. Virtually no regular or irregular armed force is equipped with a comprehensive range of arms that is self-produced in its entirety. Instead, the rule is that self-produced weapons are complemented by weapons imported from elsewhere. Even "self-produced" weapons rely in some measure on imported components or services such as specialized materials, metals, blueprints, software, training, maintenance, repair, and other goods and services. Consequently, trade is invariably part of modern arms industries' business.

Complete weapons or weapon systems once were produced in one state and then transferred to another. The phrase "arms trade" made sense in that context and is referred to here as "whole unit" arms trade. Increasingly, however, trade in arms-related components and services dominates trade in complete systems [Sprague (2004), UK Government (2004)]. It is "people, ideas, and technologies, rather than weapons [that] move across national borders" [Markusen (1999, p. 40)]. A firm in one state may produce a weapons platform, to be stocked with weapons acquired from one or more other states. Training, maintenance, and repair, even financing, are yet different parts of the overall system and can be supplied in many ways. Modern arms production and arms trade now resemble counterparts in other globalized industrial activities such as automobiles, an equally fragmented and transnational industry that includes many developing states as part of the overall production system [Bitzinger (1994)]. Markusen (2004) suggests that the commonly employed phrase "military industrial complex" be replaced with "international military industrial complex". By way of example, the American F-16 fighter jet is assembled in the United States, South Korea, Taiwan, and Turkey with high-tech components supplied by Germany, Israel, Japan, and Russia, and price-sensitive, commercial parts coming from Brazil, Poland, Spain, and South Africa [Markusen and DiGiovanna (2003)].

The industry's transnationalization carries dramatic implications for arms production and arms trade data collection efforts. Twenty years ago, a sale originating in any one state would most likely also have been produced in that state. Today, a sale originating in any one state may still be *credited* to that state but *production* is as likely to take place in a variety of locations around the globe, including the recipient state. Arms production statistics, always having been poor, do not systematically track this "outsourcing". Likewise, arms trade statistics are imputed values that do not necessarily correspond to financial flows and economic burdens. Arms production and trade statistics offered by governments and international organizations are sparse in coverage and detail, and although Revision 3 of the International Standard Industrial Classification (ISIC) code contains a category for weapons and ammunition production, reporting compliance by states is spotty. In some respects, less can be said today than in the past about the volume, location, and flow of arms production and arms trade [Dunne and Surry (2006)].[1]

Another difficulty arises in that today many developing states are bifurcated, exhibiting both extremely well developed economic sectors as well as extremely undeveloped ones. Examples include Brazil, China, India, Russia, Malaysia, Mexico, and Turkey, all with potential or actual arms production levels on par with or exceeding that of states such as Australia, Austria, Belgium, Canada, the Netherlands, Sweden, and Switzerland (see Section 2.2). Additionally, states that 20 or 30 years ago were classified by an average per capita income criterion as developing states, such as Greece, Israel, South Korea, Spain, and Taiwan are now classified as developed or high income states. In contrast, states formerly classified as "industrialized" include Albania and desperately poor former Soviet republics such as Kyrgyzstan. The movement across income categories complicates comparisons to be made among states and over time, a difficulty compounded by the emergence of non-conventional and small arms production and trade activities that have yet to command economists' full attention. This chapter treats all non-high income states, as defined by the World Bank's 2004 per capita gross national income rankings, as developing states.[2]

This chapter reviews what is known about non-high income states' arms industries and arms trade. Section 2 discusses these states' participation in the production and trade of major conventional weapons, their integration into the transnationalized arms industry, and the industrial prerequisites that make that participation possible. This section also offers a new theory of arms production that would explain certain shifts in production location and composition observed in the post-Cold War period. Section 3

[1] In other respects, more can be said. For instance, within the European Union national arms export reports have become the norm, although the quality of the reports is not always to researchers' liking. For updates, see SIPRI's arms transfer web site at www.sipri.org/contents/armstrad/atlinks_gov.html [accessed 28 September 2005]. On arms industry definition, data, and transparency, also see Bauer (2006), Hartley (this volume), and Surry (2006).

[2] The World Bank classifies economies by income. Based on 2004 GNI data, economies with per capita income of US$825 or less are low-income economies. Other categories are lower-middle income economies (US$826–3,255), upper-middle income economies (US$3,255–10,065), and high income economies (above US$10,065). The 55 political entities in the high income category are Andorra, Aruba, Australia, Austria, the Bahamas, Bahrain, Belgium, Bermuda, Brunei, Canada, Cayman Islands, Channel Islands, Cyprus, Denmark, Faeroe Islands, Finland, France, French Polynesia, Germany, Greece, Greenland, Guam, Hong Kong, Iceland, Ireland, Isle of Man, Italy, Japan, South Korea, Kuwait, Liechtenstein, Luxembourg, Macao, Malta, Monaco, the Netherlands, the Netherlands Antilles, New Caledonia, New Zealand, Norway, Portugal, Puerto Rico, Qatar, San Marino, Saudi Arabia, Singapore, Slovenia, Spain, Sweden, Switzerland, the United Arab Emirates, the United Kingdom, the United States, and the Virgin Islands (US). The special political status of Taiwan prevents the World Bank from listing it but it is treated as a high income economy. Traditionally, researchers refer to all other states as "developing" economies.

addresses the small arms and light weapons (SALW) industry. Highly lethal, it produces far-ranging adverse effects on personal safety, public health, physical infrastructure, and institutions of law and order and therefore on work incentives and investment climate. Economists have studied civil wars [e.g., Collier and Sambanis (2005)] but as yet have not particularly studied the SALW industry that has fueled them. Section 4 examines the widening presence of non-high income states in the production of weapons of mass destruction (atomic, biological, and chemical), also as yet little studied by economists. Section 5 concludes.[3] Chapter 29 in this volume discusses arms trade and arms race theory [García-Alonso and Levine (this volume)], and Chapter 33 studies arms industry procurement and policy issues [Hartley (this volume)]. In contrast, the present chapter emphasizes data-related issues with respect to non-high income states, although some theory is also presented. Arms production, acquisition, trade, or use by non-state actors are not addressed.[4]

2. Major conventional weapons

2.1. Arms transfers

Regarding arms transfers, three major data sources are available. They are, first, an annual publication entitled "Conventional Arms Transfers to Developing Nations", produced for the United States Congress by its Congressional Research Service [CRS (2005)]; second, the formerly annual but now irregularly issued *World Military Expenditures and Arms Transfers* (WMEAT), published by the Bureau of Verification and Compliance [BVC (2002)], an agency of the United States Department of State; and, third, the annual *SIPRI Yearbook*, issued by the Stockholm International Peace Research Institute [SIPRI (2005)].[5] Of the three, CRS and WMEAT claim to measure financial values of trade in *all* arms and arms-related goods and services. For example, the CRS

---

[3] So-called non-lethal weapons are not studied here. Exploratory research for a draft of this chapter found that their development and deployment appears as yet limited to a handful of high income states [see, e.g., Dando (2002, 2005), Davis (2005), Lewer and Davison (2005)]. It should be noted that non-lethal weapons are not necessarily non-lethal. For instance, a hostage taking event in Moscow on 23 October 2002 ended in the deaths of about 120 of 800 hostages when Russia authorized the use of a non-lethal chemical (fentanyl) that depresses respiration. Instead, all weapons operate along a continuum of lethality [Lewer and Davison (2005, p. 49)].

[4] For this, see, e.g., Collier and Hoeffler (this volume), Enders (this volume), and Sandler and Arce (this volume).

[5] Among economic researchers, WMEAT and SIPRI have been the most popular data sources. Since the former is not regularly produced anymore (the last data point is for 1999) it is not discussed here. Suffice it to say that the WMEAT data, should a new edition be issued, will not be comparable to earlier editions as major database valuation changes were made in 1997. London's International Institute for Strategic Studies, IISS, annually publishes *The Military Balance* [e.g., IISS (2004)]. It does not provide its own arms trade data; instead, it reproduces some CRS numbers.

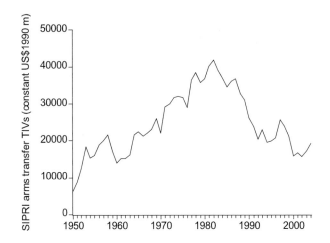

Figure 1. World arms transfer volume, 1950–2004, in constant 1990 US$ million, SIPRI trend-indicator values. *Source*: SIPRI (unpublished data).

defines its scope as pertaining to "all categories of weapons and ammunition, military spare parts, military construction, military assistance and training programs, and all associated services" [CRS (2005, p. 2)]. Transfer data for major conventional weapons are not separated from transfers in other arms. SIPRI is the world's only data source with regard to major conventional weapons alone.

Recognizing that arms transfer volumes, although expressed in US dollars, do not necessarily reflect financial flows, SIPRI refers to its data as "trend-indicator values" (TIVs) and generally refers to arms *transfers* rather than to arms *trade*. SIPRI's arms transfers database tracks deliveries of six categories of major conventional weapons. They are: aircraft, armored vehicles, artillery, radar systems, missiles, and ships [precise definitions are in SIPRI (2005, p. 523)]. Specifically excluded are small arms and light weapons, trucks, artillery under 100 mm caliber, ammunition, support equipment and components, and services and technology transfers. Figure 1 shows world arms transfer volumes, 1950–2004, as measured by TIVs, in constant 1990 US millions of dollars.[6] The high point of the global arms transfer volume as tracked by SIPRI was reached in 1982, at nearly US$42 billion (in constant 1990 US$).[7]

---

[6] The data for Figure 1 were kindly made available by SIPRI and are published here for the first time. In contrast, the annual SIPRI Yearbook contains data for only 10 years at a time.

[7] Until 1998, SIPRI did not attempt to calculate the annual *financial* value of arms transfers. Calculated from official government data, for calendar year 2003 – the latest estimate available – SIPRI deems that value to lie between US$38–43 billion, or about 0.5 to 0.6 percent of world trade for all goods and services [SIPRI (2005, p. 442)], a relatively modest number. For background information, see www.sipri.org/contents/armstrad/at_gov_ind_data.html [accessed 28 September 2005].

Table 1

World rank and volume of transfers in major conventional weapons, leading suppliers, 1950–2004, selected years (in constant 1990 US$m, SIPRI trend-indicator values)

Country rank/ supplier	Sum 2000– 2004	1950	1960	1970	1980	1990	2000	2004	Sum 1950– 2004	
01/Russia	26,925	0	0	0	0	0	4,016	6,197	49,169	[1992–2004]
02/USA	25,930	1,446	5,074	7,138	8,588	7,901	6,400	5,453	465,685	
03/France	6,358	15	889	1,608	2,958	1,605	717	2,122	86,230	
04/FR Germany	4,878	0	135	1,096	1,249	1,468	1,195**	1,091**	47,640**	
05/UK	4,450	1,456	1,804	478	1,040	1,569	1,121	985	80,470	
† 06/Ukraine	2,118	0	0	0	0	0	326	452	5,316	[1992–2004]
* 08/China	1,436	0	282	699	828	848	157	125	35,739	
‡ 10/Israel	1,258	0	0	13	227	46	272	283	5,598	
† 13/Belarus	744	0	0	0	0	0	261	50	1,837	[1993–2004]
† 14/Uzbekistan	595	0	0	0	0	0	0	170	595	[2002–2004]
‡ 15/Spain	479	0	4	70	11	130	50	75	4,546	
‡ 19/South Korea	313	0	0	0	71	44	6	50	1,328	
† 21/Georgia	248	0	0	0	0	0	54	20	320	[1999–2004]
* 24/Brazil	131	0	2	0	158	65	0	100	2,578	
* 25/Indonesia	130	0	0	5	4	0	0	50	443	
* 27/South Africa	122	0	25	3	24	0	17	35	641	
* 28/Turkey	117	0	0	0	11	0	21	18	181	
* 29/North Korea	96	0	0	0	5	4	0	0	1,996	
† 30/Kyrgyzstan	92	0	0	0	0	0	0	0	153	[1995–2004]
‡ 33/Singapore	73	0	0	0	0	5	1	70	616	
* 34/Jordan	72	0	0	0	0	0	0	72	435	
* 37/Libya	50	0	0	0	65	36	0	0	919	
* 38/Lebanon	45	0	0	0	0	0	0	0	48	
* 39/India	44	0	0	0	0	2	16	22	190	
World total	84,479	6,358	14,006	22,069	36,744	26,053	15,838	19,156	1,341,671	

Source: SIPRI (unpublished data).

Note: Numbers preceding states' names are arms export volume ranks (out of 117 states or entities) for the years 2000–2004.

†Formerly part of the USSR.

‡Formerly non-high income states.

***Non-high income states** other than Russia.

**For reunified Germany. Non/high-income state status as per World Bank's 2004 per capita gross national income (GNI) rankings.

In addition to the world's top-5 suppliers for 2000–2004, Table 1 presents arms transfer volume data on the leading arms suppliers among current or former non-high income states (apart from Russia). They include five former republics of the Soviet Union (Belarus, Georgia, Kyrgyzstan, Ukraine, and Uzbekistan), all of whom are non-high income states; four formerly non-high income states that now are high income economies (Israel, Singapore, Spain, and South Korea); and the top-ten non-high income states that are neither former Soviet republics nor states that have progressed to the status of high income economies (highlighted in **bold** type face). Following SIPRI practice, for the listed states the table is rank-ordered by the values for the last five years, 2000–2004.

According to Table 1, apart from Russia, non-high income states as *suppliers* play a minor role in the world arms market. In total, for 2000–2004, the top-10 former and current non-high income states (Ukraine through Indonesia) commanded a modest 8.8 percent of the world market for major conventional weapons. If Israel, Spain, and South Korea are removed from this calculation on the ground that by 2004 all had become high income economies (and if South Africa, Turkey, and North Korea are added to remain at a total of 10 non-high income states), the percentage drops to 6.8. If one further excludes the now independent non-Russian republics of the former Soviet Union to arrive at the 10 states that have been non-high income states for the entire 1950–2004 time-period, then the percentage of arms transfer participation of non-high income states as suppliers drops to a small 2.7 percent of the total for the 2000–2004 period, and about two-thirds of that is accounted for by China alone. This compares to over eighty percent for the world's top-5 arms suppliers. For the 55 year time-period summarized in Table 1, it is clear that supplies to the world arms market by former and current non-high income states are puny, the only exception being Russia. The snapshot listing by decade shows that only China and South Africa have a continuous history of arms exports. The record for the other non-high income states is spotty and small in value. The combined exports of major conventional weapons by Brazil, Indonesia, South Africa, Turkey, North Korea, Jordan, Libya, Lebanon, and India for the entire 55-year time-period are about equal to that of the United States for 2004 alone.

Figure 2 displays arms export volume data from 1950–2004 for 10 selected former and current non-high income states. Drawn to the same scale except for China and Spain, a number of observations may be made. First, Brazil, China, and Israel all appear to have suffered from arms export bubbles. The case of Brazil's short-lived success due to the Iran–Iraq war of the 1980s is well known[8]; those of China and Israel are not. Of the three, only Israel has recovered its arms export volume, in part by managing the post-Cold War conversion process better than most other states [Lewis (2003), Chen (2003)]. Second, most of the depicted states' arms export volumes are subject to severe swings in amplitude, e.g., the Koreas, Singapore, and Spain. Third, the Koreas appear to have entered the export market at about the same time. Fourth, only China, Israel,

---

[8] Brazil's arms industry has since then collapsed, and so has its arms trade. From 1985–1989, Brazil's TIV was US$1,385m, world-rank #11 [SIPRI (1990, p. 221)]; for 1990–1994, this dropped to US$262m, rank #19 [SIPRI (1995, p. 493)]; and for 1995–1999 to US$99m, rank #30 [SIPRI (2000, p. 372)]. Its US$131m, #24 ranking for 2000–2004 is due to US$100m TIV in 2004 alone. It may, however, be possible to argue that Brazil's successful production of commercial regional passenger aircraft is an outgrowth of its erstwhile military aircraft ambitions [Perlo-Freeman (2004)]. Similarly, from ca. 1975 to ca. 1990, Egypt was a reasonably prominent arms exporting non-high income state, but not since then.

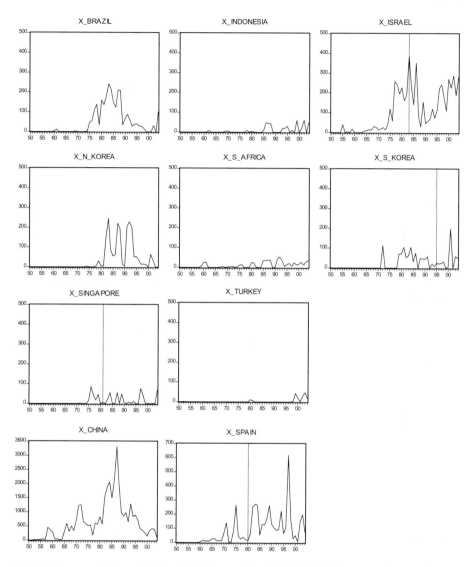

Figure 2. Arms supplies by selected non-high income states, 1950–2004; all figures are drawn to the same scale except for Spain and China; all values are constant 1990 US$ million SIPRI trend-indicator values (TIVs). *Source*: SIPRI (unpublished data). *Note*: The vertical lines for Israel (1983), South Korea (1995), Singapore (1981), and Spain (1980) are set at the years during which they achieved per capita GNP sufficient to count them among industrialized or high income states, as reported in the World Bank's annual *World Development Report*.

South Africa, and Spain have been consistent exporters for most of the time-period. Fifth, Turkey has been a dedicated arms manufacturer since the early 1980s but its lack of arms export performance suggests that its products are not deemed competitive. (Likewise, India – not displayed in Figure 2, but listed in Table 1 – is a minor player in the arms export market.) And sixth, there is no immediately obvious relation between arms transfer volume and transition from non-high income to high income state for the four now-high income states in Figure 2, namely Israel, Singapore, South Korea, and Spain.

Since the main interest in this chapter concerns non-high income economies as arms producers and suppliers, data on arms *recipients* are not presented. Suffice it to say that the top-10 non-high income states received, for 2000–2004, about 41.1 percent of all major conventional weapons shipments,[9] whereas the top-10 high income economies[10] jointly received about 28.6 percent. Six former or current non-high income states – China, India, Israel, Singapore, South Korea, and Turkey – appear as top suppliers and as top recipients. For 2000–2004, all six imported substantially more, in arms transfer volume terms, than they exported. That even the most active former and current non-high income states play but a small part in the international arms market as suppliers of whole unit major conventional weapons stems, in part, from their poverty and small size – so that their overall heft in the market is necessarily minimal – but also from a lack of international competitiveness of their products: Why for example purchase a helicopter made in South Africa when numerous high income states offer more advanced wares at competitive prices?

Even though non-high income states are not particularly successful as arms *sellers*, they nonetheless have undertaken substantial efforts as arms *producers*. These efforts, and the reasons therefore, are discussed in the ensuing section.

2.2. Arms production

States produce arms for ostensibly defensive purposes, namely the preservation of territorial integrity and the maintenance of spheres of influence. Underlying this are acute or precautionary political motives [Brauer (2002)]. But the specific form and volume of arms production are more nearly a matter of economics. First, arms export control and supply restrictions impose a constraint that can compel domestic production of arms components or of whole units by otherwise arms-importing states, even if it is economically inefficient to do so. Supply restrictions merely raise the cost of achieving the objective [García-Alonso and Levine (this volume)]. States such as Brazil, China, Egypt, India, Iran, Iraq, Pakistan, South Africa, and Turkey all have been subject to such cost-increasing export-supply restrictions. A competitive market model would reflect a supply restriction as a rise in marginal cost, thus increasing the market price of

---

[9] They are: China, India, Turkey, Egypt, Pakistan, Iran, Algeria, Yemen, Poland, and Brazil.

[10] Greece, the United Kingdom, South Korea, the United Arab Emirates, Australia, the United States, Israel, Canada, Saudi Arabia, and Italy.

major conventional arms, and hence providing an incentive for market entry either by the restriction-affected state or by other states for whom market entry may now become profitable.

A related, and second, reason for entering domestic arms production is to mitigate or remove uncertainties with regard to the reliability of supply lines so that credible threats of supply interruptions lose their sting. If the recipient were to turn elsewhere, it would be subject to the same threat from a new supplier. In the absence of an effective supply guarantee, the recipient state may thus choose to engage in a minimum of arms self-production. Note that all states mentioned in the preceding paragraph either have or had status ambitions as regional powers (Brazil, China, Egypt, South Africa, Turkey) or were or are engaged in regional conflict (India and Pakistan, Iran and Iraq), i.e., all are cases in which supply restrictions might have proved particularly onerous, thus spurring indigenous arms production efforts. These first two reasons suggest that arms production and trade may be jointly determined [Alexander, Butz and Mihalka (1981)].

Third, it is hoped that domestic arms production might stimulate the domestic economy. Appeal has been made (a) to potential arms export earnings and export-promotion industrialization,[11] (b) to foreign exchange savings from foregone arms imports and import-substitution industrialization, (c) to employment effects stemming from domestic arms production (growth-pole industrialization), and (d) in conjunction with co-production agreements, to military and non-military technology transfers that are to benefit the domestic economy at large (human capital imports embodied in technology). As an empirical matter, these goals do not appear to have been fulfilled [Brauer and Dunne (2004)].

Fourth, arms demand is a function of security preferences, national income, and the price of arms as well as the price of complementary and substitute goods [García-Alonso and Levine (this volume)]. The influence of security preferences on arms demand (imports) has been addressed in the preceding paragraphs. The influence of national income on arms demand is ambiguous. In the absence of domestic arms production data, studies can only measure the effect on the arms import component of overall arms demand. In a recent panel regression study, Smith and Tasiran (2005) found no systematic effect of income on arms imports but did find a non-linear effect of military expenditure (a proxy for security perceptions) on arms imports. As to the third item, prices, Smith and Tasiran (2005) report evidence that arms imports are price sensitive on the order of minus one: a one percent rise in price is associated with a one percent reduction in arms import quantities. Whether a higher arms trade price leads to compensating self-production or co-production (or to displacement into black market trade) or, conversely, whether a price reduction is symmetrically associated with declines in self-production are questions not as yet investigated.[12]

---

[11] Both President Vaclav Havel of then-Czechoslovakia and President Nelson Mandela of South Africa used this hope as an argument to continue to subsidize domestic arms industries following the overthrow (in 1989 and 1994, respectively) of their predecessor governments [Brauer (2002)].

[12] Also not investigated is the question of the influence on arms import demand of prices of complementary (e.g., weapons training) and substitute (e.g., diplomacy) goods and services.

As is true for the case of transfers in major conventional weapons, SIPRI is also the world's major comprehensive source of information for the production of such weapons.[13] However, data with respect to non-high income states are scarce as data collection efforts are focused on the world's largest arms producing companies.[14] For instance, for 2003 the only non-high income states represented among SIPRI's top-100 arms producing companies are Russia (first appearing at rank 29), India (35), and South Africa (80) [SIPRI (2005, Table 9A.1)]. Data for Chinese companies are unavailable, and they are spotty for Taiwan. Bauer (2006) has proposed six criteria by which to assess arms industry transparency. They are: availability, reliability, comprehensiveness, comparability, disaggregation, and relevance, but an assessment by Surry (2006) finds that even for high income states, usable arms industry data along Bauer's criteria are sparse, in part because reporting obligations that states routinely place on other industries are frequently not placed on arms makers.

Such as they are, the data suggest that, as with arms trade, substantial shifts have occurred with regard to arms production. In the 1950s and 1960s, "First World" and "Second World" states produced whole unit arms and traded a surplus to those who could not produce them (the "Third World"), at least in part to shore up regional spheres of influence. Several fundamental shifts have upset this once straightforward First-to-Third World and Second-to-Third World relation. First, during the 1970s and 1980s, an increasing number of non-high income states made economic progress enabling them to devote some of their improved capacity toward the indigenous production of major conventional weapons. Table 2 shows a quadrupling in the number of non-high income states as exporters of major conventional weapons from the 1950s to the 1980s. (The increasing number of high income states in Table 2 is the result of former non-high income states becoming high income states over time.)

Second, the number of non-high income arms producing states was greater in the 1980s than in the 1950s. But the number of suppliers in the early 2000s is less than that for the 1960s, and that of the 1990s is less than those for the 1970s and 1980s. Although there does not appear to exist any explicit theory on the matter, it is plausible that the "bubble" of non-high income arms producing states from the 1950s through the 1980s was the combined result of improved domestic production capacity and the exigencies of the bi-polar Cold War years that encouraged domestic arms production

---

[13] The *production* of weapons is a flow variable and differs from the *stock* of weapons. According to BICC (2003, p. 158), the stock of major conventional weapons held by "industrialized" states fell from an index of 183 in 1991 to an index of 100 in 2001. In contrast, non-high income states' stock of such weapons remained essentially constant: an index of 105 in 1991 as against an index of 100 in 2001. In absolute numbers, the stock of major conventional weapons in non-high income states of 208,800 pieces is larger than the 199,500 items in possession of industrialized states. A reasonable composite index of weapons *lethality* has not yet been developed. Such an index would need to include not merely the potential lethality of the weapon itself, but also the probability of successful deployment which hinges, among other things, on the training of the attending military personnel.

[14] Thus, while we have some knowledge about states' arms *transfers*, we cannot infer states' arms *retention* as our knowledge of states' arms *production* is incomplete.

Table 2
Count of states as exporters of major conventional weapons, by decade

	1950s	1960s	1970s	1980s	1990s*	2000s* ('00–'04)
High-income	20	25	27	30	32 [32]	26 [26]
Non-high income	9	23	38	37	27 [43]	21 [39]
Total	29	48	65	67	59 [75]	47 [65]
TIVs**	154,688	196,828	315,884	365,873	223,919	84,479

Source: computed from SIPRI (unpublished data).
*Numbers before brackets exclude states formerly part of the Soviet Union, Czechoslovakia, and Yugoslavia, all of which are classified by the World Bank as non-high income states (using 2004 GNI per capita as the criterion). Numbers in brackets include the successor states.
**The TIVs are in constant 1990 US$m.

efforts, even if economically inefficient [Markusen and DiGiovanna (2003, p. 10)]. For example, the Movement of Non-aligned States, founded in the 1950s, included Egypt, India, Indonesia, Pakistan, and then-Yugoslavia and, for a time, China. Brazil, although never a member of the Movement, generally expressed similar policy positions. All entered substantial arms production efforts during the Cold War years.

Third, with the end of the Cold War, the drive for "indigenization" faltered; fixed-cost driven "structural disarmament" [Dunne and Surry (2006)] makes completely indigenous development and production of major conventional weapons unaffordable to all but the United States. Instead, the industry globalized to generate cost savings via specialization in component production, niche market targeting, and supply-chain integration [Dunne and Surry (2006)]. Arms-offset deals proliferate and have become a standard feature of virtually all arms-trade deals, with heavy emphasis placed on co-production, licensing, and – especially – technology transfers [Brauer and Dunne (2004)]. The *raison d'être* motivating indigenous arms production is moving from the politically determined end of the spectrum toward the commercially determined end. Whereas states' defense industrial base used to be defined primarily in terms of home-state based prime and subcontractors [Dunne (1995)], post-Cold War it has become defined in global terms, frequently involving firms that at their core are decidedly civilian producers such as information technology firms [Dunne and Surry (2006)]. Major arms-producing corporations may still be headquartered in the United Kingdom and the United States in particular but various aspects of production are "outsourced", frequently at the demand of buying states (arms trade offsets).

The relative paucity of quantitative state-specific arms production data, as compared to arms transfer data, has led some scholars to take a different tack to learn about non-high income states' arms production. Reasoning that the production of major conventional weapons requires advanced human and physical capital inputs, Kennedy (1974), Wulf (1983), and Brauer (1991, 2000) constructed potential defense capacity (PDC) indices from International Standard Industrial Classification code data and matched these

Table 3
Potential defense capacity (PDC) index for selected high income and non-high income states (1986–1995)*

Group 1**		Group 2**		Group 3**	
Argentina	33.6	Chile	19.4	Australia	33.6
Brazil	51.6	Egypt	24.7	Belgium	34.3
Bulgaria	53.7	Hungary	68.6	Canada	31.5
China	32.5	India	42.1	France	59.7
Czech Republic	37.1	Indonesia	57.2	Greece	44.2
Mexico	61.8	Iran	18.0	South Korea	54.4
Pakistan	13.1	Romania	60.8	Netherlands	26.5
Poland	66.4	Ukraine	55.1	Spain	86.2
Russia	54.1	Yugoslavia	62.9	Sweden	59.0
South Africa	23.0			Switzerland	10.3
Turkey	55.5			USA	64.7

Source: unpublished data based on Brauer (2000).
*The PDC index refers to a percentage that measures in how many of 283 arms-production relevant industrial categories a state recorded production in any year (1986–1995). The categories consist of nine major industry groups: industrial chemicals; other chemicals; iron and steel; non-ferrous metals; metal products; non-electrical machinery; electrical machinery; transportation equipment; scientific, measuring, controlling equipment.
**Group 1 states are non-high income states with continuous, high-level arms production; Group 2 states are non-high income states with continuous, low-level arms production; Group 3 states are high-income arms producing states.

with qualitative, rank-ordered indices of arms production. Covering the mid-1970s to mid-1990s, Brauer (1991, 2000) has shown that the higher is a state's potential to produce arms, the higher is its rank-ordered actual arms production (Spearman rank-correlation coefficient of 0.6). Remarkably, the PDC index for the most arms-production engaged non-high income states exceeded that of the average high income state. Even second-tier arms producers among non-high income states reached an average PDC index lying within 10 percent of that of the high income states. (A selection of states is listed in Table 3.)

A comparison of PDC indices for the group of low-level but continuously engaged arms producers to that of high-level and very engaged arms producers among non-high income states proved statistically equivalent, suggesting that the difference in actual arms production levels, despite comparable potential, is explained by factors such as location: the former group consists of states located in relatively "tranquil" world regions, the latter are in relatively "hostile" world regions. Following the trajectory from the 1970s to the 1990s, the studies further showed that non-high income states engage in domestic arms production as they advance their human and physical capital and reach a PDC level that lies on par with the average high income state. Some non-high income states have arms production potentials they do not fully use (e.g., Mexico, Turkey), others have strained local capacities beyond what they can sustainably deliver (e.g., India,

Indonesia), and still others could conceivably produce at a higher level than they have in the past (e.g., Greece, Singapore; both now are high income economies).

2.3. Transnationalization of arms production and trade

In the mid-1990s, it was customary to speak of "tiers" of arms production and of an arms production "ladder" that non-high income states could climb as their indigenous capacities improved [Krause (1992), Bitzinger (1994)]. But with the end of the Cold War, non-high income states have been brought into a transnationalized system that includes all products, including arms. Comprehensive data to demonstrate this point are not available. Instead, this view is a judgment based on numerous country, firm, and product-specific case studies [Brauer and Dunne (2002, 2004), Markusen, DiGiovanna and Leary (2003), Dunne and Surry (2006)]. A theoretical explanation is offered in Section 2.4.

Some non-high income states simply abandoned arms production aspirations, for instance Argentina [Cavicchia (2003), Scheetz (2004)], or otherwise significantly retooled their arms production efforts. Conversion from military to civilian products in the 1990s proved much harder for example for non-high income states' platform producers than for subsystem and component producers who more easily adapted to the world arms component market or shifted activity into world commercial markets, or both [see the cases in Markusen, DiGiovanna and Leary (2003)].

Although no guarantee for sustained success, competitively sourced, made-to-order component production, enabled by targeted technology transfer and indigenous technology development, is the key to this diffusion of arms production [Conca (1998), Schwartz (1987), Bitzinger (1994)]. Like the "world car", the "world weapon" [Markusen (1999)] permits non-high income states to enter the industry as parts suppliers at lower entry costs than full-scale, whole unit self-production would require. The 1990s saw spectacular geographic shifts in manufacturing location from high income to former and current non-high income states, resulting in huge investments in technology transfers and skill development. World manufacturing has become modularized and dispersed, and yet systems integrated. Although not to the same degree, the same trend applies to the world armaments market. We now see non-high income states, for example South Africa, exiting certain full-line arms production efforts in favor of entering tailored component production tied to transnational producers headquartered in high income states [Dunne and Lamb (2004)].[15] Consequently, the erstwhile twin monopolies of design and production held by the "West" and "East" (primarily the United States and the former Soviet Union) have eroded. While weapon design remains dominated by high income states, especially the United States – in part because requisite

---

[15] Other states, such as India, that resist this integration and continue with an indigenous arms production program virtually unchanged from the Cold War years, appear to pay a heavy economic, and potentially military, price for that resistance [Maheshwari (2003), Baskaran (2004)].

R&D expenditures are so burdensome – component, assembly, and fully independent (even if licensed) production is being relocated to former and current non-high income states. This has sparked, certainly in the United States, a debate over arms-offset related production relocation, and Congress now requires of the Administration to provide an annual report detailing, *inter alia*, the economic and employment effects of arms trade offsets on the US economy. For the year 2002, for instance, the United States estimates a loss of 25,450 work-years due to offset agreements it signed that year [BXA (2005, p. 3-2)].

Transnationalization increases the difficulty of putting monetary values to the arms trade. This need not be so as a matter of principle, but appears to hold true for the arms industry [Bauer (2006), Surry (2006)]. A particular trade package may originate in the United Kingdom or the United States and be assigned an arms export value but may be produced in considerable part in the recipient state or another state or states. The average offset *agreement* asked of the United States in 2003 was 121.8 percent of the arms export contract value [BXA (2005, p. v)].[16] Offset *transactions* – in fulfillment of previously incurred obligations – amounted to US$3.6 billion that year, the highest value recorded for the 1993–2003 period. For this time-period, US companies reported 6,593 offset transactions with 46 states for a total value of US$27.1 billion [BXA (2005, p. vi)]. World-wide numbers are not available, but a large number of recent case studies, drawn from every continent, indicate that since the end of the Cold War the industry has seen a spectacular rise in arms trade offset deals through licenses, co-production, and unrelated trade by second-tier high income and non-high income states alike [Brauer and Dunne (2004)]. While the practical details of offset mechanics are inventive, the available evidence suggests that the hoped-for results – cost reduction vis-à-vis arms imports, employment generation via new and sustainable work placement, technology transfer that would spin off to the civilian sector, and consequent generalized economic development – can be documented only in rare cases. Opportunity costs associated with mandated arms trade offsets, to force or compel the development of an indigenous arms industry, appear to be higher than voluntarily negotiated arms trade offsets between supplier company and recipient buyer state [Markowski and Hall (2004)].

Regarding arms production, some small high income states such as Austria and Norway are hardly distinguishable from big non-high income states such as Indonesia or bifurcated states such as South Africa. High income and non-high income states alike are jointly integrated into a *common second tier* dominated by system designers in the first tier [Markusen (1999, 2004), Bitzinger (2003)]. This trend is likely to continue. Yet other tiers are formed by capable non-high income states that do not wish to produce arms (e.g., Mexico) and "stagnating" rather than "developing" states that continue to fall behind in capacity development (e.g., Nigeria). In all, it is questionable whether the

---

[16] This was due to an unusually high requirement for a single high-valued contract that year. The average offset agreement requirement for the eleven years 1993 to 2003 was 71.4 percent (US$50.7 billion worth of offset agreements out of US$70.9 billion in arms export contracts) [BXA (2005, Table 2-1, p. 2-2)], but with a rising trend.

formerly strict distinction between high income and non-high income arms producing states should still be kept.

It would also appear that the "ladder" model of arms production needs to be abandoned. The point of the "ladder" was to measure how far a state had progressed on the road to arms self-production, even self-sufficiency. During the Cold War period, this served a useful function as states attempted go-it-alone, whole unit production of major conventional arms, but with the end of the Cold War and the transnationalization of the industry a new arms production model would seem to revolve around the diffusion of arms-related technology transfers and foreign direct investment transmitted through various forms of offset work, i.e., issues related to economies of scale, scope, agglomeration and, ultimately, to cost rather than to location. High income and non-high income states alike "pick and choose" just how they wish to participate in the market. Section 2.4 offers a theory that explains some of the observations made thus far.

2.4. A theory of arms production

Relatively little work has been done on theoretical models of arms production and trade. A supply-and-demand model by Alexander, Butz and Mihalka (1981) is reviewed in Anderton (1995), as are a Heckscher–Olin based neoclassical trade model, an economies-of-scale model, an economies-of-learning (dynamic increasing returns) model, and models of imperfect competition and arms trade. Anderton (1996) adds a supply-and-demand model with externalities, a small game-theory model, and a product-cycle model. The extensive theoretical work over the past 10 years of a British research group revolving around Paul Dunne, Maria García-Alonso, Paul Levine, and Ron Smith is reviewed by García-Alonso and Levine (this volume). Depending on the research question, each of these theories has its uses. This subsection outlines a new theory. It is based on the "boundaries of the firm" literature [Williamson (1985)][17] and proposes an explanation for the observed shifts in the location and composition of arms production discussed in the prior sections.

Define *vertical integration* in the arms manufacturing sector as an activity that takes place within the confines of a single state, rather than within those of a single firm. A make-decision then is the decision to retain all pertinent weapons production activity within the state (in-state), and a buy-decision is the decision to engage in a cross-border purchase for all or part of a state's weapons needs (out-of-state). A state thus faces a make-or-buy decision-making problem comparable to that a firm within a state faces.

Assuming output to be constant, define, further, *technical efficiency* as the degree to which a state uses least-cost *production* processes – "the steady state production cost difference between producing to one's own requirements and the steady state cost of procuring the same item in the market" [Williamson (1985, p. 92)] – and *agency efficiency* as the degree to which *exchange* processes have been organized to minimize

---

[17] A textbook version is in Besanko et al. (2004).

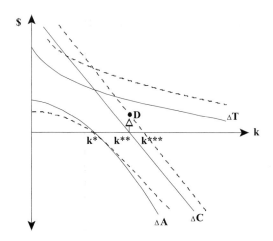

Figure 3. A theory of arms production. *Source*: Based on Besanko et al. (2004, p. 144).

agency, coordination, and transaction costs. For example, when a buy-decision exposes a state to substantial hold-up risk, agency costs of market exchange as opposed to those posed by exchange in a vertically integrated organization (in-state) may not have been minimized. Markets aggregate orders and, on account of the resulting economies of scale, scope, and agglomeration, excel in the direction of minimizing production costs but at the expense of potentially significant agency risks. In contrast, vertical integration excels in the direction of minimizing agency costs [Coase (1937)] but loses the unique advantages competitive markets deliver in terms of production efficiencies. For example, buying critical components from out-of-state because the world market can exploit economies of scale beyond what can be achieved in-state may enhance technical efficiency but perhaps only at considerable contracting costs, including those of contract monitoring and enforcement. Conversely, vertical integration may deliver tighter control over agency-related costs but lose scale efficiencies. Thus, technical and agency efficiency need to be balanced to minimize the sum of both kinds of costs.

Figure 3 [based on Besanko et al. (2004, p. 142)] measures on the vertical axis make-minus-buy cost differences. A positive (negative) value denotes that the make-decision is more (less) expensive than the buy-decision, i.e., vertical integration of a production activity in-state is more (less) costly than using out-of-state exchange. The horizontal axis measures asset specificity, k. Assets can be (a) specific to a location (e.g., an aircraft hangar located near an airfield and flight-training airspace), (b) specific to a particular production purpose (e.g., materials tailored to certain heat-resistance tolerances), (c) specific to physical assets (e.g., a guided-missile production facility), and (d) specific to human resources (e.g., investment in skills training dedicated to military-production related tasks). The more specific the asset, the further out along the horizontal axis it is measured, and the less malleable the asset is for redeployment into alternative uses.

Ignoring all dashed curves for now, in the figure the solid curve marked ΔT is the locus of all make-minus-buy technical efficiency cost minima. Likewise, the curve marked ΔA is the locus of all make-minus-buy agency efficiency cost minima. The first, ΔT, declines as asset specificity k increases. For low values of k, in-state production incurs a cost penalty for "standardized transactions for which market aggregation economies are great" [Williamson (1985, p. 92)]. At low k, it is thus preferable to purchase out-of-state. For example, competitive market firms specializing in the production of heat-resistant materials to high tolerances can spread the necessary R&D over many customers (states), conferring cost advantages relative to vertically integrated in-state production. In contrast, if asset specificity is high (e.g., warhead shockwave-modeling as an input to blast munitions production or nuclear-powered aircraft carriers as an input into the production of national security), then the more specialized uses for the input imply fewer sales outlets for outside suppliers. Consequently, the advantages of scale, scope, and agglomeration dissipate and become less prominent. The cost difference – ΔT – assumes only a small positive value and becomes asymptotic to the asset specificity axis. In other words, the cost disadvantage of in-state production relative to out-of-state acquisition is smaller the larger is asset specificity, k. In the extreme case, an input is unique to the firm (state) and the market's scale economies are exhausted.[18] One important implication is that a firm (state) "will never integrate for production cost reasons alone" [Williamson (1985, p. 94)]. Agency costs drive the integration decision.

Regarding ΔA – agency or governance costs – vertically integrated production is more costly than market exchange (positive values) when asset specificity is low ($k < k^*$) and less costly when asset specificity is high ($k > k^*$). For example, when technology developed in-state is transferred to an out-of-state supplier to produce propellers for military submarines (a highly specific asset), the risk of leakage of critical national security information to third parties rises. In the judgment of decision-makers, this may make ΔA assume a negative value (the agency cost of using the market outweighs the agency cost of in-state production), wherefore vertical integration might be preferred over outsourcing.

The final curve in the figure – ΔC – is the vertical sum of ΔT and ΔA at each k. Thus, to the left of k^{**}, the combined technical and agency costs of in-state production exceed those of out-of-state production ($\Delta C > 0$). Consequently, for low asset specificity, a state should acquire inputs from out-of-state.[19] To the right of k^{**}, the use of highly asset specific inputs argues for in-state production ($\Delta C < 0$). At k^{**} a point of indifference between in-state production and out-of-state acquisition is reached ($\Delta C = 0$). A joint downward (upward) shift of ΔT, ΔA, and ΔC results in a movement of k^{**} to the left (right) and would reduce (enlarge) the range of out-of-state acquisition

---

[18] Even when scale economies are exhausted, the market may retain scope and agglomeration advantages.

[19] Whether this refers to component inputs into arms production or to arms inputs into national security production does not matter for the theoretical argument.

and correspondingly expand (limit) the range of asset specificity over which in-state production is preferred. In the extreme, k^{**} lies at the origin so that $\Delta C \leqslant 0$ over all feasible k (since k cannot be negative). All arms production would then be contracted in-state.

Consider now a highly adverse international security environment (e.g., the Cold War period) where even allies cannot be fully trusted and agency costs attributable to out-of-state exchange are particularly high, reflecting, for instance, the risk of losing technology secrets through offset production in another, even if notionally friendly, state. Holding ΔT constant, ΔA shifts downward. This would capture a situation in which a state believes that agency costs are so high that no out-of-state producer can be trusted to deliver on a contract. Trusting the market then is *always* perceived to be more costly than in-state production. Consequently, ΔC also shifts downward and moves k^{**} to the left along the k-axis, reducing to zero the range of asset specific inputs acquired out-of-state. All inputs of any specificity necessary for weapons production are now produced in-state.

Technical and agency efficiency may not be independent of each other. For example, since 1982, the demand for, or at least trade in, major conventional weapons worldwide decreased and reduced economies-of-scale benefits. In-state production would be disadvantaged relative to out-of-state purchases, resulting in an upward shift of ΔT for each level of k (the dashed ΔT in the figure). But for low levels of asset specificity, $k < k^*$, the agency efficiency advantages of the market may now be less pronounced as decreased scale may reduce the agency cost of vertical integration while increasing the agency cost of more reliance on the market (additional layers of contracting, for example). In contrast, for high asset specificity, $k > k^*$, the agency advantages of out-of-state relative to in-state production may become more pronounced (for example, hold-up problems within vertical integration may become more serious whereas it may be possible to hedge market hold-up problems against a large number of potential out-of-state suppliers). As a consequence, ΔA *rotates* counter-clockwise around k^* (the dashed ΔA curve in the figure), the slope of ΔC becomes steeper, and k^{**} moves rightward to become k^{***}. Decreased post-1982 demand therefore would have been predicted to increase the range of asset specificity over which out-of-state procurement would occur.[20]

Even if agency effects were symmetric for all k, the combined cost – the dashed ΔC – would shift k^{**} to k^{***} if lower agency costs associated with market exchange relative to the agency costs of vertical integration shifted ΔA uniformly upward. The *threshold* up to which a state should then entrust acquisition of arms production inputs to the market (out-of-state) rises. This may also be seen by comparing k^{**} with point D. For a *given k*, namely k^{**}, the positive value of point D on ΔC represents an excess of make over buy costs. In-state production has become dearer. Insisting, nonetheless, on in-state

---

[20] For the United States, especially since 11 September 2001, the opposite conclusion would be drawn as demand for military-related goods and services has increased.

production only emphasizes the inefficiency of domestic arms production efforts that some non-high income states appear to insist on even in the post-Cold War world. This, then, would provide an explanation for certain observations made in Sections 2.2 and 2.3, namely (a) that the number and location of arms production by non-high income states has changed in the post-Cold War world (fewer whole unit suppliers) and (b) that the product palette of the remaining non-high income state producers is changing toward supply-chain integration rather than vertically-integrated, in-state, domestic production of whole unit major conventional weapons.

While this model may not be empirically testable (e.g., because of the difficulty of operationalizing a concept such as "asset specificity"), its heuristic usefulness lies in capturing many factors relevant to a state's make-or-buy arms procurement decision. For the defense industry as a whole, and arms production specifically, agency efficiency, technical efficiency, and asset specificity drive the decision-making behavior.

3. Small arms and light weapons

Conventional arms present an enormous potential for concentrated destruction. Yet states use such arms infrequently. In contrast, small arms and light weapons (SALW) are used frequently, by state and non-state actors alike. Today, they are the primary arms to cause injury and death among civilians and military personnel [Bourne (2005, p. 156)]. The *Small Arms Survey*, an annual report of the eponymous project of the Graduate Institute of International Studies in Geneva, Switzerland, estimated that "at least 500,000 people are killed each year by small arms and light weapons" and calls these weapons "the real weapons of mass destruction" [SAS (2001, p. 1)]. As compared to the last major war fought with major conventional weapons – the United States–Iraq war of 2003 – this death toll would be equivalent to a series of major wars being fought each year.[21]

As compared to major conventional weapons, SALW – like land mines – are relatively easy to manufacture (even in home production/craft industry), and because of their low weight they are easily transported, smuggled, and concealed. It has been suggested that the improvement in small arms technology (lighter, hardier, deadlier, simpler, cheaper) is one factor explaining the rise in the number of child soldiers recruited and deployed [Singer (2005, p. 38)].[22] The abuse of SALW causes severe short

---

[21] The Small Arms Survey 2005 [SAS (2005)] devotes a chapter to estimating conflict deaths (rather than overall SALW-related deaths). Using pre/post-conflict crude mortality rates (CMRs) to calculate "excess" deaths, and using estimates of deaths directly related to violent armed conflict, it finds that for sub-Saharan Africa in the early 2000s, roughly 25 percent of all conflict deaths are "direct" deaths and 75 percent "indirect" deaths (due to conflict-related privation). Of all "direct" conflict deaths, in turn, between 60–90 percent are attributable to SALW. The total (direct and indirect) conflict death toll may be larger than 300,000 people annually.

[22] This combines with an increased "labor pool" of potential child soldiers, generated by factors such as continuous war and the AIDS epidemic that has left millions of orphaned children.

and long-term economic consequences in non-high income states, principally through microeconomic effects on health, education, work incentives, and investment climate that cumulate into adverse macroeconomic outcomes [Collier et al. (2003)]. Magnified through institutional uncertainty or failure (e.g., regarding law and order, and the administration of justice), the result is lagging tax-revenue collection and insufficient economic development [SAS (2003, 2004), Florquin (2005)]. Private and public humanitarian and development aid is made more difficult or altogether impossible by the presence of small arms, with many reported instances of private charities and public agencies withdrawing from field work on account of tangible threats to their workers and the communities within which they work [Godnick, Laurance and Stohl (2005), SAS (2005, p. 251)]. Among the costs of small arms one must therefore count avoidance, prevention, or defensive behavior by those charities and agencies that remain in the field as well as the foregone benefits of work made impossible. Likewise, private corporations operating in non-high income states have seen security expenditures rise, and a burgeoning industry of "private military companies" has sprung up to provide security services [Leander (2005)]. Laurance (2005) provides an overview of the newly emerging small arms research field.

3.1. Definition, data, and market characteristics

Small arms are "revolvers and self-loading pistols, rifles and carbines, assault rifles, sub-machine guns, and light machine guns." Light weapons are "heavy machine guns, hand-held under-barrel and mounted grenade launchers, portable anti-tank and anti-aircraft guns, recoilless rifles, portable launchers of anti-tank and anti-aircraft missile systems, and mortars of less than 100 mm calibre" [SAS (2001, p. 8)]. SALW are long-lasting capital items, wherefore stockpiles are large in relation to the annual flows of weapons production and withdrawal. Correspondingly, the market for ammunition – the most obvious firearms complement – is large as well. (Stockpiles and ammunition are discussed in Section 3.2.)

The Small Arms Survey is the world's foremost data collector and analyst on SALW, fulfilling for small arms the role that SIPRI fulfills for major conventional weapons. The *Survey* provides annually updated information on small arms and light weapons products, producers, stockpiles, trade, and related issues. Since the *Survey* began publishing only in 2001, time-series data that could be used for purposes of inferential statistics are not yet available.

The SALW industry is the most widely distributed segment of the arms industry. Producers of small arms, light weapons, or associated ammunition comprise at least 1,249 companies in more than 90 states [SAS (2004)], including many non-high income states. At least 25 states host illicit (as opposed to legal or legally licensed) small arms manufacturing sites, including such unlikely states as Trinidad and Tobago. Craft or homemade small arms production is not uncommon, for example in Afghanistan and Pakistan. In South Africa, between 1994 and 1999, of 106,000 illegally owned weapons seized by government authorities, 16 percent were homemade.

During the Cold War, the SALW market was duopolistic, dominated by the United States and the Soviet Union. Since then the market has fragmented [Duffield (2001, p. 172)]. Major producers now are high income states such as Austria, Belgium, France, Germany, the United Kingdom, Israel, Italy, Switzerland, and the United States, and non-high income states such as Russia and probably China. The precise reasons for the industry's fragmentation remain uninvestigated, but reasonable hypotheses would include, on the demand-side, the explosion of civil wars, usually fought with SALW, and, on the supply-side, the pursuit of new markets for high income states' weapons products. From the 1980s to the 1990s the number of states and the number of companies producing SALW has been growing. Formerly stable supplier-recipient relations in the legal SALW market have become unstable as selling and acquisition have shifted from political to economic motives [Mussington (1994, p. 163)]. Even the covert small arms market has shifted from global suppliers to regional suppliers (e.g., from Uganda to Rwanda; from Uzbekistan to Tajikistan). One economic reason for this is that the conduct of covert trade carries political risks (e.g., the Iran-Contra arms trade scandal in the United States in the 1980s). That risk is mitigated when arms flow through other countries, and neighbors to states in conflict are best placed to facilitate such flows. Another reason pertains to the complex of issues related to regime security, the provision of security services, and violence-based natural resource extraction and wealth creation, all of which are highly localized affairs that correspondingly encourage the "localization" of the SALW trade [Duffield (2001), Cooper (2006)].

3.2. Trade values, production volumes, stockpiles, and prices

Market value estimates are difficult to establish as even the legal part of the market lacks transparency. Some data for the legal SALW trade (including ammunition) can be obtained from national export reports and from the United Nation's COMTRADE database which, however, relies on voluntary national customs reports and suffers from known defects that result in an understatement of the size of the legal trade. North American and west European states tend to report with some regularity but other major SALW exporters and importers do not. For 2001, the value of documented legal SALW exports amounted to US$2.4 billion [SAS (2004, p. 100)].[23] This is based on the UN's Harmonized System (HS) of reporting. Another estimate for 2001, based on the UN's SITC (Standard Industrial Trade Classification) code, arrives at a US$2.8 billion estimate [SAS (2004, p. 107)], the difference being accounted for by slightly varying definitions used in the HS and SITC codes. Both definitions are more restrictive than the SALW definition offered at the beginning of Section 3.1. When one includes additional SITC codes to capture additional customs transactions related to small arms, the average annual value of the legal SALW trade is thought to lie between US$5–7 billion for 1994–2001 (in constant 2001 US$), similar to the annual world trade in sports

---

[23] The Small Arms Survey numbers are based on the Norwegian Initiative on Small Arms Transfers (see www.nisat.org).

footwear or frozen fish [SAS (2004, p. 107)]. While this would capture certain military and non-military weaponry in addition to SALW, and would therefore overstate the legal SALW trade, it is also strongly suspected that states hide substantial weapon transfers in innocuous-sounding SITC codes. For example, the SITC "C2" group records customs transactions for swords, cutlasses, bayonets, lances, and parts thereof, in addition to air-guns, rifles, pistols, and truncheons. But it is not credible that between 1994 and 2001, the Netherlands, Germany, the United Kingdom, and others would have traded hundreds of millions of dollars worth of swords and bayonets, as the SITC transaction records suggest. In addition to the annual legal US\$5–7 billion SALW trade, the covert, grey, and black markets are thought to constitute an additional 10–20 percent, say, US\$1 billion [SAS (2001, pp. 165–168)]. Of the entire trade, the annual global ammunition market is thought to be worth more than the annual global market of the weaponry itself [SAS (2001, p. 15)].

SALW production volume estimates suggest at least 120 million units produced from 1980–1998 [SAS (2001, p. 13)]. The number of SALW products is multiplying and new weapon designs are introduced in part to facilitate the modernization of armed forces in the post-Cold War world. The shrinking size of post-Cold War armies, moreover, has led to surplus weapons being sold (to recover revenue in an era of shrinking defense budgets) and thus being recycled into a burgeoning secondary market [SAS (2004, p. 57)]. Prices of the AK47 assault rifle have been recorded as low as US\$15 [Duffield (2001, p. 172)].[24] However, unlike other commodity prices, weapon prices are not systematically collected, foreclosing certain research avenues. A welcome exception is Killicoat's data collection effort [Killicoat (2006))] which reports that AK47 prices in civil-war afflicted states have been constant in current terms (or falling in real terms) between 1990 and 2005, while prices in non-civil war states have increased in current terms. (See Table 4 for a listing of black market prices in selected states.)

The SALW global stockpile has grown to about 640 million units for small arms alone (i.e., not counting light weapons), even as the market for annual production has fallen in size and value [Khakee and Wulf (2005)]. Intentional weapon collection and destruction programs, such as those conducted in association with combatant disarmament, demobilization, and reintegration (DDR), snare relatively few weapons.[25] On occasion, DDR processes have been mismanaged and collected weapons recycled onto the market [SAS (2005, p. 284)]. Stockpile security is exceptionally low. Catastrophic state collapse, such as in Somalia 1991–2 and Iraq 2003, have resulted in the looting of millions of military, police, border, intelligence, and other service weapons. In Albania, in 1997, some 750,000 weapons were thus looted, about 80 percent of the national stockpile [Duffield (2001, p. 171)], an important precursor to the arming of ethnic Albanians in neighboring Kosovo and the ensuing war there that ended with a 78-day US-led NATO air war campaign in early 1999. Even in stable but otherwise poor states, hundreds of thousands of

---

[24] At one point in 2003, an Arab source reports that in Basra, in southern Iraq, AK47's briefly "traded" for a price of zero [SAS (2004, p. 48)].

[25] From the mid-1990s to the mid-2000s, only about 8 million out of 640 million [see SAS (2004, p. 58)].

Table 4
Black market prices for AK47 assault rifle, selected states, current US$ (1990–2005)*

State/year	1990	1995	2000	2005	State/year	1990	1995	2000	2005
Afghanistan	80	100	100	150	Liberia	100	100	100	45
Algeria	400	400	300	200	Mozambique	160	60	15	30
Argentina	800	700	1,000	1,200	Pakistan	120	200	200	280
Belarus	150	250	140	160	Philippines	250	300	300	328
Botswana	200	250	200	200	Sierra Leone	270	150	120	100
Colombia	609	800	350	400	Singapore	1,200	1,200	1,500	1,500
Congo, DR	200	215	120	50	Somalia	165	200	120	160
Cote d'Ivoire	180	100	100	120	South Africa	160	200	195	180
Croatia	330	180	250	300	Sudan	150	150	100	86
Iraq	300	250	250	150	United States	420	450	480	500
Israel	2,500	3,000	2,800	3,000	Zimbabwe	200	250	200	150
Kenya	500	100	200	150					
All states**	448	425	559	534					
– civil war	382	376	378	348					
– no civil war	530	464	669	655					
– all African states	235	177	139	140					

Source: Killicoat (2006).
*The data were kindly provided by Mr. Killicoat.
**Sample size varies by year.

weapons are lost annually through graft and theft by officials and uniformed personnel alike [SAS (2004, p. 56)]. Further numbers are stolen from civilian homes and recycled onto the black market. Governments are only slowly instituting reform measures to track ownership, possession, and trade.

Ammunition production, like weapons production, is widely dispersed across the globe. At least 76 states produce small-caliber munitions [SAS (2005, p. 13)]. The companies that produce ammunition are generally not those that produce the weapons [SAS (2005, p. 13)]. The two industries are separate from each other (as is the small arms industry from the light weapons industry). Small arms ammunition consists of primer, propellent, projectile, and a casing, each of which in turn tends to be produced in distinct industries; ammunition factories are often no more than assemblers of the final product [SAS (2005, chapter 1)]. Technologically, ammunition production is generally simpler than the production of the corresponding weapon, requiring little more than simple explosives and basic metal fabrication skills, even if to some tolerances. Production machinery is widely available on the world manufacturing market. This suggests low industry-entry costs and considerable scope for competitive pricing. Nonetheless, the number of primer producers worldwide is small, apparently in part because primer production involves more complex skills and tools than other ammunition components [SAS (2005, pp. 13, 30)]. There is some evidence that, as for the case of major conventional weapons, the more industrially capable a state, the more likely that it will be engaged in ammunition production.

3.3. *Supply, technology, diffusion*

In spite of falling annual production runs, SALW production is dispersing across more suppliers and more states. The requisite technology is often simple (more so for small arms than for light weapons), and production costs can be quite low. The AK47 assault rifle for instance, designed in 1947, received a much disregarded patent only in 1999; its design simplicity – it has only nine moving parts – has spawned widespread design copying, and it can be manufactured for well below US$100/unit [SAS (2001, p. 17)]. Few specifics are known about the underlying production technology and its diffusion over time and geography. Licensing of SALW appears commonplace, perhaps more so than for major conventional weapons, and in a number of cases has led to the complete transfer of production lines overseas. By way of example, production of man-portable air defense systems (MANPADS) – a relatively sophisticated product – has migrated in the form of derivatives, copies, or licensed production from China to Pakistan and North Korea, from Russia to China, Egypt, Romania, Bulgaria, North Korea, Poland, and Vietnam, and from Sweden to Pakistan [SAS (2004, Table 3.2, p. 82)]. Among assault rifles, the Kalashnikov AK series has been licensed to at least 19 states, Hechler & Koch's G3 to at least 18 states, and Herstal's FN-FAL to at least 15 states [SAS (2001, Table 1.4, p. 20) where additional examples may be found]. Unlike for the case of major conventional arms, a large number of non-high income states have become successful exporters of SALW produced under license [SAS (2002, pp. 40–54)].

SALW production and diffusion do not appear to have been specifically theorized in the economics literature. An initial hypothesis might simply pose that firms in high income states run against "horizontal boundaries". Economies of scale and scope having been exploited at home, the profit-maximizing move might be to transfer mature product lines overseas.[26] The original manufacturer gains license fees, increasing the return on the initial R&D, while freeing up limited design and production capacity for new product lines and redeploying skilled personnel to higher-valued pursuits. Vernon (1966) emphasized that mature product lines also migrate out-of-state to better capture information available in local markets and thus to adapt the product to local needs: "... producers in any market are more likely to be aware of the possibility of introducing new products in that market than producers located elsewhere would be" [Vernon (1966, p. 192)]. Licensing can also be used to circumvent home-state export restrictions and to compete for market share overseas. For the licensee, advantages include domestic production using proven design and technology, thus curtailing the economic risk of self-production or the economic cost of imports.

The product life-cycle hypothesis hints at why the thought that small arms technology has reached a technological plateau and is "likely to remain on this plateau for years to come" [SAS (2004, p. 20)] is perhaps wrong. The basic firearm platform may not have changed much in 50 years, but innovations and add-ons have drastically increased the portability, durability, range, accuracy, and penetrating power of firearms

---

[26] This is Vernon's (1966) product life-cycle hypothesis.

[see also SAS (2003, pp. 20–25)]. The trajectory may instead be one of incremental advance within a mature technology, similar to the way that innovations in complementary electronics have enhanced performance for example of unmanned aerial vehicles. Significant advances in materials science, precision production processes, and weapons and ammunition design include innovations such as sound and flash suppression technology, night scopes, armor-piercing ammunition, and fragmenting munitions. Moreover, add-ons such as range finders, laser targeting, and rapid fire mechanisms enhance the weapon as well. For armed forces, all such innovations are associated with the search for increased battlefield flexibility and higher kill-per-shot "productivity", but for R&D-intensive *producers* they represent the employment of scarce resources better not spent on maintaining mature product lines. It is thus likely that these innovations, once they in turn mature, will find their way from producers in high income states to those located in non-high income states. In addition to the assault rifle and MANPAD cases mentioned earlier, another example is that of the RPG-7, a more than 40-year old rocket-propelled grenade launcher design, variants and derivatives of and ammunition for which now are produced by at least 11 non-high income states. The low cost of the weapon (used: US$10), its rugged design, light weight, and easy upgradability for a variety of cheap munitions make it a preferred weapon for state and non-state actors alike.[27]

Ammunition is a complement to SALW. It is frequently the ammunition, not the weapon, that is the limiting factor to SALW use, misuse, and abuse [SAS (2005)]. For instance, during the 1994 Rwandan genocide, victims often were rounded up with firearms but slaughtered with bladed weapons to conserve ammunition (i.e., the lack of the firearms complement induced weapons substitution). Groups elsewhere, for example in Mali, have been documented to source or craft-produce weapons to fit munitions stolen from police or military depots. Ammunition has limited shelf-life as propellents degrade, especially when improperly stored in the more extreme environmental conditions found in many non-high income states. Also, the cost of ammunition – a consumable – can quickly outweigh the cost of the weapon, so much so that cash-strapped groups have been documented to severely punish group members for injudicious ammunition use [SAS (2005, pp. 18–20)]. Not much is known about SALW training, maintenance, and repair (TMR) requirements, another complement to SALW. One would predict that the higher the TMR cost, the less pervasive the spread and penetration of SALW throughout the world. Anecdotal evidence would support this view. A case study on MANPADS for instance suggests that training requirements for proper operation are extensive [SAS (2004, p. 85)].

Supplier, intermediary, and recipient states – or actors in those states – each need to deal with different, if any, small-arms related laws and regulations. It is not straightforward to determine whether any particular SALW trade is a legal, covert, grey, or black market activity. An arms transfer from a state to a broker may be legal under the transferring state's laws, but the broker's follow-on trade through intermediaries may not be

---

[27] Non-high income state RPG-7 producers: Bulgaria, China, Egypt, Iran, Iraq, Pakistan, Poland, Romania, Russia, Slovakia, and Thailand [SAS (2004, pp. 35–37, especially Table 1.11)].

well regulated (a grey market), and the arms may be imported altogether illegally into the ultimate recipient state (a black market). One commentator writes that the market relies as much on powerful law-breakers as on weak law-makers [Bourne (2005)]. For example, only 25 states have implemented explicit laws or regulations regarding arms brokering [SAS (2004, pp. 142, 161)], and they differ widely in reporting requirements, monitoring, verification, compliance, and enforcement. At the international level, only in July 2001 did some member states of the United Nations agree on a "Programme of Action to Prevent, Combat and Eradicate the Illicit Trade in Small Arms and Light Weapons in All Its Aspects". Biennial meetings of states in 2003 and 2005 have resulted in limited progress on agreed-upon actions. The overall regulatory environment remains weak. There would be opportunities to apply economic theory developed with regard to other global challenges, say on international environmental regulation, to the case of international arms trade regulation but this does not appear to have been done to date [see, e.g., Sandler (1997)].

3.4. The demand for small arms and light weapons

Until the mid-2000s, the SALW demand side was ignored with virtually no economics papers available even as the standard neoclassical theory of consumer demand suffices to generate a first cut at understanding the demand side.[28] At the level of the individual, the primary determinants of demand are preferences, resources, and the prices of SALW and their complements and substitutes.[29] To understand why people acquire small arms is as important as to understand why they do not. From the difference in the choice behavior we may expect to learn what accounts for the switched state. For example, the removal of certain constraints associated with the end of apartheid in South Africa in 1994 unleashed an explosive expression of previously "hidden" demand for small arms. This has been difficult to reverse. In contrast, some communities have been penetrated with arms to only a small extent [e.g., Kyrgyzstan; see SAS (2004, chapter 10)].

A gun is most "productive" in defensive or predatory situations when it is cycled among several users, but groups of people (families, clans, gangs, police forces, etc.) must develop an effective internal control mechanism to prevent gun abuse within the group. Research on how groups maintain internal cohesion and prevent within-group gun abuse may provide important clues to unraveling SALW demand in larger social entities. The huge literature on the economics of crime has yet to be exploited to learn what lessons may be transferable to the small arms demand research field [see, e.g., Cook and Ludwig (2000), Hemenway (2004)].

Final demand for self-defense, recreation, or sport-hunting purposes needs to be separated from derived demand by those for whom weapons are an input into the production

---

[28] This section relies on Brauer and Muggah (2006).

[29] Collier et al. (2003) discuss demand factors such as the relation of natural resource wealth to civil war and hence small arms demand.

of goods or services such as commercial hunting, pest-control, or security services, or the production of disservices such as banditry. These broad categories of demanders should not be conflated, not only because the underlying preferences differ but also because the means both groups bring to bear on demand are vastly different. We would expect gun collectors for instance to finance gun acquisition from earned income or by trading one asset for another, e.g., to liquidate financial holdings for a gun collection, hoping that the latter will appreciate faster than the former. Consumers need to consider the tradeoff of resource expenditure on a gun to resource expenditure on other goods and services. Thus, even in the presence of high motivation, limited resources and high gun (or ammunition) prices erect an effective barrier to acquisition. In contrast, producers, e.g., those with the intent to abuse small arms for criminal purposes, view guns as a tool that earns a return on investment. Thus, the demand for small arms by these two groups of acquirers would be expected to follow markedly different trajectories and dynamics. Theory would also suggest that producers of armed violence would search more actively than final demanders for improved technologies of violence – hardier, lighter, more easily concealed, and more powerful firearms. Effective regulation of a bad or disservice requires a capable and effective enforcement apparatus, but it is precisely the absence of this apparatus that provides the space that brings producers of violence into sustained existence.

Demand-related basic data collection and empirical studies have been carried out only as from the mid-2000s, primarily as case studies commissioned by the Small Arms Survey. Field-based research has been planned for a number of non-high income states, e.g., Burundi, Congo-Brazzaville, Macedonia, and Sudan, and initial research has been completed for non-high income states such as the Brazil, Papua New Guinea, the Solomon Islands, and South Africa [Nelson and Muggah (2004), Muggah (2004), Kirsten et al. (2004), Lessing (2005)]. Each case highlights different aspects of how motivations and means combine to stimulate or inhibit small arms acquisition or (ab)use. For example, in Papua New Guinea (PNG) the comparatively recent arrival and use of modern firearms has escalated traditional forms of violent conflict to levels that threaten to exceed local capacities to cope. While the range of types of firearms is surprisingly diverse, field study found that the numbers of such arms are comparatively modest, at least in part because of unusually high ammunition prices. This is an intriguing finding as it points to the possibility that at least in some cases policy intervention may most usefully focus not on firearms *per se* but on the supply-chain or on complementary products and services [SAS (2005, chapter 1)].

Field research has also documented interesting dynamics of local trade in small arms. In PNG, income and assets of various types (e.g., pigs, crops, and women) were found to be exchanged for firearms. Thus, the means of small arms acquisition refer not only to the exchange of earned income for arms but include grants, loans, and the depletion of unusual assets. Further, key informant interviews in PNG revealed weapon acquisition not only by individuals but also by village or tribal collectives, and surveys showed that tribes would readily rent weapons, or the services of mercenaries, to pursue violent armed conflict with neighbors. Given their high motivations and limited means, the tribes display sophisticated choice behavior to achieve their objectives. The endemic nature of violence among PNG tribes may reduce the likelihood of success for individual preference or motivations-based demand intervention. Rather, in this case initiatives may be more successful if they focus resources on raising the price of firearms, ammunition, and related repair and service, as well as raising the price of firearm (ab)use through strict and accountable law enforcement, a strategy that appears to have bourne some fruit in the Solomon Islands [see Brauer and Muggah (2006)].

Data on the distribution of SALW by user category is difficult to come by, mostly because estimation of ownership by unregistered and/or illegal owners involves large uncertainties. To cite just one example, for 2003 for 11 Latin American states one estimate suggests 8.8 million firearms in possession by uniformed (military and police) forces. This contrasts to 11.6 million civilian registered firearms and an additional estimated 25 to 60 million civilian unregistered firearms [SAS (2004, Table 2.2, p. 51)]. Similarly lop-sided distributions are obtained virtually whenever an estimate is attempted. Overall, the civilian market is estimated at 80 percent of the overall market [SAS (2004, p. 21)].

In sum, the SALW market has not been well examined theoretically or empirically. Nor is the raw material of underlying data conducive to testing whatever hypotheses theory might generate. Diplomats' work has focused – as for the case of the other weapons classes – on supply-side regulation such as arms trade and weapons registries and non-proliferation schemes. Unfortunately, as production technologies migrate, the states with the weakest capacity to create and enforce supply-side regulations are also the states where most of the SALW problems lie. This does not make supply-side research superfluous – it is certainly worth learning more about the mechanics of the diffusion of weapons production and trade and associated complements – but if effective small arms and violence control policies are to be found, research on the demand-side as well as on intermediate markets along the supply-chain will have to play a much bigger part than has been the case thus far.

4. Non-conventional weapons

4.1. Atomic weapons

A number of non-high income states are or have been engaged in the production of atomic, biological, and chemical – or ABC – weapons.[30] Economic information beyond basic count data (who produces what) is scant. For example, a certain well-stocked

---

[30] Atomic weapons belong to the larger rubric of radiological weapons. A radiological weapon is any combination of an agent and a distribution device capable of causing radiological contamination. Thus defined, release of any radioactive material (e.g., materials used in nuclear medicine) through any distribution device (e.g., dynamite) would count as a radiological weapon. In practice, such weapons still are restricted to atomic bombs, hence the limitation in this section on these weapons.

defense academy library carries over a dozen books on Pakistan's atomic program – half of them published in Pakistan – but in none of them does one find any reasonably derived program cost or budget information. One estimate, based on United Nations Special Commission (UNSCOM) mission data for Iraq, puts Pakistan's annual cost for its program, started in 1972, at between US$500–700 million, not counting the cost for delivery systems [Mian (1995, p. 63)]. Even an up-to-date encyclopedia on weapons of mass destruction [Croddy, Wirtz and Larsen (2005)], while carrying information on actual weapons and delivery types and technology, carries virtually no economic content. One can conclude only that when states do demonstrate possession of non-conventional weapons they have obviously achieved their production – at whatever cost. Regarding trade, spectacular information comes to light occasionally, as when Pakistan's Abdul Qadeer Khan's illicit nuclear proliferation network was exposed in 2003. As for the case of major conventional weapons, an arms embargo spurs the drive to find substitute suppliers. For example, Pakistan first approached the United States to acquire facilities to produce weapons-grade plutonium. Rebuffed, Pakistan redirected its efforts and eventually succeeded with technical assistance from China and North Korea and financial assistance by Libya and Saudi Arabia [Lavoy (2005, pp. 275–276)]. Abdul Qadeer Khan received training in Germany, and Germany and Canada provided pre-cursor nuclear technology [Langford (2004, p. 72)]. And US-supplied F-16 and French-supplied Mirage-5 jets provided the weapons-delivery capability. But because of an embargo placed on the F-16 in 1990, Pakistan substituted these by commencing its ballistic missile program, again with Chinese and North Korean help. By 2005, more than two dozen nations were in possession of ballistic missiles and, although an old design, almost 30 states had either purchased the SCUD missile or purchased the underlying technology to develop their own versions.

A similar story can be told for South Africa which, under an international arms trade ban, developed its own atomic weapons capability, using pre-cursor technology from the United States and France. The United States detected a low-yield, high-altitude nuclear explosion off South Africa's coast in 1979 but programs details, including suspected atomic trade relations to Israel, are unknown. South Korea also dabbled in atomic weapons manufacture but abandoned its efforts under US pressure in 1972. India's atomic program was built with pre-cursor assistance from Canada, France, Russia, and the United States. As for the case of South Africa, many of its scientists were US trained [Langford (2004, pp. 70–72)]. Before it was expelled from Iraq, UNSCOM documented Iraqi trade in atomic weapons-related equipment and physically destroyed or removed 48 operational missiles, six operational mobile launchers, 28 operational fixed launch pads, 32 fixed launch pads under construction, and other missile support equipment and materials [Segell (2005, p. 390)]. While Iraq's program strained its industrial capacity, it was able to acquire by trade much preparatory material although at unknown cost.

According to the Nuclear Threat Initiative, the following current or former non-high income states have or have had weapons-related atomic programs or functional atomic weapons: Argentina, Belarus, Brazil, China, Egypt, India, Iran, Iraq, Israel, Kazakhstan,

Libya, North Korea, Pakistan, Russia, South Africa, South Korea, Taiwan, Ukraine, Uzbekistan, and Yugoslavia.[31] Of these, Argentina, Brazil, Iraq, Libya, South Africa, South Korea, and Taiwan have withdrawn from their respective efforts[32]; Israel has never publicly acknowledged such production; Iran's efforts are widely rumored but not factually confirmed; North Korea has announced possession of atomic weapons and appears to have carried out a nuclear test explosion in October 2006; and China, India, and Pakistan all have tested atomic weapons and are known to possess delivery vehicles and targeting technology. The latter – delivery and targeting – are complementary to atomic weaponry and constitute a substantial technological hurdle to overcome (see Section 4.4).

While supply-side control of critical input technologies has slowed weapons proliferation, the idea of non-proliferation does not appear to have worked. Under perceived duress or threat even states with scant industrial and human resources have made obvious progress toward the production of such weapons. Entry into this industry is possible, even if at unknown but probably enormous cost, perhaps explaining why some states have chosen to exit this segment of the market (Brazil, Libya, and South Africa) or to rid themselves of their inheritance (Belarus, Kazakhstan, Ukraine) when their political situation and threat perception changed.

4.2. Biological weapons

Regarding biological weapons, 147 states are party to the 1972 Biological and Toxin Weapons Convention (BTWC). Entered into force in 1975, it prohibits the development, production, and stockpiling of biological weapons (BW). Some states have signed but not ratified the BTWC, e.g., Syria. Unlike the CWC (see Section 4.3), the treaty does not provide for a verification protocol, and it is not anticipated that such will be achieved during the next 10 or 20 years. This has led states to engage in confidence-building measures and to invest in biosecurity initiatives. Confidence-building measures include annual declarations and reports regarding high-risk facilities, outbreaks of unusual diseases, promotion and publication of relevant research, and cross-state scientific interaction. However, since 1986 fewer than 40 states regularly issue such declarations, with most non-high income states abstaining [Croddy (2005a, pp. 43–47)].

Iran, Iraq, Libya, South Africa, and the former Soviet Union are known to have developed and/or used biological weapons. India is known to possess a defensive bioweapons

---

[31] Syria is sometimes alleged to be among this group, but according to the Nuclear Threat Initiative there is no evidence to support this assertion. The evidence regarding Egypt is only slightly stronger. For all other states mentioned, the programs and/or weapons are either publicly known or else the evidence is deemed compelling.

[32] On 7 August 2005, former Brazilian President Jose Sarney publicly acknowledged that Brazil had an active atomic weapons program under its military dictatorship phase, 1964–1985. This was Brazil's first public acknowledgment of its erstwhile program (Andrew Hay, Reuters news story, 8 August 2005). Three weeks later, Jose Luiz Santana, former president of Brazil's nuclear energy commission publicly stated that the military were "preparing a test explosion" when the program was stopped and dismantled in August 1990 (Michael Astor, Associated Press news story, 30 August 2005).

research program. BW activity is alleged for China, Cuba, Egypt, and North Korea. Of the Soviet follow-on states, Belarus, Ukraine, and Uzbekistan have eliminated or are eliminating BW sites. The situation in Kazakhstan is unclear.[33] Brazil, Pakistan, and Russia have undisputed BW potentials but there is no convincing evidence that this has been used to research or manufacture BW agents. On Syria's and Taiwan's BW intentions and/or capabilities there are conflicting reports.

Today, the only practical (efficient) mass-dispersal method of delivering biological weapon agents – i.e., bacteria, viruses, and toxins – is thought to be through the use of infectious aerosols. But processing of biological materials to requisite diameters of between 1 and 10 microns, while maintaining viability in storage and dispersal, is considered to be "technically demanding" [Croddy (2005b, p. 53)]. Small-scale biological weapons production probably does not lie beyond the scientific and industrial capabilities of certain non-high income state-actors but as yet appears to carry little military or diplomatic value as compared to alternative applications of scarce military-related resources.

4.3. Chemical weapons

The Organization for the Prohibition of Chemical Weapons (OPCW) implements the provisions of the 1993 Convention on the Prohibition of the Development, Production, Stockpiling, and Use of Chemical Weapons and on their Destruction (CWC, for short).[34] As of 31 December 2004, 167 states have ratified the treaty. Among non-signatories are Egypt, Iraq, North Korea, and Syria. Of these, Iraq and Syria are known to have acquired (the latter through Egypt), produced, and/or used chemical weapons. So has Libya, but on 19 December 2003 it renounced the production and use of weapons of mass destruction and signed the CWC in 2004 (it still needs to ratify the treaty). Israel has signed but not ratified the treaty. The CWC includes an "anytime, anywhere" inspection provision and as of December 2002, 1,276 inspections at 5,237 declared sites had been carried out. Five states declared possession of chemical weapons stockpiles, to be destroyed within 10 to 15 years. By early 2005, twelve CWC members had declared more than 60 former chemical weapons production facilities; ten states declared possession of "old", i.e., pre-1946, chemical weapons; and three declared harboring "abandoned" chemical weapons deposited there by other states party to the CWC (the largest, over a million munitions, by Japan in China).[35]

---

[33] It has received United States funding to dismantle sites but still holds "extensive collections of virulent strains of human, animal, and plant pathogens" [Nuclear Threat Initiative; www.nti.org (accessed 31 August 2005)].

[34] Explosives are chemical weapons of course but are not covered by CWC. Military analysts consider thermobaric (fuel–air) explosives used by the United States and Russia (e.g., in the 1990s in Iraq and in Chechnya, respectively) as equivalent to low-yield tactical nuclear weapons [Clark (2005)]. Likewise, atomic weapons rely on physical properties (e.g., shockwaves) of chemical reactions and are not considered chemical weapons.

[35] Declared stockpiles: in Albania, the United States, Russia, India, and South Korea; former production facilities: in Bosnia-Herzegovina, China, France, India, Iran, Japan, Libya, Russia, Serbia and Montenegro,

Although there are limitations on what must be declared, and vigilance must be maintained regarding future chemical weapons production, it is generally thought that the CWC and its supervision, advice, and inspection regime work well.[36] The OPCW secretariat has about 500 employees and, for 2005, a €75 million budget [Hart (2005, pp. 93–96), SIPRI (2005, chapter 13)]. Nonetheless, a report in *Science* expresses concern about rapidly advancing production technology, such as "miniaturized reaction systems for chemical synthesis and production ... [with] dimensions ranging from credit card size to notebook size" [Nguyen (2005, p. 1021)]. Several lethal compounds are known to have been produced in this way. Chemical warfare agents are grouped into choking, blister, blood (systemic), and nerve agents. Other agents, such as incapacitants (riot-control agents), are considered non-lethal in the intended dosage. Their use as a method of warfare is forbidden under the CWC.

Little is known about production and delivery costs of biological and chemical weapons but as compared to atomic weapons they are generally believed to be easier and cheaper to produce. However, this does not necessarily make it easier or cheaper to deliver such weapons. For long-distance regional or intercontinental ballistic missile use for instance, in addition to solving the same long-distance delivery problems as for atomic weapons, biological agents will need to be suitably refrigerated and protected during re-entry and subsequent high-speed dispersal. Heat generated during an explosion can destroy biological or chemical agents. To prevent this, complex spray dispersal methods are needed. Furthermore, unlike for the case of atomic explosions, suitable meteorological and topological conditions must be present for CBW agents to bring about the intended effects. Some analysts thus believe that the operational utility of CBWs for state actors in state-on-state warfare is questionable [Enders and Sandler (2006), Davis (2005, p. 85), Spiers (2000, pp. 57–75)]. The general absence of their use by state actors in war is indicative.[37] However, studies in the operational use of non-conventional weapons for small-scale use in geographically limited environments (e.g., points of troop disembarkation) are advancing rapidly and are in the public domain. Combined with equally rapidly developing molecular biology, chemical, and delivery-technology engineering knowledge and its dispersion through open-access science has analysts concerned that substitution into asymmetric weaponry by non-high income states and non-state actors is attractive, even likely. The more overwhelming a potential

---

South Korea, the United Kingdom, and the United States; possession of pre-1946 CW: in Australia, Belgium, Canada, France, Germany, Italy, Japan, Slovenia, the United Kingdom, and the United States; abandoned CW: in China, Italy, Panama.

[36] Intransigent states such as Iran (atomic weapons), Iraq (atomic, biological, and chemical weapons), and North Korea (atomic weapons) can obviously delay inspection regimes which increases the burden placed on the reliability of intelligence information.

[37] Libya's prime minister reportedly cited ABC-program cost as compared to the expected military and political benefit of the resulting weapons as the reason for the country's 19 December 2003 decision to renounce weapons of mass destruction; similarly Gaddafi in a *Le Figaro* interview in November 2004 [SIPRI (2005, pp. 633–634)].

adversaries' conventional force advantage, the more compelling the option to substitute into alternative weaponry becomes. The binding constraint appears to be neither cost nor production capability but organizational and statutory: the development of a new warfare doctrine using cheap, novel, and unconventional weaponry might require a complete overhaul of the armed services partition into army, navy, and air force and would probably require formal withdrawal from the BTWC and CWC that most, but not all, states have signed and ratified.

The weapons are also attractive for state covert operations. South Africa's Project Coast (later, Project Jota) included one CW and one BW production site, the former with 120 staff members, the latter with 70. Work focused on chemical incapacitants and bioregulators to affect physiological function. The resulting agents are suspected to have been employed in Mozambique and Namibia, border states to South Africa, but the most direct application is reported to have been the use of hard-to-trace agents against individual "enemies of the state" [Bale (2005, p. 268)].

4.4. Missile technology and space-based activities

A complement to work on atomic and, although to a lesser extent, biological and chemical weapons is work on delivery technology, especially but not only with regard to missiles and missile technology. States such as Brazil, China, India, North Korea, Pakistan, Russia, and South Africa have been able to make substantial indigenous strides in this regard. Some of them have rendered assistance to states such as Syria that are thought to have tried but been unable to produce missiles with completely indigenous resources. Having no illusion about the outcome if it became entangled in a conventional war with Israel, Syria has the motivation to develop alternative war-fighting means. Yet despite 30 years of effort, it apparently does not possess the economic wherewithal to do so. Comparing Syria to states that have had a measure of success, such as Iraq, might make it possible to deduce, at least qualitatively, the relevant success threshold even in the absence of specific weapons-related cost and production data.

Cost (or export revenue) information on ballistic missiles is not reliably available. SIPRI notes scattered prices, mostly below US$2 million per unit. For these missiles, however, pay-load is small and target inaccuracy high. When fitted with conventional warheads, the weapons would therefore not be suitable for war-fighting, and their value may be psychological rather than military [SIPRI (2004, pp. 554–555)]. Fitted with ABC-weapons, target accuracy becomes less important. But if fitted with accurate guidance systems, ballistic missiles with conventional warheads become more valuable. It is generally held that such systems will shortly become widely available at commercial (i.e., market-based competitive) prices. Still, missiles are complicated devices requiring a host of inputs such as special fuels, engines, warheads, re-entry vehicles, and guidance systems so that competitive exports by non-high incomes states may yet lie a while into the future.

Quite a bit of information on non-high income states' space-related production activities is available but it is scatted and unsystematic. This information rarely comes with

any sort of cost figures or information regarding human and physical input requirements. Only three states – China, Russia, and the United States – have active military
space programs and only the United States has the capability to weaponize satellites.
This requires expensive logistics that presently no state other than the United States
can afford [UNIDIR (2003, p. 6)]. Still, as has been the case for conventional weapons,
"rapid growth in commercial space activities and the inherently dual-use nature of most
space systems" [Hays (2003, p. 22)] will increasingly subject space to economies of
scale and scope and hence primarily to economic rather than to political opportunities
and constraints. For example, high-resolution space-based photography is readily and
cheaply available from the commercial sector, whereas only a few years ago use of such
intelligence assets were restricted to the then-superpowers. Thus the militarization of
space – the use of outer space for military purposes – if not the weaponization of space
is already happening.

A typology divides military space missions into (a) space support, (b) force enhancement, (c) space control, and (d) force application missions [Hays (2003)]. By
the mid-2000s, no state has deployed weapons in space, nor can any assert control of
outer space (the ability to deny military use of space to others). But a number of states
have developed or are developing space support infrastructure to use space for force
enhancement, e.g., for integrated tactical warning and attack assessment and for intelligence, surveillance, and reconnaissance, and of course for communications, position,
velocity, time, and navigation (GPS) purposes.

Thirty-seven current or former non-high income states possess agencies, corporations, or facilities related to commercial, civilian, or military use of outer space.[38] Many
of the uses are for communication, navigation, and earth observation rather than for
military purposes and involve shared or cooperative ventures. For example, Nigeria
launched its first satellite in September 2003. While it provided little more than the
money, it is indicative of the globalized nature of even this market that it could purchase
the United Kingdom-built satellite and have it launched from Russia. Brazil curtailed its
ballistic missile research in the early 1990s and joined the Missile Technology Control
Regime but continues research on space launch vehicles. While much current space-
activity of non-high income states in benign, there is no doubt that at least some of the
current activity can be switched to military purposes.

4.5. ABC-weapons production and entry/exit theory

In the Cold War context, theoretical work was primarily directed toward nuclear arms
races and their threatened use, but this presumed the physical existence of the weapons

---

[38] They are: Algeria, Azerbaijan, Brazil, China, the Czech Republic, Egypt, Hungary, India, Indonesia, Iran,
Iraq, (Israel), Lebanon, Malaysia, Morocco, Nigeria, North Korea, Pakistan, the Philippines, Peru, Poland,
(Portugal), Russia, (Saudi Arabia), (Singapore), Slovakia, (Slovenia), South Africa, (South Korea), (Spain),
Syria, (Taiwan), Thailand, Tunisia, Turkey, Ukraine, and Uruguay. See www.globalsecurity.org [accessed 17
September 2005]. Former non-high income states are listed in parentheses.

[see, e.g., Brito and Intriligator (1995)]. The post-Cold War atomic weapons economics literature with regard to non-high income states is relatively thin. Singh and Way (2004) test a "theory of proliferation" with a model whose empirical variables include domestic political factors, the external security environment, and economic variables such as industrial capacity. Instead of a binary dependent variable, the option to "go nuclear" is stratified into four stages: (a) no interest in atomic weapons efforts, (b) exploration of an atomic weapons option, (c) active pursuit of atomic weapons acquisition, and (d) actual production of one or more atomic weapons. Covering 154 states with data from 1945 to 2000, ideally the model would predict not only the states interested in atomic weapons but also the time-path of the nuclear-weapons stage or stages any specific state may have taken. Despite some prediction misses, the model does a credible job of identifying which state enters which stage at which time. In particular, the model identifies threat perceptions (motivations) and industrial capacity (means) as the drivers in the decision to acquire atomic weapons. Not all states with the means to "go nuclear" have the motivation to do so; conversely, and worryingly, some states with the motivation to acquire nuclear arms may, in future, arrive at the means to do so.

The Singh and Way paper is a theory of entry, not of exit. Why and how a state may choose to dispose of nuclear weapons is not modeled [Singh and Way (2004, p. 883)]. Exit is modeled, even if only incidentally so, for the case of Ukraine in a paper by Jehiel, Moldovanu and Stacchetti (1996). Ukraine disposed of its nuclear inheritance by negotiations that matched the projected maintenance cost with dismantlement "aid" it could extract from Russia and the United States as against potential proliferation offers from other bidders. Part of the vertical contracting literature, the model captures a situation in which "buyers have preferences over which other agents may get the good" [Jehiel, Moldovanu and Stacchetti (1996, p. 815)] and asks about the optimal selling strategy when the ultimate buyer's acquisition generates negative externalities for non-buyers. For example, if Iran had bought Ukrainian atomic weapons, a negative externality would have been created for neighbors such as Iraq. One result of the model is that the seller can credibly commit not to sell at all. Instead of selling weapons, Ukraine sold dismantlement. The scenario is at least superficially similar to that of environmental protection groups purchasing pollution credits with the objective of removing them from circulation or of conservation societies purchasing patches of rainforest to withdraw them from potential cultivation.

Still, almost no theory work has been done with regard to the underlying production issues that bring atomic weapons into existence. One paper [Koubi (1999)] – based on the commercial R&D and patent literature – develops a three-stage military R&D race model. An important aspect of the model is that states are posited to monitor and react to their *relative* position in the race, as the outcome of the race carries implications for the distribution of military power. Unlike some commercial R&D races in which a winner-takes-all outcome may induce the losing competitor to switch resources into *another* R&D project, in the military R&D race there can be important benefits for the loser to catch up with the winner. Thus, the dynamics of the military race differ from that of the commercial race. In Koubi's model, the loser thus never concedes.

Instead, it intensifies its efforts the further behind it falls. Moreover, so long as any benefit is derived from eventual success, independent of the order of arriving at the finish line, a state will not unilaterally withdraw from the race [Koubi (1999, p. 545)].[39] An interesting application concerns the nuclear arms efforts in the non-high incomes states of China, India, and Pakistan. While the Indo-Pakistani nuclear test explosions in 1998 refocused world attention on that pair of states, India's policy is directed elsewhere: its efforts are not aimed at increasing the distance to Pakistan but at catching up with China, the more so since China assisted in the development of Pakistan's nuclear arsenal [Singh (1998)]. Koubi's model implies that if China races to catch up to the United States – possibly to snare Taiwan as the prize – then India races to catch China, and Pakistan races to catch India. Instead of viewing arms races as an n-state race where $n = 2$, as much of the literature has done (e.g., Greece–Turkey, or India–Pakistan), such races might better be viewed as n-state races where $n > 2$.

In sum, while some threat of development of biological and chemical weapons by non-high income state-actors remains, the major threat lies in the continuation of attempts to research, develop, and deploy atomic weapons atop ballistic missiles. The record is too faint to ascribe costs to the effort non-high income states undertake. But the record is clear in indicating several aspects of interest: (a) proliferation of atomic weapons-related technologies does take place; (b) some non-high income states successfully enter the industry; (c) atomic weapons arms races between and among non-high income states do take place; and (d) some non-high income states exit the atomic weapons industry, possibly irreversibly. As yet, a theory that would account for all four of these facts does not appear to have been formulated [Singh and Way (2004)].

5. Conclusion

Several themes emerge from the foregoing pages. First, data availability is poor for major conventional weapons, poorer for small arms and light weapons, and poorest for non-conventional weapons. Second, theory is not well developed regarding arms production and arms trade activities of non-high income states. An effort has been made here to show that models from outside the defense economics literature may be brought to bear to the subject matter: the vertical boundaries of the firm, the product life-cycle hypothesis, and the vertical contracting and R&D patent-race examples employed in this chapter all come from within the literature on the theory of the firm. Perhaps other field literatures may be parsed and tapped in a similar manner. Third, just as former non-high income states such as Greece, Israel, Portugal, Singapore, South Korea, Spain, and

---

[39] Koubi's model precludes consideration of a preemptive strike by the military R&D winner since this would be equivalent to a commercial winner-takes-all scenario. In this scenario, the loser is better off to stop its own efforts and redirect resources to another race. However, an avowed and credible *policy* of preemption may discourage laggards in the race from pursuit, or otherwise diminish laggards' intensity of effort, a scenario that may apply to the Middle East [Koubi (1999, p. 551)].

Taiwan graduated from low-level conventional arms production to become producers of reasonably sophisticated platforms, components, weapons, and weapon systems, so now we stand on the threshold of a number of current non-high income states being able to graduate toward the production of similarly advanced weapons. What might give pause is that the aforementioned set of states consists of small populations of inherently small economic and military weight. In contrast, current non-high income states such as Brazil, China, India, Indonesia, Malaysia, Pakistan, Russia, and South Africa pack much more potential economic and military weight. Economies of scale and scope may assume a more important role in arms production and trade dynamics than before as the internal market of these countries might now compete with those of the United States or of the European Union.

Fourth, although non-proliferation regimes have slowed weapons (or precursor-technology) proliferation, they have failed to stop it. Supply-side restrictions do not overcome demand-side pressures. We observe industry entry in all weapons categories and in future may expect to see further increases in industry participation by non-high income states, even if in a different form than hitherto (e.g., more cross-border integration of supply-chains). This is the natural consequence of the gradual development of states' human, physical, and institutional capital, i.e., the development of their production capacities. Given the means, all that is required is a motive to engage in indigenous arms production. This, fifth, puts an increasing burden on the quality of world diplomacy. The more readily available are the means to fight, and the more these means migrate to non-high income states and non-state actors, the more urgent for research and policy to address the formation of conflict-preferences and to study the design of effective self-policing or intervention mechanisms. Sixth, while all states benefit from the mutual production of mutual security, only in the rarest cases can it be said that non-high income states derive specific economic benefits from weapons production and associated trade.

References

Alexander, A.J., Butz, W.P., Mihalka, M. (1981). "Modeling the production and international trade of arms: An economic framework for analyzing policy alternatives". RAND Note N-1555-FF/RC. RAND, St. Monica, CA.

Anderton, C.H. (1995). "Economics of arms trade". In: Hartley, K., Sandler, T. (Eds.), Handbook of Defense Economics, vol. 1. North-Holland, Amsterdam, pp. 523–561.

Anderton, C.H. (1996). "What can international trade theory say about conventional arms trade?". Peace Economics, Peace Science and Public Policy 4 (1–2), 9–31.

Bale, J.M. (2005). "South Africa: Chemical and biological weapons programs". In: Croddy, E.A., Wirtz, J.J., Larsen, J.A. (Eds.), Weapons of Mass Destruction: An Encyclopedia of Worldwide Policy, Technology, and History, vol. 1. ABC-Clio, Santa Barbara, CA, pp. 266–269.

Baskaran, A. (2004). "The role of offsets in Indian defense procurement policy". In: Brauer, J., Dunne, J.P. (Eds.), Arms Trade and Economic Development: Theory, Policy, and Cases in Arms Trade Offsets. Routledge, London, pp. 217–232.

Bauer, S. (2006). European Arms Export Policies and Democratic Accountability. Oxford University Press, Oxford.

Besanko, D., Dranove, D., Shanley, M., Schaeffer, S. (2004). Economics of Strategy. Wiley, New York.

[BICC] Bonn International Center for Conversion (2003). Conversion Survey. Nomos, Baden-Baden.

Bitzinger, R.A. (1994). "The globalization of the arms industry: The next proliferation challenge". International Security 19, 170–198.

Bitzinger, R.A. (2003). Towards a Brave New Arms Industry? Oxford University Press, Oxford.

Bourne, M. (2005). "The proliferation of small arms and light weapons". In: Krahmann, E. (Ed.), New Threats and New Actors in International Security. Palgrave, New York, pp. 155–176.

Brauer, J. (1991). "Arms production in developing nations: The relation to industrial structure, industrial diversification, and human capital formation". Defence Economics 2, 165–175.

Brauer, J. (2000). "Potential and actual arms production: Implications for the arms trade debate". Defence and Peace Economics 11, 461–480.

Brauer, J. (2002). "The arms industry in developing nations: History and post-cold war assessment". In: Brauer, J., Dunne, J.P. (Eds.), Arming the South: The Economics of Military Expenditure, Arms Production, and Arms Trade in Developing Countries. Palgrave, New York, pp. 101–127.

Brauer, J., Dunne, J.P. (Eds.) (2002). Arming the South: The Economics of Military Expenditure, Arms Production, and Arms Trade in Developing Countries. Palgrave, New York.

Brauer, J., Dunne, J.P. (Eds.) (2004). Arms Trade and Economic Development: Theory, Policy, and Cases in Arms Trade Offsets. Routledge, London.

Brauer, J., Muggah, R. (2006). "Small arms demand: Theory and initial evidence". Contemporary Security Policy 27 (1), 138–154.

Brito, D., Intriligator, M. (1995). "Arms races and proliferation". In: Hartley, K., Sandler, T. (Eds.), Handbook of Defense Economics, vol. 1. North-Holland, Amsterdam, pp. 109–163.

[BVC] Bureau of Verification and Compliance (2002). World Military Expenditures and Arms Transfers, 1999–2000. Bureau of Verification and Compliance, US Department of State, Washington, DC.

[BXA] Bureau of Industry and Security (2005). Offsets in Defense Trade, Ninth Study. Bureau of Industry and Security, US Department of Commerce, Washington, DC.

Cavicchia, G.P. (2003). "The dismantling of the Argentine defense industry". In: Markusen, A., DiGiovanna, S., Leary, M.C. (Eds.), From Defense to Development? International Perspectives on Realizing the Peace Dividend. Routledge, London, pp. 101–120.

Chen, S. (2003). "Defense conversion in China". In: Markusen, A., DiGiovanna, S., Leary, M.C. (Eds.), From Defense to Development? International Perspectives on Realizing the Peace Dividend. Routledge, London, pp. 201–223.

Clark, W.S. (2005). "Fuel-air explosive (FAE)". In: Croddy, E.A., Wirtz, J.J., Larsen, J.A. (Eds.), Weapons of Mass Destruction: An Encyclopedia of Worldwide Policy, Technology, and History, vol. 1. ABC-Clio, Santa Barbara, CA, pp. 136–137.

Coase, R. (1937). "The nature of the firm". Economica 4 (16), 386–405.

Collier, P., Hoeffler, A. (2007). "Civil war". In: Sandler, T., Hartley, K. (Eds.), Handbook of Defense Economics, vol. 2. North-Holland, Amsterdam. This volume.

Collier, P., Sambanis, N. (2005). Understanding Civil War: Evidence and Analysis. World Bank, Washington, DC.

Collier, P., et al. (2003). Breaking the Conflict Trap: Civil War and Development Policy. World Bank and Oxford University Press, Washington, DC.

Conca, K. (1998). "Between global markets and domestic politics: Brazil's military-industrial collapse". Review of International Studies 24, 499–513.

Cook, P., Ludwig, J. (2000). Gun Violence: The Real Costs. Oxford University Press, Oxford.

Cooper, N. (2006). "Peaceful warriors and warring peacemakers". Economics of Peace and Security Journal 1 (1), 20–24.

Croddy, E.A. (2005a). "Biological and toxin weapons convention (BTWC)". In: Croddy, E.A., Wirtz, J.J., Larsen, J.A. (Eds.), Weapons of Mass Destruction: An Encyclopedia of Worldwide Policy, Technology, and History, vol. 1. ABC-Clio, Santa Barbara, CA, pp. 43–47.

Croddy, E.A. (2005b). "Biological warfare". In: Croddy, E.A., Wirtz, J.J., Larsen, J.A. (Eds.), Weapons of Mass Destruction: An Encyclopedia of Worldwide Policy, Technology, and History, vol. 1. ABC-Clio, Santa Barbara, CA, pp. 50–59.

Croddy, E.A., Wirtz, J.J., Larsen, J.A. (Eds.) (2005). Weapons of Mass Destruction: An Encyclopedia of Worldwide Policy, Technology, and History. ABC-Clio, Santa Barbara, CA. 2 vols.

[CRS] Congressional Research Service (2005). Conventional Arms Transfers to Developing Nations, 1997–2004. Congressional Research Service, Washington, DC.

Dando, M. (2002). "Scientific and technological change and the future of the CWC: The problem of non-lethal weapons". Disarmament Forum 4, 33–44.

Dando, M. (2005). "The malign use of neuroscience". Disarmament Forum 1, 17–24.

Davis, M. (2005). "Chemical and biological munitions and military operations". In: Croddy, E.A., Wirtz, J.J., Larsen, J.A. (Eds.), Weapons of Mass Destruction: An Encyclopedia of Worldwide Policy, Technology, and History, vol. 1. ABC-Clio, Santa Barbara, CA, pp. 80–85.

Duffield, M. (2001). Global Governance and the New Wars: The Merging of Development and Security. Zed Books, London.

Dunne, J.P. (1995). "The defense industrial base". In: Hartley, K., Sandler, T. (Eds.), Handbook of Defense Economics, vol. 1. North-Holland, Amsterdam, pp. 399–429.

Dunne, J.P., Lamb, G. (2004). "Defense industrial participation: The South African experience". In: Brauer, J., Dunne, J.P. (Eds.), Arms Trade and Economic Development. Routledge, London, pp. 284–298.

Dunne, J.P., Surry, E. (2006). "Arms production". In: SIPRI Yearbook. Oxford University Press, Oxford, pp. 387–418.

Enders, W. (2007). "Terrorism: An empirical analysis". In: Sandler, T., Hartley, K. (Eds.), Handbook of Defense Economics, vol. 2. North-Holland, Amsterdam. This volume.

Enders, W., Sandler, T. (2006). The Political Economy of Terrorism. Cambridge University Press, Cambridge.

Florquin, N. (2005). "Guns in crime". HFG Review: 21–25. http://www.hfg.org/hfg_review/5/hfgsmallarms.pdf [accessed 11 September 2005].

García-Alonso, M., Levine, P. (2007). "Arms trade and arms races: A strategic analysis". In: Sandler, T., Hartley, K. (Eds.), Handbook of Defense Economics, vol. 2. North-Holland, Amsterdam. This volume.

Godnick, W., Laurance, E.J., Stohl, R., Small Arms Survey (2005). "Effects of small arms misuse". HFG Review: 10–20. http://www.hfg.org/hfg_review/5/hfgsmallarms.pdf [accessed 11 September 2005].

Hart, J. (2005). "Chemical weapons convention (CWC)". In: Croddy, E.A., Wirtz, J.J., Larsen, J.A. (Eds.), Weapons of Mass Destruction: An Encyclopedia of Worldwide Policy, Technology, and History, vol. 1. ABC-Clio, Santa Barbara, CA, pp. 93–96.

Hartley, K. (2007). "The arms industry, procurement and industrial policies". In: Sandler, T., Hartley, K., (Eds.), Handbook of Defense Economics, vol. 2. North-Holland, Amsterdam. This volume.

Hays, P.L. (2003). Current and future military uses of space. In: United Nations Institute for Disarmament Research, Outer Space and Global Security. UNIDIR, Geneva, pp. 21–64.

Hemenway, D. (2004). Private Guns, Public Health. The University of Michigan Press, Ann Arbor, MI.

[IISS] International Institute for Strategic Studies (2004). The Military Balance, 2004–2005. Oxford University Press, London.

Jehiel, P., Moldovanu, B., Stacchetti, E. (1996). "How (not) to sell nuclear weapons". American Economic Review 86 (4), 814–829.

Kennedy, G. (1974). The Military in the Third World. Scribner's, New York.

Khakee, A., Wulf, H. (2005). "Following the trail: Production, arsenals, and transfers of small arms". HFG Review: 26–30. http://www.hfg.org/hfg_review/5/hfgsmallarms.pdf [accessed 11 September 2005].

Killicoat, P. (2006). "Cheap guns, more war? The economics of small arms". MPhil Economics Thesis. Oxford University.

Kirsten, A., Mashike, L., Matshedisho, K.R., Cock, J. (2004). "Islands of safety in a sea of guns". Mimeo. Small Arms Survey, Geneva.

Koubi, V. (1999). "Military technology races". International Organization 53 (3), 537–565.

Krause, K. (1992). Arms and the State: Patterns of Military Production and Trade. Cambridge University Press, Cambridge.

Langford, R.E. (2004). Introduction to Weapons of Mass Destruction: Radiological, Chemical, and Biological. Wiley–Interscience, Hoboken, NJ.

Laurance, E.J. (2005). "Small arms research: where we are and where we need to go". HFG Review: 3–9. http://www.hfg.org/hfg_review/5/hfgsmallarms.pdf [accessed 11 September 2005].

Lavoy, P. (2005). "Syria: chemical and biological weapons programs". In: Croddy, E.A., Wirtz, J.J., Larsen, J.A. (Eds.), Weapons of Mass Destruction: An Encyclopedia of Worldwide Policy, Technology, and History, vol. 1. ABC-Clio, Santa Barbara, CA, pp. 275–277.

Leander, A. (2005). "The market for force and public security: The destabilizing consequences of private military companies". Journal of Peace Research 42, 605–622.

Lessing, B. (2005). "A case study on firearms demand in Rio de Janeiro". Mimeo. VivaRio, Rio de Janeiro.

Lewer, N., Davison, N. (2005). "Non-lethal technologies – an overview". Disarmament Forum 1, 37–51.

Lewis, D.A. (2003). "Diversification and niche market exporting: The restructuring of Israel's defense industry in the post-Cold War era". In: Markusen, A., DiGiovanna, S., Leary, M.C. (Eds.), From Defense to Development? International Perspectives on Realizing the Peace Dividend. Routledge, London, pp. 121–150.

Maheswhari, S. (2003). "Diversification of defense-based industries in India". In: Markusen, A., DiGiovanna, S., Leary, M.C. (Eds.), From Defense to Development? International Perspectives on Realizing the Peace Dividend. Routledge, London, pp. 179–200.

Markowski, S., Hall, P. (2004). "Mandatory defense offsets – conceptual foundations". In: Brauer, J., Dunne, J.P. (Eds.), Arms Trade and Economic Development: Theory, Policy, and Cases in Arms Trade Offsets. Routledge, London, pp. 44–53.

Markusen, A. (1999). "The rise of world weapons". Foreign Policy 114, 40–51.

Markusen, A. (2004). "Arms trade as illiberal trade". In: Brauer, J., Dunne, J.P. (Eds.), Arms Trade and Economic Development. Routledge, London, pp. 66–88.

Markusen, A., DiGiovanna, S. (2003). "From defense to development?". In: Markusen, A., DiGiovanna, S., Leary, M.C. (Eds.), From Defense to Development? International Perspectives on Realizing the Peace Dividend. Routledge, London, pp. 1–14.

Markusen, A., DiGiovanna, S., Leary, M.C. (2003). From Defense to Development? International Perspectives on Realizing the Peace Dividend. Routledge, London.

Mian, Z. (1995). "The costs of nuclear security". In: Mian, Z. (Ed.), Pakistan's Atomic Bomb and the Search for Security. Gautam Publishers, Lahore, pp. 39–81.

Muggah, R. (2004). "Diagnosing demand: Assessing the motivations and means for firearms acquisition in the Solomon Islands and Papua New Guinea". Technical Report Discussion Paper 2004/7. State Society and Governance in Melanesia Project, Research School of Pacific and Asian Studies. Australian National University, Canberra.

Mussington, D. (1994). Understanding Contemporary Arms Transfers. Brassey's, London.

Nelson, C., Muggah, R. (2004). Solomon Islands: Evaluating the Weapons Free Village Campaign. Small Arms Survey, Geneva.

Nguyen, T.H. (2005). "Microchallenges of chemical weapons proliferation". Science 309, 1021.

Perlo-Freeman, S. (2004). "Offsets and the development of the Brazilian arms industry". In: Brauer, J., Dunne, J.P. (Eds.), Arms Trade and Economic Development: Theory, Policy, and Cases in Arms Trade Offsets. Routledge, London, pp. 187–204.

Sandler, T. (1997). Global Challenges: An Approach to Environmental, Political, and Economic Problems. Cambridge University Press, Cambridge.

Sandler, T., Arce, D.G. (2007). "Terrorism: A game-theoretic approach". In: Sandler, T., Hartley, K. (Eds.), Handbook of Defense Economics, vol. 2. North-Holland, Amsterdam, This volume.

[SAS] Small Arms Survey (various years). "Small Arms Survey". Oxford University Press, Oxford.

Scheetz, T. (2004). "The Argentine defense industry: An evaluation". In: Brauer, J., Dunne, J.P. (Eds.), Arms Trade and Economic Development: Theory, Policy, and Cases in Arms Trade Offsets. Routledge, London, pp. 205–216.

Schwartz, A.N. (1987). "Arms transfers and the development of second-level arms industries". In: Louscher, D.J., Salomone, M.D. (Eds.), Marketing Security Assistance: New Perspectives on Arms Sales. Lexington Books, Lexington, MA, pp. 101–130.

Segell, G. (2005). "United Nations Special Commission on Iraq (UNSCOM)". In: Croddy, E.A., Wirtz, J.J., Larsen, J.A. (Eds.), Weapons of Mass Destruction: An Encyclopedia of Worldwide Policy, Technology, and History, vol. 2. ABC-Clio, Santa Barbara, CA, pp. 389–390.

Singer, P. (2005). Children at War. Pantheon, New York.

Singh, J. (1998). "Against nuclear apartheid". Foreign Affairs 77 (5), 41–52.

Singh, S., Way, C.R. (2004). "The correlates of nuclear proliferation". Journal of Conflict Resolution 48 (6), 859–885.

[SIPRI] Stockholm International Peace Research Institute (various years). SIPRI Yearbook: Armaments, Disarmament and International Security. Oxford University Press, Oxford.

Smith, R., Tasiran, A. (2005). "The demand for arms imports". Journal of Peace Research 42, 167–181.

Spiers, E.M. (2000). Weapons of Mass Destruction: Prospects for Proliferation. St. Martin's, New York.

Sprague, O. (2004). Lock, Stock, and Barrel: How British Arms Components Add up to Deadly Weapons. Oxfam, London.

Surry, E. (2006). "Transparency in the arms industry". SIPRI Policy Paper No. 12. Stockholm International Peace Research Institute, Stockholm.

[UK Government] Foreign and Commonwealth Office (2004). Response to Sprague, 2004. http://www.the-dma.org.uk/Topical/tiDets.asp?ItemID=159 [accessed 20 April 2005].

[UNIDIR] United Nations Institute for Disarmament Research (2003). Outer Space and Global Security. UNIDIR, Geneva.

Vernon, R. (1966). "International investment and international trade in the product cycle". Quarterly Journal of Economics 80 (2), 190–207.

Williamson, O. (1985). The Economic Institutions of Capitalism. Free Press, New York.

Wulf, H. (1983). "Developing countries". In: Ball, N., Leitenberg, M. (Eds.), The Structure of the Defence Industry: An International Survey. St. Martin's Press, New York, pp. 310–343.

Chapter 31

TRADE, PEACE AND DEMOCRACY: AN ANALYSIS OF DYADIC DISPUTE[*]

SOLOMON W. POLACHEK

Department of Economics and Department of Political Science, State University of New York at Binghamton, Binghamton, NY 13902-6000, USA
e-mail: Polachek@binghamton.edu

CARLOS SEIGLIE

Department of Economics, Rutgers University, 360 King Boulevard, Newark, NJ 07102, USA
e-mail: seiglie@andromeda.rutgers.edu

Contents

Abstract	1018
Keywords	1019
1. Introduction	1020
1.1. The setting: Monadic versus dyadic analysis	1020
1.2. Defining peace: A trade theory perspective	1021
1.3. Requirement for peace: A lasting peace – Notions of a stable equilibrium	1021
2. Modeling how trade affects conflict and cooperation	1023
2.1. An economics model of the "peace-through-trade" liberal hypothesis	1023
2.1.1. Verbal explanation	1023
2.1.2. Mathematical depiction	1024
2.1.3. Trade gone awry: Three conditions for inadequate trade gains	1028
2.2. Alternative conflict–trade theories	1028
2.2.1. Marxian-based theories	1028
2.2.2. Gains from trade and military expenditures	1029
2.2.3. Game-theory: Signalling models	1030
3. Testing the theory	1031
3.1. Data	1031
3.1.1. Measuring conflict	1031
3.1.2. Measuring trade	1039

[*] We thank Jun (Jeff) Xiang for valuable research assistance, as well as Chuck Anderton and Todd Sandler for perceptive comments. Many of the findings reported here emanate from Polachek's collaborative research with Mark Gasiorowski, Judith McDonald, and John Robst. We thank each for their insights.

Handbook of Defense Economics, Volume 2
Edited by Todd Sandler and Keith Hartley
© 2007 Elsevier B.V.   All rights reserved
DOI: 10.1016/S1574-0013(06)02031-X

    3.1.3. Quantifying other country attributes   1040
  3.2. Statistical analysis: Testing the trade–conflict theory   1041
    3.2.1. Single equation cross-sectional analysis   1041
    3.2.2. Cross-sectional causality: The trade–conflict relationship with trade treated endoge-
        nously   1043
    3.2.3. Time-series analysis   1043
    3.2.4. Fixed effects   1046
    3.2.5. The trade–conflict relationship augmented by bilateral import demand elasticities 1047
4. An application – The democratic peace: Why democracies do not fight each
  other   1051
  4.1. The issue   1051
  4.2. The evidence   1053
    4.2.1. Measuring democracy: Ted Gurr data   1053
  4.3. Conclusions from the trade–conflict model regarding the democratic peace   1054
5. Extensions of the conflict–trade model   1057
  5.1. Commodity-specific trade   1058
  5.2. Foreign direct investment   1058
  5.3. Country size   1059
  5.4. Multilateral interactions   1061
    5.4.1. An application to tariffs   1063
    5.4.2. An application to foreign aid   1064
    5.4.3. An application to contiguity   1064
6. Conclusion   1065
References   1066

Abstract

At least since 1750 when Baron de Montesquieu declared "peace is the natural effect of trade," a number of economists and political scientists espoused the notion that trade among nations leads to peace. Employing resources more efficiently to produce some commodities rather than others is the foundation for comparative advantage. Specialization based on comparative advantage leads to gains from trade. If political conflict leads to a diminution of trade, then at least a portion of the costs of conflict can be measured by a nation's lost gains from trade. The greater two nations' gains from trade the more costly is bilateral (dyadic) conflict. This notion forms the basis of Baron de Montesquieu's assertion regarding dyadic dispute. This chapter develops an analytical framework showing that higher gains from trade between two trading partners (dyads) lowers the level of conflict between them. It describes data necessary to test this hypothesis, and it outlines current developments and extensions taking place in the resulting trade–conflict literature. Cross-sectional evidence using various data on political interactions confirms that trading nations cooperate more and fight less. A doubling of trade leads to a 20% diminution of belligerence. This result is robust under various specifications, and it is upheld when adjusting for causality using cross-section and time-series techniques. Further, the impact of trade is strengthened when bilateral import demand elasticities are incorporated to better measure gains from trade. Because democratic dyads trade more than non-democratic dyads, democracies cooperate with each other relatively more, thereby explaining the "democratic peace" that democracies rarely fight each other. The chapter then goes on to examine further extensions of the trade–conflict model regarding specific commodity trade, foreign direct investment, tariffs, foreign aid, country contiguity, and multilateral interactions.

Keywords

trade, conflict, cooperation, interdependence, gains from trade, dyadic conflict, democratic peace, democracy

JEL classification: F01, F51, F59, D74

1. Introduction

1.1. The setting: Monadic versus dyadic analysis

On January 1, 1959, Fidel Castro assumed the leadership of Cuba, following a revolution that deposed General Fulgencio Batista. A little over one-year later, the then Soviet First Deputy Prime Minister Anastas Mikpyan negotiated a trade agreement to wean Cuba from her dependence on the United States. Soon thereafter, the Soviet Union and Cuba established full diplomatic relations. The United States responded with an economic and political offensive leading to the Bay of Pigs, and eventually the Cuban Missile Crisis. Whereas Cuban–US relations soured during this time period, the United States and Canada became more economically and politically tied.

Fast forward to 2005. Cuban–US economic and political relations were still poor and Cuba became less economically and politically reliant on Russia. In contrast since the early 1990s Cuba has received direct investment from Canada and continued to engage in trade as it had since 1959, and Canadian–Cuban political relations have been relatively good. Also not only have economic ties between the United States and Russia improved, but political relations between these two countries became more cooperative. Finally, Canadian–US relations continue to be strong.

What do we learn from the above? First, any one country (such as the United States, Russia, or Cuba) can have both cooperative *and* conflictive international relations *at the same time*; witness each country above has both friends and enemies. Second, economic *and* political relations are intrinsically intertwined. In this chapter, we argue that the "trade and conflict" literature is motivated by these two lessons. Any given country can be both cooperating with *some* countries *and* in a state of conflict with *another* set of nations, both at the same time. Furthermore, economic and political relations go hand-in-hand. Aside from the countries mentioned above, there are countless other examples. The questions we want to address are why a particular country, like the United States has good relations with Canada yet poor relations with a country like Cuba; and why, at the same time, does a country like Cuba have good relations with Canada, yet poor relations with the United States. Clearly looking at the attributes of only *one* country in isolation, rather than *both* the countries comprising the bilateral relationship (i.e., the dyad) would not provide a full answer. Nor would systemic variables, i.e., variables common to the entire international political system, provide an answer. Systemic variables would not be able to explain how cooperation and hostility coexist simultaneously between two members of the system. For this reason, at a minimum, it makes sense to concentrate on dyads rather than countries as the unit of observation. In fact, this is precisely the approach of the conflict–trade literature, though now some have begun to extend the theory to incorporate multilateral situations.[1]

---

[1] Progress on this latter work is reported in Polachek, Robst and Chang (1999). Also see Dorussen (1999), and Hegre (2003) for other analyses of trade and conflict in a multi-country environment.

1.2. Defining peace: A trade theory perspective[2]

In the context of dyadic relations, we hope to show that *conflict* can be defined as *trade gone awry*. It is well known that nations (or for that matter other economic entities such as households) can raise their well-being through trade (if there is a difference in the relative prices each faces prior to trade). This increase in their welfare from an initial autarkic state is referred to as the "gains from trade". It results from gains due to specialization in production, which leads to higher levels of income and therefore greater consumption opportunities arising from the ability to exchange at more favorable prices, even if the level of production remains unchanged from its pre-trade level. Empirical evidence indicates that gains from trade can be substantial. For example, Acemoglu, Johnson and Robinson (2003) demonstrate that access to the Atlantic is responsible for the rise of (Western) Europe between 1500 and 1850, and this is especially true for nations engaged in long distance oceanic trade.

But what happens when a particular economic entity's gains from trade are not as high as it thinks it should receive? Often in such a circumstance the entity uses force to achieve redistribution through various means of coercion. Using force to coerce is *conflict*. Since force can be viewed as a type of trade ("I'll be violent if you don't give me what I want"), conflict is a form, as well as symptom, of "trade gone awry". As such, conflict occurs when parties fight over economic rents. When conflict lasts over a long period, it is known as protracted conflict. From a normative perspective, the control and eradication of conflict is an area of interest in the field of defense economics and peace science. Economists in this area study ways to achieve peace through eradication of conflict, while also exploring the more positive aspect of assessing war and peace's impact on society. But to control and eradicate conflict, one must know how and why inadequate trade gains come about.

1.3. Requirement for peace: A lasting peace – Notions of a stable equilibrium

Eradicating hostility and promoting cooperation is an important step leading to peace. One method of diminishing hostility and bringing about cooperation is by legalistic dictum often initiated by third parties. The problem is that attempts at peace imposed by others may be innately unstable, especially when the underlying differences originally separating the countries remain. For this reason, it seems reasonable that a viable peace is a natural peace based on mutual dependence. In his criticism of the Treaty of Versailles, Keynes (1920) argued that Germany be allowed to have economic relations with the rest of Europe or the prospects for peace would be dim. For example in *The Economic Consequences of the Peace* he writes "If we oppose in detail every means by which Germany or Russia can recover their material well-being, ... we must be prepared to face the consequences of such feelings". We similarly argue that

---

[2] This section is based on Polachek (1994) who describes conflict as trade gone awry.

only through mutual dependence can an equilibrium come about where peace remains solid and secure, so that neither party is motivated to change the status quo. Mutual dependence makes conflict more costly, and as such, it increases incentives for cooperation.

Probably many types of *mutual dependence* affect international relations. In many instances, political motivations form the basis of mutual dependence. When Willy Brandt became Foreign Minister in the Federal Republic of Germany in 1966, he developed the policy of Neue Ostpolitik (reconciliation between eastern and western Europe) eventually leading to a 1970 agreement accepting the borders of Berlin. Henry Kissinger pioneered the policy of détente that led to a considerable reduction in US–Soviet tensions, including the SALT I strategic arms reduction talks, and the "opening" of China leading to an anti-Soviet Sino–American alliance. But underlying most instances of mutual dependence are economic considerations. Willy Brandt sought closer trading relations with Eastern Europe and the Soviet Union. This helped prop up the weak communist economies, but it also highlighted the contrasting wealth and poverty between the east and west and probably ultimately set the stage for reunification. Certainly from the Soviet viewpoint decelerating the arms race reduced the drain on social and economic resources, but equally America's vulnerability to nuclear holocaust was reduced. Certainly from China, Kissinger and Nixon sought trade in one of the fastest growing world markets. Finally, more recently, mutual dependence based on economics served as justification for the European nations to come together to form the European Union.

In this chapter, we concentrate on *economic interdependence* and in particular what political scientists refer to as "vulnerability interdependence" in the international relations literature [see Mansfield and Pollins (2001) for a discussion]. This type of interdependence attempts to capture the cost of rupturing economic relations with another country. In fact, most quantitative studies of interdependence and conflict concentrate solely on *economic* aspects because economic aspects are more easily measured. As will be explained later, most use bilateral trade (or some trade-related measure such as trade-share or a trade-relative-to-GNP statistic) as the measure for interdependence, but even this is a simplification. As will be explained, theory predicts "gains from trade" to be the most relevant indicator of economic interdependence. However, because of the difficulty of measuring trade *gains*, almost all research uses some variation of trade *level* to measure mutual economic dependence. But before we jump ahead, we examine the trade (interdependence)–conflict model.[3]

---

[3] See Blainey (1988), Sayrs (1990), McMillan (1997), Barbieri and Schneider (1999), Reuveny (1999), Mansfield and Pollins (2001, 2003), and Schneider, Barbieri and Gleditsch (2003) for recent surveys on the literature emanating from the trade (interdependence)–conflict model. See Mansfield (2004) for classic reading on the topic.

2. Modeling how trade affects conflict and cooperation

The proposition that trade deters conflict has roots as far back as the sixteenth century. First, theologian philosophers such as Erasmus (1981) [*Enchiridion Militis Christiani*, the "Handbook of the Christian Soldier" originally published in 1503] realized that war was "bad". Later, the French monk Crucé (1623) sought international bodies to arbitrate international disputes. This point of view was later taken up by Rousseau (2005, originally published circa 1756) who realized that using organizations designed to arbitrate disputes would bring nations closer through communication. Related to arbitration, Immanuel Kant (1795, Perpetual Peace: A Philosophical Sketch) argued that perpetual peace could be achieved through appropriate governance in which all means used to wage war should be prohibited in order to establish mutual trust among nations. But whereas Kant believed mutual trust must be legislated, forty-five years earlier, in 1750, Baron de Montesquieu provided an economics approach to achieve mutual trust. He stated that "peace is the natural effect of trade" because "two nations who traffic with each other become reciprocally dependent" leading to "their union . . . founded on their mutual necessities" [de Montesquieu (1900, p. 316)]. Much later, British statesmen Cobden (1995, originally published in 1846), Bright (1883), as well as economists Angell (1913) and Viner (1937) espoused these same views. Perhaps, for this reason Hirschman (1945, v, xvi) emphasized 'the politics of foreign trade' by which he spelled out "the possibility of using trade as a means of political pressure . . . in the pursuit of power". Cutting existing trade for political reasons reduces gains from trade, though these losses can be somewhat mitigated if other trading partners can be found. But even here, finding other trading partners is costly.

2.1. An economics model of the "peace-through-trade" liberal hypothesis

2.1.1. Verbal explanation

These notions about how mutual dependence leads to peace can be formalized. No individual produces everything he or she needs. Instead each individual finds it advantageous to specialize. Division of labor comes about because persons work at what they do best, and trade for what they produce in a relatively more expensive way. International trade occurs for the same reason. One country alone is not able to produce all it needs efficiently. A country is said to have a comparative advantage over another when it is relatively more productive in the production of a particular commodity. Comparative advantage enables both countries to increase their welfare through trade. Thus trade is welfare enhancing.

Define conflict to be an unfriendly political action from one country to another that is hostile enough to lead the second country to cease or at least diminish trade. Generally, loss of existing trade implies a welfare loss. It is these potential welfare losses that can deter conflict. More specifically, a country that is trading with another at international prices must be better off than in autarky, otherwise it would have chosen not to trade and instead face autarkic prices. Conflict reduces trade and forces the country towards prices that are closer to where they would be in autarky. Therefore, the more that conflict changes prices towards their pre-trade level the more countries will attempt to avoid conflict. This in a nutshell is the basis for the trade–conflict model.

2.1.2. Mathematical depiction[4]

Polachek (1980, 1992) developed a framework to analyze the trade–conflict nexus. In his model, a country's preferences can be represented by a utility function over the consumption, C, of m-goods that are produced in a k-country world. Furthermore, each of these countries can initiate conflict or cooperation on any of the $k - 1$ countries towards which the level of intensity is denoted by a $1 \times (k - 1)$ vector Z. Preferences for the level of conflict or cooperation to achieve outcomes deemed important by a country generate a derived demand for it. Furthermore, conflict has effects on the terms of trade or prices in the world markets.

Formally, a country seeks to maximize

$$U = U(C, Z),\tag{1}$$

with $C = \{c_1, c_2, \ldots, c_m\}$ and $Z = \{z_1, z_2, \ldots, z_{k-1}\}$.

In order to simplify the analysis, we assume that there are two commodities which are produced in the country, q_1 and q_2 with their respective levels of consumption and prices in the country denoted by c_1, c_2 and p_1, p_2, respectively. Assume that the country interacts with only one other country in the world and we denote the level of intensity directed at this country by z. Therefore, the utility function for the country's decision-maker is now

$$U(c_1, c_2, z)\tag{1'}$$

and is assumed to be defined based on the preferences of the entire population.[5]

In a one-period world, the budget constraint for the country is

$$p_1 c_1 + p_2 c_2 + p_z z = p_1 q_1 + p_2 q_2,\tag{2}$$

where the cost of the resources used to generate conflict or cooperation is p_z. Conflict is assumed to affect prices. More specifically,

$$p_i = p_i(z, z^*),\tag{3}$$

where z is the intensity of conflict or aggression of country 1 targeted at country 2 and z^* is the level of aggression of country 2 towards 1. Assuming that country 1 exports

---

[4] Polachek (1980) first formalized this model. A more general derivation is given in Martin, Mayer and Thoenig (2005). Also see Caruso (2006).

[5] In this paper we ignore how special interest groups affect trade. See Robbins (1968) and Grossman and Helpman (2002) for valuable insights here.

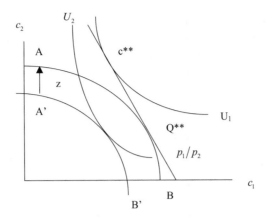

Figure 1. Gains from trade.

commodity 1 and imports commodity 2, conflict affects prices in the following manner:

$$\frac{\partial p_1}{\partial z} \leqslant 0 \quad \text{and} \quad \frac{\partial p_2}{\partial z} \geqslant 0. \tag{4}$$

In other words, we assume that conflict directed towards the other country reduces or has no impact on the price the country obtains for its export commodity and increases or has no impact on the price the country pays for its imported goods. Greater conflict by the actor towards the target requires the actor to reduce the price of their exports to induce them to purchase the good and leads to them being charged a higher price for the imports from the target country. The smaller either country is, the smaller the impact that conflict will have on prices since the elasticity of demand for imports will be greater. In the extreme case, both countries are prices takers in the international market and the cost of trade diversion is negligible.

The problem for the actor country is to maximize Equation ($1'$) subject to their resource constraint and the country's level of technology. Figure 1 depicts the problem graphically. The production possibility curve for the country is given by AB and in a world without conflict ($z = 0$), the country would choose to consume at c^{**} and produce at Q^{**} when faced with the ratio, p_1/p_2 yielding a level of utility of U_1. If the actor chooses to allocate $z > 0$ resources to conflict, then the country's consumption possibilities are reduced to $A'B'$ since there are less resources available for consumption and the terms of trade are worsened. We assume that the new equilibrium in the $c_2 c_1$ space is given by U_2. The country trades off the gains from trade for the gains from engaging in conflict. Then the implicit cost of conflict is the lost gains from trade $U_1 - U_2$ associated with decreased trade.[6] Obviously, the greater the welfare loss the greater the costs of conflict, and the greater the incentive for cooperation, independent of the country's innate preference for peace. Even if conflict does not directly diminish trade, but instead

---

[6] At this point we assume no direct costs of conflict.

leads to trade restrictions that ultimately affect the terms of trade, the same result applies. In this case, less desirable terms of trade result (e.g., a flatter terms of trade line in Figure 1) implying a new equilibrium and lower welfare. Again, the implicit price of conflict is the lost welfare associated with diminished trade brought about by conflict.

Algebraically, the problem for the actor country is to maximize

$$L = U(c_1, c_2, z) + \lambda[p_1 q_1 + p_2 q_2 - p_1 c_1 - p_2 c_2 - p_z z], \tag{5}$$

by choosing the amount of consumption of the two goods and the level of conflict to initiate against the target country while taking into account the effects that this has on prices. One could think of the problem as being solved in two stages. In the first stage, individuals decide on the amounts to consume of the different commodities, yielding the composition of imports and exports. In the second stage, the government decides on the level of conflict, z, to undertake. We can rewrite the problem as

$$\text{Max} \quad L = U(c_1, c_2, z) + \lambda[p_1 x_1 + p_2 m_2 - p_z z], \tag{6}$$

where exports $x_1 = q_1 - c_1$ and imports $m_2 = q_2 - c_2$. The first order conditions are:

$$\frac{\partial U}{\partial c_1} - \lambda p_1 = 0, \tag{7}$$

$$\frac{\partial U}{\partial c_2} - \lambda p_2 = 0, \tag{8}$$

$$\frac{\partial U}{\partial z} + \lambda\left[\left(x_1 + p_1 \frac{\partial x_1}{\partial p_1}\right)\frac{\partial p_1}{\partial z} + \left(m_2 + p_2 \frac{\partial m_2}{\partial p_2}\right)\frac{\partial p_2}{\partial z} - p_z\right] = 0. \tag{9}$$

These can be rearranged as:

$$\frac{\partial U}{\partial c_1} \Big/ \frac{\partial U}{\partial c_2} = \frac{p_1}{p_2}, \tag{10}$$

$$\frac{\partial U}{\partial z} = \lambda\left[p_z - \left(x_1 + p_1 \frac{\partial x_1}{\partial p_1}\right)\frac{\partial p_1}{\partial z} - \left(m_2 + p_2 \frac{\partial m_2}{\partial p_2}\right)\frac{\partial p_2}{\partial z}\right]. \tag{11}$$

Equation (10) is the standard condition for utility maximization in the consumption of the two goods. Whereas, Equation (11) is the additional condition that must be satisfied. The left-hand side of this equation is the marginal benefit from engaging in conflictual activity. The marginal cost is given by the right-hand side and includes the direct cost of allocating a unit of consumption to z evaluated at the price of z, p_z, as well as the indirect cost of reduction in import and export revenues resulting from the changes in prices as a consequence of international conflict,

$$\left(x_1 + p_1 \frac{\partial x_1}{\partial p_1}\right)\frac{\partial p_1}{\partial z} - \left(m_2 + p_2 \frac{\partial m_2}{\partial p_2}\right)\frac{\partial p_2}{\partial z}.$$

Therefore, Equation (11) describes the mechanism by which a country decides on the amount of belligerence. Since the bracketed term is the explicit cost as well as the implicit one of receiving less revenue for exports while at the same time having to pay

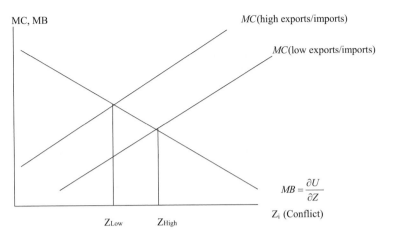

Figure 2. Equilibrium conflict.

more for imports, it represents the cost associated with extra hostility (MC). This term can be represented graphically (Figure 2) as an upward sloping curve whose position depends on the levels of imports and exports, m_2 and x_1. In equilibrium, this cost of hostility must just balance the welfare benefit of added hostility ($\frac{\partial U}{\partial z}$) so that the intersection of the ($\frac{\partial U}{\partial z}$) curve and the MC curve depicts the equilibrium conflict/cooperation. Note that equilibrium conflict/cooperation levels still arise even if hostility or cooperation implies no welfare gain ($\frac{\partial U}{\partial z} = 0$). In this case, optimal conflict is determined at the point where the MC curve intersects the horizontal axis. If imports or exports are increased, the MC shifts up, thereby implying lower levels of conflict. Thus,

PROPOSITION ONE. *The greater is an actor country's level of trade with a target, the smaller the amount of conflict that the actor will have with the target country.*

If international borrowing and lending is assumed not to be available, then conflict induces a change in optimal imports and exports. The more unfavorable the relative prices of trade induced by conflict, the more exports are forced to increase, and imports decrease. From the above one can show that welfare losses are largest, the more inelastic the import and exports demand and supply curves. Hence,

PROPOSITION TWO. *The more inelastic (elastic) an actor country's import and export demand and supply to a target country, the smaller (larger) will be the amount of conflict initiated by the actor towards the target country.*

There are other propositions that follow from the model. However, due to the lack of data for conducting the appropriate statistical tests, researchers generally concentrate on these two propositions, which form the basis of most tests of the conflict–trade model. Therefore, we hypothesize a relationship between bilateral international conflict and the welfare gains associated with bilateral trade. More precisely, the greater the welfare gains, the smaller the level of conflict that we expect. Since welfare gains increase with the level of trade, yet decrease with the import and export demand and supply elasticities, we argue that countries with the most trade (and the greatest gains from trade) have the most to lose from conflict. *Ceteris paribus* these countries have lesser amounts of conflict. Countries with the most elastic import demand and export supply curves gain the least from trade, and hence *ceteris paribus*, these countries engage in greater conflict.

To test these propositions, most empirical analyses concentrate solely on the conflict–trade relationship, but neglect gains from trade. As such, they utilize measures of conflict (which will be discussed later) and trade *levels*, and test for an inverse relationship. By limiting themselves strictly to trade levels, they implicitly assume each country's import demand and export supply curves are comparable. But clearly these import and export demand and supply curves may differ. Only a few studies get at actual gains from trade. Although imperfect, they do so by including information on import demand elasticity. We discuss more of the estimation problems that arise later in the chapter.

2.1.3. Trade gone awry: Three conditions for inadequate trade gains

There are at least three causes for inadequate trade gains. First, nations do not trade when possibly they should. Reduced trade because of tariffs would be an example. Second, two non-trading nations may be competing for the same trade, and hence the same pool of economic rents. Competition in oil sales leading OPEC members to cheat on cartel production allocations might be an example of this type condition. Third, trading partners may believe their particular terms of trade are inequitable. This generally arises when bilateral bargaining between nations determine price, but other systemic global forces determine other conditions regarding exchange.

Finally, we should note that not all theorists affirm that trade reduces conflict. Amongst these, some question whether both trading partners actually achieve positive gains from trade in many international transactions. If there are no gains from trade then conflict would not be mitigated. Others argue that trade gains provide an increase in real resources that can have a positive income effect, thereby providing an impetus for increased military spending. Finally, based on asymmetric information some argue that trade can increase conflict. We review each in turn below.

2.2. Alternative conflict–trade theories

2.2.1. Marxian-based theories[7]

Marxian-based theories contend that colonialism and imperialism go hand in hand with trade. They argue countries essentially use military force to expand trade. Viewed in this

---

[7] Barbieri (2002) is the prime advocate of this approach.

framework, trade implies an oppressor nation and an oppressed nation, with the powerful oppressor exploiting the weaker oppressed nation. Under this approach, since trade is coerced by the use or threat of force, it becomes involuntary leading to asymmetric strictly one-sided trade gains. One side wins all, and as such, the other side actually suffers major economic and other losses from trade.

Clearly a nation losing resources based on involuntary exploitative trade is far different than a nation engaged in mutually beneficial bilateral trade, where both sides gain. Both types of nations face far different circumstances. One gains from trade, and the other loses. But even a liberal theorist would find it reasonable for a nation to fight exploitation were trade gains really negative. In such a situation neither Marxian nor liberal theories contradict each other. The real question becomes whether trade is involuntary, and if so whether it exploits a nation thus rendering gains from trade to be negative, as Marxists claim; or conversely whether trade is mutually beneficial, as certainly most economists believe. Only if the former exploitation is true, can trade lead to conflict, but this circumstance is an empirical question – *not* a counterexample to the liberal hypothesis. Thus there is no contradiction, only the need for researchers to evaluate trade gains. But, according to some, even in the context of neoclassical economic models, positive gains from trade can lead to conflict.

2.2.2. Gains from trade and military expenditures

Whereas the conflict–trade model uses a Ricardian (1981, 1817) framework to show how countries engage in cooperation to protect trade gains, another approach developed by Seiglie (1992, 1996, 2005) and Findlay (2001) adopts the gains-from-trade framework to show how conflict can *rise* with trade. In these latter models, rather than trade partners acting cooperatively to protect trade gains, each trading partner utilizes newly acquired gains-from-trade wealth to purchase more of *all* goods and services, including military equipment. More specifically, as an economy opens to trade and real income rises, a country will spend more on weapons to protect these gains. Empirically, this leads to testing whether there is a positive association between the size of international trade (as a proxy for the gains from trade) and military spending. Indeed, historically nations used their navy to protect themselves from pirates, which probably was the navy's prime raison d'être. On the other hand, it is not clear that augmenting military expenditures to protect trade, or even to augment other aspects of a nation's security, implies more dyadic conflict.

Military expenditures, addressed by these theories, need not necessarily be equated with conflict. Although military equipment resulting from military expenditures often is used in combat, it can be employed for other purposes, such as augmenting national security. However, even if used for conflictive purposes, the resulting conflict most likely would *not* be directed towards trading partners, but more likely directed at third parties from whom protecting trade gains is not an issue. As such, gains-from-trade induced military expenditures would not contradict the liberal trade–conflict model that more trade increases cooperation, since any belligerence, if it even occurs, most likely would not be directed towards trading partners. Simply put, military expenditures are an aggregate measure encompassing far more than dyadic conflict. Indeed, bilateral inter-actions among trading partners should improve to protect the trade gains, which enable spending some of the gains from trade on higher military expenditures to ensure greater security. Thus theories propounding trade to induce higher military expenditures do not contradict the trade–conflict model. As will be illustrated next, the same is true for game theoretic models.

2.2.3. Game-theory: Signalling models

In the typical game theory model, parties vie to split contested resources. As already indicated, trade produces gains, which must be divided between two (or more) trading partners. Accordingly, trade gains becomes the contested resource and game theory is invoked to determine how each party behaves to determine the division. But, in the process of dividing a given resource, it becomes obvious that what one party gains, the other loses, so that the process itself has a conflictive nature. In fact, Schelling (1960) and later on Hirshleifer (1995) view conflict in this manner. Thus to game theorists the logic is simple: first, trade creates trade gains; second, trade gains must be divided; finally, dividing trade gains leads to conflict. Following the logic through, trade leads to conflict [see Morrow (1997, 1999) for example].

Again there is no contradiction with the liberal trade–conflict model which states that trade yields more cooperation than conflict. Two issues are involved: (1) whether dividing trade gains necessarily yields conflict as game theoretic models imply, and (2) whether the conflict emanating from splitting trade gains outweighs the necessary cooperation needed to protect the trade, which created the gains in the first place.

Take the first issue. A country's output can be visualized by a production-possibilities-frontier representing all goods and services a country can produce under autarky. Comparative advantage occurs when there exists differences in relative costs result-ing from varying factor endowments or technology. Under such circumstances it pays for each country to trade by exporting what it produces most efficiently and import-ing what it produces less efficiently. Thus if country A has a comparative advantage in agriculture and country B in manufacturing, each can specialize; and both can be made better off. Clearly each country gains, but the extent of the gains are determined by rel-ative prices. With only two countries and imperfect information about their preferences it might pay for each to send a signal to mislead the other in order to eke out a better terms of trade. Such gamesmanship can lead to conflict ex post; but nevertheless, it does not pay to have so much conflict so as to deter trade, since such action eliminating trade would eradicate trade gains completely. This is essentially the conclusion reached by Krugman (1995). Thus even if (1) above is correct, dividing trade gains need not im-ply an amount of conflict that exceeds the amount of cooperation necessary to protect trade in the first place. But it is not obvious that game theory is even always relevant in splitting trade gains.

Trade gains are determined by prices. Clearly the higher the export price, the greater a country's revenues from selling its products, especially if the commodity's demand is inelastic; as a result, trade gains are higher, all else constant. In the world, prices are usually set in the market. Market determined prices mean that posturing for the best price is not a viable option for the typical (small) country, because a small country must simply take prices as given. In this case there are no contested resources. Gains from trade are fixed, since each trading partner cannot change world prices. Indeed the only option is to take one's trade elsewhere, but here too the market basically sets the price. So game theory is essentially not applicable, because except for countries with monopolistic power the market determines price.

In summary there is no real contradiction between the above three approaches and the conflict–trade model itself. As such, because there is no contradiction, these three models cannot serve as an alternative explanation for the non-trivial instances of a positive trade–conflict relationship. For this reason, one needs to better understand the conflict–trade model and its implications, in order to better understand the seemingly contradictory findings relating trade and conflict. The remainder of this chapter examines the empirical findings in the conflict–trade literature.

3. Testing the theory

3.1. Data

3.1.1. Measuring conflict

Usually when one thinks of conflict, one thinks of large economic entities such as countries or groups of countries. In large-scale conflicts that take place among sizable entities, the degree of destruction is overwhelming. Over 34 million were injured in World War II, over 22 million died, and over $15 trillion (2004 dollars) were expended militarily. However, in the original conflict literature by Richardson (1960), the inventor of arms race models and whose work is the forerunner of modern peace economics research, conflict was defined more broadly even to include everyday criminal activities. Richardson understood that conflict can take many forms.

3.1.1.1. War data. As devastating as they may be, wars are actually relatively rare, and hard to define. Currently there are numerous data sets that compile information on wars. Perhaps the oldest is Richardson's (1960), containing data on 779 deadly quarrels during 1809–1949. Wright's (1942) *A Study of War* contains data on approximately 300 wars between 1480 and 1941. Other studies include Singer and Small (1972) *Wages of War* data, containing data on 79 interstate wars (more than 1000 fatalities) between 1816 and 1980. These data are continually updated under the Correlates of War Project and now contain information on other relevant variables. Also there are Levy's (1983) major power war study, the Stockholm International Peace Research Institute data (which can be obtained from its annual yearbook containing armed conflict data), and the Gochman and Maoz (1984) militarized dispute data containing interstate events involving threats or actual use of force. Many of these data are available on the Internet.

3.1.1.2. Militarized interstate dispute (MIDS) data. One problem is that wars are particularly intensive but relatively rare. The number dead or wounded varies with technology as well as country size. Similarly war data deal only with extreme hostility. They neglect acts less hostile than war as well as instances of cooperation. Militarized interstate dispute data from the Correlates of War (COW) project contain 2331 interstate disputes (conflicts in which one or more states threaten, display, or use force against one or more other states) between 1816 and 2001. But even these military dispute data represent a fraction of all interactions. Other data such as defense expenditures can indicate general hostility levels, yet defense expenditures need not reflect hostility at all since such expenditures could be viewed as a warning to other nations, and thus serve more as a measure of deterrence. Alternatively, defense expenditures can measure repression of domestic unrest. Similarly such measures as UN voting data are often deemed inadequate since they might measure political attitudes or the results of foreign aid investments rather than actual country conflict.

3.1.1.3. Events data. To alleviate some of these deficiencies several scholars have taken a different approach by compiling events data. Events data comprise bilateral interactions reported in newspapers. While clearly not all interactions are reported in newspapers, these type of data have the advantage of being able to incorporate conflictive interactions short of war, as well as cooperative type political exchanges. McClelland (1999) was the first to compile events data in the 1960s. His World Events Interaction Survey (WEIS) uses information solely from the *New York Times.* McClelland (1999) originally distinguished 22 classes and seven types of bilateral actions [Azar and Ben-Dak (1975)]. Shortly thereafter, Azar (1980) classified information from almost 50 newspapers from all over the world to report on bilateral interactions of 115 countries from 1948 to 1978 in his Cooperation and Peace Data Bank (COPDAB).[8] Finally, more recent events data are computer driven. They use computer software to read and machine-code wire service reports, particularly Reuters. Originally developed

---

[8] Also during the late 1970s and early 1980s, the United States Department of State, Department of Defense and various intelligence agencies as well as private political consulting firms such as CACI Inc. collected events data. In this regard, in 1971, the Department of State's Foreign Relations Indicator Project (FRIP) coded events data for a small set of states. Similarly, early in the Reagan administration, the Pentagon's Defense Advanced Research Project Agency (DARPA) and the National Security Council staff in the White House supported a large-scale project to develop events data for crisis forecasting. These efforts apparently had little long-term impact on the formulation of foreign policy. Domestic and international event data were also collected by Rummel (1975) and Taylor and Hudson (1972), Hermann et al. (1973) as well as Gurr (1974). However, their focus was limited [see Philip Schrodt (1995)]. For a more complete listing of conflict data see: http://www.pcr.uu.se/research/UCDP/confliktdatasetcatalog.pdf. On the other hand, see Kegley (1975) for problems that arise in using events data.

at the University of Kansas, these data are known as the Kansas Events Data Study (KEDS). Beginning in 1992 a group of researchers headed by Doug Bond at Harvard University's Center for International Affairs joined with scholars at the University of Kansas. The Harvard team developed a protocol to classify events, which they called PANDA (Protocol for the Assessment of Nonviolent Direct Action). Subsequently, Virtual Research Associates, Inc. was established in 1996. They later partnered with several University-based research teams to expand their original protocol. This second-generation protocol is called IDEA (Integrated Data for Events Analysis). Currently, the Harvard-MIT Virtual Data Center distributes historical events data developed by VRA for use by scholars.

COPDAB: The conflict and Peace Data Bank (COBDAB) is an extensive longitudinal collection of about one million daily events reported from forty-seven newspaper sources between 1948 and 1978 [Azar (1980)]. These events are coded on a 15-point scale representing different kinds of conflict and cooperation. COPDAB events in categories 1 (voluntary unification) through 7 (minor official exchanges) represent cooperation. Categories 9 (mild verbal expressions displaying discord) through 15 (extensive war acts causing deaths) represent conflict. Included in COPDAB is a numerical weighting of the amount of conflict and cooperation as determined by 18 scholars and practitioners of international relations. These are given in Table 1. To come up with a composite number, Polachek (1980) defined NETF as the weighted (taken from Table 1) frequency of conflictive events (those in category 9 to 15) minus the weighted

Table 1
Scale weights for COPDAB

Scale point	Description	Weighted value
15	Extensive war acts	102
14	Limited war acts	65
13	Small scale military acts	50
12	Political–military hostile actions	44
11	Diplomatic–economic hostile actions	29
10	Strong verbal hostile expressions	16
9	Mild verbal hostile expressions	6
8	Neutral acts	1
7	Minor official exchanges	6
6	Official verbal support	10
5	Cultural or scientific agreements	14
4	Non-military agreements	27
3	Military support	31
2	Major strategic alliance	47
1	Voluntary unification	92

Source: Azar (1980).

frequency of cooperative events (those in category 1 to 7). Here, a negative value of NETF implies that more (weighted) cooperation occurs than conflict, hence that on balance international interactions would be more cooperative than hostile. There are over 105 countries in the sample, and hence about 11 thousand possible dyadic interactions per year.

WEIS: The World Events Interaction Survey (WEIS) is a compilation of bilateral international interactions occurring between 1966–1992 reported in the New York Times. The events are coded using IDEA (Integrated Data for Events Analysis). This framework fits every reported event into one of 22 broad categories ranging from extending aid (code 7) to military assaults using force (code 22). Specific definitions for each type of cooperation and conflict event are given in Table 2, column 2 (labeled IDEA). They are weighted based on Goldstein's (1992) scale that converts the IDEA code to one that better classifies each event's intensity. In order to be consistent with COPDAB, we multiplied Goldstein's weights by minus one to give conflictive events positive values and cooperative events negative values. Thus, as can be seen from Table 2, the positive scale values represent conflict and the negative ones cooperation, while zeros are basically natural disasters and neutral social activities. The maximum positive value is 10, which corresponds to extreme conflict cases. Negative values indicate cooperation. The maximum negative value is −8.3. Since the scale includes 55 categories, it makes the use of a count model inappropriate. It is possible to divide these into smaller subcategories, but the problem is how to capture nuance differences within each category. A more useful method is to compute the weighted sum of all events for each dyad by year (weighted by the modified Goldstein scale for each type of event form). Given that their signs differentiate conflict and cooperation, a positive weighted sum means net conflict. Conversely, a negative sign implies net cooperation.

Virtual Research Associates (VRA) Data: The Virtual Research Associates (VRA) data are derived from dyadic events reported in the wire services. Rather than being read and transcribed from newspapers, they are based on computer driven formulae that analyze the first sentence of each news report. From these first sentences, the computer determines an actor, a target as well as an action [see King and Lowe (2003) for examples and more details]. This event data set is coded by IDEA so that the classification scheme is comparable to that used in WEIS. As with WEIS, the weighted sum of all events for each dyad by year, weighted by the Goldstein scale for each type of event is computed.

Because the scaling codes are the same for VRA and WEIS it makes sense to compare conflict measures for these two data sets. To do so, we take the average severity weighted level of conflict and cooperation using the Goldstein scale weights given in Table 2. Note that the WEIS data is from 1966–1992 and the VRA is from 1990–2001. The average value for WEIS for net conflict was −0.82 during the recorded period while for VRA it was 0.55. A negative number indicates more conflict than cooperation, while a positive number indicates more cooperation. This is the case for the VRA

Table 2
Goldstein weighting scale for events reported in WEIS and VRA

Goldstein	IDEA	Definition
−8.3	072	Extend military aid
−7.6	074	rally support
−7.6	073	extend humanitarian aid
−7.4	071	extend economic aid
−6.5	081	make substantial agreement
−5.4	064	improve relations
−5.2	0523	promise humanitarian support
−5.2	0522	promise military support
−5.2	0521	promise economic support
−5.2	052	promise material support
−4.8	083	collaborate
−4.8	08	agree
−4.7	05	promise
−4.5	051	promise policy or non-material support
−3.5	0432	forgive
−3.5	04	endorse or approve
−3.4	093	ask for material aid
−3.4	092	solicit support
−3.4	043	empathize
−3.4	041	praise
−3	082	agree or accept
−2.9	065	ease sanctions
−2.8	054	assure
−2.8	033	host meeting
−2.5	062	extend invitation
−2.2	0655	relax curfew
−2.2	0654	demobilize armed forces
−2.2	0653	relax administrative sanction
−2.2	0652	relax censorship
−2.2	0651	observe truce
−2.2	0632	evacuate victims
−2.2	063	provide shelter
−2.2	06	grant
−2.2	0431	apologize
−2	013	acknowledge responsibility
−1.9	066	release or return
−1.9	032	travel to meet
−1.6	0933	ask for humanitarian aid
−1.6	0932	ask for military aid
−1.6	0931	ask for economic aid
−1.6	09	request
−1.5	1011	offer peace proposal
−1.5	101	peace proposal
−1.5	03	consult
−1.2	102	call for action

(*continued on next page*)

Table 2
(*continued*)

Goldstein	IDEA	Definition
−1.1	01	yield
−1	031	discussions
−0.8	10	propose
−0.6	012	yield position
−0.6	011	yield to order
−0.1	091	ask for information
−0.1	024	optimistic comment
0	99	sports contest
0	98	A and E performance
0	97	accident
0	96	natural disaster
0	95	human death
0	94	human illness
0	72	animal death
0	27	economic status
0	26	adjust
0	25	vote
0	24	adjudicate
0	2321	government default on payments
0	2312	private transactions
0	2311	government transactions
0	231	transactions
0	23	economic activity
0.1	094	ask for protection
0.1	022	pessimistic comment
0.1	021	decline comment
0.1	02	comment
0.9	141	deny responsibility
1	14	deny
1.1	0631	grant asylum
2.2	192	reduce routine activity
2.2	121	criticize or blame
2.4	132	formally complain
2.4	131	informally complain
2.4	13	complain
2.8	12	accuse
3	161	warn
3	16	warn
3.4	122	denounce or denigrate
3.8	194	halt negotiations
4	1134	break law
4	1132	disclose information
4	1131	political flight
4	113	defy norms
4	1123	veto

(*continued on next page*)

Table 2
(*continued*)

Goldstein	IDEA	Definition
4	1122	censor media
4	1121	impose curfew
4	112	refuse to allow
4	111	reject proposal
4	11	reject
4.4	2122	political arrest and detention
4.4	2121	criminal arrest and detention
4.4	212	arrest and detention
4.4	171	non-specific threats
4.5	1963	administrative sanctions
4.5	1961	strike
4.5	196	strikes and boycotts
4.5	19	sanction
4.9	151	demand
4.9	15	demand
5	201	expel
5	20	expel
5.2	1813	protest defacement and art
5.2	1812	protest procession
5.2	1811	protest obstruction
5.2	181	protest demonstrations
5.6	193	reduce or stop aid
5.8	172	sanctions threat
6.4	175	non-military force threats
6.4	17	threaten
6.8	2112	guerrilla seizure
6.8	2111	police seizure
6.8	21	seize
6.9	183	control crowds
6.9	1814	protest altruism
6.9	18	protest
6.9	174	give ultimatum
7	2231	military clash
7	195	break relations
7	1734	threaten military war
7	1733	threaten military occupation
7	1732	threaten military blockade
7	1731	threaten military attack
7	173	military force threat
7.6	1827	military border violation
7.6	1826	military border fortification
7.6	1825	military mobilization
7.6	1824	military troops display
7.6	1823	military naval display
7.6	1821	military alert

(*continued on next page*)

Table 2
(*continued*)

Goldstein	IDEA	Definition
7.6	182	military demonstration
8.3	224	riot or political turmoil
8.7	221	bombings
9.2	2236	military seizure
9.2	2123	abduction
9.2	211	seize possession
9.6	2228	assassination
9.6	2227	guerrilla assault
9.6	2226	paramilitary assault
9.6	2225	torture
9.6	2224	sexual assault
9.6	2223	bodily punishment
9.6	2222	shooting
9.6	2221	beatings
9.6	222	physical assault
9.6	22	force
10	2237	biological weapons use
10	2235	assault
10	2234	military occupation
10	2233	coups and mutinies
10	2232	military raid
10	223	military engagements

Note: Goldstein weights are scaled (i.e., multiplied) by -1.0 to give conflictive events positive values and cooperative events negative values.
Source: King and Lowe (2003, pp. 622–623).

data. Apparently in the 1990s there was more cooperation than conflict. Although, the conflict-cooperation scale differs, the same pattern is also true for COPDAB. So it appears that between 1948 and 1978 there also was more cooperation reported than conflict.

On the other hand, the WEIS data from 1966-1993 exhibits more conflict than co-operation. To give some indication of annual conflict, we plot these data disaggregated by year in Figure 3. Note for the years in common (1990–1993) the WEIS and VRA levels differ, but move in the same direction. We attribute the differences in levels to dissimilar news sources and dissimilar countries between the two data sets. Probably this observed difference between data sets most likely results because WEIS uses the New York Times as its sole source of international relations information. Conflict can easily dominate if the New York Times emphasizes conflict over cooperation in its news reporting or if the New York Times concentrates on a narrower set of (most likely larger more populated) countries. This potential bias could raise concern regarding comparability between datasets. When using data for the United States as actor as it interacts

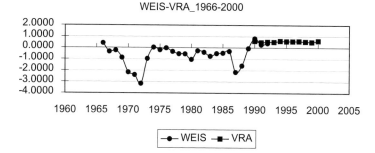

Figure 3. WEIS and VRA aggregate conflict data by year.

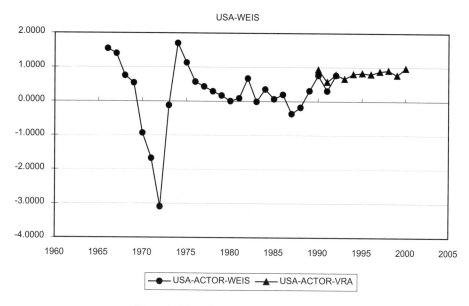

Figure 4. US conflict based on WEIS and VRA.

with other nations as shown in Figure 4 we find smaller differences in levels but not direction change for the years in common to both data sets.

3.1.2. Measuring trade

The dyadic trade variable is usually measured in terms of trade volume in millions of current US dollars. Generally dyadic trade is defined as the sum of imports and exports between the actor and target countries. When expressed as a proportion of a country's GDP it attempts to measure the dependence between dyads. Another measure that is constructed is dyadic trade shares (dyadic trade as a proportion of a country's total trade). The empirical findings that use this variable are difficult to interpret. For example, one does not know whether a negative coefficient for a trade share variable arises because of a negative relationship between the numerator (dyadic trade) and the dependent variable (conflict) or a positive relationship between the denominator (total trade) and the dependent variable. Indeed the coefficient tends towards zero if both dyadic and total trade are inversely related to conflict. We believe that it is better to adjust for each country's attribute variables separately, rather than to use composite variable like the latter.

3.1.3. Quantifying other country attributes

In most empirical studies of trade and conflict, a host of other variables are used as controls. Political scientists often control for a country's power and polity. Economists often control for the level of development. One method of measuring power is to construct a variable based on the COW military capabilities index for each country within the dyad. For example, a common approach is to identify the country with the maximum power and the one with the minimum power within a dyad, i.e., the stronger country and the weaker country. Then the ratio of these two values measures the relative capability of the stronger country over the weaker. Political science theorists predict that the more unbalanced the powers, the less likely they are to engage in conflict. Generally, a categorical variable is also included to indicate whether the dyad includes a major power.

Other variables include regime type. One standard approach to define regime type is obtained by using the Jaggers and Gurr (1995) index. Following Oneal and Russett (1999), to normalize regime type scores to be non-negative, a constant is added to each score. This variable is also used to test whether democracies are less prone to fight with each other. A joint democracy variable is defined by multiplying the dyad's two regime scores. Higher scores indicate more democratic dyads. Another control variable is a political dissimilarity variable based on Henderson (2002) who argues that dyads comprised of similar regime types share peace. This enables one to control whether autocratic states share peace as do joint democracies. Political dissimilarity is defined as the absolute distance between two countries' regime types. In addition, many control for the distance between countries. This is usually done by means of a contiguity categorical dummy variable. This variable measures whether two countries within a dyad share a land border, or share a water border separated by 400 miles or less. Much current research, e.g., Vasquez (1995) argues that contiguous dyads conflict more. Finally, some researchers include World Trade Organization (WTO) membership, given that mutual benefits associate with WTO membership arguably reduces conflict. WTO is coded one if both countries are WTO members, and zero otherwise.

Table 3 presents descriptive statistics for many of these variables over the three time-periods encompassing the events data mentioned above. Consistent with globalization, dyadic trade trends upward. During 1950–2000 average trade rose from $205 million to $2.4 billion. We also see two additional secular trends related to globalization. First, de-

Table 3
Descriptive statistics (mean variable values)

Variables	COPDAB (1948–1978)	WEIS (1966–1992)	VRA (1990–2000)
Trade	205.0965	2007.158	2376.502
Maximum power	0.0274	0.0571	0.0311
Minimum power	0.0029	0.0057	0.0041
Joint democracy	105.4562	144.09	229.0424
Political dissimilarity	7.4171	8.7586	6.8849
Contiguity dummy	0.1391	0.2321	0.1523
Major power dummy	0.1851	0.4656	0.2587
GATT/WTO membership dummy	0.3382	0.4295	0.5732
Observations	76,705	15,702	36,434

Note: Computed for country pairs (dyads) contained in COPDAB, WEIS, and VRA.
Variable definitions:

  Trade: dyadic trade volume in millions of current US dollars;

  Maximum power: Composite index of national capabilities (CINC) score (ranging from 0 to 1) of the stronger country within dyads (see: Correlates of War Project National Material Capabilities Data Documentation Version 3.0, last update: May 2005);

  Minimum power: CINC score of the weaker country within dyads;

  Joint democracy: multiplication of regime type scores (obtained from the Polity IV Survey) within dyads (1–441);

  Political dissimilarity: distance between regime type scores within dyads (0–20);

  Contiguity dummy: one if borders by land or by water within 400 miles, zero otherwise;

  Major power dummy: one if China, France, Great Britain, Russia/USSR or United States is within dyads, zero otherwise;

  GATT/WTO membership: one if both countries were GATT or WTO members, zero otherwise.

mocratization is increasing. The average level of joint democracy was measured at 105 between 1948–1978, whereas it was 229 between 1990–2000. With a score of 105 we can say that the average country is slightly autocratic, but with a score of 229 the average country is mid-way democratic. This implies that overall democratic levels throughout the world increased substantially over this time period. Second, membership in GATT and the WTO increased from 34% in COPDAB (1945–1978) to 57% in VRA (1990–2000). Countries contained in the WEIS data might somewhat overstate trade because the WEIS data rely only on countries reported in the New York Times. As already mentioned, these countries are probably politically and economically more viable.

3.2. Statistical analysis: Testing the trade–conflict theory

3.2.1. Single equation cross-sectional analysis

Polachek (1978) was the original test of this model. His, as well as most current research address the conflict–trade relationship using a single-equation framework. Typically some measure of bilateral conflict is regressed on a measure of bilateral trade holding country attributes constant. His model was

$$z_{ij} = \alpha_0 + \alpha_1 X_{ij} + \alpha_2 A_i + \alpha_3 A_j + \varepsilon_{ij}, \tag{12}$$

where z_{ij} represents conflict from country i to country j, X_{ij} depicts trade from i to j, and A_i and A_j reflect attributes of each country. These included population density, percentage GNP originating in industry, highway vehicles, secondary school enrollments, university enrollments, GNP per capita, yearly percentage changes in population, total imports and exports, and university enrollments. These regressions yielded a strong inverse relationship. A 10% increase in trade was associated with about a 1.5% decrease in conflict.

Currently numerous other papers provide empirical support for this result. All are single equation, but employ various models ranging from OLS, to GLS, logit and probit as well as Cox regression models. Various measures of conflict and varying sets of independent variables are used. They include Wallenstein (1973), Domke (1988), Kim (1995), Oneal et al. (1996), Oneal and Ray (1997), Oneal and Russett (1996, 1999), Sayrs (1990), Mansfield (1994), Mansfield and Pevehouse (2000), Crescenzi (2000), Anderton and Carter (2001), Gartzke and Li (2001), Bearce and Fisher (2002), Beck (2003), Gelpi and Grieco (2003), Hegre (2003), McDonald (2004), Bearce and Omori (2005) and Martin, Mayer and Thoenig (2005). On the other hand, only a limited number of articles do not lend support to this specification. They include Barbieri (1996, 2002), Barbieri and Levy (1999), Keshk, Pollins and Reuveny (2004), and Russett (1967).

With the exception of Polachek (1980) and Arad and Hirsch (1981) this model largely went unexplored until Pollins' (1989a, 1989b) important articles examining the opposite, namely whether trade is affected by conflict. He estimates the following model:

$$\ln M_{ijt} = \ln \beta_0 + \beta_1 \ln D_{ijt} + \beta_2 \ln D_{ijt-1} + \beta_3 \ln P_{ijt} + \beta_4 \ln P_{it}$$
$$+ \beta_5 \ln Y_{it} + \beta_5 u_{ijt}, \tag{13}$$

which denotes imports as a function of current and lagged diplomatic cooperation (D), bilateral and world import prices (P), as well as aggregate importer economic activity (Y). For each nation studied, diplomatic cooperation strongly enhances trade. From this, Pollins concludes that "nations adjust trade ties to satisfy security as well as economic welfare goals and that a formal political economy of trade should reflect this fact" [Pollins (1989b, p. 737)]. Of course, this is consistent with the conflict–trade model because the model predicts that trading nations engage in less conflict (more cooperation) because conflict leads to the diminution of trade. Traders thus cooperate in order to protect trade gains. As such, the conflict–trade relationship is simultaneous: conflict reduces trade, *and at the same time* trade reduces conflict. The problem is that single equation models do not distinguish whether both causal relationships hold. One method used to assess this dual causality has been to employ simultaneous equations techniques.

3.2.2. Cross-sectional causality: The trade–conflict relationship with trade treated endogenously

Does trade reduce conflict, does conflict reduce trade, or are both occurring simultaneously? To address this problem a number of studies examine the conflict–trade relationship using a simultaneous equations approach. The first was Polachek (1980) who used a simple two-stage least squares approach to estimate (12). Here the inverse trade conflict-elasticity more than doubled from about 0.15 to 0.35. Thus a 10% increase in trade was predicted to decrease conflict by 3.5%. Later Polachek (1992) utilized three-stage least-squares to estimate both equations simultaneously. In one equation, he assumed that conflict affects trade, while in the other he assumed trade affects conflict. However, the approach is limited because of the inherent difficulty in choosing exogenous variables to identify each equation. Essentially, Polachek used defense expenditures to identify conflict and cooperation, and development-type variables such as highway vehicles per capita, secondary school enrollments and electrical production to identify trade. Here he found that a 10% increase in trade led to a 39% decrease in conflict, but that a 10% increase in conflict had insignificant effects on trade. But he did not perform any robustness checks. Later, the issue of simultaneity was again addressed by Reuveny (2001) and Reuveny and Kang (2003). Reuveny and Kang (2003) fit equations separately for ten dyads. They found conflict and cooperation to be a significant determinant of trade and trade to be a significant determinant of conflict and cooperation. However, the signs of the effects varied by dyad. Here too, the strength of the particular relationships depended crucially on exogenous variables. As is often the case, there is little theory determining which exogenous variables are most appropriate. For this reason it is also useful to analyze causality in a time-series rather than a cross-sectional framework.

3.2.3. Time-series analysis[9]

Time-series data are important for two reasons. First such data can establish whether the inverse conflict–trade relationship obtained in the cross-section is valid over longer time periods. Second, time-series data can disentangle causality. If changes in trade levels are associated with corresponding changes in political behavior, or vice versa, then one can establish causality based on leads and lags in the time-series data.

3.2.3.1. A case study: US/Warsaw pact interactions. To illustrate, Gasiorowski and Polachek (1982) chose US/Warsaw pact countries between 1967 and 1979 as a case study.[10] These countries and the time period are important because of the volatility in

---

[9] This section borrows heavily from Gasiorowski and Polachek (1982). In addition, Polachek (2002a) performed the same analysis for US-China with similar results. Also see Reuveny and Kang (1996) for additional evidence.

[10] They also replicated the analysis for the US and Soviet Union. However, these results were not reported.

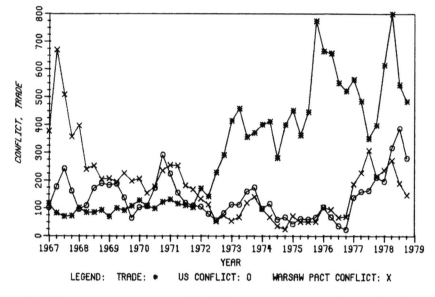

Figure 5. US–Warsaw pact trade and conflict 1967–1978 (quarterly data). *Source*: Gasiorowski and Polachek (1982).

US–Soviet relations during this timeframe. Recall the easing of US–Soviet hostilities in the big détente period of the late sixties and early seventies, and the abrupt shift that began to take place in the mid-1970s.

A time-series plot of US–Warsaw Pact trade and conflict from 1967 through 1978 are given in Figure 5. The trade measures, consisting of the sum of imports and exports, are given in real quarterly dollars. The conflict measures are intensity-weighted sums of conflictive events, aggregated quarterly from the COPDAB data. (Relative conflict measures are not needed in time-series analysis because the selectivity issues occur in each nation's reporting, but not in one nation's reporting over time.) The trends are in accord with prediction. Conflict declines as trade rises in the 1971–1972 period, then levels off until late 1975, as trade remains fairly constant. Both conflict measures show a fairly strong inverse correlation with trade before 1976. This is particularly apparent for Warsaw Pact conflict directed at the United States, which is substantially higher than United States conflict directed at the Pact before mid-1968. These inverse relationships support the contention that greater levels of trade are associated with lower levels of conflict.

The inverse trade/conflict relationship becomes more apparent when the trade and conflict data are plotted directly independent of time-period (Figure 6). Warsaw Pact conflict directed at the United States is given on the vertical axis and US–Warsaw pact trade is on the horizontal axis. The solid lines are linear and hyperbolic fits of the 1967–1975 data. The inverse relationship between conflict and trade becomes clear in this figure. In addition, it is evident that the relationship is non-linear, probably hyperbolic.

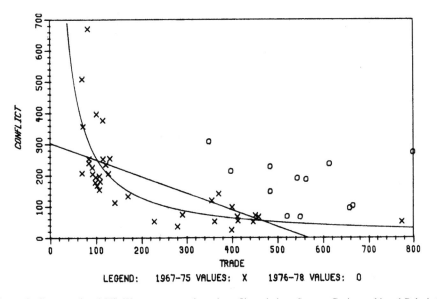

Figure 6. Cross-sectional US–Warsaw pact trade and conflict relation. *Source*: Gasiorowski and Polachek (1982).

3.2.3.2. Time-series causality. Time-series data enable one to compute Granger type causality tests. To do this, simply ascertain whether trade in one time period affects future conflict, and vice versa. Put simply, increases in explanatory power induced by lagged trade values in a regression of conflict as a function of trade indicates causality running from trade to conflict. With T representing trade and Z representing conflict, there is Granger causality if past values of T affect present values of Z. The Granger method thus involves a test of the joint hypothesis that $c_{-i} = 0$ for $i = 1$ to j, where c_{-i} is the coefficient of T lagged i periods in the following equation:

$$Z = c_0 + at + bt + (c_{-1}T_{-1} + \cdots + c_{-j}T_{-j}) + (d_{-1}Z_{-1} + \cdots + d_{-j}Z_{-j}),$$

(14)

where c_0 is the constant term, t is the time trend, T and Z are the lagged values of T and Z, and c and d are coefficients. The null hypothesis that $c_{-i} = 0$ for $i = 1$ to j implies that the past values of trade do not predict (and hence "cause") current conflict. This hypothesis can be tested with Fischer's F-test.

Rejection of this hypothesis implies that some past values of T significantly affect present Z. Thus, the condition for Granger causality to hold is to reject the null hypothesis. By the same token one can also test the reverse, which is whether past conflict "causes" current trade by re-specifying the above equation as follows:

$$T = T_0 + a't + b't + \left(c'_{-1}T_{-1} + \cdots + c'_{-j}T_{-j}\right) + \left(d'_{-1}Z_{-1} + \cdots + d'_{-j}Z_{-j}\right).$$

(15)

In this case, rejection of the null hypothesis that $d'_{-i} = 0$ for $i = 1$ to j implies that past conflict affects current trade.

Probability values for Granger F-tests of the null hypotheses that trade does not cause conflict and that conflict does not cause trade for this dyadic relationship during the 1967–1978 time period are consistent with the hypothesis that trade affects conflict. Furthermore, there seems to exist complex lagged structures in the relationship. These results can be viewed as strengthening cross-sectional findings. Specifically, one can improve on the ability of contemporaneous trade to predict conflict by incorporating lagged trade values. Thus, the underlying relationship between trade and conflict is not strictly contemporaneous, but corresponds to a distributed lagged framework. Further work on the appropriate lagged structure is obviously necessary. Research by Reuveny and Kang (1996) extends this work by examining Granger causality for sixteen dyads. Using COPDAB and WEIS quarterly data from 1960 to the early 1990s to measure conflict and IMF trade data, they show that causality generally runs in both directions. However, the strength of causality differs by the particular dyad. Thus, examining particular bilateral relationships might lead one to ponder whether the conflict–trade relationship is dyad specific. If so, it is likely that dyad-specific effects influence the conflict–trade relationship.

3.2.4. Fixed effects

The usual procedure to get at the above dyad-specific type heterogeneity is to re-specify the empirical model by adding a dyad-specific constant. In the linear form

$$NCONF_{ijt} = x_{ijt}\beta + A_{it}\gamma_i + A_{jt}\gamma_j + \alpha_{ij} + \varepsilon_{ijt}, \tag{16}$$

where β is the common effect of trade, α_{ij} the unobservable dyad-specific effects, and γ the effect of individual country attributes. One problem with this usual fixed-effects specification is that it assumes the dyad specific effect acts only through the intercept. However, the fixed effects can operate through the other coefficients, as well. For example, if

$$NCONF_{ijt} = x_{ijt}\beta_{ij} + A_{it}\gamma_i + A_{jt}\gamma_j + \alpha_{ij} + \varepsilon_{ijt}, \tag{17}$$

one could estimate dyad-specific coefficients for the trade variable (β).[11] An alternative is to run regressions for each dyad separately, especially since all coefficients can vary by dyad. Given the large number of possible dyads, we present a graph taken from Polachek (2002b) of the conflict–trade relation between the US and 115 countries for 1948–1978 in Figure 7. Each line (or curve) represents the best between a linear and hyperbolic bi-variate fit (based on R^2) between US conflict with a specific country and the US and each other country. On the vertical axis is an index of US conflict towards

---

[11] The technique Polachek and Kim (1994) develop for estimating gender wage differences could be applied to estimate such individual-specific slope coefficients.

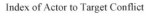

Index of Actor to Target Conflict

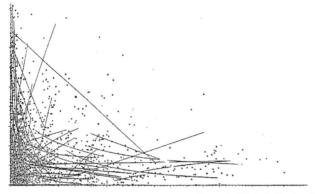

Percent of Actor's Trade with Target

Figure 7. Conflict–trade relationships between US and each country. *Note*: Each curve depicts the fitted (linear or hyperbolic) conflict–trade relationship between US (as actor) and each target country. The dots depict raw data. *Source*: Polachek (2002b).

each other country. On the horizontal axis is the percent of US trade with each specific target country. Interestingly, not all conflict–trade curves are negatively sloped. While most dyads show an inverse relationship between trade and conflict, a significant number exhibit a positive sign. Do these fixed-effect (fixed-dyad) results contradict the conflict–trade model?

One possibility is that the trade–conflict model is not tested adequately. All empirical results presented relate measures of conflict to *levels* of trade. However, the theory deals with trade *gains*, not trade levels. Trade *levels* and trade *gains* are proportional when each country exhibits similar import demand and export supply curves. However, it is not clear one can safely assume import demand and export supply curves are so similar, particularly across heterogeneous countries. Basing all empirical work on this crucial assumption may be erroneous. Of course, this assumption does not negate the theory, just the empirical implementation. Thus, one can modify the empirical implementation to rid the analysis of this assumption. If one does this, the results strengthen dramatically.

3.2.5. The trade–conflict relationship augmented by bilateral import demand elasticities[12]

Recall that the conflict–trade model hypothesizes that the welfare gains from trade induce bilateral cooperation and diminish conflict. The above empirical tests use trade to proxy welfare gains. However, as just indicated above, trade is an imperfect measure

---

[12] This section is based on research with Judith McDonald. See Polachek and McDonald (1992).

of welfare gains. Welfare gains are the sum of each trading partner's respective producer and consumer surpluses. Indeed, producer and consumer surplus are proportional to trade, but they are also inversely related to import and export demand and supply price elasticities. The more inelastic these import demand and export supply functions, the greater the trade gains, holding trade levels constant. Failing to utilize demand and supply elasticities implies an omitted variable bias. Even the sign of this bias is impossible to determine since one cannot predict the correlation between trade level and trade elasticity. Neglecting these elasticities can bias the statistical work used in current tests of the trade conflict hypothesis, thus making them unreliable. For this reason, incorporating elasticities to get at trade gains might shed light on some of the perverse results from the above fixed-effect analysis.

To incorporate these gains from trade measures, Polachek and McDonald (1992) augment the basic conflict–trade equation (12) by incorporating import demand elasticities to get at trade gains. Letting g_{ij} represent trade gains arising from actor i's trade with j, they rewrite the trade–conflict equation as

$$z_{ij} = \alpha_0 + \alpha_1 g_{ij} + \alpha_2 A_i + \alpha_3 A_j + \varepsilon_{ij}. \tag{18}$$

Here,

$$g_{ij} = \int_0^{\text{imports}} p_m(m_{ij}) \, dm_{ij} + \int_0^{\text{exports}} p_x(x_{ij}) \, dx_{ij}.$$

Solving the integral implies that gains from trade are proportional to trade levels but inversely related to trade elasticities. Thus, the gains from trade are proportional to the sum of imports and exports, weighted by the inverse of their respective import demand and export supply elasticities, as indicated below:

$$g_{ij} = m_{ij}/\varepsilon_{m_{ij}} + x_{ij}/\varepsilon_{x_{ij}}.$$

Relating trade and price elasticity to gains from trade means that incorporating these data in the conflict–trade model implies trade and conflict to be inversely related, as previously observed. But in addition, conflict is *positively* related to import demand (and export supply) price elasticities. Thus one should incorporate these elasticities to test the conflict–trade hypothesis.

Ideally one would desire commodity-specific elasticities to test whether trade in specific commodities affects international relations. However, to date, no comprehensive commodity-specific bilateral elasticities are available.[13] Nor are there any export supply price elasticities readily available, even on the aggregate level. So Polachek and McDonald (1992) concentrated on augmenting the conflict–trade model with demand elasticities computed by Marquez (1988, 1990) and Hooper, Johnson and Marquez (1998) obtained from the existing empirical international trade literature. Adopting

---

[13] Haas and Turner (1988) present information on three broad merchandise trade categories for 14 OECD countries. We will refer to these estimates shortly.

Goldstein and Kahn's (1985) imperfect substitute model, Marquez (1988, 1990) estimated income and price elasticities for bilateral import demand equations by utilizing
a world trade model he developed with data from 1970 to 1984. To incorporate these
elasticities, the empirical specification is further modified as follows:

$$z_{ij} = \alpha_0 + \alpha_1 m_{ij} + \alpha_2 x_{ij} + \alpha_3 \varepsilon_{m_{ij}} + \alpha_4 \varepsilon_{x_{ij}} + \alpha_5 A_i + \alpha_6 T_j + \varepsilon_{ij}, \qquad (19)$$

where m_{ij} and x_{ij} represent dyadic imports and exports, $\varepsilon_{m_{ij}}$ and $\varepsilon_{x_{ij}}$ represent import and export demand and supply elasticities and A and T depict actor and target
attributes.

Regression results for the Marquez elasticity augmented conflict–trade model using
country trade and attribute data for 1973 to maintain time period compatibility with the
1970–1984 Marquez elasticities are given in Table 4. They show conflict to be inversely
related to trade, but interestingly the magnitude is far stronger than in past estimates.
A doubling of imports leads to a 50% conflict reduction. Similarly, a doubling of exports
leads to a 30% decline in conflict. (Recall previous estimates yield about a 15% reduction in conflict.) To enhance the gains from trade argument, the difference in actor-target
gross national product (GNP) is used as an exogenous proxy for differences in factor
endowment. If actor and target GNP differences (GNPDIF) imply differences in actor-

Table 4
The trade–conflict relation

Variable	Mean[1]	Coefficient[2]	Elasticity[3]
Constant		−50.49	
		(3.12)	
Dyadic trade elasticity	0.83	37.62	0.47
	(0.04)	(2.63)	
Exports (billions US$)	4.13	−4.49	0.28
	(0.67)	(4.47)	0.28
Imports (billions of US$)	4.02	−8.21	0.50
	(0.67)	(−6.86)	
GNP (actor)	232.8	0.0178	
	(26.1)	(0.46)	
GNP (actor)–GNP (target)	3.93	−0.056	0.003
	(39.0)	(2.20)	
Net conflict	−66.63		
	(9.66)		
R^2		0.35	
Number of observations		178	

Note: The dependent variable is net-conflict computed from COPDAB.
Source: Polachek and McDonald (1992).

[1] Standard error of mean in parentheses.

[2] *t*-values in parentheses.

[3] Computed at mean values.

target factor endowments, then a larger GNPDIF should raise the gains from trade and diminish conflict. Here the regression result (−0.56) is also consistent with the trade–conflict hypothesis.

The result for import demand elasticity is most important. Here, as mentioned earlier, theory predicts a positive relation between the import demand elasticity and conflict, and indeed this positive relation is observed. The 37.62 coefficient implies that a 10 percent more inelastic demand is associated with a 4.7% lower level of conflict. What is significant is that incorporating import demand elasticities not only yields the predicted sign, but strengthens previous finding regarding trade's effects on conflict, as well. But the analysis can be extended even further.

Albeit for only 14 of the largest OECD countries, Polachek and McDonald (1992) exploit the International Monetary Fund's (IMF) World Trade Model (WTM) to devise import and export price elasticities for three important commodity groups: manufactures, agricultural goods, and raw materials [see Haas and Turner (1988) for a description of the model]. The WTM emphasizes the demand for a country's exports as the weighted sum of its trading partners' imports. Import demand functions depend on domestic activity and relative prices. Export supply is determined by the foreign market size, relative export prices, and capacity utilization. These equations are estimated for 1962–1983. Bilateral trade elasticities can be obtained using trade share matrix methodology outlined by Armington (1969). According to Armington, country i's demand elasticity is proportional to a share-weighted sum of a country's elasticity of substitution for a commodity (between any pair of countries) and the partial elasticity of demand buyers in country i have for the commodity in general, irrespective of the source of supply. Specifically,

$$N_{ij} = (1 - S_{ij})e_i + S_{ij}n_i,$$

where, N_{ij} = the ith country buyers' partial elasticity of demand for the commodity produced by the jth country, S_{ij} = the share of the jth country's expenditures for the commodity in the ith country's total expenditures on the commodity, e_i = the elasticity of substitution in the ith market between the commodity and any pair of countries (including the ith), and n_i = the partial elasticity of demand country i's buyers have for the commodity irrespective of the source of supply. When $i \neq j$, n_{ij} is the ith country's import demand elasticity from j. Using the above equation, demand elasticities obtained from the WTM can be converted into bilateral elasticities. The shares s_{ij} are calculated from a square trade matrix for each of the three commodities (again, manufactures, agricultural products, and raw materials) using detailed OECD trade flow information. The elasticity of substitution can be obtained by using related estimates available from Marquez (1988).

Using this methodology and concentrating on manufactures shows the trade–conflict relationship holds. All the empirical work find the signs are consistent with expectations. In addition, this research has shown that the export and the import elasticities continue to be important determinants of net conflict. Yet, under this specification exports appear to be more important to reducing conflict than imports. The results for the trade–conflict relationship using bilateral elasticities for raw materials show less variation in these elasticities than for manufactures. As before, all signs are consistent with the trade–conflict hypothesis. A doubling of exports leads to a 43% decrease in conflict. GDP differences are associated with less conflict and the Armington coefficients are consistent with less conflict when bilateral import demand curves are more inelastic.

4. An application – The democratic peace: Why democracies do not fight each other[14]

4.1. The issue

Ever since 1979 when Rummel (1979b) cited Babst's relatively obscure article analyzing Wright's (1942) war data that "no wars have been fought between independent nations with elective governments" interest intensified to test the proposition that democracies do not fight each other. Earlier work such as by Wright (1942), Greggs and Banks (1965), Haas (1965), Russett and Monsen (1975), Small and Singer (1976) and even Rummel (1968) himself, considered democracies to be equally war prone as other states. Even research scholars pursuing their work immediately after Rummel's claim were skeptical. For example, based on data in the 1960s and 1970s, Weede (1984) demonstrates that democracy and war "are not consistently and significantly correlated with each other." According to him, only in the late seventies – "a period that seems rather exceptional" – did democracies succeed in avoiding involvement in wars. Domke (1988) using Gurr's Polity I data set "failed to find any consistent association between the degree of democracy and the likelihood of war" [Bremer (1992a, p. 316)]. Similarly Dixon (1989) failed to find an association between democracy and the frequency of war over the time span 1816–1971. Additionally, though hotly contested by Rummel (1987), Vincent (1987) presents regression equations claiming "virtually no relation between dyadic freedom and dyadic conflict."

In contrast to this skepticism, there is other evidence providing ample reason to suspect that democracies in fact do deter conflict. Wright (1942) followed later by Doyle (1986) argue based on political theory dating back to Kant (1795) that "democracies must favor development of peaceful modes of international settlement because they are dependent upon law." In addition, Doyle (1986) cites empirical evidence dating back to Streit (1940) that democracies deter conflict. In espousing the need for a union of nations with fifteen democracies as the nucleus to foster peace, Streit states "No two of the fifteen have fought each other since the Belgian–Dutch war of 1830. There is no parallel in politics to this achievement of democracy in maintaining peace so long among so many powerful, independent and often rival peoples, burdened with hatreds

---

[14] This section borrows heavily from Polachek and Robst (1998). See Polachek (2002b) and Polachek (2004) for an application regarding union membership and strike activity.

and prejudices left behind by all the previous fighting among them before they achieved democracy" [Streit (1940, pp. 66–67)]. Further Watkins (1942) found that democracies cooperated overwhelmingly more than non-democracies in the League of Nations. As evidence, he finds that "whereas 23 (55 per cent) of the non-democracies have a poor record of cooperation in international organization, only one (5 per cent) of the democracies can be classed with them."

In a well cited paper, Chan (1984) rectified these paradoxical differences regarding whether or not democracies deter conflict. His solution to the problem was mostly methodological: Monadic studies using single countries as the unit of observation fail to support the contention that democracies rarely fight. On the other hand, strong support emerges using dyads as units of observations. Indeed using the Small and Singer (1982) Correlates of War (COW) data, Chan finds overwhelming support that "the more libertarian two states [are] the less the mutual violence" [Chan (1984, p. 620)] while he finds little support that "the more libertarian a state, the less its foreign violence" [Chan (1984, p. 620)]. Chan's study thus served as an impetus for a number of dyadic-based tests of the hypothesis. These, in turn, have led to a number of further studies seeking reasons why the relationship holds. These studies include: Maoz and Abdelali (1989), Levy (1989), Morgan and Campbell (1991), Morgan and Schwebach (1992), Siverson and Emmons (1991), Ray (1993), Ember, Ember and Russett (1992), Bremer (1992a, 1993), Russett and Antholis (1992), Mintz and Geva (1993), Maoz and Russett (1993), Farber and Gowa (1997), Kegley and Hermann (1996), Eyerman and Hart (1996), Thompson and Tucker (1997), Gartzke (1998), Dixon (1998), Mousseau and Shi (1999), Cederman and Penubarti (2001), Doyle (2005), Slantchev, Alexandrova and Gartzke (2005), and Kinsella (2005). Noteworthy among these studies is the consistency of the findings; so much so that Levy (1989) calls the "democracies rarely fight" phenomena a "law", and Bremer (1992b) indicates that an "ISA Atlanta Panel composed of Bruce Bueno de Mesquita, Steve Chan, T. Clifton Morgan, Harvey Starr, Eric Weede and ... [himself] ... gave unanimous support to the proposition" [Bremer (1992b, p. 1)]. Nevertheless these papers reveal that the strength of the relationship depends on how wars are defined (i.e., whether one uses Correlates of War or MIDS data), whether one is talking about originating a war or merely joining a war, whether one is talking of "covert" activity, and finally on which time period one is considering.

Given these latter qualifications, it is essential to determine how the relationship holds up both with respect to conflict less severe than militarized disputes as well as with respect to cooperative behavior. Neither COW, MIDS nor alliance data, used in virtually all current studies, can answer this question fully because they include only specific and narrow types of conflict and cooperation. In addition, with war data the direction of conflict, i.e., who is the aggressor and who is the defender, is often difficult to discern. While not without shortcomings, events data contain a wide range of dyadic interactions which are more suitable for testing the impact of democracy. These data include both the severity of conflict and the extent of cooperation, as well as the directionality of each. In addition, because of the relatively large variation in the degree of conflict and cooperation across dyads, one can look not only at democracies and non-democracies, but also one can separate out non-democracies into cases where only the actor is a democracy, cases where only the target is a democracy, and cases where neither actor nor target are democracies. For this reason, it is useful to review more broadly the "do democracies 'fight' each other" question using events data.

Once it is established that these data show democracies exhibit less conflict with each other, we analyze the deeper question of why democracies fight less, a question about which there is now also a burgeoning literature. The innovation here by Polachek (1997) was to show that democracies are richer and have more trade. To protect this wealth, democracies conflict somewhat less and cooperate considerably more. Non-democracies have less to protect and as a consequence conflict more and cooperate less. This is the theme we emphasized earlier in the gains-from-trade argument.

4.2. The evidence

4.2.1. Measuring democracy: Ted Gurr data

The Gurr data codes countries' structural and institutional characteristics as they change over time. Central to the data are measures of democracy, autocracy, and power concentration. The consensus measure of democracy is the "institutionalized democracy" variable which is an amalgamation of three independent elements: (1) citizens' abilities to express their preferences to country leaders, (2) checks and balances on the executive branch, and (3) the degree to which citizen civil liberties are protected. Gurr provides a composite scale, which ranges in value from 0 to 10, with 10 denoting the most democratic country.

Most studies use a dichotomous version of this variable, but it seems to make sense that rather than throw away information on fine gradations, one should treat the democracy variable as continuous. Yet sometimes in order to anchor one's results to past studies, we must also present outcomes with a dichotomous democracy specification. We recommend the use of two dichotomous specifications: one being more stringent with a country being classified as a democracy if it achieves a Gurr index of 7 or higher; and a less stringent measure allowing for a Gurr index of 5 or higher. Note that Bremer (1992a) uses the less stringent definition. Farber and Gowa (1997) define a democracy as 6 or higher. Generally, there are only small differences in results whether democracy is treated continuously or dichotomously. Similarly, virtually the same results emerge for both dichotomous specifications of democracy.

As for the empirical findings, regression results uphold the finding that democratic dyads have 1.51 units less conflict on the COBDAB scale than non-democratic dyads, and that mixed dyads (one democracy and one non-democracy) have between 0.85 and 2.58 units more conflict depending on whether the pair contains a non-democratic actor and democratic target (2.58) or a democratic actor and non-democratic target (the comparison group). One should note too that these results hold up even if the US is eliminated as a target. This implies that US vented conflict is not driving the results, as one might have expected during the 1960s.

4.3. Conclusions from the trade–conflict model regarding the democratic peace

Two theories are given to explain why democracies rarely fight each other. The first theory is billed as cultural-normative, and the second as structural. In reality both are related because in part structural determinants are possibly culturally induced. Cultural-normative theories are based on Kant (1795), Wright (1942), and Doyle (1986), and advanced by Russett (1989) and others. They claim that adjudication and bargaining are so embedded within democratic societal norms that democracies are able to solve disputes peacefully, especially with other democracies (though the logic is a bit murky why democracies do not do better against non-democracies, as well). Structural theories, espoused by Morgan and Campbell (1991), and based on Rummel (1979a), Hagan (1987), Domke (1988), and Bueno de Mesquita and Lalman (1992), argue that there are so many checks and balances in the democratic decision process that making the decision to fight is difficult and not taken lightly, though one might have difficulty using this logic to explain why democratic actors do not fare much better against non-democratic targets than non-democracies. Non-democracies such as dictatorships need less justification to go to war. Zinnes (2004) uses propositional calculus to provide an explanation based on normative as well as these structural factors.

Distinguishing these two theories requires isolating identifiable structural characteristics defining decision constraints which explain why democracies rarely fight each other. Failing to find such characteristics would lead one to conclude in favor of innate cultural/normative characteristics of democracies. In this vain Morgan and Campbell (1991) favor the structural characteristics interpretation by showing that at least for major powers "higher levels of decisional constraints lead to a lower probability that conflict will escalate to war." However, being bothered by "weak statistical significance" [(1991, p. 206)] they temper their conclusion indicating the possible validity of cultural norms as well. In contrast, Maoz and Russett (1992, 1993), while arguing that "both the normative and structural models are supported by the data [(1993, p. 624)]", conclude in favor of cultural-normative theories because democracies seem to have an independent effect in their statistical analysis even after controlling for other variables. They use GDP per capita relative to the US (wealth), percent GDP change (growth), contiguity, COW alliance data, and Gurr political stability data.

Finding that democracy significantly deters conflict in a regression does not rule out spurious effects. In fact, finding democracy to be significant might merely indicate that researchers have not as yet found the appropriate determinants of conflict. In this case the democracy variable serves as a proxy for underlying factors not accounted for in the data. It is in this vain that Polachek (1997) tries to build on past theories of how international trade is related to conflict to forge a possible explanation for why "democracies rarely fight each other." His explanation differs from Starr (1992) who presents a game theoretic model of dove and non-dove nations, and from Lake (1992) who adopts a public choice type model in which the pacifism of democracies emerges among non-imperialist nations interested in maintaining security.

Before turning to the conflict among democracies question, we anchor this issue to the past results relating trade and conflict: To be applicable, one would have to show that democratic dyads exhibit greater trade (or greater gains from trade) than non-democratic dyads, and that as a consequence the greater trade contributes to greater cooperation and less conflict. Democracies cooperate more and conflict less to protect greater welfare levels arising from trade gains. By cooperating rather than fighting, trade is protected and individual welfare is enhanced by per capita increases in GNP attributable in part to these gains from trade.

To test the validity of this scenario one must show first that democratic dyads in fact trade more, and show second that this greater trade is related to lower amounts of conflict. In fact, imports average \$341 billion and exports \$314.13 billion for democratic dyads, and only \$14.2 to \$15.6 billion for non-democratic dyads. Consistent with the above hypothesis, democratic dyads exhibit far greater levels of trade. The mixed dyads have trade levels in between. This might be somewhat puzzling to the above hypothesis that trade is directly related to conflict since as one would expect conflict to be in between the purely democratic and purely non-democratic dyads. However, as indicated, trade may be an inappropriate measure of gains from trade. These results are upheld when looking at correlations between democracy and trade. Democratic dyads engage in more trade: The correlation between trade and the Gurr democracy index is strongly positive varying between 0.21 and 0.36 depending on the trade index. This positive correlation is roughly the same magnitude when using the dichotomous democracy index: 0.17 to 0.31 for the stringent definition of democracy and between 0.23 and 0.32 for the weaker democracy definition. Non-democratic dyads have lower dollar trade levels. The correlation here is -0.14. However, GNP weighted trade is not significantly lower for non-democracy pairs. The correlation is between -0.01 and 0.02, and not statistically different from zero. For the mixed democracy/non-democracy dyads, trade is significantly lower for both dollar and GNP-weighted trade measures. Thus these correlations are consistent with trade being the underlying reason democracies fight less with each other: Nation pairs with more trade exhibit less conflict, and democracy-pairs exhibit more trade. Thus it is possible that the greater trade between democracies is the underlying cause for less conflict among democratic dyads. Similarly the lower relative trade associated with mixed democracy/non-democracy pairs might be responsible for the greater conflict between these mixed country pairs.

Regression analysis yields almost the same story. Modeling conflict as a function of the continuous democracy score yields that the higher the product of both country's Gurr democracy scores, the more democratic the dyad and the lower the level of net conflict (-0.028). Also consistent with the above is an inverse relationship between conflict and trade since the coefficient for trade is generally found to be significantly negative. Thus it appears that trade deters conflict as reported in previous research, and more democratic dyads exhibit less conflict. One might argue that the negative democracy coefficient is possibly spurious if democracy proxies some other underlying factor. For example, if democracies have greater levels of trade which in turn decrease conflict, then omitting trade from the analysis could cause an omitted variable bias. One way to test for this is to consider whether conflict is jointly determined by democracy as well as trade. If rather than democracy per se decreasing conflict, one finds that higher levels of trade cause lower levels of conflict then the democracy coefficient will become insignificant once one includes trade in the regression model. This approach has been used and it is found that the democracy coefficient decreases in magnitude when trade is introduced linearly, and decreases further to a statistically insignificant level when trade is introduced in a quadratic form. Thus introducing trade explains away democracy's impact. It is important to note that the trade coefficient remains exactly the same magnitude and significance. This is consistent with democracy being a proxy for trade rather than trade for democracy. This result is invariant to the use of the categorical democracy variables rather than democracy measured continuously. As before, democratic-democratic dyads exhibit less conflict. Furthermore, adding trade reduces the magnitude and statistical significance of the democracy coefficient. Here too, it is important to note that the trade coefficient remains exactly the same. Thus again democracy is a proxy for trade rather than the reverse.

Obviously it is possible that trade too might not be an independent factor. Perhaps larger more developed countries are the ones with greater trade. To test this possibility, introducing GNP and population for both the actor and target leaves the trade coefficient the same. Introducing the dyadic democracy variables raises the dyadic democracy coefficient but leaves unaltered its statistical insignificance. Thus even when accounting explicitly for country size (both in terms of the economy and population) trade decreases dyadic conflict, but democracy pairs no longer exhibit lower levels of conflict. In fact, it could argue that once controlling for trade and country attributes democracies seem to exhibit greater conflict.

Yet, non-democracies have 2.6 units more conflict when dealing with democracies than non-democracies. Trade per se explains little of this difference in conflict. However, trade and wealth differences when taken together explain 54% of this difference and adding GNP non-linearly with trade virtually explains the whole difference. Going further, by accounting for the greater conflict levels democracies exhibit towards non-democracies, the research shows that non-democracies actually exhibit less conflict towards democracies than non-democracies.[15] In conclusion, these results together imply that all levels of inter-dyadic conflict can be explained. In short, at least using events data sets, democracy is not the relevant variable in explaining conflict. Dyadic differences in conflict are essentially fully accounted for by trade and wealth differences across nations. Encouraging free trade which through "gains from trade" tends to

---

[15] There are other explanations. For example, Levy and Razin (2004) use a game theoretic model to show that information asymmetries and strategic complements cause the strategic interaction between two democracies to differ from that of any other dyad. On the other hand Zeng (2004) uses game theory to show how trade competitiveness between democracies creates stronger domestic pressure for the use of threat tactics, increasing the risk of trade war. Hess and Athanasios (2001) argue that poorly performing incumbent leaders seek to hold on to power thereby generating an incentive to initiate conflict.

increase each nation's wealth appears to be the key to decreasing conflict and increasing cooperation.

Not all political scientists agree that trade represents the underlying foundation of the democratic peace. For example, Russett and Oneal (2001) claim that the "20th century has been marked by a hopeful evolution of a zone of peace" because nations are better able to triangulate peace based on democracy, trade, and the increased role of international governmental and non-governmental organizations. While it is possible democracy and trade can instigate peace, it is not clear they act independently. Because democracies tend to be more open and to engage in more trade than autocracies, greater trade may induce their pacific role. The theories that advocate the view that democracies are more peace prone largely fail to explain why liberal states achieve peace solely with other democracies.[16] For this reason a number of articles are skeptical of democracy's independent role. Rosato (2003) argues that whereas there is peace among democracies, it is not a result of their democratic nature. He claims democracies do not trust one another more, elected leaders are not "peace loving" and democracies are not particularly slow to mobilize. Further he claims that democracies are just as prone as other countries to avoid revealing private information about its level of resolve regarding disputes. Mousseau (2005) argues that the democratic peace is contingent on levels of development. He finds that democracies appear to be a significant war deterrent only in the richest 45% of the dyads. Based on theoretical game theory models, Bueno de Mesquita, Koch and Siverson (2004), argue one cannot determine *a priori* the pacific effects of democracies. On the one hand, the bargaining model predicts democracies draw out disputes so that diplomats have time to find non-war solutions. On the other hand, the way democracies select the disputes to participate in make disputes between democracies shorter. Zeng (2004) uses a two-level game approach to show how the democratic peace does not hold with regard to US trade wars. It is possible that trade competitiveness between democratic regimes creates an impetus to use threats, thereby increasing the likelihood of a trade war.

5. Extensions of the conflict–trade model

A number of factors influence gains from trade. These include type of trade, country size, market competition, country contiguity, tariffs, foreign aid, and the number of countries in the international system. Just recently, a number of authors have begun to examine some of these aspects of the conflict–trade relationship. In this section, we briefly touch on these issues.

---

[16] See MacMillan (2003) for an extensive survey on this issue covering over 25 articles on this topic.

5.1. Commodity-specific trade

A number of papers examine how the conflict–trade relation differs depending on the commodities traded. Polachek (1980) finds that oil importers are more cooperative toward oil exporters. Polachek and McDonald (1992) show that conflict decreases when OECD nations trade manufactured goods and raw materials. This inverse relation is enhanced the more price inelastic are these imports. Using 1963–1980 trade data for several OECD countries in five commodity categories (agriculture-fishery, energy, ores-minerals, manufactured goods, and miscellaneous consumer goods), Reuveny and Kang (1996, 1998) find that the strength of the conflict–trade relation depends on the specific commodities. A rise in trade generates cooperation in 15 cases they examine and conflict in nine. They find a rise in agriculture-fishery and energy trade generates cooperation, whereas the effect for ores-minerals, manufactured goods, and miscellaneous consumer goods is mixed. As Reuveny and Kang recommend, more research is warranted in this area.

5.2. Foreign direct investment

Not only is trade increasing, but the amount of capital flows is as well. As global integration has expanded, countries have moved into a more complicated interdependent network. Foreign direct investment's annual growth rate exceeded the growth of international trade over the past decade and broke through the trillion US dollar level in 2000. This contrasts with the period of the 1960s and 1970s when countries were concerned with the possibility that their sovereignty would be reduced by multinational foreign direct investment. The focus now is on the positive effects of FDI and other types of capital flows on the home and host countries' economies. This change in attitude was complemented by the adoption of favorable policies by many countries to attract FDI. These developments raise the possibility that the role of direct investment in determining interstate relationships has increased in importance.

Research on the impact of foreign investments by multinational corporations (MNC) on the international system predates the recent increase in globalization. The more conventional literature [Vernon (1971), Gilpin (1975) and Nye (1974)] takes the view that multinational corporations (MNC) are tied to their home countries and that nation states are still the principal actors in the international system. However, if multinational firms are essentially national firms competing with one another around the globe, as Gilpin (2001) points out, then one would expect some correlation between the direct investments of multinationals and the foreign policy of their home countries.

There is now a literature examining the determinants of FDI.[17] But FDI's effects on international relations is still at its infancy. Thompson (2003) argues that direct investment draws countries closer to each other thereby decreasing the probability of deadly

---

[17] See Froot (1995), Rayome and Baker (1995), Saggi (2002), and Blonigen (2005) for surveys of the literature on the determinants of FDI.

conflicts. In empirical work using post World War II data, he illustrates that reciprocal FDI flows leads to fewer instances of conflict. Using the current political atmosphere he argues that United States, China, and Taiwan are drawn closer together because FDI flows between countries instigates the necessity to maintain stability. Based on information from World War I, Thompson argues that the warring countries had little or no FDI leading to diminished integration. In a sense this latter finding helps explain the paradox that trading nations participated in World War I whereas conflict–trade theory argues that trade should have deterred conflictive activity.

Polachek, Seiglie and Xiang (2005) also examine how FDI affects conflict and cooperation. They invoke a three-stage least squares simultaneous equations model using bilateral FDI flows from 1990–2000 and the VRA data mentioned earlier. One equation models FDI as a function of actor and target cooperation (actually net cooperation defined as the weighted cooperation minus conflict directed from an actor to target nation) and such country attributes as population, school enrollment, telephone mainlines, and gross capital formation – all of which measure levels of development. The other equation specifies net cooperation as a function of FDI, actor and target GDP, joint democracy and contiguity.

According to their results (Table 5), FDI has a significant positive effect on the net cooperation variable (0.014). For a one million US dollar increase in FDI within a dyad, on average net conflict will be reduced by 0.014 units (i.e., net cooperation will increase by 0.014 units). Translating this to an elasticity measure yields 0.31 meaning that increasing FDI by 1% yields an increase in cooperation by 0.31%, on average. The coefficient on the net cooperation variable (23.0 in column 2) also confirms that cooperation has a significant positive impact on FDI. This coefficient is consistent with FDI enhancing dyadic relationships. In this case, a one-unit change in net cooperation will increase one FDI by about $23.0 million. The elasticity for this relationship is 1.036. Thus a 1% increase in net cooperation will increase FDI by 1.04%.

5.3. Country size

Alesina and Spolaore (2003) develop a brilliant yet parsimonious model, capable of cogently addressing country size. They define nations as powerful entities whose prime purpose is to ensure well-being for their citizens. Larger countries permit economies of scale, so per citizen costs for public goods, such as defense, diminish; but by becoming large, a nation grows more heterogeneous, making the country more difficult to manage. Bigger populations imply diversity, but diversity complicates how leaders provide public goods because a wide-ranging citizenry often have conflicting interests. The tradeoff between these two, i.e., scale and heterogeneity, determines any particular nation's size. Any factor that alters this tradeoff influences a nation's size.

As an illustration, large countries need not trade as much as small countries because their size brings a greater variety of resources and more self-sufficiency. At the same time larger countries possess economies of scale in providing a powerful military. A world environment that encourages free and open trade leads to more trade.

Table 5
Three-stage least square estimation of FDI-conflict relationship-FDI inflow (Z-score in parentheses)

Independent variables	Dependent variables	
	Total (net cooperation)	FDI inflow
Constant	−0.260	−1827.978***
	(−0.16)	(−4.61)
FDI inflow	0.014***	
	(7.72)	
GDP actor	9.03e–06***	−4.36e–05
	(14.77)	(−1.35)
GDP target	6.18e–06***	−3.57e–07
	(11.05)	(−0.01)
Power ratio	−0.142***	
	(−8.59)	
Joint democracy	−0.014***	
	(−3.68)	
Contiguity	7.103***	
	(4.67)	
Total (net cooperation)		23.000***
		(8.59)
WTO		128.576*
		(1.97)
Population actor		3.91e–04***
		(3.36)
Population target		0.001***
		(4.03)
Telephone mainlines actor		0.442**
		(2.75)
Telephone mainlines target		0.357*
		(2.35)
School enrollment, primary actor		4.169*
		(2.02)
School enrollment, primary target		1.772
		(0.83)
School enrollment, secondary actor		3.231**
		(2.87)
School enrollment, secondary target		5.873***
		(4.68)
Gross capital formation actor		−2.761
		(−0.83)
Gross capital formation target		−5.200
		(−1.53)
R^2	0.2730	0.1756
N	5449	5449

Source: Polachek, Seiglie and Xiang (2005).
  * $p < 0.05$;
 ** $p < 0.01$;
*** $p < 0.001$.

At the same time, greater trade implies a lesser need for self-sufficiency, and results in smaller countries [Alesina and Spolaore (2003, Chapter 6)]. In contrast, a more belligerent world with more conflict leads countries to demand a larger military. To accomplish this, nations seek economies of scale to finance defense. As such, countries become relatively large [Alesina and Spolaore (2003, Chapter 7)]. According to Alesina and Spolaore (2003, p. 127) "these two effects are not unrelated once . . . [one considers the] connection between conflict and trade". Conflict induces larger countries that trade less, but less trade brings about more conflict. On the other hand, smaller countries trade more, but greater trade enhances peace.

5.4. Multilateral interactions[18]

Bilateral trade is not independent of other countries. Feng (1994) relates trade to alliance conflict. He finds that the relationship between trade and alliance conflict depends upon what he calls externality cost. Externality costs implies that conflict with friends of allies is more costly than with friends of foes. As such, post-World War II trade between the United States and an ally (e.g., Britain, Canada, France, West Germany, Italy and Japan) increased in direct proportion to conflict between the United States and Soviet Union. How alliances form and how third parties intervene in ongoing conflicts form a large political science literature [e.g., see Altfield and Bueno de Mesquita (1979), Holsti, Hopmann and Sullivan (1973), Kim (1991), Sabrosky (1980), Singer and Small (1966a, 1966b), Siverson and King (1979, 1980)]. In this vein, Altfield (1984), Morrow (1991), Powell (1991), and Simon and Gartzke (1996) among others base alliances on security gains from joining a coalition. Altfield and Bueno de Mesquita (1979) use an expected-utility model to predict that intervention depends on the utility gained from one or the other party winning. As such intervention is more likely if a third party gains considerable utility from one country winning, instead of another.

One can incorporate multilateral interactions into the conflict–trade framework described above. Going back to a country's objective function (specified in (1)), simply denote all possible targets as $i = 1, \ldots, n$. In this framework, we now denote actor A's utility function as

$$U_A = U_A(C, Z_1, Z_2, \ldots, Z_n; U_1, U_2, \ldots, U_n), \tag{20}$$

where $i = 1, \ldots, n$ denotes each of the world's n countries actor A faces. The variable Z_i reflects conflict with each country i. The variable U_i depicts welfare levels of each other country. As before, $\partial U_A / \partial Z_i > 0$ depicts the welfare gain from conflict with country i. But now, $\partial U_A / \partial U_i$ designates how country i's welfare affects the actor. $\partial U_A / \partial U_i > 0$ implies i is a friend, while $\partial U_A / \partial U_i < 0$ implies i is an enemy. As such, an actor's welfare is higher the higher the welfare of a friend, and smaller the higher the welfare of a foe. More generally, for any two nations i and j $\partial U_i / \partial U_j > 0$ implies i and j are friends and $\partial U_i / \partial U_j < 0$ implies i and j are enemies.

---

[18] This section borrows heavily from Polachek (2003).

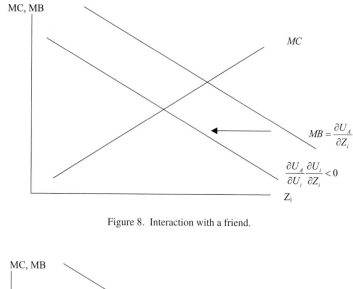

Figure 8. Interaction with a friend.

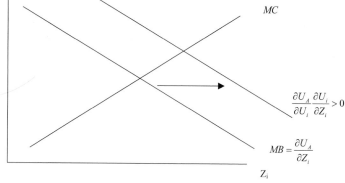

Figure 9. Interaction with a rival.

Whereas an actor's conflict toward country i can increase actor welfare $\partial U_A / \partial Z_i \geqslant 0$, it most certainly decreases the target's welfare since no country likes to be the recipient of conflict. Thus, $\partial U_i / \partial Z_i < 0$. Based on these inequalities, one can show that friendship mitigates conflict while rivalry increases conflict. To illustrate, recall that the marginal benefit of conflict $\partial U_A / \partial Z_i$ equals $\partial U_A / \partial U_i \cdot \partial U_i / \partial Z_i$. This term is negative when actor A and target i are friends ($\partial U_A / \partial U_i > 0$ and $\partial U_i / \partial Z_i < 0$). Based on the previous analysis, the marginal benefit curve shifts down implying less conflict between friends (Figure 8). Conversely, the marginal benefit curve shifts up (Figure 9) leading to more conflict when A and i are rivals ($\partial U_A / \partial U_i < 0$ and $\partial U_i / \partial Z_i < 0$). Thus friendships and rivalries affect dyadic relations.

But friendships and rivalries also affect multilateral interactions. Consider three countries: (1) an actor A, (2) a target i, and (3) a country j that can either be a friend or foe of i. Examine how an actor's conflict with country i changes when its trade with country j rises. Here an actor's conflict with country i declines if country j is a friend of i, and increases if countries i and j are rivals. Trade with a friend-of-a-friend decreases conflict, while trade with a foe-of-a-friend increases conflict.

To see this, recall that bilateral trade increases cooperation and decreases conflict. Thus an actor's conflict with j would decrease if its trade with j increases $(\partial Z_j / \partial x_j < 0)$. A lower conflict level with j raises country j's welfare because $\partial U_j / \partial Z_j < 0$, but in turn a higher welfare for country j raises country i's welfare when countries i and j are friends. Finally, an increase in country i's welfare raises the actor's welfare, thereby implying that conflict with country i decreases. As such, trade with a friend-of-a-friend decreases conflict. This would be illustrated in Figure 8 by a downward shift in conflict's marginal benefit curve, thereby decreasing conflict. The scenario for a foe-of-a-friend is the opposite.

Trade with an enemy-of-a-friend raises conflict. To see this, follow the same logic as above. An actor's conflict with j decreases as its trade with j increases. Thus $\partial Z_j / \partial x_j < 0$. Decreased conflict with j raises country j's welfare because $\partial U_j / \partial Z_j < 0$. But increased country j's welfare decreases country i's welfare, when countries i and j are enemies. Because of this decreased welfare the actor country increases conflict with i. This phenomenon would be illustrated in Figure 9 by an upward shift of the marginal benefit curve and thus imply that conflict with country i increases. One can apply the above notions about how trading with a third party affects bilateral political interactions to other situations.

5.4.1. An application to tariffs

An import duty country i imposes on an actor's exports is a tariff. As a result, trade decreases because of the higher prices paid by importers. Based on the previous gains from trade analysis, decreased trade means increased conflict. But it is possible that tariffs can also affect third party conflict. Whereas most literature deals with multilateral sanctions in the sense that several countries impose a tariff, e.g., Mansfield (1995), Martin (1992) and Mastanduno (1992), the analysis used here assesses how a tariff affects conflict even on countries that do not impose a tariff. As shown above, trade between an actor and target can alter conflict between the actor and third parties. Since tariffs alter actor-target trade, they may also influence an actor's conflict with third parties. According to the theory, actor-target conflict depends on the relationship between the target and the third party. Recall that trade with a foe-of-a-friend increases conflict while trade with a friend-of-a-friend diminishes conflict. As such, a third-party imposed tariff can decrease conflict if the target and third party are enemies, whereas conflict can increase if the target and third party are friends.

5.4.2. An application to foreign aid

How foreign aid influences political relations is a topic often considered by political scientists and economists [e.g., Abegunrin (1990), Cashel-Cordo and Craig (1997), Holsti (1982), Orr (1989/1990), Richardson (1978)]. Most view foreign aid in a bilateral setting, a framework in which foreign aid is simply considered a transfer payment from one country to another but often with requirements to purchase imports from the aid provider. To the extent that foreign aid simply becomes a subsidy to purchase a beneficiary's products, one can analyze foreign aid through its impact augmenting trade. Again applying the analysis, increased trade implies decreased conflict, but just like with tariffs it is possible that foreign aid can alter third party political interactions.

Again refer to the theory behind Figures 8 and 9. Actor-target conflict depends on the relationship between the target and the third party. Trade with a foe-of-a-friend increases conflict while trade with a friend-of-a-friend diminishes conflict. As such, third party foreign aid can increase conflict if the target and third party are enemies, whereas conflict can decrease if the target and third party are friends. The extent depends on the gains from trade and degree of friendship.

5.4.3. An application to contiguity

Many find that contiguity increases war proneness [Barbieri (1996), Bremer (1992a), Diehl (1985), Gleditsch (1995), Gochman (1991), and Goertz and Diehl (1992)]. Indeed, one would be hard pressed to find non-contiguous countries that engaged in militarized dispute prior to the 18th century. The relationship is so well established that some current research addresses *why* neighbors fight, rather than *whether* they fight [i.e., Vasquez (1995)]. On the other hand, it is well known that neighboring nations take advantage of small transportation costs to engage in more bilateral trade [Anderson (1979); Arad and Hirsch (1981); Deardorff (1984); Gowa (1994); Tinbergen (1962)]. According to the trade–conflict model, greater trade induces less conflict, thus appearing to contradict the empirical findings regarding contiguity and war. However, rather than contradicting each other, the two models may be complementary.

Analyzing the effects of contiguity is difficult because ignoring the effects of trade can lead to an omitted variable bias. One must isolate each effect, otherwise one runs the risk of underestimating conflict between neighboring countries. Despite appearing high to begin with, current conflict measures might underestimate true conflict among neighboring states because they ignore the mitigating effects of trade. Thus while neighbors fight, they might engage in even more conflict were it not for the greater trade levels induced by their proximity to each other. But greater trade between neighboring countries can affect relations with more distant countries, as well.

Again refer back to the analysis regarding third parties. Trade with a friend-of-a-friend fosters less conflict than otherwise, while trade with a foe-of-a-friend brings greater conflict. As such, given the greater trade exhibited between neighbors, an actor should display less conflict towards friends of neighboring countries and more conflict towards a neighbor's rivals.

6. Conclusion

The proposition that international trade specifically, and economic interdependence in general, reduces conflict between nations has a long tradition in the history of economic thought. The argument proposed is that trade leads to welfare gains that countries do not want to jeopardize losing by engaging in trade-disruptive activities such as wars or other forms of conflict. Yet, until fairly recent times economists have not applied some of the modern tools of economics to explore this proposition. This is surprising given the large cost to society of diverting resources towards a purely predatory or redistributive motive instead of productive activity. Given the slow pace of economic development in large parts of the world ravaged by conflict, and the dim prospects of a convergence of their income with those of the developed world, it seems the incentives to explore this topic is of some urgency.

Our review of the empirical literature on the conflict–trade relationship indicates that researchers use several different historical data sets to measure conflict. These are the COW, MIDS, COPDAB and more recently VRA. There are also different ways that trade is measured. Yet, the overwhelming evidence indicates that trade reduces conflict regardless of the proxies used to capture the gains from trade and conflict. Our preference is for using events data because this data contain both information on conflict, as well as on cooperation between nations. As such, it allows for exploring a continuum of international interactions and not just the extreme endpoint of outright war.

We also conclude that to a large extent the empirical evidence that has been found that democracies are less prone to fight with other democracies can be explained by accounting for the larger trade relationship between democracies. Furthermore, recent empirical results show that foreign direct investment plays a similar role as trade in affecting international interactions. More specifically, we find that the flow of FDI has reduced the degree of international conflict and encouraged cooperation between dyads during the period of the late 1980s and the decade of the 1990s. This is an especially important result since one of the main characteristics of globalization has been the reduction of barriers to international capital flows and as a consequence the amounts of capital flows have expanded enormously dwarfing those of trade flows.

The policy implication of our finding is that further international cooperation in reducing barriers to both trade and capital flows can promote a more peaceful world. Furthermore, efforts at democracy while laudable should not have the expected pacifying effects between neighbors unless the appropriate institutions are developed simultaneously to promote trade and capital flows between nations. It is by this vehicle that resources will be freed to address more urgent needs in the international system.

References

Abegunrin, O. (1990). Economic Dependence and Regional Cooperation in Southern Africa: SADCC and South Africa in Confrontation. Edwin Mellen Press, Lewiston, NY.

Acemoglu, D., Johnson, S., Robinson, J. (2003). "The rise of Europe: Atlantic trade, institutional change and economic growth". CEPR Discussion Papers. CEPR Discussion Papers: 3712.

Alesina, A., Spolaore, E. (2003). The Size of Nations. MIT Press, Cambridge, MA.

Altfield, M. (1984). "The decision to ally: A theory and test". Western Political Quarterly 37, 523–544.

Altfield, M., Bueno de Mesquita, B. (1979). "Choosing sides in wars". International Studies Quarterly 23, 87–112.

Anderson, J. (1979). "A theoretical foundation for the gravity equation". American Economic Review 69, 106–116.

Anderton, C.H., Carter, J. (2001). "The impact of war on trade: An interrupted time-series study". Journal of Peace Research 38, 445–457.

Angell, Sir N. (1913). The Great Illusion: A Study of the Relation of Military Power To National Advantage. Garland Publishing, New York.

Arad, R.W., Hirsch, S. (1981). "Peacemaking and vested interests: International economic transactions". International Studies Quarterly 25, 439–468.

Armington, P. (1969). "The geographic pattern of trade and the effects of price changes". IMF Staff Papers 16, 179–199.

Azar, E. (1980). "The conflict and peace data bank (COPDAB) project". Journal of Conflict Resolution 24, 143–152.

Azar, E., Ben-Dak, J.D. (1975). Theory and Practice of Events Research: Studies in Inter-nation Actions and Interactions. Gordon and Breach Science Publishers, New York.

Barbieri, K. (1996). "Economic interdependence: A path to peace or a source of interstate conflict?". Journal of Peace Research 33, 29–50.

Barbieri, K. (2002). The Liberal Illusion: Does Trade Promote Peace? University of Michigan Press, Ann Arbor.

Barbieri, K., Levy, J.S. (1999). "Sleeping with the enemy: The impact of war on trade". Journal of Peace Research 36, 463–479.

Barbieri, K., Schneider, G. (1999). "Globalization and peace: Assessing new directions in the study of trade and conflict". Journal of Peace Research 36, 387–404.

Bearce, D., Fisher, E. (2002). "Economic geography, trade, and war". Journal of Conflict Resolution 46, 365–393.

Bearce, D.H., Omori, S. (2005). "How do commercial institutions promote peace?". Journal of Peace Research 42, 659–678.

Beck, N. (2003). "Modeling dynamics in the study of conflict: A comment on Oneal and Russett". In: Schneider, G., Barbieri, K., Gleditsch, P. (Eds.), Globalization and Armed Conflict. Rowman & Littlefield, New York.

Blainey, G. (1988). The Causes of War. Macmillan Press, Basingstoke.

Blonigen, B. (2005). "A review of the empirical literature on FDI determinants". NBER Working Paper No. 11299.

Bremer, S. (1992a). "Dangerous dyads: Conditions affecting the likelihood of interstate war, 1816–1965". Journal of Conflict Resolution 36, 309–341.

Bremer, S. (1992b). "Are democracies less likely to win wars?". Paper Presented at the Annual Meetings of the American Political Science Association, Chicago.

Bremer, S. (1993). "Democracy and militarized interstate conflict, 1816–1965". International Interactions 18, 231–249.

Bright, J. (1883). Speeches on Questions of Public Policy. Macmillan, London.

Bueno de Mesquita, B., Lalman, D. (1992). War and Reason: Domestic and International Imperatives. Yale University Press, New Haven.

Bueno de Mesquita, B., Koch, M.T., Siverson, R.M. (2004). "Testing competing institutional explanations of the democratic peace: The case of dispute duration". Conflict Management and Peace Science 21, 255–267.

Caruso, R. (2006). "A trade institution as a peaceful institution? A contribution to integrative theory". Conflict Management and Peace Science 23, 53–72.

Cashel-Cordo, P., Craig, S.G. (1997). "Donor preferences and recipient fiscal behavior: A simultaneous analysis of foreign aid". Economic Inquiry 35, 653–671.

Cederman, L.E., Penubarti, R.M. (2001). "Exploring the dynamics of the democratic peace". Journal of Conflict Resolution 45, 818–833.

Chan, S. (1984). "Mirror, mirror on the wall, are the freer countries more pacific?". Journal of Conflict Resolution 28, 617–648.

Cobden, R. (1995). The Political and Economic Works of Richard Cobden. Routledge/Thoemmes Press, London.

Crescenzi, M. (2000). "Exit stage market: Market structure, interstate economic interdependence and conflict". PhD Dissertation. University of Illinois, Urbana-Champaign.

Crucé, E. (1623). Le Nouveau Cynee, ou, Discours des Occasions et Moyens d'establir une Paix Generale et la Liberté du Commerce par tout le Monde. Chez Jacques Villery, Paris.

de Montesquieu, B. (1900). The Spirit of Laws, translated by Thomas Nugent. Collier Press, New York. (originally written in 1750).

Deardorff, A.V. (1984). "Testing trade theories and predicting trade flows". In: Jones, Ronald W., Kenen, Peter B. (Eds.), Handbook of International Economics. North-Holland, Amsterdam, pp. 467–517.

Diehl, P.F. (1985). "Contiguity and military escalation in major power rivalries, 1816–1980". Journal of Politics 47, 1203–1211.

Dixon, W.J. (1989). "Political democracy and war: A new look at an old problem". Paper presented at the International Studies Association Conference, London, England.

Dixon, W.J. (1998). "Dyads, disputes and the democratic peace". In: Wolfson, Murray (Eds.), The Political Economy of War and Peace. Kluwer Academic, Boston, pp. 103–126.

Domke, W.K. (1988). War and the Changing Global System. Yale University Press, New Haven.

Dorussen, H. (1999). "Balance of power revisited, multi-actor models of trade and conflict". Journal of Peace Research 36, 443–462.

Doyle, M.W. (1986). "Liberalism and world politics". American Political Science Review 80, 1151–1169.

Doyle, M.W. (2005). "Three pillars of the liberal peace". American Political Science Review 99, 463–466.

Ember, C., Ember, M., Russett, B. (1992). "Peace between participatory polities: A cross-cultural test of the democracies rarely fight each other hypothesis". World Politics 44, 573–599.

Erasmus, D. (1981). In: O'Donnell, A.M. (Ed.), Enchiridion militis Christiani: An English version. Published for the Early English Text Society by the Oxford University Press, Oxford.

Eyerman, J., Hart, R. (1996). "An empirical test of the audience cost proposition: Democracy speaks louder than words". Journal of Conflict Resolution 40, 597–616.

Farber, H., Gowa, J. (1997). "Common interests or common polities: Reinterpreting the democratic peace". Journal of Politics 59, 393–417.

Feng, Y. (1994). "Trade, conflict, and alliances". Defence and Peace Economics 5, 301–313.

Findlay, R. (2001). "Trade and conflict". Paper presented at the American Economic Association Annual Conference, New Orleans.

Froot, K. (1995). Foreign Direct Investment. University of Chicago Press, Chicago.

Gartzke, E. (1998). "Kant we all just get along? Opportunity, willingness, and the origins of the democratic peace". American Journal of Political Science 42, 1–27.

Gartzke, E., Li, Q. (2001). "War and the invisible hand: Positive political externalities of economic globalization". Paper presented on the International Relations Workshop, University of Michigan.

Gasiorowski, M., Polachek, S. (1982). "Conflict and interdependence: East–West trade and linkages in the era of detente". Journal of Conflict Resolution 26, 709–730.

Gelpi, C., Grieco, J. (2003). Economic interdependence, the democratic state, and the liberal peace. In: Mansfield, E., Pollins, B. (Eds.), Economic Interdependence and International Conflict: New Perspectives on an Enduring Debate. University of Michigan Press, Ann Arbor.

Gilpin, R. (1975). US Power and the Multinational Corporation: The Political Economy of Foreign Direct Investment. Basic Books, New York.

Gilpin, R. (2001). Global Political Economy: Understanding the International Economic Order. Princeton University Press, Princeton.

Gleditsch, N.P. (1995). "Geography, democracy and peace". International Interactions 20, 297–324.

Gochman, C.S. (1991). "Interstate metrics: Conceptualizing, operationalizing and measuring the geographic proximity of states since the Congress of Vienna". International Interactions 17, 93–112.

Gochman, C.S., Maoz, Z. (1984). "Militarized interstate disputes, 1816–1976". Journal of Conflict Resolution 28, 585–615.

Goertz, G., Diehl, P.F. (1992). Territorial Changes and International Conflict. Routledge, London.

Goldstein, J.S. (1992). "A conflict-cooperation scale for WEIS event data". Journal of Conflict Resolution 36, 369–385.

Goldstein, M., Kahn, M. (1985). "Income and price elasticities in foreign trade". In: Jones, T., Kenen, P. (Eds.), Handbook of International Trade, vol. 2. North-Holland, Amsterdam.

Gowa, J. (1994). Allies, Adversaries, and International Trade. Princeton University Press, Princeton.

Greggs, P., Banks, A. (1965). "Dimensions of political systems: Factor analysis of a cross-polity survey". American Political Science Review, 602–614.

Grossman, G., Helpman, E. (2002). Interest Groups and Trade Policy. Princeton University Press, Princeton.

Gurr, T.R. (1974). Civil Strife Events, 1955–1970 (ICPSR 7531). Inter-University Consortium for Political and Social Research, Ann Arbor.

Haas, M. (1965). "Societal approaches to the study of war". Journal of Peace Research 2, 307–323.

Haas, R.D., Turner, A.G. (1988). "The world trade model: Revised estimates". International Monetary Fund Working Paper WP/8/850.

Hagan, J. (1987). "Regimes, political oppositions and the comparative analysis of foreign policy". In: Hermann, Charles, et al. (Eds.), New Directions in the Study of Foreign Policy. Allen and Unwin, Boston, pp. 339–365.

Hegre, H. (2003). "Development and the liberal peace: What does it take to be a trading state". In: Schneider, G., Barbieri, K., Gleditsch, N.P. (Eds.), Globalization and Armed Conflict. Rowman & Littlefield, New York, pp. 205–232.

Henderson, E. (2002). Democracy and War: The End of an Illusion? Lynne Rienner, Boulder, CO.

Hermann, C., East, M.A., Hermann, M.G., Salmore, B.G., Salmore, S.A. (1973). CREON: A Foreign Events Data Set. Sage Publications, Beverly Hills.

Hess, G.D., Athanasios, O. (2001). "War and democracy". Journal of Political Economy 109, 776–810.

Hirschman, A.O. (1945). National Power and the Struggle of Foreign Trade. University of California Press, Berkeley.

Hirshleifer, J. (1995). "Anarchy and its breakdown". Journal of Political Economy 103, 26–52.

Holsti, K.J. (1982). Why Nations Realign: Foreign Policy Restructuring in the Post War World. Allen and Unwin, Boston.

Holsti, O., Hopmann, T., Sullivan, J. (1973). Unity and Disintegration in International Alliances: Comparative Studies. Wiley, New York.

Hooper, P., Johnson, K., Marquez, J. (1998). "Trade elasticities for G-7 countries". International Finance Discussion Paper Number 609. Board of Governors of the Federal Reserve.

Jaggers, K., Gurr, T. (1995). "Tracking democracy's Third Wave with the Polity III data". Journal of Peace Research 32, 469–482.

Kant, I. (1795). Eternal Peace and Other International Essays. The World Peace Foundation, Boston. Translated by W. Hastie.

Kegley, C. (1975). International Events and the Comparative Analysis of Foreign Policy. University of South Carolina Press, Columbia.

Kegley, C.W. Jr., Hermann, M. (1996). "How democracies use intervention: A neglected dimension in studies of the democratic peace". Journal of Peace Research 33, 309–322.

Keshk, O., Pollins, B., Reuveny, R. (2004). "Trade still follows the flag: The primacy of politics in a simultaneous model of interdependence and armed conflict". The Journal of Politics 66, 1155–1179.

Keynes, J.M. (1920). The Economic Consequences of the Peace. Harcourt, Brace and Howe, New York.

Kim, C.H. (1991). "Third-party participation in wars". Journal of Conflict Resolution 35, 659–677.

Kim, S.Y. (1995). "Bilateral conflict and trade, 1948–86: The role of economic interdependence in conflict processes". Paper presented at the American Political Science Association Conference, Chicago, IL.

King, G., Lowe, W. (2003). "An automated information extraction tool for international conflict data with performance as good as human coders: A rare events evaluation design". International Organization 57, 617–642.

Kinsella, D. (2005). "No rest for the democratic peace". American Political Science Review 99, 453–457.

Krugman, P. (1995). "Economic conflicts among nations: Perceptions and reality". Paper presented at the AEA Convention, Washington, DC.

Lake, D. (1992). "Powerful pacifists: Democratic states and war". American Political Science Review 86, 24–37.

Levy, J. (1983). War in the Modern Great Power System, 1495–1975. University of Kentucky Press, Lexington.

Levy, J. (1989). "The causes of war: A review of theories and evidence". In: Tetlock, P.C., et al. (Eds.), Behavior, Society and Nuclear War, vol. 1. Oxford University Press, Oxford, pp. 209–333.

Levy, G., Razin, R. (2004). "It takes two: An explanation for the democratic peace". Journal of the European Economic Association 2, 1–29.

MacMillan, J. (2003). "Beyond the separate democratic peace: Review essay". Journal of Peace Research 40, 233–243.

Mansfield, E.D. (1994). Power, Trade and War. Princeton University Press, Princeton.

Mansfield, E.D. (1995). "International institutions and economic sanctions". World Politics 47, 575–605.

Mansfield, E.D. (2004). International Conflict and the Global Economy. Cheltenham, UK.

Mansfield, E.D., Pevehouse, J. (2000). "Trade blocs, trade flows, and international conflict". International Organization 54, 775–808.

Mansfield, E.D., Pollins, B.M. (2001). "The study of interdependence and conflict: Recent advances, open questions, and directions for future research". Journal of Conflict Resolution 45, 834–859.

Mansfield, E.D., Pollins, B.M. (2003). New Perspectives on Economic Exchange and Armed Conflict. University of Michigan Press, Ann Arbor.

Maoz, Z., Abdelali, N. (1989). "Regime types and international conflict: 1816–1976". Journal of Conflict Resolution 33, 3–35.

Maoz, Z., Russett, B. (1992). "Alliances, contiguity, wealth, and political stability: Is the lack of conflict between democracies a statistical artifact?". International Interactions 17, 245–267.

Maoz, Z., Russett, B. (1993). "Normative and structural causes of democratic peace". American Political Science Review 87, 624–638.

Marquez, J. (1988). "Income and price elasticities of foreign trade flows: Econometric estimation and analysis of the US trade deficit". Board of Governors of the Federal Reserve System International Finance discussion Papers, No. 324.

Marquez, J. (1990). "Bilateral trade elasticities". Review of Economics and Statistics 72, 70–77.

Martin, L. (1992). Coercive Cooperation: Explaining Multilateral Economic Sanctions. Princeton University Press, Princeton.

Martin, P., Mayer, T., Thoenig, M. (2005). "Make trade not war?". CEPR Discussion Papers. CEPR Discussion Papers: 5218.

Mastanduno, M. (1992). Economic Containment: COCOM and the Politics of East–West Trade. Cornell University Press, Ithaca, NY.

McClelland, C. (1999). World Event/Interaction Survey (Weis) Project, 1966–1978 [computer file]. Conducted by Charles McClelland, University of Southern California, third ICPSR ed. Inter-university Consortium for Political and Social Research, Ann Arbor, MI.

McDonald, P. (2004). "Peace through trade or free trade?". Journal of Conflict Resolution 48, 547–572.

McMillan, S. (1997). "Interdependence and conflict". Mershon International Studies Review 41, 33–58.

Mintz, A., Geva, N. (1993). "Why don't democracies fight each other? An experimental study". Journal of Conflict Resolution 37, 484–503.

Morgan, T.C., Campbell, S.H. (1991). "Domestic structure, decisional constraints, and war". Journal of Conflict Resolution 35, 187–211.

Morgan, T.C., Schwebach, V. (1992). "Take two democracies and call me in the morning: A prescription for peace". International Interactions 17, 305–320.

Morrow, J.D. (1991). "Alliances and asymmetry: An alternative to the capability aggregation model of alliances". American Journal of Political Science 35, 904–933.

Morrow, J.D. (1997). "When do 'relative gains' impede trade?". Journal of Conflict Resolution 41, 12–37.

Morrow, J.D. (1999). "How could trade affect conflict?". Journal of Peace Research 36, 481–489.

Mousseau, M. (2005). "Comparing new theory with prior beliefs: Market civilization and the democratic peace". Conflict Management and Peace Science 22, 63–77.

Mousseau, M., Shi, Y. (1999). "A test for reverse causality in the democratic peace relationship". Journal of Peace Research 36, 639–663.

Nye, J.S. (1974). "Multinationals: The game and the rules: Multinational corporations in world politics". Foreign Affairs.

Oneal, J.R., Ray, J.L. (1997). "New tests of the democratic peace: Controlling for economic interdependence, 1950–1985". Political Research Quarterly 50, 751–775.

Oneal, J.R., Russett, B.M. (1996). "The classical liberals were right: Democracy, interdependence, and conflict, 1950–1985". International Studies Quarterly 41, 267–294.

Oneal, J.R., Russett, B.M. (1999). "Assessing the liberal peace with alternative specifications: Trade still reduces conflict". Journal of Peace Research 36, 423–442.

Oneal, J.R., Oneal, F.H., Maoz, Z., Russett, B. (1996). "The liberal peace: Interdependence, democracy, and international conflict, 1950–86". Journal of Peace Research 33, 11–28.

Orr, R.M. (1989/1990). "Collaboration or conflict? Foreign aid and US–Japan relations". Pacific Affairs 62, 476–489.

Polachek, S.W. (1978). "Dyadic dispute: An economic perspective". Papers of the Peace Science Society 28, 67–80.

Polachek, S.W. (1980). "Conflict and trade". Journal of Conflict Resolution 24, 55–78.

Polachek, S.W. (1992). "Conflict and trade: An economics approach to political international interactions". In: Isard, W., Anderton, C.H. (Eds.), Economics of Arms Reduction and the Peace Process. Elsevier Science Publishers, New York, pp. 89–120.

Polachek, S.W. (1994). "Peace economics: A trade theory perspective". Peace Economics, Peace Science and Public Policy 1, 12–15.

Polachek, S.W. (1997). "Why democracies cooperate more and fight less: The relationship between international trade and cooperation". Review of International Economics 5, 295–309.

Polachek, S.W. (2002a). "Conflict and trade: An economics approach to political international interactions with special reference to US–China relations". Paper presented at the Sino–American Economic Relations under the WTO Conference, Lingnam University, Hong Kong.

Polachek, S.W. (2002b). "Trade-based interactions: An interdisciplinary perspective". Conflict Management and Peace Science 19, 1–21.

Polachek, S.W. (2003). "Multilateral interactions in the trade–conflict model". In: Schneider, G., Barbieri, K., Gleditsch, N.P. (Eds.), Globalization and Armed Conflict. Rowman & Littlefield, New York.

Polachek, S.W. (2004). "What can we learn about the decline in U.S. union membership from international data". In: Wunnava, P.V. (Ed.), The Changing Role of Unions. M.E. Sharpe, Armonk, NY, pp. 362–377.

Polachek, S.W., Kim, M.K. (1994). "Panel estimates of the gender earnings gap: Individual-specific intercept and individual-specific slope models". Journal of Econometrics 61, 23–42.

Polachek, S.W., McDonald, J.A. (1992). "Strategic trade and the incentive for cooperation". In: Chatterji, M., Forcey, L. (Eds.), Disarmament, Economic Conversion, and the Management of Peace. Praeger Press, New York, pp. 273–284.

Polachek, S.W., Robst, J. (1998). "Cooperation and conflict among democracies: Why do democracies cooperate more and fight less". In: Wolfson, M. (Ed.), The Political Economy of War and Peace. Kluwer, Boston, pp. 127–154.

Polachek, S.W., Robst, J., Chang, Y.C. (1999). "Liberalism and interdependence: Extending the trade–conflict model". Journal of Peace Research 36, 405–422.

Polachek, S., Seiglie, C., Xiang, J. (2005). "Globalization and international conflict: Can FDI increase peace?". Working Paper Rutgers University, Newark: 1-35.

Pollins, B. (1989a). "Does trade still follow the flag?". American Political Science Review 83, 465–480.

Pollins, B. (1989b). "Conflict cooperation and commerce: The effect of international political interactions". American Journal of Political Science 33, 737–761.

Powell, R. (1991). "Absolute and relative gains in international relations". American Political Science Review 85, 1303–1320.

Ray, J.L. (1993). "War between democracies: Rare or nonexistent?". International Interactions 18, 251–276.

Rayome, D., Baker, J.C. (1995). "Foreign direct investment: A review and analysis of the literature". International Trade Journal 9, 3–37.

Reuveny, R. (1999). "The trade conflict debate: A survey of theory, evidence and future research". Peace Economics, Peace Science and Public Policy 6, 23–49.

Reuveny, R. (2001). "Disaggregated trade and conflict: Eexploring propositions in a simultaneous framework". International Politics 38, 401–428.

Reuveny, R., Kang, H. (1996). "International trade, political conflict/cooperation, and granger causality". American Journal of Political Science 40, 943–970.

Reuveny, R., Kang, H. (1998). "Bilateral trade and political conflict/cooperation: Do goods matter?". Journal of Peace Research 35, 581–602.

Reuveny, R., Kang, H. (2003). "A simultaneous-equations model of trade, conflict, and cooperation". Review of International Economics 11, 279–295.

Ricardo, D. (1981). The Principles of Political Economy and Taxation. Cambridge University Press, Cambridge (originally published in 1817).

Richardson, L.F. (1960). Arms and Insecurity, A Mathematical Study of the Causes and Origins of War. The Boxwood Press/Quadrangle Books, Pittsburgh/Chicago.

Richardson, N.R. (1978). Foreign Policy and Economic Dependence. The University of Texas Press, Austin.

Robbins, L. (1968). The Economic Causes of War. Howard Fertig Press, New York.

Rosato, S. (2003). "The flawed logic of democratic peace theory". American Political Science Review 97, 585–602.

Rousseau, J.J. (2005). The Plan for Perpetual Peace, On the Government of Poland, and Other Writings on History and Politics. Dartmouth College Press and University Press of New England, Hanover, N.H..

Rummel, R. (1968). "The relationship between national attributes and foreign conflict behavior". In: Singer, J.D. (Ed.), Quantitative International Politics: Insights and Evidence. Free Press, New York, pp. 187–214.

Rummel, R.J. (1975). National Attributes and Behavior. Sage Publications, Beverly Hills.

Rummel, R.J. (1979a). The Dimensions of Nations. Sage Publications, Beverly Hills.

Rummel, R.J. (1979b). "War, power, peace". In: Understanding Conflict and War, vol. 4. Sage Press, Beverly Hills.

Rummel, R.J. (1987). "On Vincent's view of freedom and international conflict". International Studies Quarterly 31, 113–117.

Russett, B. (1967). International Regions and the International System. Rand McNally, Chicago.

Russett, B. (1989). "Democracy and peace". In: Russett, B., et al. (Eds.), Choices in World Politics. W.H. Freeman, New York.

Russett, B., Antholis, W. (1992). "Do democracies fight each other? Evidence from the Peloponnesian War". Journal of Peace Research 29, 415–434.

Russett, B., Monsen, R.J. (1975). "Bureaucracy and polyarchy as predictors of performance: A cross-national examination". Comparative Political Studies 8, 5–31.

Russett, B., Oneal, J. (2001). Triangulating Peace: Democracy, Interdependence, and International Organizations. Norton, New York.

Sabrosky, A.N. (1980). "Interstate alliances: Their reliability and the expansion of war". In: Singer, J. David (Ed.), The Correlates of War: II. Free Press, New York, pp. 161–198.

Saggi, K. (2002). "Trade, foreign direct investment, and international technology transfer: A survey". World Bank Research Observer 17, 191–235.

Sayrs, L.W. (1990). "Expected utility and peace science: An assessment of trade and conflict". Conflict Management and Peace Science 11, 17–44.

Schelling, T.C. (1960). The Strategy of Conflict. Harvard University Press, Cambridge, MA.

Schneider, G., Barbieri, K., Gleditsch, N.P. (2003). "Does globalization contribute to peace? A critical survey of the literature". In: Schneider, G., Barbieri, K., Gleditsch, N.P. (Eds.), Globalization and Armed Conflict. Rowman & Littlefield, New York, pp. 3–29.

Schrodt, P. (1995). "Event data in foreign policy analysis". In: Neack, Laura, Hey, Jeanne A.K., Haney, Patrick J. (Eds.), Foreign policy analysis: Continuity and change in its second generation. Prentice Hall, Englewood Cliffs, NJ.

Seiglie, C. (1992). "Determinants of military expenditures". In: Isard, W., Anderton, C. (Eds.), Economics of Arms Reduction and the Peace Process. North-Holland, Amsterdam, pp. 183–202.

Seiglie, C. (1996). "The effects of trade on military spending". Paper presented at the PSSI meetings. Rice University, Houston.

Seiglie, C. (2005). "Openness of the economy, terms of trade and arms". Rutgers University Newark Working Paper #2005-008:1-37.

Simon, M., Gartzke, E. (1996). "Political system similarity and the choice of allies". Journal of Conflict Resolution 40, 617–635.

Singer, J.D., Small, M. (1966a). "Formal alliances, 1815–1939: A qualitative description". Journal of Peace Research 3, 1–32.

Singer, J.D., Small, M. (1966b). "National alliance commitments and war involvement, 1815–1945". Peace Research Society (International) Papers 5, 109–140.

Singer, J.D., Small, M. (1972). The Wages of War, 1816–1965: A Statistical Handbook. Wiley, New York.

Siverson, R., Emmons, J. (1991). "Birds of a feather: Democratic political systems and alliance choices in the twentieth century". Journal of Conflict Resolution 35, 285–306.

Siverson, R., King, J. (1979). "Alliances and the expansion of war". In: Singer, J. David, Wallace, Michael D. (Eds.), To Augur Well: Early Warning Indicators in World Politics. Sage, Beverly Hills, CA, pp. 37–50.

Siverson, R., King, J. (1980). "Attributes of national alliance membership and war participation, 1815–1965". American Journal of Political Science 24, 1–15.

Slantchev, B., Alexandrova, A., Gartzke, E. (2005). "Probabilistic causality, selection bias, and the logic of the democratic peace". American Political Science Review 99, 459–462.

Small, M., Singer, J.D. (1976). "The war proneness of democratic regimes, 1816–1965". Jerusalem Journal of International Relations 1, 50–69.

Small, M., Singer, J.D. (1982). Resort to Arms: International and Civil Wars, 1816–1980. Sage Publications, Beverly Hills.

Starr, H. (1992). "Democracy and war: Choice, learning, and security communities". Journal of Peace Research 29, 207–213.

Streit, C. (1940). Union Now: A Proposal for a Federal Union of the Leading Democracies. Harper Press, New York.

Taylor, C.L., Hudson, M.C. (1972). World Handbook of Political and Social Indicators, second ed. Yale University Press, New Haven, CT.

Thompson, P.G. (2003). "Foreign direct investment and war: Economic deterrence to armed conflict". PhD Dissertation, UCLA.

Thompson, W.R., Tucker, R. (1997). "A tale of two democratic peace critiques". Journal of Conflict Resolution 41, 428–454.

Tinbergen, J. (1962). Shaping the World Economy: Suggestions for an International Policy. Twentieth Century Fund, New York.

Vasquez, J. (1995). "Why do neighbors fight? Proximity, interaction, or territoriality". Journal of Peace Research 32, 277–293.

Vernon, R. (1971). Sovereignty at Bay: The Multinational Spread of US Enterprises. Basic Books, New York.

Vincent, J. (1987). "On Rummel's omnipresent theory". International Studies Quarterly 31, 119–126.

Viner, J. (1937). Studies in the Theory of International Trade, first ed. Harper & Brothers, New York.

Wallenstein, P. (1973). Structure and War: On International Relations 1920–1968. Raben and Sjögren, Stockholm.

Watkins, J. (1942). "Democracy and international organization: The experience of the League of Nations". American Political Science Review 36, 1136–1141.

Weede, E. (1984). "Democracy and war involvement". Journal of Conflict Resolution 28, 56–69.

Wright, Q. (1942). A Study of War. University of Chicago Press, Chicago.

Zeng, K. (2004). Trade Threats, Trade Wars: Bargaining, Retaliation, and American Coercive Diplomacy. University of Michigan Press, Ann Arbor.

Zinnes, D.A. (2004). "Constructing political logic: The democratic peace puzzle". Journal of Conflict Resolution 48, 430–454.

Chapter 32

NEW ECONOMICS OF MANPOWER IN THE POST-COLD WAR ERA

BETH J. ASCH and JAMES R. HOSEK

RAND, Santa Monica, CA, USA

JOHN T. WARNER

Clemson University, USA

Contents

Abstract	1076
Keywords	1076
1. Introduction	1077
2. Supply of defense manpower in the post-Cold War era	1078
2.1. Enlistment supply	1080
2.1.1. Overview of models	1081
2.1.2. US enlistment supply	1082
2.2. Retention: Models and recent evidence	1091
2.2.1. Overview of models	1091
2.2.2. Empirical evidence	1094
2.3. Deployment: Theory and evidence	1097
2.3.1. Model of deployment and reenlistment	1097
2.3.2. Empirical evidence	1101
2.4. Spouses and families: Effect of military on the earnings of spouses	1103
3. Demand for manpower and force management in post-Cold War era	1105
3.1. Personnel productivity and efficient force mixes	1105
3.2. Personnel management in the post-Cold War era	1109
3.2.1. The US drawdown as a case study in force management	1109
3.2.2. Recent developments in force management	1110
4. Issues in compensation	1112
4.1. Pay adequacy to attract a quality force	1112
4.2. Gaining added pay flexibility	1115
4.3. Civilian earnings of military retirees	1117
4.4. Rising cost of entitlements	1118

Handbook of Defense Economics, Volume 2
Edited by Todd Sandler and Keith Hartley
© 2007 Elsevier B.V.   *All rights reserved*
DOI: 10.1016/S1574-0013(06)02032-1

   4.5. Addressing obstacles to compensation reform   1120
5. New contributions to the economics of the draft   1120
   5.1. Recent contributions   1121
   5.2. Ending conscription in Europe   1127
6. Summary   1131
References   1133

Abstract

Since the publication of Volume 1 of the *Handbook of Defense Economics*, key events have shaped the defense manpower research agenda and called for research to help policymakers deal with the challenges that these factors presented. One event was the end of the Cold War, which permitted drastic force reductions in the USA and elsewhere and enabled many NATO members to eliminate conscription. A second event was a rise in college attendance in the USA, which led to recruiting difficulties despite the reduction in accession demand. A third event was increased operational tempo of US forces abroad. Fourth is the rising cost of US military entitlements and a shift toward a greater share of military compensation being deferred. This chapter reviews the recent work that economists have supplied in response to these events. Studies have analyzed the dramatic trend toward volunteer forces in Europe, seeking to explain why some countries chose to end conscription while others did not. Studies of US enlistment supply have estimated the effect of rising college attendance on enlistment and evaluated strategies for mitigating its effect. Studies of operational tempo have provided new theoretical insights about the relationship between operational tempo and retention and empirical evidence about this linkage. Improvements have been made to models relating compensation to retention, and the models been used to address issues relating to the structure of compensation. This chapter reviews these studies and other new contributions to the defense manpower literature. Reserve force issues remain a neglected research area. Despite the heavy reliance on reserve forces in recent US operations abroad, little is known about how changes in activation expectations and activation duration affect reserve recruiting and retention. Such analysis is needed to guide reserve compensation and personnel policy, and this topic represents an important area for future research.

Keywords

military, manpower, enlistment supply, retention, draft, conscription, volunteer force, military compensation, reserves, productivity, Cold War, downsizing, deployment, dynamic programming, operational tempo

JEL classification: J24, J31, J41, M51

1. Introduction

Since the publication of Volume 1 of the *Handbook of Defense Economics*, several key factors on the demand and supply sides of military labor markets have shaped the recent defense manpower research agenda and called for research to help inform policymakers. The main event on the demand side was the end of the Cold War, which permitted a drastic reduction of forces in the United States and elsewhere. The US active duty force was reduced from 2.1 million to 1.3 million, a 38 percent reduction; NATO countries reduced their manpower levels by a similar percentage. The reduction in force levels enabled many European countries to eliminate conscription and implement volunteer forces.

Downsizing in the United States was accompanied by a significant reorganization of the roles and missions of US active and reserve forces, assigning to the reserve forces many missions and functions previously given to the active forces. But after the downsizing and reorganization of US forces was completed, deployments to Bosnia and Kosovo in the mid-to-late 1990s and to Afghanistan and Iraq in the wake of September 11, 2001, put stress on US forces, causing some to question whether US downsizing went too far.

Several trends in the US economy have affected the supply of personnel to the US armed forces. One of these trends is the increased return to a college degree, which has induced a larger percentage of youth to pursue college degrees rather than enter military service immediately after graduation from high school. This trend has increased the difficulty of recruiting in the United States. A potential offset to this trend is the rapidly growing Hispanic population. Hispanics have a higher propensity to serve in the US military than most other demographic groups, but are less likely to meet US military entrance standards. Adjusting to these changes in supply has been a challenge for US military personnel managers.

The purpose of this survey is to review contributions to the literature on military manpower economics that have been published since the first volume of the *Handbook* and place them in the context of the post-Cold War market for military manpower. This survey is organized as follows. Section 2 reviews recent analyses of enlistment supply. In light of post-drawdown events, pre-drawdown models of the supply of military manpower have been extended to incorporate factors relevant in the new environment such as the effect of rising college attendance on enlistment supply and the effect of deployment on military retention. Section 3 studies the demand for manpower and personnel management in the post-Cold War era. The major theme of this section is the impact of technological change and its implications for personnel management. Section 4 discusses recent issues in compensation management in light of the expansion of US operations abroad. Section 5 discusses recent developments in the economics of conscription and examines the trend toward volunteer forces in Europe. Section 6 closes the survey.

2. Supply of defense manpower in the post-Cold War era

The end of the Cold War, the rise in operations other than war in the 1990s, and the war on terrorism after September 11, 2001, may have caused the supply of military manpower, both for enlistment and reenlistment, to undergo a structural shift, as those who joined or stayed in the military reassessed the value of the military option in light of dramatically changed missions. If the decision to enlist or reenlist is described using standard occupational choice theory with two sectors, military and civilian [Rosen (1986), Warner and Asch (1995)], individuals decide whether to join or stay in the military by comparing the pay and non-pecuniary benefits in each sector. If U^{M} and U^{C} are the utility of each choice, W^{M} and W^{C} are military and civilian wages, respectively, and τ^{M} and τ^{C} are the value of non-pecuniaries in each sector, then individuals join or choose the military only if $U^{\mathrm{M}} = W^{\mathrm{M}} + \tau^{\mathrm{M}} > U^{\mathrm{C}} = W^{\mathrm{C}} + \tau^{\mathrm{C}}$, or $W^{\mathrm{M}} - W^{\mathrm{C}} > \tau^{\mathrm{C}} - \tau^{\mathrm{M}}$. That is, they join if the utility of military employment exceeds civilian employment, or the pay differential exceeds their net preferences for civilian life, $\tau = \tau^{\mathrm{C}} - \tau^{\mathrm{M}}$. The distribution of τ over the relevant population determines the level of the supply curve and its elasticity with respect to pay. Included in the value of non-pecuniaries are factors such as the value of serving one's country, which for most prospective recruits is a positive factor, and the risk of injury or death, which is usually a negative factor. Tastes for military and civilian service are distinct owing to the uniqueness of the military employment contract; members often work long, irregular hours, may spend weeks or months away from home during deployments, are on call to travel any where in the world on short notice, and face the risk of injury and death. In addition, active members and their families are relocated every few years, due to permanent change of station moves, and may be sent abroad. Deployments may be frequent, long, and uncertain. And, of course, service means adapting to a regimented lifestyle and the discipline associated with the hierarchical rank structure.

Changes in the national security environment will shift the supply curve of military personnel by changing the perceived value of non-pecuniaries. But the direction of the shift is theoretically ambiguous. An increase in the heterogeneity of preferences for the military implies a greater variance in $\tau(\sigma^2)$ and a less elastic supply curve of manpower. More generally, the end of the Cold War could mean that elasticity estimates for military pay, advertising, bonuses, civilian opportunities, and other factors affecting supply differ using data post-1990. Beyond changes in elasticities, the factors affecting supply changed in the 1990s, and several had a negative impact on manpower supply. First, the US economy underwent an unusually robust and long-lasting growth period that saw the civilian unemployment rate fall to its lowest level in 30 years, from 7 percent in 1992 to 4 percent in 2000, and that resulted in a dramatic expansion in the civilian employment opportunities of "high-quality" youth. The US services target the recruitment of high-quality youth, defined as high school diploma graduates who score in the upper half of the Armed Forces Qualification (AFQT) distribution. During this period of economic growth, real wages in the US economy rose steadily for many groups [Hosek and Sharp (2001)]. Although military pay also grew, civilian pay grew at a faster rate than did military pay between 1994 and 1999. Over this five-year period, enlisted pay grew about 6 percent less quickly than civilian pay of similar civilian high school graduates, and officer pay grew about 8 percent less quickly than the civilian pay of similar college graduates. Beginning in 2000, the US economy weakened and the unemployment rate trended upward, from a low of 4.0 percent to a high of 6.1 percent in July 2003 for those ages 16 and older. Since 2003 unemployment declined, albeit more slowly for those ages 16 to 19.

Second, college attendance rates and college expectations among the military's prime recruiting market – high-school seniors and graduates within 12 months of graduation – and had risen substantially in the 1980s and continued to rise in the 1990s, though more slowly, stabilizing since 2000. The attendance rate among male high school graduates within 12 months of completing high school in the United States rose from 46.7 percent in 1980 to 61.2 percent in 2003 [US Department of Education (2004, Table 183)] and for females the increase was from 51.8 percent to 66.5 percent. All else equal, the military has faced increased competition from colleges for high-quality youth, especially females.

Another factor affecting supply is the population of veterans who positively recommend military service. Declines are due to reduction in manpower requirements after the Cold War and the resulting reduction in veterans leaving active duty, as well as the aging of the WWII generation and the resulting reduction in veterans due to morbidity. In 1987, 49 percent of US males over the age of 34 were military veterans; by 2003 the percentage had declined to 29 percent (authors' calculations from Current Population Survey data).

Other factors that changed dramatically were the policy levers defense planners use to manage supply, including military pay, retirement, bonuses and allowances, and in the case of recruiting, advertising, recruiters, educational benefits and other recruiting resources. Following the post-Cold War downsizing, resources declined given the smaller required force size of the military, though not as fast as the decline in enlistment goals. Consequently, and with the help of a mild recession in the early 1990s, recruit quality skyrocketed to an all-time high of 72 percent of recruits who were deemed high quality (Figure 1). But resources were later increased because both recruiting and retention targets became more difficult to achieve in the late 1990s. Recruit quality was still reasonably high, above the 60 percent floor set by the US DoD on percent of recruits who are required to be in the top half of the AFQT distribution, and the 90 percent floor on the percent who have a high school diploma. However, the Army and Air Force failed to reach their recruiting goals in 1999 and both the Army and Navy missed their recruiting goals in 1998. All of the services had difficulty retaining experienced personnel in technical skill areas, and the Air Force and Navy struggled with the outflow of aviators to the private sector. In part, these difficulties reflected the negative effects of declines in relative pay and the veterans' population and the impact of a robust economy. Recruiting difficulties also reflected the fact that enlistment goals had increased from the mid-1990s when they were low as part of the services' manpower drawdown

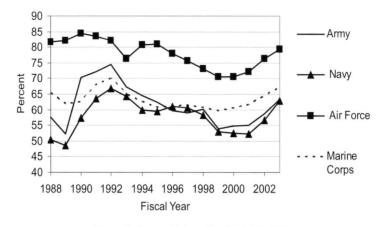

Figure 1. Percent high-quality, FY 1988–2003.

strategy that cut the number below the level required to sustain the force size in the steady state.

In the case of retention, an issue related to the inter-cohort equity of the military re-tirement system arose in the late 1990s. Military personnel who entered service after July 1986 were under a reduced retirement structure, known by the acronym REDUX. By the late 1990s, when they had been in service for more than a dozen years and were deciding whether to stay for twenty years, the vesting age, they realized their retirement benefits would be less than those of peers who had entered service only a few months or years ahead of them. Ultimately, equity was restored by giving members under RE-DUX the choice of the pre-REDUX retirement benefit structure (known as High-Three) or receiving a $30,000 bonus at year of service 15 in exchange for a pledge to remain in service for five more years. The pressure for the change resulted not from evidence showing that REDUX distorted the efficient allocation of manpower or reduced pro-ficiency in performing mission-essential tasks, but rather from a growing consensus within the services that REDUX eroded morale, and therefore negatively affected reten-tion and capability.

2.1. Enlistment supply

As the previous discussion makes clear, numerous factors affecting enlistment supply changed after the end of the Cold War. Of particular concern was what appeared to be a decline in youth tastes for the military, as measured by DoD-surveys of US youth on how likely they would be to join to the military. Between 1990 and 1998, the fraction of male high school seniors responding definitely or probably to the question of joining fell by about one-third. Warner, Simon and Payne (2001, 2003b) analyze the extent to which the decline reflects a shift in preferences or is due to other factors such as the state of the economy, changes in military pay, recruiting effort as measured by recruiters and advertising, declines in military service among the parents of US youth, and other family-related factors. Using data from the DoD-sponsored Youth Attitude Tracking Study, they find that youth propensity does not respond to or reflect the intensity of the services' recruiting efforts, as measured by advertising awareness and expenditures as well as numbers of recruiters. Family background, such as whether the father is a college graduate, geographic region, as well as metrics of academic achievement, such as grades in high school, have a more pronounced effect on propensity. These changes in youth attitudes call into question whether enlistment models of the 1980s are robust or new models are needed.

2.1.1. Overview of models

Two general approaches are used to model enlistment supply. The first approach specifies a logit or probit model of individuals' decisions to enlist, where demographic (e.g., age, family background) and environmental characteristics (e.g., location) are used to predict the probability eligible youth would select the military versus civilian opportunities. These models are estimated with individual level data and are useful for targeting recruiting effort, such as numbers of recruiters, toward youth with the greatest prospect of enlistment. Earlier studies using this approach used the National Longitudinal Survey data on enlistment decisions in the 1980s and include Hosek and Peterson (1985a, 1990), Gorman and Thomas (1993), and Kilburn (1992). Kilburn and Klerman (1999) re-estimated the Hosek and Peterson (1985a) model using post-Cold War data on enlistment decisions in the early 1990s from the National Educational Longitudinal Survey (NELS) to determine whether the same characteristics were associated with enlistment in the more recent data as in the earlier study. They find that similar variables were associated with enlistment in the two periods. For high school seniors, variables that might be expected to be associated with college attendance were the strongest influences on enlistment decisions. In the Kilburn and Klerman study, these included a negative effect of AFQT score, mother's education, family income, and a positive effect of number of siblings. For high school graduates, variables associated with civilian job opportunities had the strongest influence. These include the negative effect on enlistment decisions of civilian wages and being unemployed. Marriage had a positive influence on enlistment decisions but the presence of children had a negative influence. Kilburn and Klerman modified the Hosek and Peterson specification by adding more variables available in the NELS that might be relevant to the enlistment decision, including whether a parent is in the military, whether English is not the first language, whether the individual had used marijuana or had been arrested, and average in-state college tuition. For seniors, only the coefficient estimate for English not being the first language was negative and statistically significant. For graduates, having a parent in the military and having been arrested were both positively related to the enlistment decision.

Kilburn and Klerman also expanded the choice set to include a third choice, the decision to attend college. Thus, they estimate a multinomial logit model of the decisions to enlist, attend college, or be a civilian. The advantage of including the college choice is that the expanded model provides more information about whether a particular variable affects enlistment via the choice between the military and college or the choice between military and civilian work. They find that variables that influence the expected returns to education like AFQT score, age when a senior, and mother's education reduce enlistment rates because they increase the likelihood of attending college. Variables associated with availability of resources to pay for college were strong predictors of which high-quality youth attended college and which enlisted. In general, their analysis shows a high degree of substitutability between college and enlistment among high-aptitude youth and between work and enlistment for other young men.

The other approach to modeling enlistment supply is to specify an aggregate enlistment model. Dertouzos (1985) developed the approach currently used. The structural enlistment supply model is given as $\ln H = \lambda \ln L + \beta \ln X + \ln E$ where H is the number of high-quality enlistments in a given geographic area in a given period, L is the number of low quality enlistments, X is a vector of variables representing the factors that determine the recruiting market, and E is recruiter effort. Recruiters face monthly quotas, Q_H and Q_L for high and low-quality enlistments, respectively, and are managed by incentive plans to motivate them to achieve the quotas. Low-quality quotas are easier to meet than high-quality ones, and given the enlistment potential of a given recruiting market, recruiters trade off the production of low for high-quality enlistments along the production possibility frontier. Recruiters are assumed to choose the levels of L and H yielding the level of effort that maximizes their utility, given the potential of the recruiting market represented by the variables in X. Effort is unobserved and is posited to depend on performance relative to quotas, or $\ln E = \gamma_1 \ln(H/Q_H) + \gamma_2 \ln(L/Q_L)$. Substituting $\ln E$ into the structural enlistment equation, and recognizing that H and L are jointly determined through the recruiter's constrained optimization problem, gives the following two equation system for enlistment:

$$\ln H = \alpha_1 \ln L + \alpha_2 \ln X + \alpha_3 \ln Q_H + \alpha_4 \ln Q_L,$$
$$\ln L = \theta + \pi_1 \ln X + \pi_2 \ln Q_H + \pi_3 \ln Q_L. \tag{1}$$

Simultaneous estimation of these equations gives coefficient estimates for γ_1 and γ_2 allowing identification of the underlying structural parameters λ and β. Substituting the second equation into the first gives a reduced form equation for high-quality enlistments. In fact, most studies of high-quality enlistment supply have estimated the reduced equation for $\ln H$ and not the structural model in equation system (1).

2.1.2. US enlistment supply

Table 1 presents elasticity and effects estimated by studies of US enlistments for studies that use post-Cold War data for the Army unless otherwise noted. For the sake of comparison, it also summarizes pre-Cold War estimates (panel 2 in the table), drawn from two reviews of the literature, the first from Warner and Asch (1995) and the second from Warner, Simon and Payne (2001, Appendix B). In addition, three studies [Warner,

Table 1
Army high-quality enlistment elasticity estimates

	Recruiters	Own quota	Advertising[c]	Bonus	Ed benefits	M/C pay	U-rate	Cross service	College	Vets	Youth pop
1. Using post-drawdown data											
W&S[1]	0.41[a]										
W&S[1]	0.56[b]					0.93	0.49				
WS&P[2]	0.50	0.15	0.16	0.12	0.47	1.05	0.26	−0.12	−0.87	1.44	N/A
B & S[3]	0.14	N/A	N/A		0.08	1.64	0.19	N/A			
HDMM[4]	0.29	N/A	0.02 (Radio); 0.03 (TV)		N/A	0.55	0.18	N/A			0.50
2. Using pre-drawdown data											
WS&P lit. review[2]	0.15 to 1.65	0.15 to 0.46	0.028 to 0.72	−0.19 to 0.09	−0.041 to 0.37	0.13 to 1.92	0.15 to 0.52				
WS&P lit rev. mean	0.76	0.30	0.10	0.057	0.09	0.75	0.62				0.67
W & A lit review[5]	0.15 to 1.15	0.19 to 0.41	0.07 to 0.72	−0.29 to −0.46	−0.04 to 0.17	0.15 to 1.89	0.49 to 1.36	N/A	N/A	N/A	
W & A lit rev. mean	0.65	0.29	0.22	0.09	0.11	0.64	0.77	N/A	N/A	N/A	
3. Pre- and post-drawdown comparisons											
WS&P[1]											
Pre	0.55	0.2	N/A	N/A	N/A	N/A	0.22	−0.13	N/A	N/A	N/A
Post	0.41	0.07	N/A	N/A	N/A	N/A	0.34	−0.13	N/A	N/A	N/A
M&M[6]											
Pre	0.51	0.16	N/A	N/A	0.07	0.19	0.11		N/A	N/A	0.08
Post	0.6	0.08	N/A	N/A	0.01	0.31	0.16		N/A	N/A	0.16

(continued on next page)

Table 1
(continued)

	Recruiters	Own quota	Advertising[c]	Bonus	Ed benefits	M/C pay	U-rate	Cross service	College	Vets	Youth pop
D&G[7]											
Pre	0.166	−0.16	See later discussion	−0.07 to 0.01	N/A	1.01	0.59				
Post	0.11	0.21				−0.36^d	0.15				

[1] Warner and Simon (2005).
[2] Warner, Simon and Payne (2001).
[3] Bohn and Schmitz (1996); estimates using Navy recruiting districts and month dummies.
[4] Hogan et al. (1996); shows median estimates for Navy.
[5] Warner and Asch (1995).
[6] Murray and McDonald (1999).
[7] Dertouzos and Garber (2003).
[a] Elasticity with respect to increase in recruiters.
[b] Elasticity with respect to decrease in recruiters.
[c] Elasticity with respect to national own-service advertising.
[d] Elasticity with respect to civilian wages.

Simon and Payne (2001), Murray and McDonald (1999), and Dertouzos and Garber (2003)] explicitly compare estimates from the 1980s and 1990s for evidence of shifts in the enlistment model, and results from these studies are included in Table 1.

Estimates from Warner, Simon and Payne (2001, 2003a) and Warner and Simon (2005) show the effects of post-Cold War trends and provide preliminary estimates of the enlistment effects of recent operations in Iraq and Afghanistan. These studies find that the growth in college attendance, the decline of the veteran influencer population and combat operations and fatalities in Afghanistan and Iraq had negative and statistically significant effects on high-quality enlistments. College attendance is measured as the fraction of a state's high school graduate population, aged 17 to 21, enrolled in college. For the Army, each 10 percent increase in college attendance is estimated to reduce high quality enlistments by 8.7 percent. Thus, they estimate that the 11 percent increase in college attendance between 1987 and 1997 reduced high-quality enlistments for the Army by 9.8 percent. The percent veterans' population elasticity is positive, large, and statistically significant, equal to 1.44 for the Army. Thus, the 19 percent decline in the percent of the population that is a veteran is estimated to reduce Army high-quality enlistments by 27.4 percent. Arguably, this estimate is too large, and overstates the effects of a decline in veteran influencers because of correlation with the state fixed effects. States with significant veterans' populations may also be states with values or cultural factors that produce more high-quality enlistments. Some evidence of different cultural values is found in the later Warner and Simon (2005) analysis, using data extending from 1987 to 2005. They show that states where the 2004 presidential election results favored the Republican candidate George Bush – the so-called "red states" – produced more high-quality Army enlistments in 2004 and 2005 than did "blue" states.

The Iraqi war has taken a sizable toll on Army recruiting, as evidenced in the Warner and Simon (2005) analysis by the negative and statistically significant effects of the Operation Iraqi Freedom (OIF) effect and number of fatalities per quarter during that operation. OIF is estimated to have reduced Army high-quality enlistments by 34 percent, with 16 percentage points attributable to the OIF effect and 18 percentage points due to an average fatality rate of 186 deaths per quarter. The added risks and stresses associated with extended combat operations has reduced Army high-quality enlistments and bodes problems in the future to the extent such operations continue. Notably, youth propensity to serve in the military initially surged following the attacks of September 2001, with the exception of African–American youth who initially showed a slight decline in propensity. Black youth showed an increase in propensity between November 2001 and 2003, followed by a sharp decline between November 2003 and 2004. Combat operations in support of OIF began in the spring of 2003. The fraction of male enlistments that are African Americans fell from 20 to about 10 percent between 2000 and 2005. While it is not clear yet whether these declines are attributable to the anticipated risks and stresses of combat operations should they enlist, the weaker support for the war among African–American parents – 80 percent stating that they would not recommend service because of the war relative to 59 percent of white parents – suggests that the war has had a negative impact.

Comparison of pre- and post-Cold War Army elasticity estimates in panels 1 and 2 of Table 1 indicates recent elasticity estimates for relative military and civilian pay are within the range of pre-drawdown estimates, as are the recent estimates for the unemployment rate. Warner and Simon (2005) estimate a relative pay elasticity of 0.93 while their previous analysis for the Army [Warner, Simon and Payne (2001)] produced an estimate of 1.05. Bohn and Schmitz estimate a higher elasticity of 1.64 while Hogan et al. (1996) estimate a lower one of 0.55. These estimates are within the range found in the Warner, Simon and Payne (2001) literature review and the range discussed in the first volume of the *Handbook*. Warner and Simon (2005) estimate that relative pay rose by 8 percent over the 1996 to 2005 period, implying an increase in Army enlistments over that period of 7 percent. Recent unemployment elasticities range from 0.177 in the Hogan et al. study to 0.49 in the Warner and Simon (2005) study. The later study estimates that the 20 percent drop in the unemployment rate between 2003 and 2005 implied a 10 percent drop in high-quality enlistments over that period.

Recruiter productivity appears to have declined in the Army in the post-Cold War years. While more recent estimates of the recruiter elasticity are within the range found in earlier studies, they are invariably on the low end of the range. Furthermore, Warner, Simon and Payne (2001), Murray and McDonald (1999), and Dertouzos and Garber (2003) all find post-Cold War estimates that are lower than pre-Cold War estimates. The first study finds an Army recruiter elasticity of 0.50 while the latter two found elasticities of 0.139 and 0.28, respectively. Past studies reviewed by Warner, Simon and Payne (2001) found a range for the recruiter elasticity of 0.15 to 1.647, with a mean value of 0.763. The mean elasticity in the studies reviewed in Warner and Asch (1995) was 0.648. Murray and McDonald (1999) find smaller recruiter elasticities in the 1990s period than in the 1980s period for both the Army and Air Force. As they note, the reason for the decline is unclear. It may be due to a decline in youth interest in these services, changes in how recruiters were used and managed or simply to less effort exerted by recruiters because resources were reduced more slowly than were recruiting goals in the initial years of the drawdown. Recruiter management issues are discussed below. Interestingly, Warner and Simon use a spline specification that allows the recruiter elasticity to differ if the number of recruiters is increasing or decreasing. They estimate a 0.4 recruiter elasticity if recruiters are increasing but 0.6 if they are decreasing. Thus, the 30 percent decline in Army recruiters between 2001 and 2004 is estimated to have reduced Army high-quality enlistments by 18 percent.

Advertising is the other key input into the recruiting process. Table 1 also shows that post-Cold War elasticity estimates of own Army national advertising, measured in 2000 dollars, are in the general range of pre-Cold War studies. Thus, Warner, Simon and Payne (2001) estimate that a 10 percent increase in total Army advertising increases enlistments by 1.63 percent while Hogan et al. find elasticities that range from 0.021 for radio to 0.028 for television. Past studies find elasticities of around 0.10 on average.

However, Dertouzos and Garber (2003) argue that advertising was considerably different in the 1990s, and they call into question both past as well as recent studies of military advertising. They argue that past econometric models of advertising effectiveness are flawed because they are overly restrictive in key respects. First, the logarithmic functional form that is generally used embeds the assumption that the advertising elasticity is the same regardless of the baseline level of advertising. However, it seems likely that advertising will be ineffective if too little is spent because insufficient advertising impressions are made to influence youths' attitudes about military service. Likewise, after some saturation point advertising expenditures are ineffective because youths have received the same advertising message many times. Second, advertising is likely to have dynamic effects beyond the time period when an ad is first placed, but the effects are likely to diminish over time as the target audience forgets the initial advertising impression. Some past studies have used restrictive functional forms in addressing the dynamic aspects of advertising. Dertouzos and Garber modify the basic enlistment supply model and use a flexible functional form in the specification of the potential effects of advertising to allow the elasticity of different media to vary with the scale of advertising and so permits thresholds and saturation points that vary with media type and month. Their model permits an S-shaped (logistic) relationship between enlistments and advertising with effects that are spread out over the course of several months and depend on the combination of parameters estimated for the given media type.

Dertouzos and Garber estimate their model using data from the mid-1980s and data over the 1993–1997 period and distinguish between television, radio, and magazine advertising. Their estimates suggest that the S-curves differ by media type. If only a small budget were available, such as $20 per 1000 young males, magazine advertising would be the most cost-effective medium because it is the one is estimated to have a noticeable enlistment effect for such a small spending level. For larger budgets, say $75 per 1000 young males, a mix of magazine and radio advertising is the best choice. Only for large budgets does television advertising make sense.

Because of threshold effects of advertising expenditures, advertising budgets that are too low may be less efficient than larger budgets. Dertouzos and Garber argue that at the budget levels that prevailed in the 1980s, advertising was cost-effective, but the budget levels in the period 1993 to 1997 were too low to be in the part of the S-curve where expenditures would have their maximum effect at the margin. The policy implication is that the services should not cut their advertising budgets too deeply during periods of low demand for recruits, lest they operate in the least efficient part of the S-curve.

Success in recruiting depends on recruiter effort incentives and productivity. Dertouzos (1985) and Polich, Dertouzos and Press (1986) find that the full market expansion effect of a change in pay or other recruiting resources such as enlistment bonuses will not be realized if recruiters reduce their effort because their jobs become easier as a result of the expansion in resources. To achieve the full effect, quotas must also increase, as should the incentive to achieve them. Moreover, they show that recruiters will pursue low-quality enlistments unless they are rewarded sufficiently to allocate their effort toward high-quality enlistments. The services have used various incentive schemes to motivate recruiter performance. These schemes reward recruiters who meet quotas with points that lead to rewards, including faster promotions. These schemes have varied over time within and across services, in terms of whether they reward individual or group performance (such as station-level performance), absolute performance or performance relative to another group or a standard, whether they are based on monthly performance or performance over a longer time horizon, and what types of enlistments are rewarded. Oken and Asch (1997) review the history of these schemes from the 1980s through the late 1990s.

Dertouzos and Garber (2004) examine the role of Army recruiter management and specifically, the effects of recruiter selection and assignment, and mission allocation, and recruiter rewards on enlistments using data from 1998 to 2003. They find that younger recruiters and recruiters assigned to locations with similar backgrounds in terms of race, gender, and home state, are more effective. For example, an African–American recruiter produces 10 percent more enlistments than non-African–American recruiters also located in urban markets. They also find that successful recruiters are rewarded in terms of faster promotions. Less successful recruiters have career paths similar to those of non-recruiters. They also find evidence that group-level goals improved performance substantially relative to individual-level goals, suggesting that the gains from cooperation, specialization, and peer-pressure that can occur under team incentive schemes outweigh any losses from free riding.

Elasticity estimates for educational benefits and bonuses are in the range of estimates from the 1980s. Warner, Simon and Payne (2001) estimate elasticities of 0.12 and 0.47 for the present value of bonuses and educational benefits, respectively. Just as past studies find a significant channeling effect of these targeted benefits on enlistments in hard-to-fill skills, Warner et al. find evidence of their effect on channeling recruits to longer terms of service. Warner and Simon (2005) investigate the channeling effect of bonuses by the Air Force to 6-year enlistment contracts. Prior to 1999, 85 percent of recruits signed up for 4 year contracts and few received bonuses. They found that recruits' term choices were highly responsive to the bonus spread between 4-year and 6-year enlistment contracts. A $2500 spread is estimated to increase 6-year contracts by 15 percentage points.

Hansen, Wills and Reese (2004) studies the Navy's nuclear field bonus program. Since the late 1980s, the US Navy has varied enlistment bonuses for nuclear field recruits by season of entry, and Hansen studies whether the program has been successful in smoothing the flow of recruits into training. He finds that larger bonuses the less popular months of entry do in fact induce recruits to enter the Navy in off-peak months. Hansen finds that a 1 percent increase in off-peak bonuses decreases the proportion of nuclear field recruits entering the Navy in the peak summer season by 1.9 percent. With 37 percent of nuclear field recruits entering the Navy in the peak season over the 1988 to 2002 time period, a 5.3 percent increase in the off-peak bonus would reduce this rate to 33 percent and result in a level-loaded seasonal profile. The seasonal bonus program has reduced training costs by smoothing the flow of recruits into training over the course of the year.

   The studies reported in Table 1 rely on natural variation in the factors associated with enlistment to identify their effects on enlistment. However, to assess the effects of new incentives, controlled national experiments were conducted. In the Army's "2 + 2 + 4" experiment, recruits were offered an $8000 Army College Fund (ACF) benefit for enlisting in a non-combat specialty for a period of two years on active duty (plus training time), plus two years in the Selected Reserve, plus four years in the Individual Ready Reserve. The program was targeted to about 20 percent of high-quality recruits and represented a modest enhancement to an already well-established ACF program. Not surprisingly, then, Buddin (1991) estimated a modest market expansion effect for male high-quality recruits of 3 percent. He found little evidence that the program induced recruits away from longer enlistment terms of service but did find that enlistments in hard-to-fill non-combat skills rose by 16 percent. Thus, the program had a skill-channeling effect. In the Army's "College-First" experiment, eligible recruits in the test cell could attend college prior to enlistment. These participants were required to join the Delayed Entry Program while enrolled in college up to 2 years. Upon completion of 2 years of college, they could enter the Army in paygrade E-4 with a bonus payment. Furthermore, these recruits could receive incentives to cover school costs such as loan repayment funds. Orvis and McDonald (2004) find that College-First has a significant high-quality market expansion effect among high school graduates including those with college, with the largest effect among those with less than a year of college.

   An alternative to national tests, which are expensive and only permit testing of the enlistment effects of a limited number of new incentives, is the use survey methods that query potential enlistees about their preferences for a broad array of hypothetical new incentives. Relying on hedonic theory [Rosen (1986)], the approach produces information about the value of attributes of different choices based on the preferences for choices characterized as bundles of attributes. Also known as a factorial design in the statistics literature and as conjoint analysis in the market research literature, the survey involves presenting respondents with numerous multi-dimensional choices and asking them to indicate their choice, or preference, based on the attributes of those choices. In the case of enlistment, past studies have offered prospective recruits enlistment options with new incentives and asked them about their interest in the new options. Conditional logit or ordered logit model estimation then provides estimates of the effects of different new incentives on enlistment.

   Kraus, Griffis and Golfin (2000) analyzed alternative new Navy enlistment incentives that would offer college credit as well as enlistment bonuses and Navy College Fund incentives for alternative Navy jobs and obligation lengths. They find that "medium propensity" respondents have a stronger relative preference for college fund benefits than high propensity respondents, while offering college credit for Navy training was found to have a large positive effect on propensity. In contrast, increasing obligation length by one year had a substantial negative effect on propensity. Asch, Schonlau and Du (2004) analyzed alternative college-first incentive designs; each hypothetical incentive would allow college market recruits to attend college before entering the military. They considered programs that would offer higher military pay, enlistment bonuses, tuition stipends, and student loan repayment, as well as programs that would require recruits to major in a field related to their military occupation, like medical technology for hospital corpsman. They found that the loan repayment program had the largest effect on the propensity of college market youth, followed by pay and stipend benefits, where the college market was defined as those who were college-bound high school seniors, currently enrolled college students, or recent college dropouts. Loan repayment programs were also estimated to be the most cost-effective because, based on past Army experience with loan repayment, the average loan amount is relatively small, about $16,000 in 2000.

Given the growing Hispanic youth population and rising college expectations among eligible youth, greater attention is being paid to the enlistment potential of the Hispanic and college market. Economic theory implies that the military should equalize the marginal cost of recruiting youth in the traditional markets such as high-school graduates, and those in non-traditional markets such as the college market to meet a given mission. Asch and Kilburn (2003) examine which segments of the college markets have the greatest enlistment potential. They find that individuals who attend 2-year colleges as well as those who drop out of 2-year colleges have the greatest potential, given their family background, demographics and employment profiles. Kraus et al. (2004) reach similar conclusions about the 2-year college market.

While college students generally have a weaker preference for the military, Hispanic youth have a higher propensity to enlist than their white counterparts. Nonetheless, Hispanics are underrepresented among enlistments; they comprised 17 percent of the 18 to 24 year-old civilian population in 2004 but only 15 percent of accessions. Lower high-school graduation rates are a key reason Hispanic youth fail to qualify for military service. However, even conditional on graduation, Asch et al. (2005) find that a sizable percentage of Hispanic as well as African–American youth fail to meet the services' AFQT standards or they exceed their standards for weight. About a third of Hispanic youth who exceed the weight standard are within 10 pounds, suggesting that a large fraction far exceed the standard. While the services can and do grant waivers and allow overweight youth to enlist, exceeding the weight standard is associated with higher attrition rates. Also, because of a correlation between weight and other disqualifying characteristics, relaxing the weight standard, by say 10 percent, will not necessarily result in a 10 percent increase in those who qualify for service. As for disqualifying because of AFQT scores, presumably Hispanic youth would improve their test score performance by improving their English language proficiency. Representation might also improve through improved recruiter management of Hispanic recruiting. Hattiangadi, Lee and Quester (2004) find that the Marine Corps is more successful than the other services in recruiting Hispanics because, among other actions, recruiters reach out to parents and family and are required to stay in touch with recruits and parents throughout basic training. The United States is not the only country with an underrepresentation of some minority groups. Bellany (2003) analyzes the underrepresentation of ethnic minorities among enlistments to the British army using data from 1987 to 2000. He finds that, although application rates are lower among ethnic minorities, these rates are somewhat more responsive to changes in the unemployment rate and relative military pay than are white application rates.

Compared to active duty recruiting, reserve recruiting has received relatively little attention. Arkes and Kilburn (2005) provide some post-Cold War evidence about reserve enlisted supply. They estimate a joint active-reserve enlistment model that incorporates the role of college in civilian opportunity as an alternative to enlistment. They find a large positive unemployment effect: a one percentage point increase in the unemployment rate is estimated to increase the fraction of a state's youth population that chooses active duty by 1.4 percent and chooses reserve duty by about 7 percent. Active duty recruiters are estimated to have a positive effect on reserve recruiting, but only up to a point. At higher levels of active recruiter density, recruiters are estimated to have a negative effect on reserve recruiting.

Since September 2001 the reserve forces have participated more and have experienced frequent and longer deployments. Furthermore, many reservists have suffered injuries, and there have been numerous casualties among members of the reserve components. How activations and deployments have affected reserve supply is only beginning to be studied.

2.2. Retention: Models and recent evidence

2.2.1. Overview of models

The development of retention theory was spurred by the need to account systematically for present and future compensation in the empirical analysis of retention. Increasingly, however, retention theory has become intertwined with the analysis of alternative compensation structures and their role in inducing individuals to exert effort and self-select in a way consistent with the goals of the organization, i.e., the military service. That is, compensation policy has become a focal point of retention analysis.

The empirical analysis of retention is based on several types of models. Probably most common is a one-period model in which reenlistment depends on a measure of military/civilian pay such as the current pay ratio or the current value of the annualized cost of leaving (ACOL). The ACOL model was discussed at some length in Warner and Asch (1995); readers are referred back to that discussion. Theoretically, the model is a random utility model consistent with one-time occupational choice, in that the individual weighs current pay and the stream of future pay for each occupational pathway under consideration. The error term in the random utility model may be viewed as representing heterogeneous taste for military service, a transitory shock, or both combined. Such models are well suited to cross-sectional data, including a time series of cross-sections. The models are easy to estimate with commonly available software and readily handle a large number of explanatory variables, often including the availability and amount of a reenlistment bonus, the unemployment rate, and controls for pay grade, occupational specialty, AFQT, education level, race, ethnicity, gender, and marital status.

A generalization of the ACOL model to panel data, the ACOL-2 model extends the one-period, random utility model by introducing separate terms for taste (preference for the military) and for the transitory shock. Panel data are necessary to identify the error structure. An attractive feature of ACOL-2 is its ability to account for the selective nature of retention: as personnel are buffeted by transitory shocks in period after period, those with a higher taste for military service are the ones who tend to remain. Although it improves on the ACOL model, the ACOL-2 model has some conceptual limitations [Warner and Asch (1995) and Goldberg (2001)] that the dynamic programming approach addresses. Gotz and McCall (1984) were the first to apply dynamic programming to retention. Their path-breaking work led to a theoretical model of Air Force officer retention and to empirical estimates of its parameters. Their work heralded the application of dynamic programming models to topics in many branches of economics including retirement, occupational choice, job tenure and wages, industrial structure (entry, exit, and market equilibrium of firms), and further applications to military retention.

The dynamic programming model of retention has the following basic structure. Following the notation of Berkovec and Stern (1991), define $V(M, t, s)$ as the value at time t of having entered the military at time s, $V(C, t, s)$ as the value at time t of a civilian job that started at time s, and β as the individual's personal discount factor ($\beta = 1/(1 + \rho)$):

$$V(M, t, s) = W_t^M + \tau^m + \beta E Z_M(t, s) + \varepsilon_t^m \equiv \overline{V}(M, t, s) + \varepsilon_t^m,$$

$$V(C, t, s) = W_t^C + \tau^c + \beta E Z_C(t, s) + \varepsilon_t^c \equiv \overline{V}(C, t, s) + \varepsilon_t^c,$$

$$E Z_M(t, s) = E \operatorname{Max}\left(\overline{V}(M, t+1, s) + \varepsilon_{t+1}^m, \overline{V}(C, t+1, t+1) + \varepsilon_{t+1}^c\right),$$

$$E Z_C(t, s) = E \operatorname{Max}\left(\overline{V}(C, t+1, s) + \varepsilon_{t+1}^c, \overline{V}(M, t+1, t+1) + \varepsilon_{t+1}^m\right). \qquad (2)$$

The individual chooses to stay in the military at t if $\overline{V}(M, t, s) + \varepsilon_t^m > \overline{V}(C, t, t) + \varepsilon_t^c$. The terms with over bars are non-stochastic and include not only current-period pay and taste, but also the discounted value of following the optimal program next period. That is, the individual can re-optimize depending on the conditions in that period, including the revelation of the transitory shock. Recognizing this in the current period, the individual takes the expected value of choosing the optimum program in the next period – that is, the individual takes the expected value of the maximum. The opportunity for re-optimization carries forward to the final period of choice. As a result, the solution of finite-length, discrete choice dynamic programs such as these involves defining the conditions in the terminal period (e.g., an individual with 30 years of service must transition to the civilian state at that point), and applying backward recursion from the final period to the present period. The recursion produces optimal rules of motion and, in particular, produces expressions for the $\overline{V}$ terms for each period and state.

The shock terms are usually assumed to have an extreme value distribution or a normal distribution. The extreme value distribution produces closed-form expressions for the expected value of the maximum and the probability of staying in the military. Specifically, the extreme value distribution is $F(\varepsilon_t^i) = \exp(-\exp(-\varepsilon_t^i/s))$, where i is the choice {M, C} and s is the shape parameter, which is related to the variance by the formula $\sigma^2 = s^2\pi^2/6$. The extreme value distribution also has a location parameter, and in this application it is represented by the value function. The expected value of the maximum is:

$$E \max_i[\overline{V}_i + \varepsilon_i] = \iint \text{Max}(\overline{V}_m + \varepsilon_m, \overline{V}_c + \varepsilon_c)\, dF(\varepsilon)$$
$$= s(\gamma + \log[\exp(\overline{V}_m/s) + \exp(\overline{V}_c/s)]), \tag{3}$$

where γ is Euler's constant (≈ 0.577216). The probability of a particular choice, given one's present state, has a multinomial logit form because the ε's follow an extreme value distribution. For example, the probability of staying in the military at t given that one is in the military at $t-1$ is the logistic function

$$\frac{\exp(\overline{V}(M, t, s))}{\exp(\overline{V}(M, t, s)) + \exp(\overline{V}(C, t, t))}.$$

A similar expression can be derived for each period, and the probability of staying in the military for k consecutive periods is the product of such probabilities for the k periods. The probabilities for a sample of individuals can be used to create a maximum likelihood function, opening the path to estimate the model parameters.

Structure can be introduced into the dynamic programming model to handle a rich variety of environments. Once the key parameters of the model have been assumed, calibrated, or estimated on the basis of the current environment, the parameters and the model can be used to simulate alternative compensation and personnel policies. The key parameters in the model above are the mean and variance of the net preference for military service $\tau^m - \tau^c$, and the variance of the transitory shock ε. Perhaps the most obvious restriction to introduce, at least for the US military, is that of *no re-entry*. The military prohibits re-entering active duty after leaving it, except at the most junior grades. This restriction is present in stochastic dynamic programming models in the following way. The value of leaving equals the present discounted value of civilian wages, civilian taste, and retirement benefits; military pay does not appear because de facto it is not possible to re-enter the military. $\overline{V}(C, t, s)$ may be defined in the same way. Alternatively, it may be defined such that $V(M, t+1, t+1)$ in the expression above for $EZ_C(t, s)$ is set to negative infinity, so that continuation in the civilian state would always be chosen by a civilian. The probability of *promotion* is introduced by writing V_{t+1}^M as an expected value depending on the probability of promotion from current rank r to rank $r + 1$: $\pi_{r,r+1}V_{t+1}^M(r+1) + (1 - \pi_{r,r+1})V_{t+1}^M(r)$. (Demotions can be introduced by allowing for downward movement in rank.) With the model programmed to keep track of rank and year of service, *up-or-out rules* can be introduced. Under such a rule, when the individual has not been promoted by the time the rule applies, the value of continuing in the military can be set to minus infinity, which forces the probability of transitioning to the civilian state to equal one.

Asch and Warner (2001b) augment the model by adding individual ability and individual effort and simulate the effect of alternative compensation structures, characterizing the results in terms of expected years of service, retention of high ability individuals, incentive to exert effort, and cost. Asch and Warner (2001b) and Asch, Johnson and Warner (1998) simulate alternative retirement benefit systems coupled with changes to the structure of basic pay. Daula and Moffitt (1995) estimate a dynamic programming model of Army reenlistment by means of repeated application of probit. Hosek et al. (2002) extend the model backward to include the enlistment decision, add a switching cost associated with breaching the military contract and leaving before the end of term (attrition), and allow the civilian wage to depend on military training, in their case, information technology training. Asch, Hosek and Clendenning (in press) extend the model to include participation in the reserves after leaving active duty. Their model shows, for example, how changes in active or reserve compensation or retirement benefits affect active-duty retention, percentage qualifying for active-duty retirement, affiliation with reserve units after leaving active duty, reserve retention, and percentage qualifying for reserve retirement.

2.2.2. Empirical evidence

Empirical studies of enlisted retention have focused on first-term reenlistment, and second-term reenlistment, and those of officers have focused on retention at the initial service obligation (6 to 10 years of service) and at the time of promotion to major (at 10 to 12 years of service). Warner and Asch (1995) and Goldberg (2001) summarized the pay elasticity estimates from ten studies of enlisted retention and two studies of officer retention. The data for these studies came largely from the period 1975–1990. The enlisted pay elasticity mostly fell in the range of 1.0 to 2.5, with a few lower estimates and a few higher, and the officer pay elasticity was in the range from 0.8 to 1.6. Some more recent estimates of the enlisted pay elasticity tended to be lower, i.e., 0.5 to 1.5. Hansen and Wenger (2005) addressed the question of whether the pay elasticity has declined in recent years; see below. Some enlisted studies also estimated the effect of reenlistment bonuses [see the summary in Goldberg (2001) and a study by Hattiangadi, Lee and Quester (2004)]. Reenlistment bonuses are paid in selected military specialties, and the amount of the bonus equals the individual's basic pay times the number of years of reenlistment times a bonus multiplier (integer values from one to six). Because the term length of reenlistment contract is the individual's choice, the studies used a bonus variable based on an assumed term of four years. The studies found that a one-step increase in the bonus multiplier led to an increase in the reenlistment probability mostly in the range of 0.02 to 0.03 points; the range was the same for first- and second-term reenlistment. Lump sum payment of bonuses was found to be more cost effective than payment by installment [Hosek and Peterson (1985b), Hattiangadi, Lee and Quester (2004)].

Fullerton (2003) used two military pay variables in his study of Air Force pilot retention. The first was a pilot's expected lifetime earnings from the present period forward if he left immediately for a job in the airlines, compared with staying in the Air Force to complete 20 years of service – and becoming eligible for immediate receipt of military retirement benefits – and then joining the airlines. The comparison shows that as of 1999, at 15 years of service or more the payoff from staying in the Air Force until retirement at 20 years is greater than the payoff from leaving. Therefore, experienced pilots would have an incentive to stay until 20 years of service. But before 15 years this measure indicates that it pays to leave and join the airlines, suggesting that junior pilots have an incentive to leave. However, Fullerton's second pay variable tends to counteract that incentive. This variable was the size of the initial pay cut from leaving the Air Force at the ninth year of service and joining the airlines. The cut in pay results because of losing the pilot bonus, an amount up to $25,000, and because military pay was higher than starting pay in the airlines. According to Fullerton, a pilot faced a pay cut of about $60,000, or nearly 60 percent, in the first year in the airlines after departing at year of service nine. Airline pay grew rapidly, however, and within a few years it equaled military pay including the bonus. The second pay variable can be interpreted as a type of switching cost. Both pay variables have the expected effect and are statistically significant in Fullerton's retention regression. Fullerton also finds that airline hiring, measured by the number of pilots the airlines hired as a percentage of the size of the USAF pilot force, significantly affects pilot retention, as does economic activity, measured by the unemployment rate. A one-percentage increase in airline hiring increases the probability of separation by 1.13 percent, while a one-percentage point increase in the male unemployment rate reduces the probability of separation by 20 percent. Fullerton measured operational tempo by the number of pilot deployments relative to the size of the USAF pilot force. A 22 percent increase in tempo – similar to the increase from operations over Serbia and Kosovo – increases the separation probability by 3 percent. Elliott, Kapur and Gresenz (2004) also find that increases in airline hiring increase pilot separations.

Hansen and Wenger (2005) were interested in whether the military pay elasticity had decreased in the 1990s compared with earlier years of the all-volunteer force. Ultimately, they found no evidence in support of a decrease, and they discovered that the apparent differences in pay elasticity estimates, including the possible decrease in the elasticity, could be laid to differences in methodology. These differences included whether the data were individual-level or grouped; how military pay was defined (e.g., current military/civilian pay ratio, ACOL); what model was estimated (ACOL, ACOL-2, stay/leave or extend/re-enlist/leave); and what additional explanatory variables were included [e.g., sea duty/non-sea duty expected next term; whether a separation incentive was offered – voluntary separation incentive (VSI) and special separation benefit (SSB) were offered during the drawdown in the early 1990s; occupation type (called "rating" in the US Navy)]; eligibility to re-enlist (ineligibles included/excluded). In their baseline model – a logit model of first-term reenlistment for 3 years or more versus not doing so, with military pay measured by ACOL – Hansen and Wenger estimate a pay elasticity of 1.6, which is in the middle of the range of previous estimates. In addition, in a series of separate excursions that change the measure of military pay, include extensions, alter the mix of included variables, use grouped data, and exclude those not eligible to reenlist, they generate elasticity estimates that range from 0.3 to 2.8, much like the range found in the body of past studies. Moreover, they find that models based on the ACOL pay variable predict reenlistment "much more accurately" than those based on the military/civilian pay ratio (p. 42).

Golding and Gregory (2002) analyzed the relationship between career sea pay (CSP) and the willingness of sailors to remain or extend on sea duty. CSP applied to the ranks of E-4 and higher in their data, although in FY 2001 CSP was extended to cover E-1 to E-3. The results of regression analysis showed that sea pay had a positive effect on completing a year of an obligated sea tour and on encouraging extensions on sea duty. An increase of $50 per month in sea pay increased the predicted completion rate of a 48-month sea tour by 3.3 percentage points, or 11 percent, and increased extensions of 48-month tours by 2.9 percentage points, or 5.8 percent. Overall, the $50 per month increase in sea pay would produce 1425 work-years of sea duty. This works out to a cost of $31,600 per additional work-year and is less than the cost of having another Petty Office Third Class or someone in pay grade E-4 ($37,200 in 2002).

Kraus, Lien and Orme (2003) offer further evidence of sailors' preferences for non-pecuniary aspects of service. These include guarantees of location and assignment for a particular type of duty; survey respondents indicated that a 4 to 6 percent increase in pay would be required to achieve the same increase in reenlistment intention as caused by the guarantees. Two aspects of service having a negative effect on reenlistment intentions were "requiring sailors to live on ship or in group housing rather than in civilian housing during in-port sea duty." Pay increases could neutralize the decrease in reenlistment intentions, e.g., a 13 percent pay increase for sailors living on ship rather than in civilian housing would hold their reenlistment intention constant.

Educational benefits are a powerful recruiting incentive, as discussed above. But educational benefits such as the Montgomery GI Bill that increase enlistment also create an incentive to leave military service once the individual has qualified to receive the full benefit (e.g., after 24 months on active duty). Tuition assistance (TA), however, pays the cost of college classes while on active duty, which might be expected to blunt the incentive to leave service. However, Buddin and Kapur (2002) find that TA recipients have lower first-term retention than non-users who are also eligible for TA. The reason appears to be that TA recipients, like non-TA recipients, also have GI bill benefits, and use of TA signals a strong preference for college, which may be completed faster – and often with additional financial assistance – by becoming a full-time student in the civilian world.

Hosek et al. (2004) analyzed the supply and retention of enlisted information technology (IT) personnel. During the 1990s, as the IT market boomed, the military was not expected to compete well against private sector opportunities. But in fact the services were able to meet IT recruiting goals and attract high-quality recruits into IT, even though enlistment incentives (bonuses, educational benefits) were about the same in IT and non-IT specialties. Also, attrition in IT was lower even after controlling for education and AFQT, and first-term retention was similar in IT and non-IT specialties. Hosek et al. documented these outcomes and developed a dynamic programming model to rationalize them. The model extends the Gotz/McCall model by including the enlistment decision, allowing the accumulation of IT human capital to increase the civilian opportunity wage, and including a switching cost if the service member leaves before completing the term of service. The analysis suggests that by providing valuable, transferable training in many military specialties and offering pathways for career advancement, the services can compete for individuals who might otherwise be drawn to college (e.g., two-year colleges) or to employers offering on-the-job training.

2.3. Deployment: Theory and evidence

2.3.1. Model of deployment and reenlistment

The widespread growth in operations has resulted in an increased pace of military operations and an increase in deployments. Several models [e.g., Hosek and Totten (1998, 2002), and Hosek, Kavanagh and Miller (2006)] address the question of how deployments affect reenlistment. At the core of these models is the individual's preference for time at home station relative to time deployed and the factors that affect the individual's willingness to tradeoff time at home station for time away. The models also raise the question of why current deployment should affect reenlistment, which often occurs in the future. If current deployment accords with one's expectations and if deployment draws are independent, then one might argue that it has no bearing on future reenlistment just as an outcome of "heads" from the toss of a fair coin toss should not affect the willingness to accept a new bet at even odds.

Assume the individual's utility depends on income, time at home station (home time), and time away including deployment (time deployed). The fraction of the period spent at home station is $(1-d)$ and fraction of time deployed is d. Base pay is m, and letting w be the amount of deployment pay if the individual were deployed for the entire period, wd is the deployment pay received for the fraction of the period d. Utility depends on income $m + wd$, home time $(1 - d)$, and deployment time d: $U(m + wd, 1 - d, d)$. [Hosek and Totten (2002) also include the number of deployments in their model but the basic insight is much the same as here.]

Assume deployment time is distributed uniformly between d_1 and d_2; that is, when deployment occurs, the length of the deployment will be d_1 or more, but no more than d_2. Define $\delta = (d_1 - d_2)/2$, so mean deployment time, given deployment, is $\mu = d_1 + \delta$. It can be shown that the variance of deployment time, given deployment, is $\sigma^2 = \delta^2/3$.

Expected utility equals the utility when at home, which occurs with probability $(1 - p)$, plus expected utility when deployed, which occurs with probability p. Expected utility when deployed is an average of the utility at each deployment length times the likelihood of that length. For the uniform distribution, the probability density equals $1/(2\delta)$ throughout the deployment range. Therefore expected utility is

$$EU = (1 - p)U(m, 1, 0) + p \int_{\mu-\delta}^{\mu+\delta} \frac{1}{2\delta} U(m + wd, 1 - d, d)\, \mathrm{d}d. \tag{4}$$

An increase in δ increases the variance of deployment time. To isolate the effect of an increase in variance from that of an increase in the mean, assume d_2 increases and d_1 decreases by the same amount. This increases δ but leaves mean deployment time unaffected. To isolate the effect of increasing the mean, assume d_1 and d_2 increase by the same amount. This increases the mean but keeps the difference $d_2 - d_1 = 2\delta$ constant, and so the variance stays the same.

If the individual could choose, he would maximize expected utility by finding the optimal values p^*, μ^* and δ^*. The perspective in this case has the individual looking ahead to the future and, in effect, choosing among distributions of deployment. The individual weighs the expected utility from a high or low probability of the occurrence of deployment, a long or short average length of deployment, and a large or small variance in deployment length. The derivatives of expected utility with respect to p, μ and δ are:

$$
\begin{aligned}
EU_p &= -U(m, 1, 0) + \int_{\mu-\delta}^{\mu+\delta} \frac{1}{2\delta} U(m + wd, 1 - d, d)\, dd, \\
EU_\mu &= \frac{p}{2\delta} \big[U(m + w(\mu + \delta), 1 - (\mu + \delta), \mu + \delta) \\
&\quad - U\big(m + w(\mu - \delta), 1 - (\mu - \delta), \mu - \delta\big) \big], \\
EU_\delta &= \frac{p}{2\delta} \bigg[U\big(m + w(\mu + \delta), 1 - (\mu + \delta), \mu + \delta\big) \\
&\quad + U\big(m + w(\mu - \delta), 1 - (\mu - \delta), \mu - \delta\big) \\
&\quad - \int_{\mu-\delta}^{\mu+\delta} \frac{1}{2\delta} U(m + wd, 1 - d, d)\, dd \bigg].
\end{aligned}
$$
(5)

The derivative of expected utility with respect to p does not depend on p, and the optimal value p^* must be inferred by logic. If the derivative is positive, expected utility given deployment exceeds utility without deployment, so some deployment is preferred to no deployment, implying $p^* = 1$. Similarly, if the derivative is negative, then no deployment is preferred to some deployment. Because preferences differ, some individuals prefer deployment ($p^* = 1$), others prefer none ($p^* = 0$), and others might be indifferent ($0 \leqslant p^* \leqslant 1$). Although service members typically cannot control whether they deploy, they can satisfy their preferences to some extent when joining the military by choosing the branch and occupational area closest to their preferences.

The derivative of expected utility with respect to mean deployment time μ depends on utility at the longest deployment time minus utility at the shortest. The optimal value of μ occurs where these utilities are equal; the derivative is zero at that point (assuming it is attainable). With diminishing marginal utility of both home time and time deployed, utility can increase with deployment time and then decrease. For instance, at low time deployed the marginal utility of deployment time is high and the marginal utility of home time is low, so utility increases as deployment time increases. But with high time deployed the reverse is true. At some point in between, expected utility reaches a maximum ($0 < \mu^* < 1$). However, depending on preferences, utility can increase monotonically with deployment time, in which case the derivative is always positive and $\mu^* = 1$, or utility can decrease monotonically with deployment time, implying $\mu^* = 0$. When $\mu^* > 0$ we have $p^* = 1$, and when $\mu^* = 0$ we have $p^* = 0$.

The third derivative shows the effect of an increase in the variance of time deployed. If utility is concave in deployment time, the individual is risk averse to variation in deployment time and an increase in variance reduces expected utility. Concavity is consistent with the argument that at low levels of deployment time, an increase in deployment time increases utility, while at high levels of deployment time an increase in deployment time decreases utility (or at least increases it at a lower rate). Under concavity, the preferred variance of deployment time is zero ($\delta^* = 0$). Furthermore, if utility is maximized at no deployment ($\mu^* = 0$) or full deployment ($\mu^* = 1$), then any variance in deployment time moves the individual to a lower level of expected utility. Again, the optimal variance is zero. Even if an exact length cannot credibly be given, the model implies that the individual would prefer to have information that reduced the variance.

In an all-volunteer force, it is reasonable to expect that most members prefer some deployment to none. For those preferring deployment, probably most prefer to be deployed part of the period ($0 < \mu^* < 1$). Assuming utility is concave in deployment time (risk aversion), the optimal variance in time deployed is zero. In a conscripted force, there is no reason to believe that the individual enters the service and occupation closest to his preferred values p^*, μ^* and δ^*. Because of concavity, conscripts, like volunteers, probably prefer no variance in deployment length. However, on average conscripts are likely to have lower values of p^* and μ^* than those of volunteers, i.e., less likely to prefer deployment.

The service member is not always free to choose the parameters of deployment and as a result the actual values may not equal the preferred values. Any difference between the preferred and actual values of the probability of deployment, mean length of deployment, and variance of deployment length of course reduces expected utility relative to the individual's optimum.

The typical member probably prefers some deployment for part of the period ($p^* = 1$, $0 < \mu^* < 1$). If so, then increases in μ beyond the median value of μ^* utility will decrease for more and more members. For example, if the distribution of μ^* among individuals centers at 0.25 (deployed one-fourth of the time), increases in μ from this level would increasingly tend to reduce members' expected utility. This could reduce some members' expected utility below expected utility at their best alternative and they would want to leave the military.

The military could respond by increasing base pay, deployment pay, or factors affecting the marginal utility of time deployed and home time. In particular, the deployment pay rate could be written as a schedule with higher pay the greater the amount of time deployed. Policy can also address factors affecting the marginal utility of time deployed such as the training for deployment, the quality of unit leadership, unit cohesion, living conditions, food, facilities to communicate back home, and provision of supplies and equipment (e.g., body armor). For service members with families, the model can be expanded to allow for the positive effect on member's marginal utility of time deployed from factors that assure the member that his or her family is taken care of, e.g., the quality of housing, schools, health care, family support, recreational facilities, day care, and spouse employment opportunities [Huffman et al. (2005)]. In addition, the military could place more weight on deployment in promotion decisions.

The model can be expanded to divide home time into time at military work and "leisure" time. This is an important distinction because during periods of high deployment non-deployed members frequently work unusually long duty days to support deployments. This can be expected to decrease the marginal utility of time spent in military activities and reduce the intention to stay in the military. It too can be offset by family-oriented policies and higher pay, although currently there is no higher pay for non-deployed members whose work schedules are unusually hard. The model can also be expanded along the lines of a two-person labor-leisure model to consider how rigidity and uncertainty in the service member's work schedule affects the spouse's time allocation, including labor force participation, type of job chosen, and hours of work. This extension is relevant to understanding how deployments affect the military family – a broader context than how deployments affect reenlistment – and is applicable to both active and reserve families. Further, the model can be embedded in a dynamic programming model of retention, with service members assumed to have a taste for deployment in addition to their taste for military service.

Expected utility is independent of a specific draw of deployment d. That is, the derivative of expected utility with respect to d is zero. Therefore, the current realization of deployment has no effect on expected utility. Although some members may be highly satisfied (or dissatisfied) with their current deployment and quite vocal in saying so, this may have no effect on expected future utility and hence no effect on retention.

However, if the current realization of deployment causes the individual to revise the estimates of p, μ or δ, or the factors mentioned above, expected utility will change. [Hosek and Totten (2002) model this with Bayesian learning.] For instance, US soldiers' expectations about the frequency and duration of deployment may have changed markedly because of the operations in Iraq and Afghanistan. This in turn might require a change in compensation policy, the management of deployments (e.g., realigning units to broaden the rotation base and stabilize the rotation pattern), or an increase in force size.

Actual deployment experience might also cause a revision in preferences. A specific example of this is post-traumatic stress syndrome. This point is especially relevant to first term enlisted personnel and junior officers who, as civilians, never experienced deployment and who have naïve priors on p, μ and δ, and the marginal utility of deployment time and home time. Based on comments in focus groups of junior enlisted personnel who had been deployed to Iraq or Afghanistan, Hosek, Kavanagh and Miller (2006) heard from individuals who had been deployed more frequently and much longer than they had expected, and who had come to anticipate frequent deployments in the future if they remained in service. Also, many individuals had expected more certainty in the start and end dates of their deployment, and were surprised when dates were changed and re-changed. They were also surprised to perform tasks that they had not trained for, such as hunting insurgents and taking part in rebuilding the infrastructure, and when inexpensive, reliable communication back home was not available. Others found it painful to miss family events like births or first steps, yet found deployment missions to be meaningful and fulfilling. Individuals were surprised by the strong bonds created among unit members who had shared danger.

2.3.2. Empirical evidence

Studies of the effect of deployments on retention have found both positive and negative effects. For example, in the area of naval deployments, Golding and Griffis (2004) found that retention in "zone A", one to six years of service, increased among Navy personnel during Operation Desert Storm/Desert Shield, and the increase occurred despite deployments being longer than in the period before the operation. However, retention after the operation decreased, suggesting that the increase was transitory and simply delayed the outflow of personnel. Cooke, Marcus and Quester (1992) distinguished time underway on a vessel but not deployed on a mission, from time underway and deployed. Looking at reenlistments before 1986, they found that sailors with more time away from home-port had lower retention, as did sailors with longer deployments. However, Golding and Griffis (2004) conclude that longer deployments have not adversely affected reenlistment rates in the post-1986 period, at least when the deployments do not last so long that morale suffers. But quick re-deployments do reduce reenlistments.

Hosek and Totten (1998, 2002) studied all four services and on the whole found a positive or zero effect of deployments on reenlistment. They differentiate between deployments that involve hostile duty and those that do not. They consider reenlistments in the years 1996–1999 and define reenlistment to mean a new service obligation of 24 months or more. Episodes and months of deployment were counted over the three-year period ending three months before the reenlistment decision. Episodes and months of deployments were inferred from special pays, namely, family separation allowance and hostile fire pay. The vast majority of service members had a total of two or fewer deployments, e.g., one non-hostile and zero hostile, one hostile and zero non-hostile, one of each, two hostile, or two non-hostile. Also, 46 percent and 57 percent of first-term soldiers and airmen had no deployment, compared with 24 percent and 37 percent of sailors and Marines; second-term percentages were similar. Regression results showed that first-term reenlistment increased as the number of non-hostile episodes increased from zero. First-term reenlistment remained roughly constant in the Air Force and Marines as the number of hostile episodes increased, though in the Army reenlistment increased from 39 to 45 percent with the first hostile episode whereas in the Navy it decreased from 40 to 38 percent. Compared to the first-term, the results for second-term reenlistment showed larger increases in reenlistment as non-hostile episodes increased and also showed increases as hostile episodes increased. Further analysis showed that the results for first-term personnel depended on whether they were married at the time of reenlistment. The deployment effects for married first-term personnel were similar to those of second-term personnel, whereas for unmarried first-term personnel deployments, whether hostile or not, had little effect on reenlistment. Soldiers were an exception; non-hostile deployments increased the reenlistment of unmarried first-term soldiers. The difference in the effect of deployments on second-term versus first-term personnel probably arises from self-selection. First-term service members who experience deployment directly or learn about it by talking with other service members can make a more informed decision than when they first entered the military, and those service members who expect deployment to be satisfying and meaningful element of their military experience are more likely to choose to remain in the military. Further, the positive effects of deployment on first-term personnel also may represent self-selection; service members who choose to marry (and their spouses) may be comfortable with the military lifestyle, including deployments.

Another possible hypothesis for why deployments, especially non-hostile deployments, have a positive effect on reenlistment is that deployment speeds up promotion to higher ranks, and that faster promotion increases reenlistment. Hosek and Totten (2002) analyzed this hypothesis via a two-equation model like that used by Buddin et al. (1992), with equations for time to Sergeant (or pay grade E-5) promotion and for reenlistment. Separate models were estimated for first- and second-term reenlistment. Results showed that non-hostile deployments did speed up promotion to E-5 by a few months (relative to an average of about 60 months total time in service to E-5) and hostile deployments had practically no effect. However, the deployment-driven effect of faster promotion on reenlistment, although statistically significant, was too small to be of practical importance. Thus, there was little support for the hypothesis that deployments increased reenlistment because they speeded up promotion.

Fricker (2002) used the same database to analyze the relationship between deployments and officer continuation at two major phases of their careers: at the end of the initial service obligation (junior officers at roughly four to five years of service), and during the period after that (mid-grade officers between five and ten years of service). Paralleling the analysis of enlisted personnel, Fricker found a positive association between non-hostile deployments and officer retention. Selection effects also appear to be present; for mid-grade officers in three of the four services, the relationship between hostile deployments and retention was positive.

A different vein of empirical work concerns the effect of deployment on the earnings of reservists. Studies based on self-reports of earnings gain or loss in surveys of military personnel found that many reservists experienced a net loss in earnings. Using the May 2004 Status of Forces Survey of Reserve Component Members, Klerman, Loughran and Martin (2005) estimate that sixty percent of the reservists surveyed report an earnings loss, and 44 percent have an earnings loss of ten percent or more. This estimate was based on a comparison of monthly earnings before and during the respondent's most recent activation. But such estimates may suffer from recall bias, inaccurate knowledge of one's monthly earnings, and incomplete or inaccurate adjustment for the tax advantage owing to favorable tax treatment of military allowances (e.g., family separation allowance, subsistence allowance), and the non-taxability of earnings when serving in an area designated as a combat zone tax exclusion area. To surmount these concerns,

Klerman, Loughran, and Martin arranged to link service personnel records with Social Security Administration (SSA) records. SSA records include both military earnings and earnings from the reservist's civilian employer; the use of Medicare taxable earnings in the SSA record meant that earnings were not capped at a taxable limit. Using data for 2001–2003, Klerman, Loughran, and Martin find that only 28 percent of activated reservists have a loss in earnings, with 20 percent having a loss of ten percent or more. Broadly speaking, the longer a reservist is deployed, the more likely there is an earnings gain and the larger the earnings gain. The fact that many reservists' earnings increase when deployed is a piece of a larger puzzle: do reservist expenses also increase, and even if earnings increase net of expenses, is the increase sufficient to sustain the retention of reservists who are deployed? These questions remain open.

2.4. Spouses and families: Effect of military on the earnings of spouses

About half of US military personnel are married. Although past retention studies do not recognize retention as a family decision process, recent studies do address questions about how military service affects the employment and earnings of military spouses, and whether lower military family earnings are due to the lower earnings of the spouses. These issues are investigated by Hosek et al. (2002), Harrell et al. (2004), and Payne, Warner and Little (1992).

Hosek et al. (2002) use data from the 1988 to 2000 Current Population Surveys on the employment and earnings of civilian wives of military and non-military families, where both of the military and non-military subsamples were weighted each year to reflect the male, education, race/ethnicity composition of the active duty force in that year. Military wives were found to earn $5640 less per year than civilian wives with similar attributes. The lower earnings of military wives arise from differences in labor supply and differences in wage rates. Using a regression framework to analyze different aspects of wives labor supply and to estimate wage models for wives who worked, Hosek et al. found that military wives are less likely to work in a year (0.74 predicted probability versus 0.82 predicted probability for civilian spouses); less likely to work full-time (0.48 predicted probability versus 0.59 predicted probability for civilian spouses); have fewer weeks of work; and have similar, though slightly lower, hours of work per week. Together these factors imply that military wives work fewer hours per year. Weekly wages were also found to be lower. The weekly wage if the wife worked full-time was $308 for the civilian wife "look-alike" but $268 for the military wife. Harrell et al. (2004) also find lower earnings and less employment among military wives using 1990 Census data, as does Payne, Warner and Little (1992) using 1985 CPS data for civilian wives and 1985 DoD personnel survey data for military wives.

A number of hypotheses might explain these military spouse outcomes, but one possibility consistent with several of the observed patterns is that military wives with lower tastes for work are increasingly self-selected as the military career of her husband progresses. Military wives know that they are likely to move frequently, and may be willing to accept lower wage jobs rather than use their remaining time to search for high-wage jobs. Similarly employers may not be willing to offer training or other contracts that lead to higher wages, given the expectation that wives will not be with the firm for a long period of time. Also, the military is demanding of the member's time, and the wife's labor supply takes these demands into account. Furthermore, the military may be demanding of the wife's time, and officers' wives may be called to provide voluntary support activities.

Consistent with these ideas is the finding that the probability that a wife works in a year declines with age in the military, but not in the civilian sector. Such a pattern is consistent with the selective departure from the military of families with wives who have a stronger attachment to the labor force. Also, the probability declines more for military wives with a college education, most of whom are officers' wives. Both Hosek et al. (2002) and Payne, Warner and Little (1992) find that differences in weeks worked per year, among wives who work, are an important factor explaining the lower earnings of military wives. This difference in weeks is undoubtedly due to the frequent long distance moves experienced by military families due to the military's rotation cycle. Hosek et al. find that military families are three times as likely as civilian families to have an out-of-county move in a year. Military wives who move suffer a larger wage rate and weeks of work loss than civilians who move (3.8 weeks for military wives versus 1.2 weeks for civilian wives) because they are more likely to move longer distances including overseas. Harrell et al. (2004) use 1990 census data, permitting an analysis by service branch, and finds that relocation across states reduces the likelihood of employment the most for Army wives relative to civilian wives while relocation from abroad reduces the likelihood of employment the most for Navy and Air Force wives. One surprising result is the relatively small difference in the location of military and civilian families. It is often assumed that military families live in rural areas, but Hosek et al. find that both military and civilian families are more likely to live in suburban than rural areas while a relatively large percentage of military families state their location as missing, probably reflecting the fact that their duty location differs from their permanent location.

Payne, Warner and Little (1992) estimate the effect of longer rotations on military wives' earnings and finds that relative to a 6-year rotation policy, a 3-year policy reduces military spouse earnings by 40 percent of what the wife would have earned had she been able to stay in the same location for 6 years. Fifteen of this 40 percent is attributable to lost employment time (fewer months on the job) and 25 percent is due to lost seniority and the associated higher pay that comes with greater seniority.

It remains for future studies to sort out whether the lower wages and weaker attachment to the labor force of military wives have adverse effects on husband retention decisions. If these spouse labor market outcomes reflect the result of self-selection as the husbands' careers progress, then they should have no effect on retention. If, on the other hand, military wives face barriers to supplying labor or to higher wages, relative to their expectations, then these outcomes should have a negative effect on retention.

Finally, it should be noted that the services have spouse employment assistance programs that provide career counseling and limited job placement. The effectiveness of these programs has yet to be evaluated in terms of their effects on spouse employment or in terms of their effects on readiness, such as their effect on retention.

3. Demand for manpower and force management in post-Cold War era

Manpower is a key ingredient into the production of military readiness. Understanding how manpower affects readiness and estimating the most efficient mix of manpower and other inputs to military readiness has been a major challenge for researchers, for several reasons. The first is that the demand for manpower is a derived demand, and the desired level of the "final product" – military readiness – is not easily quantified, especially in an era when a military force must prepare for a wide spectrum of challenges ranging from traditional war to nuclear, chemical, and biological, to counter-terrorism and counter-insurgency. The second reason is the many dimensions along which the military manpower input may be measured, including experience, quality, skill (occupation). The third reason is that in the Total Force era the definition of manpower must be expanded to include reserve forces and civilian substitutes. The fourth reason is that ongoing, rapid technical change tends to reduce the overall demand for manpower but increase the demand for experience, quality, and skill. This section updates what research in the past decade has contributed to our understanding of the relationship between the various dimensions of readiness and manpower input.

Given the productivity relationships, the goal of force management is to continually balance the force along the multiple dimensions of experience, quality, skill, and active/reserve/civilian status to achieve the most readiness at least cost. Given the rapid pace of technical change and changes in the threat spectrum, military planners have shifted from the paradigm of preparing for certain types of engagements, e.g., protracted traditional war in one or two pre-specified theaters, to emphasizing the creation of military capabilities that can be drawn up and combined into ensembles appropriate for contingencies as they materialize. As a result, military personnel managers must manage the force in a fluid, dynamic environment. This section also deals with force management issues that have arisen since the end of the Cold War. The main theme here is that US force managers need increased flexibility to manage the force in a rapidly changing environment, but are often constrained by outmoded "legacy" systems and personnel practices that inhibit movement toward more efficient force mixes.

3.1. Personnel productivity and efficient force mixes

Personnel productivity studies are typically performed at the individual or unit levels. At the individual level, studies relate individual performance measures such as supervisor ratings or performance on skills-qualification tests to individual characteristics such as years of military experience, amount of training, education level, and entry test score (AFQT). Unit-level studies relate unit performance to unit-level manpower measures (manning level, average experience level, etc.) and other inputs. At the individual level, studies attempt to determine whether individual performance improvement, due to increased experience or improved personal characteristics, is worth the cost. At the unit level, studies attempt to answer the question of what input combination is most efficient.[1]

Warner and Asch (1995) survey the pre-1995 literature on the relationship between manpower and readiness. The pre-1995 studies yielded the following broad conclusions. First, experience is a key component of productivity. Individual productivity rises sharply within the first term of enlistment and continues to rise thereafter. Units with more senior personnel mixes are more productive. Second, quality matters: individual performance measures are strongly related to both education and entry test scores. Third, productivity varies more by experience level and by quality measure the more complex the tasks being performed and the more complicated the equipment with which personnel work. More senior forces and higher quality forces become more cost-effective as these complexity factors increase.

Studies performed since 1995 reinforce these conclusions.[2] Junor and Oi (1996) study the relationship between personnel quality and various readiness indicators (supply, equipment failure and repair rates, equipment condition, and training) for US Navy surface ships using 1974–1994 data from the US Navy's Status of Resources and Training Systems (SORTS) database. Junor et al. (1997) perform similar analyses using SORTS data for Naval air squadrons. The unit of observation is a ship or aircraft squadron in a fiscal year quarter. These studies both develop a Personnel Quality Index (PQI) that is defined as the first principal component of the following variables: the percentage of the unit with a high school degree, the percentage in mental groups I-IIIA, the percentage of personnel demoted in the previous time period, the percentage of personnel in the unit who were promoted to the rank of sergeant or E-5 by their 4th year of service, and average years of service in the unit. Using limited dependent variable methods, the discrete unit readiness indicators are regressed on the PQI, unit manning (ratio of actual to authorized manning), crew turnover, and controls for other factors such as time period and unit characteristics (deployment status, age, and class of ship or aircraft).

For both US Navy ships and aircraft, the manning level and PQI are the two factors most related, both statistically and in terms of magnitude of effect, to the various readiness indicators. Several of the readiness indicators are almost proportional to the

---

[1] Unit-level readiness studies typically specify a production function of the form $R = R(M, K; T)$ where R denotes readiness, M denotes manpower inputs, K denotes capital (equipment) inputs, and the function is conditional on the state of technology (T). The optimal resource mix between manpower and equipment (the mix that delivers a given readiness at least cost) depends on the marginal products of the inputs (i.e., $MP_M = \partial R/\partial M$ and $MP_K = \partial R/\partial K$) and their marginal costs (i.e., MC_M and MC_K). The most efficient (cost-effective) mix occurs where, for a given input mix, the relative marginal product of manpower (MP_M/MP_K) equals the relative marginal cost (MC_M/MC_K). When manpower is disaggregated by manpower input category (e.g., experience level), the optimal mix equates each category's relative marginal productivity with its relative marginal cost.

[2] See Kavanagh (2005) for a detailed discussion of pre- and post-1995 productivity studies.

manning level, implying a strong effect of quantitative level of manpower input – high readiness depends on ships being fully manned. Further, according to the PQI, the quality of US Navy manpower rose dramatically after 1981.[3] Junor and Oi (1996) estimate that this personnel quality improvement reduced the equipment failure rate on ships by 50 percent and equipment repair time by 36 percent. The "fully mission capable" rate for Navy aircraft was 68 percent in 1995. Junor et al. (1997) estimate that, had the 1995 aircraft inventory been maintained by 1982 quality personnel, the fully mission capable rate would decline to 47 percent, a reduction of 31 percent. These results imply that personnel quality can be substituted for quantity to keep readiness constant, although another implication is that, holding the manning level constant, a ship's readiness depends strongly on personnel quality. Neither study, however, attempted to estimate the most efficient, cost-effective mix of manning and personnel quality.

Doyle (1998) uses activity analysis to study trade-offs between manning and experience. Activity analysis defines sets of tasks to be completed and specifies experience-learning curves for these various tasks. Task sets include training, supervisory work, and regular work. Within each task set, there are a number of specific tasks that must be performed ranging from simple to complex. Regular work has direct military value; training and supervisory work have value only as they support the accomplishment of regular work. Activity analysis uses linear programming to solve for the various experience mixes that can accomplish a given amount of regular work given the learning curves for various tasks.

Using learning curves estimated for US Air Force enlisted personnel by earlier studies, Doyle estimates the manpower mixes required to meet a specified level of regular work while also performing training and supervisory tasks. A representative mix is shown in Table 2. Since a more junior force requires more training and supervisory

Table 2
Various experience mixes

First-term/ career mix	Unit size	Number of personnel 1–4 YOS	Number of personnel 5–8 YOS	Number of personnel 9–12 YOS	Number of personnel 13+ YOS
30–70	95	30	20	15	30
40–60	97	38	21	13	25
50–50	100	50	18	12	20
60–40	102	60	16	10	16
70–30	105	75	10	8	12

Source: Doyle (1998). [From Kavanagh (2005).]

---

[3] The PQI is normalized to have a mean of 0 and a standard deviation of 1. In 1981, the typical United States Navy ship had a PQI of -1.5 in 1981; by 1994 the typical ship had a PQI of $+2.5$.

work from the more experienced personnel, a given size force accomplishes less regular work the more junior it is and therefore requires more personnel to accomplish the same level of regular work. A force comprised of 70 percent careerists requires only 95 people to perform the same tasks as a force of 105 people comprised of 70 percent first-term personnel. More experienced personnel do tasks faster than more junior personnel, but Doyle finds that it is the reduction in supervisory time that permits the bulk of the reduction in overall manning when the average experience level increases.

More complex tasks have steeper learning curves (i.e., learning continues over a longer time) than less complex tasks, implying that the trade-off between experience and force size is larger in skill (occupational) areas that have a larger number of complex tasks relative to the number of simple tasks.

Moore, Golding and Griffis (2000) and Hansen et al. (2003) study the mix of first-term and career personnel in the US Navy. Reenlistments in the US Navy soared in the late 1990s and early 2000s, leading to significant experience growth. The Navy responded to this growth by reducing accessions. These studies ask whether first-term retention had become too high. They construct the marginal costs of first-term and second-term personnel and then compare the relative marginal costs of careerists in different skills with estimates of their relative marginal productivity (as discussed below). The studies are notable for the detail of their cost considerations and incorporate many "drag-along" costs that are often ignored. They reach the conclusion that first-term Navy reenlistment was too high in many skill areas and that the Navy should reduce reenlistment bonuses in many skills. Only in some skills characterized by high training costs and high productivity growth was the experience mix about right.

The conclusions of these studies, though, are questionable. First, rather than use estimates of the experience-productivity relationship from military studies, they estimate the relationship from civilian experience-earning profiles. It is not obvious that civilian earnings profiles usefully estimate the marginal productivity of military personnel by experience level. Second, the studies assume a constant total force size and therefore do not allow the total force size to be reduced to maintain a constant readiness level as the average experience level increases.

DiTrapani and Keenan (2005) and Kleinman and Hansen (2005) provide evidence indicating that smaller, but more experienced, crews are considerably more productive than larger, less experienced crews on Navy ships. A natural experiment was provided when the crews on US Navy converted some support ships from military to civilian crews. The civilian crews were only half of the size of the Navy crews they replaced, but had much more overall experience (25 percent of the civilian crews had more than 10 years of experience versus only 11 percent of military crews) and, importantly, more experience at sea for any given overall experience level. This study found that the smaller civilian crews performed as well or better than the larger Navy crews in all areas of performance.

3.2. Personnel management in the post-Cold War era

3.2.1. The US drawdown as a case study in force management

During the drawdown of US forces after the end of the Cold War, the active duty force was reduced by 38 percent, from 2.1 to 1.3 million personnel. How to effect such a substantial force reduction raised difficult force management issues. Initially, many in the US military services and the US department of defense wanted to accomplish the drawdown by reducing new accessions. But the large accession declines implied by this strategy would mean insufficient numbers of personnel to staff the higher ranks and experience levels in future years. It became apparent that the drawdown would require a balanced force reduction in all ranks and year groups. But how to accomplish a balanced force reduction was problematic. Careerists who were not yet vested in the 20-year retirement system would not leave voluntarily, and to separate them involuntarily would be seen as a break of faith of an implicit contract, especially those with 10–19 years of service. This posed the problem of how to induce personnel to leave voluntarily and to do so in a way that was not detrimental to force quality.

To induce voluntary separation, the US department of defense originally devised a plan called the Voluntary Separation Incentive (VSI). The VSI offered an annuity payment to eligible personnel based on the formula $0.025 *$ years of service $*$ final basic pay for twice the individual's current years of service. Individuals in groups designated to be in excess supply who had between 7 and 19 years of service were eligible for the VSI. Groups were defined on the basis of occupation, rank, and service. Many more personnel in the Army and Air Force than personnel in the Navy and Marine Corps were eligible for the VSI. Later, Congress added a lump-sum payment alternative called the Selective Separation Bonus (SSB). The SSB was set at 1.5 times the lump-sum payment for involuntary separation already in law. [See Table 1 of Warner and Pleeter (2001) for a comparison of VSI and SSB benefit amounts to personnel in various ranks and years of service.] Finally, because neither of these options was attractive to personnel with more than 15 years of service, Congress allowed early retirement with a lifetime annuity for personnel with more than 15 years of service beginning in 1993.

How effective were these drawdown programs in inducing voluntary separation and did they induce the right personnel to leave? Analyses by Moore, Griffis and Cavaluzzo (1996), Mehay and Hogan (1998) and Asch and Warner (2001a) indicate that the programs were successful in both inducing sufficient numbers of personnel, and the right personnel, to separate. Because separations increased among personnel ineligible for the payments as well as those eligible for them, the increase in separations as a percentage of eligible personnel overstates the effect of the programs. Using a difference-in-differences approach that contrasted the change in separation rates between 1992 and 1988 of Army enlisted personnel eligible for the payments with the change in separation for ineligible personnel, Asch and Warner estimated that the programs induced a 16–20 percentage-point increase in separation among eligible personnel. To be sure, the programs paid rents to personnel who would have left without them, but they were effective in inducing higher separation.

Studying Navy second-term retention between 1992 and 1994, Moore, Griffis and Cavaluzzo (1996) treat eligibility for separation payments as an endogenous right-hand side variable and develop instruments based on the difference between personnel inventories and personnel requirements. They estimate that the separation rate of personnel eligible for the program was 22 percentage points higher than the separation rate of non-eligible personnel. Treating eligibility as an endogenous variable gave a larger estimate than treating it as exogenous.

One reason the programs were effective is that personnel were told that if the programs did not induce enough voluntary separation during certain eligibility windows, personnel would be involuntarily separated (with a separation payment of 2/3 of the SSB) until force targets were met. The Air Force in fact published a table informing personnel in eligible skills of their probability of involuntary separation in the event the voluntary separation programs did not induce enough voluntary separation. Mehay and Hogan (1998) estimate a significant effect of this announcement: separations were significantly higher in groups at higher risk of involuntary separation. In the end, the programs induced enough voluntary separation that virtually no personnel had to be involuntarily separated. But there was clearly an involuntary component because many personnel left knowing that they were at risk of eventual involuntary separation.

One potential problem with separation programs is that they might induce adverse selection whereby the best and brightest leave and the less able stay. But Asch and Warner (2001a) find that the program was in fact pro-selective – it induced lower-quality personnel, as measured by education level and AFQT score, to leave at higher rates. Presumably, these personnel made rational forecasts that they would be at higher risk of involuntary separation in the future.

Finally, the choice between the lump-sum and annuity payments offered during the drawdown program reveals information about personal discount rates. Warner and Pleeter (2001) use drawdown data to estimate personal discount rates, controlling for potential selection bias that might arise if the program induced personnel with higher discount rates to separate at higher rates. Controlling for such bias in a sequential probit model of separation and incentive choice, they estimate that the typical officer has a personal discount rate of around 10–12 percent while the typical enlisted person has a personal discount rate well over 20 percent. Discount rates decline as age, education level, and AFQT score increase and are lower for whites, females, and those without dependents. Personnel apply lower discount rates to larger choice amounts, which explained part of the difference between the discount rates between officers and enlisted personnel.

3.2.2. Recent developments in force management

The US drawdown period demonstrated the value of flexible force management tools that can be targeted quickly to adjust personnel supply with manpower demand. Unfortunately, many of the legacy policies, including compensation and personnel policies, remain in place. Authority for the US services to offer voluntary separation payments to mid-careerists not yet vested in the retirement system expired on September 30, 2001 and has not been renewed. But such authority is needed again because the combined Navy and Air Force strength was reduced in 2005 by 30,000 and these services are now confronted with force imbalances. As during the drawdown, these services are again reluctant to separate mid-careerists involuntarily and, without adequate force management tools, have resorted to reduced accessions to meet strength targets. The Air Force recruited only about 18,000 in FY 2005, down from 30,000 in previous years. It will potentially experience "holes in the force" in future years.

Hansen and Husted (2005) study voluntary separation payment options including administratively fixed payment schemes such as the VSI and SSB and an auction in which personnel would bid the payment that would induce them to leave, with the separation payment set at the highest or second-highest offer price that induces the required number of separations. The recommendation to explore an auction option is an outgrowth of the Assignment Incentive Pay (AIP) system implemented by the US Navy in 2003. Historically, military assignments to different geographic areas have been like a lottery and based on the philosophy that everyone share the pain of bad assignments from time to time. But like a draft, random selection for geographic assignment fails to exploit heterogeneity in individual preferences. Hogan and Mackin (2003) analyzed the then-existing Navy assignment system and demonstrated that assignment pay can substitute for reenlistment bonuses and reduce overall manpower costs when geographic preferences are heterogeneous.

In developing an AIP, the problem arose how to implement such a pay. Assignment pay rates could be set administratively. But a more innovative and more efficient solution would be to set AIP rates by using a market. As early as 1999, economists advising the Navy had recommended an Internet-based auction in which sailors could go on-line and submit bids to go to different locations, with AIP rates to different locations established by the first or second marginal bids. Golding and Cox (2003) discussed issues in auction system design. In 2003 the Navy implemented an Internet auction system in which sailors can bid for assignments at selected overseas locations, and the Navy plans to expand the system to include all locations by 2007.[4] Preliminary indications are that the system is working well [Golfin, Lien and Gregory (2004)]. There is still institutional resistance to using market-based incentives in the other US military services, especially the Air Force, but that resistance may diminish based on the success of the Navy AIP system.

---

[4] The AIP system currently applies to only about 10,000 personnel in selected overseas locations. Although the system will be Navy-wide by 2007, commanding officers at various locations must demonstrate that their billets are hard to fill for the AIP system to be available at their location. The United States Navy does not appear to be carrying an AIP system to its logical extreme, whereby the system would apply to all locations and personnel might pay to go to desirable locations as well as be paid to go to undesirable ones.

4. Issues in compensation

4.1. Pay adequacy to attract a quality force

From an efficiency standpoint, the adequacy of military pay is judged in terms of the ability of the armed forces to attract, retain, develop, sort, motivate, and eventually separate personnel cost-effectively. Furthermore, as became even clearer in the post-Cold War environment and the new post-September 11, 2001 national security environment, it must also be judged in terms of its ability to facilitate the flexible use and management of personnel when threats and the manpower requirements to meet those threats are less certain. Military pay lagged behind civilian pay in the early 1990s, and recruiting problems arose in the late 1990s as did pockets of retention problems. In response, members received an across-the-board pay raise in January 2000 and another pay raise in July 2000 targeted to specific pay grades and year of service groups, and recruiting and retention resources were expanded, as discussed earlier. Recruiting and retention outcomes improved, at least until 2005 when Army accessions fell short of the goal. Beyond enlisted supply, there is the question of the adequacy of military compensation since the end of the Cold War from the standpoint of effort and sorting incentives, enhanced management flexibility, cost-effectiveness, and feasibility of reform.

With respect to effort and sorting incentives, the structure of military basic pay has become somewhat more skewed, in accordance with economic theory. Skewness means the pay gap between grades rises with grade. Table 3, reproduced from Asch et al.

Table 3
Basic pay by pay grade relative to pay of an E-5 or O-3 (in percent), by year

Pay grade	Median years of service	1949	1958	1971	1981	1995	July 2000	2005
E-1	1	49	40	63	59	59	59	56
E-2	1	51	41	70	67	67	66	63
E-3	2	59	47	73	69	69	68	66
E-4	4	77	76	85	82	82	84	77
E-5	8	100	100	100	100	100	100	100
E-6	13	127	126	125	125	125	124	126
E-7	17	155	150	147	148	148	147	151
E-8	20		171	169	170	170	171	174
E-9	25		210	208	209	217	218	224
O-1	2	63	51	55	55	55	55	54
O-2	3	77	66	69	69	69	72	70
O-3	7	100	100	100	100	100	100	100
O-4	14	125	125	121	121	121	127	128
O-5	20	154	164	152	152	152	154	151
O-6	24	188	207	184	183	183	186	182

Sources: Congressional Budget Office (1995, p. 41), Asch, Romley and Totten (2005).

(2005), shows how basic pay varies with promotion. The Career Compensation Act of 1949 established the general structure of the pay table. For example, in 2005, pay relative to the pay of an E-5 (sergeant) ranged from 56 percent for an E-1 (private) to 224 percent for an E-9 (sergeant major). Except for the pay raises for junior enlisted personnel in 1971 in anticipation of the end of the draft in 1973, the structure of the pay table has remained relatively stable, especially for officers. As a result of the targeted pay raises, the structure in 2005 is more skewed for enlisted personnel than it was in 1995. The pay of an E-7 (sergeant first class) is 51 percent greater than that of an E-5 in 2005 but was 48 percent higher in 1995. For an E-9, it is 124 percent higher rather than 117 percent higher. The 2005 structure is more similar to the 1940s design. It remains to be seen if empirical work bears out whether effort incentives have been greater as a result of the increased skewness of the pay table. Such an analysis would need to account for how effort supply varies with promotion probabilities and how promotion probabilities vary with pay grade.

Until 2000, targeted pay raises were rare, but between 2000 and 2005 were made in general accordance with economic theory, as shown in Table 3. Initially, in 2000, the targeted pay raise was intended to rectify anomalies in the pay table, such as automatic longevity raises that were greater than raises associated with promotion. That is, the raises were set to ensure that junior personnel had a stronger incentive to seek promotion by supplying effort rather than holding back effort to get an automatic longevity raise. [The theory of effort incentives provided by the structure of the pay table is summarized in Warner and Asch (1995).] Later, the targeted raises were paid to mid-career and senior personnel and were intended to recognize that most enlisted personnel had some college (typically one to two years of post-secondary coursework) or planned to attain some college, and had better external wage opportunities than a high school graduate. Although most enlisted personnel do not stay for an entire career, military planners recognized that, to maintain the proper skewness of the pay table, the pay of senior grade enlistees had to increase if mid-career pay was increased.

Military compensation consists of an array of pays and allowances (Table 4). Regular military compensation (RMC) is the sum of basic pay, basic allowance for housing, basic allowance for subsistence and the tax advantage of receiving these allowances tax-free, and is considered the metric of military pay that is most comparable to civilian pay. For enlisted personnel, basic pay is about 60 percent of enlisted cash compensation, while the basic allowance for housing and subsistence are about 28 percent. For officers, the corresponding figures are around 68 percent and 19 percent, respectively.

The array of special and incentive pays as well as bonuses are policy variables that can facilitate management flexibility by offering an efficient means of varying the level of compensation in response to differences in the desirability of different locations or duties (e.g., sea pay), risks (e.g., Toxic Fuels Duty Pay), skills (e.g., Foreign Language Pay), exposure to danger during military operations (Hostile Fire Pay) and recruiting or retention conditions (enlistment and reenlistment bonuses). Though offering the possibility of management flexibility, in actuality they average to relatively small amounts

Table 4
Average US military compensation, FY 1999

Category of cash compensation	Army	Air force	Marine corps	Navy
Enlisted personnel				
Regular military compensation	$30,509	$31,398	$28,241	$30,655
Special and incentive pays	482	301	317	1345
Bonuses	372	381	11	777
Miscellaneous allowances and COLAs	832	1015	785	967
Total	32,195	33,095	29,355	33,743
Officers				
Regular military compensation	$61,689	$61,599	$58,707	$59,761
Special and incentive pays	927	2810	1889	3134
Bonuses	673	1695	756	2172
Miscellaneous allowances and COLAs	837	779	810	872
Total	64,125	66,883	62,161	65,940

Source: Asch, Hosek and Martin (2005).

because the incidence and/or average amounts of special and incentive pays as well as bonuses are generally small, as seen in Table 4.

On the other hand, these pays account for most of the variation in cash compensation. Hosek et al. (2002) construct percentiles of total cash pay by years of service for officers and enlisted personnel using 1999 data and find that the variation in pay at each YOS is remarkably small. The first is the common foundation of pay across services and occupations, namely RMC. As shown in Table 4, RMC accounts for $30,000 of the (approximate) $32,000 average enlisted pay and $60,000 of the (approximate) $64,000 average officer pay. Second, the services have similar promotion criteria, though they have different systems. Third, special and incentive pays and bonuses do not average out to large amounts. Fourth, as a result of the first three factors, pay profiles show very little variation across occupation categories; a result is common retention patterns by occupation.

Asch, Hosek and Warner (2001) show percentiles of civilian earnings for males with various levels of education and experience. At each level, the variation in civilian pay is generally much larger than the variation in military pay. One reason for the larger variation is that civilian earnings are averaged across many civilian firms that may differ in their hiring requirements and industry conditions, and the military is more likely to be more homogeneous in terms of factors that affect earnings than is the civilian economy at large. Nonetheless, it is likely that much of the variation in civilian earnings at a given year of experience is due to differences in the rewards to ability, education, training, and experience. Thus, the source of variation in pay in the civilian economy is in marked contrast to the military where the variation is small and is due to sustaining similar retention profiles across occupational areas.

4.2. Gaining added pay flexibility

Since the end of the Cold War, many observers, including studies, commissions, study groups and senior military leaders, have noted the conformity of military careers produced by the military compensation system and retirement system in particular [Asch and Warner (2001b), US Department of Defense (2000, 2002), Schirmer et al. (2004), Rostker (2002), Warner (2006)]. The 20-year military retirement system induces a very high percentage of mid-career personnel to stay until they are vested at 20 years and then induces them (together with more stringent up-or-out rules) to leave at 20 when the retirement system's immediate annuity begins. The retirement system induces highly similar careers, regardless of occupational area [Hosek et al. (2002)]. These observers have called for more flexible management of military personnel, involving more variable retention patterns and career lengths across occupational areas, longer assignments and fewer rotations, and reform of the up-or-out system.

For example, as described in the Defense Science Board report (2000), 20 years is not the optimal career for all military career fields. Some occupations, such as infantry, have a 12 to 14 year productive career, while others, such as lawyers, should have a career that spans well beyond 20 years. Furthermore, military skills are obtained by gaining breadth of experience from a sequence of assignments. The requirement for assignments that are more "joint" has increased in the post-Cold War period, implying more frequent rotations within the fixed 20-year career, and shorter rotations in the key billets that lead to senior leadership positions. More frequent rotations also divorce the link between actions today and the consequences of those actions, and hampers effective evaluation of personnel based on outcomes. They also mean that individuals, ceteris paribus, are more likely to take actions that look good, are easy, or have an immediate payoff, and are not necessarily the most beneficial to the unit or service in the long run.

As for up-or-out, the current system does not accommodate task specialization too well and allow individuals who do not want command responsibility to remain in operator jobs for extended periods. In addition, the promotion system together with the up-or-out provision, as the primary incentive for high performance in the military, embeds incentives for predictable job behavior ("playing it safe") and penalizes even minor blemishes on one's record, given the lack of variation in promotion probabilities across eligible personnel. Thus, the system discourages desirable risk-taking, innovation, and entrepreneurship, that is, the types of behaviors and skills demanded by a transformed military operating in a post-September 11 national security environment.

Gaining added management flexibility requires restructuring the retirement system. The restructured system should allow for different service lengths and retirement ages depending on military needs, while at the same time helping members accumulate savings when they exit from the labor force at older ages. To meet members' needs to save for retirement, the restructured system should vest all personnel relatively early, say between 5 and 10 years of service, in an old-age annuity. Some commissions, such as the Defense Science Board, have argued that the old-age benefit should be a defined contribution plan. Others have discussed the advantages of the two-part US federal employee retirement system that includes both a defined contribution plan and a basic defined benefit plan. To meet the services' need for variable career lengths, the restructured system should provide a separation pay in the form of an early annuity or a set of lump sum payments, for which the timing of the first payment may be varied by skill area. Thus, payments would be early for skills like combat arms in which the military wanted to increase early separations, and later (or no payments) for those skills in which the military wanted to increase retention.

Analyses have found that retention generally falls when the compensation system is restructured to "backload" more compensation later in a member's career. Given that a typical member is relatively young and with a high personal discount rate, a backloaded system is less valuable relative to the civilian alternative. To maintain retention, current compensation must increase. Asch and Warner (2001b) and Asch, Johnson and Warner (1998) recommend a skewed increase in basic pay to increase effort incentives and a cash separation payment to ease the transition to the civilian sector. As discussed in Asch, Johnson and Warner (1998) and Warner (2006), the restructured retirement systems offer the opportunity for more flexible management of personnel because the eligibility for the separation payment can be targeted by skill area. With vesting shifted to an earlier point than 20 years, benefits grow in a smoother, more continuous manner over a military career that can span a longer time frame than 20 years, if such a long career is desired. Alternatively, if a short career is desired, separation payments could begin earlier.

Much of the focus on military retirement reform has been on the active duty system. The extensive use of reserve forces in Iraq and Afghanistan has raised questions about the adequacy of reserve compensation. If reservists now expect to be used more frequently and for longer periods than ever before and to be used side by side with active duty forces, some argue they should be paid the same as their active duty counterparts. In fact, this is already largely true when it comes to basic pay, allowances, and many special and incentive pays, but it is not true of retirement benefits. Active-duty members begin receiving military retirement benefits as soon as they leave active-duty after completing 20 years of service. Like actives, reservists are vested after 20 years of creditable service, but they must wait until age 60 to receive military retirement benefits. Some critics of the current system fear that benefit inequity will hurt morale, reduce the supply of reservists, and jeopardize future force strength and readiness.

The US Congress has proposed several bills to make reserve retirement benefits more equitable with the active benefit by reducing the age of first receipt of retirement benefits. For example, one bill would reduce the age of first receipt to age 55 from 60 while another would reduce the age by one year for every two years of creditable service beyond twenty. Asch et al. (2005) use the active-reserve dynamic retention model to simulate the active retention and retirement effects, the reserve affiliation, retention, and retirement effects, and the basic pay and retirement accrual cost implications of these proposals. They find that, overall, proposals to reduce age of first receipt are not cost-effective because they increase costs but have little impact on the recruitment of departing active-duty members into the reserves and have a negative or small impact on overall reserve retention relative to the current system. The reason for the increase in cost but not in retention is that individual reservists are relatively young on average, so their personal discount rates exceed the government discount rate. Reservists do not value the increases to their future retirement benefit as highly as it costs the government to provide those increases.

Asch, Hosek, and Clendenning also note that the concept of active and reserve equity extends beyond the simple issue of the age of retirement entitlement. Among these are the demands of full-time active duty service in terms of readiness, deployment, frequent absences, permanent change of station moves, the inability to have a full-time civilian job, and the impact of the military regimen on the family and the negative effects on the employment and earning opportunities of the military spouse. In addition, the calculation of basic pay in determining retirement benefits favors reservists. Basic pay for a retired reservist is the value of basic pay in effect when the reservist turns 60, not the value of basic pay in effect in the year when the reservist separated plus the cost of living adjustment to age 60. This favors the reservists because basic pay typically rises faster than the cost of living. Furthermore, one purpose of active-duty retirement benefits is to help the retired active-duty member establish a civilian career, whereas reservists typically already have a civilian career and a retirement benefit plan with their employer.

Finally, Asch, Hosek, and Clendenning argue that increasing the generosity of reserve retirement benefits is an inefficient, poorly targeted, and unfair way of compensating reservists for the higher burden of deployment. It is poorly targeted because the reservists who have been activated are concentrated in specific occupations and reserve components such as the Army National Guard, and not all reservists have been activated. It is unfair because not all reservists will achieve 20 years of creditable service and qualify for reserve retirement. Compensation policies, such as higher bonuses and special pays that directly target reservists who are likely to be activated, are more cost-effective force management tools.

4.3. Civilian earnings of military retirees

Active duty members who retire from the military generally enter the civilian work force for a "second career" until they exit the labor force. A question of interest is whether their military service yields a return in the civilian sector.

Evidence on the civilian returns to military service for military retirees from the 1970s was discussed in Warner and Asch (1995). The key study by Borjas and Welch (1986) used survey data on military retirees in 1977 with data on civilian veterans from the 1977 current population survey and found that initially during their second career in the civilian sector, military retirees earned less than their civilian counterparts, presumably because some of their human capital was military-specific. However, over time the gap in earnings converged as retirees "retool" and accumulate more civilian-sector human capital. Nonetheless, over the span of the second career, officer retirees earned 14 percent less and enlisted retirees earned 20 percent less than their veteran counterparts in the civilian sector.

Two surveys of military retirees, one in 1996 and another in 2003 provide more recent information on post-service earnings. Cardell et al. (1997) analyze the 1996 survey of military retirees, employ an approach identical to that of Borjas and Welch, and obtain similar results, especially for enlisted personnel: military retirees experience an initial earnings gap compared to civilian veterans but eventually catch up. Loughran (2002) argues that both the Borjas and Welch and the Cardell et al. findings are the result of failing to control for cohort effects in their cross-sectional data. Because Loughran uses information on two points in time – recalled earnings on the first full-time job following retirement and reported earnings in 1995, he is able to control for cohort effects in his analysis. He finds strong evidence of cohort effects. Specifically, more recent retirees in the 1990s earned civilian wages that were 25 percent less than non-retirees, while retirees who left the military in the 1970s earned comparable earnings to civilian non-retirees, thereby explaining the apparent "catchup" observed by Cardell et al. and Borjas and Welch. Conditional on age, education, race, marital status, occupation, and geographic location, wages of recent retirees were even lower – 32 percent below mean civilian earnings. After controlling for cohort effects, he finds little evidence of convergence; post-service civilian earnings improve slightly over time for older cohorts relative to non-retirees, but remain essentially unchanged for more recent cohorts.

More recently, Mackin and Darling (2005) use the 2003 survey of military retirees and find that retirees do not experience an earnings gap relative to civilians, a result that differs from previous efforts. However, it is unclear whether their findings indicate a shift in the civilian earnings of military retirees or the confounding effects of aging and cohort effects.

4.4. Rising cost of entitlements

A large fraction of military compensation is in the form of non-cash benefits, especially health care benefits. About 57 percent of average total compensation budget costs is non-cash compensation with health care accounting for 29 percent of total compensation budget costs [Congressional Budget Office (2004)]. Beginning in the 1990s, the military health care benefit underwent a change; it established a system, known as TRI-CARE, to finance a menu of health care options, each provided in the private sector for military members and their dependents as well as retirees and their dependents. The growth in the cost of military health care has been substantial; between 1988 and 2003 the inflation-adjusted growth in cost has been around 4 percent, excluding cost growth for TRICARE for Life, the health benefit introduced for post-age 65 military retirees in 2002 [Hosek (2005), Congressional Budget Office (2003)]. This rate is similar to the rate of increase experienced in the civilian sector for the same period, according to Hosek. Nonetheless, TRICARE for Life, the new program for post-65 retirees will increase costs significantly in the future, if no other change is made. By 2013, the Congressional Budget Office estimates that TRICARE for Life will increase health care costs by 44 percent.

As discussed by Hosek (2005), TRICARE compares favorably overall with civilian health plans in terms of the benefits it provides. For beneficiaries who are eligible for employer benefits, especially military retirees who are under the age of 65 and are employed in the civilian economy, the major advantage of TRICARE is that its premiums are lower on average than civilian premiums, and employer plans typically charge twice what TRICARE charges for prescription drugs. Consequently, the pre-age 65 military health benefit has the potential to "crowd out" civilian health benefits as pre-age 65 military retirees have an incentive to switch to the TRICARE benefit. According to Hosek, 72 percent of military retirees under age 65 working full time worked for employers who provided health insurance. Among those with access to an employer health plan, 35 percent paid to enroll in TRICARE. When a retiree with dependents gives up employer insurance and uses TRICARE, employers save about $7000 per year at current premium rates and the employee saves about $2500. DoD assumes both costs. Thus, most of the benefit of offering TRICARE to pre-65 retirees is likely to accrue to employers, not retirees. As noted by Hosek, if current trends continue, DoD risks becoming the primary insurer for all of its beneficiaries, picking up an even higher share of costs.

The growth in health care benefits for military retirees represents a shift toward a greater share of military compensation being deferred. It is not likely that retention or recruiting is affected as much by improvements in health benefits for pre- or post-age 65 retirees, as they would be by changes in cash bonuses targeted to junior and mid-career active duty and reserve personnel. On the other hand, no doubt the comprehensive nature of military health care benefit has value to the military member and serves to improve the attractiveness of military service. Therefore, recent studies have recommended increasing the cost-effectiveness of the military health benefit, by introducing cost-share arrangements, increasing premium contributions and fees, financing health care for retirees under age 65 through an accrual fund, as is currently done for retirees over age 65, and introducing tax-advantage health savings accounts.

As stated above, current cash compensation budget costs now comprise less than half of total military compensation costs. In the private sector, the figure is closer to 80 percent [Bureau of Labor Statistics (2000)]. Available evidence for the private sector suggests that employees place an average value of less than $.50 on each dollar of benefit cost to employers [Royalty (2000)]. Economic theory leads to the conclusion that it is most efficient to compensate in cash because cash gives employees the most choice to purchase goods and services providing the highest value, unless there are other reasons that improve overall social welfare. For example, in-kind benefits might improve productivity (e.g., child care or health clubs), attract workers with desirable characteristics, or reduce costs. Although there is little evidence available on the effectiveness of military in-kind benefits and their impact on metrics of readiness or productivity, military compensation could be more efficiently provided if members were allowed more choice in the mix of benefits versus cash and in the allocation of compensation between deferred versus current compensation.

4.5. Addressing obstacles to compensation reform

Asch and Hosek (2004) argue that a major obstacle to compensation reform is the lack of demand for reform on the part of the services. As noted, observers have called for reform of military compensation and of the military retirement system in particular to permit greater flexibility in managing personnel. Yet, little change has occurred. Therefore, Asch and Hosek argue that derivation of the optimal compensation reform must incorporate that specifically address the lack of incentives of the services and service members to support reform because they prefer the status quo on equity grounds.

To explore what these elements are, Asch et al. (2005) apply a model developed by Demange and Geoffard (2003) of reforming incentive schemes under political constraints. The application of the model assumes three parties: taxpayers, service members, and Congress. Service members are heterogeneous in terms of their taste for service. The first-best compensation scheme is the one where members choose effort and career lengths that maximize the total expected joint welfare of the triad. However, if the status quo scheme is not the first-best scheme, a politically feasible reform is a new scheme that increases efficiency over the status quo (or does not reduce it), makes a large enough proportion of service members better off that they do not block reform, and balances the budget (the sum of taxes collected equals total expenditures paid to service members). Given the proportion of members, q, required to make the reform feasible, the marginal member, defined over the distribution of taste for service, such that q percent of members accept the new scheme, determines the compensating variation required to "buy off" support for reform. Clearly, it is possible that some members earn a rent because they would have been willing to accept a smaller buyoff or perhaps been made even better off under the reform.

At some point, the total cost of the buyoff to members exceeds the efficiency gain to taxpayers of lower taxes or better national defense, at which point the reform is no longer sensible. It is useful to consider the conditions when reform will occur. Political reform is more likely to be successful when the total cost of the buyoff is smaller. This outcome occurs when service members have less political power, are more homogeneous, and their career lengths or effort is more responsive to financial incentives. Finally, given heterogeneity of members, a menu of reforms, much like a cafeteria plan can improve the feasibility of reform and reduce the necessary compensating variation.

5. New contributions to the economics of the draft

Outside of Great Britain, conscription was almost universal in Europe prior to the end of the Cold War [Jehn and Selden (2002)]. Perhaps the most remarkable event in the post-Cold War era has been the decisions of many European countries to end conscription. Jehn and Selden (2002) argued that the decisions of different countries to end conscription were based on country-specific factors and that no single factor could explain the decisions to end conscription. And they thought at the time of publication of their paper that the trend toward volunteer forces had run its course. But since 2000, six more European countries – the Czech Republic, Hungary, Latvia, Romania, Slovakia, and Slovenia have moved to implement volunteer forces. So it is useful to analyze the choice of system of military manpower procurement and identify the factors most likely related to the decisions of European countries to move toward volunteerism. This section reviews recent contributions to the literature on conscription and then examines the trend in Europe toward volunteer forces in light of these contributions.

5.1. Recent contributions

Economists have a natural bias in favor of a volunteer system for providing military personnel. But work in the early 1990s cited in Warner and Asch (1995) showed that the case for volunteer forces over conscripted forces is not ironclad. Extending this work, Warner and Asch (1996, 2001), and Warner and Negrusa (2005) have built models in which the real resource cost of a military force is the sum of four separate costs: (1) the opportunity costs of the military personnel in the force, (2) the cost of recruiting and training the force, (3) individuals' costs of attempting to avoid or evade military service together with the government's costs of preventing evasion (evasion costs), and (4) deadweight costs of taxation.

The first three costs all tend to be smaller in a volunteer force than a conscripted force of equal size. Consider first opportunity cost. The opportunity cost of military service is the military member's foregone civilian wage plus the member's tastes for civilian life. Tastes incorporate all of the non-pecuniary differences between military and civilian life and are measured by the military wage premium necessary to make the individual indifferent between military and civilian life. The supply curve of personnel to the military arrays individuals in the civilian population by their opportunity cost from lowest to highest; it slopes upward due to variation in both civilian wage opportunities and non-pecuniary taste factors. In a volunteer force, all volunteers have opportunity cost less than or equal to the military wage. A conscripted force has a higher opportunity cost than a volunteer force of equal size when draftees are obtained in a random draft due to the fact that randomly conscripted individuals will have higher average opportunity costs than the marginal volunteer.[5] However, drafts that conscript individuals in order of their civilian opportunity costs (called 'least-value drafted first') as well as drafts that permit draftees to buy replacements or opt out by paying a commutation fee, can reduce

---

[5] Although the model is static, the opportunity cost of military service includes long-run, dynamic effects on lifecycle earnings, as several papers reviewed below make evident.

or even eliminate the opportunity cost differential between conscripted and volunteer forces [Warner and Asch (2001)].[6]

The US military experienced a significant rise in retention after the move to volunteerism. Turnover averaged 21 percent under the draft; in the all-volunteer force (AVF) era, turnover has averaged 15 percent [Warner and Asch (2001)]. The result has been a higher average experience level, more years per accession (rising from 4.7 to 6.5), and an increase in the average age of the enlisted force (rising from 25 to 27.6). Lower turnover reduces training costs and permits a higher return on training investment. However, recruiting costs may be higher in the volunteer system due to the need for extra recruiters and advertising.

Evasion costs are zero under a volunteer system, but may be a significant cost under conscription. Warner and Negrusa (2005) formally analyze evasion costs. Individuals attempt to evade the draft when the expected benefit of evasion exceeds the expected personal cost of evasion. Evasion is more likely the higher is the opportunity cost of military service, the easier it is to evade conscription, and the smaller the penalties for evasion. Evasion is less likely when the period of military service is short and when the citizenry willingly accepts the need for some period of compulsory service.[7]

The equilibrium amount of evasion depends not only on individuals' costs and benefits of evasion but on the government's cost of preventing it. The easier it is for individuals to evade conscription by going underground or by going to another country, the more costly a government's efforts at policing evasion will be. Factors such as geographic isolation and better governmental systems for tracking its citizens reduce evasion costs and increase the likelihood of conscription; proximity to other countries and porous borders increase governmental evasion costs and reduce the likelihood of conscription.

The deadweight tax loss cost of providing a military force arises from the fact that the government must raise tax revenue to pay military personnel. Taxes distort economic activity; estimates for the United States of the deadweight loss per dollar of tax revenue are about 20–30 percent of tax revenue [Browning (1987)]. Because the supply curve of personnel to the military slopes upward, the military payroll, and hence the deadweight tax loss, rises exponentially under a volunteer force. But under conscription the payroll only rises linearly due to the fact that additional personnel are brought in at a fixed wage. Hence conscripted forces have lower deadweight tax losses than volunteer forces of equal size.

---

[6] The World War I draft in the United States was essentially a least-value drafted first draft. Hiring replacements and allowing draftees to opt out with a commutation fee were common practices during the Revolutionary and Civil Wars. More recent drafts in the United States have been by random lottery. Mulligan and Schleifer (2004) found that 13 countries practicing conscription as of 1998 permitted buyouts.

[7] Thus, during the Cold War period, conscription in Europe did not promote much effort at evasion because the service periods were relatively short (generally less than a year) and because need for a high percentage of the adult male population to have military training in the event of a conflict with the Soviet Union was well accepted. By contrast, many US youth sought to evade the draft during the Vietnam War period because of the longer duration of conscripted service (2 years) and because they did not view the war as vital to US interests.

Since the social cost of volunteer forces rises at a faster rate with respect to force size than the cost of conscripted forces, there will be a force size F^* below which volunteer forces are cheaper and beyond which a volunteer system is more costly. However, the choice of manpower procurement system should not be made on the cost of a given size force, but the capability a given force provides. Studies surveyed in Warner and Asch (1995) and Section 3 above indicate that military readiness improves with reduced turnover and greater average experience. An implication is that volunteer forces do not need to be as large as conscripted forces to provide the same level of military capability. Furthermore, the payoff to experience depends positively on the complexity of military hardware, so the productivity differential between volunteer and conscripted forces widens with the complexity of military equipment.

When productivity considerations are taken into account, the higher productivity of the volunteer system reinforces its lower social cost when the required capability calls for a volunteer force smaller than F^*. When the required capability calls for a volunteer (or draft) force size bigger than F^*, the volunteer system will still be the preferred system if the (smaller) volunteer force can provide a given capability at lower social cost. Two conditions are necessary for conscription to dominate: a very large required force size and a small productivity differential between conscripted and volunteer forces.

Comparative statics available in Warner and Asch (1996) show that the switch point F^* at which conscription becomes the cheaper system for a given force size increases with the elasticity of labor supply (which implies less dispersion in opportunity costs in the population of individuals available for military service). But a leftward shift in the supply curve, caused for instance by an unpopular war or civilian sector productivity (wage) growth, would reduce F^*. Warner and Negrusa (2005) show that F^* usually decreases when evasion is easier or when the government's cost of preventing it increases.[8] A higher deadweight tax loss per unit of taxation causes F^* to decrease.

Mulligan and Schleifer (2004) provide a different reason for why, under certain circumstances, conscription may be the preferred manpower procurement system. They argue that the cost of implementing a system of conscription – including costs associated with establishing induction centers, identifying, calling, and screening prospective inductees for service, and preventing evasion – is a fixed cost. The larger this fixed cost (relative to volunteer system costs, which vary with force size), the less inclined countries will be to conscript. But countries that already have a large government bureaucracy already in place, as in France during the 19th century, will have a lower cost of incorporating conscription into the administrative system.

---

[8] F^* tends to fall because, at any given force size, easier evasion and higher government costs of preventing it usually raises the cost of a conscripted force relative to the cost of a volunteer force. However, Warner and Negrusa (2005) identify a special case in which the reverse occurs. Such happens when the supply of personnel to the military is highly inelastic and successful evasion leaves a potential pool of conscripts who have lower average opportunity costs than the pool would have had without evasion. See Warner and Negrusa (2005) for details.

Two main predictions follow from their analysis. The first is that highly regulated economies with a large government bureaucracy already in place will be more likely to conscript than less regulated economies. Second, because the per-taxpayer cost of conscription varies inversely with population, more populated countries will be more likely to conscript. A larger demand for military manpower increases the likelihood of conscription because the fixed cost of conscription is thereby spread over a larger number of conscripts. Their model thus also predicts a greater likelihood of conscription the larger the demand for military manpower, but for different reasons from the models discussed above.

Mulligan and Schleifer explain the availability of exemptions from service and the permission to hire replacements within the context of fixed costs. A system of exemptions adds another fixed cost to the system of conscription, and allowing replacements (buyouts) adds yet another fixed administrative cost. Below a certain population size, conscription will be universal or random due to the higher per-capita cost of permitting exemptions or replacements. Between this population size and a larger threshold, a system of exemptions will be adopted (after the per-capita cost falls enough) but buyouts will not be allowed. Finally, above the last threshold, buyouts as well as exemptions will be allowed.

To test their model, Mulligan and Schleifer develop a database containing about 130 countries and estimate models for procurement system that include the size of the military relative to the population aged 16–24, a measure of fixed conscription cost, the total population, per-capita real GDP, the fraction of the population over the age of 64, and type of political system.[9] The size of the military relative to the 15–24 year-old population is found to be strongly related to the likelihood of conscription, a result supportive of their model but also with the discussion above.

Mulligan and Schleifer measure the fixed cost of conscription by whether the country is an English legal origin country. Countries whose legal origin is English common law are presumed to have smaller government bureaucracies than other countries and hence a larger cost of implementing conscription on top of existing administrative bureaucracies. Results in fact indicate that being an English legal origin country reduces the probability of conscription about 50 percent, an extremely large effect. Using their large sample of countries, population is estimated to have a positive effect on the likelihood of conscription, a result they argue is consistent with the fixed conscription cost hypothesis. But analysis of a subset of 32 countries for which the force size exceeds 10 percent of the 15–24 year-old male population does not find a relationship between population and likelihood of conscription.

Per-capita real GDP and the fraction of the population over the age of 65 are hypothesized to be proxies for deadweight tax loss. Analysis with the full sample of countries finds no relationship between their proxies for deadweight tax loss and the likelihood of

---

[9] Data were collected for the years 1985, 1990, and 1995 and the sample size varied with year. See Mulligan and Schleifer (2004) for details.

conscription. But analysis of the subset of 32 countries for which the force size exceeds 10 percent of the 15–24 year-old male population indicates that higher-income countries are less likely to conscript and countries with a larger fraction of the population over the age of 64 are more likely to conscript. They conclude that deadweight tax losses are more likely to affect the choice of system when the demand for military manpower is relatively high.

According to some theories, democracies are more likely to rely on volunteer systems. But according to other theories, the reverse is true [see Mulligan and Schleifer (2004) for discussion]. In any event, Mulligan and Schleifer find little support that form of government affects the choice of manpower procurement system.

Mulligan and Schleifer find that only 2 of 49 English origin countries in their sample allowed students to postpone service and none allowed exemptions from service, shorter terms of service, or buyouts. However, 43 of the 86 non-English legal origin countries had some form of student postponement or exemption from service and 13 allowed buyouts. They take the much lower likelihood that English legal origin countries had something other than a pure random draft as evidence of higher fixed costs of administering a non-random draft in those countries.

Conscription is an implicit tax on draftees. Several recent studies have examined the allocative and distributive effects of the conscription tax. Most existing discussions of the allocative effects of the conscription tax are static. But in addition to the tax a conscript pays during the period of service due to lower military pay (plus the non-pecuniary differential τ), military service may have more long-lasting consequences. Lau, Poutvaara and Wagener (2004) address these long-term consequences by building a lifecycle model of a representative agent that compares effects on labor supply, consumption, saving, and human capital accumulation of volunteerism versus conscription. The model contrasts the life cycle of an individual who is conscripted for the first period of working life with an individual who never serves but who pays taxes throughout the lifecycle to pay volunteers who serve. The conscription tax is paid in the military service period while in the volunteer system the tax is spread evenly over the life cycle. The analysis shows that, compared with explicit taxation, the draft tax is more distortionary, causing a significant reduction in human capital accumulation, wealth, and lifetime utility. The draft tax becomes more distortionary when individuals confront borrowing constraints that limit human capital investment.

Kim (2005) and Frank (2004) study the long-term, human capital consequences of conscription in the United States. Kim utilizes panel data from the Wisconsin Longitudinal Survey, which has tracked a large sample of 1957 Wisconsin high school graduates and their siblings, and seeks to control for selection bias that occurs due to military entry standards by using siblings as controls in some analyses and non-draftee veterans in others. Draftees eventually accumulate about 2/3 of a year less education than their siblings or non-draftee veterans and earn less throughout their lifetimes. A treatment-effect-on-the-treated analysis finds that in 1976 draftees earned about 11 percent less than non-draftee veterans and 6 percent less than non-veterans. (The difference in these estimates most likely reflects a positive selection effect due to military entrance standards.) By 1992 the draftee/non-draftee difference had widened to 17 percent while the draftee/non-veteran difference remained essentially unchanged. Kim attributes much of the effect of conscription to career disruption: draftees were less likely to enter the occupations they planned to enter prior to military service (in particular, professional and managerial occupations).

Frank (2004) performs a novel analysis of the long-term consequences of conscription by studying whether there is a difference in the representation in large corporations of executives who were subject to the 1970 draft lottery and those who were not. The annual reports of publicly traded corporations identify executives in the first four or five levels by name and give their ages. Frank used everybirthday.com to identify the birthdates of corporate executives born in the interval 1944–1947 and in the interval 1948–1951. He then matched birthdates to draft sequence number. He found that men born in the years 1948–1950 on dates that were called were underrepresented in the top managerial ranks of large corporations while men with birth dates that were not called were overrepresented. No difference was found for men born between 1944 and 1947, possibly because most men born prior to 1948 had already been taken if they were fit for service. Therefore, Frank's analysis suggests that conscription can have a long-term impact on careers.

Imbens and van der Klaauw (1995) present evidence about the human capital effects of military service using data from the Netherlands. They do not observe earnings at the individual level, only the aggregate level for those that did, and did not, enter military service. Because selection for service is endogenous, they use various instruments for military service, including fraction of a birth cohort that served, which varied substantially across cohorts. They estimate that draftees earn about 5 percent less than non-draftees. And since conscripts in the Netherlands serve for about a year, the earnings penalty for military service is similar to the loss of a year of labor market experience.

But in a detailed analysis of earnings data from the volunteer force era in the United States, Angrist (1998) finds very little net human capital effect of military service. The earnings effect of military service was estimated from cohort earnings of individuals who entered military service between 1976 and 1982 and individuals who applied for service but did not enter. Earnings data came from Social Security earnings records from the period of entry through 1991. Angrist developed several instrumental variable estimation strategies to control for the selection biases arising from the fact that individuals who enter service are not randomly sampled from the youth population. Most entrants had left service by 1988. Angrist finds generally small and statistically insignificant earnings differences between veterans and non-veterans in the 1988–1991 (post-service) period [for detailed estimates by race, see Table V of Angrist (1998)].

Hirsch and Mehay (2003) provide additional evidence about the earnings effect of military service. In a novel analysis, they use the Reserve Components Survey for 1986 and 1992 to compare the earnings of veterans who departed from active military duty and then associated with reserve units with reservists who had never had active service. Since these two types of reservists should be very similar in unobservable attributes, using reservists with no active service as a control group for veteran reservists with active duty should reduce or eliminate selection bias in an even better way than Angrist's use of individuals who applied for, but did not enter, active service. Using regression and matched comparison methods, they find minor overall differences in earnings between the two groups. Their results mirror Angrist's findings. In the United States at least, military service appears to add as much to future civilian earnings as a year of civilian experience.[10] In the volunteer context, the lack of earnings difference between veterans and non-veterans may be due to the fact that the career decisions of volunteers are not distorted in the way that draftee career decisions would be.

There has been much discussion in the United States of who pays the conscription tax. Related to this discussion is the question of whether the volunteer system attracts recruits disproportionately from low income classes. Proponents of conscription have argued that it spreads the burden of military service (i.e., the conscription tax) more evenly across the spectrum of income classes and leavens the military force. Furthermore, proponents have maintained that the volunteer system in the United States has drawn disproportionately from low income classes and resulted in an unrepresentative force. Recent analysis of US data indicates that the US enlisted forces are drawn from all income classes and that the enlisted forces are not drawn disproportionately from low income households (although it draws more heavily from rural areas than from urban areas and, geographically, more from the South and West than from the North) [see Kane (2005)].

5.2. Ending conscription in Europe

Why have a number of European countries made the decision to end conscription while others have not? As the models discussed in Section 5.1 suggest, the primary factor is the demand for manpower. Reduction in military manpower demand increases the likelihood that a volunteer system will be the more cost-effective system of military manpower procurement. Table 5 shows that since the 1980s defense spending in current and future NATO countries has declined as a percentage of GDP. This decline has translated into a decline in defense manpower (uniformed military plus civilian) as a percentage of the labor force.

For each current or future NATO member, Figure 2 shows the active duty force as a percentage of the male population ages 16–49 deemed fit for military service according to each country's mental and physical entry standards. Countries are grouped by their current or intended future method of manpower procurement as of December 2005. The figure reveals a tendency for countries with larger military manpower requirements relative to the recruitable male population, Greece and Turkey being the highest, to

---

[10] While Angrist (1998) and Hirsch and Mehay (2003) were unable to control for military occupation, past studies surveyed in Warner and Asch (1995) have found the post-service return to military service to depend on military occupation. Some skills (e.g., electronics) have been estimated to provide more transferable human capital than others (e.g., combat arms).

Table 5
Measures of defense effort by selected NATO members, 1980–1984 and 2003

Country	Defense as a percent of GDP		Defense manpower as a percent of labor force[a]	
	1980–1984	2003	1980–1984	2003
Belgium	3.2	1.3	2.8	1.0
Czech Republic	//[b]	2.2	//	1.1
Denmark	2.4	1.6	1.5	1.0
France	4.0	2.6	2.8	1.6
Germany	3.3	1.4	2.4	0.9
Greece	5.4	4.2	6.1	5.1
Hungary	//	1.9	//	1.4
Italy	2.1	1.9	2.5	1.5
Luxembourg	1.0	0.9	0.9	0.8
Netherlands	3.0	1.6	2.5	0.9
Norway	2.7	2.0	2.5	1.4
Poland	//	2.0	//	1.2
Portugal	2.9	2.1	2.5	1.4
Spain	2.3	1.2	2.9	0.9
Turkey	4.0	4.8	4.6	3.9
United Kingdom	5.2	2.4	2.1	1.1
NATO Europe	**3.5**	**2.0**	**2.8**	**1.6**
Canada	2.0	1.2	1.0	0.5
United States	5.3	3.5	2.9	1.5
North America	**5.6**	**3.4**	**2.7**	**1.4**
NATO total	**4.5**	**2.7**	**2.7**	**1.5**

Source: NATO website http://www.nato.int/docu/pr/2003/table3.pdf.
[a]Includes uniformed military personnel and civilian personnel.

[b]// indicates not a NATO member at the time.

continue conscription. Among the countries continuing conscription, the average force requirement as a percentage of the total number of military personnel on hand is 2.96. The average for the countries that currently have, or plan to implement, a volunteer force is 1.67.

It is clear, however, that the downsizing brought about by the end of the Cold War is not the only factor influencing the choice between conscription or an AVF. Figure 2 indicates that some of the countries deciding to maintain conscription have a comparable, or even lower, demand for manpower than the countries choosing voluntarism, including the United States and United Kingdom (which both have forces equal to about 2 percent of the fit male population). Other factors identified by the analysis above may be affecting decisions to maintain, or end, conscription.

First, and probably most important, changing roles and missions of military forces in many countries has raised the productivity of volunteer forces relative to conscripted forces. Prior to the collapse of communism, the military forces of some Scandinavian members of NATO were militia-based forces whose purpose was homeland defense. Rather than maintain large active forces, these countries conscripted a large percent-

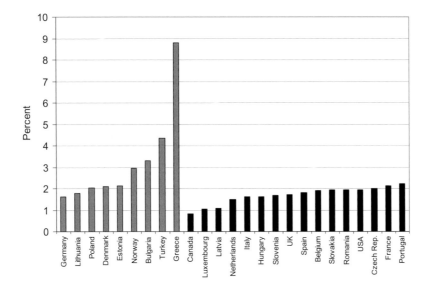

Figure 2. Active force as a percent of males aged 15–49 fit for military service. Note: Grey bar = conscription, Black bar = volunteer.

age of the male youth population for short periods of training and then required these personnel to undergo periodic refresher training well into middle age. For example, Norway had a reserve force over ten times the size of its active force [see Table 3 of Jehn and Selden (2002)]. The homeland defense forces of these countries are largely ground combat forces, which may be suitable for conscripts and for which there may be little productivity gain from conversion to volunteerism.

While large militia-based forces might be necessary for homeland defense against a potential invasion, they are not as useful in the roles and missions that NATO has embraced as priorities in recent years. Aside from legal restrictions that prohibit many European countries from deploying short-term conscripts outside of their borders [Williams (2004)], rapid-deployment and peacekeeping are activities that require training and skill-sets beyond the scope given to conscripts. Furthermore, volunteerism allows individual countries within NATO to specialize in the performance of specific tasks within the overall mission in ways that could not be accomplished in armies in which draftees predominate. Decisions by Belgium, France, Italy, and Spain to end conscription were motivated in large part by such productivity considerations.[11]

[11] The United States Department of Defense sponsored a conference in Brussels, Belgium on June 15–17, 2004 on the end of conscription in Europe. Conference papers by Daffix, Medina and Nidier on the end of conscription in France, Diaz on the end of conscription in Spain, and Villani on the end of conscription in Italy all stressed changing roles and missions of NATO member forces and the need to integrate those forces as the primary reason (aside from downsizing) for ending conscription in those countries. Papers by these and other authors are due to be published in an MIT Press book edited by Cindy Williams and Curtis Gilroy [Williams and Gilroy (2006)].

Equity issues also seem to be playing a role in European decisions to end conscription. Conscription has had a long tradition in Europe, especially in countries with almost universal conscription for training in militia-based homeland defense forces. When conscription is universal, it will not be seen as inequitable. And when the service period is short, less than a year in most European countries [see Table 2 of Jehn and Selden (2002)], the conscription tax is relatively small (compared to the United States, where the service period for draftees was two years). Both of these factors reduced the inequities of conscription in Europe. But declining force requirements and the need to have those who serve do so for longer periods has brought home the inequities to European publics. In Spain, for example, the Partido Popular won an absolute majority in the Spanish Congress in 1997 after it promised to end conscription [Jehn and Selden (2002)].[12]

When the external threat is high and the political support for conscription is broad, draft evasion is less likely. Evasion becomes more likely with a decline in the perceived external threat, which lessens the belief that a high rate of participation in the military, which can be readily achieved by conscription, is necessary for national survival. After the fall of communism, the perceived level of military threat declined across Europe. As a result, it is likely that both the demand for security and the belief that citizens have a moral obligation to serve have decreased, making evasion more likely. Furthermore, countries with porous borders and from which migration is easier – such as Romania those on the eastern border of NATO – may find evasion more difficult to detect and prevent while countries from which migration is more difficult – such as Turkey – may have a lower cost of enforcing conscription.

Probably the most subtle factor influencing a country's choice about how to procure military manpower is the deadweight loss from taxation. Countries with less developed tax systems, in which the costs of collecting taxes and the economic distortions from taxation are high, will have a lower cost of conscription relative to volunteerism. Several cases illustrate this idea. Denmark and Norway, two countries planning to continue conscription, already have high levels of taxation; deadweight tax losses due to additional direct taxation may be high in those countries, tilting the balance away from a volunteer force. By contrast, due to its less developed system of direct taxation and difficulty in collecting direct taxes, Turkey has relied heavily on the inflation tax (by printing money to finance government spending), and may have found that collecting taxes implicitly through conscription, as well as through inflation, was easier than collecting taxes directly.

Despite the large sample analysis by Mulligan and Schleifer indicating that large countries are more likely to maintain conscription, for the 22 continental European countries there is no relationship between the population size and the decision to end conscription. Large countries as well as small decided to end conscription, and a pro-

[12] The NATO conference papers cited in the previous footnote all pointed to declining political support for conscription as a driving factor behind the end of conscription in Europe.

bit analysis of manpower procurement method as a function of manpower requirement, real GDP per-capita, and population shows that the only significant variable is manpower requirement as a fraction of the male population fit for service.[13] As discussed above, changing roles and missions of European military forces (which raised the relative productivity of volunteer forces) and declining political support for conscription (arising from growing awareness of the inequity of the conscription tax when fewer have to pay it) appear to be at the heart of the decisions of some countries to end conscription.

The basic question for European countries that have ended conscription is whether volunteer forces will be sustainable in the face of looming population declines. In Spain, for instance, the male population between the ages of 18 and 27 is projected to decline about 20 percent between 2004 and 2020. Recruiting of young people will become more difficult, and force managers will have to find ways to accommodate the population declines. Fortunately, two factors indicate that the decline is manageable. The first is that the military manpower requirement is currently a much smaller percentage of the recruitable male population than it is in the United States (Table 5) and will remain so in the future. The second is that the forces of European countries are currently much younger and less experienced than the US force. Retention increases that will naturally occur as these countries gain experience managing volunteer forces will be productivity-enhancing, permitting reductions in overall force size and in accession requirements. A related observation regarding the affordability of a volunteer force in the face of declining population comes from recognizing the difference between the cost of a volunteer force to the government versus the cost to society. If, as studies have found, conscription reduces lifetime earnings but volunteerism does not, then the cost of shifting to volunteerism may create a gain for society even if it is accompanied by higher governmental cost paid for by a higher tax burden.

6. Summary

The last decade has seen the emergence of the volunteer system in many European countries and a continuation of the volunteer force in the United States. Research indicates that the overall increasing reliance on volunteerism as a method of procuring defense manpower may be attributed to several factors. These include an end of the Cold War, which resulted in a diminished threat of worldwide conventional war and a reduction in the demand for military manpower, and a recognition that at lower levels of demand, the governmental budgetary cost and the social cost of a voluntary force are likely to be lower than the costs under a system of conscription. In addition, the accumulation of evidence from US experience under an all-volunteer force indicates that the cost-effectiveness of a volunteer force depends not only on the initial cost of

---

[13] Data for population and real GDP per capita were drawn from the Penn World Table for the year 2000.

recruitment, which might be lower or higher under volunteerism depending on the circumstances, but also on the retention and productivity of volunteers. The self-selection of volunteers led to lower initial attrition and higher first- and second-term reenlistment as compared with conscripts. This resulted in higher retention, greater unit cohesion because of lower turnover, and improved performance attributable to increased experience in the military. Furthermore, the volunteer force succeeded in attracting recruits who were better educated – over 90 percent were high school graduates – and had higher AFQT scores than the youth population. Research also showed that education and AFQT score had a positive effect on performance. The improvement in experience, education, and AFQT scores produced an armed force with greater capability to perform any given task, greater versatility to perform a range of tasks, and greater capacity to make intelligent resource allocation decisions under uncertainty. The gains in retention and productivity came as a bonus to the original advocates of the volunteer force. In their time, the late 1960s and early 1970s, the debate over ending conscription swirled around displeasure with the Vietnam war, the inequity of a conscription tax borne by conscripts but not by society at large, the unfairness of the draft system in place at that time and the draft-evasion behavior it induced, and the argument that individuals in a free society should be free to choose whether to serve in the military. But research has shown that the gains in retention and productivity, along with the decreased demand for manpower and demand for greater specialization of force roles, are key factors to consider in weighing the shift from conscription to volunteerism.

Recruiting and retention research underscores the importance of understanding behavior at the individual level. Economic models of occupational choice form the basis of analyses of military pay, enlistment bonuses, educational benefits, and advertising as factors that affect an individual's decision to enlist, choice of occupational area, and term of service length. The formal inclusion of individual heterogeneity in the models provides leverage for understanding why certain incentives appeal to certain individuals but not others, and equally if not more important, for understanding the huge importance of self-selection as a factor supporting higher retention among volunteers versus conscripts. Heterogeneity and self-selection also explain why retention rates increase with years of military service, and this is exploited in ACOL-2 and dynamic programming models of retention. Similarly, economic models of individual behavior are at the heart of research on recruiter performance and the structure of recruiter incentives. Finally, individual choice models provide a basis for understanding the role of the military compensation, personnel management, and retirement benefit systems in shaping retention by year of service. The similarity of these systems across occupations within a service goes a long way in explaining the similarity in retention patterns across occupations. By the same token, it is now understood that changes in these systems will be necessary if the services are to seek greater variation in career lengths across occupations or among individuals within an occupation, or to seek retaining personnel at a certain skill level (e.g., master level), for a longer time. A related aspect of this concerns the use of reserve forces. If the anticipated shift in the United States to an "operational" reserve means that reservists and prospective recruits into the reserves should now credibly expect more deployment than in the past, reservist compensation and retirement benefits may need to be adjusted. Similarly, if European nations anticipate using their forces more frequently in multi-national efforts to quell small-scale contingencies or combat terrorism, their compensation packages may need to be adjusted.

In the United States, the volunteer military has become a military of families. Roughly three-fourths of military personnel beyond the first term of service are married and many have children. Research on military spouses, in particular, military wives, has shown that they earn less, work fewer weeks, and have lower wage rates than do observationally comparable civilian wives. But for the most part, spouses have not been integrated into the analysis of retention. Neither theoretical models nor empirical work on retention has taken a husband-and-wife perspective despite the high marriage rate among career military personnel. Spouse career concerns, childcare, school quality, health care, and frequent moves all seem likely to affect the member's – i.e., the family's – choice to stay in the military. However, most data sets do not combine these family variables along with data on the service member. In addition, the family is likely to be affected by high operational tempo and by frequent or long deployment of the member. Much remains to be done on understanding how these factors affect the retention of active duty members, and a parallel set of questions arises for reservists and their families.

Finally, the reserve forces are being relied upon as an operational force and not just as a strategic resource to be used in times of emergencies. Since September 2001, a large fraction of US reservists have been activated, many have been activated multiple times, and many have been activated for over a year. As a consequence, reservists can expect to be activated more often and for a longer duration than before September 2001. The Department of Defense is exploring a new concept of reserve duty, called a "continuum of service", to bring skills into the reserves more rapidly and flexibly. Under this concept reservists can be called upon to serve in a variety of capacities from 0 to 365 days per year on an as-needed basis. The continuum of service concept constitutes a significant departure from the traditional two-days per month, and two-weeks per year concept of reserve service. How changes in activation expectations, the operations in Iraq and Afghanistan, as well as new concepts of service affect reserve recruiting and retention outcomes, and how these outcomes respond to traditional reserve recruiting and retention resources in the post 9/11 environment, are only beginning to be studied. Such analysis is needed to guide reserve compensation and personnel policy, and this topic represents an important area for future research.

References

Angrist, J. (1998). "Estimating the labor market impact of voluntary military service using social security data on military applicants". Econometrica 66, 249–288.

Arkes, J., Kilburn, M.R. (2005). Modeling Reserve Recruiting, MG-202-OSD. RAND, Santa Monica, CA.

Asch, B., Hosek, J. (2004). "Looking to the future: What does transformation mean for military manpower and personnel policy?". In: Bicksler, B., Gilroy, C., Warner, J. (Eds.), The All-Volunteer Force, Thirty Years of Service. Brassey's, Washington, DC, pp. 57–89.

Asch, B., Kilburn, M. (2003). "The enlistment potential of college students". In: Kilburn, M., Asch, B. (Eds.), Recruiting Youth in the College Market, Current Practices and Future Policy Options, MR-1093-OSD. RAND, Santa Monica, CA.

Asch, B., Warner, J. (2001a). An Examination of the Effects of Voluntary Separation Incentives. RAND, Santa Monica, CA.

Asch, B., Warner, J. (2001b). "A theory of compensation and personnel policy in hierarchical organizations with application to the US military". Journal of Labor Economics 19, 523–562.

Asch, B., Johnson, R., Warner, J. (1998). Reforming the Military Retirement System, MR-748-OSD. RAND, Santa Monica, CA.

Asch, B., Hosek, J., Warner, J. (2001). An Analysis of Pay for Enlisted Personnel, DB-344-OSD. RAND, Santa Monica, CA.

Asch, B., Schonlau, M., Du, C. (2004). Policy Options for Military Recruiting in the College Market: Results from a National Survey, MG-105-OSD. RAND, Santa Monica, CA.

Asch, B., Hosek, J., Clendenning, D. (2007). A Policy Analysis of Reserve Retirement Reform, MG-378-OSD. RAND, Santa Monica, CA. In press.

Asch, B., Hosek, J., Martin, C. (2005). A Look at Cash Compensation for Active Duty Personnel, MR-1492-OSD. RAND, Santa Monica, CA.

Asch, B., Romley, J., Totten, M. (2005). The Quality of Personnel in the Enlisted Ranks, MG-324-OSD. RAND, Santa Monica, CA.

Asch, B., Buck, C., Klerman, J., Kleykamp, M., Loughran, D. (2005). What Factors Affect the Military Enlistment of Hispanic Youth? A Look at Enlistment Qualifications, DB-484-OSD. RAND, Santa Monica, CA.

Bellany, I. (2003). "Accounting for Army recruitment: White and non-white soldiers and the British army". Defence and Peace Economics 14, 281–292.

Berkovec, J., Stern, S. (1991). "Job exit behavior of older men". Econometrica 59, 189–210.

Bohn, D., Schmitz, E. (1996). The Expansion of the Navy College Fund: An Evaluation of the FY 1995 Program Impacts. Navy Recruiting Command, Arlington, VA.

Borjas, G., Welch, F. (1986). "The post-service earnings of military retirees". In: Gilroy, C. (Ed.), Army Manpower Economics. Westview Press, Boulder, CO, pp. 295–319.

Browning, E. (1987). "On the marginal welfare cost of taxation". American Economic Review 77, 11–23.

Buddin, R. (1991). Enlistment Effects of the 2 + 2 + 4 Recruiting Experiment, R-4097-A. RAND, Santa Monica, CA.

Buddin, R., Kapur, K. (2002). Tuition Assistance Usage and First-Term Military Retention. MR-1295-OSD. RAND, Santa Monica, CA.

Buddin, R., Levy, D., Hanley, J., Waldman, D. (1992). Promotion Tempo and Enlisted Retention, R-4135-FMP. RAND, Santa Monica, CA.

Bureau of Labor Statistics (2000). "Employer costs for employee compensation 1986–1999". Bulletin 2526. Bureau of Labor Statistics, Washington, DC.

Cardell, S., Lamoreaux, D., Stromsdorfer, E., Wang, B., Weeks, G. (1997). "The post-service earnings of military retirees: A comparison of the 1996 retired military personnel sample with a statistically comparable sample from the march 1994 Current Population Survey". Unpublished manuscript. Washington State University.

Congressional Budget Office (1995). Military Pay and the Rewards for Performance. Congressional Budget Office, Washington DC.

Congressional Budget Office (2003). Growth in Medical Spending by the Department of Defense. Congressional Budget Office, Washington, DC.

Congressional Budget Office (2004). "Military compensation: Balancing cash and noncash benefits". Economic and Budget Issue Brief. Congressional Budget Office, Washington, DC.

Cooke, T., Marcus, A., Quester, A.O. (1992). Personnel Tempo of Operations and Navy Enlisted Retention, CRM 91-150. Center for Naval Analyses, Alexandria, VA.

Daula, T., Moffit, R. (1995). "Estimating dynamic models of quit behavior: The case of military reenlistment". Journal of Labor Economics 13, 449–523.

Demange, G., Geoffard, P. (2003). Reforming Incentive Schemes Under Political Constraint: The Physician Agency. Centre for Economic, Policy Research. http://www.delta.ens.fr/demange/physicians.pdf.

Dertouzos, J. (1985). Recruiter Incentives and Enlistment Supply. R-3065-MIL. RAND, Santa Monica, CA.

Dertouzos, J., Garber, S. (2003). Is Military Advertising Effective? An Estimation Methodology and Applications to Recruiting in the 1980s and 1990s, MR-1591-OSD. RAND, Santa Monica, CA.

Dertouzos, J., Garber, S. (2004). Human Resource Management and Army Recruiting, Analyses of Policy Options, DRR-3305-A. RAND, Santa Monica, CA.

DiTrapani, A., Keenan, J. (2005). Applying Civilian Manning Practice to Navy Ships, Research Memorandum D0011501. Center for Naval Analyses, Alexandria, VA.

Doyle, M. (1998). Youth vs. Experience in the Enlisted Air Force: Productivity Estimates and Policy Analysis, RGSD-139. RAND, Santa Monica, CA.

Elliott, M., Kapur, K., Gresenz, C. (2004). Modeling the Departure of Military Pilots from the Service, MR-1327-OSD. RAND, Santa Monica, CA.

Frank, D. (2004). As Luck would Have It: The Effect of the Vietnam Draft Lottery on the Future Corporate Leaders of America. Kellogg School of Management, Northwestern University, Evanston, IL.

Fricker, R. (2002). The Effects of Perstempo on Officer Retention in the US Military, MR-1556-OSD. RAND, Santa Monica, CA.

Fullerton, R. (2003). "An empirical assessment of us Air Force attrition". Defence and Peace Economics 14, 343–356.

Goldberg, M. (2001). A Survey of Enlisted Retention: Models and Findings, CRM D0004085.A2/Final. Center for Naval Analyses, Alexandria, VA.

Golding, H., Cox, G. (2003). Design and Implementation of AIP, CAB D0007827. Center for Naval Analyses, Alexandria, VA.

Golding, H., Gregory, D. (2002). Sailors' Willingness to Complete Sea Tours: Does Money Matter? CRM D0006886.A2/Final. Center for Naval Analyses, Alexandria, VA.

Golding, H., Griffis, H. (2004). How has Perstempo's Effect on Reenlistment Changed since the 1986 Navy Policy? CAB D0008863. Center for Naval Analyses, Alexandria, VA.

Golfin, P., Lien, D., Gregory, D. (2004). Evaluation of the Assignment Incentive Pay (AIP) System, CAB D0010240.A2/Final. Center for Naval Analyses, Alexandria, VA.

Gorman, L., Thomas, G. (1993). "General intellectual achievement, enlistment intentions, and racial representation in the US military". Armed Forces and Society 19, 611–624.

Gotz, G., McCall, J. (1984). A Dynamic Model Retention Model of Air Force Officer Retention: Theory and Estimation, R-03028-AF. RAND, Santa Monica, CA.

Hansen, M., Husted, T. (2005). The Case for Voluntary Separation Pay, CRM D0011959.A2/Final. Center for Naval Analyses, Alexandria, VA.

Hansen, M., Wenger, J. (2005). "Is the pay responsiveness of enlisted personnel decreasing?". Defense and Peace Economics 16, 29–43.

Hansen, M., Wenger, J., Monroe, A., Griffis, H. (2003). Is Enlisted Retention too High? CRM D0008594.A2/Final. Center for Naval Analyses, Alexandria, VA.

Hansen, M., Wills, J.K., Reese, D. (2004). Level-Loading of Enlisted Accessions, CRM D0010352.A2/Final. Center for Naval Analyses, Alexandria, VA.

Harrell, M., Lim, N., Werber Castenada, L., Golinelli, D. (2004). Working Around the Military: Challenges to Military Spouse Employment and Education, MG-196-OSD. RAND, Santa Monica, CA.

Hattiangadi, A., Lee, G., Quester, A. (2004). Recruiting Hispanics: The Marine Corps Experience Final Report, CRM D0009071.A2/Final. Center for Naval Analyses, Alexandria, VA.

Hirsch, B., Mehay, S. (2003). "Evaluating the labor market performance of veterans using a matched comparison group design". Journal of Human Resources 38, 673–700.

Hogan, P., Mackin, P. (2003). "Volunteer assignments and economic efficiency". Presented at Western Economic Association Meetings, San Francisco, CA.

Hogan, P., Dali, T., Mackin, P., Mackie, C. (1996). An Econometric Analysis of Navy Television Advertising Effectiveness. Systems Analytic Group, Falls Church, VA.

Hosek, S. (2005). Military Health Benefits: Defense Advisory Committee on Military Compensation. RAND, Santa Monica, CA.

Hosek, J., Peterson, C. (1985a). Enlistment Decisions of Young Men, R-3238-MIL. RAND, Santa Monica, CA.

Hosek, J., Peterson, C. (1985b). Reenlistment Bonuses and Retention Behavior, R-3199-MIL. RAND, Santa Monica, CA.

Hosek, J., Peterson, C. (1990). Serving Her Country: An Analysis of Women's Enlistment. R-3853-FMP. RAND, Santa Monica, CA.

Hosek, J., Sharp, J. (2001). Keeping Military Pay Competitive: The Outlook for Civilian Wage Growth and its Consequences, IP-205. RAND, Santa Monica, CA.

Hosek, J., Totten, M. (1998). Does Perstempo Hurt Reenlistment?: The Effect of Long or Hostile Perstempo on Reenlistment, MR-990-OSD. RAND, Santa Monica, CA.

Hosek, J., Totten, M. (2002). Serving Away from Home: How Deployments Influence Reenlistment, MR-1594-OSD. RAND, Santa Monica, CA.

Hosek, J., Asch, B., Fair, C., Martin, C., Mattock, M. (2002). Married to the Military: The Employment and Earnings of Military Wives Compared with Those of Civilian Wives, MR-1565-OSD. RAND, Santa Monica, CA.

Hosek, J., Mattock, M., Fair, C., Kavanagh, J., Sharp, J., Totten, M. (2004). Attracting the Best: How the Military Competes for Information Technology Personnel, MG-108-OSD. RAND, Santa Monica, CA.

Hosek, J., Kavanagh, J., Miller, L. (2006). How Deployments Affect Service Members, MG-432-RC. RAND, Santa Monica, CA.

Huffman, A., Adler, A., Castro, C., Dolan, C. (2005). "The impact of operations tempo on turnovers intentions of Army personnel". Military Psychology 17, 175–202.

Imbens, G., van der Klaauw, W. (1995). "Evaluating the cost of conscription in the Netherlands". Journal of Business and Economic Statistics 13, 207–215.

Jehn, C., Selden, Z. (2002). "The end of conscription in Europe?". Contemporary Economic Policy 20, 93–100.

Junor, L., Oi, J. (1996). A New Approach for Modeling Ship Readiness, CRM 95-239. Center for Naval Analyses, Alexandria, VA.

Junor, L., Jondrow, J., Francis, P., Oi, J. (1997). Understanding Aircraft Readiness: An Empirical Approach, CRM 97-014. Center for Naval Analyses, Alexandria, VA.

Kane, T. (2005). Who Bears the Burden? Demographic Characteristics of US Military Recruits Before and After 9/11, CDA05-08. The Heritage Foundation, Washington, DC.

Kavanagh, J. (2005). Determinants of Productivity for Military Personnel: A Review of Findings on the Contributions of Experience, Training, and Aptitude to Military Performance, TR-193. RAND, Santa Monica, CA.

Kilburn, M.R. (1992). "Minority representation in the US military". PhD dissertation, Department of Economics, University of Chicago, Chicago, IL.

Kilburn, R., Klerman, J. (1999). Enlistment Decisions in the 1990s: Evidence from Individual-Level Data, MR-944-OSD/A. RAND, Santa Monica, CA.

Kim, H. (2005). The Military Draft and Career Disruption. Department of Economics, University of Wisconsin at Madison, Madison, WI.

Kleinman, S., Hansen, M. (2005). Setting Military Compensation: When 50-Year-olds Decide What 20-Year-olds Want. DRM D0012938A1/Final. Center for Naval Analyses, Alexandria, VA.

Klerman, J., Loughran, D., Martin, C. (2005). Early Results on Activations and the Earnings of Reservists, TR-274-OSD. RAND, Santa Monica, CA.

Kraus, A., Griffis, H., Golfin, P. (2000). Choice-Based Conjoint Study of Recruitment Incentives, CRM D0001428.A2/Final. Center for Naval Analyses, Alexandria, VA.

Kraus, A., Lien, D., Orme, B. (2003). The Navy Survey on Reenlistment and Quality of Service: Using Choice-Based Conjoint to Quantify Relative Preferences for Pay and Nonpay Aspects of Naval Service, CRM D0008146.A2/Final. Center for Naval Analyses, Alexandria, VA.

Kraus, A., Wenger, J., Houck, L., Gregory, D. (2004). College Recruits in the Enlisted Navy: Navy Outcomes and Civilian Opportunities, CRM D0010405.A2/Final. Center for Naval Analyses, Alexandria, VA.

Lau, M., Poutvaara, P., Wagener, A. (2004). "Dynamic costs of the draft". German Economic Review 5, 381–406.

Loughran, D. (2002). Wage Growth in the Civilian Careers of Military Retirees, MR-1363-OSD. RAND, Santa Monica, CA.

Mackin, P., Darling, K. (2005). The Post-Service Earnings of Military Retirees: Evidence from the 2003 Survey of Retired Military, DMDC Report No. 2004-011. Defense Manpower Data Center, Arlington, VA.

Mehay, S., Hogan, P. (1998). "The effects of bonuses on voluntary quits: Evidence from the military's downsizing". Southern Economic Journal 65, 127–139.

Moore, C., Griffis, H., Cavaluzzo, L. (1996). A Predictive Model of Navy Second-term Retention, CRM 95-245. Center for Naval Analyses, Alexandria, VA.

Moore, C., Golding, S., Griffis, H. (2000). Manpower and Personnel IWAR 2000: Aging the Force. CNA Annotated Briefing D0003079. Center for Naval Analyses, Alexandria, VA.

Mulligan, C., Schleifer, A. (2004). "Conscription as regulation". NBER Working Paper. National Bureau of Economic Research, Cambridge, MA.

Murray, M., McDonald, L. (1999). Recent Recruiting Trends and Their Implications for Models of Enlistment Supply, MR-847-OSD/A. RAND, Santa Monica, CA.

Oken, C., Asch, B. (1997). Encouraging Recruiter Achievement: A Recent History of Military Recruiter Incentive Programs, MR-845-OSD/A. RAND, Santa Monica, CA.

Orvis, B., McDonald, L. (2004). Strengthening Army Recruiting: The College First and GED Plus Test, DRR-3426-A. RAND, Santa Monica, CA.

Payne, D., Warner, J., Little, R. (1992). "Tied migration decision and returns to human capital: The case of military wives". Social Science Quarterly 73, 324–339.

Polich, M., Dertouzos, J., Press, J. (1986). The Enlistment Bonus Experiment, R-3353-FMP. RAND, Santa Monica, CA.

Rosen, S. (1986). "The theory of equalizing differences". In: Ashenfelter, O., Layard, R. (Eds.), Handbook of Labor Economics. North-Holland, Amsterdam, pp. 641–692.

Rostker, B. (2002). Time for a Change: Developing a New Officer Military Personnel System for the 21st Century. RAND, Santa Monica, CA.

Royalty, A. (2000). "A discrete choice approach to estimating workers' marginal valuation of fringe benefits". Working paper. Indiana University, Purdue University, Indianapolis and Stanford University.

Schirmer, P., Levy, D., Thie, H., et al. (2004). New Paths to Success: Determining Career Alternatives for Field-grade Officers, MG-117. RAND, Santa Monica, CA.

US Department of Defense (2000). Report of the Defense Science Board Task Force on Human Resources Strategy. Office of the Under Secretary of Defense, Acquisition, Technology, and Logistics, Washington, DC.

US Department of Defense (2002). Report of the Ninth Quadrennial Review of Military Compensation. Office of the Under Secretary of Defense, Personnel and Readiness, Washington, DC.

US Department of Education (2004). Digest of Education Statistics. National Center for Education Statistics. http://nces.ed.gov/programs/digest/d04/tables/dt04_183.asp, accessed January 10, 2006.

Warner, J. (2006). Thinking About Military Retirement, CRM D0013583.A1/Final. Center for Naval Analyses, Alexandria, VA.

Warner, J., Asch, B. (1995). "The economics of military manpower". In: Hartley, K., Sandler, T. (Eds.), Handbook of Defense Economics, vol. 1. Elsevier, Amsterdam, pp. 347–398.

Warner, J., Asch, B. (1996). "The economic theory of conscription reconsidered". Defence and Peace Economics 7, 297–312.

Warner, J., Asch, B. (2001). "The record and prospects of the all-volunteer military in the United States". Journal of Economic Perspectives 15, 169–192.

Warner, J., Negrusa, S. (2005). "Evasion costs and the theory of conscription". Defence and Peace Economics 16, 83–100.

Warner, J., Pleeter, S. (2001). "The personal discount rate: Evidence from military downsizing programs". American Economic Review 91, 33–53.

Warner, J., Simon, C. (2005). "Estimates of army enlistment supply 1988–2005". Briefing presented to the military recruiting summit, November 2, 2005, Clemson University, SC, Arlington, VA.

Warner, J., Simon, C., Payne, D. (2001). "Enlistment supply in the 1990s: A study of the Navy college fund and other enlistment incentive programs". DMDC Report No. 2000-015. Defense Manpower Data Center, Arlington, VA.

Warner, J., Simon, C., Payne, D. (2003a). "The military recruiting productivity slowdown: The roles of resources, opportunity cost, and tastes of youth". Defence and Peace Economics 14, 329–342.

Warner, J., Simon, C., Payne, D. (2003b). Propensity, Application, and Enlistment: Evidence from the Youth Attitudinal Tracking Study. Department of Economics, Clemson University, Clemson, SC.

Williams, C., (2004). "Filling NATO's ranks: Military personnel policies in transition". Report of transatlantic roundtable, 8–9 September 2003. Transatlantic Center of the German Marshall Fund of the United States, Brussels, Belgium.

Williams, C., Gilroy, C. (2006). Service to Country: Personnel Policy and the Transformation of Western Militaries. MIT Press, Cambridge, MA.

Chapter 33

THE ARMS INDUSTRY, PROCUREMENT AND INDUSTRIAL POLICIES

KEITH HARTLEY

Centre for Defence Economics, University of York, England, UK

Contents

Abstract	1140
Keywords	1140
1. Introduction	1141
2. Arms industries	1141
2.1. Definitions	1141
2.2. Facts on the world's arms industries	1144
2.3. The economics of arms industries	1148
2.4. Market conduct: Competition and the military–industrial complex	1151
2.4.1. Defense R&D	1152
2.4.2. The military–industrial–political complex	1155
2.5. Market performance	1156
2.5.1. Contract performance	1157
2.5.2. Productivity and profitability	1158
2.5.3. Exports	1160
3. Procurement: Theory and policy issues	1161
3.1. Assessing arms industries: Benefit–cost analysis	1166
3.2. Some policy issues and challenges	1168
3.2.1. Military outsourcing	1169
3.2.2. Determining the profitability of non-competitive contracts	1170
4. Industrial policies	1171
5. Conclusion	1173
References	1174

Handbook of Defense Economics, Volume 2
Edited by Todd Sandler and Keith Hartley
© *2007 Elsevier B.V.   All rights reserved*
DOI: 10.1016/S1574-0013(06)02033-3

Abstract

Weapons programs are criticized for cost overruns, delays in delivery and failure to meet their operational requirements. Critics focus on the power and influence of the military–industrial–political complex. This chapter addresses these controversial areas involving arms industries, alternative procurement policies and industrial policy. Arms industries are defined and statistics are presented on the world's arms industries. They can be analyzed as economically strategic industries where both R&D and production quantities are important and lead to decreasing cost industries reflecting economies of scale and learning. A structure-conduct-performance approach is applied. Market conduct is assessed including defense R&D and the role of the military–industrial–political complex. Market performance is reviewed by assessing contract performance, firm productivity and profitability and exports. Governments are central to understanding arms markets and weapons procurement raises both theory and policy issues. There are principal-agent problems and issues of adverse selection, moral hazard, risk sharing and bilateral monopoly. Various types of contract are available, each with different efficiency incentives. Governments can also use their buying power to determine the size, structure and performance of a nation's defense industrial base (DIB). The benefits and costs of a national DIB are assessed and three policy issues and challenges are reviewed. These are the role of competition in arms procurement, its extension to military outsourcing and the profitability of non-competitive contracts. Alternative industrial policies are a further aspect of procurement policy. Guidelines for a defense industrial policy in a military alliance are outlined together with an assessment of European collaborative programs. The Chapter concludes by speculating on the future of the defense firm and proposing an agenda for future research in the field.

Keywords

arms industries, procurement, industrial policies, contract types, the defense industrial base, competition, collaborative programs

JEL classification: H4, H57, L1, L5

1. Introduction

This is a controversial area. Critics point to the power and influence of the 'military–industrial and political complex' and its impact on existing and new weapons programs. These programs are then criticized for their cost overruns, delays in delivery and unsatisfactory performance on entry into service. Accusations are made of inefficiencies and excessive profits in defense industries and poor project management by procurement agencies. Firms are condemned for their arms exports to less developed nations which are believed to contribute to regional arms races, international debt and poverty and are reputed to be characterized by bribery and corruption. Nor are industrial policies immune from controversy. Buying from a national defense industry can be a form of protectionism through preferential purchasing which is then justified by governments pointing to the 'substantial' economic and industrial benefits from such procurement choices. Alternative policies such as international collaboration are also criticized for their inefficiencies in work-sharing and for their bureaucratic management and industrial arrangements.

The world's arms industries are dominated by American firms and such household names as Boeing, Lockheed Martin and Northrop Grumman. But the United States defense industry is not an example of the competitive model. Critics have compared the way the US Department of Defense (DoD) does business and buys its weapons to Soviet central planning. The United States defense industry has a state – owned component (e.g., government laboratories, shipyards, depots, and arsenals); the private sector is subject to DoD's industrial policy and excessive regulation; there remains excess capacity; and the US defense market is closed to foreign competition [Eland (2001)].

This chapter addresses these issues. It seeks to subject myths, emotion and special pleading to economic analysis and empirical evidence. What do we know; what do we not know; and what do we need to know for sensible debates and public choices on arms industries, procurement policies and industrial policies? Each of these topics is the subject of separate sections.

2. Arms industries

2.1. Definitions

Various definitions of arms or defense industries have been offered. Examples include: "the defense industrial base consists of those industrial assets which provide key elements of military power and national security: such assets demand special consideration by government" [HCP (1986, p. xxxvii)]; or the nation's defense industry "embraces all defense suppliers that create value, employment, technology or intellectual assets in the country" [MoD (2002)]; or the defense industrial base "constitutes those companies which provide defense and defense related equipment to the defense ministry" [Dunne (1995, p. 402)].

Problems arise in operationalizing and measuring these definitions. Consider the apparently simple definition of the defense industry comprising those firms supplying weapons (i.e., lethal equipment such as combat aircraft, tanks and warships) to the nation's defense ministry and its armed forces. This definition captures the demand and supply aspects of weapons markets with defense ministries and armed forces as buyers or procurement agencies and firms as suppliers and contractors to the defense ministry. But here the simplicity ends. There are questions about the ownership and location of firms, about other non-weapons items supplied to the armed forces and whether national defense ministries are the only customers for arms industries. Firms can be state-or privately-owned, national or foreign-owned and located at home or overseas. Similarly, armed forces and defense ministries buy a range of products and services in addition to weapons. Examples include clothing, food, fuel, office equipment, computers, furniture and motor cars. A range of services are also purchased including catering, cleaning, construction, consultancy, design, legal advice, repair and maintenance of equipment, research, telecommunications, training and transport. Many of these goods and services are dual-use items which are bought and sold in civilian markets. Some of the services are examples of military outsourcing (i.e., where private contractors are used to provide services traditionally undertaken 'in-house' by the armed forces). Nor is the national defense ministry the only customer for its arms industries: weapons are exported to foreign defense ministries and parts and components are also exported to foreign defense industries (e.g., aero-engines, electronics).

There are further problems in defining defense industries. The definition needs to embrace research and development activities, in-service support, mid-life updates and disposal (e.g., nuclear weapons) as well as production. Nor should the focus be solely on prime contractors: there is an extensive and complex network of suppliers to the primes. One of the few studies on defense industry supply chains found that on UK armored fighting vehicles, the prime contractor had some 200 first level suppliers, each of which had an average of 18 suppliers; in turn, the second level suppliers each had an average of 7 suppliers; and the third level suppliers had an average of 2–3 suppliers with many of the second and third tier suppliers unaware of their involvement on defense work (e.g., firms supplied general inputs and raw materials such as glass, rubber and steel: Hartley et al. (1997)).

Definitions also give a misleading impression that the defense industry is a single, homogenous entity. The supply side of the defense market comprises varying numbers of small to large-sized firms, either publicly- or privately-owned with different degrees of specialization and dependence on defense and civil sales. In fact, there are a set of related markets for nuclear and conventional equipment and for air, land and sea systems including services supplied by firms some of which are involved in a variety of markets with others specializing in one sector or in a sub-sector (e.g., aero-engines, avionics, defense electronics, components). Examples include BAE Systems (UK) and Northrop Grumman (USA) each involved in aircraft, electronics, missiles, small arms/ammunition and warships; MBDA (Europe) specializes in missiles; General Electric and Pratt and Whitney (USA) together with Rolls-Royce specialize in aero-engines; and defense electronics firms include Honeywell International and ITT (USA: see Table 2).

Data problems abound with official government statistics varying in both quality and coverage between nations. Estimates of *industry* output and employment require that all firms in the defense industrial base be identified, including the network of suppliers involved in sub-contracting and the suppliers of materials, parts and components (i.e., the supply chain). Some suppliers might not be aware that they are involved in defense production. Similar data problems arise at the *company* level. Even at the prime contractor level, it is difficult to obtain published data showing the proportion of a firm's labor force involved in defense work. Often major defense contractors are large conglomerates with a range of military and civil products; and where companies publish defense sales data, they usually report sales for a range of military products for both home and export markets. Other firms might be involved in dual-use technologies and production, making it even more difficult to identify defense output. Here, a definition of defense firms and industries has to determine the boundaries between military and civil business and whether to classify firms as part of the defense industrial base on the basis of the *absolute value of sales* to defense ministries and/or on the basis of the *proportion of arms in total company sales*. For example, firms with only defense sales are clearly in the national defense industrial base; but should firms with a low proportion of defense sales be included (e.g., under 10%)? Such a low share criterion might exclude important components of a nation's defense effort which are required during emergencies and conflict, such as civil airlines and merchant shipping which provide a crucial re-supply capability for the armed forces [Hartley and Hooper (1995)].

Defense firms and industries have a history of change reflecting new threats and new technology. The major arms companies of the late nineteenth century, namely, Armstrong, Gatling, Maxim, Krupp and Vickers (e.g., machine guns, armor, battleships) have been replaced by such companies as Boeing, Lockheed Martin, EADS and BAE Systems (e.g., aerospace, missiles, electronics). The future defense firm will be subject to similar changes so that the defense firm of 2050 is likely to be as different from today's defense firm as today's firms are from those of 1950 and 1915. New threats in the form of international terrorism together with 'failed and rogue' states with weapons of mass destruction will create demands for new weapons systems to be developed by existing or new entry defense firms. Responding to terrorism will require intelligence and surveillance systems, airport anti-terrorist security devices (supplied by security firms), small arms and stun grenades, some of which can be supplied by small firms in competitive markets (c.f., combat aircraft, submarines). Other threats will require such systems as ballistic missile defense and firms able to respond to biological/chemical threats (e.g., chemicals-pharmaceutical firms). New technology is a further source of change and uncertainty. For example, modern military strategy requires network enabled capability (NEC) which provides rapid and more accurate information exchange in order to speed-up the decision/action cycle. In turn, this requires intelligence, surveillance and reconnaissance systems with increasing demands on the defense electronics industry. The growing importance of electronics in modern weapons systems can be illustrated with examples from the aerospace industry. In a 1960s combat aircraft, avionics represented about 25% of unit flyaway costs; for a 1980s combat aircraft the corresponding figure was some 33%; for a 2005 generation aircraft the share was 35–40% of unit flyaway costs; and forecasts suggest that for future unmanned combat air vehicles (UCAVs), electronics systems might be about 50% of unit costs [Hartley, Braddon and Dowdall (2004)]. Such changes in technology and threats need to be reflected in the definition and measurement of defense industries [Braddon (2004), Hartley and Sandler (2003)].

2.2. Facts on the world's arms industries

Published data are available on employment in the world's defense industries and in the top 100 largest arms producing companies. In 2003, employment in the world's arms industries was almost 7.5 million with over 60% of the total in the industrialized nations. Employment declined substantially following the end of the Cold War when the world's arms industries employed over 16 million people in 1990. Amongst the world's leading arms industries, there were major employment reductions in the Ukraine, Russia and Germany between 1990 and 2003. In contrast, there was a relatively small employment reduction in the United States which might reflect its world power status and the influence of its military–industrial–political complex; whilst alone amongst the leading nations, North Korea did not reduce employment in its arms industry.[1] Defense industry employment is also concentrated in a few nations with the USA accounting for 36% of the world total and the top ten nations accounting for almost 90% of world arms industry employment in 2003 (see Table 1).

Defense industry employment estimates are sensitive to the definitions of arms industries and to the methodology used to estimate employment. Ideally, estimates need to include both direct and indirect employment in full-time equivalents. Direct employment comprises employment in the companies receiving contracts from the national defense ministry and indirect comprises the personnel employed by suppliers to the direct contractors throughout the supply chain; but it does not include induced employment reflecting the multiplier effects from spending by defense industry workers (e.g., in local shops, restaurants and garages). The methodology for deriving employment estimates also needs to be specified. Various methods are used, including the aggregation of information about individual defense companies, calculations based on procurement and export data and country case studies. Another more rigorous method uses national input–output tables which assumes homogeneity in the product groups involved: it assumes that defense output from a specific product group (e.g., aircraft) will have similar characteristics (e.g., import intensity; intermediate to final output relationship) as total output in that sector which comprises civil and military sales. Output data for each sector are then converted to direct employment estimates by using a single value of

---

[1] For the period 1990–2003, North Korea arms industry employment increased over the years 1990–1993 and then remained stable at 120 000 personnel whilst South Korea reduced employment in its arms industry from 50 000 to 45 000 personnel [BICC (2001, 2005)].

Table 1
Employment in world's arms industries

Nation/region	Index 1990 (2003 = 100)	Numbers 1990 (000s)	Numbers 2003 (000s)
World total	217	16 230	7479
Developing	*181*	*5012*	*2769*
Industrialized	*239*	*11 257*	*4710*
Ten leading nations:			
USA	115	3105	2700
China	191	4011	2100
Russia	326	2543	780
France	160	384	240
UK	220	440	200
Ukraine	666	1199	180
India	147	250	170
North Korea	83	100	120
Germany	300	240	80
Japan	121	97	80

Note: Ukraine index is for 1992; figures for China are unreliable [BICC (2005, p. 145)].
Source: BICC (2001, 2005).

turnover per full-time employee for each product group: this also assumes homogeneity between civil and defense products in each product group [Turner, Chalmers and Hartley (2003)]. Not surprisingly, different sources provide different employment estimates. For example, Table 1 shows UK defense industry employment of 200 000 personnel in 2003 [BICC (2005); see also SIPRI (2003, p. 404)] whilst the UK official figures show an estimate of 305000 personnel for the same year (comprising 165 000 direct and 140 000 indirect employed on Ministry of Defence equipment and non-equipment expenditures and defense exports: MoD (2005)).

Data are also available on the world's leading arms companies. Since 1990 and the end of the Cold War, there has been major re-structuring involving mergers and acquisitions leading to larger defense firms and increased market concentration. There has also been the emergence of military service companies reflecting military outsourcing, especially in the United States and parts of Europe (e.g., UK). Some American service companies have obtained contracts as a result of the Iraq war (e.g., KBR/Halliburton) and some of these contract awards have raised issues of 'favoritism' and preferential treatment. Over the period 1990 to 2003, total arms sales for the top 100 companies rose from an aggregate $162.6 billion to $235.7 billion (2003 constant prices) representing a real increase of some 45%.

Table 2 shows the world's leading arms companies for the period 1990–2003. Whilst the top 10 companies are dominated by United States firms, the share of European firms in the top 10 has doubled from 20% in 1990 to 40% in 2003, with the United States share declining from 80% to 60% (based on numbers of firms in top10). Over the period 1990–2003, the top 10 show major changes in rankings, exits, new entrants and product range. Some of the changes in rankings reflect mergers and acquisitions.

Table 2
Top 10 arms companies (sales in US$ millions at current prices and exchange rates)

| Company | 1990 | | | Company | 2003 | | |
	Sector	Arms sales	Arms share in total sales (%)		Sector	Arms sales	Arms share in total sales (%)
McDonnell–Douglas	Ac; El; Mi	9890	55	Lockheed Martin	Ac; El; Mi; Sp	24910	78
General Dynamics	Ac; El; Mi; Mv; Sh	8300	82	Boeing	Ac; El; Mi; Sp	24370	48
British Aerospace (UK)	Ac; A; El; Mi; SA/O	7520	40	Northrop Grumman	Ac; El; Mi; SA/A; Sh	22720	87
Lockheed	Ac	7500	75	BAE Systems (UK)	A; Ac; El; Mi; SA/A; Sh	15760	77
General Motors	Ac; Eng; El; Mi	7380	6	Raytheon	El; Mi	15450	85
General Electric	Eng	6450	11	General Dynamics	A; El; Mv; Sh	13100	79
Raytheon	El; Mi	5500	57	Thales (F)	El; Mi; SA/A	8350	70
Thomson-CSF (F)	El;Mi	5250	77	United Technologies (UTC)	El;Eng	6210	20
Boeing	Ac; El; Mi	5100	18	EADS (EU)	Ac; El; Mi; Sp	8010	24
Northrop	Ac	4930	86	Finmeccanica (It)	A; Ac; El; Mv; Mi; SA/A	5290	57

Notes:
   (i) EU = Europe; F = France; It = Italy; UK = United Kingdom; all other companies are US companies.
  (ii) 1990 data are based on top 100 arms companies in OECD and developing countries; 2003 data based on top 100 arms companies excluding China.
 (iii) A = artillery; Ac = aircraft; El = electronics; Eng = engines; Mi = missiles; Mv = military vehicles; SA/O = small arms/ordinance; Sh = ships; Sp = space; Oth = other.
 (iv) If the list were extended to include the top 12 firms, then in 2003 the 12th rank would be Halliburton (a military service company, not listed in the top firms in 1990).
Source: SIPRI (1992, 1993, 2005).

Examples include Lockheed's merger with Martin Marietta and its acquisition of Loral and General Dynamics military aircraft business; Boeing acquired McDonnell Douglas and Rockwell; and EADS was an international merger involving Aerospatiale Matra (France), Daimler Chrysler Aerospace (Germany) and CASA (Spain). Also, within the top 10, since 1990, single product companies no longer exist and have been replaced by multi-product arms companies, each with more defense products. Within the top 10 in 1990 there was an average of 2.8 products per company; in 2003, the corresponding average was 4.1. By 2003, some firms supplied a range of air, land and sea systems (e.g., Northrop Grumman; BAE) compared with 1990 when all the top 10 were focused mostly on the aerospace industry (i.e., aircraft, aero-engines and missiles). There has also been a marked growth in defense electronics: in 1990, 70% of the top 10 arms companies had electronics divisions; in 2003, all firms in the top 10 were involved in defense electronics.

The structural changes since the 1990s have led to larger firms and increased industrial concentration. Between 1990 and 2003, the largest firm increased its share of the top 10 arms sales from 13.5 to 17.2% and its share of the top 100 arms sales also increased from 7.8 to 10.6%; and corresponding share figures for the three largest firms in the top 10 rose from 37.2 to 49.8% and their share of the top 100 increased from 21.5 to 30.5%. Admittedly, these are non-conventional measures of concentration but they are indicative of the general trend towards increased concentration. The trend is more apparent in national defense markets, which are typically characterized by domestic monopoly, duopoly or by oligopoly in some products.

Over the period 1990–2003, arms companies amongst the top 10 became more defense-dependent: arms sales as a share of total sales rose from an average of 23% in 1990 to 58% in 2003 for the top 10. Within the top 100, defense dependence also increased. In 1990, there were 29 firms in the top 100 with arms sales of 75% or more; by 2003, the corresponding figure was 44 firms. By 2003, there were also more companies which were totally dependent on arms sales: in 1990, there were 5 firms with 100% arms sales and the figure rose to 11 firms in 2003 with four of the 11 being in the motor vehicles sector (including subsidiaries).

Firms have also become larger. In real terms, the average size of arms company sales in the top 10 increased by over 50%, but the average size of the overall company as measured by total real sales (i.e., military and civil of top 10) declined by some 40% over this period. Table 3 shows the average size of company by ranking and the trend towards larger firms. Between 1990 and 2003, the average size of arms company almost doubled within the top 5 group and more than trebled in the top 20 group. Also, within the top 5, whilst both United States and European firms increased their average size, the size gap between the top US and European firms increased substantially (i.e., from 1.6 in 1990 to 2.5 in 2003 for the relative size of United States to European firms in the top 5). This suggests that if the European defense industry is to remain internationally competitive, there is substantial scope for more mergers and re-structuring in Europe [Mantin and Tishler (2004), Markusen and Serfati (2000)].

Table 3
Average size of arms company, 1990–2003 (average size in $ billions at constant
2003 prices)

Ranking of largest firms	1990	2003
Top 5	11.2	20.7
Top 10	9.4	14.5
Top 20	2.6	8.7
Top 50	2.4	4.2
Top 100	1.6	2.4
Top 5: USA	10.9	20.1
Top 5: European	6.9	8.1

Notes:
　　(i) Based on 100 largest arms companies in OECD and developing countries
　　　　in 1990; and on 100 largest arms companies, excluding China in 2003.
　　(ii) Constant prices based on US consumer price index for 1990 and 2003.
Source: SIPRI (1992, 2005).

The creation of larger arms firms and increased industrial concentration has two policy implications. First, the trade-off between monopoly and competition where the standard neo-classical model predicts that monopoly is associated with higher prices, abnormal profits and inefficiency. Here, the definition of a monopoly is dependent on the definition of the market. Procurement agencies and governments are often subject to monopoly if they are unwilling to allow foreign firms to bid for national defense contracts (e.g., the Buy American Act; Article 296 of the European Union). Second, larger arms companies should be seen as a major producer groups in the 'military–industrial–political' complex. Such companies possess bargaining power which they will seek to use to influence government policy in their favor (e.g., in the award of procurement contracts and the continuation rather than cancellation of projects). Small numbers of large arms companies can be modelled using game theory where there will be strategic behaviour and interaction between companies in procurement competitions and between producer groups and governments as buyers of arms. Compared with the competitive model, game theory predicts that with small numbers the pursuit of self-interest might not result in a socially desirable outcome. In such situations, major producer groups and procurement agencies will be involved in games of bluff, chicken and 'tit for tat'. The behavior of both principal (buyer) and agent (contractor) will be affected by asymmetric information which allows contractors opportunities for both inefficiency and rents [Laffont and Tirole (1993)].

2.3. The economics of arms industries

Arms industries are often regarded as *economically* strategic industries characterized by monopoly/oligopoly structures, decreasing costs, R&D-intensity and associated spinoffs. The possibility of monopoly rents provides a role for government in capturing some of these rents. These characteristics define the central economic features of arms industries, namely:

(i) *The importance of R&D as a fixed cost.* For major weapons systems, R&D is costly and these costs have risen in real terms. Also, for weapons such as combat aircraft, development periods are lengthy and can take over 15 years. For example, the US F/A-22 Raptor is the world's most advanced combat aircraft. Since the acquisition programme started in 1986, cost and delivery schedule estimates have grown significantly. By 2004, development costs were estimated at $28.7 billion which was a 127% increase over the 1986 estimate; the planned development cycle had grown from 9 years to 19 years; the initial operational capability date had slipped over 9 years; and estimated unit procurement costs had risen from $69 million in 1988 to $153 million in 2004, which was a 122% increase (and the 2006 unit procurement costs were an estimated $174.3 million per aircraft). Not surprisingly, the US Air Force purchase plans have changed from an initial request for 750 aircraft to a 2006 estimated purchase of 183 aircraft [GAO (2004), GAO (2006a, 2006b)]. Reductions in procurement numbers means rising R&D costs per aircraft as fixed R&D costs are spread over smaller numbers. However, new weapons are 'more capable' and one squadron of F-22A aircraft will replace two squadrons of F-15s and will also lead to savings in annual operating and support costs [GAO (2006a)].

(ii) *Production: the importance of quantity, scale and learning economies.* Large-scale production allows economies of scale and learning so giving rise to decreasing unit costs. Conceptually, scale relates to the output per time-period for a single product, whereas learning is based on cumulative output per product.[2] Whilst the concepts are clear, there are empirical difficulties in distinguishing between scale and learning. Studies suggest that the median unit production cost saving by increasing scale from the minimum efficient scale to the ideal level was 10–20%: tanks and warships showed unit cost reductions of 10% or less; combat aircraft gave unit cost reductions of 20%; conventional munitions 20–30%; and missiles some 25 to 40% [Hartley (2006a)]. Traditionally, learning was associated with aircraft production and learning curve slopes of 75 to 80%; but it also applies to other defense industries such as aero-engines, avionics, electronics, missiles, main battle tanks and warships with slopes ranging from 75 to 96% [Sandler and Hartley (1995, p. 125)]. Whilst labor learning remains important, it has been affected by modern manufacturing methods, new materials and business practices Examples of new methods include computer-aided design and computer-aided manufacturing; capital-intensive production including numerically controlled laser alignment

---

[2] For example, scale might be based on an annual output of 100 000 units of a tank; learning applies to cumulative output so that if a tank has been produced at an annual rate of 100 000 units for 10 years, its cumulative output is 1 million. Evidence reported in this chapter is based on interview studies. Scale curves were based on unit cost reductions in moving from minimum efficient scale to ideal scale where there would be no further reductions in unit production costs.

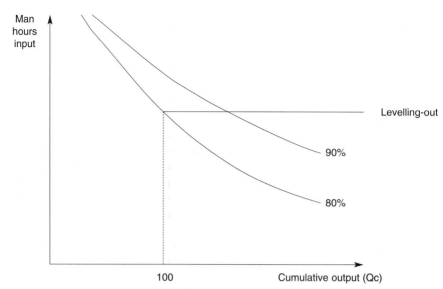

Figure 1. Labor learning curves.

systems; lean methods; supply chain changes; major assemblies arrive for final assembly already 'pre-packed' with all components and avionics which do not have to be installed during final assembly [Rand (2002, p. 10)]. For European aerospace industries, typical labor learning curves are now 85 to 90% compared with the traditional 80% curve. Moreover, European aerospace firms are now achieving continuous learning on military and civil aircraft projects compared with the 1950s/60s experience of 'flat' learning curves at some 100 units (whereas US experience showed continuous learning: Hartley (2006a)). Examples of learning curves with slopes of 80% and 90% and a curve which levels out after some 100 units are shown in Figure 1. Nonetheless, there remain substantial differences in the scale of output between US and European Union (EU) arms firms in air, land and sea systems with American firms having a scale advantage. For example, on the Joint Strike Fighter (Lockheed Martin F-35), the initial planned order was for 3002 units comprising 2852 aircraft for the US Forces and a UK requirement for 150 aircraft. Decreasing unit costs from scale and learning result in smaller numbers of larger firms and increased industry concentration.

(iii) *Imperfect markets*. Typically, for major weapons systems, national arms markets are dominated by monopoly, duopoly and oligopolies on the supply side. The major prime contractors are also large firms in an absolute sense. Furthermore, the demand side is imperfect with national governments as major or monopsony buyers (see Section 3).

(iv) *Forms of organization*. The major arms firms have developed different forms of organization to respond to new and changing market environments. Multi-product firms have replaced the traditional single product specialists whereby arms firms used to specialize in one product, such as combat aircraft, naval aircraft, large aircraft or main battle tanks. The modern arms company has to cope with limited and uncertain defense budgets together with new and costly technologies requiring substantial R&D resources. Firms will choose a form of organization which will adjust to these market developments, build on their comparative advantage whilst economizing on transaction costs and exploiting any economies of scope. Amongst the major prime contractors, two types of organization have emerged. First, defense specialists supplying a range of air, land and sea systems, including defense electronics and a capability of supporting these systems during their 'in-service' life (e.g., via military outsourcing). BAE Systems, Lockheed Martin and Northrop Grumman are examples of such defense specialists, with arms accounting for over 75% of their sales. Second, an alternative organization 'model' is based around aerospace companies specializing in military and civil aircraft and helicopters, space systems and defense electronics. Boeing and EADS are examples of such aerospace specialists, each with a substantial business in large civil jet airliners with arms accounting for under 50% of their sales [see Table 2: Hayward (2005)]. These defense-civil companies are not dependent on winning large arms contracts and their civil business supports their industrial capability for re-entering defense markets in the future.

2.4. Market conduct: Competition and the military–industrial complex

The size of the home market and the trend to a smaller number of larger arms firms affects the form and extent of competition. Europe is characterized by domestic monopolies whilst the United States has more duopolies and oligopolies in major weapons systems. In such markets, rivalry takes both price and non-price forms with their relative importance related to the stage of the weapons acquisition process. In the development stage of major weapons systems, much emphasis is placed on technical and performance features of contractor proposals (e.g., the extent to which a proposal will meet the Armed Forces mission requirements). At this stage, the technical risks and uncertainties are substantial so that initial price estimates are usually unreliable. Price becomes a more reliable allocative mechanism once the technical risks of development have been reduced (e.g., for production work). Previous efforts to subject a contractor to a fixed price contract for both development and production work for a major high technology project have been associated with losses and the threat of bankruptcy for a major contractor. Examples of losses under total package procurement occurred in the early 1970s with the US Grumman F-14 combat aircraft and Lockheed C-5 transport aircraft [Burnett and Kovacic (1989)]. More recently, the UK's experience with its purchase of the Nimrod MR4 maritime reconnaissance and attack aircraft confirms the financial risks of fixed price contracts for combined development and production work.

In 1996, following an international competition, British Aerospace (now BAE Systems) was awarded a fixed price contract for the design, development and production of 21 Nimrod MR4 aircraft, including training and initial support for the whole system. There were continued technical and resource problems which led to a series of re-negotiations and reviews, culminating in a 2003 agreement between the UK Ministry of Defense and BAE Systems to change from a fixed price contract to a target cost incentive fee contract for design and development including three trials aircraft. Under the revised contract, series production was suspended pending definition of a satisfactory design standard, planned procurement was reduced to 18 aircraft and further reduced to about 12 aircraft in 2004. Under the 2003 agreement, BAE also made provisions in its accounts of £500 million against this contract, in addition to earlier provisions of £300 million. In 2005, the forecast cost for the program was £3.81 billion against an original estimate of £2.8 billion with a cost overrun of £995 million; and the in-service date was forecast at September 2010 against an original estimate of April 2003 representing a slippage of 89 months [NAO (2005)]. A feature of this programme is its change from a competitively-determined fixed price for development and production to a target cost incentive fee contract for design and development only, with a separate contract for production aircraft and financial penalties incurred by the prime contractor. It also shows how competitive procurement can be modified subsequently to a non-competitive procurement.

2.4.1. Defense R&D

The focus on defense R&D as a major aspect of non-price rivalry in arms acquisition raises questions about what is known about such spending.

Data on defense R&D are valuable sources of information on a nation's military technological capability and its commitment to a national defense industrial base. Defense R&D increases a nation's military capability by improving its national security through using technology (quality) rather than increasing the quantity of arms. Such R&D might also contribute to a technological arms race and to the rising costs of defense equipment so creating pressures for higher defense spending.

US and UK evidence shows that for combat aircraft, real unit production costs have risen by about 10% per year which is equivalent to a factor of 2.5 per decade [Kirkpatrick (1995)]. Similar percentage increases of about 10% apply to other defense equipment resulting in a doubling in unit production costs every 7.25 years and the end of the Cold War has made no difference to unit cost escalation [Pugh (1993, 2006)]. This rising cost–time relationship for combat aircraft is illustrated in Figure 2, which also shows examples of aircraft which departed from the trend line (e.g., Tornado, Typhoon: BAe (1997)). These cost increases reflect the technical arms race: next generation arms are more effective than their predecessors and tend to have higher development and higher unit production costs. Higher unit costs mean that fewer units can be purchased from a limited defense budget, leading to numerically smaller Armed Forces and forecasts of a single tank army, a single ship navy and Starship Enterprise for the air force! Similarly, higher development and production costs impact on arms industries leading to fewer new programmes and smaller numbers to be manufactured so reducing the scope for learning and scale economies and further increasing unit production costs

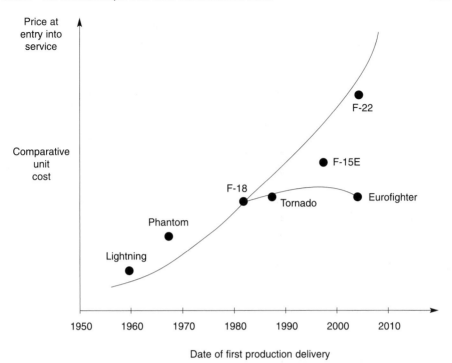

Figure 2. Unit costs and time-trends.

[Kirkpatrick (1995)]. Development of current generations of combat aircraft and their engines costs about the same as manufacturing 200 units of the aircraft; but what currently is enough to develop and produce 200 units is unlikely to be sufficient to complete the development of its successor [Pugh (2006)]. Improvements in the efficiency of procurement and in industrial productivity can alleviate the effects of unit cost escalation, but only on a transitory short-run basis. For example, with unit cost escalation of 10% per annum, competitive procurement leading to cost reductions of some 20% would provide relief from cost escalation for only 23 months. Similarly, Unmanned Air Vehicles (UAVs) are unlikely to provide a technological revolution to break this cost escalation trend: the rapid growth in their capability is being reflected in a correspondingly rapid growth in their costs so that they will eventually be unaffordable [Pugh (2006)]. As a result, unit cost escalation is a major determinant of both military and industrial capabilities and their structures [Pugh (1993, p. 182), Pugh (2006)]. Such unit cost escalation reflects the nature of military competition rather than inefficiencies in procurement.

Data on defense R&D spending for the period 1981–2004 are shown in Table 4. These data are for government-funded defense R&D, excluding privately-funded defense R&D. China is a notable omission, but there are estimates suggesting China's defense R&D budget of $2.9 billion in 2001. During part of the Cold War 1981–1991, the USSR was the leading defense R&D spending nation. However, following the end

Table 4
Defense R&D, 1981–2004 (2001 prices and 2001 PPP rates: $ millions)

Nation	1981	1991	2001	2004	Defense industry employment 2003 (000s)	Defense R&D share of defense budget, 2001 (%)
USA	34 751	51 105	46 210	67 464	2700	14.6
Russia	64 100	68 500	4800	6100	780	11.5
UK	6465	4593	3267	4681	200	9.1
France	4936	6899	3708	4061	240	11.1
Germany	1258	2030	1231	1410	80	4.6
Japan	272	807	996	1148	80	2.2
Italy	334	748	407	Na	26	1.8
Spain	28	519	2215	Na	20	31.2
Sweden	269	636	295	667	25	6.8
Total EU	13 290	15 425	11 123	13 441	645	6.9
Total (All above)	112 413	135 837	63 129	88 153	4151	9.1

Notes:
   (i) Defense R&D data from SIPRI Yearbooks. Russian/USSR data from Chris Davis (Oxford).
   (ii) Defense industry employment data from BICC (2005).
   (iii) Column 2004 shows latest data from OECD (2004): US data for 2004; Germany, Japan, Sweden and UK latest data are for 2003; France is for 2002; Italy and Spain are for 2001.
   (iv) Defense R&D shares for EU and All Nations are based on medians.
Sources: BICC (2005), OECD (2004).

of the Cold War and for 2001–2004, the USA became the major spending nation, accounting for almost 70% of world defense R&D spending in 2001 (including China). After the end of the Cold War in 1990, most Western nations reduced their defense R&D spending, especially in Russia. Spain was a notable exception with a marked long-run increase in defense R&D spending reflected in its aerospace and defense electronics programs (e.g., Eurofighter Typhoon).

Table 4 confirms the R&D scale differences between the United States and EU arms industries, with defense R&D determining technological capability and competitiveness. In 2001, no EU nation achieved a defense R&D effort approaching 10% of the US level of defense R&D. Nations differed in the share of their defense budgets allocated to R&D. The United States. was amongst the highest with a share of some 15% in 2001, compared with shares of 11.5% for Russia and about 7% for the EU. Spain was an outlier with a share figure of some 31%, further reflecting the nation's efforts to develop its defense industrial base. Table 4 also shows defense industry employment which might be expected to be positively associated with defense R&D. The rank correlation coefficient between defense R&D in 2001 and defense industry employment in 2003 was positive at 0.81 which was significant at the 1% level.

Defense R&D spending buys equipment capability which can be expressed as a time advantage and in turn is a determinant of international competitiveness. A study of ten nations found that there is a positive relationship between equipment capability

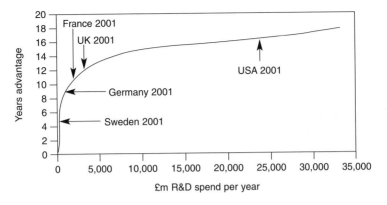

Figure 3. R&D and equipment capabilities.

and R&D spending with the relationship subject to diminishing returns, as shown in Figure 3. The United States has a time advantage of some 6 years reflected in its equipment capability compared with France and the UK; but such advantage is achieved by spending ten-times as much on defense R&D. Moreover, it was found that equipment quality was most highly correlated with R&D spend 10–15 years earlier [Middleton et al. (2006)].

For 2001, total world defense R&D spending was almost $68 billion providing a further indication of its importance as a non-price factor in the competitive process (i.e., comprising Table 4 nations, plus China, Korea, Canada and other OECD nations: Hartley (2006b)). Such expenditure has obvious opportunity costs through the use of scarce scientific personnel and assets which could be used on civilian research; but there are possible beneficial externalities through technical spillovers for the civilian economy. There is no shortage of examples of such spillovers. They include military aircraft and jet engine technology applied to civil aircraft (e.g., Airbus and Boeing airliners), to the motor car industries, including Formula 1 racing cars, and to supply chains. Whilst such examples are useful, they are no substitute for quantitative data on the market value of spillovers. Further problems arise in identifying the counter-factual: what would have happened to technology spinoffs in the absence of defense R&D? Evaluating technology benefits must also address the transmission mechanism and allow for the long time-lags from R&D on defense projects (e.g., 18 year development programme for Typhoon) and the application of such technology elsewhere in the economy. On transmission mechanisms, it appears that defense technology is transferred to other sectors via staff turnover, consultancy (e.g., Formula 1 racing car industry) through the supply chain and through links with universities [Hartley (2006b)].

2.4.2. The military–industrial–political complex

From a public choice perspective, the military–industrial–political complex comprises interest groups of the Armed Forces and national Defense Departments, producer groups of major prime contractors and politicians with an interest in defense spending in their constituencies. Such groups have vested interests in lobbying governments to influence the award of contracts and so seek to affect the competitive process in arms procurement.

The trend towards larger defense contractors, some of whom are national monopolies, has created even more powerful and influential producer groups. These groups will try to persuade governments to allocate contracts in their favour using various arguments about support for jobs and plants in high unemployment areas, the need to support the national defense industrial base, the importance of retaining 'key' technologies and the export potential of a new arms programme. Such arguments are often dominated by myths, emotion and special pleading, lacking economic analysis, critical evaluation and empirical evidence (see Section 3 below).

A public choice view of arms procurement sees interest groups rather than efficiency determining contract awards. Politicians are reluctant to close military bases and defense industrial plants in their constituencies with associated job losses so leading to the retention of excess industrial capacity. Lobbying by defense contractors for business replaces even limited competition. Prime contractors allocate sub-contracts to embrace as many political constituencies (states) as possible whilst vote-maximizing governments and their staffs will allocate defense contracts to marginal constituencies (states) and those constituencies most likely to vote for the government. Armed Forces and Defense Departments will co-operate with defense companies and politicians in accepting cost overruns, retaining excess industrial capacity and in imposing industrial policy which allows government interference to achieve outcomes which depart from efficient competitive market solutions. For example, budget-maximizing bureaucracies (i.e., Armed Forces and Defense Departments) have every incentive to support defense contractors' optimistic cost, time and performance estimates for new weapons programs; and once started, projects are difficult to stop (see Figure 4). The Armed Forces might also seek to persuade government of the budget benefits of multiyear procurement when, in reality, such funding may fail to reveal the full cost of decisions at the time they are made [CBO (2006)]. Similarly, losers in a competition often receive compensating work to allow them to remain in the industry on grounds of retaining both competition and the national defense industrial base. Finally, national defense monopolies and their rents are often protected from new entrants either in the form of national firms from non-defense sectors or from foreign competition (e.g., Buy American Act, Article 296 of the EU). The result is that political markets have replaced competition for arms procurement [Eland (2001)].

2.5. Market performance

An evaluation of the performance of arms industries is part of the standard structure-conduct-performance paradigm. Various indicators can be used to measure the performance of arms companies and industries. These include performance against contracts, labour productivity, profitability and export performance.

2.5.1. Contract performance

Modern weapons projects are costly and are characterized by cost overruns, delays in delivery and by failures to achieve required mission performance specifications. Some examples for UK and US major weapons projects are given in Table 5. This shows cost escalation of 35% for the UK Astute and Nimrod programs and delays of 43 and 89 months, respectively. The collaborative Typhoon aircraft had cost escalation of 14% and delays in the Astute-Nimrod range. Overall, on 19 major UK weapons projects, cost escalation was some 10% with delays averaging about 20 months per project [NAO (2005)]. Similarly, a US General Accountability Office Report estimated a 37% cost increase on 26 US weapons programs since the initial business case, with time delays of nearly 17% equivalent to some 26 months [GAO (2006b)]. Cost overruns mean that the buying power of the weapon system investment dollar is reduced resulting in smaller quantities. For example, the initial planned quantity for the US F-22A Raptor was 750 aircraft compared with a 2006 estimated buy of 183 aircraft; similarly, for the US Joint Strike Fighter the corresponding numbers are 2852 aircraft and 2443 units, respectively.

Questions arise as to the causes of such cost and delivery slippages. Figure 4 provides a framework for assessing these features. Each iso-quant shows various time-cost combinations for given levels of performance. Consider a major weapon with estimated development costs of C_1 and an expected completion date of T_1. Figure 4 shows that cost slippages can result from procurement agencies demanding that equipment be de-

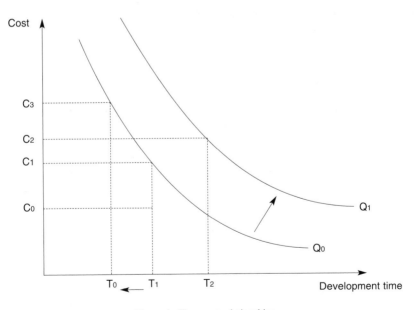

Figure 4. Time-cost relationships.

Table 5
Examples of cost escalation and delays: UK and US experience

Project	Initial cost estimate ($ billions)	2005 cost estimate ($ billions)	Delay (months)
A400M airlifter (7-nation collaboration)	4.8	4.6	15
Astute nuclear-powered submarine	4.5	6.1	43
Nimrod MR4 aircraft	4.9	6.7	89
Type 45 destroyer	9.6	10.3	18
Eurofighter Typhoon (4-nation collaboration)	29.2	33.3	54
US sample of 26 weapons projects: R&D costs	120.4	164.9	26
US Joint Strike Fighter	189.8	206.3	18
US Expeditionary Fighting Vehicle	8.1	11.1	Na

Notes:
  (i) For the UK, the initial cost estimate is approved cost at main gate. All UK costs in 2004/2005 prices; US costs in 2006 prices.
  (ii) Typhoon costs for 2005 were not reported by NAO: the estimates were derived from data in NAO (2005).
Source: NAO (2005), GAO (2006b).

livered faster (T_0 at cost C_3); or where increased performance is required (Q_1 at cost C_2 and time T_2); or where iso-quants might be 'blobs' and indeterminate reflecting uncertainty rather than clearly-defined frontiers; and where contractors might initially bid low (C_0) to buy into a project and then increase their cost estimates once the project has started and becomes more difficult to stop. However, whatever the causes of cost and delivery slippages, there is a more fundamental issue of the optimality of such changes. One view is that some changes might be optimal in providing a preferred weapon at least-cost (e.g., modifications might be cost-effective even though costs increase over their initial estimate). This view requires evidence on the cost of alternative solutions, the valuation of marginal improvements in performance and ultimately, the effectiveness of the weapon in combat. An alternative view is that slippages reflect inefficiencies amongst both arms companies and procurement agencies. Here, there is a presumption that arms companies are inefficient, operating in imperfect markets and supplying under long-term contracts where they are effectively monopoly suppliers.

2.5.2. Productivity and profitability

Few studies are available comparing the performance of defense and civilian companies. One US study compared similar manufacturing processes across manufacturing plants with and without defense prime or sub-contracts in the same industries. It found that manufacturing establishments in the defense and commercial sectors did not differ statistically in scale or production volumes [Watkins and Kelley (2001)].

Table 6 presents an example of the available data for comparing the performance of defense and civilian firms. It shows productivity, R&D and profitability data for a group of European and United States aerospace and defense firms together with an all companies average which is used to represent civilian companies. Within Europe, most aerospace and defense firms had value added productivity figures which exceeded the all companies composite. Dassault achieved the highest value added productivity as well as profitability for the European group. On labour productivity (sales per employee) and profitability, almost all European and United States aerospace and defense firms were below the all companies composite. If the relatively lower profitability figures are maintained over the long run, they raise questions as to why firms remain in the defense sector. Possible reasons might be that profitability on capital employed is more attractive (compared with profits on sales); or that government-funded defense R&D provides valuable spillovers to other parts of a defense contractor's business. Furthermore, the R&D performance indicators confirm aerospace and defense as R&D-

Table 6

Productivity and profitability of arms companies, 2005

Company	Sales per employee (£000s)	Value added per employee (£000s)	R&D as share of sales (%)	R&D per employee (£000s)	Profits as share of sales (%)
European aerospace and defense:		57.7			4.5
EADS, Netherlands	203.2	67.2	7.2	14.7	1.9
BAE Systems, UK	131.1	60.0	12.2	16.0	5.1
Thales, France	131.3	54.1	4.2	5.6	2.3
Rolls-Royce, UK	168.7	58.1	4.7	8.0	4.4
Snecma, France	136.0	48.6	11.1	15.1	6.0
Finmeccanica, Italy	114.9	49.2	19.3	22.2	5.6
SAAB, Sweden	115.5	58.5	4.5	5.2	7.1
Dassault Aviation France	193.7	77.7	1.9	3.7	12.1
USA aerospace and defense:					
Lockheed Martin	142.3	na	2.7	3.9	5.7
Boeing	171.8	na	3.6	6.2	4.3
Raytheon	133.5	na	2.4	3.2	4.5
Northrop Grumman	124.0	na	1.7	2.1	6.7
All companies composite	193.4	51.5	3.8	7.3	9.6

Notes:

(i) Value added data are published by DTI for top 600 European companies only; there are no comparable figures for the US companies. For value added, the All Companies Composite is based on the top 600 European firms.

(ii) Data for R&D, labour productivity and US firm's profitability are from DTI (2005a); remaining data are from DTI (2005b).

(iii) All Companies Composite data based on top 1000 global companies except for value added data.

(iv) Snecma is now part of SAFRAN. For Dassault, the R&D figures are based on R&D plus depreciation.

Source: DTI (2005a, 2005b).

intensive sectors compared with the all companies average. Of course, cross-section company data of the type shown in Table 6 have their limitations. They do not show long-run trends; they are for aerospace and defense firms only; they also reflect a company's total sales comprising military and civil business (e.g., Boeing and EADS with their civil aircraft businesses); companies differ in their mix of military business; and the R&D data are based on figures disclosed in annual company accounts, excluding government-provided R&D funds which dominate military R&D work.

2.5.3. Exports

Exports are often used as an indicator of international competitiveness; but arms exports are frequently influenced by a variety of non-economic factors (e.g., arms embargos; allies/friends; regional conflict; human rights concerns: Levine, Sen and Smith (2000); see also Chapter 29). Nonetheless, data are available on arms exports by country which allows a broad assessment of international competitiveness. Table 7 shows the top 10 suppliers of major conventional weapons for the period 2000 to 2004. Over the period, Russia and the United States accounted for over 60% of world arms exports and the major EU nations accounted for a further 20%. The United States arms industry's competitiveness compared with the EU reflects the scale differences in R&D and output.

Arms exports provoke considerable ethical and political controversy. Yet, there is an economic dimension in terms of the benefits and costs of arms exports which needs to be injected into such debates. Both benefits and costs have to be identified and estimated. This was the focus of a study which estimated the economic costs and benefits of a 50% cut in UK arms exports from the average level of 1998 and 1999. Unlike some polemical work in this area, the study used a welfare economics framework and general equilibrium model, it carefully identified all relevant assumptions and focused on the

Table 7
Suppliers of major conventional weapons (US$ millions at 1990 prices)

Supplier	2000	2004	Total: 2000–2004
Russia	4016	6197	26 925
USA	6400	5453	25 930
France	717	2122	6358
Germany	1195	1091	4878
UK	1121	985	4450
Ukraine	326	452	2118
Canada	124	543	1692
China	157	125	1436
Sweden	280	260	1290
Israel	272	283	1258
World Total	15 840	19 162	84 490

Source: SIPRI (2005).

adjustment impacts on four groups, namely, defense workers, other UK workers, UK-resident shareholders and the government [Chalmers et al. (2002)].

Arms exports are believed to provide economic benefits to the exporting nation in the form of jobs, export earnings and the maintenance of defense industrial capacity. The study estimated that a 50% reduction in UK defense exports would result in a net financial loss to the Exchequer of some £40 million to £100 million a year on a continuing basis. Such a reduction would also involve a one-off adjustment cost cumulatively estimated to range from £0.9 billion to £1.4 billion. If possible terms of trade effects were included, the estimated cumulative cost of economic adjustment would rise to some £2 billion to £2.5 billion. The bulk of these costs would be borne in the first few years. Compared with other industries, the decline of UK coal mining and of the UK defense industry following the end of the Cold War involved much larger adjustment costs. Overall, it was concluded that the economic costs of reducing UK arms exports are relatively small and largely one-off [Chalmers et al. (2002)].

3. Procurement: Theory and policy issues

Governments are central to understanding arms markets. They are major buyers and sometimes monopsony buyers as well as regulators of such variables as profits and exports. Government buying power can be used to determine the size, structure, conduct, performance and ownership of arms industries. Examples include changes in defense spending (e.g., wars; disarmament) affecting the size of a nation's defense industrial base. Governments influence industry structure by allowing or preventing mergers and by controlling entry and exit (e.g., bail-outs: Liston-Heyes (1995)); they determine market conduct by specifying the form and terms of competitions; they affect performance by regulating profits on non-competitive contracts and controlling arms exports (both the quantity and quality of arms exports: see Chapter 29); and they can determine whether firms and the industry will be state- or privately-owned.

Buying arms involves the government's procurement agency in a complex set of choices under uncertainty. Arms procurement involves choices about:

(i) *Product requirements: what to buy?* Equipment performance requirements for a weapon system have to be specified. Such specifications determine the technical progress, risks and uncertainties of the procurement programme. One extreme involves the procurement of equipment which exists and is being bought and sold in reasonably competitive markets (e.g., off-the-shelf purchases of computers; lorries; office equipment; transport aircraft). The opposite extreme involves the procurement of advanced weapons systems which do not exist and have to be developed specifically for one government customer and where there are only one or a few national firms with the technical and industrial capability to undertake and complete the program (e.g., advanced combat aircraft; missiles; nuclear-powered aircraft carriers and submarines; satellite communication systems). Such market situations are characterized by information asymmetries between the buyer and contractor and where the buyer-seller relationship is governed by incomplete contracting [Bos (1996)]. This results in the hold-up problem where the R&D and other resources required for the programme are costly, highly-specific and worthless if the government does not buy the weapon (similar losses might occur for the government if it invests in the project). The contractual relationship between buyer and seller is further complicated by issues of adverse selection, moral hazard and risk sharing. Procurement agencies are at an informational disadvantage in contract negotiations since firms are experts with private information on their technological and production possibilities (adverse selection arises where the firm has more information than the procurement agency about some exogenous variables); and firms know the amount of effort they will devote to the work (moral hazard refers to endogenous variables that are not observed by the procurement agency: Laffont and Tirole (1993, p. 1)). Firms also know the likely risks and they know their minimum supply price for the contract.

(ii) *The contractor: who to buy from?* A contractor has to be selected where the options are between using competition and direct negotiation with a preferred supplier. Competition requires more choices. It might be based on a selected list of firms determined by technical, financial and performance criteria. Further choices are needed between competition restricted to national firms or open to foreign firms; and whether price and/or non-price factors will determine contract awards. Competition can determine prices and 'police' profits whereas negotiation with a preferred supplier requires that both prices and profits be agreed between buyer and seller. Such bilateral monopoly bargaining between a monopsony government buyer and monopoly seller involves two 'sticking points' namely, the buyer's maximum price or willingness to pay and the firm's minimum supply price below which it will not undertake the work. Negotiation occurs where the maximum price exceeds the minimum supply price. Generally, in such negotiations, adverse selection allows the firm to extract rents from the government buyer and moral hazard allows the firm to take discretionary action affecting its costs or the quality of its products (e.g., effort levels might not be maximized reflected in labor hoarding and 'on-the-job' leisure).

(iii) *Contract type: how to buy?* Procurement agencies have to select a contract type ranging between the extremes of firm/fixed prices and cost-plus contracts and the 'intermediate' case of target cost incentive contracts. Each has different risk sharing arrangements between the buyer and seller; each has different efficiency incentive, rent and equity properties; and each has different opportunities for strategic behaviour in contract negotiations. Bos (1996) analyzes the optimality of target-cost and fixed price contracts and shows that target cost pricing can achieve a first best where both fixed price and cost reimbursement contracts fail to do so. He concludes that under incomplete contracting, optimality may sometimes be achieved by contracts which combine several formulae which, individually, would fail to achieve efficiency.

Contracts differ in their incentive features. Cost-plus contracts have very low-powered incentives, whilst fixed price contracts offer extremely high-powered incen-

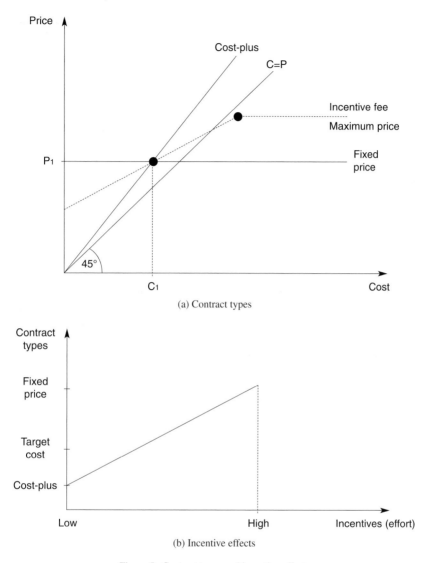

(a) Contract types

(b) Incentive effects

Figure 5. Contract types and incentive effects.

tives. Figure 5 shows the various types of contracts and their incentive features. Figure 5(a) illustrates three contract types based on an estimated cost of C_1: a fixed price contract is based on estimated cost plus a profit margin to give a fixed price of P_1 which remains unchanged regardless of actual costs. With a cost-plus contract, the price rises to reflect actual costs and a profit margin; whilst a target cost incentive fee contract shares any cost under-runs and over-runs between the government and contractor on an agreed basis, subject to a maximum price liability. Figure 5(b) summarizes the incentive features of these contracts.

(iv) *Timing: when to buy*? Choices are needed as to where in the development-production life-cycle to make decisions about the type of equipment to be bought. Decisions can be made at the initial design stage or during development or at the prototype stage or before the start of production. Competition can continue through these various stages (and can extend to mid-life up-dates and in-service support). Choices at the various stages have different risk and efficiency implications. Project and contractor selection at the initial design stage maximizes program risks and removes efficiency incentives from the contractor who is awarded a contract for development and production. In contrast, delaying project selection and maintaining competition reduces risks and provides efficiency incentives but at a cost. For example, at the initial design stage, two competing designs might be selected to proceed to a prototype competition with the winner awarded a development contract. Such a policy maintains competition to the prototype stage but at the cost to the government of funding rival projects after which the successful firm is no longer subject to rivalry.

Contracts are costly to write and enforce. They can involve substantial transaction costs, especially for costly, high technology weapons with long development periods and their associated uncertainties. Contracts for development work in the weapons acquisition cycle are likely to be incomplete and poorly specified simply because at the early stage, it is difficult to define the product ex ante. In such circumstances, incremental acquisition allows the buyer to acquire information to specify the product in more detail.

The United States Joint Strike Fighter aircraft (JSF) is an example of a 'fly-before-you-buy' competitive procurement and its impact on industry structure. It was also aimed at breaking the upward spiral of weapons costs through designing an affordable combat aircraft to meet the requirements of three US services (US Air Force, Navy, and Marine Corps) with commonality of parts for the three aircraft. Initially, it was estimated that some 80% of the aircraft would be common leading to cost savings of some 18 to 25% for development, production and operation over the life-cycle compared with the cost of three independently-developed aircraft types [CBO (1997, p. 42)]. Further cost savings came from combining the requirements of the three US services resulting in an initial planned order for 2852 aircraft plus a further requirement for 150 aircraft from the UK giving a total order for 3002 units with opportunities for economies of scale and learning. Estimated exports ranged from a lower-bound figure of 1500 aircraft to an optimistic estimate of 3000 units or more. This was a massive contract in the post-Cold War era and was subject to intensive lobbying by contractors and politicians.

Initially, three US companies submitted competing designs for the program (i.e., Boeing, Lockheed Martin, McDonnell–Douglas in partnership with Northrop Grumman and British Aerospace) and in late 1996, Boeing and Lockheed Martin were selected to proceed to the Concept Demonstration Phase of the program. Following its elimination from the JSF competition, McDonnell Douglas merged with Boeing in August 1997. Meanwhile, Lockheed Martin arranged with the former McDonnell–Douglas partners, Northrop Grumman and British Aerospace (now BAE Systems) to form a team to bid for the JSF contract in competition with Boeing (merged with McDonnell–Douglas). The rivals were each awarded a government cost-plus a fixed fee contract subject to a maximum price. Boeing received a contract of $661.8 million and Lockheed Martin a contract of $718.8 million (1996 prices) with each firm required to build two proto-types (i.e., Boeing X-32, Lockheed Martin X-35). This prototype competition involved two contrasting designs and technical solutions, especially for the vertical take-off vari-ants.

The JSF prototype competition was a 'winner-takes-all' competition. In October 2001, the JSF contract was awarded to Lockheed Martin. The contract was for the System Development and Demonstration Phase to test the validity and design to cer-tification and the total capability of the aircraft prior to entering production which was initially expected to be in 2008. The estimated 12 year development phase was ex-pected to cost $41.5 billion with a total estimated cost of over $250 billion for both development and production. Of course, once the winner was announced, it became a monopolist. Boeing was sufficiently diversified with other military and civil aircraft business to survive the loss of the JSF contract; and its existing fighter aircraft contracts (i.e., F-18E/F, F-22) will allow it to remain in the combat aircraft business for some time.

Competition in the JSF program also extended to the aircraft engine and into its pro-duction phase. Pratt and Whitney was initial choice of engine (F-135) but an alternative engine was also developed for the JSF program, namely, the General Electric F-136 engine The UK Rolls-Royce aero-engine company was involved in both engines. The alternative General Electric engine was designed to stimulate competition in price and quality by providing a second source of supply and to provide an insurance in the event of technical or operational problems with the Pratt and Whitney engine. Initial plans were for the General Electric engine to compete with the Pratt and Whitney engine from the 72nd production aircraft onwards. By late 2005, the General Electric-Rolls-Royce team was awarded a $2.4 billion development contract; but in early 2006, the rival Gen-eral Electric engine was threatened with cancellation. The DoD believed that there was no cost benefit or savings from an engine competition for the JSF and that there was a low operational risk from relying upon a single engine supplier. Critics of the rival engine, including Pratt and Whitney, claimed that technical advance and improved reli-ability meant that there was no longer a need for an insurance engine; that the costs of developing the rival engine would never be recovered; and that sharing purchases over two engines would mean that neither supplier would achieve maximum cost savings from scale economies. Predictably, General Electric took a different view claiming that relying on a sole source would create a monopoly (achieving short-term cost savings of $1.8 billion against claimed benefits of some $16 billion from competition) and that cancellation would lead General Electric to exit the fighter engine business. A GAO Report was critical of the Department of Defense analysis of the economic case for cancellation suggesting that it was flawed. It assumed a buy of 3036 engines when the most likely number was 8400 engines so that the Pentagon under-estimated cost savings by a factor of three; the analysis ignored cost savings over the life-cycle on spares and maintenance; and it was motivated by the desire to find immediate budget savings at the DoD [GAO (2006a)].

(v) *Choice criteria*. In selecting projects and contractors, the procurement agency has to decide whether to base its choices on military criteria such as cost, quality and delivery dates, or on the basis of wider economic and industrial criteria (e.g., jobs, technology, exports). There is the related issue of *who chooses*: the procurement agency or ultimately, the government with its concerns about local jobs and re-election?

(vi) *Regulation, corruption and monitoring of contracts and arms firms*. Arms procurement involves public interest issues, with taxpayer's representatives concerned about the efficiency and profitability of arms contracts. The result has been the creation of regulatory regimes to monitor arms contracts, contractors and procurement agencies. These range from formal legal arrangements whereby arms firms and procurement agencies are subject to prosecutions and court proceedings to more informal ad hoc arrangements with each case treated on its merits. The public interest scandals associated with arms contracts often arise with non-competitive contracts where there is an absence of rivalry and opportunities for 'organizational slack' and excessive profits: such outcomes might result where there is an absence of 'truth in contract negotiations.' But competition is not without its opportunities for corruption and misbehavior. Contract awards are made by officials who might be influenced by side payments and/or by the offer of future lucrative employment with a major and successful bidder. Some procurement regimes allow contractors to appeal to the courts as a mechanism for policing the buying process [Arrowsmith and Hartley (2002), Schooner (2001), Laffont and Tirole (1993)].

An example of illegal actions in procurement occurred in the United States involving the Air Force Principal Deputy Assistant Secretary in the DoD (Darleen Druyun) who admitted to the favourable treatment of the Boeing Corporation in key contract awards and negotiations. An official investigation in 2005 found that in this case too much control and management of too many functions with insufficient oversight resided in one person. This individual had exceptional expertise in contracting; she had long tenure in her position; there was little oversight because of no immediate supervisor; there were 'behind closed doors' decisions; and her daughter and future son-in-law were employed by Boeing [DSB (2005)].

3.1. Assessing arms industries: Benefit–cost analysis

Governments can use their buying powers to determine the size and structure of a nation's defense industrial base (DIB). Support might take the form of preferential purchasing and/or favorable contract terms (e.g., cost-based contracts; guaranteed and abnormal profit rates). A national defense industrial base offers both military-strategic and wider economic and industrial benefits. The military benefits include independence and security of supply and re-supply, especially during a conflict. Arms can be designed for the specific requirements of a nation's armed forces; a national DIB enables the procurement agency to be a more informed buyer as well as providing a degree of bargaining power when considering foreign acquisitions. There are wider economic benefits in the form of jobs, many of which can be highly-skilled and hence, high wage jobs; there are technology and spinoff benefits; and possible balance of payments contributions from export earnings and import-savings.

But these benefits are not without costs. Resources used in the DIB have alternative uses which invites the question: would the resources used in the nation's DIB make a greater contribution to jobs, technology and the balance of payments if they were used elsewhere in the economy (e.g., construction projects such as roads and buildings create jobs)? What are the extra costs, if any, of supporting the DIB (e.g., an extra 10 or 20% in unit costs?) and how highly does society value its national DIB (i.e., how much is it willing to pay)? There are also alternative means of achieving the military-strategic benefits of a DIB. For example, security of supply can be achieved by purchasing from overseas and by buying sufficient stocks to be stored for any crisis. Choices are then required between the costs of a DIB and the costs of importing and storage. Similarly, a procurement agency can be an informed buyer by maintaining a research capability to provide scientific appraisal of different types of weapons without the need to support a large DIB comprising design, development and production capabilities.

There is a more fundamental criticism of the concern with the wider economic benefits of a national DIB. Typically, the standard economic case for government intervention at the micro-level is based on market failure which usually involves imperfections and externalities, including public goods. State intervention based on jobs and balance of payments benefits suggests failures in both labor markets and foreign exchange rate markets; but policy-makers rarely identify the causes of these market failures and the appropriateness of DIB policy as a means of 'correcting' any such failures. Technology spillovers provide a more valid economic case for state intervention. R&D and technology markets are likely to create beneficial externalities in the form of spillovers for other sectors of the economy and these could be a basis for state intervention in arms industries to 'correct' such market failures. Examples of spillovers from military projects such as Eurofighter Typhoon include carbon fibre technology, avionics and aero-engine technology with some of these technologies applied to civil aircraft, motor cars (including Formula 1 racing cars) and to the health sector (e.g., surgery; joints; cameras used to inspect aero-engines applied to dentistry). However, there might be alternative and lower-cost policies for achieving spillovers rather than supporting the DIB; but there is the distinctive feature that spillovers from arms procurement are in the form of a 'free gift' resulting from the acquisition of weapons systems whose primary purpose is national defense and security.

3.2. Some policy issues and challenges

Three policy issues represent challenges to procurement agencies, namely, the role of competition in procurement, its extension to military outsourcing and determining the profitability of non-competitive contracts. The trend towards larger firms and increasingly imperfect markets has adverse impacts on the role of competition in arms procurement. Many European states have to choose between supporting a national monopoly or opening their national defense markets to allow foreign firms to bid for arms contracts. In theory, competition promotes efficiency leading to lower prices, better products and the 'policing' of profits. In reality, firms can 'play any games' and various strategies have emerged to thwart the intentions of competitive procurement. For example, competitively-determined fixed price contracts can be re-negotiated where the buyer makes major changes to the contract specification (with some changes motivated and initiated by contractors via procurement officials so appearing to come from the buyer). Or, modifications to a fixed price contract can occur where the technology risks and rising costs confront the contractor with the prospect of bankruptcy, especially where the contractor is a 'national champion' and a major employer; or where because of rising costs on a fixed price contract, the contractor threatens to withdraw from the defense market. In cases where rivalry is maintained through competitive prototyping, it is not unknown for the rival firms to merge and share the work rather than take a win/lose gamble. Governments might also subject their domestic monopolies to competition by allowing foreign firms to bid for national defense contracts. But such a policy is not costless: at some stage a foreign firm will have to be awarded a contract since without the prospect of success, foreign arms firms are unlikely to bear the substantial costs of continued bidding for major weapons contracts.

Competition has further limitations. Sometimes it can lead to unintended and undesirable behavior and consequences for both the buyer and contractors. These may include over-optimistic cost and time estimates and the potential loss of flexibility for timely insertions of technology in the future. Also, competitions can be costly to organize; their benefits might not exceed such costs; and they might fail to sustain key national defense industrial capabilities. The competition for the US Joint Strike Fighter is an example of the limitations of competition and competitive prototyping. Since the start of the development phase, JSF has increased its cost estimate and delayed deliveries despite a re-planning effort which added over $7 billion and 18 months to the development program. Uncertainties in developing the JSF have prevented the pricing of initial production orders on a fixed price basis with cost reimbursement contracts used for initial procurement so placing greater cost risk on the DoD [GAO (2006a)].

Concerns about the limitations of competition have led to the search for alternative approaches to arms procurement. One option is partnering, especially where a nation wishes to retain key defense industrial capabilities for military-strategic reasons. In such cases, governments might offer guaranteed business to national firms under a long-term partnership where the contractors agree to share cost data and accept gainshare mechanisms, including target cost incentive fee pricing and the use of risk-adjusted profit rates according to the type of work undertaken on the contract. Partnering requires a spirit of openness, transparency and trust between the contracting parties. However, the result is to create national monopolies with protected and guaranteed markets requiring procurement agencies to negotiate contracts which provide efficiency incentives and control over potential monopoly profits [DIS (2005)].

3.2.1. Military outsourcing

In recent years, competition in procurement has been extended to military outsourcing which is known variously as contractorization, contracting-out, private finance initiatives and public–private partnerships. Typically, military outsourcing involves private firms bidding for work previously undertaken 'in-house' by the armed forces. As a result, traditional armed forces monopolies are subjected to competition allowing procurement agencies to improve technical and allocative efficiency through re-contracting for different levels of service. Examples include training, repair and maintenance, transport, the provision of air tanker services and buildings financed by the private sector and leased to the military on long-term contracts [Fredland (2004), Hartley (2002)]. As always, choices and trade-offs cannot be avoided. Private firms offer high-powered efficiency incentives but there are the transaction costs of contracting. In contrast, public agencies offer low-powered efficiency incentives but they might better on loyalty and trust (i.e., sovereign transactions).

Military outsourcing is an aspect of public procurement combining the skills of economists and lawyers. It is claimed to offer benefits of cost savings, risk transfer from the public to private sectors and it encourages private firms to be innovative. One fallacy needs to be addressed. Where outsourcing takes the form of private finance replacing public finance (e.g., construction of buildings for the armed forces), there is no effect on efficiency if the same resources are used. Indeed, since governments can always borrow more cheaply than the private sector, if private finance is to lead to cost savings, the extra financing costs for the private sector must be offset by savings elsewhere on the project (e.g., over the life-cycle of the project). Interestingly, private finance initiatives show opportunities for both private finance and private provision of defense activities.

Some military outsourcing contracts can be long-term (e.g., 20–30 years). UK experience claims cost savings of 5 to 40% from military outsourcing, but it is difficult to assess the reliability of these claims over such long-term contracts. There are also problems in writing and enforcing long duration contracts which deliver a range of services of approved quality for a variety of unknown and unknowable future contingencies ranging from peace to war (and war with unknown enemies in different locations). Such contracts require trust, commitment and partnership between both buyer and contractor. Furthermore, once awarded a long-term contract, firms will seek to exploit their monopoly power and earn monopoly rents. As a result, contractors have incentives to economize or default on those parts of the contract which are difficult (costly) to specify and enforce and such behavior might have serious implications for military capability (success versus failure in conflict).[3] In principle, military outsourcing offers gains to taxpayers, firms, shareholders, financiers and lawyers. If the benefits of outsourcing fail to be achieved, then taxpayers, the armed forces and society could be losers.

Proposals to extend private firms into combat operations are much more controversial. This raises the more general question of the limits to military outsourcing which need to be evaluated in terms of its costs and benefits. Consider the problems of private military firms undertaking military operations. There would be demanding problems of writing and enforcing contracts for unforeseen contingencies and various threats, so that firms would not know the resources needed for the contract. There would be asset specificity and hold-up issues where military equipment and training has little value in alternative civilian uses. Loyalty and trustworthiness cannot be ignored. Heads of state need to be confident of the loyalty of their military forces: private firms can withdraw from combat contracts and might change sides although such behavior would affect the reputation of the firm. Finally, contracts and associated performance indicators can give unexpected and undesirable results. For example, cost-minimizing behavior by private contractors might impose substantial collateral damage and costs on civilians; there might be incentives to prolong a conflict; and firms might aim to avoid losing their costly assets (e.g., new, costly weapons).

3.2.2. Determining the profitability of non-competitive contracts

Competitive procurement is not always possible nor desirable. Examples occur where a firm which has designed and developed a weapon system is awarded a production contract; or there might be an urgent requirement (e.g., war); or where a government's preferred supplier is a national monopoly contractor; or it might reflect a government's desire to maintain a national industrial capability in areas such as nuclear-powered submarines, aircraft carriers, manned bomber aircraft and main battle tanks. In such situations, problems arise in determining prices and profits on non-competitive contracts. This is an under-researched field of defense economics.

Theory suggests that the prices for non-competitive contracts should be based on estimated costs assuming efficient behavior and a government-determined profit margin reflecting normal profits. Estimating costs requires reliable estimating techniques otherwise 'excessive' profits can arise from estimating errors or the use of false data in cost-estimating rather than from efficiency improvements [Hartley (1969)]. There is the additional task of assessing whether the firm is operating as a cost-minimizer. Here, there are information asymmetries with private contractors possessing detailed knowledge on their production possibilities and their effort levels for the contract. In these circumstances, procurement agencies often require either 'equality of information' between buyer and seller or 'truth in negotiations' legislation reinforced with a legal right

---

[3] There is the casualty issue about private contractors. In Iraq, the deaths of private contractors did not count as soldiers lost. This gave the US administration political benefits which induced it to hire private security staff at many times the cost of a US soldier.

to 'post-cost' and/or renegotiate contracts (i.e., requiring contractor to make refunds to the defense department).

The profit rates for non-competitive contracts also have to be determined. Inevitably, there are criticisms that profit rates on non-competitive contracts are 'too high' especially for work which is viewed by procurement agencies as less risky compared with other work and that such contracts fail to provide firms with sufficient efficiency incentives. There are further criticisms that non-competitive contracts create a 'cosy' relationship between the procurement agency, the defense industry and the regulatory body (i.e., capture). In the UK, profits on non-competitive contracts were traditionally based on providing contractors with a 'fair' return on capital which was defined as the rate of return equal on average to the return earned by British industry. The reference group for the application of this comparability principle comprised a group of UK industrial and commercial companies operating in a fully competitive environment representing the alternative use value of capital (e.g., in 1996, the target rate of return on capital was 19.3% on an historic cost basis: Review Board (1996)). The UK profit formula was further complicated by the need to convert the target return on capital to a rate of return based on the cost of production.

An alternative UK profit formula was proposed whereby the rate of return would be based on a weighted average cost of capital comprising the cost of equity and the cost of debt with the cost of equity based on the capital asset pricing model (CAPM). Using the CAPM model, the weighted cost of capital for 1998 was estimated at 12.1% compared with a target rate of return recommended by the Review Board for non-competitive contracts of 15.7% on capital giving a differential of 3.6% points. However, the UK profit formula was modified in 2003 to allow profits on non-competitive contracts to be based on both capital employed and costs of production (with a target profit rate on cost of production of 5.67%). The revised profit formula was introduced to reflect the changing nature of the procurement environment, to provide a mechanism for recognizing varying degrees of risk; to develop some method for determining the weighting between capital and costs of production; and the need for simplicity of administration [Review Board (2004)].

4. Industrial policies

A further aspect of procurement policy has to be considered, namely, alternative industrial policies. These involve procurement choices between the extremes of support for a national DIB or importing foreign arms (either with or without offsets) or the 'intermediate' solutions of international collaboration and licensed/co-production. Each option involves varying degrees of work-sharing and technology for the buying nation with corresponding alternative prices [Hartley (1995)].

Economic theory offers some guidelines for defense industrial policy in an established military alliance such as NATO or the EU as a developing military alliance.

There are two key guidelines, namely, gains from trade and gains from scale and learning economies. Most NATO and EU defense markets are protected with preferential purchasing and support for national champions (e.g., Buy American Act, Article 296 of EU Treaty). Free trade between member states of a military alliance would lead to gains from specialization with trade based on comparative advantage. This requires abolition of tariff barriers, subsidies and preferential purchasing by member states so allowing free entry and competition for national defense contracts. Firms from member states would be allowed to bid for defense contracts in each nation state. In late 2005, EU member states agreed to a voluntary code of conduct for defense procurement to encourage competition in the EU defense equipment market where arms contracts were exempt from the normal EU internal market rules [EU (2005)].

Additional cost savings are available where arms industries are decreasing cost industries (e.g., aerospace). Greater output reduces unit R&D costs and leads to economies of scale, learning and scope: such economies are not achieved in small scale EU national defense markets but are available in a single arms market embracing all member states of a military alliance. Estimates suggest that competition effects might lead to unit cost savings of 10 to 25% with scale and learning economies probably contributing a 15 to 25% reduction in unit costs [Hartley (2006a)].

Policies to introduce an efficient defense industrial policy will, like all policies, involve gainers and losers. Potential gainers include those industries and firms which are privately-owned and have already been exposed to competition and competitively-determined fixed price contracts. Possible losers will be state-owned firms which operated in protected markets receiving subsidies and cost-plus contracts. Changes to establish a more efficient industrial policy will involve adjustment costs and will take time. There will be some unemployment and under-employment of resources, reflected in job losses, plant closures, exits from the industry and local unemployment. Potential losers will oppose change and will lobby for 'fair and managed' competition with work allocated on a *juste retour* basis and protection for alliance defense industries (e.g., Fortress Europe). With such pressures from producer groups, the ideal of an efficient defense industrial policy will soon be transformed into cartels, collusive tendering, a lack of rivalry and inefficient alliance defense industries.

Within Europe, collaboration has been the most distinctive of its defense industrial policies, especially in aerospace systems (e.g., 3-nation Tornado, 4-nation Eurofighter Typhoon).[4] In theory, perfect international collaboration leads to savings in development and unit production costs. However, actual collaboration involves departures from the 'ideal' case with work-sharing based on political, equity and bargaining criteria

---

[4] JSF is an international co-operative program consisting of the USA and eight foreign partners (UK, Italy, Netherlands, Turkey, Denmark, Norway, Canada and Australia). The partners have made various financial contributions to the development phase in return for an involvement in the program. However, the aircraft is a US design with Lockheed Martin as prime contractor for the program. Problems have arisen over the work allocated to the foreign partners, especially access to advanced technology (technology transfer).

(*juste retour*) rather than efficiency criteria, resulting in inefficiencies in both development and production and longer development times. An official UK study provided evidence on the inefficiencies of collaboration. It estimated that total development costs on collaborative projects were some 140% to almost 200% higher than comparable national programmes depending on the number of partner nations; but the UKs cost share on collaborative programmes was about one third of total development costs. On production, it was found that collaboration achieved scale and learning economies in the region of half of those on national projects with collaboration causing an average of 11 months delay [NAO (2001)]. A comparison of cost escalation and delays for the 4-nation Eurofighter Typhoon and other major UK weapons projects is shown in Table 5. Other projects show considerable cost escalation and delays compared with Typhoon. Such cost escalation and delays reflect the transaction costs of international contracting including the management of collaborative programs, the co-operative industrial arrangements and changed order quantities as well as budget constraints and delayed approvals by national partners [NAO (2001)].

5. Conclusion

Arms are one input into the military production function. Efficiency requires that inputs of capital (arms) and personnel (labour) are converted into the maximum available military output from these inputs. Here, there are issues about the incentives for individuals and groups in the armed forces and the procurement agency to behave efficiently as well as problems of measuring output. Ultimately, the armed forces determine the demand for arms, including new technology, and the procurement agency acting as an agent for the armed forces has to convert this demand into procurement and industrial policy with their impact on the national DIB. Questions arise as to whether the armed forces behave efficiently or whether they are inefficient budget-maximizing bureaucratic interest groups protecting their traditional monopoly property rights (e.g., air forces always demanding state of the art manned combat aircraft); and whether there is scope for efficiency-improving rivalry between each of the armed forces?

Defense firms have a long history of change and uncertainty. New technology has resulted in revolutions in arms and armed forces. Examples include the emergence in the twentieth century of manned aircraft, missiles and nuclear weapons. Continued technical change and the emergence of new threats (e.g., international terrorism: see Chapters 25 and 26) means that the future defense firm will be different from today's defense firm. Not all existing arms firms will survive and adjust to new technologies. Future aerospace firms will shift from manned combat aircraft to unmanned combat air vehicles, missiles and space systems and the electronics industry is likely to become more important providing the next generation of new entrants, systems integrators and prime contractors. New forms of industrial organization will also emerge characterized by buying rather than making, using international supply chains in a global economy leading to more international arms firms [Hartley and Sandler (2003)].

Costly, defense specific arms will create further challenges for governments and the DIB. Examples include aircraft carriers, main battle tanks, manned strategic bomber aircraft and nuclear-powered submarines. Increasingly, these are purchased in small numbers with long gaps in development between new generations of equipment. Where such systems require highly specific human and physical capital, there will be problems and costs in maintaining such assets during gaps in development. The absence of competition for these weapons means that their prime contractors will have to be treated as regulated firms requiring procurement agencies to review their regulatory policies for non-competitive contracts (c.f., regulation of natural monopolies).

Continued industry re-structuring amongst both prime contractors and suppliers means that national markets will be dominated by larger firms and monopolies. Competition remains an efficient 'policing' mechanism, but it will require a government's willingness to 'open-up' its national defense market to allow foreign firms to bid for arms contracts with possible adverse impacts on the domestic DIB.

For the future, there is no shortage of research questions in this area. More information is needed on the cost structure of arms companies in both development and production and the opportunities for economies of scale, learning and scope. The trade-offs for alternative industrial policies need to be identified and estimated. Further modelling work is needed of arms companies as regulated firms and the economics of non-competitive contracts and the profitability of such contracts. Comparisons are needed between the performance of arms companies and civilian firms. Project case studies are needed to compare, contrast and evaluate various procurement policies. Such studies need to include the major arms programs within each nation (e.g., F-22A, JSF, Typhoon, aircraft carriers, nuclear-powered submarines). Finally, there is a major research agenda studying technology spillovers in the defense and civil sectors, their transmission mechanisms and their market value.

References

Arrowsmith, S., Hartley, K. (Eds.) (2002). Public Procurement. International Library of Critical Writings in Economics, vol. 144. Elgar, Cheltenham.

BAe (1997). British Aerospace Annual Report and Accounts 1997. British Aerospace, Registered Office, Farnborogh.

BICC (2001). Conversion Survey 2001. Bonn International Centre for Conversion, Nomos Verlagsgesellschaft, Baden-Baden.

BICC (2005). Conversion Survey 2005. Bonn International Centre for Conversion, Nomos Verlagsgesellschaft, Baden-Baden.

Bos, D. (1996). "Incomplete contracting and target-cost pricing". Defence and Peace Economics 7, 279–296.

Braddon, D. (2004). "The future of the defence firm". Defence and Peace Economics 15, 499–586.

Burnett, W.B., Kovacic, W.E. (1989). "Reform of United States weapons acquisition policy: Competition, teaming agreements and dual sourcing". Yale Journal on Regulation 6, 249–317.

CBO (1997). A Look at Tomorrow's Tactical Airforces. Congressional Budget Office, Washington, DC.

CBO (2006). The Air Force's Proposal for Procuring F-22 Fighters. Congressional Budget Office, Washington, DC (March).

Chalmers, M., Davies, N.V., Hartley, K., Wilkinson, C. (2002). "The economic costs and benefits of UK defence exports". Fiscal Studies 23, 343–368.

DIS (2005). Defence Industrial Strategy. Ministry of Defence, The Stationery Office, Cmnd 6697, London (December).

DSB (2005). Management Oversight in Acquisition in Organizations. Report of the Defense Science Board Task Force, Department of Defense, Washington, DC (March).

DTI (2005a). The 2005 R&D Scoreboard: The Top 750 UK and 1000 Global Companies by R&D Investment. Department of Trade and Industry, London.

DTI (2005b). The Value Added Scoreboard: The Top 800 UK and 600 European Companies by Value Added. Department of Trade and Industry, London.

Dunne, P. (1995). "The defense industrial base". In: Hartley, K., Sandler, T. (Eds.), Handbook of Defense Economics, vol. 1. North-Holland, Amsterdam.

Eland, I. (2001). "Reforming a defense industry rife with socialism, industrial policy and excessive regulation". Policy Analysis 421, 1–18. December.

EU (2005). EU Governments Agree Voluntary Code for Cross-Border Competition in Defence Equipment Markets. European Defence Agency, Brussels. 21st November.

Fredland, J.E. (2004). "Outsourcing military force: a transaction cost perspective on the role of military companies". Defence and Peace Economics 15, 205–220.

GAO (2004). Tactical Aircraft: Changing Conditions Drive Need for New F/A-22 Business Case. US General Accounting Office, Washington, DC (March).

GAO (2006a). "Tactical aircraft. Recapitalization Goals are not Supported by Knowledge-Based F-22A and JSF Business Cases". US Government Accountability Office, Washington, DC (March).

GAO (2006b). Defence Acquisitions: Assessments of Selected Major Weapons Programs. US Government Accountability Office, Washington, DC (March).

Hartley, K. (1969). "Estimating military aircraft production outlays: The British experience". Economic Journal 79, 861–881.

Hartley, K. (1995). "Industrial policies in the defense sector". In: Hartley, K., Sandler, T. (Eds.), Handbook of Defense Economics, vol. 1. North-Holland, Amsterdam, pp. 459–489.

Hartley, K. (2002). "The economics of military outsourcing". Public Procurement Law Review 5, 287–297.

Hartley, K. (2006a). "Defence industrial policy in a military alliance". Journal of Peace Research 43, 473–489.

Hartley, K. (2006b). "Defence R&D: Data issues". Defence and Peace Economics 17, 169–175.

Hartley, K., Hooper, N. (1995). Study of the Value of the Defence Industry to the UK Economy: A Statistical Analysis for DTI, MoD, SBAC and DMA. Centre for Defence Economics, University of York and DTI, London.

Hartley, K., Sandler, T. (2003). "The future of the defence firm". Kyklos 56, 361–380.

Hartley, K., Hooper, N., Sweeney, M., Matthews, R., Braddon, D., Dowdall, P., Bradley, J. (1997). Armored Fighting Vehicle Supply Chain Analysis. Centre for Defence Economics, University of York and DTI, London (September).

Hartley, K., Braddon, D., Dowdall, P. (2004). "The UK defence electronics industry: Adjusting to change". Defence and Peace Economics 15, 565–586.

Hayward, K. (2005). "I have seen the future and it works: The US defence industry transformation – Lessons for the UK defence industrial base". Defence and Peace Economics 16, 127–141.

HCP (1986). The Defence Implications of the Future of Westland plc. Defence Committee, House of Commons Paper, HMSO, London.

Kirkpatrick, D.L. (1995). "The rising unit cost of defence equipment – The reasons and results". Defence and Peace Economics 6, 263–288.

Laffont, J., Tirole, J. (1993). The Theory of Incentives in Procurement and Regulation. MIT Press, Cambridge, MA.

Levine, P., Sen, S., Smith, R. (2000). "Arms exports, controls and production". Defence and Peace Economics 11, 443–548.

Liston-Heyes, C. (1995). "Bailouts and defence contracting: A necessary evil?". Defence and Peace Economics 6, 289–294.

Mantin, B., Tishler, A. (2004). "The structure of the defence industry and the security needs of the country: A differentiated products model". Defence and Peace Economics 15, 397–419.

Markusen, A., Serfati, C. (2000). "Remaking the military industrial relationship: A French–American comparison". Defence and Peace Economics 11, 271–299.

Middleton, A., Bowns, S., Hartley, K., Reid, J. (2006). "The effects of defense R&D on military equipment quality". Defence and Peace Economics 17, 117–139.

MoD (2002). "Defence industrial policy". Policy Paper 5. Ministry of Defence, London.

MoD (2005). UK Defence Statistics 2005. DASA, Ministry of Defence, London.

NAO (2001). Maximising the Benefits of Defence Equipment Co-operation. National Audit Office, London, HC 300 (March).

NAO (2005). Ministry of Defence: Major Projects Report 2005. National Audit Office, The Stationery Office, London.

OECD (2004). Main Science and Technology Indicators. OECD, Paris.

Pugh, P.G. (1993). "The procurement nexus". Defence Economics 4, 179–194.

Pugh, P.G. (2006). "Retrospect and prospect: Trends in cost and their implications for UK aerospace". Lecture to Royal Aeronautical Society, London.

Rand (2002). Final Assembly and Checkout Alternatives for the Joint Strike Fighter. Rand Corporation, Santa Monica, CA.

Review Board (1996). Report on the 1996 General Review of the Profit Formula for Non-Competitive Government Contracts. Review Board for Government Contracts, The Stationery Office, London (March).

Review Board (2004). Report on the 2003 General Review of the Profit Formula for Non-Competitive Government Contracts. Review Board for Government Contracts, The Stationery Office, London (March).

Sandler, T., Hartley, K. (1995). The Economics of Defense. Cambridge University Press, Cambridge.

Schooner, S. (2001). "The fear of oversight: the fundamental failure of businesslike government". American University of Law Review 50, 627–722.

SIPRI (1992). SIPRI Yearbook 1992. Oxford University Press, Oxford.

SIPRI (1993). SIPRI Yearbook 1993. Oxford University Press, Oxford.

SIPRI (2003). SIPRI. Yearbook 2003. Oxford University Press, Oxford.

SIPRI (2005). SIPRI Yearbook 2005. Oxford University Press, Oxford.

Turner, A.J.W., Chalmers, M.G., Hartley, K. (2003). "Estimated UK employment dependent on ministry of defence expenditure and defence exports". Defence Statistics Bulletin No. 5. DASA, Ministry of Defence, London.

Watkins, T.A., Kelley, M.R. (2001). "Manufacturing scale, lot sizes and product complexity In defense and commercial manufacturing". Defence and Peace Economics 12, 229–247.

Chapter 34

SUCCESS AND FAILURE IN DEFENSE CONVERSION IN THE 'LONG DECADE OF DISARMAMENT'

MICHAEL BRZOSKA

Institute for Peace Research and Security Policy at the University of Hamburg, Germany
e-mail: brzoska@ifsh.de

Contents

Abstract   1178
Keywords   1178
1. Introduction   1179
2. Elements for the analysis of defense conversion   1180
   2.1. Definitions of defense conversion   1180
   2.2. Post-Cold War resource release   1181
   2.3. Conversion as a class of transformations   1184
   2.4. Measures of conversion   1186
   2.5. Conversion and grand theories of economics   1188
3. Economic benefits and costs of conversion after the Cold War   1190
   3.1. Reorientation of government budgets   1190
   3.2. Reuse of military know-how as well as research and development facilities   1192
   3.3. Industrial conversion on the level of the firm   1194
   3.4. Re-employment of former soldiers and military personnel   1199
   3.5. Base conversion   1200
   3.6. Regional conversion effects   1201
   3.7. Net costs of weapons destruction   1202
4. Government policies for conversion   1203
5. Conclusions   1205
References   1206

Handbook of Defense Economics, Volume 2
Edited by Todd Sandler and Keith Hartley
© 2007 Elsevier B.V.   All rights reserved
DOI: 10.1016/S1574-0013(06)02034-5

Abstract

The 'long decade of disarmament' between the mid-1980s and the late 1990s provides ample evidence of the effects of a substantial defense downturn. The chapter starts out with a brief discussion of various concepts of conversion, focusing on a resource-reuse perspective. This is followed by sections on measuring success and failure in the conversion of resources and putting such measures into the perspectives of broader economic theories of change and growth. The body of the chapter is a review of the analytical and comparative literature analyzing the benefits and costs of the reuse of six types of resources, namely government spending, military research and development facilities, defense production facilities, armed forces and defense industry personnel, military land and military equipment, including chemical weapons and nuclear material. The chapter concludes with a brief analysis of various government policies aiming at improving the rate of success of conversion.

Keywords

defense conversion, allocative efficiency, industrial change, labor force and employment, land use, cost-benefit analysis

JEL classification: N40, O10, O19, P20

1. Introduction

Defense efforts have long been marked by cycles on ever-increasing plateaus of military spending. Resources are mobilized for military efforts in preparation for and during major conflict. After the end of major conflict, or the preparation of major conflict, armed forces and their supporting infrastructures, which can be called the 'military sector', are built down. The latest such built-down began in the late 1980s. Between 1986 and 1999, global military spending sank by about 34 percent, world-wide defense procurement spending was almost halved, global employment in the defense industry shrank from over 17 million to less than 9 million and the number of soldiers was reduced from 29 to 22 million [BICC (2003, pp. 151–153)].

This sharp reduction in demand for military services made large amounts of resources available for civilian reuse. However, such reuse is neither automatic, nor always economically efficient and sometimes not even possible. Still, there was great hope in the late 1980s and early 1990s in many countries of a 'peace dividend', a stimulus to economic and social development resulting from a shift of resources from military to civilian use. Such expectations were, at least partly, based upon the perception of such stimuli in earlier periods of large military built-downs, particularly in the US and Russia after the end of World War II [Albrecht (1979), Alexander (1994)].

The majority view of the 'long decade of disarmament', the period of large-scale reduction in military expenditures between the mid-1980s and the late-1990s, is disappointment. Expectations of major economic benefits of disarmament have not been met. However, shifts in resource use have occurred and have had identifiable benefits. The detailed analysis of conversion reveals different outcomes of resource reuse, depending on resource types, the particular region or country in question and specific circumstances of the resource transfer. Conversion has been successful, albeit not everywhere, with respect to all resources earlier employed in the military sector and not to the extent expected by many in the late 1980s and early 1990s.

This chapter is a review of the analytical literature on conversion, which flourished during the long decade of disarmament. It only sporadically takes note of narrative accounts of individual cases of successful conversion. While there is a wealth of such accounts in many countries, they are of only limited value for the more general assessment of the conditions and factors shaping the successes and failures of conversion, the focus of this chapter. The chapters thus attempts to provide an overview over what happened in the late 1980s and the 1990s, an assessment of prospects and options which might be helpful during the next downward cycle of armaments.

Section 2 sets the stage for the discussion of the challenges and outcomes of the conversion of particular categories of resources in Section 3. Section 2 begins with a brief discussion of definitions of conversion, followed by a subsection addressing the question whether conversion is different from other types of major shifts in resource use between economic sectors. In the next subsection I look at concepts of measuring success and failure in conversion before outlining why it is important to put the analysis of conversion within a broader perspective of economic thinking. Section 3 is an overview of the literature analyzing success and failure in various types of resource conversion. Most of the relevant literature is from the 1990s, when conversion attracted considerable attention, including in academic research. With the end of the long decade of disarmament, the interest in the topic dropped markedly. In Section 4, I briefly look at various attempts of government policies to affect the course of conversion, before concluding in Section 5.

2. Elements for the analysis of defense conversion

2.1. Definitions of defense conversion

While the core of defense conversion as transitions from military to civilian use of resources is universally accepted, conversion has been defined in various ways in the past, starting from a narrow to a very wide conception. The most useful of these for economic analysis is a resource-reuse perspective of inputs into military sectors.

In the late 1970s and early 1980s, that is before the post-Cold War military downsizing occurred, conversion was predominantly equated with the conversion of industries, or to be more exact, the substitution of military with civilian goods in production. Authors in various Western countries thought about the difficulties and likely effects of changing defense industries to civilian production, generally predicting smooth transitions and economic gains [Cooley (1980), Thorsson (1984), Schomacker, Wilke and Wulf (1987), Melman (1988)]. In planned economies, such as the Soviet Union, it was assumed that conversion could simply be ordered by the central planning organization and would result in major increases in civilian production as the defense sector was generally thought to be more efficient and technologically advanced than civilian sectors [Melman (1988), Albrecht (1979)].

When military downsizing seriously got under way in the late 1980s, it quickly became obvious that more was changing than just the demand for defense production. Other areas of potential and actual transfer of resources from military to civilian use began to receive attention, including from economists. Three areas stand out:

- the civilian reuse of land formerly occupied by armed forces, including the facilities on this land (military bases);
- the demobilization and reintegration of former soldiers;
- the civilian re-use of research capacities and know-how formerly in the military sector.

In the end, however, the economic analysis of these elements of conversion remained more limited than that of industrial conversion. Throughout the 1990s, the conversion of both military land and military personnel did not receive much analytical attention even though it was extensive in practice, as reviewed below in Section 3. More was written on the civilian reuse of know-how and research facilities, though with a strong focus on the United States and Russia, the two countries with by far the largest defense research efforts during the Cold War. But defense industry conversion remained the core of conversion studies, partly because there was the body of earlier literature which had already begun to analyze important features of conversion, such as the need to overcome specific military 'cultures', and partly because political interest was largest in industrial conversion as a result of large decreases in employment in many countries (see below, Section 4). However, civilian reuse of resources was considerably less in industrial production than in other types of conversion. The focus on industrial conversion both in much of the academic literature and in public perception contributed to the predominantly negative image of conversion mentioned in Section 1.

The partial approaches to the study of various types of conversion were first aggregated into a comprehensive approach by Edward Laurance and Herbert Wulf [Laurance and Wulf (1995), see also Brauer and Marlin (1992) and Fontanel (1994)]. They describe the military sector as using resources for the production of military output, that can equally well also be used to produce civilian goods and services. Resources they identify are money (government spending), technical know-how, people, land and weaponry. This is obviously quite similar to a traditional economic view of production combining factors such as land, labor, capital and know-how, with government spending added as a kind of subsidy to a production process not producing goods or services to be sold on markets.

A more fundamental approach to conversion is implicit in the work of Seymour Melman (1988) and some of his students, such as Lloyd Dummas (1995) and Michael Renner (1992). Melman argued that the specific style of working for military customers, such as long-term planning of production, secure profits and little competition, had infected large parts of industry and the economy in countries with high levels of military spending such as the Soviet Union and the United States. Conversion of the defense industries alone would therefore be neither sufficient nor, indeed, possible; rather conversion would have to encompass all of industry and the way it was doing business. While this describes pretty well what was needed in former socialist economies with high military spending, Melman's views were not confirmed for Western market economies in the 1990s.

Even further expansions of the concept of military conversion have been discussed, encompassing changes in belief systems ("conversion of the mind") or the way armed forces operate. Such broad conceptions may be closer to the original usage of the term conversion as a change in the religious conviction of a person, but they do not easily lend themselves to economic analysis [Laurance and Wulf (1995)]. The best definition for economic analysis, and therefore used here, is that of the actual civilian reuse of resources earlier employed in the military sector.

2.2. Post-Cold War resource release

Data are available for some of the resources used in military sectors worldwide. Data on the global military spending, the number of soldiers in armed forces and employment, is presented in Tables 1 to 3. The numbers indicate the extent of resource release in the

Table 1
Global military spending, 1987–2002 (military spending in billion US $, prices of 1999)

	1987	1992	1997	2002
World	1109	844	723	802
United States	417	357	287	321
Soviet Union/CIS	217	35	18	20
EU members	204	190	168	172
OPEC members	53	62	36	52
China	14	19	27	40
ASEAN members	13	13	15	14

Source: BICC (1996, 2004).

Table 2
Employment in arms production, 1987–2002 (million employees)

	1987	1992	1997	2002
World	17.8	14.1	8.9	7.7
EU members	1.4	1.2	0.8	0.7
Soviet Union/CIS	6.1	4.4	1.5	1.1
China	4.5	4.0	3.1	2.3
United States	3.6	2.8	2.2	2.6

Source: BICC (1996, 2004).

Table 3
Armed forces personnel, 1987–2002 (million soldiers)

	1987	1992	1997	2002
World	28.8	25.8	22.1	20.5
Asia except China and India	7.4	7.8	7.2	7.2
China	4.0	3.2	2.8	2.3
Africa	2.2	2.1	2.0	2.2
EU members	2.9	2.6	2.2	1.9
USSR/CIS incl. Russia	3.9	3.6	2.0	1.5
United States	2.3	1.9	1.5	1.5
India	1.3	1.3	1.2	1.2
America, South	1.2	0.9	1.0	0.9
Europe, East, except USSR/CIS	1.5	1.1	0.8	0.5

Source: BICC (1996, 2004).

'decade of disarmament'. They also give some information on sequences in the decline in military resource use and its geographical distribution.

Global military spending started to decline first and deepest (Table 1). The most important element of this decline was the collapse of defense spending in the former Soviet Union. The decline was also marked in other regions, such as Eastern Europe and the Middle East [BICC (1996, 2003)], but not universal. China, for instance, did not reduce military spending.

Global military spending began to increase again in the late 1990s. A large share of the increase is due to the growth in US defense spending beginning in 1990. While other major countries, such as China and Russia, also raised their military spending in the new decade, many other states did not. Member countries of the European Union and Asean, for instance, kept their levels of military spending.

Global arms production did not decline as rapidly as defense spending in the late 1980s and early 1990s, as measured by employment data (Table 2). However, in the mid-1990s, it started to shrink more than other indicators of military resource use. Global defense employment in 2002 was less than 40 percent of what it had been in 1987. Again, the reduction was most pronounced in the former Soviet Union and Eastern Europe. The reduction in employment in defense production continued into the new decade in all major arms producing countries and regions. The data indicates that capacities were not reduced proportionally to the reduction in demand, as expressed by military expenditures, in the late 1980s and early 1990s. A major cause of the continuing decline is improvements in labor productivity, particularly in China and, to a lesser degree, among EU member countries. The increase in defense spending in the United States led to increased employment in arms production, while in China more military demand was met with shrinking labor forces in defense industries. Chinese defense production was, and to a lesser extent continues to be, over-bloated at very low levels of productivity [Brömmelhörster and Frankenstein (1997)].

Military sectors in industrialized and developing countries are marked by quite different capital–labor ratios. Trends in global data on armed forces personnel are dominated by developments in Asia, and to lesser extent, Africa. Because the aggregate number of soldiers in these regions remained more or less constant over the 1990s, global totals did not shrink proportionally to decreases in military spending. Still, major force reductions occurred in many countries. Large scale reductions were recorded in the former Soviet Union, in Eastern Europe, among EU member countries, the United States, and also in some countries in Asia, such as China, and Africa, such as South Africa. In addition, large reductions in armed forces compared to the total number of soldiers occurred in many smaller countries, particularly after the end of local wars. In many of these countries, reintegration programs for former soldiers were conducted (see below).

The decline in resource use in the 'long decade of disarmament' of the late 1980s and early 1990s can be compared to other periods of major reduction in military spending. The post-World War II reductions were much more extensive in almost all aspects than the post-Cold War decline. For instance, the number of civilian

Table 4
Cycles in United States defense burden, 1940–2005

	First year of cycle	Defense burden in first year of cycle period	Last year of cycle	Defense burden in last year of cycle period
World War II	1940	1.7	1944	37.8
Post-Word War II built down	1945	37.5	1948	3.6
Korean War	1949	4.9	1953	14.2
Post-Korean War period	1954	13.1	1965	7.4
Vietnam War	1966	7.7	1968	9.5
Post-Vietnam War period	1969	8.7	1979	4.7
Second Cold-War build-up	1980	4.9	1986	6.2
Post-Cold War period	1987	6.1	1998	3.1
Global War on Terror build-up	1999	3.0	2005	3.9

Note: Defense cycles are defined by changes in the trend of the defense burden, that is the percentage share of defense outlays in national income.
Source: United States, Budget of the United States Government: Historical Tables Fiscal Year 2006, Washington, DC, 2005, http://www.gpoaccess.gov/usbudget/fy06/hist.html.

defense-related employees (government officials and employees in government-run arsenals) in the United States shrank from 2.6 million to 0.7 million between 1945 and 1950, while it only shrank from 1.1 million to 0.7 million between 1987 and 1997 [http://www.gpoaccess.gov/usbudget/fy06/hist.html, Table 17.2]. The comparison of the two cases is similar for West European countries. The situation was different, however, for Eastern Europe, particularly the Soviet Union. The Soviet post-World War II reductions were smaller than those in the West, while the post-Cold War cuts were considerably larger than in the West, as indicated in Tables 1–3.

Table 4 gives additional data useful for scaling the extent of military resource release in the 1990s, by listing cycles in defense spending in the United States. Cycles are defined through turning-points in the share of defense spending in national income, or defense burdens. During the first defense built-down period after the World War II between 1945 and 1948, the defense burden shrank by 90 percent. The second period of reduction occurred after the Korean War, with defense burdens falling from 13.1 percent to 7.4 percent. Defense burdens fell again post-Vietnam War between 1969 and 1979 by about 40 percent. The post-Cold War 'long decade of disarmament' was the fourth period of defense built-down noted in Table 4. It was somewhat deeper, measured by relative defense burdens, than the post-Korean War and the post-Vietnam War reductions, but less so than the post-World War II reductions.

2.3. Conversion as a class of transformations

A resource reuse definition of conversion makes it similar to other forms of resource shifts, for instance from agriculture to industry. Such transformations are occurring all the time, and are thus familiar to economic actors and standard to economic analysis, so why devote special attention to the reorientation of resources formerly used in military sectors?

Before this question is answered, it makes sense to further differentiate the concept of resource reuse. Resource reuse can occur at various levels of aggregation of resources, ranging from the asset to the whole economy. In the analysis of conversion, several such levels of aggregation have been used:

- The basic level is that of factors of production, namely, land, labor, know-how and capital, as embodied in physical assets, persons and particular pieces of land. These factors of production are used in the production of the goods that the military needs, such as tanks and airplanes as well as in the production of the service 'security', which the military itself is in the business of producing. The same factors, with the exception of weapons, are used for the production of civilian goods, such as cars, and services, such as health care, albeit in different mix and quality.

- Instead of looking at assets, people and land, researchers have also looked at higher levels of aggregation of resources, such as companies, military bases, sectors of the economy or even the whole economy. Different from conversion at the level of assets, persons and land, conversion will often only be partial at this level. In a company, for instance, some assets and some employees may change to the production of civilian goods, while military production continues in the company. The conversion literature is divided over calling such diversification in production conversion, with some authors contending that only the complete change-over of a company, in the example chosen here, constitutes conversion and others more willing to give it the label of partial conversion. In the end, this is a question of semantics.

- Another high level of aggregation used in the conversion literature is that of government spending. Military sectors are, for all practical purposes, dependent on government spending; without government spending the militaries of all countries cannot buy the factors of production they need. Obviously, if the money was not given to defense, it could be used for civilian purposes, for instance to pay for civilian activities, such as health care.

I now turn to the above-mentioned question of the difference between military conversion and other forms of resource transformation. How, for instance, is turning an arms-producing factory into one producing car tires different from transforming a shoe factory into one producing car tires?

Since the 1950s, a large body of literature has described and analyzed the differences in the production of goods and services between the military and the civilian sectors in Western countries [Alic et al. (1992), Markusen and Yudken (1992), Gansler (1995)], as well as in the former socialist countries [Cooper (1991), Gaddy (1996), Sapir (2000)]. There are various differences:

(a) Some differences are notable *cum grano salis* on the level of factors of production. Examples include higher pay for workers employed in arms production, considering their level of training and competence, highly polluted military land, including by dangerous things such as unexploded ammunition. Military capital, such as weaponry, tends to be technologically more complex, more expensive and less economical to use than comparable civilian capital (compare for instance the average military communication system with encryption and security measures to an average civilian telephone system). The primary reason is that in the military, and as a consequence often also in the defense industry and other elements of the military sector, the relationship between performance and cost differs from that in civilian sectors (with the exception of some civilian sectors with a high premium of performance, such as car racing): performance takes clear precedence over cost. An aircraft that is only marginally more agile than another one is vastly superior in a dog fight among fighter aircraft.

(b) Differences are also notable on the level of the production unit and the company. These differences largely stem, in addition to the performance/cost relationship, from other often-found characteristics of the military sector. One is the secrecy requirements. These lead to the compartmentalization of work and the separation of production activities. Another difference is that production is often performance but not cost-oriented. The lack of cost control via market performance is often compensated by control through large bureaucracies. As a consequence, labor forces, and in particular the mix of management capabilities, are different from that of a civilian production unit. The pervasiveness and effects of the differences between civilian and military production on the level of the production unit are disputed by some authors [Kelley and Watkins (1995), Watkins (1998)]. This is a major issue particular in the literature on industrial conversion which will be reviewed below.

(c) Can there be differences between government spending for military and civilian purposes? On this level of aggregation of resource use, the answer is particularly contested and dependent on assumptions about macroeconomic effects of government spending in general and the relations between income and investment in particular. This will also be reviewed below.

2.4. Measures of conversion

In the conversion literature, two main approaches are offered to measure whether conversion has occurred, one input-oriented and the other output-oriented. Again, it is quite useful to illustrate the differences with the help of the three levels of aggregation of resources developed above:

(a) On the level of production factors, an input-oriented approach makes much sense. Conversion has occurred when land formerly used by the military is now used for civilian purposes, whether as an industrial park or as a nature reserve; when people formerly with the military are now in civilian jobs; or when a machine earlier used to produce tanks is now used to produce trucks. Conversion is not occurring when the land stays idle, the people are unemployed and the machines are rusting away.

(b) On the level of government spending, a highly fungible form of 'resource', the focus of analysis generally is on the outcome of changes. A reduction in military spending signals that fewer factors of production are used for military purposes. However, this does not imply that labor, land, know-how and capital formerly employed in the military sector will now be used in the civilian sector. They may stay idle. Still, the economy can have benefited because the shift in spending may have led to increased demand for unemployed factors of production. This will happen whenever the productivity of the civilian factors of production is higher than those coming from the military sector. Successful conversion in the form of a higher rate of growth of national income after a shift in government spending can occur without transition of factors of production from military to civilian purposes.

(c) There are various ways to measure conversion on the level of the production unit or company. This can be illustrated with the simple example of the closure of a military base. A base comprises of land but also superstructures, such as roads and buildings, and employs people, for instance in services. Fairly often, civilian reuse of the land is accompanied by the destruction of at least part of the superstructure and a reduction in employment related to the use of land but an increase in economic activity due to more productive use of the land. What is the appropriate measure here? The extent of the reuse of physical assets and former employees? Or the higher income resulting from the civilian reuse of the land?

Both measures – the physical reuse of assets and employees and change in output – have been used in the analysis of the success conversion. There is no agreement in the literature which is to be preferred, as these measures address partly differing concerns. Physical reuse is of particular interest for those interested in demilitarization. Even if it does not result in increased economic activity, a reduction in military land-use is an indicator of a smaller military. Re-employment of individuals is the measure employees in the military sector and their unions are most interested in. For the overall fate of an economy, however, the output of goods and services is what is most relevant. And, as mentioned, the civilian reuse of resources may be less productive than the use of other available factors of production, and the combination of factors in a military production unit less productive than an alternative combination. This is most obvious in the case of industrial conversion. To turn an industrial plant producing weapons into a factory competitively producing civilian goods may require a complete change in production machinery as well as the work-force. With very little of the resources reused, the production unit may still be successful in terms of the change of output from weapons to civilian goods: in fact, the likelihood of such success is much higher. But conversion on the level of the company is not paralleled by much conversion on the level of production factors.

Debates about the proper measure for industrial conversion were particularly heated in the 1990s in the case of production units or companies only partially changing over to civilian production. A particularly interesting example of large-scale partial change-over to civilian production, the Chinese defense industry, is briefly discussed below in Section 3.3. Such diversification of production may be economically quite successful in terms of output but it can occur without much reuse of assets or people formerly used in military production and without demilitarization in terms of a reduced capacity to produce military goods. A decidedly 'demilitarization' view of conversion requires that military production is curtailed in a way to make resumption of such production costly. A decidedly 'economic' point of view of conversion is to look at the commercial success of a company. A decidedly 'social' point of view is to look at whether assets, but particularly people, are reemployed in civilian production. In addition to providing fodder to academic debate, the various points of view on how to measure success in conversion have also been important for the public perception of conversion, which has been dominated by the 'social' view of conversion, as well as for government policies (an issue I will come back to in Section 4).

The diversity of views on the measurement of conversion in production units and companies producing both civilian and military goods is symptomatic of a larger issue whose importance has been growing over time, namely the separation between civilian and military activities, which is at the core of the concept of conversion. The increasing importance of dual-use technologies and the changing nature of the production of military goods [Hartley and Sandler (2003)] as well as the changing tasks of armed forces (with peacekeeping and homeland defense becoming more important) lead to a growing share of what are essentially civilian goods and technologies in the procurement budgets of defense ministries. Armed forces are increasingly using 'off-the-shelf' civilian products, for instance electronics, and many tasks, such as logistics, that used to be performed within armed forces, are successively privatized [Wulf (2005)]. Economists have generally argued in favor of such 'commercialization' of military activities, with some warning about the substitution of public with private monopolies [Markusen (2003)]. In a world where dual-use and multiple-purpose is dominant, the resource-reuse perspective of conversion loses its relevance. If resources, assets and services rendered by armed forces are not military-specific any more, the only transaction costs or other 'friction' resulting from a reduction in defense spending would result from shifts in demand. Interestingly, this is rather similar to the prevalent ideas on the prospects of industrial conversion in command economies during the Cold War, which, however, proved to be wrong, as described in the following section.

2.5. Conversion and grand theories of economics

The discussion of measures of conversion and its success contains some elements of larger debates in economics such as on the putty-clay nature of capital and on the relations between demand and supply.

During the 1960s and 1970s, much thinking on conversion in Western market economies was Keynesian in the sense that the primary concern was with the effects of reduced demand. Supply-side issues, such as transaction costs of transferring resources from military to civilian use, received little attention. One of the reasons for this was the differing experience post World War II in the United States, where the end of the war initiated an economic boom, and in the United Kingdom, where this did not occur. The difference cannot be told as well as a supply side story – companies were largely geared towards military production on both sides of the Atlantic and a good deal of new technology had been developed in the United Kingdom as well as in the US – but is rather convincing in macroeconomic terms. The British consumers and government were broke, while in the US the release of forced savings and an expanding capital market allowed consumers to satisfy pent-up demand for goods. Post-World War II was also fairly successful in the Soviet Union, where planners ordered entities to produce civilian goods instead of military ones [Alexander (1990, 1994)].

When post-Cold War reductions of armed forces began, in the mid 1980s, economic analysis had predominantly shifted to a supply-side view. This showed in various strands of the conversion discourse. For instance, the 'peace dividend' analysis had little interest in macroeconomic imbalances resulting from reductions in defense spending. Furthermore, companies trying to convert from military to civilian production found that they were not competitive on civilian markets, neither in terms of technology nor in terms of cost. Much of the land that the military wanted to get rid of was not attractive to civilian investors, as it was polluted or lacked good connection to far away industrial centers. Soldiers retiring from armed forces found little demand for their particular skills and so on. Obviously, there were costs involved in conversion, but, so it was generally argued in the early 1990s, not resulting from macro- but from microeconomic 'frictions' [Brauer and Marlin (1992), Isard and Anderton (1992), Klein, Lo and McKibbin (1995), Fontanel (1994)].

Based on such supply-side considerations, an important conceptual innovation to thinking on conversion was made, seeing conversion as an investment process [Hartley et al. (1993), Fontanel, Samson and Spalanzani (1995), Intriligator (1996)]. Obviously, companies needed money and time to investigate civilian markets, reassess their production facilities, retool, retrain work forces and, above all, market their products and earn reputations in civilian markets. Land needed to be cleaned-up and, if necessary, connected by road to major industrial centers, former soldiers retrained. Not strictly conversion, but also of importance for government spending on defense versus civilian purposes: disarmament is a costly process, particularly with respect to chemical and nuclear weapons (see below). Because of all these investments, costs of conversion would first outbalance benefits, but, after some time, conversion would make a positive contribution to economic growth.

Other authors were concerned with the behavior of major actors, in particular defense companies, employing approaches borrowed from political economy. For producers of military goods, for instance, investment into improving factors of production and removing other barriers of entry into civilian markets is not the only option to deal with the problem of reduced military demand. Another option is to try to take a larger share of the shrinking market for military goods. The market for military goods remains highly politicized in most countries, and thus subject to lobbying. Avoiding the cost and effort to convert to civilian production is an attractive option for those producers who can exploit political rents resulting from political protection. This was extensively done in the Soviet Union, including during its final phase, when conversion was ordered by the leadership and at least some Soviet defense producing companies adopted seemingly strange but rational behavior [Gaddy (1996), Gonchar (2000)]. Ordered, for instance, to produce prams, they did so, but made from special steels, very heavy and expensive. Proving that they were not able to produce competitive goods, they continued to lobby the government for large military orders. A similar phenomenon of rent-seeking behavior can be detected in Western market economies. Some defense producing companies found it more lucrative to focus on lobbying in politicized, closed defense markets rather than to try to convert production lines to civilian use [Sapolsky and Gholz (1999), Markusen (1999)]. In some cases, companies even choose to close or sell profitable civilian production units in order to focus on defense production even in times of declining defense markets [Sapolsky and Gholz (1999)]. Managers at least partly acted on the advice of well-known defense industry executives, such as Norman Augustine of Lockheed-Martin as well as private consultants that conversion was "unblemished by success" [Adelman and Augustine (1992, p. 28)] while the particular expertise of defense companies lay in their technology niche and marketing skills [Lundquist (1992)].

3. Economic benefits and costs of conversion after the Cold War

In the following sections, the extent of post-Cold War conversion success will be briefly discussed on the major levels of conversion identified above.

3.1. Reorientation of government budgets

The reduction of military budgets in the late 1980s and early 1990s provided parliamentarians and governments in many countries with a range of options on how to reallocate the future savings in government spending. The predominant reaction was to use the savings to shrink government debt, followed by increasing other civilian budget lines, while reductions in taxes were not a frequent measure. A UN study, for instance, found that of 36 countries reducing their share of military spending in national income between 1985 and 1990 only 7 increased their shares of civilian government spending in national income over this period [United Nations (1995)]. Similar results were found for later periods [BICC (1996)]. In a few cases, the savings from reduced military spending were used for special projects or programs. In Germany, for instance, annual transfer of more than US $100 billion per year of public money to support the economy and social systems in the East was partly financed from reductions in defense spending. Working with budget figures and with shares of military spending for the United States in the 1990s, Gold estimated that about 60 percent of the drop in defense spending was converted into reducing the budget deficit and 40 percent into civilian spending [Gold (2000)]. In some countries, particularly former socialist states, economies contracted to such an extent that there were no savings which could be redistributed. After much hope in the late 1980s and early 1990s in a 'peace dividend' to be spent for favored purposes such as social or development assistance, the pendulum of popular opinion swung in the other direction. Instead of a 'peace dividend' some spoke of a 'peace penalty' of reduced economic activity [Brömmelhörster (2000)].

Results from econometric work with national income growth as an independent variable generally find positive contributions from reductions in military spending, but are highly dependent on modeling. The major exception to the general trend is the group of former socialist countries, where reductions in military spending contributed to the general downturn of the economy.

Summarizing a series of national country econometric studies [Gleditsch et al. (1996)], most of which used LINK-associated models to estimate macro-economic relationships, Bjerkholt writes: "Some of the early studies may have tended to exaggerate the economic benefits to be gained from reducing military expenditure, underestimating conversion problems and the short-term reallocations necessary to put resources tied up in military production and establishment to other uses. As the national studies show there are for most countries rather limited (or even negative!) short-run gains to be reaped from reduced armaments" [Bjerkholt (1996, p. 19)]. Smith, summarizing cross-national and international studies adds: "Like the national simulations, the overall conclusions of the comparative econometric studies and the global simulations are quite positive. There may be short-term adjustment costs, though these may be reduced by forward-looking behavior by private sector agents and financial markets, but there are long-term economic benefits as resources are reallocated from military to civilian uses" [Smith (1996, p. 357)]. Using their standard economic growth model, researchers associated with the International Monetary Fund found: "Recent data on military spending indicate a sizable peace dividend has been achieved since 1985. Results suggest that countries that have made sharp cuts in military spending typically have also reduced non-military spending as well as their fiscal deficit, thereby potentially encouraging private investment. There is indirect evidence that military spending cuts have also allowed countries to maintain or increase their social spending in the face of total spending cuts. In contrast, countries that have increased their military spending have also increased their other spending and sharply increased their deficits" [Clements, Gupta and Schiff (1996, p. 33), see also Bayoumi, Hewitt and Schiff (1995) and Knight, Loayza and Villanueva (1996)]. Estimating standard macroeconomic relationships for the United States in the 1990s and including the military burden as a variable, Gold estimated that about one fourth of the increase in income in the US in the 1990s was the result of the reallocation of military spending to other civilian spending categories, including debt reduction [Gold (2000)].

Comparative empirical studies of the 'peace dividend' suggest that the effects of reductions in military spending are predominantly positive, but are highly contingent on overall economic conditions and policies. The reductions of military spending – about 3 percentage points of national income in the global average between the mid-1980s and the mid-1990s – were not large enough to determine the fate of economies. Still, available econometric evidence suggests that in a large number of countries the reductions in military spending were associated with some, albeit often small, short-term increases in national income and larger long-term increases. However, because of the dependence on modeling and overall economic conditions, exact figures are not reliable. Most of the growth effect occurred through reductions in government budgets, while redistribution of government spending to civilian purposes, such as development assistance or social spending, remained exceptional.

3.2. Reuse of military know-how as well as research and development facilities

A large part of the stock of technical knowledge and know-how was used, during the last decades, for military purposes. During the Cold War somewhere between 20 and 25 percent of all public research and development spending was for such purposes [Albrecht (1979)]. Similar shares were noted for research facilities as well as scientists and technicians. Much of the military research effort was concentrated in the Soviet Union and the United States [Gummett et al. (1996)].

After the end of the Cold War, the demand for military know-how dropped considerably in many countries. In the United States, military research and development (R&D) spending was reduced by about 30 percent between the late 1980s and the late 1990s (when it began to grow again). In Russia, military R&D spending practically collapsed, to less than 10 percent of its earlier level during the same period of time [Gonchar (2000)]. So naturally questions were asked such as: can the know-how, the facilities and the scientists be used for civilian purposes, and how?

Several issues are shaping the answers, and will be discussed below. One is the comparative level of technological achievement in the military versus in the civilian sphere. Because of the special requirements of the military for secrecy, civilian and military technology often progressed separately and at differing speeds. A second issue is institutional barriers between military and civilian technology. To the extent that such barriers were high during the Cold War, and could be dismantled after the end of the Cold War, a large stock of know-how became available for civilian use. A third is the difference in direction between civilian and military research and development. Some of the knowledge acquired through military funding will only be useful for military purposes, and not for civilian ones. A fourth issue is the demand for civilian know-how – the reuse of facilities and reemployment of researchers will depend on such demand.

Practical experience in Western countries in the late 1980s demonstrated that the military sector was in front in some areas of technology, such as composite fiber structures and metal coating, while in most others civilian research had outpaced the military effort. This was particularly true for electronics but also for important frontiers of material science and aerospace. This finding contrasted with earlier experiences of a broad superiority of military R&D, leading to 'spin-off' from military to civilian applications, including in electronics and aerospace [Alic et al. (1992)]. The difference was largely due to the large increase in civilian R&D spending in the West after the end of World War II which had outpaced military R&D [United States Congress Office of Technology Assessment (1993)]. In the Soviet Union, military research was generally ahead of civilian effort, but only competitive with Western efforts in some areas of military technology [Bernstein (1994), Sapir (2000)].

Barriers between military and civilian research and development differed between types of technology, economic sectors and countries during the Cold War, depending on secrecy requirements but also institutional arrangements. For instance, in Germany most of military research and development was conducted in companies producing both for civilian and military markets, while in the US separation dominated with dedicated government research facilities doing most of the military research. In the Soviet command economy, the two spheres were strictly kept apart with the military side highly privileged in terms of resource allocation. The strict separation of military research and development had fostered technological solutions without any consideration of possible civilian use [Gonchar (1997)].

In most Western countries, much of the research and development effort became more integrated in the 1970s and 1980s. 'Spin-in' of know-how and technology developed for civilian purposes into military applications became more prominent. As a consequence, military R&D was redirected to focus more on those areas of technology lines with few civilian applications [Alic et al. (1992)]. As a result, many of those technologies, where military research facilities had an edge in the 1980s were defense-specific. One example would be stealth technology, which has few civilian applications [United States Congress Office of Technology Assessment (1993)]. No such 'spin-in' occurred in the Soviet Union, which in the 1970s and 1980s experienced an increasingly serious decline in its capability to produce civilian technological advances [Sapir (2000)].

While it has been argued that military research and development crowded-out civilian research and development during periods of the Cold War [Lichtenberg (1995)], the 1990s were a period of slack demand for civilian research and development in many countries. This was most dramatic in Russia, where public R&D spending during the 1990s dropped to less than half of its earlier level [Gonchar (2000)], but it also happened in other countries. In Germany, Japan and the United States, for instance, the share of civilian R&D in national income dropped in the early 1990s. Contrary to earlier cycles of reduced military spending, such as after World War II (adaptation of military technology to civilian goods) and during the post-Korean and post-Vietnam war built downs in the late-1950s and early 1970s (electronics, space), there were no similarly large new technology projects which could have led to a surge in demand for civilian research and development efforts. Political efforts to establish such projects in the early 1990s, for instance for energy-saving technologies, failed [United States Congress Office of Technology Assessment (1993)].

These considerations help to explain why the extent of reuse of knowledge, technical know-how and research facilities as well as the civilian reemployment of researchers earlier working for military purposes was, judging by the scant evidence available, rather limited. Examples of institutions struggling with finding customers for its civilian R&D include US government research facilities, where such efforts remained marginal despite dedicated government programs such as Cooperative Research and Development Agreements (CRADA), the German Fraunhofer Institute and the British Defence Evaluation and Research Agency (DERA) [BICC (1996, chapter 2)]. The latter became somewhat more successful when it was split up into a pure military research institutions and the commercially-oriented company QuinetiQ. In Russia, only small parts of the earlier vast military R&D complex have found civilian uses and unemployment remained very high throughout the 1990s [Gonchar (2000)].

The 1990s were no good period for the successful application of know-how earlier funded for defense-purpose. The specific characteristics of the defense sector, but even more so the tremendous growth of civilian R&D spending in the decades prior to the late 1980s, had made a good part of defense R&D lagging behind civilian efforts or highly focused on defense applications. This was particularly devastating for the large post-Soviet defense R&D sector, little of which could find useful civilian application.

3.3. Industrial conversion on the level of the firm

At its core, industrial conversion is industrial structural change but with some additional difficulties. Civilian production has to be expanded and new civilian markets have to be found. However, as mentioned above, since the 1950s a large body of literature has identified factors which make arms production different from civilian industries in Western countries as well as in former socialist countries. Secrecy requirements, performance orientation, cost negligence and narrow markets can combine to something like a 'defense industry culture', a set of mentalities but also organizational features of many typical defense firms [Markusen and Yudken (1992), Gansler (1995)]. Defense-typical organizational set-ups also set high barriers of exit from defense markets and entry into civilian markets. Defense production entities generally have larger research and development and administration departments than comparable civilian companies. Marketing departments are smaller. Customer orientation, cost awareness, etc. are underdeveloped. In the view of some analysts, socio-cultural factors, such as expectations of manager and workers, have been a major impediment to successful conversion [Feldman (1998, 1999)].

Differences between typical defense and civilian firms are greater in some countries than in others, as they are reified by bureaucratic procedures and company practices. As mentioned before, separation was pervasive in the Soviet Union. In Germany, the government has tried to encourage civil–military interactions within companies since the mid-1950s, without eliminating tight control over production [Brzoska, Wilke and Wulf (1999)]. For the United States, differing claims are made. While the majority of authors [Markusen et al. (1991), Lundquist (1992), Adelman and Augustine (1992), Gansler (1995)] argued that civilian and military production was separated by 'firewalls', Kelley and Watkins (1995) maintained that there was hardly any difference and production largely integrated. The main cause for these differing views is the focus of attention on large defense versus small multi-market companies. Much of the work of Markusen and associates was on prime contractors of the Pentagon that is mostly larger companies with high shares in defense production while Kelley and Watkins (1995) took a broader view, with most of their empirical evidence dominated by smaller companies.

Distinct differences can also be noted for particular branches of the defense industry and firms in different positions in the supply chain. For instance, because of the prevalence of dual-use technologies, companies in defense electronics are generally rather similar to civilian firms in the same industrial sector, at least more so than producers of artillery or heavy vehicles which primarily produce defense-specific goods [Alic et al. (1992)]. Down the supply chain, secrecy and administrative requirements decrease while cost-consciousness increases [Feldman (1997)].

Transition from socialist economies to market economies has created additional problems for conversion, especially in Russia, Ukraine and Belarus which had highly militarized industrial sectors. Defense companies undergoing conversion suffered from the same problems of transition as civilian companies: weak local demand, strong international competition, unclear legal environments, volatile political structures and low levels of government support. In addition, however, they had to cope with the particular problems inherited from the Cold War period described above. For a time, the privatization of defense industries was seen as the best way to cope with these structural problems. However, privatization was often incomplete and inconsistent as the government was not willing, for social and military reasons, to yield full control of defense companies to private entrepreneurs. The organizational inconsistencies, the sheer size of conglomerates and conflicting policies on conversion and defense production encouraged rent-seeking by company managers. Whether to pursue arms production or conversion sometimes depended more on the signals received from those capable of distributing favors and money, than on what might be economically efficient. However, it also created a different kind of civil–military integration. More than in Western countries, the capability to invest in conversion was often linked to continued weapons production, especially for export markets. As a result, instead of being a boon for civilian economic development, as was expected during socialist times, defense firms in the former socialist countries turned out to be a burden, with only few exceptions, such as the technologically-advanced Russian space industry and companies quick and able to adopt new Western technologies for Eastern European markets [on Eastern Europe see for instance Kiss (1997); on Russia: Gaddy (1996), Sapir (2000), Gonchar (2000)].

Most studies of industrial conversion rely on single cases or a few case-studies. A great many case-studies were published in the 1990s [Gleditsch et al. (1999)], including cases where the change-over from military to civilian production resulted in growth at the company, such as US electronics company Texas Instruments, GPS-system innovator Magellan in the United States, Oerkikon-Bührle of Switzerland or EPRO of Germany [BICC (1997)]. There were also cases where it was accompanied by hard times and even bankruptcy, as in the case of Deutsche System Technik in Germany and many companies throughout Eastern Europe [BICC (1997)].

Qualitative studies based on larger datasets are rare; even less frequent are quantitative studies. A major reason is the scarcity of appropriate data. Markusen and collaborators collected data on a large number of US defense producers [Markusen and Yudken

Table 5
Changes in military and civilian sales for the largest arms-producing companies, 1990–1995

Groups of companies	Number of companies	Changes in sales 1990–1995, in billion current US dollars	
		Military	Civilian
Companies which lost arms sales 1990–1995:			
Companies which were able to fully compensate lost arms sales with increased civilian sales	27	−16	+155
Companies which were able to partly compensate lost arms sales with increased civilian sales	10	−3	+1
Companies which lost both arms sales and civilian sales	13	−13	−47
Sub-total	*50*	*−31*	*+109*
Companies which gained arms sales 1990–1995:			
Companies which increased both arms sales and civilian sales	30	+13	+162
Companies which increased arms sales and lost civilian sales	10	+8	−14
Sub-total	*40*	*+20*	*+148*
Total for the above companies	**90**	**−11**	**+257**

Note: Data for 90 of the 100 hundred largest arms producers worldwide in 1995 in the SIPRI arms industry database for which sufficient data was available.
Source: BICC (1998, p. 198).

(1992), Oden and Bischak (1995), Feldman (1997), Oden (1999)]. They found a mixed picture of both defense firms diversifying into civilian markets and firms focusing on defense production in shrinking markets as 'pure play' companies only active in defense markets. Their analysis stresses the choice of managements, as well as incentives set by the US government. Kelley and Watkins (1995) collected data from a sample of almost 1000 randomly selected companies from what they called the 'machine-intensive durable goods sector' (MDG) which included all the major branches of conventional arms production. Based on their data, they argue: "If our findings for the MDG sector hold true for manufacturing as a whole, we see few technical or organizational barriers to converting most defense plants to further serve commercial markets" [Kelley and Watkins (1995, p. 530)]. Another type of data which has been used to analyze conversion on the level of companies is the SIPRI data for the largest 100 arms producers worldwide [BICC (1996, 1998), Brzoska, Wilke and Wulf (1999), Sköns and Weidacher (1999)]. Using these data, Table 5 shows that companies raised their sales of civilian goods by 257 percent in the first half of the 1990s, while sales of military goods shrank by 11 percent. This would indicate an overwhelming conversion success. But this is a premature judgment. When sales data are accumulated according to whether companies reduced or increased arms production between 1990 and 1995, as is also done in Table 5, not much of a difference is noted between companies reducing or increasing

Table 6
Output dynamics across defense industrial branches in Russia, 1991–1999

	1999 as a percentage of 1991	
	Military output	Civilian output
Aircraft	16	32
Shipbuilding	50	39
Radio	34	33
Communications	9	14
Electronics	7	23
Ammunition and special chemicals	17	16
Space	41	78
Nuclear	34	104
Defense complex total	*19*	*39*

Source: Adopted from BICC (2001, p. 61).

military sales. 40 companies, which did not reduce arms sales, were able to increase their civilian sales by a total of 148 percent while 50 companies reducing their military sales increased their civilian sales by only 109 percent. The lower increase in civilian sales by companies losing arms sales than by companies increasing arms sales is largely caused by 13 companies losing both military and civilian sales. It seems that success in expanding civilian sales was not influenced by changes in the civilian–military production mix of companies but rather by others factors, discussed below.

A few countries have official statistics on conversion, or conversion-related indicators. These are countries with an administratively distinct defense industry. Russia publishes data for the 'military industrial complex', the bureaucratically designated defense industry, distinguishing between military and civilian production. Table 6 reports data for the 1990s, which show a decline in both military and civilian production. Civilian sales had in 1999 contracted to 39 percent of their 1991 volume, while defense sales were down to 19 percent of what they had been in the early 1991. The end of government protection revealed that the military–industrial complex was only competitive in few civilian markets, particularly those served by nuclear and space industries.

A conversion world by itself was created in China beginning in the 1980s. China has published official numbers on various aspects of conversion, such as the share of goods produced in 'conversion companies' in particular markets, or the share of civilian production in defense companies [Brömmelhörster and Frankenstein (1997)]. Judging by these numbers, conversion has been highly successful. According to Chinese data, civilian output in defense companies in 1979 was 8 percent, rising to 40 percent by 1985, and for 1997 it was announced that 80 percent of the defense industries output were civilian goods [Wie (1997)]. However, it is far from clear what these figures imply [Berthélemy and Deger (1995), Brömmelhörster and Frankenstein (1997)]. Companies producing and selling in 'conversion markets' are generally subsidized. The rationale for such subsidies is to maintain surge capacities in case of war – leading Brömmelhörster and

Frankenstein (1997) to the suspicion that conversion in China is an instrument to keep levels of military–industrial preparedness high.

For the general picture of industrial conversion, the following factors, drawn from the work of the group around Ann Markusen [Bischak (1997), Markusen and Costigan (1999), Markusen, DiGiovanna and Leary (2003)] and at BICC [BICC (1998), Brzoska (1999, 2001)] seem particularly relevant for explaining the differences in the success of industrial conversion among countries, sectors and companies:

- *General economic setting.* Conversion as general industrial change was highly dependent upon new opportunities and markets which are the signs of healthy, growing economies.
- *Market position.* Arms producers were better in some markets – government markets, for instance, where marketing is similar to the defense market, or those for large-scale complex systems, such as space. Technology monopolies were an obvious advantage for entering civilian markets.
- *Prior exposure to civilian markets.* It seems to have helped if companies already have experience in civilian markets, in terms of marketing, management and 'company culture.' Related to this is the nature of technology produced in the firm and whether or not it was directly applicable to civilian markets or needs costly adaptation.
- *Flexibility.* Since organizational structures, company culture, etc. have to be changed, a high degree of flexibility of those in the organization was required. Alternatively, change had to be brought about by an exchange of personnel – for instance, fewer administrators and more marketing personnel. Inflexibility is often cited as a major factor inhibiting conversion success.
- *Investment.* More detailed analysis of the success and failures of industrial conversion confirm the view of disarmament as an investment process [Hartley et al. (1993)]. Money was needed for new machinery, training, etc., and to bridge periods of slow sales. Often, outside funding was needed for investment, so the willingness of outside creditors, such as banks, to finance conversion became crucial. In the Russian case, arms exports were used by some companies to fund conversion.
- *Commitment.* Commitment by management and employees has been found to be of significant importance in case studies. The opposite position, an unwillingness to pursue conversion for ideological reasons, or because it runs counter to strategic decisions of a company, was a major inhibition for conversion.

Overall, industrial conversion in the 1990s presents a mixed picture, in at least two senses. First, there is a large variety of outcomes of conversion efforts, ranging from bankruptcy of firms to major success in civilian markets. Second, few firms opted for complete conversion in the sense of exiting the military market. The predominant strategy of companies trying to compensate for shrinking defense sales was one of diversification. Companies stayed as much as possible in defense markets, not the least in order to be able to fund the costly and time-consuming change-over from military to defense production.

3.4. Re-employment of former soldiers and military personnel

Resettlement from military service to civilian life can involve considerable upheaval extending across all aspects of the life not only of the individual but also of their family. Different armed forces have different traditions with respect to exposing personnel to such change. In most Western armed forces, for the majority of soldiers service is seen as only temporary employment, which should be followed by a civilian job, for which it is a task of the armed forces to prepare personnel. An extensive literature exists on the question how military service affects later civilian earnings in the civilian sector. However, results are not conclusive [Warner and Asch (1995), Loughran (2002)]. 'Bridging' a military career through training relevant for civilian jobs seems to result in improving the job-market prospects of soldiers [Goldberg and Warner (1987), Lakhani (1998)]. In the former socialist countries, as well as many developing states, professional soldiers tended to be in the services for their whole working life. In the 1990s, these regular patterns were in upheaval. Both in Western and Eastern countries armed forces drastically reduced personnel, including through early termination of contracts.

The chances of reemployment in the civilian economy are highly dependent on civilian labor markets as well as the skills of former military personnel. Studies of Western industrialized countries generally have found high rates of former military personnel finding civilian jobs within comparatively short periods of time. In a survey of 764 former army and navy personnel by Hooper and Stephens in the mid-1990s, over 80 percent of respondents had found a civilian job within 6 months (see Table 7). However, skills attained in the armed forces were only useful in a majority of cases, but not for all respondents [Hooper and Stephens (2000)]. Re-employment prospects of former military personnel in Eastern Europe have been much worse, even though former military personnel, according to anecdotal evidence, had a better chance of finding a job than similarly educated former employees in civilian positions [Pauwels (2000), Heinemann-Grüder (2002)].

A particular challenge to conversion is the reintegration of former combatants into civilian economies after the end of wars in developing countries. Demobilization, Disarmament and Reintegration (DDR) programs have been designed and implemented

Table 7

Source of skills used in civilian job, sample of former United Kingdom military personnel

Civilian job compared with service job	Royal navy		Army	
	No.	%	No.	%
Not use service skills	40	20.7	86	24.1
Use general skills	38	19.2	133	37.2
Use specific skills	116	60.1	138	38.6
Number of responses	193	100.0	357	100.0

Source: Hooper and Stephens (2000).

in a large number of post-War situations. Evaluations of such programs confirm the importance of general economic improvements as the prime condition for successful economic reintegration of former combatants [Colletta, Kostner and Wiederhofer (1996), Kingma (2000), Pauwels (2000)].

3.5. Base conversion

Base closures are predominantly motivated by the savings resulting from a streamlined base structure for defense budgets. The United States General Accounting Office (2002, p. 42), for instance, estimated net savings of US $16 billion for four rounds of base closures up to Fiscal Year 2002. Often, base closures are strongly opposed by local communities because of their local economic effects. Bases generally offer employment opportunities for locals and local economies benefit from purchases by soldiers stationed on a base. The civilian reuse of bases therefore often is measured by the contribution it makes to the local economy in terms of employment and purchases of goods and services.

The economic costs and benefits of the reuse of military land and superstructures is the least researched area of conversion. Still, it seems safe to say that in some respects it has been the most successful in terms of contributions to economic growth, at least in Western industrialized countries. Studies for the United States [Dardia et al. (1996), Accordino (2000)] as well as countries in Western Europe [Jauhiainen et al. (1999), Baltes (2004)] show high degrees of economically productive civilian re-use of military land, particularly by the manufacturing and service sectors. In the German State of North-Rhine Westphalia, for instance, 271 military sites comprising 8350 ha were transferred to civilian users in the 1990s. 84,000 soldiers had been stationed on these bases. In addition to the employment effects resulting from reduced demand, 26,000 civilian employment positions were directly lost through base closure. Nearly all of the former military land had been converted to some civilian use, ranging from a railway test facility to university dormitories within five years. In a survey of all 'conversion communities' in the State made in 2000, the creation of 9480 new jobs on the conversion sites was recorded, with the expectation of increasing this number substantially as more private investment was attracted to various sites. However, this had required substantial funding of about €300 million for planning and zoning, environmental clean-up and rebuilding of infrastructure The exact cost is difficult to note as in many cases, such as housing, improvements in superstructure were funded that would not have been necessary for conversion to occur but improved the market value of the converted land [Schirowki (2000)]. Even more impressive results are reported for the United States. The United States General Accounting Office confirmed data from the Department of Defense showing that by 2001 about 62 percent (79,740 jobs) of the 129,649 jobs lost at major bases closed in four rounds of base closures since 1998 had been replaced at these sites. These figures did not include jobs lost or created in the areas surrounding the realigning or closing bases [United States General Accounting Office (2002, p. 42), see also Dardia et al. (1996)]. An attempt to measure all employment effects was made by Hooker and Knetter (1999). They used a counter-factual approach, comparing actual county-level employment with the trend prior to changes in base locations. Differences were not statistically significant, suggesting no net job losses. Poppert and Herzog (2003) examined the indirect employment effects of major base closure using a model of private non-farm employment growth at the county level. They concluded that the civilian re-use of land led to both higher direct employment on the former bases and higher indirect employment in the surrounding communities. Theses effects already started to take root prior to the actual release of military land, which Poppert and Herzog explain with "community optimism (following apprehension) and BRAC-related federal assistance" (2003, pp. 479–480).

Land re-use in Eastern Europe and developing countries has been much slower, largely because land was abundant and the costs of making military land usable were often high [Cunnigham (1997), Jauhiainen et al. (1999)]. However, there are important exceptions, such as Subic Bay, a former US military base in the Philippines, which became a major trade hub and production zone, or military bases in the former US occupied Panama Canal Zone, which have attracted major investment [BICC (1996, chapter 5)].

The re-use of military land is a prime example for the general dependence of the success of conversion on the combination of general economic factors, in particular the scarcity of a resource with the capital invested in it. Where land was scarce, such as in many regions surrounding bases in Western Europe and the United States, it was in high demand when it was released for civilian use. In other regions, of the world, conversion success was also possible, however, mostly because of the reuse of infrastructure, such as building and harbor facilities.

3.6. Regional conversion effects

Both the defense industry and bases of armed forces worldwide have traditionally been concentrated in specific regions within states for a variety of security, political and functional reasons. In Germany, for instance, defense industry concentration is relatively high in Baden-Württemberg, Bavaria and Bremen, while military bases are concentrated in Schleswig-Holstein, Rhineland-Palatinate and Lower Saxony. In Slovakia, defense industrial activity has been highly concentrated in the 'military triangle' formed by large enterprises in Dubnica, Detva and Martin in central Slovakia. Russian defense industry was concentrated in St. Petersburg, around Moscow and in the Urals. Chinese defense industry is particularly dense in Beijing, Hubei and Liaoning [Markusen and Oden (1994), Kapstein (1995)].

Communities with high concentrations of defense-related activities and employment are, on the one hand, over-proportionally affected by reductions in defense expenditure but often can also provide cushioning effects, depending on the general state of the economy in the region, the flexibility of labor markets and the structure of employment [Elsner (1995), Brzoska and Markusen (2000)]. Economic research on regional conversion has focused on overall employment effects, generally including secondary effects on local employment for sub-contractors and local suppliers and tertiary effects on local retail and service jobs through the use of 'regional multipliers'. Estimates of such regional multipliers in Western countries for the 1990s are in the 1.5–2.0 range [Commission of the European Communities (1992, pp. 97–98), Brömmelhörster (1994), Braddon and Dowdall (1996)].

Studies on the regional reemployment of persons formerly in the defense sector have also been done, for instance in the United Kingdom, in Germany, the United States and Russia. They show that former defense industrial workers had a higher success rate in finding reemployment than other workers of similar qualification [Markusen and Oden (1994), Brzoska and Markusen (2000)]. Reasons for this labor market observation may include a perception by employers that the former defense workers had worked in highly bureaucratized environments and with comparatively new machinery. However, skills developed or required for defense work are not always transferable to alternative employment. A study of defense industry redundancies in the Southwest England region, for example, concluded that relatively few people were able to find jobs either of the same type as their previous defense job or which enabled them to use defense skills. In particular, the study found that in core defense skill areas of engineers and technologists – such as metal machining, electronics and metal working trades – between 40 and 60 percent were re-employed in less skilled jobs [Hooper et al. (1996)). In the United States, nearly across the board, the impact of cuts in defense industry employment in heavily defense-dependent regions – such as Los Angeles–Long Beach and St. Louis – was mitigated by the growth of the service sector [Oden (1999)].

3.7. Net costs of weapons destruction

The reduction of military spending and armed forces after the end of the Cold War made large numbers of conventional weapons redundant. In addition, agreements on limitations of the numbers of heavy weapons in Europe, the elimination of chemical weapons worldwide and for reductions of nuclear weapons became possible. The disposal of these surplus weapons can also be considered part of the overall conversion balance of the 'long decade of disarmament'.

The destruction of conventional weapons is fairly cheap. Small arms, such as rifles, can be crushed by steam rollers, and even heavy equipment, such as tanks, can be taken apart for a few thousand dollars a piece. On the other hand, little money can be made from selling scrap metal because many different materials are used. Ships are more expensive to destroy, largely because of their use of hazardous material, such as asbestos, but also have some scrap value. A medium-sized warship, for instance, consists of several thousands tons of steel which can be sold. The cost of the destruction of ammunition depends on how environmentally safe the disposal is done [Renner (1996), BICC (1997), Kopte and Wilke (1998)].

Much higher costs are associated with the disposal of chemical and nuclear weapons. In 2004, it was estimated by the US General Accounting Office (US GAO) that the overall cost of destruction of 31,000 tons of chemical agents in the US arsenal in the early 1990s would accumulate to over $25 billion [US GAO (2004a)]. The price tag for the destruction of the even larger Russian stockpile was estimated at about half this amount, though destruction had only started and cost estimates were less reliable than in the US case. Direct economic benefits of chemical weapons disposal, for instance through reduced costs of guarding facilities, are very limited but the elimination of chemical weapons precludes potentially high costs of illegal use or unintentional leakage [Patel (2005)]. The cost of the disposal of nuclear weapons cannot be estimated with any certainty, partly because civilian re-use of weapons-grated plutonium and uranium is technically possible [Willett (2003)]. While large quantities of highly-enriched uranium have been diluted and used in civilian power reactors, the future of plutonium is more open. Due to proliferation risks, it is unlikely that it will be politically acceptable to use plutonium in the civilian nuclear industry outside of the major nuclear weapons powers. However, all methods for disposal of weapons-grade plutonium are very costly [US National Academy of Sciences (1994)]. The largest price tags related to nuclear weapons, however, are put on nuclear clean-ups of production facilities. The cost of the clean up of the largest facility in the US nuclear weapons complex, the Hanford site in Washington State alone, has been estimate at US $56 billion [US GAO (2004b)].

4. Government policies for conversion

A number of countries had specific conversion policies in the 1990s and a few, such as China and Russia, continued to have them into the new century. Western countries also supported conversion in former Warsaw Treaty member countries. The prime rationale for conversion programs worldwide was to counter adverse effects of the reduction in military spending on local and regional economies, particularly and their outcomes. Interestingly, support for the conversion of land, and former soldiers, has been more frequent than support for industrial conversion in Western states while the opposite is true for former socialist states.

Fundamental views on the proper role of government in the economy have also shaped the assessment on the necessity, usefulness or futility of government programs for the support of conversion. Government intervention justified on the basis of 'disarmament as an investment process' will focus on high risks and other areas of conversion where private actors are not providing amounts of capital to be judged by public decision-makers as sufficient, for instance, for the civilian re-use of contaminated former military land. From a political economy perspective, additional government intervention is justified where actors are seeking private gains only where there are social benefits, for instance in the civilian application of technology developed for military purposes in defense companies. Those who are skeptical of the governments' capability to redress market failures of the kind described will also be wary of conversion policies. The predominance of neo-liberal economic policies in most countries in the late 1980s and 1990s partly explains why conversion programs remained marginal, with very few exceptions.

The Soviet leadership made conversion a focus of industrial policy in the late 1980s, with poor results [Cooper (1991), Sapir (2000)]. The civilian goods that defense companies produced in fulfillment of plans often were not competitive on civilian markets. Russia, and during the early 1990s the Ukraine, continued to issue conversion programs, setting indicative goals of civilian production for the defense industry but not providing adequate funding for investments needed to fulfill the goals [Gonchar (1997, 2000)]. China, as mentioned, has had the most extensive conversion program worldwide, mixing regulations for and subsidies to state-owned defense companies with protection of some market to achieve a high rate of conversion albeit at unknown economic costs [Brömmelhörster and Frankenstein (1997)].

The largest program in monetary terms promoting the transfer of technology from military to civilian applications was launched by the Clinton Administration in early 1993. Its central element was the Technology Reinvestment Program (TRP) which aimed at helping defense companies to market their technologies in civilian markets [Bischak (1997)]. Other countries with similar, albeit much smaller, programs, include the United Kingdom, which created a Defence Diversification Agency in 1998 and France, where the government has supported the creation of 'societées de conversion' to help companies market civilian technology spinoffs [Serfati et al. (2001)]. No systematic evaluations of these programs seem to have been made. Positive assessments found in the literature [Bischak (1997), Reppy (1999)] are based primarily on anecdotal evidence and interviews with representatives of companies benefiting from these programs.

In addition to national, there were regional programs to support conversion. A number of Western industrialized countries had programs to support regions in distress due to defense downsizing, funded from national or regional governments. The largest of such programs were those of the European Union (PERIFRA, KONVER I, KONVER II) amounting to more than €1 billion between 1992 and 1999. These programs were able to cushion some of the effects of base closures through a variety of measures, but less so with respect to defense industry downsizing [Brömmelhörster (1999)].

While studies comparing different conversion policies are rare it seems that those among countries in Western Europe which had more active government policies, such as France and Germany, had a higher rate of re-use of both land and industrial facilities than the United Kingdom with less active policies [Brömmelhörster (1999), Brzoska, Wilke and Wulf (1999)]. However, it is unclear whether this was not offset in terms of employment by a greater flexibility in local labor markets. Comparisons of regions with more or less active conversion policies in the United States yield similar inconclusive results with employment resulting from government assistance in some cases surpassed by unassisted conversion success in other regions [Oden (1999), Accordino (2000)]. The comparison between China and Russia clearly shows that the active policy in China led to more conversion than the policy chaos in the 1990s in Russia. However, this came at some cost to the Chinese economy [Brömmelhörster and Frankenstein (1997)].

Except for the case of China, conversion programs in the 1990s were too small to have more than marginal effect on conversion success. Still, there is than some evidence from those cases where support was provided, such as in the US dual-use program and the EU KONVER program that more dedicated government assistance would have resulted in more conversion, particularly in economically-disadvantaged regions.

5. Conclusions

Downsizing of military sectors in the late 1980s and 1990s, the 'long decade of disarmament' was deeper than at any other period since the post-World War II cuts. Disarmament was global, with Eastern Europe and particularly the countries of the former Soviet Union experiencing the most extensive reductions in relation to the earlier sizes of military sectors.

Post-Cold War cuts in global military spending allowed for major savings compared to what would have been spent at the Cold-War levels. The share of defense expenditures in global income shrank from just over 6 percent to just over 3 percent between the mid-1980s and the late-1990s. In many countries, the savings on defense expenditures could be used for civilian purposes. The predominant use was for the reduction of government spending and public debt. In other countries, however, particularly in Eastern Europe and the countries of the former Soviet Union, the cuts in military spending contributed to the general down-turn of the economies.

Large-scale reductions in military spending and armed forces made resources of various types available for civilian reuse, ranging from land to facilities for research and development. Overall, the conversion record of the 'long decade of disarmament' beginning in the mid-1980s and ending in the late 1990s is mixed. Conversion seldom proved to be an automatic transfer of resources. Rather, investments had to be made into the reuse of land, the retooling of factories and the retraining of personnel prior to civilian use. Successful cases of conversion, defined as the productive re-use of resources for civilian purposes, can particularly be found in the area of base conversion. But there are also millions of former soldiers and employees in defense production who found gainful employment in the civilian sector of the economy, and numerous companies which expanded civilian sales by reusing machinery, land and people earlier employed for the production of military goods.

Still, expectations in the late 1980s and early 1990s of a big peace dividend, or a major economic push through the civilian use of military technology proved illusory. In the end, conversion was much less spectacular, much more 'normal' transition and therefore much more dependent on general economic conditions, than had been assumed. Resource reuse was most successful in Western economies, particularly the United States, which had expanding economies. It was least successful in former socialist countries where economies contracted. Where resources, such as land, were scarce, they were used; where they were abundant, or where investment for civilian use were high, they were abandoned. Compared with such fundamentals, the specifics of military conversion only had minor influence on the rate of conversion success in the 1990s.

The study of conversion, which had its heyday in the 1990s, was good in describing what happened in the 'long decade of disarmament' but less so in analyzing the causes of why conversion was successful in some cases and not in others. A major reason for the inconclusiveness of much of the analytical research is the relative small scale of conversion compared to other changes, such as transformation of former socialist economies and the globalization of production. In the end, after more than a decade of research, even basic questions, such as how different defense sectors are from the rest of the economy, remained contentious.

Still, some results of conversion research from the 1990s will be helpful for the next period of downsizing. Hopes for an identifiable 'peace dividend' beyond the savings from reduced defense spending should be lower than they were in the late 1980s and early 1990s. In particular, it should be clear that benefits from civilian exploitation of military research and technology and the change-over of companies from civilian to military production will be limited and dependent on favorable macro-economic circumstances, the availability of money for investment and the dedicated will of those responsible to make such a transformation.

Not much conversion research has occurred after the end of the 'long decade of disarmament'. However, there is scope for additional analysis of that period, for instance with respect to the long-term macro-economic effects of military downsizing and the long-term fate of companies attempting industrial conversion. Cases which warrant particular attention are conversion in China and the re-use of military land after base closures.

References

Accordino, J. (2000). Captives of the Cold War Economy. The Struggle for Defense Conversion in American Communities. Westport, Praeger.

Adelman, K.L., Augustine, N.R. (1992). "Defense conversion: Bulldozing the management". Foreign Affairs 71, 26–47.

Albrecht, U. (1979). Rüstungskonversionsforschung: Eine Literaturstudie mit Forschungsempfehlungen (Arms Conversion Research: A Literature Review with Recommendations for Research). Nomos, Baden-Baden.

Alexander, A.J. (1990). The Conversion of Soviet Defense Industry. RAND, Santa Monica.

Alexander, J.D. (1994). "Military conversion policies in the USA: 1940s and 1990s". Journal of Peace Research 31, 19–33.

Alic, J.A., Branscomb, L.M., Brooks, H., Carter, A.B., Epstein, G.L. (1992). Beyond Spinoff: Military and Commercial Technologies in a Changing World. Harvard Business School Press, Boston.

Baltes, P.T. (2004). Handlungsökonomie und neue Institutionenökonomie. Eine theoretische Auseinandersetzung anhand der Transktionsmechanismen zur Liegenschaftskonversion (Actor-oriented Economics and Institution Economics. A Theoretical Discussion Using the Example of Transaction Mechanisms in Site Conversion). BWV Berliner Wissenschafts-Verlag, Berlin.

Bayoumi, T., Hewitt, D.P., Schiff, J. (1995). "Economic consequences of lower military spending: Some simulation results". In: Klein, L.R., Lo, F., McKibbin, W.J. (Eds.), Arms Reduction: Economic Implications in the Post-Cold War Era. UNU Press, Tokyo, pp. 172–219.

Bernstein, D. (1994). Defense Industry Restructuring in Russia: Case Studies and Analysis. CISAC, Stanford University, Stanford, CA.

Berthélemy, J.C., Deger, S. (1995). Conversion of Military Industries in China. OECD Development Center, Paris.

BICC (Bonn International Center for Conversion) (annually 1996–1998). BICC Conversion Survey. Oxford University, Oxford.

BICC (Bonn International Center for Conversion) (annually from 1999). BICC Conversion Survey. Nomos, Baden-Baden.

Bischak, G. (1997). US Conversion after the Cold War, 1990–1997. BICC, Bonn.

Bjerkholt, O. (1996). "The National Peace Dividend". In: Gleditsch, N.P., et al. (Eds.), The Peace Dividend. Elsevier, Amsterdam, pp. 17–26.

Braddon, D., Dowdall, P. (1996). "Flexible networks and the restructuring of the regional defence industrial base: The case of South West England". Defence and Peace Economics 7, 47–59.

Brauer, J., Marlin, J.T. (1992). "Converting resources from military to non-military uses". Journal of Economic Perspectives 6, 145–164.

Brömmelhörster, J. (1994). Ökonomie der Konversion: Wirkungen, Barrieren und Erfordernisse für die Bundesrepublik Deutschland (Economics of Conversion: Effects, Barriers and Requirements in the Federal Republic of Germany). Campus, Frankfurt.

Brömmelhörster, J. (1999). KONVER II – Fostering of Conversion by the European Union. BICC, Bonn.

Brömmelhörster, J. (Ed.) (2000). Paying the Peace Dividend: Declining Military Expenditures After the Cold War. Nomos, Baden-Baden.

Brömmelhörster, J., Frankenstein, J. (Eds.) (1997). Mixed Motives, Uncertain Outcomes: Defense Conversion in China. Lynne Rienner, Boulder.

Brzoska, M. (1999). "Military conversion: The balance sheet". Journal of Peace Research 36, 131–140.

Brzoska, M. (2001). "Defense industry conversion". In: Gleditsch, N.P., et al. (Eds.), Making Peace Pay – A Bibliography on Disarmament & Conversion. Regina Books, Claremont, pp. 133–156.

Brzoska, M., Markusen, A.R. (Eds.) (2000). "Military industrial conversion". International Regional Science Review (Special Issue) 23 1–131.

Brzoska, M., Wilke, P., Wulf, H. (1999). "The changing civil–military production mix in Western Europe's Defense Industry". In: Markusen, A.R., Costigan, S. (Eds.), Arming the Future: A Defense Industry for the 21st Century. Council on Foreign Relations Press, New York, pp. 371–408.

Clements, B., Gupta, S., Schiff, J. (1996). "Worldwide military spending, 1990–1995". IMF Working Paper No. 96/64, Washington.

Colletta, N.J., Kostner, M., Wiederhofer, I. (1996). Case Studies in War-to-Peace Transition. The Demobilization and Reintegration of Ex-combatants in Ethiopia, Namibia, and Uganda. World Bank, Washington, DC.

Commission of the European Communities (1992). The Economic and Social Impact of Reductions in Defence Spending and Military Forces on the Regions of the Community. Office for Official Publications of the European Communities, Luxembourg.

Cooley, M. (1980). Architect or Bee? The Human/Technology Relationship. Slough, Hand and Brain.

Cooper, J. (1991). "Military cuts and conversion in the defence industry". Soviet Economy 7, 121–135.

Cunnigham, K. (1997). Base Closure and Redevelopment in Central and Eastern Europe. BICC, Bonn.

Dardia, M., McCarthy, K., Malkin, J., Vernez, G. (1996). The Effects of Military Base Closures on Local Communities: A Short-Term Perspective. RAND, Santa Monica.

Dumas, L.J. (Ed.) (1995). The Socio-Economics of Conversion from War to Peace. Sharpe, Armonk, NY.

Elsner, W. (1995). "Instruments and institutions of industrial policy at the regional level in Germany: The example of industrial defense conversion". Journal of Economic Issues 29, 503–516.

Feldman, J.M. (1997). Diversification after the Cold War: Results of the National Defense Economy Survey. Center for Urban Policy Research, Rutgers University, New Brunswick, NJ.

Feldman, J.M. (1998). "The conversion of defense engineers' skills: Explaining success and failure through customer-based learning, teaming, and managerial integration". In: Susman, G.I., Sean O'Keefe, O. (Eds.), The Defense Industry in the Post-Cold War Era: Corporate Strategies and Public Policy Perspectives. Pergamon, Oxford, pp. 281–318.

Feldman, J.M. (1999). "Civilian diversification, learning, and institutional change: Growth through knowledge and power". Environment and Planning A 31, 1805–1824.

Fontanel, J. (1994). La conversion économique du secteur militaire (The Economic Conversion of the Military Sector). Economica, Paris.

Fontanel, J., Samson, I., Spalanzani, A. (1995). "Conversion for the 1990s: "Peace cost" against "peace dividend"". Defence and Peace Economics 6, 169–184.

Gaddy, C. (1996). The Price of the Past: Russia's Struggle With the Legacy of a Militarized Economy. Brookings, Washington, DC.

Gansler, J.S. (1995). Defense Conversion: Transforming the Arsenal of Democracy. MIT Press, Cambridge, MA.

Gleditsch, N.P., Bjerkholt, O., Cappelen, A., Smith, R.P., Dunne, J.P. (Eds.) (1996). The Peace Dividend. Elsevier, Amsterdam.

Gleditsch, N.P., Lindgren, G., Mouhleb, N., Smit, S., de Soysa, I. (Eds.) (1999). Making Peace Pay – A Bibliography on Disarmament & Conversion. Regina Books, Claremont.

Gold, D. (2000). "Whatever happened to the peace dividend? The economic consequences of the post-Cold War decline in military expenditures in the United States". In: Brömmelhörster, J. (Ed.), Paying the Peace Dividend: Declining Military Expenditures After the Cold War. Nomos, Baden-Baden, pp. 47–68.

Goldberg, M., Warner, J. (1987). "Military experience, civilian experience, and the earnings of veterans". Journal of Human Resources 22, 62–81.

Gonchar, K. (1997). Research and Development (R&D) Conversion in Russia. BICC, Bonn.

Gonchar, K. (2000). Russia's Defense Industry at the Turn of the Century. BICC, Bonn.

Gummett, P., et al. (Eds.) (1996). Military R&D After the Cold War: Conversion and Technology Transfer in Eastern and Western Europe. Kluwer, Dordrecht.

Hartley, K., Sandler, T. (2003). "The future of the defence firm". Kyklos 56, 361–380.

Hartley, K., et al. (1993). Economic Aspects of Disarmament: Disarmament as an Investment Process. United Nations, New York.

Heinemann-Grüder, A. (2002). Becoming an Ex-military Man: Demobilization and Reintegration of Military Professionals in Eastern Europe. BICC, Bonn.

Hooker, M.A., Knetter, M. (1999). Measuring the Economic Effects of Military Base Closures. National Bureau of Economic Research, Cambridge.

Hooper, N., Stephens, E. (2000). "Civilian employment of service leavers". In: Pauwels, N. (Ed.), From War Force to Workforce. Nomos, Baden-Baden, pp. 121–144.

Hooper, N., et al. (1996). Defense Industry Redundancies in the South West Region. University of York, Centre for Defence Economics, Heslington.

Intriligator, M.D. (1996). "The peace dividend: Myth or reality?". In: Gleditsch, N.P., et al. (Eds.), The Peace Dividend. Elsevier, Amsterdam, pp. 1–16.

Isard, W., Anderton, C.H. (1992). "A survey of the peace economics literature". In: Isard, W., Anderton, C.H. (Eds.), Economics of Arms Reduction and the Peace Process: Contributions From Peace Economics and Peace Science. North-Holland, Amsterdam, pp. 1–55.

Jauhiainen, J.S., Mampaey, L., Schuster, J.S., de Penanros, R., Goudie, I.S., Tamás, P., Ferencz, Z. (1999). Post-Cold War Conversion in Europe: Defense Restructuring in the 1990s and the Regional Dimension. GRIP, Brussels.

Kapstein, E.B. (1995). "The economic transition in defense-dependent regions of Russia". Defence and Peace Economics 6, 253–261.

Kelley, M.R., Watkins, T.A. (1995). "In from the cold: Prospects for conversion of the defense industrial base". Science 268, 525–532.

Kingma, K. (Ed.) (2000). Demobilization in Sub-Saharan Africa: The Development and Security Impacts. Macmillan Publishers, Basingstoke.

Kiss, J. (1997). The Defence Industry in East-Central Europe: Restructuring and Conversion. Oxford University Press, Oxford.

Klein, L.R., Lo, F., McKibbin, W.J. (Eds.) (1995). Arms Reduction: Economic Implications in the Post-Cold War Era. UNU Press, Tokyo.

Knight, M., Loayza, D., Villanueva, N. (1996). "The peace dividend: Military spending cuts and economic growth". International Monetary Fund Staff Papers 43, 1–37.

Kopte, S., Wilke, P. (1998). "Disarmament and the disposal of surplus weapons: A Survey of the dismantling, destruction and transfer of surplus weapons and ammunition". In: Kaldor, M., Albrecht, U., Schméder, G. (Eds.), Restructuring the Global Military Sector: The End of Military Fordism. Pinter, London, pp. 67–100.

Lakhani, H. (1998). "The socioeconomic benefits of active military service to reservists". Armed Forces and Society 24, 549–565.

Laurance, E.J., Wulf, H. (1995). Conversion and the Integration of Economic and Security Dimensions. BICC, Bonn.

Lichtenberg, F. (1995). "Economics of defense r&d". In: Hartley, K., Sandler, T. (Eds.), Handbook of Defense Economics, vol. 1. Elsevier, Amsterdam, pp. 431–457.

Loughran, D. (2002). Wage Growth in the Civilian Careers of Military Retirees David. RAND, Santa Monica.

Lundquist, J.T. (1992). "Shrinking fast and smart. Hang on to what you've got to have and throw the rest away". Harvard Business Review 70, 74–85.

Markusen, A.R. (1999). "The rise of world weapons". Foreign Policy 114, 130–152.

Markusen, A.R. (2003). "The case against privatizing national security". Governance 16, 471–502.

Markusen, A.R., Costigan, S. (Eds.) (1999). Arming the Future: A Defense Industry for the 21st Century. Council on Foreign Relations Press, New York.

Markusen, A.R., Oden, M.D. (1994). Regional Adjustment of Defense Dependent Regions in the Post-Cold War Era. OECD, Paris.

Markusen, A.R., Yudken, J. (1992). Dismantling the Cold War Economy. Basic Books, New York.

Markusen, A.R., Campbell, S., Hall, P., Deitrick, S. (1991). The Rise of the Gunbelt: The Military Remapping of Industrial America. Oxford University Press, New York.

Markusen, A.R., DiGiovanna, S., Leary, M.C. (2003). From Defense to Development? International Perspectives on Realizing the Peace Dividend. Routledge, London.

Melman, S. (1988). The Demilitarized Society: Disarmament and Conversion. Harvest House, Montreal.

Oden, M.D. (1999). "Cashing In, Cashing Out, and Converting: Restructuring of the Defense Industrial Base in the 1990s". In: Markusen, A.R., Costigan, S. (Eds.), Arming the Future: A Defense Industry for the 21st Century. Council on Foreign Relations Press, New York, pp. 74–105.

Oden, M.D., Bischak, G.A. (1995). Coming in From the Cold: Arms Industry Restructuring and Economic Conversion Policies in the United States, 1989–1993. ILO Employment Department, Geneva.

Patel, B. (2005). Peace Dividend through Chemical Weapons Disarmament. BICC, Bonn.

Pauwels, N. (Ed.) (2000). War Force to Work Force: Global Perspectives on Demobilization and Reintegration. Nomos, Baden-Baden.

Poppert, P.E., Herzog, H.W. Jr. (2003). "Force Reduction, Base Closure, and the Indirect Effects of Military Installations on Local Employment Growth". Journal of Regional Science 43, 459–481.

Renner, M. (Ed.) (1992). Economic Adjustment after the Cold War: Strategies for Conversion. Aldershot, Dartmouth.

Renner, M. (1996). Cost of Disarmament: An Overview of the Economic Costs of the Dismantlement of Weapons and the Disposal of Military Surplus. BICC, Bonn.

Reppy, J. (1999). "Dual-use technology: Back to the future". In: Markusen, A., Costigan, S. (Eds.), Arming the Future: A Defense Industry for the 21st Century. Council on Foreign Relations Press, New York, pp. 269–284.

Sapir, O. (2000). L'URSS au tournant. Une économie en transition (Turning the USSR Around. An Economy in Transition). Harmattan, Paris.

Sapolsky, H., Gholz, E. (1999). "Private arsenals: Americas post Cold War burden". In: Markusen, A., Costigan, S. (Eds.), Arming the Future A Defense Industry for the 21st Century. Council on Foreign Relations Press, New York.

Schirowki, U. (2000). Zehn Jahre Truppenabzug und Konversion in Nordrhein-Westfalen-Bilanz und Perspektiven (Ten Years of Troop Reduction and Conversion in North-Rhein Westphalia – Balance Sheet and

Perspectives). Ministerium für Wirtschaft und Mittelstand, Energie und Verkehr des Landes Nordrhein-Westfalen, Düsseldorf.

Schomacker, K., Wilke, P., Wulf, H. (1987). Alternative Produktion statt Rüstung. Gewerkschaftliche Initiativen für sinnvolle Arbeit und sozial nützliche Produkte (Alternative Production Instead of Arms: Trade Union Initiatives for Meaningful Work and Socially Useful Products). Bund Verlag, Köln.

Serfati, C., Brzoska, M., Hagelin, B., Sköns, E., Smit, W. (Eds.) (2001). "The future of defence production". In: The Restructuring of the European Defence Industry. Publishing House of the European Commission, Luxembourg.

Sköns, E., Weidacher, R. (1999). "Arms Production". In: SIPRI Yearbook 1999. Armaments, Disarmament and International Security. Oxford University Press, Oxford, pp. 387–420.

Smith, R. (1996). "The international peace dividend". In: Gleditsch, N.P., et al. (Eds.), The Peace Dividend. Elsevier, Amsterdam, pp. 351–357.

Thorsson, I. (1984). In Pursuit of Disarmament. Conversion from Military to Civil Production in Sweden. Liber, Stockholm.

United Nations (1995). World Economic and Social Survey 1995. Current Trends and Policies in the World Economy. United Nations, New York.

United States Congress Office of Technology Assessment (1993). Defense Conversion: Redirecting R&D, OTA-ITE-552. Washington, DC, 1993.

United States General Accounting Office (2002). Military Base Closures: Progress in Completing Actions from Prior Realignments and Closures. GAO-02-433, April 5.

United States General Accounting Office (2004a). Chemical Weapons: Destruction Schedule Delays and Cost Growth Continue to Challenge Program Management. GAO-04-634T, April 1.

United States General Accounting Office (2004b). Nuclear Waste: Absence of Key Management Reforms on Hanford's Cleanup Project Adds to Challenges of Achieving Cost and Schedule Goals. GAO-04-611, June 9.

United States National Academy of Sciences (1994). Management and Disposition of Excess Weapons Plutonium. National Academy Press, Washington, DC.

Warner, J., Asch, B. (1995). "The economics of military manpower". In: Hartley, K., Sandler, T. (Eds.), Handbook of Defense Economics, vol. 1. Elsevier Science, Amsterdam.

Watkins, T.A. (1998). "Are defense and non-defense manufacturing industries really all that different?". In: Susman, G., O'Keefe, S. (Eds.), The Defense Industry in the Post Cold War Era. Elsevier Science, Oxford.

Wie, K. (1997). "Army re-tools commercial production". China Daily (Business Weekly) A17-23 (in FBIS-CHI-97-230).

Willett, S. (2003). Costs of Disarmament – Disarming the Costs: Nuclear Arms Control and Nuclear Rearmament. UNIDIR, Geneva.

Wulf, H. (2005). Internationalizing and Privatizing War and Peace: The Bumpy Ride to Peace Building. Macmillan, London.

Chapter 35

A SURVEY OF PEACE ECONOMICS[*]

CHARLES H. ANDERTON and JOHN R. CARTER

Department of Economics, College of the Holy Cross, 1 College Street, Worcester, MA 01610, USA
e-mails: canderto@holycross.edu; jcarter@holycross.edu

Contents

Abstract   1212
Keywords   1212
1. Introduction   1213
2. Nature and scope of peace economics   1213
  2.1. Definition of peace economics   1213
  2.2. Patterns of conflict in the international system   1216
3. Determinants of interstate armed conflict   1221
  3.1. Conflict cycle   1221
  3.2. Wittman's expected utility model of war   1223
  3.3. Assessing the risk of interstate armed conflict   1224
    3.3.1. Geography of interstate conflict   1224
    3.3.2. Economic development   1226
    3.3.3. Economic interdependence   1227
  3.4. Assessing war duration   1227
4. Arms rivalry, proliferation, and arms control   1229
  4.1. Definitions   1229
  4.2. Models of arms rivalry   1229
    4.2.1. Prisoner's dilemma interpretation of arms rivalry   1229
    4.2.2. Richardson model   1231
    4.2.3. The Intriligator–Brito model   1231
    4.2.4. Arms rivalry as economic choice   1234
  4.3. Selected empirical studies of arms rivalry and proliferation   1234
    4.3.1. Arms rivalry and the risk of war   1234
    4.3.2. Determinants of nuclear weapons proliferation   1235
5. Technological and geographic dimensions of conflict   1236
  5.1. The inherent propensity toward peace or war   1236

[*] The authors are indebted to Jurgen Brauer, Keith Hartley, Michael Intriligator, and Todd Sandler for valuable comments on an earlier draft. Any errors are the sole responsibility of the authors.

Handbook of Defense Economics, Volume 2
Edited by Todd Sandler and Keith Hartley
© 2007 Elsevier B.V. All rights reserved
DOI: 10.1016/S1574-0013(06)02035-7

5.2. Lanchester theory and the inherent propensity toward peace or war	1236
5.2.1. Basic Lanchester model of war attrition	1236
5.2.2. Lanchester war with mobilization advantage and re-supply	1237
5.2.3. Lanchester attack/defend model	1238
5.3. Offense/defense theory and evidence	1240
6. Appropriation and exchange theory	1242
6.1. Edgeworth box model of vulnerable trade	1242
6.2. General equilibrium model of production, appropriation, and exchange	1245
7. Experiments in peace economics	1247
7.1. Experimental methods	1247
7.2. Early experiments	1248
7.3. Recent experiments	1250
8. Concluding remarks	1251
References	1254

Abstract

Peace economics can be defined as the use of economics to understand the causes and effects of violent conflict in the international system and the ways that conflict can be avoided, managed, or resolved. This chapter surveys major subject areas of peace economics, highlighting seminal as well as current contributions. Particularly noteworthy among the newer developments is how major datasets like the Correlates of War Project have fostered a rapid growth of econometric studies based on relatively large cross-country panels.

The topics surveyed include: the relation of peace economics to both defense economics and peace studies; data sources and trends for interstate, intrastate, and extra-state conflict; the costs of conflict; the conflict life cycle; the determinants of interstate armed conflict, with emphasis on the role of territory, economic development, and economic interdependence; arms rivalry, proliferation, and arms control, with particular attention given to the foundational models of Richardson and Intriligator and Brito; the technological and geographic dimensions of conflict, including their connections with Schelling's inherent propensity toward war or peace, various Lanchester war models, and the offense–defense balance; appropriation and exchange theory, wherein appropriation undermines the security of exchange at the same time that exchange shapes the incentives for appropriation; experiments in peace economics, most notably the pathbreaking prisoner's dilemma experiments of the 1950s; and future directions in the field.

Keywords

war, conflict cycle, arms rivalry, arms control, proliferation, offense–defense balance, appropriation, exchange, game theory, experimental economics

JEL classification: C70, C90, D74, H56

1. Introduction

Philosophers and sages have pondered the causes and effects of war for millennia, but only within the last century have scholars begun to study war with the formal methods of social science. Building on the work of Lewis Richardson (1939, 1960a, 1960b), Pitirim Sorokin (1937), and Quincy Wright (1942), the scientific study of war became firmly established by the mid-1960s around a community of scholars associated with the Correlates of War Project, the Peace Science Society (International), and the *Journal of Conflict Resolution*. Most early scholars involved in the scientific study of war were political scientists, but there were a few economists among the pioneers, most notably Kenneth Boulding, Walter Isard, and Thomas Schelling. By the late 1960s a small group of economists had emerged who were applying economic methods to better understand the causes, effects, and possible amelioration of violent conflict in the international system. Their legacy was the emergence of a subfield of economics that has been referred to in recent decades as "peace economics". Peace economics utilizes economic methods and principles to understand the causes and effects of conflict in the international system and ways that conflict can be avoided, managed, or resolved.

This chapter identifies selected major subject areas of peace economics, highlighting seminal contributions and current research in each area. We begin with a definition of peace economics, a comparison of peace economics with defense economics and peace studies, and an empirical overview of the frequency and cost of violent conflict in the international system (Section 2). We then turn to selected topics including determinants of interstate armed conflict (Section 3); arms rivalry, proliferation, and arms control (Section 4); technological and geographic dimensions of conflict (Section 5); appropriation and exchange theory (Section 6); and experiments in peace economics (Section 7). Other major topics in peace economics are omitted or covered only briefly because they are reviewed elsewhere in Volumes 1 and 2 of this *Handbook*. In the conclusion we briefly assess the current state of peace economics and note directions for future research (Section 8).

2. Nature and scope of peace economics

2.1. Definition of peace economics

According to Isard (1994, p. 9) peace economics

> ... is generally concerned with: (1) resolution, management or reduction of conflict in the economic sphere ...; (2) the use of economic measures and policy to cope with and control conflicts ...; and (3) the impact of conflict on the economic behavior and welfare of firms, consumers, organizations, government and society. Central to the field are: analyses of conflicts among nations, regions and other communities ...; measures to control (deescalate) arms races and achieve reduction in

military expenditures and weaponry; and programs and policies to utilize resources thus released for more constructive purposes . . . . It draws upon utility, production, public choice and welfare theories . . . . Behaving units are taken to engage in appropriative (e.g., military ventures) as well as productive activities, with war often viewed as a rational, purposeful choice of decision makers.

Isard identifies the primary concern of peace economics as conflict management, reduction, or resolution. He refers to numerous forms of inter-group conflict (among nations, regions, or communities) and a variety of motivations (economic or not). He highlights the interdependence of conflict and economics, the analytical tools of economics, and the rationality assumption, and thus asserts the economic focus of the field as well as its quantitative and scientific nature. Finally, Isard acknowledges that scholars working in peace economics often have normative commitments that they expect their research to support (e.g., reduction in military expenditures).

Another field devoted to the study of conflict is defense economics. There is substantial overlap between defense economics and peace economics, but there are also differences. The most important difference centers on normative issues. In its early years, defense economics viewed "*all* military problems as, in one of their aspects, economic problems in the efficient allocation and use of resources" [Hitch and McKean (1960, p. v)]. Hence, the primary focus of early pioneers of defense economics was the efficiency of the military sector. This included identification and implementation of efficiency conditions for military spending, weapons contracting, recruitment of military labor, allocation of resources in war, and the like. Peace economists, on the other hand, tend to be committed to reductions in defense spending, a lessening of war as an option in international affairs, and the application of economic methods to promote peace, not military efficiency. In our view, defense economics has broadened its focus over the years to include many of the topics of interest to peace economists, while also retaining its historic interest in military efficiency issues.

Peace economics is also related to but distinct from the field known as peace studies. In one of the few wide-ranging textbooks in peace studies, Barash (1991, p. 25) states: "In fact, Peace Studies has a clearly stated value orientation: It is opposed to war and biased toward peace (although not necessarily toward pacifism)." Barash (1991, p. 67) also states that "military expenditures diminish a country's opportunity to invest money in other, socially more productive ways." Most peace economists share Barash's value orientation about war and military spending, so there is a kinship between peace economics and peace studies.

Nevertheless, peace economics differs from peace studies in three important respects. First, as Isard's definition shows, peace economics emphasizes economic methods, principles, and variables in studying the causes and consequences of violent conflict. Although peace economics draws upon the perspectives of multiple disciplines, there remains a strong emphasis on economic aspects of conflict. Hence, peace economics is viewed by many of its practitioners as a subfield of economics. Peace studies, on the other hand, draws upon the tools and perspectives of many disciplines and is not viewed as a subfield of any one discipline.

A second difference is that peace studies adopts a broader conception of violence. In peace studies, the notion of peace includes not only the absence of war but also of structural violence that involves "denying people important rights such as economic opportunity, social and political equality, a sense of fulfillment and self worth, and so on" [Barash (1991, p. 8)]. Hence, problems of poverty, environmental degradation, preventable diseases, lack of free expression, and most other harms that might afflict people represent "a kind of violence . . . , even if bullets or clubs are not used" [Barash (1991, p. 8)]. Many peace economists are sympathetic to the concerns of peace studies, but they tend to have a more limited domain of analysis that focuses upon the threat or use of physical force between groups. We suspect the main reasons for this more limited domain are that it maintains a well-defined identity for the field and fosters depth of analysis and accumulation of knowledge around a relatively small number of topics.

A third difference is that peace studies involves both scholarship and activism, whereas peace economics is almost exclusively devoted to scholarship. Of course, all applied scholarship is activist to the extent that policy prescriptions are offered. But activism in peace studies includes protests, peace marches, letter writing campaigns, and the like, in which many peace economists are not involved.

Following Isard (1994) and others in peace and defense economics, we offer the following definition: Peace economics utilizes economic methods and principles to understand the causes and effects of potential and actual violent conflict in the international system and ways that violent conflict can be avoided, managed, or resolved. This definition encompasses economic methods (e.g., mathematics, game theory, statistical inference, and experimentation) and principles (e.g., scarcity, opportunity cost, rationality, equilibrium, and strategic interdependence) [Intriligator (1982)]. It also highlights the major objectives of peace economics, namely, to identify and explain the causes of violent conflict and its effects (e.g., casualties, refugees, impacts on trade, and impacts on growth). The conflicts studied are generally between groups in the international system (e.g., states and non-national groups) as opposed to individuals (e.g., common crime) and involve war and crises that portend war. Finally, our definition highlights the applied and policy objectives of peace economics, namely to find ways to reduce the prevalence and severity of threatened or actual inter-group violence.

Our definition is consistent with what we regard as the seminal contributions in peace economics. Following Richardson (1960a), a number of economists developed oligopoly perspectives on arms rivalry and arms control in the context of the Cold War [Boulding (1962), Schelling and Halperin (1961), McGuire (1965), Intriligator (1975)]. Isard (1969) utilized economic concepts and methods to develop conflict management procedures, while Boulding (1962) did the same in studying a broad range of action–reaction processes in conflict systems. Schelling (1960, 1966) pioneered the application of game theory to conflict escalation, continuation, and de-escalation. Other important contributions include Olson and Zeckhauser (1966) and Sandler and Cauley (1975) on alliance behavior, Tullock (1974) on intrastate conflict, and Benoit (1973) on the economic impact of defense spending in developing countries. Isard and Boulding are also regarded for their respective roles in establishing the Peace Science Society (originally the Peace Research Society) in the early 1960s and *The Journal of Conflict Resolution* in 1957.

2.2. Patterns of conflict in the international system

Interstate, intrastate, and extra-state conflicts constitute the principal subject matter in peace economics. Interstate conflict occurs between two or more states. Intrastate conflict occurs between two or more groups within the internationally recognized territory of a state. This encompasses both civil conflict (between the state government and one or more non-state actors) and inter-communal conflict (between two or more groups, none of which is the state government). Extra-state conflict occurs between a state and a non-sovereign entity outside the border of the state.

Figure 1 summarizes three well-known conflict datasets used in peace research. The first is the Correlates of War (COW) Project's dataset on *wars* (labeled COW Wars in Figure 1). The second is the dataset of *armed conflicts* developed jointly by the International Peace Research Institute in Oslo (PRIO) and the Uppsala Conflict Data Program (UCDP) (labeled PRIO/UCDP Armed Conflicts). The third is COW's dataset on *militarized interstate disputes* (labeled COW MIDs). The figure shows that all three datasets recognize a fatality level of 1000 as the demarcation between war and sub-war conflict. The COW War and PRIO/UCDP Armed Conflicts datasets record interstate, intrastate, and extra-state wars, while PRIO/UCDP also covers interstate, intrastate, and extra-state conflicts short of war with fatalities between 25 and 999. The COW MID dataset includes interstate conflict only, with fatalities ranging from zero to 999. Note that the temporal domains of the three datasets vary: 1816–1997 for COW Wars, 1946–2004 for PRIO/UCDP Armed Conflicts, and 1816–2001 for COW MIDs.

While the major distinctions among the three datasets are summarized in the top of Figure 1, more subtle differences within and among them are revealed in the definitions in the bottom part. The bases for counting fatalities (military only vs. military plus civilian, per war vs. per year) differ between COW and PRIO/UCDP and even within COW for the three types of wars. COW and PRIO also differ on the specification of intrastate war: PRIO/UCDP counts only wars between a state and one or more internal groups, whereas COW counts also inter-communal wars in which the state is not among the combatants. The differences in definitions across datasets will, of course, lead to coding differences in some cases. For example, the September 11, 2001 attack by al Qaeda against the USA is ignored by COW because COW counts only military fatalities in the definition of extra-state war, whereas PRIO/UCDP includes the case as extra-state war because it counts military plus civilian fatalities.

Drawing upon COW data, Table 1 shows the frequency of war onsets from 1816–1997 by war type. War onsets refer to wars initiated during a given time period. Table 1 shows that there was a total of 400 war onsets in the international system from 1816–1997. More than half of the wars were intrastate (213 or 53.3%), followed by extra-state (108 or 27.0%) and interstate (79 or 19.8%). Table 1 shows

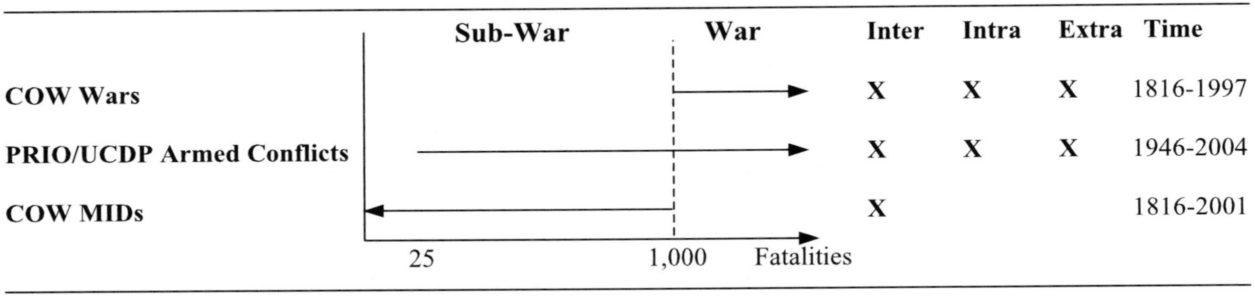

	Sub-War	War	Inter	Intra	Extra	Time
COW Wars			X	X	X	1816–1997
PRIO/UCDP Armed Conflicts			X	X	X	1946–2004
COW MIDs			X			1816–2001

25   1,000   Fatalities

COW Wars:

Interstate war – combat between states involving a minimum of 1000 battle deaths (military only) for the whole war among all states involved.

Intrastate war – combat between two or more groups within the internationally recognized territory of the state leading to 1000 battle-related deaths (military and civilian, excluding massacres) per year. Intrastate wars encompass civil wars (between the state government and one or more non-state actors) and inter-communal wars (between two or more groups, none of which is the state government).

Extra-state war – combat between a state and a non-sovereign entity outside the border of the state leading to 1000 battle deaths (military only) per year among the parties involved.

PRIO/UCDP Wars:

Interstate war – combat between states leading to a minimum of 1000 battle-related deaths (military and civilian) per year among all states involved.

Intrastate war – combat between a state and one or more internal groups leading to a minimum of 1000 battle-related deaths (military and civilian) per year among the parties involved.

Extra-state war – combat between a state and a non-sovereign entity outside the border of the state leading to 1000 battle-related deaths (military and civilian) per year among the parties involved.

PRIO/UCDP Armed Conflicts:

Apply PRIO/UCDP's war definitions, but with battle-related casualties (military and civilian) between 25 and 999.

COW MIDs:

Militarized interstate dispute – united historical case in which the "threat, display or use of military force short of war by one member state is explicitly directed towards the government, official representatives, official forces, property, or territory of another state" [Jones, Bremer and Singer (1996, p. 168)].

Figure 1. COW and PRIO/UCDP conflict datasets.

Table 1
War onsets per decade by war type, 1816–1997

Period	Interstate wars	Intrastate wars	Extra-state wars	Total per period
1816–1819	0	1	2	3
1820–1829	2	7	6	15
1830–1839	0	11	5	16
1840–1849	4	9	8	21
1850–1859	5	8	9	22
1860–1869	8	14	5	27
1870–1879	4	9	10	23
1880–1889	3	3	12	18
1890–1899	4	9	16	29
1900–1909	6	7	4	17
1910–1919	8	11	6	25
1920–1929	2	12	6	20
1930–1939	9	8	2	19
1940–1949	3	9	5	17
1950–1959	3	11	6	20
1960–1969	6	16	3	25
1970–1979	7	25	3	35
1980–1989	4	19	0	23
1990–1997	1	24	0	25
1816–1899	30	71	73	174
1900–1997	49	142	35	226
1816–1997	79	213	108	400

Source: Sarkees (2000).

that interstate and intrastate wars were more frequent in the twentieth century relative to the nineteenth century (49 and 142 compared to 30 and 71), while extra-state wars were less frequent (35 compared to 73). In recent decades, intrastate wars have become more frequent while extra-state wars as coded by COW have virtually disappeared. Sarkees, Wayman and Singer (2003) attribute the reduction in extra-state wars to the substantial decline of colonies and dependencies in the international system. Table 1 also suggests that the hoped for global peace following the end of the Cold War in 1989 did not generally materialize in the 1990s. Only three other time periods in Table 1 have more total war onsets than the 1990–1997 period.

Peace economists are also concerned with conflicts that may portend war or that involve relatively low levels of potential or actual violence. COW MID data are useful for studying *interstate* conflict short of war. Two points need emphasizing about MIDs. First, according to the COW definitions in Figure 1, a MID is not a war. The threat, display, or use of military force constitute three categories of conflict that fall short of war in the COW dataset. When a MID reaches the point where military combat is sufficiently sustained that it will lead to a minimum of 1000 total battle deaths, then the MID becomes an interstate war [Jones, Bremer and Singer (1996, p. 168)]. Second, some scholars treat the *use* of military force between states as interstate war even though battle deaths are less than the 1000 threshold.

Figure 2 shows the frequency of MID onsets in the international system from 1816–2000 by five year periods. MID onsets refer to MIDs that are begun in a given year. Figure 2 also shows the number of MID onsets that involved the use of military force (labeled MIDs-Use-Force) and the number of MID onsets that eventually rose to the level of interstate war (labeled MIDs-to-War). Also labeled in Figure 2 are time periods identified as important by historians of international relations [Gochman and Moaz (1990, p. 198)]. Three observations follow. First, the twentieth century witnessed far more MIDs than the nineteenth century: of the 2297 MID onsets from 1816–2000, 86.5% occurred in the twentieth century (1900–1999). Second, a substantial percentage of MID onsets involved the use of military force, although the percentage varies considerably across historical periods. For the entire period 1816–2000, 71.6% of MID onsets involved the use of military force. During the Bismarkian era (1871–1890), 42.4% of MID onsets involved military force, compared to 77.1% during the Cold War (1946–1989). Third, the percent of MID onsets that crossed the threshold for COW's definition of war is small. Of the 2297 MIDs that arose in the entire period 1816–2000, only 106 (4.6%) escalated to war.

Over the past few decades, and especially since September 11, 2001, peace economists have become increasingly interested in terrorism. Figure 3 shows the time paths for international terrorist incidents and for domestic terrorist incidents (divided by 10). According to the data source, the Terrorism Knowledge Base (TKB), "international terrorism includes incidents in which the perpetrators go abroad to strike their targets, select domestic targets associated with a foreign state, or create an international incident by attacking airline passengers or equipment." Domestic terrorism is defined by the TKB as "incidents perpetrated by local nationals against a purely domestic target," such as the 1995 bombing of the Murrah Federal Building in Oklahoma City. Three observations follow. First, contrary to popular impression, no upward (linear) trend is evident in the international incidents series for the full period 1989–2004. Nevertheless, the number of terrorist incidents appears to be rising in recent years, and the severity of terrorism as measured by casualties per incident (not shown) has been rising [Enders and Sandler (2000)]. Second, domestic incidents around the world are much more numerous than international incidents (approximately 8 times so), at least for the limited period of 1998–2004. Third, there appears to be a positive correlation between movements in the number of international and domestic incidents per year, again for the limited period for which data are available.

The conflicts summarized in Table 1 and Figures 1–3 involve economic costs of three sorts. First, when nations and groups allocate resources to conflict activities, alternative goods that could be produced with those resources are forgone. Real military expenditures serve as a crude proxy for the direct opportunity costs of resources employed in potential or actual conflict involving nation states [Brzoska (1995)]. Note that this economic cost is borne even when conflict activities are purely defensive and no violence

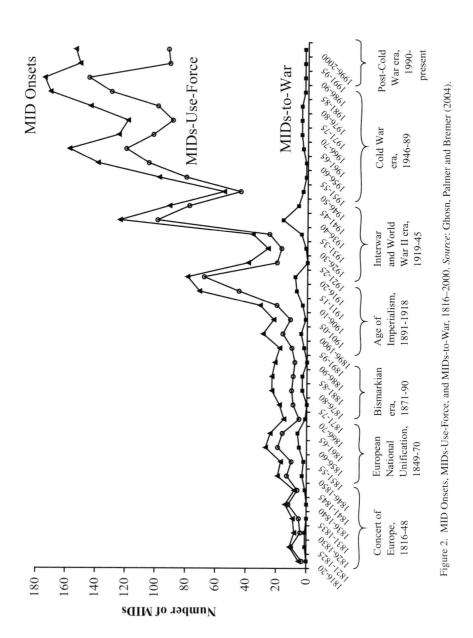

Figure 2. MID Onsets, MIDs-Use-Force, and MIDs-to-War, 1816–2000. *Source:* Ghosn, Palmer and Bremer (2004).

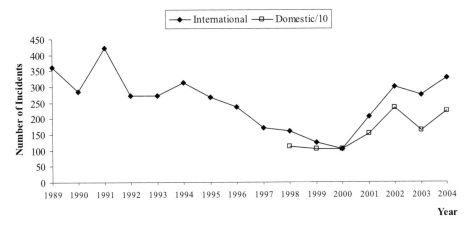

Figure 3. International and domestic terrorist incidents worldwide. *Source*: Terrorism Knowledge Base (http://www.thb.org).

occurs. Second, when conflict does turn violent, resources (including human lives) are destroyed, causing the loss of future production of goods and services. Harrison (2000) documented the destruction of human and physical capital for the allied and axis powers during World War II. For additional studies on the destruction of assets from war, see Harris (1997) on the Iran–Iraq war of 1980–1988, Mohammed (1997) on Sudan's civil war of 1983–1993, and Enders and Sandler (2006) on the September 11, 2001 terrorist attack on the USA. Third, when conflict is threatened or realized, some ordinary production and exchange activities are rendered uneconomical and hence lost. For example, Anderton and Carter (2003) and Glick and Taylor (2005) document the substantial disruption to trade caused by interstate wars, while Bayer and Rupert (2004) and Nitsch and Schumacher (2004) demonstrate the same for civil wars and terrorism, respectively. Other studies show the effects of war on economic growth [see, e.g., Koubi (2005) for interstate wars, Murdoch and Sandler (2004) for civil wars, and Blomberg, Hess and Weerapana (2004) on terrorism].

3. Determinants of interstate armed conflict

3.1. Conflict cycle

Conflicts ordinarily pass through phases, as depicted nicely in Lund's (1996) life-cycle diagram, reproduced here as Figure 4. The bell-shaped curve depicts the course of a typical conflict as hostility rises and falls over time. The far left column indicates phases of the cycle that range from peace (durable, stable, and unstable) to crisis and war. Placed around the outside are terms used for third-party interventions. The "P series" (preventive diplomacy, peacemaking, etc.) is found in discussions associated with the United Nations, while the "C series" (conflict prevention, conflict management, etc.) is

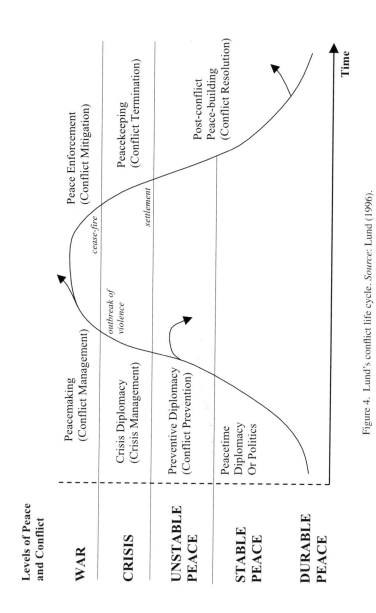

Figure 4. Lund's conflict life cycle. *Source:* Lund (1996).

used in the scholarly literature [Lund (1996, p. 385)]. The arrows along the curve show that wars can be prevented, escalate, or recur.

Social scientists have tended to specialize in their study of conflict by focusing on various aspects of the conflict cycle. Boulding (1978) emphasized non-violent political and legal actions, trade, and grants as means of preserving stable peace, shown in the lower left portion of the conflict curve. In the crisis and war phases (upper left), Schelling (1966) explored the strategic threat or use of violence as part of a bargaining process, while Richardson (1960a) and Boulding (1962, chapter 2) considered action–reaction processes that might move parties from crisis to war. Isard (1969) and Isard and Smith (1982) developed conflict management procedures for managing violent conflict (upper left) and for mitigating or terminating ongoing conflict (upper right). Wittman (1979) developed necessary conditions for war termination (right side) in the context of an expected utility model.

3.2. Wittman's expected utility model of war

Wittman's (1979) expected utility model provides a general framework for thinking about various aspects of the conflict cycle, including war onset, duration, termination, and recurrence. Here we focus on onset. Assume two states A and B involved in a potentially violent dispute but with a common interest in reaching an outcome that is not highly destructive to their respective interests. This assumption treats the conflict between A and B as part of what Schelling (1960, pp. 5–6, 89) calls a bargaining or mixed motive game. The bargaining context is apparent in the Wittman model where various possible settlements stand as alternatives to war. Let variable s represent the settlement possibilities between A and B, which are involved in a territorial dispute, for example. Total acquiescence by B (with A obtaining all of the disputed territory) occurs when $s = 0$; the opposite extreme occurs when $s = 1$. Let $U_i^t(s)$ denote player i's present discounted utility for settlement s, and let $EU_i^t(w)$ denote i's expected utility of fighting a war over the disputed territory. The superscript t in the utility functions indicates that utility assessments occur at time t and thus can change as the dispute unfolds and new information is acquired.

In Figure 5 we show utility functions over settlements for A and B. Settlements are measured on the X axis ranging from total acquiescence by B to the same by A. Hence, $U_A^t(s)$ is a decreasing function and $U_B^t(s)$ an increasing function of s. On the Y axis we show expected utilities of war for each player, where in this case they are assumed to be high relative to the settlement utility functions. A prefers a war over any settlement that offers less utility than $EU_A^t(w)$. Hence, A will accept settlements only to the left of s_A. By similar logic, B will accept settlements only to the right of s_B. Because no mutually agreeable settlements exist, war is the predicted outcome, given the utilities shown in Figure 5. On the other hand, as can be seen, if the expected utility of one or both players fall sufficiently relative to the corresponding settlement utility functions, then war can be expected to be avoided. For elaboration and critique of the expected utility approach, see Bueno de Mesquita (1981) and Singer (2000).

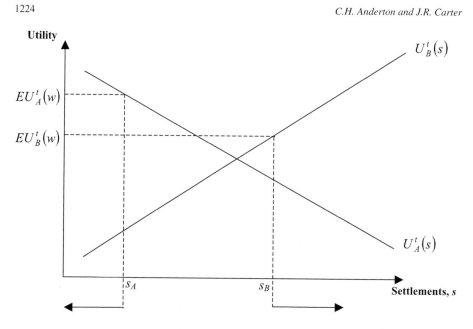

Figure 5. Wittman's expected utility model of war. *Source*: Wittman (1979).

In the Wittman model, higher expected utilities from war and lower utilities from settlements increase the likelihood of war onset. The question that naturally follows is what factors increase expected utilities of war and decrease utilities of settlement, thus making war more likely. Another question pertains to conflict management and asks how third-party mediators might influence the same utilities in the opposite direction so as to reduce the likelihood of war or terminate a war that is underway. The related literatures on the risk of interstate armed conflict and on conflict management and termination attempt to provide answers to these and other questions.

3.3. Assessing the risk of interstate armed conflict

The empirical literature on the determinants of interstate armed conflict is vast, with the number of studies now easily exceeding 500 [Geller and Singer (1998)]. Pushed by advancements in data sources, computing power, and econometrics, these studies have become increasingly sophisticated and ambitious. In most cases they apply regression methods to pooled time-series of countries (monads) or country-pairs (dyads). Depending on their particular hypotheses and concerns, they include an assortment of geographic, economic, political, and military capability variables.

3.3.1. Geography of interstate conflict

Geography properly belongs in any discussion of the economics of interstate armed conflict. This is because geography can affect the economic cost of conflict, but also because conflict can involve the appropriation of economic wealth in the form of land and other natural resources. Under the heading of geography we include here considerations of proximity, contiguity, and territory. Proximity refers to the spatial closeness of two countries, often operationalized as the distance between their respective capitals. It is conjectured that the closer are two countries, the lower is the cost of projecting military power in an interstate conflict [Boulding (1962)]. Contiguity refers to whether two countries are spatially adjacent. Because of the frequency and multiplicity of their interactions, contiguous countries are conjectured to be more apt to find themselves in disputes over territory, policy, regime, or other matters [Bremer (2000), Senese (2005)]. Territory (or territoriality) refers to whether claims to a geographic area are disputed between the countries. Territorial disputes are believed to have comparatively high stakes and hence are conjectured to be more likely to lead to armed conflict than non-territorial disputes. This is due not only to the value that land has in terms of use, resource extraction, or security, but also to its psychological value in terms of national identity, culture, and reputation [Hensel (2000), Huth (2000)].

A recent empirical analysis of the geography of conflict is Senese's (2005) dyadic study of the effects of contiguity and territory on MID and war onsets over the period 1919–1995. For each year and each country-pair, Senese first recorded whether a MID began. Then, for each of these MID onsets, he recorded whether the MID escalated to war. This procedure yielded two qualitative dependent variables, one measuring MID onset and the other war onset. Right-hand variables included indicators for contiguity, territorial disagreement, and the product of the two indicators. Additional variables controlled for alliances, democracy, major power status, economic development, and relative capability.

Separate probits were estimated for MID and war onsets, based on a sample of 494,613 dyad years with 1348 MID onsets and 96 wars. The results showed a direct positive impact for both contiguity and territory in the MID onset equation. Allowing for the contiguity-territory interaction, the risk of a MID onset was estimated to increase from 0.001 for non-contiguous dyads with no territorial disagreements to 0.038 for contiguous pairs with territorial disagreements. Probabilities for the mixed dyads fell in between. In the war onset equation, again territory had a direct positive effect. The estimated impact of territorial disagreement was to increase the probability of war onset from 0.030 to 0.282 for non-contiguous dyads and from 0.020 to 0.094 for contiguous dyads. Surprisingly, the estimated effect of contiguity was to decrease the probability of war onset. This was particularly the case for dyads with territorial disagreement, where the probability dropped from 0.282 to 0.094. Senese's interpretation of this last set of probabilities was that the presence of a territorial MID without a shared border might imply a greater difficulty of resolving such a dispute by means short of war. For ourselves, we wonder if the effect of contiguity was underestimated in both equations due to the omission of a dyadic trade variable, which may be positively correlated with contiguity and negatively correlated with conflict.

3.3.2. Economic development

It seems a truism that almost any review of economic literature will include a reference to Adam Smith. Here the call is answered with Book V, Chapter 1 of the *Wealth of Nations*, in which Smith (1976) provided an insightful account of the effect of economic development on armed conflict. Smith distinguished four levels of economic development: hunting, pastoral, agricultural, and manufacturing. In Smith's view, the least developed (hunting) and most developed (manufacturing) societies would be less likely to initiate war due to high opportunity costs. For hunter societies, their armies would be limited in scale because time away from the chase would severely tax their means of livelihood. For developed societies, warriors would have to be drawn away from manufacturing, leading to a direct and substantial loss of output. For moderately developed pastoral and agricultural societies, however, the opportunity cost of war was comparatively low in Smith's view. Shepherds could bring their herds with them to war, allowing them to maintain the flocks during war. In agricultural societies, once the seeds were planted, men of military age could go to war with only a small loss in output, leaving maintenance of crops to the women, children, and older men. Across the four levels of development, Smith's ideas thus suggested an inverted-U-shaped relationship between the level of economic development and the risk of war.

Smith's account of the likelihood of war is remarkable. As noted by Goodwin (1991, p. 25), "It is striking that despite the century and more of bloody conflict based on religious intolerance and issues of dynastic succession that Europe had just been through at the time Smith wrote, he was able to present an explanation for the likelihood of peace or war rooted in the consequences of economic growth alone." Smith's originality is evidenced also by the fact that modern scholarship has generally assumed a linear relationship between development and interstate conflict [see, e.g., East and Gregg (1967), Hegre (2000)]. Only with the recent contribution of Boehmer and Sobek (2005) has current thinking caught up with Smith's expectation of a nonlinear relationship.

Boehmer and Sobek (2005, p. 5) hypothesized an inverted-U relationship between development and conflict because the "changing orientation of economies from agricultural and extractive activities eventually to service-based economies alters the cost–benefit calculations concerning territorial acquisition." Poor states lack the military resources while developed states lack the economic motivation, leaving states at an intermediate level of development as those most likely to enter militarized interstate disputes. Boehmer and Sobek tested their hypothesis using country-level data for all states from 1870 to 1992. They used successively three dependent variables, measuring whether a country initiated a new MID, whether it was involved in a new MID over territory, and whether it participated in a new MID with fatalities. To permit a nonlinear effect for development, energy consumption per capita was entered in both log and log-squared forms. Control variables included democracy, population growth and density, economic openness, and military capability. Logit results showed a significant and substantial nonlinear effect of development for all three measures of armed conflict. For example, as the level of development increased from its minimum to its maximum sample value, the estimated probability of initiating a MID rose from 0.0014 to 0.0275 before falling to 0.0088. Based on their analysis, Boehmer and Sobek projected that the countries most prone to armed conflict today are moderately developed states like China, India, Iran, Pakistan, and Nigeria, while in the future the risk will rise with continued development by states like Liberia, Sudan, and the Democratic Republic of Congo.

3.3.3. Economic interdependence

Bilateral trade brings economic gains; these gains add to the opportunity cost of armed conflict when conflict disrupts trade. Hence, according to the liberal peace hypothesis, increased trade reduces the likelihood of armed conflict between trading countries, other things equal [Polachek (1980)]. During a period of rising globalization, the literature on trade and conflict has advanced rapidly in terms of both quantity and quality. We look briefly here at estimates of the effect of bilateral trade provided by Russett and Oneal (2001), whose research has been central in this area. For more comprehensive reviews see Schneider, Barbieri and Gleditsch (2003) and Polachek and Seiglie (Chapter 31 in this *Handbook*).

Russett and Oneal (2001) tested the liberal peace hypothesis for a sample of roughly 40,000 dyad-years spanning most of the period 1886–1992. The sample was restricted to dyads that were contiguous or contained at least one major power. Conflict was measured by a qualitative dependent variable indicating whether a dyad was involved in a MID that year. For each country in a dyad, economic dependence was gauged by how much the country traded with its dyadic partner relative to its GDP. The country in the dyad with the lower dependence was considered the weak link; hence, its dependence was treated as determinant of the likelihood of militarized disputes. Other independent variables included democracy, intergovernmental organizations, alliances, distance, and relative power.

Based on their logit analysis, Russett and Oneal (2001, p. 171) estimated the risk of involvement in a militarized dispute to be 0.03 for the typical dyad. From this baseline they found that the risk decreased by 43 percent when the trade dependence of the less dependent country increased by one standard deviation above the sample mean. Responding to challenges, Oneal and Russett (2003a, 2003b) have reported estimates of the pacific effect of trade based on alternative specifications, samples, and estimation methods. These estimates of risk reduction typically fall in a range of 20 to 40 percent, and they rise to about 60 percent or higher when the dependent variable is narrowed from MID involvement to MID onset with fatalities.

3.4. Assessing war duration

War duration concerns the width of the upper portion of the conflict cycle in Figure 4 corresponding to conflict management, mitigation, and termination. Note that war duration and termination are conceptually linked since termination is the endpoint of duration. War termination can be caused by military, political, or economic factors as well as third party intervention [Massoud (1996)]. Schelling's (1960, 1966) classic works treated conflict initiation, management, and termination as expectations formation among players within a mixed motive bargaining game. Isard (1969) and Isard and Smith (1982) utilized oligopoly principles to develop numerous theoretical procedures for preventing, shortening, or terminating conflict. Raiffa (1982) presented practical procedures for managing business conflicts, with obvious parallels to interstate conflicts. Boulding (1962) explored a number of ways in which conflicts end. Wittman (1979) presented necessary conditions for war termination, while Cross (1977) emphasized the role of learning in conflict bargaining. Each of these contributions treated the duration and termination of conflict as the result of players' rational cost–benefit calculations in the context of changing circumstances and information.

Consistent with this perspective, Slantchev (2004, p. 814) began his empirical study of war duration by assuming that leaders "form expectations about what they can gain from war and weigh these benefits against the costs of obtaining them through fighting." Once war is underway, leaders update their beliefs about relative strength, settlement possibilities, and risks of continued fighting. Information is gained during the course of the war until expectations about the outcome converge, thus permitting a successful settlement proposal. Based on this view of endogenous war termination, Slantchev derived a series of hypotheses, such as the prediction that initial military parity would increase uncertainty of the outcome and therefore tend to lengthen a war. He tested the hypotheses with hazard and ordered probit methods for a sample of 104 interstate wars between 1816 and 1991. Slantchev found that initial military parity, more difficult war terrain, and number of states involved lengthen expected duration, while contiguity and war initiation by a democratic state shorten expected duration. Slantchev also found that long wars tended to result in defeat or concessions for initiators, and initiators with advantages in prewar reserve forces and with lower casualty rates tended to demand and receive better settlements.

Greig (2001) studied the empirical determinants of short and long-term mediation success among enduring interstate rivals. Using hazard and ordered logit analysis, he analyzed 202 mediation attempts involving 19 enduring rivalries during the period 1946–1992. Regarding short-term mediation outcomes, Greig found that the probability of full or partial settlement success was greater when mediation occurred earlier in a rivalry, when mediation was initiated by one or both rivals, and when the dispute involved a territorial issue. Greig gauged long-term outcomes in terms of the comparative severity of the next dispute and the elapsed time until the next militarized dispute involving force. He found that long-term success was more likely when at least one of the rivals had moved toward democracy within the past two years, when the rivals' previous disputes had tended to end in stalemate, and when their previous disputes were more severe in terms of hostility and fatalities. Greig (2001, p. 710) drew the policy lesson that "mediation efforts are best able to facilitate improvement in the rivalry relationship and reduce the frequency of the most conflictual types of activities after enduring rivals have had sufficient opportunity to experience an extended pattern of high-cost disputes that fail to yield a change in the rivalry status quo."

4. Arms rivalry, proliferation, and arms control

4.1. Definitions

Born in the Cold War, peace economics has long been concerned with issues of arms rivalry, proliferation, and arms control. An *arms rivalry* is a competitive increase in weapons quantities or qualities of two or more parties. The parties might be states, intrastate groups (e.g., rebel factions), or transnational groups (e.g., terrorist organizations). Although the expressions arms rivalry and arms race are often used synonymously, an *arms race* is more properly thought of as a special case of arms rivalry distinguished by an unusually rapid rate of increase in armaments. *Proliferation* is an increase in the number of parties possessing weapons of mass destruction (WMD), namely nuclear, biological, chemical, or radiological weapons. Proliferation often grows out of an arms rivalry and can easily spawn new rivalries.

Following Schelling and Halperin (1961, p. 2), *arms control* refers to all forms of military cooperation between potential adversaries designed to reduce (1) the risk of war, (2) damage should war occur, and (3) the political and economic costs of military preparation. This conception of arms control asserts a common interest between adversaries, once again placing war and rivalry in the context of a mixed motive game. The forms of cooperation are varied and include changes in lines of communication, location of forces, quantity or technological capacity of weapons, and rates of weapons accumulation. Note also that the three goals of arms control are distinct, raising the possibility of tradeoffs among them.

4.2. Models of arms rivalry

Many foundational contributions in peace economics focused partly or wholly on arms rivalry and arms control. We return to the historical roots of peace economics by surveying four seminal models of arms rivalry. The models are distinguished by their mathematical approach and theoretical focus. The prisoner's dilemma model is a basic game theoretic analysis of the mixed motive nature of arms rivalry among strategically interdependent players. Richardson's (1960a) arms rivalry model uses differential equations to identify conditions that could give rise to an unstable arms race. Intriligator and Brito's dynamic model of a missile war leads to various strategic implications of arms rivalry and arms control [Intriligator (1975), Intriligator and Brito (1986)]. McGuire's (1965) optimization model draws on oligopoly theory to explore the interdependent resource allocation decisions of two armed rivals.

4.2.1. Prisoner's dilemma interpretation of arms rivalry

Assume two rivals *A* and *B* choose between the strategies of low armaments or high armaments. Each rival prefers to have relative military advantage, but armaments are costly. The ordinal payoffs generate the prisoner's dilemma game shown in Figure 6.

Player *B*

	Low Armaments	High Armaments
Low Armaments	3, 3	1, 4
High Armaments	4, 1	2, 2

Player *A*

Figure 6. Prisoner's dilemma game of arms rivalry.

For each player, it is better to choose high armaments, regardless of the other player's choice. If both players choose their dominant strategy, the payoff outcome is (2, 2). The outcome is a Nash equilibrium, meaning that neither player has the incentive to unilaterally switch to low armaments. The outcome is also Pareto inefficient, which is the impetus for arms control. If *A* and *B* abide by an arms agreement to lower armaments, the payoff outcome is (3, 3) rather than (2, 2), because resources are available for non-military activities with no change in relative advantage. Note that the diversion of resources from weapons supports Schelling and Halperin's second and third arms control goals: because weapons stocks are lower, damage is lower if war occurs, and the cost of military preparation is reduced.

If the prisoner's dilemma shows that the impetus for arms control is efficiency, it also shows that the bane of arms control is cheating. If *A* increases its armaments while *B* abides by the agreement, then *A* increases its payoff from 3 to 4. *B* has the same incentive to cheat. If both cheat, there is in effect no arms agreement, and the outcome returns to the Nash equilibrium. To guard against cheating, most arms control agreements contain verification and compliance measures. When the basic prisoner's dilemma game is extended to allow for detection of cheating, it can be shown that a Nash equilibrium can include abidance if the probability of detection is sufficiently high [see, e.g., Sandler and Hartley (1995, pp. 78–79)].

Arms rivalries typically involve repeated rounds of action and reaction, which means that the potential for cooperation is greater than in a one-shot prisoner's dilemma. For example, if *A* cheats on an arms control agreement and is detected, *B* might cease to maintain low armaments in future rounds, thereby punishing *A* by lowering *A*'s payoff. Hence, *A* (and by similar logic, *B*) may be less prone to cheat given the on-going nature and uncertain length of the relationship. In formal repeated prisoner's dilemma games of unknown length, it can be shown that if the players value the future sufficiently, then there exist (subgame perfect) Nash equilibriums that yield low armaments in every round [see, e.g., Fudenberg and Maskin (1986)].

The prisoner's dilemma by itself does not speak to Schelling and Halperin's first arms control objective, namely a reduction in the risk of war. To connect armaments to the risk of war, a link must be made between weapons accumulations and the likelihood of war between the rivals, such as done by Richardson.

4.2.2. Richardson model

Mathematical modeling of arms rivalry began with Richardson (1960a) who, more than any other, initiated and inspired the quantitative study of arms rivalry and war. The basic Richardson model for two players A and B is defined by two differential equations:

$$\dot{M}_A = kM_B - \alpha M_A + g, \tag{1}$$

$$\dot{M}_B = rM_A - \beta M_B + h. \tag{2}$$

Richardson assumed that each player's time rate of change in military capability, $\dot{M}_i$ $(i = A, B)$, is positively related to the rival's military stock and negatively related to its own military stock. Parameters k and r are reaction coefficients of A and B, which show how sensitive each nation is to the military capability of the other. Parameters α and β are fatigue coefficients, which reflect the economic or political costs of a player's own military stock. Parameters g and h are grievance terms, representing sources of change in military capability independent of own and adversary military stocks. A steady-state equilibrium of military capability (M_A^*, M_B^*) is found when $\dot{M}_A = \dot{M}_B = 0$:

$$M_A^* = (kh + \beta g)/(\alpha\beta - kr), \tag{3}$$

$$M_B^* = (rg + \alpha h)/(\alpha\beta - kr). \tag{4}$$

The equilibrium is stable if and only if $\alpha\beta > kr$, meaning roughly that the degree of fatigue in the system $(\alpha\beta)$ outweighs the degree of reactivity (kr).

Note that the Richardson model lacks any strategic elements that might determine the degree of reactivity and it is silent about when an arms rivalry might lead to war. However, it is clear from his writings that Richardson was particularly troubled about the possible absence of a stable equilibrium. Without stability, an arms rivalry could become a true arms race, with accelerating armaments increasing fears and suspicions and with them the risk of war [Richardson (1960a, p. 61)]. Hence, in Richardson's view, mitigating an unstable arms rivalry could contribute to all three of Schelling and Halperin's arms control objectives.

An important extension of the Richardson model was provided by Boulding (1962, chapter 2), who generalized the concept of action–reaction processes to include states, non-state groups, and individuals. The actions of the players in their various domains involve many possible forms of hostility and friendliness, not just arms rivalry. Hence, Boulding's work suggests applications of the Richardson model to non-interstate arms rivalries and to a broader class of action–reaction processes in conflict settings. For a review of additional extensions of the Richardson model, see Sandler and Hartley (1995, pp. 82–89).

4.2.3. The Intriligator–Brito model

Whereas Richardson's major concern was the stability of arms rivalry, Intriligator and Brito were interested in crisis stability, meaning the potential for the risk of war to remain low even in a period of rising tension (including arms escalation) between rivals. The Intriligator–Brito (I–B) model therefore focused on the strategic implications of the deterrent and attack capabilities of the rivals' missile holdings, M_i $(i = A, B)$. Here we present a simplified version of the I–B model [Intriligator (1975), Intriligator and Brito (1986), Wolfson (1985)].

In an all-out attack by nation B, $f_B M_B$ of A's missiles could be destroyed, where the parameter f_B is the number of A missiles destroyed by one B counterforce missile. If A has enough surviving missiles to create an unacceptable level of casualties in B, $\overline{C}_B$, then B could be deterred. The number of surviving missiles that A perceives it needs to deter B is $\overline{C}_B/v_A$, where v_A is the number of casualties in B caused by one A countervalue missile. Applying similar logic to B's deterrence of A implies the following deterrence conditions for A and B:

$$M_A \geqslant f_B M_B + \overline{C}_B/v_A, \tag{5}$$

$$M_B \geqslant f_A M_A + \overline{C}_A/v_B. \tag{6}$$

Assume that A and B also consider using their missiles to attack. In an all-out attack by A, $f_A M_A$ of B's missiles could be destroyed. If B's surviving missiles could cause no more than $\widehat{C}_A$ casualties in retaliation, then A could attack. Applying similar logic to B's attack potential implies the following attack conditions for A and B:

$$(M_B - f_A M_A)v_B \leqslant \widehat{C}_A \quad \text{or equivalently} \quad M_A \geqslant M_B/f_A - (\widehat{C}_A/f_A v_B), \tag{7}$$

$$(M_A - f_B M_B)v_A \leqslant \widehat{C}_B \quad \text{or equivalently} \quad M_B \geqslant M_A/f_B - (\widehat{C}_B/f_B v_A), \tag{8}$$

where v_i $(i = A, B)$ is casualties caused by one i countervalue missile.

Conditions (5)–(8) carry various strategic implications for alternative missile vectors (M_A, M_B) as shown in Figure 7. Combinations of M_A and M_B on or to the right of the "A deters" line (in regions 1, 2A, and 4A) are missile vectors that imply A can deter B. Vectors on or to the left of the "B deters" line (in regions 1, 2B and 4B) imply that B can deter A. The shaded area (region 1) is the cone of mutual deterrence. Combinations of M_A and M_B on or to the right of the "A can attack" line (in regions 4A, 5A and 6) imply that A can attack B, while points on or to the left of the "B can attack" line (in regions 4B, 5B and 6) imply that B can attack A. Figure 7 also shows a region of jittery deterrence (region 3) where A and B can neither attack nor deter. Areas 5A, 5B and 6 are regions of war initiation. In regions 5A and 5B one side can attack and neither can deter. In region 6 each side can attack and neither can deter.

The I–B model can be used to explore the effects of arms rivalry and arms control on the risk of war [Intriligator and Brito (1986)]. Starting from the origin in Figure 7, arms trajectory T1 moves the missile vector into region 6 where each can attack and neither can deter, thus generating a high risk of war. Trajectory T1 is consistent with Richardson's view that an arms rivalry increases the risk of war. But the Richardson view is not the only one that emerges in the I–B model. Suppose an arms rivalry occurs along trajectory T2, which Intriligator and Brito believed was reasonably descriptive of the post-World War II rivalry between the USA and the USSR. The rivalry pushes the

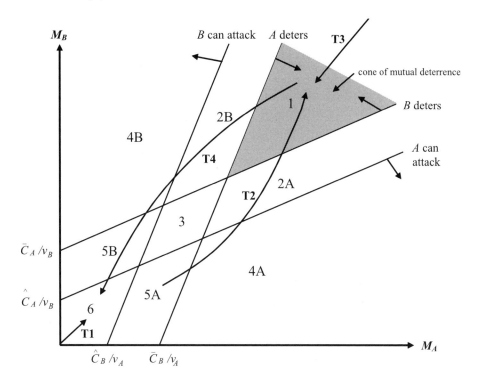

Figure 7. The Intriligator–Brito model.

missile vector into region 1 where both players can deter and hence lowers the risk of war. Notice that along trajectory T2 the risk of war is lowered through an *increase in weapons*. At the same time, the damage should war occur and the cost of military preparation are both higher, indicating that in some scenarios tradeoffs exist among the goals of arms control. Arms reduction trajectory T3 moves the missile vector further down in the cone of mutual deterrence, implying reduced weapons costs with no increase in the risk of war. Trajectory T3 also implies lower damage in the event of war. Trajectory T4 is a different matter, however. A substantial weapons reduction moves the missile vector into the dangerous region 6 where the risk of war is high.

Other scenarios can be explored with the I–B model, including cases of weapons proliferation when a trajectory moves the missile vector off the horizontal or vertical axis, changes in the missile effectiveness terms, f_i and v_i, and changes in acceptable casualties, $\bar{C}_i$ and $\widehat{C}_i$. Anderton (1992) criticized the attack conditions of the I–B model. His reformulation of the I–B model suggested that a missile rivalry contained to low weapons levels would not be associated with an excessively high risk of war, everything else the same.

4.2.4. Arms rivalry as economic choice

McGuire's (1965) model of arms rivalry is important because it embedded the strategic concerns of attack and deterrence in a rational choice framework. In his basic model McGuire assumed nations A and B maximized their respective utilities as functions of security and consumption subject to a resource constraint. Security was determined by a nation's attack and deterrence capabilities, which in turn depended on the two countries' weapons stocks along with other factors like information. Reaction functions were derived and then solved for the Cournot/Nash equilibrium of armaments.

McGuire's theoretical study of arms rivalry was remarkably wide ranging. In extensions he explored the contract curve available under bilateral arms control, the Stackelberg solution available under unilateral arms control, and survival/extinction solutions. He also analyzed the role of information (and secrecy) and showed how incomplete information can radically alter the rate and direction of arms rivalry and the opportunities for mutually beneficial arms control. Because uncertainty could affect the relative marginal returns for attack and deterrence, McGuire maintained that information could be manipulated unilaterally or multilaterally so as to shift an arms rivalry toward a lower-risk equilibrium. Lastly, McGuire emphasized the multidimensional nature of arms rivalry and arms control, recognizing the substitution possibilities among weapons quantities, qualities (e.g., accuracy, yield), and intelligence effort.

4.3. Selected empirical studies of arms rivalry and proliferation

4.3.1. Arms rivalry and the risk of war

Richardson's (1939, 1960a) studies of military expenditures prior to World Wars I and II led him to believe that arms buildups increase the risk of war. It was not until the I–B model raised questions about the generality of Richardson's view that a debate existed in peace economics about the relationship between arms rivalries and the risk of war. The first empirical test of the issue was conducted by Wallace (1979), who found that arms rivalries between major states exerted a strong positive effect on the escalation of militarized disputes to war. The robustness of this finding was questioned in studies that followed [e.g., see Diehl (1983)].

Building upon this earlier literature, Sample (2002) used all MID dyads from 1816 to 1992 to investigate the effect of military buildups on the likelihood of escalation to war. Her dependent variable measured whether a MID escalated to war, and her key right-hand variable indicated whether both nations in the dyad were involved in rapid military buildups. Other independent variables controlled for comparative military capabilities, high defense burdens, territorial disputes, contiguity, and nuclear capability on the part of one or both nations. In contrast to the early studies, Sample's dataset included both major and minor powers. Of 2304 dispute dyads, 267 involved major states, 1196 involved minor states, and 841 involved a major and a minor state.

Using all dyads for the full period 1816–1992, Sample found a significant positive relationship between military buildups and escalation to war. Based on logit analysis, disputes involving dyads with rapid buildups were estimated to be more than twice as likely to escalate to war, other things equal. Among other significant effects, Sample also found that the presence of nuclear weapons reduced the likelihood of escalation by about half. When she estimated her model separately for the three types of dyads, she again found a large significant effect of buildups for both major power dyads and minor power dyads but no effect for mixed dyads. Also, when she restricted her analysis to post-World War II, she found no significant effect for buildups among any of the three dyad types, while nuclear capability continued to have a negative effect for major and mixed dyads. In Sample's view, the results suggest that disputants in mixed dyads read one another's buildups differently than do disputants in major and minor dyads, and that all dyads perception of deterrence has changed since the use of nuclear weapons in World War II. We would add that the results are broadly consistent with Richardson's view on arms rivalry leading up to the two world wars as well as Intriligator and Brito's interpretation of the deterrence effect of nuclear armaments.

4.3.2. Determinants of nuclear weapons proliferation

While most studies have been restricted to case study methods, Singh and Way (2004) recently provided a rigorous large-scale analysis of the risk factors of nuclear weapons proliferation. Their work is an important addition to peace economics, not only because of the latter's long interest in proliferation, but also because Singh and Way found that economic variables have an important influence on nuclear proliferation. Also, their work suggests that quantitative study of the proliferation of other weapons of mass destruction (biological, chemical, radiological) might be possible in the future.

Using hazard models as well as multinomial logit, Singh and Way estimated the effects of various economic and political variables on the likelihood of nuclear proliferation. They began by defining four stages or levels of proliferation, ranging from no interest to serious exploration to program launch to weapons acquisition. Of their sample of 154 countries over the period 1945–2000, 23 countries seriously explored the nuclear option, of which 16 proceeded to launch programs, and of which 9 (including South Africa) actually acquired nuclear weapons. Indicator variables for these three active stages were coded for each country-year and served as dependent variables. Primary independent variables related to per capita GDP, industrial capacity, security, political organization, and trade policy. Singh and Way found that external security issues exerted a powerful influence on proliferation. Participation in long-lived rivalries and frequent MIDs increased substantially the risk that a nation would move toward nuclear weapons, whereas alliance with a nuclear-armed major power decreased the risk. Economic development generally had a positive effect, but the likelihood of proliferation actually dropped off at higher income levels. Lastly, consistent with the liberal peace hypothesis, trade openness was found to lower the risk of proliferation.

5. Technological and geographic dimensions of conflict

5.1. The inherent propensity toward peace or war

A major theme in Schelling's early work in peace economics was that there exist characteristics inherent in weaponry, geography, and military organization that push adversaries toward peace or war, independent of the personalities and goals of the leaders, the nature of the disagreement between the rivals, and misperceptions about resolve or hostility [Schelling (1960, chapters 9 and 10, 1966, chapter 6) and Schelling and Halperin (1961, chapters 1 and 2)]. Schelling (1966, p. 234) wrote: "There is, then, something that we might call the 'inherent propensity toward peace or war' embodied in the weaponry, the geography, and the military organization of the time. Arms and military organizations can hardly be considered the exclusively determining factors in international conflict, but neither can they be considered neutral." Note that Schelling does not overstate the applicability of the concept of inherent propensity. The elements of weapons technology, geography, and organization are not necessarily dominant or even most important in explaining the risk of war, but neither are they irrelevant.

5.2. Lanchester theory and the inherent propensity toward peace or war

Whereas the Richardson model involved the *accumulation* of weapons in an arms rivalry, the Lanchester (1916) model pertained to the *attrition* of weapons in a war. Throughout much of the twentieth century, the Lanchester model constituted the foundation of mathematical war modeling [Taylor (1983)]. Lanchester theory has been subject to criticism among war modelers [Epstein (1985), Ancker (1995, p. 182)], but it is still used to assess some of the dynamic aspects of war in military service organizations [Epstein (1985, p. 3)].

5.2.1. Basic Lanchester model of war attrition

Suppose players A and B fight a war, with military stocks $M_i(t)$ $(i = A, B)$ at time t during the war. The basic Lanchester model describes the attrition of military stocks for the two sides with the following differential equations:

$$\dot{M}_A = -\beta M_B, \tag{9}$$
$$\dot{M}_B = -\alpha M_A, \tag{10}$$

where the notation for time has been suppressed for convenience. The parameters α and β, called attrition-rate coefficients, describe the effectiveness of A and B's military stocks in destroying the stock of the other. The coefficients can reflect the speed or accuracy of weapons, geographical impediments or enhancements to fighting ability, and the effectiveness of military organization and training. Given the pre-war or time-zero stocks M_i^0 $(i = A, B)$, Equations (9) and (10) determine the winner in a fight-to-the-finish war in accordance with the well-known Lanchester square law [Taylor (1983,

v. 1, pp. 72–74)]:

$$\alpha\left(M_A^0\right)^2 > \beta\left(M_B^0\right)^2 \quad \Rightarrow \quad A \text{ wins,}$$
$$\alpha\left(M_A^0\right)^2 < \beta\left(M_B^0\right)^2 \quad \Rightarrow \quad B \text{ wins.} \qquad (11)$$

As an example, suppose A has 1000 soldiers armed with assault rifles with effectiveness $\alpha = 0.02$, and B has 500 soldiers with machine guns with effectiveness $\beta = 0.10$. Substituting the coefficient values into condition (11) implies that B will win a war with A, even though B is outnumbered two-to-one.

5.2.2. Lanchester war with mobilization advantage and re-supply

We extend the basic Lanchester model by introducing two factors, mobilization advantage and weapons re-supply. Weapons technology, geography, and military organization affect whether a first-mover attack advantage exists. If so, the attacker will have some period of extra-normal military success relative to its rival. We call this the mobilization advantage period. Suppose player A assumes that if B attacks, B's effectiveness would be β_a and would have a surprise attack advantage lasting for θ_B units of time. The subscript on β_a indicates that B is the attacker. The mobilization advantage period is assumed to be a time during which B can attack A, but A cannot strike back. This is Stage 1 of the Lanchester war. Once the mobilization advantage period ends, the model enters Stage 2 where A fights with effectiveness α_d against B, where the subscript on α_d indicates that A is the defender. Assume that once the war enters Stage 2, each player acquires additional weapons P_i $(i = A, B)$ from indigenous production or the arms market.

The two-stage Lanchester model with mobilization advantage and weapons re-supply under the assumption that B attacks is then:

Stage 1 $(t = 0$ to $t = \theta_B)$

$$\dot{M}_A = -\beta_a M_B,$$
$$\dot{M}_B = 0; \qquad (12)$$

Stage 2 $(t = \theta_B$ to $t = $ end of war)

$$\dot{M}_A = -\beta_a M_B + P_A,$$
$$\dot{M}_B = -\alpha_d M_A + P_B. \qquad (13)$$

Based upon mathematical manipulations of Taylor's (1983, v. 2, pp. 338–43) general linear Lanchester model with replacements, and given the pre-war military stocks, (12) and (13) determine the winner in a fight-to-the-finish war according to:

$$\alpha_d\left[M_A^0 - \beta_a\theta_B M_B^0 - (P_B/\alpha_d)\right]^2 > \beta_a\left[M_B^0 - (P_A/\beta_a)\right]^2 \quad \Rightarrow \quad A \text{ wins,}$$
$$\alpha_d\left[M_A^0 - \beta_a\theta_B M_B^0 - (P_B/\alpha_d)\right]^2 < \beta_a\left[M_B^0 - (P_A/\beta_a)\right]^2 \quad \Rightarrow \quad B \text{ wins.} \quad (14)$$

Note that if mobilization advantages and weapons re-supply during war are absent ($\theta_i = P_i = 0$, $i = A, B$), condition (14) collapses to the victory condition of the basic Lanchester model in (11).

5.2.3. Lanchester attack/defend model

Solving the top half of (14) for M_A^0 defines the "*A* defends" condition:

$$M_A^0 \geqslant \left[(\beta_a/\alpha_d)^{0.5} + \beta_a\theta_B\right]M_B^0 + \left(\frac{P_B}{\alpha_d} - \frac{P_A}{(\alpha_d\beta_a)^{0.5}}\right) \quad \Rightarrow \quad A \text{ defends.} \quad (15)$$

Similar methods give the "*B* defends" condition:

$$M_B^0 \geqslant \left[(\alpha_a/\beta_d)^{0.5} + \alpha_a\theta_A\right]M_A^0 + \left(\frac{P_A}{\beta_d} - \frac{P_B}{(\alpha_a\beta_d)^{0.5}}\right) \quad \Rightarrow \quad B \text{ defends.} \quad (16)$$

When the defend condition in (15) is not satisfied, then B can attack and defeat A. Likewise, when (16) is not satisfied, A can attack and defeat B. Conditions (15) and (16) highlight four elements that affect a player's ability to defend in the event of war: (1) own and rival weapons stocks, M_A^0 and M_B^0; (2) weapons capabilities (e.g., speed, accuracy), α and β; (3) mobilization advantages, θ_A and θ_B; and (4) re-supply abilities, P_A and P_B.

Various cases that arise under conditions (15) and (16) can be depicted in a graph with M_A plotted horizontally and M_B vertically. Treating (16) as an equality, B's defend line is plotted as a straight line with slope equal to the bracketed term and vertical intercept equal to the parenthetical term. B can defend at points on or above this line. A's defend line is plotted similarly from (15), but with slope equal to the inverse of the bracketed term and horizontal intercept equal to the parenthetical term. A can defend at points on or below its line.

Assume for now that any war between A and B would be quick, so that re-supply of weapons is irrelevant ($P_i = 0$, $i = A, B$). Both defend lines pass through the origin as in Figure 8. Figure 8a is drawn under the condition that B's defend line has a smaller slope than does A's, thereby creating a zone of mutual defense. After a simple rearrangement, the slope condition for a zone of mutual defense can be written algebraically as:

$$\left[(\beta_a/\alpha_d)^{0.5} + \beta_a\theta_B\right]\left[(\alpha_a/\beta_d)^{0.5} + \alpha_a\theta_A\right] < 1. \quad (17a)$$

This condition tends to hold when technological, geographic, and organizational factors combine to cause low attack parameters α_a and β_a, high defense parameters α_d and β_d, and low mobilization advantages θ_A and θ_B. Given an initial weapons stocks at point q, neither side can successfully attack, implying a relatively low risk of war. In Schelling's terminology, Figure 8a depicts an inherent propensity toward peace. This contrasts with Figure 8b, where the comparative magnitudes of the parameters are reversed, creating a mutual region of attack under the condition:

$$\left[(\beta_a/\alpha_d)^{0.5} + \beta_a\theta_B\right]\left[(\alpha_a/\beta_d)^{0.5} + \alpha_a\theta_A\right] > 1. \quad (17b)$$

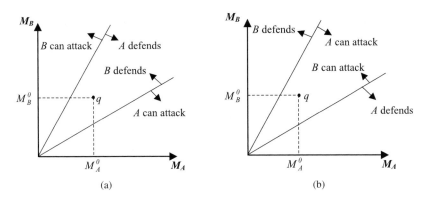

Figure 8. Mutual defense and mutual attack regions in the Lanchester attack/defend model.

A problem arises at point q in Figure 8b due to the common knowledge that the first mover will win. Even rivals that fundamentally wish to avoid war may nevertheless be compelled to attack before their rival does [Schelling (1966, chapter 6), Fischer (1984)]. In Schelling's terminology, Figure 8b depicts an inherent propensity toward war [Anderton (1990)].

Figure 8 highlights the importance of qualitative arms control. In Figure 8b, geographic repositioning of forces or placement of peacekeepers between the rivals could reduce mobilization advantages (lower θ_A and θ_B). Reconfigurations of weapons technologies and military organization away from attack and toward defense could reduce relative attack effectiveness (lower β_a/α_d and α_a/β_d). Such qualitative arms control could change the rivalry from an inherent propensity toward war in Figure 8b to an inherent propensity toward peace in Figure 8a.

In wars of long duration, weapons re-supply is generally operative ($P_i > 0$, $i = A, B$). Weapons re-supply ability is presumably rooted in economic strength, access to the arms market, or both. There are a number of possible effects and implications of weapons re-supply on inherent propensities in Figure 8. Other things equal, if P_B was substantially larger than P_A, the defend lines would have their same slopes but negative vertical intercepts, as dictated by conditions (15) and (16). If the weapons re-supply abilities were sufficiently asymmetric, at a balanced initial weapons point q in Figure 8a, B could defend but A could not. In such a scenario, A could be expected to resist arms reductions more than B due to B's relative strength in weapons re-supply. Hence, relative economic strength can be an important dimension of arms control broadly conceived. Turning to Figure 8b, downward shifts of the defend lines under B's relative superiority of weapons re-supply could cause point q to lie again in a region where B could defend but A could not. In such a scenario, there would still be a mutual attack region in the graph and thus an inherent propensity toward war based upon intrinsic weapons characteristics and geography. Nevertheless, the reciprocal fear of attack would be removed based upon B's superior weapons re-supply ability.

5.3. Offense/defense theory and evidence

Offense–defense theory (ODT) maintains that the character of international relations is influenced by the ease or difficulty of offensive relative to defensive military operations [Lynn-Jones (2004, p. xi)]. ODT has been applied to many aspects of international relations, including the risk of war, alliance formation, arms control, crisis behavior, size of states, and structure of the international system [Adams (2003/2004, p. 46)]. ODT's central prediction is that war is more likely when offense has the advantage over defense in military operations [Van Evera (1999)]. Here we liken Schelling's concept of an inherent propensity toward peace or war with an offense–defense balance in favor of the defense and offense, respectively.

ODT is an active and controversial research topic in international relations [Adams (2003/2004), Gortzak, Haftel and Sweeney (2005)]. One area of debate is how to conceptualize and measure the offensive/defensive balance (ODB) [Gortzak, Haftel and Sweeney (2005, p. 72)]. Van Evera (1998) conceptualizes the ODB broadly to include military technology, geography, collective security systems, defensive alliances, behavior of neutral states, and perceptions of the actors. Adams (2003/2004) defines the ODB narrowly in terms of military technology alone. In the Lanchester models above, the ODB is conceptualized narrowly based on military technology and organization alone when mobilization advantages and weapons re-supply are set to zero, but more broadly when mobilization advantages and weapons re-supply are included. Schelling's original conception of inherent propensity is relatively narrow, encompassing military technology, military organization, and geography, but not weapons re-supply and the additional factors included by Van Evera.

How broadly the ODB is defined will affect the explanatory scope claimed for ODT. Given Van Evera's broad conceptualization, it is not surprising that he views ODT as an encompassing theory of war risk and other international relations phenomena. Indeed, Van Evera (1999, p. 190) claims that ODT should be viewed as the "master key to the causes of conflict." In contrast to Van Evera, Schelling (1966, p. 234) maintained that the elements that determine the inherent propensity toward peace or war "can hardly be considered the exclusively determining factors in international conflict." Schelling's more narrow approach suggests that the ODB is just one among other factors purported to explain war risk and that the empirical challenge is to determine the relative importance of the ODB.

An empirical test of ODT that is consistent with Schelling's more narrow approach was recently provided by Adams (2003/2004), who defined the ODB based upon military technology alone. In testing the effects of the ODB, Adams (2003/2004, p. 47) argued that it is important to observe the incidence of attack and conquest rather than of war because the ODB can be expected to generate less variance in the incidence of war than in attack and conquest. Adams also distinguished between offense, defense, and deterrence. An offensive operation occurs when a state uses force to conquer another state's territory or to compel it to comply with policy directives. A defensive operation occurs when a state uses force against another state's military to fend off and limit the damage of that state's offensive operation. A deterrent operation occurs when a state prepares or shows an ability to use force against another state's non-military assets to discourage that state from initiating or continuing an offensive operation [Adams (2003/2004, p. 53)]. Adams' use of these terms is broadly consistent with Schelling's (1966, pp. 78–80) conceptions of defense, deterrence, offense, and compellence, although there are some distinctions.

Based on her systematic review of the best technologies available since 1800, Adams determined that offense was dominant during 1800–1849 and 1934–1945, defense was dominant during 1850–1933, and deterrence was dominant in the nuclear era beginning in 1946. She hypothesized that attacks and conquests would be most frequent in offense-dominant eras, less frequent in the defense-dominant era, and rare in the deterrence-dominant era. Adams tested these hypotheses on a dataset she constructed on attacks and conquests by great powers and nuclear states from 1800–1997. For each state and year, Adams coded three dependent variables, indicating whether the state's territory was conquered, whether it attacked another great power, and whether it attacked a non-great power. The key independent variable was the offense–defense–deterrence balance, which was coded 0 in the deterrence-dominant era, 1 in the defense-dominant era, and 2 in the offense-dominant eras. Additional variables included relative military capability, number of years a state had been a great power or a nuclear state, and a time trend. Using logit analysis, Adams found strong support for her hypotheses about the effects of the offense–defense–deterrence balance on great power attacks and conquests. Adams (2003/2004, p. 76) estimated that attacks on other great powers were 12 times more likely each year under offensive dominance (probability 0.156) than under defensive dominance (probability 0.013), and they were 13 times more likely each year under defensive dominance than under deterrence dominance (probability 0.001). Smaller but significant effects with the predicted pattern were found for conquests and attacks on non-great powers.

Adams' research seems broadly supportive of the Lanchester modeling exercises summarized in Figure 8. When the ODB favors the defense, Figure 8a pertains, and great power attacks and conquests are relatively unlikely. When the ODB favors the offense, Figure 8b obtains, and great power attacks and conquests are more likely. In addition to the results on the ODB, Adams (2003/2004, p. 77) found that the least capable great powers (those with capability indexes in the 10th percentile) were 2.5 times less likely to attack (probability 0.006) than the most capable great powers (those in the 90th percentile, probability 0.015). For conquests, she found that the probability that the least capable great powers would be conquered was 40 times higher (probability 0.008) than that of the most capable great powers (probability 0.0002). These results on relative capability pertain to the position of the initial weapons vector in Figure 8. When a state's relative capability is sufficiently weak, the initial weapons stock is in a zone where its rival can attack and win. This condition can hold irrespective of the ODB. Hence, the ODB is just one element that affects the risk of attack in the Lanchester model; the relative capability of the rivals also matters as Adams found.

Finally, note that an intermediate conception of the ODB would incorporate geographic elements of war as implied by Schelling. In the Lanchester model, the presence of mobilization advantages tilts attack/defense possibilities toward the offense. One aspect of mobilization advantage is the geographic closeness of states, measured by proximity or contiguity. Empirical research has shown that proximity and contiguity are significant risk factors for interstate war [see, e.g., Russett and Oneal (2001), Senese (2005)]. In our view, this lends empirical support to the Lanchester exercises above and to the value of incorporating geography in conceptualizations of the ODB.

6. Appropriation and exchange theory

Previous sections of this survey have emphasized the place of economic concepts, variables, and methods in understanding risk factors for war, arms rivalry, proliferation, and arms control, and conflict management and termination. Research in peace economics also evaluates the effects of military spending on the economy and the effects of conflict on economic variables such as trade, growth, and investment. While peace economics will continue to advance our understanding of these topics, a new branch of inquiry has emerged that focuses on a decidedly different objective, namely the introduction of appropriation possibilities into mainstream economic theory. This relatively new branch grows out of the seminal work of Bush (1972), Hirshleifer (1988, 1991), Garfinkel (1990), Skaperdas (1992), and Grossman and Kim (1995), who developed models of appropriation and production (see Chapter 22 of this *Handbook* for a review). More recent work has introduced appropriation into economic models of exchange [Anderton, Anderton and Carter (1999), Rider (1999), Hausken (2004), Anderson and Marcouiller (2005)]. The central premise of this literature is that appropriation, like production and exchange, is a fundamental category of economic behavior that profoundly affects economic incentives and outcomes. These models reveal how conflict both shapes and is shaped by the traditional economic activities of production and exchange.

6.1. Edgeworth box model of vulnerable trade

Following Anderton and Carter (2006), assume two players A and B, which can be individuals or groups (including nations). There are two goods X and Y, and the initial endowments E_i^X and E_i^Y ($i = A, B$) of the goods are such that if trade occurs, A will import X and export Y. For simplicity, assume that A and B have equal cross endowments ($E_A^X = E_B^Y$ and $E_A^Y = E_B^X$). This gives rise to a square Edgeworth box and an initial endowment point on the negative diagonal, as shown by point a in Figure 9. Assume the players have identical and homothetic preferences over goods X and Y, such that the contract curve is the positive diagonal. Also assume that the goods are weighted equally in the utility function ($MRS|_{X=Y} = 1$). The square Edgeworth box, identical homothetic preferences, equal weight together imply that the absolute slope of the negative diagonal in Figure 9 is the relative world price of X and equals 1 ($P = P^X/P^Y = 1$).

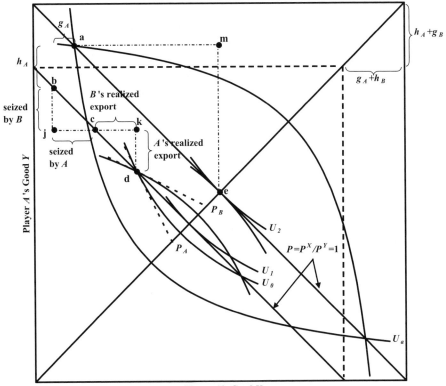

Figure 9. Exchange and appropriation in an Edgeworth box.

Absent appropriation possibilities, player A imports am units of X and exports me units of Y (with B the other side of the trade), and consumption occurs at point e.

To introduce trade vulnerability into the Edgeworth box, assume that goods designated for trade are subject to appropriation and are called gross exports. Exports remaining after appropriation are called realized exports and are exchanged at Walrasian prices P^X and P^Y. For simplicity assume that each good is attacked and defended out of initial endowments of that good. Hence, player A uses g_A^X of its X endowment to appropriate B's gross exports of X, which B protects by diverting h_B^X of its X endowment to defense. Likewise, B allocates g_B^Y of its Y endowment to appropriate A's gross exports, which A protects with h_A^Y of its Y endowment. To help follow the notation, think of g as guns for attack and h as height of defensive fortification.

Assume that appropriation of each traded good is determined by a ratio-form contest success function such that the proportion of gross exports realized in exchange depends on the levels of defense and attack and a vulnerability parameter Z^j ($j = X, Y$). Given equal vulnerabilities ($Z^X = Z^Y$) along with the other symmetry assumptions, each player will allocate an equal amount of resources to defend exports ($h_A^Y = h_B^X = h$) and to attack imports ($g_A^X = g_B^Y = g$). Resources allocated to defense and attack are not available for consumption, so the Edgeworth box shrinks by $h+g$ along each dimension, giving rise to the dashed box in Figure 9. The use of resources for defense and attack also shifts the endowment point from a to b. Given the symmetry assumptions, point b will likewise lie on the negative diagonal of the reduced box. The shrinkage of the Edgeworth box shows the *resource cost effect* of trade vulnerability and is determined endogenously.

The two fundamental activities of appropriation and exchange combine to determine the final consumption point d in Figure 9. Appropriation moves the economy from b to c, while realized trade moves the economy from c to d. Player A's gross exports of good Y consist of bj units seized by B and kd units sold to B. Given symmetry, identical amounts apply to player B for good X. Because d lies on the negative diagonal of the reduced box, the players have equal cross consumptions and P continues to equal 1. The location of points c and d are determined endogenously.

A region of mutual gain remains at the final consumption point d in Figure 9. This reflects the *wedge effect* of appropriation possibilities, which prevents the effective relative prices of X observed by A and B from converging. This is because the anticipated piracy of Y exports raises A's effective relative price P_A above 1, while the anticipated piracy of X exports lowers B's effective relative price P_B below 1. Consequently, the players' marginal values are unequal at equilibrium point d, but neither player has an incentive to extend trade farther. In short, appropriation possibilities restrain trade, much like tariffs.

The utility losses associated with the resource cost and wedge effects are also shown in Figure 9. Focusing on player A, the resource cost effect reduces utility from U_2 to U_1, and the wedge effect further reduces it from U_1 to U_0. By symmetry, the same utility losses hold for player B. Note in Figure 9 that player A's indifference curve through point d is higher than A's indifference curve through point a. Hence, player A (and by symmetry, player B) prefers vulnerable trade to autarky ($U_0 > U_a$). However, if appropriation possibilities are sufficiently strong, the resource cost and wedge effects can result in indifference curve U_0 lying below the indifference curve through point a. In this case trade would not occur as an equilibrium outcome.

Anderton and Carter (2006) use numerical simulations of their model to explore the effects of symmetric and asymmetric changes in vulnerability and resource endowments and the conditions under which trade equilibrium is foreclosed. The main lesson is that appropriation possibilities can profoundly reshape an economy and threaten the existence of exchange itself. The model also shows that a motive for the accumulation of the tools of conflict can be rooted in the protection or appropriation of wealth, in this case the wealth embodied in trade. At a broader level, Figure 9 demonstrates that the classic Edgeworth box economy is a special case, not just because it abstracts from production, but also because it ignores the complicating effects of appropriation possibilities on the economy.

6.2. General equilibrium model of production, appropriation, and exchange

Anderton, Anderton and Carter (1999) model a one-time interaction between two players as a sequential predator–prey game with the potential for trade. The two players, called Defender and Attacker, begin the game with resource endowments R_D and R_A. Defender moves first, allocating its resources between production of consumption goods X and Y and production of military goods M_D used to defend its resources. Attacker moves second, allocating its resources to the production of consumption goods and, if it chooses to attack Defender's resources, military goods M_A. Any seizure of resources by Attacker forecloses the possibility of trade. Hence, given Defender's level of defense, either Attacker produces military goods and engages in appropriation or Attacker produces no military goods and engages in trade. The combined decisions of Defender and Attacker result in either conflict or trade. As first mover, Defender anticipates Attacker's reaction and chooses a level of military goods that brings about the state of the world (conflict or trade) that yields Defender the higher utility. If conflict is better for Defender, it strategically chooses M_D to maximize utility in the conflict world. If trade is better for Defender, it strategically chooses M_D such that Attacker will trade and set attack effort M_A to zero. Anderton, Anderton and Carter (1999) adapt Grossman and Kim's (1996) predator–prey model of production and appropriation to define the conflict utilities, and they use a standard Ricardian model of production and exchange to specify the trade utilities.

Anderton, Anderton and Carter (1999) focus their analysis on two key parameters: the relative technological advantage of attack over defense, Z, and the relative resource endowment, $R = R_D/R_A$. Figure 10 depicts how Z and R typically combine to determine the existence of conflict or trade. For the moment, ignore the bold locus and focus on the light lines that demarcate the Z–R space into three zones. These three zones depict combinations of Z and R that lead Attacker to allocate zero (no predation), some (partial predation), or all (pure predation) of its resources to attack Defender's resources in the Grossman–Kim model of conflict. There are no exchange possibilities in that model, so the central issue is whether Attacker will allocate resources to attack Defender's resources and, if so, whether Attacker will partially or fully specialize in predation. Intuitively, when Z is high, attack is effective, and when R is high, Defender is a lucrative target to attack. As shown in Figure 10, when attack effectiveness and relative resource endowment (Z and R) are both low, it is comparatively easy for Defender to completely deter Attacker (no predation). If Z and R are sufficiently high, it pays Attacker to completely specialize in predation (pure predation). For sufficiently high levels of Z but moderate levels of R, Attacker can appropriate a substantial portion of Defender's resources with only a modest level of weapons, leaving some of its resources for production (partial predation) [Anderton, Anderton and Carter (1999, pp. 171–172)].

Assume now that specialized production and exchange is possible between Defender and Attacker. When profitable to do so, Defender will induce Attacker to trade by choosing the lowest level of weapons consistent with Attacker accepting trade. When it is

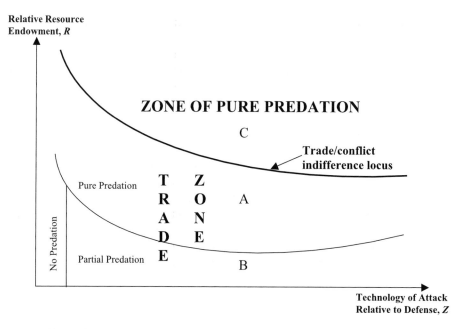

Figure 10. Trade and predation in a model of production, exchange, and appropriation.

not profitable to induce trade, Defender will choose a level of weapons that minimizes its loss from Attacker's predation. The dark curve in Figure 10 represents a typical *trade/conflict indifference locus* that emerges in the model. For $Z–R$ points below the locus (in the Trade Zone), trade occurs rather than conflict. For $Z–R$ points above the locus (in the Zone of Pure Predation), pure predation occurs. For $Z–R$ points on the locus, both Defender and Attacker are indifferent between trade and conflict [Anderton, Anderton and Carter (1999, pp. 172–174)].

Several implications follow from Figure 10. First, exchange forestalls appropriation over a wide range of combinations of relative attack effectiveness and relative resource endowment. Figure 10 shows $Z–R$ points of trade that would otherwise be points of pure predation (set A) or partial predation (set B). Sets A and B demonstrate how pure conflict models miss the conflict-reducing potential of specialized production and exchange. Figure 10 also demonstrates how standard trade models, which ignore appropriation possibilities, overstate trade potential. When relative attack effectiveness and relative resources of Defender are sufficiently high, incentives for predation are so strong that pure predation results, and specialized production and exchange disappear. Thus, appropriation possibilities foreclose trade in the zone of pure predation. Finally, note that in standard trade theory, such as the Ricardian model, the existence of exchange is *presumed* when the players' opportunity costs of production differ. In models of pure conflict, the existence of exchange is *precluded* by assumption. In Anderton, Anderton and Carter's (1999) integrated model, the existence of exchange is *derived* based on the interdependence of the three fundamental categories of economic activity: production, exchange, and appropriation. The broad lesson here is that production, exchange, and appropriation are in truth profoundly intertwined, because appropriation possibilities determine the security of production and exchange at the same time that production and exchange possibilities shape incentives for appropriation.

7. Experiments in peace economics

With early peace economics came the application of game theory, and with game theory came the use of experimental methods. As we have seen in this survey and elsewhere in this volume, focus on cooperation and conflict leads naturally to the formulation of game theoretic models. These models, when formalized, consist of behavioral assumptions (rationality, self-regarding preferences, etc.) and game structures (number of players, available actions, order of play, payoffs, etc.). The explicit game structures in turn provide much if not most of the design whereby experiments are staged to test the models' predictions.

7.1. Experimental methods

In order to understand an empirical phenomenon, economists withdraw to the abstract world of models, bringing with them what are believed to be the phenomenon's essential features as captured in assumptions of behavior and structure. Rules of logic are applied to generate hypotheses and predictions, which are then tested against empirical observations. In the laboratory, data are generated ordinarily by a process in which the structural assumptions are made true by design, hence leaving the behavioral assumptions as targets for testing. The advantages of laboratory-generated data derive from two basic characteristics of experimentation: manipulation and control. In the typical experiment, two treatments are used to force a change in an exogenous variable while leaving an endogenous variable free to change. The temporal sequence of the two changes establishes the direction of influence in a causal relationship between the two variables. Possible effects of extraneous variables are controlled by holding other observable variables fixed and by randomizing subjects between treatments. The result is the avoidance of econometric issues involving functional form, multicollinearity, and errors in variables, which typically arise in analyses of naturally-occurring data. For further discussion of experimental methods see Smith (1989) and Singleton and Straits (2005).

Economic experiments yield meaningful data when they are designed and executed in accordance with certain principles. Some of these principles are common to all disciplines. For example, procedures should be sufficiently clear to permit replication by others, and between two treatments only one exogenous variable should be changed. More notable in economic experiments are three precepts that when satisfied establish control over subjects' preferences. Due to Smith (1982), these are known as non-satiation, saliency, and dominance. Stated informally, these precepts hold that experimental rewards matter to subjects' utility, that rewards are determined by subjects' choices during the experiment, and that rewards matter most in determining these choices. Practical implications for conducting economic experiments include using cash rewards, keeping the experiment as clear and simple as the model permits, using generic and value-neutral language, offering higher payoff scales for more complex decision tasks, and preserving subjects' privacy [see Friedman and Sunder (1994)].

7.2. Early experiments

To a considerable degree the shared history of peace economics, game theory, and experimental methods flows from the now famous prisoner's dilemma experiment conducted by Dresher and Flood at the Rand Corporation in 1950 [Flood (1958)]. The experiment set off an immense growth in game-theory experiments in general and prisoner's dilemma experiments in particular. These experiments were of keen interest to scholars concerned with issues of peace and conflict, leading the editors of *The Journal of Conflict Resolution* to initiate a regular section dedicated to "gaming" in 1965. Representative of the early prisoner's dilemma experiments was the work of research teams at Ohio State University [Scodel et al. (1959), Minas et al. (1960)] and the University of Michigan [Pilisuk and Rapoport (1963), Pilisuk et al. (1965), Rapoport and Chammah (1965)].

In the basic Ohio State experiment [Scodel et al. (1959)], fixed pairs of subjects played a repeated game without communication. The number of trials equaled 50 and was known in advance by subjects. The choice between cooperation (C) and defection (D) was operationalized by pressing a black or red button. Subjects played for real cash payments, which accumulated at the end of each trial. The payoffs in pennies were $(C, C) = (3, 3)$, $(D, C) = (5, 0)$, $(C, D) = (0, 5)$, and $(D, D) = (1, 1)$. Hence, the opportunity cost of cooperating rather than defecting was 2 cents if the other player cooperated and 1 cent if the other player defected. Under standard assumptions, the formal backward induction argument predicted that subjects would defect on all trials. The alternative "intuitive" prediction, attributed to game theorists Luce and Raiffa (1957, p. 101), was that intelligent subjects would come to cooperate in the repeated game. The experimental results fell between the two predictions, showing a mix of cooperation and defection, with choices to defect being more frequent. Also, over the course of 50 trials, the relative frequency of defection increased, a result confirmed in follow-up experiments [Minas et al. (1960)].

The Michigan experiments [Pilisuk and Rapoport (1963), Pilisuk et al. (1965)] are particularly noteworthy because of the adaptations that were introduced to explore issues of disarmament. The researchers began with a finitely repeated prisoner's dilemma, much like the design used at Ohio State. The point payoffs were $(C, C) = (20, 20)$, $(D, C) = (40, -20)$, $(C, D) = (-20, 40)$, and $(D, D) = (0, 0)$, where each point was worth 0.2 cents. The first adaptation was to allow degrees of cooperation, thereby transforming the game from a prisoner's dilemma into what would now be recognized as a public–goods game with alternative levels of contribution. Subjects began a trial with 20 colored chips, white side up and blue side down. They then chose a degree of cooperation by deciding how many chips to turn over to blue side up. Each subject earned points equal to two times the other player's blue chips minus one times the player's own blue chips. The result was a 21×21 payoff matrix, with payoffs in the four corners identical to those described above. Again, by backward induction, the formal prediction was that subjects would defect fully by leaving all chips white side up. As a treatment variable, in some sessions the decision process was framed explicitly in disarmament terms: white chips carried a missile icon and were called weapons, blue chips carried a factory icon and were called economic units, and subjects were told that the experiment simulated a disarmament problem.

The second adaptation was to divide each trial into a sequence of 20 moves, where each move consisted of turning over as many as two chips, either from white to blue or vice versa. Because payoffs were determined only by the final distribution of colors at the end of a trial, the formal game structure was left unchanged by this adaptation. This incorporation of moves, however, permitted additional manipulations whereby the experimenter could announce the distribution of chips at some predetermined point in the sequence of moves [Pilisuk and Rapoport (1963), Pilisuk (1984)]. In the disarmament frame, these announcements constituted arms inspections, which could be either mandatory or optional. Because the distributions could still be changed in subsequent moves, the announcements amounted to cheap talk.

The results of the Michigan experiments are not easily summarized, given the large number of experimental conditions generated by crossing various treatment variables. It suffices to say that, consistent with the Ohio State experiments, the observed play in all treatments included both cooperation and defection. Also, the disarmament frame yielded the same or more cooperation than a neutral frame, and inspections tended to decrease cooperation, apparently due to increased armament during the post-inspection moves.

A more complete review would reveal a surprisingly diverse range of early experiments that could be properly placed under the heading of peace economics. It is certainly true that the quality of the research was limited by the newness of both the theory and methodology. When the experiments were designed to test specific predictions, they usually relied on conjecture and intuition rather than on formally derived hypotheses. Relevant details of design and procedure were frequently omitted, instructions were seldom offered, and the results were often presented in a sketchy and uneven manner. Also, subjects remained in fixed pairs in multiple-trial experiments like the prisoner's dilemmas above, thus conflating the effects of learning and reputation. That said, there is in the early experiments much that impresses. First and foremost, performance-based cash payments were used, often by scholars who were trained psychologists, not economists. Second, the designs were wonderfully imaginative, as illustrated by the Michigan experiments, but also by the extensive use of programmed strategies. Finally, the researchers asked questions that still capture the interest of experimentalists, like does communication matter, how do subjects learn, and is the behavioral assumption of self interest sufficient.

7.3. Recent experiments

Experimentation in peace economics, as in all of social science, has continued to grow unabated over the past half century. Assisted by computer technology, experiments have matured in terms of methodology and scope. Most important, experiments have contributed mightily to the interplay between theory and observation. Here we are content to review two experiments that we believe are illustrative of modern experiments relevant to peace economics.

To see how the literature has advanced since the early prisoner's dilemma experiments, consider two groups facing militarized conflict over a public good. Each group has a dominant strategy to participate in the conflict, but both groups are better off if neither participates than if both participate. Moreover, because the outcome is a public good, each individual within a group has a dominant strategy to not participate, even though all members are better off if all members participate than if none participates. Hence, an intergroup prisoner's dilemma is created such that a free-rider incentive arises both between and within the two groups. Note that free riding by all individuals yields the Pareto efficient outcome for the two groups. Hence, efforts to reduce within-group free riding can worsen the prospects of a peaceful resolution of conflict between the groups [Bornstein (1992)].

Goren and Bornstein (2000) conducted a repeated intergroup prisoner's dilemma experiment with and without within-group communication. Fixed pairs of 3-person groups played 60 rounds of the stage game, with payoffs presented in table form. For each group, the level of participation was equivalent to the number of group members that individually chose to participate. Hence, the level of participation for a 3-person group was 0, 1, 2, or 3. The experiment was framed in neutral terms. Because the number of rounds was unknown by the subjects, the logic of backward induction did not apply, thus permitting theoretical equilibriums to include cooperative play. In the no-communication treatment, the average rate of participation across subjects decreased from about 40 percent in earlier rounds to less than 20 percent in later rounds, which is characteristic of repeated prisoner's dilemma experiments. In the within-group communication treatment, the average participation rate was significantly higher, but it decayed similarly from about 80 percent to less than 60 percent. Interestingly, the variance of participation across groups increased with successive rounds. As the repeated game progressed, roughly one-third of the paired groups succeeded in combining within-group communication and between-group reciprocity to attain the Pareto efficient outcome of zero participation, whereas another one-third used the communication to intensify between-group competition to full participation. The authors conclude that groups can often resolve their conflicts by signaling their willingness to cooperate contingent on the reciprocal cooperation of the other group.

As discussed previously in this survey, conflict between persons or groups often involves appropriation. Attention to this basic fact has resulted in a number of models that attempt to integrate appropriation with production and/or exchange opportunities [see, e.g., Hirshleifer (1991), Grossman and Kim (1995), and Anderton, Anderton and Carter (1999)]. Because the models are formal, they tend to be well suited for testing with controlled experiments [see Durham, Hirshleifer and Smith (1998), Carter and Anderton (2001), and Duffy and Kim (2005)]. Perhaps best known is Hirshleifer's (1991) paradox-of-power model. The model assumes that two players divide their respective resource endowments between productive and fighting efforts. Their productive efforts combine to yield a social income, which is divided between the players in accordance with their relative fighting efforts and the technology of conflict. Central to the technology of conflict is the decisiveness parameter m, which measures the sensitivity of the division of income to increases in the disparity of fighting efforts. The model generates two predictions under Nash equilibrium play. The first is that an increase in m will increase the fighting efforts of both players and hence reduce aggregate income. The second gives the model its name: if the decisiveness parameter is not too high, the equilibrium ratio of final incomes will be less than the ratio of resource endowments, meaning that conflict will leave the poor relatively richer.

Durham, Hirshleifer and Smith (1998) tested the paradox-of-power model with a large-scale experiment in which 139 subject pairs played 16 rounds of the stage game. The experiment was framed in neutral terms. The number of rounds was unknown to the subjects, and available payoffs were presented in matrix form. The design involved 12 experimental conditions formed from 3 treatment variables – matching protocol (wherein pairs were either fixed or varied from round to round), decisiveness parameter m (either 1 or 4), and endowment ratio (1, 1.67, or 4). Two sessions of 10 to 12 pairs were run for each treatment condition. The empirical results were largely supportive of the model's predictions. Average fighting efforts approximated Nash equilibrium levels, but deviations toward cooperation and less fighting were evident in the final rounds, particularly is those sessions where pairs were fixed. The prediction that an increase in the decisiveness parameter would increase both players' fighting was strongly supported, with 45 of 48 available comparisons between sessions showing the expected pattern. Regarding the paradox of power, the correct pattern between endowment and income ratios was observed in 9 of the 12 sessions where the paradox was predicted to hold. Equally important, the paradox was not observed in all four sessions where it was expected not to hold, given the high decisiveness and relative endowments in those sessions.

8. Concluding remarks

Science is characterized by the interplay between theory and observation. Ideally, an empirical question stimulates theory, which yields hypotheses, which generate tests, which then lead to revisions, extensions, and more questions. In actuality, the scientific process works in a variety of ways. Sometimes, for example, there is no general theory and the hypotheses are little more than plausible conjectures. Also, while the scientific process is cyclical, its periods are not like the seasons of a year. For long periods, the focus can be on theory and modeling with little or no empirical testing; or the reverse, empirical study can flourish despite a paucity of theoretical guidance. Lastly, science can be episodic, at various times pulled by events and pushed by new theories, data sources, or methodologies.

This description of science is also a description of peace economics. Some areas of peace economics, such as the study of appropriation possibilities, are largely theoretical with comparatively little empirical work. Other areas, like the determinants of interstate war, have advanced primarily through empirical analysis. Still others, like the investigation of terrorism, include a robust presence of both theoretical models and empirical analysis. Consistent with the scientific process, historical events or seminal contributions have often spurred an area's development. Richardson's (1960a, 1960b) theoretical and empirical analysis of arms rivalries and deadly quarrels, discovered by economists and political scientists during the first tense decades of the Cold War, inspired an explosive growth in the scientific study of war and peace that continues to this day. Also, the impetus for empirical analysis provided by the Correlates of War project and the construction of other large datasets cannot be overstated. As we consider the future of peace economics, we envision a field that continues to be scientific, with empirical work leading the way in some areas and theoretical models in others, and catalytic events and contributions inspiring new research.

We expect peace economics to continue to be identified by the use of economic assumptions, principles, methods, and variables in the study of interstate, intrastate, and extra-state conflict (Section 2). Despite the multi-disciplinary nature of peace economics, we believe it is important for the field's identity that more graduate programs in economics and other disciplines offer specialty fields in the economics of conflict. We are encouraged by the rapid growth of empirical work in many areas of peace economics. Besides COW and PRIO/UCDP, there are now over 50 conflict datasets available to researchers [Eck (2004)]. On the downside, we are struck by the lack of standardization in the definition of variables. Examples include the substantial variations in definitions of war between COW and PRIO/UCDP and even within COW across different types of wars. We might hope that the demands of future research lead to greater convergence in definitions and measures.

In the study of the determinants of interstate armed conflict (Section 3), we are hopeful that more formal theoretical modeling will eventually complement the impressive empirical work that has been done. The empirical literature on territory and the theoretical literature on appropriation possibilities have been separate, but we believe they could be joined in productive ways. The appropriation possibilities literature treats the seizure of resources including territory as a fundamental category of economic behavior. Appropriation models could shed new light on empirical studies of territorial conflicts, while the empirical studies could provide data and cases pertinent to the theory of appropriation possibilities. Regarding economic development, recall that Boehmer and Sobek

(2005) presented evidence of an inverted-U-shaped effect on the risk of interstate war. It is interesting to note that a similar effect on the risk of nuclear proliferation was found by Singh and Way (2004) as reviewed in Section 4. Add to these Hegre, Gissinger and Gleditsch's (2003) finding of an inverted-U relationship between per capita GDP and the risk of civil wars, and there emerges the suggestion of an empirical regularity across different conflict domains that might deserve more general treatment. Lastly, with regard to economic interdependence, the liberal peace debate is certain to remain central to the field of peace economics. Polachek (1994, p. 12) once characterized conflict as "trade gone awry." Since his influential study of trade and interstate hostility [Polachek (1980)], there has developed a huge literature which now is being extended to include intrastate conflict [Hegre, Gissinger and Gleditsch (2003)] and extra-state conflict [Li and Schaub (2004)].

Most research on arms rivalry, proliferation, arms control, and the offense–defense balance focuses on interstate conflict (Sections 4 and 5). An important aspect of many contemporary conflicts, however, is rivalry between groups within a state (intrastate rivalry), between states and transnational entities such as terrorist organizations or criminal syndicates (extra-state rivalry), or even between transnational entities themselves (trans-state rivalry). Most non-interstate rivalries involve accumulation and potential use of small arms and light weapons, although the risk looms large that transnational organizations such as al Qaeda might acquire WMD [Intriligator and Toukan (2005)]. The prominence of non-interstate rivalries can be expected to intensify in immediate decades ahead. Although the literature surveyed in Sections 4 and 5 is interstate in focus, the concepts and methods developed therein are broadly applicable to non-interstate arms rivalries. Perhaps the most important challenge for the study of non-interstate arms rivalry and conflict is the creation of new datasets on the access and accumulation of weapons by non-national entities. Such efforts are already underway, for example, at the Norwegian Initiative on Small Arms Transfers, the Graduate Institute of International Studies (Geneva) Small Arms Survey, and the Monterey Institute's Center for Nonproliferation Studies.

As reviewed in Section 7, experiments involving strategic interaction have a long and rich tradition in peace economics. With the continued development of formal models and game-theoretic applications, as in the area of appropriation possibilities (Section 6), we expect that experimentation in peace economics will likely grow. We also expect that new experiments will emerge that in many ways recall the concerns of early researchers in peace economics. Schelling (1960, p. 164) conjectured that people "can do better than a purely deductive game theory would predict," and countless dilemma and bargaining experiments have since shown Schelling to be right. As a consequence, there is much exciting research now being done in new fields like behavioral economics and neuroeconomics, whose insights will naturally find their way into peace economics [see, e.g., Smith (2003)].

We conclude with final thoughts on the fundamental purpose of peace economics. Richardson (1939, 1960a) viewed his research as important for understanding the occurrence of World Wars I and II and what might have been done to forestall these wars.

Scholars since Richardson have maintained that focus on the causes and consequences of violent conflicts and on how scientific knowledge might promote alternatives to violence. Hence, as abstract and technical as much of the research in peace economics may be, its fundamental purpose is to generate knowledge that can affect policy in Pareto-improving directions. For dissemination of such knowledge, generally accessible treatments in peace economics are available in the classic works of Schelling (1960, 1966), Schelling and Halperin (1961), and Boulding (1962) and in the more recent works of Raiffa (1982), Fischer (1984), Isard (1992), Sandler and Hartley (1995), Hirshleifer (2001), Collier et al. (2003), Coulomb (2004), Vahabi (2004), and Enders and Sandler (2006). We anticipate a future of vigorous and important research, as peace economics continues to build an understanding of the causes, consequences, and possible amelioration of violent conflict.

References

Adams, K.R. (2003/2004). "Attack and conquer? International anarchy and the offense–defense–deterrence balance". International Security 28, 45–83.

Ancker, C.J. (1995). "A proposed foundation for a theory of combat". In: Bracken, J., Kress, M., Rosenthal, R.E. (Eds.), Warfare Modeling. Military Operations Research Society, pp. 165–197.

Anderson, J.E., Marcouiller, D. (2005). "Anarchy and autarky: Endogenous predation as a barrier to trade". International Economic Review 46, 189–213.

Anderton, C.H. (1990). "The inherent propensity toward peace or war embodied in weaponry". Defence and Peace Economics 1, 197–219.

Anderton, C.H. (1992). "A new look at the relationship among arms races, disarmament, and the probability of war". In: Chatterji, M., Forcey, L.R. (Eds.), Disarmament, Economic Conversion and Management of Peace. Praeger, New York, pp. 75–87.

Anderton, C.H., Carter, J.R. (2003). "Does war disrupt trade?". In: Schneider, G., Barbieri, K., Gleditsch, N.P. (Eds.), Globalization and Armed Conflict. Rowman & Littlefield, Boulder, pp. 299–310.

Anderton, C.H., Carter, J.R. (2006). "Vulnerable trade: The dark side of an Edgeworth box". Unpublished manuscript. College of the Holy Cross, Worcester, MA.

Anderton, C.H., Anderton, R.A., Carter, J.R. (1999). "Economic activity in the shadow of conflict". Economic Inquiry 37, 166–179.

Barash, D.P. (1991). Introduction to Peace Studies. Wadsworth, Belmont, CA.

Bayer, R., Rupert, M.C. (2004). "Effects of civil wars on international trade, 1950–1992". Journal of Peace Research 41, 699–713.

Benoit, E. (1973). Defense and Economic Growth in Developing Countries. D.C. Heath, Boston.

Blomberg, S.B., Hess, G.D., Weerapana, A. (2004). "Economic conditions and terrorism". European Journal of Political Economy 20, 463–478.

Boehmer, C.R., Sobek, D. (2005). "Violent adolescence: State development and the propensity for militarized interstate conflict". Journal of Peace Research 42, 5–26.

Bornstein, G. (1992). "The free-rider problem in intergroup conflicts over step-level and continuous public goods". Journal of Personality and Social Psychology 62, 597–606.

Boulding, K.E. (1962). Conflict and Defense: A General Theory. Harper, New York.

Boulding, K.E. (1978). Stable Peace. University of Texas Press, Austin.

Bremer, S.A. (2000). "Who fights whom, when, where, and why?". In: Vasquez, J.A. (Ed.), What Do We Know About War? Rowman & Littlefield, New York, pp. 23–36.

Brzoska, M. (1995). "World military expenditures". In: Hartley, K., Sandler, T. (Eds.), Handbook of Defense Economics, vol. 1. Elsevier, New York, pp. 45–67.

Bueno de Mesquita, B. (1981). The War Trap. Yale University Press, New Haven.

Bush, W.C. (1972). "Individual welfare in anarchy". In: Tullock, G. (Ed.), Explorations in the Theory of Anarchy. Center for Study of Public Choice, Blacksburg, VA, pp. 5–18.

Carter, J.R., Anderton, C.H. (2001). "An experimental test of a predator–prey model of appropriation". Journal of Economic Behavior & Organization 45, 83–97.

Collier, P., Elliott, L., Hegre, H., Hoeffler, A., Reynal-Querol, M., Sambanis, N. (2003). Breaking the Conflict Trap: Civil War and Development Policy. Oxford University Press, New York.

Coulomb, F. (2004). Economic Theories of Peace and War. Routledge, New York.

Cross, J.G. (1977). "Negotiation as a learning process". Journal of Conflict Resolution 21, 581–606.

Diehl, P.F. (1983). "Arms races and escalation: A closer look". Journal of Peace Research 20, 205–212.

Duffy, J., Kim, M. (2005). "Anarchy in the laboratory (and the role of the state)". Journal of Economic Behavior & Organization 56, 297–329.

Durham, Y., Hirshleifer, J., Smith, V.L. (1998). "Do the rich get richer and the poor poorer? Experimental tests of a model of power". American Economic Review 88, 970–983.

East, M.A., Gregg, P.M. (1967). "Factors influencing cooperation and conflict in the international system". International Studies Quarterly 11, 244–269.

Eck, K. (2004). "Conflict dataset catalog". Mimeo. Department of Peace and Conflict Research. Uppsala University.

Enders, W., Sandler, T. (2000). "Is transnational terrorism becoming more threatening? A times series investigation". Journal of Conflict Resolution 44, 307–332.

Enders, W., Sandler, T. (2006). The Political Economy of Terrorism. Cambridge University Press, Cambridge, UK.

Epstein, J.M. (1985). The Calculus of Conventional War: Dynamic Analysis Without Lanchester Theory. The Brookings Institution, Washington, DC.

Fischer, D. (1984). Preventing War in the Nuclear Age. Rowman & Allanheld, Totowa, NJ.

Flood, M.M. (1958). "Some experimental games". Management Science 5, 5–26.

Friedman, D., Sunder, S. (1994). Experimental Methods: A Primer for Economists. Cambridge University Press, Cambridge.

Fudenberg, D., Maskin, E. (1986). "The folk theorem in repeated games with discounting or with incomplete information". Econometrica 54, 532–554.

Garfinkel, M.R. (1990). "Arming as a strategic investment in a cooperative equilibrium". American Economic Review 80, 50–68.

Geller, D.S., Singer, J.D. (1998). Nations at War: A Scientific Study of International Conflict. Cambridge University Press, Cambridge, UK.

Ghosn, F., Palmer, G., Bremer, S.A. (2004). "The MID3 data set, 1993–2001: Procedures, coding rules, and description". Conflict Management and Peace Science 21, 133–154.

Glick, R., Taylor, A.M. (2005). "Collateral damage: The economic impact of war, 1870–1997". Mimeo.

Gochman, C.S., Moaz, Z. (1990). "Militarized interstate disputes, 1816–1976". In: Singer, J.D., Diehl, P.F. (Eds.), Measuring the Correlates of War. University of Michigan Press, Ann Arbor, pp. 193–221.

Goodwin, C.D. (1991). "National security in classical political economy". In: Goodwin, C.D. (Ed.), Economics and National Security: A History of Their Interaction. Duke University Press, Durham, pp. 23–35.

Goren, H., Bornstein, G. (2000). "The effects of intragroup communication on intergroup cooperation in the repeated intergroup prisoner's dilemma (IPD) game". Journal of Conflict Resolution 44, 700–719.

Gortzak, Y., Haftel, Y.Z., Sweeney, K. (2005). "Offense–defense theory: An empirical assessment". Journal of Conflict Resolution 49, 67–89.

Greig, J.M. (2001). "Moments of opportunity: Recognizing conditions of ripeness for international mediation between enduring rivals". Journal of Conflict Resolution 45, 691–718.

Grossman, H.I., Kim, M. (1995). "Swords or plowshares? A theory of the security of claims to property". Journal of Political Economy 103, 1275–1288.

Grossman, H.I., Kim, M. (1996). "Predation and production". In: Garfinkel, M.R., Skaperdas, S. (Eds.), The Political Economy of Conflict and Appropriation. Cambridge University Press, New York, pp. 57–71.

Harris, G. (1997). "Estimates of the economic cost of armed conflict: The Iran–Iraq war and the Sri Lankan civil war". In: Brauer, J., Gissy, W.G. (Eds.), Economics of Conflict and Peace. Avebury, Aldershot, pp. 269–291.

Harrison, M. (2000). "The economics of World War II: An overview". In: Harrison, M. (Ed.), The Economics of World War II. Cambridge University Press, Cambridge, UK, pp. 1–42.

Hausken, K. (2004). "Mutual raiding of production and the emergence of exchange". Economic Inquiry 42, 572–586.

Hegre, H. (2000). "Development and the liberal peace: What does it take to be a trading state?". Journal of Peace Research 37, 5–30.

Hegre, H., Gissinger, R., Gleditsch, N.P. (2003). "Globalization and internal conflict". In: Schneider, G., Barbieri, K., Gleditsch, N.P. (Eds.), Globalization and Armed Conflict. Rowman & Littlefield, Boulder, pp. 251–275.

Hensel, P.R. (2000). "Territory: Theory and evidence on geography and conflict". In: Vasquez, J.A. (Ed.), What Do We Know About War? Rowman & Littlefield, New York, pp. 57–84.

Hirshleifer, J. (1988). "The analytics of continuing conflict". Synthese 76, 201–233.

Hirshleifer, J. (1991). "The paradox of power". Economics and Politics 3, 177–200.

Hirshleifer, J. (2001). The Dark Side of the Force: Economic Foundations of Conflict Theory. Cambridge University Press, Cambridge, UK.

Hitch, C.J., McKean, R.N. (1960). The Economics of Defense in the Nuclear Age. Harvard University Press, Cambridge.

Huth, P.K. (2000). "Territory: Why are territorial disputes between states a central cause of international conflict?". In: Vasquez, J.A. (Ed.), What Do We Know About War? Rowman & Littlefield, New York, pp. 85–110.

Intriligator, M.D. (1975). "Strategic consideration in the Richardson model of arms races". Journal of Political Economy 83, 339–353.

Intriligator, M.D. (1982). "Research on conflict theory: Analytic approaches and areas of application". Journal of Conflict Resolution 26, 307–327.

Intriligator, M.D., Brito, D.L. (1986). "Arms races and instability". Journal of Strategic Studies 9, 113–131.

Intriligator, M.D., Toukan, A. (2005). "Terrorism and weapons of mass destruction". Mimeo.

Isard, W. (1969). General Theory: Social, Political, Economic, and Regional with Particular Reference to Decision-Making Analysis. MIT Press, Cambridge, MA.

Isard, W. (1992). Understanding Conflict & the Science of Peace. Blackwell, Cambridge, MA.

Isard, W. (1994). "Peace economics: A topical perspective". Peace Economics, Peace Science, and Public Policy 1, 9–11.

Isard, W., Smith, C. (1982). Conflict Analysis and Practical Conflict Management Procedures. Ballinger, Cambridge, MA.

Jones, D.M., Bremer, S.A., Singer, J.D. (1996). "Militarized interstate disputes, 1816–1992: Rationale, coding rules, and empirical patterns". Conflict Management and Peace Science 15, 163–212.

Koubi, V. (2005). "War and economic performance". Journal of Peace Research 42, 67–82.

Lanchester, F. (1916). Aircraft in Warfare, the Dawn of the Fourth Arm. Constable, London.

Li, Q., Schaub, D. (2004). "Economic globalization and transnational terrorism: A pooled times-series analysis". Journal of Conflict Resolution 48, 230–258.

Luce, R.D., Raiffa, H. (1957). Games and Decisions. Wiley, New York.

Lund, M.S. (1996). "Early warning and preventive diplomacy". In: Crocker, C.A., Hampson, F.O., Aall, P. (Eds.), Managing Global Chaos: Sources of and Responses to International Conflict. US Institute of Peace, Washington, pp. 379–402.

Lynn-Jones, S.M. (2004). "Preface". In: Brown, M.E., Cote, O.R., Lynn-Jones, S.M., Miller, S.E. (Eds.), Offense, Defense, and War. MIT Press, Cambridge, MA, pp. xi–xxxvii.

Massoud, T.G. (1996). "War termination". Journal of Peace Research 33, 491–496.

McGuire, M.C. (1965). Secrecy and the Arms Race. Harvard University Press, Cambridge.

Minas, J.S., Scodel, A., Marlowe, D., Rawson, H. (1960). "Some descriptive aspects of two-person non-zero-sum games II". Journal of Conflict Resolution 4, 193–197.

Mohammed, N.A.L. (1997). "The Sudan: The cost of the second civil war (1983–1993)". In: Brauer, J., Gissy, W.G. (Eds.), Economics of Conflict and Peace. Avebury, Aldershot, pp. 229–247.

Murdoch, J.C., Sandler, T. (2004). "Civil wars and economic growth: Spatial dispersion". American Journal of Political Science 48, 138–151.

Nitsch, V., Schumacher, D. (2004). "Terrorism and international trade: An empirical investigation". European Journal of Political Economy 20, 423–434.

Olson, M., Zeckhauser, R. Jr. (1966). "An economic theory of alliances". Review of Economics and Statistics 48, 25–48.

Oneal, J.R., Russett, B.M. (2003a). "Assessing the liberal peace with alternative specifications: Trade still reduces conflict". In: Schneider, G., Barbieri, K., Gleditsch, N.P. (Eds.), Globalization and Armed Conflict. Roman & Littlefield Publishers, Lanham, MD, pp. 143–163.

Oneal, J.R., Russett, B.M. (2003b). "Modeling conflict while studying dynamics: A response to Nathaniel Beck". In: Schneider, G., Barbieri, K., Gleditsch, N.P. (Eds.), Globalization and Armed Conflict. Roman & Littlefield Publishers, Lanham, MD, pp. 179–188.

Pilisuk, M. (1984). "Experimenting with the arms race". Journal of Conflict Resolution 28, 296–315.

Pilisuk, M., Rapoport, A. (1963). "A non-zero-sum game model of some disarmament problems". Peace Research Society (International), Papers 1, 57–78.

Pilisuk, M., Potter, P., Rapoport, A., Winter, J.A. (1965). "War hawks and peace doves: Alternative resolutions of experimental conflicts". Journal of Conflict Resolution 9, 491–508.

Polachek, S.W. (1980). "Conflict and trade". Journal of Conflict Resolution 24, 55–78.

Polachek, S.W. (1994). "Peace economics: A trade theory perspective". Peace Economics. Peace Science, and Public Policy 1, 12–15.

Raiffa, H. (1982). The Art and Science of Negotiation. Harvard University Press, Cambridge.

Rapoport, A., Chammah, A.M. (1965). Prisoner's Dilemma: A Study in Conflict and Cooperation. University of Michigan Press, Ann Arbor.

Richardson, L.F. (1939). Generalized Foreign Politics. Cambridge University Press, London.

Richardson, L.F. (1960a). Arms and Insecurity: A Mathematical Study of the Causes and Origins of War. Homewood, Pittsburgh.

Richardson, L.F. (1960b). Statistics of Deadly Quarrels. Boxwood Press, Pacific Grove, CA.

Rider, R. (1999). "Conflict, the sire of exchange". Journal of Economic Behavior & Organization 40, 217–232.

Russett, B.M., Oneal, J.R. (2001). Triangulating Peace: Democracy, Interdependence, and International Organization. Norton, New York.

Sample, S.G. (2002). "The outcomes of military buildups: Minor states vs. major powers". Journal of Peace Research 39, 669–691.

Sandler, T., Cauley, J. (1975). "On the economic theory of alliances". Journal of Conflict Resolution 19, 330–348.

Sandler, T., Hartley, K. (1995). The Economics of Defense. Cambridge University Press, Cambridge, UK.

Sarkees, M.R. (2000). "The correlates of war data on war: An update to 1997". Conflict Management and Peace Science 18, 123–144.

Sarkees, M.R., Wayman, F.W., Singer, J.D. (2003). "Inter-state, intra-state, and extra-state wars: A comprehensive look at their distribution over time, 1816–1997". International Studies Quarterly 47, 49–70.

Schelling, T.C. (1960). The Strategy of Conflict. Harvard University Press, Cambridge.

Schelling, T.C. (1966). Arms and Influence. Yale University Press, New Haven.

Schelling, T.C., Halperin, M.H. (1961). Strategy and Arms Control. Pergamon–Brassey's, London.

Schneider, G., Barbieri, K., Gleditsch, N.P. (2003). "Does globalization contribute to peace? A critical survey of the literature". In: Schneider, G., Barbieri, K., Gleditsch, N.P. (Eds.), Globalization and Armed Conflict. Roman & Littlefield Publishers, Lanham, MD, pp. 3–29.

Scodel, A., Minas, J.S., Ratoosh, P., Lipetz, M. (1959). "Some descriptive aspects of two-person non-zero-sum games". Journal of Conflict Resolution 3, 114–119.

Senese, P.D. (2005). "Territory, contiguity, and international conflict: Assessing a new joint explanation". American Journal of Political Science 49, 769–779.

Singer, J.D. (2000). "The etiology of interstate war: A natural history approach". In: Vasquez, J.A. (Ed.), What Do We Know About War? Rowman & Littlefield, New York, pp. 3–21.

Singh, S., Way, C.R. (2004). "The correlates of nuclear proliferation". Journal of Conflict Resolution 48, 859–885.

Singleton, R.A., Straits, B.C. (2005). Approaches to Social Research, fourth ed. Oxford University Press, New York.

Skaperdas, S. (1992). "Cooperation, conflict, and power in the absence of property rights". American Economic Review 82, 720–739.

Slantchev, B.L. (2004). "How initiators end their wars: The duration of warfare and the terms of peace". American Journal of Political Science 48, 813–829.

Smith, A. (1976). The Wealth of Nations. University of Chicago Press, Chicago.

Smith, V.L. (1982). "Microeconomic systems as an experimental science". American Economic Review 72, 923–955.

Smith, V.L. (1989). "Theory, experiment and economics". Journal of Economic Perspectives 3, 151–169.

Smith, V.L. (2003). "Constructivist and ecological rationality in economics". American Economic Review 93, 465–508.

Sorokin, P. (1937). Social and Cultural Dynamics. American Book Company, New York.

Taylor, J.G. (1983). Lanchester Models of Warfare, Volumes 1 and 2. Operations Research Society of America, Arlington.

Tullock, G. (1974). The Social Dilemma: The Economics of War and Revolution. Center for the Study of Public Choice, Blacksburg, VA.

Vahabi, M. (2004). The Political Economy of Destructive Power. Edward Elgar, Cheltenham.

Van Evera, S. (1998). "Offense, defense, and the causes of war". International Security 22, 5–43.

Van Evera, S. (1999). Causes of War: Power and the Roots of Conflict. Cornell University Press, Ithaca, NY.

Wallace, M. (1979). "Arms races and escalation: Some new evidence". Journal of Conflict Resolution 23, 3–16.

Wittman, D. (1979). "How a war ends: A rational model approach". Journal of Conflict Resolution 23, 743–763.

Wolfson, M. (1985). "Notes on economic warfare". Conflict Management and Peace Science 8, 1–20.

Wright, Q. (1942). A Study of War, Volumes 1 and 2. University of Chicago Press, Chicago.

AUTHOR INDEX OF VOLUME 2

n indicates citation in a footnote.

Abadie, A.   854

Abdelali, N., *see* Maoz, Z.   1052

Abegunrin, O.   1064

Accordino, J.   1200, 1204

Acemoglu, D.   704, 905n, 1021

Adams, K.R.   1240, 1241

Addison, T.   724

Adelman, K.L.   1190, 1194

Adler, A., *see* Huffman, A.   1100

Al-Sowayel, D., *see* Bolks, S.M.   894, 894n, 895–897, 898n, 901–903

Albrecht, U.   1179, 1180, 1192

Alerassool, M.   888n, 898

Alesina, A.   633, 691n, 1059, 1061

Alexander, A.J.   983, 989, 1189

Alexander, J.D.   1179, 1189

Alexandrova, A., *see* Slantchev, B.   1052

Alic, J.A.   1185, 1192, 1193, 1195

Allen, S.H.   898n

Altfield, M.   1061

Amegashie, J.A.   764

Amin, M., *see* Findlay, R.   689

Anbarci, N.   672n, 676, 676n

Ancker, C.J.   1236

Anderson, J.   1064

Anderson, J.E.   685, 1242

Anderton, C.H.   628, 629, 685, 943, 959, 989, 1042, 1221, 1233, 1239, 1242, 1244–1246, 1251

Anderton, C.H., *see* Carter, J.R.   1251

Anderton, C.H., *see* Isard, W.   1189

Anderton, R.A., *see* Anderton, C.H.   685, 1242, 1245, 1246, 1251

Andreou, A.S.   916

Angell, N.   627, 1023

Angrist, J.   1126, 1127n

Antholis, W., *see* Russett, B.M.   1052

Arad, R.W.   1042, 1064

Arce, D.G.   778, 779, 782–785, 788, 789, 793, 810

Arce, D.G., *see* Sandler, T.   782, 784, 789, 796, 977n

Arkes, J.   1091

Armington, P.   1050

Arquilla, J.   779

Arreguin-Toft, I.   938

Arrowsmith, S.   1166

Asch, B.   1089, 1090, 1093, 1094, 1109, 1110, 1112–1116, 1120

Asch, B., *see* Hosek, J.   1094, 1103, 1104, 1114, 1115

Asch, B., *see* Oken, C.   1088

Asch, B., *see* Warner, J.   1078, 1082, 1084, 1086, 1091, 1092, 1094, 1106, 1113, 1117, 1121–1123, 1127n, 1199

Askari, H.G.   871n

Athanasios, O., *see* Hess, G.D.   1056n

Atkinson, S.E.   780

Augustine, N.R., *see* Adelman, K.L.   1190, 1194

Axelrod, R.   676

Azam, J.-P.   677, 719, 733

Azar, E.   1032, 1033

Bai, J.   842, 843

Baik, K.H.   693

Bailey, M.J.   642

Baker, J.C., *see* Rayome, D.   1058n

Baldwin, D.A.   871

Bale, J.M.   1007

Baliga, S.   920

Baltes, P.T.   1200

Banks, A.   730

Banks, A., *see* Greggs, P.   1051

Barash, D.P.   1214, 1215

Barbieri, K.   898n, 1022n, 1028n, 1042, 1064

Barbieri, K., *see* Schneider, G.   1022n, 1227

Barelli, P.   699, 699n

Baskaran, A.   987n

Basuchoudhary, A.   810

Bates, R.   722

Bauer, S.   976n, 984, 988
Baumol, W.J.   700
Bayer, R.   1221
Bayoumi, T.   1191
Bearce, D.H.   1042
Beck, N.   1042
Becker, G.S.   832, 879n, 881–883
Becker, G.S., *see* Ehrlich, I.   643
Bellany, I.   1090
Ben-Dak, J.D., *see* Azar, E.   1032
Benassy, J.P.   964
Benoit, E.   1215
Berbaum, M.L., *see* Oneal, J.R.   898n
Berkovec, J.   1092
Bernheim, B.D.   796
Bernstein, D.   1193
Berryman, J.   947
Berthélemy, J.C.   1197
Besanko, D.   989n, 990
Bester, H.   670, 677, 678n
Bhattacharya, R., *see* Gupta, S.   852, 853
Bier, V.   793
Bischak, G.A.   1198, 1204
Bischak, G.A., *see* Oden, M.D.   1196
Bitzinger, R.A.   975, 987, 988
Bjerkholt, O.   1191
Bjerkholt, O., *see* Gleditsch, N.P.   1191
Black, P.A.   875n
Blainey, G.   1022n
Blake, D., *see* Desai, M.   917
Blanton, S.L.   950
Blavatsky, P.   657, 658
Bloch, F.   693, 698, 699
Blomberg, S.B.   726n, 850, 861, 864, 1221
Blonigen, B.   1058n
Blume, A.   957
Bobrow, D.B.   749, 754, 759
Boehmer, C.R.   1226, 1252, 1253
Bohn, D.   1084
Bolks, S.M.   894, 894n, 895–897, 898n,
   901–903
Bonetti, S.   892, 892n, 893, 893n, 894, 896, 897
Bonn International Center for Conversion
   (BICC)   984n, 1144n, 1145, 1154, 1179,
   1182, 1183, 1190, 1194–1198, 1201, 1202
Borjas, G.   1117
Bornstein, G.   1250
Bornstein, G., *see* Goren, H.   1250
Bos, D.   1162
Boulding, K.E.   627, 1215, 1223, 1225, 1228,
   1231, 1254

Bourne, M.   993, 1000
Boutros-Ghali, B.   744, 745, 748, 752
Bowns, S., *see* Middleton, A.   1155
Boyer, M.A., *see* Bobrow, D.B.   749, 754, 759
Braddon, D.   1144, 1202
Braddon, D., *see* Hartley, K.   1142, 1144
Bradley, J., *see* Hartley, K.   1142
Brady, L.J.   894
Branscomb, L.M., *see* Alic, J.A.   1185, 1192,
   1193, 1195
Brauer, J.   916, 919, 920, 926, 944n, 955, 982,
   983, 983n, 985–988, 1000n, 1002, 1181, 1189
Bremer, S.A.   1051–1053, 1064, 1225
Bremer, S.A., *see* Ghosn, F.   1220
Bremer, S.A., *see* Jones, D.M.   1219
Bright, J.   1023
Brito, D.L.   617, 670, 677, 915, 923, 960, 1009
Brito, D.L., *see* Intriligator, M.D.   915, 917,
   920, 1229, 1232
Brömmelhörster, J.   1183, 1191, 1197, 1198,
   1202, 1204
Brooks, H., *see* Alic, J.A.   1185, 1192, 1193,
   1195
Browning, E.   1122
Brzoska, M.   943n, 944n, 954, 1194, 1196,
   1198, 1201, 1202, 1204, 1219
Brzoska, M., *see* Serfati, C.   1204
Buck, C., *see* Asch, B.   1090, 1112, 1113,
   1116, 1120
Buddin, R.   1089, 1096, 1102
Bueno de Mesquita, B.   899, 1054, 1057, 1223
Bueno de Mesquita, B., *see* Altfield, M.   1061
Bueno de Mesquita, E.   779, 782, 797
Buhaug, H.   718
Bureau of Economic Analysis   849
Bureau of Industry and Security (BIS)   988
Bureau of Labor Statistics   1119
Bureau of Verification and Compliance (BVC)
   977
Burnett, W.B.   1151
Bush, W.C.   1242
Butz, W.P., *see* Alexander, A.J.   983, 989
Buzan, B.   951

Cairns, E.   717
Campbell, S., *see* Markusen, A.R.   1194
Campbell, S.H., *see* Morgan, T.C.   1052, 1054
Cappelen, A., *see* Gleditsch, N.P.   1191

Carballo, M. 728
Cardell, S. 1118
Carment, D. 762
Carter, A.B., *see* Alic, J.A. 1185, 1192, 1193, 1195
Carter, J.R. 1251
Carter, J.R., *see* Anderton, C.H. 685, 1042, 1221, 1242, 1244–1246, 1251
Caruso, R. 1024n
Cashel-Cordo, P. 1064
Castro, C., *see* Huffman, A. 1100
Cauley, J., *see* Enders, W. 803
Cauley, J., *see* Sandler, T. 778, 780, 1215
Cavaluzzo, L., *see* Moore, C. 1109, 1110
Cavicchia, G.P. 987
Cederman, L.E. 1052
Chakravarti, S., *see* Gupta, S. 852, 853
Chalmers, M.G. 735, 951, 1161
Chalmers, M.G., *see* Turner, A.J.W. 1145
Chammah, A.M., *see* Rapoport, A. 1248
Chan, S. 1052
Chang, Y.C., *see* Polachek, S.W. 1020n
Chen, A.H. 858
Chen, S. 980
Chwe, M.S.Y. 698
Cingranelli, D. 730
Clark, D.J. 657
Clark, W.S. 1005n
Clements, B. 1191
Clements, B., *see* Gupta, S. 852, 853
Clendenning, D., *see* Asch, B. 1094
Coase, R. 990
Cobden, R. 1023
Cock, J., *see* Kirsten, A. 1001
Colletta, N.J. 1200
Collier, P. 612, 690, 700, 704, 716, 720–725, 726n, 732–735, 902n, 932–934, 937, 938, 977, 977n, 994, 1000n, 1254
Commission of the European Communities 1202
Conca, K. 987
Congressional Budget Office (CBO) 1112, 1118, 1156, 1164
Congressional Research Service (CRS) 944, 944n, 945, 946, 977, 978
Cook, P. 1000
Cooke, T. 1101
Cooley, M. 1180
Cooper, H., *see* Black, P.A. 875n
Cooper, J. 1185, 1204
Cooper, N. 995

Corbett, L. 730
Cornes, R. 642, 793, 883, 883n
Cortright, D. 871n, 888n, 902, 903
Cortright, D., *see* Lopez, G.A. 871n
Costigan, S., *see* Markusen, A.R. 1198
Coulomb, F. 1254
Cox, D.G. 900, 903
Cox, G., *see* Golding, H. 1111
Craft, C.B. 917, 950
Craig, S.G., *see* Cashel-Cordo, P. 1064
Crescenzi, M. 1042
Croddy, E.A. 1003–1005
Cross, J.G. 1228
Crucé, E. 1023
Cunnigham, K. 1201

Dadak, C. 871n
Dajani, M.S., *see* Daoudi, M.S. 894
Dal Bo, E. 690
Dal Bo, P., *see* Dal Bo, E. 690
Dali, T., *see* Hogan, P. 1084, 1086
Damrosch, L.F. 902, 903
Dando, M. 977n
Daoudi, M.S. 894
Dardia, M. 1200
Darling, K., *see* Mackin, P. 1118
Dashti-Gibson, J. 888n, 893, 894, 896–898
Daula, T. 1094
Davidson, J. 903n
Davies, N.V., *see* Chalmers, M.G. 951, 1161
Davis, C. 943n
Davis, D., *see* Woodcock, T. 771
Davis, M. 977n, 1006
Davis, P., *see* Dashti-Gibson, J. 888n, 893, 894, 896–898
Davison, N., *see* Lewer, N. 977n
De Mello, L., *see* Gupta, S. 947
de Montesquieu, B. 1023
de Penanros, R., *see* Jauhiainen, J.S. 1200, 1201
de Soysa, I., *see* Gleditsch, N.P. 1195
Deardorff, A.V. 1064
Defence Industrial Strategy (DIS) 1169
Defense Science Board (DSB) 1166
Deger, S. 927
Deger, S., *see* Berthélemy, J.C. 1197
Dehejia, R.H. 893, 893n, 896, 897
Deitrick, S., *see* Markusen, A.R. 1194
Demange, G. 1120
Department of Trade and Industry (DTI) 1159
DeRouen Jr., K. 764, 765

Dertouzos, J. 1082, 1084–1088
Dertouzos, J., *see* Polich, M. 1087
Desai, M. 917
Diehl, P.F. 1064, 1234
Diehl, P.F., *see* Goertz, G. 1064
DiGiovanna, S., *see* Markusen, A.R. 975, 985, 987, 1198
DiTrapani, A. 1108
Dixit, A.K. 684, 963n
Dixon, W.J. 898n, 1051, 1052
Dodd, R. 766
Dolan, C., *see* Huffman, A. 1100
Dollery, B.E. 875n
Domke, W.K. 1042, 1051, 1054
Dorussen, H. 891n, 1020n
Dowdall, P., *see* Braddon, D. 1202
Dowdall, P., *see* Hartley, K. 1142, 1144
Doxey, M.P. 870n
Doyle, M. 1107
Doyle, M.W. 746, 764, 1051, 1052, 1054
Drakos, K. 856, 859
Dranove, D., *see* Besanko, D. 989n, 990
Drezner, D.W. 890, 894, 903n
Drury, A.C. 893, 893n, 894, 896–898
Drury, A.C., *see* Cox, D.G. 900, 903
Du, C., *see* Asch, B. 1089
Duffield, M. 995, 996
Duffy, J. 1251
Dumas, L.J. 1181
Dunne, J.P. 918, 927, 934, 936, 948, 949, 953–957, 963, 966, 967, 976, 985, 987, 1141
Dunne, J.P., *see* Brauer, J. 944n, 983, 985, 987, 988
Dunne, J.P., *see* Gleditsch, N.P. 1191
Dunne, J.P., *see* Smith, R.P. 915
Durch, W.J. 747, 749
Durham, Y. 1251

East, M.A. 1226
East, M.A., *see* Hermann, C. 1032n
Eaton, J. 890–892, 895
Eck, K. 1252
Eckstein, Z. 853, 854, 864
Ehrlich, I. 643
Eland, I. 1141, 1156
Elbadawi, I. 723n
Eldor, R. 858
Ellingsen, T., *see* Hegre, H. 722
Elliott, K.A., *see* Hufbauer, G.C. 869, 871, 893, 893n, 894, 896–898
Elliott, M. 1095

Elliott, V.L., *see* Collier, P. 612, 690, 700, 704, 732, 1254
Elsner, W. 1201
Ember, C. 1052
Ember, M., *see* Ember, C. 1052
Emmons, J., *see* Siverson, R.M. 899n, 1052
Enders, W. 610, 645, 778, 782, 798, 803, 810, 811, 817, 832–836, 839–842, 844, 845, 849, 852, 855, 856, 856n, 857, 863, 864, 977n, 1006, 1219, 1221, 1254
Enders, W., *see* Sandler, T. 779, 799
Engers, M., *see* Eaton, J. 890–892, 895
Enthoven, A. 630
Epstein, G.L., *see* Alic, J.A. 1185, 1192, 1193, 1195
Epstein, J.M. 714, 1236
Erasmus, D. 1023
Eriksson, M., *see* Gleditsch, N.P. 713–715, 717
Esteban, J.M. 660n, 662n, 692, 696n, 698, 703n
Eubank, W.L., *see* Weinberg, L.B. 860
European Union (EU) 1172
Everett, H.M. 645
Eyerman, J. 1052

Fair, C., *see* Hosek, J. 1094, 1096, 1103, 1104, 1114, 1115
Farber, H. 1052, 1053
Farnham, B. 899n
Fearon, J.D. 677, 678, 713, 716, 721–723, 894, 901
Feldman, J.M. 1194–1196
Felix, D. 753
Feng, Y. 1061
Ferencz, Z., *see* Jauhiainen, J.S. 1200, 1201
Findlay, R. 689, 702, 887n, 1029
Fischer, D. 753n, 1239, 1254
Fischer, D., *see* Isard, W. 753n
Fisher, E., *see* Bearce, D.H. 1042
Flemming, P., *see* Mickolus, E.F. 818
Flood, M.M. 1248
Florquin, N. 994
Fontanel, J. 1181, 1189
Forbes, J.F., *see* Sandler, T. 755
Forrer, J., *see* Askari, H.G. 871n
Francis, P., *see* Junor, L. 1106, 1107
Frank, D. 1125, 1126
Frankenstein, J., *see* Brömmelhörster, J. 1183, 1197, 1198, 1204
Fredland, E. 772
Fredland, J.E. 1169

Fricker, R. 1102
Friedman, D. 1248
Froot, K. 1058n
Fudenberg, D. 1230
Fuertes, A.-M. 935
Fullerton, R. 1094

Gaddy, C. 1185, 1190, 1195
Gadea, M.D. 936
Galtung, J. 869n, 870, 894n, 901
Gansler, J.S. 1185, 1194
Garber, S., *see* Dertouzos, J. 1084–1086, 1088
García-Alonso, M.D.C. 950, 950n, 953, 954, 956, 968, 977, 982, 983, 989
García-Alonso, M.D.C., *see* Dunne, J.P. 918, 948, 949, 953–957, 963, 966, 967
Gardeazabal, J., *see* Abadie, A. 854
Garfinkel, M.R. 629, 662n, 676n, 678, 678n, 685, 692n, 693n, 695n, 699, 1242
Gartzke, E. 899n, 1042, 1052
Gartzke, E., *see* Simon, M. 1061
Gartzke, E., *see* Slantchev, B. 1052
Gasiorowski, M. 1043, 1043n, 1044, 1045
Gates, S. 720
Gates, S., *see* Buhaug, H. 718
Gates, S., *see* Hegre, H. 722
Geller, D.S. 1224
Gelpi, C. 1042
Genicot, G. 693n, 699n
Geoffard, P., *see* Demange, G. 1120
Gerges, F.A. 840
Geva, N., *see* Mintz, A. 1052
Ghobarah, H., *see* Russett, B.M. 727, 730
Gholz, E., *see* Sapolsky, H. 1190
Ghosn, F. 1220
Gibler, D.M. 915
Gibney, M., *see* Corbett, L. 730
Gilmore, E., *see* Lujala, P. 722
Gilpin, R. 1058
Gilroy, C., *see* Williams, C. 1129n
Gissinger, R., *see* Hegre, H. 1253
Gleditsch, N.P. 713–715, 717, 915, 1064, 1191, 1195
Gleditsch, N.P., *see* Hegre, H. 722, 1253
Gleditsch, N.P., *see* Lacina, B. 716, 717
Gleditsch, N.P., *see* Lujala, P. 722
Gleditsch, N.P., *see* Schneider, G. 1022n, 1227
Glick, R. 1221
Gochman, C.S. 1032, 1064, 1219
Godnick, W. 994
Goertz, G. 1064

Gold, D. 1190, 1191
Goldberg, M. 1092, 1094, 1199
Golde, S. 955, 957
Golding, H. 1096, 1101, 1111
Golding, S., *see* Moore, C. 1108
Goldstein, J.S. 1034
Goldstein, M. 1049
Golfin, P. 1111
Golfin, P., *see* Kraus, A. 1089
Golinelli, D., *see* Harrell, M. 1103, 1104
Gonchar, K. 1190, 1192–1195, 1204
Gonzalez, F.M. 699n, 700, 701
Goodwin, C.D. 1226
Goren, H. 1250
Gorman, L. 1081
Gortzak, Y. 1240
Gotz, G. 1092
Goudie, I.S., *see* Jauhiainen, J.S. 1200, 1201
Gowa, J. 1064
Gowa, J., *see* Farber, H. 1052, 1053
Gray, C.S. 610
Gregg, P.M., *see* East, M.A. 1226
Greggs, P. 1051
Gregory, D., *see* Golding, H. 1096
Gregory, D., *see* Golfin, P. 1111
Gregory, D., *see* Kraus, A. 1090
Greif, A. 704
Greig, J.M. 1228
Gresenz, C., *see* Elliott, M. 1095
Grieco, J., *see* Gelpi, C. 1042
Griffis, H., *see* Golding, H. 1101
Griffis, H., *see* Hansen, M. 1108
Griffis, H., *see* Kraus, A. 1089
Griffis, H., *see* Moore, C. 1108–1110
Grossman, G. 1024n
Grossman, H.I. 627, 629, 634, 657, 662n, 663n, 690, 699n, 702, 720, 1242, 1245, 1251
Guha-Sapir, D. 727
Gummett, P. 1192
Gupta, S. 852, 853, 947
Gupta, S., *see* Clements, B. 1191
Gurr, T.R. 722, 1032n
Gurr, T.R., *see* Jaggers, K. 1040

Haas, M. 1051
Haas, R.D. 1048n, 1050
Haass, R.N. 888n
Haavelmo, T. 652, 662n, 704
Haftel, Y.Z., *see* Gortzak, Y. 1240
Hagan, J. 1054
Hagelin, B., *see* Serfati, C. 1204

Hall, P., *see* Markowski, S. 988
Hall, P., *see* Markusen, A.R. 1194
Halperin, M.H., *see* Schelling, T.C. 1215, 1229, 1236, 1254
Hamilton, J.D. 930
Han, T., *see* Grossman, H.I. 634
Hanley, J., *see* Buddin, R. 1102
Hanlon, J. 888n
Hansen, M. 1088, 1094, 1095, 1108, 1111
Hansen, M., *see* Kleinman, S. 1108
Harkness, J. 875n
Harrell, M. 1103, 1104
Harris, G. 1221
Harrison, M. 1221
Hart, J. 1006
Hart, R., *see* Eyerman, J. 1052
Hart, R.A. 893, 893n, 894–897, 901n, 903
Hartley, K. 613, 752, 754, 755n, 948, 976n, 977, 1142–1144, 1149, 1150, 1155, 1169–1173, 1188, 1189, 1198
Hartley, K., *see* Arrowsmith, S. 1166
Hartley, K., *see* Chalmers, M.G. 951, 1161
Hartley, K., *see* García-Alonso, M.D.C. 950n, 953
Hartley, K., *see* Middleton, A. 1155
Hartley, K., *see* Sandler, T. 610, 642, 691n, 916, 920, 948, 1149, 1230, 1231, 1254
Hartley, K., *see* Turner, A.J.W. 1145
Hattiangadi, A. 1090, 1094
Hattori, A., *see* Fischer, D. 753n
Hausken, K. 685, 1242
Hays, P.L. 1008
Hayward, K. 1151
Heal, G. 778, 789
Heal, G., *see* Kunreuther, H. 778
Hegre, H. 641, 722, 723, 1020n, 1042, 1226, 1253
Hegre, H., *see* Collier, P. 612, 690, 700, 704, 732, 1254
Heinemann-Grüder, A. 1199
Helpman, E., *see* Grossman, G. 1024n
Hemenway, D. 1000
Henderson, E.A. 900n, 1040
Henderson, H. 753
Hensel, P.R. 1225
Herbst, J.I. 717, 721
Hermann, C. 1032n
Hermann, M.G., *see* Kegley Jr., C.W. 1052
Hermann, M.G., *see* Hermann, C. 1032n
Herring, E., *see* Buzan, B. 951
Herzog Jr., H.W., *see* Poppert, P.E. 1201

Hess, G.D. 693n, 700, 700n, 704, 900n, 1056n
Hess, G.D., *see* Blomberg, S.B. 726n, 850, 861, 864, 1221
Hewitt, D.P., *see* Bayoumi, T. 1191
Hickson, C., *see* Thompson, E.A. 628, 629
Hirsch, B. 1126, 1127n
Hirsch, S., *see* Arad, R.W. 1042, 1064
Hirschman, A.O. 1023
Hirshleifer, J. 611, 627, 641, 642, 654–656, 656n, 662n, 665, 699n, 701, 719, 762, 918, 1030, 1242, 1251, 1254
Hirshleifer, J., *see* Durham, Y. 1251
Hitch, C.J. 1214
Hoeffler, A., *see* Collier, P. 612, 690, 700, 704, 716, 721–725, 726n, 732–735, 902n, 932–934, 937, 938, 977n, 1254
Hoffman, B. 778, 779, 807, 810, 860
Hoffman, F. 871n
Hogan, P. 1084, 1086, 1111
Hogan, P., *see* Mehay, S. 1109, 1110
Holsti, K.J. 1064
Holsti, O. 1061
Hooker, M.A. 1201
Hooper, N. 1199, 1202
Hooper, N., *see* Hartley, K. 1142, 1143
Hooper, P. 1048
Hopmann, T., *see* Holsti, O. 1061
Horowitz, A.W. 690
Hosek, J. 1078, 1081, 1094, 1096, 1097, 1100–1104, 1114, 1115
Hosek, J., *see* Asch, B. 1094, 1114, 1120
Hosek, S. 1118, 1119
Houck, L., *see* Kraus, A. 1090
House of Commons Paper (HCP) 1141
Hudson, M.C., *see* Taylor, C.L. 1032n
Hufbauer, G.C. 869, 871, 893, 893n, 894, 896–898, 904n
Huffman, A. 1100
Humphreys, M. 722
Huntington, S.P. 640, 721
Husted, T., *see* Hansen, M. 1111
Hutchison, M., *see* Gibler, D.M. 915
Huth, P.K. 1225
Huth, P.K., *see* Russett, B.M. 727, 730

Ihori, T. 643
Imbens, G. 1126
Ingram, P. 951
International Institute for Strategic Studies (IISS) 977n
International Policy Institute for Counterterrorism 824, 828

Intriligator, M.D.   620, 915, 917, 920, 1189,
1215, 1229, 1232, 1253
Intriligator, M.D., *see* Brito, D.L.   617, 670,
677, 915, 923, 960, 1009
Isard, W.   753n, 1189, 1213, 1215, 1223, 1228,
1254
Isbister, R., *see* Ingram, P.   951
Isham, C., *see* Gerges, F.A.   840

Jaggers, K.   1040
Jalalighajar, M., *see* Willett, T.D.   902n
James, P.   899n
Jauhiainen, J.S.   1200, 1201
Jehiel, P.   1009
Jehn, C.   1120, 1121, 1129, 1130
Jia, H.   656
Jing, C.   893n, 895–898
Johansen, S.   926
Johnson, K., *see* Hooper, P.   1048
Johnson, R., *see* Asch, B.   1094, 1116
Johnson, S.H., *see* Acemoglu, D.   704, 905n,
1021
Jondrow, J., *see* Junor, L.   1106, 1107
Jones, D.M.   1219
Junor, L.   1106, 1107

Kaempfer, W.H.   869n, 872, 875, 875n, 876,
876n, 877n, 878, 879n, 883n, 886, 886n, 888,
888n, 889, 890n, 893n, 900n
Kaempfer, W.H., *see* Jing, C.   893n, 895–898
Kaempfer, W.H., *see* Lowenberg, A.D.   877n,
878, 879n
Kahn, H.   636
Kahn, M., *see* Goldstein, M.   1049
Kammler, H.   755n
Kane, T.   1127
Kang, H., *see* Reuveny, R.   1043, 1043n, 1046,
1058
Kant, I.   627, 1023, 1051, 1054
Kapstein, E.B.   1201
Kapur, K., *see* Buddin, R.   1096
Kapur, K., *see* Elliott, M.   1095
Kavanagh, J.   1106n, 1107
Kavanagh, J., *see* Hosek, J.   1096, 1097, 1100
Kay, A.F., *see* Henderson, H.   753
Keely, C.B.   727
Keenan, J., *see* DiTrapani, A.   1108
Kegley Jr., C.W.   1032n, 1052
Kelley, M.R.   1186, 1194, 1196
Kelley, M.R., *see* Watkins, T.A.   1158
Kennedy, G.   985

Keshk, O.   1042
Keynes, J.M.   1021
Khakee, A.   996
Khan, A., *see* Mack, A.   869n, 870
Khanna, J.   754–759, 761
Kilburn, M.R.   1081
Kilburn, M.R., *see* Arkes, J.   1091
Kilburn, M.R., *see* Asch, B.   1090
Kilburn, R.   1081
Killicoat, P.   996, 997
Kim, C.H.   1061
Kim, H.   1125
Kim, M., *see* Duffy, J.   1251
Kim, M., *see* Grossman, H.I.   627, 629, 657,
662n, 663n, 699n, 1242, 1245, 1251
Kim, M.K., *see* Polachek, S.W.   1046n
Kim, S.Y.   1042
King, G.   1034, 1038
King, J., *see* Siverson, R.M.   1061
Kingma, K.   1200
Kinsella, D.   943n, 950n, 951, 1052
Kirkpatrick, D.L.   948n, 1152, 1153
Kirshner, J.   869n, 888n
Kirsten, A.   1001
Kiss, J.   1195
Klare, M.T.   685
Klein, H.   948, 968
Klein, L.R.   753, 754, 1189
Kleinman, S.   1108
Klerman, J.   1102
Klerman, J., *see* Asch, B.   1090, 1112, 1113,
1116, 1120
Klerman, J., *see* Kilburn, R.   1081
Kleykamp, M., *see* Asch, B.   1090, 1112, 1113,
1116, 1120
Knetter, M., *see* Hooker, M.A.   1201
Knight, M.   1191
Koch, M.T., *see* Bueno de Mesquita, B.   1057
Konrad, K.A.   627, 655, 670n, 702, 703
Konrad, K.A., *see* Bester, H.   678n
Koopmans, T.C., *see* Samuelson, P.A.   915n
Kopte, S.   1202
Kostner, M., *see* Colletta, N.J.   1200
Koubi, V.   1009, 1010, 1010n, 1221
Kovacic, W.E., *see* Burnett, W.B.   1151
Kraus, A.   1089, 1090, 1096
Krause, K.   987
Krueger, A.B.   860
Krugman, P.   1030
Kulve, H.   948, 968
Kunreuther, H.   778

Kunreuther, H., *see* Heal, G.   778, 789
Kuran, T.   714, 720, 887n
Kutan, A.M., *see* Drakos, K.   856
Kutsoati, E., *see* Amegashie, J.A.   764

La Porta, R.   905n
Lacina, B.   716, 717
Lacy, D.   891, 895
Laffont, J.J.   956n, 1148, 1162, 1166
Laitin, D., *see* Fearon, J.D.   713, 721, 723
Lake, D.   1054
Lakhani, H.   1199
Lalman, D., *see* Bueno de Mesquita, B.   1054
Lam, S.L.   892n, 893, 893n, 896, 897
Lamb, G., *see* Dunne, J.P.   987
Lamoreaux, D., *see* Cardell, S.   1118
Lanchester, F.   620, 1236
Landes, W.M.   798
Langford, R.E.   1003
Lapan, H.E.   779, 781, 782, 803, 806, 807, 810
Lapan, H.E., *see* Sandler, T.   781, 789, 793, 811
Larsen, J.A., *see* Croddy, E.A.   1003
Lau, M.   1125
Laurance, E.J.   994, 1181
Laurance, E.J., *see* Godnick, W.   994
Lavoy, P.   1003
Leander, A.   994
Leary, M.C., *see* Markusen, A.R.   987, 1198
Lebovic, J.H.   919
Lee, D.R.   781, 793
Lee, G., *see* Hattiangadi, A.   1090, 1094
Lee, J.   699n, 700
Lee, S., *see* Baik, K.H.   693
Lehman, J.A., *see* Kaempfer, W.H.   886n
Leibbrandt, M.V., *see* Dollery, B.E.   875n
Leitzel, J.   892
Lektzian, D.   899, 900, 900n, 901, 901n, 902n, 903
Lessing, B.   1001
Levine, P.   920, 922, 948, 953, 954, 954n, 955, 957, 959, 960, 960n, 962, 963, 970, 1160
Levine, P., *see* Brauer, J.   955
Levine, P., *see* Dunne, J.P.   918, 948, 949, 953–957, 963, 966, 967
Levine, P., *see* García-Alonso, M.D.C.   953, 954, 956, 977, 982, 983, 989
Levine, P., *see* Sandler, T.   953, 962
Levine, P., *see* Smith, R.P.   951, 953
Levitt, M.   800
Levitt, S.D.   737
Levy, D., *see* Buddin, R.   1102

Levy, D., *see* Schirmer, P.   1115
Levy, G.   1056n
Levy, J.S.   1031, 1052
Levy, J.S., *see* Barbieri, K.   1042
Lewer, N.   977n
Lewis, D.A.   980
Leyton-Brown, D.   870, 870n, 894, 894n
Li, Q.   779, 860, 1253
Li, Q., *see* Gartzke, E.   1042
Li, Q., *see* Reuveny, R.   899n
Lichtenberg, F.   1193
Lien, D., *see* Golfin, P.   1111
Lien, D., *see* Kraus, A.   1096
Lim, N., *see* Harrell, M.   1103, 1104
Lindgren, G., *see* Gleditsch, N.P.   1195
Lipetz, M., *see* Scodel, A.   1248
Liston-Heyes, C.   1161
Little, R., *see* Payne, D.   1103, 1104
Liu, P., *see* Seiglie, C.   925
Lo, F., *see* Klein, L.R.   1189
Loayza, D., *see* Knight, M.   1191
Lopez, G.A.   871n, 888n
Lopez, G.A., *see* Cortright, D.   871n, 888n, 902, 903
Lopez-de-Silanes, F., *see* La Porta, R.   905n
Loughran, D.   1118, 1199
Loughran, D., *see* Asch, B.   1090, 1112, 1113, 1116, 1120
Loughran, D., *see* Klerman, J.   1102
Lowe, W., *see* King, G.   1034, 1038
Lowenberg, A.D.   877n, 878, 879n
Lowenberg, A.D., *see* Jing, C.   893n, 895–898
Lowenberg, A.D., *see* Kaempfer, W.H.   869n, 872, 875, 875n, 876, 876n, 877n, 878, 879n, 883n, 886, 886n, 888, 888n, 889, 890n, 893n, 900n
Luce, R.D.   655, 1248
Ludwig, J., *see* Cook, P.   1000
Lujala, P.   722
Lund, M.S.   1221–1223
Lundahl, M., *see* Findlay, R.   887n
Lundborg, P.   870
Lundquist, J.T.   1190, 1194
Lynn-Jones, S.M.   1240

MacCulloch, R., *see* Pezzini, S.   722
Mack, A.   869n, 870
Mackie, C., *see* Hogan, P.   1084, 1086
Mackin, P.   1118
Mackin, P., *see* Hogan, P.   1084, 1086, 1111
MacMillan, J.   1057n
Maheswhari, S.   987n

Major, S. 888n, 900
Maleckova, J., *see* Krueger, A.B. 860
Malkin, J., *see* Dardia, M. 1200
Mampaey, L., *see* Jauhiainen, J.S. 1200, 1201
Mansfield, E.D. 1022, 1022n, 1042, 1063
Mantin, B. 955, 957, 1147
Maoz, Z. 1052, 1054
Maoz, Z., *see* Gochman, C.S. 1032
Maoz, Z., *see* Oneal, J.R. 1042
Marcouiller, D., *see* Anderson, J.E. 685, 1242
Marcus, A., *see* Cooke, T. 1101
Marinov, N. 902n
Markose, S.M. 917, 938
Markowski, S. 988
Markusen, A.R. 943n, 950, 975, 985, 987, 988,
    1147, 1185, 1188, 1190, 1194–1196, 1198,
    1201, 1202
Markusen, A.R., *see* Brzoska, M. 1201, 1202
Marlin, J.T., *see* Brauer, J. 1181, 1189
Marlowe, D., *see* Minas, J.S. 1248
Marquez, J. 1048–1050
Marquez, J., *see* Hooper, P. 1048
Marshall, M., *see* Gurr, T.R. 722
Martin, C., *see* Asch, B. 1114
Martin, C., *see* Hosek, J. 1094, 1103, 1104,
    1114, 1115
Martin, C., *see* Klerman, J. 1102
Martin, L.L. 894, 894n, 1063
Martin, P. 1024n, 1042
Martin, S. 951
Marwah, K., *see* Klein, L.R. 753, 754
Mashike, L., *see* Kirsten, A. 1001
Maskin, E., *see* Fudenberg, D. 1230
Massoud, T.G. 1228
Mastanduno, M. 1063
Mateou, N.H., *see* Andreou, A.S. 916
Matshedisho, K.R., *see* Kirsten, A. 1001
Matthews, R., *see* Hartley, K. 1142
Mattock, M., *see* Hosek, J. 1094, 1096, 1103,
    1104, 1114, 1115
Maxwell, J.W., *see* Reuveny, R. 701n
Mayall, J. 870
Mayer, T., *see* Martin, P. 1024n, 1042
McBride, M. 678n
McCall, J., *see* Gotz, G. 1092
McCarthy, K., *see* Dardia, M. 1200
McClelland, C. 1032
McDonald, J.A., *see* Polachek, S.W. 1047n,
    1048–1050, 1058
McDonald, L. 730
McDonald, L., *see* Murray, M. 1084–1086

McDonald, L., *see* Orvis, B. 1089
McDonald, P. 1042
McFadden, D.L. 656n
McGann, A.J., *see* Major, S. 888n, 900
McGillivray, F. 899, 900, 900n
McGuire, M.C. 627, 628, 642, 644, 702, 917,
    1215, 1229, 1234
McGuire, M.C., *see* Ihori, T. 643
McKean, R.N., *see* Hitch, C.J. 1214
McKibbin, W.J., *see* Klein, L.R. 1189
McMillan, S. 1022n
McNamara, R.S. 610, 752
Mehay, S. 1109, 1110
Mehay, S., *see* Hirsch, B. 1126, 1127n
Mehlum, H. 662n, 690
Melman, S. 1180, 1181
Melnick, R., *see* Eldor, R. 858
Mendez, R.P. 753
Mendoza, J., *see* Grossman, H.I. 627
Mertens, W., *see* Kaempfer, W.H. 889
Mesnard, A., *see* Azam, J.-P. 677
Mian, Z. 1003
Mickolus, E.F. 799, 818
Middleton, A. 1155
Miers, A.C. 893n
Miers, A.C., *see* Morgan, T.C. 894, 895
Miguel, E. 721
Mihalka, M., *see* Alexander, A.J. 983, 989
Milgrom, P. 667
Millar, A., *see* Cortright, D. 888n
Miller, L., *see* Hosek, J. 1097, 1100
Minas, J.S. 1248
Minas, J.S., *see* Scodel, A. 1248
Ministry of Defence (MoD) 1141, 1145
Mintz, A. 1052
Miyagawa, M. 893, 894, 894n
Mo, J., *see* Dorussen, H. 891n
Moaz, Z., *see* Gochman, C.S. 1219
Moene, K., *see* Mehlum, H. 662n, 690
Moffett, M.H., *see* Kaempfer, W.H. 877n
Moffit, R., *see* Daula, T. 1094
Mohammed, N.A.L. 1221
Moldovanu, B., *see* Jehiel, P. 1009
Monroe, A., *see* Hansen, M. 1108
Monsen, R.J., *see* Russett, B.M. 1051
Moore, C. 1108–1110
Morga, A., *see* García-Alonso, M.D.C. 956
Morgan, T.C. 875n, 888, 892n, 894, 895, 903,
    1052, 1054
Morgan, T.C., *see* Miers, A.C. 893n
Morgan, T.C., *see* Palmer, G. 903

Morrison, A. 752, 753
Morrow, J.D. 1030, 1061
Morrow, J.D., *see* Bueno de Mesquita, B. 899
Moselle, B. 702
Mouhleb, N., *see* Gleditsch, N.P. 1195
Mousseau, M. 898n, 899n, 1052, 1057
Mouzakis, F. 955
Mouzakis, F., *see* Levine, P. 948, 955, 960, 963
Mueller, D. 643
Muggah, R. 1001
Muggah, R., *see* Brauer, J. 1000n, 1002
Muggah, R., *see* Nelson, C. 1001
Mulligan, C. 1122n, 1123, 1124n, 1125
Murdoch, J.C. 609, 726n, 915, 923, 933, 1221
Murdoch, J.C., *see* Sandler, T. 755n
Murdock, J.M., *see* Mickolus, E.F. 799, 818
Murray, M. 1084–1086
Murshed, S.M., *see* Addison, T. 724
Mussington, D. 995
Muthoo, A. 674

Nalebuff, B. 637
National Audit Office (NAO) 950n, 1152,
    1157, 1158, 1173
National Memorial Institute for the Prevention
    of Terrorism 824
NATO 609, 619
Navarro, P. 849
Neal, L. 634
Neary, H.M. 663n
Negrusa, S., *see* Warner, J. 1121–1123, 1123n
Nelson, C. 1001
Nguyen, T.H. 1006
Nikolaidou, E., *see* Dunne, J.P. 927
Nikolaidou, E., *see* Smith, R.P. 915
Nincic, M. 894
Niou, E.M.S. 693n
Niou, E.M.S., *see* Lacy, D. 891, 895
Nitsch, V. 857, 864, 1221
Nitzan, S. 655, 659
Njolstad, O., *see* Gleditsch, N.P. 915
Noh, S.J. 691, 692n, 693, 698
Noh, S.J., *see* Grossman, H.I. 702
Nooruddin, I. 894, 895, 895n, 896, 897, 901,
    902, 902n, 903
Nordhaus, W. 640
North, D.C. 704
Nossal, K.R. 871n, 902, 903
Nye, J.S. 1058

Ocal, N. 927
Oden, M.D. 1196, 1202, 1204

Oden, M.D., *see* Markusen, A.R. 1201, 1202
Oi, J., *see* Junor, L. 1106, 1107
Oken, C. 1088
Oliveros, S., *see* Bier, V. 793
Olson, M. 627, 633, 691, 691n, 881, 1215
Olson, M., *see* McGuire, M.C. 627, 702
Omond, R., *see* Hanlon, J. 888n
Omori, S., *see* Bearce, D.H. 1042
Oneal, F.H., *see* Oneal, J.R. 1042
Oneal, J.R. 898n, 1040, 1042, 1227
Oneal, J.R., *see* Russett, B.M. 898n, 1057,
    1227, 1242
O'Neill, B. 637
Organization for Economic Cooperation and
    Development (OECD) 1154
Orme, B., *see* Kraus, A. 1096
Orphanides, A., *see* Blomberg, S.B. 850, 864
Orphanides, A., *see* Hess, G.D. 693n, 900n
Orr, R.M. 1064
Orvis, B. 1089
Osborne, M.J. 674
O'Sullivan, M.L. 871n
Overgaard, P.B. 779, 782, 806, 807

Paarlberg, R. 894
Palmer, G. 903
Palmer, G., *see* Ghosn, F. 1220
Palmer, G., *see* Morgan, T.C. 903
Palmer, G., *see* Partell, P.J. 901n
Panofsky, W. 950n
Pape, R.A. 871, 902, 902n, 903
Parai, L. 753, 768
Pardos, E., *see* Gadea, M.D. 936
Parise, G.F., *see* Enders, W. 855, 856n
Partell, P.J. 901n
Patel, B. 1203
Pauwels, N. 1199, 1200
Payne, D. 1103, 1104
Payne, D., *see* Warner, J. 1080, 1082,
    1084–1086, 1088
Peltzman, S. 879n, 882
Penubarti, R.M., *see* Cederman, L.E. 1052
Perez-Forniez, C., *see* Gadea, M.D. 936
Perlo-Freeman, S. 980n
Perlo-Freeman, S., *see* Dunne, J.P. 934, 936
Perron, P., *see* Bai, J. 842, 843
Pesaran, M.H. 916, 934, 936
Pessoa, S.D., *see* Barelli, P. 699, 699n
Peterson, C., *see* Hosek, J. 1081, 1094
Pevehouse, J., *see* Mansfield, E.D. 1042
Pezzini, S. 722

Pilisuk, M. 1248, 1249
Pindyck, R.S., *see* Dixit, A.K. 963n
Pleeter, S., *see* Warner, J. 1109, 1110
Polachek, S.W. 627, 1020n, 1021n, 1024, 1024n, 1033, 1041–1043, 1043n, 1046, 1046n, 1047, 1047n, 1048–1050, 1051n, 1053, 1054, 1058, 1059, 1060, 1061n, 1227, 1253
Polachek, S.W., *see* Gasiorowski, M. 1043, 1043n, 1044, 1045
Polak, B., *see* Moselle, B. 702
Polich, M. 1087
Pollins, B.M. 1042
Pollins, B.M., *see* Keshk, O. 1042
Pollins, B.M., *see* Mansfield, E.D. 1022, 1022n
Poppert, P.E. 1201
Porter, R.C. 878, 885n
Potter, P., *see* Pilisuk, M. 1248
Poutvaara, P., *see* Lau, M. 1125
Powell, R. 676, 678, 1061
Press, J., *see* Polich, M. 1087
Pugh, G.E. 645
Pugh, P.G. 1152, 1153

Quester, A.O., *see* Cooke, T. 1101
Quester, A.O., *see* Hattiangadi, A. 1090, 1094

Radcliff, B., *see* Dashti-Gibson, J. 888n, 893, 894, 896–898
Raiffa, H. 1228, 1254
Raiffa, H., *see* Luce, R.D. 1248
Rajan, R.G. 667
Rapoport, A. 1248
Rapoport, A., *see* Pilisuk, M. 1248, 1249
Ratoosh, P., *see* Scodel, A. 1248
Rawson, H., *see* Minas, J.S. 1248
Ray, D. 698
Ray, D., *see* Esteban, J.M. 660n, 662n, 696n
Ray, J.L. 1052
Ray, J.L., *see* Oneal, J.R. 1042
Rayome, D. 1058n
Razin, R., *see* Levy, G. 1056n
Razzolini, L., *see* Basuchoudhary, A. 810
Reed, H.E., *see* Keely, C.B. 727
Reese, D., *see* Hansen, M. 1088
Regan, P.M. 718n, 764, 765
Reid, J., *see* Middleton, A. 1155
Reiter, D. 918, 938
Renner, M. 1181, 1202
Renwick, R. 870, 870n, 894n
Reppy, J. 1204

Reuveny, R. 701n, 899n, 1022n, 1043, 1043n, 1046, 1058
Reuveny, R., *see* Keshk, O. 1042
Review Board 1171
Reynal-Querol, M. 722, 723n
Reynal-Querol, M., *see* Collier, P. 612, 690, 700, 704, 732, 1254
Ricardo, D. 1029
Richards, D., *see* Cingranelli, D. 730
Richardson, L.F. 620, 920, 924, 1031, 1213, 1215, 1223, 1229, 1231, 1234, 1252, 1253
Richardson, N.R. 1064
Rider, R. 685, 1242
Rider, T.J., *see* Gibler, D.M. 915
Riis, C., *see* Clark, D.J. 657
Riley, J., *see* Hirshleifer, J. 656
Robbins, L. 1024n
Robinson, J.A. 702, 722
Robinson, J.A., *see* Acemoglu, D. 704, 905n, 1021
Robson, A.J. 916
Robst, J., *see* Polachek, S.W. 1020n, 1051n
Rodrik, D. 905n
Roemer, J.E. 719
Rogers, E.S. 871n
Rogers, E.S., *see* Cortright, D. 888n
Romley, J., *see* Asch, B. 1112
Ronfeldt, D., *see* Arquilla, J. 779
Rosato, S. 900n, 1057
Rosen, S. 1078, 1089
Rosendorff, B.P. 638, 641, 704, 782, 788, 789
Rosh, R.M. 932
Ross, M. 724
Rostker, B. 1115
Rotte, R. 918
Rousseau, J.J. 1023
Rowe, D.M. 876n
Rowlands, D., *see* Carment, D. 762
Royalty, A. 1119
Rubinstein, A., *see* Osborne, M.J. 674
Rummel, R.J. 1032n, 1051, 1054
Rupert, M.C., *see* Bayer, R. 1221
Russett, B.M. 727, 730, 898n, 1042, 1051, 1052, 1054, 1057, 1227, 1242
Russett, B.M., *see* Ember, C. 1052
Russett, B.M., *see* Maoz, Z. 1052, 1054
Russett, B.M., *see* Oneal, J.R. 898n, 1040, 1042, 1227

Sabrosky, A.N. 1061
Sageman, M. 860

Saggi, K.   1058n
Sákovics, J., *see* Esteban, J.M.   692, 698, 703n
Sala-i-Martin, X.   723
Salmore, B.G., *see* Hermann, C.   1032n
Salmore, S.A., *see* Hermann, C.   1032n
Sambanis, N.   716, 723
Sambanis, N., *see* Collier, P.   612, 690, 700,
    704, 732, 977, 1254
Sambanis, N., *see* Doyle, M.W.   746, 764
Sambanis, N., *see* Elbadawi, I.   723n
Sambanis, N., *see* Hegre, H.   723
Sample, S.G.   1234
Samson, I., *see* Fontanel, J.   1189
Samuelson, L., *see* Bier, V.   793
Samuelson, P.A.   915n
Sánchez-Pagés, S.   677
Sánchez-Pagés, S., *see* Bloch, F.   693, 699
Sandler, T.   610, 627, 642, 691n, 736, 755,
    755n, 778–782, 784, 789–791, 793, 795–797,
    799, 802, 811, 916, 920, 948, 953, 962, 977n,
    1000, 1149, 1215, 1230, 1231, 1254
Sandler, T., *see* Arce, D.G.   778, 779, 782–785,
    788, 789, 793, 810
Sandler, T., *see* Atkinson, S.E.   780
Sandler, T., *see* Cornes, R.   642, 793, 883, 883n
Sandler, T., *see* Enders, W.   610, 645, 778, 782,
    798, 803, 810, 811, 817, 832–836, 839–842,
    844, 845, 849, 852, 855, 856n, 857, 863, 864,
    1006, 1219, 1221, 1254
Sandler, T., *see* Hartley, K.   613, 754, 755n,
    948, 1144, 1173, 1188
Sandler, T., *see* Hegre, H.   641
Sandler, T., *see* Khanna, J.   754–759, 761
Sandler, T., *see* Lapan, H.E.   779, 781, 782,
    803, 806, 807, 810
Sandler, T., *see* Lee, D.R.   781, 793
Sandler, T., *see* Mickolus, E.F.   799, 818
Sandler, T., *see* Murdoch, J.C.   609, 726n, 923,
    933, 1221
Sandler, T., *see* Rosendorff, B.P.   638, 641, 782,
    788, 789
Sandler, T., *see* Shimizu, H.   749, 749n, 751,
    760
Sandler, T., *see* Siqueira, K.   798
Sanjian, G.S.   950
Sapir, O.   1185, 1193, 1195, 1204
Sapolsky, H.   1190
Sargent, K., *see* Sandler, T.   802
Sarkees, M.R.   1218
Satyanath, S., *see* Miguel, E.   721
Sayrs, L.W.   1022n, 1042

Schaeffer, S., *see* Besanko, D.   989n, 990
Schaub, D., *see* Li, Q.   1253
Scheetz, T.   987
Schelling, T.C.   627, 645, 1030, 1215, 1223,
    1228, 1229, 1236, 1239–1241, 1253, 1254
Schiff, J., *see* Bayoumi, T.   1191
Schiff, J., *see* Clements, B.   1191
Schirmer, P.   1115
Schirowki, U.   1200
Schleifer, A., *see* Mulligan, C.   1122n, 1123,
    1124n, 1125
Schlesinger, H., *see* Konrad, K.A.   670n
Schmalensee, R.   655
Schmidt, C.M., *see* Rotte, R.   918
Schmitz, E., *see* Bohn, D.   1084
Schneider, G.   1022n, 1227
Schneider, G., *see* Barbieri, K.   1022n
Schomacker, K.   1180
Schonlau, M., *see* Asch, B.   1089
Schooner, S.   1166
Schott, J.J., *see* Hufbauer, G.C.   869, 871, 893,
    893n, 894, 896–898
Schrodt, P.   1032n
Schumacher, D., *see* Nitsch, V.   857, 864, 1221
Schuster, J.S., *see* Jauhiainen, J.S.   1200, 1201
Schwartz, A.N.   987
Schwebach, V.L., *see* Morgan, T.C.   875n, 888,
    892n, 1052
Scodel, A.   1248
Scodel, A., *see* Minas, J.S.   1248
Segell, G.   1003
Seiglie, C.   749, 761–765, 925, 1029
Seiglie, C., *see* Polachek, S.W.   1059, 1060
Selden, Z.   870, 885n, 888n, 898
Selden, Z., *see* Jehn, C.   1120, 1121, 1129,
    1130
Selten, R.   780, 789
Sen, A.K.   721
Sen, S., *see* Deger, S.   927
Sen, S., *see* Levine, P.   962, 1160
Senese, P.D.   900n, 1225, 1242
Senese, P.D., *see* Dixon, W.J.   898n
Serfati, C.   1204
Serfati, C., *see* Markusen, A.R.   1147
Sergenti, E., *see* Miguel, E.   721
Setter, O.   964, 964n
Shambaugh, G., *see* Davidson, J.   903n
Shanley, M., *see* Besanko, D.   989n, 990
Sharan, R., *see* Gupta, S.   947
Sharp, J., *see* Hosek, J.   1078, 1096
Shefi, Y.   947, 955n

Shi, Y., *see* Mousseau, M. 899n, 1052
Shimizu, H. 749, 749n, 751, 760, 761
Shimizu, H., *see* Khanna, J. 754–759, 761
Shleifer, A., *see* La Porta, R. 905n
Siems, T.F., *see* Chen, A.H. 858
Simon, C., *see* Warner, J. 1080, 1082, 1084–1086, 1088
Simon, M. 1061
Singer, D.J. 713
Singer, J.D. 1031, 1061, 1223
Singer, J.D., *see* Geller, D.S. 1224
Singer, J.D., *see* Jones, D.M. 1219
Singer, J.D., *see* Sarkees, M.R. 1218
Singer, J.D., *see* Small, M. 713, 1051, 1052
Singer, P. 993
Singh, J. 1010
Singh, S. 1009, 1010, 1235, 1253
Singleton, R.A. 1247
Siqueira, K. 762–764, 796, 798
Siqueira, K., *see* Sandler, T. 781, 789–791, 793, 795
Siverson, R.M. 899n, 1052, 1061
Siverson, R.M., *see* Bueno de Mesquita, B. 899, 1057
Sjostrom, T., *see* Baliga, S. 920
Skaperdas, S. 629, 655, 661n–664n, 665, 666n, 667n, 670n, 676, 678n, 685, 689, 691, 692, 692n, 698, 1242
Skaperdas, S., *see* Anbarci, N. 672n, 676, 676n
Skaperdas, S., *see* Garfinkel, M.R. 629, 678, 678n, 685
Skaperdas, S., *see* Genicot, G. 693n, 699n
Skaperdas, S., *see* Konrad, K.A. 627, 702, 703
Skaperdas, S., *see* Lee, J. 699n, 700
Skaperdas, S., *see* McBride, M. 678n
Sköns, E. 1196
Sköns, E., *see* Serfati, C. 1204
Slantchev, B.L. 1052, 1228
Smaldone, J.P., *see* Craft, C.B. 950
Small Arms Survey (SAS) 993, 993n, 994–996, 996n, 997–999, 999n, 1000–1002
Small, M. 713, 1051, 1052
Small, M., *see* Singer, D.J. 713
Small, M., *see* Singer, J.D. 1031, 1061
Smit, S., *see* Gleditsch, N.P. 1195
Smit, W.A., *see* Kulve, H. 948, 968
Smit, W.A., *see* Serfati, C. 1204
Smith, A. 888n, 895, 1226
Smith, A., *see* Bueno de Mesquita, B. 899
Smith, A., *see* McGillivray, F. 899, 900
Smith, C., *see* Isard, W. 1223, 1228

Smith, R.P. 915, 919, 923, 929, 935, 945, 948, 951, 953, 962, 983, 1191
Smith, R.P., *see* Brauer, J. 955
Smith, R.P., *see* Dunne, J.P. 918, 927, 948, 949, 953–957, 963, 966, 967
Smith, R.P., *see* Fuertes, A.-M. 935
Smith, R.P., *see* García-Alonso, M.D.C. 950n
Smith, R.P., *see* Gleditsch, N.P. 1191
Smith, R.P., *see* Levine, P. 920, 922, 948, 953, 954, 954n, 955, 957, 959, 960, 960n, 962, 963, 970, 1160
Smith, R.P., *see* Pesaran, M.H. 916, 934, 936
Smith, V.L. 1247, 1253
Smith, V.L., *see* Durham, Y. 1251
Smith, W.Y., *see* Enthoven, A. 630
Sobek, D., *see* Boehmer, C.R. 1226, 1252, 1253
Sobel, R.S. 766, 767, 769
Söderbom, M., *see* Collier, P. 716, 723–725, 734
Sola, M., *see* Smith, R.P. 915, 929
Solberg, E., *see* James, P. 899n
Solby, S., *see* Carballo, M. 728
Sollenberg, M., *see* Gleditsch, N.P. 713–715, 717
Solomon, B. 746, 754, 766–769, 771
Solomon, B., *see* Parai, L. 768
Sorokin, P. 1213
Soubeyran, R., *see* Bloch, F. 693, 699
Souva, M. 905, 905n
Souva, M., *see* Lektzian, D. 899, 900, 900n, 901, 901n, 902n, 903
Spagnolo, F., *see* Smith, R.P. 915, 929
Spalanzani, A., *see* Fontanel, J. 1189
Spencer, A., *see* Navarro, P. 849
Spiers, E.M. 1006
Spolaore, E., *see* Alesina, A. 633, 691n, 1059, 1061
Sprague, O. 975
Stacchetti, E., *see* Jehiel, P. 1009
Stam, A.C., *see* McGillivray, F. 900n
Starr, H. 1054
Starr, H., *see* Russett, B.M. 898n
Stephens, E., *see* Hooper, N. 1199
Stern, S., *see* Berkovec, J. 1092
Stewart, F. 722
Stigler, G.J. 879n, 881
Stockholm International Peace Research Institute (SIPRI) 919, 945, 977, 978, 978n, 980n, 984, 1006n, 1007, 1145, 1146, 1148, 1160

Stohl, R., *see* Godnick, W.   994
Stone, J.R.N., *see* Samuelson, P.A.   915n
Stowsky, J.   951, 968
Straits, B.C., *see* Singleton, R.A.   1247
Strand, H., *see* Gleditsch, N.P.   713–715, 717
Streit, C.   1051, 1052
Stromsdorfer, E., *see* Cardell, S.   1118
Sturzenegger, F.   699, 699n, 701
Subramanian, A., *see* Rodrik, D.   905n
Sullivan, J., *see* Holsti, O.   1061
Sunder, S., *see* Friedman, D.   1248
Surry, E.   976n, 984, 988
Surry, E., *see* Dunne, J.P.   976, 985, 987
Sweeney, K., *see* Gortzak, Y.   1240
Sweeney, M., *see* Hartley, K.   1142
Syropoulos, C., *see* Anbarci, N.   672n, 676, 676n
Syropoulos, C., *see* Garfinkel, M.R.   685
Syropoulos, C., *see* Skaperdas, S.   629, 661n, 663n, 664n, 665, 666n, 667n, 676, 678n, 685, 689
Szymanski, S.   655

Tabellini, G.   905n
Tamás, P., *see* Jauhiainen, J.S.   1200, 1201
Tan, G., *see* Niou, E.M.S.   693n
Tanzi, V.   627
Tasiran, A., *see* Smith, R.P.   935, 945, 948, 983
Tavares, J.   851, 864
Taylor, A.M., *see* Glick, R.   1221
Taylor, C.L.   1032n
Taylor, J.G.   1236, 1237
Teegen, H., *see* Askari, H.G.   871n
Thie, H., *see* Schirmer, P.   1115
Thoenig, M., *see* Martin, P.   1024n, 1042
Thomas, G., *see* Gorman, L.   1081
Thompson, E.A.   628, 629
Thompson, P.G.   1058
Thompson, W.R.   1052
Thorsson, I.   1180
Tinbergen, J.   1064
Tirole, J., *see* Laffont, J.J.   1148, 1162, 1166
Tishler, A., *see* Blume, A.   957
Tishler, A., *see* Golde, S.   955, 957
Tishler, A., *see* Mantin, B.   955, 957, 1147
Tishler, A., *see* Setter, O.   964, 964n
Tishler, A., *see* Shefi, Y.   947, 955n
Tommasi, M., *see* Sturzenegger, F.   699, 699n, 701
Torbat, A.E.   888n
Torvik, R., *see* Mehlum, H.   662n, 690

Torvik, R., *see* Robinson, J.A.   722
Totten, M., *see* Asch, B.   1112
Totten, M., *see* Hosek, J.   1096, 1097, 1100–1102
Toukan, A., *see* Intriligator, M.D.   1253
Tschirhart, J., *see* Atkinson, S.E.   780
Tschirhart, J., *see* Sandler, T.   778, 780
Tsebelis, G.   870, 870n
Tsiddon, D., *see* Eckstein, Z.   853, 854, 864
Tucker, R., *see* Thompson, W.R.   1052
Tullock, G.   627, 655, 882n, 886, 1215
Turner, A.G., *see* Haas, R.D.   1048n, 1050
Turner, A.J.W.   1145

Udis, B., *see* Smith, R.P.   951, 953
United Kingdom Government: Foreign and Commonwealth Office   975
United Kingdom Parliament   869n
United Nations   743, 745, 747, 748, 750, 768, 1190
United Nations General Assembly   768
United Nations High Commissioner for Refugees (UNHCR)   729
United Nations Institute for Disarmament Research (UNIDIR)   1008
United Nations Security Council   746
United States Congress Office of Technology Assessment   1192, 1193
United States Department of Commerce   634
United States Department of Defense   1115
United States Department of Education   1079
United States Department of State   828
United States General Accounting Office   1149, 1157, 1158, 1166, 1168, 1200, 1203
United States National Academy of Sciences   1203

Vahabi, M.   1254
van Bergeijk, P.A.G.   875n, 892, 892n, 893, 893n, 894, 896, 897
van der Klaauw, W., *see* Imbens, G.   1126
Van Evera, S.   1240
van Panhuis, W.G., *see* Guha-Sapir, D.   727
Vasquez, J.   1040, 1064
Venkatesh, S.A., *see* Levitt, S.D.   737
Verdier, D.   871n, 904n
Verdier, T., *see* Robinson, J.A.   722
Vernez, G., *see* Dardia, M.   1200
Vernon, R.   998, 998n, 1058
Villanueva, N., *see* Knight, M.   1191
Vincent, J.   1051

Viner, J.   1023
Vishny, R., *see* La Porta, R.   905n
Vohra, R., *see* Ray, D.   698

Wagener, A., *see* Lau, M.   1125
Wait, T., *see* Parai, L.   768
Waldman, D., *see* Buddin, R.   1102
Waldman, R.J., *see* Keely, C.B.   727
Wall Street Journal   876n
Wallace, M.   1234
Wallensteen, P.   1042
Wallensteen, P., *see* Gleditsch, N.P.   713–715, 717
Wallensteen, P., *see* Nincic, M.   894
Walter, B.F.   716, 725
Wang, B., *see* Cardell, S.   1118
Wang, T.Y.   950
Warner, J.   1078, 1080, 1082, 1084–1086, 1088, 1091, 1092, 1094, 1106, 1109, 1110, 1113, 1115–1117, 1121–1123, 1123n, 1127n, 1199
Warner, J., *see* Asch, B.   1093, 1094, 1109, 1110, 1114–1116
Warner, J., *see* Goldberg, M.   1199
Warner, J., *see* Payne, D.   1103, 1104
Wärneryd, K.   677n, 692
Wärneryd, K., *see* Bester, H.   670, 677
Watkins, J.   1052
Watkins, T.A.   1158, 1186
Watkins, T.A., *see* Kelley, M.R.   1186, 1194, 1196
Way, C.R., *see* Singh, S.   1009, 1010, 1235, 1253
Wayman, F.W., *see* Sarkees, M.R.   1218
Weede, E.   898n, 899n, 1051
Weeks, G., *see* Cardell, S.   1118
Weerapana, A., *see* Blomberg, S.B.   861, 1221
Weidacher, R., *see* Sköns, E.   1196
Weinberg, L.B.   860
Weingast, B., *see* North, D.C.   704
Weinstein, J.M.   720, 722
Weiss, T.G.   888n
Welch, F., *see* Borjas, G.   1117
Wenger, J., *see* Hansen, M.   1094, 1095, 1108
Wenger, J., *see* Kraus, A.   1090
Werber Casteneda, L., *see* Harrell, M.   1103, 1104

Whinston, M., *see* Bernheim, B.D.   796
White, J.R.   778
White House, the   800, 840
Wie, K.   1197
Wiederhofer, I., *see* Colletta, N.J.   1200
Wilke, P., *see* Brzoska, M.   1194, 1196, 1204
Wilke, P., *see* Kopte, S.   1202
Wilke, P., *see* Schomacker, K.   1180
Wilkinson, C., *see* Chalmers, M.G.   951, 1161
Wilkinson, P.   779
Willett, S.   1203
Willett, T.D.   902n
Williams, C.   1129, 1129n
Williamson, O.   989, 991
Wills, J.K., *see* Hansen, M.   1088
Winter, J.A., *see* Pilisuk, M.   1248
Wintrobe, R.   889
Wirtz, J.J., *see* Croddy, E.A.   1003
Wittman, D.   662n, 1223, 1224, 1228
Wohlander, S.B., *see* Palmer, G.   903
Wolfson, M.   1232
Wolfson, M., *see* James, P.   899n
Wood, B., *see* Dehejia, R.H.   893, 893n, 896, 897
Woodcock, T.   771
World Health Organization (WHO)   727n
World Bank   849
Wright, Q.   1031, 1051, 1054, 1213
Wulf, H.   985, 1188
Wulf, H., *see* Brzoska, M.   1194, 1196, 1204
Wulf, H., *see* Khakee, A.   996
Wulf, H., *see* Laurance, E.J.   1181
Wulf, H., *see* Schomacker, K.   1180

Xiang, J., *see* Polachek, S.   1059, 1060

Yang, J., *see* Askari, H.G.   871n
Yi, S.-S.   698
Yudken, J., *see* Markusen, A.R.   1185, 1194–1196

Zak, P.J.   690, 699n
Zeckhauser, R., *see* Olson, M.   627, 691n, 1215
Zeng, K.   1056n, 1057
Zingales, L., *see* Rajan, R.G.   667
Zinnes, D.A.   898n, 1054
Zombanakis, G.A., *see* Andreou, A.S.   916

SUBJECT INDEX OF VOLUME 2

9/11   831, 840–845, 848, 849, 858, 859, 863

ability to pay   747, 761
action–reaction processes   924, 1215, 1223
adjustment costs   1161, 1172
adverse selection   1162
aerospace   1154, 1160, 1172, 1173
Afghanistan   749
Afghanistan and Pakistan   747
Africa   1182, 1183
African Union   754
agent   1148
aid   721, 728, 731, 733–735
aircraft carriers   1174
al-Qaida   840, 842, 863
all-volunteer force   1131
alliances   624, 628, 635, 637, 638, 640, 642,
    643, 1215
alternative uses   1167
America, South   1182
ammunition   976, 978, 994–997, 999, 1001,
    1002
anarchy   658, 661, 662, 668, 669, 676, 701
appropriation   762, 1213, 1242
Armed Forces   613–615, 619, 620, 1181
– monopolies   1169
– personnel   1183
arms agreement   1230
arms companies   1143, 1158, 1174
arms control   960, 1213
Arms Control and Disarmament Agency
    (ACDA)   945
arms exports   950, 1141
arms export's tax   954
arms industries   610, 615, 618, 955, 976, 977,
    984, 988, 994, 1141
arms inspections   1249
arms markets   1161
arms procurement   1161
arms production   975, 976, 982–989, 992, 993,
    1010, 1011, 1183
arms proliferation   957
arms race between India and Pakistan   927

arms races   610, 611, 614, 615, 617, 920, 937,
    952, 1213
arms rivalry   1213
arms trade   610, 611, 613, 615, 618, 975–978,
    983, 984, 988, 989, 995, 1000, 1002, 1003,
    1010
arms trade offsets   985, 988
arms transfers   944, 945, 977, 978
arms-producing countries   952
Article 296 of EU Treaty   1148, 1156, 1172
ASEAN   1182, 1183
Asia   1183
assessment scale   747
asset specificity   1170
assistance in kind   761
assurance game   785, 788, 789, 800–803
asymmetric information   779, 782, 806–812,
    917, 949, 954, 956, 1161, 1170
asymptotic analysis   935
attack   1232
autarky   1244
average size of arms company   1147

backward induction   1248
Baden-Württemberg   1201
BAE Systems   1142, 1151, 1152, 1165
bail-outs   1161
balance of trade   767
bankruptcy   1168
bargaining   652, 653, 657, 673, 674, 676–678,
    689, 703, 1223
Bavaria   1201
behavioral assumptions   1247
Beijing   1201
Belarus   1195
benefit principle   761
benefit–cost analysis   1166, 1228
benefits and costs of arms exports   1160
benefits and costs of maintaining UK defense ex-
    ports   951
benefits of coordination   957
biased intervention   763
bilateral monopoly   1162
Boeing   1147, 1151, 1160, 1164

Bonn International Centre for Conversion
(BICC) 1144, 1145, 1179, 1190, 1202
Bosnia 749
Boutros-Ghali 744, 748, 752
Brazil 955
bribery and corruption 947
British Aerospace 1164
budget constraints 968
budget-maximizing bureaucracies 1156, 1173
burden sharing 744, 760
Buy American Act 1148, 1156, 1172

C-5 transport aircraft 1151
Canada 750
cancellation 1166
capital asset pricing model (CAPM) 1171
capture 1171
cartel agreements 954, 961
cartels, collusive tendering 1172
case studies 766
Central Intelligence Agency 919
cheap talk 1249
cheating 1230
chemical weapons 1202, 1203
China 915, 928, 932, 1182, 1183, 1197, 1198,
1203, 1204
Chinese defense industry 1188, 1201
choice criteria 1166
civil airlines 1143
civil wars 713–721, 723–728, 730–734, 736,
737, 762, 765, 1216
civilian markets 1142
civilian reemployment 1193
Clinton Administration 1204
club good 750
cointegration 926
Cold War 743, 748, 750, 765, 915, 934, 937,
943, 948, 949, 951, 1077, 1078, 1082,
1085, 1086, 1105, 1109, 1112, 1115,
1120–1122, 1218
Cold War arms race 917
collaboration 947, 1172
collective action problems 609, 610, 617, 618,
620, 961, 962
collusion 771
command economies 1188
company accounts 1160
compellence 1241
competition 1148, 1151, 1162, 1164, 1168,
1174
competition effects 1172

competitive procurement 1170
competitively-determined fixed price contracts
1152, 1168, 1172
concentration in the defense industry 943, 956
cone of mutual deterrence 1232
conflict 611–616, 618–620, 624–626, 627,
629–635, 638–641, 645, 1020–1034, 1038,
1040, 1042–1059, 1061–1065, 1213
– civil wars 765
– management 765
– Gulf War I 765
– inter-state 765
– intra-state 765
– Korea 765
conflict cycle 1221
conflict management procedures 1214, 1215,
1221, 1223
conflict prevention 1221
conflict technology 655, 658, 660, 661, 663,
664, 672, 674, 682, 687, 691, 694, 695,
698, 701
conflict-cooperation 1027, 1038
conglomerates 1143
Congo 748
conscription 1076, 1077, 1121–1132
conscription-adjusted data 755
contest success function 1243
contestable-income production function 762
contiguity 1225
contract curve 1234
contract performance 1157
contracting-out 1169
contracts 944
contributor-specific benefits 761
contributor-specific damage 761
conversion 1180, 1187
cooperation 1020–1025, 1027, 1029, 1030,
1032–1034, 1038, 1042, 1043, 1052, 1053,
1055, 1057–1059, 1063, 1065
cooperative agreements 954
Cooperative Research and Development Agreements (CRADA) 1194
Correlates of War Project 1213
corruption 1141, 1166
cost escalation 1141, 1152, 1153, 1156, 1157,
1173
cost of violent conflict 1213
cost reimbursement contracts 1168
cost structure 1174
cost–time relationship 1152
cost-effectiveness 956

cost-minimizer   1170
cost-plus contracts   1162, 1163
costs   713, 716, 717, 719, 720, 724–728, 730,
    732–735, 737
counter-factual evidence   771
counter-interventions   765
counterterrorism   782, 785, 789, 795–798, 806,
    811, 817, 818, 832, 840, 842, 863
countertrade   944
country-specific benefits   750
covariance   934
credibility of commitment   962
crisis stability   1231
Croatia   748
cross-section regressions   932–934, 938

data   947
– collection   713, 714
– for arms race   916
– for arms trade   968
– for conflicts   771
– on defense R&D spending   1153
– problems   1143
– sets   817–819, 824, 828, 831, 832, 844, 851,
    857, 862, 863, 1216
debt   624, 634, 635
decreasing cost industries   1148, 1150, 1172
defection   1248
Defence Diversification Agency   1204
Defence Evaluation and Research Agency
    (DERA, UK)   1194
defense and civilian firms   1159
defense burdens   1234
Defense Departments   1156
defense economics   1214
defense electronics industry   1143, 1147, 1151,
    1154, 1195
defense employment   1183
defense firms   1143, 1160, 1173
defense industrial base   619, 1143
– definition of the defense industry   1141, 1142
– defense industry culture   1194
– defense industry employment   1144, 1154
– defense industrial policy   1171
defense industries   610, 611, 613, 619, 620,
    948, 1180, 1202
defense R&D   1152
defense spending   1181, 1183, 1184, 1191
defense-related employees   1184
defensive measures   779, 781–783, 787, 788,
    791, 793, 811

delays in delivery   1157, 1173
demand for weapons   947, 948
demand functions   934, 960
Demobilization, Disarmament and Reintegration
    (DDR)   1199
democracies   1040, 1041, 1051–1057, 1059,
    1065, 1225
democracy/non-democracy   1055
democratic peace   1054, 1057
deployments   1077, 1078, 1091, 1095, 1097–
    1102, 1117, 1129, 1133
detection   1230
determinants of interstate armed conflict   1224
deterrence   624, 632, 637, 640, 783, 784, 785,
    787, 789–793, 795, 804, 805, 810
Deutsche System Technik   1195
developing states   975, 976
development   722, 723, 725, 728, 733–735
development contract   1164
diminishing returns   1155
direct negotiation   1162
disarmament   1189, 1205, 1248
disruption to trade   1221
Dixit–Stiglitz *CES* utility function   963
domestic monopoly   1147
domestic procurement   949, 964
domestic production   963
domestic terrorism   832, 850, 855, 857, 863
dominance   1248
dominant strategy   1230
downsizing   1077
draft   1120–1122, 1125, 1126, 1132
drawdown   1077
dual-use technologies   951, 1142, 1143, 1188,
    1205
duopoly   1147
dyadic conflict   1029, 1030
dynamic game   921
dynamic models   935
dynamic programming   1092–1094, 1096, 1100
dynamics   937

EADS   1147, 1151, 1160
Eastern Europe   1184
econometrics   915
economic and industrial benefits   1141
economic consequences   817
economic dependence   1227
economic development   1225
economic growth   654, 701, 702, 704, 1221

economic impacts of terrorism
– direct 769
– indirect 768
– induced 768
economic methods 1214
economic openness 1226
economic sanctions 869, 871, 872, 883, 888, 900, 902, 905
economically strategic industries 948, 1148
economics of arms industries 1148
economies of scope 1151
Edgeworth box 1242
efficiency incentive 1156, 1162, 1168, 1214
efficient defense industrial policy 1172
elasticity of substitution 923, 958
electronics industry 1173
employment 1144
endogenous policy 872, 879, 880, 884, 888
enduring interstate rivals 1228
enlistment supply 1076, 1077, 1080–1082, 1087
entry 1161
EPRO 1195
equality of information 1170
equilibrium 1215
equipment capability 1154
equity 1162
estimating costs 1170
EU defense equipment market 1172
EU KONVER program 1205
EU members 1182
EU PERIFRA program 1204
Euler equation 922
Eurofighter Typhoon 1154
Europe 957
Europe, East, except USSR/CIS 1182
European aerospace industries 1150
European Union (EU) 750, 1183
excess industrial capacity 1156
excessive profits 1141, 1170
exchange 652, 653, 682–685, 690, 1213
exchange rate 767
– floating 767
exit 1161
expected utility model 1223
experiments 1213
export control policies 943, 954, 955, 957
export earnings 1161
export subsidies 943, 950, 954
exports 1160
exports tax 954

externalities 778, 779, 781, 782, 789, 790, 792, 795–799, 811, 1155, 1167
extra-state conflict 1216

F-14 combat aircraft 1151
F-22A Raptor 1149, 1157, 1174
'fair and managed' competition 1172
fatigue coefficients 1231
favorable contract terms 1166
financial penalties 1152
financial sanctions 888, 895, 897, 898, 901
firm/fixed prices 1162
fiscal balance 767
fixed price contract 1151, 1163
fixed-proportion technology 756
'fly-before-you-buy' competitive procurement 1164
for-profit firms 772
foreign aid 755
foreign direct investment 818, 857
former Yugoslavia 746, 960
free gift 1167
free riding 752, 755, 1250

gains from scale and learning economies 1172
gains from trade 1021, 1022, 1028, 1029, 1047, 1048, 1053, 1055, 1056, 1172
game theory 719, 889, 890, 929, 930, 932, 949, 1148, 1215
– complete information 764
– incomplete information 764
General Electric 1142, 1165
general equilibrium 762
geography 1224
German Fraunhofer Institute 1194
Germany 760, 1190, 1194, 1202
global arms trade models 952
global military spending 1179, 1183
globalization 609, 610, 615, 617–620, 624, 627, 630–633, 641, 938
globalized arms trade market 948
governance 624, 627, 629, 630, 633, 637, 641, 654, 659, 690, 691, 700–705
government statistics 1143
GPS-system 1195
Granger causality 771, 925
Greece 915, 930–932, 938
Greece and Turkey 958
Greek–Turkish arms race 916, 919, 920, 926, 929
grievance 1231

group formation   653, 654, 659, 660, 691, 696–699, 705
Gulf War   960

habit forming   760
Haiti   742, 768, 769
health costs   726–728, 730, 731, 736
heterogeneity   935
heterogeneous panel model   936
highly-enriched uranium   1203
hold-up problem   1162, 1170
Honeywell International   1143
hostage-taking events   779–781, 803–806
human and physical capital   1221
human military capital   918

illegal actions   1166
imperfectly competitive   943, 1150, 1158, 1167, 1168
import   947
importing foreign arms   1171
impure public good   754
incentives   761, 762, 953, 956, 1162, 1173
income distribution function   762
incomplete contracting   1162
incomplete information   797
incremental acquisition   1164
India   915, 927, 938, 1182
India and Pakistan   958
indifference curves   959
indirect export subsidy   950
industrial concentration   1147, 1148
industrial organization   943, 1161, 1173
industrial policies   943, 950, 951, 1171, 1174
industry supply chains   1142
inefficiencies   1141
inefficiencies of collaboration   1173
inefficient alliance defense industries   1172
inflation   767
information   1228
information asymmetries
   see asymmetric information
inherent propensity toward peace or war   1236
input–output (I–O) model   766
– tables   1144
instrumental variable estimators   936
inter-communal conflict   1216
interdependence   1022, 1065
interdependent risks   789, 798
interest groups   872, 879, 880, 882–890, 900, 1156

intergovernmental organizations   1227
international collaboration   1141, 1171
international competitiveness   1160
international contracting   1173
international cooperation   779, 799–803, 811
International Monetary Fund   1191
International Peace Research Institute in Oslo   1216
international supply chains   1173
international terrorism   1143
interstate armed conflict   1213
interventions   717, 718, 733–736
intrastate conflict   1215, 1216
investment   1198
irreversible investment   963
iso-quant   1157
ITT   1143

Japan   760
jobs   1161
Joint Strike Fighter aircraft   1150, 1157, 1164, 1168, 1174
joint-product model   755
juste retour   1172, 1173

KBR/Halliburton   1145
Keynesian   1188
KONVER I   1204
KONVER II   1204
Korean War   1184
Kosovo   749

Lanchester model   1236
larger defense contractors   1148, 1156, 1168, 1174
leader–follower model   923
learning and scale economies   1149, 1152, 1228
Lebanon   748, 767
Letter of Assistance (LOA)   748
liberal peace hypothesis   1227
license systems   947
licensed/co-production   1171
life-cycle   1166
likelihood ratio tests   932
limits to military outsourcing   1170
LINK-associated models   1191
lobby   1172, 1156
Lockheed Martin   1151, 1164, 1190
Long Beach   1202
long decade of disarmament   1179
long duration contracts   1169
Los Angeles   1202

Lower Saxony   1201
Lucas Critique   923

macroeconomic costs   818, 851, 855, 863, 864
Magellan   1195
maintenance of defense industrial capacity
      1161
major conventional weapons   976, 978, 980,
      982, 984, 985, 992–994, 997, 998, 1003,
      1010
major power   1225
marginal constituencies   1156
market conduct   1151, 1161
market failure   1167
market performance   1156
Markov processes   916, 920
matching protocol   1251
mathematical statistics   916
mathematical war modeling   1236
Matra–BAE Dynamics–Alenia (MBDA)   1142
McDonnell–Douglas   1164
measure of arms   916
measures of conversion   1186, 1188
median voter   762
mediation   1228
merchant shipping   1143
mergers and acquisitions   1145, 1161
middle power   750
militarized interstate disputes   1216
military   1076–1082, 1085–1087, 1089–1095,
      1099, 1103–1105, 1108, 1111–1119,
      1121–1128, 1131, 1133
military alliance   1172
military benefits   1167
military budgets   1190
military capability   918, 1226
military compensation   1076, 1112, 1113, 1115,
      1118–1120, 1132
military 'cultures'   1181
military expenditures   918, 1214
military labor   1214
military manpower   1076–1078, 1105, 1106,
      1121, 1123–1125, 1127, 1128, 1130–1132
military organization   1236
military outsourcing   1142, 1169
military production function   1173
military retention   1077, 1092
military service companies   1145
military–civilian partnerships   951
military–industrial–political complex   1141,
      1144, 1148, 1155, 1197

misperceptions   1236
Missile Technology Control Regime   955
mission creep   746
– horizontal   746
– vertical   746
mixed motive game   1223
mixed strategies   929
mobilization advantage   1237
monitoring of contracts   1166
monopolistic competition   965
monopoly   1148, 1158, 1174
– power   1169
– rents   1148
monopsony buyers   1161
moral hazard   1162
Moscow   1201
multi-product firms   1150
multilateral interventions   765
multiple equilibria   960
multiple stage games   952

Nash equilibrium   757, 921, 959, 960, 962,
      1230
national champions   943, 956, 1168
national defense industrial base   1152, 1167
national monopolies   1169
national security   943
national welfare   951
natural monopolies   1174
natural resources   721, 722, 724
NBC   944
negotiations   805, 806
Nepal   933
neutral policy   763
new technologies   609, 610, 613, 614, 619,
      1143, 1173
New Trade literature   952
new trade theory   943
Nimrod MR4   1151, 1157
non-competitive   1174
– contracts   1170
non-conventional weapons   1003, 1006, 1010
non-cooperation   967
non-cooperative equilibrium   953
non-excludable   960
Non-Governmental Organizations (NGO)   746
non-linear reaction functions   923, 925
non-price rivalry   1152, 1155
non-rival   961
non-satiation   1247
non-UN-financed missions   751
normal good   758

Norman Augustine   1190
North Atlantic Treaty Organization (NATO)
   751, 756, 758
North Korea   915
North-Rhine Westphalia   1200
Northrop Grumman   1142, 1151, 1164
Norway   750
nuclear weapons   1202, 1203
nuclear weapons proliferation
   see proliferation
nuclear-powered submarines   1174

observer mission   770
offense–defense theory   1240
offsets   944, 988, 1171
oligopoly   1147, 1148, 1215, 1229
OPEC members   1182
open conflict   653, 668–678
operational tempo   1076, 1095, 1133
Operations and Maintenance (O&M)   768
opportunity costs   1155, 1215
organization   1150

Pakistan   915, 927, 938
Panama Canal Zone   1201
panel estimates   721, 733, 932, 935, 936, 938
paradox-of-power   1251
Pareto efficient   1250
Pareto inefficient   1230
partnership   1168, 1169
peace agreement   948
peace building   745
peace dividend   752, 1179, 1205
peace enforcement   746
peace making   744
Peace Science Society   1213
peace studies   1214
peacekeeping   610–613, 615, 616, 619
– financing   744
– operations   744
– multi-dimensional   764
– spill-ins   758
peacemaking   1221
performance measures   766, 1161
PERIFRA   1204
perverse incentives   769
Philippines   1201
plutonium   1203
political-economy calculation   919
pooled static panel   937
population growth   1226

post-Cold War   934, 937, 951, 960, 1180
post-conflict   713, 721, 725–728, 731–733,
   735–737, 754
'post-cost' and/or renegotiate contracts   1171
power   652, 658–660, 662, 665, 667, 673, 674,
   702–704
predator–prey game   1245
preferences   1242
preferential purchasing   1141, 1166, 1172
prevention   728, 733, 734
preventive diplomacy   1221
price contract   1168
price estimates   1151
prime contractors   1142, 1150–1152, 1156,
   1173
principal   1148
Prisoner's dilemma   781, 783, 784, 785, 802,
   920, 929, 1229
– repeated   1248
private benefits   759
private finance initiatives   1169
private military firms   1170
private security provision   772
privatization   751, 1195
proactive measures   778, 779, 782, 787, 788,
   798, 799
procurement   610, 611, 613, 619, 620, 943
procurement rules   952
procurement: theory and policy issues   967,
   1161
producer groups   1148, 1156, 1172
production   950, 1214
productivity   1087, 1105, 1106, 1108, 1119,
   1123, 1128, 1129, 1131, 1132, 1159
profit rates on non-competitive contracts   1171
profitability   1159
proliferation   1213, 1235
prototype competition   1164
proximity   1225
public benefits   760
public choice   760, 1155, 1214
public good   759, 770, 943, 1250
– pure   744
public interest   1166
public–goods game   1249
public–private partnerships   1169
publicly-owned   949

qualitative and asymmetric arms race   917, 938
qualitative arms control   1239

qualitative export controls   950, 954
quality of weapons   953
quantitative export controls   950
quantitative symmetric arms races   917, 938
QinetiQ   1194

R&D   918, 948, 950, 952, 954, 956, 964, 966,
    968, 1149, 1159, 1192–1194
– subsidies   951, 953
– intensity   1148
Rand Corporation   1150, 1248
rational-actor model   832, 863
rationality   1214
re-deployments   1101
reaction coefficients   1231
reaction functions   925, 1234
– linear   959
real option theory   963
real unit production costs   1152
rebel groups   764
reciprocity   1250
reduced form   925
refugees   728–730
regimes   931
regional conversion effects   1201
regional multipliers   1202
regulated firms   1174
regulating the arms industry   950
regulation   943, 1166
relative capability   1225
rent-seeking   763
rents   1162, 1169
repeated game without communication   1248
reputational equilibria   962
reserve forces   1076, 1077, 1091, 1094, 1105,
    1116, 1132, 1133
reserve retention   1094
resettlement   1199
residual contribution   759
resource cost effect   1244
retention   1091, 1092, 1094, 1096, 1101–1104,
    1108, 1110, 1114, 1116, 1117, 1122,
    1131–1133
Review Board   1171
revised profit formula   1171
Ricardian model   1245
Richardson model   917, 922–924, 926, 928, 929
rising costs of defense equipment   1152
risk aversion   762
risk sharing   1162
risk-adjusted profit rates   1168

risks   624, 629, 635, 636, 638, 641, 643, 645
Rolls-Royce   1142, 1165
Russia   946, 1179, 1180, 1183, 1192–1195,
    1197, 1202–1204

saliency   1248
sanctions   767
scale and learning economies   1149, 1172, 1173
scale of output   1150
scarcity   1215
Schleswig-Holstein   1201
scientific study of war   1213
security   1234
Security Council   745
security perceptions   943
security sensitive products   944
Security Web   932
shadow of the future   676, 677, 681, 682, 705
Sierra Leone   748
signaling   1250
SIPRI   931, 945, 1145
Slovakia   1201
small arms and light weapons   977, 978, 993,
    994, 1000, 1010, 1202, 1253
societées de conversion   1204
Somalia   748
South Africa   767, 1183
South Korea   915
Southwest England   1202
Soviet military spending   919
Soviet Union   915, 943, 1180–1184, 1190,
    1192–1194, 1204, 1205
spillovers   757–759, 933, 938, 1155
spinoffs   769, 1148
spurious regression   925
St. Louis   1202
St. Petersburg   1201
stable   1231
Stackelberg solution   1234
stalemate   1228
Stand-by Forces High Readiness Brigade (SHIR-
    BRIG)   753
statistical inference   1215
stock of arms   958
strategic context   924
strategic interaction   943, 949, 952, 1215
strategic trade theory   967
structural breaks   928, 936
structural instability of arms race models   923
structural shocks   924, 925
structural stability   923, 937
structural violence   1215

structure of the defense industry   943, 948
structure of the global arms industry   957
Subic Bay   1201
subsidies   749, 967
substitution possibilities   1234
supplier cartels   951
supply chain   1143
supply side regulation   957
support for a national DIB   1171
switching   931
symmetric equilibrium   966

tailored response   764
Taiwan   915
target cost incentive contracts   1152, 1162,
     1163, 1168
target rate of return   1171
taste-shifting parameter   757
taxation policy   761
taxation schemes   753
technical and allocative efficiency   1169
technological arms race   1152
technological change   612
technology   948, 951
technology of conflict   654, 655, 657, 658, 668,
     685
Technology Reinvestment Program (TRP)
     1204
technology spillovers   1155, 1167, 1174
technology-intensive   761
terms of trade   961, 1161
territorial dispute   1223
territory   1225
terrorism   610–617, 620, 778–780, 782, 787,
     789, 792, 793, 797–799, 803, 811, 1219
Texas Instruments   1195
theoretical   920
theory of arms races   915
thinning of benefits   759
third-party intervention   744
threats   624, 631, 632, 635–637, 639–641, 644,
     645, 948
tied-aid   752
time-lags   1155
time-series analysis   759, 917
tit for tat   929, 932
Tobin Tax   753
top 100 largest arms producing companies
     1144
total package procurement   1151
tourism   818, 855, 856

tradable obligations   761
trade   615, 618, 758, 1020–1031, 1039–1050,
     1053–1059, 1061, 1063–1065
trade and conflict   1020, 1024, 1027–1031,
     1041–1043, 1044, 1046–1051, 1054,
     1057–1059, 1064, 1065
trade gains   1022
trade (interdependence)   1022
trade sanctions   869, 872, 875, 892, 895, 897,
     898, 900, 901
trade-offs   949, 966, 968, 1148, 1169, 1174
trade/conflict indifference locus   1246
transaction costs   772, 1151, 1164, 1169, 1173
transfer function modeling   769
transition matrices   930
transmission mechanism   1155
transparency   956, 1169
troop contribution   749
trust   1023, 1169
truth in negotiations   1170
Turkey   915, 930–932, 938
two-agent two-choice games   929
Typhoon   1155, 1157, 1167, 1173, 1174

UAVs   1153
UK defense industry employment   1145
UK profit formula   1171
UK weapons projects   1157
Ukraine   1195, 1204
UN   743, 1190
– charter   745
– Mission in Haiti   766
– peacekeeping   743
– peacekeeping budget   750
– reimbursement   749
– scale of assessments   747
– standing force   753
– financial arrangements   761
– Protection Force   746
unbalanced panel   937
uncertainty   949, 957, 963
unit root tests   926
United Kingdom   1189, 1202
United States   915, 946, 957, 1179–1184, 1189,
     1191–1193, 1195, 1200, 1202
United States defense industry   1141
United States General Accounting Office   1200,
     1202
unstable arms race   1229, 1231
Uppsala Conflict Data Program   1216
Ural   1201
US weapons programs   1157

utility   1214
utility function   966

VAR (Vector Autoregression)   925–927
VECM (Vector Error Correction Model)   923–925, 927, 928
verification and compliance measures   1230
Vietnam War   1184, 1193
voluntary code of conduct   1172
voluntary contributions   758
volunteer forces   1076, 1077, 1095, 1099, 1121–1123, 1126, 1130–1132
vote-maximizing governments   1156

war   1213
war onset, duration, termination, and recurrence   1223
warring factions   770
Warsaw Treaty   1203
warship   1202
weapons contracting   1214
weapons costs   1164

weapons of mass destruction (WMD)   944, 977, 993, 1003, 1005, 1229
weapons programs   1141
weapons re-supply   1237
wedge effect   1244
welfare of importer countries   954, 955, 1214
Western Europe   957, 1184
Western market economies   1181
wider economic benefits   1167
'winner-takes-all' competition   1165
within and between regressions   935
world arms exports   1160
World Gross Product (WGP)   754
World Military Expenditures and Arms Transfers (WMEAT)   919, 945
world power status   1144
World Trade Organization (WTO)   950, 954
World War II   1183, 1184, 1189, 1192, 1193
world's defense industries   1144
world's leading arms companies   1145

zone of mutual defense   1238